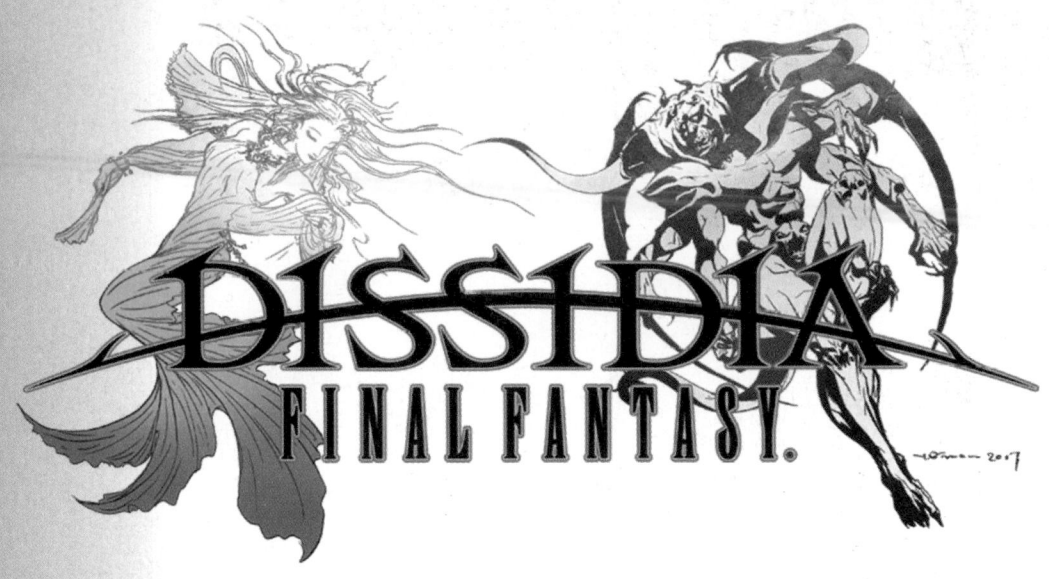

DISSIDIA FINAL FANTASY.

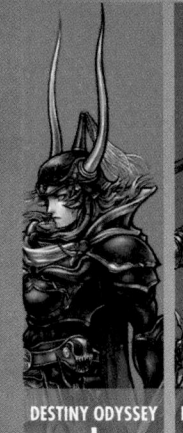
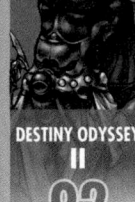
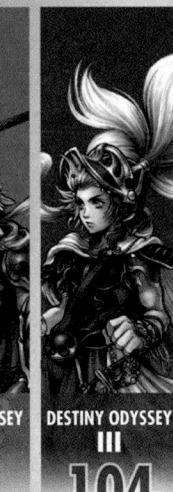
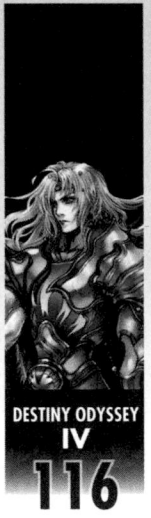
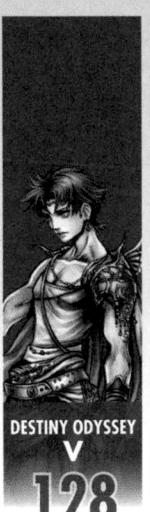
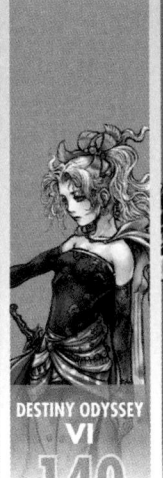
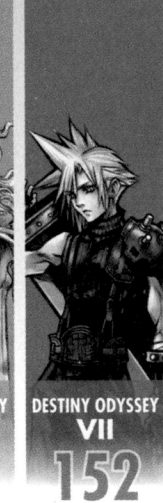
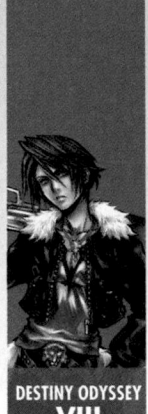
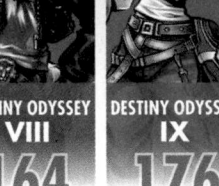
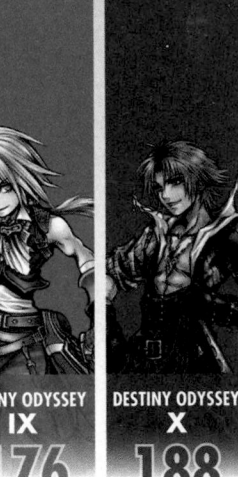

WARRIOR OF LIGHT

Paragon—Crushes enemies with deft, balanced sword techniques.

A legendary warrior blessed by the light. Bearing sword and shield, he is skilled in all aspects of combat.
In Final Fantasy I, the Warrior of Light set out to rescue Princess Sarah of Cornelia, but ended up saving the world.

His origins, his destination, his goals, and his motivations are unknown—even to him.

BASIC MOBILITY*

Ground Movement Speed	⭐⭐
Innate Number of Jumps	1
Jump Height	⭐⭐
Jump Rising Speed	⭐⭐
Air Dash Speed	⭐⭐
Quickmove Speed	⭐⭐

*Mobility can be increased with the abilities
Speed Boost, Jump Boost, Jump Times
Boost, and Precision Jump.

EQUIPMENT

Weapon	Swords, Greatswords, Axes
Hands	Shields, Gauntlets
Head	Helms
Body	Light Armor, Heavy Armor

STAT PROGRESSION

LV	HP	CP	BRV	ATK	DEF	LUK
1	1000	330	95	11	14	10
5	1242	335	118	15	18	12
10	1545	341	147	20	23	15
20	2151	353	205	30	33	20
30	2757	365	263	40	43	25
40	3363	377	320	50	53	30
50	3969	389	378	60	63	35
60	4575	401	436	70	73	40
70	5181	413	493	80	83	45
80	5787	425	551	90	93	50
90	6393	437	609	100	103	55
100	6999	450	667	110	113	60

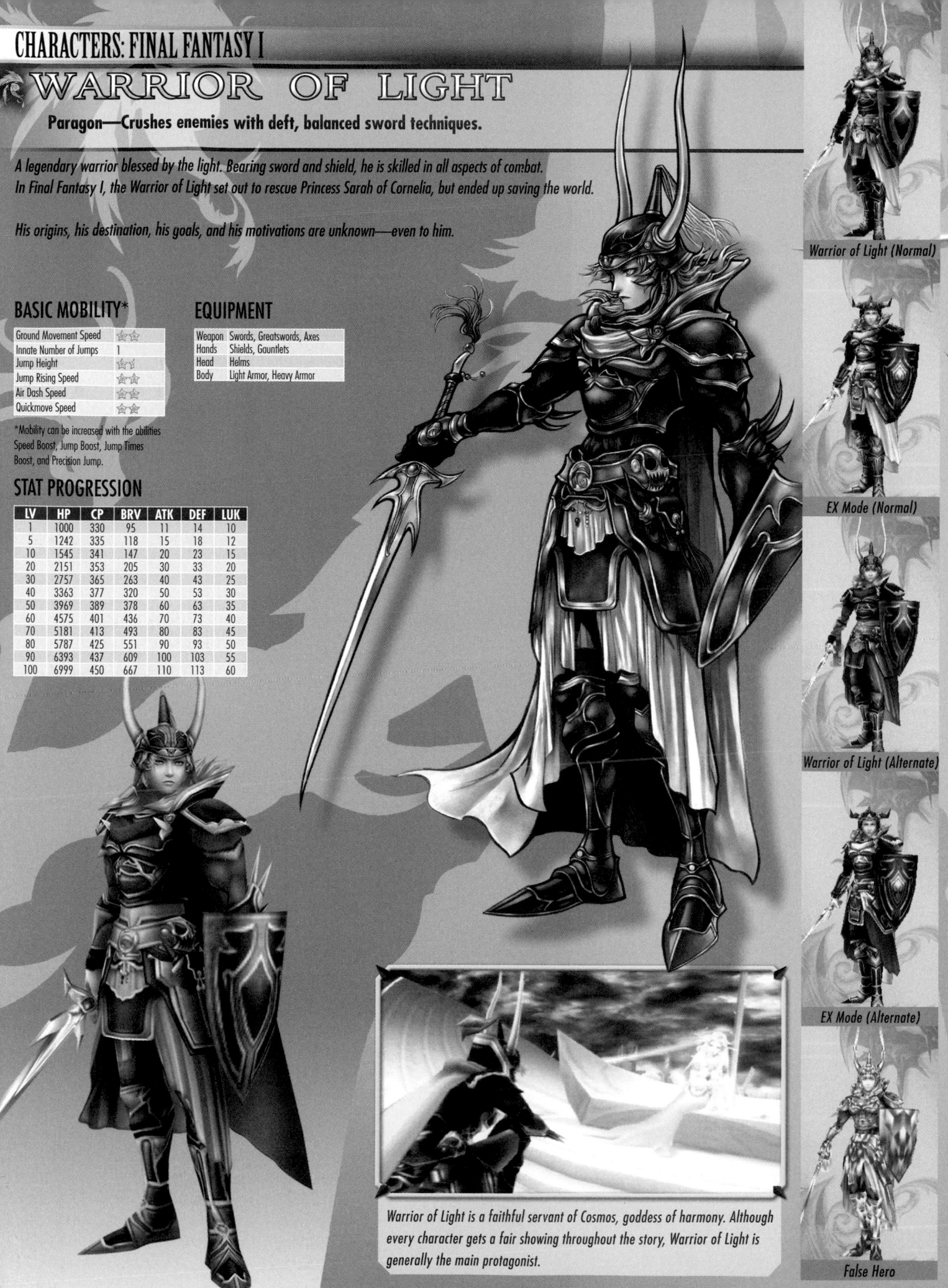

Warrior of Light (Normal)

EX Mode (Normal)

Warrior of Light (Alternate)

EX Mode (Alternate)

False Hero

Warrior of Light is a faithful servant of Cosmos, goddess of harmony. Although every character gets a fair showing throughout the story, Warrior of Light is generally the main protagonist.

ABILITY PROGRESSION

LEVEL	SKILL	TYPE	CP (N)	CP (M)	AP TO MASTER	ATTACK COMMANDS & EFFECTS*
01	Crossover	Bravery Attack (Air)	30	15	120	◎ ◎ (Map Break, Wall Rush, Chase)
(Mastery)	Rune Saber (midair)	Combo Attack	40	20	300	◉ after Crossover (Map Break, Wall Rush, Guard Crush)
01	Dayflash	Bravery Attack (Land)	30	15	90	◎ ◎ ◎ (Map Break, Wall Rush)
01	Red Fang	Bravery Attack (Land)	20	10	120	◉
01	Shield of Light (ground)	HP Attack (Land)	40	20	180	◉ (Guard, Wall Rush, Guard Crush, Map Break)
01	Shield of Light (midair)	HP Attack (Air)	40	20	180	◉ (Guard, Wall Rush, Guard Crush, Map Break)
01	Shining Wave	HP Attack (Land)	40	20	180	◉ (Guard Crush, Map Break)
03	Sword Thrust	Bravery Attack (Land)	30	15	180	◉ (Map Break) ◉ (Wall Rush, Map Break)
04	Air Dash	Action	10	5	100	▲ during Quickmove
07	Jump Boost	Action	10	5	150	-
(Mastery)	Jump Boost+	Action	20	10	150	-
(Mastery)	Jump Boost++	Action	40	20	150	-
09	Rising Buckler	Bravery Attack (Air)	30	15	120	◎ ◎ (Wall Rush, Map Break)
(Mastery)	Bitter End A	Combo Attack	40	20	300	◉ after Rising Buckler (Guard Crush, Wall Rush, Map Break)
11	Auto Recovery	Support	20	5	250	
11	Auto Chase	Support	20	5	250	
13	Shield Strike	Bravery Attack (Air)	30	15	120	◎ ◎ (Wall Rush, Map Break)
(Mastery)	Bitter End B	Combo Attack	40	20	300	◉ after Shield Strike (Guard Crush, Wall Rush, Map Break)
15	Auto EX Command	Support	30	10	300	
15	Auto EX Burst	Support	20	5	150	
18	Reverse Air Dash	Action	10	5	100	▲ during Quickmove
19	Blue Fang	Bravery Attack (Land)	20	10	120	◉
21	Speed Boost	Action	20	10	150	
(Mastery)	Speed Boost+	Action	40	20	150	
(Mastery)	Speed Boost++	Action	70	35	150	
24	White Fang	Bravery Attack (Land)	20	10	120	◉ (Map Break)
25	EX Critical Boost	Extra	45	40	300	-
(Mastery)	Disable EX Critical Boost	Extra	20	10	300	-
26	Auto EX Defense	Support	30	10	300	-
29	Reverse Free Air Dash	Action	30	15	200	■ + ▲
30	Ascension	Bravery Attack (Land)	30	15	90	◎ ◎ ◎ (Wall Rush, Chase, Map Break)
(Mastery)	Rune Saber (ground)	Combo Attack	40	20	300	◉ after Ascension (Guard Crush, Wall Rush, Map Break)
32	Recovery Attack	Action	20	10	120	◉ or ◉ while reeling
32	Controlled Recovery	Action	10	5	120	Analog Stick during Recovery
35	Riposte	Extra	45	40	300	-
(Mastery)	Disable Riposte	Extra	20	10	300	-
38	Radiant Sword	HP Attack (Air)	40	20	180	■ (Wall Rush)
39	Jump Times Boost	Action	20	10	150	-
(Mastery)	Jump Times Boost+	Action	40	20	150	-
(Mastery)	Jump Times Boost++	Action	70	30	150	-
40	Omni Air Dash	Action	40	20	300	Analog Stick + ■ + ▲
43	Sneak Attack	Extra	50	45	360	-
(Mastery)	Disable Sneak Attack	Extra	30	15	360	-
47	Physical Shield	Extra	20	10	280	-
50	Magic Shield	Extra	20	10	280	-
53	Multi-Air Slide	Action	10	5	250	Analog Stick + ✕ after expending jumps. See Multi-Air Slide
(Mastery)	Multi-Air Slide+	Action	30	15	300	
57	Midair Evasion Boost	Action	20	10	150	-
60	Bravery Regen	Extra	20	10	280	-
64	Evasion Time Boost	Support	20	10	220	-
67	First Strike	Extra	40	35	360	-
(Mastery)	Disable First Strike	Extra	20	10	360	-
71	Concentration	Extra	30	15	250	-
(Mastery)	Concentration+	Extra	60	30	250	-
(Mastery)	Concentration++	Extra	100	50	250	-
74	Cat Nip	Extra	30	25	300	-
(Mastery)	Disable Cat Nip	Extra	20	10	300	-
78	Anti-EX	Extra	30	20	300	-
(Mastery)	Disable Anti-EX	Extra	20	10	300	-
81	Achy	Extra	30	15	250	-
(Mastery)	Achy+	Extra	60	30	250	-
85	Counterattack	Extra	50	45	360	-
(Mastery)	Disable Counterattack	Extra	30	15	360	-
88	Gambler's Spirit	Extra	30	15	300	-
(Mastery)	Disable Gambler's Spirit	Extra	20	10	300	-
92	Back to the Wall	Extra	30	25	300	-
(Mastery)	Disable Back to the Wall	Extra	20	10	300	-
95	Precision Jump	Extra	10	5	180	-
98	Snooze and Lose	Extra	100	50	250	-
100	EXP to HP	Extra	20	0	500	-
100	EXP to Bravery	Extra	20	0	500	-
100	EXP to EX Force	Extra	20	0	500	-

*Initial commands may require directional presses, depending on the slot to which abilities are assigned.

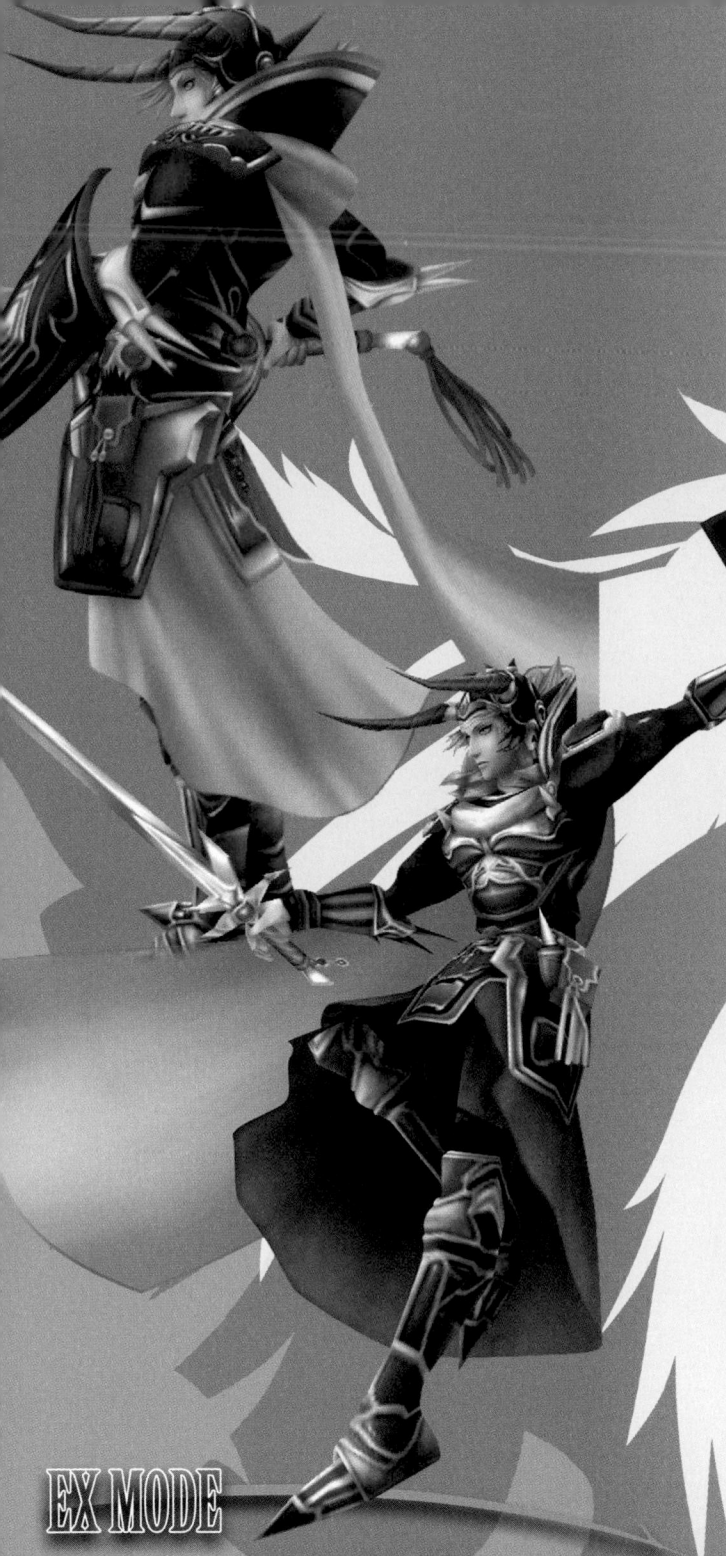

EX MODE

EX BURST

Oversoul: A sharp, repeated strike like a flash of light. (Press D-pad directions as indicated on screen to attack, up to six times total.)

EX EFFECTS

Regen: Vigor and stamina recover little by little, restoring HP.

Mirror Attack: A wall of light appears while attacking, repelling weak magical attacks.

Protect: An aura of light covers the body, raising defense.

Light's Blessing: A sword of light appears, dealing additional damage.

GARLAND

Nemesis—Destroys foes with heavy attacks from a multiform weapon.

Garland becomes a playable character after you finish any Destiny Odyssey, then purchase him from the PP Catalog.

A knight sworn to face the Warrior of Light. He wields a powerful, adaptive weapon. In Final Fantasy I, he was a famed knight of Cornelia when he suddenly went rogue, kidnapping the Princess of Cornelia and taking her to the ruins of the Chaos Shrine. Just before dying, he was transported 2000 years into the past, where he robbed the future of its strength as he survived in solitude. Chained by time and growing continuously hateful, one can only imagine what sort of eternity he dreams of…

BASIC MOBILITY*

Ground Movement Speed	☆
Innate Number of Jumps	1
Jump Height	☆
Jump Rising Speed	☆
Air Dash Speed	☆☆
Quickmove Speed	☆☆

*Mobility can be increased with the abilities Speed Boost, Jump Boost, Jump Times Boost, and Precision Jump.

EQUIPMENT

Weapon	Greatswords, Katana, Spears, Axes
Hands	Shields, Gauntlets
Head	Helms
Body	Light Armor, Heavy Armor

STAT PROGRESSION

LV	HP	CP	BRV	ATK	DEF	LUK
1	1000	330	95	13	14	10
5	1242	335	118	17	18	12
10	1545	341	147	22	23	15
20	2151	353	205	32	33	20
30	2757	365	263	42	43	25
40	3363	377	320	52	53	30
50	3969	389	378	62	63	35
60	4575	401	436	72	73	40
70	5181	413	493	82	83	45
80	5787	425	551	92	93	50
90	6393	437	609	102	103	55
100	6999	450	667	112	113	60

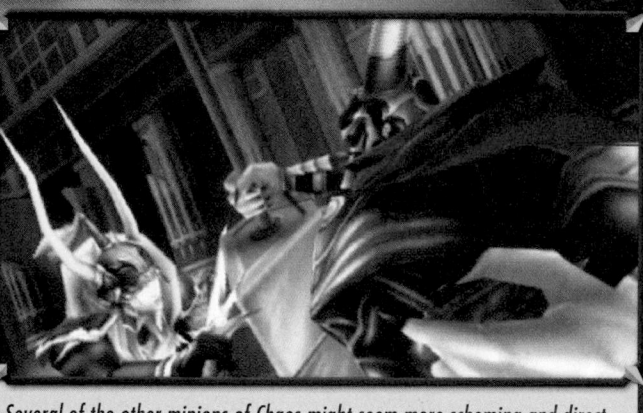

Several of the other minions of Chaos might seem more scheming and direct than the more reserved Garland, but he holds deep secrets that will shock even his evil allies…

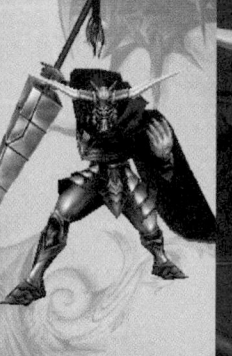

Garland (Normal)

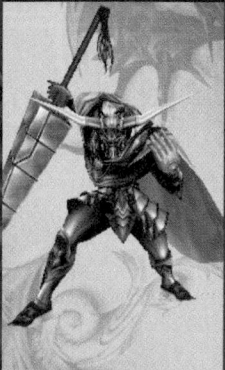

EX Mode (Normal)

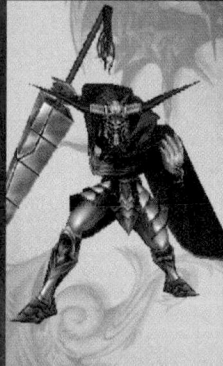

Garland (Alternate)

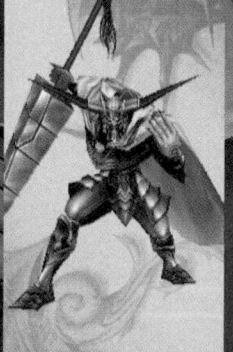

EX Mode (Alternate)

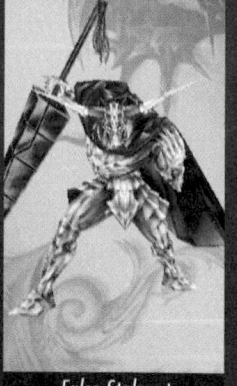

False Stalwart

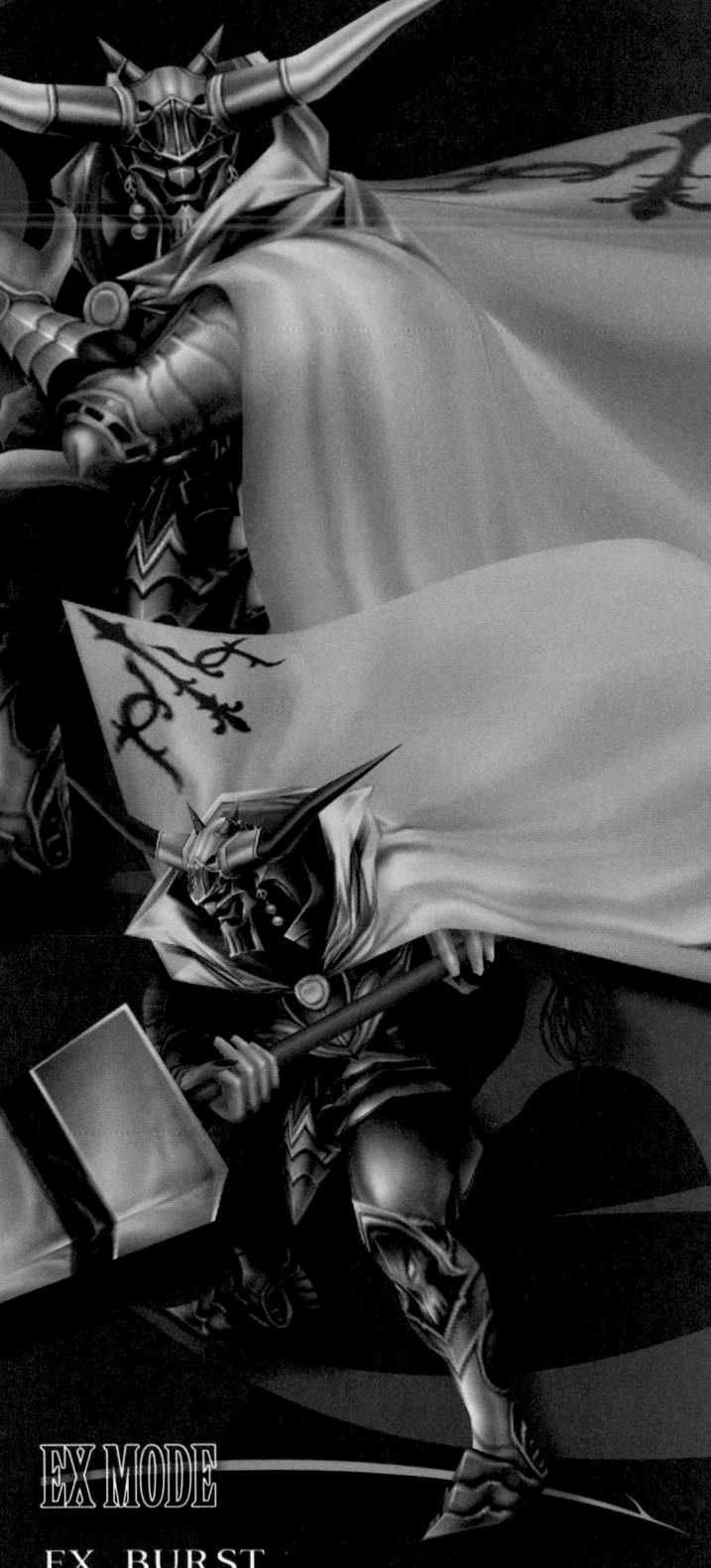

ABILITY PROGRESSION

LEVEL	SKILL	TYPE	CP (N)	CP (M)	AP TO MASTER	ATTACK COMMANDS & EFFECTS*
01	Blaze (midair)	HP Attack (Air)	40	20	180	● (Map Break)
01	Deathblow	Bravery Attack (Land)	20	10	90	● (Map Break)
01	Chain Cast	Bravery Attack (Air)	30	15	180	● (Map Break, Chase)
01	Earthquake	HP Attack (Land)	40	20	180	● (Guard Crush, Map Break, Wall Rush)
01	Round Edge	Bravery Attack (Land)	30	15	120	● (Movement OK, Map Break) ● (Map Break) ● (Map Break)
01	Twin Swords	Bravery Attack (Air)	30	15	180	● (Map Break, Wall Rush)
03	Bardiche	Bravery Attack (Air)	30	15	180	● (Map Break, Wall Rush)
04	Air Dash	Action	10	5	100	● during Quickmove
07	Speed Boost	Action	20	10	150	
(Mastery)	Speed Boost+	Action	40	20	150	-
(Mastery)	Speed Boost++	Action	70	35	150	-
08	Lance Charge	Bravery Attack (Land)	30	15	120	● (Map Break) ● (Map Break, Wall Rush)
11	Auto Recovery	Support	20	5	250	
11	Auto Chase	Support	20	5	250	-
13	Blaze (ground)	HP Attack (Land)	40	20	180	● (Map Break)
15	Auto EX Burst	Support	20	5	150	
15	Auto EX Command	Support	30	10	300	
18	Reverse Air Dash	Action	10	5	100	● during Quickmove
19	Twist Drill	Bravery Attack (Air)	30	15	180	● (Map Break) ● (Map Break, Chase)
21	Jump Boost	Action	10	5	150	-
(Mastery)	Jump Boost+	Action	20	10	150	-
(Mastery)	Jump Boost++	Action	40	20	150	-
24	Highbringer	Bravery Attack (Land)	30	15	120	● (Map Break) ● (Map Break, Chase) ● (Precise timing, Map Break) ● (Map Break, Wall Rush)
25	EX Critical Boost	Extra	45	40	300	-
26	Auto EX Defense	Support	30	10	300	
29	Reverse Free Air Dash	Action	10	5	100	■ + ▲
30	Cyclone	HP Attack (Air)	40	20	300	● (Pulls in, Guard Crush, Map Break)
32	Recovery Attack	Action	20	10	120	● or ● while reeling
32	Controlled Recovery	Action	10	5	120	Analog Stick during Recovery
35	Riposte	Extra	45	40	300	-
(Mastery)	Disable Riposte	Extra	20	10	300	
38	Tsunami	HP Attack (Land)	40	20	300	● (Guard Crush, Map Break)
39	Jump Times Boost	Action	20	10	150	-
(Mastery)	Jump Times Boost+	Action	40	20	150	-
(Mastery)	Jump Times Boost++	Action	70	30	150	-
40	Omni Air Dash	Action	40	20	300	Analog Stick ┃ ●
43	Sneak Attack	Extra	50	45	360	-
(Mastery)	Disable Sneak Attack	Extra	30	15	360	-
47	Physical Shield	Extra	20	10	280	-
50	Magic Shield	Extra	20	10	280	-
53	Multi-Air Slide	Action	10	5	250	Analog Stick + ✕ after expending jumps
(Mastery)	Multi-Air Slide+	Action	30	15	300	See Multi-Air Slide
57	Midair Evasion Boost	Action	20	10	150	-
60	Bravery Regen	Extra	20	10	280	-
64	Evasion Time Boost	Support	20	10	220	-
67	First Strike	Extra	40	35	360	-
(Mastery)	Disable First Strike	Extra	20	10	360	-
71	Concentration	Extra	30	15	250	
(Mastery)	Concentration+	Extra	60	30	250	
(Mastery)	Concentration++	Extra	100	50	250	
74	Cat Nip	Extra	30	25	300	
(Mastery)	Disable Cat Nip	Extra	20	10	300	
78	Anti-EX	Extra	30	20	300	
(Mastery)	Disable Anti-EX	Extra	20	10	300	
81	Achy	Extra	30	15	250	
(Mastery)	Achy+	Extra	60	30	250	
85	Counterattack	Extra	50	45	360	
(Mastery)	Disable Counterattack	Extra	30	15	360	
88	Gambler's Spirit	Extra	30	15	300	
(Mastery)	Disable Gambler's Spirit	Extra	20	10	300	
92	Back to the Wall	Extra	30	25	300	
(Mastery)	Disable Back to the Wall	Extra	20	10	300	
95	Precision Jump	Extra	10	5	180	
98	Snooze and Lose	Extra	100	50	250	
100	EXP to HP	Extra	20	0	500	
100	EXP to Bravery	Extra	20	0	500	
100	EXP to EX Force	Extra	20	0	500	

*Initial commands may require directional presses, depending on the slot to which abilities are assigned.

EX MODE

EX BURST

Soul of Chaos: An attack terrible enough to shake the heavens. (Repeatedly press ● to add strength to the attack.)

EX EFFECTS

Regen: Vigor and stamina recover little by little, restoring HP.

Indomitable Resolve: Even while taking damage, attacks can be performed without flinching.

FIRION

Weapons Specialist—Reels distant and aerial opponents in for melee combat on solid ground.

A young warrior skilled in many types of weaponry. He is hot-blooded, with a strong sense of duty. In Final Fantasy II, his hometown of Fynn was invaded by the Empire of Palamecia, killing his parents and severely wounding him. Later he joined a resistance group identifying themselves by the watchword "Wild Rose." This reference to his hometown holds deep meaning for him, but he is reluctant to speak it aloud for fear of attracting imperial soldiers.

BASIC MOBILITY*

Ground Movement Speed	⭐⭐✰
Innate Number of Jumps	1
Jump Height	⭐
Jump Rising Speed	⭐⭐✰
Air Dash Speed	⭐⭐✰
Quickmove Speed	⭐⭐✰

*Mobility can be increased with the abilities Speed Boost, Jump Boost, Jump Times Boost, and Precision Jump.

EQUIPMENT

Weapon	All
Hands	Parrying Weapons, Shields, Bangles
Head	Hats, Helms
Body	Clothing, Light Armor

STAT PROGRESSION

LV	HP	CP	BRV	ATK	DEF	LUK
1	1000	330	95	12	13	10
5	1242	335	118	16	17	12
10	1545	341	147	21	22	15
20	2151	353	205	31	32	20
30	2757	365	263	41	42	25
40	3363	377	320	51	52	30
50	3969	389	378	61	62	35
60	4575	401	436	71	72	40
70	5181	413	493	81	82	45
80	5787	425	551	91	92	50
90	6393	437	609	101	102	55
100	6999	450	667	111	112	60

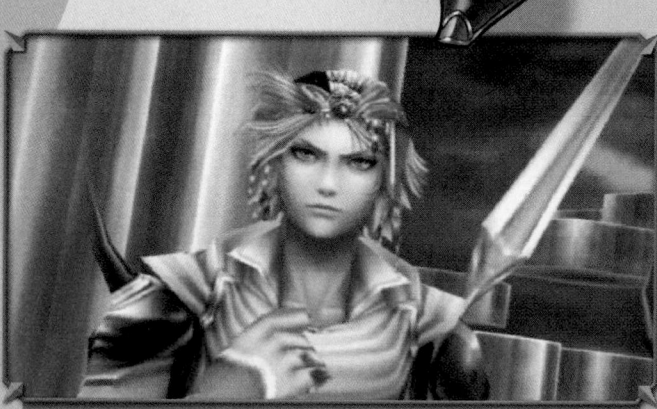

Firion is driven by a dream he is almost embarrassed to admit to his comrades.

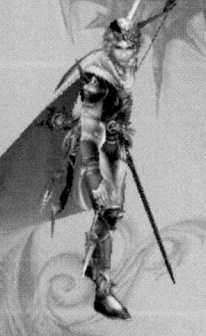

Firion (Normal)

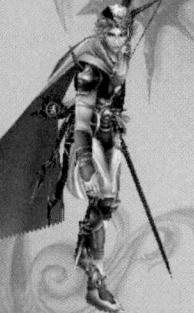

EX Mode (Normal)

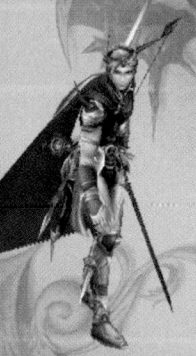

Firon (Alternate)

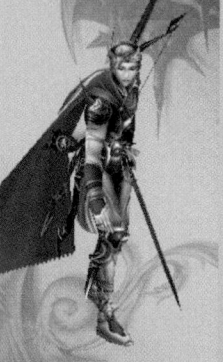

EX Mode (Alternate)

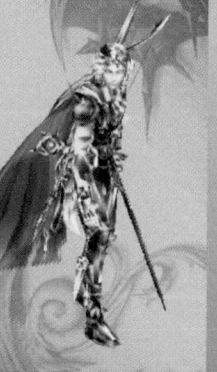

Imitation Liegeman

ABILITY PROGRESSION

LEVEL	SKILL	TYPE	CP (N)	CP (M)	AP TO MASTER	ATTACK COMMAND & EFFECTS*
01	Blizzard	Bravery Attack (Air)	20	10	120	◉
01	Fire	Bravery Attack (Air)	20	10	120	◉
01	Reel Axe	Bravery Attack (Land)	30	15	90	◉ (Pull in, Guard Crush) ◉ (Map Break, Wall Rush)
(Mastery)	Double Trouble C	Combo Attack	40	20	300	◉ after first ◉ press during Reel Axe (Guard Crush, Map Break, Wall Rush)
01	Rope Knife	Bravery Attack (Land)	30	15	90	◉ (Pull in, Map Break) ◉ (Wall Rush)
(Mastery)	Double Trouble B	Combo Attack	40	20	300	◉ after first ◉ press during Rope Knife (Guard Crush, Map Break, Wall Rush)
01	Straightarrow (ground)	HP Attack (Land)	40	20	180	◉ (can be held; Map Break, Wall Rush)
01	Straightarrow (midair)	HP Attack (Air)	40	20	180	◉ (can be held; Map Break, Wall Rush)
03	Lance Combo	Bravery Attack (Land)	30	15	90	◉ (Pull in) ◉ (Map Break, Chase) ◉ (Map Break, Wall Rush)
(Mastery)	Double Trouble A	Combo Attack	40	20	300	◉ after first ◉ press during Lance Combo (Guard Crush, Map Break, Wall Rush)
04	Air Dash	Action	10	5	100	▲ during Quickmove
07	Speed Boost	Action	20	10	150	-
(Mastery)	Speed Boost+	Action	40	20	150	-
(Mastery)	Speed Boost++	Action	70	35	150	-
09	Swordslash (ground)	Bravery Attack (Land)	20	10	120	◉ (Chase)
11	Auto Recovery	Support	20	5	250	-
11	Auto Chase	Support	20	5	250	-
15	Auto EX Burst	Support	20	5	150	-
15	Auto EX Command	Support	30	10	300	-
16	Thunder	Bravery Attack (Air)	20	10	120	◉
18	Reverse Air Dash	Action	10	5	100	▲ during Quickmove
21	Jump Boost	Action	10	5	150	-
(Mastery)	Jump Boost+	Action	20	10	150	-
(Mastery)	Jump Boost++	Action	40	20	150	-
23	Swordslash (midair)	Bravery Attack (Air)	20	10	80	◉ (Chase)
25	EX Critical Boost	Extra	45	40	300	-
26	Auto EX Defense	Support	30	10	300	-
29	Reverse Free Air Dash	Action	10	5	100	◼ + ▲
30	Shield Bash	HP Attack (Land)	40	20	180	◉ (Guard; if Guard activates, Guard Crush and Map Break)
32	Recovery Attack	Action	20	10	120	◉ or ◼ while reeling
32	Controlled Recovery	Action	10	5	120	Analog Stick after Recovery
35	Riposte	Extra	45	40	300	-
(Mastery)	Disable Riposte	Extra	20	10	300	-
38	Weaponsmaster	HP Attack (Air)	40	20	300	◉ (Guard Crush, Map Break, Wall Rush)
39	Jump Times Boost	Action	20	10	150	-
(Mastery)	Jump Times Boost+	Action	40	20	150	-
(Mastery)	Jump Times Boost++	Action	70	30	150	-
40	Omni Air Dash	Action	40	20	300	Analog Stick + ◼ + ▲
43	Sneak Attack	Extra	50	45	360	-
(Mastery)	Disable Sneak Attack	Extra	30	15	360	-
47	Physical Shield	Extra	20	10	280	-
50	Magic Shield	Extra	20	10	280	-
53	Multi-Air Slide	Action	10	5	250	Analog Stick + ✖ after expending jumps
(Mastery)	Multi-Air Slide+	Action	30	15	300	See Multi-Air Slide
57	Midair Evasion Boost	Action	20	10	150	-
60	Bravery Regen	Extra	20	10	280	-
64	Evasion Time Boost	Support	20	10	220	-
67	First Strike	Extra	40	35	360	-
(Mastery)	Disable First Strike	Extra	20	10	360	-
71	Concentration	Extra	30	15	250	-
(Mastery)	Concentration+	Extra	60	30	250	-
(Mastery)	Concentration++	Extra	100	50	250	-
74	Cat Nip	Extra	30	25	300	-
(Mastery)	Disable Cat Nip	Extra	20	10	300	-
78	Anti-EX	Extra	30	20	300	-
(Mastery)	Disable Anti-EX	Extra	20	10	300	-
81	Achy	Extra	30	15	250	-
(Mastery)	Achy+	Extra	60	30	250	-
85	Counterattack	Extra	50	45	360	-
(Mastery)	Disable Counterattack	Extra	30	15	360	-
88	Gambler's Spirit	Extra	30	15	300	-
(Mastery)	Disable Gambler's Spirit	Extra	20	10	300	-
92	Back to the Wall	Extra	30	25	300	-
(Mastery)	Disable Back to the Wall	Extra	20	10	300	-
95	Precision Jump	Extra	10	5	180	-
98	Snooze and Lose	Extra	100	50	250	-
100	EXP to HP	Extra	20	0	500	-
100	EXP to Bravery	Extra	20	0	500	-
100	EXP to EX Force	Extra	20	0	500	-

*Initial commands may require directional presses, depending on the slot to which abilities are assigned.

EX MODE

EX BURST

Fervid Blazer: A chain of attacks releasing the power of his weapons. Damage dealt adds to his own HP. (Enter the commands that display before the attack.)

EX EFFECTS

Regen: Vigor and stamina recover little by little, restoring HP.

Blood Weapon: Absorbs HP equivalent to damage dealt.

CHARACTERS

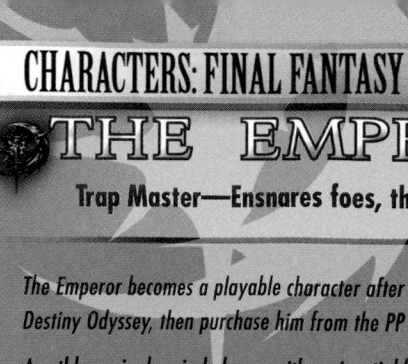

THE EMPEROR

Trap Master—Ensnares foes, then batters them with HP attacks.

The Emperor becomes a playable character after you finish any Destiny Odyssey, then purchase him from the PP Catalog.

A ruthless, single-minded man with an insatiable lust for power. In Final Fantasy II, he led the military empire of Palamecia, bringing country after country under his heel. With his incredible sorcery, he was even able to command demons and the Cyclone. He will do anything for power—including selling his soul. His pride is almost fearsome in its intensity.

BASIC MOBILITY*

Ground Movement Speed	⭐⭐
Innate Number of Jumps	1
Jump Height	⭐
Jump Rising Speed	⭐
Air Dash Speed	⭐⭐
Quickmove Speed	⭐⭐

EQUIPMENT

Weapon	Swords, Daggers, Rods, Staves
Hands	Bangles
Head	Hats, Hairpins
Body	Clothing, Robes

*Mobility can be increased with the abilities Speed Boost, Jump Boost, Jump Times Boost, and Precision Jump.

STAT PROGRESSION

LV	HP	CP	BRV	ATK	DEF	LUK
1	1000	330	95	11	13	10
5	1242	335	118	15	17	12
10	1545	341	147	20	22	15
20	2151	353	205	30	32	20
30	2757	365	263	40	42	25
40	3363	377	320	50	52	30
50	3969	389	378	60	62	35
60	4575	401	436	70	72	40
70	5181	413	493	80	82	45
80	5787	425	551	90	92	50
90	6393	437	609	100	102	55
100	6999	450	667	110	112	60

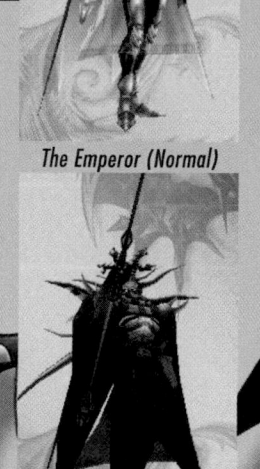

The Emperor (Normal)

EX Mode (Normal)

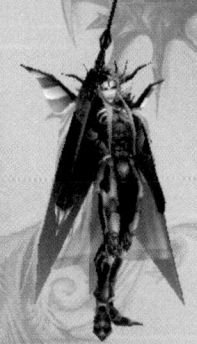

The Emperor (Alternate)

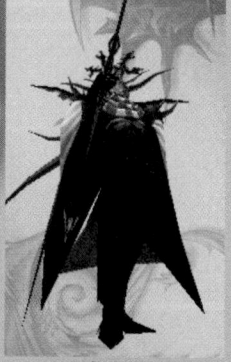

EX Mode (Alternate)

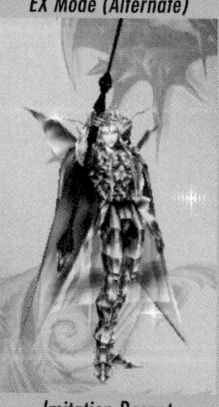

Imitation Despot

> Tremble in fear... Now I have powers the likes of which even gods can only dream!

The Emperor thinks himself the puppetmaster of the whole ordeal, and imagines he can bend even the whim of the gods to his will. Whether that's true remains to be seen...

ABILITY PROGRESSION

LEVEL	SKILL	TYPE	CP (N)	CP (M)	AP TO MASTER	ATTACK COMMANDS & EFFECTS*
01	Flare (ground)	HP Attack (Land)	40	20	180	◉ (Guard Crush, Map Break)
01	Flare (midair)	HP Attack (Air)	40	20	180	◉ (Guard Crush, Map Break)
01	Landmine	Bravery Attack (Land)	20	10	90	◉ (Pull-in, Map Break)
01	Light Crest (midair)	Bravery Attack (Air)	30	15	180	◉ (Map Break)
01	Mine	Bravery Attack (Air)	20	10	90	◉ (Pull-in, Map Break)
01	Thunder Crest	Bravery Attack (Land)	30	15	120	◉ (Pull-in, Map Break)
02	Reverse Free Air Dash	Action	10	5	100	▰▰ + ⬤
03	Bombard	Bravery Attack (Land)	30	15	120	◉ (Guard Crush, Map Break, Chase)
04	Air Dash	Action	10	5	100	⬤ during Quickmove
07	Jump Boost	Action	10	5	150	-
(Mastery)	Jump Boost+	Action	20	10	150	-
(Mastery)	Jump Boost++	Action	40	20	150	-
08	Dynamite (ground)	Bravery Attack (Land)	30	15	120	◉ hold longer for larger explosive; gains power after holding for 1.7 and 2.7 seconds (Pull-in, Map Break)
11	Auto Recovery	Support	20	5	250	-
11	Auto Chase	Support	20	5	250	-
14	Light Crest (ground)	Bravery Attack (Land)	30	15	120	◉ (Map Break)
15	Auto EX Burst	Support	20	5	150	-
15	Auto EX Command	Support	30	10	300	-
18	Reverse Air Dash	Action	10	5	100	⬤ during Quickmove
20	Starfall (ground)	HP Attack (Land)	40	20	300	◉ (Move OK, Pull-in, Map Break)
21	Speed Boost	Action	20	10	150	-
(Mastery)	Speed Boost+	Action	40	20	150	-
(Mastery)	Speed Boost++	Action	70	35	150	-
25	EX Critical Boost	Extra	45	40	300	-
26	Auto EX Defense	Support	30	10	300	-
28	Dynamite (midair)	Bravery Attack (Air)	30	15	180	◉ hold longer for larger explosive; gains power after holding for 1.7 and 2.7 seconds (Pull-in, Map Break)
32	Recovery Attack	Action	20	10	120	◉ or ⬤ while reeling
32	Controlled Recovery	Action	10	5	120	Analog Stick during Recovery
35	Riposte	Extra	45	40	300	-
(Mastery)	Disable Riposte	Extra	20	10	300	-
38	Starfall (midair)	HP Attack (Air)	40	20	300	-
39	Jump Times Boost	Action	20	10	150	-
(Mastery)	Jump Times Boost+	Action	40	20	150	-
(Mastery)	Jump Times Boost++	Action	70	30	150	-
40	Omni Air Dash	Action	40	20	300	Analog Stick + ▰▰ + ⬤
43	Sneak Attack	Extra	50	45	360	-
(Mastery)	Disable Sneak Attack	Extra	30	15	360	-
47	Physical Shield	Extra	20	10	280	-
50	Magic Shield	Extra	20	10	280	-
53	Multi-Air Slide	Action	10	5	250	✕ after expending jumps
(Mastery)	Multi-Air Slide+	Action	30	15	300	See Multi-Air Slide
57	Midair Evasion Boost	Action	20	10	150	-
60	Bravery Regen	Extra	20	10	280	-
64	Evasion Time Boost	Support	20	10	220	-
67	First Strike	Extra	40	35	360	-
(Mastery)	Disable First Strike	Extra	20	10	360	-
71	Concentration	Extra	30	15	250	-
(Mastery)	Concentration+	Extra	60	30	250	-
(Mastery)	Concentration++	Extra	100	50	250	-
74	Cat Nip	Extra	30	25	300	-
(Mastery)	Disable Cat Nip	Extra	20	10	300	-
78	Anti-EX	Extra	30	20	300	-
(Mastery)	Disable Anti-EX	Extra	20	10	300	-
81	Achy	Extra	30	15	250	-
(Mastery)	Achy+	Extra	60	30	250	-
85	Counterattack	Extra	50	45	360	-
(Mastery)	Disable Counterattack	Extra	30	15	360	-
88	Gambler's Spirit	Extra	30	15	300	-
(Mastery)	Disable Gambler's Spirit	Extra	20	10	300	-
92	Back to the Wall	Extra	30	25	300	-
(Mastery)	Disable Back to the Wall	Extra	20	10	300	-
95	Precision Jump	Extra	10	5	180	-
98	Snooze and Lose	Extra	100	50	250	-
100	EXP to HP	Extra	20	0	500	-
100	EXP to Bravery	Extra	20	0	500	-
100	EXP to EX Force	Extra	20	0	500	-

*Initial commands may require directional presses, depending on the slot to which abilities are assigned.

EX MODE

EX BURST

Absolute Dominion: An attack that takes over the opponent's mind. HP damage dealt is absorbed. (Enter the commands that display on the screen.)

EX EFFECTS

Regen: Vigor and stamina recover little by little, restoring HP.

Blood Magic: Absorbs HP equivalent to damage dealt.

ONION KNIGHT

Mystic Fencer—Hails light, speedy attacks down upon opponents.

A youth bearing the title of Onion Knight. Intelligent and mischievous, he unquestionably believes he can accomplish anything in the world. In Final Fantasy III, he was an orphan raised by Topapa, the Ur village elder. After a sudden earthquake opened a cavern in the ground, the boy and his friends went to investigate and fell into the Altar Cave. Eventually, they were chosen as Warriors of the Light by the Wind Crystal.

BASIC MOBILITY*

Ground Movement Speed	★★★
Innate Number of Jumps	4
Jump Height	★
Jump Rising Speed	★★
Air Dash Speed	★★
Quickmove Speed	★★★

EQUIPMENT

Weapon	Swords, Daggers, Rods, Staves, Thrown Weapons
Hands	Parrying Weapons, Bangles, Gauntlets
Head	Hats, Hairpins
Body	Clothing, Light Armor

*Mobility can be increased with the abilities Speed Boost, Jump Boost, Jump Times Boost, and Precision Jump.

STAT PROGRESSION

LV	HP	CP	BRV	ATK	DEF	LUK
1	1000	350	95	8	12	10
5	1242	354	118	12	16	12
10	1545	359	147	17	21	15
20	2151	369	205	27	31	20
30	2757	379	263	37	41	25
40	3363	389	320	47	51	30
50	3969	399	378	57	61	35
60	4575	409	436	67	71	40
70	5181	419	493	77	81	45
80	5787	429	551	87	91	50
90	6393	439	609	97	101	55
100	6999	450	667	107	111	60

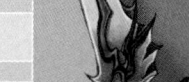

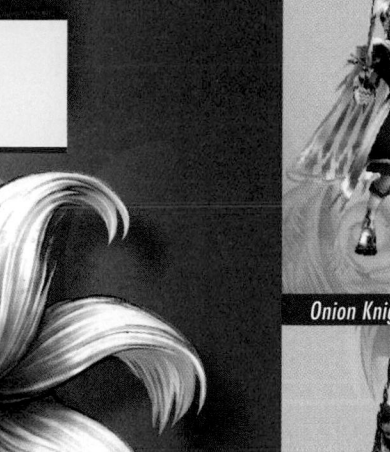

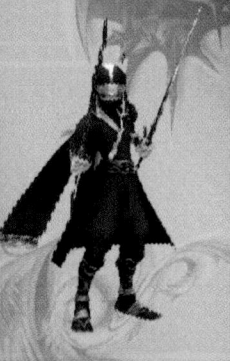
Onion Knight (Normal)

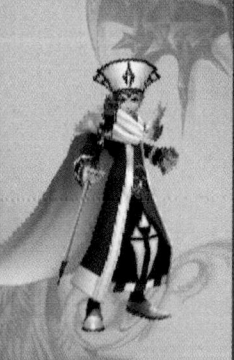
EX Mode - Ninja (Normal)

EX Mode – Sage (Normal)

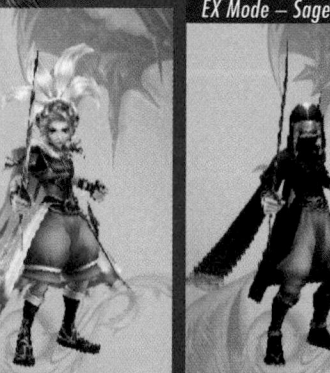

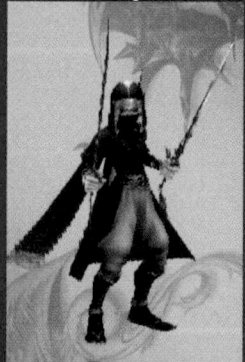
Onion Knight (Alternate)

EX Mode – Ninja (Alternate)

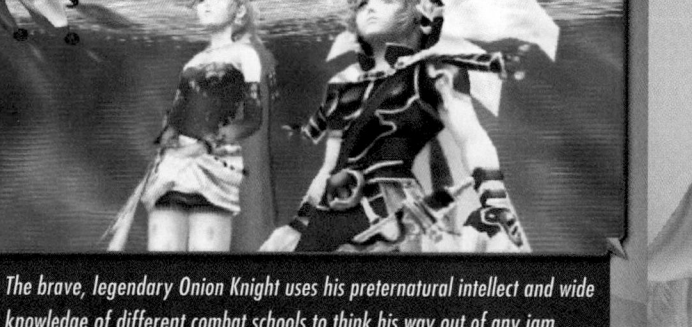
The brave, legendary Onion Knight uses his preternatural intellect and wide knowledge of different combat schools to think his way out of any jam.

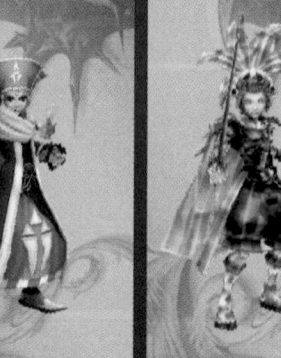
EX Mode – Sage (Alternate)

Counterfeit Youth

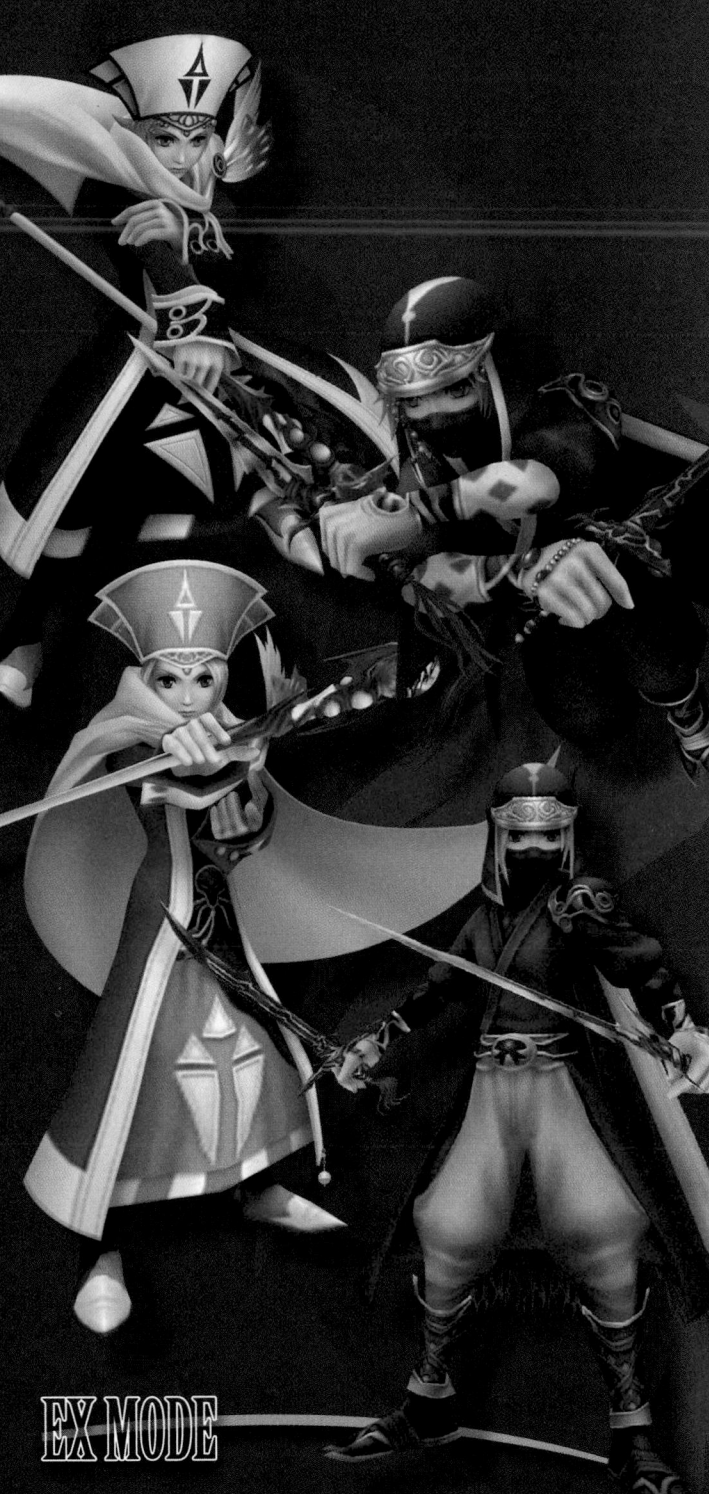

ABILITY PROGRESSION

LEVEL	SKILL	TYPE	CP (N)	CP (M)	AP TO MASTER	ATTACK COMMANDS & EFFECTS*
01	Blade Torrent	HP Attack (Land)	40	20	180	◉ (Guard Crush, Map Break, Wall Rush)
01	Blizzard	Bravery Attack (Land)	20	10	30	◉ (Map Break in EX Mode)
(Mastery)	Blizzaga	Combo Attack	30	15	120	◉ after Blizzard (Map Break, Wall Rush)
(Mastery)	Quake	Combo Attack	40	20	300	◉ after Blizzard (Guard Crush, Map Break)
01	Comet	HP Attack (Air)	40	20	180	◉ (Move OK, Guard Crush, Map Break)
01	Multi-Hit	Bravery Attack (Land)	30	15	60	◉
(Mastery)	Extra Slice	Combo Attack	30	15	90	◉ after Multi-Hit (Map Break, Wall Rush)
(Mastery)	Swordshower	Combo Attack	40	20	300	◉ after Multi-Hit (Guard Crush, Map Break, Wall Rush)
01	Thunder	Bravery Attack (Air)	20	10	60	◉ (Map Break in EX Mode)
(Mastery)	Thundaga	Combo Attack	30	15	180	◉ after Thunder (Map Break, Chase)
(Mastery)	Flare	Combo Attack	40	20	300	◉ after Thunder (Guard Crush, Map Break)
01	Turbo-Hit	Bravery Attack (Air)	30	15	15	◉
(Mastery)	Extra Lunge	Combo Attack	30	15	120	◉ after Turbo-Hit (Map Break, Chase)
(Mastery)	Guiding Swipe	Combo Attack	40	20	300	◉ after Turbo-Hit (Guard Crush, Map Break, Wall Rush)
04	Air Dash	Action	10	5	100	◉ during Quickmove
07	Jump Boost	Action	10	5	150	-
(Mastery)	Jump Boost+	Action	20	10	150	-
(Mastery)	Jump Boost++	Action	40	20	150	-
11	Auto Recovery	Support	20	5	250	-
11	Auto Chase	Support	20	5	250	-
13	Firaga	HP Attack (Land)	40	20	180	◉ (Guard Crush, Map Break)
15	Auto EX Burst	Support	20	5	150	-
15	Auto EX Command	Support	30	10	300	-
18	Reverse Air Dash	Action	10	5	100	▲ during Quickmove
21	Speed Boost	Action	20	10	150	-
(Mastery)	Speed Boost+	Action	40	20	150	-
(Mastery)	Speed Boost++	Action	70	35	150	-
25	EX Critical Boost	Extra	45	40	300	-
26	Auto EX Defense	Support	30	10	300	-
28	Wind Shear	HP Attack (Air)	40	20	180	◉ (Move OK, Guard Crush, Pull-in, Map Break, Wall Rush)
29	Reverse Free Air Dash	Action	10	5	100	▣ + ▲
32	Recovery Attack	Action	20	10	120	◎ or ◉ while reeling
32	Controlled Recovery	Action	10	5	120	Analog Stick during Recovery
35	Riposte	Extra	45	40	300	-
(Mastery)	Disable Riposte	Extra	20	10	300	-
39	Jump Times Boost	Action	20	10	150	-
(Mastery)	Jump Times Boost+	Action	40	20	150	-
(Mastery)	Jump Times Boost++	Action	70	30	150	-
40	Omni Air Dash	Action	40	20	300	Analog Stick + ▣ + ▲
43	Sneak Attack	Extra	50	45	360	-
(Mastery)	Disable Sneak Attack	Extra	30	15	360	-
47	Physical Shield	Extra	20	10	280	-
50	Magic Shield	Extra	20	10	280	-
53	Multi-Air Slide	Action	10	5	250	Analog Stick + ✕ after expending jumps
(Mastery)	Multi-Air Slide+	Action	30	15	300	See Multi-Air Slide
57	Midair Evasion Boost	Action	20	10	150	-
60	Bravery Regen	Extra	20	10	280	-
64	Evasion Time Boost	Support	20	10	220	-
67	First Strike	Extra	40	35	360	-
(Mastery)	Disable First Strike	Extra	20	10	360	-
71	Concentration	Extra	30	15	250	-
(Mastery)	Concentration+	Extra	60	30	250	-
(Mastery)	Concentration++	Extra	100	50	250	-
74	Cat Nip	Extra	30	25	300	-
(Mastery)	Disable Cat Nip	Extra	20	10	300	-
78	Anti-EX	Extra	30	20	300	-
(Mastery)	Disable Anti-EX	Extra	20	10	300	-
81	Achy	Extra	30	15	250	-
(Mastery)	Achy+	Extra	60	30	250	-
85	Counterattack	Extra	50	45	360	-
(Mastery)	Disable Counterattack	Extra	30	15	360	-
88	Gambler's Spirit	Extra	30	15	300	-
(Mastery)	Disable Gambler's Spirit	Extra	20	10	300	-
92	Back to the Wall	Extra	30	25	300	-
(Mastery)	Disable Back to the Wall	Extra	20	10	300	-
95	Precision Jump	Extra	10	5	180	-
98	Snooze and Lose	Extra	100	50	250	-
100	EXP to HP	Extra	20	0	500	-
100	EXP to Bravery	Extra	20	0	500	-
100	EXP to EX Force	Extra	20	0	500	-

*Initial commands may require directional presses, depending on the slot to which abilities are assigned.

EX MODE

EX BURST

Ninjutsu: Throw the ninja's strongest weapon—the shuriken. (From the menu that displays, find and select "Shuriken.")

Spellbook: Cast the sage's strongest spell—Holy. (From the menu that displays, find and select "Holy.")

EX EFFECTS

Regen: Vigor and stamina recover little by little, restoring HP.

Dual Wield: Attacks move faster than the eye can see to snatch a greater amount of bravery. (Job change to Ninja when performing physical attack.)

Sage's Wisdom: Releases sealed mystic power, making spells stronger. (Job changes to Sage when performing a magic attack.)

CLOUD OF DARKNESS

Bane of Life—Harries foes from afar with a wide variety of HP-attacking energy beams.

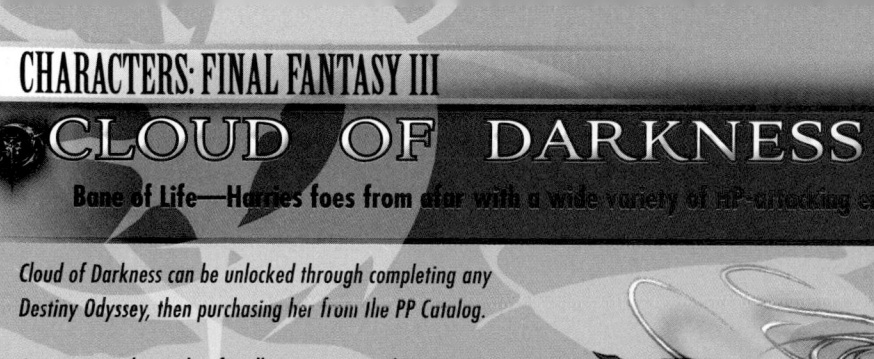

Cloud of Darkness can be unlocked through completing any Destiny Odyssey, then purchasing her from the PP Catalog.

An existence that wishes for all to return to nothingness. She has transcended the abstract and is the embodiment of fear. In Final Fantasy III, she had been defeated by a flood of light 1000 years earlier. However, a flood of darkness created by Master Xande allowed her to return. Seeing the imbalances of light and darkness in the world, she decided to destroy all existence. The two tentacles at her right and left have differing special abilities. It is rumored their personalities are different as well.

BASIC MOBILITY*

Ground Movement Speed	★★☆
Innate Number of Jumps	1
Jump Height	★★☆
Jump Rising Speed	★
Air Dash Speed	★
Quickmove Speed	★

*Mobility can be increased with the abilities Speed Boost, Jump Boost, Jump Times Boost, and Precision Jump.

EQUIPMENT

Weapon	Rods, Staves
Hands	Bangles
Head	Hats, Hairpins
Body	Clothing, Robes

STAT PROGRESSION

LV	HP	CP	BRV	ATK	DEF	LUK
1	1000	330	95	10	12	10
5	1242	335	118	14	16	12
10	1545	341	147	19	21	15
20	2151	353	205	29	31	20
30	2757	365	263	39	41	25
40	3363	377	320	49	51	30
50	3969	389	378	59	61	35
60	4575	401	436	69	71	40
70	5181	413	493	79	81	45
80	5787	425	551	89	91	50
90	6393	437	609	99	101	55
100	6999	450	667	109	111	60

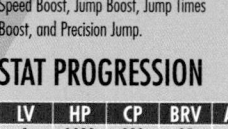

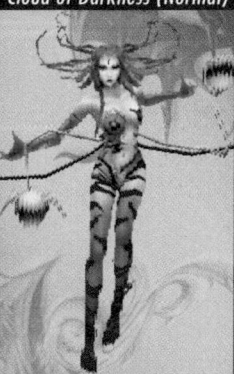

Cloud of Darkness (Normal)

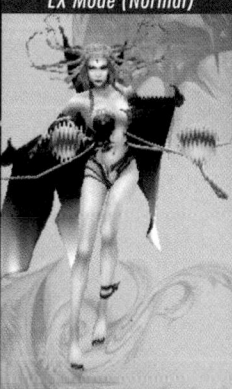

EX Mode (Normal)

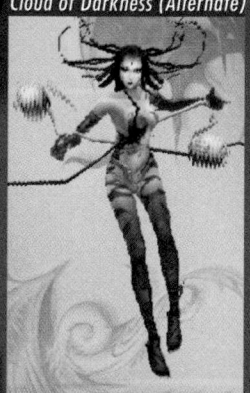

Cloud of Darkness (Alternate)

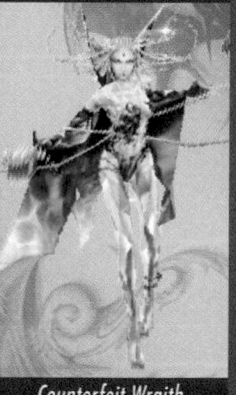

EX Mode (Alternate)

Counterfeit Wraith

Many minions of Chaos are Machiavellian schemers with their own agendas. Cloud of Darkness, like Exdeath, is more elemental and single-minded—she simply wishes for the return of all to nothing.

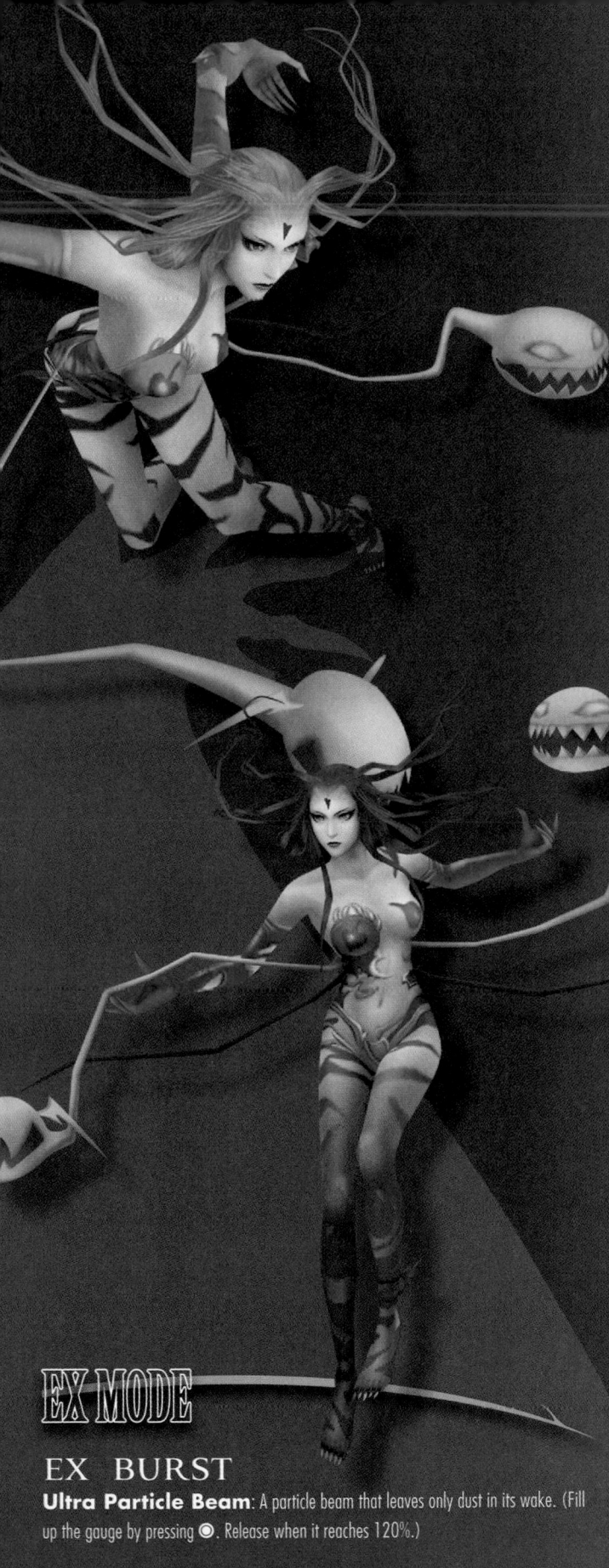

ABILITY PROGRESSION

LEVEL	SKILL	TYPE	CP (N)	CP (M)	AP TO MASTER	ATTACK COMMANDS & EFFECTS*
01	Tentacle of Pain	Bravery Attack (Land)	50	25	140	◉ for triple swipe (Move OK) then ◉ during first swipe (Map Break, Chase) or ◉ during second swipe (Map Break, Wall Rush) or ◉ during third swipe
01	Tentacle of Suffering	Bravery Attack (Air)	50	25	120	◉ for triple swipe (Move OK) then ◉ during first swipe (Map Break, Chase) or ◉ during second swipe (Map Break) or ◉ during third swipe
01	[Anti-Air] Particle Beam	HP Attack (Land)	40	20	180	◉ (Guard Crush, Map Break)
01	[Long-Range] Particle Beam	HP Attack (Land)	40	20	300	◉ (Guard Crush, Map Break)
01	Aura Ball	HP Attack (Air)	40	20	180	Press and hold ◉ (charge to generate up to five spheres, release to detonate, Move OK, Guard Crush, Map Break)
01	[Wrath] Particle Bream (midair)	HP Attack (Air)	40	20	180	◉ (Guard, if incoming attack guarded, then Guard Crush and Map Break)
04	Air Dash	Action	10	5	100	◉ during Quickmove
07	Jump Boost	Action	10	5	150	-
(Mastery)	Jump Boost+	Action	20	10	150	-
(Mastery)	Jump Boost++	Action	40	20	150	-
11	Auto Recovery	Support	20	5	250	-
11	Auto Chase	Support	20	5	250	-
12	[Wrath] Particle Bream (ground)	HP Attack (Land)	40	20	180	◉ (Guard, if incoming attack guarded, then Guard Crush and Map Break)
15	Auto EX Burst	Support	20	5	150	-
15	Auto EX Command	Support	30	10	300	-
17	[Fusillade] Particle Beam		40	20	180	-
18	Reverse Air Dash	Action	10	5	100	◉ during Quickmove
21	Speed Boost	Action	20	10	150	-
(Mastery)	Speed Boost+	Action	40	20	150	-
(Mastery)	Speed Boost++	Action	70	35	150	-
24	[Feint] Particle Beam	HP Attack (Land)	40	20	180	◉ (Guard Crush, Wall Rush, Map Break, Evades attacks)
25	EX Critical Boost	Extra	45	40	300	-
26	Auto EX Defense	Support	30	10	300	-
29	Reverse Free Air Dash	Action	10	5	100	■ + ▲
32	Recovery Attack	Action	20	10	120	◉ or ◉ while reeling
32	Controlled Recovery	Action	10	5	120	◉ during Recovery
35	Riposte	Extra	45	40	300	-
(Mastery)	Disable Riposte	Extra	20	10	300	-
38	[O-Form] Particle Beam	HP Attack (Air)	40	20	300	◉ Guard Crush, Map Break, Wall Rush
39	Jump Times Boost	Action	20	10	150	-
(Mastery)	Jump Times Boost+	Action	40	20	150	-
(Mastery)	Jump Times Boost++	Action	70	30	150	-
40	Omni Air Dash	Action	40	20	300	● + ■ + ▲
43	Sneak Attack	Extra	50	45	360	-
(Mastery)	Disable Sneak Attack	Extra	30	15	360	-
47	Physical Shield	Extra	20	10	280	-
50	Magic Shield	Extra	20	10	280	-
53	Multi-Air Slide	Action	10	5	250	● + ✕ after expending jumps
(Mastery)	Multi-Air Slide+	Action	30	15	300	See Multi-Air Slide
57	Midair Evasion Boost	Action	20	10	150	-
60	Bravery Regen	Extra	20	10	280	-
64	Evasion Time Boost	Support	20	10	220	-
67	First Strike	Extra	40	35	360	-
(Mastery)	Disable First Strike	Extra	20	10	360	-
71	Concentration	Extra	30	15	250	-
(Mastery)	Concentration+	Extra	60	30	250	-
(Mastery)	Concentration++	Extra	100	50	250	-
74	Cat Nip	Extra	30	25	300	-
(Mastery)	Disable Cat Nip	Extra	20	10	300	-
78	Anti-EX	Extra	30	20	300	-
(Mastery)	Disable Anti-EX	Extra	20	10	300	-
81	Achy	Extra	30	15	250	-
(Mastery)	Achy+	Extra	60	30	250	-
85	Counterattack	Extra	50	45	360	-
(Mastery)	Disable Counterattack	Extra	30	15	360	-
88	Gambler's Spirit	Extra	30	15	300	-
(Mastery)	Disable Gambler's Spirit	Extra	20	10	300	-
92	Back to the Wall	Extra	30	25	300	-
(Mastery)	Disable Back to the Wall	Extra	20	10	300	-
95	Precision Jump	Extra	10	5	180	-
98	Snooze and Lose	Extra	100	50	250	-
100	EXP to HP	Extra	20	0	500	-
100	EXP to Bravery	Extra	20	0	500	-
100	EXP to EX Force	Extra	20	0	500	-

*Initial commands may require directional presses, depending on the slot to which abilities are assigned.

EX MODE

EX BURST

Ultra Particle Beam: A particle beam that leaves only dust in its wake. (Fill up the gauge by pressing ◉. Release when it reaches 120%.)

EX EFFECTS

Regen: Vigor and stamina recover little by little, restoring HP.

[Null] Particle Beam: The recovery time after all attacks can be canceled by performing an HP attack.

CECIL HARVEY

Split Soul—Shifts between the opposing strengths of paladin and dark knight.

A kind-hearted knight who wields the accursed power of darkness. In Final Fantasy IV, he was Lord Captain of Baron's airship force, the Red Wings, until circumstances led to his dismissal and embarkation on a journey of self-discovery. Eventually he was able to overcome his dark past and start down the path of a paladin. He is gentle and humble towards everyone, including children such as Porom and Palom.

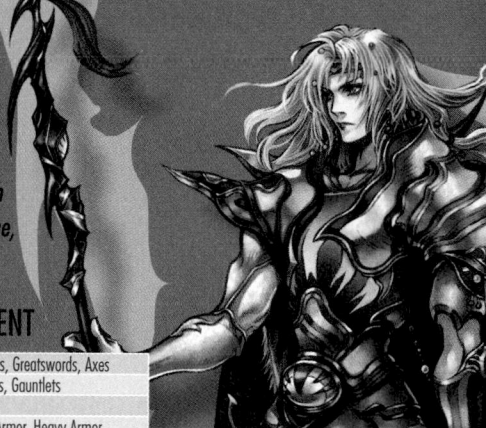

BASIC MOBILITY*

MOVEMENT	DARK KNIGHT	PALADIN
Ground Movement Speed	★☆	★★
Innate Number of Jumps	1	1
Jump Height	★	★★★
Jump Rising Speed	★	★★
Air Dash Speed	★☆	★★
Quickmove Speed	★☆	★★

*Mobility can be increased with the abilities Speed Boost, Jump Boost, Jump Times Boost, and Precision Jump.

EQUIPMENT

Weapon	Swords, Greatswords, Axes
Hands	Shields, Gauntlets
Head	Helms
Body	Light Armor, Heavy Armor

STAT PROGRESSION

LV	HP	CP	BRV	ATK	DEF	LUK
1	1000	330	95	10	11	10
5	1242	335	118	14	15	12
10	1545	341	147	19	20	15
20	2151	353	205	29	30	20
30	2757	365	263	39	40	25
40	3363	377	320	49	50	30
50	3969	389	378	59	60	35
60	4575	401	436	69	70	40
70	5181	413	493	79	80	45
80	5787	425	551	89	90	50
90	6393	437	609	99	100	55
100	6999	450	667	109	110	60

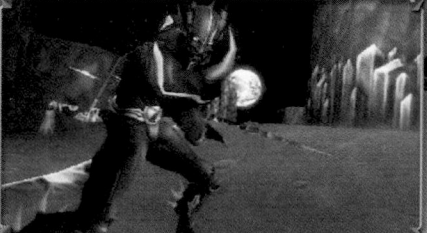

Like Jecht, Sephiroth, and his brother Golbez, Cecil has been on both sides of justice. Though he's left behind the dark, he remembers his dark knight training, and is able to move freely between dark knight and paladin disciplines.

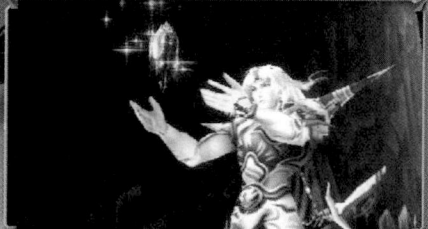

Midair HP attacks change Cecil into a paladin, while ground-based HP attacks transform him into a dark knight. The bravery attacks Dark Step and Paladin Arts also change his current job. During EX Mode, swap at will with ▬ + ⬤.

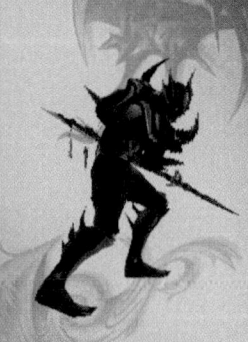
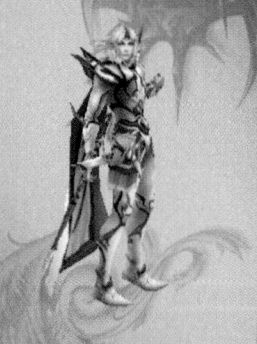
Dark Knight Cecil (Normal) — Dark Knight Cecil (Alternate)

Paladin Cecil (Normal) — Paladin Cecil (Alternate)

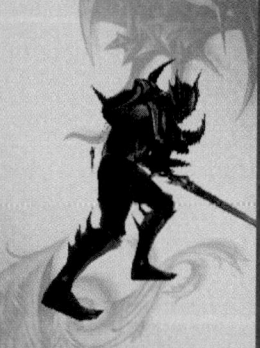
Dark Knight EX Mode (Normal) — Dark Knight EX Mode (Alternate)

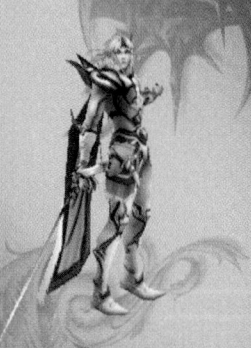
Paladin EX Mode (Normal) — Paladin EX Mode (Alternate)

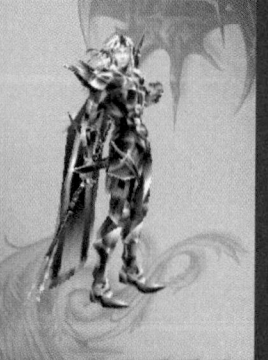
Dark Knight Delusory Knight — Paladin Delusory Knight

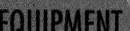

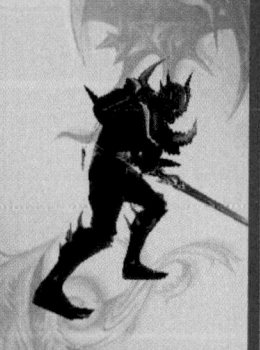
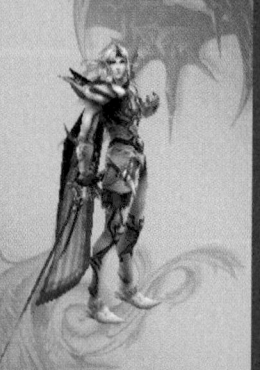
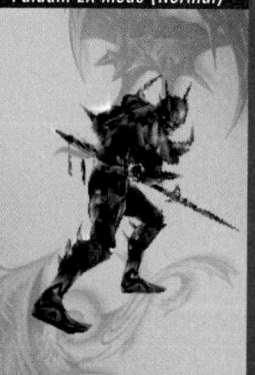

ABILITY PROGRESSION

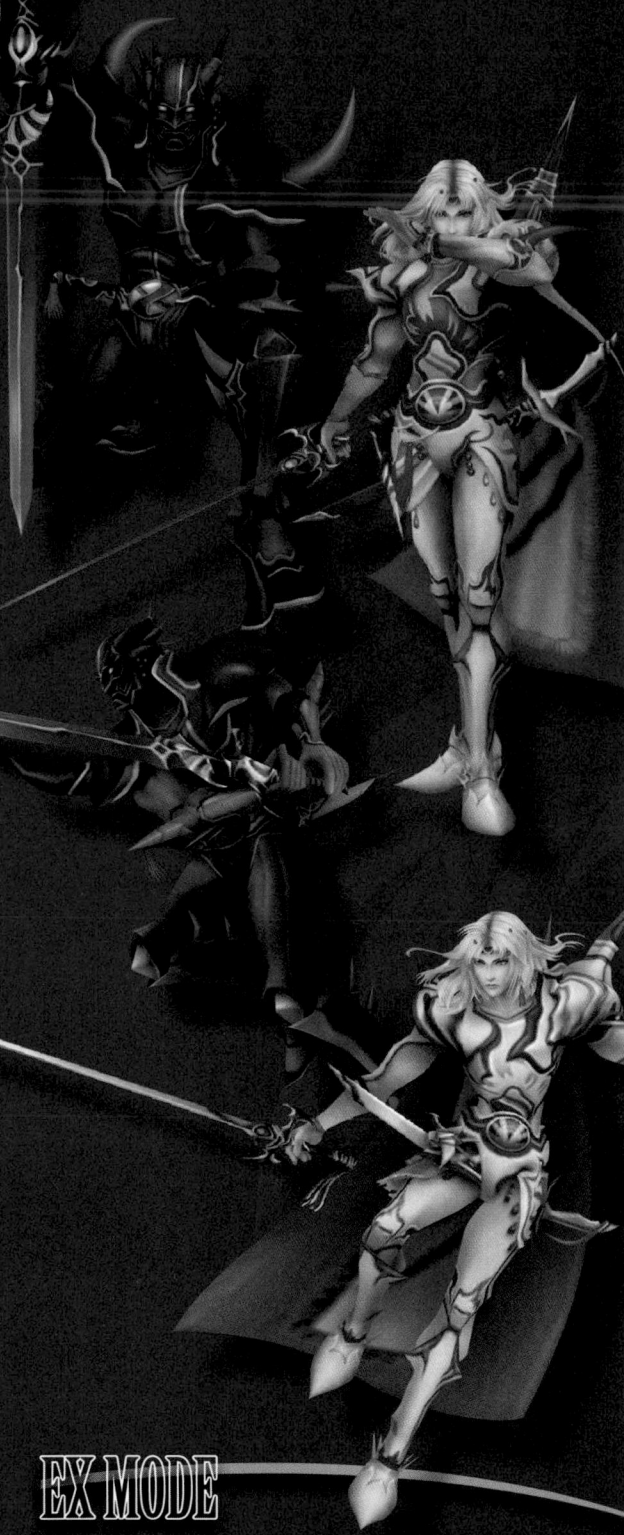

LEVEL	SKILL	TYPE	CP (N)	CP (M)	AP TO MASTER	ATTACK COMMANDS & EFFECTS*
01	Dark Cannon	Bravery Attack (Land-Dark Knight)	20	10	180	⊚ (Guard, Map Break)
01	Gravity Ball	Bravery Attack (Air-Dark Knight)	20	10	140	⊚ (Wall Rush, Map Break)
01	Radiant Wings	Bravery Attack (Air-Paladin)	20	10	120	⊚ ⊚ (Map Break, Wall Rush)
01	Saint's Fall	HP Attack (Air)	40	20	360	⊚ (Guard Crush, Wall Rush, Map Break, job change: Paladin)
01	Slash	Bravery Attack (Land-Paladin)	20	10	180	⊚ (Chase)
01	Soul Eater	HP Attack (Land)	40	20	360	⊚ (Guard Crush, Wall Rush, Map Break, job change: Dark Knight)
01	Valiant Blow	Bravery Attack (Land-Dark Knight)	20	10	140	(Map Break) ⊚ (Wall Rush, Map Break)
03	Shadow Lance	Bravery Attack (Land- Dark Knight)	20	10	90	⊚ (Map Break, Wall Rush)
04	Air Dash	Action	10	5	100	⊚ during Quickmove
07	Speed Boost	Action	20	10	150	-
(Mastery)	Speed Boost+	Action	40	20	150	-
(Mastery)	Speed Boost++	Action	70	35	150	-
08	Sacred Cross	Bravery Attack (Air-Paladin)	20	10	120	⊚ (Chase)
11	Auto Recovery	Support	20	5	250	-
11	Auto Chase	Support	20	5	250	-
13	Nightfall	Bravery Attack (Air- Dark Knight)	20	10	180	⊚ (Chase, Map Break)
15	Auto EX Burst	Support	20	5	150	-
15	Auto EX Command	Support	30	10	300	-
17	Searchlight	Bravery Attack (Air-Paladin)	20	10	90	⊚
18	Reverse Air Dash	Action	10	5	100	⊚ during Quickmove
21	Jump Boost	Action	10	5	150	-
(Mastery)	Jump Boost+	Action	20	10	150	-
(Mastery)	Jump Boost++	Action	40	20	150	-
22	Dark Flame	HP Attack (Land)	40	20	360	⊚ (Guard Crush, Wall Rush, Map Break, job change: Dark Knight)
25	EX Critical Boost	Extra	45	40	300	-
26	Auto EX Defense	Support	30	10	300	-
27	Lightning Rise	Bravery Attack (Land-Paladin)	20	10	180	⊚ (Guard, Map Break, Chase)
29	Reverse Free Air Dash	Action	10	5	100	▣ + ⊚
32	Recovery Attack	Action	20	10	120	⊚ or [square] while reeling
32	Controlled Recovery	Action	10	5	120	Analog Stick during Recovery
33	Paladin Force	HP Attack (Air)	40	20	360	⊚ (Guard Crush, Wall Rush, Map Break, job change: Paladin)
35	Riposte	Extra	45	40	300	-
(Mastery)	Disable Riposte	Extra	20	10	300	-
38	Paladin Arts	Bravery Attack (Air- Dark Knight)	30	15	300	⊚ (Map Break) ⊚ (job change: Paladin)
39	Jump Times Boost	Action	20	10	150	-
(Mastery)	Jump Times Boost+	Action	40	20	150	-
(Mastery)	Jump Times Boost++	Action	70	30	150	-
40	Omni Air Dash	Action	40	20	300	Analog Stick + ▣ + ⊚
43	Sneak Attack	Extra	50	45	360	-
(Mastery)	Disable Sneak Attack	Extra	30	15	360	-
44	Dark Step	Bravery Attack (Land-Paladin)	30	15	200	⊚ ⊚ (job change: Paladin, Chase, Map Break)
47	Physical Shield	Extra	20	10	280	-
50	Magic Shield	Extra	20	10	280	-
53	Multi-Air Slide	Action	10	5	250	Analog Stick + ⊗ after expending jumps See Multi-Air Slide
(Mastery)	Multi-Air Slide+	Action	30	15	300	-
57	Midair Evasion Boost	Action	20	10	150	-
60	Bravery Regen	Extra	20	10	280	-
64	Evasion Time Boost	Support	20	10	220	-
67	First Strike	Extra	40	35	360	-
(Mastery)	Disable First Strike	Extra	20	10	360	-
71	Concentration	Extra	30	15	250	-
(Mastery)	Concentration+	Extra	60	30	250	-
(Mastery)	Concentration++	Extra	100	50	250	-
74	Cat Nip	Extra	30	25	300	-
(Mastery)	Disable Cat Nip	Extra	20	10	300	-
78	Anti-EX	Extra	30	20	300	-
(Mastery)	Disable Anti-EX	Extra	20	10	300	-
81	Achy	Extra	30	15	250	-
(Mastery)	Achy+	Extra	60	30	250	-
85	Counterattack	Extra	50	45	360	-
(Mastery)	Disable Counterattack	Extra	30	15	360	-
88	Gambler's Spirit	Extra	30	15	300	-
(Mastery)	Disable Gambler's Spirit	Extra	20	10	300	-
92	Back to the Wall	Extra	30	25	300	-
(Mastery)	Disable Back to the Wall	Extra	20	10	300	-
95	Precision Jump	Extra	10	5	180	-
98	Snooze and Lose	Extra	100	50	250	-
100	EXP to HP	Extra	20	0	500	-
100	EXP to Bravery	Extra	20	0	500	-
100	EXP to EX Force	Extra	20	0	500	-

*Initial commands may require directional presses, depending on the slot to which abilities are assigned.

EX MODE

EX BURST

Soul Shift: A chain of attacks combining the power of light and darkness. (Enter the commands that appear on both sides of the screen at the same time.)

EX EFFECTS

Regen: Vigor and stamina recover little by little, restoring HP.

Proteus: Bridles light and darkness to instantly change jobs without attacking. (Activate with ▣ + ⊙.)

Inner Strength: Each attack is 1.5 times as powerful.

GOLBEZ

Thaumaturge—Uses techniques that simultaneously strike physically and magically.

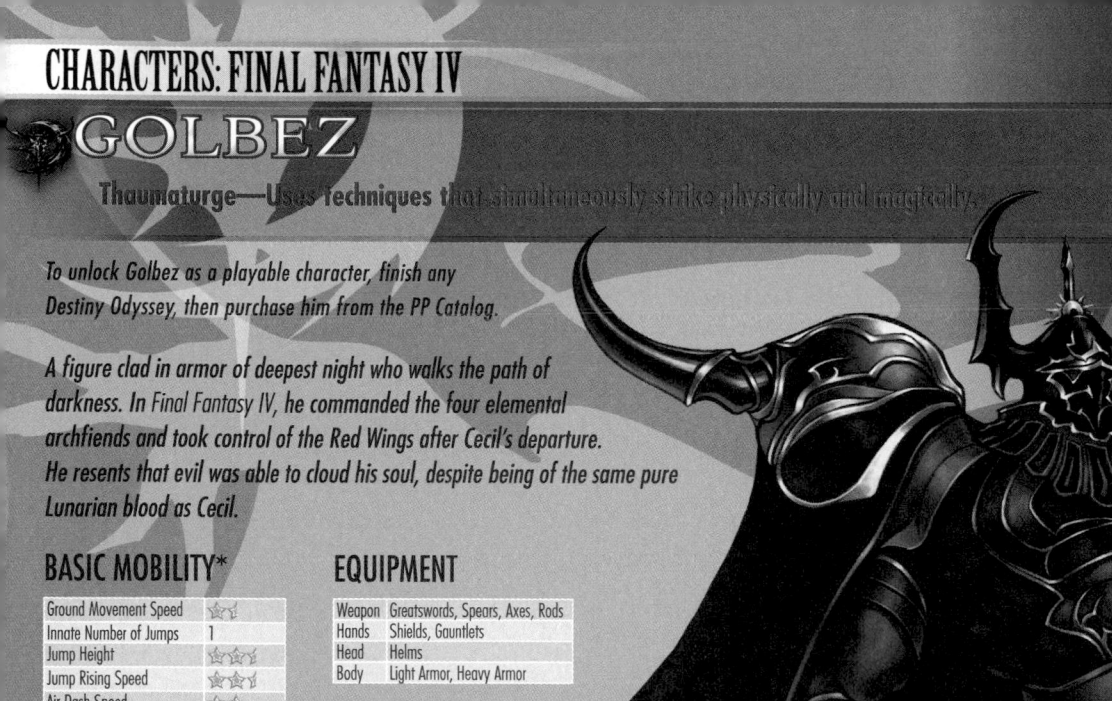

To unlock Golbez as a playable character, finish any
Destiny Odyssey, then purchase him from the PP Catalog.

A figure clad in armor of deepest night who walks the path of
darkness. In *Final Fantasy IV*, he commanded the four elemental
archfiends and took control of the Red Wings after Cecil's departure.
He resents that evil was able to cloud his soul, despite being of the same pure
Lunarian blood as Cecil.

BASIC MOBILITY*

Ground Movement Speed	★☆☆
Innate Number of Jumps	1
Jump Height	★★☆
Jump Rising Speed	★★☆
Air Dash Speed	★★☆
Quickmove Speed	★★☆

*Mobility can be increased with the abilities
Speed Boost, Jump Boost, Jump Times
Boost, and Precision Jump.

EQUIPMENT

Weapon	Greatswords, Spears, Axes, Rods
Hands	Shields, Gauntlets
Head	Helms
Body	Light Armor, Heavy Armor

STAT PROGRESSION

LV	HP	CP	BRV	ATK	DEF	LUK
1	1000	330	95	11	13	10
5	1242	335	118	15	17	12
10	1545	341	147	20	22	15
20	2151	353	205	30	32	20
30	2757	365	263	40	42	25
40	3363	377	320	50	52	30
50	3969	389	378	60	62	35
60	4575	401	436	70	72	40
70	5181	413	493	80	82	45
80	5787	425	551	90	92	50
90	6393	437	609	100	102	55
100	6999	450	667	110	112	60

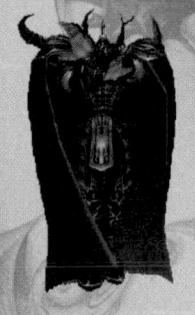

Golbez (Normal)

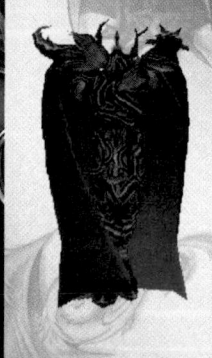

EX Mode (Normal)

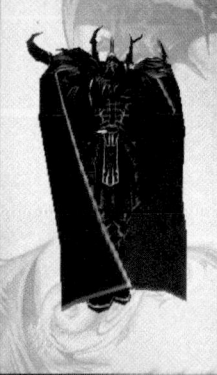

Golbez (Alternate)

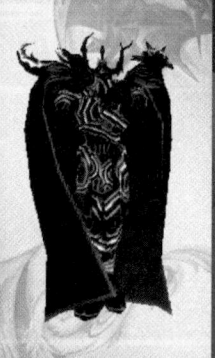

EX Mode (Alternate)

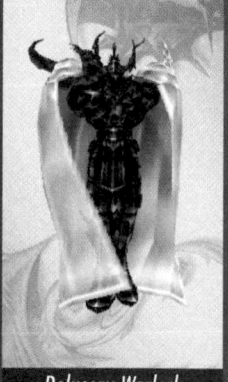

Delusory Warlock

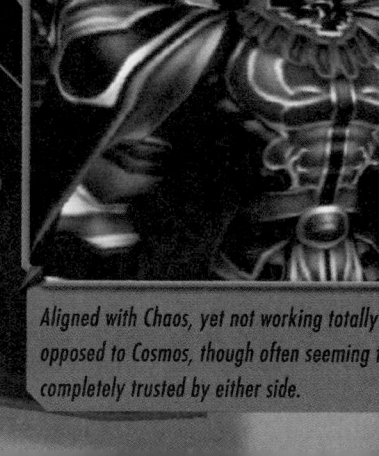

Aligned with Chaos, yet not working totally in concert with other villains, and
opposed to Cosmos, though often seeming to aid her followers, Golbez is not
completely trusted by either side.

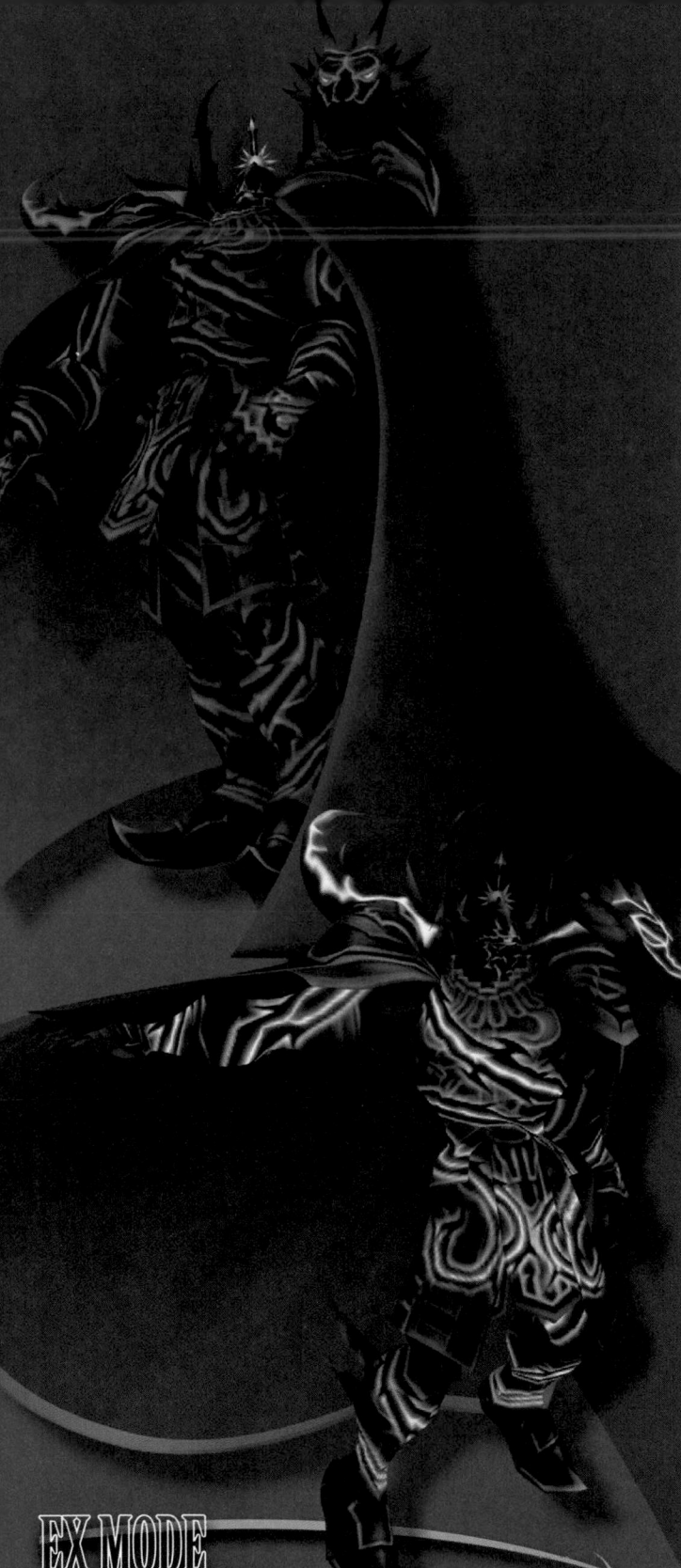

ABILITY PROGRESSION

LEVEL	SKILL	TYPE	CP (N)	CP (M)	AP TO MASTER	ATTACK COMMANDS & EFFECTS*
01	Attack System	Bravery Attack (Land)	30	15	180	●
01	Genesis Rock	HP Attack (Air)	40	20	180	● (Move OK, Guard Crush, Wall Rush, Map Break)
01	Gravity Force	Bravery Attack (Air)	30	15	120	● (Move OK, Pull-in, Map Break)
01	Nightglow	HP Attack (Land)	40	20	180	● (Move OK, Guard Crush, Wall Rush, Map Break)
01	Rising Wave	Bravery Attack (Land)	30	15	180	● (Map Break) ● (Wall Rush, Map Break) ●
(Mastery)	Cosmic Ray A	Combo Attack	40	20	300	● after first ● press in Rising Wave (Guard Crush, Map Break)
04	Air Dash	Action	10	5	100	● during Quickmove
07	Speed Boost	Action	20	10	150	-
(Mastery)	Speed Boost+	Action	40	20	150	-
(Mastery)	Speed Boost++	Action	70	35	150	-
08	Float System	Bravery Attack (Air)	30	15	120	● (Map Break) ● (Map Break, Chase) ● (Wall Rush)
(Mastery)	Cosmic Ray D	Combo Attack	40	20	300	● after first ● press in Float System (Wall Rush, Guard Crush, Map Break)
11	Auto Recovery	Support	20	5	250	-
11	Auto Chase	Support	20	5	250	-
13	Gravity System	Bravery Attack (Air)	30	15	120	● (Map Break) ● (Map Break, Chase) ● (Wall Rush)
(Mastery)	Cosmic Ray C	Combo Attack	40	20	300	● after first ● press in Gravity System (Wall Rush, Guard Crush, Map Break)
15	Auto EX Burst	Support	20	5	150	-
15	Auto EX Command	Support	30	10	300	-
18	Reverse Air Dash	Action	10	5	100	● during Quickmove
21	Jump Boost	Action	10	5	150	-
(Mastery)	Jump Boost+	Action	20	10	150	-
(Mastery)	Jump Boost++	Action	40	20	150	-
25	EX Critical Boost	Extra	45	40	300	-
26	Auto EX Defense	Support	30	10	300	-
29	Reverse Free Air Dash	Action	10	5	100	▣ + ●
32	Recovery Attack	Action	20	10	120	● or ● while reeling
32	Controlled Recovery	Action	10	5	120	Analog Stick during Recovery
33	Glare Hand	Bravery Attack (Land)	30	15	180	● (Chase, Map Break) ● Wall Rush, Map Break)
(Mastery)	Cosmic Ray B	Combo Attack	40	20	300	● after first ● press in Glare Hand (Wall Rush, Guard Crush, Map Break)
35	Riposte	Extra	45	40	300	-
(Mastery)	Disable Riposte	Extra	20	10	300	-
39	Jump Times Boost	Action	20	10	150	-
(Mastery)	Jump Times Boost+	Action	40	20	150	-
(Mastery)	Jump Times Boost++	Action	70	30	150	-
40	Omni Air Dash	Action	40	20	300	Analog Stick + ▣ + ●
43	Sneak Attack	Action	50	45	360	-
(Mastery)	Disable Sneak Attack	Extra	30	15	360	-
47	Physical Shield	Extra	20	10	280	-
50	Magic Shield	Extra	20	10	280	-
53	Multi-Air Slide	Action	10	5	250	Analog Stick + ✖ once jumps are expended
(Mastery)	Multi-Air Slide+	Action	30	15	300	See Multi-Air Slide
57	Midair Evasion Boost	Action	20	10	150	-
60	Bravery Regen	Extra	20	10	280	-
64	Evasion Time Boost	Support	20	10	220	-
67	First Strike	Extra	40	35	360	-
(Mastery)	Disable First Strike	Extra	20	10	360	-
71	Concentration	Extra	30	15	250	-
(Mastery)	Concentration+	Extra	60	30	250	-
(Mastery)	Concentration++	Extra	100	50	250	-
74	Cat Nip	Extra	30	25	300	-
(Mastery)	Disable Cat Nip	Extra	20	10	300	-
78	Anti-EX	Extra	30	20	300	-
(Mastery)	Disable Anti-EX	Extra	20	10	300	-
81	Achy	Extra	30	15	250	-
(Mastery)	Achy+	Extra	60	30	250	-
85	Counterattack	Extra	50	45	360	-
(Mastery)	Disable Counterattack	Extra	30	15	360	-
88	Gambler's Spirit	Extra	30	15	300	-
(Mastery)	Disable Gambler's Spirit	Extra	20	10	300	-
92	Back to the Wall	Extra	30	25	300	-
(Mastery)	Disable Back to the Wall	Extra	20	10	300	-
95	Precision Jump	Extra	10	5	180	-
98	Snooze and Lose	Extra	100	50	250	-
100	EXP to HP	Extra	20	0	500	-
100	EXP to Bravery	Extra	20	0	500	-
100	EXP to EX Force	Extra	20	0	500	-

*Initial commands may require directional presses, depending on the slot to which abilities are assigned.

EX MODE

EX BURST

Twin Moon: Casts a powerful spell along with a Shadow Dragon. (Enter the commands that appear on both sides of the screen at the same time.)

EX EFFECTS

Regen: Vigor and stamina recover little by little, restoring HP.

Black Fang: Breaks opponent in one hit, although you only gain stage bravery as a result. (Activate with ▣ + ●.)

BARTZ KLAUSER

Mimic—Mimes the attacks of his companions, adding his own special touches.

A cheerful man with a strong sense of justice and the inability to ignore those in trouble. In Final Fantasy V, at his father's dying wish, he traveled the world along with his chocobo, Boko. Free-spirited and spunky, one would never know that a childhood trauma left him with a paralyzing fear of high places. For good or ill, this too is part of his innocent, youthful personality.

BASIC MOBILITY*

Ground Movement Speed	☆☆
Innate Number of Jumps	1
Jump Height	☆☆
Jump Rising Speed	☆☆
Air Dash Speed	☆☆
Quickmove Speed	☆☆

*Mobility can be increased with the abilities Speed Boost, Jump Boost, Jump Times Boost, and Precision Jump.

EQUIPMENT

Weapon	All
Hands	All
Head	All
Body	All

STAT PROGRESSION

LV	HP	CP	BRV	ATK	DEF	LUK
1	1000	350	95	11	12	10
5	1242	354	118	15	16	12
10	1545	359	147	20	21	15
20	2151	369	205	30	31	20
30	2757	379	263	40	41	25
40	3363	389	320	50	51	30
50	3969	399	378	60	61	35
60	4575	409	436	70	71	40
70	5181	419	493	80	81	45
80	5787	429	551	90	91	50
90	6393	439	609	100	101	55
100	6999	450	667	110	111	60

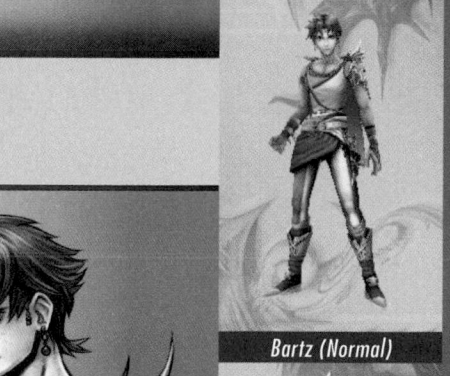
Bartz (Normal)

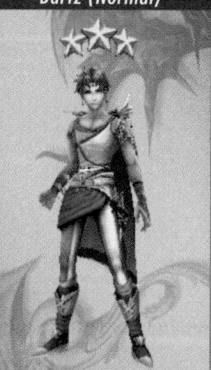
EX Mode (Normal)

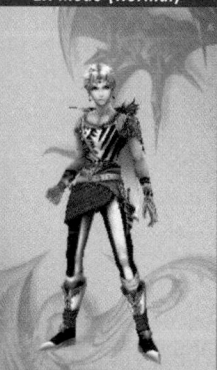
Bartz (Alternate)

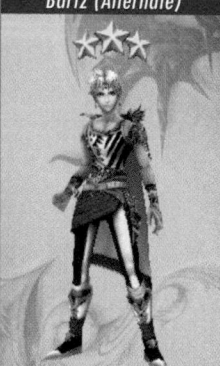
EX Mode (Alternate)

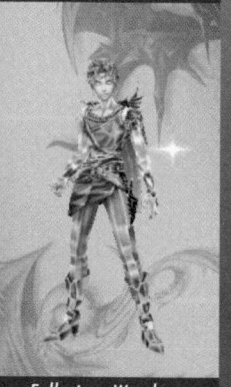
Fallacious Wanderer

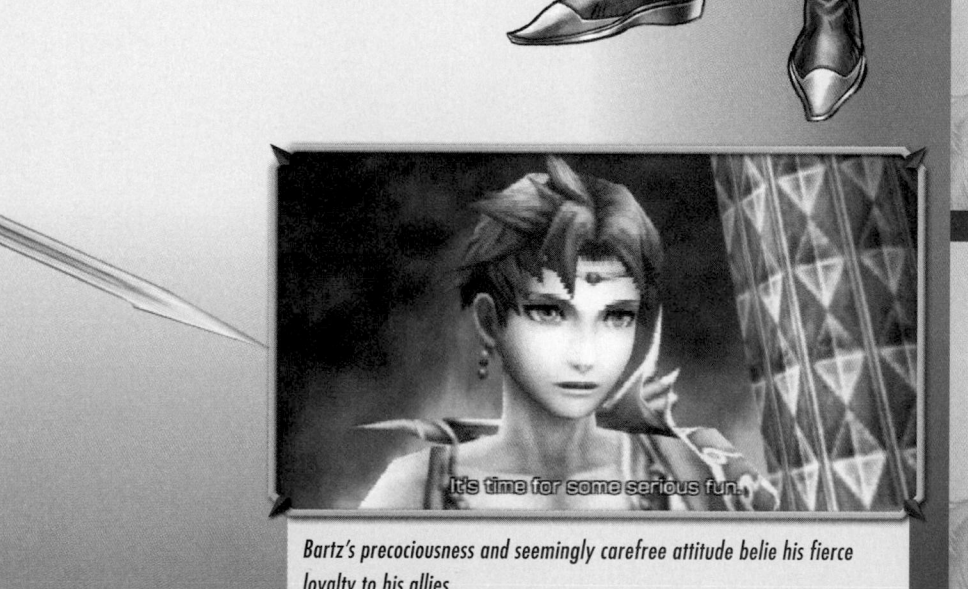
It's time for some serious fun.

Bartz's precociousness and seemingly carefree attitude belie his fierce loyalty to his allies.

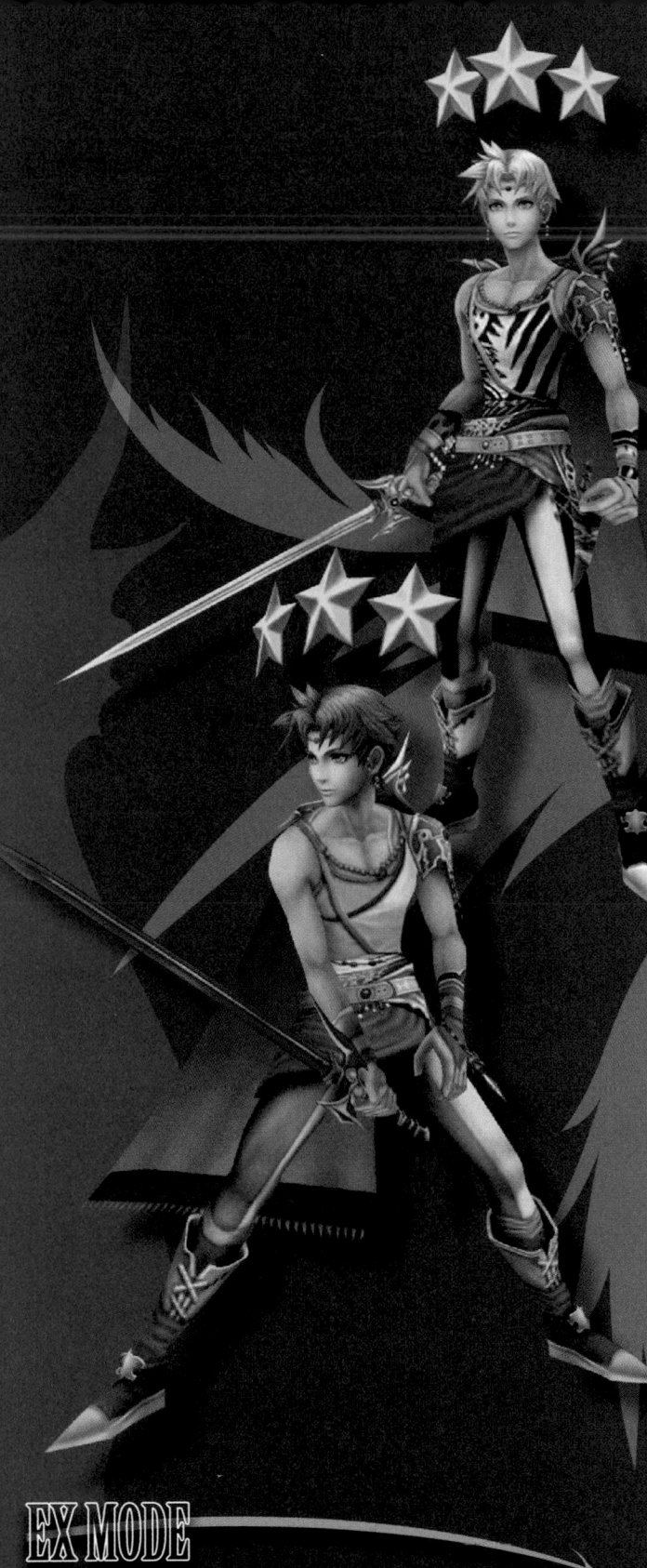

ABILITY PROGRESSION

LEVEL	SKILL	TYPE	CP (N)	CP (M)	AP TO MASTER	ATTACK COMMANDS & EFFECTS*
01	Ascendent Lance	Bravery Attack (Land)	30	15	120	◎◎ (Wall Rush, Map Break)
01	Holy	Bravery Attack (Air)	20	10	120	◎◎ (Map Break, Chase)
(Mastery)	Flare	Combo Attack	50	25	300	● after Holy (Guard Crush, Map Break)
01	Reel Impulse	Bravery Attack (Land)	30	15	120	◎ (Guard Crush) ◎ (Wall Rush, Map Break)
01	Soul Eater	HP Attack (Land)	50	25	180	● (Guard Crush, Wall Break)
01	Storm Shot	Bravery Attack (Air)	30	15	180	◎◎ (Map Break, Wall Rush)
01	Wind Shear	HP Attack (Air)	50	25	300	● (Move OK, Guard Crush, Pull-in, Map Break)
03	Climbarrel	Bravery Attack (Land)	40	20	120	◎ (Map Break) ◎ (Map Break, Chase)
04	Air Dash	Action	10	5	100	● during Quickmove
07	Speed Boost	Action	20	10	150	-
(Mastery)	Speed Boost+	Action	40	20	150	-
(Mastery)	Speed Boost++	Action	70	35	150	-
10	Solid Ascension	Bravery Attack (Land)	40	20	120	◎◎◎◎◎ (Map Break)
11	Auto Recovery	Support	20	5	250	-
11	Auto Chase	Support	20	5	250	-
15	Auto EX Burst	Support	20	5	150	-
15	Auto EX Command	Support	30	10	300	-
18	Reverse Air Dash	Action	10	5	100	● during Quickmove
19	Flood	HP Attack (Land)	50	25	180	● (Map Break)
21	Jump Boost	Action	10	5	150	-
(Mastery)	Jump Boost+	Action	20	10	150	-
(Mastery)	Jump Boost++	Action	40	20	150	-
25	EX Critical Boost	Extra	45	40	300	-
26	Auto EX Defense	Support	30	10	300	-
28	Slidehazzard	Bravery Attack (Air)	30	15	180	◎ (Map Break) ◎ (Map Break) ◎ ◎ (Map Break, Wall Rush)
29	Reverse Free Air Dash	Action	10	5	100	■ + ▲
32	Recovery Attack	Action	20	10	120	● or ● while reeling
32	Controlled Recovery	Action	10	5	120	Analog Stick during Recovery
35	Riposte	Extra	45	40	300	-
(Mastery)	Disable Riposte	Extra	20	10	300	-
38	Paladin Force	HP Attack (Air)	50	25	180	
39	Jump Times Boost	Action	20	10	150	-
(Mastery)	Jump Times Boost+	Action	40	20	150	-
(Mastery)	Jump Times Boost++	Action	70	30	150	-
40	Omni Air Dash	Action	40	20	300	Analog Stick + ■ + ▲
43	Sneak Attack	Extra	50	45	360	-
(Mastery)	Disable Sneak Attack	Extra	30	15	360	-
47	Physical Shield	Extra	20	10	280	-
50	Magic Shield	Extra	20	10	280	-
53	Multi-Air Slide	Action	10	5	250	✕ after expending jumps
(Mastery)	Multi-Air Slide+	Action	30	15	300	See Multi-Air Slide
57	Midair Evasion Boost	Action	20	10	150	-
60	Bravery Regen	Extra	20	10	280	-
64	Evasion Time Boost	Support	20	10	220	-
67	First Strike	Extra	40	35	360	-
(Mastery)	Disable First Strike	Extra	20	10	360	-
71	Concentration	Extra	30	15	250	-
(Mastery)	Concentration+	Extra	60	30	250	-
(Mastery)	Concentration++	Extra	100	50	250	-
74	Cat Nip	Extra	30	25	300	-
(Mastery)	Disable Cat Nip	Extra	20	10	300	-
78	Anti-EX	Extra	30	20	300	-
(Mastery)	Disable Anti-EX	Extra	20	10	300	-
81	Achy	Extra	30	15	250	-
(Mastery)	Achy+	Extra	60	30	250	-
85	Counterattack	Extra	50	45	360	-
(Mastery)	Disable Counterattack	Extra	30	15	360	-
88	Gambler's Spirit	Extra	30	15	300	-
(Mastery)	Disable Gambler's Spirit	Extra	20	10	300	-
92	Back to the Wall	Extra	30	25	300	-
(Mastery)	Disable Back to the Wall	Extra	20	10	300	-
95	Precision Jump	Extra	10	5	180	-
98	Snooze and Lose	Extra	100	50	250	-
100	EXP to HP	Extra	20	0	500	-
100	EXP to Bravery	Extra	20	0	500	-
100	EXP to EX Force	Extra	20	0	500	-

*Initial commands may require directional presses, depending on the slot to which abilities are assigned.

EX MODE

EX BURST

Master Mime: Adds the strength of his allies to his own job abilities for a series of masterful blows. (Press D-pad directions as indicated on screen to attack.)

EX EFFECTS

Regen: Vigor and stamina recover little by little, restoring HP.

Goblin Punch: Attack bravery, then perform an HP attack. If you are the same level as the foe, your power massively increases. (Activate with ■ + ◎.)

EXDEATH

Entropic Adversary—Unmatched in guards and counters, he draws foes to inevitable defeat.

Exdeath becomes playable after you finish any Destiny Odyssey, then purchase him from the PP Catalog.

A magus of supreme darkness, born from a great evil sealed into a tree. In Final Fantasy V, his soul was sealed away by the sage Ghido and the four Dawn Warriors, but he was still able to use the power of darkness to be reborn. By joining the world's two dimensions into one, he desired to gain the power of the Void.

BASIC MOBILITY*

Ground Movement Speed	
Innate Number of Jumps	1
Jump Height	
Jump Rising Speed	
Air Dash Speed	
Quickmove Speed	

*Mobility can be increased with the abilities Speed Boost, Jump Boost, Jump Times Boost, and Precision Jump.

EQUIPMENT

Weapon	Rods, Staves
Hands	Shields, Gauntlets
Head	Helms
Body	Light Armor, Heavy Armor

STAT PROGRESSION

LV	HP	CP	BRV	ATK	DEF	LUK
1	1000	350	95	11	14	10
5	1242	354	118	15	18	12
10	1545	359	147	20	23	15
20	2151	369	205	30	33	20
30	2757	379	263	40	43	25
40	3363	389	320	50	53	30
50	3969	399	378	60	63	35
60	4575	409	436	70	73	40
70	5181	419	493	80	83	45
80	5787	429	551	90	93	50
90	6393	439	609	100	103	55
100	6999	450	667	110	113	60

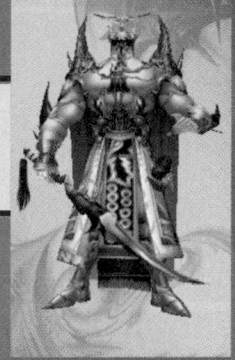

Exdeath (Normal)

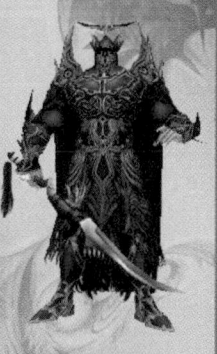

EX Mode (Normal)

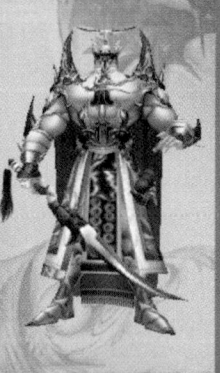

Exdeath (Alternate)

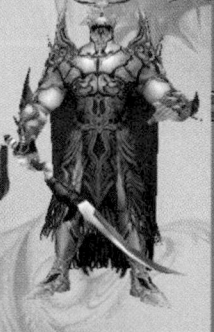

EX Mode (Alternate)

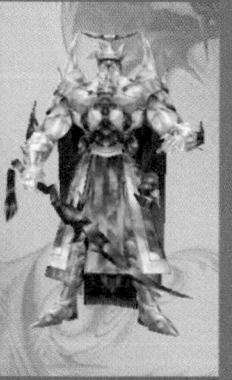

Fallacious Tree

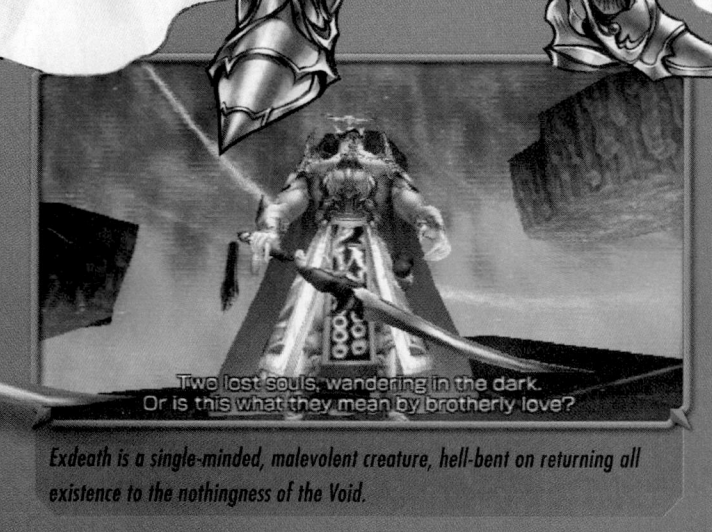

Two lost souls, wandering in the dark. Or is this what they mean by brotherly love?

Exdeath is a single-minded, malevolent creature, hell-bent on returning all existence to the nothingness of the Void.

ABILITY PROGRESSION

LEVEL	SKILL	TYPE	CP (N)	CP (M)	AP TO MASTER	ATTACK COMMANDS & EFFECTS*
01	Black Hole (ground)	Bravery Attack (Land)	30	15	180	◉ (Pull-in, Map Break)
01	Delta Attack (ground)	HP Attack (Land)	40	20	180	◉ (Guard, Guard Crush, Map Break, Wall Rush)
01	Delta Attack (midair)	HP Attack (Air)	40	20	180	◉ (Guard, Guard Crush, Map Break, Wall Rush)
01	Low Block (midair)	Bravery Attack (Air)	20	10	90	◉ (Guard); if successful, ◉ (Move OK, Guard Crush, Map Break) or [toward opponent] + ◉ ◉ or [away from opponent] + ◉ (Map Break) ◉ (Map Break) or ◉ (Guard Crush, Map Break) or [away from opponent] + ◉
01	Mid Block (midair)	Bravery Attack (Air)	20	10	90	◉ (Guard); if successful, ◉ (Move OK, Guard Crush, Map Break) or [toward opponent] + ◉ ◉ or [away from opponent] + ◉ (Map Break) ◉ (Map Break) or ◉ (Guard Crush, Map Break) or [away from opponent] + ◉
01	Reverse Polarity (ground)	Bravery Attack (Land)	30	15	180	Hold and release ◉ (Wall Rush, Map Break)
01	Reverse Polarity (midair)	Bravery Attack (Air)	30	15	140	Hold and release ◉ (Wall Rush, Map Break)
01	Vacuum Wave (ground)	Bravery Attack (Land)	30	15	180	◉ (Map Break, Chase)
03	High Block (midair)	Bravery Attack (Air)	20	10	90	◉ (Guard); if successful, ◉ (Move OK, Guard Crush, Map Break) or [toward opponent] + ◉ ◉ or [away from opponent] + ◉ (Map Break) ◉ (Map Break) or ◉ (Guard Crush, Map Break) or [away from opponent] + ◉
03	Sword Dance (ground)	Bravery Attack (Land)	20	10	120	◉ (Wall Rush)
04	Air Dash	Action	10	5	100	◉ during Quickmove
07	Speed Boost	Action	20	10	150	-
(Mastery)	Speed Boost+	Action	40	20	150	-
(Mastery)	Speed Boost++	Action	70	35	150	-
08	Almagest (ground)	HP Attack (Land)	40	20	300	◉ (Guard Crush, Map Break, Wall Rush)
11	Auto Recovery	Support	20	5	250	-
11	Auto Chase	Support	20	5	250	-
12	Omni Block (midair)	Bravery Attack (Air)	30	15	140	◉ (Guard); if successful, ◉ (Move OK, Guard Crush, Map Break) or [toward opponent] + ◉ ◉ or [away from opponent] + ◉ (Map Break) ◉ (Map Break) or ◉ (Guard Crush, Map Break) or [away from opponent] + ◉
12	Hurricane (ground)	Bravery Attack (Land)	30	15	180	◉ (Move OK, Pull-in, Map Break)
15	Auto EX Burst	Support	20	5	150	-
15	Auto EX Command	Support	30	10	300	-
16	Black Hole (midair)	Bravery Attack (Air)	30	15	140	◉ (Pull-in, Map Break)
16	Grand Cross (ground)	HP Attack (Land)	40	20	300	-
18	Reverse Air Dash	Action	10	5	100	◉ during Quickmove
20	Sword Dance (midair)	Bravery Attack (Air)	20	10	90	◉ (Wall Rush)
20	Low Block (ground)	Bravery Attack (Land)	20	10	120	◉ (Guard); if successful, ◉ (Move OK, Guard Crush, Map Break) or [toward opponent] + ◉ ◉ or [away from opponent] + ◉ (Map Break) ◉ (Map Break) or ◉ (Guard Crush, Map Break) or [away from opponent] + ◉
21	Jump Boost	Action	10	5	150	-
(Mastery)	Jump Boost+	Action	20	10	150	-
(Mastery)	Jump Boost++	Action	40	20	150	-
24	Vacuum Wave (midair)	Bravery Attack (Air)	30	15	140	◉ (Map Break, Chase)
24	Mid Block (ground)	Bravery Attack (Land)	20	10	120	◉ (Guard); if successful, ◉ (Move OK, Guard Crush, Map Break) or [toward opponent] + ◉ ◉ or [away from opponent] + ◉ (Map Break) ◉ (Map Break) or ◉ (Guard Crush, Map Break) or [away from opponent] + ◉
25	EX Critical Boost	Extra	45	40	300	-
26	Auto EX Defense	Support	30	10	300	-
29	Reverse Free Air Dash	Action	10	5	100	◼ + ◎
30	Almagest (midair)	HP Attack (Air)	40	20	300	◉ (Guard Crush, Map Break, Wall Rush)
30	High Block (ground)	Bravery Attack (Land)	20	10	120	◉ (Guard); if successful, ◉ (Move OK, Guard Crush, Map Break) or [toward opponent] + ◉ ◉ or [away from opponent] + ◉ (Map Break) ◉ (Map Break) or ◉ (Guard Crush, Map Break) or [away from opponent] + ◉
32	Recovery Attack	Action	20	10	120	◉ or ◉ while reeling
32	Controlled Recovery	Action	10	5	120	Analog Stick during Recovery
34	Hurricane (midair)	Bravery Attack (Air)	30	15	140	◉ (Move OK, Pull-in, Map Break)
35	Riposte	Extra	45	40	300	-
(Mastery)	Disable Riposte	Extra	20	10	300	-
38	Grand Cross (midair)	HP Attack (Air)	40	20	300	◉
38	Omni Block (ground)	Bravery Attack (Land)	30	15	180	◉ (Guard); if successful, ◉ (Move OK, Guard Crush, Map Break) or [toward opponent] + ◉ ◉ or [away from opponent] + ◉ (Map Break) ◉ (Map Break) or ◉ (Guard Crush, Map Break) or [away from opponent] + ◉
39	Jump Times Boost	Action	20	10	150	-
(Mastery)	Jump Times Boost+	Action	40	20	150	-
(Mastery)	Jump Times Boost++	Action	70	35	150	-
40	Omni Air Dash	Action	40	20	300	Analog Stick + ◼ + ◎
43	Sneak Attack	Extra	50	45	360	-
(Mastery)	Disable Sneak Attack	Extra	30	15	360	-
47	Physical Shield	Extra	20	10	280	-
50	Magic Shield	Extra	20	10	280	-
53	Multi-Air Slide	Action	10	5	250	Analog Stick + ◎ after expending jumps
(Mastery)	Multi-Air Slide+	Action	30	15	300	See Multi-Air Slide
57	Midair Evasion Boost	Action	20	10	150	-
60	Bravery Regen	Extra	20	10	280	-
64	Evasion Time Boost	Support	20	10	220	-
67	First Strike	Extra	40	35	360	-
(Mastery)	Disable First Strike	Extra	20	10	360	-
71	Concentration	Extra	30	15	250	-
(Mastery)	Concentration+	Extra	60	30	250	-
(Mastery)	Concentration++	Extra	100	50	250	-
74	Cat Nip	Extra	30	25	300	-
(Mastery)	Disable Cat Nip	Extra	20	10	300	-
78	Anti-EX	Extra	30	20	300	-
(Mastery)	Disable Anti-EX	Extra	20	10	300	-
81	Achy	Extra	30	15	250	-
(Mastery)	Achy+	Extra	60	30	250	-
85	Counterattack	Extra	50	45	360	-
(Mastery)	Disable Counterattack	Extra	30	15	360	-
88	Gambler's Spirit	Extra	30	15	300	-
(Mastery)	Disable Gambler's Spirit	Extra	20	10	300	-
92	Back to the Wall	Extra	30	25	300	-
(Mastery)	Disable Back to the Wall	Extra	20	10	300	-
95	Precision Jump	Extra	10	5	180	-
98	Snooze and Lose	Extra	100	50	250	-
100	EXP to HP	Extra	20	0	500	-
100	EXP to Bravery	Extra	20	0	500	-
100	EXP to EX Force	Extra	20	0	500	-

*Initial commands may require directional presses, depending on the slot to which abilities are assigned.

EX MODE

EX BURST

Power of the Void: At his command, all is absorbed by darkness and returned to the Void. (Fill the gauge by pressing ◉. Release when it reaches 0.)

EX EFFECTS

Regen: Vigor and stamina recover little by little, restoring HP.

Speed Guard: Time necessary to block an attack decreases. Counterattack chance increases.

TERRA BRANFORD

Esperkin—Fires spells that always find their mark.

A pure, innocent girl born with the power of magic. In *Final Fantasy VI*, she was a soldier for the Gestahlian Empire, which aimed to take over the world. In reality, her mind and actions were controlled by a hypnotic device. Upon traveling to the snow-covered mining town of Narshe, she met a man named Locke and was stolen away to the Returners, a resistance group. She has a fondness for moogles and enjoys fluffing their fur, especially as she drifts off to sleep.

BASIC MOBILITY*

Ground Movement Speed	⭐
Innate Number of Jumps	1
Jump Height	⭐⭐⭐
Jump Rising Speed	⭐⭐
Air Dash Speed	⭐½
Quickmove Speed	⭐½

EQUIPMENT

Weapon	Daggers, Rods, Staves
Hands	Bangles
Head	Hats, Hairpins
Body	Clothing, Robes

*Mobility can be increased with the abilities Speed Boost, Jump Boost, Jump Times Boost, and Precision Jump.

STAT PROGRESSION

LV	HP	CP	BRV	ATK	DEF	LUK
1	1000	330	95	12	11	10
5	1242	335	118	16	15	12
10	1545	341	147	21	20	15
20	2151	353	205	31	30	20
30	2757	365	263	41	40	25
40	3363	377	320	51	50	30
50	3969	389	378	61	60	35
60	4575	401	436	71	70	40
70	5181	413	493	81	80	45
80	5787	425	551	91	90	50
90	6393	437	609	101	100	55
100	6999	450	667	111	110	60

I'm afraid of my powers.

Terra fears her own destructive magical potential.

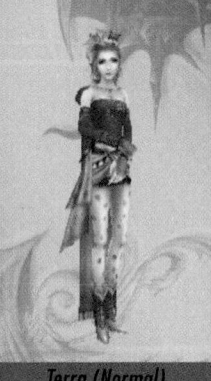

Terra (Normal)

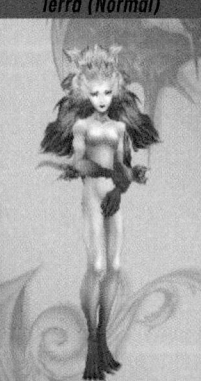

EX Mode (Normal)

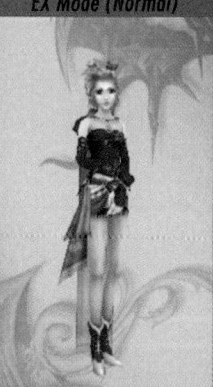

Terra (Alternate)

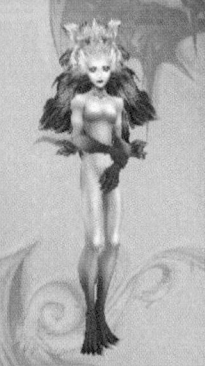

EX Mode (Alternate)

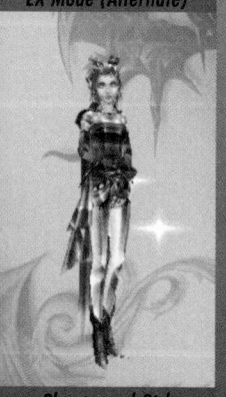

Phantasmal Girl

ABILITY PROGRESSION

LEVEL	SKILL	TYPE	CP (N)	CP (M)	AP TO MASTER	ATTACK COMMANDS & EFFECTS*
01	Blizzara (midair)	Bravery Attack (Air)	30	15	140	◉ (Guard, Map Break, Wall Rush)
01	Blizzard Combo (ground)	Bravery Attack (Land)	30	15	180	◉ ◉ (Map Break, Wall Rush) or Analog Stick Up + ◉ (Map Break, Wall Rush)
01	Fire	Bravery Attack (Land)	20	10	120	◉ (Map Break, Chase)
01	Flood	HP Attack (Ground)	40	20	180	◉ (Map Break)
01	Thundara	Bravery Attack (Air)	20	10	90	◉ (Map Break)
01	Tornado (midair)	HP Attack (Air)	40	20	180	◉ (Move OK, Pull-in, Guard Crush, Map Break, Wall Rush)
02	Reverse Free Air Dash	Action	10	5	100	▭ + △
03	Blizzara (ground)	Bravery Attack (Land)	30	15	180	◉ (Guard, Map Break, Wall Rush)
04	Air Dash	Action	10	5	100	△ during Quickmove
06	Blizzard Combo (midair)	Bravery Attack (Air)	30	15	140	◉ ◉ (Map Break, Wall Rush) or Analog Stick Up + ◉ (Map Break, Wall Rush)
07	Jump Boost	Action	10	5	150	-
(Mastery)	Jump Boost+	Action	20	10	150	-
(Mastery)	Jump Boost++	Action	40	20	150	-
10	Holy	Bravery Attack (Air)	20	10	140	◉ (Map Break, Chase)
11	Auto Recovery	Support	20	5	250	-
11	Auto Chase	Support	20	5	250	-
14	Tornado (ground)	HP Attack (Land)	40	20	180	◉ (Move OK, Pull-in, Guard Crush, Map Break, Wall Rush)
15	Auto EX Burst	Support	20	5	150	-
15	Auto EX Command	Support	30	10	300	-
18	Reverse Air Dash	Action	10	5	100	△ during Quickmove
20	Holy Combo	Bravery Attack (Air)	30	15	200	◉ (Map Break, Chase) ◉ (Map Break)
(Mastery)	Ultima	Combo Attack	40	20	300	◉ after Holy Combo (Pull-in, Map Break, Wall Rush)
21	Speed Boost	Action	20	10	150	-
(Mastery)	Speed Boost+	Action	40	20	150	-
(Mastery)	Speed Boost++	Action	70	35	150	-
24	Graviga	Bravery Attack (Land)	30	15	180	◉ (Move OK, Pull-in, Map Break, Wall Rush)
25	EX Critical Boost	Extra	45	40	300	-
26	Auto EX Defense	Support	30	10	300	-
29	Meteor	Bravery Attack (Land)	30	15	180	◉ (Map Break)
32	Recovery Attack	Action	20	10	120	◉ or ◉ while reeling
32	Controlled Recovery	Action	10	5	120	Analog Stick during Recovery
35	Riposte	Extra	45	40	300	-
(Mastery)	Disable Riposte	Extra	20	10	300	-
38	Meltdown	HP Attack (Air)	40	20	300	
39	Jump Times Boost	Action	20	10	150	-
(Mastery)	Jump Times Boost+	Action	40	20	150	-
(Mastery)	Jump Times Boost++	Action	70	30	150	-
40	Omni Air Dash	Action	40	20	300	Analog Stick + ▭ + △
43	Sneak Attack	Extra	50	45	360	-
(Mastery)	Disable Sneak Attack	Extra	30	15	360	-
47	Physical Shield	Extra	20	10	280	-
50	Magic Shield	Extra	20	10	280	-
53	Multi-Air Slide	Action	10	5	250	Analog Stick + ✕ after expending jumps
(Mastery)	Multi-Air Slide+	Action	30	15	300	See Multi-Air Slide
57	Midair Evasion Boost	Action	20	10	150	-
60	Bravery Regen	Extra	20	10	280	-
64	Evasion Time Boost	Support	20	10	220	-
67	First Strike	Extra	40	35	360	-
(Mastery)	Disable First Strike	Extra	20	10	360	-
71	Concentration	Extra	30	15	250	-
(Mastery)	Concentration+	Extra	60	30	250	-
(Mastery)	Concentration++	Extra	100	50	250	-
74	Cat Nip	Extra	30	25	300	-
(Mastery)	Disable Cat Nip	Extra	20	10	300	-
78	Anti-EX	Extra	30	20	300	-
(Mastery)	Disable Anti-EX	Extra	20	10	300	-
81	Achy	Extra	30	15	250	-
(Mastery)	Achy+	Extra	60	30	250	-
85	Counterattack	Extra	50	45	360	-
(Mastery)	Disable Counterattack	Extra	30	15	360	-
88	Gambler's Spirit	Extra	30	15	300	-
(Mastery)	Disable Gambler's Spirit	Extra	20	10	300	-
92	Back to the Wall	Extra	30	25	300	-
(Mastery)	Disable Back to the Wall	Extra	20	10	300	-
95	Precision Jump	Extra	10	5	180	-
98	Snooze and Lose	Extra	100	50	250	-
100	EXP to HP	Extra	20	0	500	-
100	EXP to Bravery	Extra	20	0	500	-
100	EXP to EX Force	Extra	20	0	500	-

*Mobility can be increased with the abilities Speed Boost, Jump Boost, Jump Times Boost, and Precision Jump.

EX MODE

EX BURST

Riot Blade: Power is focused in both hands and fired as countless blades. (Repeatedly press left and ◉ to raise the gauges on the left and right.)

EX EFFECTS

Regen: Vigor and stamina recover little by little, restoring HP.

Glide: Uses the esper power hidden within to move freely through the air. (Activate by holding ◉ in midair.)

Chainspell: Embraces the spirit of a magus to raise magical power and cast the same spell again. (Press ◉ or ◉ after casting to activate.)

KEFKA PALAZZO

Mad Mage—Bewitches opponents, confusing them with unpredictable spells.

To unlock Kefka as a playable character, finish any Destiny Odyssey, then purchase him from the PP Catalog.

A mage who finds no greater joy than in destruction. In *Final Fantasy VI*, he was the right hand of Emperor Gestahl. A proven military strategist, he favored effective (if inhumane) methods that caused countless casualties. His pushy methods left him disliked by anyone unlucky enough to work under him. Infusions of Magitek power have caused him to lose his grip on sanity. Thirty-five years old, he is known for his high, lingering laugh.

BASIC MOBILITY*

Ground Movement Speed	☆
Innate Number of Jumps	1
Jump Height	☆☆☆
Jump Rising Speed	☆☆☆
Air Dash Speed	☆☆
Quickmove Speed	☆☆

*Mobility can be increased with the abilities Speed Boost, Jump Boost, Jump Times Boost, and Precision Jump.

EQUIPMENT

Weapon	Rods, Staves, Instruments
Hands	Bangles
Head	Hats, Hairpins
Body	Clothing, Robes

STAT PROGRESSION

LV	HP	CP	BRV	ATK	DEF	LUK
1	1000	350	95	12	11	10
5	1242	354	118	16	15	12
10	1545	359	147	21	20	15
20	2151	369	205	31	30	20
30	2757	379	263	41	40	25
40	3363	389	320	51	50	30
50	3969	399	378	61	60	35
60	4575	409	436	71	70	40
70	5181	419	493	81	80	45
80	5787	429	551	91	90	50
90	6393	439	609	101	100	55
100	6999	450	667	110	110	60

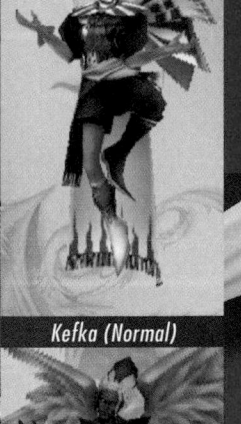

Kefka (Normal)

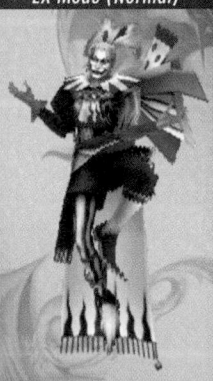

EX Mode (Normal)

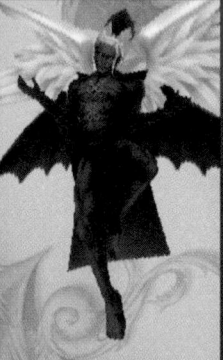

Kefka (Alternate)

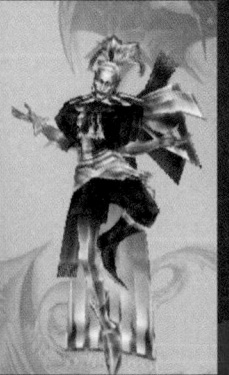

EX Mode (Alternate)

Phantasmal Harlequin

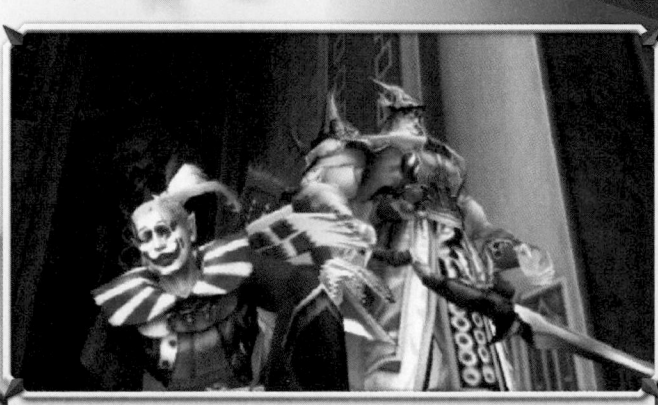

This mad jester wants everything to burn. He's frequently seen assisting other Chaos-aligned characters simply to contribute to havoc.

ABILITY PROGRESSION

LEVEL	SKILL	TYPE	CP (N)	CP (M)	AP TO MASTER	ATTACK COMMANDS & EFFECTS*
01	Havoc Wing (ground)	HP Attack (Land)	40	20	180	◉ (Guard Crush, Map Break, Wall Rush)
01	Lickety-Split Thundaga (ground)	Bravery Attack (Land)	20	10	90	◉ (Map Break, Wall Rush, Chase)
01	Trine (midair)	HP Attack (Air)	40	20	180	◉ (Map Break)
01	Twisty-Turny Blizzaga (ground)	Bravery Attack (Land)	30	15	180	◉ (Map Break, Wall Rush)
01	Waggle-Wobbly Firaga (midair)	Bravery Attack (Air)	20	10	90	◉ (Map Break)
01	Zap-Trap Thundaga (midair)	Bravery Attack (Air)	30	15	120	◉ (Map Break, Chase)
02	Reverse Free Air Dash	Action	10	5	100	▥ + ⬟
03	Wuggle-Wobbly Firaga (ground)	Bravery Attack (Land)	20	10	140	◉ (Map Break)
03	Extra-Crispy Firaga (midair)	Bravery Attack (Air)	30	15	120	◉ (Map Break, Chase)
04	Air Dash	Action	10	5	100	⬟ during Quickmove
06	Extra-Crispy Firaga (ground)	Bravery Attack (Land)	30	15	180	◉ (Map Break, Chase)
07	Jump Boost	Action	10	5	150	-
(Mastery)	Jump Boost+	Action	20	10	150	-
(Mastery)	Jump Boost++	Action	40	20	150	-
09	Scatter Spray Blizzaga (ground)	Bravery Attack (Land)	30	15	180	◉ (Map Break)
09	Scatter Spray Blizzaga (midair)	Bravery Attack (Air)	30	15	120	◉ (Map Break)
11	Auto Recovery	Support	20	5	250	-
11	Auto Chase	Support	20	5	250	-
12	Trine (ground)	HP Attack (Land)	40	20	180	◉ (Map Break)
15	Auto EX Burst	Support	20	5	150	-
15	Auto EX Command	Support	30	10	300	-
16	Lickety-Split Thundaga (midair)	Bravery Attack (Air)	20	10	180	◉ (Map Break, Wall Rush, Chase)
16	Zap-Trap Thundaga (ground)	Bravery Attack (Land)	30	15	180	◉ (Map Break, Chase)
18	Reverse Air Dash	Action	10	5	100	⬟ during Quickmove
20	Havoc Wing (midair)	HP Attack (Air)	40	20	180	◉ (Guard Crush, Map Break, Wall Rush)
21	Speed Boost	Action	20	10	150	-
(Mastery)	Speed Boost+	Action	40	20	150	-
(Mastery)	Speed Boost++	Action	70	35	150	-
24	Twisty-Turny Blizzaga (midair)	Bravery Attack (Air)	30	15	120	◉ (Map Break, Wall Rush)
25	EX Critical Boost	Extra	45	40	300	-
26	Auto EX Defense	Support	30	10	300	-
28	Ultima (ground)	Bravery Attack (Land)	30	15	180	◉ (Map Break, Wall Rush)
28	Ultima (midair)	Bravery Attack (Air)	30	15	120	◉ (Map Break, Wall Rush)
31	Meteor (ground)	Bravery Attack (Land)	30	15	180	◉ (Map Break, Chase)
31	Meteor (midair)	Bravery Attack (Air)	30	15	120	◉ (Map Break, Chase)
32	Recovery Attack	Action	20	10	120	⬟ or ◉ while reeling
32	Controlled Recovery	Action	10	5	120	Analog Stick during Recovery
34	Hyperdrive	HP Attack (Land)	40	20	300	Hold and release ◉ (Grows more powerful after 2.4 and 3.4 seconds; Map Break)
35	Riposte	Extra	45	40	300	-
(Mastery)	Disable Riposte	Extra	20	10	300	-
38	Forsaken (ground)	HP Attack (Land)	40	20	300	Hold ◉ (Guard Crush, Map Break)
38	Forsaken (midair)	HP Attack (Air)	40	20	300	Hold ◉ (Guard Crush, Map Break)
39	Jump Times Boost	Action	20	10	150	-
(Mastery)	Jump Times Boost+	Action	40	20	150	-
(Mastery)	Jump Times Boost++	Action	70	30	150	-
40	Omni Air Dash	Action	40	20	300	Analog Stick + ▥ + ⬟
43	Sneak Attack	Extra	50	45	360	-
(Mastery)	Disable Sneak Attack	Extra	30	15	360	-
47	Physical Shield	Extra	20	10	280	-
50	Magic Shield	Extra	20	10	280	-
53	Multi-Air Slide	Action	10	5	250	Analog Stick + ✕ after expending jumps
(Mastery)	Multi-Air Slide+	Action	30	15	300	See Multi-Air Slide
57	Midair Evasion Boost	Action	20	10	150	-
60	Bravery Regen	Extra	20	10	280	-
60	Glide Boost	Action	20	10	150	-
64	Evasion Time Boost	Support	20	10	220	-
67	First Strike	Extra	40	35	360	-
(Mastery)	Disable First Strike	Extra	20	10	360	-
71	Concentration	Extra	30	15	250	-
(Mastery)	Concentration+	Extra	60	30	250	-
(Mastery)	Concentration++	Extra	100	50	250	-
74	Cat Nip	Extra	30	25	300	-
(Mastery)	Disable Cat Nip	Extra	20	10	300	-
78	Anti-EX	Extra	30	20	300	-
(Mastery)	Disable Anti-EX	Extra	20	10	300	-
81	Achy	Extra	30	15	250	-
(Mastery)	Achy+	Extra	60	30	250	-
85	Counterattack	Extra	50	45	360	-
(Mastery)	Disable Counterattack	Extra	30	15	360	-
88	Gambler's Spirit	Extra	30	15	300	-
(Mastery)	Disable Gambler's Spirit	Extra	20	10	300	-
92	Back to the Wall	Extra	30	25	300	-
(Mastery)	Disable Back to the Wall	Extra	20	10	300	-
95	Precision Jump	Extra	10	5	180	-
98	Snooze and Lose	Extra	100	50	250	-
100	EXP to HP	Extra	20	0	500	-
100	EXP to Bravery	Extra	20	0	500	-
100	EXP to EX Force	Extra	20	0	500	-

*Initial commands may require directional presses, depending on the slot to which abilities are assigned.

EX MODE

EX BURST

Light of Judgment: A light comes from the heavens, cleansing all in its wake. (Memorize the commands that display, then enter them in order.)

EX EFFECTS

Regen: Vigor and stamina recover little by little, restoring HP.

Glide: Increases the magus power within to move freely through the air. (Activate by holding ✕ in midair.)

Exhilarating Magic: All spells become more chaotic—projectiles multiply, magic rebounds, and other unpredictable effects occur.

CHARACTERS

CLOUD STRIFE

Buster Basher—Can send foes flying with a single swipe of his massive sword.

An acerbic young swordsman with glowing eyes who wields a blade as large as he is. In *Final Fantasy VII*, after leaving the Shinra Company, he started working as a jack-of-all-trades in the city of Midgar. After joining the anti-Shinra group Avalanche, he became entangled in a battle for the future of the planet. On the surface he looks disaffected with most everything, but he is quite a fan of extreme sports such as snowboarding, motorcycling, and chocobo riding.

BASIC MOBILITY*

Ground Movement Speed	⭐⭐☆
Innate Number of Jumps	1
Jump Height	⭐⭐☆
Jump Rising Speed	⭐⭐☆
Air Dash Speed	⭐⭐⭐
Quickmove Speed	⭐⭐⭐

*Mobility can be increased with the abilities Speed Boost, Jump Boost, Jump Times Boost, and Precision Jump.

EQUIPMENT

Weapon	Swords, Greatswords
Hands	Shields, Bangles
Head	Hats, Helms
Body	Clothing, Light Armor

STAT PROGRESSION

LV	HP	CP	BRV	ATK	DEF	LUK
1	1000	330	95	11	13	10
5	1242	335	118	15	17	12
10	1545	341	147	20	22	15
20	2151	353	205	30	32	20
30	2757	365	263	40	42	25
40	3363	377	320	50	52	30
50	3969	389	378	60	62	35
60	4575	401	436	70	72	40
70	5181	413	493	80	82	45
80	5787	425	551	90	92	50
90	6393	437	609	100	102	55
100	6999	450	667	110	112	60

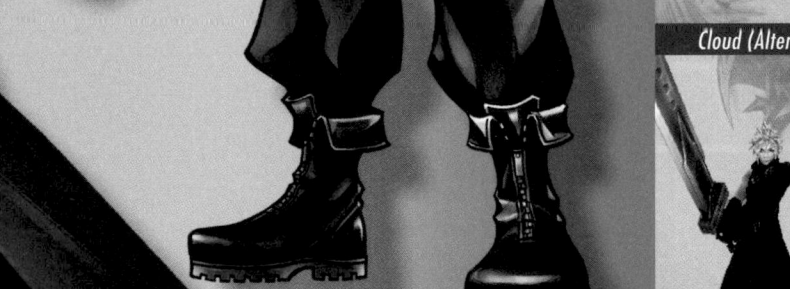

To his companions, Cloud seems unmotivated and aloof. They do not suspect how much he worries for and looks after them.

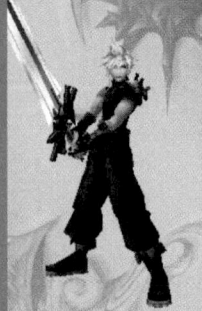

Cloud (Normal)

EX Mode (Normal)

Cloud (Alternate)

EX Mode (Alternate)

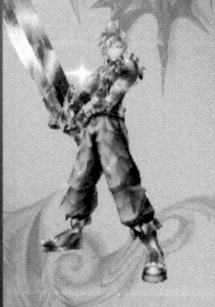

Imaginary Soldier

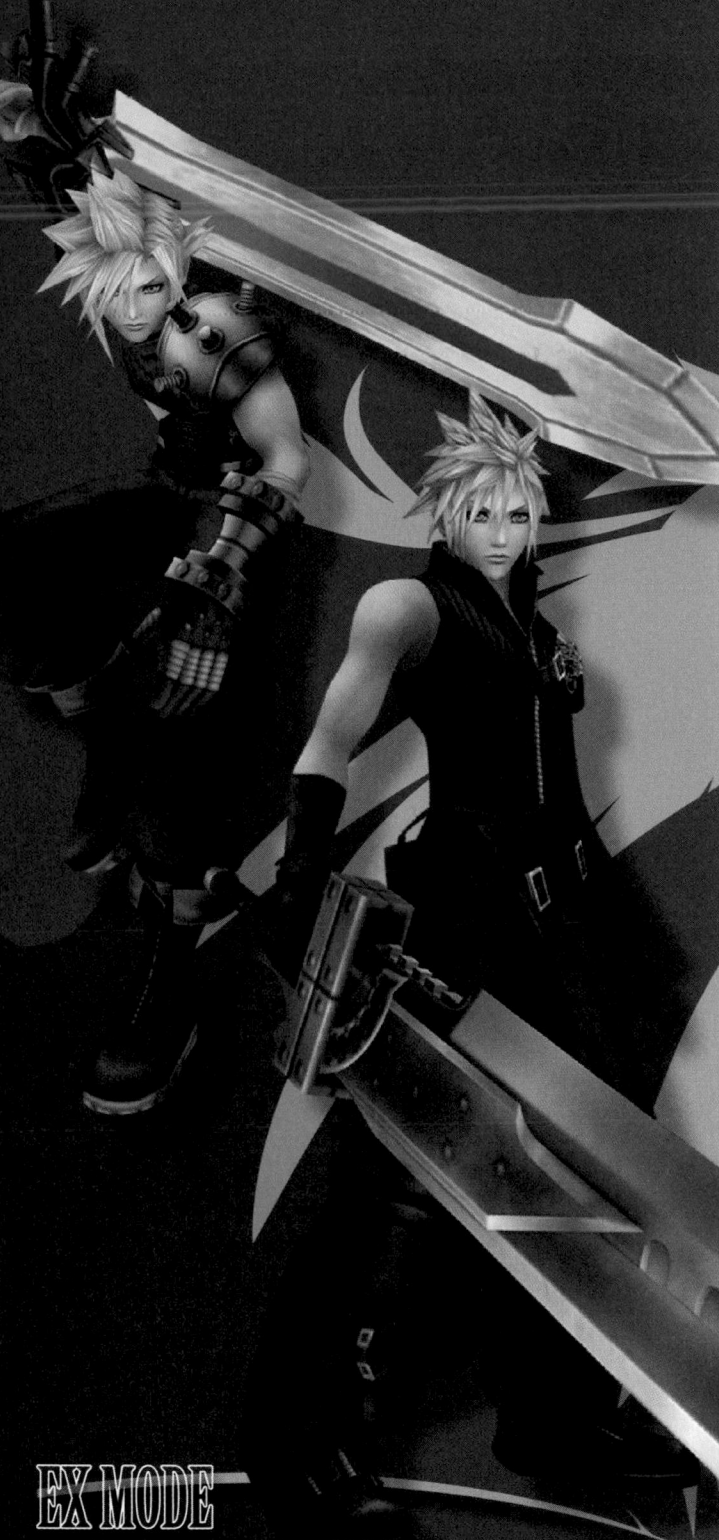

ABILITY PROGRESSION

LEVEL	SKILL	TYPE	CP (N)	CP (M)	AP TO MASTER	ATTACK COMMANDS & EFFECTS*
01	Braver	HP Attack (Air)	40	20	180	● (Guard Crush, Map Break, Wall Rush)
01	Climhazzard	Bravery Attack (Land)	30	15	120	● (Map Break) ● (Map Break) ● (Map Break, Wall Rush)
01	Cross-Slash	HP Attack (Land)	40	20	180	● (Guard Crush, Map Break, Wall Rush)
01	Double Cut	Bravery Attack (Land)	30	15	120	● ● (Chase)
01	Fire	Bravery Attack (Land)	20	10	90	● ●
01	Slashing Blow	Bravery Attack (Air)	30	15	300	● ● (Map Break, Wall Rush) or Analog Stick Up + ● (Map Break, Wall Rush)
(Mastery)	Omnislash Version 5	Combo Attack	40	20	300	● after first ● press in Slashing Blow (Guard Crush, Map Break, Wall Rush)
03	Sonic Break	Bravery Attack (Land)	30	15	180	● ● ● (Wall Rush, Map Break)
(Mastery)	Finishing Touch	Combo Attack	40	20	300	● after second ● press in Sonic Break (Guard Crush, Map Break, Wall Rush)
04	Air Dash	Action	10	5	100	▲ during Quickmove
07	Speed Boost	Action	20	10	150	-
(Mastery)	Speed Boost+	Action	40	20	150	-
(Mastery)	Speed Boost++	Action	70	35	150	-
08	Fira	Bravery Attack (Land)	20	10	90	●
11	Auto Recovery	Support	20	5	250	-
11	Auto Chase	Support	20	5	250	-
13	Aerial Fang	Bravery Attack (Air)	30	15	140	● (Chase, Map Break)
15	Auto EX Burst	Support	20	5	150	-
15	Auto EX Command	Support	30	10	300	-
17	Rising Fang	Bravery Attack (Air)	30	15	150	● (Map Break, Wall Rush)
18	Reverse Air Dash	Action	10	5	100	▲ during Quickmove
21	Jump Boost	Action	10	5	150	-
(Mastery)	Jump Boost+	Action	20	10	150	-
(Mastery)	Jump Boost++	Action	40	20	150	-
23	Firaga	Bravery Attack (Land)	30	15	120	● (Map Break)
25	EX Critical Boost	Extra	45	40	300	-
26	Auto EX Defense	Support	30	10	300	-
29	Reverse Free Air Dash	Action	10	5	100	■ + ▲
30	Blade Beam	Bravery Attack (Land)	30	15	120	● (Chase, Map Break)
32	Recovery Attack	Action	20	10	120	● or ● while reeling
32	Controlled Recovery	Action	10	5	120	Analog Stick during Recovery
35	Riposte	Extra	45	40	300	-
(Mastery)	Disable Riposte	Extra	20	10	300	-
38	Meteorain	HP Attack (Land)	40	20	300	● (Guard Crush, Map Break)
39	Jump Times Boost	Action	20	10	150	-
(Mastery)	Jump Times Boost+	Action	40	20	150	-
(Mastery)	Jump Times Boost++	Action	70	30	150	-
40	Omni Air Dash	Action	40	20	300	Analog Stick + ■ + ▲
43	Sneak Attack	Extra	50	45	360	-
(Mastery)	Disable Sneak Attack	Extra	30	15	360	-
47	Physical Shield	Extra	20	10	280	-
50	Magic Shield	Extra	20	10	280	-
53	Multi-Air Slide	Action	10	5	250	Analog Stick + ✕ after expending jumps
(Mastery)	Multi-Air Slide+	Action	30	15	300	See Multi-Air Slide
57	Midair Evasion Boost	Action	20	10	150	-
60	Bravery Regen	Extra	20	10	280	-
64	Evasion Time Boost	Support	20	10	220	-
67	First Strike	Extra	40	35	360	-
(Mastery)	Disable First Strike	Extra	20	10	360	-
71	Concentration	Extra	30	15	250	-
(Mastery)	Concentration+	Extra	60	30	250	-
(Mastery)	Concentration++	Extra	100	50	250	-
74	Cat Nip	Extra	30	25	300	-
(Mastery)	Disable Cat Nip	Extra	20	10	300	-
78	Anti-EX	Extra	30	20	300	-
(Mastery)	Disable Anti-EX	Extra	20	10	300	-
81	Achy	Extra	30	15	250	-
(Mastery)	Achy+	Extra	60	30	250	-
85	Counterattack	Extra	50	45	360	-
(Mastery)	Disable Counterattack	Extra	30	15	360	-
88	Gambler's Spirit	Extra	30	15	300	-
(Mastery)	Disable Gambler's Spirit	Extra	20	10	300	-
92	Back to the Wall	Extra	30	25	300	-
(Mastery)	Disable Back to the Wall	Extra	20	10	300	-
95	Precision Jump	Extra	10	5	180	-
98	Snooze and Lose	Extra	100	50	250	-
100	EXP to HP	Extra	20	0	500	-
100	EXP to Bravery	Extra	20	0	500	-
100	EXP to EX Force	Extra	20	0	500	-

*Initial commands may require directional presses, depending on the slot to which abilities are assigned.

EX MODE

EX BURST

Omnislash: An attack slicing the opponent over and over. (Repeatedly press ● to raise the gauge.)

EX EFFECTS

Regen: Vigor and stamina recover little by little, restoring HP.

Ultima Weapon (CRUSH): Each attack becomes even heavier, crushing all attempts at blocking.

Ultima Weapon (ATK): The higher the user's HP, the sharper the weapon's blade.

SEPHIROTH

Focused Blade—Uses peerless swordsmanship to deliver precise strikes.

Unlock Sephiroth as a playable character by first finishing any Destiny Odyssey, then purchasing Sephiroth from the PP Catalog.

A legendary member of SOLDIER once revered as a hero. In Final Fantasy VII, after learning that he was the product of genetic experimentation, he decided he was fated to destroy the planet—and he had more than enough power to do so. During his stint in SOLDIER, he adeptly learned how to slash enemies with an impossibly long sword. His fighting prowess is perhaps the only thing he values as a token from the time he considered himself to be human.

BASIC MOBILITY*

Ground Movement Speed	★★☆
Innate Number of Jumps	1
Jump Height	★★☆
Jump Rising Speed	★★☆
Air Dash Speed	★★☆
Quickmove Speed	★★☆

*Mobility can be increased with the abilities Speed Boost, Jump Boost, Jump Times Boost, and Precision Jump.

EQUIPMENT

Weapon	Katana, Spears
Hands	Shields, Gauntlets
Head	Helms
Body	Light Armor, Heavy Armor

STAT PROGRESSION

LV	HP	CP	BRV	ATK	DEF	LUK
1	1000	330	95	11	12	10
5	1242	335	118	15	16	12
10	1545	341	147	20	21	15
20	2151	353	205	30	31	20
30	2757	369	263	40	41	25
40	3363	377	320	50	51	30
50	3969	389	378	60	61	35
60	4575	401	436	70	71	40
70	5181	413	493	80	81	45
80	5787	425	551	90	91	50
90	6393	437	609	100	101	55
100	6999	450	667	110	111	60

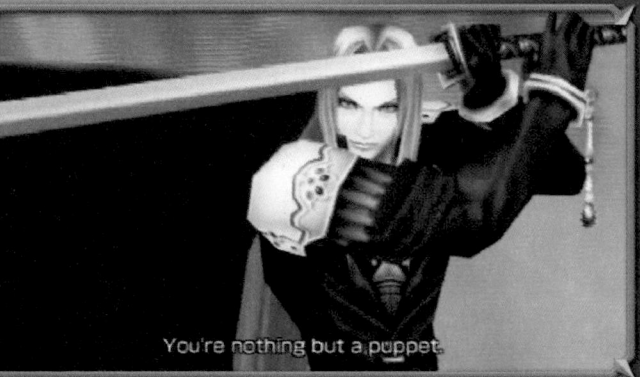

You're nothing but a puppet.

Once the star agent of SOLDIER, revelations regarding his origin have infected Sephiroth's judgment and turned his view of the world rotten.

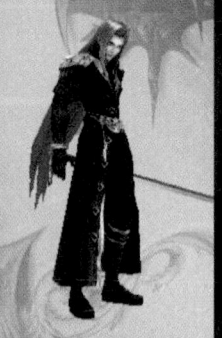

Sephiroth (Normal)

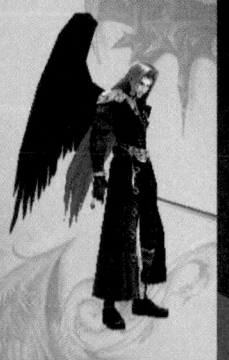

EX Mode (Normal)

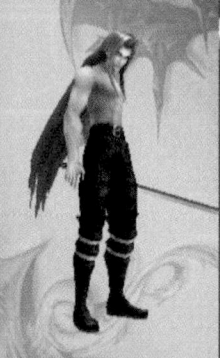

Sephiroth (Alternate)

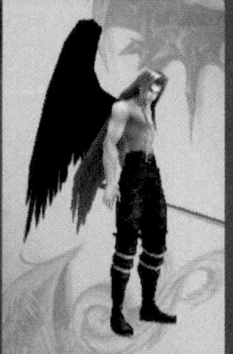

EX Mode (Alternate)

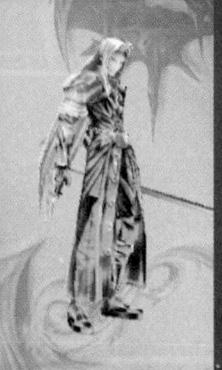

Imaginary Soldier

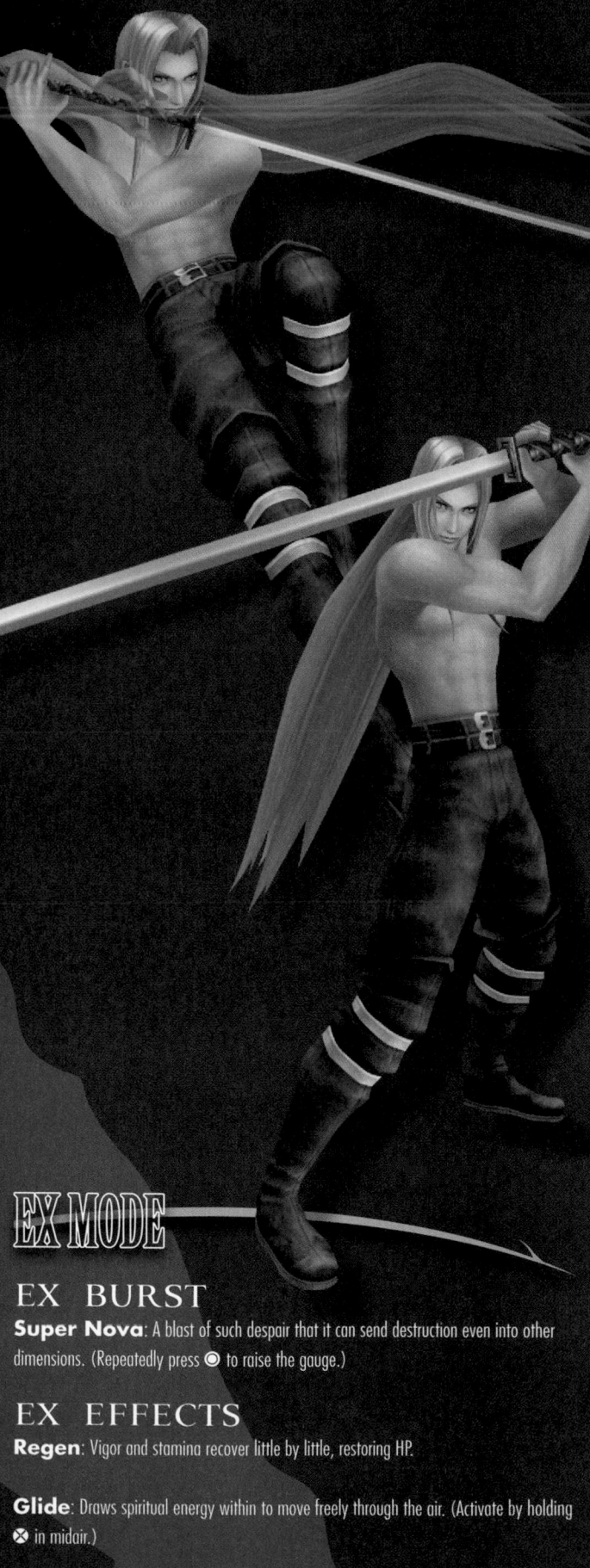

ABILITY PROGRESSION

LEVEL	SKILL	TYPE	CP (N)	CP (M)	AP TO MASTER	ATTACK COMMANDS & EFFECTS*
01	Hell's Gate (midair)	HP Attack (Air)	40	20	300	Hold and release ● (Move OK, Guard Crush, Map Break)
01	Octaslash (ground)	HP Attack (Land)	40	20	300	● (Guard Crush, Map Break, Wall Rush)
01	Shadow Flare (ground)	Bravery Attack (Land)	30	15	120	●
01	Reaper	Bravery Attack (Land)	30	15	120	● (Map Break) ● (Map Break) ● (Map Break, Chase)
01	Scintilla (ground)	HP Attack (Land)	40	20	300	● (Guard, Guard Crush, Map Break, Wall Rush)
01	Sudden Cruelty	Bravery Attack (Air)	30	15	180	● (Map Break) ● (Map Break, Chase)
03	Oblivion	Bravery Attack (Air)	30	15	180	● (Wall Rush, Map Break)
04	Air Dash	Action	10	5	100	● during Quickmove
07	Speed Boost	Action	20	10	150	-
(Mastery)	Speed Boost+	Action	40	20	150	-
(Mastery)	Speed Boost++	Action	70	35	150	-
08	Godspeed	Bravery Attack (Air)	30	15	180	● (Map Break) ● (Map Break, Wall Rush)
11	Auto Recovery	Support	20	5	250	-
11	Auto Chase	Support	20	5	250	-
13	Octaslash (midair)	HP Attack (Air)	40	20	300	● (Guard Crush, Map Break, Wall Rush)
15	Auto EX Burst	Support	20	5	150	-
15	Auto EX Command	Support	30	10	300	-
18	Reverse Air Dash	Action	10	5	100	● during Quickmove
19	Shadow Flare (midair)	Bravery Attack (Air)	30	15	180	●
21	Jump Boost	Action	10	5	150	-
(Mastery)	Jump Boost+	Action	20	10	150	-
(Mastery)	Jump Boost++	Action	40	20	150	-
24	Fervent Blow	Bravery Attack (Land)	30	15	120	● (Map Break) ● (Map Break, Wall Rush)
25	EX Critical Boost	Extra	45	40	300	-
26	Auto EX Defense	Support	30	10	300	-
28	Scintilla (midair)	HP Attack (Air)	40	20	300	● (Guard, Guard Crush, Map Break, Wall Rush)
29	Reverse Free Air Dash	Action	10	5	100	▪ + ▲
32	Recovery Attack	Action	20	10	120	● or ● while reeling
32	Controlled Recovery	Action	10	5	120	Analog Stick during Recovery
33	Black Materia	HP Attack (Land)	40	20	300	Hold and release ● (Grows in power after holding for 1.5 and 3.0 seconds, Guard Crush, Map Break, Pull-in and Wall Rush at max power)
35	Riposte	Extra	45	40	300	-
(Mastery)	Disable Riposte	Extra	20	10	300	-
38	Heaven's Light	HP Attack (Air)	40	20	300	● (Guard Crush, Map Break, Wall Rush)
39	Jump Times Boost	Action	20	10	150	-
(Mastery)	Jump Times Boost+	Action	40	20	150	-
(Mastery)	Jump Times Boost++	Action	70	30	150	-
40	Omni Air Dash	Action	40	20	300	Analog Stick + ▪ + ▲
43	Sneak Attack	Extra	50	45	360	-
(Mastery)	Disable Sneak Attack	Extra	30	15	360	-
47	Physical Shield	Extra	20	10	280	-
50	Magic Shield	Extra	20	10	280	-
53	Multi-Air Slide	Action	10	5	250	Analog Stick + ✕ after expending jumps
(Mastery)	Multi-Air Slide+	Action	30	15	300	See Multi-Air Slide
57	Midair Evasion Boost	Action	20	10	150	-
60	Bravery Regen	Extra	20	10	280	-
60	Glide Boost	Action	20	10	150	-
64	Evasion Time Boost	Support	20	10	220	-
67	First Strike	Extra	40	35	360	-
(Mastery)	Disable First Strike	Extra	20	10	360	-
71	Concentration	Extra	30	15	250	-
(Mastery)	Concentration+	Extra	60	30	250	-
(Mastery)	Concentration++	Extra	100	50	250	-
74	Cat Nip	Extra	30	25	300	-
(Mastery)	Disable Cat Nip	Extra	20	10	300	-
78	Anti-EX	Extra	30	20	300	-
(Mastery)	Disable Anti-EX	Extra	20	10	300	-
81	Achy	Extra	30	15	250	-
(Mastery)	Achy+	Extra	60	30	250	-
85	Counterattack	Extra	50	45	360	-
(Mastery)	Disable Counterattack	Extra	30	15	360	-
88	Gambler's Spirit	Extra	30	15	300	-
(Mastery)	Disable Gambler's Spirit	Extra	20	10	300	-
92	Back to the Wall	Extra	30	25	300	-
(Mastery)	Disable Back to the Wall	Extra	20	10	300	-
95	Precision Jump	Extra	10	5	180	-
98	Snooze and Lose	Extra	100	50	250	-
100	EXP to HP	Extra	20	0	500	-
100	EXP to Bravery	Extra	20	0	500	-
100	EXP to EX Force	Extra	20	0	500	-

*Initial commands may require directional presses, depending on the slot to which abilities are assigned.

EX MODE

EX BURST

Super Nova: A blast of such despair that it can send destruction even into other dimensions. (Repeatedly press ● to raise the gauge.)

EX EFFECTS

Regen: Vigor and stamina recover little by little, restoring HP.

Glide: Draws spiritual energy within to move freely through the air. (Activate by holding ✕ in midair.)

Heartless Angel: Bravery cannot be gained, but opponent's bravery falls to 1. (Activate with ▪ + ●.)

SQUALL LEONHART

Relentless Revolver—Corners enemies with chained combos.

A cold, taciturn youth who wields a gunblade, a weapon consisting of part sword and part gun. In Final Fantasy VIII, he was raised as a mercenary at the Balamb Garden Military Academy and belonged to the special military force, SeeD. It is arguable whether his decision to train with the old-fashioned and notoriously difficult to master gunblade is more a show of strength or of stubbornness.

BASIC MOBILITY*

Ground Movement Speed	⭐⭐
Innate Number of Jumps	1
Jump Height	⭐⭐
Jump Rising Speed	⭐⭐
Air Dash Speed	⭐⭐
Quickmove Speed	⭐⭐

*Mobility can be increased with the abilities Speed Boost, Jump Boost, Jump Times Boost, and Precision Jump.

EQUIPMENT

Weapon	Swords, Thrown Weapons
Hands	Shields, Bangles
Head	Hats, Helms
Body	Clothing, Light Armor

STAT PROGRESSION

LV	HP	CP	BRV	ATK	DEF	LUK
1	1000	330	95	10	12	10
5	1242	335	118	14	16	12
10	1545	341	147	19	21	15
20	2151	353	205	29	31	20
30	2757	365	263	39	41	25
40	3363	377	320	49	51	30
50	3969	389	378	59	61	35
60	4575	401	436	69	71	40
70	5181	413	493	79	81	45
80	5787	425	551	89	91	50
90	6393	437	609	99	101	55
100	6999	450	667	109	111	60

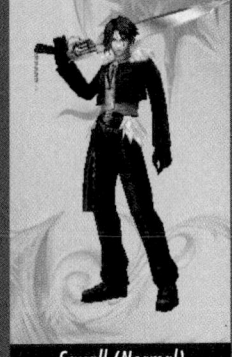

Squall (Normal)

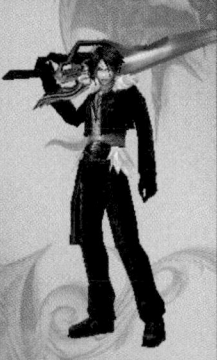

EX Mode (Normal)

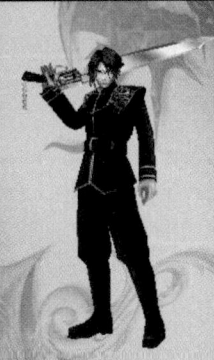

Squall (Alternate)

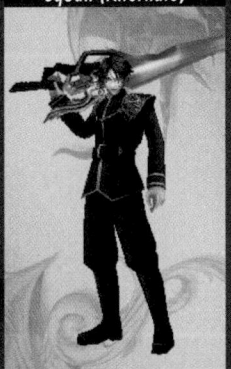

EX Mode (Alternate)

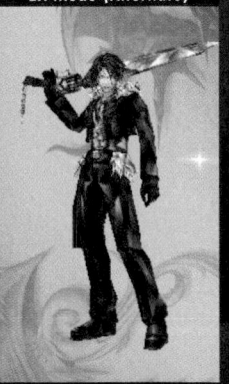

Transient Lion

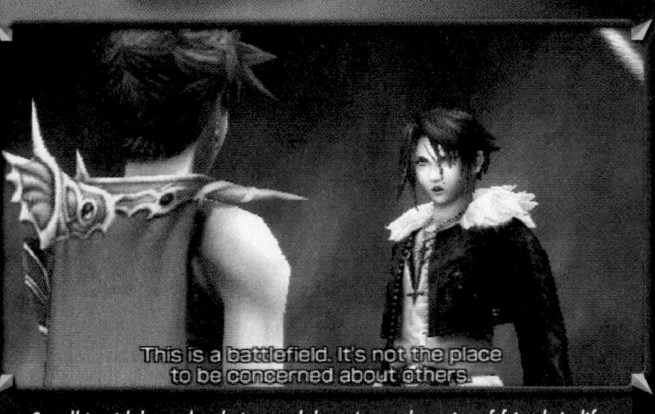

This is a battlefield. It's not the place to be concerned about others.

Squall is withdrawn by choice, and doesn't see the point of friends in life, or allies in combat. He's allowed life to harden him, but he forgets that others struggle too...

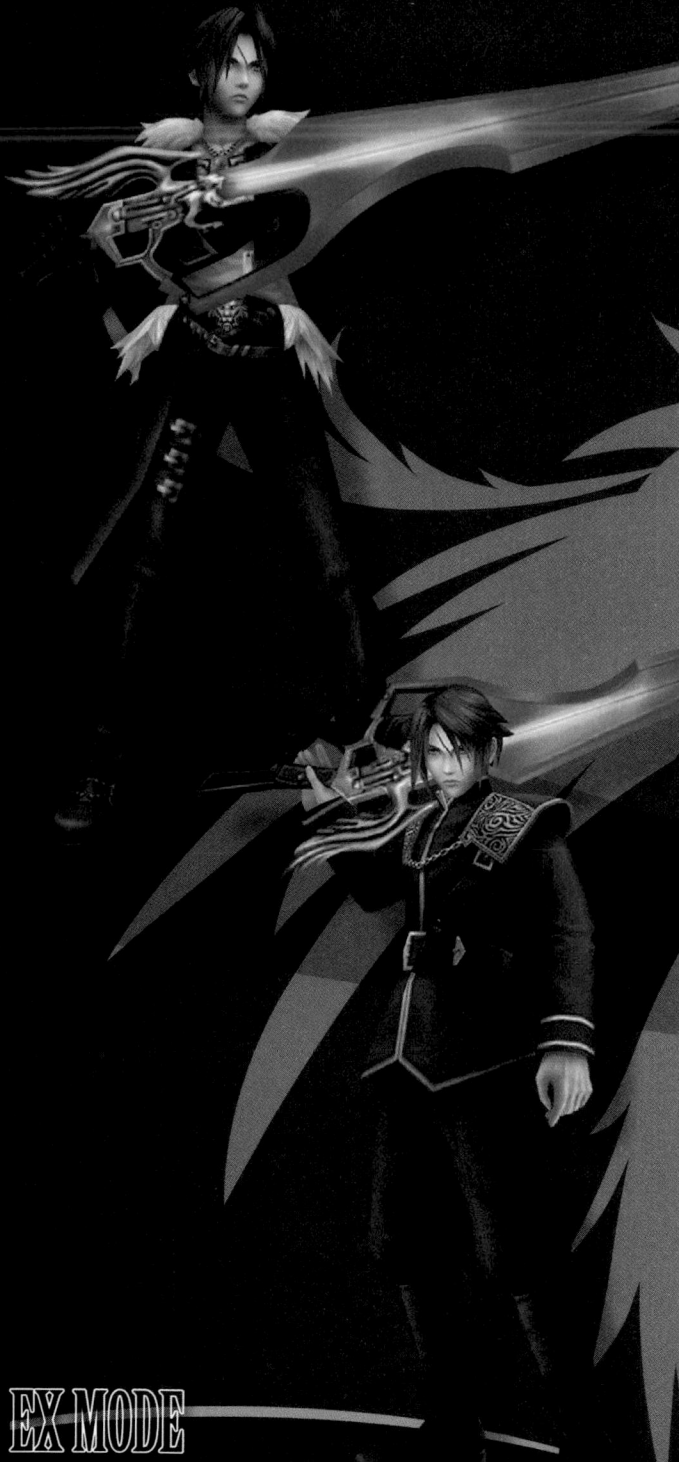

ABILITY PROGRESSION

LEVEL	SKILL	TYPE	CP (N)	CP (M)	AP TO MASTER	ATTACK COMMANDS & EFFECTS*
01	Aerial Circle	HP Attack (Air)	40	20	180	● (Guard, Guard Crush, Pull-in, Map Break, Wall Rush)
01	Blizzard Barret	Bravery Attack (Land)	20	10	90	●
01	Fated Circle	HP Attack (Land)	40	20	180	● (Guard, Guard Crush, Pull-in, Wall Rush)
01	Heel Crush	Bravery Attack (Air)	30	15	180	● (Map Break, Wall Rush)
01	Rough Divide (ground)	HP Attack (Land)	40	20	300	● (Guard Crush, Map Break, Wall Rush)
01	Upper Blues	Bravery Attack (Land)	30	15	120	● ● ● ● (Map Break, Wall Rush)
03	Solid Barret	Bravery Attack (Land)	30	15	120	● ● ● ● ● (Chase, Map Break)
04	Air Dash	Action	10	5	100	▲ during Quickmove
06	Thunder Barret	Bravery Attack (Land)	30	15	120	● (Map Break)
07	Speed Boost	Action	20	10	150	-
(Mastery)	Speed Boost+	Action	40	20	150	-
(Mastery)	Speed Boost++	Action	70	35	150	-
10	Beat Fang	Bravery Attack (Air)	30	15	180	● ● ● (Map Break) ● (Map Break, Wall Rush)
11	Auto Recovery	Support	20	5	250	-
11	Auto Chase	Support	20	5	250	-
15	Auto EX Burst	Support	20	5	150	-
15	Auto EX Command	Support	30	10	300	-
16	Rough Divide (midair)	HP Attack (Air)	40	20	300	● (Guard Crush, Map Break, Wall Rush)
18	Reverse Air Dash	Action	10	5	100	▲ during Quickmove
21	Jump Boost	Action	10	5	150	-
(Mastery)	Jump Boost+	Action	20	10	150	-
(Mastery)	Jump Boost++	Action	40	20	150	-
22	Fusillade	Bravery Attack (Land)	30	15	120	● ● ● ● ● (Chase, Map Break)
25	EX Critical Boost	Extra	45	40	300	-
26	Auto EX Defense	Support	30	10	300	-
28	Blasting Zone	HP Attack (Land)	40	20	300	● (Guard Crush, Map Break)
29	Reverse Free Air Dash	Action	10	5	100	■ + ▲
32	Recovery Attack	Action	20	10	120	● or ● while reeling
32	Controlled Recovery	Action	10	5	120	Analog Stick during Recovery
33	Mystic Flurry	Bravery Attack (Air)	30	15	180	● ● ● ● ● (Map Break, Wall Rush)
35	Riposte	Extra	45	40	300	-
(Mastery)	Disable Riposte	Extra	20	10	300	-
38	Revolver Drive	HP Attack (Land)	40	20	180	Hold and release ● (Guard Crush, Map Break, Wall Rush)
39	Jump Times Boost	Action	20	10	150	-
(Mastery)	Jump Times Boost+	Action	40	20	150	-
(Mastery)	Jump Times Boost++	Action	70	30	150	-
40	Omni Air Dash	Action	40	20	300	Analog Stick + ■ + ▲
43	Sneak Attack	Extra	50	45	360	-
(Mastery)	Disable Sneak Attack	Extra	30	15	360	-
47	Physical Shield	Extra	20	10	280	-
50	Magic Shield	Extra	20	10	280	-
53	Multi-Air Slide	Action	10	5	250	Analog Stick + ✖ after expending jumps
(Mastery)	Multi-Air Slide+	Action	30	15	300	See Multi-Air Slide
57	Midair Evasion Boost	Action	20	10	150	-
60	Bravery Regen	Extra	20	10	280	-
64	Evasion Time Boost	Support	20	10	220	-
67	First Strike	Extra	40	35	360	-
(Mastery)	Disable First Strike	Extra	20	10	360	-
71	Concentration	Extra	30	15	250	-
(Mastery)	Concentration+	Extra	60	30	250	-
(Mastery)	Concentration++	Extra	100	50	250	-
74	Cat Nip	Extra	30	25	300	-
(Mastery)	Disable Cat Nip	Extra	20	10	300	-
78	Anti-EX	Extra	30	10	300	-
(Mastery)	Disable Anti-EX	Extra	20	10	300	-
81	Achy	Extra	30	15	250	-
(Mastery)	Achy+	Extra	60	30	250	-
85	Counterattack	Extra	50	45	360	-
(Mastery)	Disable Counterattack	Extra	30	15	360	-
88	Gambler's Spirit	Extra	30	15	300	-
(Mastery)	Disable Gambler's Spirit	Extra	20	10	300	-
92	Back to the Wall	Extra	30	25	300	-
(Mastery)	Disable Back to the Wall	Extra	20	10	300	-
95	Precision Jump	Extra	10	5	180	-
98	Snooze and Lose	Extra	100	50	250	-
100	EXP to HP	Extra	20	0	500	-
100	EXP to Bravery	Extra	20	0	500	-
100	EXP to EX Force	Extra	20	0	500	-

*Initial commands may require directional presses, depending on the slot to which abilities are assigned.

EX MODE

EX BURST

Renzokuken: A flurry of attacks ending in one shattering blow. (Watch your timing and press ■ when the cursor is in the frame.)

EX EFFECTS

Regen: Vigor and stamina recover little by little, restoring HP.

Lion Heart (RANGE): Transfers the heart of a lion to the weapon, increasing its range.

Lion Heart (HIT): Pushes the weapon's specs to the limit, increasing the force of each blast.

ULTIMECIA

Sorcerous Fusileer—Keeps opponents at a distance with magical barrages.

Ultimecia becomes a playable character after you finish any Destiny Odyssey, then purchase her from the PP Catalog.

A powerful sorceress possessing a deep-seated rage and the ability to control space and time. In *Final Fantasy VIII*, she reigned over the far future. Using time compression magic, she aimed to create a world where the past, present, and future were one, and only she might exist.

BASIC MOBILITY*

Ground Movement Speed	☆
Innate Number of Jumps	4
Jump Height	☆
Jump Rising Speed	☆
Air Dash Speed	☆☆
Quickmove Speed	☆

*Mobility can be increased with the abilities Speed Boost, Jump Boost, Jump Times Boost, and Precision Jump.

EQUIPMENT

Weapon	Daggers, Rods, Staves, Instruments
Hands	Bangles
Head	Hats, Hairpins
Body	Clothing, Robes

STAT PROGRESSION

LV	HP	CP	BRV	ATK	DEF	LUK
1	1000	330	95	12	10	10
5	1242	335	118	16	14	12
10	1545	341	147	21	19	15
20	2151	353	205	31	29	20
30	2757	365	263	41	39	25
40	3363	377	320	51	49	30
50	3969	389	378	61	59	35
60	4575	401	436	71	69	40
70	5181	413	493	81	79	45
80	5787	425	551	91	89	50
90	6393	437	609	101	99	55
100	6999	450	667	111	109	60

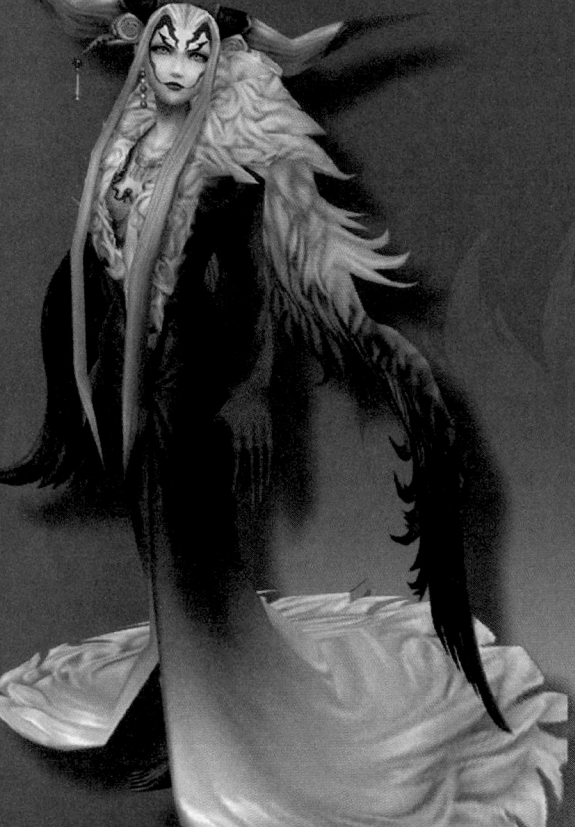

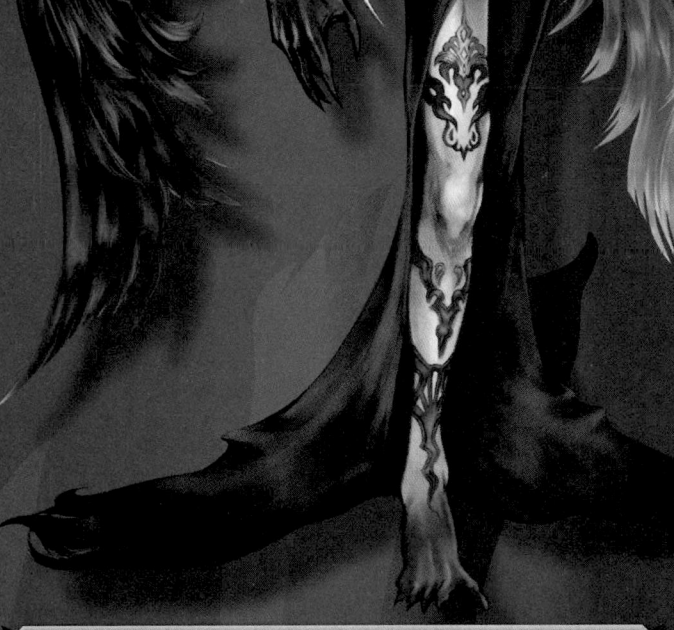

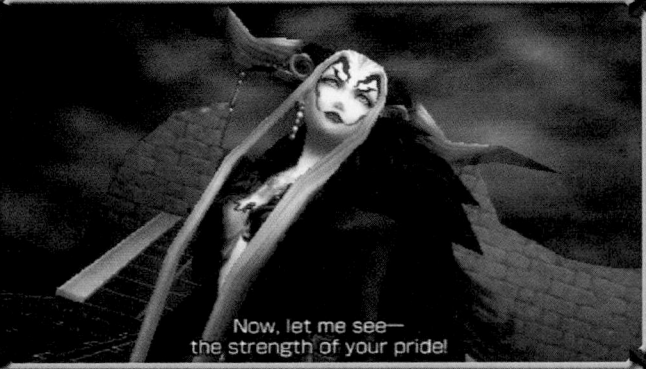

Now, let me see— the strength of your pride!

Ultimecia, crazed and staggeringly powerful, schemes with The Emperor and other emissaries of Chaos toward the unknotting of it all.

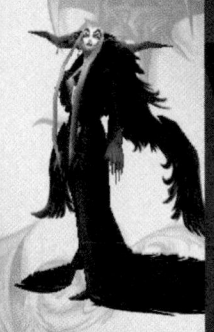

Ultimecia (Normal)

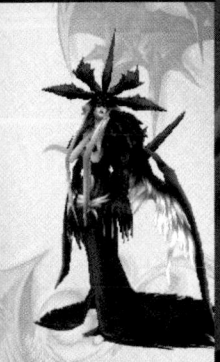

EX Mode (Normal)

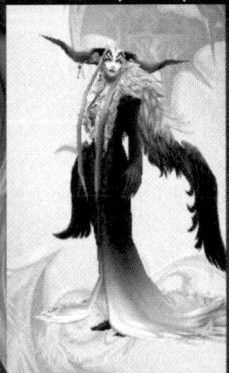

Ultimecia (Alternate)

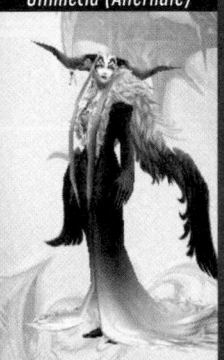

EX Mode (Alternate)

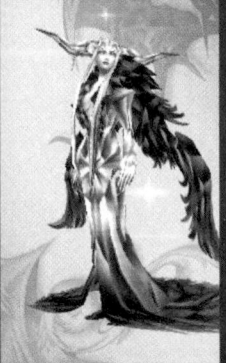

Transient Witch

LEVEL	SKILL	TYPE	CP (N)	CP (M)	AP TO MASTER	ATTACK COMMANDS & EFFECTS*
01	Great Attractor (midair)	HP Attack (Air)	40	20	180	Press and release ⬤ (Move OK, power increases after holding for longer than 3.0, 4.5, and 6.0 seconds, Map Break, hold at least 3.0 seconds for Guard Crush)
01	Knight's Arrow (ground)	Bravery Attack (Land)	30	15	180	Press ⬤ repeatedly (Move OK) hold ⬤ (Move OK, Map Break)
01	Knight's Arrow (midair)	Bravery Attack (Air)	30	15	140	Press ⬤ repeatedly (Move OK) hold ⬤ (Move OK, Map Break)
01	Knight's Axe (midair)	Bravery Attack (Air)	30	15	140	Press ⬤ repeatedly (Move OK, Chase) hold ⬤ (Move OK, Guard Crush, Map Break)
01	Knight's Blade (ground)	Bravery Attack (Land)	20	10	120	Press ⬤ repeatedly (Move OK) hold ⬤ (Move OK, Map Break)
01	Shockwave Pulsar (ground)	HP Attack (Land)	40	20	180	Press and release ⬤ (Move OK, power increases after holding for longer than 2.0 and 4.5 seconds, Guard Crush, Map Break)
02	Reverse Free Air Dash	Action	10	5	100	🔘 + 🅐
04	Air Dash	Action	10	5	100	🅐 during Quickmove
06	Knight's Blade (midair)	Bravery Attack (Air)	20	10	90	Press ⬤ repeatedly (Move OK) hold ⬤ (Move OK, Map Break)
07	Jump Boost	Action	10	5	150	-
(Mastery)	Jump Boost+	Action	20	10	150	-
(Mastery)	Jump Boost++	Action	40	20	150	-
11	Auto Recovery	Support	20	5	250	-
11	Auto Chase	Support	20	5	250	-
12	Knight's Axe (ground)	Bravery Attack (Land)	30	15	180	Press ⬤ repeatedly (Move OK, Chase) hold ⬤ (Move OK, Guard Crush, Map Break)
15	Auto EX Burst	Support	20	5	150	-
15	Auto EX Command	Support	30	10	300	-
17	Great Attractor (ground)	HP Attack (Land)	40	20	180	Press and release ⬤ (Move OK, power increases after holding for longer than 3.0, 4.5, and 6.0 seconds, Map Break, hold at least 3.0 seconds for Guard Crush)
18	Reverse Air Dash	Action	10	5	100	🅐 during Quickmove
21	Speed Boost	Action	20	10	150	-
(Mastery)	Speed Boost+	Action	40	20	150	-
(Mastery)	Speed Boost++	Action	70	35	150	-
23	Apocalypse (ground)	HP Attack (Land)	40	20	300	
25	EX Critical Boost	Extra	45	40	300	-
26	Auto EX Defense	Support	30	10	300	
29	Shockwave Pulsar (midair)	HP Attack (Air)	40	20	180	Press and release ⬤ (Move OK, power increases after holding for longer than 2.0 and 4.5 seconds, Guard Crush, Map Break)
32	Recovery Attack	Action	20	10	120	⬤ or ⬤ while reeling
32	Controlled Recovery	Action	10	5	120	Analog Stick during Recovery
35	Riposte	Extra	45	40	300	-
(Mastery)	Disable Riposte	Extra	20	10	300	-
38	Apocalypse (midair)	HP Attack (Air)	40	20	300	Hold and release ⬤ (Guard Crush, Map Break)
39	Jump Times Boost	Action	20	10	150	-
(Mastery)	Jump Times Boost+	Action	40	20	150	-
(Mastery)	Jump Times Boost++	Action	70	30	150	-
40	Omni Air Dash	Action	40	20	300	Analog Stick + 🔘 + 🅐
43	Sneak Attack	Extra	50	45	360	-
(Mastery)	Disable Sneak Attack	Extra	30	15	360	-
47	Physical Shield	Extra	20	10	280	-
50	Magic Shield	Extra	20	10	280	-
53	Multi-Air Slide	Action	10	5	250	Analog Stick + ❌ after expending jumps
(Mastery)	Multi-Air Slide+	Action	30	15	300	See Multi-Air Slide
57	Midair Evasion Boost	Action	20	10	150	-
60	Bravery Regen	Extra	20	10	280	-
64	Evasion Time Boost	Support	20	10	220	-
67	First Strike	Extra	40	35	360	-
(Mastery)	Disable First Strike	Extra	20	10	360	-
71	Concentration	Extra	30	15	250	-
(Mastery)	Concentration+	Extra	60	30	250	-
(Mastery)	Concentration++	Extra	100	50	250	-
74	Cat Nip	Extra	30	25	300	-
(Mastery)	Disable Cat Nip	Extra	20	10	300	-
78	Anti-EX	Extra	30	20	300	-
(Mastery)	Disable Anti-EX	Extra	20	10	300	-
81	Achy	Extra	30	15	250	-
(Mastery)	Achy+	Extra	60	30	250	-
85	Counterattack	Extra	50	45	360	-
(Mastery)	Disable Counterattack	Extra	30	15	360	-
88	Gambler's Spirit	Extra	30	15	300	-
(Mastery)	Disable Gambler's Spirit	Extra	20	10	300	-
92	Back to the Wall	Extra	30	25	300	-
(Mastery)	Disable Back to the Wall	Extra	20	10	300	-
95	Precision Jump	Extra	10	5	180	-
98	Snooze and Lose	Extra	100	50	250	-
100	EXP to HP	Extra	20	0	500	-
100	EXP to Bravery	Extra	20	0	500	-
100	EXP to EX Force	Extra	20	0	500	-

EX MODE

EX BURST

Time Compression: A flurry of attacks ending in one crushing blow. (Watch your timing and press ⬤ when the cursor is in the frame.)

EX EFFECTS

Regen: Vigor and stamina recover little by little, restoring HP.

Time Crush: Opponent's movements are completely frozen for a set time. Keep in mind that this has a long casting time. (Activate with 🔘 + 🔘.)

*Some commands may require directional presses, depending on the slot to which abilities are assigned.

ZIDANE TRIBAL

Aerial Ace—Unequaled in midair combat.

A thief with great energy and a sharp wit, though all is lost when it comes to women. In Final Fantasy IX, *he was a member of Tantalus, a gang of thieves masquerading as a traveling theater group. After kidnapping the beguiling Princess Garnet, he was drawn into a conflict that concerned his very birth. While usually cheerful and waggish, he does have bouts of despair. However, this may be another part of his charm.*

BASIC MOBILITY*

Ground Movement Speed	⭐⭐½
Innate Number of Jumps	2
Jump Height	⭐⭐
Jump Rising Speed	⭐⭐⭐
Air Dash Speed	⭐⭐½
Quickmove Speed	⭐⭐½

*Mobility can be increased with the abilities Speed Boost, Jump Boost, Jump Times Boost, and Precision Jump.

EQUIPMENT

Weapon	Daggers, Thrown Weapons
Hands	Parrying Weapons, Bangles, Gauntlets
Head	Hats, Hairpins
Body	Clothing, Light Armor

STAT PROGRESSION

LV	HP	CP	BRV	ATK	DEF	LUK
1	1000	330	95	9	11	10
5	1242	335	118	13	15	12
10	1545	341	147	18	20	15
20	2151	353	205	28	30	20
30	2757	365	263	38	40	25
40	3363	377	320	48	50	30
50	3969	389	378	58	60	35
60	4575	401	436	68	70	40
70	5181	413	493	78	80	45
80	5787	425	551	88	90	50
90	6393	437	609	98	100	55
100	6999	450	667	108	110	60

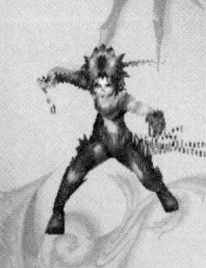

Zidane (Normal)

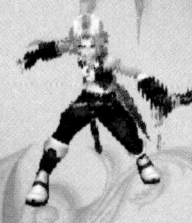

EX Mode (Normal)

Zidane (Alternate)

EX Mode (Alternate)

Capricious Thief

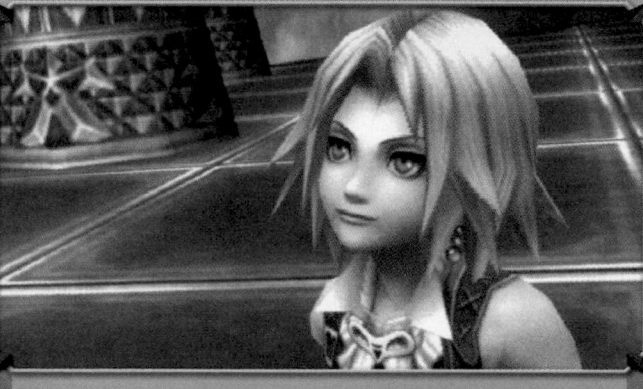

Zidane, like his pal Bartz, is considerably lighter-of-heart than the majority of the cast.

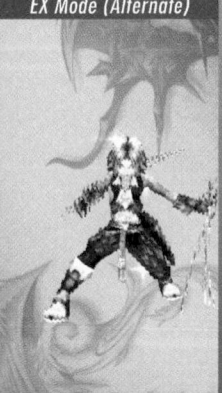

ABILITY PROGRESSION

LEVEL	SKILL	TYPE	CP (N)	CP (M)	AP TO MASTER	ATTACK COMMANDS & EFFECTS*
01	Free Energy	HP Attack (Air)	40	20	180	●
01	Rumble Rush	Bravery Attack (Land)	30	15	180	●● (Map Break, Chase)
(Mastery)	Meo Twister (ground) A	Combo Attack	40	20	300	● after second ● press of Rumble Rush (Map Break)
01	Scoop Art (midair)	Bravery Attack (Air)	20	10	120	●●●
01	Shift Break	HP Attack (Air)	40	20	180	● (Pull-in, Map Break)
01	Swift Attack (midair)	Bravery Attack (Air)	30	15	160	● (Map Break, Chase)
(Mastery)	Meo Twister (ground) B	Combo Attack	40	20	300	● after second ● press of Swift Attack (Map Break)
01	Tidal Flame	HP Attack (Land)	40	20	180	● Map Break
03	Tempest	Bravery Attack (Air)	30	15	180	● (Map Break, Chase)
(Mastery)	Meo Twister (midair) A	Combo Attack	40	20	300	● after second ● press of Tempest (Map Break)
04	Air Dash	Action	10	5	100	▲ during Quickmove
07	Jump Boost	Action	10	5	150	-
(Mastery)	Jump Boost+	Action	20	10	150	-
(Mastery)	Jump Boost++	Action	40	20	150	-
08	Vortex	Bravery Attack (Air)	30	15	180	●● (Map Break, Wall Rush)
10	Storm Impulse	Bravery Attack (Air)	30	15	180	●● (Map Break, Wall Rush)
11	Auto Recovery	Support	20	5	250	-
11	Auto Chase	Support	20	5	250	-
14	Scoop Art (ground)	Bravery Attack (Land)	20	10	120	●●●
15	Auto EX Burst	Support	20	5	150	-
15	Auto EX Command	Support	30	10	300	-
18	Reverse Air Dash	Action	10	5	100	▲ during Quickmove
19	Swift Attack (ground)	Bravery Attack (Land)	30	15	200	●● (Map Break, Chase)
(Mastery)	Meo Twister (ground) B	Combo Attack	40	20	300	● after second ● press of Swift Attack (Map Break)
21	Speed Boost	Action	20	10	150	-
(Mastery)	Speed Boost+	Action	40	20	150	-
(Mastery)	Speed Boost++	Action	70	35	150	-
24	Solution 9	Bravery Attack (Air)	30	15	140	●
25	EX Critical Boost	Extra	45	40	300	-
26	Auto EX Defense	Support	30	10	300	-
29	Reverse Free Air Dash	Action	10	5	100	■ + ▲
31	Stellar Circle 5	HP Attack (Land)	40	20	180	● (Guard Crush, Pull-in, Map Break)
32	Recovery Attack	Action	20	10	120	● or ● while reeling
32	Controlled Recovery	Action	10	5	120	Analog Stick during Recovery
35	Riposte	Extra	45	40	300	-
(Mastery)	Disable Riposte	Extra	20	10	300	-
37	Grand Lethal	HP Attack (Air)	40	20	300	● (Guard Crush, Map Break, Wall Rush)
39	Jump Times Boost	Action	20	10	150	-
(Mastery)	Jump Times Boost+	Action	40	20	150	-
(Mastery)	Jump Times Boost++	Action	70	30	150	-
40	Omni Air Dash	Action	40	20	300	Analog Stick + ■ + ▲
43	Sneak Attack	Extra	50	45	360	-
(Mastery)	Disable Sneak Attack	Extra	30	15	360	-
47	Physical Shield	Extra	20	10	280	-
50	Magic Shield	Extra	20	10	280	-
53	Multi-Air Slide	Action	10	5	250	Analog Stick + ✕ after expending jumps
(Mastery)	Multi-Air Slide+	Action	30	15	300	See Multi-Air Slide
57	Midair Evasion Boost	Action	20	10	150	-
60	Bravery Regen	Extra	20	10	280	-
64	Evasion Time Boost	Support	20	10	220	-
67	First Strike	Extra	40	35	360	-
(Mastery)	Disable First Strike	Extra	20	10	360	-
71	Concentration	Extra	30	15	250	-
(Mastery)	Concentration+	Extra	60	30	250	-
(Mastery)	Concentration++	Extra	100	50	250	-
74	Cat Nip	Extra	30	25	300	-
(Mastery)	Disable Cat Nip	Extra	20	10	300	-
78	Anti-EX	Extra	30	20	300	-
(Mastery)	Disable Anti-EX	Extra	20	10	300	-
81	Achy	Extra	30	15	250	-
(Mastery)	Achy+	Extra	60	30	250	-
85	Counterattack	Extra	50	45	360	-
(Mastery)	Disable Counterattack	Extra	30	15	360	-
88	Gambler's Spirit	Extra	30	15	300	-
(Mastery)	Disable Gambler's Spirit	Extra	20	10	300	-
92	Back to the Wall	Extra	30	25	300	-
(Mastery)	Disable Back to the Wall	Extra	20	10	300	-
95	Precision Jump	Extra	10	5	180	-
98	Snooze and Lose	Extra	100	50	250	-
100	EXP to HP	Extra	20	0	500	-
100	EXP to Bravery	Extra	20	0	500	-
100	EXP to EX Force	Extra	20	0	500	-

*Initial commands may require directional presses, depending on the slot to which abilities are assigned.

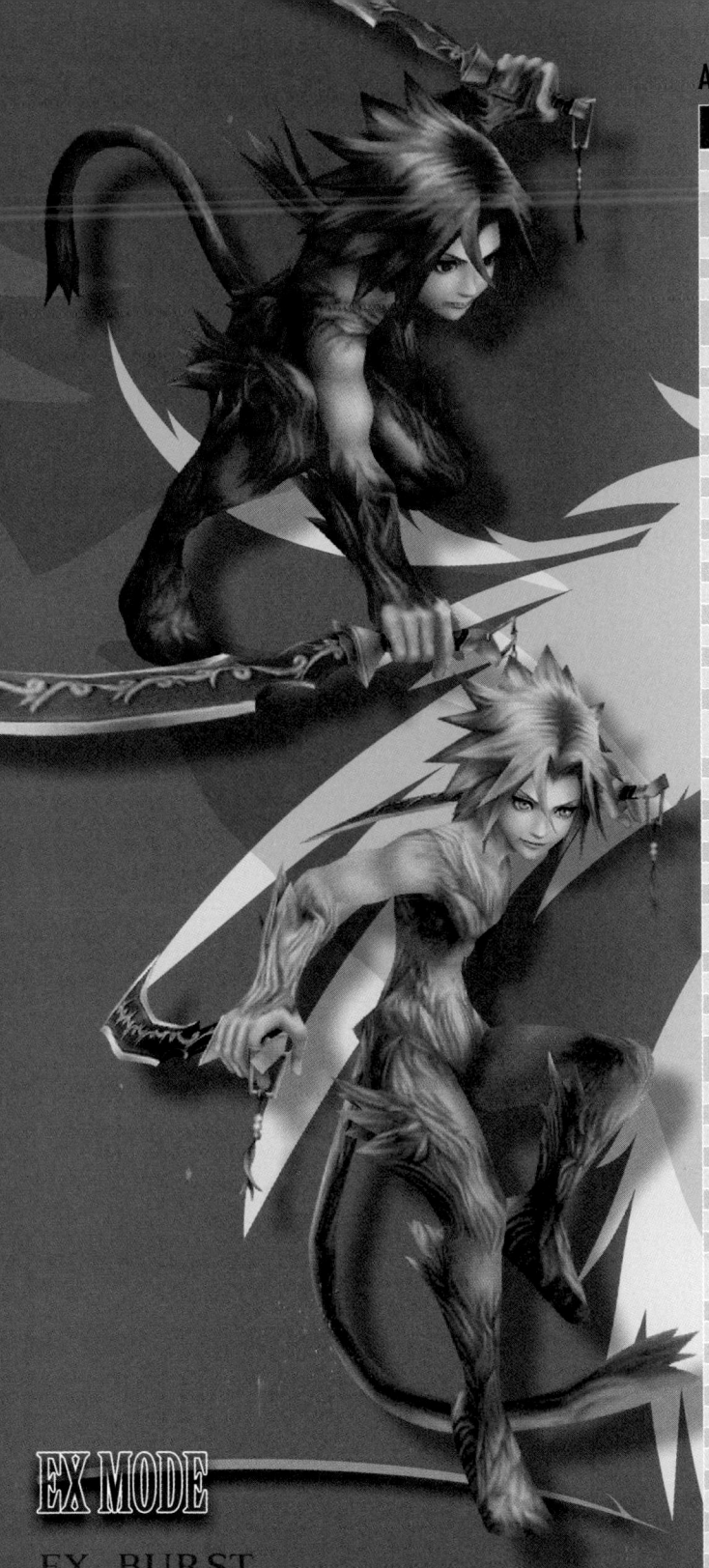

EX MODE

EX BURST

Reverse Gaia: A chain of attacks that grows faster with each blow. (Repeatedly press ● to increase the number of hits.)

EX EFFECTS

Regen: Vigor and stamina recover little by little, restoring HP.

Aerial Jump: Dormant potential is unlocked, enabling nimble leaps to be performed while in midair.

Dodge Jump: Grants invincibility for the period between touching the ground and leaping into the air.

KUJA

Graceful Glider—Can freely change his distance from foes to set up devastating attacks

Kuja becomes a playable character after you finish any Destiny Odyssey, then purchase him from the PP Catalog.

A sadistic, narcissistic silver-haired man of a delicate, epicene beauty. In *Final Fantasy IX*, he threw the continent into disarray by providing black mages, mass-produced soldiers created from Mist, to Alexandria's Queen Brahne. Born for the stage, he has a tendency to get carried away with his own flowery speech. On the other hand, those who get on his bad side are treated with bitter venom.

BASIC MOBILITY*

Ground Movement Speed	⭐⯪
Innate Number of Jumps	1
Jump Height	⭐⭐⯪
Jump Rising Speed	⭐⭐
Air Dash Speed	⭐⭐⯪
Quickmove Speed	⭐⭐

*Mobility can be increased with the abilities Speed Boost, Jump Boost, Jump Times Boost, and Precision Jump.

EQUIPMENT

Weapon	Daggers, Rods, Staves
Hands	Bangles
Head	Hats, Hairpins
Body	Clothing, Robes

STAT PROGRESSION

LV	HP	CP	BRV	ATK	DEF	LUK
1	1000	330	95	10	12	10
5	1242	335	118	14	16	12
10	1545	341	147	19	21	15
20	2151	353	205	29	31	20
30	2757	365	263	39	41	25
40	3363	377	320	49	51	30
50	3969	389	378	59	61	35
60	4575	401	436	69	71	40
70	5181	413	493	79	81	45
80	5787	425	551	89	91	50
90	6393	437	609	99	101	55
100	6999	450	667	109	111	60

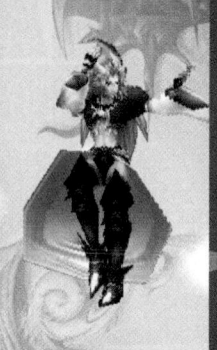
Kuja (Normal)

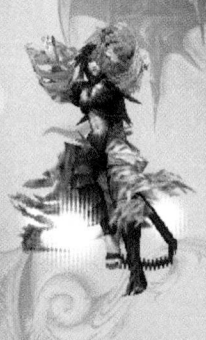
EX Mode (Normal)

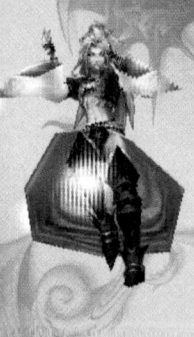
Kuja (Alternate)

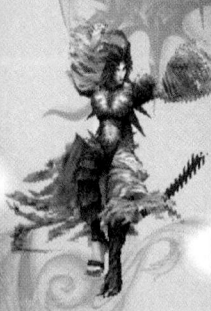
EX Mode (Alternate)

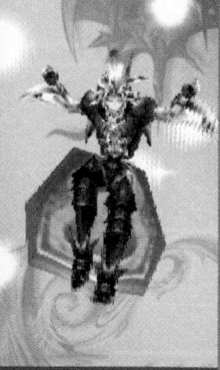
Capricious Reaper

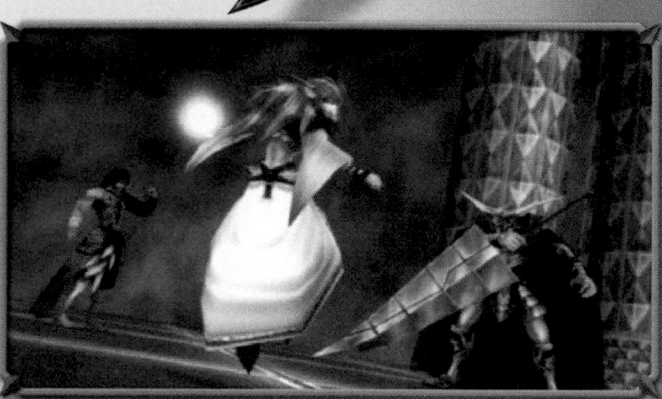
The theatrical Kuja can seem just as harried by his allies alongside Chaos as he is by Zidane and other agents of Cosmos.

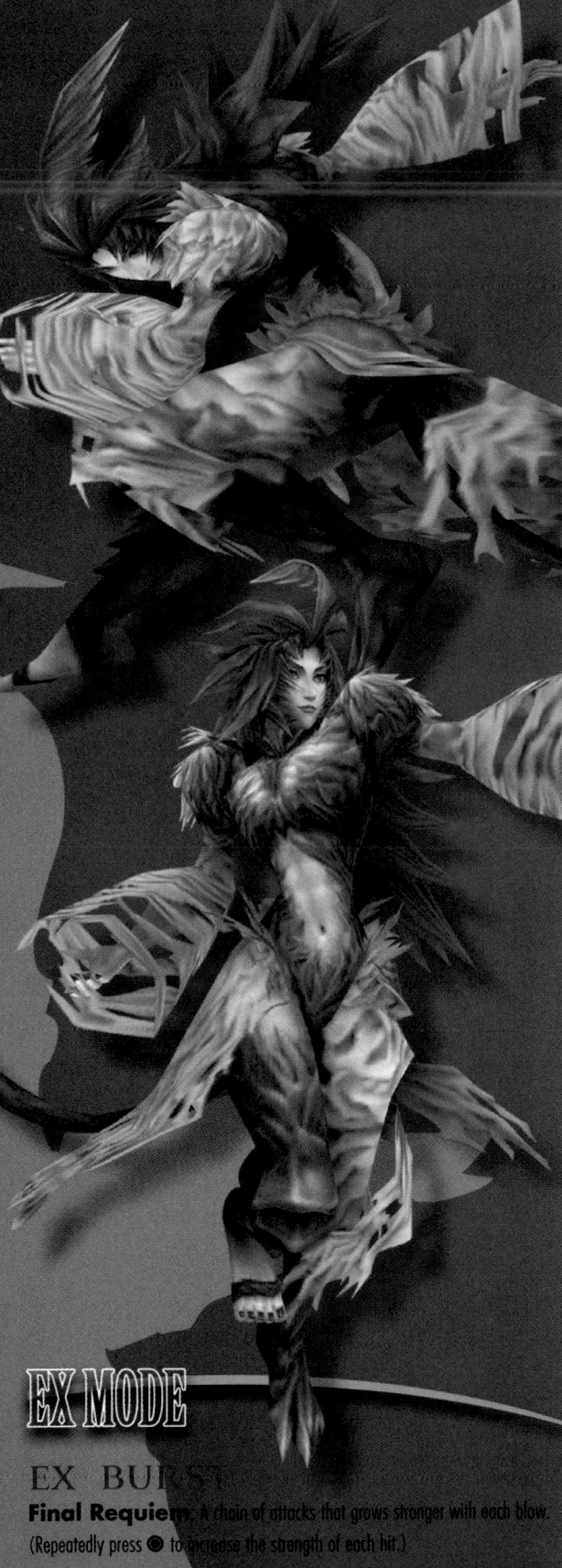

ABILITY PROGRESSION

LEVEL	SKILL	TYPE	CP (N)	CP (M)	AP TO MASTER	ATTACK COMMANDS & EFFECTS*
01	Flare Star (midair)	HP Attack (Air)	40	20	180	◉ (Move OK, Guard Crush, Map Break, Wall Rush)
01	Remote Flare (ground)	Bravery Attack (Land)	30	15	180	◉ (Move OK, Map Break, Wall Rush)
01	Ring Holy (midair)	Bravery Attack (Air)	20	10	90	◉ (Move OK)
01	Seraphic Star (ground)	HP Attack (Land)	40	20	180	◉ (Guard Crush, Pull-in, Map Break)
01	Snatch Shot (midair)	Bravery Attack (Air)	30	15	120	◉ (Move OK, Map Break) ◉ (Move OK, Map Break, Chase up close, Wall Rush from far)
01	Strike Energy (ground)	Bravery Attack (Land)	30	15	180	◉ (Move OK, Map Break) ◉ (Move OK, Map Break, Chase up close, Wall Rush from far)
02	Reverse Free Air Dash	Action	10	5	100	▬ + ◉
03	Snatch Blow (ground)	Bravery Attack (Land)	30	15	180	◉ (Move OK, Map Break) ◉ (Move OK, Map Break, Wall Rush up close, Chase from far)
04	Air Dash	Action	10	5	100	▲ during Quickmove
06	Strike Energy (midair)	Bravery Attack (Air)	30	15	120	◉ (Move OK, Map Break) ◉ (Move OK, Map Break, Chase up close, Wall Rush from far)
07	Jump Boost	Action	10	5	150	-
(Mastery)	Jump Boost+	Action	20	10	150	-
(Mastery)	Jump Boost++	Action	40	20	150	-
09	Seraphic Star (midair)	HP Attack (Air)	40	20	180	◉ (Guard Crush, Pull-in, Map Break)
11	Auto Recovery	Support	20	5	250	-
11	Auto Chase	Support	20	5	250	-
12	Snatch Shot (ground)	Bravery Attack (Land)	30	15	180	◉ (Move OK, Map Break) ◉ (Move OK, Map Break, Chase up close, Wall Rush from far)
15	Auto EX Burst	Support	20	5	150	-
15	Auto EX Command	Support	30	10	300	-
16	Burst Energy (midair)	Bravery Attack (Air)	30	15	120	◉ (Move OK, Map Break) ◉ (Move OK, Map Break)
18	Reverse Air Dash	Action	10	5	100	▲ during Quickmove
20	Snatch Blow (midair)	Bravery Attack (Air)	30	15	120	◉ (Move OK, Map Break) ◉ (Move OK, Map Break, Wall Rush up close, Chase from far)
21	Speed Boost	Action	20	10	150	-
(Mastery)	Speed Boost+	Action	40	20	150	-
(Mastery)	Speed Boost++	Action	70	35	150	-
21	EX Glide Boost	Action	20	10	200	-
24	Flare Star (ground)	HP Attack (Land)	40	20	180	◉ (Move OK, Guard Crush, Map Break, Wall Rush)
25	EX Critical Boost	Extra	45	40	300	-
26	Auto EX Defense	Support	30	10	300	-
29	Burst Energy (ground)	Bravery Attack (Land)	30	15	180	◉ (Move OK, Map Break) ◉ (Move OK, Map Break, Wall Rush up close, Chase from far)
32	Recovery Attack	Action	20	10	120	◉ or ◉ while reeling
32	Controlled Recovery	Action	10	5	120	Analog Stick during Recovery
33	Ring Holy (ground)	Bravery Attack (Land)	20	10	120	◉ (Move OK)
33	Remote Flare (midair)	Bravery Attack (Air)	30	15	120	◉ (Move OK, Map Break, Wall Rush)
35	Riposte	Extra	45	40	300	-
(Mastery)	Disable Riposte	Extra	20	10	300	-
38	Ultima (ground)	HP Attack (Land)	40	20	300	◉ (Move OK, Guard Crush, Map Break)
39	Jump Times Boost	Action	20	10	150	-
(Mastery)	Jump Times Boost+	Action	40	20	150	-
(Mastery)	Jump Times Boost++	Action	70	30	150	-
40	Omni Air Dash	Action	40	20	300	Analog Stick + ▬ + ⬅
43	Sneak Attack	Extra	50	45	360	-
(Mastery)	Disable Sneak Attack	Extra	30	15	360	-
44	Ultima (midair)	HP Attack (Air)	40	20	300	◉ (Move OK, Guard Crush, Map Break)
47	Physical Shield	Extra	20	10	280	-
50	Magic Shield	Extra	20	10	280	-
53	Multi-Air Slide	Action	10	5	250	Analog Stick + ✕ after expending jumps
(Mastery)	Multi-Air Slide+	Action	30	15	300	See Multi-Air Slide
57	Midair Evasion Boost	Action	20	10	150	-
60	Bravery Regen	Extra	20	10	280	-
60	Glide Boost	Action	20	10	150	-
64	Evasion Time Boost	Support	20	10	220	-
67	First Strike	Extra	40	35	360	-
(Mastery)	Disable First Strike	Extra	20	10	360	-
71	Concentration	Extra	30	15	250	-
(Mastery)	Concentration+	Extra	60	30	250	-
(Mastery)	Concentration++	Extra	100	50	250	-
74	Cat Nip	Extra	30	25	300	-
(Mastery)	Disable Cat Nip	Extra	20	10	300	-
78	Anti-EX	Extra	30	15	300	-
(Mastery)	Disable Anti-EX	Extra	20	10	300	-
81	Achy	Extra	30	15	250	-
(Mastery)	Achy+	Extra	60	30	250	-
85	Counterattack	Extra	50	45	360	-
(Mastery)	Disable Counterattack	Extra	30	15	360	-
88	Gambler's Spirit	Extra	30	15	300	-
(Mastery)	Disable Gambler's Spirit	Extra	20	10	300	-
92	Back to the Wall	Extra	30	25	300	-
(Mastery)	Disable Back to the Wall	Extra	20	10	300	-
95	Precision Jump	Extra	10	5	180	-
98	Snooze and Lose	Extra	100	50	250	-
100	EXP to HP	Extra	20	0	500	-
100	EXP to Bravery	Extra	20	0	500	-
100	EXP to EX Force	Extra	20	0	500	-

*Initial commands may require directional presses, depending on the slot to which abilities are assigned.

EX MODE

EX BURST

Final Requiem: A chain of attacks that grows stronger with each blow. (Repeatedly press ◉ to increase the strength of each hit.)

EX EFFECTS

Regen: Vigor and stamina recover little by little, restoring HP.

Hyper Glide: Maintains altitude longer than the normal Glide. (Activate by holding ✕ in midair.)

Auto Magic: Casts Holy and Flare while jumping, falling, touching down, or gliding.

TIDUS

Spry Striker—Dazzles opponents with swift dodges and speedy counters.

A light-hearted, cheerful youth able to calm others even through the most trying of situations. In Final Fantasy X, he was an ace blitzball player for the Zanarkand Abes. After an assault from the monster Sin, he found himself in a world called Spira and began traveling with Yuna, a summoner.

BASIC MOBILITY*

-	NORMAL	EX MODE
Ground Movement Speed	★★★☆	★★★★
Innate Number of Jumps	1	1
Jump Height	★★★☆	★★★☆
Jump Rising Speed	★★★☆	★★★★
Air Dash Speed	★★★☆	★★★★
Quickmove Speed	★★★☆	★★★★

Mobility can be increased with the abilities Speed Boost, Jump Boost, Jump Times Boost, and Precision Jump.

EQUIPMENT

Weapon	Swords, Grappling Weapons
Hands	Shields, Bangles
Head	Hats, Helms
Body	Clothing, Light Armor

STAT PROGRESSION

LV	HP	CP	BRV	ATK	DEF	LUK
1	1000	330	95	11	12	10
5	1242	335	118	15	16	12
10	1545	341	147	20	21	15
20	2151	353	205	30	31	20
30	2757	365	263	40	41	25
40	3363	377	320	50	51	30
50	3969	389	378	60	61	35
60	4575	401	436	70	71	40
70	5181	413	493	80	81	45
80	5787	425	551	90	91	50
90	6393	437	609	100	101	55
100	6999	450	667	110	111	60

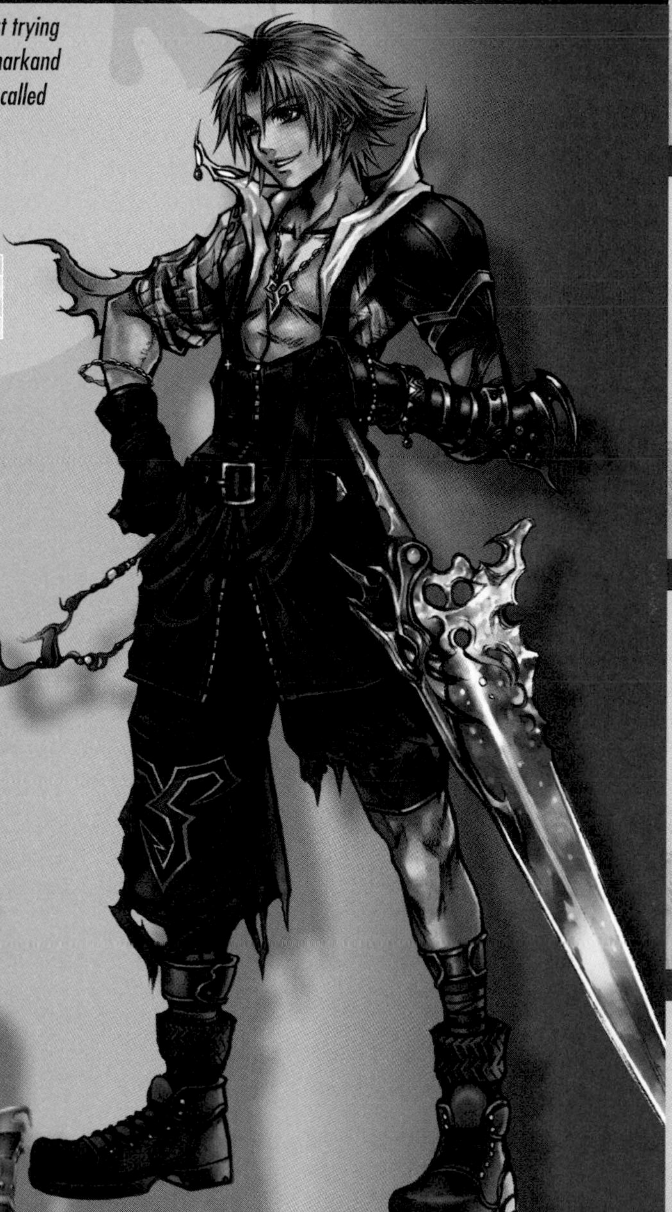

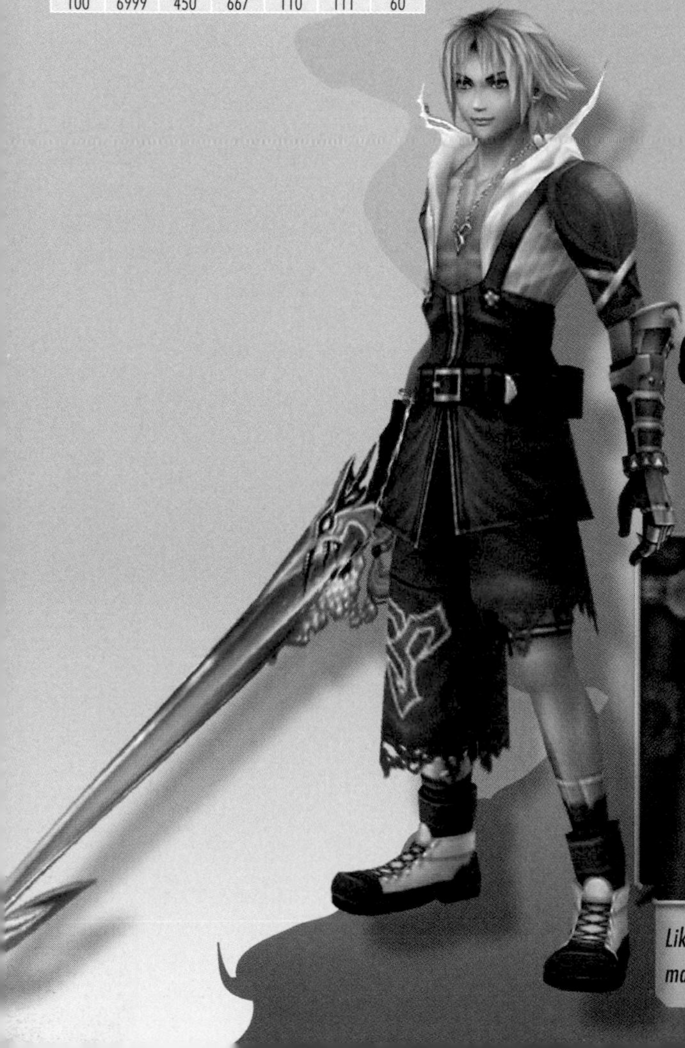

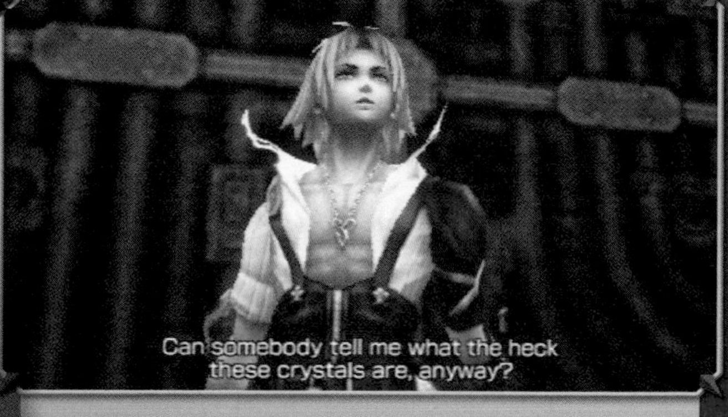

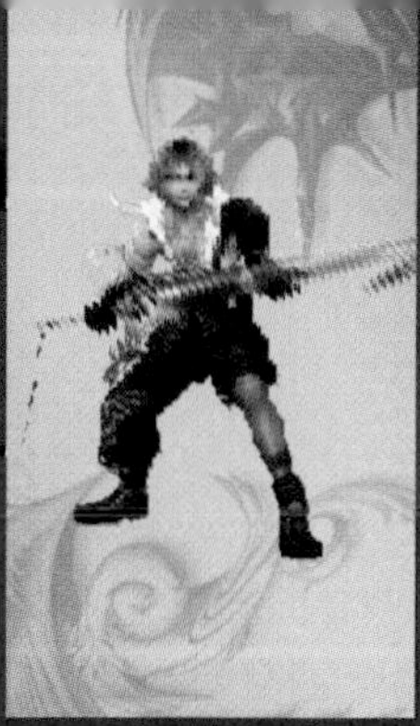

Tidus (Normal)

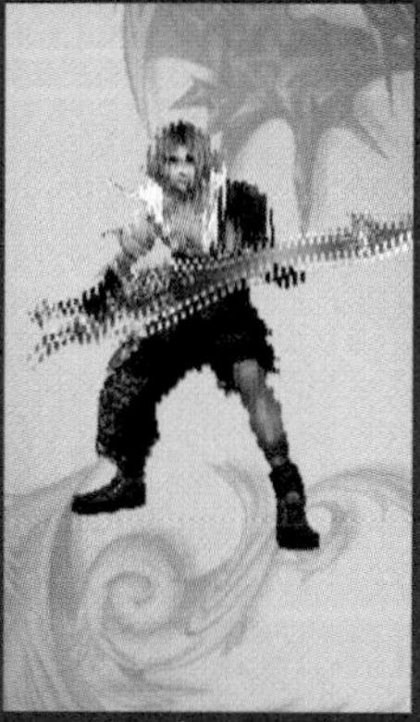

EX Mode (Normal)

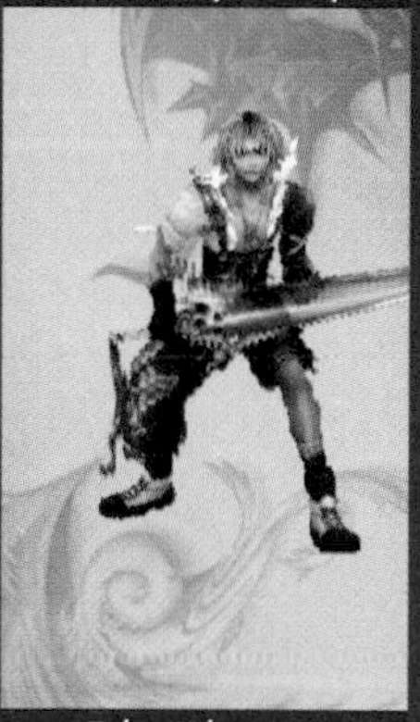

Tidus (Alternate)

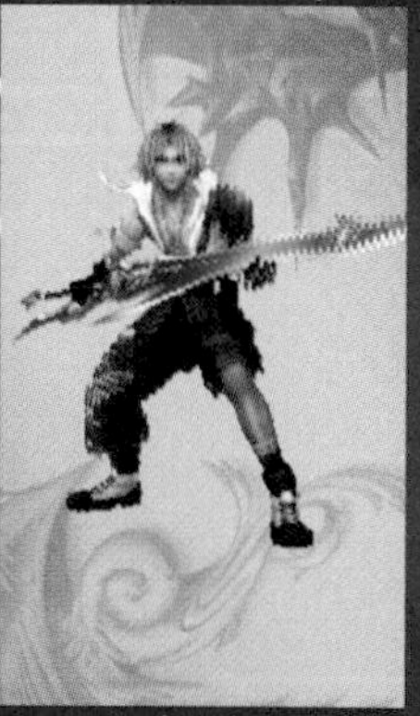

EX Mode (Alternate)

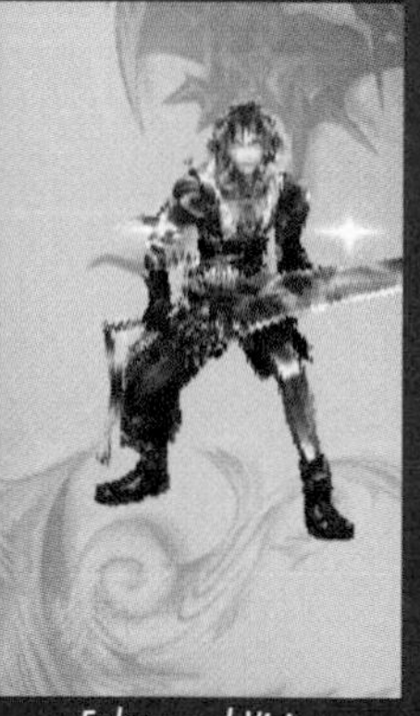

Ephemeral Vision

Can somebody tell me what the heck these crystals are, anyway?

Like Bartz and Zidane, Tidus brings a lighter mood to the proceedings. This masks his deep resentment of his father, Jecht.

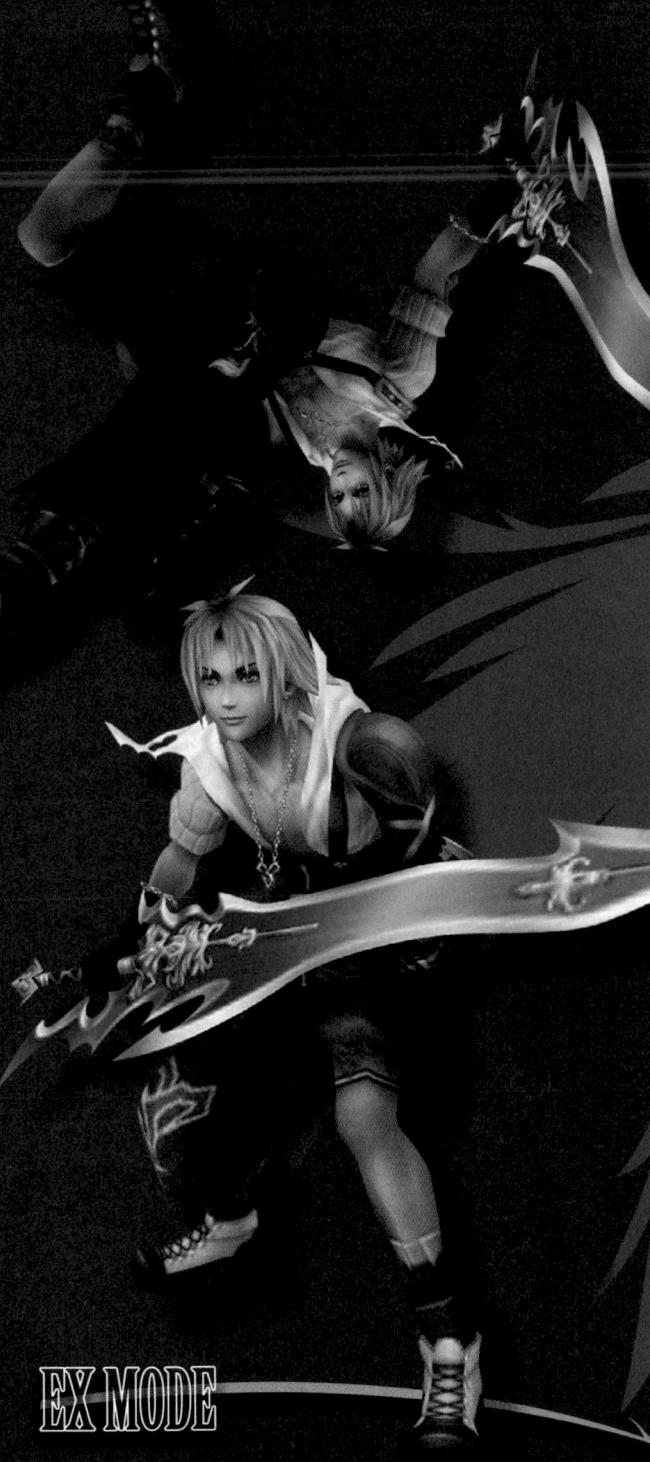

ABILITY PROGRESSION

LEVEL	SKILL	TYPE	CP (N)	CP (M)	AP TO MASTER	ATTACK COMMANDS & EFFECTS*
01	Energy Rain (midair)	HP Attack (Air)	40	20	180	◎ Guard Crush, Map Break
01	Hop Step (midair)	Bravery Attack (Air)	30	15	140	◎ ◎ (Chase)
01	Sonic Buster	Bravery Attack (Land)	30	15	140	◎ (Map Break) ◎ (Map Break) ◎ (Map Break, Wall Rush)
01	Spiral Cut	HP Attack (Land)	40	20	180	◎ Guard Crush, Map Break
01	Stick & Move	Bravery Attack (Air)	30	15	180	◎ (Move OK, evades attacks, Map Break, Chase)
(Mastery)	Quick Hit D	Combo Attack	40	20	300	◎ after Stick & Move (Guard Crush, Map Break, Wall Rush)
01	Wither Shot (ground)	Bravery Attack (Land)	20	10	90	◎ (Chase)
03	Dart & Weave (ground)	Bravery Attack (Land)	30	15	120	◎ (Evades attacks, Map Break, Chase)
(Mastery)	Quick Hit B	Combo Attack	40	20	300	◎ after Dart & Weave (Guard Crush, Map Break, Wall Rush)
04	Air Dash	Action	10	5	100	◎ during Quickmove
06	Full Slide	Bravery Attack (Air)	30	15	180	◎ (Map Break) ◎ (Map Break) ◎ (Map Break, Wall Rush)
07	Jump Boost	Action	10	5	150	-
(Mastery)	Jump Boost+	Action	20	10	150	-
(Mastery)	Jump Boost++	Action	40	20	150	-
09	Sphere Shot	Bravery Attack (Land)	20	10	90	◎ (Map Break, Wall Rush)
11	Auto Recovery	Support	20	5	250	-
11	Auto Chase	Support	20	5	250	-
12	Hop Step (ground)	Bravery Attack (Land)	30	15	120	◎ ◎ (Chase)
15	Auto EX Burst	Support	20	5	150	-
15	Auto EX Command	Support	30	10	300	-
16	Wither Shot (midair)	Bravery Attack (Air)	20	10	120	◎ (Chase)
18	Reverse Air Dash	Action	10	5	100	◎ during Quickmove
20	Dart & Weave (midair)	Bravery Attack (Air)	30	15	180	◎ (Evades attacks, Map Break, Chase)
(Mastery)	Quick Hit E	Combo Attack	40	20	300	◎ after Dart & Weave (Guard Crush, Map Break, Wall Rush)
21	Speed Boost	Action	20	10	150	-
(Mastery)	Speed Boost+	Action	40	20	150	-
(Mastery)	Speed Boost++	Action	70	35	150	-
24	Stick & Move (ground)	Bravery Attack (Land)	30	15	120	◎ (Move OK, evades attacks, Map Break, Chase)
(Mastery)	Quick Hit A	Combo Attack	40	20	300	◎ after Stick & Move (Guard Crush, Map Break, Wall Rush)
25	EX Critical Boost	Extra	45	40	300	-
26	Auto EX Defense	Support	30	10	300	-
28	Cut & Run	Bravery Attack (Land)	30	15	140	◎ (Guard, evades attacks, Map Break, Chase)
(Mastery)	Quick Hit C	Combo Attack	40	20	300	◎ after Cut & Run (Guard Crush, Map Break, Wall Rush)
29	Reverse Free Air Dash	Action	10	5	100	▣ + △
32	Recovery Attack	Action	20	10	120	◎ or ◎ while reeling
32	Controlled Recovery	Action	10	5	120	Analog Stick during Recovery
33	Charge & Assault	HP Attack (Air)	40	20	300	◎ (Guard Crush, Map Break)
35	Riposte	Extra	45	40	300	-
(Mastery)	Disable Riposte	Extra	20	10	300	-
38	Energy Rain (ground)	HP Attack (Land)	40	20	180	
39	Jump Times Boost	Action	20	10	150	-
(Mastery)	Jump Times Boost+	Action	40	20	150	-
(Mastery)	Jump Times Boost++	Action	70	30	150	-
40	Omni Air Dash	Action	40	20	300	Analog Stick + ▣ + △
43	Sneak Attack	Extra	50	45	360	-
(Mastery)	Disable Sneak Attack	Extra	30	15	360	-
44	Jecht Shot	HP Attack (Air)	40	20	300	◎ (Guard Crush, Map Break, Wall Rush)
47	Physical Shield	Extra	20	10	280	-
50	Magic Shield	Extra	20	10	280	-
53	Multi-Air Slide	Action	10	5	250	Analog Stick + ✕ after expending jumps
(Mastery)	Multi-Air Slide+	Action	30	15	300	See Multi-Air Slide
57	Midair Evasion Boost	Action	20	10	150	-
60	Bravery Regen	Extra	20	10	280	-
64	Evasion Time Boost	Support	20	10	220	-
67	First Strike	Extra	40	35	360	-
(Mastery)	Disable First Strike	Extra	20	10	360	-
71	Concentration	Extra	30	15	250	-
(Mastery)	Concentration+	Extra	60	30	250	-
(Mastery)	Concentration++	Extra	100	50	250	-
74	Cat Nip	Extra	30	25	300	-
(Mastery)	Disable Cat Nip	Extra	20	10	300	-
78	Anti-EX	Extra	30	20	300	-
(Mastery)	Disable Anti-EX	Extra	20	10	300	-
81	Achy	Extra	30	15	250	-
(Mastery)	Achy+	Extra	60	30	250	-
85	Counterattack	Extra	50	45	360	-
(Mastery)	Disable Counterattack	Extra	30	15	360	-
88	Gambler's Spirit	Extra	30	15	300	-
(Mastery)	Disable Gambler's Spirit	Extra	20	10	300	-
92	Back to the Wall	Extra	30	25	300	-
(Mastery)	Disable Back to the Wall	Extra	20	10	300	-
95	Precision Jump	Extra	10	5	180	-
98	Snooze and Lose	Extra	100	50	250	-
100	EXP to HP	Extra	20	0	500	-
100	EXP to Bravery	Extra	20	0	500	-
100	EXP to EX Force	Extra	20	0	500	-

*Initial commands may require directional presses, depending on the slot to which abilities are assigned.

EX MODE

EX BURST

Blitz Ace: A flurry of attacks leading to a magnificent shot. (Watch your timing and press ◎ when the cursor hits the center.)

EX EFFECTS

Regen: Vigor and stamina recover little by little, restoring HP.

Mirror Dash: Top running speed increases, deflecting weak magical attacks.

Caladbolg (ATK): The higher the user's HP, the sharper the weapon's blade.

Caladbolg (DODGE): The period of invincibility between dodging and attacking increases.

CHARACTERS

JECHT

Brutal Blitzer—His ferocious melee strikes can be charged to savage extremes.

Jecht becomes a playable character after you finish any Destiny Odyssey, then purchase him from the PP Catalog.

A former blitzball star, and Tidus's father. His surly and rough-spoken nature belies a much gentler heart. In Final Fantasy X, he accidentally came into contact with Sin while training out at sea—an event that doomed him for eternity. Tidus's signature move, the Jecht Shot, was originally named the "Sublimely Magnificent Jecht Shot Mark III." Until Tidus, no one else could successfully perform it.

BASIC MOBILITY*

Ground Movement Speed	⭐⭐☆
Innate Number of Jumps	1
Jump Height	⭐⭐⭐
Jump Rising Speed	⭐⭐☆
Air Dash Speed	⭐⭐☆
Quickmove Speed	⭐⭐☆

*Mobility can be increased with the abilities Speed Boost, Jump Boost, Jump Times Boost, and Precision Jump.

EQUIPMENT

Weapon	Greatswords, Axes, Grappling Weapons
Hands	Shields, Bangles
Head	Hats, Helms
Body	Clothing, Light Armor

STAT PROGRESSION

LV	HP	CP	BRV	ATK	DEF	LUK
1	1000	330	95	13	13	10
5	1242	335	118	17	17	12
10	1545	341	147	22	22	15
20	2151	353	205	32	32	20
30	2757	365	263	42	42	25
40	3363	377	320	52	52	30
50	3969	389	378	62	62	35
60	4575	401	436	72	72	40
70	5181	413	493	82	82	45
80	5787	425	551	92	92	50
90	6393	437	609	102	102	55
100	6999	450	667	112	112	60

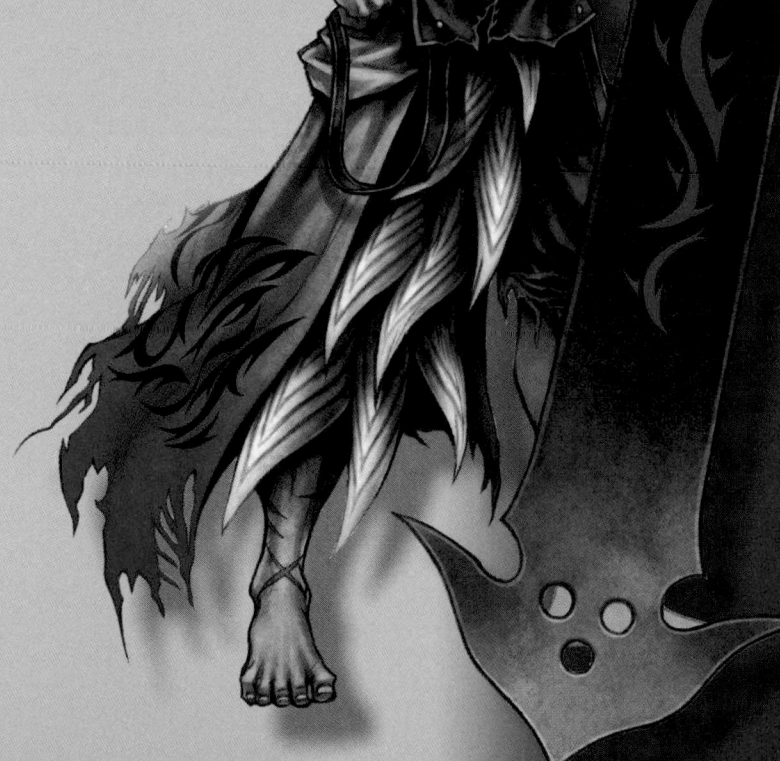

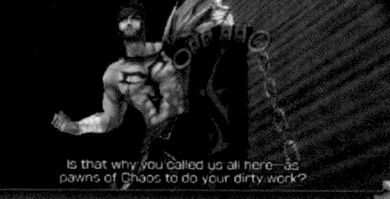

Is that why you called us all here—as pawns of Chaos to do your dirty work?

Jecht's turn toward the darkness wasn't all his doing, so the gruff warrior and ex-athlete is more out for himself than anything else.

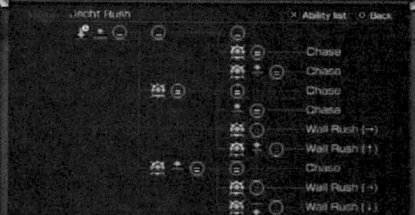

Jecht's attacks can be charged to increase their power, and his Jecht Rush bravery attack leads to a wide array of potential combos depending on follow-up inputs.

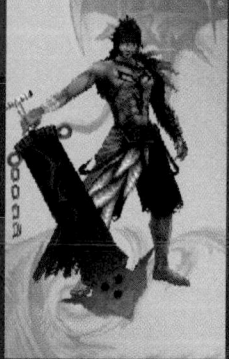

Jecht (Normal)

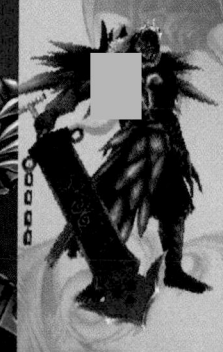

EX Mode (Normal)

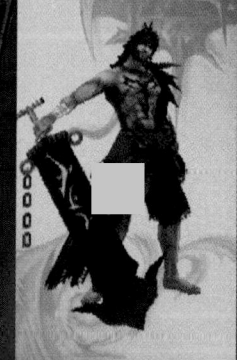

Jecht (Alternate)

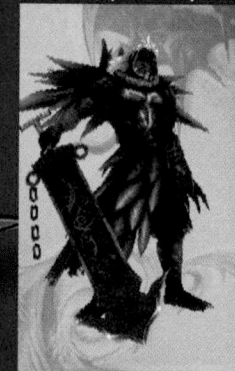

EX Mode (Alternate)

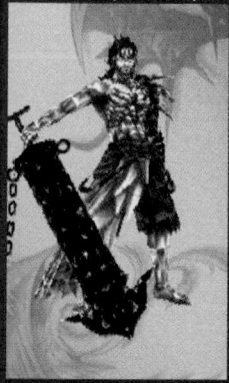

Ephemeral Phantom

ABILITY PROGRESSION

LEVEL	SKILL	TYPE	CP (N)	CP (M)	AP TO MASTER	ATTACK COMMANDS & EFFECTS*
01	Jecht Blade (ground)	HP Attack (Land)	40	20	180	Hold and release ● (Grows in power at 1.0 and 1.5 seconds, Guard Crush, Map Break, Wall Rush)
01	Jecht Rush	Bravery Attack (Land)	45	25	90	Hold and release ● (Grows in power after 0.3 and 0.8 seconds, Map Break, many combos possible when charging less than 0.8 seconds as per nearby screenshot, Guard Break after holding longer than 0.8 seconds)
01	Jecht Stream	Bravery Attack (Air)	45	25	180	Hold and release ● (Increases in power after 0.3 and 0.8 seconds, Map Break)
01	Triumphant Grasp	HP Attack (Air)	40	20	180	Press and release ● (Grows in power after 0.8 and 1.3 seconds, Guard Crush, Map Break, Wall Rush)
04	Air Dash	Action	10	5	100	▲ during Quickmove
05	Jecht Block (ground)	Bravery Attack (Land)	30	15	120	● (Guard)
07	Speed Boost	Action	20	10	150	-
(Mastery)	Speed Boost+	Action	40	20	150	-
(Mastery)	Speed Boost++	Action	70	35	150	-
11	Auto Recovery	Support	20	5	250	-
11	Auto Chase	Support	20	5	250	-
12	Jecht Block (midair)	Bravery Attack (Air)	30	15	120	● (Guard)
15	Auto EX Burst	Support	20	5	150	-
15	Auto EX Command	Support	30	10	300	-
18	Reverse Air Dash	Action	10	5	100	▲ during Quickmove
21	Jump Boost	Action	10	5	150	-
(Mastery)	Jump Boost+	Action	20	10	150	-
(Mastery)	Jump Boost++	Action	40	20	150	-
23	Jecht Blade (midair)	HP Attack (Air)	40	20	180	-
25	EX Critical Boost	Extra	45	40	300	-
26	Auto EX Defense	Support	30	10	300	-
29	Reverse Free Air Dash	Action	10	5	100	▣ + ▲
32	Recovery Attack	Action	20	10	120	● or ● while reeling
32	Controlled Recovery	Action	10	5	120	Analog Stick during Recovery
35	Riposte	Extra	45	40	300	-
(Mastery)	Disable Riposte	Extra	20	10	300	-
38	Ultimate Jecht Shot	HP Attack (Land)	40	20	300	Hold and release ● (Grows in power after 1.0 and 1.5 seconds, Guard Crush, Map Break, Wall Rush)
39	Jump Times Boost	Action	20	10	150	-
(Mastery)	Jump Times Boost+	Action	40	20	150	-
(Mastery)	Jump Times Boost++	Action	70	30	150	-
40	Omni Air Dash	Action	40	20	300	Analog Stick + ▣ + ▲
43	Sneak Attack	Extra	50	45	360	-
(Mastery)	Disable Sneak Attack	Extra	30	15	360	-
47	Physical Shield	Extra	20	10	280	-
50	Magic Shield	Extra	20	10	280	-
53	Multi-Air Slide	Action	10	5	250	Analog Stick + ✕ after expending jumps
(Mastery)	Multi-Air Slide+	Action	30	15	300	See Multi-Air Slide
57	Midair Evasion Boost	Action	20	10	150	-
60	Bravery Regen	Extra	20	10	280	-
64	Evasion Time Boost	Support	20	10	220	-
67	First Strike	Extra	40	35	360	-
(Mastery)	Disable First Strike	Extra	20	10	360	-
71	Concentration	Extra	30	15	250	-
(Mastery)	Concentration+	Extra	60	30	250	-
(Mastery)	Concentration++	Extra	100	50	250	-
74	Cat Nip	Extra	30	25	300	-
(Mastery)	Disable Cat Nip	Extra	20	10	300	-
78	Anti-EX	Extra	30	20	300	-
(Mastery)	Disable Anti-EX	Extra	20	10	300	-
81	Achy	Extra	30	15	250	-
(Mastery)	Achy+	Extra	60	30	250	-
85	Counterattack	Extra	50	45	360	-
(Mastery)	Disable Counterattack	Extra	30	15	360	-
88	Gambler's Spirit	Extra	30	15	300	-
(Mastery)	Disable Gambler's Spirit	Extra	20	10	300	-
92	Back to the Wall	Extra	30	25	300	-
(Mastery)	Disable Back to the Wall	Extra	20	10	300	-
95	Precision Jump	Extra	10	5	180	-
98	Snooze and Lose	Extra	100	50	250	-
100	EXP to HP	Extra	20	0	500	-
100	EXP to Bravery	Extra	20	0	500	-
100	EXP to EX Force	Extra	20	0	500	-

*Initial commands may require directional presses, depending on the slot to which abilities are assigned.

EX MODE

[...] Recovery: [...] recover little by little, restoring HP.

[...] Combos: [...] if the first hit misses the opponent, combos can nevertheless [...]

[...] a flurry of attacks leading to a splendidly impressive shot. (Watch your [...] when the cursor hits the center.)

SHANTOTTO

Chainspeller—Batters foes with incredibly powerful magical HP attacks.

Finish Distant Glory: Lady of Legend to unlock Shantotto for purchase in the PP Catalog.

A war hero with immeasurable magical power. Former minister of the Orastery, then head of the Parliament of Patriarchs, in the original game, Shantotto was one of the top minds in the Federation of Windurst. It's said her pride is higher than the pinnacles of the Gustaberg range, and her temper hotter than the magma flowing forth from the mighty Mount Yuhtunga. Her age is unknown, and her only regret in life seems to be having thus far neglected to marry.

BASIC MOBILITY*

Ground Movement Speed	☆☆
Innate Number of Jumps	2
Jump Height	☆
Jump Rising Speed	☆
Air Dash Speed	☆☆
Quickmove Speed	☆☆

*Mobility can be increased with the abilities Speed Boost, Jump Boost, Jump Times Boost, and Precision Jump.

EQUIPMENT

Weapon	Rods, Staves
Hands	Bangles
Head	Hats, Hairpins
Body	Clothing, Robes

STAT PROGRESSION

LV	HP	CP	BRV	ATK	DEF	LUK
1	1000	400	95	13	10	10
5	1242	402	118	17	14	12
10	1545	405	147	22	19	15
20	2151	410	205	32	29	20
30	2757	415	263	42	39	25
40	3363	420	320	52	49	30
50	3969	425	378	62	59	35
60	4575	430	436	72	69	40
70	5181	435	493	82	79	45
80	5787	440	551	92	89	50
90	6393	445	609	102	99	55
100	6999	450	667	112	109	60

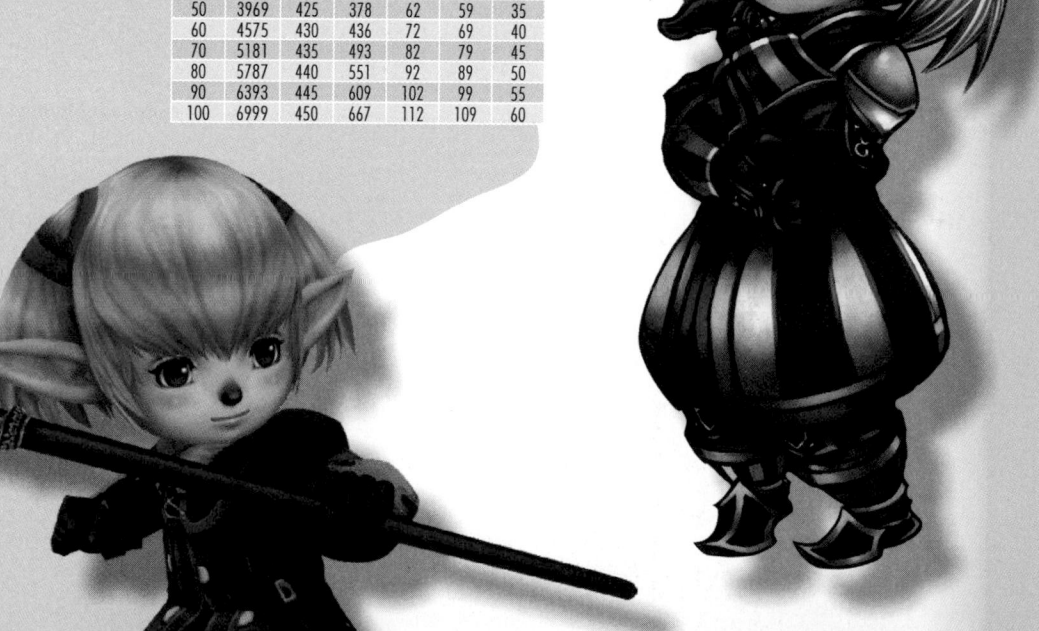

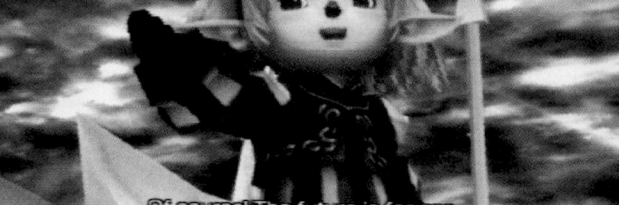

Of course! The future is for one to take by brute force!

While this Taru boasts in coupled verse, her magic rules the multiverse.

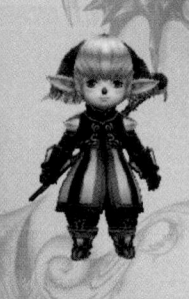

Shantotto (Normal)

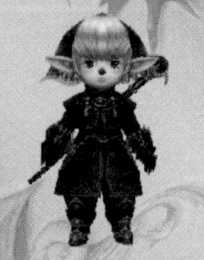

EX Mode (Normal)

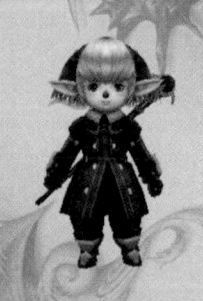

Shantotto (Alternate)

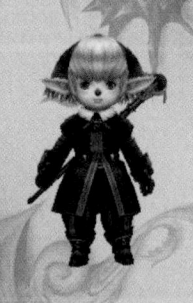

EX Mode (Alternate)

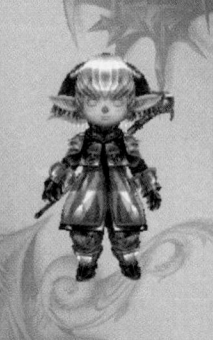

Lady of Antiquity

PROGRESSION

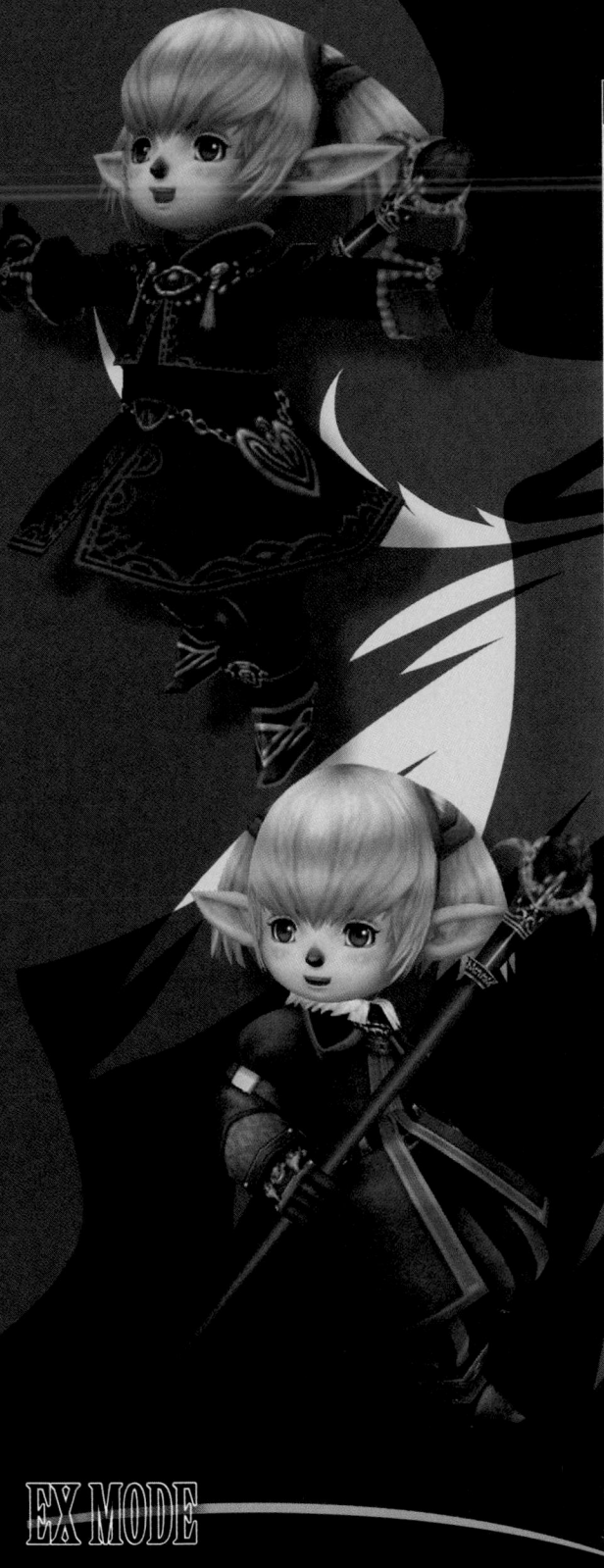

LEVEL	SKILL	TYPE	CP (N)	CP (M)	AP TO MASTER	ATTACK COMMANDS & EFFECTS*
01	A Couple Attacks	Bravery Attack (Land)	30	15	90	◎◎◎ (Wall Rush, Chase, Map Break)
01	Retribution	Bravery Attack (Air)	30	15	180	◎ (Guard, Map Break, Chase)
01	Spirit Magic: Air	HP Attack (Air)	40	20	240	◎ (More powerful when bravery exceeds 2999 and 5999; Pull-in, Mid-power version: Map Break; Full power version: Guard Crush, Map Break)
01	Spirit Magic: Earth	HP Attack (Land)	40	20	200	◎ (More powerful when bravery exceeds 2999 and 5999; Mid-power version: Map Break; Full power version: Guard Crush, Map Break)
01	Spirit Magic: Fire	HP Attack (Land)	40	20	260	◎ (More powerful when bravery exceeds 2999 and 5999; Mid-power version: Map Break; Full power version: Guard Crush, Map Break)
01	Spirit Magic: Ice	HP Attack (Air)	40	20	280	◎ (More powerful when bravery exceeds 2999 and 5999; Mid-power version: Map Break; Full power version: Guard Crush, Map Break)
01	Spirit Magic: Thunder	HP Attack (Land)	40	20	300	◎ (More powerful when bravery exceeds 2999 and 5999; Mid-power version: Map Break; Full power version: Guard Crush, Map Break)
01	Spirit Magic: Water	HP Attack (Air)	40	20	220	◎ (More powerful when bravery exceeds 2999 and 5999; Pull-in, Mid-power version: Map Break; Full power version: Guard Crush, Map Break)
02	Reverse Free Air Dash	Action	10	5	100	▣ + △
03	Bio (ground)	Bravery Attack (Land)	30	15	120	◎
03	Bio (midair)	Bravery Attack (Air)	30	15	120	◎
04	Air Dash	Action	10	5	100	△ during Quickmove
07	Jump Boost	Action	10	5	150	-
(Mastery)	Jump Boost+	Action	20	10	150	-
(Mastery)	Jump Boost++	Action	40	20	150	-
11	Auto Recovery	Support	20	5	250	-
11	Auto Chase	Support	20	5	250	-
13	Bind (ground)	Bravery Attack (Land)	20	10	120	◎
13	Bind (midair)	Bravery Attack (Air)	20	10	120	◎
15	Auto EX Burst	Support	20	5	150	-
15	Auto EX Command	Support	30	10	300	-
18	Reverse Air Dash	Action	10	5	100	△ during Quickmove
21	Speed Boost	Action	20	10	150	-
(Mastery)	Speed Boost+	Action	40	20	150	-
(Mastery)	Speed Boost++	Action	70	35	150	-
25	EX Critical Boost	Extra	45	40	300	-
26	Auto EX Defense	Support	30	10	300	-
29	Stun (ground)	Bravery Attack (Land)	20	10	120	◎
29	Stun (midair)	Bravery Attack (Air)	20	10	120	◎
32	Recovery Attack	Action	20	10	120	◎ or ◉ while reeling
32	Controlled Recovery	Action	10	5	120	Analog Stick during Recovery
35	Riposte	Extra	45	40	300	-
(Mastery)	Disable Riposte	Extra	20	10	300	-
39	Jump Times Boost	Action	20	10	150	-
(Mastery)	Jump Times Boost+	Action	40	20	150	-
(Mastery)	Jump Times Boost++	Action	70	30	150	-
40	Omni Air Dash	Action	40	20	300	Analog Stick + ▣ + △
43	Sneak Attack	Extra	50	45	360	-
(Mastery)	Disable Sneak Attack	Extra	30	15	360	-
47	Physical Shield	Extra	20	10	280	-
50	Magic Shield	Extra	20	10	280	-
53	Multi-Air Slide	Action	10	5	250	Analog Stick + ✕ after expending jumps
(Mastery)	Multi-Air Slide+	Action	30	15	300	See Multi-Air Slide
57	Midair Evasion Boost	Action	20	10	150	-
60	Bravery Regen	Extra	20	10	280	-
64	Evasion Time Boost	Support	20	10	220	-
67	First Strike	Extra	40	35	360	-
(Mastery)	Disable First Strike	Extra	20	10	360	-
71	Concentration	Extra	30	15	250	-
(Mastery)	Concentration+	Extra	60	30	250	-
(Mastery)	Concentration++	Extra	100	50	250	-
74	Cat Nip	Extra	30	25	300	-
(Mastery)	Disable Cat Nip	Extra	20	10	300	-
78	Anti-EX	Extra	30	20	300	-
(Mastery)	Disable Anti-EX	Extra	20	10	300	-
81	Achy	Extra	30	15	250	-
(Mastery)	Achy+	Extra	60	30	250	-
85	Counterattack	Extra	50	45	360	-
(Mastery)	Disable Counterattack	Extra	30	15	360	-
88	Gambler's Spirit	Extra	30	15	300	-
(Mastery)	Disable Gambler's Spirit	Extra	20	10	300	-
92	Back to the Wall	Extra	30	25	300	-
(Mastery)	Disable Back to the Wall	Extra	20	10	300	-
95	Precision Jump	Extra	10	5	180	-
98	Snooze and Lose	Extra	100	50	250	-
100	EXP to HP	Extra	20	0	500	-
100	EXP to Bravery	Extra	20	0	500	-
100	EXP to EX Force	Extra	20	0	500	-

*Initial commands may require directional presses, depending on the slot to which abilities are assigned.

EX MODE

EX BURST

Play Rough: A flurry of attacks leading to a blast of terribly strong magic. Select spells from the menu. Fire-Water-Thunder-Earth-Wind-Ice order deals maximum damage.

EX EFFECTS

Regen: Vigor and stamina recover little by little, restoring HP.

Manafont: Bravery does not decrease even after successfully landing HP attacks.

CHARACTERS

GABRANTH

EXecutioner—Passes sentence from beneath the Judge's helm.

Unlock Gabranth as a playable character by finishing Distant Glory: Redemption of the Warrior and purchasing him from the PP Catalog.

A warrior who swears his life to those he trusts. In *Final Fantasy XII*, he served as a Judge Magister of the Archadian Empire. Despite being non-native to the Empire, he advanced to the position of Judge at an impressive speed. However, his heart was filled with regret from being unable to protect his home country, and he despised his older brother Basch for abandoning him and their mother.

-	NORMAL	EX MODE
Ground Movement Speed	★	★★★
Innate Number of Jumps	1	1
Jump Height	★	★★★
Jump Rising Speed	★★	★★
Air Dash Speed	★	★★★
Quickmove Speed	★	★★★

*Mobility can be increased with the abilities Speed Boost, Jump Boost, Jump Times Boost, and Precision Jump

EQUIPMENT

Weapon	Swords, Daggers, Greatswords
Hands	Shields, Gauntlets
Head	Helms
Body	Light Armor, Heavy Armor

STAT PROGRESSION

LV	HP	CP	BRV	ATK	DEF	LUK
1	1000	350	95	9	10	10
5	1242	354	118	13	14	12
10	1545	359	147	18	19	15
20	2151	369	205	28	29	20
30	2757	379	263	38	39	25
40	3363	389	320	48	49	30
50	3969	399	378	58	59	35
60	4575	409	436	68	69	40
70	5181	419	493	78	79	45
80	5787	429	551	88	89	50
90	6393	439	609	98	99	55
100	6999	450	667	108	109	60

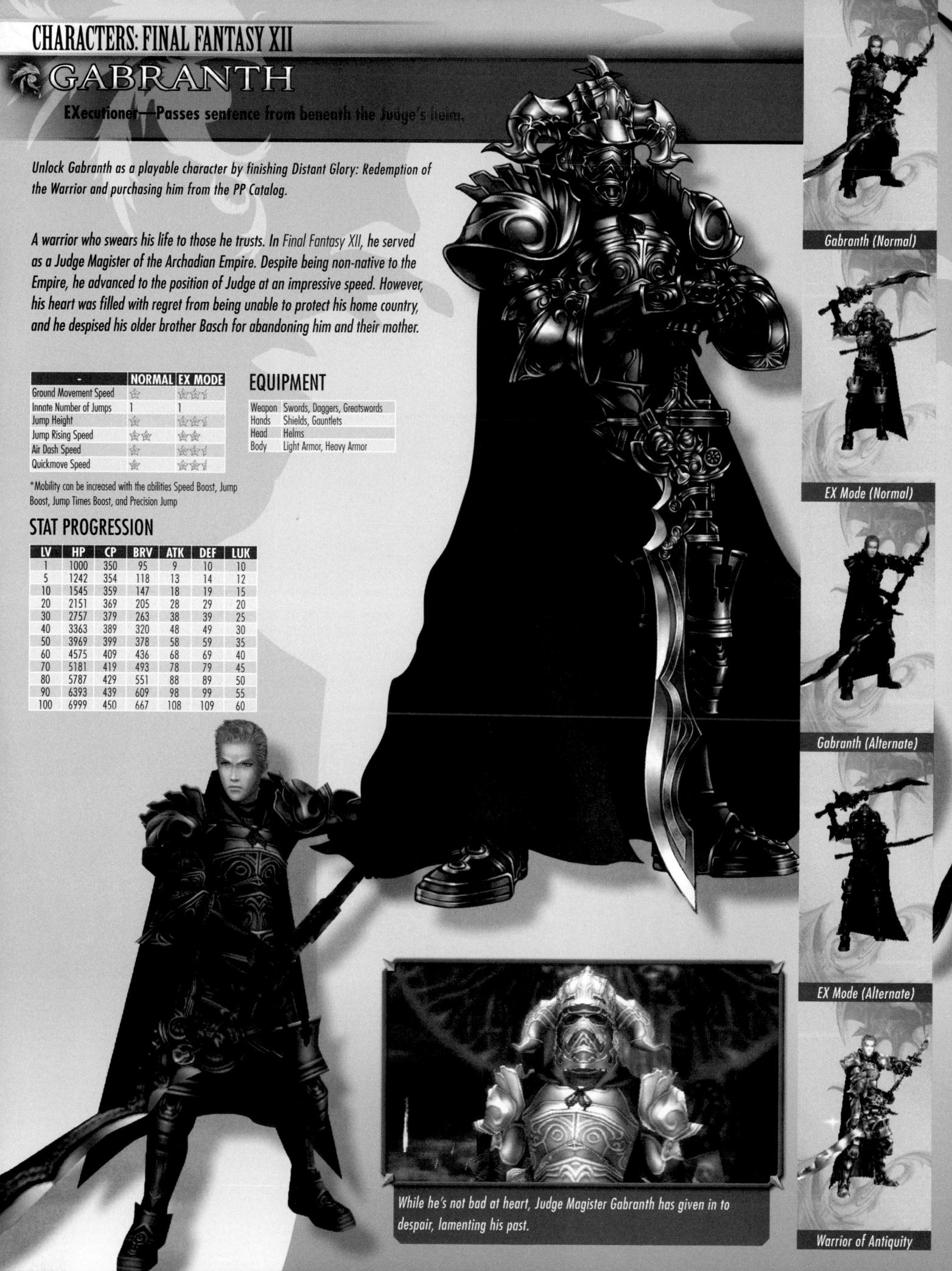

While he's not bad at heart, Judge Magister Gabranth has given in to despair, lamenting his past.

Gabranth (Normal)

EX Mode (Normal)

Gabranth (Alternate)

EX Mode (Alternate)

Warrior of Antiquity

ABILITY PROGRESSION

LEVEL	SKILL	TYPE	CP (N)	CP (M)	AP TO MASTER	ATTACK COMMANDS & EFFECTS*
01	Aero (ground)	Bravery Attack (Land-EX Mode)	20	10	140	● (Pull-in, Map Break, Chase)
01	Aero (midair)	Bravery Attack (Air-EX Mode)	20	10	140	● (Pull-in, Map Break, Chase)
01	Circle of Judgment	Bravery Attack (Air-Normal)	20	10	180	● (Move OK, Pull-in, Map Break)
01	Enrage	Bravery Attack (Land-EX Mode)	30	15	140	● (Map Break) ● (Map Break) ● (Map Break) ● (Map Break) ● (Map Break, Wall Rush)
01	EX Charge (ground)	HP Attack (Land-Normal)	20	10	300	Hold ● (Fills EX Gauge)
01	EX Charge (midair)	HP Attack (Air-Normal)	20	10	300	Hold ● (Fills EX Gauge)
01	Hatred	HP Attack (Air-EX Mode)	40	20	180	Hold and release ● (Guard Crush, Pull-in, Map Break, Wall Rush)
01	Innocence (ground)	HP Attack (Land-EX Mode)	40	20	180	● (Guard, Guard Crush, Map Break, Wall Rush)
01	Sentence (ground)	Bravery Attack (Land-Normal)	20	10	120	● (Map Break) ● (Map Break)
01	Vortex of Judgment	Bravery Attack (Air-EX Mode)	30	15	140	● (Move OK, Guard, Pull-in, Map Break) ● (Move OK, Guard, Pull-in, Map Break) ● (Move OK, Guard, Pull-in, Map Break, Chase)
03	Lunge	Bravery Attack (Land-Normal)	20	10	120	● (Map Break)
04	Air Dash	Action	10	5	100	● during Quickmove
06	Sentence (midair)	Bravery Attack (Air-Normal)	20	10	180	● (Map Break) ● (Map Break)
07	Speed Boost	Action	20	10	150	-
(Mastery)	Speed Boost+	Action	40	20	150	-
(Mastery)	Speed Boost++	Action	70	35	150	-
10	Rupture	Bravery Attack (Air-EX Mode)	30	15	140	● (Map Break, Wall Rush)
11	Auto Recovery	Support	20	5	250	-
11	Auto Chase	Support	20	5	250	-
15	Auto EX Burst	Support	20	5	150	-
15	Auto EX Command	Support	30	10	300	-
16	Relentless Lunge	Bravery Attack (Land-EX Mode)	30	15	140	● (Map Break) ● (Map Break) ● (Map Break, Chase)
18	Reverse Air Dash	Action	10	5	100	● during Quickmove
21	Jump Boost	Action	10	5	150	-
(Mastery)	Jump Boost+	Action	20	10	150	-
(Mastery)	Jump Boost++	Action	40	20	150	-
23	Innocence (midair)	HP Attack (Air-EX Mode)	40	20	180	● (Guard, Guard Crush, Map Break, Wall Rush)
25	EX Critical Boost	Extra	45	40	300	-
26	Auto EX Defense	Support	30	10	300	-
29	Reverse Free Air Dash	Action	10	5	100	■ + ●
30	Dual Rend	Bravery Attack (Air-EX Mode)	30	15	140	● (Map Break, Wall Rush)
32	Recovery Attack	Action	20	10	120	● or ● while reeling
32	Controlled Recovery	Action	10	5	120	Analog Stick during Recovery
35	Riposte	Extra	45	40	300	-
(Mastery)	Disable Riposte	Extra	20	10	300	-
38	Guilt	HP Attack (Land-EX Mode)	40	20	300	● (Guard, Pull-in, Map Break)
39	Jump Times Boost	Action	20	10	150	-
(Mastery)	Jump Times Boost+	Action	40	20	150	-
(Mastery)	Jump Times Boost++	Action	70	30	150	-
40	Omni Air Dash	Action	40	20	300	Analog Stick + ■ + ●
43	Sneak Attack	Extra	50	45	360	-
(Mastery)	Disable Sneak Attack	Extra	30	15	360	-
47	Physical Shield	Extra	20	10	280	-
50	Magic Shield	Extra	20	10	280	-
53	Multi-Air Slide	Action	10	5	250	Analog Stick + ✕ after expending jumps
(Mastery)	Multi-Air Slide+	Action	30	15	300	See Multi-Air Slide
57	Midair Evasion Boost	Action	20	10	150	-
60	Bravery Regen	Extra	20	10	280	-
64	Evasion Time Boost	Support	20	10	220	-
67	First Strike	Extra	40	35	360	-
(Mastery)	Disable First Strike	Extra	20	10	360	-
71	Concentration	Extra	30	15	250	-
(Mastery)	Concentration+	Extra	60	30	250	-
(Mastery)	Concentration++	Extra	100	50	250	-
74	Cat Nip	Extra	30	25	300	-
(Mastery)	Disable Cat Nip	Extra	20	10	300	-
78	Anti-EX	Extra	30	20	300	-
(Mastery)	Disable Anti-EX	Extra	20	10	300	-
81	Achy	Extra	30	15	250	-
(Mastery)	Achy+	Extra	60	30	250	-
85	Counterattack	Extra	50	45	360	-
(Mastery)	Disable Counterattack	Extra	30	15	360	-
88	Gambler's Spirit	Extra	30	15	300	-
(Mastery)	Disable Gambler's Spirit	Extra	20	10	300	-
92	Back to the Wall	Extra	30	25	300	-
(Mastery)	Disable Back to the Wall	Extra	20	10	300	-
95	Precision Jump	Extra	10	5	180	-
98	Snooze and Lose	Extra	100	50	250	-
100	EXP to HP	Extra	20	0	500	-
100	EXP to Bravery	Extra	20	0	500	-
100	EXP to EX Force	Extra	20	0	500	-

*Initial commands may require directional presses, depending on the slot to which abilities are assigned.

Gabranth is unique in that he can only access HP attacks, and therefore deal HP damage, during EX Mode. EX Charge is used while EX Mode is not active to build up EX Force. Equip Gabranth with accessories and equipment that both accelerate EX Force collection and extend EX Mode duration. When landing HP attacks during EX Mode, you may forgo using an EX Burst, to instead remain in EX Mode longer.

EX MODE

EX BURST

Quickening: Blows embodying wrath itself. (Shuffle options with ■. Press ✕ to select moves to use.)

EX EFFECTS

Regen: Vigor and stamina recover little by little, restoring HP.

Stray's Tenacity: Boosts stats and abilities, and greatly strengthens attacks.

GAME BASICS
STRUCTURE OF THE GAME

There are several ways to play *DISSIDIA FINAL FANTASY*. You can pop in for a Quick Battle or a round of Arcade Mode, or sit down for a lengthy campaign in one of several Story Mode chapters. Whatever way you choose to play, all of your progress is saved under a single profile, and all progress made in one mode carries over to the others. For example, if you're finding a character's Story Mode to be excessively difficult, you can use that character in a series of Quick Battle or Communications Mode fights, and whatever EXP, AP, and items you earn will be available to you the next time you challenge Story Mode.

The ultimate goal of the game is up to you. To view the ending, you'll need to complete Chapter 4 of the Shade Impulse Story Mode. But, if you hope to complete all 151 accomplishments (*DISSIDIA's* equivalent of achievements or trophies), or unlock all of the in-game events, you'll have a much longer road to travel.

STORY MODE

There are seventeen total chapters to *DISSIDIA's* story, divided into four categories. Completing a chapter typically unlocks new treasures and stronger enemies, so you'll need to replay each chapter multiple times to get everything.

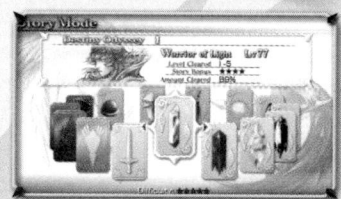

DESTINY ODYSSEY
After the Prologue, the ten chapters of Destiny Odyssey are unlocked, one for each of the ten initially selectable Cosmos heroes. You can play the Destiny Odyssey chapters in any order, but each has a difficulty ranking between one and five stars, and the game will be easier to learn if you play in order of difficulty.

SHADE IMPULSE
After completing any Destiny Odyssey chapter, you'll unlock the Shade Impulse Story Mode. There are four chapters to Shade Impulse, and unlike the Destiny Odyssey chapters, you must complete each one to unlock the next. Once unlocked, you can challenge any Shade Impulse chapter with any of the ten initially selectable Cosmos heroes. Shade Impulse Chapter 4 ends with a battle against Chaos himself; when he is bested, the ending rolls.

DISTANT GLORY
After completing Shade Impulse Chapter 4, you'll unlock the two chapters of Distant Glory. Your reward for clearing each of these challenging chapters is the opportunity to unlock a new playable character from the PP Catalog. You may challenge the Distant Glory chapters with any character, including unlocked Chaos characters.

INWARD CHAOS
Inward Chaos is the game's ultimate challenge, a single expert-level chapter where you'll face enemies as strong as level 110. You can challenge Inward Chaos with any unlocked character.

ARCADE MODE

Arcade Mode offers a simplified version of *DISSIDIA* that gives you pre-made characters and a roster of foes to battle. If you lose, you can retry as often as you like. You do not earn any combat rewards in this mode, but players who make it to the end will win 300 PP and a few useful trade accessories will be added to their collection. You may use any unlocked character in Arcade Mode.

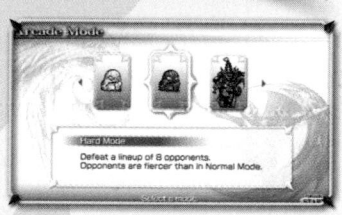

NORMAL MODE
Normal Mode pits a pre-made, level 10 version of your chosen character against a series of five random foes. Survive till the end and you'll receive a Chocobo Cologne trade accessory, which can be swapped at the shop to raise a character by a single level.

HARD MODE
You can unlock Hard Mode for 3,000 PP in the PP Catalog. Hard Mode features level 50 versions of characters, and a series of eight foes instead of five. Here, your opponents have stronger tactics, making for much tougher battles overall. Those who emerge triumphant earn PP, as well as three valuable accessories: a Wind Stone, a Water Stone, and a Lifestone.

TIME ATTACK
You may unlock the Time Attack for 10,000 PP after clearing Chapter 4 of the Shade Impulse Story Mode. The Time Attack mode has a preset course of ten opponents (ending with Chaos) instead of the randomized courses of the previous two modes. All characters are level 100, and each has a predetermined Summonstone, although you can only use yours three times throughout the entire course. Time Attack survivors will receive ten Transmogridust accessories, and may earn a set of five Elixirs, Hi-Elixirs, or Megalixirs as a reward for a low total playtime

DUEL COLOSSEUM MODE

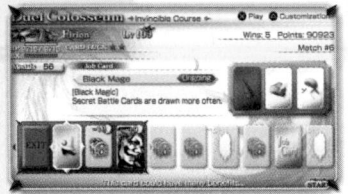

The Duel Colosseum is unlocked after completing Shade Impulse Chapter 4. It initially comes with two open courses, for level 1-30 and 31-60 characters. More challenging courses can be unlocked from the PP Catalog.

The Duel Colosseum is an endless card game in which you choose from a hand of cards that include battles (which earn you medals), treasures (which cost you medals), and jobs (which change the rules of the game). The Duel Colosseum is a great way for experienced players to rack up items quickly. See the Duel Colosseum section for more details.

QUICK BATTLE

Quick Battle allows you to play as any unlocked character in a single battle where you can set all of the terms. You choose the battlefield and the opponent, as well as the opponent's AI strength, level, and behavior. There are some limitations at the beginning of the game, but as you progress you can unlock higher CPU level caps, additional stages, and special rulesets from the PP Catalog.

Early in the game, Quick Battles are a great way to get a bit of EXP for a character you want to level up. For more advanced players, they are ideal for acquiring specific items through Battlegen, since you can choose whichever opponent or stage can generate the item you want and keep trying until you get it. You can also aim for rare item drops by setting your opponent's strength to "High (Equipment)."

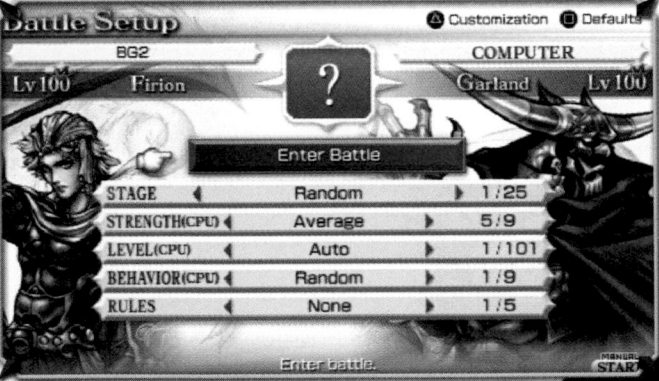

AP CHANCES

When fighting in Quick Battle, Duel Colosseum, or Communications Mode, an "AP Chance" will be announced at the beginning of each fight. If you fulfill a condition, such as striking first or hitting for more or less than your base bravery, you'll earn two additional AP at the end of the fight.

COMMUNICATIONS MODE

Communications Mode allows you to enter *DISSIDIA's* lobby system, either to battle against your friends online via a local wireless connection, or spar offline, where you can battle computer-controlled "ghost" characters recorded in Friend Cards.

Begin by selecting your opponent: a Friend Card of either a person in the same lobby, or of someone you've met previously whose Friend Card was automatically transferred to you. Then, choose your own character, a stage, and (if unlocked) a special ruleset. When battling against a live opponent, you'll have the option to set a handicap—so that if one character is of a much higher level, that character's stats become reduced to an appropriate level. When battling a ghost, you may change the behavior setting with which the computer can battle.

You can win all the usual rewards in Communications Mode, and there are special rewards for battling online against other people. You can buy options from the PP Catalog that allow you to get copies of your friends' equipment through Battlegen and even keep all acquired AP, gil, items, and accessories after a loss. Both online and offline battles allow you to create otherwise unavailable rare gems through Battlegen, and online battles also allow you to randomly generate artifacts. (Note that when an item is dropped during an online battle, the original item is not lost; the opponent merely gets a copy.)

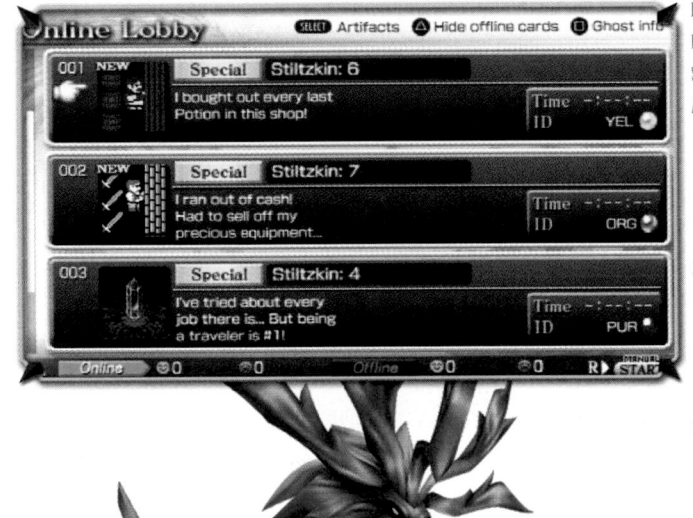

FRIEND CARDS

Every profile automatically comes with a Friend Card. To change the details on your Friend Card, choose Friend Card Settings and select the Player Icon that will represent you, the message that will be displayed on your card, and the character from your profile that will fight on your behalf as a ghost character. (The computer automatically chooses a playstyle based on the tactics you use when playing that character.) Whenever you interact with another player by meeting in an online lobby or simply walking by with both of your PSPs in sleep mode and set to "Card Exchange," you'll get a copy of each other's Friend Cards.

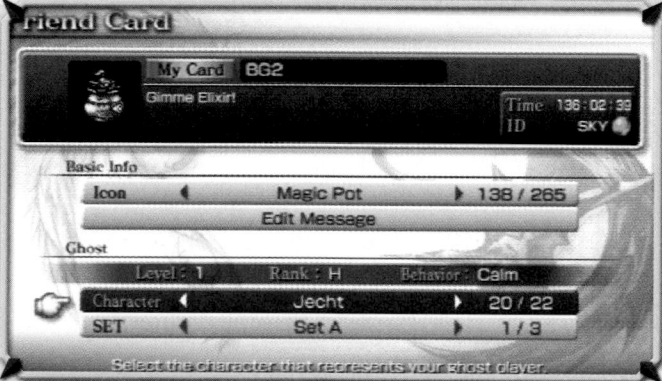

ID COLORS

All Friend Cards have a randomly assigned colored ID. This determines which rare gem accessory can be created via Battlegen when battling that player. For example, only by battling a player or ghost with a PUR ID will you have a chance to Battlegen a Purple Gem and achieve the corresponding secret accomplishment.

FRIEND REWARDS

If you re-encounter a player after he or she has battled your ghost, you'll get a reward of gil and PP. For each time your ghost won, you'll receive 1,000 gil and 100 PP. Each time it loses, you'll receive half that. However, the maximum amount you can receive is set by your Friend Reward level, which you can raise by buying the Friend Reward Boost options in the PP Catalog.

OFFLINE FRIENDS

Even if you never play online, you can get Friend Cards from Mognet or from passwords that will be distributed by the developers after the game's release. You can earn rare items and Battlegen accessories (but not artifacts) by battling the ghosts they contain.

ARTIFACTS

During online battles, sometimes your opponent may drop an artifact instead of a normal item drop. (As with any piece of equipment, raising your Luck stat and buying the Item Drop Rate Up option from the PP Catalog increases your odds of getting one.) Artifacts are armaments based on your opponent's weapon or armor, but with different abilities. All artifacts have an orange hammer icon next to their name. If there's a feather on top of the hammer, it means you may rename the artifact to change its ability. Each time an artifact is renamed, a line is added to its history. The longer its history, the more impressive its abilities may be. To unlock the game's best abilities, an artifact may need to change hands up to 50 times!

You can equip artifacts like any other equipment, but you can't sell them at shops unless you go to the Artifact menu under Communications Mode. You can only hold 20 artifacts at once, so sell the weaker ones regularly to make room for new ones.

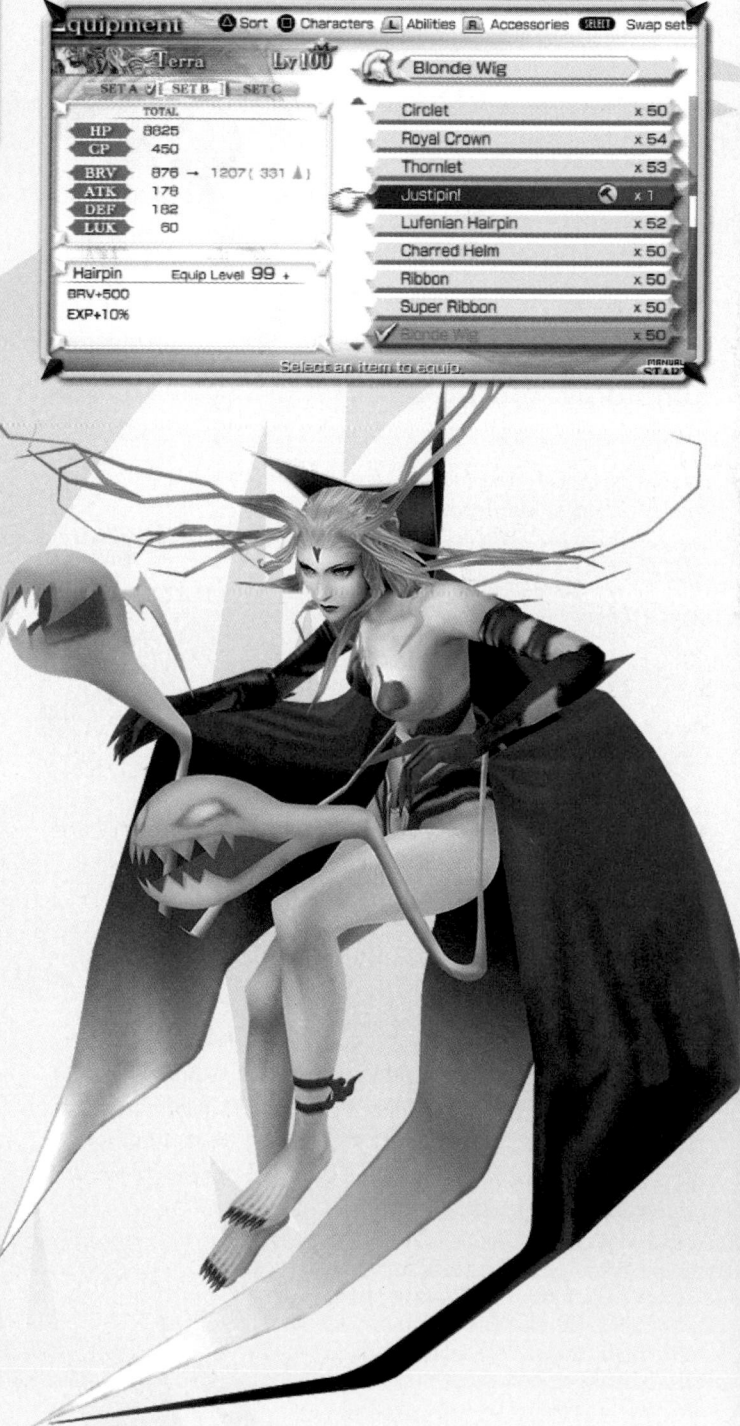

YOUR BONUS SCHEDULE

DISSIDIA FINAL FANTASY is constantly tracking the passage of time and personal play patterns in order to dish out periodic rewards. Those who take advantage of these systems can earn massive PP, EXP, AP, and gil bonuses, as well as free items and exclusive Friend Cards and Player Icons.

A PREPONDERANCE OF POINTS

There are many different points you can earn in DISSIDIA FINAL FANTASY. You'll need plenty of each to develop your roster of fighters.

EXP: Experience Points are earned whenever you deal HP damage to your foes; you do not need to win a battle to collect them. As they earn EXP, characters rise in level, which improves their stats, grants them new attacks and abilities, and allows them to equip more items.

AP: Ability Points are earned when you win a battle, and additional points are earned when you fulfill the conditions of an AP Chance in Quick Battle, Duel Colosseum, or online fights. Whatever amount of AP you earn is added to the AP bar of all abilities your character has enabled. When the bar is full, the ability will be mastered, which halves the cost to equip it and may unlock higher levels of the same ability or, in the case of certain attacks, the second stage of an ability combo.

PP: Player Points are earned after each battle in any mode (except for Arcade Mode) and can be found in chests or won as prizes in many situations. These points can be used to unlock items from the PP Catalog, which is accessible from the game's main menu.

Gil: Gil is the unit of currency in Final Fantasy, and is earned through combat victories, as prizes in Story Mode, or by selling unwanted items. It can be spent on weapons, armaments, and accessories in the shop that is accessible from any character's Customization menu.

BONUS DAYS

When you fire up a new game of DISSIDIA FINAL FANTASY, you'll be asked on what day of the week you're most likely to play. That day becomes your weekly Bonus Day, when you get extra AP, gil, PP, and EXP from battles all day long, and you may also get one of the following random bonuses: a 10% discount at the shop, a 10% bonus when selling items at the shop, a 1% higher chance of Battlegen, or a 1% higher chance of an item drop. You can also get lesser bonuses (one or more of the AP, gil, PP, and EXP bonuses) on random days throughout the week; press ● on the main menu to open up the calendar and see when these are scheduled.

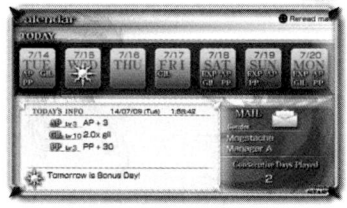

To make these random bonuses appear more often, buy the Icon Likelihood level ups from the Calendar section of the PP Catalog. To increase the bonuses themselves (from one extra AP per battle to 2 extra AP per battle, for example), buy the Icon Boost level ups. For obvious reasons, these are the very first things you should spend your PP on. And, if you beat every Destiny Odyssey chapter, you'll be able to buy even higher levels of Icon Boost and Icon Likelihood.

PLAY PLANS

At the beginning of the game, you'll also be asked to declare yourself as either a casual, average, or hardcore gamer. The option you choose determines your initial Play Plan, a system that rewards you the more you play throughout a single day.

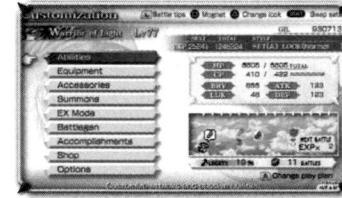

Your Play Plan is represented by the chocobo in the lower-right corner of the Customization screen. (You may change your Play Plan at any time by pressing ■ on this screen, but only do this at the beginning or end of a daily play session, since it resets your Play Plan progress.) With every battle you engage in, in any mode except Arcade Mode, the chocobo takes a step. Eventually, the chocobo takes to the sky in search of Gysahl Greens, and when it reaches one, you'll get an EXP bonus in the next fight. The more you play, the higher your "Lucky!!" rate rises, which later results in other random EXP bonuses. When the chocobo reaches the treasure chest at the end of your Play Plan, you'll get an accessory that confers an EXP bonus upon your character—the longer the Play Plan, the higher the bonus. (These accessories have a 30% chance of breaking after any battle, but don't worry, you'll rack up a bunch of them.)

BONUS DAY EVERY DAY

You can change your Bonus Day by selecting Player Settings from the main menu, but your Bonus Day will be cancelled for the next seven days to prevent cheating. However, if you wish to fool the game, you can press Home to access the PSP's Xross Media Bar, scroll left to System Settings, and down to access Date & Time Settings. By manipulating the date, you can make every day your Bonus Day.

THE FIVE COURSES

Early in the game, you should choose the longest Play Plan that you'll be able to complete; there's no point going hardcore if you can't rack up 60 battles per day. After completing all five Destiny Odyssey chapters, you'll be able to buy the Black Chocobo (Grind-lover) and Fat Chocobo (Treasure Hunter) Play Plans in the PP Catalog; these offer steady bonuses regardless of how long you can play.

CASUAL PLAN

The chocobo finds a Chocobo Down (+20% EXP, 30% chance of breaking) after every 15 battles.

AVERAGE PLAN

The chocobo finds a Chocobo Wing (+50% EXP, 30% chance of breaking) after every 30 battles.

HARDCORE PLAN

The chocobo finds a Chocobo Feather (+100% EXP, 30% chance of breaking) after every 60 battles.

GRIND-LOVER

The black chocobo finds EXP-boosting greens and earns Lucky!! bonuses more often, but does not find treasure.

TREASURE-HUNTER

The Fat Chocobo finds treasures after every three to five battles (65% chance of Chocobo Down, 30% chance of Chocobo Wing, 5% chance of Chocobo Feather), but does not find any greens or raise your Lucky!! bonus.

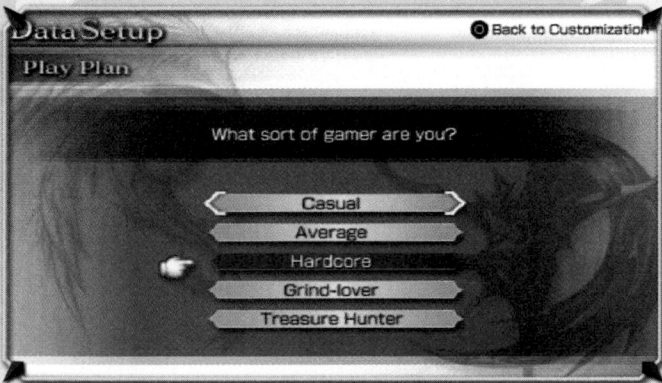

MOGNET

When you press ● on the main menu to visit the Calendar, you'll likely find a letter waiting for you. Your moogle friends will mail you every day, but only if you've taken the time to read the previous day's letters. Moogle mail is full of fun stuff; *DISSIDIA* tips, nostalgic references to old *Final Fantasy* games, *Final Fantasy* trivia quizzes, and so on. But it isn't just for fun—every letter comes with a free bonus of at least 30 PP, and if you send the right responses, you can get far more exciting prizes. The best of the lot is the Stiltzkin Friend Cards, a series of eight offline Friend Cards that provide an opportunity to challenge ghosts for rare item drops and win each of the ID-specific Battlegen accessories.

BLUE MAIL

Mail in blue envelopes comes from the Mognet Head Office. Their typical letters offer daily advice on how to get the most out of *DISSIDIA FINAL FANTASY*, but they do send out special letters with added prizes when you either play the game for many days in a row or allow a long period to lapse between play sessions. Playing for 20 days in a row (or tricking the system clock into believing you did) rewards you with a bunch of PP and seven out of eight Stiltzkin Friend Cards.

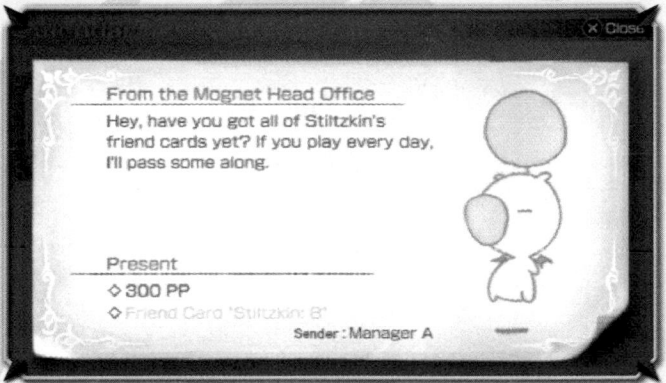

YELLOW MAIL

Mail in yellow envelopes comes from individual moogles seeking friendship, advice, or to test your knowledge of *Final Fantasy* trivia. There are several multi-letter sequences in which a moogle contacts you, asks a question to which you must send a reply, and then mails you again, usually with another question. These are mostly for fun, but these sequences can also earn you special prizes if you say the right things. See the Secrets and Cheats section of this guide for the prize-winning answers to each of the moogle mail sequences.

THE FUNDAMENTALS OF COMBAT

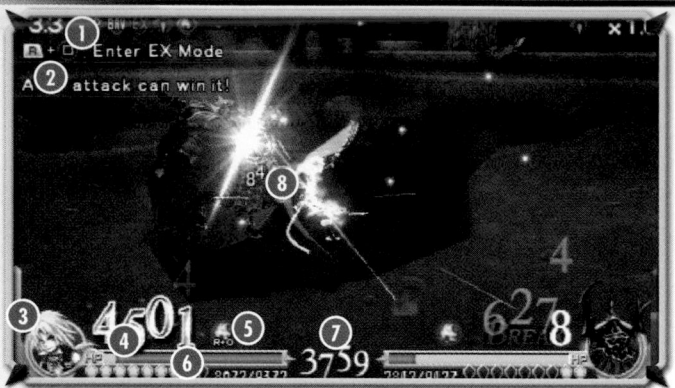

While your ultimate goal in any *DISSIDIA* battle is to reduce your foe's HP to zero, you'll expend most of your effort fighting over something called "bravery." All characters have two types of attacks: bravery attacks (executed with the ● button) and HP attacks (executed with the ● button). Bravery attacks steal bravery from your target and add it to your own bravery total. HP attacks deal damage to the target's HP bar equal to the attacker's bravery total. You'll ultimately need to land an HP attack to end each fight, but you'll spend most of the battle using bravery attacks, both to weaken your foe's offense and to build up the power necessary to finish your opponent off with a single crushing blow.

① **Accessory Bonuses:** When you've achieved the conditional bonuses on your accessories, the appropriate icons light up, and the multiplier rises. [See the Accessories section of this guide for more information.]

② **Battle Information:** Changing your Battle Information setting affects what messages appear here. For example, beginners are informed of the appearance of EX Cores and told when they are capable of delivering a lethal HP attack. In contrast, advanced players are primarily given information about battle rewards such as EXP bonuses and Battlegen successes.

③ **EX Gauge:** This meter fills as you gather EX Force and EX Cores. When it's full, you can enter EX Mode.

④ **Player's Bravery:** The combat energy that changes hands throughout the battle, determining the amount of damage you're capable of dealing with your next HP attack.

⑤ **Summonstone:** The player's equipped Summonstone. When it is lit up it is ready to use. Any bars and icons near here indicate summon-related effects.

⑥ **HP Display:** In addition to your current HP and Max HP, an HP bar provides a somewhat confusing visual diagram. The small diamonds represent HP in 1,000 HP increments, while the large upper bar shows any remaining HP. (It's easier just to look at the number.)

⑦ **Stage Bravery:** The bravery that is awarded to any player who causes a Bravery Break.

⑧ **Damage Indicator:** Whenever damage is dealt, a number showing the amount pops up on the battlefield. Damage dealt to you appears in red, while damage dealt to your foe appears in white or light blue. Bravery damage is represented by smaller digits, while HP damage numbers are significantly larger.

THE INS AND OUTS OF BRAVERY

Bravery is a little more complicated than just trading a number back and forth. It's important to understand where this resource comes from, and how to acquire and expend it in the most efficient ways possible.

BUILDING YOUR BASE BRAVERY

All fighters begin the battle with an amount of bravery determined by their base BRV stat and the equipment and accessories they have equipped. Characters also earn a bravery bonus of 10% of their base BRV stat for each level they are higher than their opponent.

The power of bravery attacks is determined by the power of the attack itself, the attacker's ATK stat, the target's DEF stat, and the effect of all damage-related bonuses granted by equipment and accessories. Whenever you connect with a bravery attack, you gain an amount of bravery equal to the amount lost by the target.

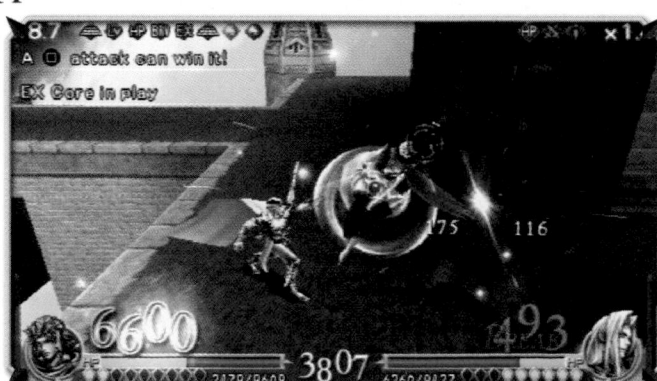

CLAIMING STAGE BRAVERY

At the bottom of the screen, between the two HP bars, you'll notice a third bravery total. This is called stage bravery, and it is typically equal to 20% of the combined Max HP of both combatants. (Later in the game, you'll encounter maps that have their own special rules for determining stage bravery.) When an attack would reduce a foe's bravery to below 0, the enemy enters the "Bravery Break" state, and the attacker earns all of the bravery from the stage bravery pool. This massive surge of bravery is often enough to fuel a lethal HP Attack. After a character claims the stage bravery, the pool quickly refills itself.

THE BRAVERY BREAK STATE

When a combatant's bravery is reduced to below 0, that character enters the "Bravery Break" state. When in this state, the character's bravery begins refilling to base bravery level, a process that usually takes around 20 seconds; however, until bravery is refilled, the broken fighter effectively has 0 bravery and is unable to deal any HP damage to foes. Since the fighter has no bravery to lose, the opponent's bravery attacks are equally ineffective, but HP attacks remain perfectly capable of dealing damage. Bravery attacks are not completely irrelevant, however; if a character in the Bravery Break state lands a bravery attack, it speeds up the process of refilling bravery. Likewise, if the broken character takes a hit from an opponent's bravery attack, it slows the process down. Similarly, a character can drastically speed up the recovery process by landing an HP attack. Though the attack won't deal any damage, it will allow the fighter to instantly break out of the Bravery Break state.

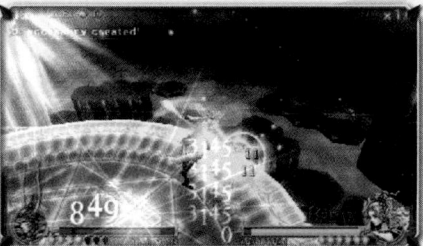

RECOVERING SPENT BRAVERY

When a character lands an HP attack, it deals HP damage equal to the attacker's bravery and then reduces the said bravery to 0. The attacker's bravery then begins to refill to base level; the more damage dealt with the HP attack, the longer it takes to recover. Unlike characters in the Bravery Break state, characters who have spent bravery on an HP attack may continue to deal damage with both bravery and HP attacks during the bravery recovery process.

EX MODE AND THE EX GAUGE

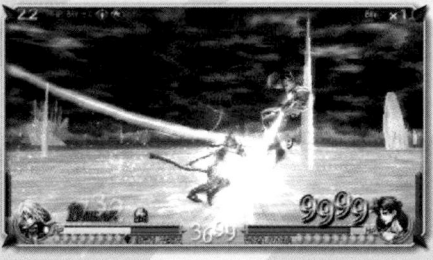

The second fundamental combat tactic involves filling your EX Gauge with EX Force. When your EX Gauge is full, you can enter EX Mode by simultaneously pressing ▬ and ⬤. Each character has powerful EX Effects that become active while in EX Mode, such as HP regeneration, improved mobility, a wider attack range, or even the ability to reduce a foe's bravery to 1. All characters also see their critical hit rate rise to 50% and gain the ability to execute a potentially deadly EX Burst after connecting with an HP attack. EX Mode doesn't last long, but it's so powerful that, if used correctly, it can turn a losing battle around completely.

Collecting EX Force

EX Force comes in two forms. In its raw form, it's the tiny shining specs that are generated by successful attacks, blocks, and midair dodges. These won't add a lot to your gauge, but when you're in desperate straits, they'll have to do. Items and accessories can increase the amount of energy you'll get from EX Force and EX Cores, as well as the distance from which you can collect raw EX Force.

EX Cores appear at random intervals in certain areas of each battlefield. EX Cores tend to appear near the combatant with the highest LUK stat, giving the luckiest characters a shot at reaching them first. When an EX Core appears the screen will flash and a distinctive sound effect will play (there may also be a text notification if Battle Information is set to beginner).

An unclaimed EX Core will absorb all of the EX Force on the battlefield. As it gathers more EX Force, the one-winged EX Core that fills only 20% of your EX Gauge grows into a two-winged core that fills 60%, and then into a four-winged core that can completely fill an EX Gauge.

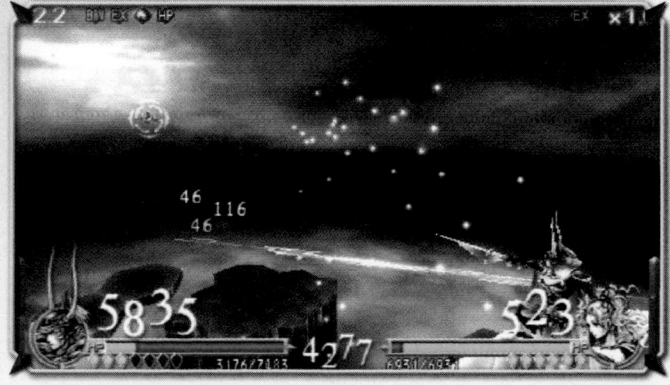

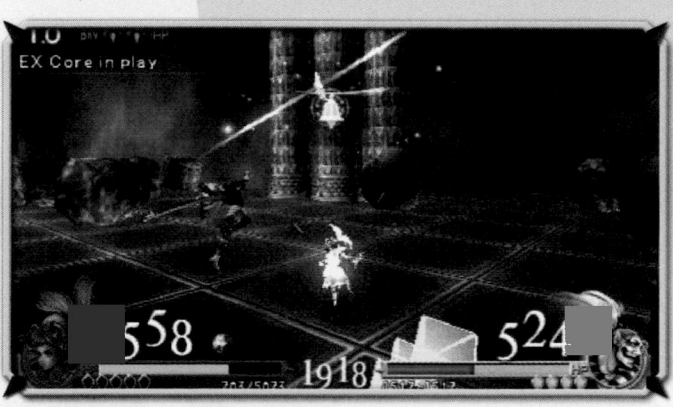

Timing Your EX Mode Activation

When your EX Gauge turns orange, indicating that it is completely full, don't activate your EX Mode immediately. One of the best things about EX Mode is that if you activate it in the middle of an opponent's attack, you can not only interrupt your enemy's combo, but in many cases you'll stagger your foe as well. Your enemy will then be ripe for either a critical hit-filled bravery combo or a potentially fatal HP attack from you.

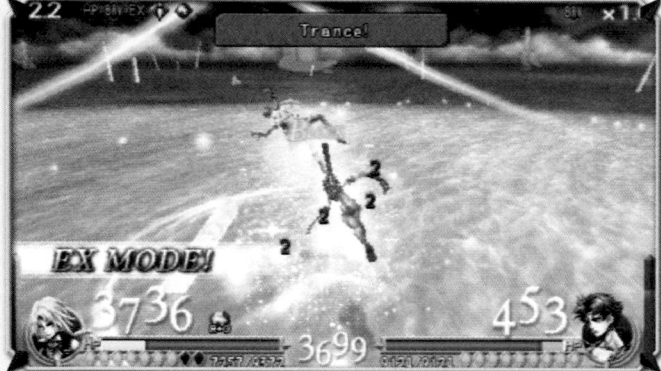

Activating Your EX Burst

To transition a successful HP attack into an EX Burst, you need only hit ● after the prompt appears on-screen. Your EX Burst will always hit, but its effectiveness varies based on your performance in an event that differs for each character. Some EX Burst activations require rapid button mashing, while others require mimicking a sequence of directions or even selecting a specific spell from a pop-up menu. The effects differ as well, but nearly all EX Bursts begin with a series of small bravery attacks that build up to a devastating HP attack finish.

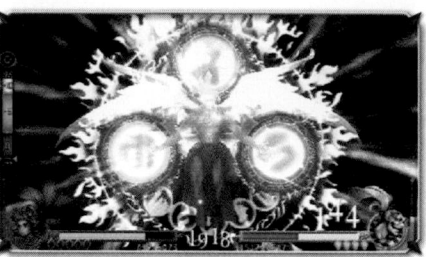

If you're on the receiving end of an EX Burst, all is not lost. You can reduce some of the damage by rapidly pressing ● when the colored meter appears on your screen. (Don't press it too rapidly; you want the arrow to hover in the yellow +10 area, not the red -5 area.) If you have trouble triggering your EX Bursts or defending against them, you can equip the Auto EX Burst and Auto EX Defense Support Abilities, respectively.

THE THREE PATHS TO VICTORY

Now let's put it all together into the three basic tactics you'll use to win battles in *DISSIDIA FINAL FANTASY*.

KILL WEAKER FOES IN ONE FELL SWOOP

When battling opponents that are of a lower level, you'll begin with significantly more starting bravery and earn more bravery with each attack. Even if you trade bravery attacks back and forth, your more effective attacks eventually inflict a Bravery Break. If the stage bravery bonus doesn't give you enough bravery to finish them in a single attack, allow them to recover their bravery and Bravery Break them again. If you attempt to beat your foe with multiple HP attacks instead of finishing them in one fell swoop, you'll give them an opportunity to turn the battle around while your bravery pool is refilling.

CHIP AWAY AT STRONGER FOES WITH HP ATTACKS

Against stronger foes, you have little hope of causing a Bravery Break. Your foe will begin with more bravery, and your attacks will do relatively little bravery damage. Instead, focus on chipping away at your enemy's health with HP attacks. Since you won't be doing much HP damage, your bravery will refill quickly, putting you in position to attack again without an extended period of vulnerability. Using HP attacks can also be a strong defensive move; when you're in danger of a Bravery Break, connecting with a low-power HP attack allows you to quickly refill your bravery to starting levels.

WHEN ALL SEEMS LOST, GO FOR THE EX HAIL MARY

Some foes are so good at defending or evading that it's difficult to connect with anything. When you can't outplay your foe, you must go for the Hail Mary tactic of filling up your EX Gauge and attempting to win with EX Bursts. When pursuing this strategy, be prepared to lock onto and claim EX Cores as soon as they appear, and pick up all the EX Force that you can while fleeing your foe's attacks. Once you have a full EX Gauge, try to enter EX Mode while your foe is striking with a close-range combo attack to cancel it and create an opening for a counterattack.

ENHANCING YOUR ATTACKS

CRITICAL HITS

Critical hits deal greatly increased bravery damage. (You cannot score critical hits on HP attacks.) The odds of randomly scoring a critical hit are less than 2%, but there are several ways that you can engineer them:

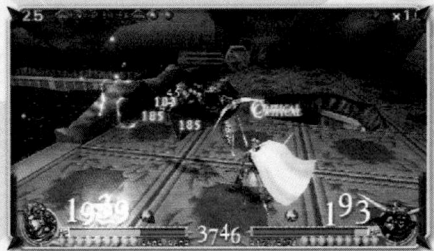

1. When in EX Mode, a character has a 50% chance of scoring a critical hit with each bravery attack. During an EX Burst, all hits are critical hits.

2. If you hit with a bravery attack immediately after a successful block, you will always execute a critical hit.

3. If you land a bravery attack during the period when your bravery is refilling after a successful HP attack, you will always execute a critical hit.

4. There are several Extra Abilities that boost your odds of landing a critical hit in certain situations, such as Riposte, Sneak Attack, and First Strike. However, these are generally not learned before level 40.

DP BONUSES

When Story Mode battles offer a DP bonus for scoring a critical hit within 10 seconds, and you don't have a skill like First Strike that would make it easy, the best tactic is to immediately drain your bravery with a successful HP attack and then execute a flurry of bravery attacks.

WALL RUSHES

Certain attacks have the "wall rush" attribute, which means they have enough force to knock their target into parts of the stage for additional damage. When the force of your attack knocks your foe into a wall, onto the floor or ceiling, or through a breakable object like a pillar, the enemy takes additional damage equal to roughly 50% of the damage dealt by the attack itself. (Some items and accessories can raise or lower wall rush damage.)

Wall rush damage is applied to both bravery attacks and HP attacks, although you can never score a killing blow with wall rush HP damage; instead, your foe is simply reduced to 1 HP.

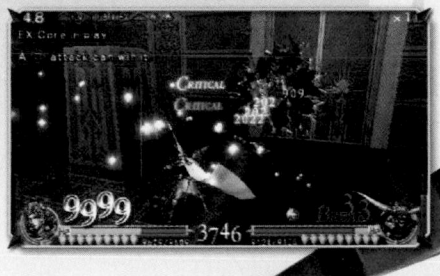

GIVING CHASE

"Chase" is another special property of attacks. After successfully landing a chase attack, your foe will be knocked a great distance away. If your foe doesn't hit a wall or the floor, an ⊗ prompt briefly appears on-screen. Hit ⊗ before it disappears and you'll leap after your foe for a chance to strike again in midair. (If you equip the Auto Chase Attack ability, you'll automatically give chase without having to press ⊗.)

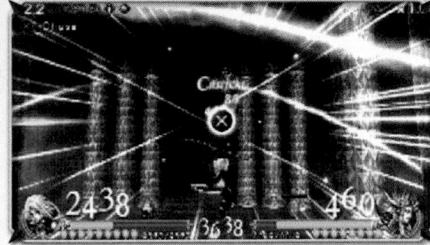

Chases are a bit of a mind game; as the attacker, you must choose between executing a bravery attack or an HP attack, both of which the defender can evade by anticipating which attack you'll use, thereby turning the tables upon the attacker. It is usually more advantageous to use one type of attack over the other, but attackers have a better chance of catching their foe off guard by selecting the less logical choice.

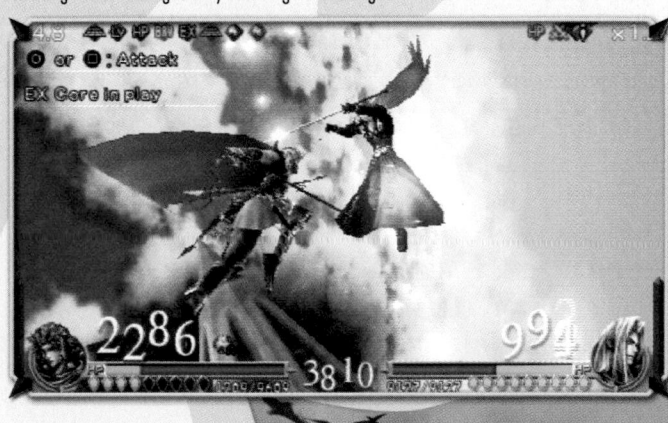

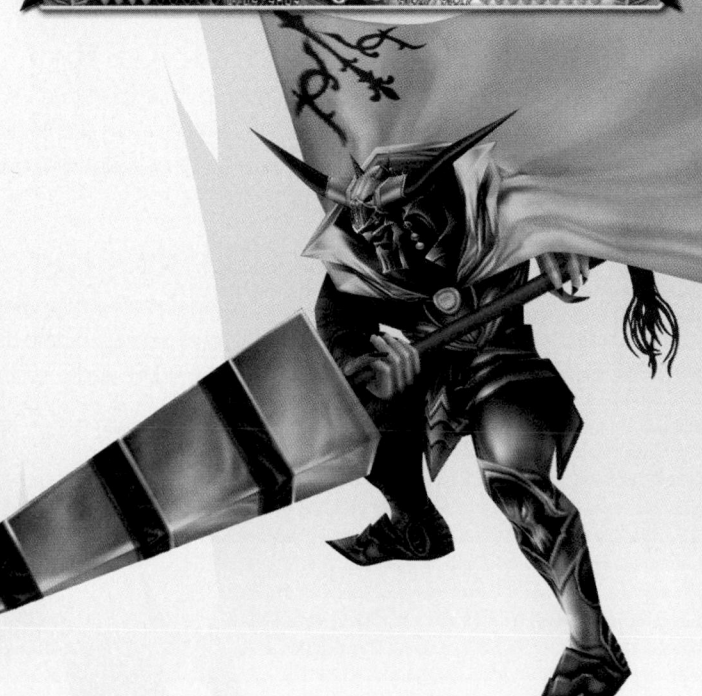

ANATOMY OF A CHASE

1. The attacker lands a hit with a chase attack, sending the opponent flying into the air.

2. The attacker presses ✕ at the prompt, leaping after the foe. Both characters are now locked into the chase sequence.

3. After the game enters slow motion, the attacker has roughly two seconds in which to assess the situation and press ⦿ for a bravery attack or ⦿ for an HP attack. You can aim your bravery attacks upward or downward with the Analog Stick.

4. The defender can dodge by pressing ✕, but must anticipate which attack is coming. To dodge a bravery attack, press ✕ immediately. To dodge an HP attack, wait for roughly one second before pressing the button.

5. If the defender failed to dodge, or dodged the wrong attack, then the defender takes the hit and gets knocked away (for a possible wall rush or second chase). However, if the defender dodged correctly, the chase continues at the start of step 3, but with the positions reversed—the defender is now the attacker, and vice versa.

6. If each player successfully evades three times, the chase sequence ends.

READING YOUR OPPONENT'S TELLS

When you're on the defending side, there are several clues that point to what sort of attack your foe will make. However, processing the information in time to make the right choice requires quick reflexes and practice. The first clue is your opponent's pose; most characters tend to hunch over before launching an HP attack, and stretch out before attempting a bravery attack. Next, each character has a brief voice sample before they execute an HP attack (there is no voice before a bravery attack), and the screen dims slightly.

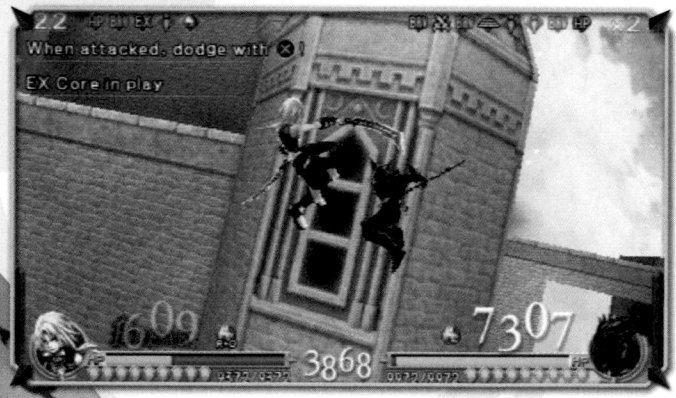

SUMMONSTONES

It wouldn't be Final Fantasy without summons. In *DISSIDIA*, summons come in the form of Summonstones that are found in the Story Mode, either as on-map treasures or DP bonus prizes. Summonstones can only be used once per battle, but have a significant effect on combat, typically by manipulating bravery values for one or both players. There are two kinds of Summonstones: ones that you trigger manually, by pressing ▬ and ⦿, and ones that trigger automatically when a certain condition is met.

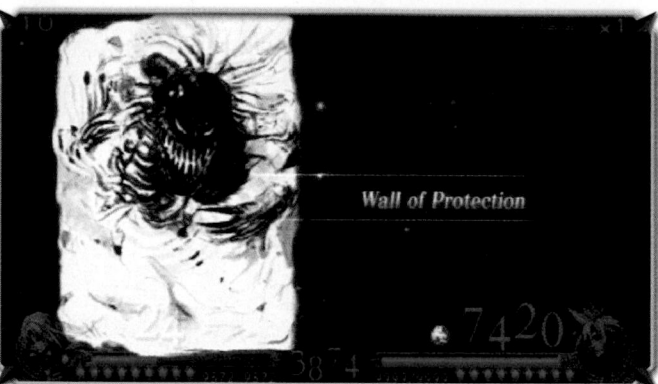

CHARGING SUMMONSTONES

After being used in one to three battles (depending on its type), your Summonstone must recharge before it can be used again. It will take you three battles before an AUTO Summonstone is recharged, and six to recharge most manual Summonstones. Summonstones only begin to recharge when they're completely used up, so a Summonstone with one remaining use does not recharge.

SETTING RESERVES

You don't want to be left without the power of summons while your favorite Summonstone is recharging, so it's important to set reserves in the Summons menu. When you have Summonstones in reserve, you'll automatically switch to the next one in line when your currently equipped stone needs to be charged. You can set up to five Summonstones in your reserve list, and players who use manual Summonstones will need to set at least four to ensure they always have a Summonstone charged and ready. (Players who use faster-charging AUTO Summonstones can set only two in their reserves and continuously rotate between them.).

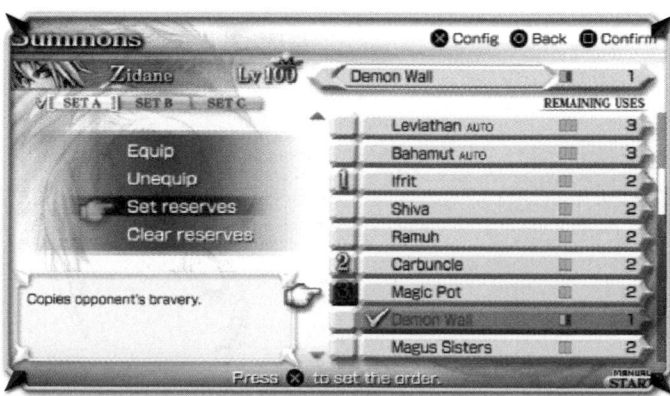

GAME BASICS

BLOCKING AND EVASION

DISSIDIA is a game best played aggressively, but there are also plenty of effective defensive options at your fingertips. Attacks can be blocked or evaded, and tumbling characters can break their falls with a well-timed recovery. Note that all of the defensive options covered here have prerequisite abilities that must be enabled before they can be used. (Each character has them pre-enabled at level 1.)

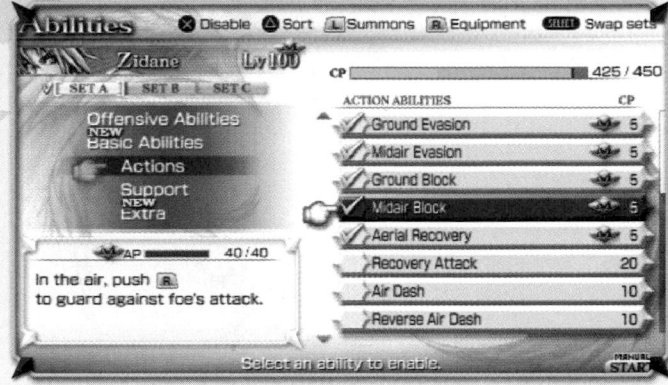

BLOCKING

You can enter a blocking pose by pressing the right trigger, if you have a blocking ability enabled. A successful block can prevent the damage from melee attacks and send the attacker reeling, allowing the defender to counterattack with an increased critical hit chance. Blocking is a great way to deal with projectiles, and in many cases blocked projectiles are reflected back at the attacker. (To increase the odds of reflecting a projectile, wait until the last possible moment to block.)

However, there are serious risks to blocking. You can't block attacks with the Block Break property, and that includes the majority of HP attacks—when you're fleeing a fatal HP strike, you'll want to evade exclusively. It's also very dangerous to block early; a block lasts for only around one second, and when you come out of a block, you'll be briefly unable to move or defend against incoming attacks in any way.

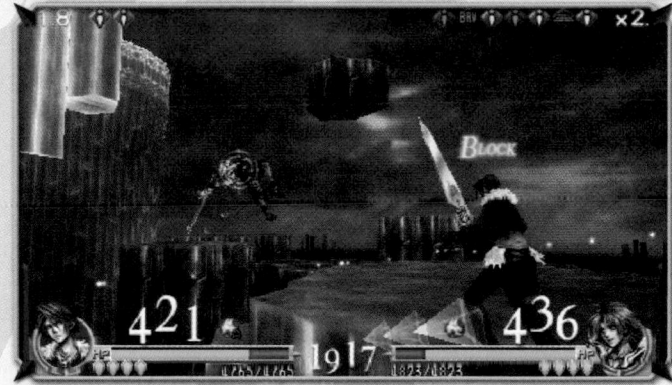

BLOCKING ENABLERS	Ground Block	Midair Block

EVASION

If you have an evasion ability enabled, you can attempt to dodge incoming attacks by pressing ▬ and ✕. As soon as you execute the evasion, you'll be invulnerable to all forms of damage for three-tenths of a second (this duration can be doubled with the Evasion Time Boost ability). Evasion is a more reliable way of avoiding attacks than blocking, but it takes a lot of practice to master the timing.

By holding the Analog Stick as you evade, you can choose the direction in which you'll roll away. Many attacks last more than three-tenths of a second, so you'll usually want to roll to either side to make sure you're out of the line of fire when your invulnerability ends. But if you know the attack is a brief one, such as an incoming projectile, consider rolling towards your foe so you'll be ready to strike while your opponent is still vulnerable.

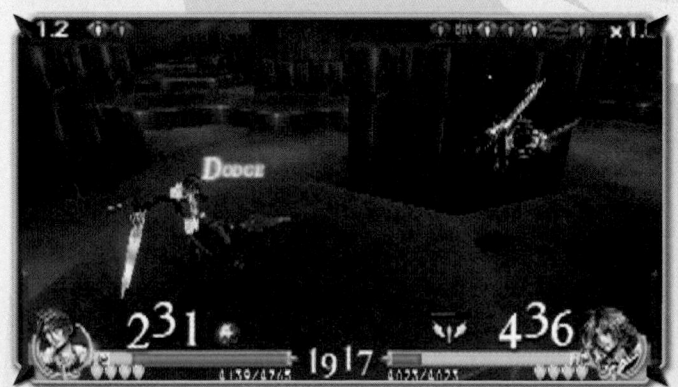

EVASION ENABLERS	Ground Evasion	Midair Evasion
EVASION ENHANCERS	Midair Evasion Boost	Evasion Time Boost

BREAKING A FALL

The final defensive option is recovery, which simply means breaking your fall with a tap of the ✖ button. You can set this to happen automatically with the Auto Recovery ability, but only the standard Aerial Recovery ability can be built off of with Recovery Attack, which turns a normal recovery into a bravery attack, and Controlled Recovery, which gives you more control of the direction in which you fall.

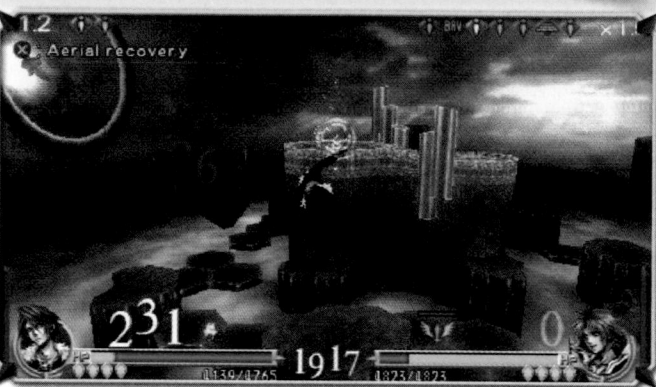

RECOVERY ENABLERS	Aerial Recovery	Auto Recovery
RECOVERY ENHANCERS	Recovery Attack	Controlled Recovery

GETTING AROUND THE BATTLEFIELD

There's a lot going on in *DISSIDIA*, and even the simple act of navigating the vast 3D battlefields can be a challenge. In addition to the basics (moving with the Analog Stick and jumping with ✖), you can Air Dash, execute Quickmoves, and double jump. In addition to letting you get where you need to be, Quickmoves and Air Dashes have defensive properties; when using them, you're immune to magical projectiles. Knowing this makes it much easier to reach foes that are barraging you with fireballs.

Quickmoves: You can execute Quickmoves by tapping ▲ wherever you see a yellow arrow in the environment. Quickmoves involve everything from running up walls and columns to sliding along magical streams of energy.

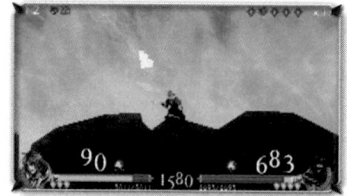

Quickmoves are particularly important when navigating the game's indoor areas.

Double Jumps and Beyond: All characters are capable of executing a second jump at the height of their first jump. Onion Knight and Ultimecia can take things a step further, jumping four times instead of the usual two. But the record holder is Zidane, who can jump ten times when in EX Mode. Every character can gain additional jumps with the Jump Times Boost ability. The Multi-Air Slide ability allows you to do a long-distance Air Dash when you press ✖ after completing your final jump.

Air Dashes: Air Dash abilities allow you to blast directly at your currently selected target (either your enemy or an EX Core; if you have the EX Core Lock On ability equipped, you can toggle between targets with ▣.) The basic Air Dash can only be used during Quickmoves. Stick with Free Air Dash, which comes pre-equipped to most level 1 characters, so you can Air Dash from anywhere, including during jumps. The final stage of Air Dash abilities is Omni Air Dash, which allows you to dash in whatever direction you hold the Analog Stick, rather than forcing you to pursue your locked-on target. The reverse versions of Air Dash skills blast you away from your target instead of towards it, and should only be of interest to characters who focus on long-range attacks.

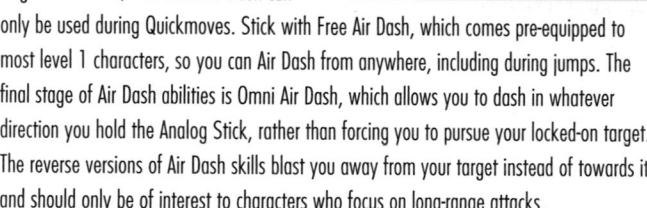

AIR DASH	During Quickmove, press ▲ to dash towards target. Hold ▲ to extend range.
REVERSE AIR DASH	During Quickmove, press ▲ to dash away from target. Hold ▲ to extend range.
FREE AIR DASH	Press ▣ + ▲ at any time to dash towards target. Hold ▲ to extend range.
REVERSE FREE AIR DASH	Press ▣ + ▲ at any time to dash away from target. Hold ▲ to extend range.
OMNI AIR DASH	Press ▣ + ▲ at any time to dash in the direction you're pressing the Analog Stick. Hold ▲ to extend range.

COMMAND-STYLE BATTLE MODE

If the complexities of DISSIDIA are too much for you, or you're just plain bad at action games, all hope is not lost. Stick with the controls for long enough to beat a single Destiny Odyssey chapter, and you'll unlock the option to switch your Battle Mode to "Command-style" in the Options menu. This transforms DISSIDIA into more of a traditional menu-driven Final Fantasy, where you never need to worry about movement and can give your character general orders with simple commands (select Fight to focus on bravery attacks, choose Finisher to execute HP attacks, pick Defend to focus on blocking and dodging, and employ Summon to use your Summonstone). Once a command is chosen, your character continuously executes it until a new command is selected. You may order your character to run away from his opponent by holding ▣ and ▣.

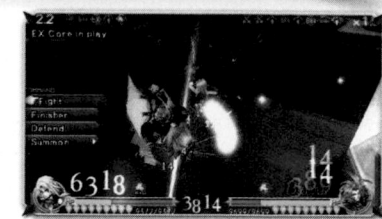

If this is a little too simple, visit the shop to purchase the "Command Battle Boost" ability at the cost of one precious Rosetta Stone. Once equipped as a Support Ability, Command Battle Boost adds certain commands related to characters' EX Modes, chasing and dodging during chases, and a few other conditional commands.

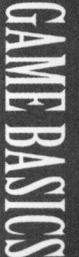

BUILDING YOUR CHARACTERS

DISSIDIA may play like a fighting game, but it's an RPG at heart. Each character can level up 99 times, learning new attacks and gaining stat boosts with higher levels. The customization options run deep, including scores of abilities to master, hundreds of weapons and armaments, and a strategic accessory system.

CHARACTER SETS

Each character can have up to three full sets of abilities, equipment, and accessories. You can toggle between Set A, Set B, and Set C with ⊞. This allows you to, for example, prepare one set with all your best gear for tough fights, and load up another set with gear that makes grinding for EXP and items easier. Note that you cannot mix and match between your sets; if you're using ability Set B, you must also use equipment Set B and accessory Set B. If you want to create multiple sets with only minor modifications, you can press ⊞ on the Customization screen to copy the content of one set to another.

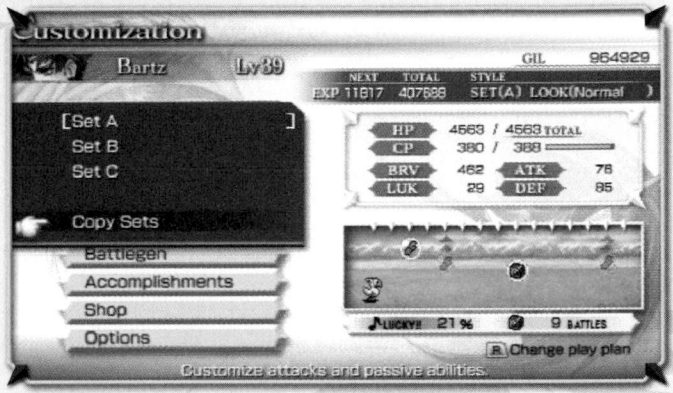

LEVELS AND MASTERY

All characters level up at the same rate. While your characters hit their level max at 100 (and are then considered "mastered"), you may encounter enemies with levels as high as 130. Leveling up raises your base stats, and at certain levels, characters can learn new abilities. All equipment has a prerequisite level that must be reached before it can be equipped.

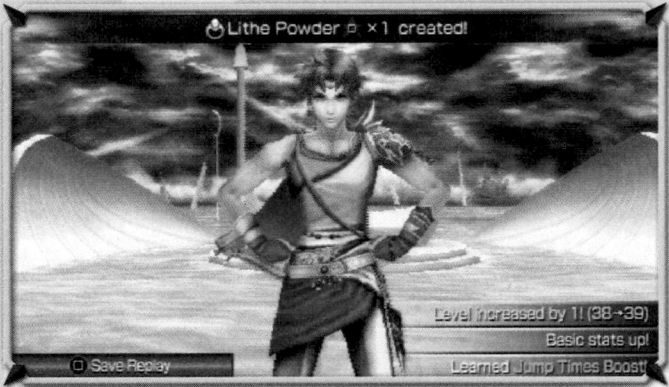

EXPLANATION OF STATS

Your characters' fundamental strengths are determined by six basic stats. These stats increase as your character gains levels, and are modified by bonuses (and occasional penalties) applied by equipment.

HP: Hit Points are a measure of your character's health. When they hit zero, the battle is lost.

CP: Capacity Points reflect the amount of abilities you can equip at one time. These are gained mainly by leveling up, and are not modified by equipment.

BRV: This determines your base bravery, a measure of how much bravery damage you can sustain and how much HP damage you can dish out.

ATK: This stat affects the amount of bravery damage you deal with bravery attacks.

DEF: Your lone defensive stat affects the amount of bravery damage you receive from enemy bravery attacks.

LUK: Luck is an important factor that affects your odds of success at Battlegen, your chances of winning item drops in battle, and how close to your character EX Cores will appear.

HOW EXP IS CALCULATED

In *DISSIDIA FINAL FANTASY*, experience points (EXP) are earned by dealing HP damage to foes, not by defeating them. In most modes, this EXP is yours to keep whether you win or lose (although if you retry a lost fight in Story Mode, you will be reset to your previous EXP levels). As a basic rule, you earn one EXP for each point of damage you deal, but this amount can be modified by a number of factors.

BONUS TYPE	BONUS AMOUNT	CONDITIONS
Calendar Bonus	10%-100%	Available on Bonus Days and EXP-icon days. Bonus varies based on your EXP Icon Boost level (which can be raised in the PP Catalog).
Play Plan Bonus	20% - 400%	Single-battle bonus that occurs when the chocobo in your Play Plan finds Gysahl Greens.
Equipment Bonuses	10%-100% each	Certain weapons and accessories offer EXP bonuses. Artifacts may also have EXP-bonus properties.
Rank Bonus	10% per rank	The game assigns each of your characters a letter rank between H (lowest) and SSS (highest) based on the skill with which you play that character. (You can view your ranks in the Friend Card Settings screen.) You'll receive EXP bonuses for each rank your opponents are above you.
Rank Penalty	1% per rank	When you defeat an opponent of a lower rank, you suffer a modest penalty of 1% of the EXP for each rank they are below you.
EX Burst Finish	Half your Max HP	When you deal the finishing blow with an EX Burst, you receive a flat-rate bonus based on your Max HP.
Story Mode Bonus	Varies	In Story Mode, extra EXP may be awarded for defeating bosses and other special opponents.
Online Bonus	150% of Max HP	Win or lose, all players receive a healthy EXP bonus for battling online.

ABILITIES

Outside of walking and jumping, nearly everything your characters can do come from their abilities. Each character's attack is an ability, as is their capability to block, evade, and even lock onto EX Cores. You can review and set your abilities in the Customization menu.

EARNING AND MASTERING ABILITIES

You typically acquire new abilities by leveling up, but some abilities can be earned through mastery of other abilities. These include the second stage of combo attacks and ability chains like Jump Boost, which unlocks Jump Boost+ when mastered, which in turn unlocks Jump Boost++. A few special skills are unlocked in the "Etc." section of the shop, including Command Mode Boost and a series of abilities that allow characters to use items they couldn't otherwise equip.

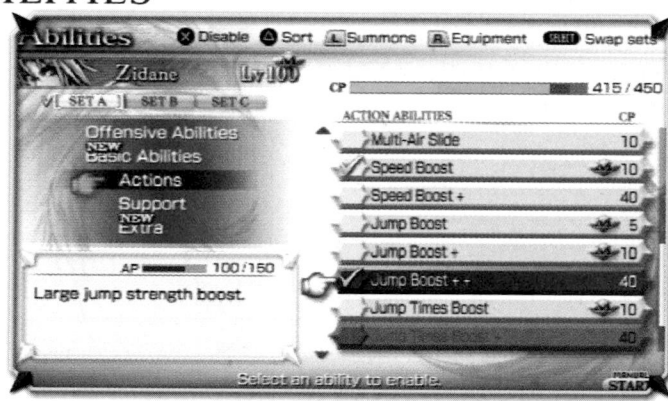

Each ability has a CP cost, and you can only enable as many abilities as your total CP will allow. Increasing your CP stat by leveling up is a great way to add more abilities, but mastering an ability decreases its CP cost, which makes doing so an equally beneficial way to gain some CP. Abilities are mastered by collecting AP; at the end of every victorious battle, AP gets added to the AP bars of each enabled ability. When the bar fills completely, the ability is then mastered.

MASTERING ATTACKS QUICKLY

You can assign the same attack to multiple attack slots. This costs a lot of CP, but an attack that's set to two slots will gain double the AP, and so on.

OFFENSIVE ABILITIES

In the Offensive Abilities sub-menu, you typically have three slots for land bravery attacks (assigned to ●+ Analog Stick neutral, ●+ Analog Stick towards foe, and ●+ Analog Stick away from foe, respectively), and three slots for air bravery attacks (assigned to ●+ Analog Stick neutral, ●+ Analog Stick up, and ●+ Analog Stick down, respectively). You have a similar set of slots for ●-based HP attacks, although many characters won't learn enough HP attacks to fill out all the slots. Attacks cost a lot of CP, so don't feel obligated to enable more attacks than you need; two land and two air bravery attacks are often enough.

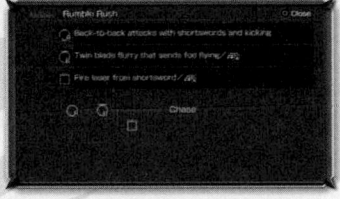

It isn't always clear what attacks do from the name and brief description alone, but you can highlight any attack and press ● to pull up a detailed list of each move in its attack sequence. The special icons reveal which attacks in each chain have special properties like breaking blocks or providing temporary invulnerability. (Press **START** to pull up a key to the Command Chart Icons.)

Branching Abilities

When mastered, some attacks evolve into combos, opening up one or more sub-slots beneath the slot in which it's equipped. You can then equip the next part of the combo into that slot. Combos are very effective in battle; if you can land the first move, you'll be able to chain it into the second combo with a tap of the button. However, combos can be expensive to equip, since each part has its own CP cost.

The most valuable property of combos is that even though they're listed under bravery attacks, many are actually HP attacks. Landing a bravery attack that combos into an HP attack is, for many characters, much easier than directly landing an HP attack. The circumstances of how this works varies by move, so highlight the combo and press ● to pull up its Command Chart for details. Some combos split in two directions, with both a bravery attack follow-up (marked with a ●) and an HP attack follow-up (marked with a ●). But combos that have only a ● follow-up may have both bravery attack and HP attack components; players who want to hold onto their bravery can press ● instead of ● to execute just the bravery parts.

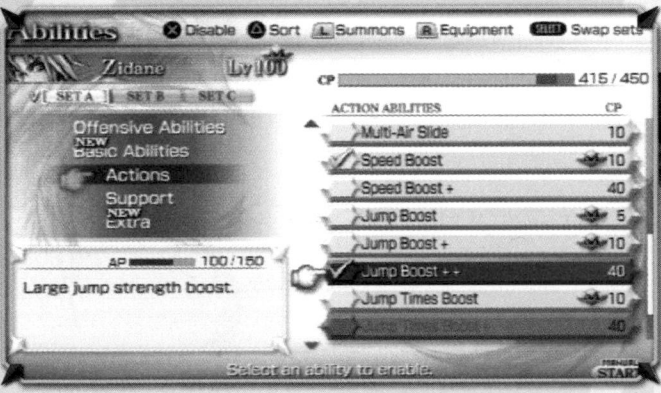

BASIC ABILITIES

The Basic Abilities menu is where you can find all of your non-attack abilities. These are just as vital as attacks, so make sure to save plenty of CP to spend on them.

Action Abilities consist of anything that enables or enhances a non-attack action. It's here that you'll find the crucial blocking, evasion, recovery, and air dash options, as well as abilities that increase speed, jump distance, and number of jumps.

Support Abilities make battles easier by allowing the game to automate functions like chasing and recovery. These are useful for beginners who are overwhelmed by the complexities of combat, or who have trouble executing specific mechanics like EX Bursts. Experienced players should try to avoid wasting CP on Support Abilities, although a few (like EX Core Lock On and Evasion Time Boost) are well worth their costs.

Extra Abilities are typically acquired late in the game, during a character's last 50 levels of growth. This section is a grab bag of abilities that allow characters to execute critical hits in certain situations, strengthen their defenses when near death, and convert EXP into some other resource (just to name a few). Players who carefully choose Extra Abilities to match their character and play style will find them to be well worth their typically high CP costs.

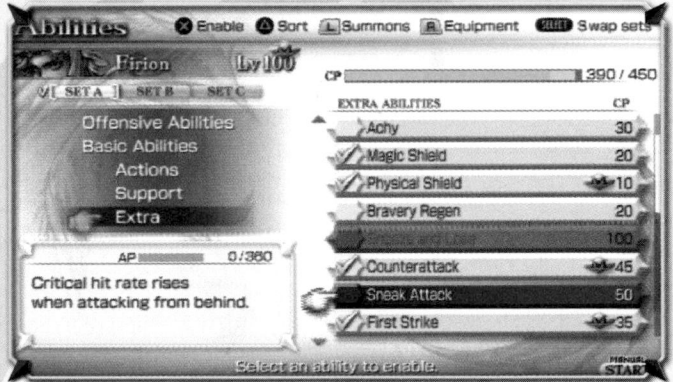

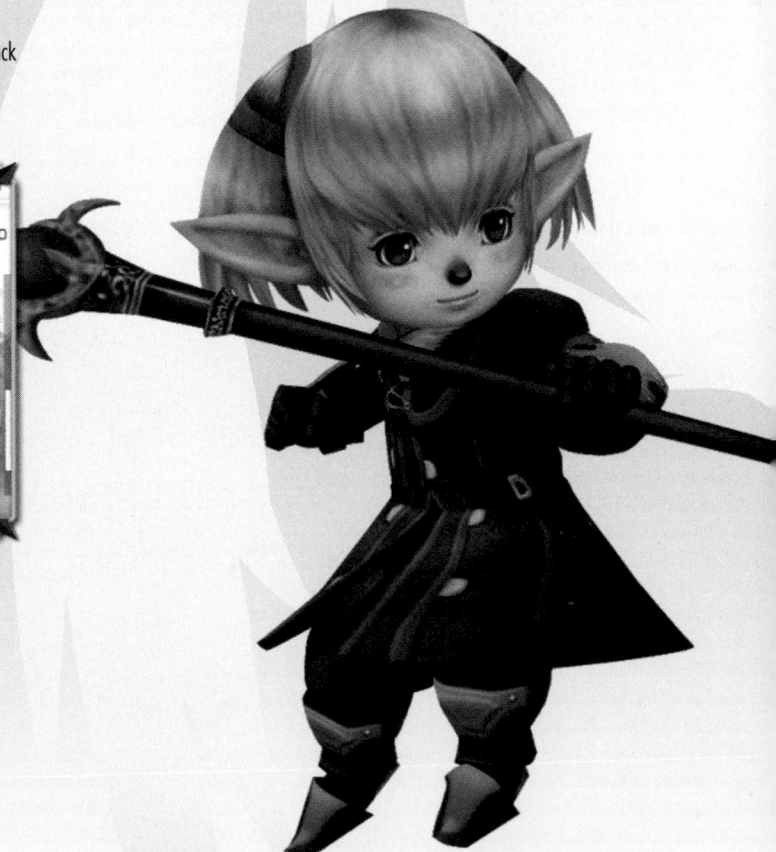

USING AND ACQUIRING ITEMS

You can outfit your characters with hundreds of different items. Each character can equip one weapon, armor for their heads, arms, and torso, and up to ten accessories. You can find these items on your quest, earn them from defeating foes, and trade for them at one of the best-stocked shops in gaming history.

WEAPONS AND ARMAMENTS

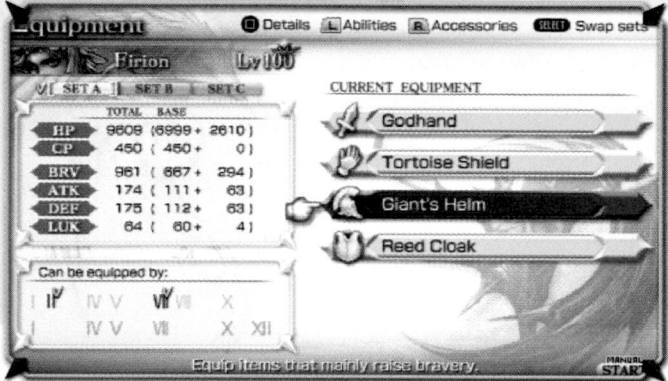

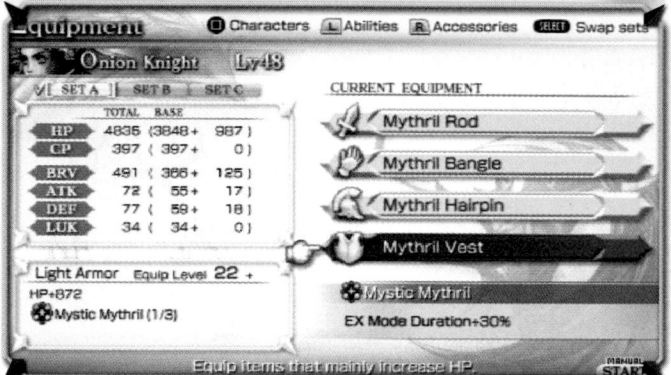

Within the four equipment categories, there are 25 different types of gear. Some characters can equip almost anything, while others are limited by an exclusive preference for robes over heavy armor, or daggers over swords. When highlighting an item, press ● to pull up a list of who can equip it. Character names are not written out, only the numbers of the games they come from, with Cosmos-side characters in light blue and Chaos-side characters in purple. Character also must reach a set character level (called the "equip level") before they can equip weapons and armaments. There is no need to stock duplicate items for multiple characters; any number of characters can equip the same single item.

EQUIPMENT COMBINATIONS

Many weapons and armaments have special abilities. Most are self-explanatory, but you'll sometimes see ones with names like "Dazzling Diamond (1/3)" or "Force of the Resolute (1/4)." These are special abilities that only become active when you're using a full set of items with the same ability (the number after the ability indicates how many you must equip). So if you scrounge up, say, a Diamond Sword, a Diamond Cuff, and a Diamond Hairpin, you can turn on the Dazzling Diamond ability that gives you a 100% AP bonus. Equipment combinations are all or nothing; wear only two out of three items and the ability has no effect.

ACCESSORIES

There are hundreds of accessories in *DISSIDIA*, and just as many viable strategies you can build out of them. The easiest option is to fill your slots with basic accessories that provide modest stat boosts and special abilities. But you can get more power by figuring out a single effect you want to push heavily—like damage, defense, or EX Core absorption—and using a few basic accessories backed up with as many booster accessories as you can pile on. If you can earn and select booster accessories that enhance your play style, you can increase the power of your basic accessories by a factor of ten or more.

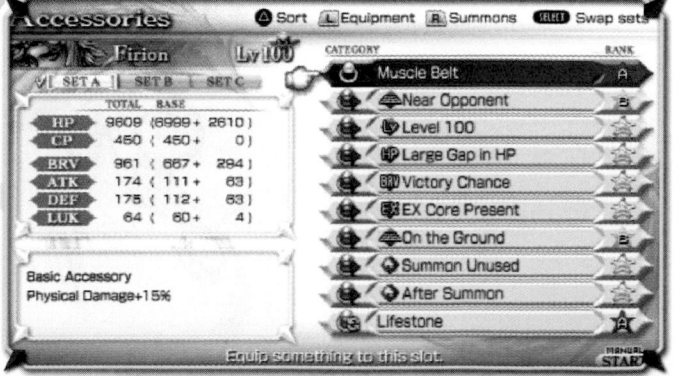

Basic Accessories provide a boost to a single attribute, like damage, speed, the distance from which you can absorb EX Force, and so on. They are rarely found and usually must be traded for at the shop.

Booster Accessories combine with basic accessories to increase their power. Each booster accessory is merely a condition, like "[Position] In Midair" or "[EX] EX Core Present." If that condition is met, you get the listed boost, which typically multiplies the original power of the accessory somewhere from 1.1 to 2.0 times. The trick is to equip lots of boosters, so that their multipliers multiply each other. If you can equip eight booster accessories with a x1.5 multiplier and meet all of their conditions at once, suddenly your basic accessory becomes 25 times as powerful as it used to be. Booster accessories are typically earned by completing accomplishments.

Special Accessories are similar to basic accessories, but cannot be modified by booster accessories. In addition to raising stats, some have unconventional effects like allowing their wearer to survive a fatal strike at 1 HP.

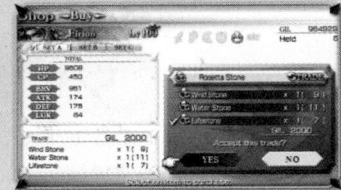

Trade Accessories typically boost stats by a few points, but mainly exist as ingredients for the shop's trade system.

ROSETTA STONES AND ACCESSORY SLOTS

Each character begins with only three accessory slots, which isn't much room to play with. You can buy new slots (for a total of up to ten slots per character) for the price of a Rosetta Stone and 1,000 gil in the shop. Early in the game, you must be careful with your Rosetta Stones. Thorough players can find two or three of them in each Destiny Odyssey chapter, but it won't be enough to max out all your characters. Fortunately, even the easiest courses of the Duel Colosseum offer plentiful amounts of Wind Stones, Water Stones, and Lifestones, the three components that can be traded for Rosetta Stones.

EQUIP LIMITATIONS

There are limits to how many of the same accessory you can equip. Accessories marked with a gold star are considered Rank S; all other accessories have their rank listed on their icon.

RANK	EQUIP LIMIT
☆	1
☆	2
☆	3
☆	4
☆	No limit

ACCESSORY BREAKABILITY

Some special accessories have a breakability rate, which reveals the odds that they'll shatter after any given battle. These are typically extremely strong effects, providing EXP bonuses, increased odds of an item drop, a big boost to your starting bravery, or a way to resurrect your character in a losing fight. There are other accessories that allow you to lower their breakability rates, but these are extremely rare.

BUILDING YOUR ARSENAL

There are a great many ways to acquire items in *DISSIDIA FINAL FANTASY*, and you'll need to use them all if you hope to build a well-stocked arsenal of weapons, armaments, and accessories.

GAME MODE PRIZES

In the Story Mode, you'll find items in treasure chests and earn them as awards for having extra Destiny Points. In the Duel Colosseum Mode, you'll earn medals that can be spent on rare items of your choice. In the Arcade Mode, you'll win preset prizes for completing a circuit of foes. Before you hit the shop, make sure you can't find the item for free!

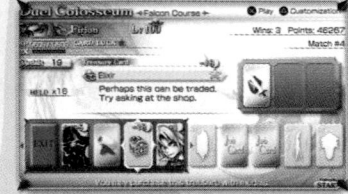

THE SHOP

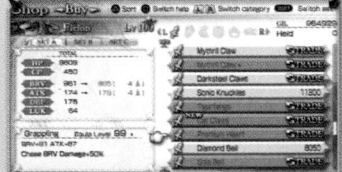

The shop is always open, and can be accessed directly from any character's Customization menu. The shop sells basic weaponry and armor, but for fancier gear and accessories, gil won't be enough. In addition to a hefty sticker price, you'll have to provide all the ingredients necessary to make the item in question. Recipes typically include a weaker item of the same type and a pair of trade accessories.

The shop is updated regularly with new stock. Basic items appear based on your characters' levels; you won't be able to see a Katana with an equip level of 78 until you have a character capable of wielding Katanas at level 71 or so. New stock also appears when you first acquire a key ingredient of its recipe, regardless of its equip level. Finally, when you acquire rare items in Story Mode or from item drops, their recipes are typically added to the shop, in case you need to make a replacement.

Battlegen

Battlegen is a unique system that generates new items right in the middle of combat. Before a battle begins, press ▬ or ▬ to pull up the Battlegen screen. You'll see a list of accessories you can generate during the fight, as well as the odds of doing so. The icons to the left of the item name reveal how you'll need to do it; the square over the sword indicates a successful HP attack, the BRV icon indicates a successful bravery attack, and the EX icon indicates an EX Burst. The map of the battlefield means that the item is located within the terrain, and you'll need to smash things apart with wall rushes and collateral damage to generate it. However, you only get to keep the items you create through Battlegen if you win the fight. (Unless you're playing online and have purchased the Online Match - Gain Accessories After Loss options.)

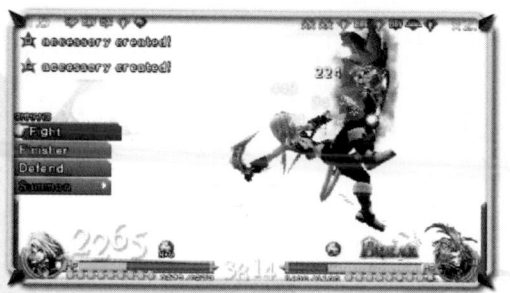

Each character has a unique list of items that you can create through Battlegen, as does each battlefield, so you'll need to fight a wide variety of foes in a wide variety of places to get everything. You can keep track of who has what and how to get it with the Battlegen menu in the Customization screen. When battling in the Communications Mode against other players online, or the ghosts from their friend cards, you can use Battlegen to get copies of any of the accessories they have equipped. (This requires the Online Match - Battlegen OK option from the PP Catalog.) When battling in any other mode, you can only create the 100 or so trade accessories that are exclusively available through Battlegen.

There are several ways to raise the listed odds of succeeding at Battlegen:

BATTLE STRONG FOES	The odds of acquiring items through Battlegen rises with your target's level; take on higher level foes via Quick Battle fights to improve your odds.
RAISE YOUR LUK	The luckier you are, the higher your odds of a successful Battlegen. You can raise your LUK with a wide variety of accessories.
BATTLEGEN-BOOSTING ACCESSORIES	The Sunrise and Moonrise basic accessories improve your odds of succeeding at Battlegen. You can raise the odds much further by attaching booster accessories. There are also special accessories (such as Superslick) that increase Battlegen odds.
BONUS DAY	A 1% boost in Battlegen rates is a randomly appearing Bonus Day bonus.
THE PP CATALOG	You can buy "Battlegen Rate Up" options from the PP Catalog to raise your odds of a successful Battlegen in the next battle by 1%.

ITEM DROPS

At the end of each victorious fight, there's a very small chance your foe might drop his weapon or one of his armaments. (Note that in an online battle, there's a chance this equipment will turn into an artifact.) Many rare pieces of equipment can only be won this way, some from foes that are generated in the Quick Battle mode, some from enemies who make fixed appearances in the Story Mode or Duel Colosseum, and even some who only appear as Friend Cards.

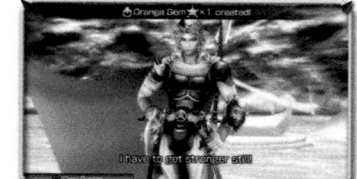

The odds of earning any one piece of equipment is very low, often less than 1% for the best items. But as with Battlegen, there are ways for item hunters to increase the odds:

BATTLE STRONG FOES	The odds of acquiring items through item drops rises not with your target's level, but its rank. The highest ranked foes offer a 1% bonus.
RAISE YOUR LUK	The luckier you are, the higher your odds of a successful item drop. You can raise your LUK with a wide variety of accessories.
DROP RATE-BOOSTING ITEMS AND ACCESSORIES	Item hunters can boost their odds of success with armaments like Thief Gloves and Thief's Cap and accessories like Mog's Amulets.
BONUS DAY	A 1% boost in item drop rates is a randomly appearing Bonus Day bonus.
THE PP CATALOG	You can buy "Item Drop Rate Up" options from the PP Catalog to raise your odds of a successful item drop in the next battle by 0.5%.
PLAY ONLINE	Online battles have a much higher rate of item drops. You can also purchase "Online Match - Gain Item After Loss" to win items after losing fights.

COLLECTIONS AND UNLOCKABLES

In addition to the items, abilities, and Summonstones that directly strengthen your character, there are several other things to collect in *DISSIDIA FINAL FANTASY*.

PP Catalog Bonuses: The PP you earn from each fight allows you to unlock items from the PP Catalog, which contains everything from new characters and stages to new combat rules and background music. See the PP Catalog appendix for a full list.

Accomplishments: There are 151 accomplishments that you can earn through your gameplay achievements. A list can be found in the Accomplishments menu of the Customization screen, but many entries do not appear until certain conditions are met, such as completing the accomplishment halfway. (You can find a full list of accomplishments and their listing conditions in the Accomplishments appendix.) Completing accomplishments earns you exclusive booster accessories and Player Icons.

Museum Entries: After completing two Destiny Odyssey chapters, you'll unlock a museum where you can enjoy the game's event scenes, music, and voices whenever you like. Additionally, you can view details on the characters and summons you've collected, and get story background from the Cosmos and Chaos Reports you find (Cosmos Reports are unlocked each time you beat Shade Impulse Chapter 4 with a new Cosmos character; Chaos Reports are unlocked when Chaos-side characters beat the Boss card of their Cosmos-side counterparts). You can also view your accumulated Player Icons and watch any battle replays you've saved.

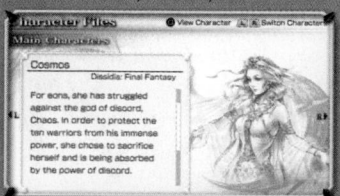

STORY MODE
INTRODUCTION

STARTING A NEW GAME

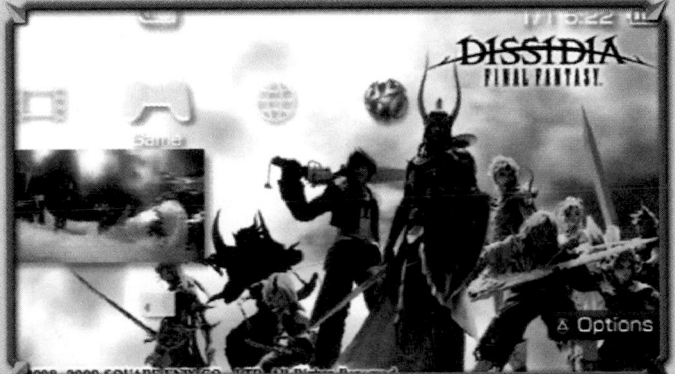
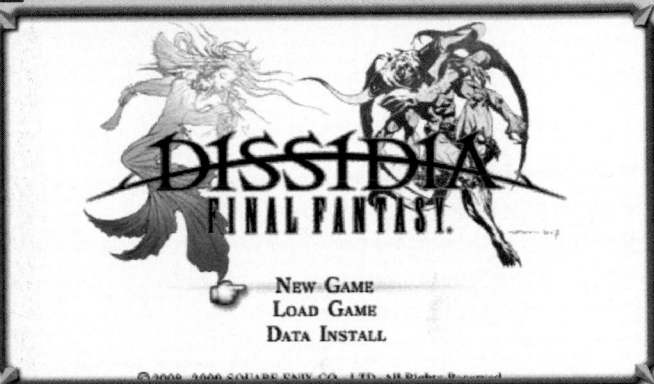

Before venturing into Story Mode, you'll first need to set up the game. If you have a ProDuo™ memory stick, you can elect to perform a Data Install before starting a new game. You can choose to use 261, 410, or 612 megabytes of memory to decrease loading times. The installation itself can take a fair bit of time—up to an hour for the 612mb installation.

After choosing whether or not to install data, proceed to New Game. The first order of business is selecting a nickname. This nickname can help you differentiate between save files, and is also visible to other players during wireless play.

BATTLE TUTORIAL

Next, you must select a Play Plan. Depending on your selection, different bonuses are earned after engaging in a certain number of battles. The Casual Play Plan grants smaller awards more frequently, while the Hardcore Play Plan gives greater awards less often. The Average Play Plan is somewhere in between—Casual grants a bonus every 15 battles, Average every 30, and Hardcore every 60. Don't worry about making an "incorrect" decision here—you can change your Play Plan later from the Start Menu. Later on, two additional Play Plans—The Grind-lover and The Treasure Hunter—can be unlocked and purchased from the PP Catalog.

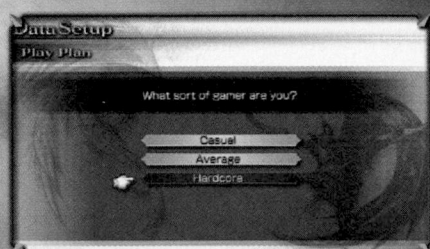

After selecting a Play Plan, you'll then pick a Bonus Day. This is a day of the week on which you receive extra bonuses. The bonuses include things like discounted shop prices, as well as increased rates for item drops, Battlegen, and EXP gained. These effects can be made more pronounced by upgrading them in the PP Catalog.

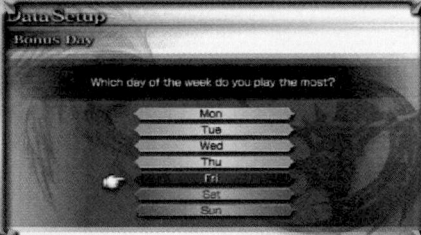

Before beginning the game, you'll have one last chance to alter any of these settings as desired. Again, don't worry about messing up, as this configuration doesn't have to be permanent. Get ready, though, because as soon as you confirm your selections, the game's battle tutorial begins!

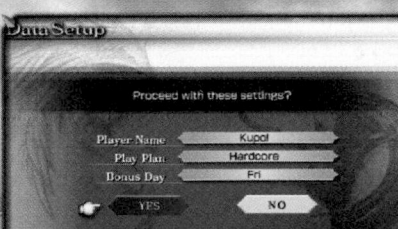

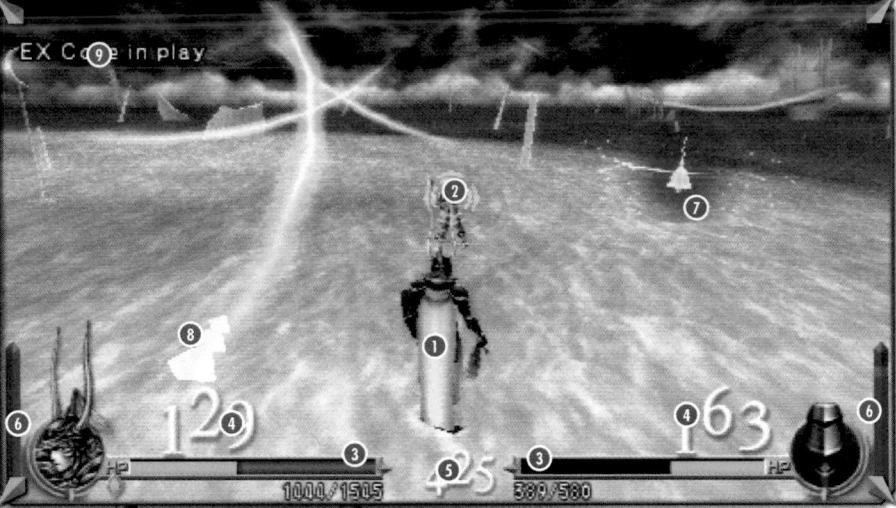

EX Core in play

① **Player Character:** The combatant you control. By default, ● controls movement, and 🕹 controls the camera. This, along with many other aspects of control, can be changed if desired. Once you can access the Start Menu after the Battle Tutorial, proceed to Options to make any modifications.

② **Enemy Character & Lock-on Cursor:** Your enemy in a given stage. As pictured here, the blue Lock-on Cursor tracks the foe.

③ **HP bars:** The visual bars represent 1000 HP. Additional multiples of 1000 are indicated under the HP bars by diamond symbols. The current and maximum totals of HP are also represented numerically.

④ **Bravery levels:** Each fighter's current bravery level. Bravery indicates how much damage HP attacks will inflict on the adversary.

⑤ **Stage bravery:** This amount of spare bravery will be added to either combatant's bravery level if Bravery Break is inflicted on the opponent.

⑥ **EX Force gauges:** These gauges show how close either combatant is to being able to activate EX Mode. The EX Gauge is built up by collecting EX Force and EX Cores throughout the battlefield.

⑦ **EX Core:** This bell-shaped concentration of EX Force greatly fills up EX Gauges when acquired.

⑧ **Quickmove Indicator:** This indicates battlefield elements that allow special movement by pressing ▲ when nearby.

⑨ **Battle Information:** The information displayed here applies directly to the current battle situation. This can be set to Beginner, Normal, or Off in Options.

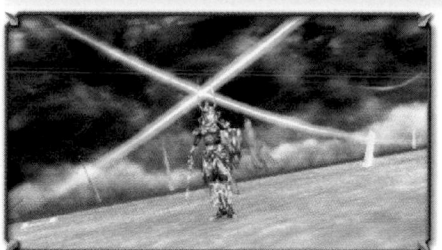
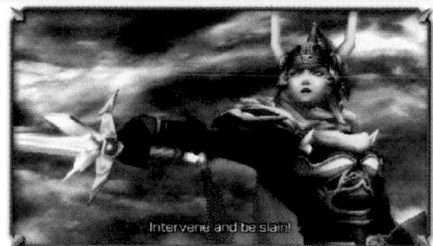
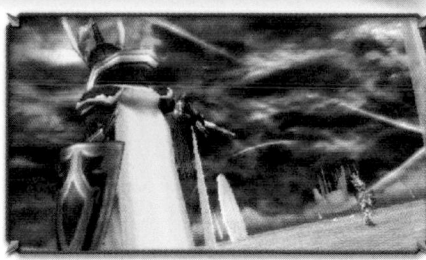

Warrior of Light, hailing from the very first *Final Fantasy*, stars in a series of battles designed to acquaint you with combat in *DISSIDIA FINAL FANTASY*. Here, Warrior of Light rushes to an urgent meeting, but is soon waylaid by an unholy doppelganger!

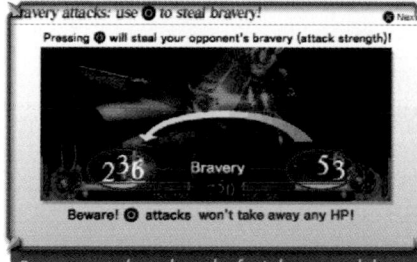

Bravery attacks reduce the foe's bravery while increasing your own.

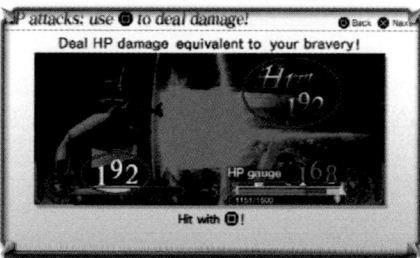

HP attacks deal HP damage equivalent to current bravery. Bravery is immediately reduced to 0 after successfully landing an HP attack, but quickly returns to the character's base bravery.

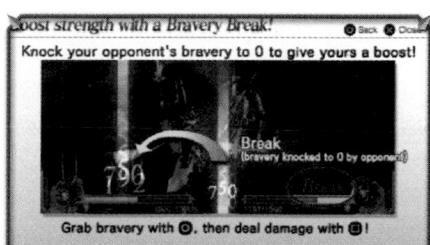

Bravery Break occurs when either combatant's bravery is reduced below 0. In so doing, the attacker gains the stage bravery. Obviously, inflicting Break on the enemy is paramount to victory, as the next HP attack benefits from a significant boost in attack power. Characters afflicted with Break will have their bravery return to their base level from 0, but only very slowly. This process is accelerated by landing an HP attack.

Warrior of Light has a well-developed arsenal in the tutorial—once you've graduated to Story Mode proper, you won't be equipped like this for a while. Bravery and HP attacks suitable for both long-range and up-close melee are available. From far away, rely on Blue Fang (on land: Analog Stick away from foe + ●) to pepper the enemy with icy projectiles. Bravery builds up if Blue Fang hits, and you may even inflict Break on your opponent. When your bravery is sufficient to make HP attacks worth using (which happens very quickly in the tutorial), both Shining Wave (on land: Analog Stick away from foe + ●) and Radiant Sword (in midair: ●) can strike from far away, dealing real damage. When closer to your foe, Shield of Light (on land: ●) also deals HP damage, and Warrior of Light can actually combo from some of his bravery attacks into Rune Saber, a devastating HP attack. After successfully striking with either Ascension (on land: ●, ●, ●), or Crossover (in midair: ●, ●), quickly press ● to initiate Rune Saber. On any stage of the tutorial, this usually wins the battle outright.

There are also other options here—instead of using Rune Saber, if you simply do nothing following these particular up-close bravery strings, a prompt for ✖ eventually appears on-screen. Pressing ✖ here initiates a chase sequence. When chasing, Warrior of Light will automatically Air Dash next to the enemy's reeling body in midair. From here, you can input any Analog Stick direction + ● or ● to make Warrior of Light smack the opponent in the chosen direction with either a bravery or HP attack.

If you use a bravery attack during a chase sequence, you'll be prompted to press ✗ to chase again (up to three times in a row). Chase sequences end prematurely if you do nothing, if you use an HP attack, or if you use a bravery attack that slams the opponent into a wall or a facet of the environment, causing a Wall Rush. The enemy can also turn the tables on you by dodging your chase attacks. A successful dodge allows a combatant to go on the offensive. However, since the enemies in the tutorial won't dodge chase attacks, this isn't a worry yet.

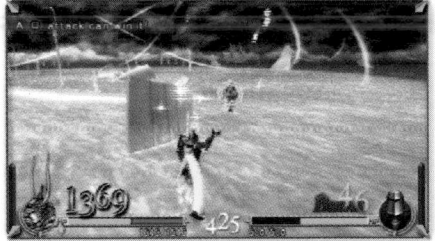

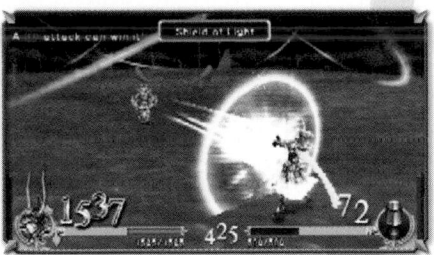

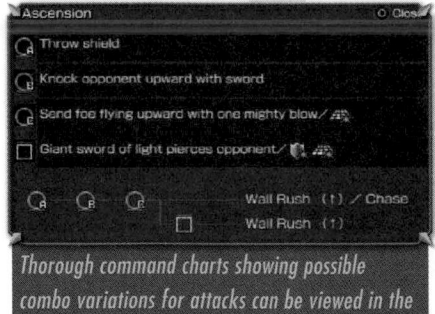

Thorough command charts showing possible combo variations for attacks can be viewed in the Abilities Menu.

SECOND BATTLE: EX MODE AND EX BURST

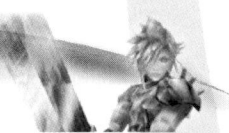

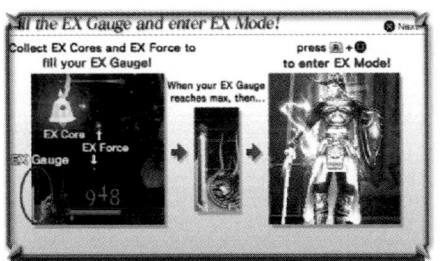

The EX Gauge is filled by collecting EX Force and EX Cores. EX Force consists of small pockets of EX energy left behind when combatants strike each other, while EX Cores are heavily concentrated sources of EX energy that resemble winged bells.

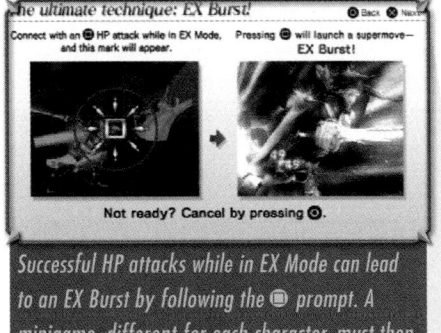

Successful HP attacks while in EX Mode can lead to an EX Burst by following the ◉ prompt. A minigame, different for each character, must then be performed to maximize the EX Burst's damage.

If you're on the wrong end of an EX Burst, press ◉ rapidly to keep the cursor in the yellow or green and boost your EX Burst defense. But beware of pressing too fast and ending up in the red; there, defense is actually lowered!

The second tutorial stage opens with an EX Core appearing right in front of Warrior of Light. This object fills the EX Gauge. With a full EX Gauge, you can initiate EX Mode by pressing ▬ + ◉. As long as the gauge is full, this is possible at any time, including during an attack or even while getting hit by the opponent! While in EX Mode, characters change in appearance and receive special bonuses. These include things like a Regen effect on HP, increased power for certain attacks, a greater rate of critical hits, special deflection properties against incoming moves, or increased defense. Most importantly, however, being in EX Mode enables an EX Burst, an extremely damaging and flashy attack initiated by following the ◉ prompt after hitting the foe with an HP attack.

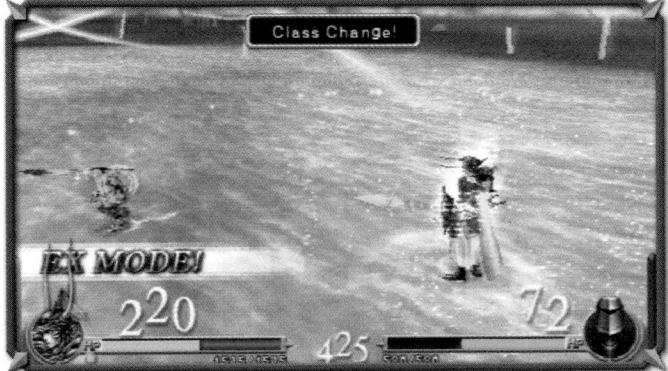

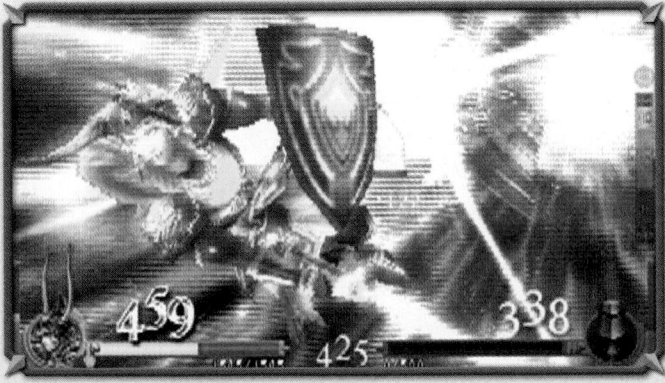

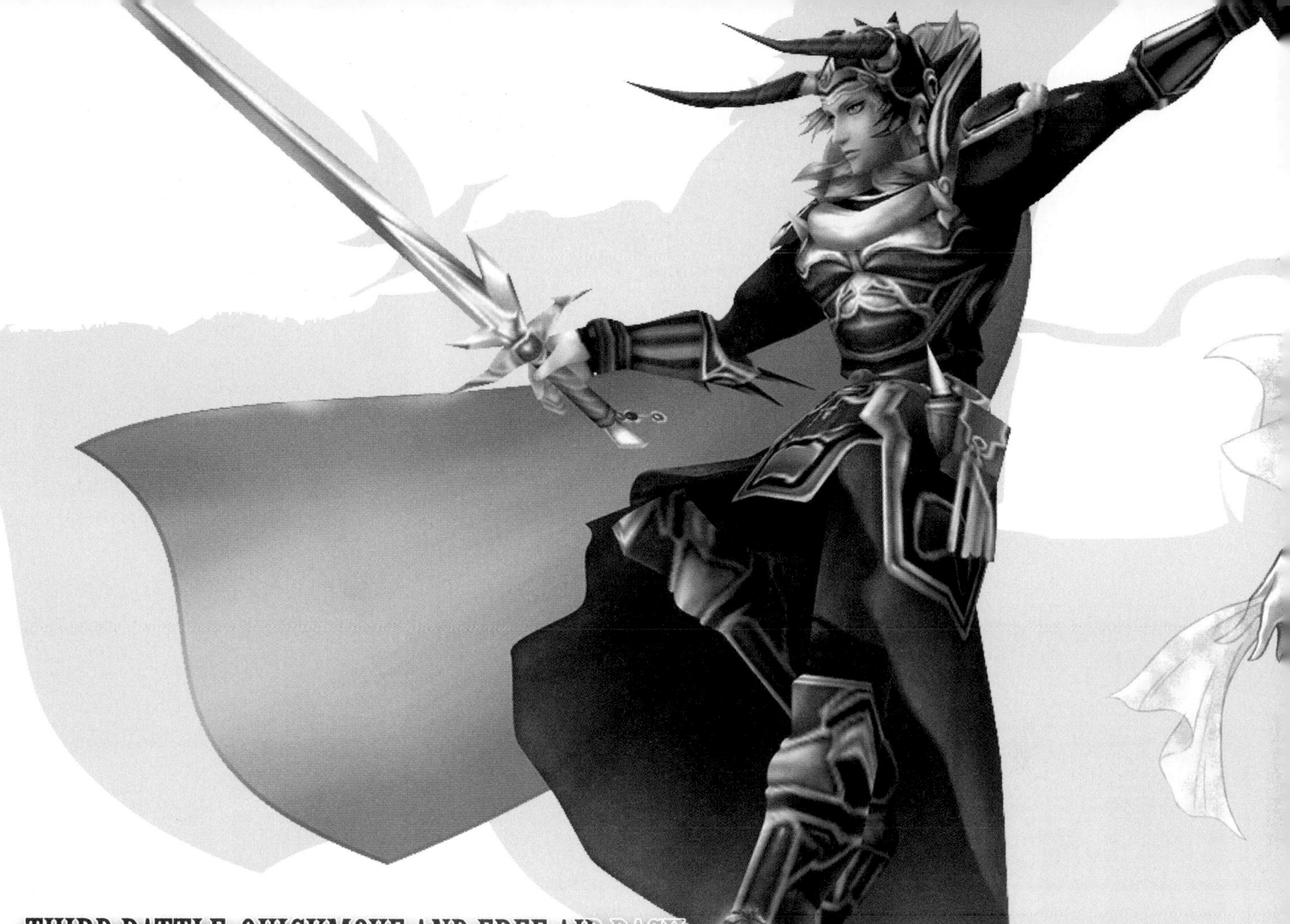

THIRD BATTLE: QUICKMOVE AND FREE AIR DASH

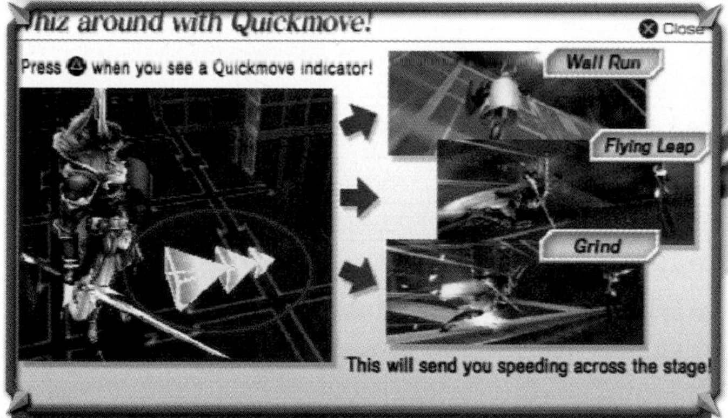

Whiz around with Quickmove!
❌ Close

Press ▲ when you see a Quickmove indicator!

Wall Run

Flying Leap

Grind

This will send you speeding across the stage!

Quickmove creates many new movement opportunities.

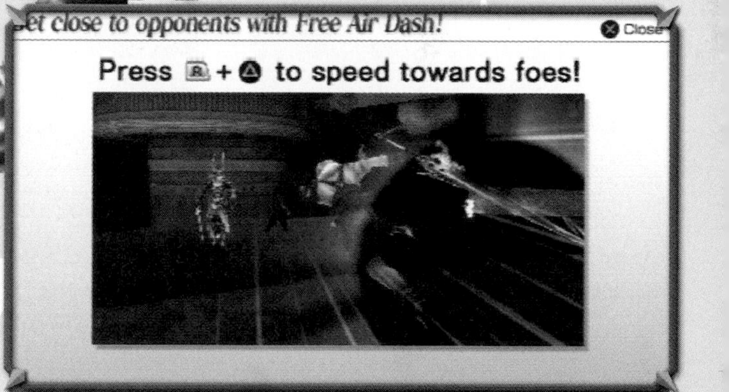

Get close to opponents with Free Air Dash!
❌ Close

Press R + ▲ to speed towards foes!

Free Air Dash allows you to close the distance between you and your target quickly.

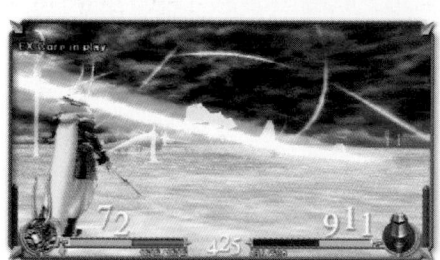

The tutorial battles take place in Order's Sanctuary, the bastion of Cosmos, goddess of harmony. Threaded around the stage are luminous green bands of light, which characters can grind along by using Quickmove. Press ▲ near a yellow Quickmove Indicator to ride the rails. It's often much faster to use Quickmove to traverse portions of a stage than it is to run or Air Dash. Use the Analog Stick to change direction during Quickmove. Quickmove can be interrupted by attacking, by pressing ▲ to Air Dash toward the target, or by hitting ✕ to jump.

FOURTH BATTLE: EX CORE LOCK-ON

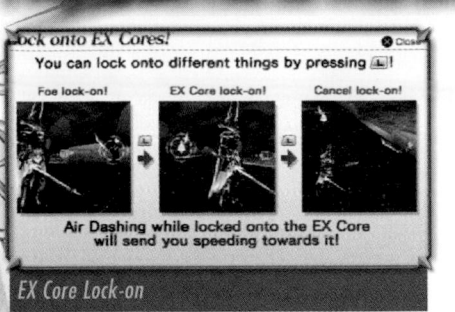

Lock onto EX Cores!
You can lock onto different things by pressing ▣!

Foe lock-on! EX Core lock-on! Cancel lock-on!

Air Dashing while locked onto the EX Core
will send you speeding towards it!

EX Core Lock-on

During the final battle of the tutorial, EX Cores appear at various points throughout the stage. Occasionally when an EX Core is being generated, you'll see the EX Force in an area being drawn in toward a central point, where the EX Core will form. Before they are acquired by one combatant or the other, existing EX Cores can also absorb nearby EX Force, garnering them more energy in the process. Pressing ▣ repeatedly toggles between locking on to the enemy, to any existing EX Cores, or to nothing at all. This is extremely useful, because in the hectic commotion of battle, you might sometimes miss spotting an EX Core available for the taking. Occasionally toggling ▣ a few times just to check for EX Cores can help you discover them before your opponent does—if you do wind up locking on to an EX Core, use Air Dash to get to it quickly!

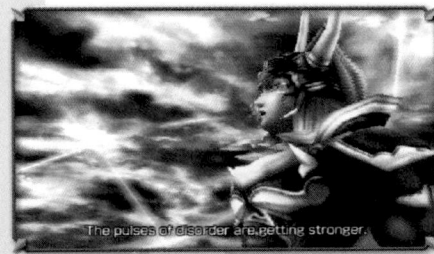

EX Core in play

Having completed the tutorial, you'll gain access to the Start Menu, where you can enter the battle and customization modes of *DISSIDIA FINAL FANTASY* in earnest. In Story Mode, only one level is available initially—the Prologue, another tutorial starring Warrior of Light, this time highlighting the boardgame-like intricacies of Story Mode. Completing the Prologue unlocks the PP Catalog, as well as the Destiny Odyssey boards, which feature past *Final Fantasy* heroes battling the forces of Chaos.

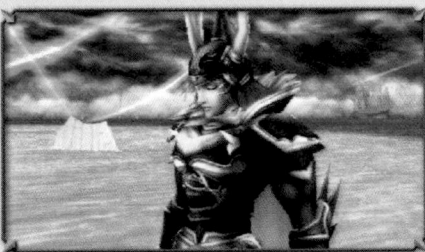

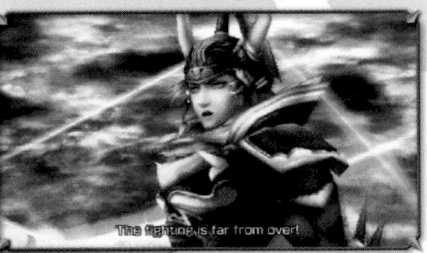

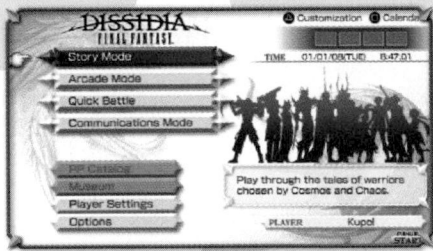

STORY MODE INTRO

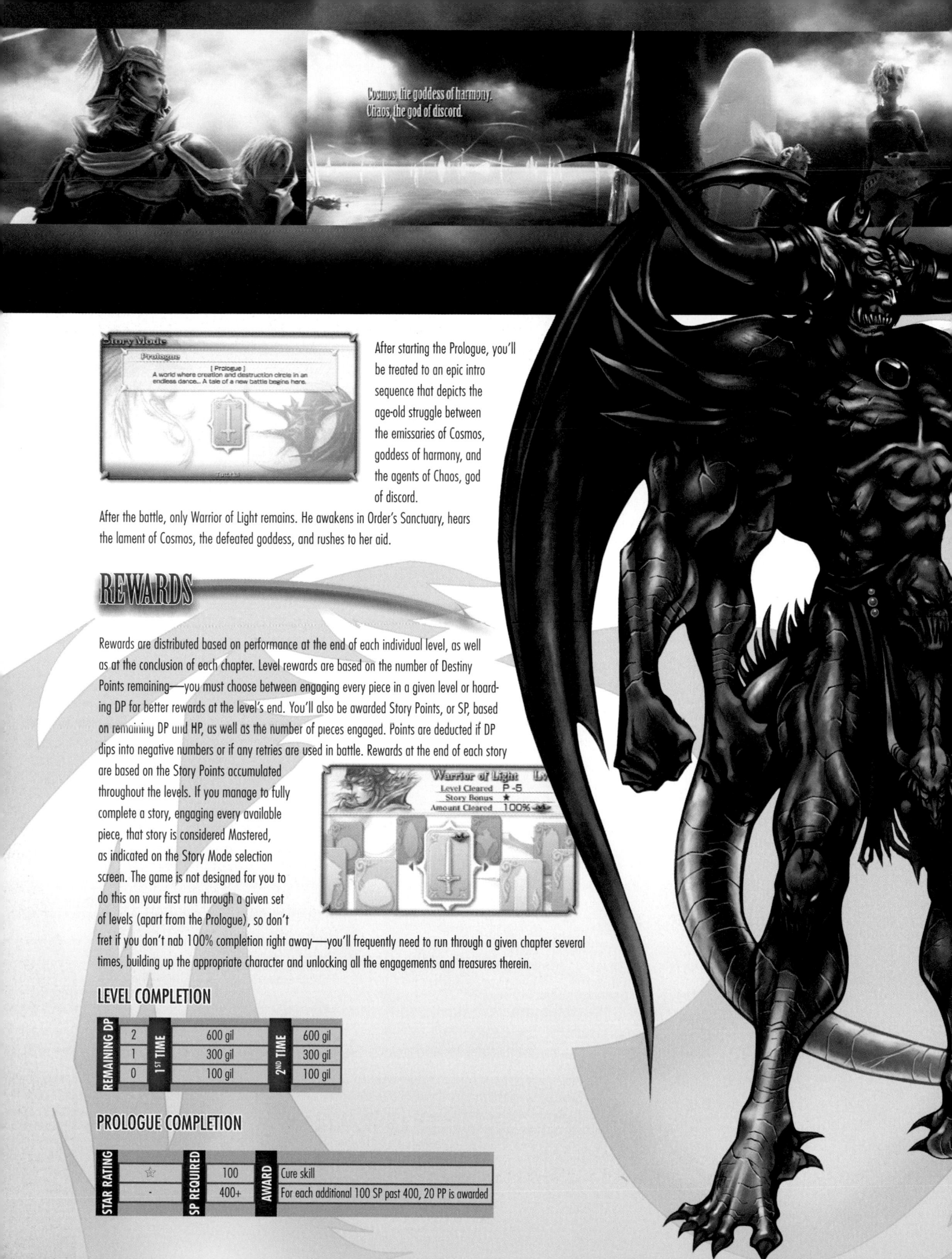

Cosmos, the goddess of harmony. Chaos, the god of discord.

After starting the Prologue, you'll be treated to an epic intro sequence that depicts the age-old struggle between the emissaries of Cosmos, goddess of harmony, and the agents of Chaos, god of discord.

After the battle, only Warrior of Light remains. He awakens in Order's Sanctuary, hears the lament of Cosmos, the defeated goddess, and rushes to her aid.

REWARDS

Rewards are distributed based on performance at the end of each individual level, as well as at the conclusion of each chapter. Level rewards are based on the number of Destiny Points remaining—you must choose between engaging every piece in a given level or hoarding DP for better rewards at the level's end. You'll also be awarded Story Points, or SP, based on remaining DP and HP, as well as the number of pieces engaged. Points are deducted if DP dips into negative numbers or if any retries are used in battle. Rewards at the end of each story are based on the Story Points accumulated throughout the levels. If you manage to fully complete a story, engaging every available piece, that story is considered Mastered, as indicated on the Story Mode selection screen. The game is not designed for you to do this on your first run through a given set of levels (apart from the Prologue), so don't fret if you don't nab 100% completion right away—you'll frequently need to run through a given chapter several times, building up the appropriate character and unlocking all the engagements and treasures therein.

LEVEL COMPLETION

REMAINING DP	1ST TIME		2ND TIME	
2		600 gil		600 gil
1		300 gil		300 gil
0		100 gil		100 gil

PROLOGUE COMPLETION

STAR RATING	SP REQUIRED	AWARD
☆	100	Cure skill
-	400+	For each additional 100 SP past 400, 20 PP is awarded

PROLOGUE 1

THE SHATTERED WORLD

STARTING DP **1** | MAX FINISHING **0** | ENGAGEMENTS **0**

Levels in Story Mode play out on grids that resemble gameboards. The goal of each level is to reach and destroy the Stigma of Chaos. While there are usually obstacles along the way, including bosses that occasionally guard the Stigma of Chaos, you'll only have to cross the board and touch the Stigma to complete the first Prologue level.

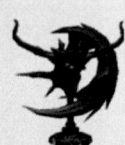

Stigma of Chaos

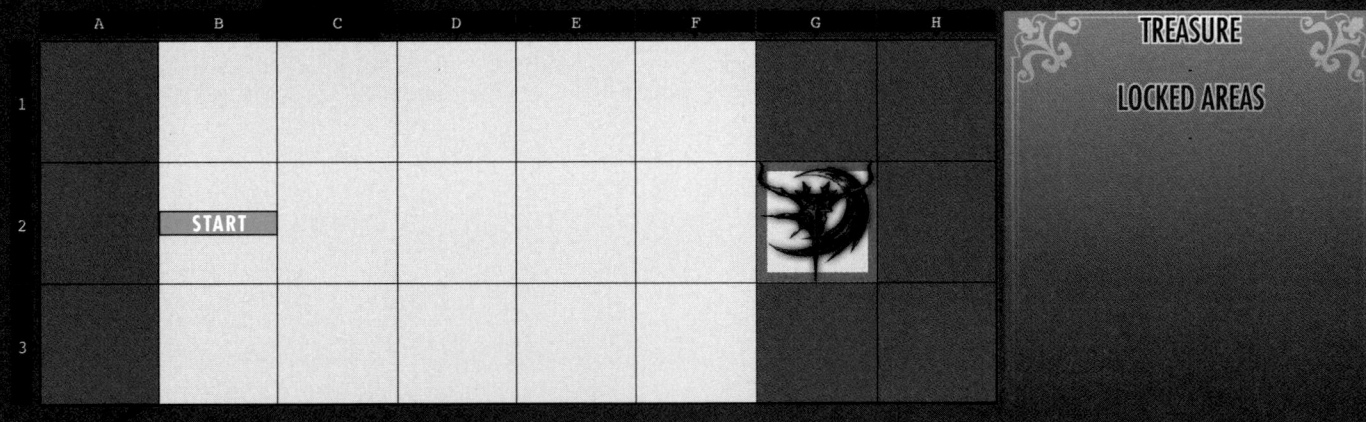

TREASURE

LOCKED AREAS

START

DP EFFICIENCY ROUTE

There's nothing to do on this first stage except cross to the Stigma of Chaos and destroy it.

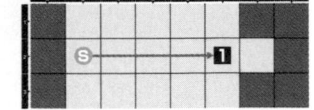

At the onset of each level, you'll have a certain amount of Destiny Points, or DP. When you move and engage a piece, the home area is changed, expending 1 DP. If you enter an engagement and lose the battle, then return to the board instead of retrying, you'll lose 2 DP! Sometimes you'll have to balance returning to the board with retrying failed encounters, an act which itself costs 1 DP, to maximize your DP when you've run into an encounter that's proving to be more difficult than anticipated. Finishing a level with as many DP remaining as possible goes a long way toward earning special rewards.

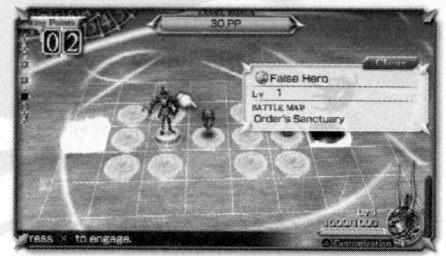
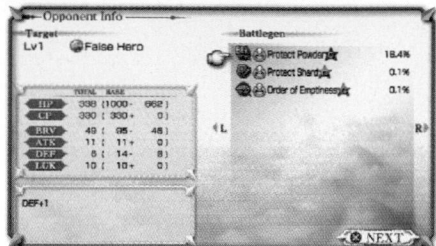

Here you'll have the first encounter with an opposing battle piece. These symbols represent manikins, evil creatures fashioned from crystal by Chaos, placed on the board to impede your progress. Engaging a battle piece results in a battle. Before the battle, you'll have a chance to view the enemy's vitals on the Opponent Info screen. Here you can check their stats and equipment, as well as any spoils you can receive through Battlegen. Battlegen is a system where the combination of two characters facing off and performing certain actions can create accessories. Thus, you can gain an item just by performing a Wall Rush, or even an HP attack. The Opponent Info screen lists the items you may create, the action necessary to create it, and the chance of receiving the item after a successful action. Obviously, Battlegen rewards with higher percentage chances are easier to obtain. Always be sure to check Battlegen rewards on the Opponent Info screen, as not only does the probability of successfully creating an accessory through Battlegen increase as you gain levels, but more rewards become available the further you progress.

TYPES OF BATTLE PIECES

There are several types of distinct battle pieces. Their visual differences tell you something about the opponent they represent even before you check the Opponent Info screen or enter battle.

 A normal battle piece. Does not have accessories equipped.

 A harder battle piece, bolstered by accessories.

 A battle piece with unusual stats, such as extreme attack power but incredibly low HP.

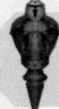 A tough battle piece with good stats, equipment, and accessories.

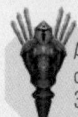 An extremely tough battle piece. Only appears on levels you've already cleared with at least a 3-star rating.

 The piece that represents the end of a level. Not always accompanied by a battle, but when it is, it's a boss fight! Beware, and prepare accordingly.

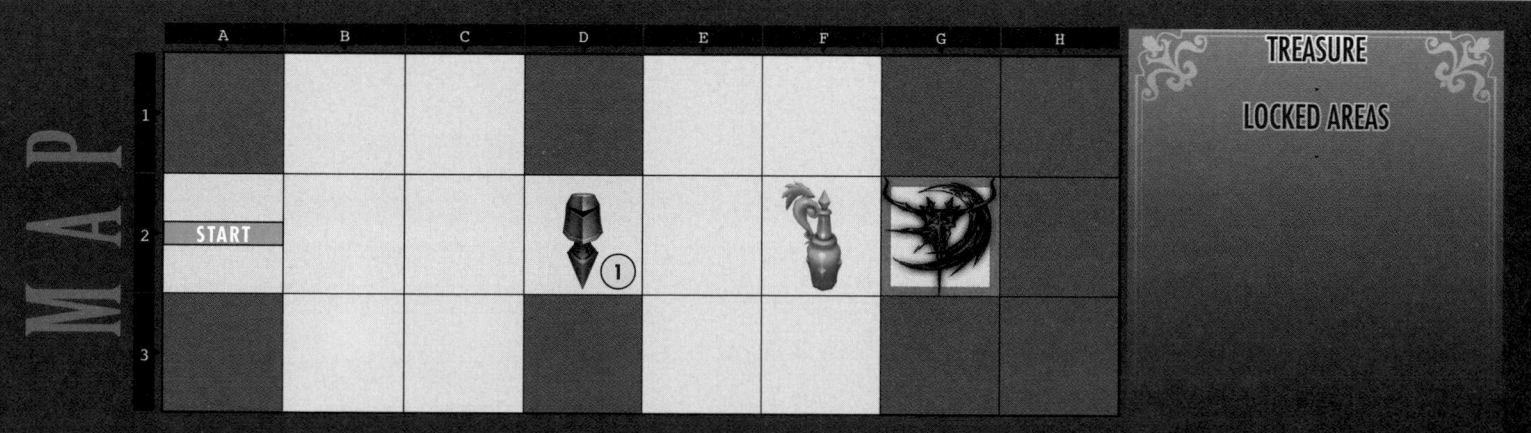

BATTLE PIECE DATA

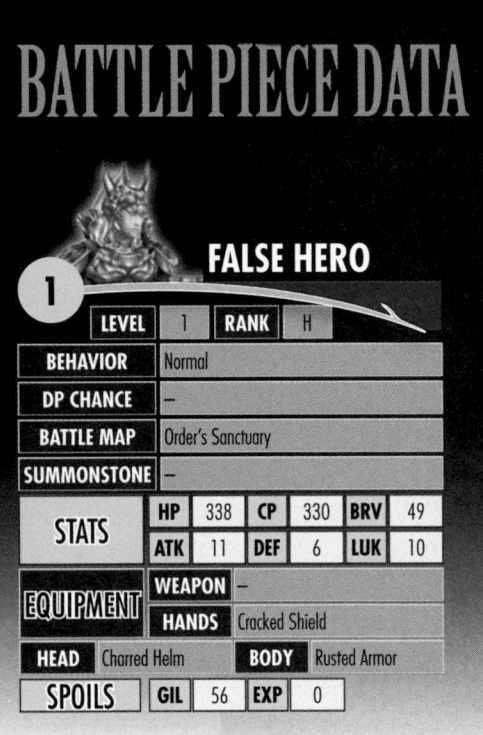

FALSE HERO

1

LEVEL	1	RANK	H

BEHAVIOR	Normal
DP CHANCE	–
BATTLE MAP	Order's Sanctuary
SUMMONSTONE	–

STATS	HP	338	CP	330	BRV	49
	ATK	11	DEF	6	LUK	10

EQUIPMENT	WEAPON	–
	HANDS	Cracked Shield

HEAD	Charred Helm	BODY	Rusted Armor

SPOILS	GIL	56	EXP	0

INTERPRETING ENEMY DATA

Battle pieces represent different enemies, each possessing different behavior, capabilities, and attributes. The Battle Piece Data section for each level breaks down each foe's level, stats, and equipment. Also revealed is the stage the battle takes place on, whether there's a DP Chance in the battle, and whether the foe is equipped with a Summonstone. Rank and Behavior are also detailed, but these require a bit more explanation.

Rank indicates the general power level of the enemy. When fighting higher-ranked foes, you'll receive bonuses to EXP gained if the enemy has a higher level than your character—10% extra for each rank, from D to SSS. EXP actually drops slightly for H to F rank enemies—1% for each rank if the foe has a lower level than your character. Drop rates are also lower for these minor ranks.

CPU RANK	EFFECT
SSS	Bonus EXP
SS	Bonus EXP
S	Bonus EXP
A	Bonus EXP
B	Bonus EXP
C	Bonus EXP
D	Bonus EXP
E	–
F	EXP Penalty, lowered drop rates
G	EXP Penalty, lowered drop rates
H	EXP Penalty, lowered drop rates

Behavior is also important. This setting is what determines the general actions of the AI for each foe. In Quick Battle, you can actually choose this setting for your opponent. In Story Mode, of course, you can't. Knowing what type of Behavior a foe will exhibit ahead of time can help greatly—for example, if your foe is a type that dodges often, you probably won't want to follow them with chase attacks; if your foe blocks often, you might get close and do nothing so they'll try to block an attack that never comes—leaving an opening you can take advantage of.

BEHAVIOR AVAILABLE IN ALL MODES:	DESCRIPTION
Tactician	Uses bravery attacks. Uses HP attacks if either HP falls below 40% of max, or bravery exceeds base bravery x3.
Valiant	Like Tactician, but more aggressive.
Survivor	Like Tactician, but attacks less often early in the fight.
Cautious	Like Tactician, but attacks less often throughout. Uses ranged attacks liberally.
Calm	Usually uses HP attacks. If HP falls below 40% of max, switches focus to bravery attacks. Seldom attacks early in the fight.
Extreme	Like Calm, but very aggressive early on. As HP dwindles, attacks become less frequent.
Conservative	Usually uses bravery attacks. When bravery exceeds foe's HP, switches focus to HP attacks.
Vicious	Almost always uses HP attacks.

STORY MODE & DUEL COLOSSEUM ONLY:	
Normal	Uses a good balance of attacks, favoring a hit-and-run strategy.
Standby	Uses a good balance of attacks, but doesn't move around much.
Blocker	Blocks frequently.
Evader	Dodges frequently.
Aggressive	Favors close combat.
Tricky	Uses a lot of feints.
Summoner	Immediately uses a Summonstone, then reverts to Normal behavior.

DP EFFICIENCY ROUTE

Simply advance toward the Stigma of Chaos, toppling the manikin and grabbing the Potion along the way.

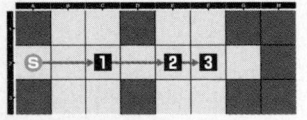

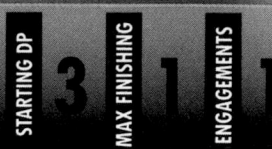

STARTING DP	MAX FINISHING	ENGAGEMENTS
3	1	1

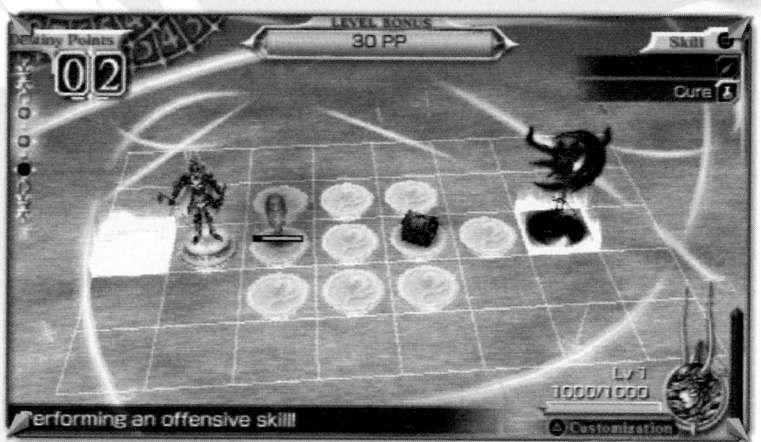

Skills are randomly assigned for use in Story Mode. Initially, only Maser Eye is available—this skill deals 20% damage to an adjacent battle piece. Further skills are unlocked by earning Story Point rewards for various Story Mode chapters, starting with the Prologue—the 1 star reward after clearing the Prologue is Cure. As there is only one battle piece on this level, the enemy before you presents a good opportunity to test out this skill. Move next to the battle piece, then select it with ● and use Maser Eye. The enemy is now softened up before battle is even initiated.

This is especially useful here, as this particular enemy is your first opportunity for a DP Chance. This is a chance to increase your Destiny Points for the level. The requirements for successfully completing the DP Chance and scoring the extra DP are listed prior to battle. The requirements range from things like simply winning the battle, to winning without taking damage, to landing a critical hit or EX Burst within 10 seconds, to a variety of other goals. Successfully converting DP Chances is crucial to getting good Story Point scores at the end of each level. Here, using Maser Eye helps achieve this DP Chance—win within 10 seconds!

DP CHANCE TYPES

DESCRIPTION	NOTES
Win battle	Simply win. This requirement is attached to some especially difficult fights.
Win without taking damage	While bravery attacks don't inflict actual damage, they do count toward negating this DP Chance! You must avoid getting hit at all.
Win without losing HP	Sustaining bravery attacks is okay. Sustaining HP attacks is not.
Keep foe from getting EX Cores	Listen keenly for the EX Core spawn noise and toggle ▣ occasionally to check if an EX Core spawned far away. If one is on the stage at any time, drop what you're doing and collect it so your foe can't.
Win within 10 seconds	If the foe's HP is less than your base bravery, you can just hit them with an HP attack. If it's higher, you'll need to get bravery high enough for a kill shot very, very quickly. This can be done through a BRV Break, or by using a combo with bravery attacks that leads to an ending HP attack. Summons that boost bravery, like Ifrit, can be used as well.
Win within 20 seconds	This might seem more lenient than the previous requirement, but it usually comes with foes who are harder, so the extra time is not as much of a blessing as you might expect.
Wall Rush within 10 seconds	Slam your foe into a wall or obstacle very quickly.
Activate Battlegen within 10 seconds	Fulfill a Battlegen requirement very quickly. Be sure to check Battlegen possibilities before every battle.
Critical hit within 10 seconds	The easiest way to accomplish this is to save EX Force on previous fights on a given level, so that you enter this fight with a full EX Gauge. The instant the fight begins, input ▬ + ● to enter EX Mode, then strike with bravery attacks. Bravery attacks during EX Mode almost always cause critical hits. Otherwise, try landing an HP attack instantly, then follow-up quickly with bravery attacks. After landing an HP attack, your bravery resets to 0 then slowly recovers to your base bravery. During this time, any bravery attacks will also cause critical hits. Simply going for bravery attacks from the get-go is not a great approach, since your rate of success will only be about 2%.
BRV Break within 10 seconds	Attack with strong bravery attacks quickly. This is one of the easier DP Chance requirements to fulfill, if the opponent is cooperative and actually lets you hit them!
EX Burst within 10 seconds	This requirement usually requires preparation—it's rare for an EX Core to not only be active at the beginning of a fight, but also near enough that you can collect it, activate EX Mode, and track your opponent down! Instead, save up EX Force during previous fights, build it up by using the Aura skill, or get it from a Potion on the level. During the actual battle, simply activate EX Mode with ▬ + ● immediately, then go for an HP attack.
Raise accessory multiplier x8.0	Booster accessories give you special bonuses in certain circumstances. Whether a boost is active will be indicated in the upper-left corner of the screen. The foe's boost, if any, is in the upper-right. You must first wear enough booster accessories to allow the possibility of hitting an 8.0 multiplier, then actually do it during the fight.

SKILLS

NAME	EFFECT
Maser Eye	Deals 20% damage to one enemy.
Cure	Recovers 30% of HP.
Scan	Identifies enemies that open locked areas.
Aura	EX Gauge + 50% at start of next battle.
Blink	Enables you to clear Berserk once. (Use before battle.)
Ray-Bomb	Deals 40% damage to one enemy.
Sight	Unlocks all Enigma Arcas.
Cura	Recovers 50% of HP.
Missile	Deals 20-50% damage to one enemy.
Curaga	Fully restores HP.
Matra Magic	Deals 10% damage to all enemies in engagement range.
Regen	Recovers 5% of total HP whenever your Home Area changes.
Invisible	Clears Berserk.
Temblor	Deals 10% damage to all enemies in the level.
Jump	Lets you leap over one piece. (Only allowed when the destination is empty.)

Maser Eye is available during the Prologue. Cure is learned after the Prologue. After that, you can tackle the ten Destiny Odyssey chapters in any order you like, but skills will be earned in the order as listed regardless, as the 1-star award for each completed chapter.

If you care more about maximizing DP Chances for a level than getting a lot of Story Points, you can press START and retry a battle if you've missed out on the DP Chance.

This level also features the first treasure chest. Upon opening it, you'll receive a Broadsword! Press ⬜ to go into the Customization menu to equip it. Many chests will have different contents if you play through a given level again—in this case, a repeat playthrough of the Prologue after completing it the first time will yield 10 Player Points for use in the PP Catalog, instead of the Broadsword. This is only one way in which you're encouraged to play levels multiple times— on subsequent trips through a level, depending on performance, new enemy battle pieces and treasure chests can appear, and some paths may be open that were blocked before.

BONUSES AVAILABLE FROM COMPLETED CHAPTERS

STAR RATING		BONUS	
☆			New skill (in order listed here)
☆☆			Special areas unlocked
☆☆☆			Rare battle pieces spawn
☆☆☆☆			Rare treasure chests spawn

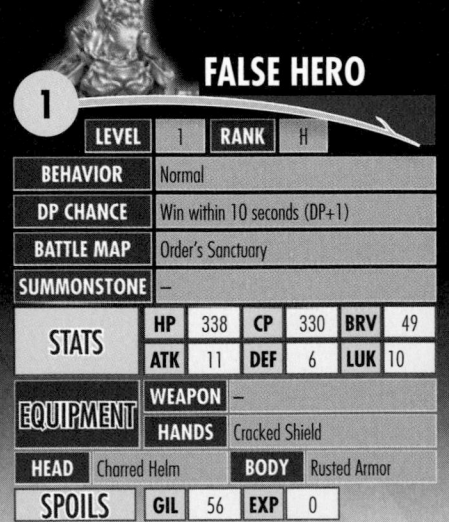

TREASURE

CHEST	1ST TIME	2ND TIME
A	Broadsword	10 PP

LOCKED AREAS

BATTLE PIECE DATA

FALSE HERO

1

LEVEL	1	RANK	H
BEHAVIOR	Normal		
DP CHANCE	Win within 10 seconds (DP+1)		
BATTLE MAP	Order's Sanctuary		
SUMMONSTONE	–		

STATS	HP	338	CP	330	BRV	49
	ATK	11	DEF	6	LUK	10

EQUIPMENT	WEAPON	–		
	HANDS	Cracked Shield		
HEAD	Charred Helm	BODY	Rusted Armor	

SPOILS	GIL	56	EXP	0

DP EFFICIENCY ROUTE

As with previous Prologue levels, advance straight to the end to use DP most efficiently, hopefully completing the DP Chance along the way.

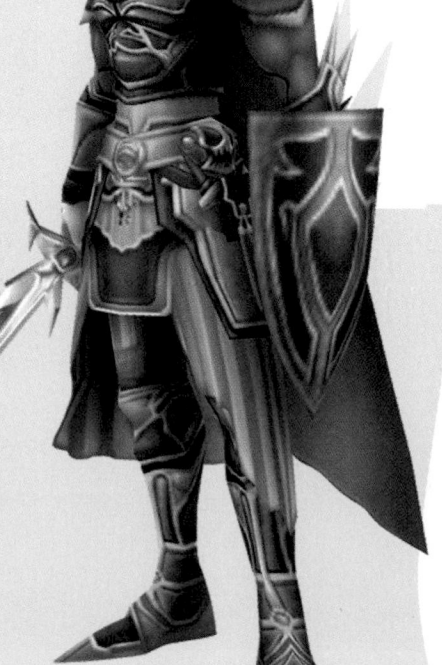

Here, two battle pieces are positioned near each other so that if you engage one, you're adjacent to the other. Positioning yourself like this before a battle results in a chained battle — you'll be forced to fight other adjacent battle pieces after defeating the first one, as they'll become Berserk upon seeing you defeat their nearby allies. Here, both battle pieces offer DP Chances—① for an EX Burst within 10 seconds, and ② for a critical hit within 10 seconds. In both battles, an EX Core immediately spawns in front of Warrior of Light. This is useful in both battles. Obviously, a full EX Gauge is needed to land an EX Burst within 10 seconds against battle piece ①, but EX Mode is also useful against ②, since Warrior of Light's standard bravery attacks during EX Mode become critical hits. Simply rush forward, grab the EX Core, then either go for an HP attack against ① for an EX Burst, or bravery attacks against ② for a critical hit. Remember, be ready to fight them one right after another!

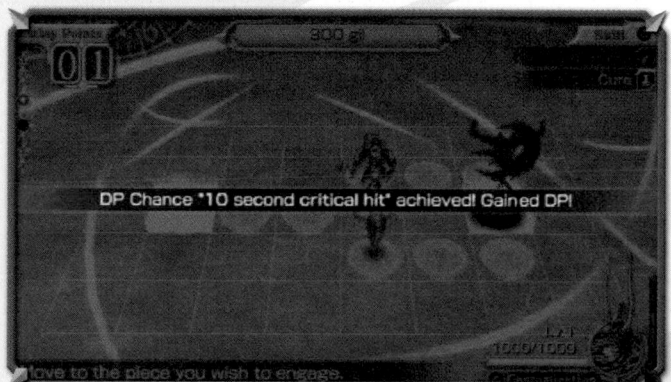
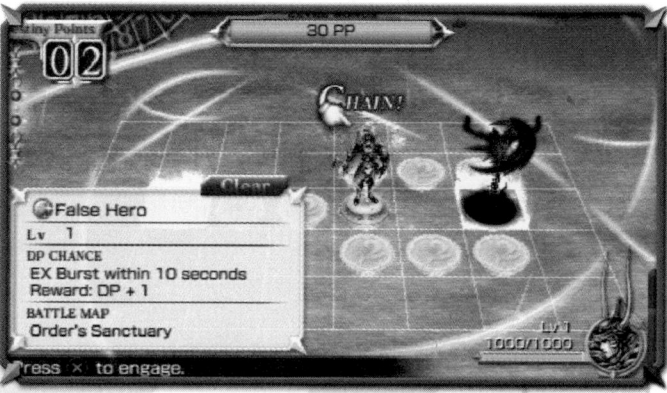

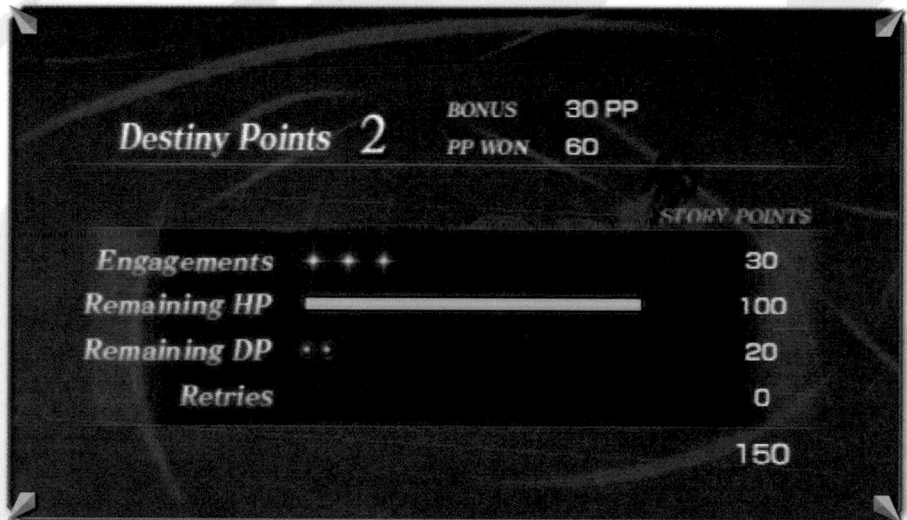

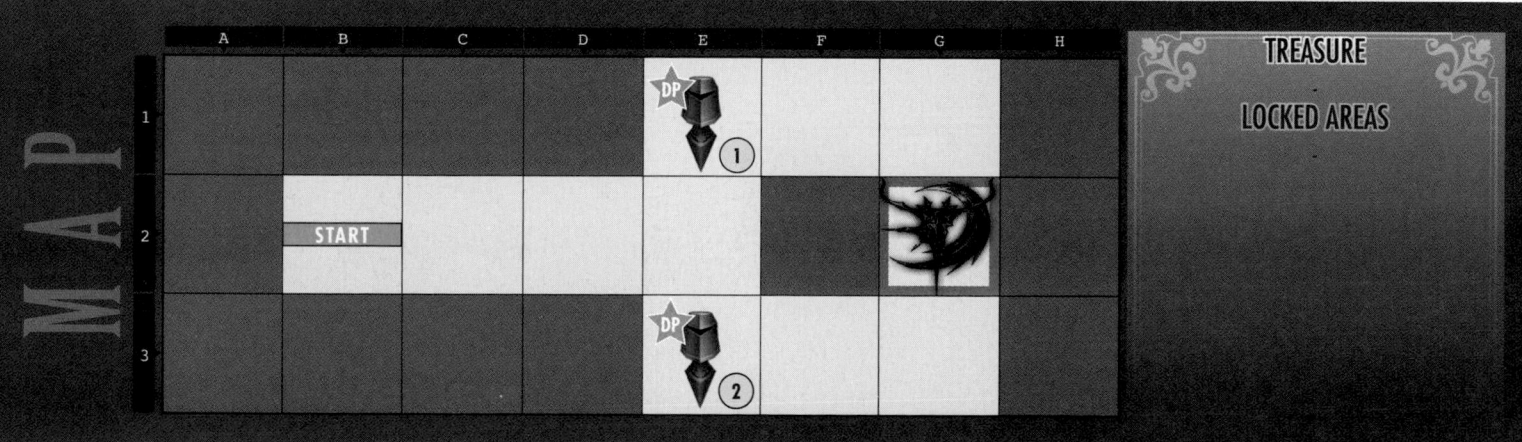

BATTLE PIECE DATA

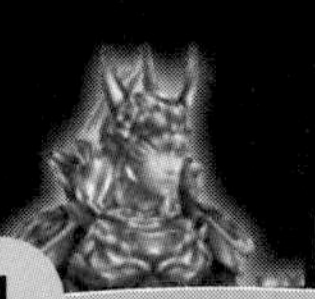

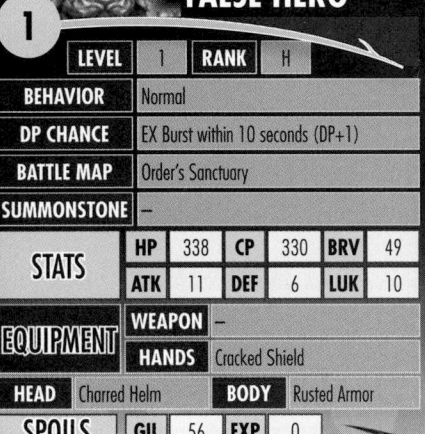

① FALSE HERO

LEVEL	1	RANK	H

BEHAVIOR	Normal
DP CHANCE	EX Burst within 10 seconds (DP+1)
BATTLE MAP	Order's Sanctuary
SUMMONSTONE	–

STATS	HP	338	CP	330	BRV	49
	ATK	11	DEF	6	LUK	10

EQUIPMENT	WEAPON	–
	HANDS	Cracked Shield

HEAD	Charred Helm	BODY	Rusted Armor

SPOILS	GIL	56	EXP	0

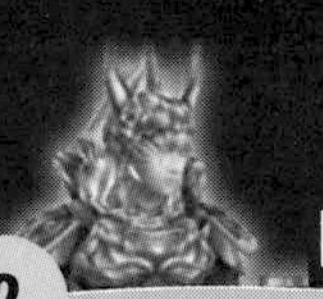

② FALSE HERO

LEVEL	1	RANK	H

BEHAVIOR	Normal
DP CHANCE	Critical hit within 10 seconds (DP+1)
BATTLE MAP	Order's Sanctuary
SUMMONSTONE	–

STATS	HP	338	CP	330	BRV	49
	ATK	11	DEF	6	LUK	10

EQUIPMENT	WEAPON	–
	HANDS	Cracked Shield

HEAD	Charred Helm	BODY	Rusted Armor

SPOILS	GIL	56	EXP	0

DP EFFICIENCY ROUTE

After completing the chained battle against ① and ②, and hopefully clearing DP Chances with both, proceed to the Stigma of Chaos.

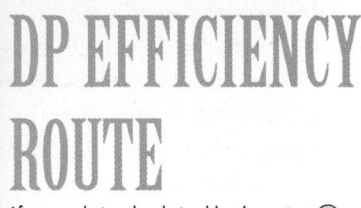

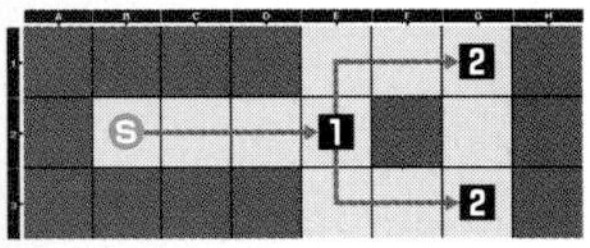

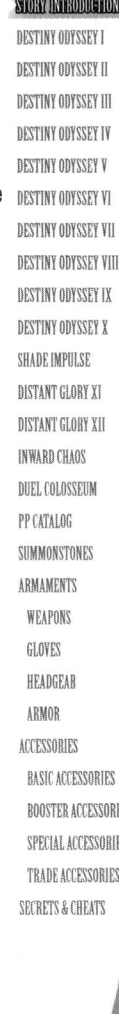

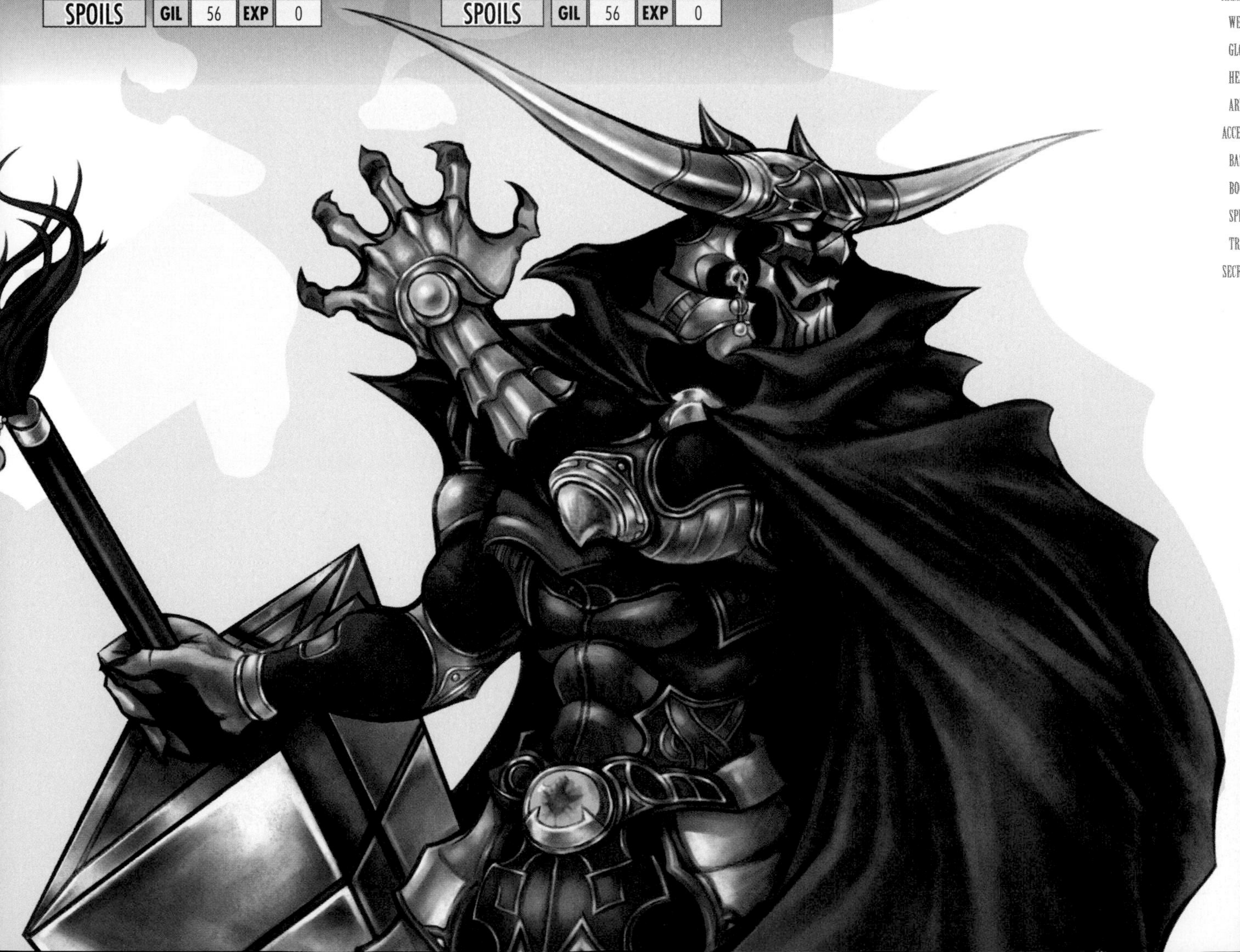

STORY MODE INTRO

The final level of the Prologue features a treasure chest along with a boss fight against a facsimile of Garland, nemesis of Warrior of Light. The main difference between this adversary and the previous ones in the Prologue is that the boss here is equipped with accessories. These special items can augment stats. In this case, the False Stalwart wears a Hyper Ring, which boosts his damage by 10%. He also wears two booster accessories, which add a multiplier of 1.2 each to the Hyper Ring's effect when he's very close to you. Different booster accessories have different requirements to enable their multipliers. Your multipliers, if any, are displayed on the top left of the screen, while your opponent's are on the top right. Equip the Power Ring you find in the treasure chest here for a little boost of your own, and enter the battle. After the battle, your performance for the entire Prologue chapter is evaluated. Scores for each level are determined based on the number of successful engagements as well as your remaining HP and Destiny Points. Any retries used penalize your final score. The more Story Points you end up with for the chapter, the better the rewards.

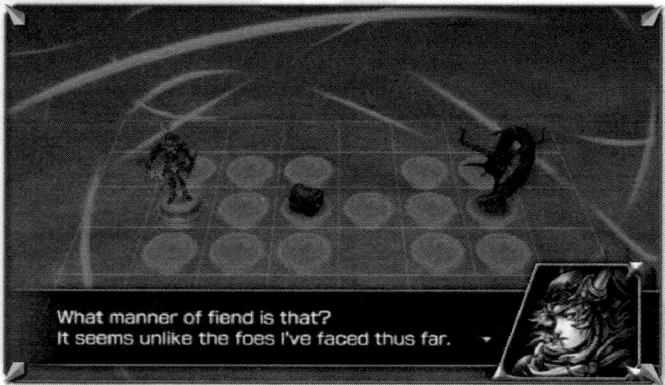

What manner of fiend is that?
It seems unlike the foes I've faced thus far.

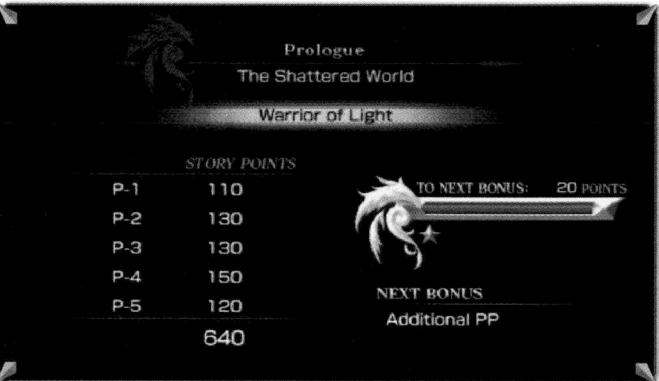

Prologue
The Shattered World

Warrior of Light

STORY POINTS

		TO NEXT BONUS:	20 POINTS
P-1	110		
P-2	130		
P-3	130		
P-4	150		
P-5	120	NEXT BONUS	
	640	Additional PP	

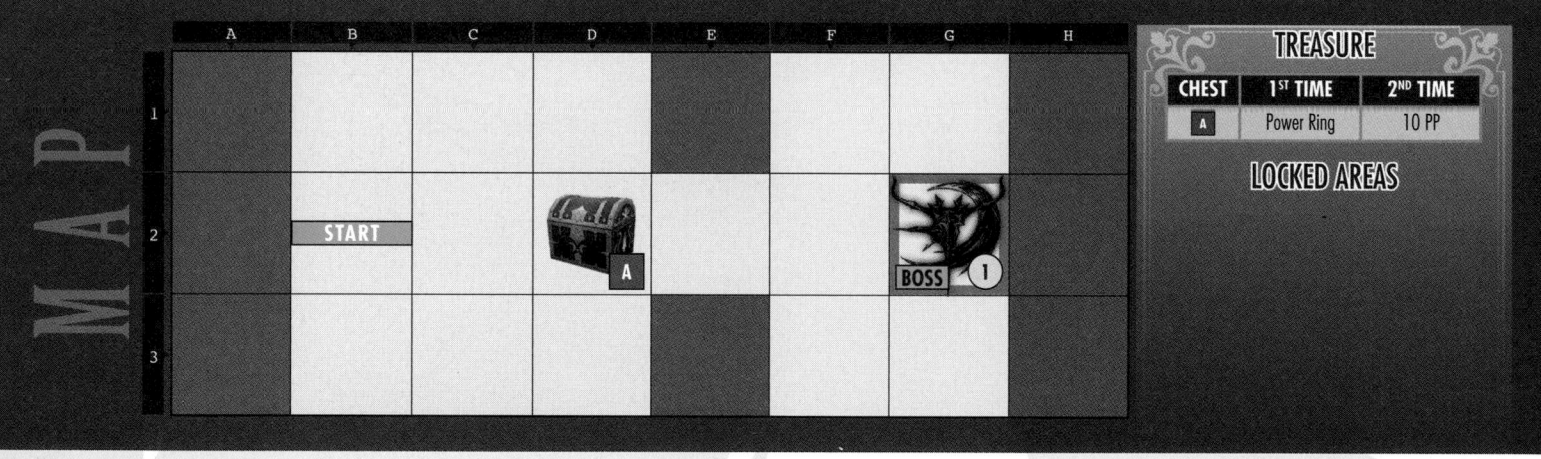

TREASURE

CHEST	1ST TIME	2ND TIME
A	Power Ring	10 PP

LOCKED AREAS

BATTLE PIECE DATA

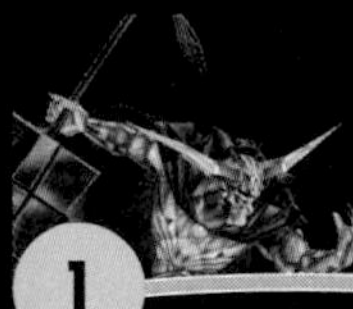

① FALSE STALWART

LEVEL	1	RANK	H

BEHAVIOR	Normal
DP CHANCE	–
BATTLE MAP	Order's Sanctuary
SUMMONSTONE	–

STATS	HP	338	CP	330	BRV	49
	ATK	13	DEF	6	LUK	10

EQUIPMENT	WEAPON	–
	HANDS	Cracked Shield

HEAD	Charred Helm	BODY	Rusted Armor

SPOILS	GIL	168	EXP	0

ACCESSORIES	Hyper Ring, [Position] Near Opponent x2

DP EFFICIENCY ROUTE

Pick up the treasure chest, then head to the boss. The Prologue is complete!

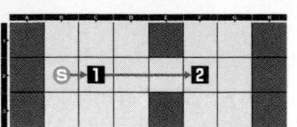

After the battle, Warrior of Light finds a depleted Cosmos trying to rest in her sanctuary. She's been defeated by Chaos, and the whole world is now at risk. While she rests, she gathers protagonists from the whole *Final Fantasy* series to seek out crystals, which can aid in the fight against Chaos. The search will surely be difficult and fraught with danger, and every hero has their own path to follow in order to help restore Cosmos…

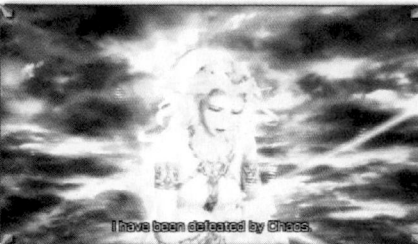

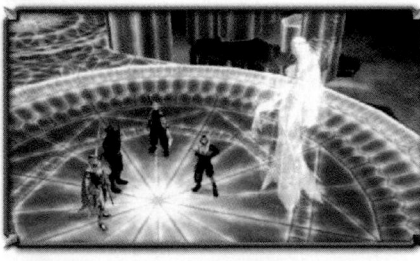

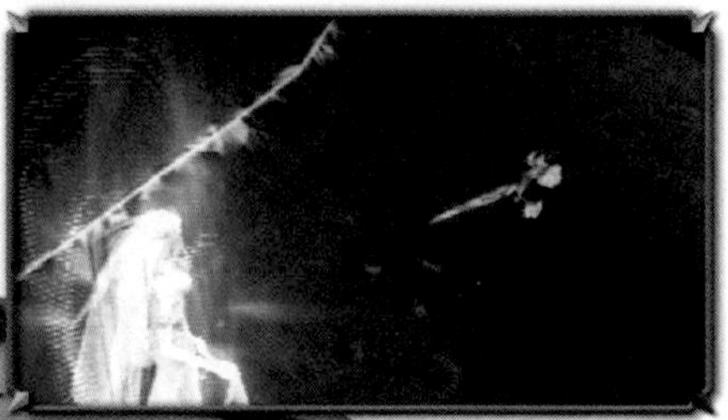

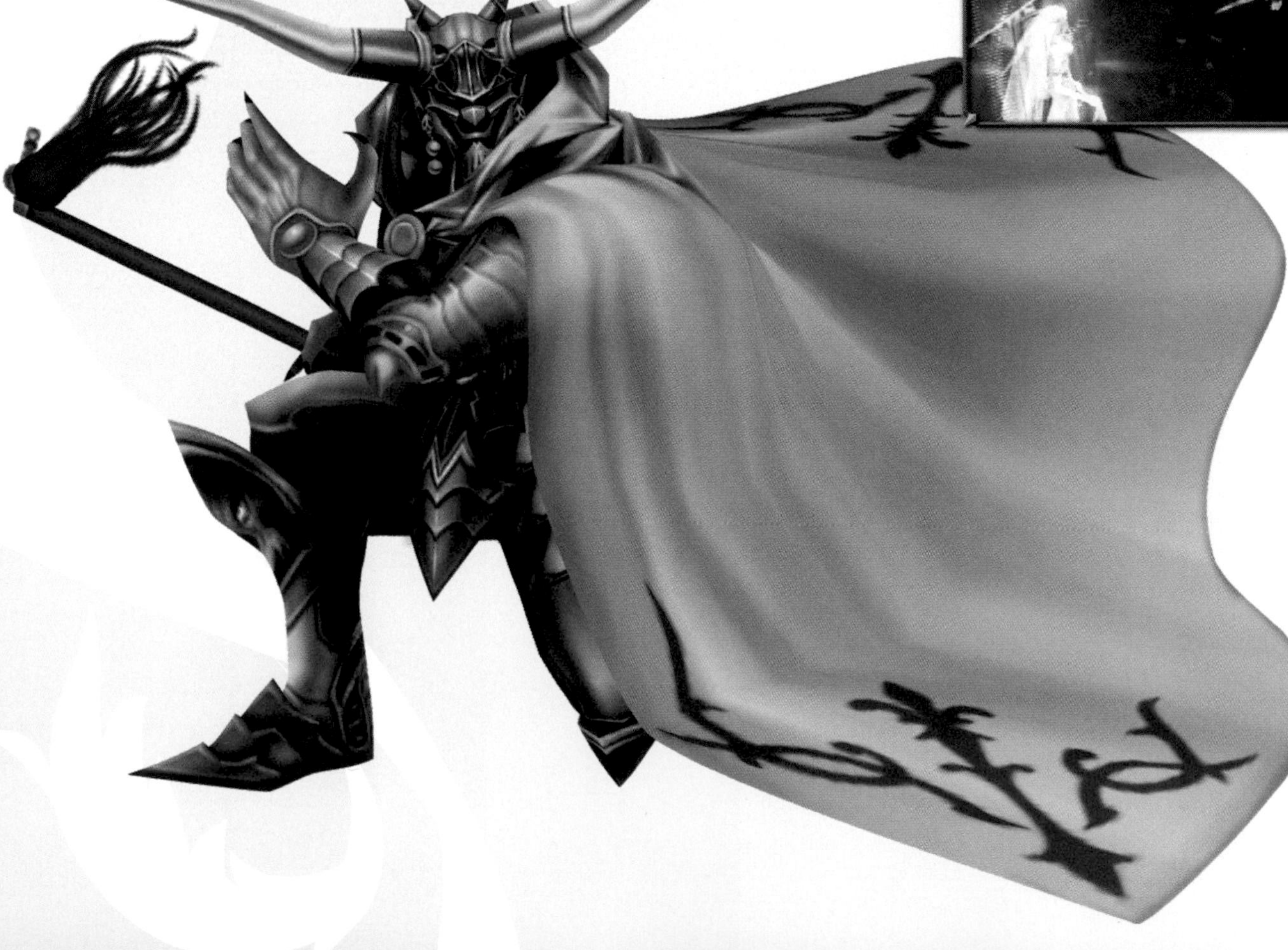

STORY MODE INTRO

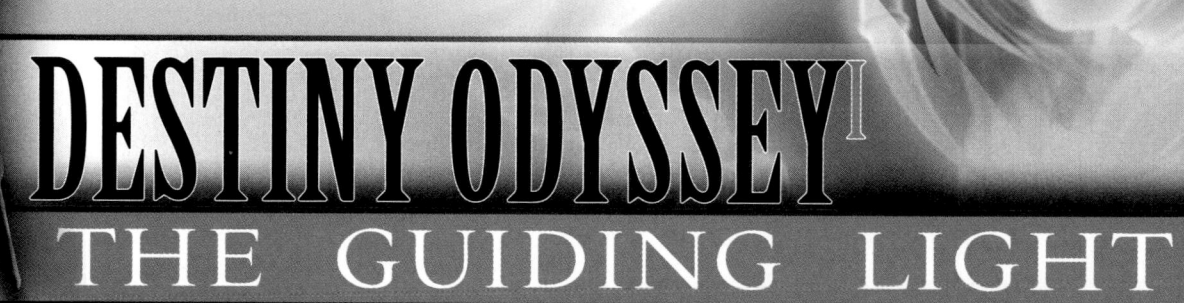

DESTINY ODYSSEY I
THE GUIDING LIGHT

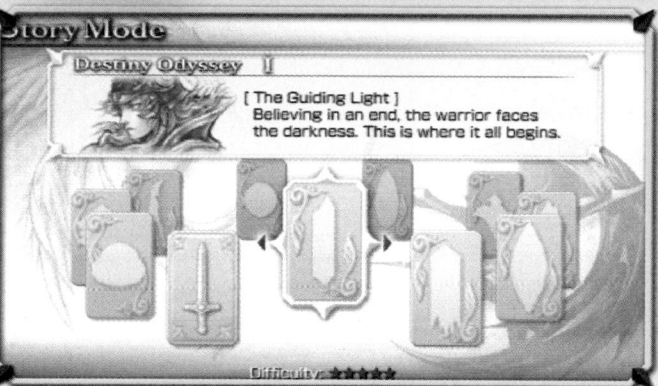

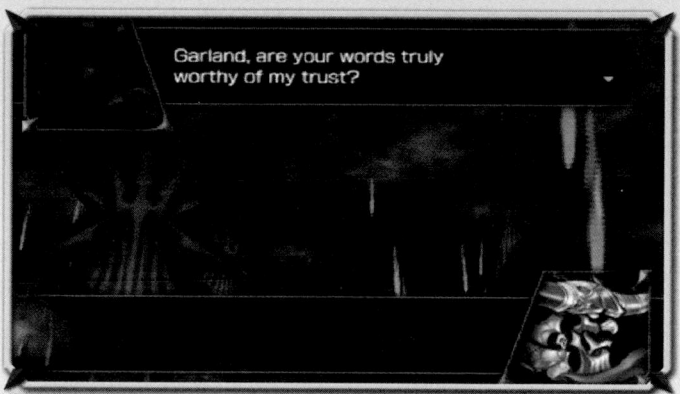

Warrior of Light sets out to aid the ailing Cosmos by finding crystals, while Chaos gathers his strength. Yet the god of discord seems mistrustful of his own minions…

REWARDS

At the end of each level, rewards are available if you finish with a positive number of Destiny Points, or DP. This walkthrough includes miniature level maps that indicate the most efficient route to take through a given level, in order to maximize DP.

LEVEL COMPLETION

REMAINING DP	1ST TIME		2ND TIME
7		Rosetta Stone	300 PP
6		Dwarven Axe	200 PP
5		Tomahawk	120 PP
4		Mandragora Summonstone	80 PP
3		1000 gil	50 PP
2		600 gil	30 PP
1		300 gil	20 PP
0		100 gil	10 PP

At the end of each set of levels, you'll receive rewards based on your performance. Story Points, or SP, are awarded after each level based on remaining DP, HP, and the number of engagements undertaken. Points are penalized for retries, or for a DP total that dips into negatives. If you miss out on a desired bonus on the first playthrough, don't fret—SP is cumulative across multiple playthroughs.

DESTINY ODYSSEY I COMPLETION

STAR RATING	SP REQUIRED	AWARD
★	100	New skill
★★	200	Special areas unlocked
★★★	300	Rare battle pieces spawned
★★★★	400	Rare treasure chests spawned
—	500 SP, then every 500 SP extra	100 PP

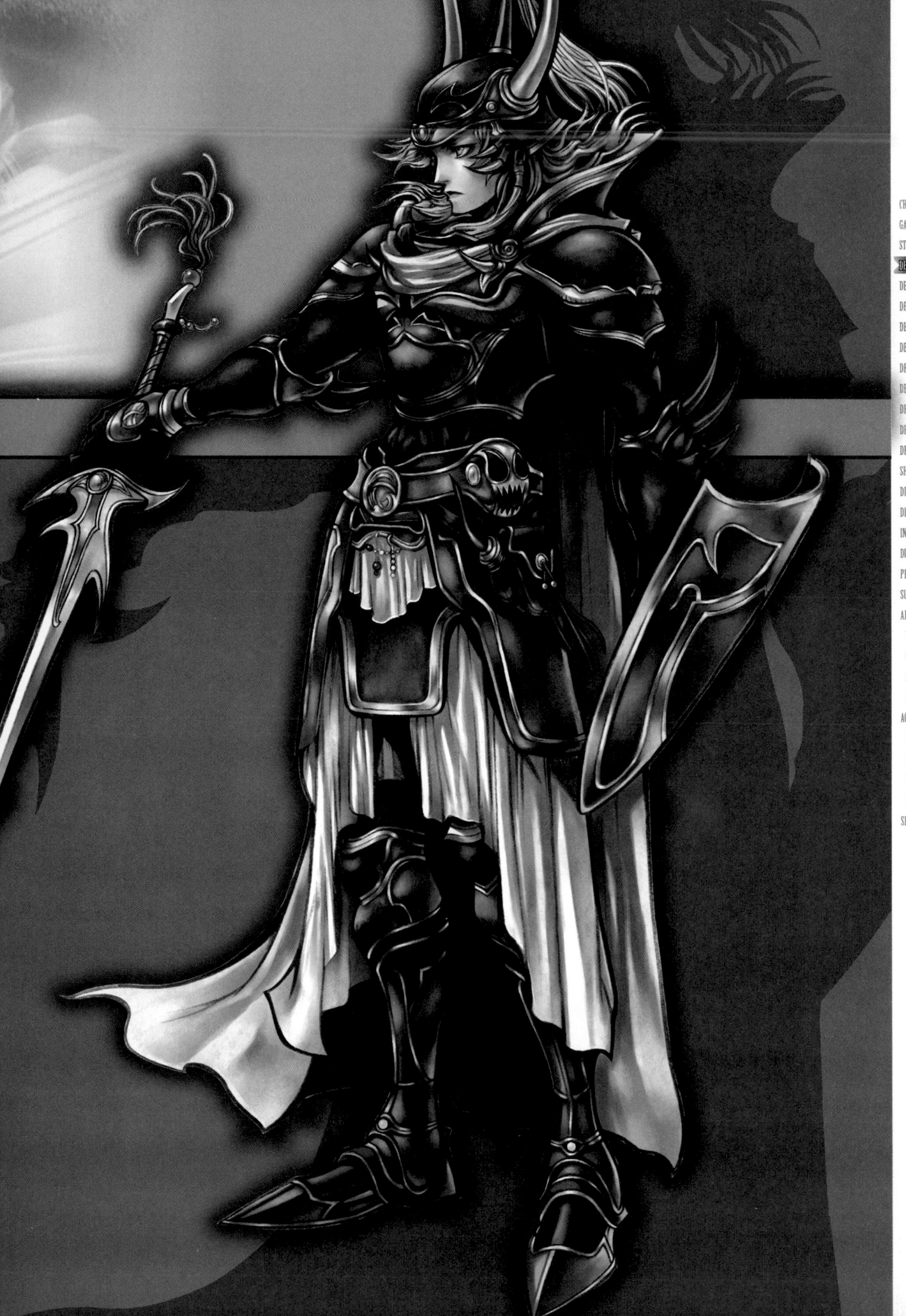

DESTINY ODYSSEY I

DESTINY ODYSSEY I-1

STARTING DP	MAX FINISHING	ENGAGEMENTS
3	3	5

In this area, you'll get your first taste of battle pieces and Locked Areas that only appear after certain conditions are fulfilled. Battle piece ④ only appears after defeating battle piece ② (indicated by the red line on the map). Depending on your board position when this happens, you may be forced into combat immediately by a battle chain. Furthermore, the Locked Area in front of the boss only disappears after defeating at least three of the battle pieces.

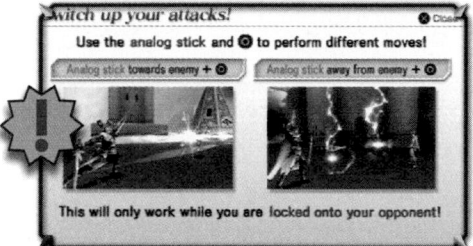

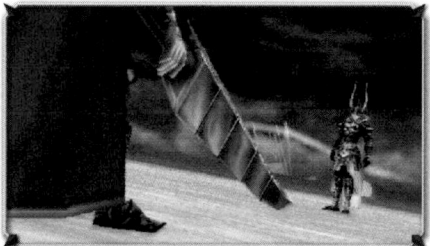

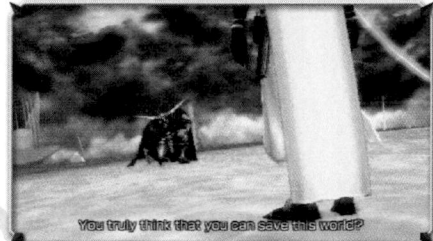

MAP

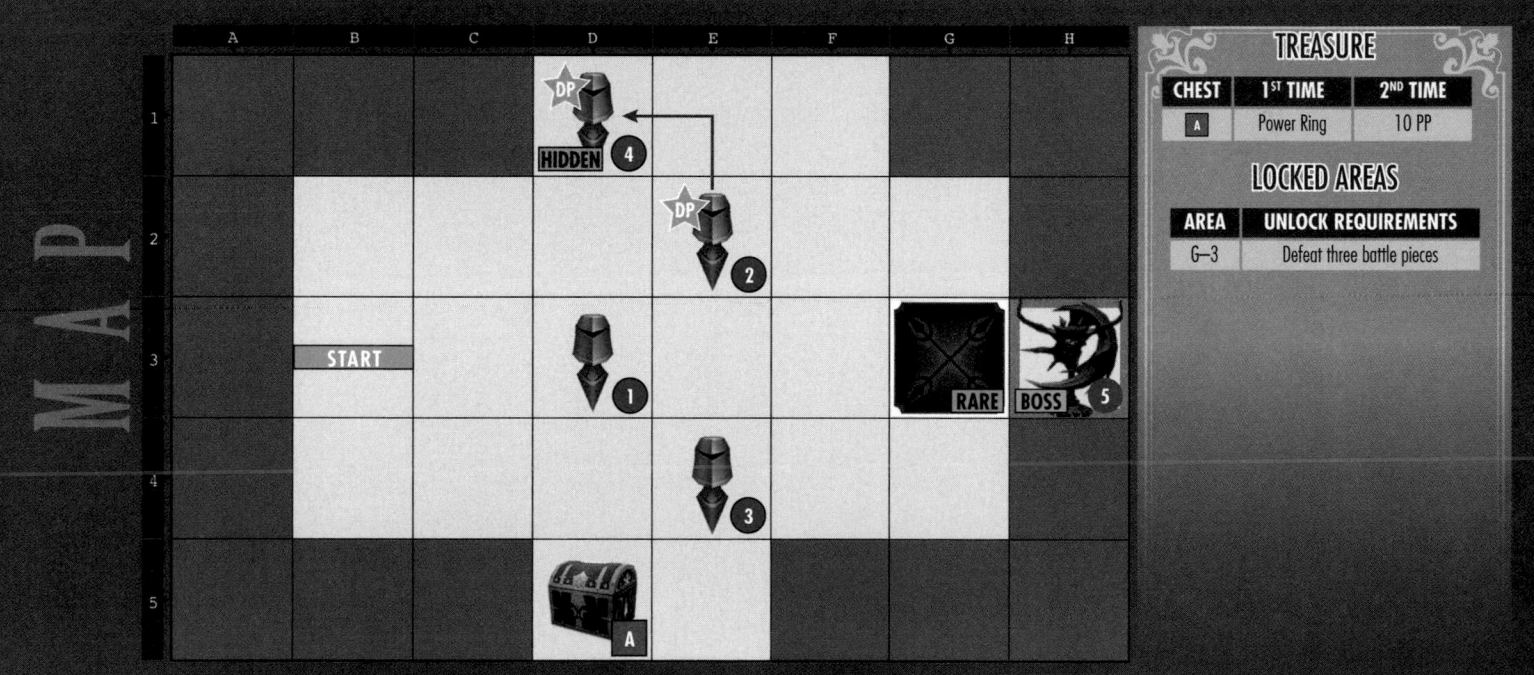

TREASURE

CHEST	1ST TIME	2ND TIME
A	Power Ring	10 PP

LOCKED AREAS

AREA	UNLOCK REQUIREMENTS
G–3	Defeat three battle pieces

DP EFFICIENCY ROUTE

You'll want to engage the three battle pieces adjacent to grid square D-2. This lets you uncover the hidden enemy, clear both DP Chances, and remove the Locked Area in front of the boss all in one fell swoop through a three-part chain. Battle piece ② requires a critical hit within 10 seconds to fulfill the DP Chance. The easiest way to do this is to engage battle piece ① first, and save up a full EX Gauge during that fight. This allows you to enter EX Mode immediately during the fight with battle piece ②—bravery attacks during EX Mode are almost guaranteed to be critical hits. Maximizing DP on this level, and many others, means skipping the treasure chest, but you can always crack it open on another run.

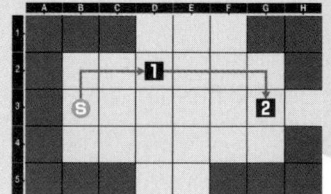

BATTLE PIECE DATA

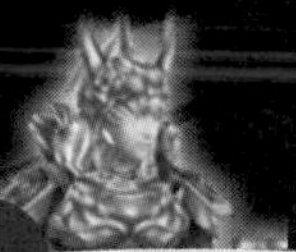

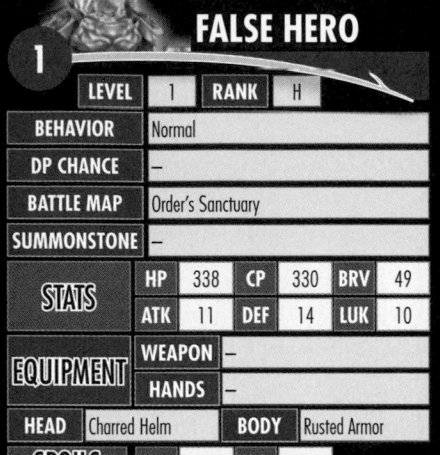

1 FALSE HERO

LEVEL	1	RANK	H

BEHAVIOR	Normal
DP CHANCE	–
BATTLE MAP	Order's Sanctuary
SUMMONSTONE	–

STATS	HP	338	CP	330	BRV	49
	ATK	11	DEF	14	LUK	10

EQUIPMENT	WEAPON	–
	HANDS	–

HEAD	Charred Helm	BODY	Rusted Armor

SPOILS	GIL	56	EXP	800

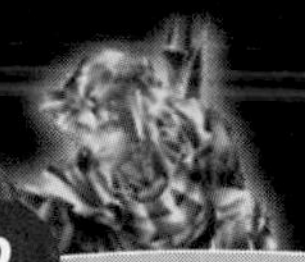

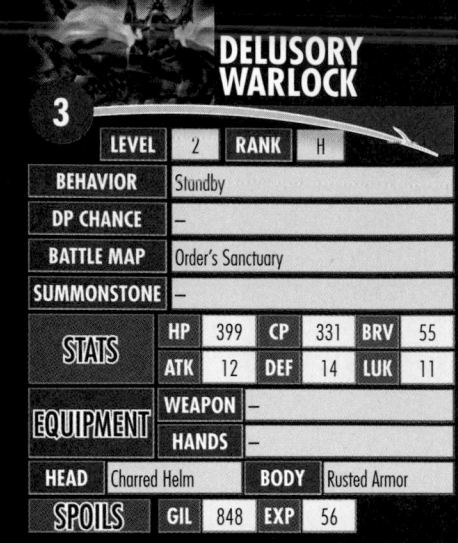

2 IMITATION LIEGEMAN

LEVEL	2	RANK	H

BEHAVIOR	Aggressive
DP CHANCE	Critical hit within 10 seconds (DP+1)
BATTLE MAP	Old Chaos Shrine
SUMMONSTONE	–

STATS	HP	399	CP	331	BRV	101
	ATK	13	DEF	14	LUK	11

EQUIPMENT	WEAPON	–
	HANDS	–

HEAD	–	BODY	Rusted Armor

SPOILS	GIL	56	EXP	848

3 DELUSORY WARLOCK

LEVEL	2	RANK	H

BEHAVIOR	Standby
DP CHANCE	–
BATTLE MAP	Order's Sanctuary
SUMMONSTONE	–

STATS	HP	399	CP	331	BRV	55
	ATK	12	DEF	14	LUK	11

EQUIPMENT	WEAPON	–
	HANDS	–

HEAD	Charred Helm	BODY	Rusted Armor

SPOILS	GIL	848	EXP	56

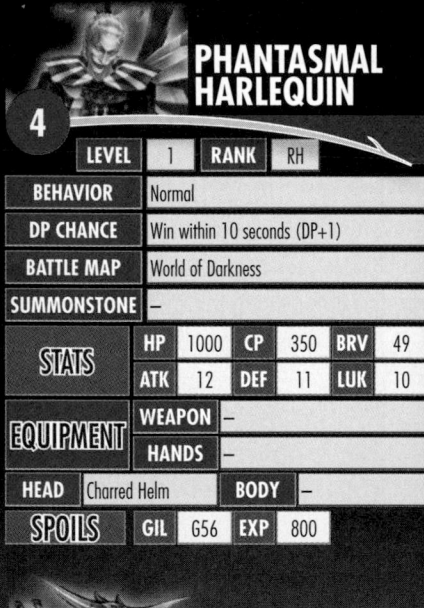

4 PHANTASMAL HARLEQUIN

LEVEL	1	RANK	RH

BEHAVIOR	Normal
DP CHANCE	Win within 10 seconds (DP+1)
BATTLE MAP	World of Darkness
SUMMONSTONE	–

STATS	HP	1000	CP	350	BRV	49
	ATK	12	DEF	11	LUK	10

EQUIPMENT	WEAPON	–
	HANDS	–

HEAD	Charred Helm	BODY	–

SPOILS	GIL	G56	EXP	800

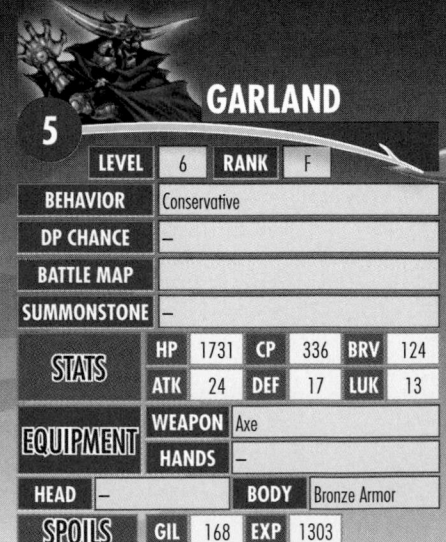

5 GARLAND

LEVEL	6	RANK	F

BEHAVIOR	Conservative
DP CHANCE	–
BATTLE MAP	
SUMMONSTONE	–

STATS	HP	1731	CP	336	BRV	124
	ATK	24	DEF	17	LUK	13

EQUIPMENT	WEAPON	Axe
	HANDS	

HEAD	–	BODY	Bronze Armor

SPOILS	GIL	168	EXP	1303

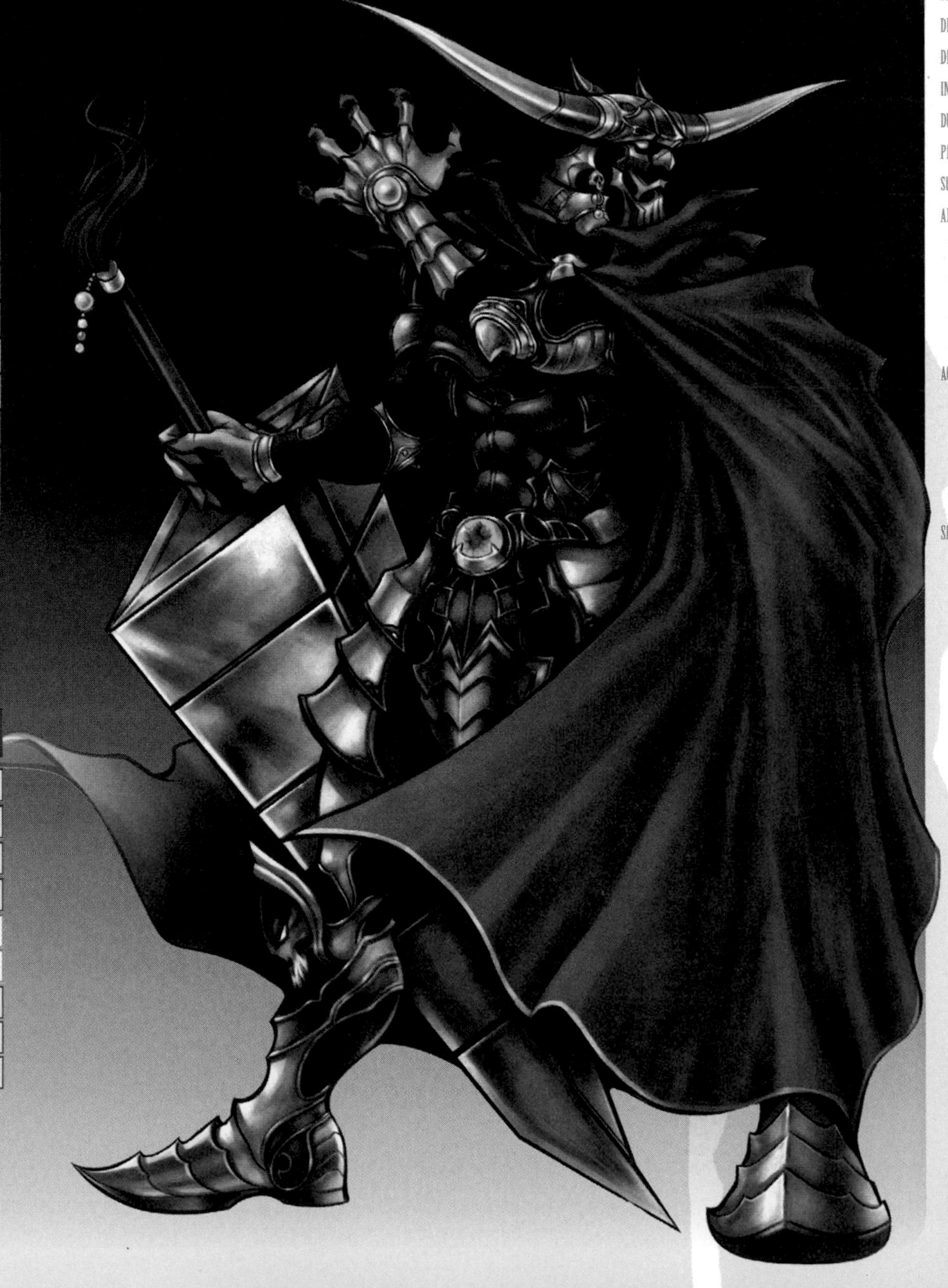

DESTINY ODYSSEY I

DESTINY ODYSSEY I-2

On this level, you'll get your first taste of areas that are blocked off during the first playthrough. The impasses at A-2 and A-4 only disappear when you've already completed Destiny Odyssey I previously with at least a 2-star rating, just as there are certain treasure chests and enemy battle pieces that only appear on other levels after an initial completion. This level also houses the first "strange" battle piece you'll fight, at E-1. This manikin adversary is wearing accessories that make it very powerful, yet also reduce its HP to 1! If you can avoid its assault and get a solid hit in, the fight should be rather short-lived. The Locked Areas on this stage are uncovered by defeating particular battle pieces. Beware the boss, Sephiroth—he is very keen to block or dodge your attacks. Wait to dodge an attack of his, then strike while he recovers!

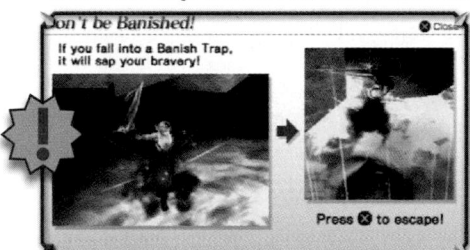
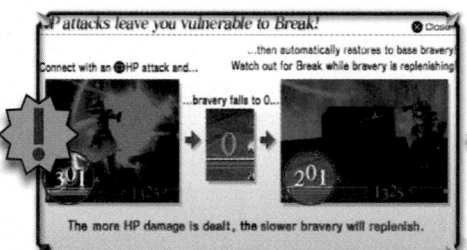
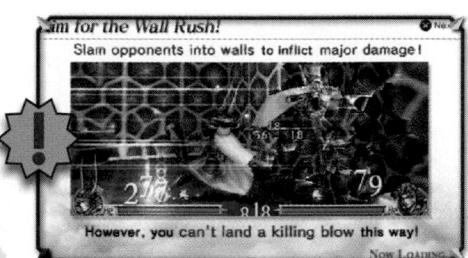

MAP

TREASURE

CHEST	1ST TIME	2ND TIME
A	Bronze Armor	10 PP
a	Ifrit Summonstone (after 2—star rating)	–

LOCKED AREAS

AREA	UNLOCK REQUIREMENTS
C–2	Defeat battle piece 4
C–4	Defeat battle piece 1
B–2	Defeat battle piece 3
B–4	Defeat battle piece 5

DP EFFICIENCY ROUTE

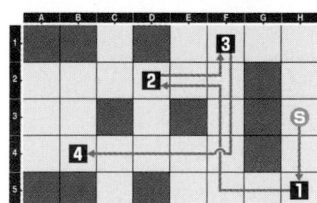

You'll want to clear all the DP Chances in the stage, while avoiding any detours. Defeat the battle pieces at G-5 and then D-3 before chaining the two battle pieces around F-1. After that, head to the boss, proceeding through the previously blocked areas.

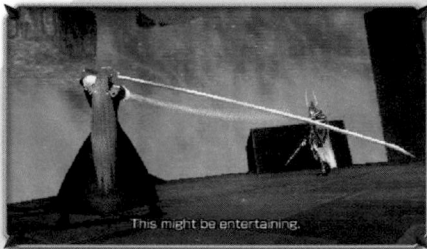

Warrior of Light finds Firion depleted after a battle with Sephiroth, and acts as the cavalry. After Warrior of Light and Sephiroth face off, Sephiroth shares some cryptic words before he escapes.

BATTLE PIECE DATA

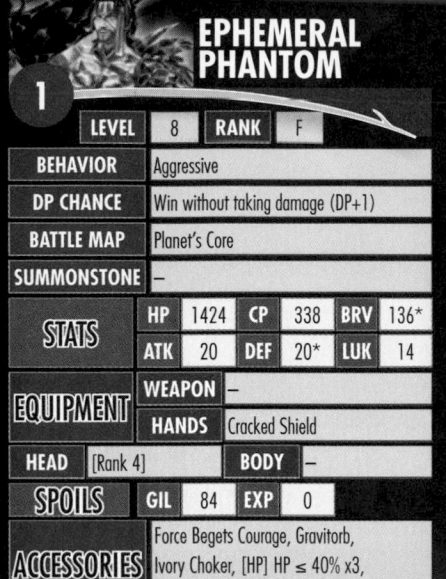

1 EPHEMERAL PHANTOM

LEVEL 8	**RANK** F

BEHAVIOR	Aggressive
DP CHANCE	Win without taking damage (DP+1)
BATTLE MAP	Planet's Core
SUMMONSTONE	–

STATS	HP	1424	CP	338	BRV	136*
	ATK	20	DEF	20*	LUK	14

EQUIPMENT	WEAPON	–
	HANDS	Cracked Shield

HEAD [Rank 4]	**BODY** –

SPOILS	GIL	84	EXP	0

ACCESSORIES	Force Begets Courage, Gravitorb, Ivory Choker, [HP] HP ≤ 40% x3, [HP] Near Death x3

2 PHANTASMAL HARLEQUIN

LEVEL 3	**RANK** G

BEHAVIOR	Aggressive
DP CHANCE	Win within 10 seconds (DP+1)
BATTLE MAP	Order's Sanctuary
SUMMONSTONE	–

STATS	HP	1121	CP	352	BRV	107
	ATK	14	DEF	13	LUK	11

EQUIPMENT	WEAPON	–
	HANDS	–

HEAD –	**BODY** –

SPOILS	GIL	84	EXP	0

3 COUNTERFEIT YOUTH

LEVEL 9	**RANK** C

BEHAVIOR	Summoner
DP CHANCE	Critical hit within 10 seconds (DP+1)
BATTLE MAP	Order's Sanctuary
SUMMONSTONE	Carbuncle

STATS	HP	1	CP	358	BRV	0
	ATK	16	DEF	12	LUK	14

EQUIPMENT	WEAPON	–
	HANDS	Cracked Shield

HEAD Tiara	**BODY** Rusted Armor

SPOILS	GIL	84	EXP	2970

ACCESSORIES	The Rotten, Soul of the Craven, Guardian Bangle, [HP] HP = 1 x3

4 CAPRICIOUS REAPER

LEVEL 3	**RANK** G

BEHAVIOR	Tricky
DP CHANCE	–
BATTLE MAP	World of Darkness
SUMMONSTONE	–

STATS	HP	1121	CP	332	BRV	107
	ATK	12	DEF	14	LUK	11

EQUIPMENT	WEAPON	–
	HANDS	–

HEAD –	**BODY** –

SPOILS	GIL	84	EXP	0

5 IMITATION LIEGEMAN

LEVEL 4	**RANK** G

BEHAVIOR	Normal
DP CHANCE	BRV Break within 10 seconds (DP+1)
BATTLE MAP	World of Darkness
SUMMONSTONE	–

STATS	HP	1182	CP	333	BRV	113
	ATK	15	DEF	16	LUK	12

EQUIPMENT	WEAPON	–
	HANDS	–

HEAD –	**BODY** –

SPOILS	GIL	84	EXP	0

6 SEPHIROTH

LEVEL 10	**RANK** E

BEHAVIOR	Calm
DP CHANCE	–
BATTLE MAP	Planet's Core
SUMMONSTONE	–

STATS	HP	1973	CP	341	BRV	147
	ATK	25	DEF	21	LUK	15

EQUIPMENT	WEAPON	Katana
	HANDS	–

HEAD –	**BODY** Bronze Armor

SPOILS	GIL	252	EXP	1545

* Denotes use of the base value (for stats that vary).

DESTINY ODYSSEY I-3

STARTING DP	**5**	
MAX FINISHING	**5** (+2 after 3-star rating)	
ENGAGEMENTS	**6** (+1 after 3-star rating)	

This is the first level to feature a battle piece and treasure chest that only appear after clearing the level once and returning for a successive playthrough (provided you score a sufficient star bonus to unlock them). There's also an extra Stigma of Chaos marker partway through, indicating a mid-boss of sorts. Toward the end, the Elixir at G-5 can randomly refill your skills, if desired. Foes are tougher here, and often dodge and punish attacks if you are aggressive and try to take the initiative. To play it safe, focus on collecting EX Cores, and wait for enemies to attack first so you can dodge their attack and counter it.

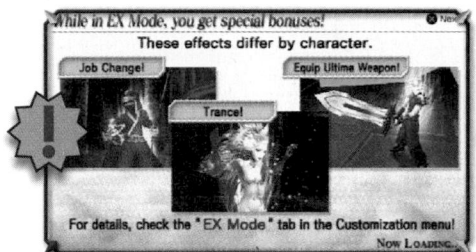

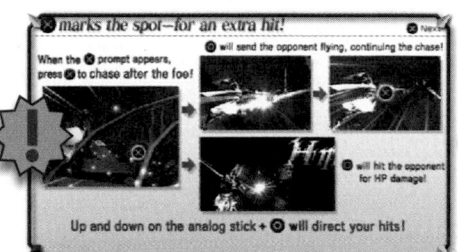

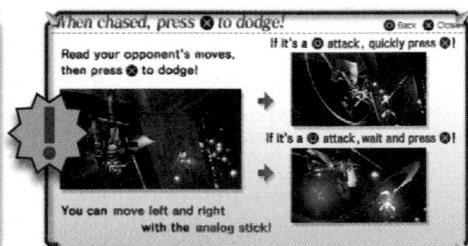

MAP

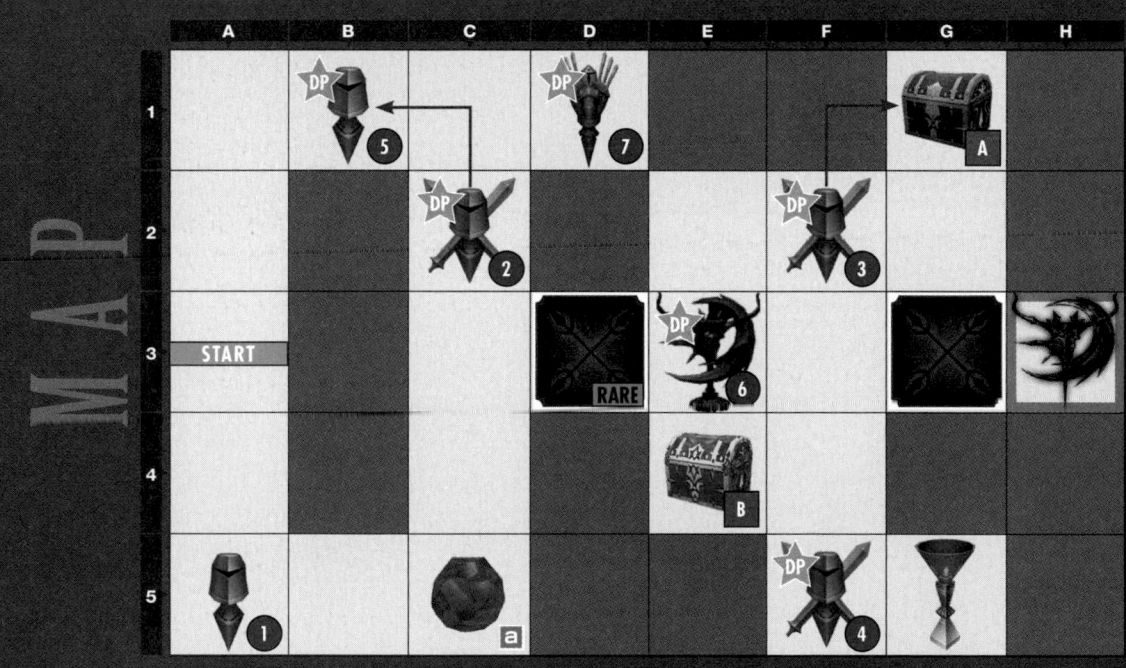

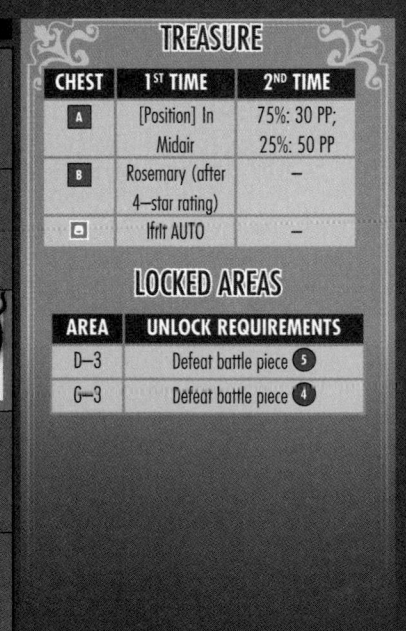

TREASURE

CHEST	1ST TIME	2ND TIME
A	[Position] In Midair	75%: 30 PP; 25%: 50 PP
B	Rosemary (after 4–star rating)	–
a	Ifrit AUTO	–

LOCKED AREAS

AREA	UNLOCK REQUIREMENTS
D–3	Defeat battle piece ⑤
G–3	Defeat battle piece ④

DP EFFICIENCY ROUTE

Max DP can only be accomplished here on a return trip. After completing Destiny Odyssey I enough times to unlock the 3-star bonus, new pieces appear on some of the levels. Here, an "ultimate" battle piece appears at D-1. From the start, head to C-1 and start a chain with both the battle piece at C-2 and the new ultimate battle piece. Next, the battle piece at B-1 appears, adding to the chain. This piece requires a critical hit within 10 seconds to score the DP, so save EX Force during the previous two fights so you can just enter EX Mode to make things simpler. Afterward, head to Ultimecia, then to F-4, where you can grab the new treasure chest that only appears on successive playthroughs after a 4-star rating is achieved. The adjacent battle piece will chain without costing you any DP. Finally, head to the Stigma of Chaos, ending the level.

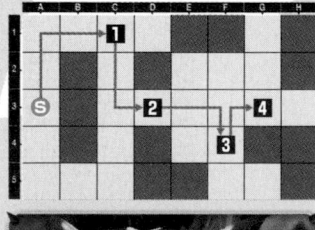

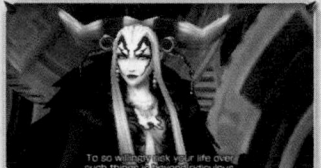

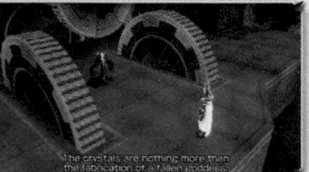

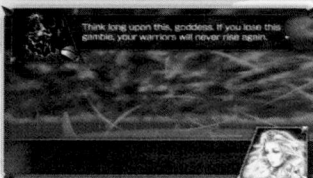

What is the goddess up to, consorting with a fiend like Golbez…?

BATTLE PIECE DATA

1 FALLACIOUS TREE

	LEVEL	5	RANK	G
BEHAVIOR	Evader			
DP CHANCE	–			
BATTLE MAP	Order's Sanctuary			
SUMMONSTONE	–			

STATS	HP	580	CP	354	BRV	118
	ATK	15	DEF	18	LUK	12

EQUIPMENT	WEAPON	–
	HANDS	

HEAD	–	BODY	Rusted Armor

SPOILS	GIL	112	EXP	0

2 DELUSORY WARLOCK

	LEVEL	10	RANK	E
BEHAVIOR	Aggressive			
DP CHANCE	Win without taking damage (DP+1)			
BATTLE MAP	Old Chaos Shrine			
SUMMONSTONE	–			

STATS	HP	1545	CP	341	BRV	180
	ATK	20	DEF	15	LUK	15

EQUIPMENT	WEAPON	–
	HANDS	Cracked Shield

HEAD	Mythril Helm	BODY	–

SPOILS	GIL	112	EXP	0

ACCESSORIES	Force Begets Courage, Gravitorb, Ivory Choker, [HP] HP ≤ 40% x3, [HP] Near Death x3

3 IMAGINARY CHAMPION

	LEVEL	10	RANK	E
BEHAVIOR	Standby			
DP CHANCE	Keep foe from getting EX Cores (DP+1)			
BATTLE MAP	Ultimecia's Castle			
SUMMONSTONE	–			

STATS	HP	1545	CP	341	BRV	180
	ATK	20	DEF	14	LUK	15

EQUIPMENT	WEAPON	–
	HANDS	Cracked Shield

HEAD	Mythril Helm	BODY	–

SPOILS	GIL	112	EXP	0

ACCESSORIES	Force Begets Courage, Gravitorb, Ivory Choker, [HP] HP ≤ 40% x3, [HP] Near Death x3

4 EPHEMERAL PHANTOM

	LEVEL	11	RANK	E
BEHAVIOR	Evader			
DP CHANCE	Wall Rush within 10 seconds (DP +1)			
BATTLE MAP	World of Darkness			
SUMMONSTONE	–			

STATS	HP	1606	CP	342	BRV	136*
	ATK	23	DEF	20*	LUK	15

EQUIPMENT	WEAPON	–
	HANDS	Cracked Shield

HEAD	[Rank 4]	BODY	–

SPOILS	GIL	112	EXP	894

5 CAPRICIOUS REAPER

	LEVEL	6	RANK	G
BEHAVIOR	Standby			
DP CHANCE	Critical hit within 10 seconds (DP+1)			
BATTLE MAP	Old Chaos Shrine			
SUMMONSTONE	–			

STATS	HP	641	CP	336	BRV	124
	ATK	15	DEF	17	LUK	13

EQUIPMENT	WEAPON	–
	HANDS	

HEAD	–	BODY	Rusted Armor

SPOILS	GIL	112	EXP	0

6 ULTIMECIA

	LEVEL	13	RANK	D
BEHAVIOR	Cautious			
DP CHANCE	BRV Break within 10 seconds			
BATTLE MAP	Ultimecia's Castle			
SUMMONSTONE	–			

STATS	HP	2042	CP	344	BRV	252
	ATK	27	DEF	23	LUK	16

EQUIPMENT	WEAPON	Rod
	HANDS	–

HEAD	Leather Hat	BODY	Robe

SPOILS	GIL	336	EXP	1727

7 FALSE STALWART

	LEVEL	26	RANK	B
BEHAVIOR	Extreme			
DP CHANCE	Win Battle (DP+2)			
BATTLE MAP	Order's Sanctuary			
SUMMONSTONE	–			

STATS	HP	2515*	CP	360	BRV	297
	ATK	56	DEF	54	LUK	23

EQUIPMENT	WEAPON	[Rank 5]
	HANDS	Knight's Shield

HEAD	Knight Helm	BODY	[Rank 4]

SPOILS	GIL	336	EXP	2113

ACCESSORIES	Force Begets Courage, Gravitorb, Ivory Choker, [HP] HP ≤ 40% x3, [HP] Near Death x3

* Denotes use of the base value (for stats that vary).

DESTINY ODYSSEY I

DESTINY ODYSSEY I-4

STARTING DP	MAX FINISHING	ENGAGEMENTS
5	5	7

Pay attention to the red battle piece, a new addition on this level—this adversary engages *you* first if you approach it on the board. Beware getting close unless you're ready for combat! This level also holds a rare treasure chest containing a Rosetta Stone, which only appears after clearing Destiny Odyssey I with a 4-star rating. This rare chest is hidden away behind a Locked Area that only disappears on a return trip, provided you've achieved at least a 2-star bonus. Rosetta Stones can be traded in the shop for more accessory slots!

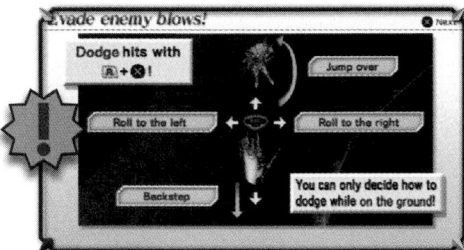

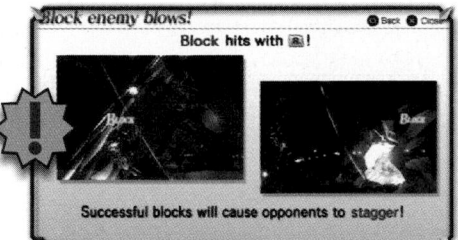

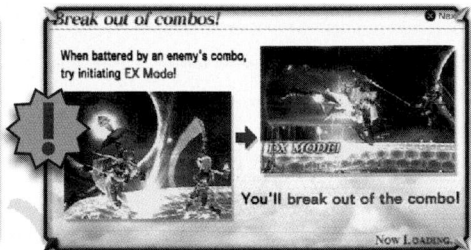

MAP

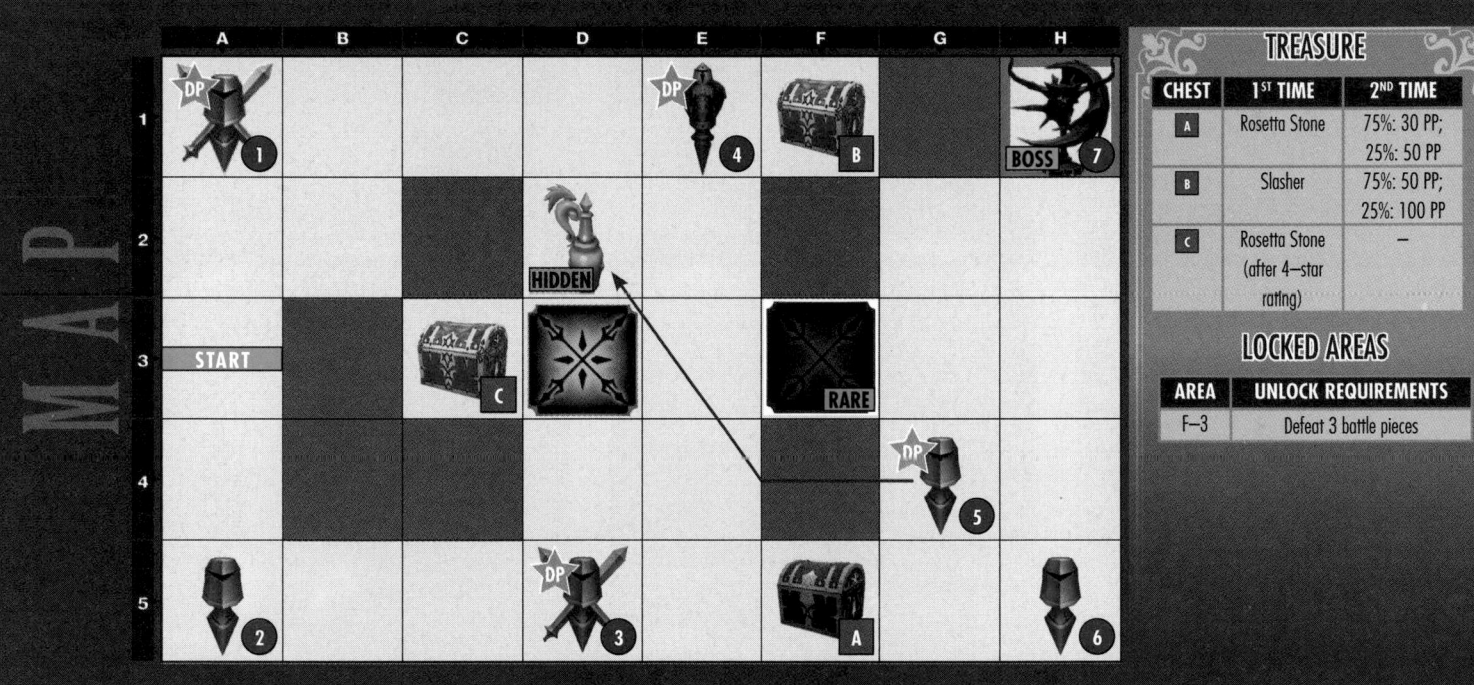

TREASURE

CHEST	1ST TIME	2ND TIME
A	Rosetta Stone	75%: 30 PP; 25%: 50 PP
B	Slasher	75%: 50 PP; 25%: 100 PP
C	Rosetta Stone (after 4-star rating)	—

LOCKED AREAS

AREA	UNLOCK REQUIREMENTS
F–3	Defeat 3 battle pieces

DP EFFICIENCY ROUTE

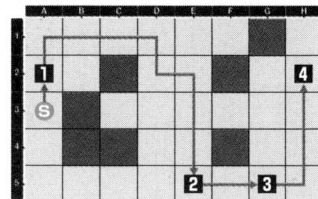

This level is relatively straightforward. You'll want to successfully clear DP Chances against battle pieces ① and ④, then open the A treasure chest while next to battle piece ③, making it go Berserk and chain you. After that, chain battle pieces ⑤ and ⑥ before heading to the boss. Note that the "win without taking damage" criteria for some DP Chances *includes* avoiding bravery attacks, even though they do not inflict HP damage.

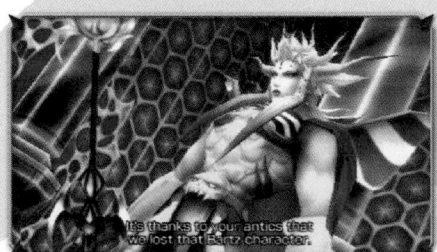

Apparently, Warrior of Light's arrival allows Bartz to slip away from The Emperor. The Emperor attempts to take his frustration out on this new hero on the scene, first through deception, then through combat.

BATTLE PIECE DATA

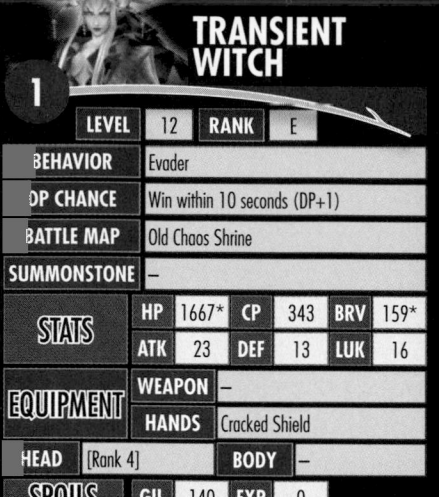

1 TRANSIENT WITCH

LEVEL	12	RANK	E

BEHAVIOR	Evader
DP CHANCE	Win within 10 seconds (DP+1)
BATTLE MAP	Old Chaos Shrine
SUMMONSTONE	—

STATS	HP	1667*	CP	343	BRV	159*
	ATK	23	DEF	13	LUK	16

EQUIPMENT	WEAPON	—
	HANDS	Cracked Shield

HEAD	[Rank 4]	BODY	—

SPOILS	GIL	140	EXP	0

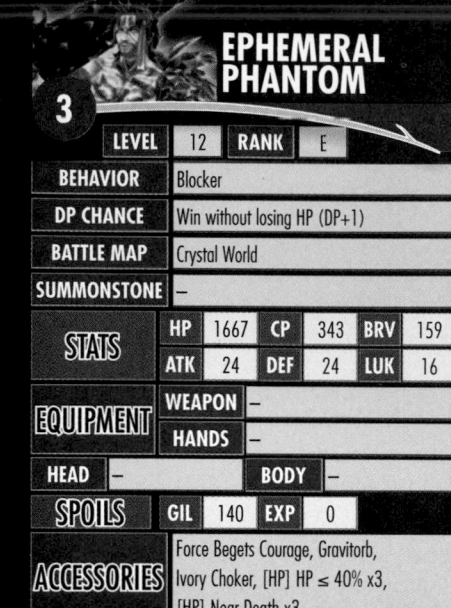

2 FALLACIOUS TREE

LEVEL	7	RANK	G

BEHAVIOR	Tricky
DP CHANCE	—
BATTLE MAP	Pandaemonium
SUMMONSTONE	—

STATS	HP	1364	CP	356	BRV	130
	ATK	17	DEF	20	LUK	13

EQUIPMENT	WEAPON	—
	HANDS	—

HEAD	—	BODY	—

SPOILS	GIL	140	EXP	0

3 EPHEMERAL PHANTOM

LEVEL	12	RANK	E

BEHAVIOR	Blocker
DP CHANCE	Win without losing HP (DP+1)
BATTLE MAP	Crystal World
SUMMONSTONE	—

STATS	HP	1667	CP	343	BRV	159
	ATK	24	DEF	24	LUK	16

EQUIPMENT	WEAPON	—
	HANDS	—

HEAD	—	BODY	—

SPOILS	GIL	140	EXP	0

ACCESSORIES	Force Begets Courage, Gravitorb, Ivory Choker, [HP] HP ≤ 40% x3, [HP] Near Death x3

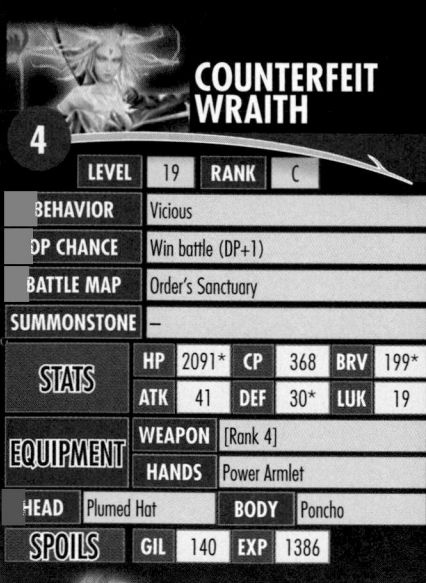

4 COUNTERFEIT WRAITH

LEVEL	19	RANK	C

BEHAVIOR	Vicious
DP CHANCE	Win battle (DP+1)
BATTLE MAP	Order's Sanctuary
SUMMONSTONE	—

STATS	HP	2091*	CP	368	BRV	199*
	ATK	41	DEF	30*	LUK	19

EQUIPMENT	WEAPON	[Rank 4]
	HANDS	Power Armlet

HEAD	Plumed Hat	BODY	Poncho

SPOILS	GIL	140	EXP	1386

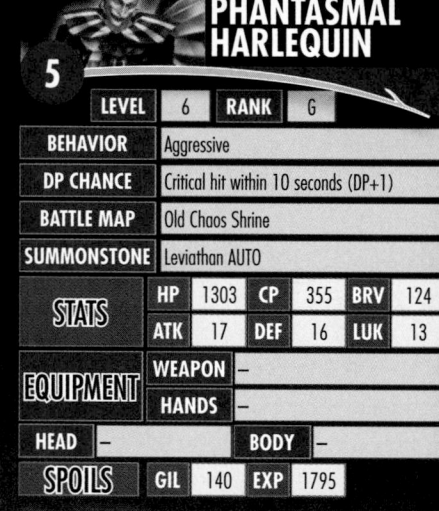

5 PHANTASMAL HARLEQUIN

LEVEL	6	RANK	G

BEHAVIOR	Aggressive
DP CHANCE	Critical hit within 10 seconds (DP+1)
BATTLE MAP	Old Chaos Shrine
SUMMONSTONE	Leviathan AUTO

STATS	HP	1303	CP	355	BRV	124
	ATK	17	DEF	16	LUK	13

EQUIPMENT	WEAPON	—
	HANDS	—

HEAD	—	BODY	—

SPOILS	GIL	140	EXP	1795

6 CAPRICIOUS REAPER

LEVEL	5	RANK	G

BEHAVIOR	Aggressive
DP CHANCE	Win without taking damage (DP+1)
BATTLE MAP	Order's Sanctuary
SUMMONSTONE	—

STATS	HP	1145	CP	335	BRV	180
	ATK	14	DEF	8	LUK	12

EQUIPMENT	WEAPON	—
	HANDS	Cracked Shield

HEAD	Hairpin	BODY	—

SPOILS	GIL	140	EXP	0

7 THE EMPEROR

LEVEL	15	RANK	D

BEHAVIOR	Calm
DP CHANCE	—
BATTLE MAP	Pandaemonium
SUMMONSTONE	Iron Giant

STATS	HP	2101	CP	347	BRV	280
	ATK	33	DEF	27	LUK	17

EQUIPMENT	WEAPON	Oak Staff
	HANDS	—

HEAD	Plumed Hat	BODY	Robe

SPOILS	GIL	420	EXP	3696

ACCESSORIES	Earring x2, Star Earring, [Position] Far from Opponent x2

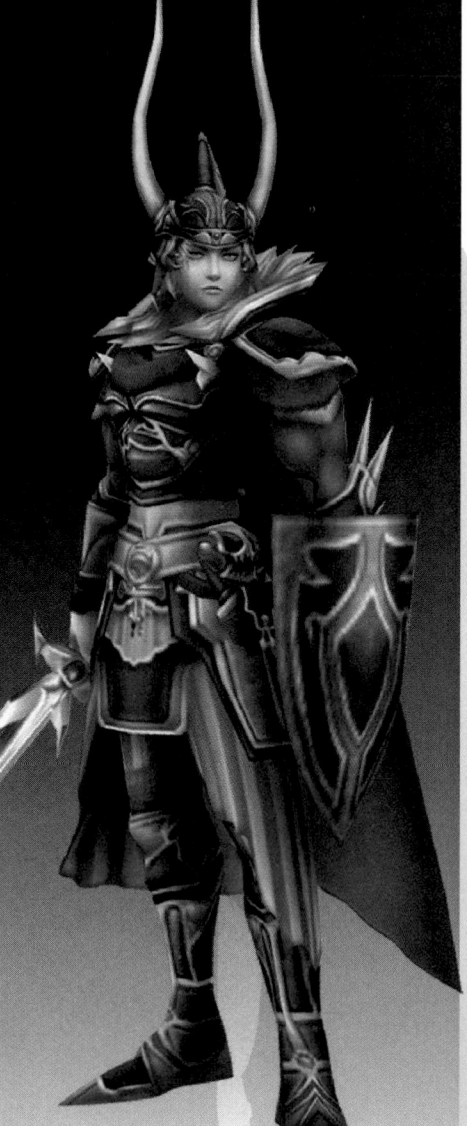

* Denotes use of the base value (for stats that vary).

DESTINY ODYSSEY I

DESTINY ODYSSEY

I-5

STARTING DP	MAX FINISHING	ENGAGEMENTS
4	5	7
	(+2 after 3–star rating)	(+1 after 3–star rating)

This stage appears barren initially, but quickly reveals itself to be laden with tricks and traps. Battle pieces ❶ and ❷, as well as treasure chest Ⓐ, all spawn more battle pieces that are likely in position to force you into a battle chain. An ultimate battle piece and a rare treasure chest only appear here after you've achieved a sufficient bonus on previous runs (3- and 4-star, respectively). The ultimate battle piece is significantly harder than anything else in Destiny Odyssey I, including bosses, so play a cautious hit-and-run style. After three battle pieces are defeated, a path opens to the boss. When you defeat four battle pieces on this level, a Potion appears at F-5.

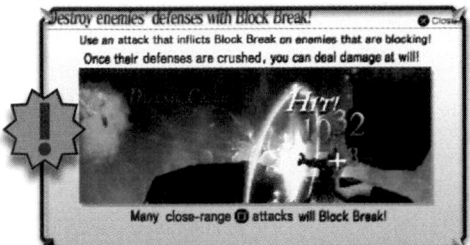
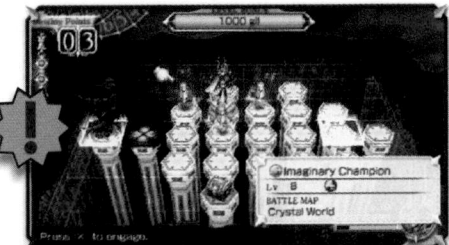
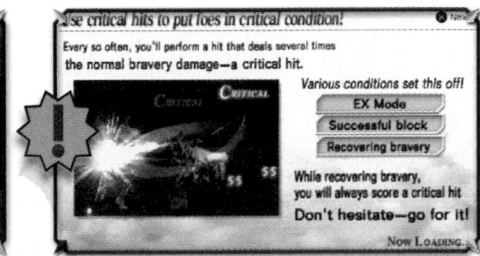

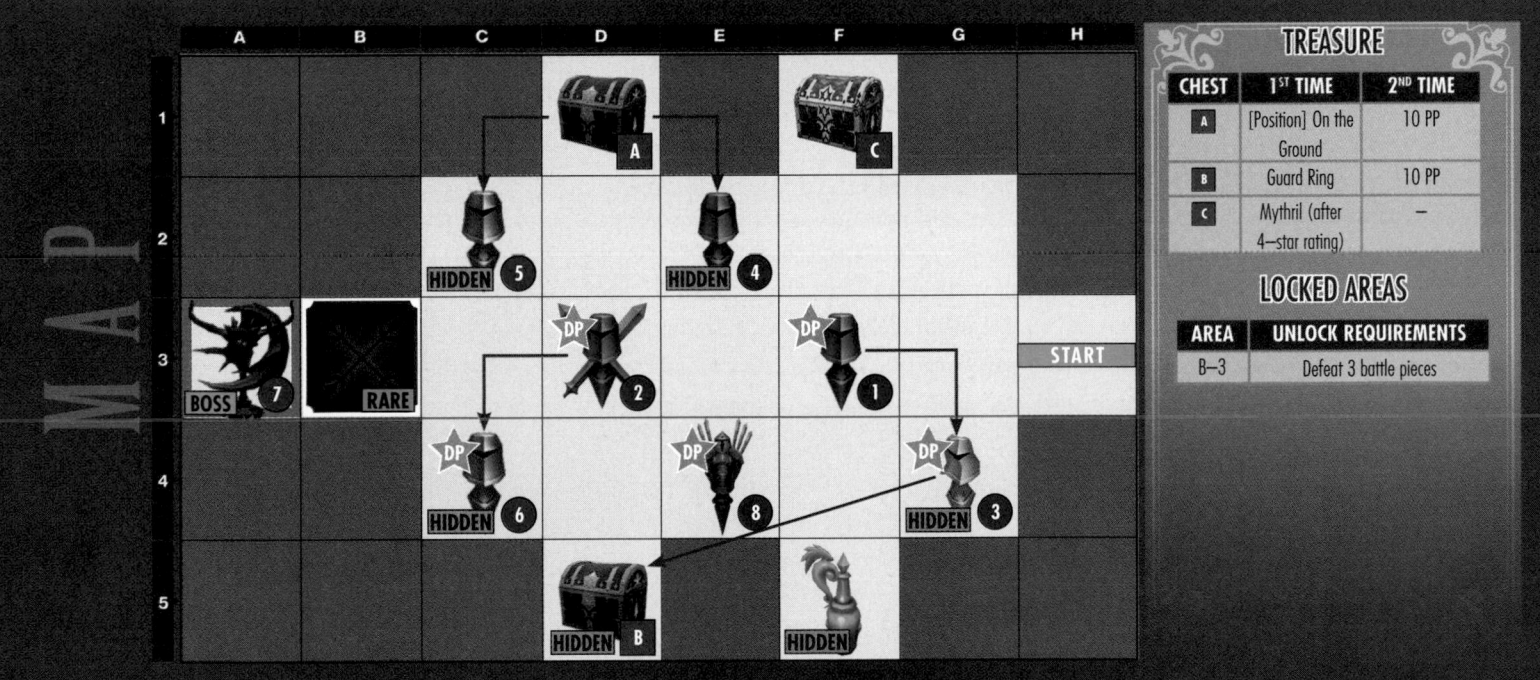

TREASURE

CHEST	1ST TIME	2ND TIME
A	[Position] On the Ground	10 PP
B	Guard Ring	10 PP
C	Mythril (after 4–star rating)	–

LOCKED AREAS

AREA	UNLOCK REQUIREMENTS
B–3	Defeat 3 battle pieces

DP EFFICIENCY ROUTE

Until you achieve a 3-star bonus on previous runs, you can't obtain the maximum DP on this final level. Once you do, though, it's a pretty linear path. Proceed to F-4 and engage either battle piece ❶ or ❽. This leads to a chain with the newly revealed battle piece ❸. Since the battle with piece ❸ requires an EX Burst within 10 seconds to fulfill the DP Chance there, stock up on EX Force during the battles with pieces ❶ and ❽, so you're ready in advance. Afterward, proceed to D-4, where you can open the treasure chest and cause a chain with battle pieces ❷ and ❻. Finally, proceed to the Stigma of Chaos for the boss battle with Garland, and the conclusion of Destiny Odyssey I.

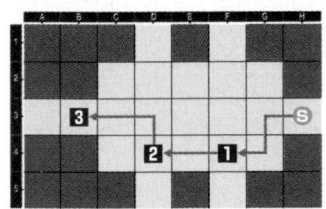
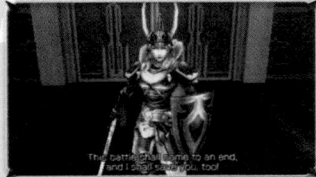
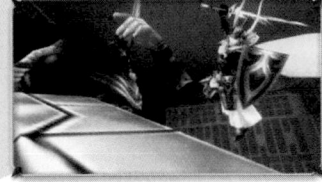
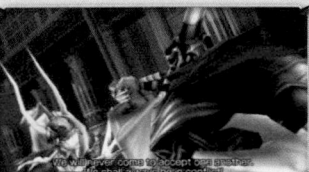
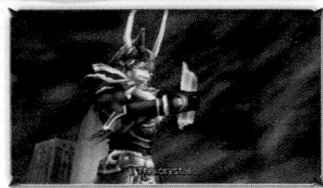

BATTLE PIECE DATA

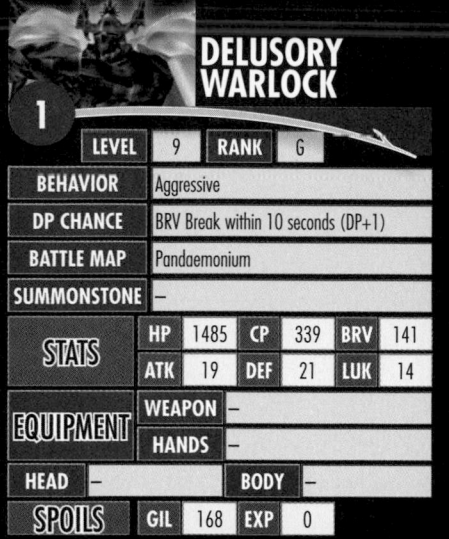

1 DELUSORY WARLOCK

LEVEL	9	RANK	G

BEHAVIOR	Aggressive
DP CHANCE	BRV Break within 10 seconds (DP+1)
BATTLE MAP	Pandaemonium
SUMMONSTONE	–

STATS	HP	1485	CP	339	BRV	141
	ATK	19	DEF	21	LUK	14

EQUIPMENT	WEAPON	–
	HANDS	–

HEAD	–	BODY	–

SPOILS	GIL	168	EXP	0

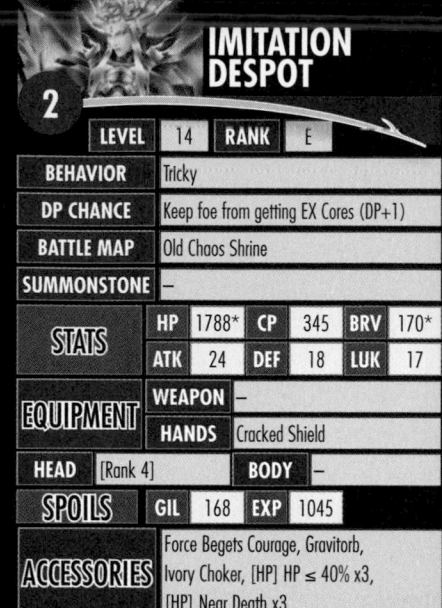

2 IMITATION DESPOT

LEVEL	14	RANK	E

BEHAVIOR	Tricky
DP CHANCE	Keep foe from getting EX Cores (DP+1)
BATTLE MAP	Old Chaos Shrine
SUMMONSTONE	–

STATS	HP	1788*	CP	345	BRV	170*
	ATK	24	DEF	18	LUK	17

EQUIPMENT	WEAPON	–
	HANDS	Cracked Shield

HEAD	[Rank 4]	BODY	–

SPOILS	GIL	168	EXP	1045

ACCESSORIES	Force Begets Courage, Gravitorb, Ivory Choker, [HP] HP ≤ 40% x3, [HP] Near Death x3

3 COUNTERFEIT YOUTH

LEVEL	15	RANK	B

BEHAVIOR	Summoner
DP CHANCE	EX Burst within 10 seconds (DP+1)
BATTLE MAP	Ultimecia's Castle
SUMMONSTONE	Carbuncle

STATS	HP	1	CP	364	BRV	0
	ATK	22	DEF	18	LUK	17

EQUIPMENT	WEAPON	–
	HANDS	Cracked Shield

HEAD	Beret	BODY	Rusted Armor

SPOILS	GIL	168	EXP	3696

ACCESSORIES	The Rotten, Soul of the Craven, Guardian Bangle, [HP] HP = 1 x3

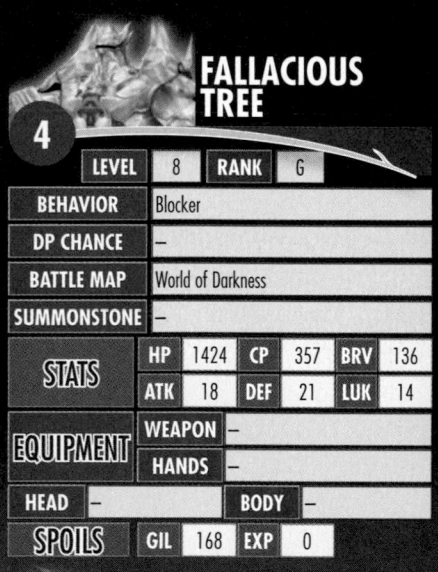

4 FALLACIOUS TREE

LEVEL	8	RANK	G

BEHAVIOR	Blocker
DP CHANCE	–
BATTLE MAP	World of Darkness
SUMMONSTONE	–

STATS	HP	1424	CP	357	BRV	136
	ATK	18	DEF	21	LUK	14

EQUIPMENT	WEAPON	–
	HANDS	–

HEAD	–	BODY	–

SPOILS	GIL	168	EXP	0

5 IMAGINARY CHAMPION

LEVEL	8	RANK	G

BEHAVIOR	Normal
DP CHANCE	–
BATTLE MAP	Crystal Map
SUMMONSTONE	Cactuar

STATS	HP	1424	CP	338	BRV	136
	ATK	18	DEF	19	LUK	14

EQUIPMENT	WEAPON	–
	HANDS	–

HEAD	–	BODY	–

SPOILS	GIL	168	EXP	0

6 TRANSIENT WITCH

LEVEL	9	RANK	G

BEHAVIOR	Tricky
DP CHANCE	Win without taking damage (DP+1)
BATTLE MAP	Pandaemonium
SUMMONSTONE	Alexander

STATS	HP	1485	CP	339	BRV	141
	ATK	20	DEF	18	LUK	14

EQUIPMENT	WEAPON	–
	HANDS	–

HEAD	–	BODY	–

SPOILS	GIL	168	EXP	0

7 GARLAND

LEVEL	18	RANK	D

BEHAVIOR	Valiant
DP CHANCE	–
BATTLE MAP	Old Chaos Shrine
SUMMONSTONE	Magic Pot

STATS	HP	2640	CP	350	BRV	234
	ATK	41	DEF	35	LUK	19

EQUIPMENT	WEAPON	Light Axe
	HANDS	Buckler

HEAD	Iron Helm	BODY	Iron Armor

SPOILS	GIL	504	EXP	5075

ACCESSORIES	Muscle Belt x2, Champion Belt, [Position] Near Opponent x2, [Combat] Attacking Bravery

8 FALSE HERO

LEVEL	30	RANK	B

BEHAVIOR	Survivor
DP CHANCE	Win battle (DP+2)
BATTLE MAP	Old Chaos Shrine
SUMMONSTONE	Ifrit

STATS	HP	2757*	CP	365	BRV	263*
	ATK	40*	DEF	43*	LUK	25

EQUIPMENT	WEAPON	[Rank 5]
	HANDS	[Rank 4]

HEAD	[Rank 6]	BODY	[Rank 4]

SPOILS	GIL	336	EXP	0

ACCESSORIES	Force Begets Courage, Gravitorb, Ivory Choker, [HP] HP ≤ 40% x3, [HP] Near Death x3

* Denotes use of the base value (for stats that vary).

DESTINY ODYSSEY I

DESTINY ODYSSEY II
THE UNENDING DREAM

REWARDS

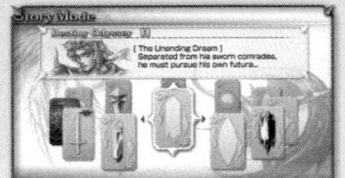

At the end of each level, rewards are available if you finish with a positive number of Destiny Points, or DP. This walkthrough includes miniature level maps that indicate the most efficient route to take through a given level in order to maximize DP.

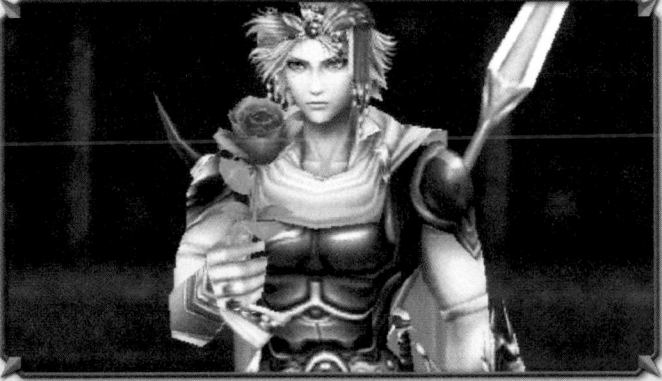

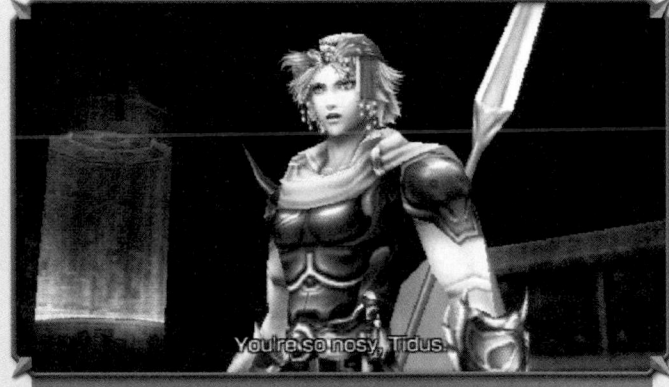

You're so nosy, Tidus.

Firion's reason to take up arms in the struggle is a simple, almost quaint dream…one he's a little embarrassed to share with his friends.

LEVEL COMPLETION

REMAINING DP		1ST TIME		2ND TIME
7		Rosetta Stone		300 PP
6		Ice Lance		200 PP
5		Flame Lance		120 PP
4		Malboro		80 PP
3		1000 gil		50 PP
2		600 gil		30 PP
1		300 gil		20 PP
0		100 gil		10 PP

DESTINY ODYSSEY II COMPLETION

STAR RATING		SP REQUIRED		AWARD
☆		100		New skill
☆☆		200		Special areas unlocked
☆☆☆		300		Rare battle pieces spawned
☆☆☆☆		400		Rare treasure chests spawned
–		500 SP, then every 500 SP extra		100 PP

At the end of each set of levels, you'll receive rewards based on your performance. Story Points, or SP, are awarded after each level based on remaining DP and HP, and on the number of engagements undertaken. Points are penalized for retries, or for a DP total that dips into negatives. If you miss out on a desired bonus on the first playthrough, don't worry—SP is cumulative across multiple playthroughs.

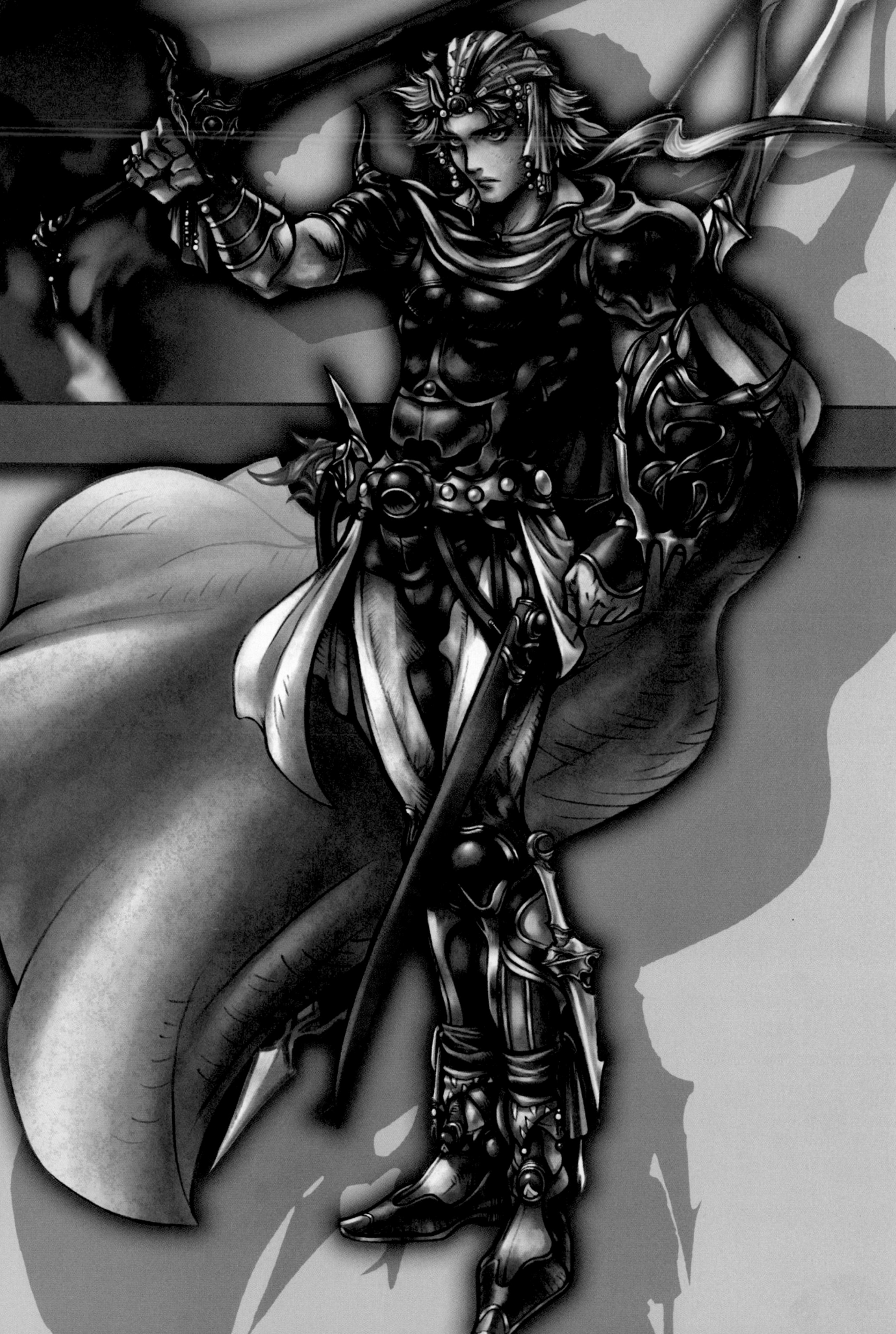

DESTINY ODYSSEY II

Firion is a master of many weapons, and uses many different kinds of attacks. In particular, his Straightarrow HP attack has enormous range, and you can get by many CPU-controlled foes by simply running away and firing Straightarrow repeatedly. While many CPU behavior types can successfully dodge it most of the time, none of them are able to dodge correctly *every* single time, making this an effective strategy. The attack can be "charged"—when you press ● to start the attack, continue holding the button down. Firion won't fire until you let go—if the enemy dodges prematurely, you can then fire the arrow into them during the tail-end of their dodge, while they are vulnerable. Firion's levels are split up into varying paths. It's up to you to select which route to take to the Stigma of Chaos. You can also opt to clear the levels out completely, but this can result in negative DP totals and poor level scores. This beginning level features a few rather weak foes, as well as a treasure chest containing a Spear for Firion. Engaging the Stigma of Chaos ends the level without a fight.

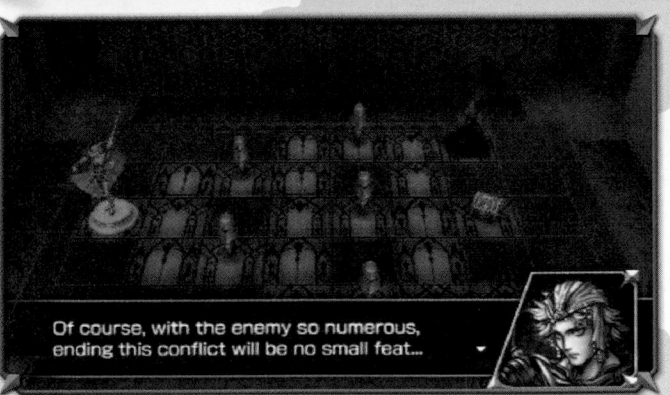

Of course, with the enemy so numerous, ending this conflict will be no small feat...

MAP

TREASURE

CHEST	1ST TIME	2ND TIME
A	Spear	75%: 30 PP; 25%: 50 PP

LOCKED AREAS

AREA	UNLOCK REQUIREMENTS
	—

DP EFFICIENCY ROUTE

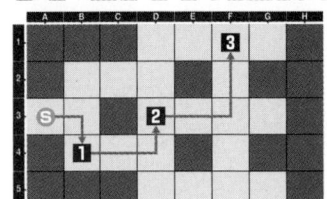

The fastest route through this level is pretty simple. Just take out battle pieces ❷ and ❹, the only fights with DP Chances, before heading to the exit.

BATTLE PIECE DATA

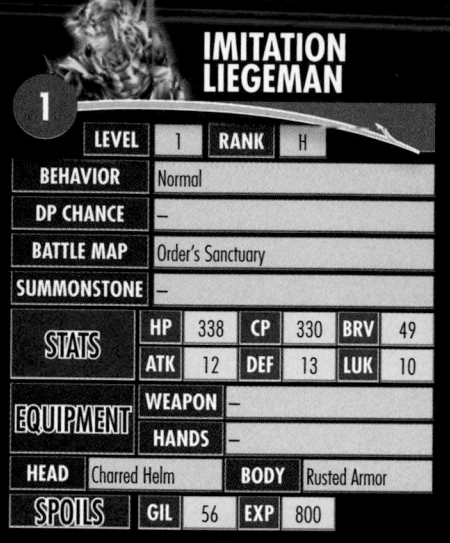

1 — IMITATION LIEGEMAN

| LEVEL | 1 | RANK | H |

BEHAVIOR	Normal
DP CHANCE	—
BATTLE MAP	Order's Sanctuary
SUMMONSTONE	—

STATS

HP	338	CP	330	BRV	49
ATK	12	DEF	13	LUK	10

EQUIPMENT

WEAPON	—
HANDS	—

| HEAD | Charred Helm | BODY | Rusted Armor |

SPOILS

| GIL | 56 | EXP | 800 |

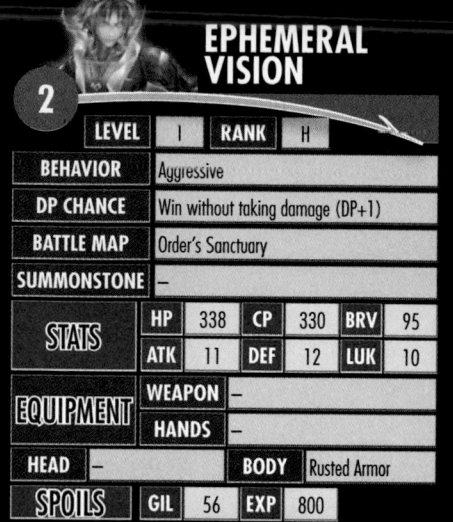

2 — EPHEMERAL VISION

| LEVEL | 1 | RANK | H |

BEHAVIOR	Aggressive
DP CHANCE	Win without taking damage (DP+1)
BATTLE MAP	Order's Sanctuary
SUMMONSTONE	—

STATS

HP	338	CP	330	BRV	95
ATK	11	DEF	12	LUK	10

EQUIPMENT

WEAPON	—
HANDS	—

| HEAD | — | BODY | Rusted Armor |

SPOILS

| GIL | 56 | EXP | 800 |

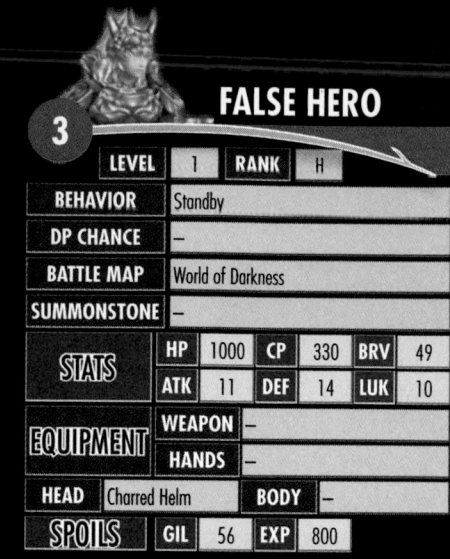

3 — FALSE HERO

| LEVEL | 1 | RANK | H |

BEHAVIOR	Standby
DP CHANCE	—
BATTLE MAP	World of Darkness
SUMMONSTONE	—

STATS

HP	1000	CP	330	BRV	49
ATK	11	DEF	14	LUK	10

EQUIPMENT

WEAPON	—
HANDS	—

| HEAD | Charred Helm | BODY | — |

SPOILS

| GIL | 56 | EXP | 800 |

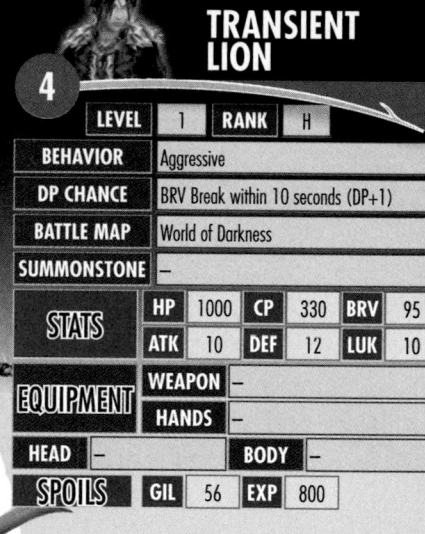

4 — TRANSIENT LION

| LEVEL | 1 | RANK | H |

BEHAVIOR	Aggressive
DP CHANCE	BRV Break within 10 seconds (DP+1)
BATTLE MAP	World of Darkness
SUMMONSTONE	—

STATS

HP	1000	CP	330	BRV	95
ATK	10	DEF	12	LUK	10

EQUIPMENT

WEAPON	—
HANDS	—

| HEAD | — | BODY | — |

SPOILS

| GIL | 56 | EXP | 800 |

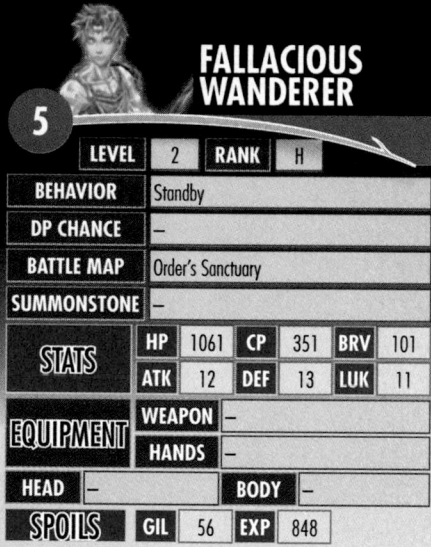

5 — FALLACIOUS WANDERER

| LEVEL | 2 | RANK | H |

BEHAVIOR	Standby
DP CHANCE	—
BATTLE MAP	Order's Sanctuary
SUMMONSTONE	—

STATS

HP	1061	CP	351	BRV	101
ATK	12	DEF	13	LUK	11

EQUIPMENT

WEAPON	—
HANDS	—

| HEAD | — | BODY | — |

SPOILS

| GIL | 56 | EXP | 848 |

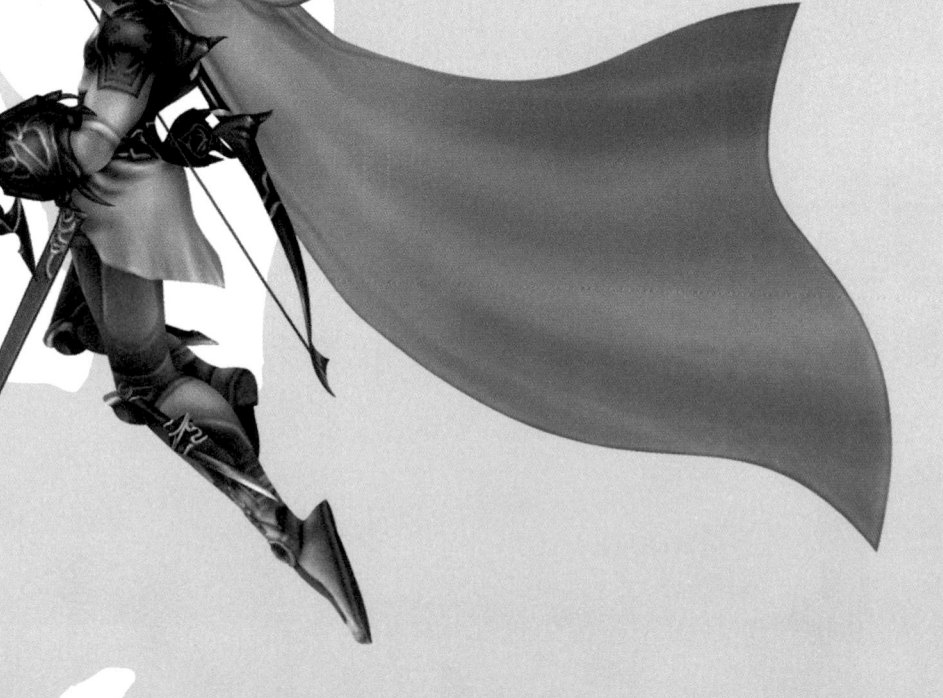

DESTINY ODYSSEY II

DESTINY ODYSSEY

II-2

STARTING DP 4   **MAX FINISHING** 4   **ENGAGEMENTS** 6

Firion's second level again contains alternate routes heading to the exit. Grab the Leather Armor from the treasure chest located at G-1. The Shiva Summonstone is also here, but it is not available until return visits, after a 2-star rating. The way to the boss is opened by defeating battle piece ④, which you'll want to do anyway since the battle offers a DP Chance. Against the boss, Jecht, keep your distance and pepper him with Firion's long-range arsenal.

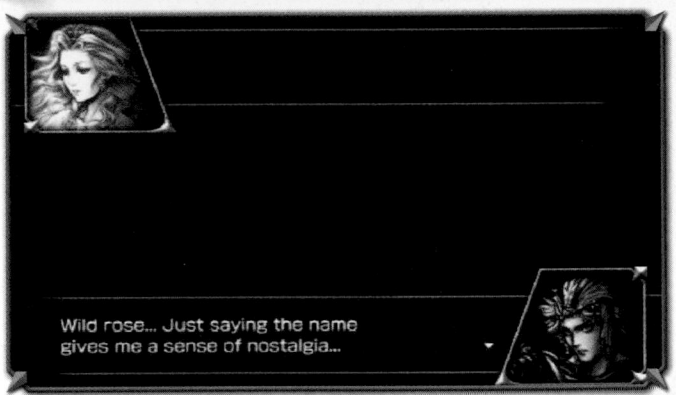

> Wild rose... Just saying the name gives me a sense of nostalgia...

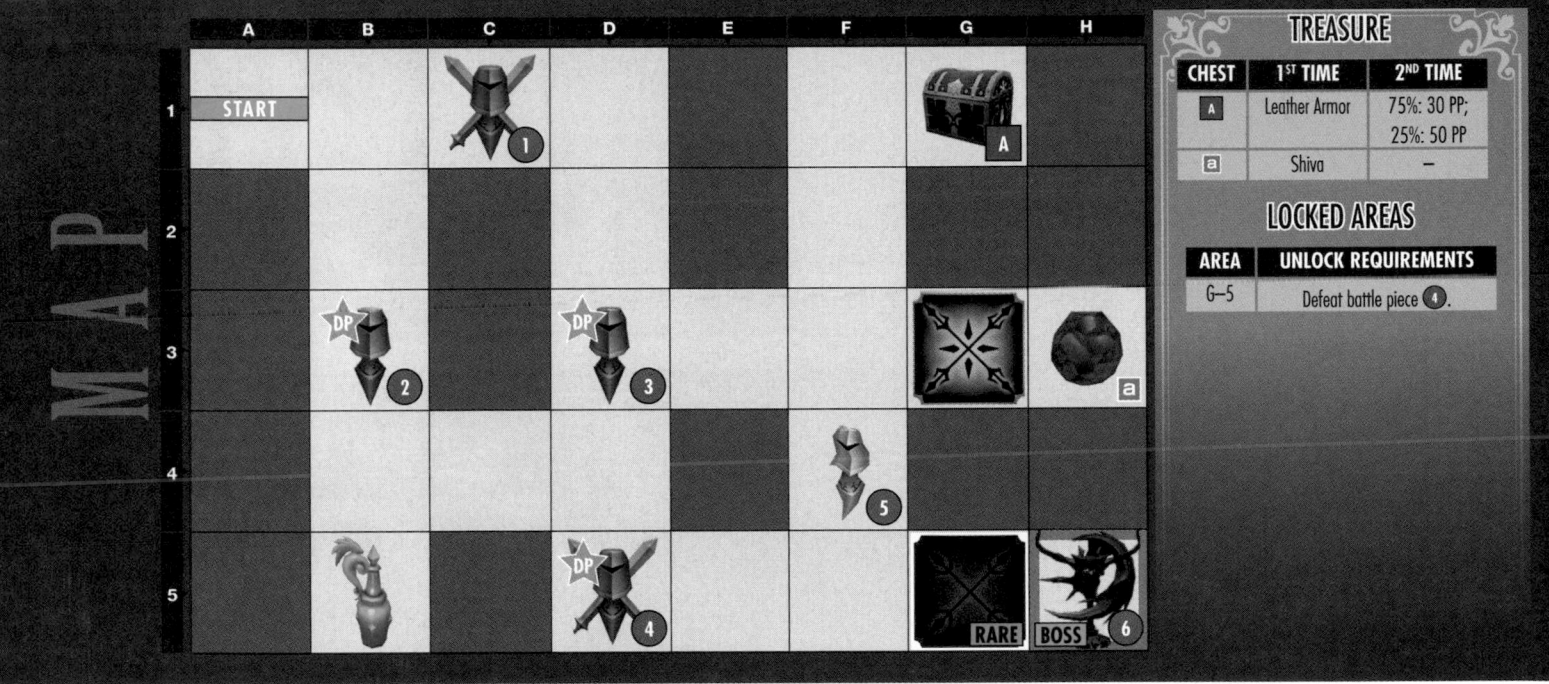

TREASURE

CHEST	1ST TIME	2ND TIME
A	Leather Armor	75%: 30 PP; 25%: 50 PP
a	Shiva	—

LOCKED AREAS

AREA	UNLOCK REQUIREMENTS
G—5	Defeat battle piece ④.

DP EFFICIENCY ROUTE

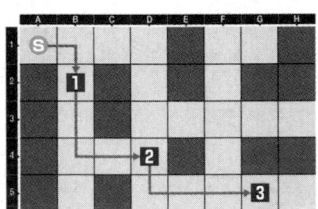

From the start, head downward and engage battle piece ②. You won't have an opportunity to build EX Force beforehand in order to guarantee critical hits in EX Mode, so instead you may want to attempt an immediate HP attack followed by a bravery attack (a guaranteed critical hit while your bravery recovers after the HP attack), or block an attack and counter. Afterward, head to D-4 and chain battle pieces ③ and ④. Save up a full EX Gauge during the fight with battle piece ③, so you'll be able to use an EX Burst immediately against battle piece ④.

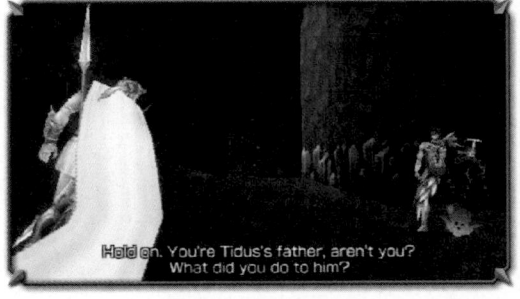

> Hold on. You're Tidus's father, aren't you? What did you do to him?

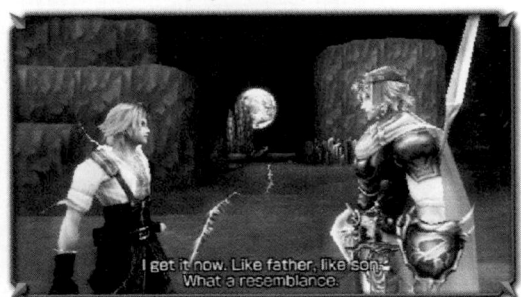

> I get it now. Like father, like son. What a resemblance.

BATTLE PIECE DATA

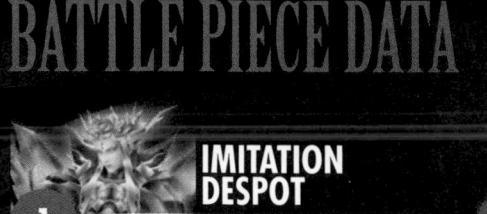

1 IMITATION DESPOT

LEVEL	4	RANK	G

BEHAVIOR	Normal
DP CHANCE	–
BATTLE MAP	World of Darkness
SUMMONSTONE	

STATS	HP	1182	CP	333	BRV	113
	ATK	14	DEF	8	LUK	12

EQUIPMENT	WEAPON	–
	HANDS	Cracked Shield

HEAD	–	BODY	–

SPOILS	GIL	84	EXP	945

ACCESSORIES	Arcane Resin, Gravitorb, Attractorb x2, [Position] Far from Opponent x6

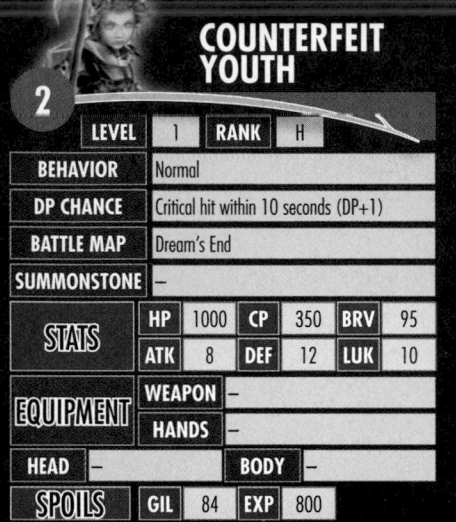

2 COUNTERFEIT YOUTH

LEVEL	1	RANK	H

BEHAVIOR	Normal
DP CHANCE	Critical hit within 10 seconds (DP+1)
BATTLE MAP	Dream's End
SUMMONSTONE	

STATS	HP	1000	CP	350	BRV	95
	ATK	8	DEF	12	LUK	10

EQUIPMENT	WEAPON	–
	HANDS	–

HEAD	–	BODY	–

SPOILS	GIL	84	EXP	800

3 PHANTASMAL GIRL

LEVEL	1	RANK	H

BEHAVIOR	Aggressive
DP CHANCE	Win within 10 seconds (DP+1)
BATTLE MAP	Dream's End
SUMMONSTONE	

STATS	HP	1000	CP	330	BRV	95
	ATK	12	DEF	11	LUK	10

EQUIPMENT	WEAPON	–
	HANDS	–

HEAD	–	BODY	–

SPOILS	GIL	84	EXP	800

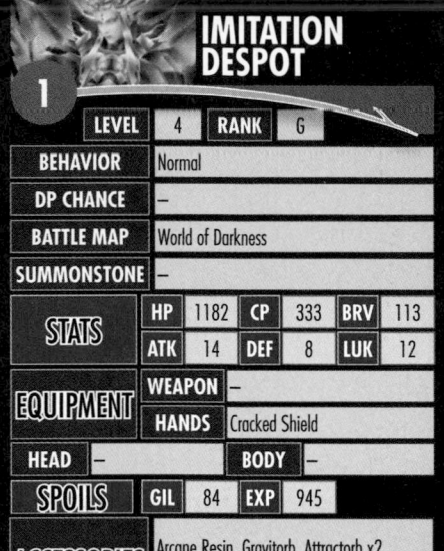

4 EPHEMERAL VISION

LEVEL	4	RANK	G

BEHAVIOR	Aggressive
DP CHANCE	EX Burst within 10 seconds (DP+1)
BATTLE MAP	Order's Sanctuary
SUMMONSTONE	

STATS	HP	1182	CP	333	BRV	113
	ATK	14	DEF	7	LUK	12

EQUIPMENT	WEAPON	–
	HANDS	Cracked Shield

HEAD	–	BODY	–

SPOILS	GIL	84	EXP	945

ACCESSORIES	Arcane Resin, Gravitorb, Attractorb x2, [Position] Far from Opponent x6

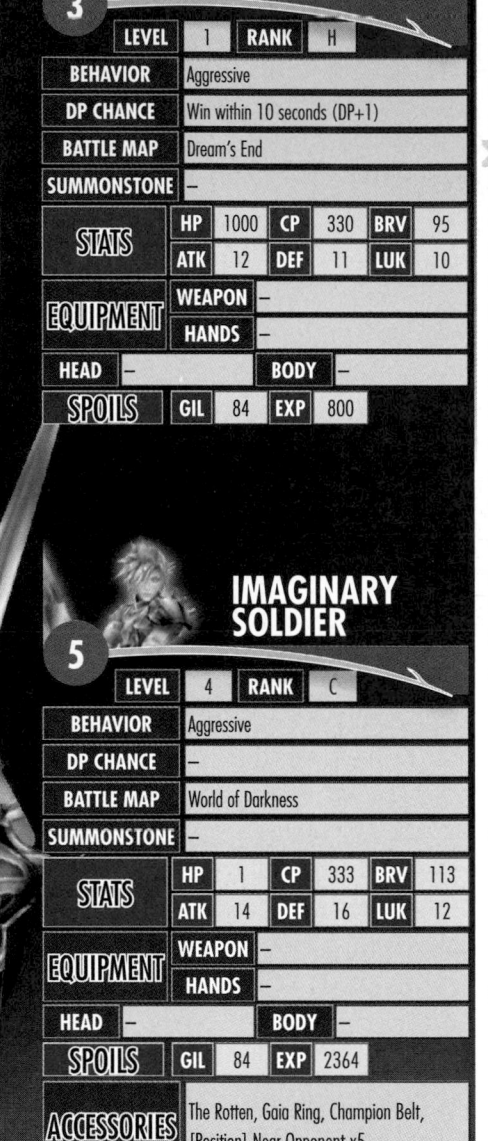

5 IMAGINARY SOLDIER

LEVEL	4	RANK	C

BEHAVIOR	Aggressive
DP CHANCE	–
BATTLE MAP	World of Darkness
SUMMONSTONE	

STATS	HP	1	CP	333	BRV	113
	ATK	14	DEF	16	LUK	12

EQUIPMENT	WEAPON	–
	HANDS	–

HEAD	–	BODY	–

SPOILS	GIL	84	EXP	2364

ACCESSORIES	The Rotten, Gaia Ring, Champion Belt, [Position] Near Opponent x5

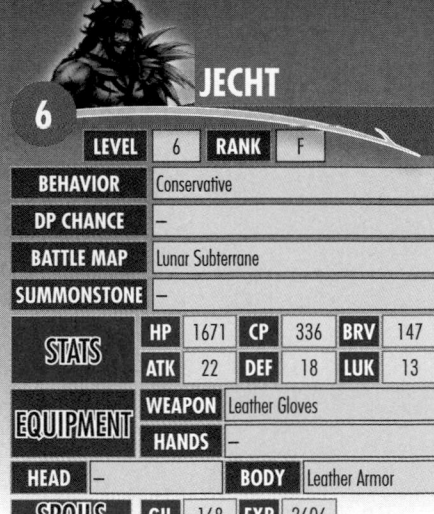

6 JECHT

LEVEL	6	RANK	F

BEHAVIOR	Conservative
DP CHANCE	–
BATTLE MAP	Lunar Subterrane
SUMMONSTONE	

STATS	HP	1671	CP	336	BRV	147
	ATK	22	DEF	18	LUK	13

EQUIPMENT	WEAPON	Leather Gloves
	HANDS	–

HEAD	–	BODY	Leather Armor

SPOILS	GIL	168	EXP	2606

DESTINY ODYSSEY II

Unlike most levels, which place you at an edge at the start, this one puts you dead center. However, opening the way to the Stigma of Chaos requires defeating battle piece **5** in the furthest bottom right corner. Along the way, battle piece **4** is an expert fight against an intimidating Exdeath manikin, but the actual battle isn't too bad—this foe falls apart against a constant, long-range barrage of Straightarrow. You can also defeat Ultimecia, the boss, in this manner.

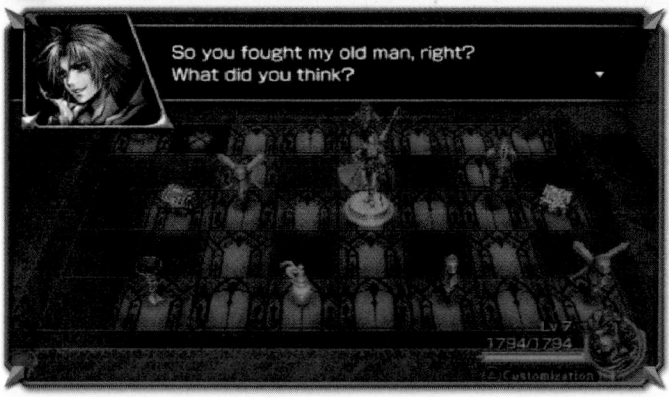

So you fought my old man, right?
What did you think?

MAP

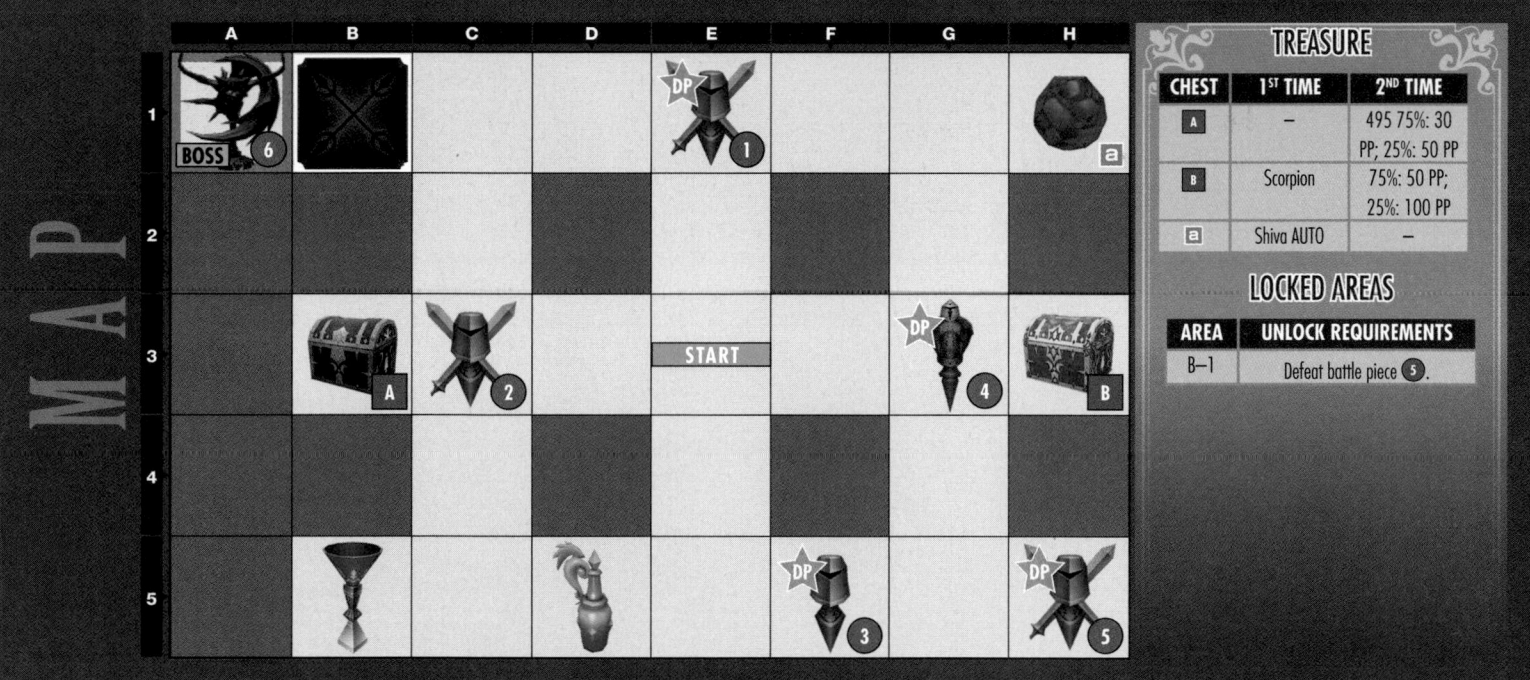

TREASURE

CHEST	1ST TIME	2ND TIME
A	–	495 75%: 30 PP; 25%: 50 PP
B	Scorpion	75%: 50 PP; 25%: 100 PP
a	Shiva AUTO	–

LOCKED AREAS

AREA	UNLOCK REQUIREMENTS
B–1	Defeat battle piece **5**.

DP EFFICIENCY ROUTE

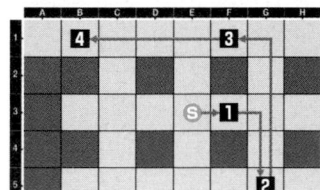

There are four DP Chances to take on here. Head right immediately and engage expert battle piece **4** before descending to chain battle pieces **3** and **5**. Afterward, take on battle piece **1** en route to the Stigma of Chaos, and the showdown with Ultimecia.

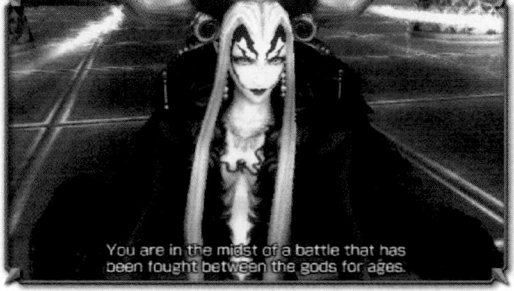

You are in the midst of a battle that has been fought between the gods for ages.

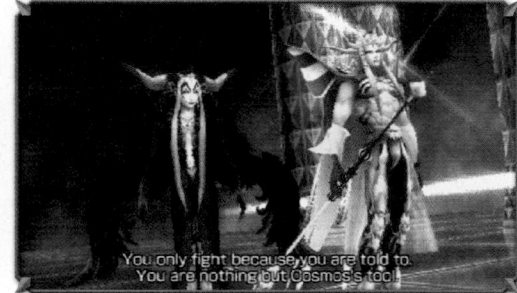

You only fight because you are told to. You are nothing but Cosmos's tool.

BATTLE PIECE DATA

1 IMITATION DESPOT

LEVEL	7	RANK	F

BEHAVIOR	Aggressive
DP CHANCE	Win within 10 seconds (DP+1)
BATTLE MAP	Dream's End
SUMMONSTONE	–

STATS	HP	1364	CP	337	BRV	130
	ATK	17	DEF	11	LUK	13

EQUIPMENT	WEAPON	–
	HANDS	Cracked Shield

HEAD	–		BODY	–

SPOILS	GIL	112	EXP	1091

ACCESSORIES	Arcane Resin, Gravitorb, Attractorb x2, [Position] Far from Opponent x6

2 TRANSIENT LION

LEVEL	6	RANK	F

BEHAVIOR	Aggressive
DP CHANCE	–
BATTLE MAP	Ultimecia's Castle
SUMMONSTONE	–

STATS	HP	1303	CP	336	BRV	124
	ATK	15	DEF	9	LUK	13

EQUIPMENT	WEAPON	–
	HANDS	Cracked Shield

HEAD	–		BODY	–

SPOILS	GIL	112	EXP	1042

ACCESSORIES	Arcane Incense, Gravitorb, Attractorb x2, [Position] Far from Opponent x6

3 PHANTASMAL GIRL

LEVEL	2	RANK	G

BEHAVIOR	Normal
DP CHANCE	Win without taking damage (DP+1)
BATTLE MAP	World of Darkness
SUMMONSTONE	–

STATS	HP	399	CP	331	BRV	101
	ATK	13	DEF	12	LUK	11

EQUIPMENT	WEAPON	–
	HANDS	–

HEAD	–		BODY	Rusted Armor

SPOILS	GIL	112	EXP	848

4 FALLACIOUS TREE

LEVEL	15	RANK	C

BEHAVIOR	Calm
DP CHANCE	Win battle (DP+1)
BATTLE MAP	Order's Sanctuary
SUMMONSTONE	–

STATS	HP	1848*	CP	364	BRV	176*
	ATK	38	DEF	28*	LUK	17

EQUIPMENT	WEAPON	[Rank 4]
	HANDS	[Rank 2]

HEAD	Iron Helm		BODY	[Rank 3]

SPOILS	GIL	112	EXP	0

* Denotes use of the base value (for stats that vary).

5 DELUSORY WARLOCK

LEVEL	6	RANK	F

BEHAVIOR	Normal
DP CHANCE	BRV Break within 10 seconds (DP+1)
BATTLE MAP	World of Darkness
SUMMONSTONE	–

STATS	HP	1303	CP	336	BRV	124
	ATK	16	DEF	10	LUK	13

EQUIPMENT	WEAPON	–
	HANDS	Cracked Shield

HEAD	–		BODY	–

SPOILS	GIL	112	EXP	1042

ACCESSORIES	Arcane Incense, Gravitorb, Attractorb x2, [Position] Far from Opponent x6

6 ULTIMECIA

LEVEL	9	RANK	E

BEHAVIOR	Vicious
DP CHANCE	–
BATTLE MAP	World of Darkness
SUMMONSTONE	–

STATS	HP	1800	CP	339	BRV	164
	ATK	23	DEF	19	LUK	14

EQUIPMENT	WEAPON	Rod
	HANDS	–

HEAD	–		BODY	Robe

SPOILS	GIL	252	EXP	2970

DESTINY ODYSSEY

II-4

Several elements of this level only appear after returning with sufficient star rating. The Rosetta Stone in treasure chest **B** can only be obtained after a 2-star rating, a rare, ultimate battle piece only appears after a 3-star rating, and a rare treasure chest only appears after a 4-star rating. The ultimate battle piece is a crystal mock-up of The Emperor. While this manikin is powerful, it is not very good at avoiding several of Firion's attacks—like many CPU-controlled opponents. The most effective attacks are Rope Knife on the ground when you are in close and Straightarrow when executed from long range.

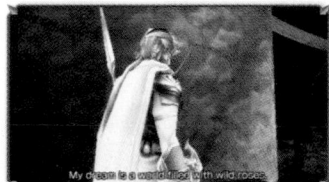
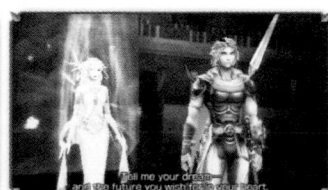
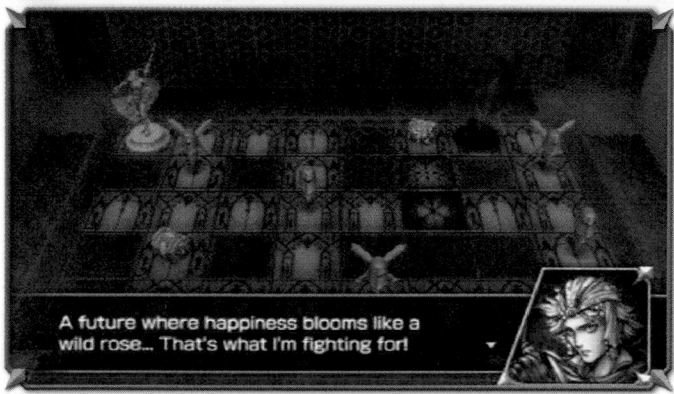

A future where happiness blooms like a wild rose... That's what I'm fighting for!

MAP

TREASURE

CHEST	1ST TIME	2ND TIME
A	Kunai	75%: 30 PP; 25%: 50 PP
B	Rosetta Stone (after 2–star rating)	–
B	Bergamot (after 4–star rating)	–

LOCKED AREAS

AREA	UNLOCK REQUIREMENTS
F–3	Defeat battle piece ①.

DP EFFICIENCY ROUTE

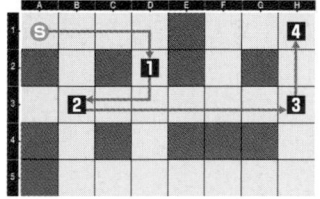

Since rare battle piece ⑥ (worth 2 DP upon defeat) only appears after a 3-star rating, you must wait to maximize DP on this level. From the outset, move to and defeat battle piece ②, then move between battle pieces ① and ⑥, chaining them. The Locked Area opens, allowing you to cross to battle pieces ④ and ⑤ and chain them as well. Afterward, you can move on to the Stigma of Chaos.

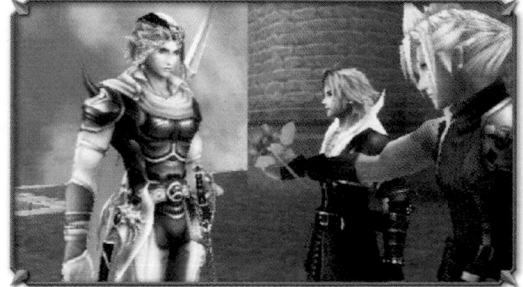
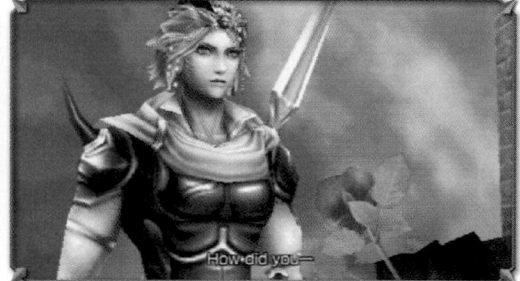

BATTLE PIECE DATA

1 FALSE HERO

LEVEL	8	RANK	F
BEHAVIOR	Aggressive		
DP CHANCE	Critical hit within 10 seconds (DP+1)		
BATTLE MAP	The Rift		
SUMMONSTONE	–		

STATS	HP	1424	CP	338	BRV	136
	ATK	18	DEF	13	LUK	14

EQUIPMENT	WEAPON	–
	HANDS	Cracked Shield

HEAD	–	BODY	–

SPOILS	GIL	140	EXP	854

ACCESSORIES	Arcane Incense, Gravitorb, Attractorb x2, [Position] Far from Opponent x6

2 COUNTERFEIT YOUTH

LEVEL	3	RANK	G
BEHAVIOR	Normal		
DP CHANCE	Win within 10 seconds (DP+1)		
BATTLE MAP	Order's Sanctuary		
SUMMONSTONE	–		

STATS	HP	1121	CP	352	BRV	107
	ATK	10	DEF	14	LUK	11

EQUIPMENT	WEAPON	–
	HANDS	

HEAD	–	BODY	–

SPOILS	GIL	140	EXP	672

3 IMITATION DESPOT

LEVEL	9	RANK	F
BEHAVIOR	Aggressive		
DP CHANCE	–		
BATTLE MAP	World of Darkness		
SUMMONSTONE	–		

STATS	HP	1485	CP	339	BRV	141
	ATK	19	DEF	13	LUK	14

EQUIPMENT	WEAPON	–
	HANDS	Cracked Shield

HEAD	–	BODY	–

SPOILS	GIL	140	EXP	891

ACCESSORIES	Arcane Resin, Gravitorb, Attractorb x2, [Position] Far from Opponent x6

4 CAPRICIOUS REAPER

LEVEL	9	RANK	F
BEHAVIOR	Aggressive		
DP CHANCE	Keep foe from getting EX Cores (DP+1)		
BATTLE MAP	The Rift		
SUMMONSTONE	–		

STATS	HP	1485	CP	339	BRV	141
	ATK	18	DEF	12	LUK	14

EQUIPMENT	WEAPON	–
	HANDS	Cracked Shield

HEAD	–	BODY	–

SPOILS	GIL	140	EXP	891

ACCESSORIES	Arcane Incense, Gravitorb, Attractorb x2, [Position] Far from Opponent x6

5 FALSE STALWART

LEVEL	3	RANK	G
BEHAVIOR	Aggressive		
DP CHANCE	Win without taking damage (DP+1)		
BATTLE MAP	Ultimecia's Castle		
SUMMONSTONE	–		

STATS	HP	1121	CP	332	BRV	107
	ATK	15	DEF	16	LUK	11

EQUIPMENT	WEAPON	–
	HANDS	–

HEAD	–	BODY	–

SPOILS	GIL	140	EXP	672

6 IMITATION DESPOT

LEVEL	24	RANK	B
BEHAVIOR	Valiant		
DP CHANCE	Win battle (DP+2)		
BATTLE MAP	Order's Sanctuary		
SUMMONSTONE	–		

STATS	HP	2394*	CP	358	BRV	228*
	ATK	34*	DEF	36*	LUK	22

EQUIPMENT	WEAPON	[Rank 5]
	HANDS	Silver Bangles

HEAD	Hairpin	BODY	[Rank 4]

SPOILS	GIL	336	EXP	0

ACCESSORIES	Arcane Incense, Gravitorb, Attractorb x2, [Position] Far from Opponent x6

* Denotes use of the base value (for stats that vary).

DESTINY ODYSSEY II

DESTINY ODYSSEY II-5

STARTING DP	MAX FINISHING	ENGAGEMENTS
5	5 (+2 after 3 star rating)	6 (+1 after 3-star rating)

Like the level before it, a treasure chest and battle piece only appear here after achieving a 3-star or better rating for Destiny Odyssey II. The rare battle piece is a fight against a fierce Firion manikin, who employs many of the same attacks that you've used to lay waste to its manikin allies. In particular, watch out for Rope Knife chaining into Double Trouble up close. This manikin is also vigilant about hunting down EX Cores the instant they appear. Try to dance on the edge of its Rope Knife range, avoiding its attacks and countering with your own. The boss battle, against The Emperor, can be won with the same tactics that have served throughout Firion's levels. The only caveat is that Straightarrow's range is less of an advantage in the cramped halls of Pandaemonium.

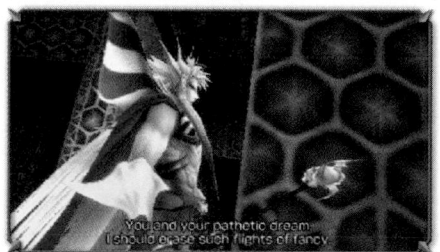
You and your pathetic dream. I should erase such flights of fancy.

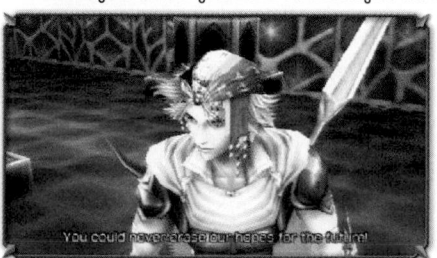
You could never erase our hopes for the future!

MAP

TREASURE

CHEST	1ST TIME	2ND TIME
A	Orange Drop	75%: 30 PP; 25%: 50 PP
B	Rosetta Stone	75%: 30 PP; 25%: 50 PP
C	Mythril (after 4–star rating)	–

LOCKED AREAS

AREA	UNLOCK REQUIREMENTS
E–3	Defeat battle piece 1.
B–3	Defeat battle piece 5.

DP EFFICIENCY ROUTE

Max DP can't be accomplished here until a 3-star or better rating has revealed the rare battle piece 7. Once it's present, begin the level by heading between battle pieces 1 and 3, chaining them. A Locked Area disappears, allowing you to then move between battle pieces 4 and 7. After chaining them as well, head to the upper left corner to defeat battle piece 5, opening the way to the boss.

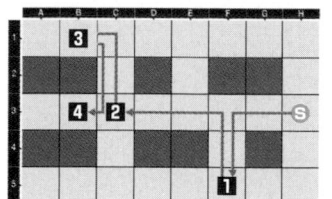

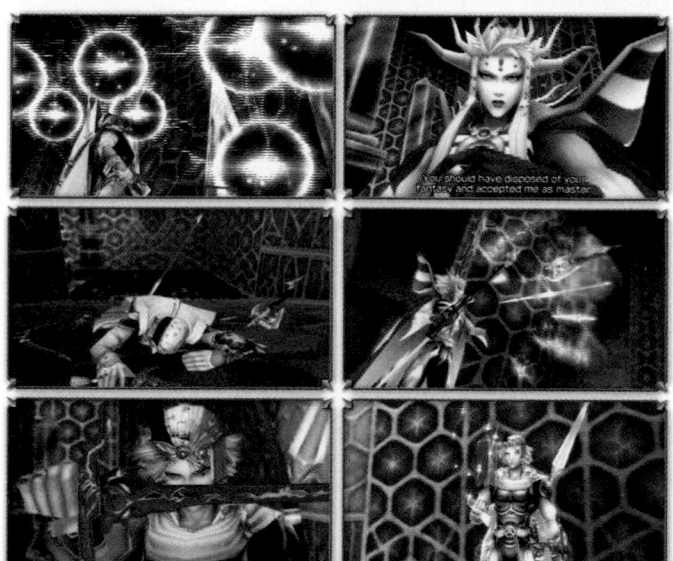
You should have disposed of your fantasy and accepted me as master.

BATTLE PIECE DATA

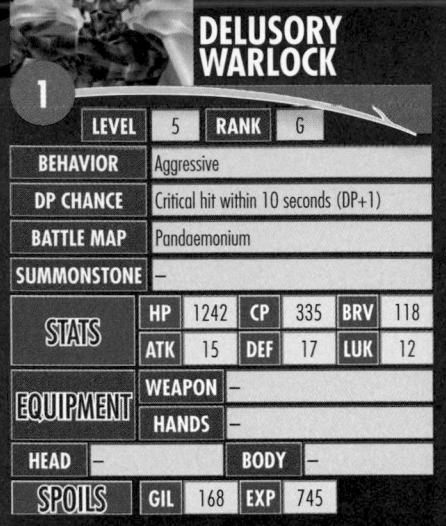

1. DELUSORY WARLOCK

LEVEL	5	RANK	G			

BEHAVIOR	Aggressive
DP CHANCE	Critical hit within 10 seconds (DP+1)
BATTLE MAP	Pandaemonium
SUMMONSTONE	–

STATS	HP	1242	CP	335	BRV	118
	ATK	15	DEF	17	LUK	12

EQUIPMENT	WEAPON	–
	HANDS	–

HEAD	–	BODY	–

SPOILS	GIL	168	EXP	745

2. FALLACIOUS WANDERER

LEVEL	10	RANK	F

BEHAVIOR	Normal
DP CHANCE	–
BATTLE MAP	Dream's End
SUMMONSTONE	–

STATS	HP	1545	CP	359	BRV	147
	ATK	20	DEF	13	LUK	15

EQUIPMENT	WEAPON	–
	HANDS	Cracked Shield

HEAD	–	BODY	–

SPOILS	GIL	168	EXP	927

ACCESSORIES	Arcane Incense, Gravitorb, Attractorb x2, [Position] Far from Opponent x6

3. IMAGINARY SOLDIER

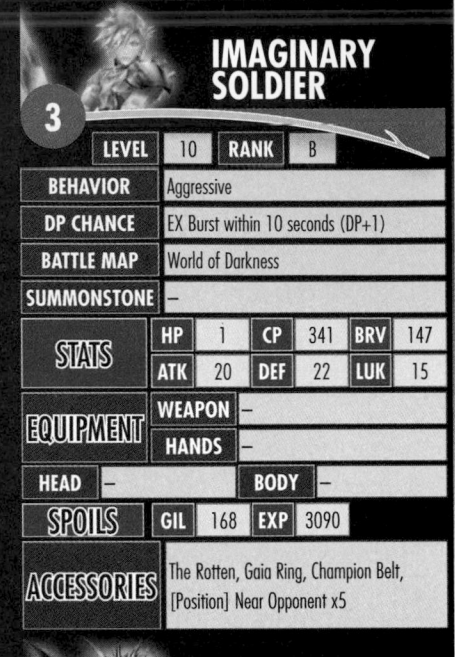

LEVEL	10	RANK	B

BEHAVIOR	Aggressive
DP CHANCE	EX Burst within 10 seconds (DP+1)
BATTLE MAP	World of Darkness
SUMMONSTONE	–

STATS	HP	1	CP	341	BRV	147
	ATK	20	DEF	22	LUK	15

EQUIPMENT	WEAPON	–
	HANDS	–

HEAD	–	BODY	–

SPOILS	GIL	168	EXP	3090

ACCESSORIES	The Rotten, Gaia Ring, Champion Belt, [Position] Near Opponent x5

4. FALSE STALWART

LEVEL	4	RANK	G

BEHAVIOR	Normal
DP CHANCE	Win within 10 seconds (DP+1)
BATTLE MAP	The Rift
SUMMONSTONE	–

STATS	HP	1182	CP	333	BRV	113
	ATK	16	DEF	17	LUK	12

EQUIPMENT	WEAPON	–
	HANDS	–

HEAD	–	BODY	–

SPOILS	GIL	168	EXP	709

5. CAPRICIOUS REAPER

LEVEL	11	RANK	F

BEHAVIOR	Normal
DP CHANCE	Win without taking damage (DP+1)
BATTLE MAP	Ultimecia's Castle
SUMMONSTONE	–

STATS	HP	1606	CP	342	BRV	153
	ATK	20	DEF	14	LUK	15

EQUIPMENT	WEAPON	–
	HANDS	Cracked Shield

HEAD	–	BODY	–

SPOILS	GIL	168	EXP	963

ACCESSORIES	Arcane Incense, Gravitorb, Attractorb x2, [Position] Far from Opponent x6

6. THE EMPEROR

LEVEL	13	RANK	D

BEHAVIOR	Tactician
DP CHANCE	–
BATTLE MAP	Pandaemonium
SUMMONSTONE	Atomos

STATS	HP	2042	CP	344	BRV	269
	ATK	31	DEF	29	LUK	16

EQUIPMENT	WEAPON	Oak Staff
	HANDS	Bronze Bangle

HEAD	Plumed Hat	BODY	Robe

SPOILS	GIL	336	EXP	4317

ACCESSORIES	Gaia Ring, Phoenix Down, [HP] HP = 1, [HP] Near Death, [HP] Near Loss

7. IMITATION LIEGEMAN

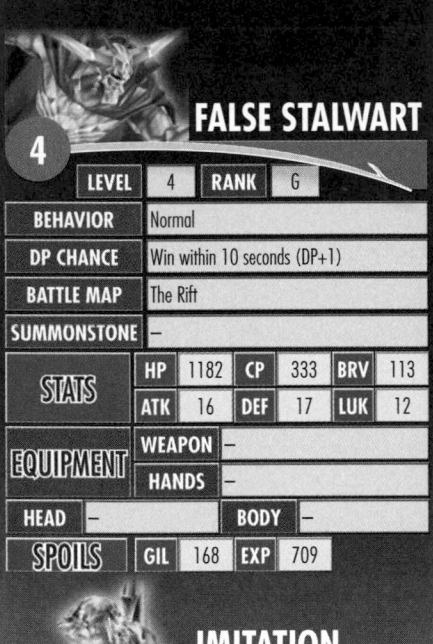

LEVEL	27	RANK	B

BEHAVIOR	Vicious
DP CHANCE	Win battle (DP+2)
BATTLE MAP	Pandaemonium
SUMMONSTONE	Shiva

STATS	HP	2575*	CP	361	BRV	245*
	ATK	38*	DEF	39*	LUK	23

EQUIPMENT	WEAPON	[Rank 4]
	HANDS	[Rank 3]

HEAD	[Rank 5]	BODY	Poncho

SPOILS	GIL	336	EXP	0

ACCESSORIES	Arcane Incense, Gravitorb, Attractorb x2, [Position] Far from Opponent x6

* Denotes use of the base value (for stats that vary).

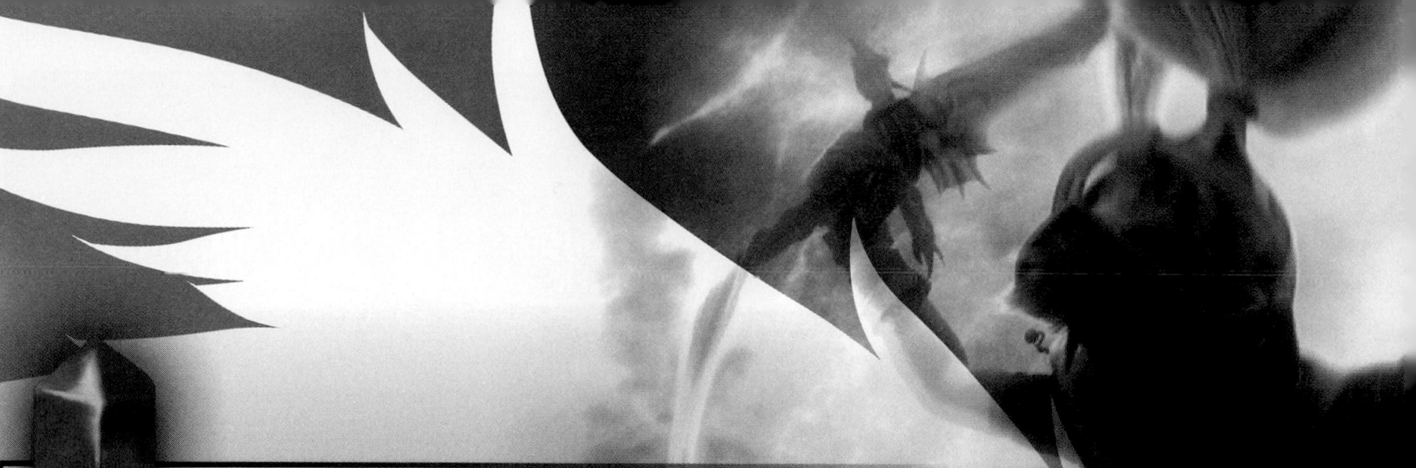

DESTINY ODYSSEY III
THE PRIDE OF YOUTH

Difficulty: ☆☆☆☆

Prerequisite: Finish Prologue

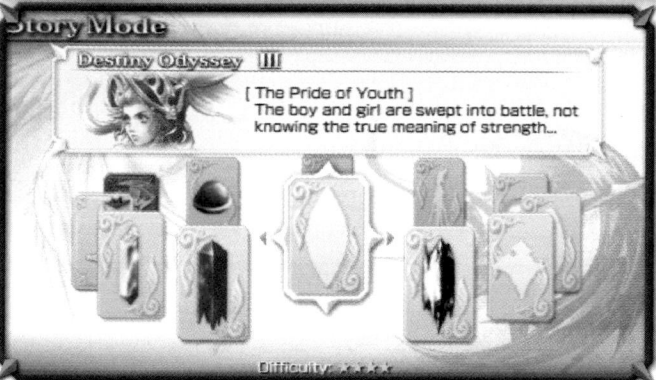

Story Mode
Destiny Odyssey III
[The Pride of Youth]
The boy and girl are swept into battle, not knowing the true meaning of strength...
Difficulty: ★★★★

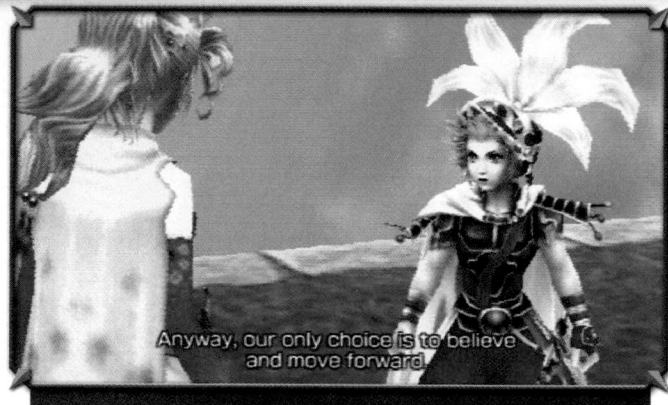

Anyway, our only choice is to believe and move forward.

Onion Knight and Terra travel together, searching for their crystals. Terra is hesitant, but Onion Knight believes that he can find the way.

REWARDS

At the end of each level, rewards are available if you finish with a positive number of Destiny Points, or DP. This walkthrough includes miniature level maps that indicate the most efficient route to take through a given level, in order to maximize DP.

LEVEL COMPLETION

REMAINING DP	1ST TIME	2ND TIME
7	Rosetta Stone	300 PP
6	Ice Rod	200 PP
5	Flame Rod	120 PP
4	Ultros	80 PP
3	1000 gil	50 PP
2	600 gil	30 PP
1	300 gil	20 PP
0	100 gil	10 PP

At the end of each set of levels, you'll receive rewards based on your performance. Story Points, or SP, are awarded after each level based on remaining DP and HP, as well as the number of engagements undertaken. Points are penalized for retries, or for a DP total that dips into negatives. If you miss out on a desired bonus on the first playthrough, don't worry—SP is cumulative across multiple playthroughs.

DESTINY ODYSSEY III COMPLETION

STAR RATING	SP REQUIRED	AWARD
☆	100	New skill
☆☆	200	Special areas unlocked
☆☆☆	300	Rare battle pieces spawned
☆☆☆☆	400	Rare treasure chests spawned
–	500 SP, then every 500 SP extra	100 PP

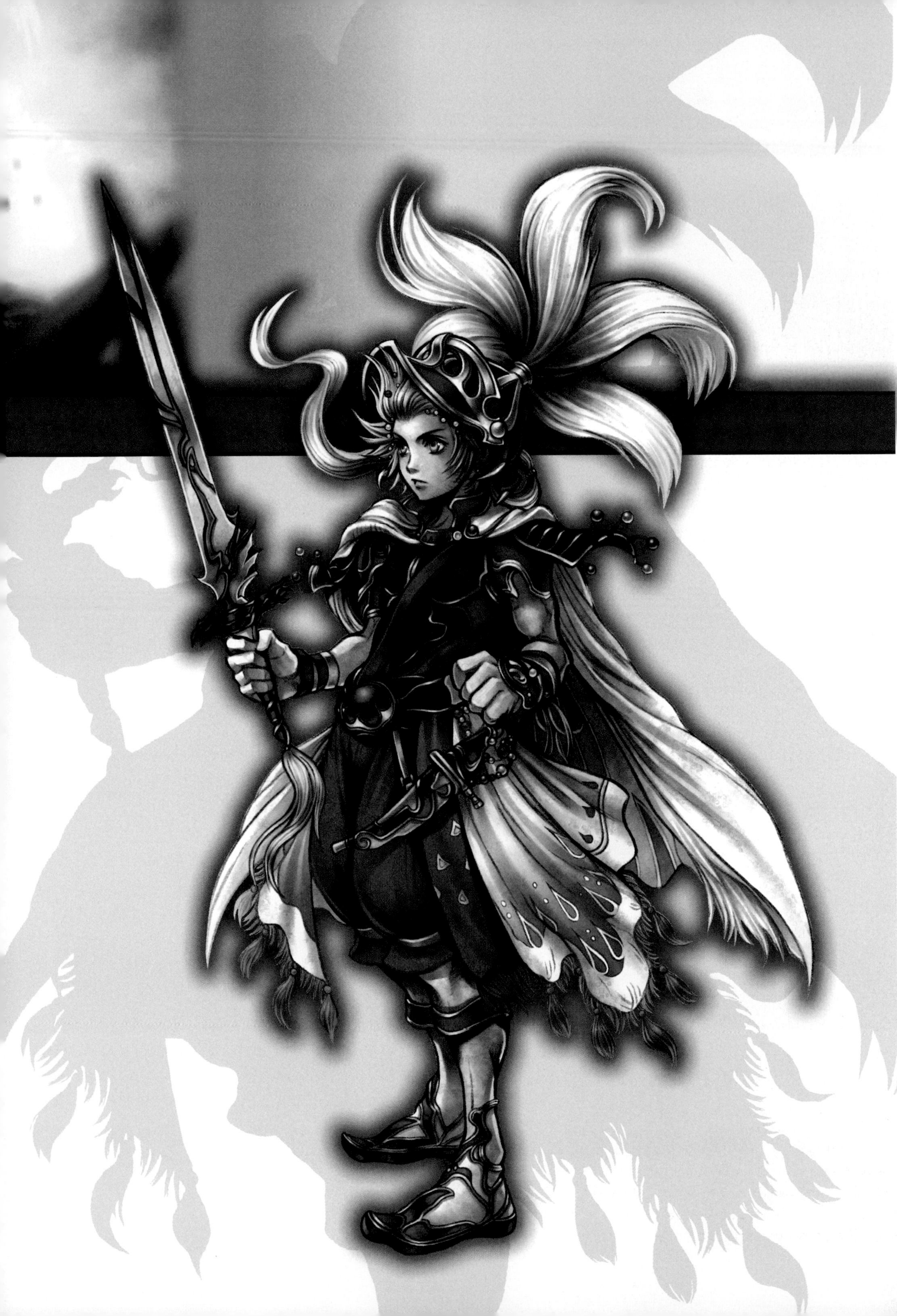

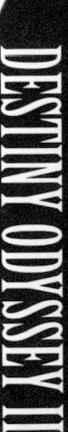

DESTINY ODYSSEY III

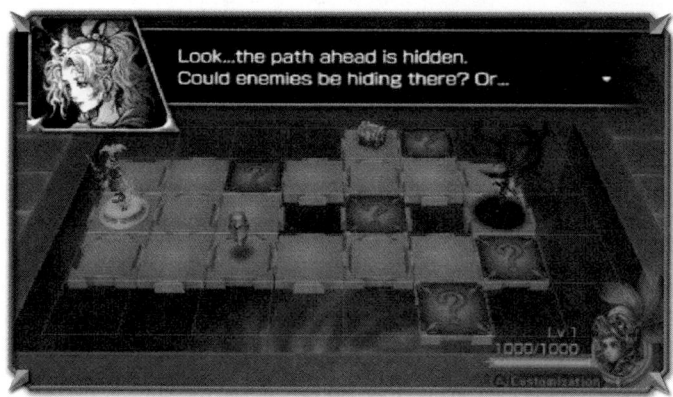

Look...the path ahead is hidden.
Could enemies be hiding there? Or...

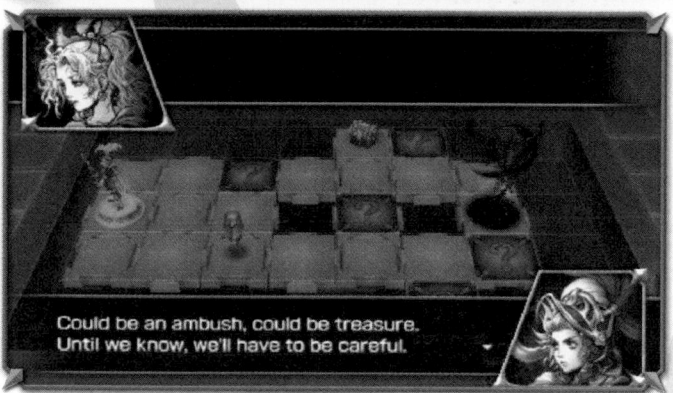

Could be an ambush, could be treasure.
Until we know, we'll have to be careful.

As the legendary Onion Knight and Terra travel across his levels, you'll notice most board pieces are obscured by blue question marks. These are called Enigma Areas. The contents of an Enigma Area can be revealed by moving next to it, or by simply following this guide! All Enigma Areas for a level can be uncovered by using the Sight skill. Onion Knight's ability set can seem a little underwhelming compared to some of his comrades at the start—he can't set up Chase mode initially, and he doesn't learn abilities very quickly by leveling up. Instead, his abilities expand by mastering the AP requirements, causing some abilities to branch. Mastering Turbo-Hit, for example, allows access to the follow-up ability Extra Lunge, which can lead to Chase mode. Only 15 AP is required for this example, so it doesn't take long to obtain.

MAP

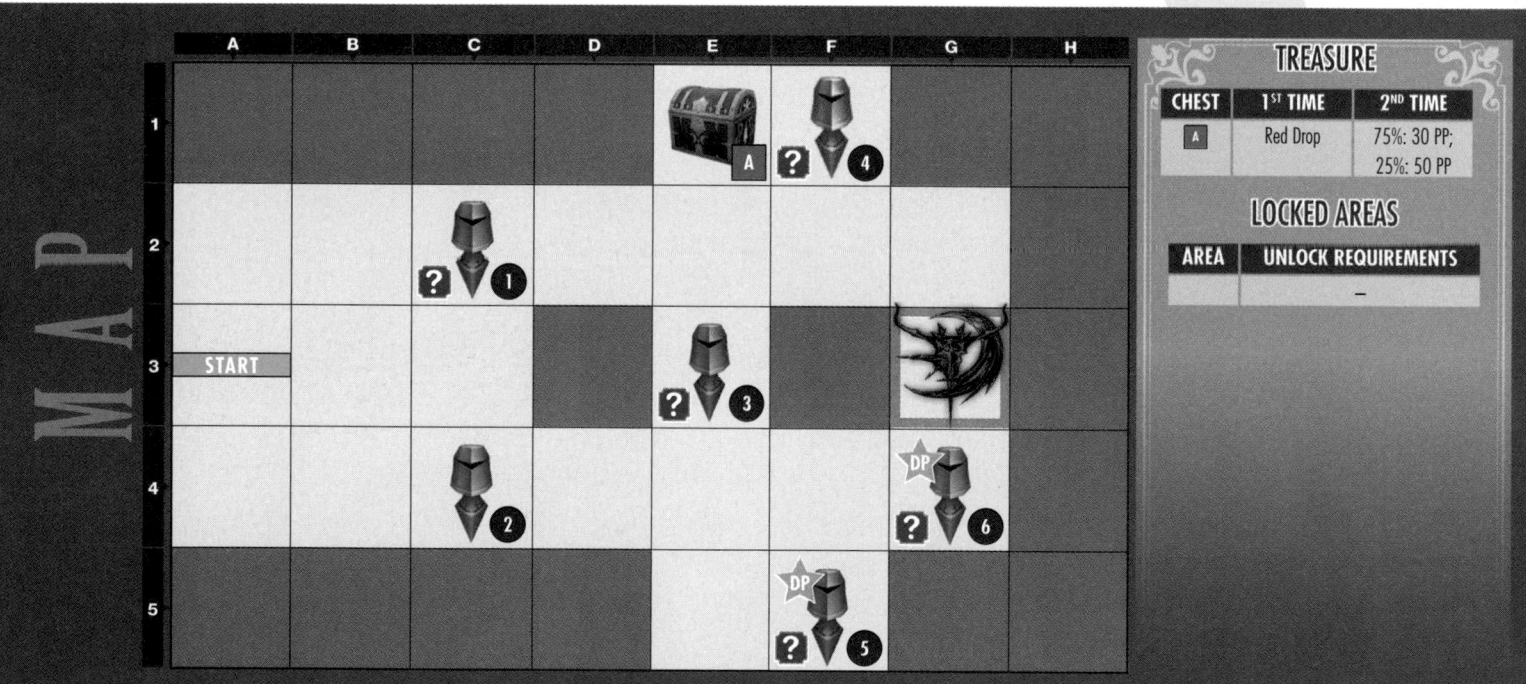

TREASURE

CHEST	1ST TIME	2ND TIME
A	Red Drop	75%: 30 PP; 25%: 50 PP

LOCKED AREAS

AREA	UNLOCK REQUIREMENTS
	—

DP EFFICIENCY ROUTE

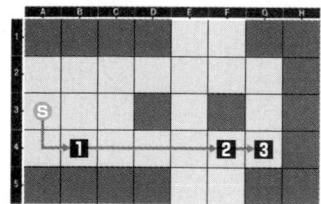

The route through this level is short and sweet, if you're looking for DP. Engage and defeat battle piece **2** (or chain battle pieces **1** and **2** ...either way costs 1 DP), then head to F-4 and chain the two battle pieces shrouded behind Enigma Areas.

BATTLE PIECE DATA

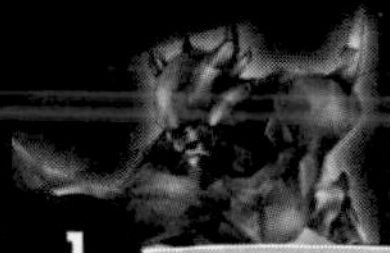

1 DELUSORY KNIGHT

LEVEL	1	RANK	H

BEHAVIOR	Aggressive
DP CHANCE	—
BATTLE MAP	Order's Sanctuary
SUMMONSTONE	—

STATS	HP	338	CP	330	BRV	49
	ATK	10	DEF	3	LUK	10

EQUIPMENT	WEAPON	—
	HANDS	Cracked Shield
HEAD	Charred Helm	BODY	Rusted Armor

SPOILS	GIL	56	EXP	1100

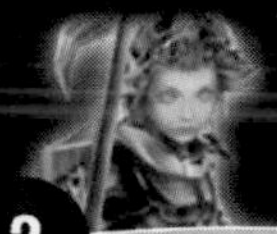

2 COUNTERFEIT YOUTH

LEVEL	1	RANK	H

BEHAVIOR	Normal
DP CHANCE	—
BATTLE MAP	Order's Sanctuary
SUMMONSTONE	—

STATS	HP	338	CP	350	BRV	49
	ATK	8	DEF	4	LUK	10

EQUIPMENT	WEAPON	—
	HANDS	Cracked Shield
HEAD	Charred Helm	BODY	Rusted Armor

SPOILS	GIL	56	EXP	1100

3 COUNTERFEIT WRAITH

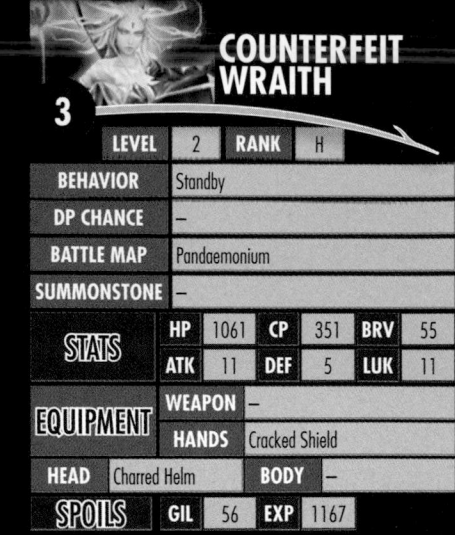

LEVEL	2	RANK	H

BEHAVIOR	Standby
DP CHANCE	—
BATTLE MAP	Pandaemonium
SUMMONSTONE	—

STATS	HP	1061	CP	351	BRV	55
	ATK	11	DEF	5	LUK	11

EQUIPMENT	WEAPON	—
	HANDS	Cracked Shield
HEAD	Charred Helm	BODY	—

SPOILS	GIL	56	EXP	1167

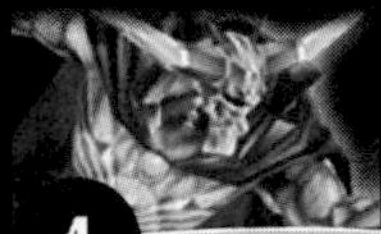

4 FALSE STALWART

LEVEL	2	RANK	H

BEHAVIOR	Standby
DP CHANCE	—
BATTLE MAP	Pandaemonium
SUMMONSTONE	—

STATS	HP	399	CP	331	BRV	55
	ATK	14	DEF	7	LUK	11

EQUIPMENT	WEAPON	—
	HANDS	Cracked Shield
HEAD	Charred Helm	BODY	Rusted Armor

SPOILS	GIL	56	EXP	1167

5 EPHEMERAL VISION

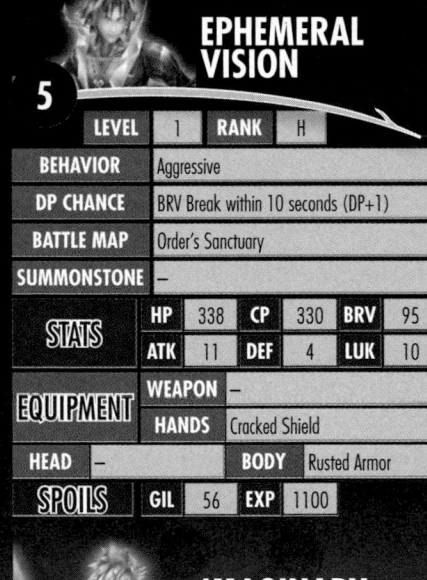

LEVEL	1	RANK	H

BEHAVIOR	Aggressive
DP CHANCE	BRV Break within 10 seconds (DP+1)
BATTLE MAP	Order's Sanctuary
SUMMONSTONE	—

STATS	HP	338	CP	330	BRV	95
	ATK	11	DEF	4	LUK	10

EQUIPMENT	WEAPON	—
	HANDS	Cracked Shield
HEAD	—	BODY	Rusted Armor

SPOILS	GIL	56	EXP	1100

6 IMAGINARY SOLDIER

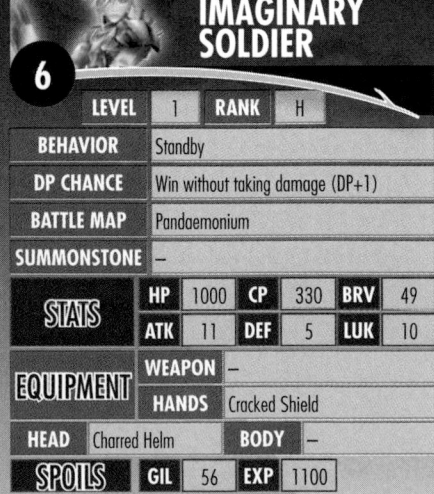

LEVEL	1	RANK	H

BEHAVIOR	Standby
DP CHANCE	Win without taking damage (DP+1)
BATTLE MAP	Pandaemonium
SUMMONSTONE	—

STATS	HP	1000	CP	330	BRV	49
	ATK	11	DEF	5	LUK	10

EQUIPMENT	WEAPON	—
	HANDS	Cracked Shield
HEAD	Charred Helm	BODY	—

SPOILS	GIL	56	EXP	1100

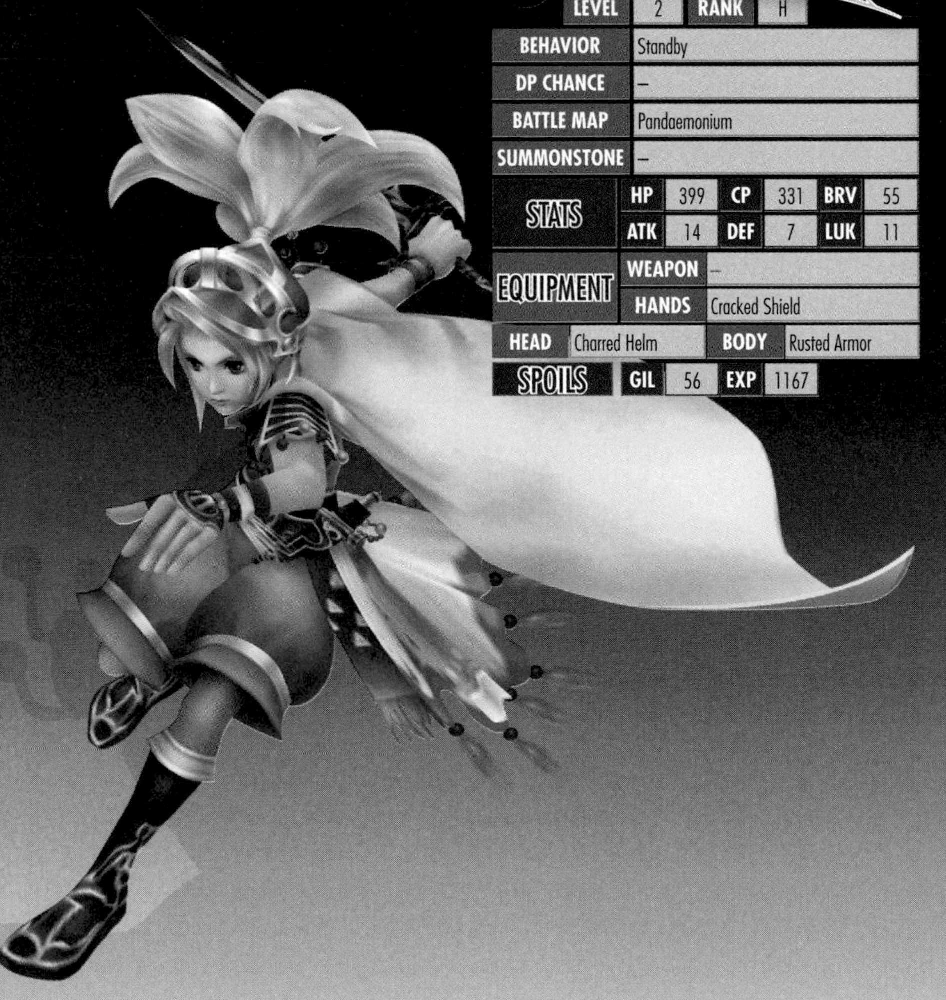

DESTINY ODYSSEY III

STARTING DP	MAX FINISHING	ENGAGEMENTS
5	4	5

This second level is also filled with Enigma Areas. Although many of them shroud battle pieces, one hides a Potion, while another masks a treasure chest. When returning after at least a 2-star rating on Destiny Odyssey III, you can also acquire the Phoenix Summonstone.

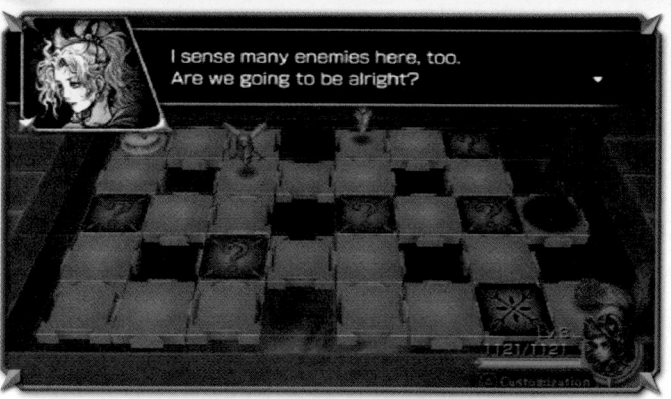

I sense many enemies here, too.
Are we going to be alright?

MAP

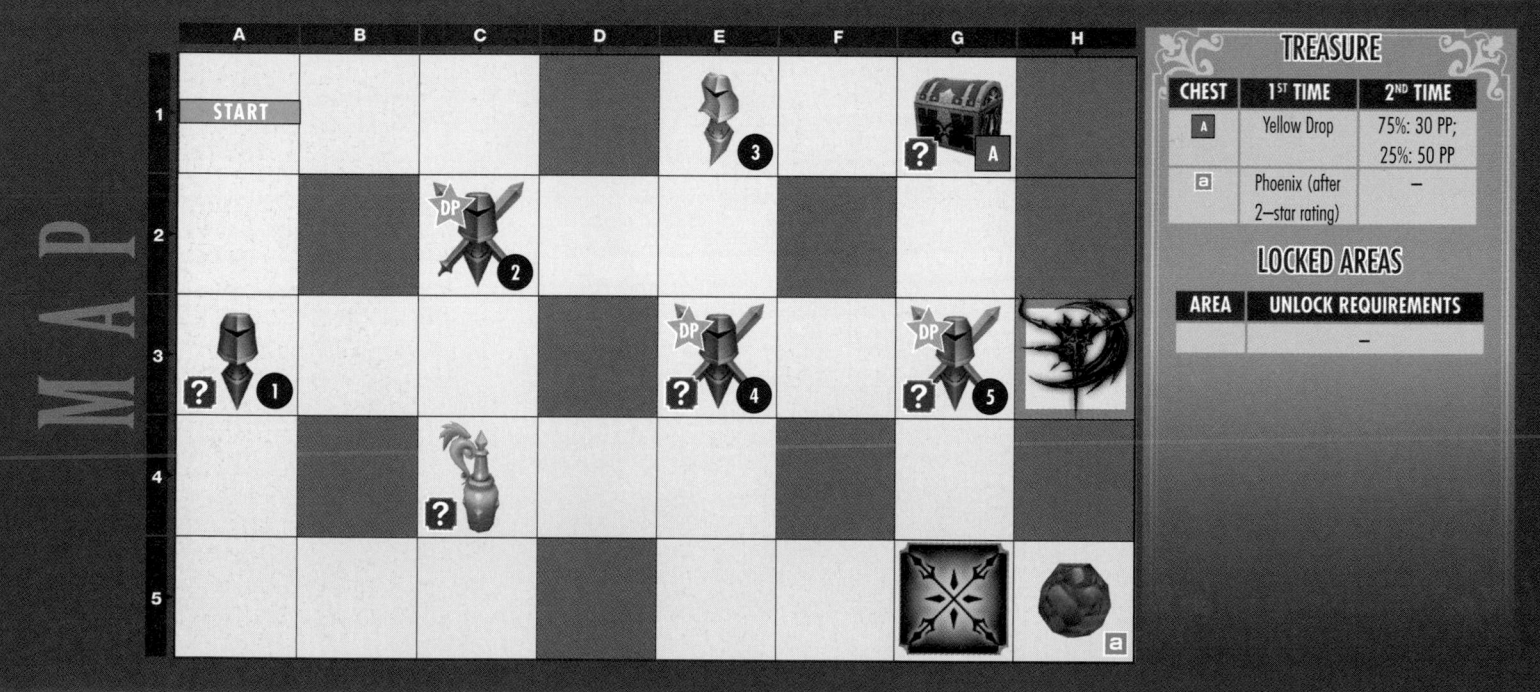

TREASURE

CHEST	1ST TIME	2ND TIME
A	Yellow Drop	75%: 30 PP; 25%: 50 PP
a	Phoenix (after 2–star rating)	–

LOCKED AREAS

AREA	UNLOCK REQUIREMENTS
	–

DP EFFICIENCY ROUTE

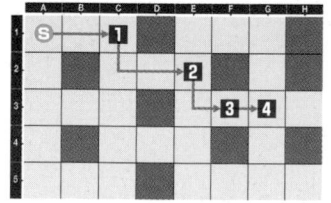

There's not much to maxing out DP here, without opportunities for DP Chance battle chains—just take a straight path to the exit. Take out battle piece ②, then head to E-2 and chain battle pieces ③ and ④. Afterward, defeat battle piece ⑤, opening access to the Stigma of Chaos.

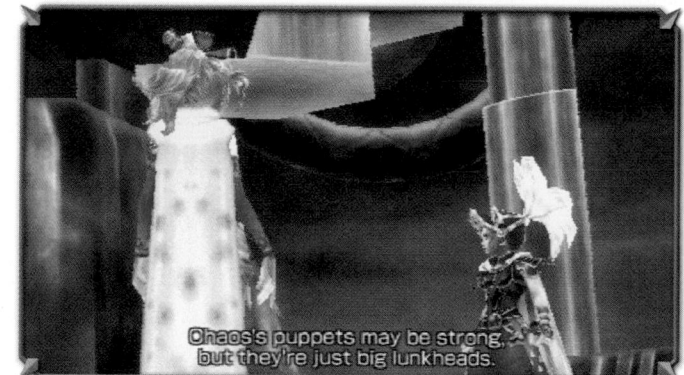

Chaos's puppets may be strong, but they're just big lunkheads.

BATTLE PIECE DATA

1. PHANTASMAL HARLEQUIN

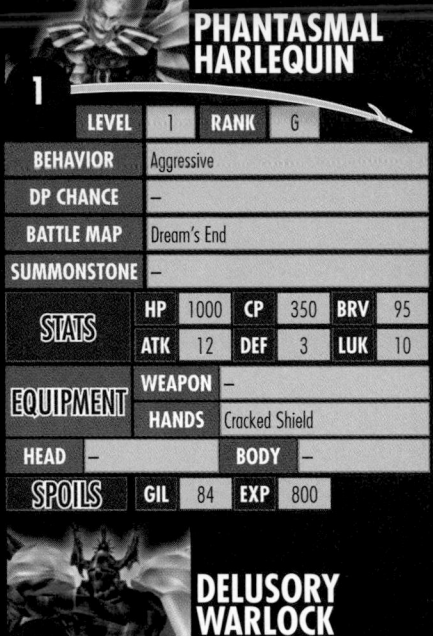

LEVEL	1	RANK	G

BEHAVIOR	Aggressive
DP CHANCE	–
BATTLE MAP	Dream's End
SUMMONSTONE	–

STATS	HP	1000	CP	350	BRV	95
	ATK	12	DEF	3	LUK	10

EQUIPMENT	WEAPON	–	
	HANDS	Cracked Shield	
HEAD	–	BODY	–

SPOILS	GIL	84	EXP	800

2. EPHEMERAL VISION

LEVEL	6	RANK	F

BEHAVIOR	Normal
DP CHANCE	Win without losing HP (DP+1)
BATTLE MAP	Dream's End
SUMMONSTONE	–

STATS	HP	1303	CP	336	BRV	124
	ATK	16	DEF	9	LUK	13

EQUIPMENT	WEAPON	–	
	HANDS	Cracked Shield	
HEAD	–	BODY	–

SPOILS	GIL	84	EXP	1042

ACCESSORIES	Defense Cuff x4, [Position] On the Ground

3. CAPRICIOUS THIEF

LEVEL	7	RANK	C

BEHAVIOR	Summoner
DP CHANCE	–
BATTLE MAP	Order's Sanctuary
SUMMONSTONE	Cactuar

STATS	HP	1	CP	337	BRV	130*
	ATK	15	DEF	9	LUK	13

EQUIPMENT	WEAPON	–	
	HANDS	Cracked Shield	
HEAD	[Rank 4]	BODY	Rusted Armor

SPOILS	GIL	84	EXP	2728

ACCESSORIES	The Rotten, Soul of the Sovereign

4. DELUSORY WARLOCK

LEVEL	5	RANK	F

BEHAVIOR	Standby
DP CHANCE	Win within 10 seconds (DP+1)
BATTLE MAP	Pandaemonium
SUMMONSTONE	–

STATS	HP	1242	CP	335	BRV	118
	ATK	15	DEF	9	LUK	12

EQUIPMENT	WEAPON	–	
	HANDS	Cracked Shield	
HEAD	–	BODY	–

SPOILS	GIL	84	EXP	993

ACCESSORIES	Black Cape x4, [Position] In Midair

5. COUNTERFEIT WRAITH

LEVEL	6	RANK	F

BEHAVIOR	Aggressive
DP CHANCE	BRV Break within 10 seconds (DP+1)
BATTLE MAP	Pandaemonium
SUMMONSTONE	–

STATS	HP	1303	CP	355	BRV	124
	ATK	15	DEF	9	LUK	13

EQUIPMENT	WEAPON	–	
	HANDS	Cracked Shield	
HEAD	–	BODY	–

SPOILS	GIL	84	EXP	1042

ACCESSORIES	Black Cape x4, [HP] Near Death x2

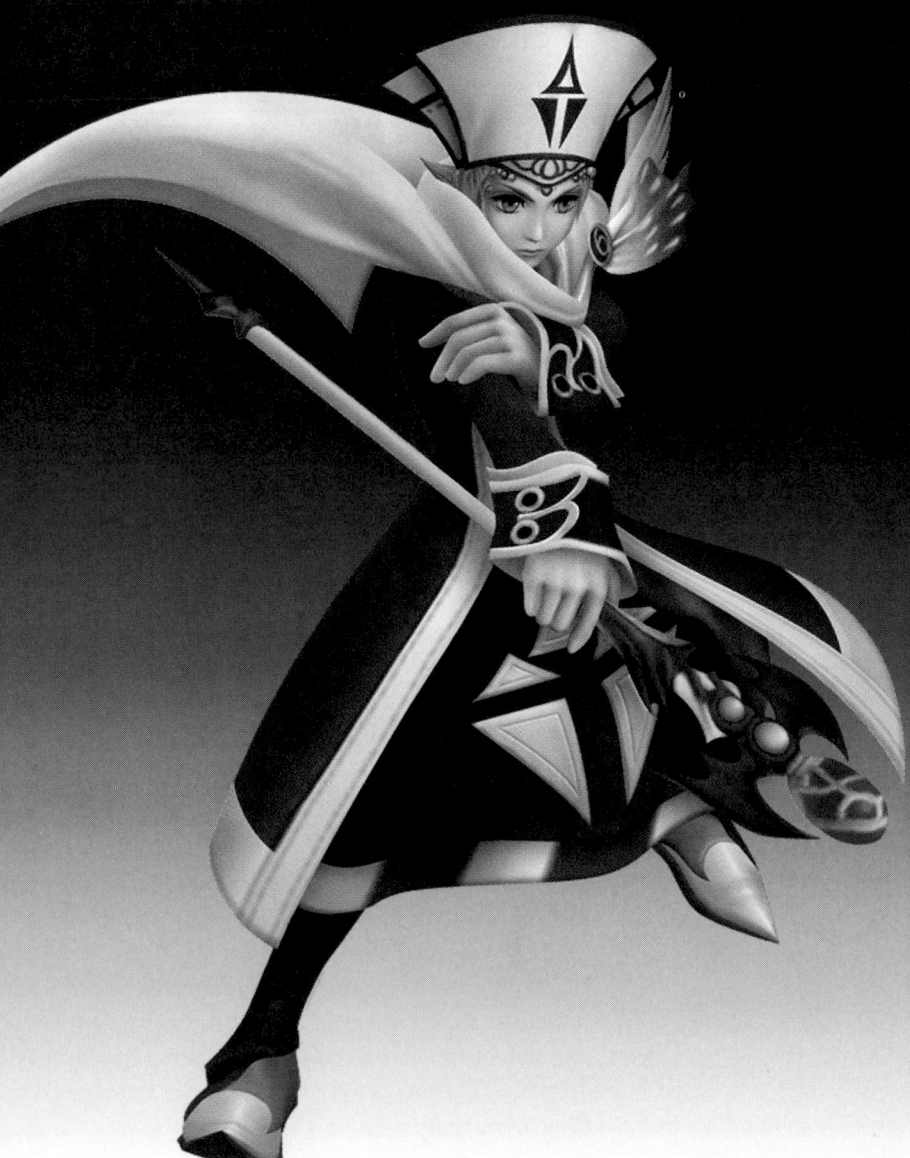

* Denotes use of the base value (for stats that vary).

DESTINY ODYSSEY III

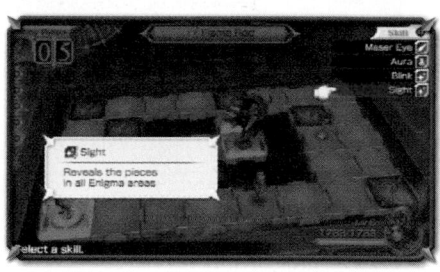

This level's perimeter route rings the road to the exit, which is blocked off initially. Getting to the Stigma of Chaos either requires defeating any four battle pieces, or dealing with expert battle piece ❸. This is an expert fight against a manikin of The Emperor. Although this foe ranks at double your level or more the first time through, it can be defeated if you stack other things in your favor. Go for a BRV Break, then use a summon like Alexander to freeze your bravery at a high level, if possible. Then, get to work nailing the foe with Comet. CPU-controlled enemies frequently dodge the beginning of Comet before eventually getting hit by the end of the attack. Likewise, ultimate battle piece ❼, only present after a previous 3-star rating, is also very tough. This Cloud of Darkness manikin assaults aggressively from all ranges. Like many foes, it can't deal with Comet from mid-range very well, and it will often dodge once or twice only to be hit by the very end of the attack.

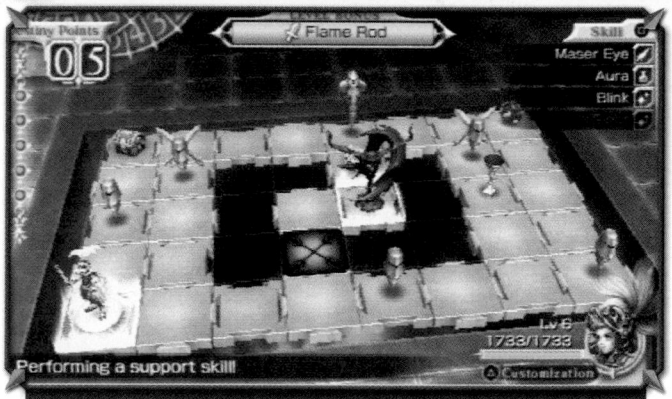

Sight, if available, can be used to uncover all the Enigma Areas. However, you can only use this once per Destiny Odyssey run-through, unless you find an Elixir to refill your skills!

MAP

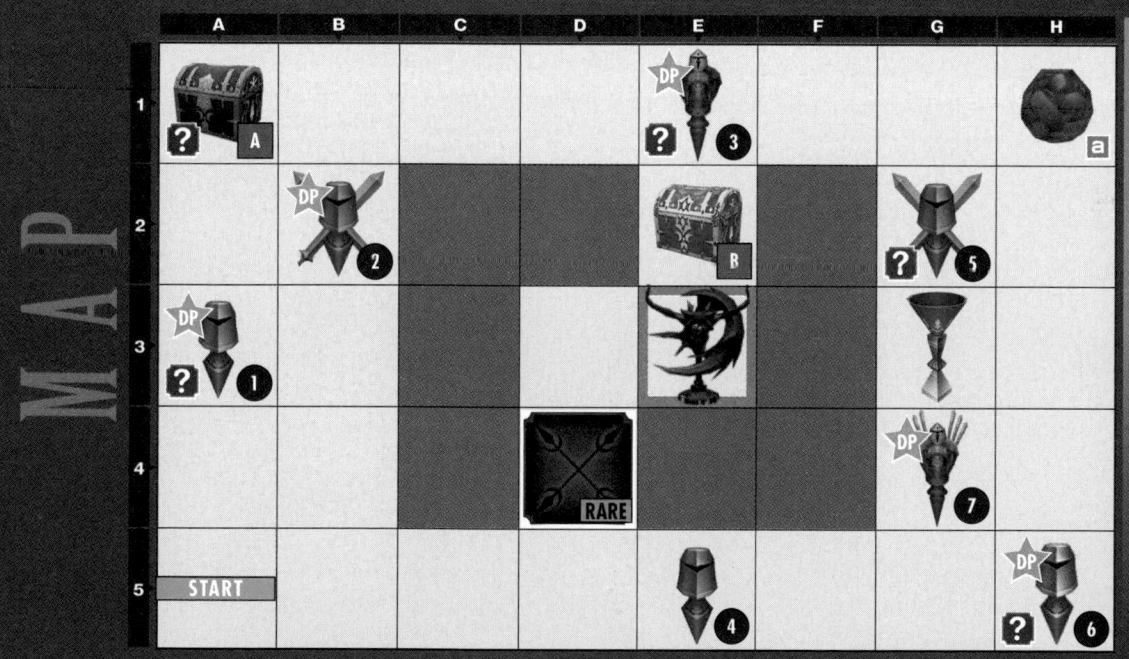

TREASURE

CHEST	1ST TIME	2ND TIME
A	Hide Armlet	75%: 30 PP; 25%: 50 PP
B	Full Metal Staff	75%: 50 PP; 25%: 100 PP
a	Phoenix AUTO	–

LOCKED AREAS

AREA	UNLOCK REQUIREMENTS
D–4	Defeat 4 battle pieces

DP EFFICIENCY ROUTE

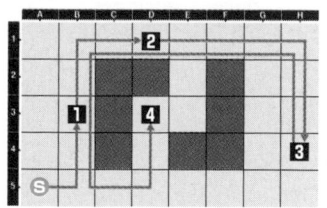

You'll be taking a roundabout route to maximize Destiny Points here, and a previous 3-star rating is required. Begin by chaining battle pieces ❶ and ❷ right near the start. This can be challenging, since the DP Chance for piece ❷ requires a win within 10 seconds, and the DP Chance for piece ❶ requires an EX Burst within 10 seconds. Basically, there is almost no time to actually build up a full EX Gauge in order to EX Burst piece ❷ right away. You can still make it, though, by using the Aura skill (if available) to fill up half your gauge on the level board. Then, wear equipment like Main Gauche along with accessories like Cyan Drop. These items boost your initial EX Force level going into battle. Play your cards right, and you can defeat battle piece ❷ and have a full EX Gauge going into the chain with battle piece ❶, even without much time to hunt down EX Cores or to fight other opponents on the level. After these pieces are dispensed with, head to D-1 to take on expert battle piece ❸. Then head to H-4, where you can chain battle piece ❻ and ultimate battle piece ❼. During this chain, the Locked Area at D-4 disappears, allowing you to loop back around the stage and approach the Stigma of Chaos from below.

BATTLE PIECE DATA

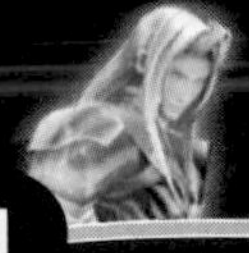

1 IMAGINARY CHAMPION

LEVEL	4	RANK	G

BEHAVIOR	Evader
DP CHANCE	EX Burst within 10 seconds (DP+1)
BATTLE MAP	Dream's End
SUMMONSTONE	—

STATS	HP	520	CP	333	BRV	113
	ATK	14	DEF	15	LUK	12

EQUIPMENT	WEAPON	—		
	HANDS	—		
HEAD	—	BODY	Rusted Armor	

SPOILS	GIL	112	EXP	709

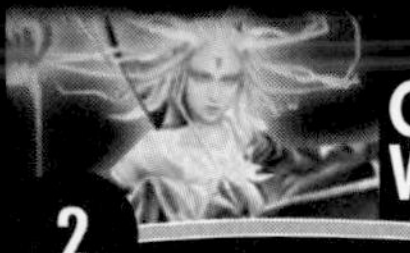

2 COUNTERFEIT WRAITH

LEVEL	7	RANK	F

BEHAVIOR	Standby
DP CHANCE	Win within 10 seconds (DP+1)
BATTLE MAP	Old Chaos Shrine
SUMMONSTONE	—

STATS	HP	1364	CP	356	BRV	130
	ATK	16	DEF	10	LUK	13

EQUIPMENT	WEAPON	—		
	HANDS	Cracked Shield		
HEAD	—	BODY	—	

SPOILS	GIL	112	EXP	818

ACCESSORIES	Defense Cuff x4, [HP] Near Death x2

3 IMITATION DESPOT

LEVEL	16	RANK	B

BEHAVIOR	Valiant
DP CHANCE	Win battle (DP+1)
BATTLE MAP	Old Chaos Shrine
SUMMONSTONE	—

STATS	HP	2624	CP	348	BRV	182*
	ATK	26*	DEF	37	LUK	18

EQUIPMENT	WEAPON	[Rank 4]		
	HANDS	Power Armlet		
HEAD	Plumed Hat	BODY	Poncho	

SPOILS	GIL	112	EXP	0

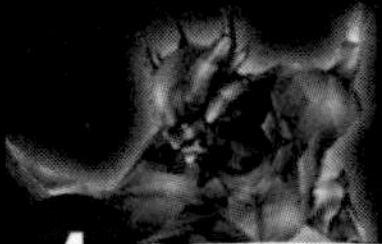

4 DELUSORY KNIGHT

LEVEL	3	RANK	G

BEHAVIOR	Aggressive
DP CHANCE	—
BATTLE MAP	World of Darkness
SUMMONSTONE	—

STATS	HP	1121	CP	332	BRV	61
	ATK	12	DEF	13	LUK	11

EQUIPMENT	WEAPON	—		
	HANDS	—		
HEAD	Charred Helm	BODY	—	

SPOILS	GIL	112	EXP	672

* Denotes use of the base value (for stats that vary).

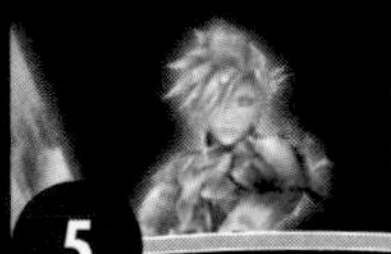

5 IMAGINARY SOLDIER

LEVEL	9	RANK	F

BEHAVIOR	Evader
DP CHANCE	—
BATTLE MAP	Pandaemonium
SUMMONSTONE	—

STATS	HP	1485	CP	339	BRV	141
	ATK	19	DEF	13	LUK	14

EQUIPMENT	WEAPON	—		
	HANDS	Cracked Shield		
HEAD	—	BODY	—	

SPOILS	GIL	112	EXP	891

ACCESSORIES	Black Cape x4, [Position] In Midair

6 DELUSORY WARLOCK

LEVEL	3	RANK	G

BEHAVIOR	Evader
DP CHANCE	Win without taking damage (DP+1)
BATTLE MAP	Order's Sanctuary
SUMMONSTONE	—

STATS	HP	1121	CP	332	BRV	61
	ATK	13	DEF	15	LUK	11

EQUIPMENT	WEAPON	—		
	HANDS	—		
HEAD	Charred Helm	BODY	—	

SPOILS	GIL	112	EXP	672

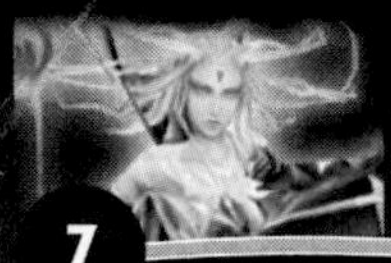

7 COUNTERFEIT WRAITH

LEVEL	26	RANK	B

BEHAVIOR	Calm
DP CHANCE	Win battle (DP+2)
BATTLE MAP	Order's Sanctuary
SUMMONSTONE	—

STATS	HP	2515*	CP	375	BRV	240*
	ATK	51	DEF	51	LUK	23

EQUIPMENT	WEAPON	Rod of Wisdom		
	HANDS	Silver Bangles		
HEAD	Hairpin	BODY	[Rank 4]	

SPOILS	GIL	336	EXP	2515

ACCESSORIES	Defense Cuff x4, [Position] On the Ground

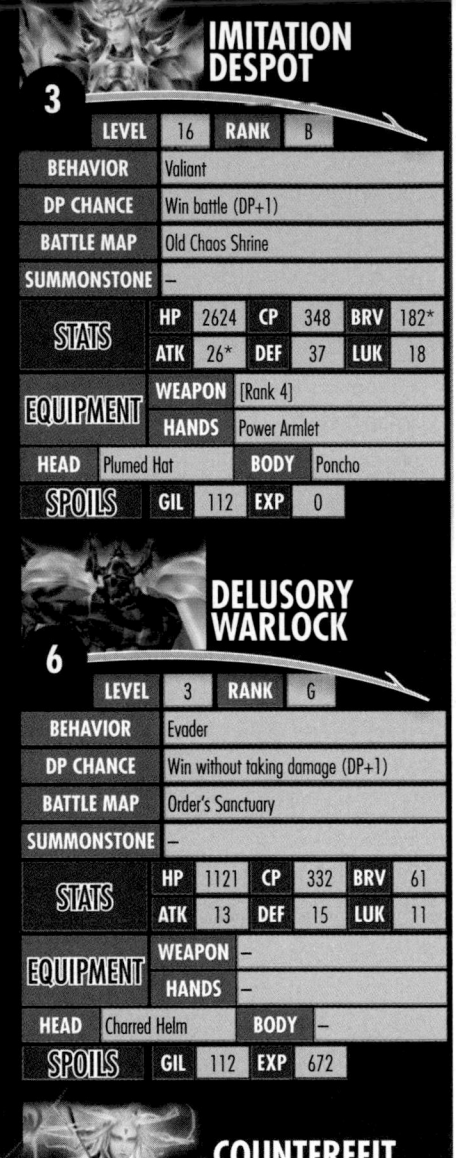

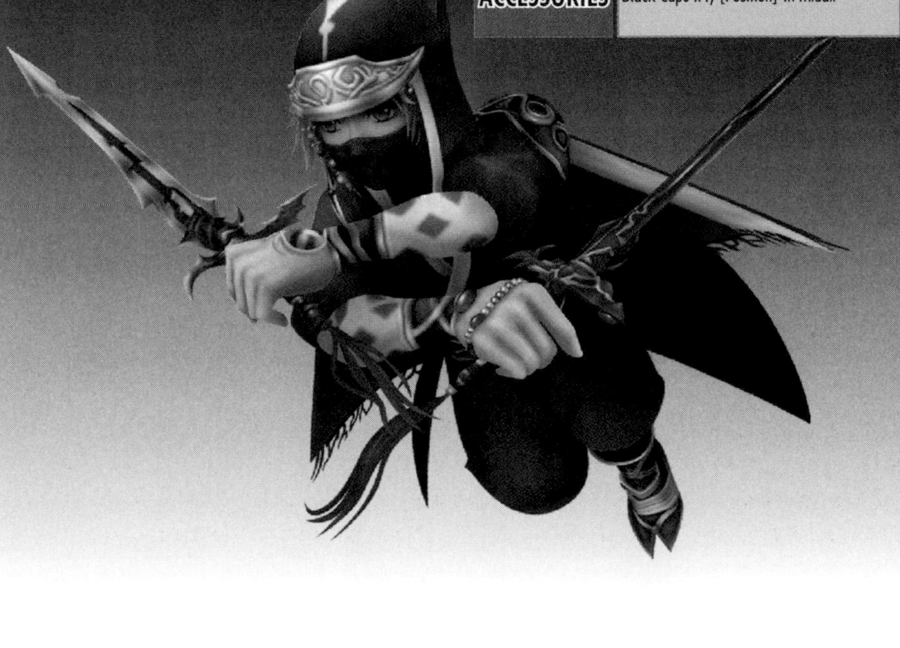

DESTINY ODYSSEY III

More Enigma Areas litter the landscape here, concealing foes, treasure chests, and a Potion. One treasure chest, behind a gold Locked Area, is only accessible after a 2-star rating, and another treasure chest only appears after a 4-star rating. When checking an Enigma Area while adjacent to another, you should always be wary that you might be forced into a battle chain you didn't anticipate, particularly if both hidden areas contain battle pieces. Similarly, if you know a treasure chest is in an Enigma Area, and another nearby Enigma Area houses a battle piece, you can position yourself adjacent to both, and use only 1 DP for both the chest and the foe. The opponent during this boss fight is a surprising one. She'll enter EX Mode almost immediately, but she is hesitant to actually use an EX Burst if she hits you with an HP attack. Be wary of Tornado up close, and use attacks like Comet and Firaga from mid- to long-range.

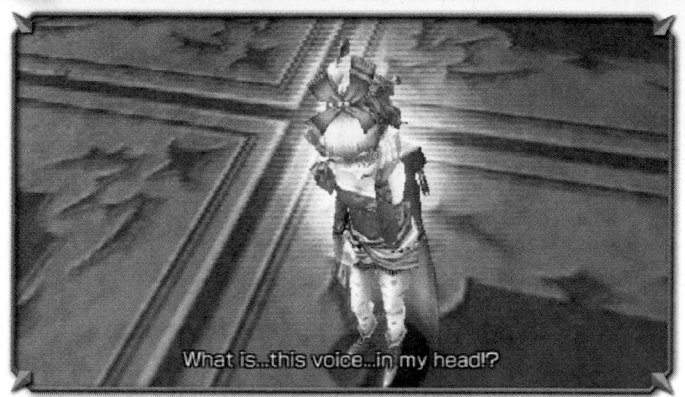

What is...this voice...in my head!?

MAP

	A	B	C	D	E	F	G	H
1			? / 2			C		BOSS 6
2					DP 4			
3	DP 1			DP ? / 3			DP ? / 5	
4	START					? / A		
5			B	✦				?

TREASURE

CHEST	1ST TIME	2ND TIME
A	Rosetta Stone	75%: 30 PP; 25%: 50 PP
B	Rosetta Stone (after 2—star rating)	—
C	Tea Tree	—

LOCKED AREAS

AREA	UNLOCK REQUIREMENTS
	—

DP EFFICIENCY ROUTE

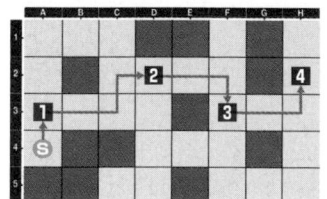

Going for DP here means cutting a straight swath across the level, fighting the four foes with DP Chances. Battle piece ①, right by the start, is first on the agenda. Next, chain battle pieces ③ and ④ from grid square D-2. Finally, defeat battle piece ⑤ before heading to the Stigma of Chaos.

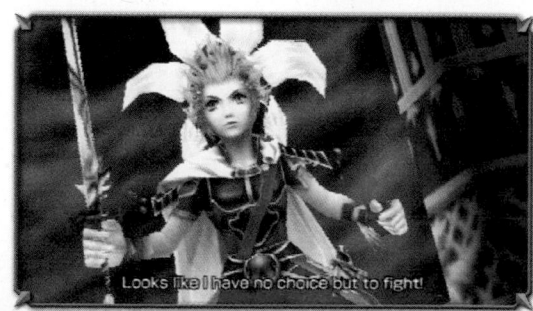

Looks like I have no choice but to fight!

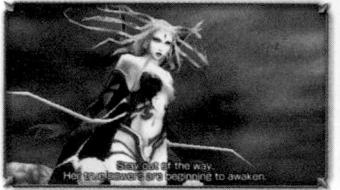

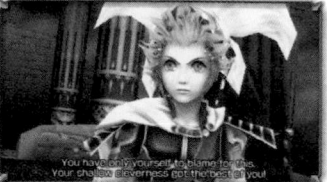

BATTLE PIECE DATA

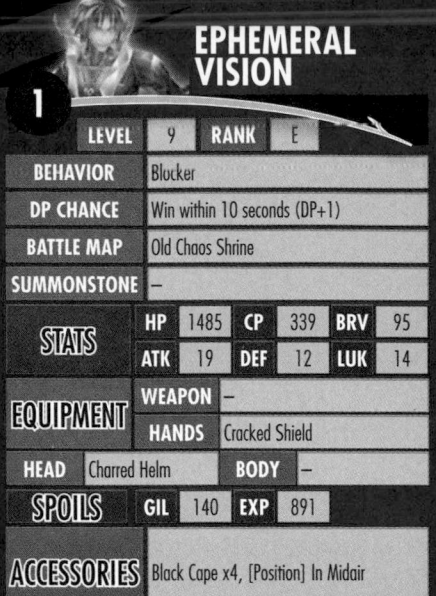

1 EPHEMERAL VISION

LEVEL	9	RANK	E

BEHAVIOR	Blocker
DP CHANCE	Win within 10 seconds (DP+1)
BATTLE MAP	Old Chaos Shrine
SUMMONSTONE	—

STATS	HP	1485	CP	339	BRV	95
	ATK	19	DEF	12	LUK	14

EQUIPMENT	WEAPON	—
	HANDS	Cracked Shield

HEAD	Charred Helm	BODY	—

SPOILS	GIL	140	EXP	891

ACCESSORIES	Black Cape x4, [Position] In Midair

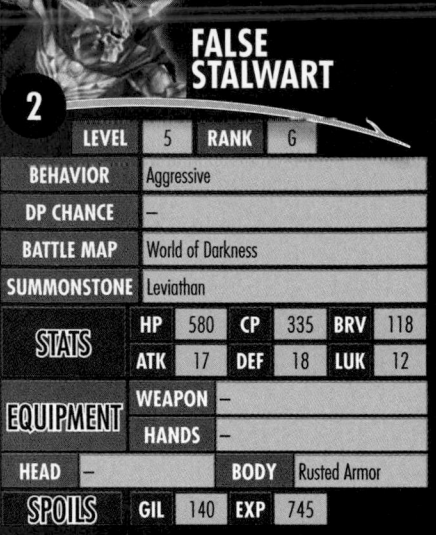

2 FALSE STALWART

LEVEL	5	RANK	G

BEHAVIOR	Aggressive
DP CHANCE	—
BATTLE MAP	World of Darkness
SUMMONSTONE	Leviathan

STATS	HP	580	CP	335	BRV	118
	ATK	17	DEF	18	LUK	12

EQUIPMENT	WEAPON	—
	HANDS	—

HEAD	—	BODY	Rusted Armor

SPOILS	GIL	140	EXP	745

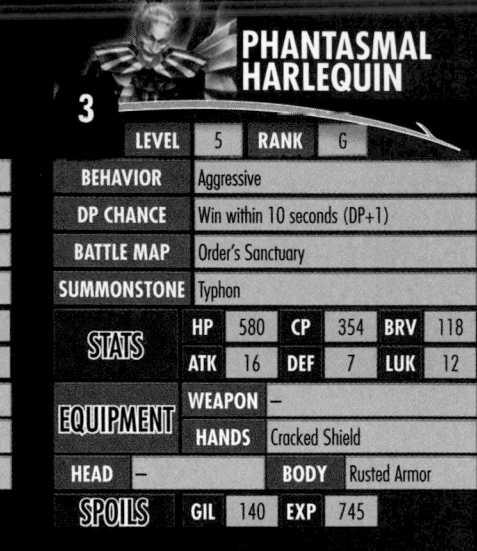

3 PHANTASMAL HARLEQUIN

LEVEL	5	RANK	G

BEHAVIOR	Aggressive
DP CHANCE	Win within 10 seconds (DP+1)
BATTLE MAP	Order's Sanctuary
SUMMONSTONE	Typhon

STATS	HP	580	CP	354	BRV	118
	ATK	16	DEF	7	LUK	12

EQUIPMENT	WEAPON	—
	HANDS	Cracked Shield

HEAD	—	BODY	Rusted Armor

SPOILS	GIL	140	EXP	745

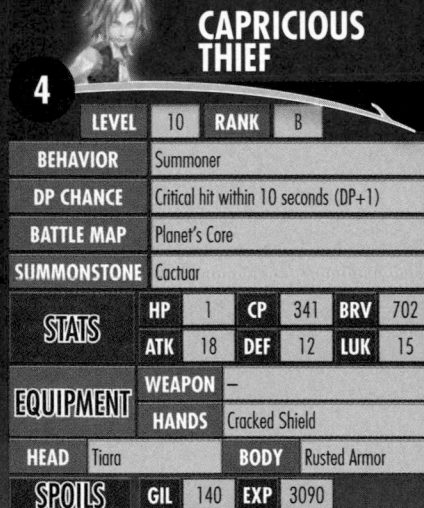

4 CAPRICIOUS THIEF

LEVEL	10	RANK	B

BEHAVIOR	Summoner
DP CHANCE	Critical hit within 10 seconds (DP+1)
BATTLE MAP	Planet's Core
SUMMONSTONE	Cactuar

STATS	HP	1	CP	341	BRV	702
	ATK	18	DEF	12	LUK	15

EQUIPMENT	WEAPON	—
	HANDS	Cracked Shield

HEAD	Tiara	BODY	Rusted Armor

SPOILS	GIL	140	EXP	3090

5 COUNTERFEIT WRAITH

LEVEL	10	RANK	G

BEHAVIOR	Blocker
DP CHANCE	Win without losing HP (DP+1)
BATTLE MAP	Pandaemonium
SUMMONSTONE	—

STATS	HP	1545	CP	359	BRV	101
	ATK	19	DEF	13	LUK	15

EQUIPMENT	WEAPON	—
	HANDS	Cracked Shield

HEAD	Charred Helm	BODY	—

SPOILS	GIL	140	EXP	927

ACCESSORIES	Defense Cuff x4, [HP] Near Death x2

6 TERRA

LEVEL	11	RANK	H

BEHAVIOR	Normal
DP CHANCE	—
BATTLE MAP	Old Chaos Shrine
SUMMONSTONE	—

STATS	HP	1859	CP	342	BRV	187
	ATK	25	DEF	21	LUK	15

EQUIPMENT	WEAPON	Staff
	HANDS	—

HEAD	—	BODY	Robe

SPOILS	GIL	168	EXP	1606

ACCESSORIES	Puppeteer's Wheel

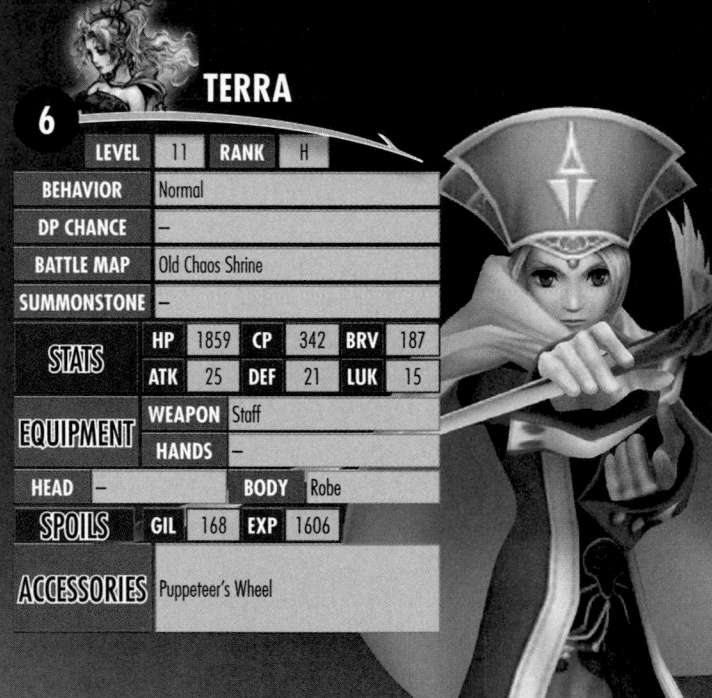

DESTINY ODYSSEY III

The last of Onion Knight's levels is also the most cluttered. As before, you can use Sight to reveal Enigma Areas. A rare battle piece and treasure chest are only revealed after a rating of 3 stars or better on previous runs. The rare, ultimate battle piece that shows up after a 3-star rating can prove to be a very difficult fight. This manikin facsimile of the Onion Knight is "Mean" with a capital M. It's extremely aggressive, Air Dashing straight for you continually; it spaces very well, staying at the edge of its attack range and punishing your mistakes; it takes off instantly for any EX Cores that appear; and it's very good at dodging incoming attacks. To make matters worse, this manikin also has Phoenix equipped, and often uses it the first time it hits you. This prevents its bravery from being broken. To win at a lower level, you'll have to play more or less perfectly: building more EX Force, using EX Mode as often as possible, and coaxing the foe into dodging Comet incorrectly (especially useful near the edges of the stage). The boss, Cloud of Darkness, is a relative pushover by comparison.

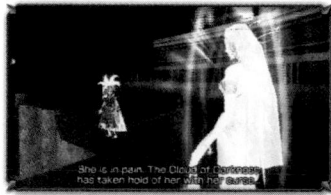
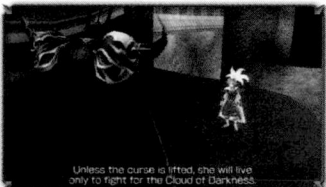
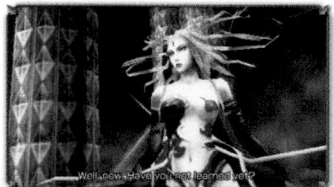
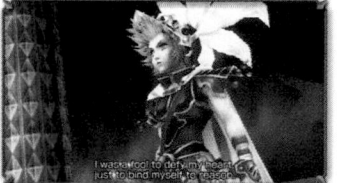

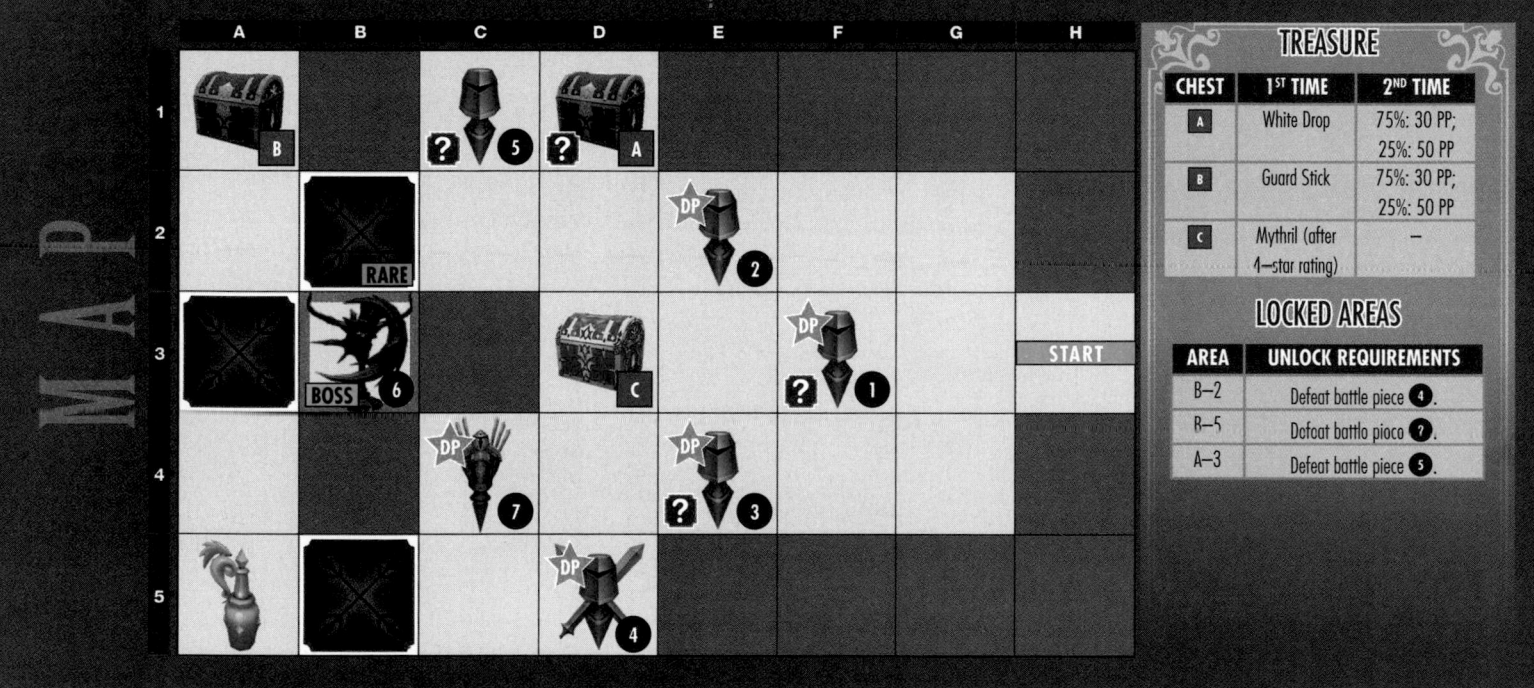

TREASURE

CHEST	1ST TIME	2ND TIME
A	White Drop	75%: 30 PP; 25%: 50 PP
B	Guard Stick	75%: 30 PP; 25%: 50 PP
C	Mythril (after 4-star rating)	—

LOCKED AREAS

AREA	UNLOCK REQUIREMENTS
B-2	Defeat battle piece ④.
B-5	Defeat battle piece ⑦.
A-3	Defeat battle piece ⑤.

DP EFFICIENCY ROUTE

After achieving a 3-star rating on this level, the rare battle piece necessary for maximum DP appears at C-4. However, after getting a 4-star rating, a rare chest appears that blocks the optimal route. So, you'll have to go for max DP either after getting a 3-star rating but before a 4-star rating, or after collecting the 4-star chest, which will not reappear on subsequent playthroughs. Once the proper scenario is laid out, head from the start to F-2. Here, you'll chain battle pieces ① and ②, both with DP Chances. Afterward, head to D-4, where you'll be sandwiched between battle pieces ③, ④, and ⑦. After chaining the lot of them, the Locked Area blocking the way to the boss disappears, allowing you to attack the boss and complete Onion Knight's Destiny Odyssey.

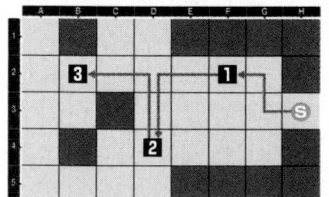

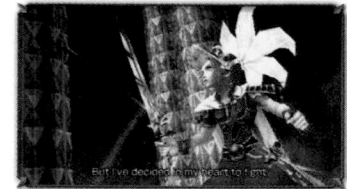
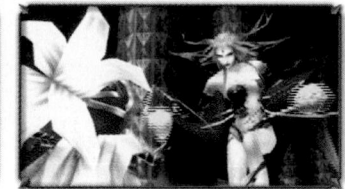
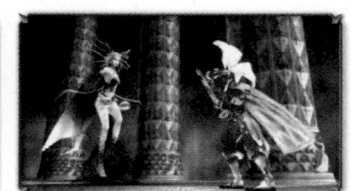
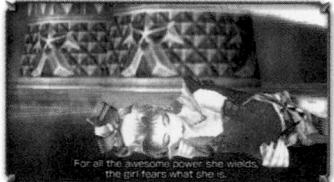

BATTLE PIECE DATA

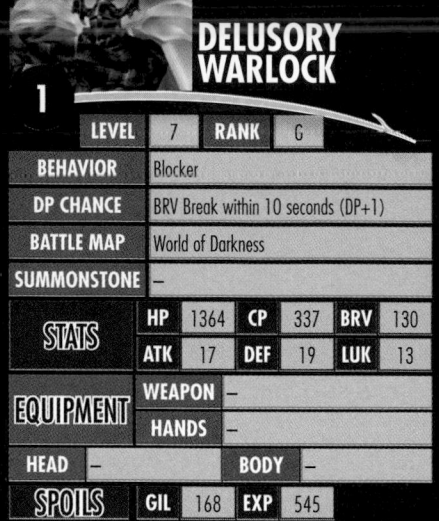

1 DELUSORY WARLOCK

LEVEL	7	RANK	G

BEHAVIOR	Blocker
DP CHANCE	BRV Break within 10 seconds (DP+1)
BATTLE MAP	World of Darkness
SUMMONSTONE	–

STATS	HP	1364	CP	337	BRV	130
	ATK	17	DEF	19	LUK	13

EQUIPMENT	WEAPON	–
	HANDS	–
HEAD	–	BODY	–

SPOILS	GIL	168	EXP	545

2 IMAGINARY CHAMPION

LEVEL	8	RANK	G

BEHAVIOR	Aggressive
DP CHANCE	Wall Rush within 10 seconds (DP+1)
BATTLE MAP	Planet's Core
SUMMONSTONE	Ultros

STATS	HP	1424	CP	338	BRV	136
	ATK	18	DEF	19	LUK	14

EQUIPMENT	WEAPON	–
	HANDS	–
HEAD	–	BODY	–

SPOILS	GIL	168	EXP	569

3 FALSE STALWART

LEVEL	6	RANK	G

BEHAVIOR	Evader
DP CHANCE	Win within 10 seconds (DP+1)
BATTLE MAP	Pandaemonium
SUMMONSTONE	–

STATS	HP	1303	CP	336	BRV	124
	ATK	18	DEF	19	LUK	13

EQUIPMENT	WEAPON	–
	HANDS	–
HEAD	–	BODY	–

SPOILS	GIL	168	EXP	521

4 IMITATION DESPOT

LEVEL	12	RANK	E

BEHAVIOR	Aggressive
DP CHANCE	Win without taking damage (DP+1)
BATTLE MAP	Order's Sanctuary
SUMMONSTONE	–

STATS	HP	1667	CP	343	BRV	159
	ATK	22	DEF	16	LUK	16

EQUIPMENT	WEAPON	–
	HANDS	Cracked Shield
HEAD	–	BODY	–

SPOILS	GIL	168	EXP	666

ACCESSORIES	Black Cape x4, [Position] In Midair

5 CAPRICIOUS REAPER

LEVEL	7	RANK	G

BEHAVIOR	Tricky
DP CHANCE	–
BATTLE MAP	Old Chaos Shrine
SUMMONSTONE	Bomb

STATS	HP	1364	CP	337	BRV	130
	ATK	16	DEF	18	LUK	13

EQUIPMENT	WEAPON	–
	HANDS	–
HEAD	–	BODY	–

SPOILS	GIL	168	EXP	545

6 CLOUD OF DARKNESS

LEVEL	15	RANK	D

BEHAVIOR	Conservative
DP CHANCE	–
BATTLE MAP	World of Darkness
SUMMONSTONE	Iron Giant

STATS	HP	2004	CP	364	BRV	315
	ATK	32	DEF	26	LUK	17

EQUIPMENT	WEAPON	Oak Staff
	HANDS	–
HEAD	Hairpin	BODY	Robe

SPOILS	GIL	252	EXP	4620

ACCESSORIES	Earring x2, Star Earring, [Position] Far from Opponent x2

7 COUNTERFEIT YOUTH

LEVEL	29	RANK	B

BEHAVIOR	Extreme
DP CHANCE	Win battle (DP+2)
BATTLE MAP	World of Darkness
SUMMONSTONE	–

STATS	HP	2697*	CP	378	BRV	257*
	ATK	36*	DEF	40*	LUK	24

EQUIPMENT	WEAPON	[Rank 5]
	HANDS	[Rank 4]
HEAD	[Rank 6]	BODY	[Rank 4]

SPOILS	GIL	336	EXP	2697

ACCESSORIES	Black Cape x4, [Position] In Midair

* Denotes use of the base value (for stats that vary).

DESTINY ODYSSEY III

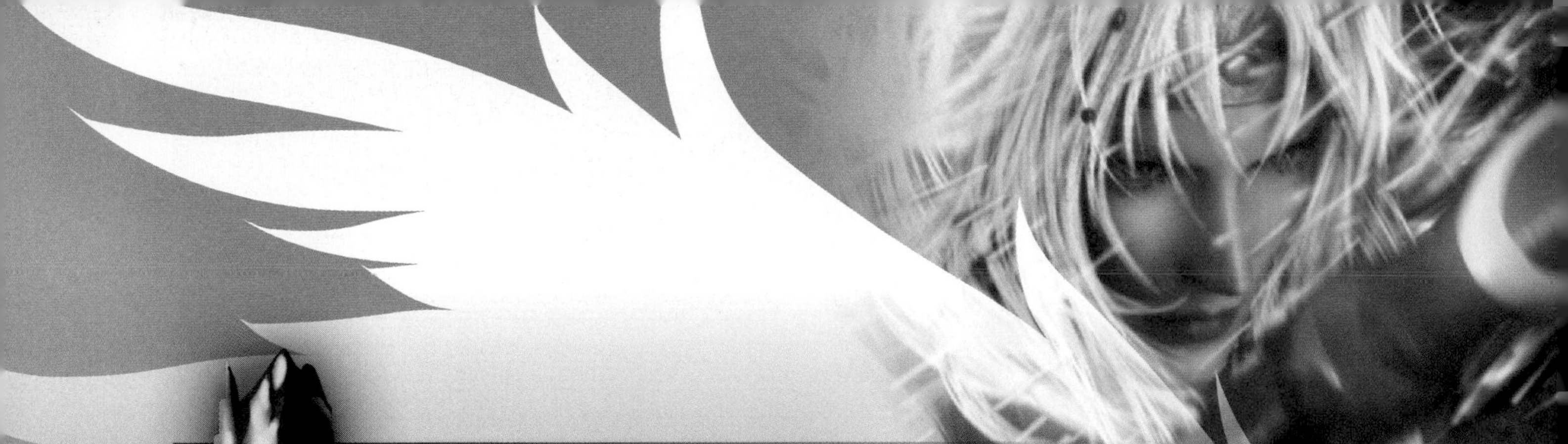

Difficulty ☆

Prerequisite
Finish Prologue

DESTINY ODYSSEY IV
MOONLIT KNIGHTS

REWARDS

At the end of each level, rewards are available if you finish with a positive number of Destiny Points, or DP. This walkthrough includes miniature level maps that indicate the most efficient route to take through a given level, in order to maximize DP.

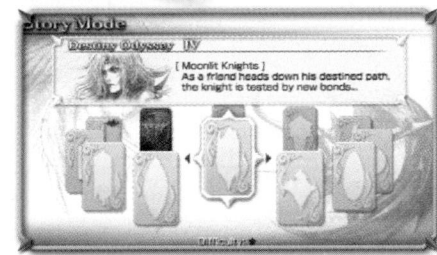

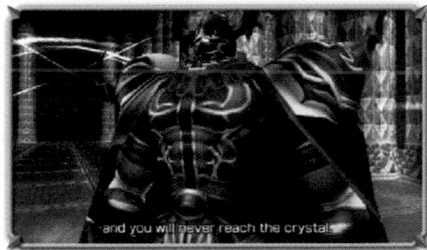

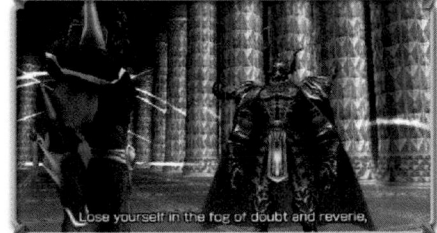

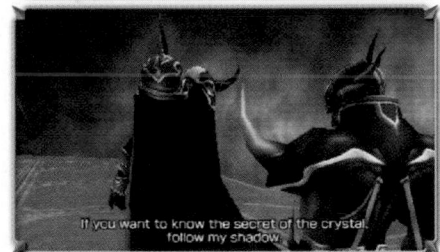

Hampered by his duality and his doubt, Cecil has made no progress toward finding his crystal. To assuage his brother's worry, Golbez beckons him to follow. But is this agent of Chaos trustworthy?

LEVEL COMPLETION

REMAINING DP		1ST TIME		2ND TIME
7		Rosetta Stone		300 PP
6		Ice Armor		200 PP
5		Flame Armor		120 PP
4		Bomb Summonstone		80 PP
3		1000 gil		50 PP
2		600 gil		30 PP
1		300 gil		20 PP
0		100 gil		10 PP

DESTINY ODYSSEY IV COMPLETION

STAR RATING	SP REQUIRED	AWARD
☆	100	New skill
☆☆	200	Special areas unlocked
☆☆☆	300	Rare battle pieces spawned
☆☆☆☆	400	Rare treasure chests spawned
–	500 SP, then every 500 SP extra	100 PP

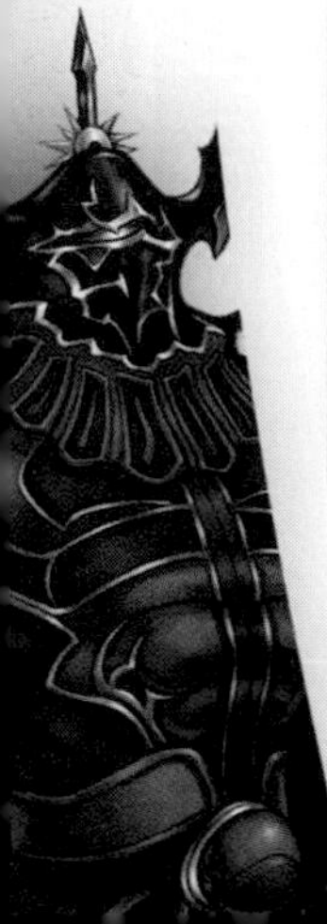

At the end of each set of levels, you'll receive rewards based on your performance. Story Points, or SP, are awarded after each level based on remaining DP, HP, and the number of engagements undertaken. Points are penalized for retries, or for a DP total that dips into negatives. If you miss out on a desired bonus on the first playthrough, don't worry—SP is cumulative across multiple playthroughs.

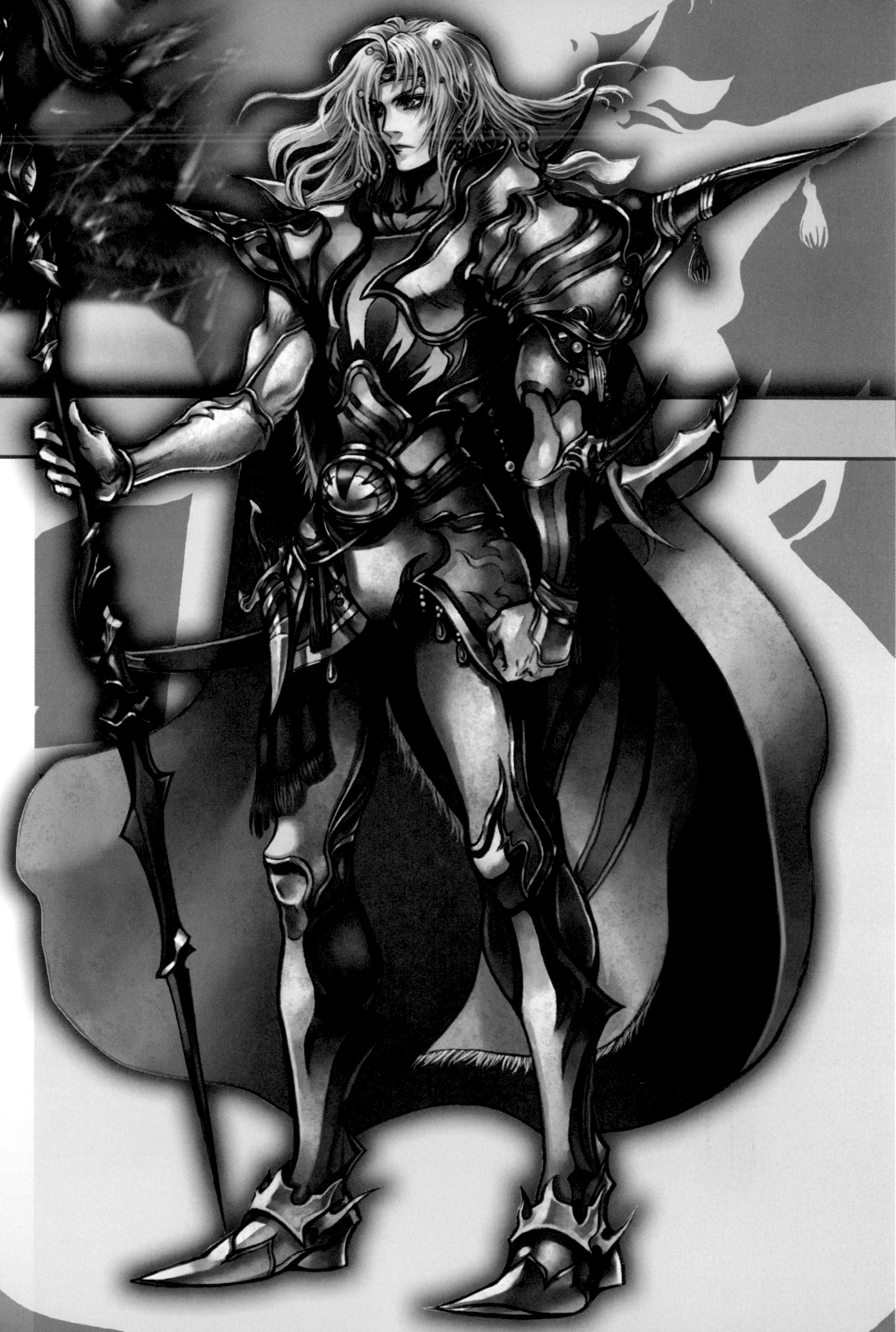

DESTINY ODYSSEY IV

Levels for the conflicted knight Cecil are pretty straightforward. The biggest issue is wrapping your head around Cecil's combat style. Both Paladin and Dark Knight jobs are available to him. As a Dark Knight, Cecil focuses on methodical ranged attacks, while as a Paladin, his attacks are better suited to close combat. Switch to Paladin by using HP attacks in mid-air, and switch to Dark Knight by using HP attacks on the ground. Each job has a unique set of bravery attacks. During EX Mode, switch freely between jobs with ▬ + ▣.

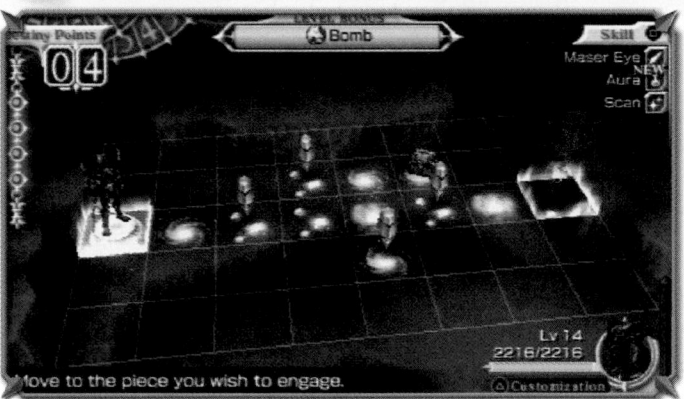

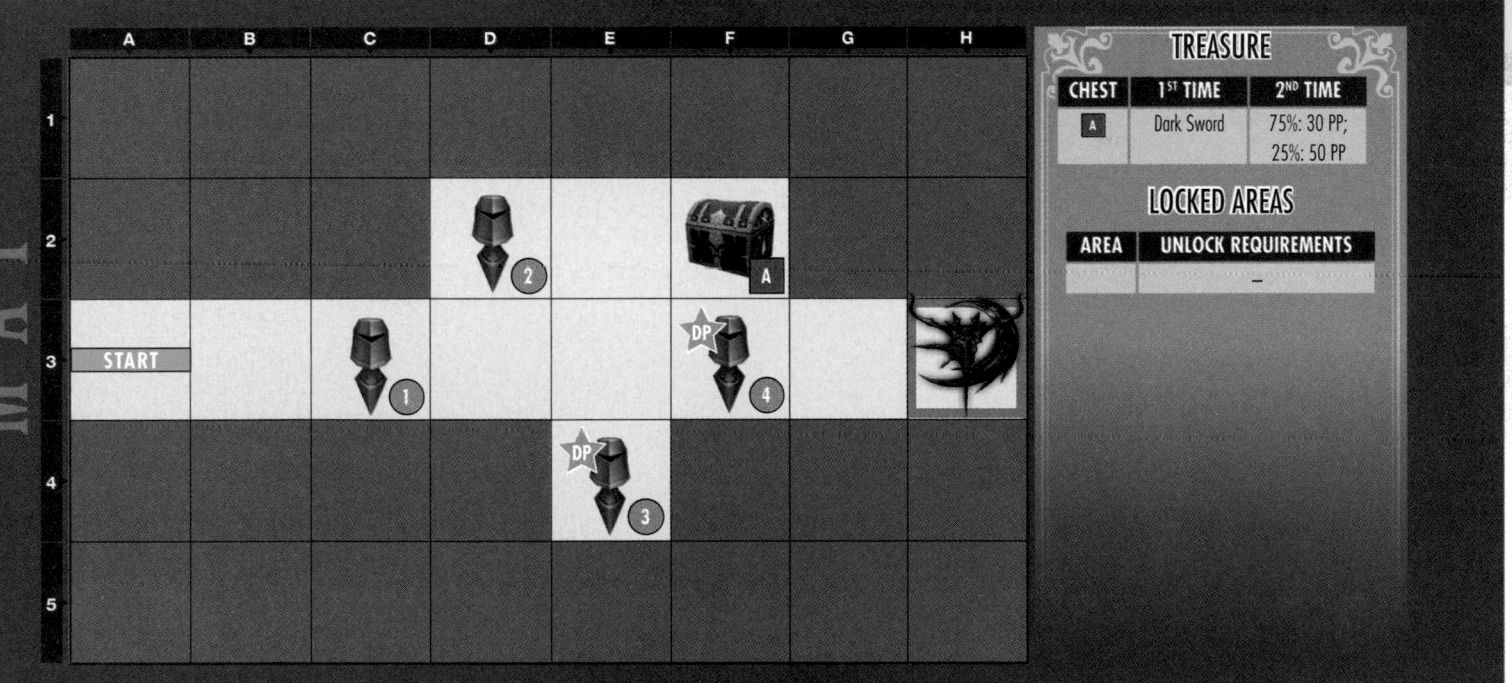

TREASURE

CHEST	1ST TIME	2ND TIME
A	Dark Sword	75%: 30 PP; 25%: 50 PP

LOCKED AREAS

AREA	UNLOCK REQUIREMENTS
	—

DP EFFICIENCY ROUTE

To maximize DP here, simply proceed in a straight line to the Stigma of Chaos. Build a full EX Gauge against battle piece ①, so you can activate EX Mode and guarantee a quick critical hit against battle piece ③. While you can attempt to build up your EX Gauge against battle piece ④, it's best to just try and finish off that battle quickly to avoid potentially taking damage and missing out on DP.

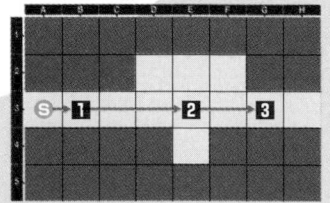

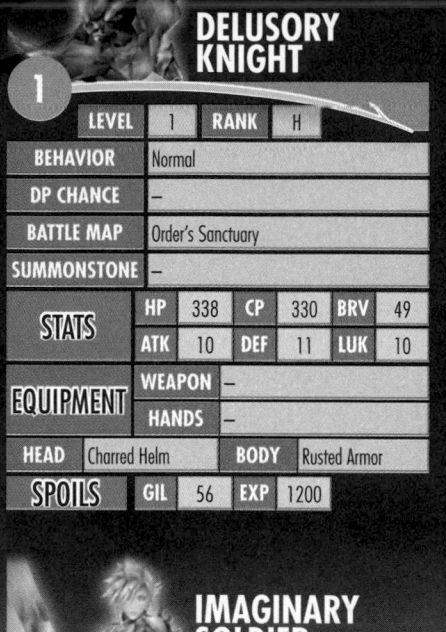

BATTLE PIECE DATA

1 DELUSORY KNIGHT

LEVEL	1	RANK	H

BEHAVIOR	Normal
DP CHANCE	–
BATTLE MAP	Order's Sanctuary
SUMMONSTONE	–

STATS	HP	338	CP	330	BRV	49
	ATK	10	DEF	11	LUK	10

EQUIPMENT	WEAPON	–
	HANDS	–

HEAD	Charred Helm	BODY	Rusted Armor

SPOILS	GIL	56	EXP	1200

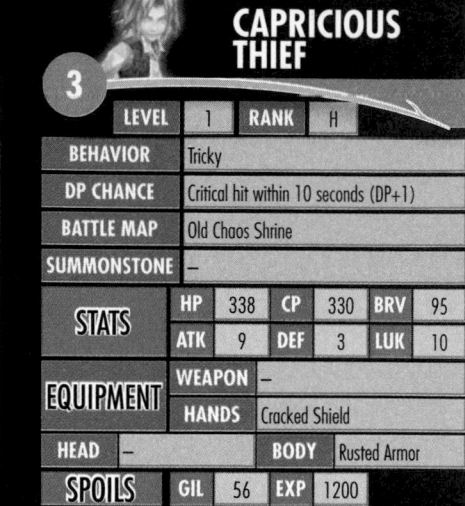

2 TRANSIENT LION

LEVEL	1	RANK	H

BEHAVIOR	Aggressive
DP CHANCE	–
BATTLE MAP	Order's Sanctuary
SUMMONSTONE	–

STATS	HP	338	CP	330	BRV	49
	ATK	10	DEF	12	LUK	10

EQUIPMENT	WEAPON	–
	HANDS	–

HEAD	Charred Helm	BODY	Rusted Armor

SPOILS	GIL	56	EXP	1200

3 CAPRICIOUS THIEF

LEVEL	1	RANK	H

BEHAVIOR	Tricky
DP CHANCE	Critical hit within 10 seconds (DP+1)
BATTLE MAP	Old Chaos Shrine
SUMMONSTONE	–

STATS	HP	338	CP	330	BRV	95
	ATK	9	DEF	3	LUK	10

EQUIPMENT	WEAPON	–
	HANDS	Cracked Shield

HEAD	–	BODY	Rusted Armor

SPOILS	GIL	56	EXP	1200

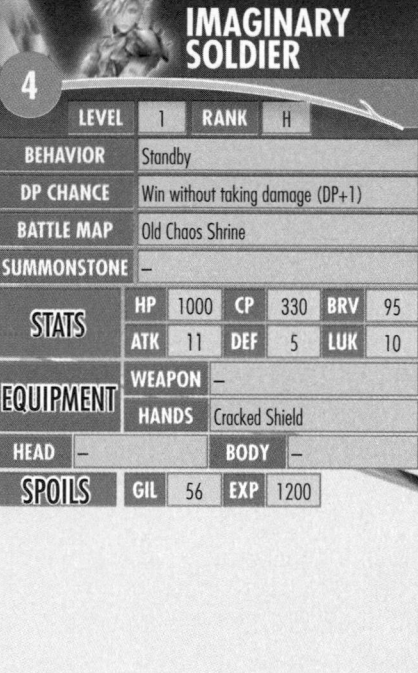

4 IMAGINARY SOLDIER

LEVEL	1	RANK	H

BEHAVIOR	Standby
DP CHANCE	Win without taking damage (DP+1)
BATTLE MAP	Old Chaos Shrine
SUMMONSTONE	–

STATS	HP	1000	CP	330	BRV	95
	ATK	11	DEF	5	LUK	10

EQUIPMENT	WEAPON	–
	HANDS	Cracked Shield

HEAD	–	BODY	–

SPOILS	GIL	56	EXP	1200

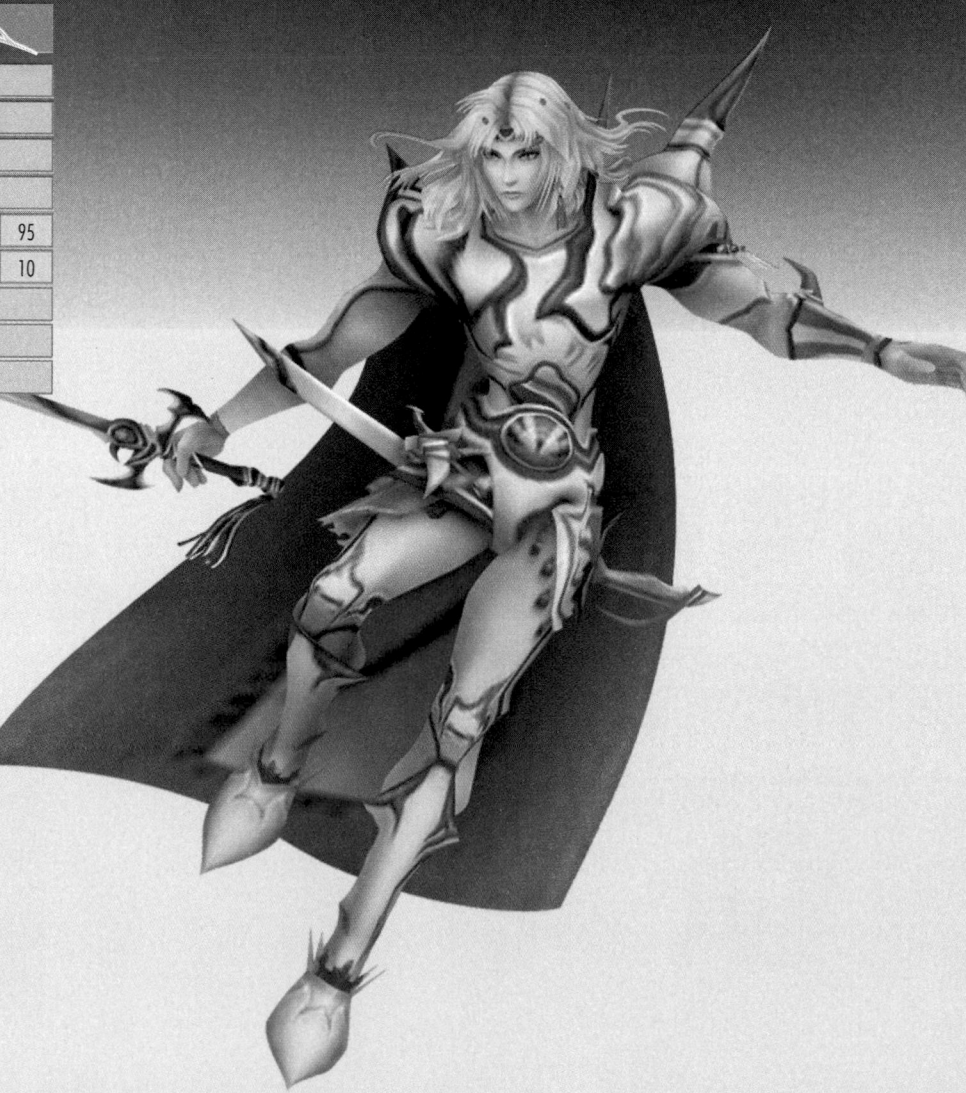

DESTINY ODYSSEY IV

This level has two routes to the Stigma of Chaos. One route has a treasure chest along with many DP Chance battles. Raid the treasure chest to obtain Dark Armor—four pieces of this set can be found in treasure chests across Destiny Odyssey IV, and wearing any three of the pieces at once grants significant bonus damage to Wall Rushes. The other route houses a Potion and Summonstone. The Carbuncle Summonstone is hidden away here behind a Locked Area that only opens after clearing Destiny Odyssey IV with at least a 2-star rating. Carbuncle can be a life-saver against powerful opponents, since it matches the opponent's bravery total to yours. Very useful when your opponent has enough bravery built up to assure a kill shot, while you're just sitting on base bravery!

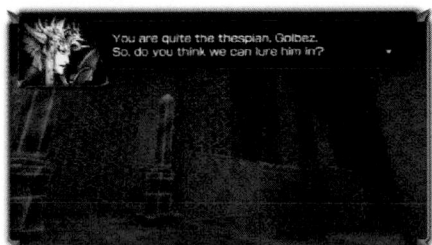
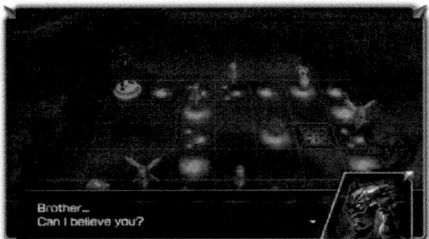
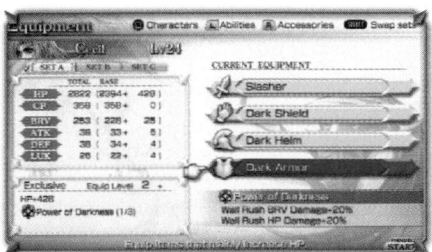

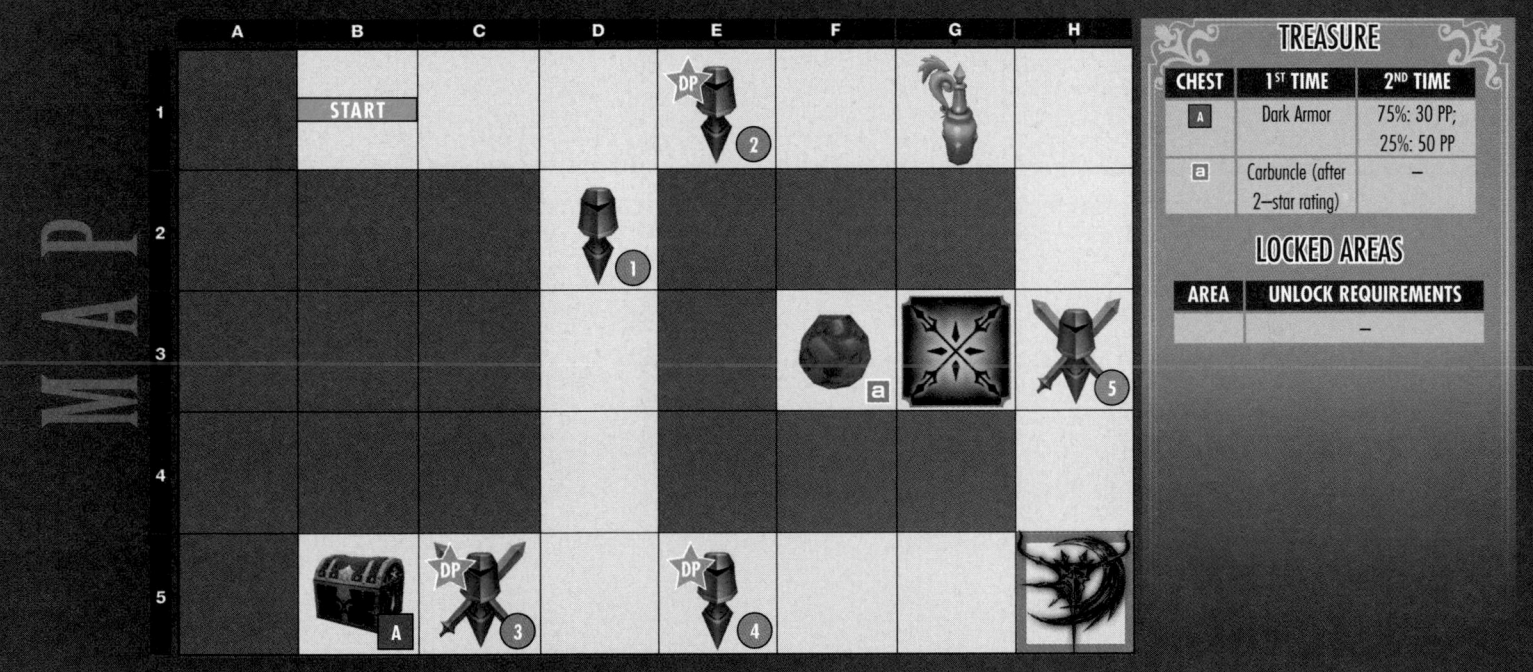

TREASURE		
CHEST	1ST TIME	2ND TIME
A	Dark Armor	75%: 30 PP; 25%: 50 PP
a	Carbuncle (after 2—star rating)	—

LOCKED AREAS	
AREA	UNLOCK REQUIREMENTS
	—

DP EFFICIENCY ROUTE

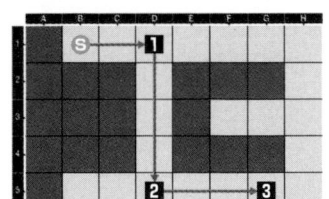

After chaining battle pieces adjacent to D-1 and D-5 (scoring all DP Chances, of course!), proceed to the Stigma of Chaos to end the level. You must skip the Potion, treasure chest, and Summonstone to do this.

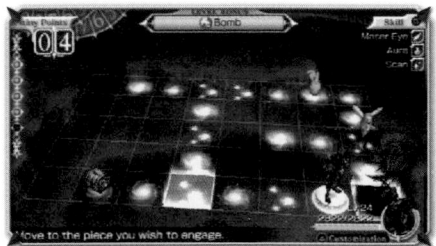

BATTLE PIECE DATA

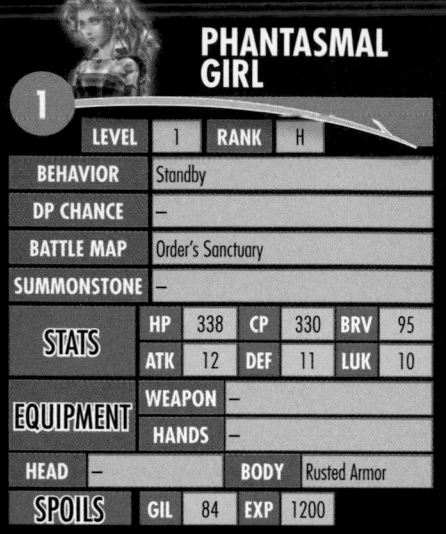

1 PHANTASMAL GIRL

LEVEL	1	RANK	H

BEHAVIOR	Standby
DP CHANCE	—
BATTLE MAP	Order's Sanctuary
SUMMONSTONE	—

STATS	HP	338	CP	330	BRV	95
	ATK	12	DEF	11	LUK	10

EQUIPMENT	WEAPON	—
	HANDS	—

HEAD	—		BODY	Rusted Armor

SPOILS	GIL	84	EXP	1200

2 IMITATION LIEGEMAN

LEVEL	1	RANK	H

BEHAVIOR	Aggressive
DP CHANCE	BRV Break within 10 seconds (DP+1)
BATTLE MAP	Old Chaos Shrine
SUMMONSTONE	—

STATS	HP	1000	CP	330	BRV	49
	ATK	12	DEF	5	LUK	10

EQUIPMENT	WEAPON	—
	HANDS	Cracked Shield

HEAD	Cracked Helm		BODY	—

SPOILS	GIL	84	EXP	1200

3 DELUSORY WARLOCK

LEVEL	3	RANK	G

BEHAVIOR	Aggressive
DP CHANCE	Win within 10 seconds (DP+1)
BATTLE MAP	World of Darkness
SUMMONSTONE	—

STATS	HP	1121	CP	332	BRV	61
	ATK	13	DEF	19	LUK	11

EQUIPMENT	WEAPON	—
	HANDS	Knight's Shield

HEAD	Charred Helm		BODY	—

SPOILS	GIL	84	EXP	1345

ACCESSORIES	Hyper Ring, Guardian Bangle, [HP] Near Loss x6

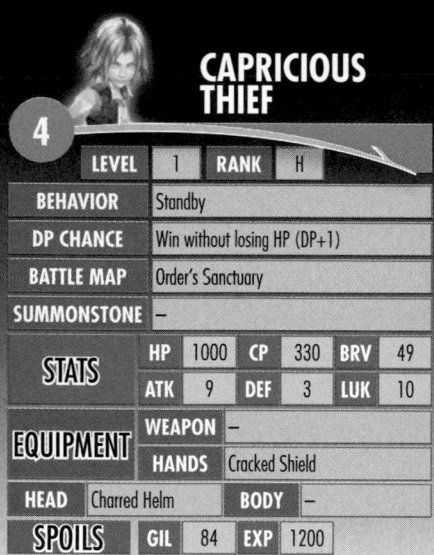

4 CAPRICIOUS THIEF

LEVEL	1	RANK	H

BEHAVIOR	Standby
DP CHANCE	Win without losing HP (DP+1)
BATTLE MAP	Order's Sanctuary
SUMMONSTONE	—

STATS	HP	1000	CP	330	BRV	49
	ATK	9	DEF	3	LUK	10

EQUIPMENT	WEAPON	—
	HANDS	Cracked Shield

HEAD	Charred Helm		BODY	—

SPOILS	GIL	84	EXP	1200

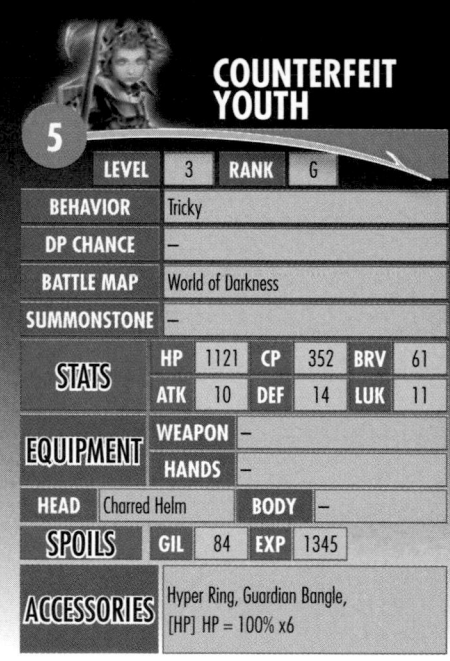

5 COUNTERFEIT YOUTH

LEVEL	3	RANK	G

BEHAVIOR	Tricky
DP CHANCE	—
BATTLE MAP	World of Darkness
SUMMONSTONE	—

STATS	HP	1121	CP	352	BRV	61
	ATK	10	DEF	14	LUK	11

EQUIPMENT	WEAPON	—
	HANDS	—

HEAD	Charred Helm		BODY	—

SPOILS	GIL	84	EXP	1345

ACCESSORIES	Hyper Ring, Guardian Bangle, [HP] HP = 100% x6

STARTING DP	MAX FINISHING	ENGAGEMENTS
6	5 (+2 after 3-star rating)	6 (+2 after 3-star rating)

This level has two routes to the Stigma of Chaos. One route has a treasure chest along with many DP Chance battles. Raid the treasure chest to obtain Dark Armor—four pieces of this set can be found in treasure chests across Destiny Odyssey IV, and wearing any three of the pieces at once grants significant bonus damage to Wall Rushes. The other route houses a Potion and Summonstone. The Carbuncle Summonstone is hidden away here behind a Locked Area that only opens after clearing Destiny Odyssey IV with at least a 2-star rating. Carbuncle can be a life-saver against powerful opponents, since it The approach to this level changes quite a bit depending on how many times you've tackled it. At first, you'll want to defeat battle piece ② to open up the Locked Area blocking off treasure chest Ⓐ. In later visits, after achieving a 3-star or higher rating, your attention should be focused on treasure chest Ⓑ and battle piece ⑦. This rare battle piece represents a tough copy of Golbez, who may be difficult to defeat until your level is higher. At least it has predictable behavior. It generally focuses on bravery attacks early on, often rushing in to apply them. Block first, then strike with attacks of your own while the foe reels. When not going for blocks, always run in wide circles around the Golbez imposter, causing its bravery attacks to miss.

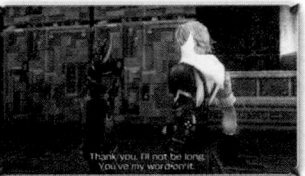
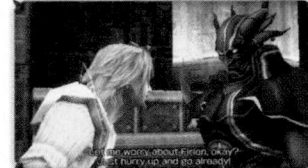
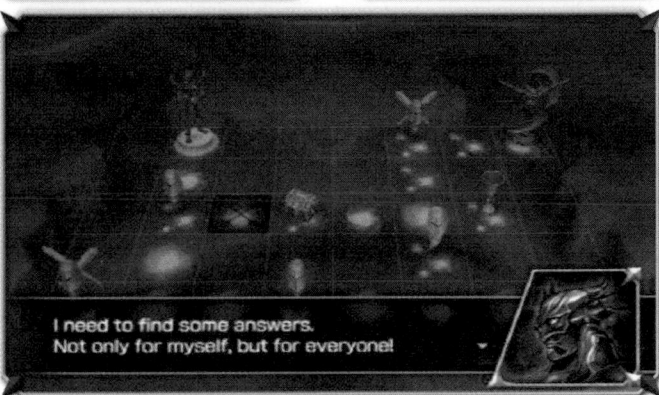

Tidus offers to cover for Cecil while he seeks out his supposedly evil brother for answers...

MAP

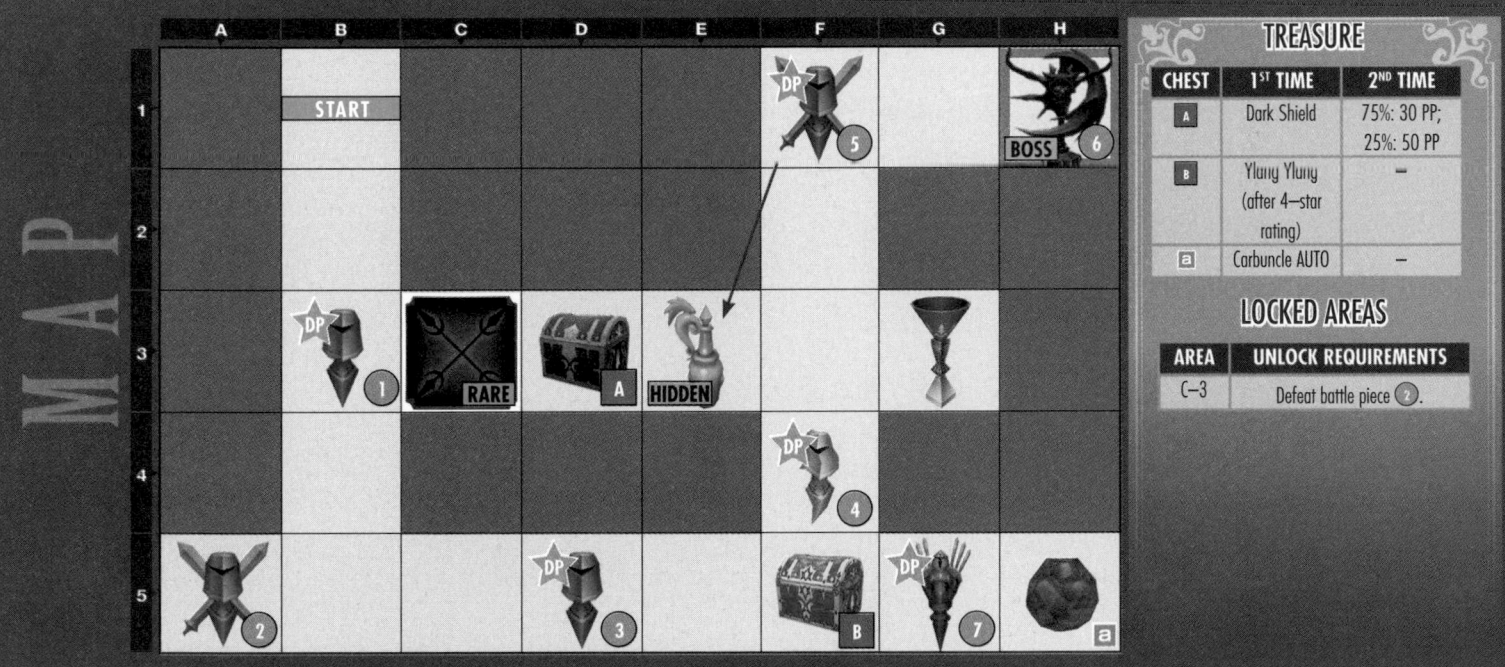

TREASURE

CHEST	1ST TIME	2ND TIME
Ⓐ	Dark Shield	75%: 30 PP; 25%: 50 PP
Ⓑ	Ylang Ylang (after 4-star rating)	—
ⓐ	Carbuncle AUTO	—

LOCKED AREAS

AREA	UNLOCK REQUIREMENTS
C–3	Defeat battle piece ②.

DP EFFICIENCY ROUTE

Before attempting max DP on this level, you'll need at least a 3-star rating on Destiny Odyssey IV, so the rare, ultimate battle piece spawns at G-5. Head down from the start, taking out battle pieces ① and ③ before engaging ④ and ⑦. If you achieve a 4-star rating, the rare treasure chest at F-5 will actually throw a monkey wrench into max DP plans, since you'll have to use up an extra Destiny Point to open it! However, once you've opened the rare chest, it won't appear on future runs, making another max DP attempt possible. After chaining pieces ④ and ⑦, head up to battle piece ⑤, then the Stigma of Chaos to finish the level.

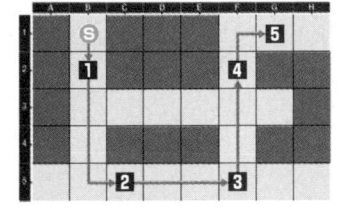
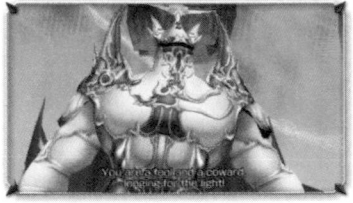

BATTLE PIECE DATA

1 TRANSIENT LION

LEVEL	1	RANK	H

BEHAVIOR	Aggressive
DP CHANCE	Win without taking damage (DP+1)
BATTLE MAP	Planet's Core
SUMMONSTONE	—

STATS	HP	1000	CP	330	BRV	95
	ATK	10	DEF	12	LUK	10

EQUIPMENT	WEAPON	—
	HANDS	—
HEAD	—	BODY	—

SPOILS	GIL	112	EXP	1200

2 COUNTERFEIT YOUTH

LEVEL	5	RANK	G

BEHAVIOR	Aggressive
DP CHANCE	—
BATTLE MAP	Order's Sanctuary
SUMMONSTONE	—

STATS	HP	1242	CP	354	BRV	72
	ATK	12	DEF	16	LUK	12

EQUIPMENT	WEAPON	—
	HANDS	—
HEAD	Charred Helm	BODY	—

SPOILS	GIL	112	EXP	1490

ACCESSORIES	Hyper Ring, Guardian Bangle, [HP] HP = 100% x6

3 COUNTERFEIT WRAITH

LEVEL	1	RANK	H

BEHAVIOR	Standby
DP CHANCE	Win within 10 seconds (DP+1)
BATTLE MAP	World of Darkness
SUMMONSTONE	—

STATS	HP	1000	CP	350	BRV	95
	ATK	10	DEF	12	LUK	10

EQUIPMENT	WEAPON	—
	HANDS	—
HEAD	—	BODY	—

SPOILS	GIL	112	EXP	1200

4 EPHEMERAL VISION

LEVEL	5	RANK	C

BEHAVIOR	Aggressive
DP CHANCE	Critical hit within 10 seconds (DP+1)
BATTLE MAP	Old Chaos Shrine
SUMMONSTONE	—

STATS	HP	1	CP	335	BRV	118*
	ATK	15	DEF	16*	LUK	12

EQUIPMENT	WEAPON	—
	HANDS	Cracked Shield
HEAD	[Rank 4]	BODY	Rusted Armor

SPOILS	GIL	112	EXP	2484

ACCESSORIES	Arcane Resin, The Rotten, Gaia Ring, [Position] Near Opponent x5

5 DELUSORY WARLOCK

LEVEL	4	RANK	G

BEHAVIOR	Standby
DP CHANCE	EX Burst within 10 seconds (DP+1)
BATTLE MAP	Old Chaos Shrine
SUMMONSTONE	—

STATS	HP	1182	CP	333	BRV	67
	ATK	14	DEF	20	LUK	12

EQUIPMENT	WEAPON	—
	HANDS	[Rank 3]
HEAD	Charred Helm	BODY	—

SPOILS	GIL	112	EXP	1418

ACCESSORIES	Hyper Ring, Guardian Bangle, [HP] Near Loss x6

6 EXDEATH

LEVEL	7	RANK	F

BEHAVIOR	Valiant
DP CHANCE	—
BATTLE MAP	Planet's Core
SUMMONSTONE	—

STATS	HP	1792	CP	356	BRV	141
	ATK	20	DEF	20	LUK	13

EQUIPMENT	WEAPON	Staff
	HANDS	—
HEAD	—	BODY	Bronze Armor

SPOILS	GIL	168	EXP	2728

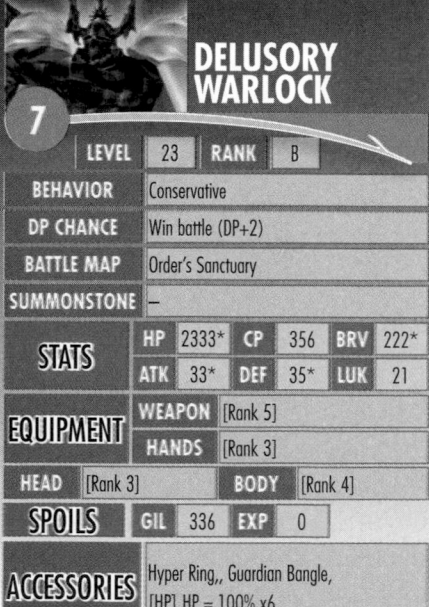

7 DELUSORY WARLOCK

LEVEL	23	RANK	B

BEHAVIOR	Conservative
DP CHANCE	Win battle (DP+2)
BATTLE MAP	Order's Sanctuary
SUMMONSTONE	—

STATS	HP	2333*	CP	356	BRV	222*
	ATK	33*	DEF	35*	LUK	21

EQUIPMENT	WEAPON	[Rank 5]
	HANDS	[Rank 3]
HEAD	[Rank 3]	BODY	[Rank 4]

SPOILS	GIL	336	EXP	0

ACCESSORIES	Hyper Ring,, Guardian Bangle, [HP] HP = 100% x6

* Denotes use of the base value (for stats that vary).

DESTINY ODYSSEY IV

Look for the Dark Helm, another piece of the dark set, here at D-1. Grabbing this item provides a good example of a method to save DP—open it before engaging the adjacent battle piece, and the battle piece will engage you instead. Opening the chest and fighting the foe together takes only one DP. Similarly, if you engage the enemy from C-1 you could open the treasure chest from your home area without expending any additional DP. Another chest, located at H-5, can only be accessed after scoring a 2-star rating for the whole chapter. Watch out for expert battle piece ⑤. This Sephiroth manikin strikes relentlessly with attacks that hit a large area. Dodge and counter the crystal creature's assault.

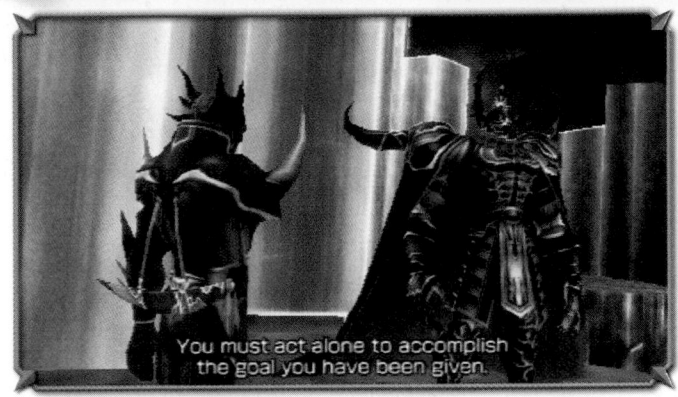

You must act alone to accomplish the goal you have been given.

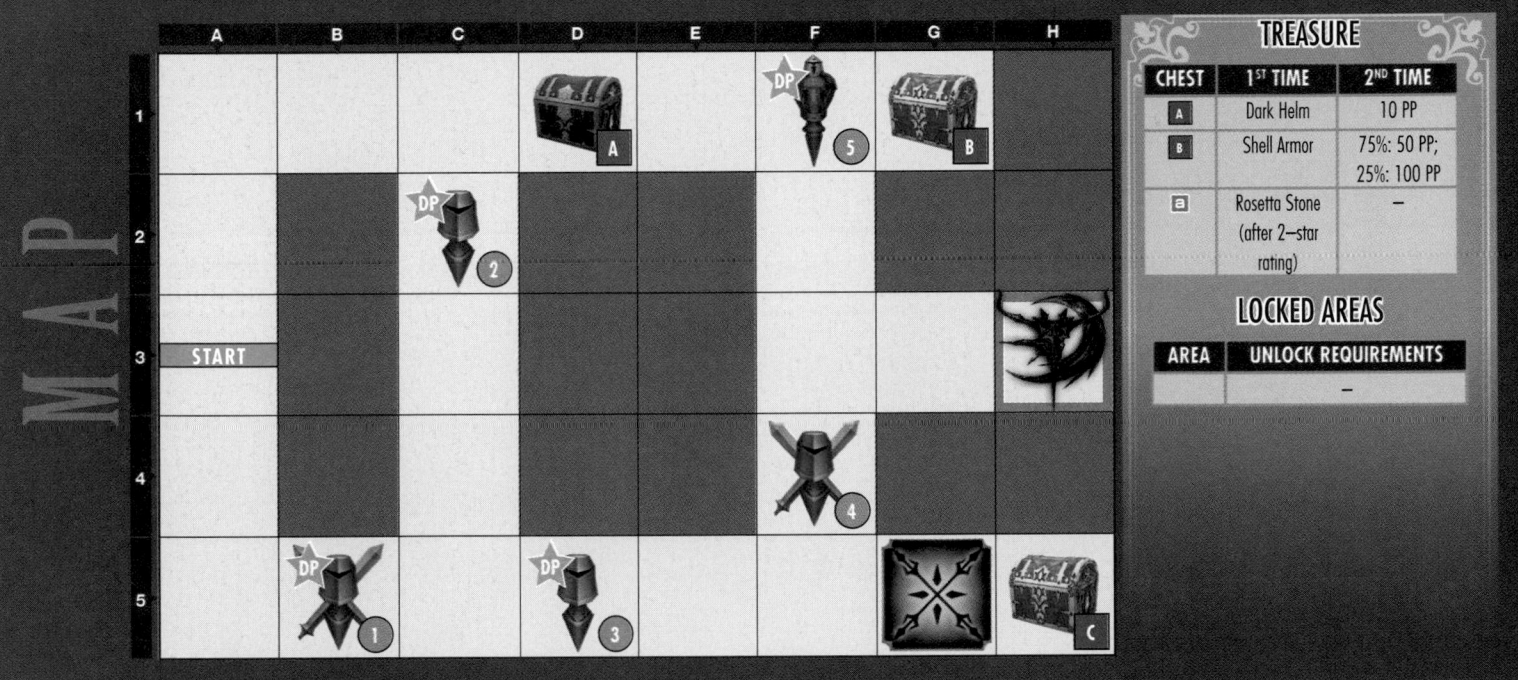

MAP

TREASURE

CHEST	1ST TIME	2ND TIME
A	Dark Helm	10 PP
B	Shell Armor	75%: 50 PP; 25%: 100 PP
a	Rosetta Stone (after 2–star rating)	–

LOCKED AREAS

AREA	UNLOCK REQUIREMENTS
	–

DP EFFICIENCY ROUTE

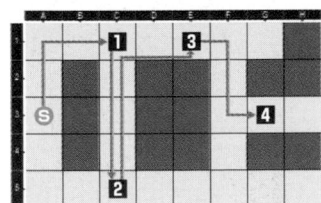

By traveling to C-1 at the outset, you can open the treasure chest and engage battle piece ②. Then, head down to C-5 and chain battle pieces ① and ③. Finally, engage battle piece ⑤ before heading to the Stigma of Chaos, completing the level.

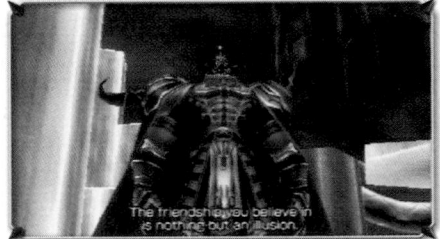

The friendship you believe in is nothing but an illusion.

BATTLE PIECE DATA

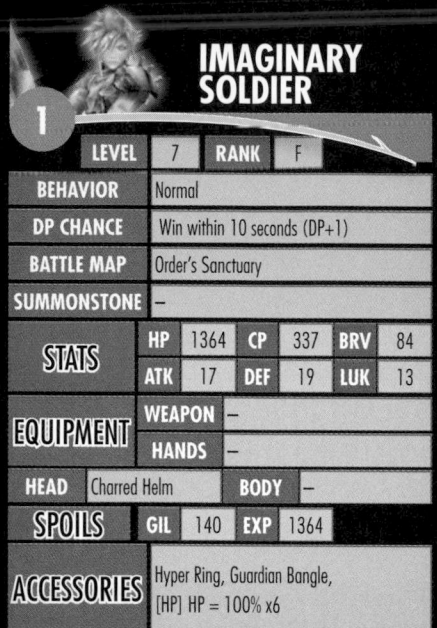

1. IMAGINARY SOLDIER

LEVEL	7	RANK F

Field	Value
BEHAVIOR	Normal
DP CHANCE	Win within 10 seconds (DP+1)
BATTLE MAP	Order's Sanctuary
SUMMONSTONE	–

STATS

HP	1364	CP	337	BRV	84
ATK	17	DEF	19	LUK	13

EQUIPMENT

WEAPON	–
HANDS	–
HEAD	Charred Helm
BODY	–

SPOILS — GIL 140 · EXP 1364

ACCESSORIES — Hyper Ring, Guardian Bangle, [HP] HP = 100% x6

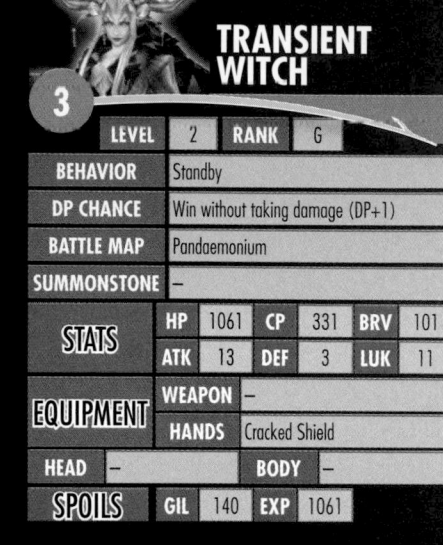

2. PHANTASMAL GIRL

LEVEL	2	RANK G

Field	Value
BEHAVIOR	Aggressive
DP CHANCE	BRV Break within 10 seconds (DP+1)
BATTLE MAP	Kefka's Tower
SUMMONSTONE	–

STATS

HP	1061	CP	331	BRV	101
ATK	13	DEF	4	LUK	11

EQUIPMENT

WEAPON	–
HANDS	Cracked Shield
HEAD	–
BODY	–

SPOILS — GIL 140 · EXP 1061

3. TRANSIENT WITCH

LEVEL	2	RANK G

Field	Value
BEHAVIOR	Standby
DP CHANCE	Win without taking damage (DP+1)
BATTLE MAP	Pandaemonium
SUMMONSTONE	–

STATS

HP	1061	CP	331	BRV	101
ATK	13	DEF	3	LUK	11

EQUIPMENT

WEAPON	–
HANDS	Cracked Shield
HEAD	–
BODY	–

SPOILS — GIL 140 · EXP 1061

4. DELUSORY WARLOCK

LEVEL	8	RANK F

Field	Value
BEHAVIOR	Normal
DP CHANCE	–
BATTLE MAP	Kefka's Tower
SUMMONSTONE	–

STATS

HP	1424	CP	338	BRV	136*
ATK	18	DEF	20*	LUK	14

EQUIPMENT

WEAPON	–
HANDS	[Rank 4]
HEAD	Charred Helm
BODY	–

SPOILS — GIL 140 · EXP 1424

ACCESSORIES — Hyper Ring, Guardian Bangle, [HP] Near Loss x6

5. IMAGINARY CHAMPION

LEVEL	15	RANK C

Field	Value
BEHAVIOR	Valiant
DP CHANCE	Win battle (DP+1)
BATTLE MAP	Old Chaos Shrine
SUMMONSTONE	–

STATS

HP	2640	CP	347	BRV	176*
ATK	40	DEF	26*	LUK	17

EQUIPMENT

WEAPON	[Rank 4]
HANDS	[Rank 2]
HEAD	Iron Helm
BODY	[Rank 3]

SPOILS — GIL 140 · EXP 0

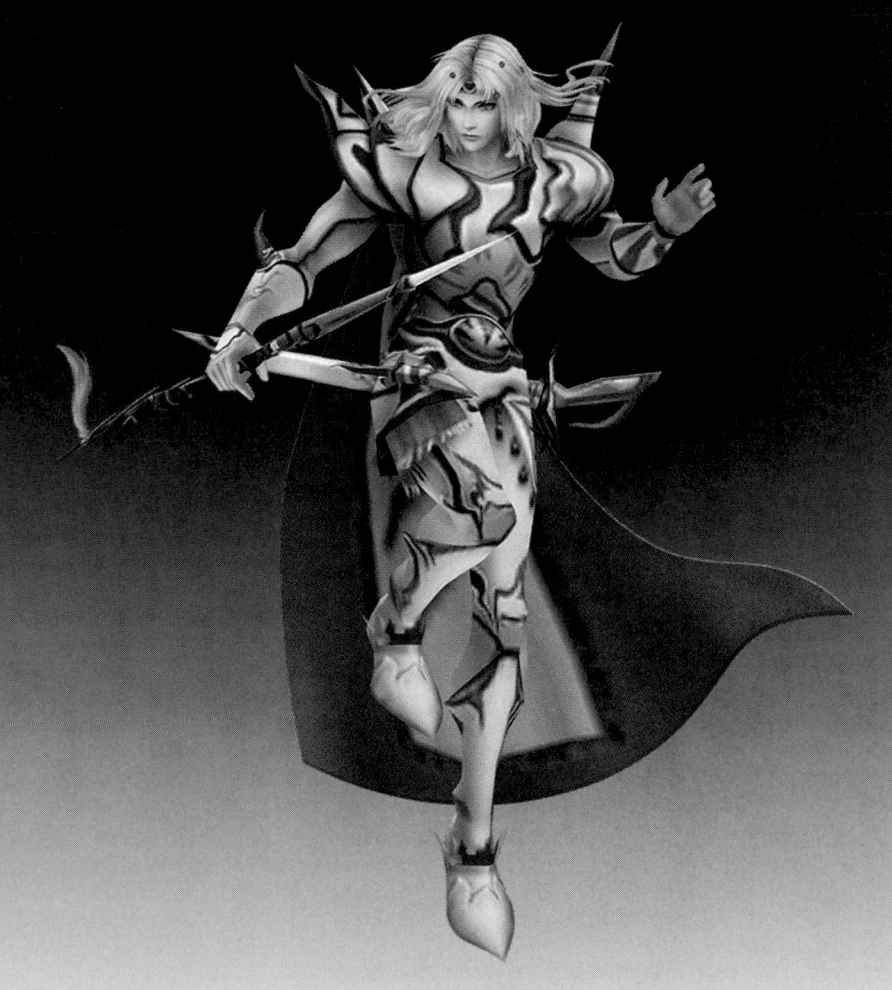

* Denotes use of the base value (for stats that vary).

DESTINY ODYSSEY IV-5

The last level here is a straight shot across to the Stigma of Chaos, with some detours along the way to open Locked Areas and scavenge treasure. A 3-star rating for Destiny Odyssey IV places a rare battle piece at F-4. The terrain of this battle makes a great ally. Hide behind the small moonrock formations and send Dark Flame HP attacks toward the Cecil manikin. Dark Flame can pass through solid structures and track the enemy, making it perfect for this environment. If you haven't yet reached level 22 and learned Dark Flame, you'll have to fight out in the open. Let your opponent miss with an attack like Saint's Fall, then strike while it recovers.

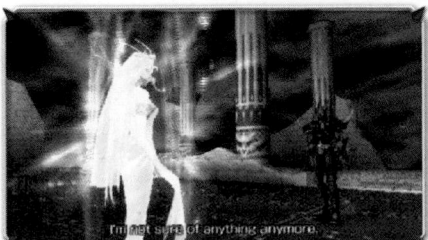
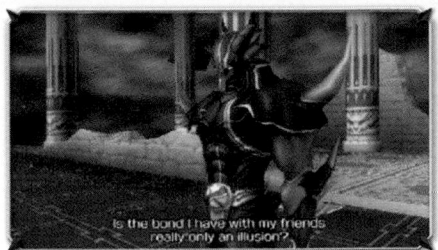

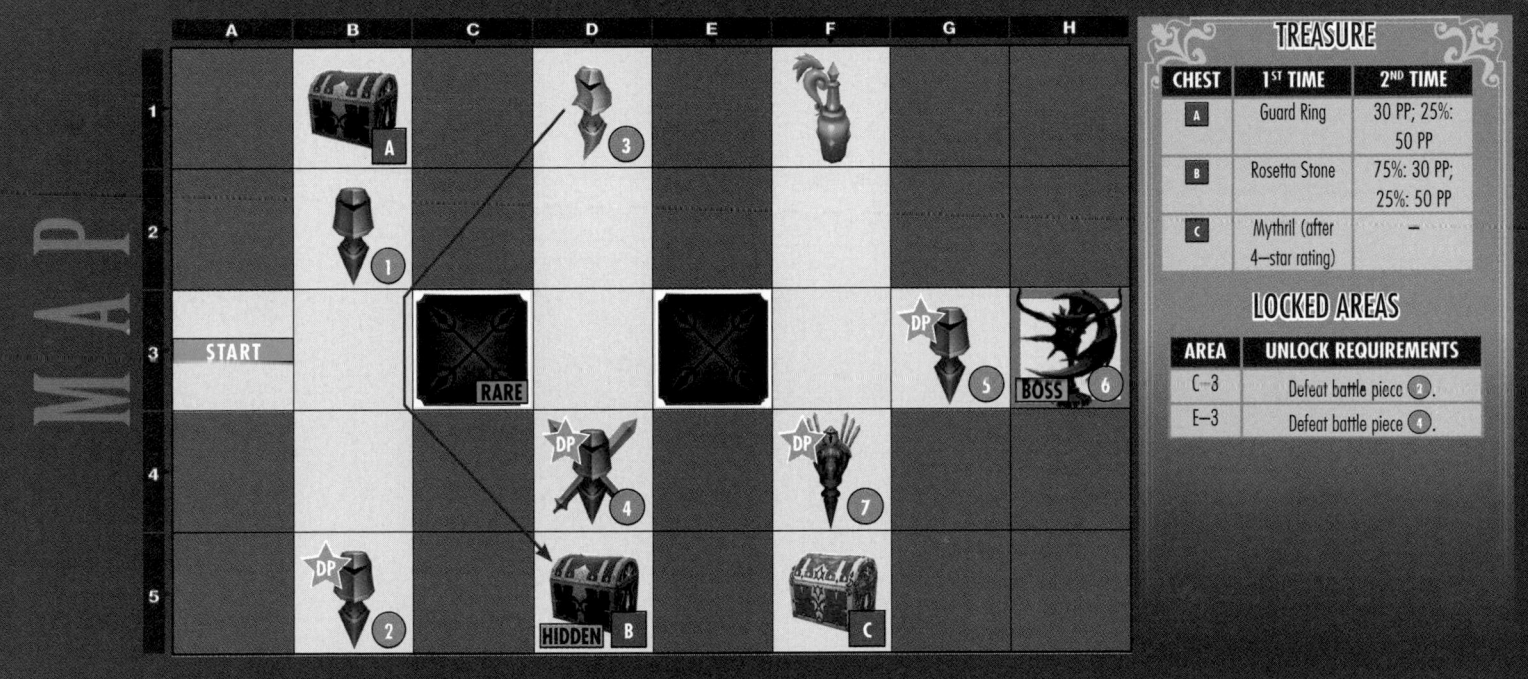

TREASURE

CHEST	1ST TIME	2ND TIME
A	Guard Ring	30 PP; 25%: 50 PP
B	Rosetta Stone	75%: 30 PP; 25%: 50 PP
C	Mythril (after 4-star rating)	—

LOCKED AREAS

AREA	UNLOCK REQUIREMENTS
C—3	Defeat battle piece ①.
E—3	Defeat battle piece ④.

DP EFFICIENCY ROUTE

Maximizing DP on this final level is straightforward, but requires that you've already cleared with at least a 3-star rating on Destiny Odyssey IV. This causes the rare ultimate battle piece to spawn, which is worth +2 DP when defeated. Apart from a slight downward detour at the beginning to defeat battle piece ②, it's a straight shot across the stage, clearing out battle pieces with a DP Chance along the way.

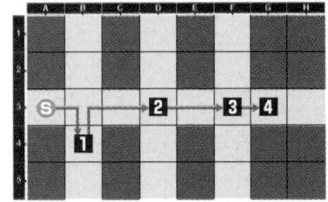
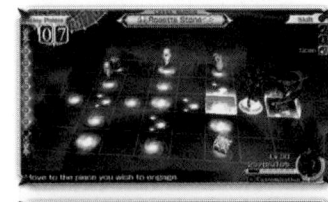
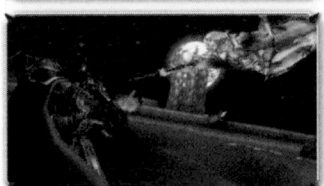
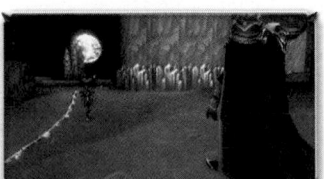
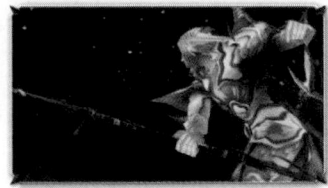

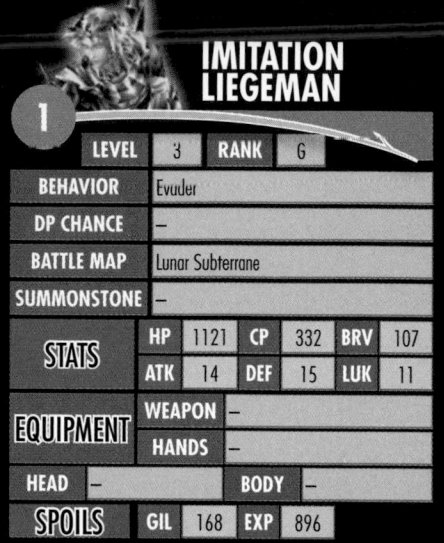

BATTLE PIECE DATA

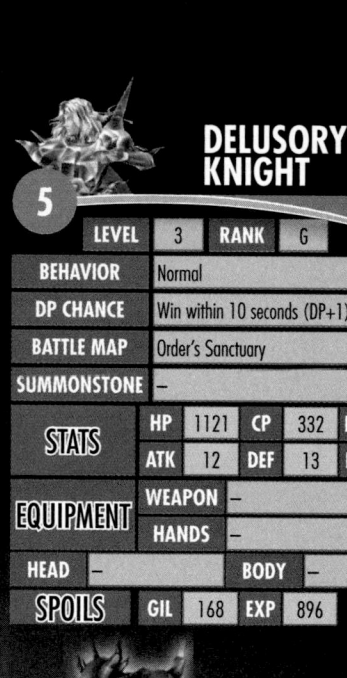

1 — IMITATION LIEGEMAN

LEVEL	3	RANK	G

BEHAVIOR	Evader
DP CHANCE	—
BATTLE MAP	Lunar Subterrane
SUMMONSTONE	—

STATS	HP	1121	CP	332	BRV	107
	ATK	14	DEF	15	LUK	11

EQUIPMENT	WEAPON	—
	HANDS	—

HEAD	—	BODY	—

SPOILS	GIL	168	EXP	896

2 — COUNTERFEIT WRAITH

LEVEL	3	RANK	G

BEHAVIOR	Evader
DP CHANCE	Win without taking damage (DP+1)
BATTLE MAP	Pandaemonium
SUMMONSTONE	—

STATS	HP	1121	CP	352	BRV	107
	ATK	12	DEF	14	LUK	11

EQUIPMENT	WEAPON	—
	HANDS	—

HEAD	—	BODY	—

SPOILS	GIL	168	EXP	896

3 — EPHEMERAL VISION

LEVEL	9	RANK	B

BEHAVIOR	Aggressive
DP CHANCE	—
BATTLE MAP	Old Chaos Shrine
SUMMONSTONE	—

STATS	HP	1	CP	339	BRV	170
	ATK	19	DEF	13	LUK	14

EQUIPMENT	WEAPON	—
	HANDS	Cracked Shield

HEAD	Heavy Helm	BODY	Rusted Armor

SPOILS	GIL	168	EXP	2970

ACCESSORIES	Arcane Resin, The Rotten, Gaia Ring, [Position] Near Opponent x5

4 — TRANSIENT WITCH

LEVEL	9	RANK	F

BEHAVIOR	Aggressive
DP CHANCE	BRV Break within 10 seconds (DP+1)
BATTLE MAP	Kefka's Tower
SUMMONSTONE	—

STATS	HP	1485	CP	339	BRV	95
	ATK	20	DEF	18	LUK	14

EQUIPMENT	WEAPON	—
	HANDS	—

HEAD	Charred Helm	BODY	—

SPOILS	GIL	168	EXP	1188

ACCESSORIES	Hyper Ring, Guardian Bangle, [HP] HP = 100% x6

5 — DELUSORY KNIGHT

LEVEL	3	RANK	G

BEHAVIOR	Normal
DP CHANCE	Win within 10 seconds (DP+1)
BATTLE MAP	Order's Sanctuary
SUMMONSTONE	—

STATS	HP	1121	CP	332	BRV	107
	ATK	12	DEF	13	LUK	11

EQUIPMENT	WEAPON	—
	HANDS	—

HEAD	—	BODY	—

SPOILS	GIL	168	EXP	896

6 — GOLBEZ

LEVEL	12	RANK	D

BEHAVIOR	Tactician
DP CHANCE	—
BATTLE MAP	Lunar Subterrane
SUMMONSTONE	Ifrit

STATS	HP	2357	CP	343	BRV	200
	ATK	30	DEF	26	LUK	16

EQUIPMENT	WEAPON	Guard Stick
	HANDS	—

HEAD	Iron Helm	BODY	Iron Armor

SPOILS	GIL	252	EXP	4167

ACCESSORIES	Booster x2, Hyperstar, [Position] Far from Opponent x2

7 — DELUSORY KNIGHT

LEVEL	27	RANK	B

BEHAVIOR	Extreme
DP CHANCE	Win battle (DP+2)
BATTLE MAP	Lunar Subterrane
SUMMONSTONE	Carbuncle

STATS	HP	3367	CP	361	BRV	314
	ATK	36*	DEF	37*	LUK	23

EQUIPMENT	WEAPON	[Rank 4]
	HANDS	[Rank 3]

HEAD	Heavy Helm	BODY	[Rank 3]

SPOILS	GIL	336	EXP	0

ACCESSORIES	Hyper Ring, Guardian Bangle, [HP] HP = 100% x6

* Denotes use of the base value (for stats that vary).

Difficulty: ☆☆☆☆

Prerequisite: Finish Prologue

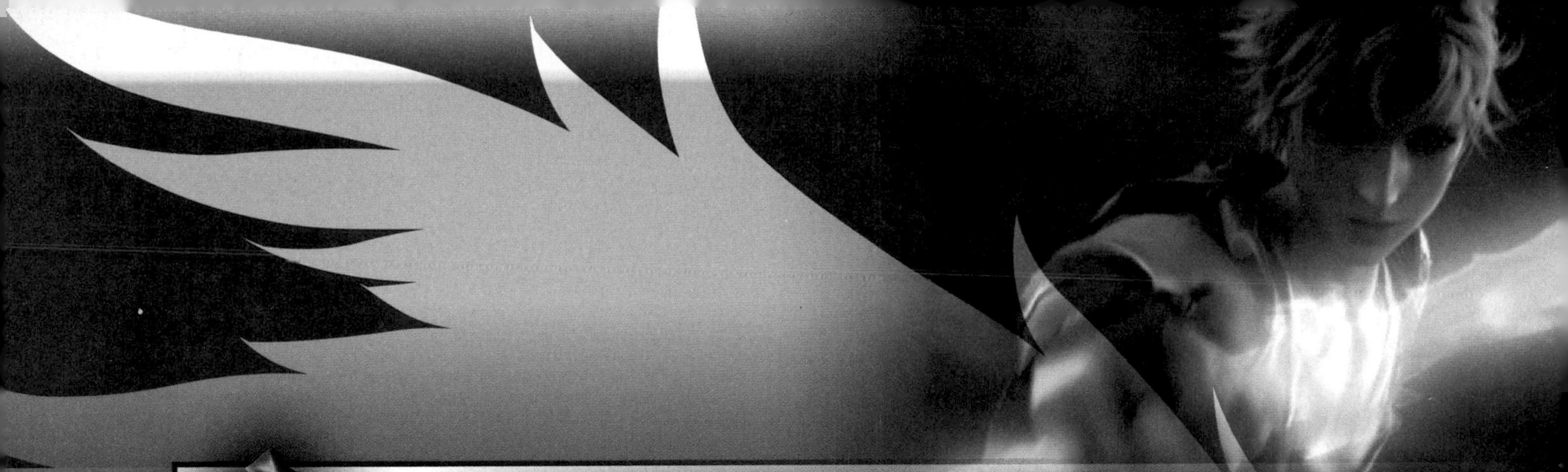

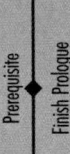

DESTINY ODYSSEY V

JOURNEY, COURAGE, FRIENDS

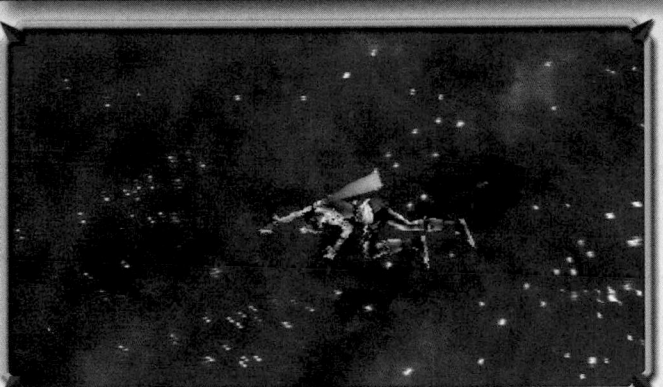

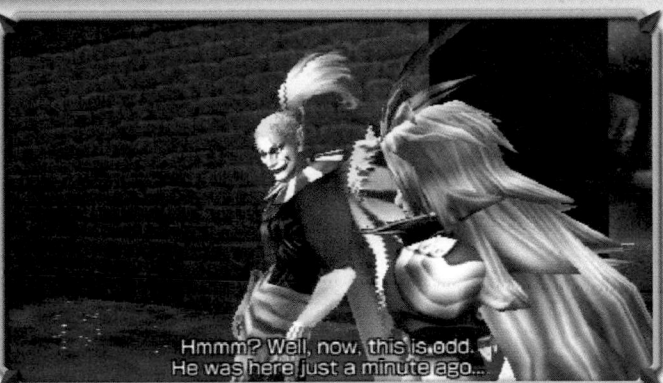

Hmmm? Well, now, this is odd.
He was here just a minute ago...

Bartz begins in strange territory, spirited away from his friends into the clutches of those sided with Chaos. He evades Kefka and Kuja, and strikes out across unfamiliar terrain...

REWARDS

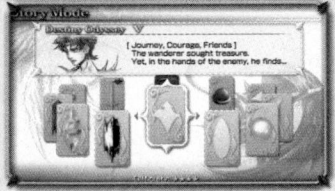

At the end of each level, rewards are available if you finish with a positive number of Destiny Points, or DP. This walkthrough includes miniature level maps that indicate the most efficient route to take through a given level, in order to maximize DP.

LEVEL COMPLETION

REMAINING DP	1ST TIME	2ND TIME
7	Rosetta Stone	300 PP
6	Ice Shield	200 PP
5	Flame Shield	120 PP
4	Tonberry	80 PP
3	1000 gil	50 PP
2	600 gil	30 PP
1	300 gil	20 PP
0	100 gil	10 PP

DESTINY ODYSSEY V COMPLETION

STAR RATING	SP REQUIRED	AWARD
☆	100	New skill
☆☆	200	Special areas unlocked
☆☆☆	300	Rare battle pieces spawned
☆☆☆☆	400	Rare treasure chests spawned
–	500 SP, then every 500 SP extra	100 PP

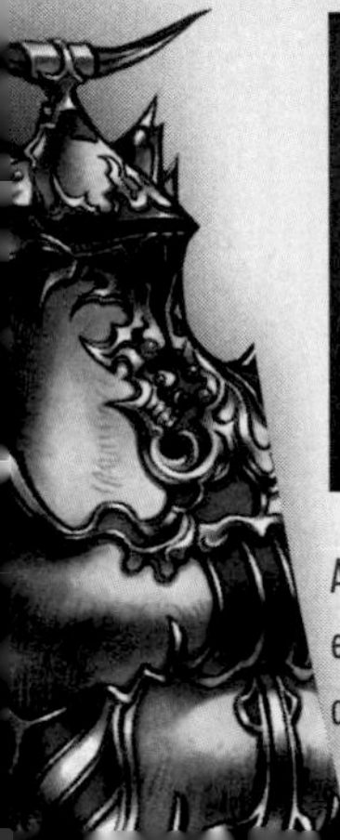

At the end of each set of levels, you'll receive rewards based on your performance. Story Points, or SP, are awarded after each level based on remaining DP and HP, as well as the number of engagements undertaken. Points are penalized for retries, or for a DP total that dips into negatives. If you miss out on a desired bonus on the first playthrough, don't worry—SP is cumulative across multiple playthroughs.

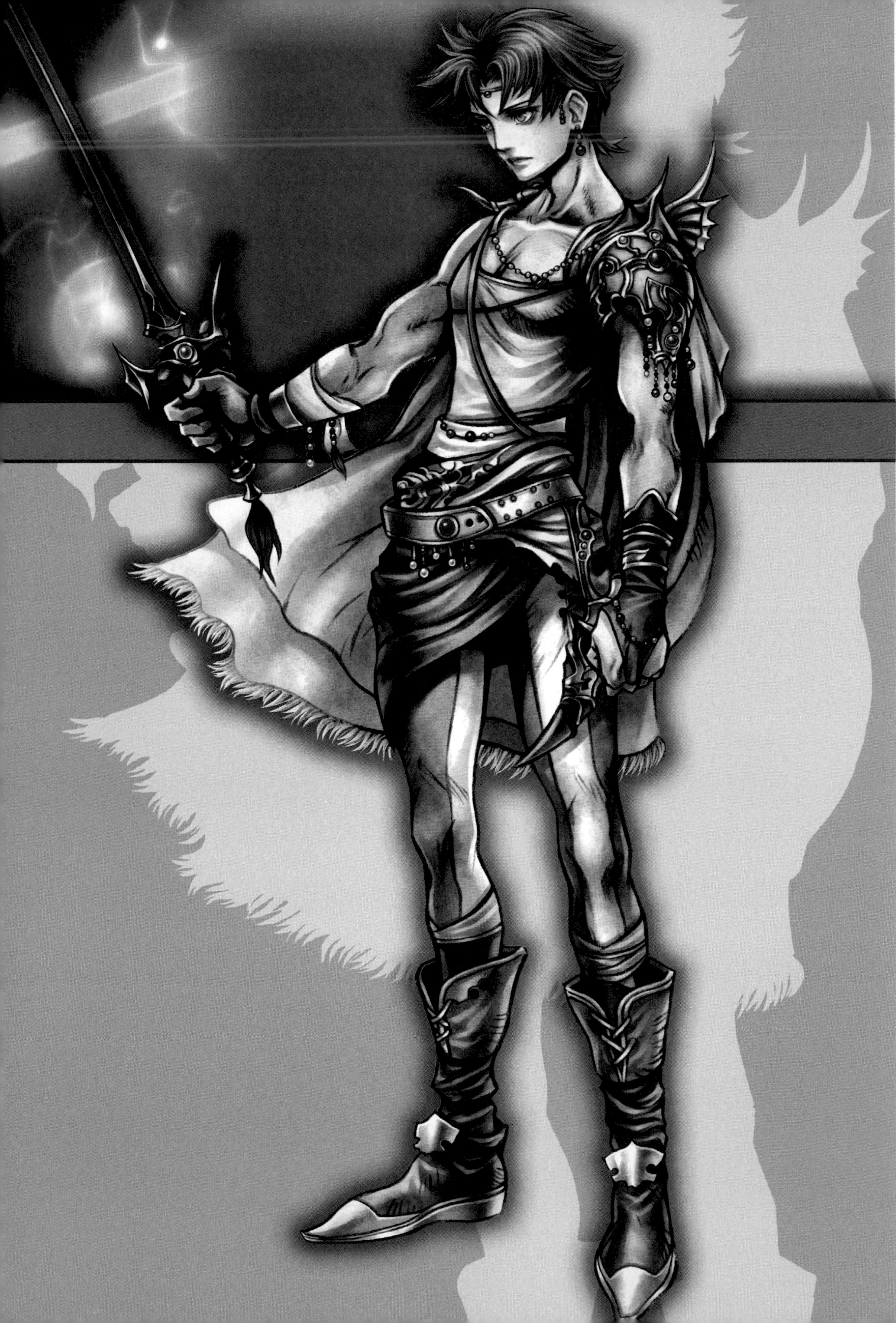

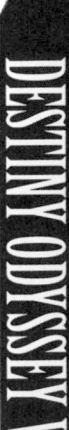

DESTINY ODYSSEY V

DESTINY ODYSSEY

Bartz draws his attacks from the arsenals of his allies. As he levels up, he learns more and more. His combat naturally seems familiar if you've cleared the Destiny Odyssey chapters of his friends. The levels Bartz will traverse are mostly wide-open spaces, filled with various battle pieces, treasure chests, and other assorted roadblocks. This brief opening level doesn't have many encounters or a boss, granting a leisurely opportunity to get acquainted with Bartz as a combatant.

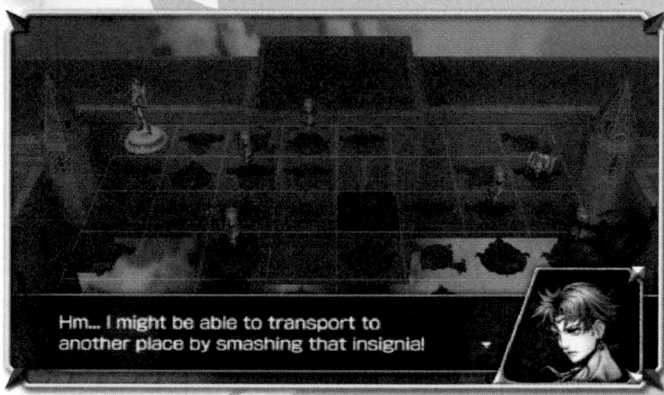

Hm... I might be able to transport to another place by smashing that insignia!

MAP

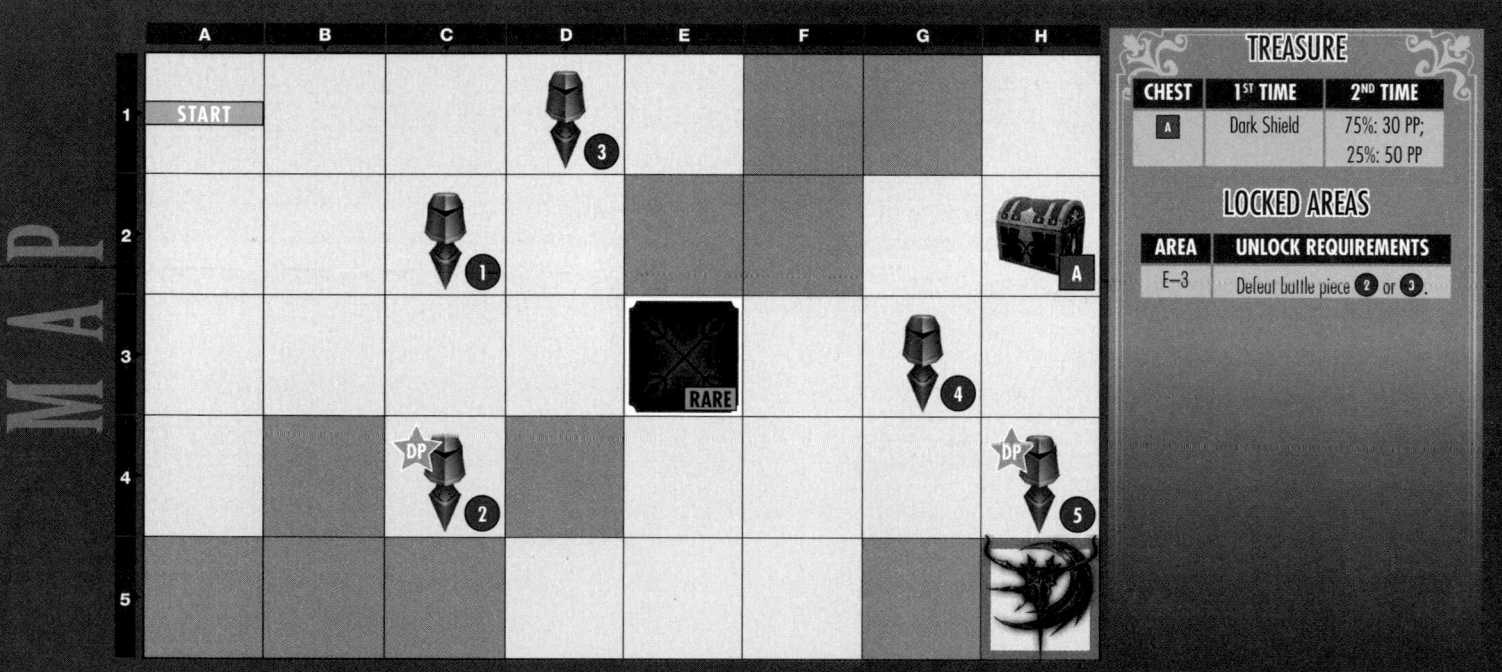

TREASURE

CHEST	1ST TIME	2ND TIME
A	Dark Shield	75%: 30 PP; 25%: 50 PP

LOCKED AREAS

AREA	UNLOCK REQUIREMENTS
E-3	Defeat battle piece ② or ③.

DP EFFICIENCY ROUTE

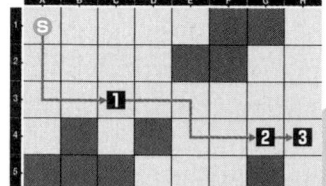

There are only two DP Chances on Bartz's first level. For the first, head to C-3 and chain battle pieces ❶ and ❷. The Locked Area disappears after defeating battle piece ❷, allowing you to cross to G-4. Chain battle pieces ❹ and ❺ here, before destroying the Stigma of Chaos and finishing the level.

BATTLE PIECE DATA

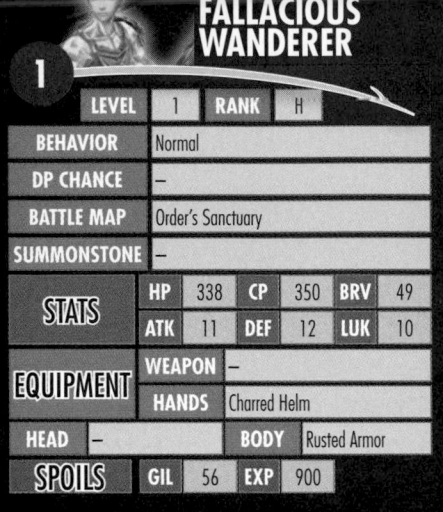

1 FALLACIOUS WANDERER

LEVEL	1	RANK	H

BEHAVIOR	Normal
DP CHANCE	—
BATTLE MAP	Order's Sanctuary
SUMMONSTONE	—

STATS	HP	338	CP	350	BRV	49
	ATK	11	DEF	12	LUK	10

EQUIPMENT	WEAPON	—	
	HANDS	Charred Helm	
HEAD	—	BODY	Rusted Armor

SPOILS	GIL	56	EXP	900

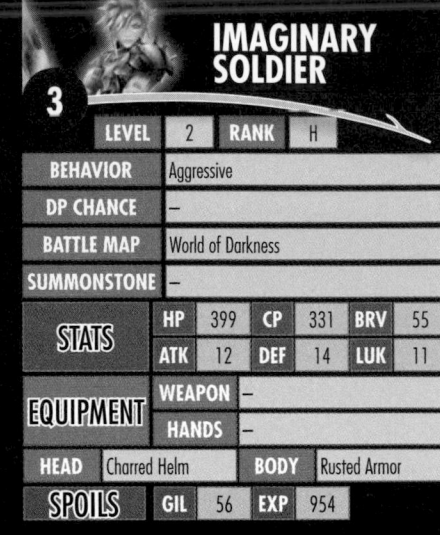

2 PHANTASMAL GIRL

LEVEL	2	RANK	H

BEHAVIOR	Tricky
DP CHANCE	BRV Break within 10 seconds (DP+1)
BATTLE MAP	Order's Sanctuary
SUMMONSTONE	—

STATS	HP	1061	CP	331	BRV	55
	ATK	13	DEF	12	LUK	11

EQUIPMENT	WEAPON	—	
	HANDS	—	
HEAD	Charred Helm	BODY	—

SPOILS	GIL	56	EXP	954

3 IMAGINARY SOLDIER

LEVEL	2	RANK	H

BEHAVIOR	Aggressive
DP CHANCE	—
BATTLE MAP	World of Darkness
SUMMONSTONE	—

STATS	HP	399	CP	331	BRV	55
	ATK	12	DEF	14	LUK	11

EQUIPMENT	WEAPON	—	
	HANDS	—	
HEAD	Charred Helm	BODY	Rusted Armor

SPOILS	GIL	56	EXP	954

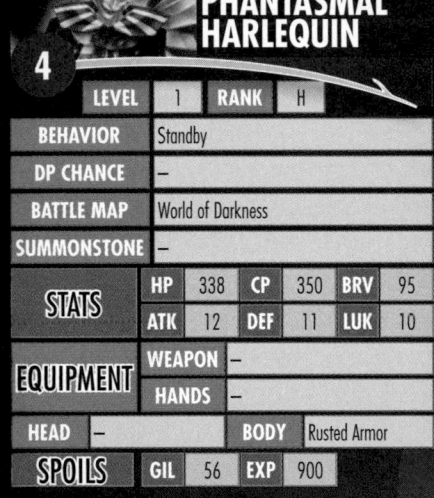

4 PHANTASMAL HARLEQUIN

LEVEL	1	RANK	H

BEHAVIOR	Standby
DP CHANCE	—
BATTLE MAP	World of Darkness
SUMMONSTONE	—

STATS	HP	338	CP	350	BRV	95
	ATK	12	DEF	11	LUK	10

EQUIPMENT	WEAPON	—	
	HANDS	—	
HEAD	—	BODY	Rusted Armor

SPOILS	GIL	56	EXP	900

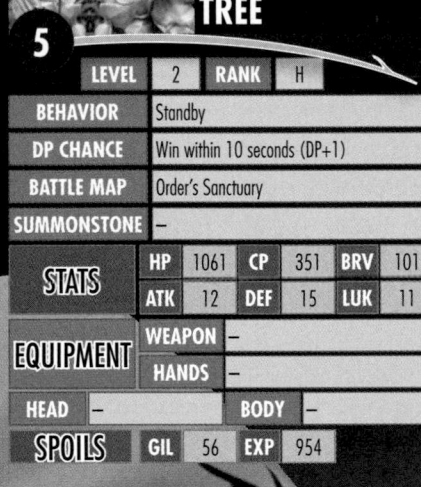

5 FALLACIOUS TREE

LEVEL	2	RANK	H

BEHAVIOR	Standby
DP CHANCE	Win within 10 seconds (DP+1)
BATTLE MAP	Order's Sanctuary
SUMMONSTONE	—

STATS	HP	1061	CP	351	BRV	101
	ATK	12	DEF	15	LUK	11

EQUIPMENT	WEAPON	—	
	HANDS	—	
HEAD	—	BODY	—

SPOILS	GIL	56	EXP	954

DESTINY ODYSSEY V

STARTING DP	MAX FINISHING	ENGAGEMENTS
5	4	6

This level is a little more complex than the first, with two Locked Areas blocking the path to the exit. There are two chances for chains against adjacent battle pieces, and defeating battle piece **2** makes a Potion appear near battle piece **3**. If needed, this Potion can be used before or after engaging battle piece **3**. The Leviathan Summonstone is found here near the Stigma of Chaos, but only after at least a 2-star rating on previous completions of Destiny Odyssey V.

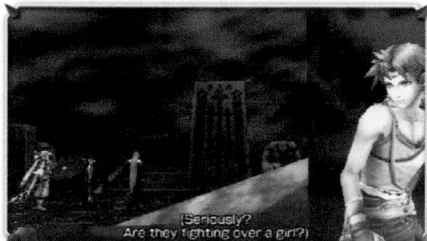
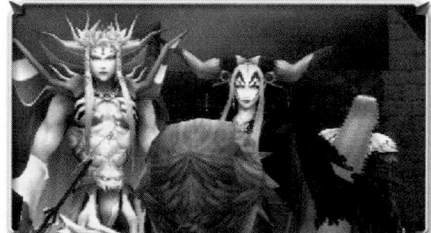
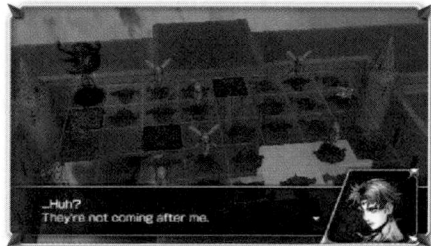

MAP

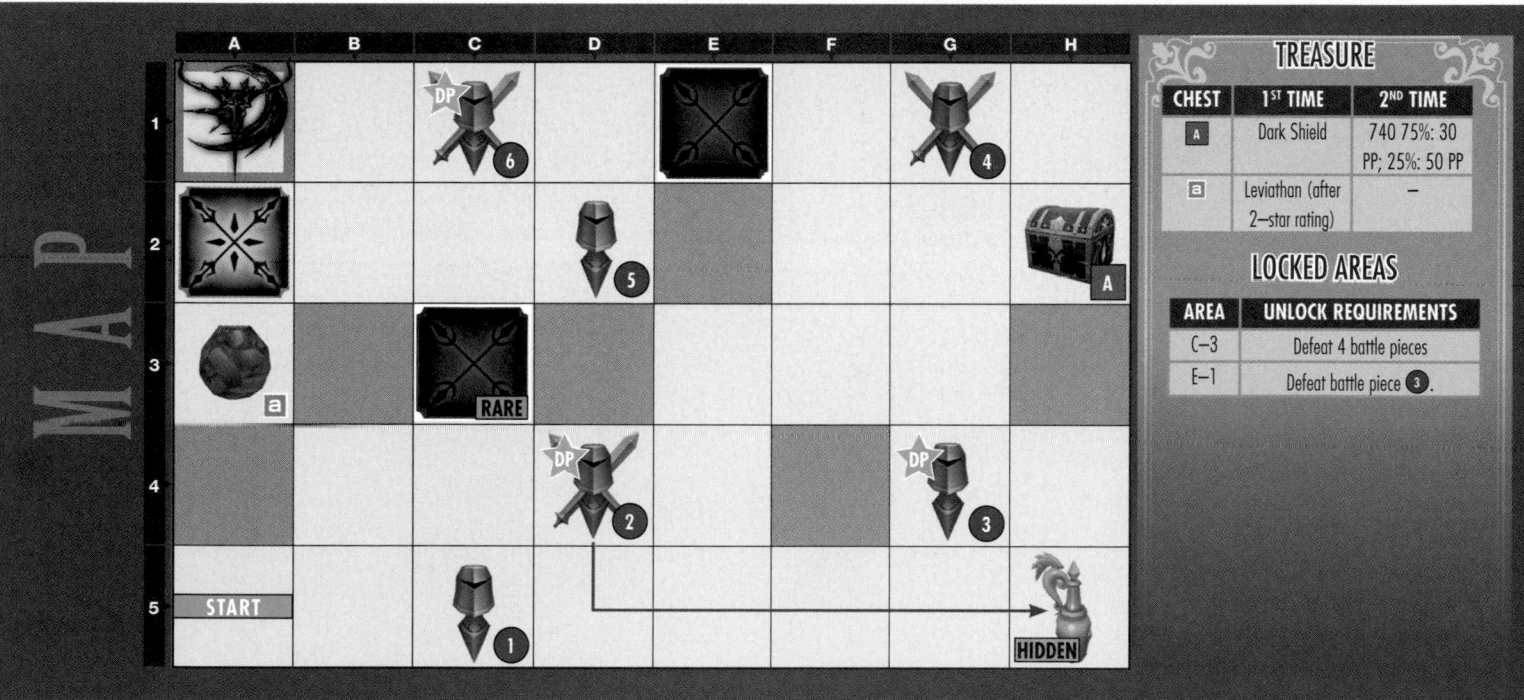

TREASURE

CHEST	1ST TIME	2ND TIME
A	Dark Shield	740 75%: 30 PP; 25%: 50 PP
a	Leviathan (after 2–star rating)	–

LOCKED AREAS

AREA	UNLOCK REQUIREMENTS
C–3	Defeat 4 battle pieces
E–1	Defeat battle piece **3**.

DP EFFICIENCY ROUTE

A circuitous route on this level leads to the most Destiny Points. Initially, you should chain battle pieces **1** and **2**, located right near the start. During these battles, hunt down EX Force and EX Cores. You'll need them against battle piece **3**, the next foe on the agenda. Scoring the DP Chance here requires an EX Burst within 10 seconds. After defeating battle piece **3**, head through the area vacated by the Locked Area at E-1, and chain battle pieces **5** and **6**. The DP Chance against battle piece **6** again requires a fast EX Burst, so take your time collecting more EX Force against piece **5**. After this chain, head to the exit.

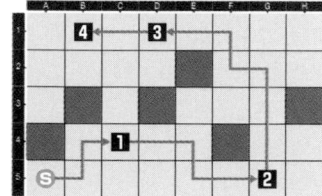

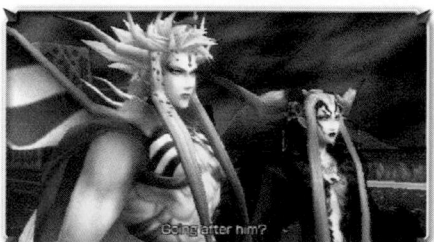

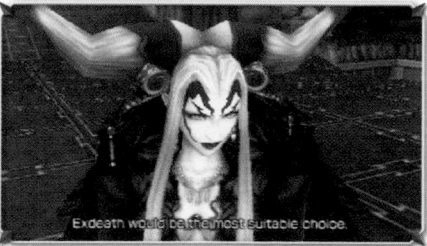

BATTLE PIECE DATA

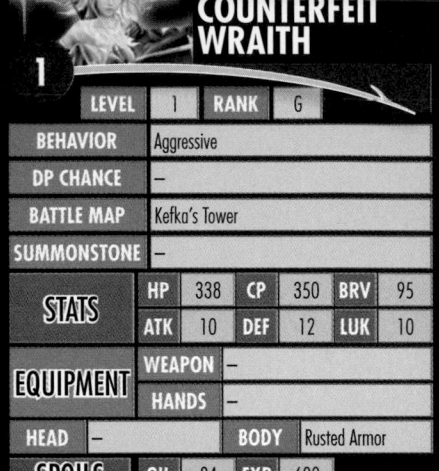

1 COUNTERFEIT WRAITH

LEVEL	1	RANK	G

BEHAVIOR	Aggressive
DP CHANCE	–
BATTLE MAP	Kefka's Tower
SUMMONSTONE	–

STATS	HP	338	CP	350	BRV	95
	ATK	10	DEF	12	LUK	10

EQUIPMENT	WEAPON	–
	HANDS	–

HEAD	–	BODY	Rusted Armor

SPOILS	GIL	84	EXP	600

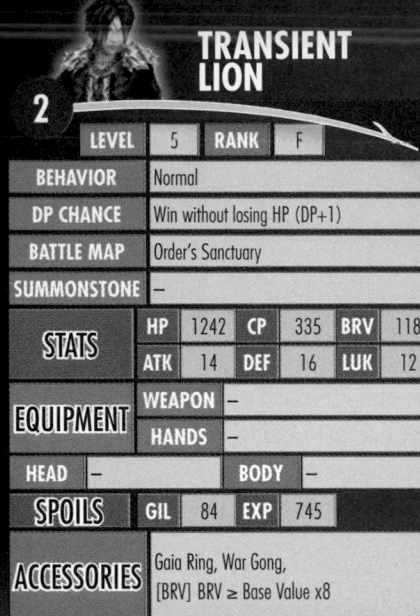

2 TRANSIENT LION

LEVEL	5	RANK	F

BEHAVIOR	Normal
DP CHANCE	Win without losing HP (DP+1)
BATTLE MAP	Order's Sanctuary
SUMMONSTONE	–

STATS	HP	1242	CP	335	BRV	118
	ATK	14	DEF	16	LUK	12

EQUIPMENT	WEAPON	–
	HANDS	–

HEAD	–	BODY	–

SPOILS	GIL	84	EXP	745

ACCESSORIES	Gaia Ring, War Gong, [BRV] BRV ≥ Base Value x8

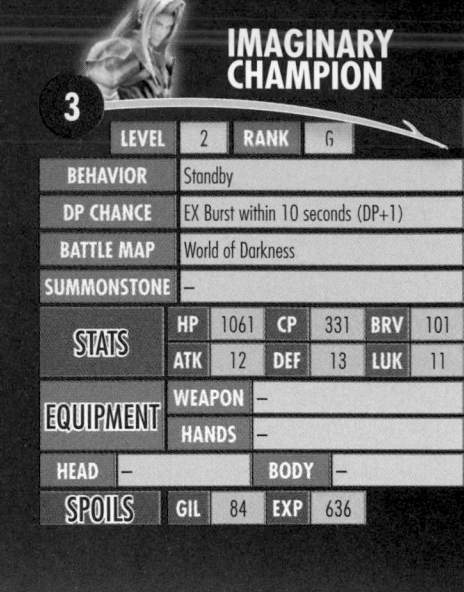

3 IMAGINARY CHAMPION

LEVEL	2	RANK	G

BEHAVIOR	Standby
DP CHANCE	EX Burst within 10 seconds (DP+1)
BATTLE MAP	World of Darkness
SUMMONSTONE	–

STATS	HP	1061	CP	331	BRV	101
	ATK	12	DEF	13	LUK	11

EQUIPMENT	WEAPON	–
	HANDS	–

HEAD	–	BODY	–

SPOILS	GIL	84	EXP	636

4 PHANTASMAL GIRL

LEVEL	5	RANK	F

BEHAVIOR	Normal
DP CHANCE	–
BATTLE MAP	World of Darkness
SUMMONSTONE	–

STATS	HP	1242	CP	335	BRV	118
	ATK	16	DEF	15	LUK	12

EQUIPMENT	WEAPON	–
	HANDS	–

HEAD	–	BODY	–

SPOILS	GIL	84	EXP	745

ACCESSORIES	Gaia Ring, War Gong, [BRV] BRV ≥ Base Value x8

5 FALSE STALWART

LEVEL	1	RANK	G

BEHAVIOR	Standby
DP CHANCE	–
BATTLE MAP	Kefka's Tower
SUMMONSTONE	–

STATS	HP	1000	CP	330	BRV	49
	ATK	13	DEF	14	LUK	10

EQUIPMENT	WEAPON	–
	HANDS	–

HEAD	Charred Helm	BODY	–

SPOILS	GIL	84	EXP	600

6 FALLACIOUS TREE

LEVEL	6	RANK	F

BEHAVIOR	Aggressive
DP CHANCE	EX Burst within 10 seconds (DP+1)
BATTLE MAP	Kefka's Tower
SUMMONSTONE	–

STATS	HP	1303	CP	355	BRV	124
	ATK	16	DEF	19	LUK	13

EQUIPMENT	WEAPON	–
	HANDS	–

HEAD	–	BODY	–

SPOILS	GIL	84	EXP	781

ACCESSORIES	Gaia Ring, War Gong, Battle Chant, [BRV] BRV ≥ Base Value x7

DESTINY ODYSSEY

V-3

STARTING DP	MAX FINISHING	ENGAGEMENTS
4	5 (+2 after 3-star rating)	7 (+1 after 3-star rating)

This level is a wide-open affair with many encounters, and it also contains a Leviathan AUTO Summonstone for the taking. Expert battle piece ⑥ is a very tough opponent that shows up during your first run through the chapter. It's nearly impossible to BRV Break this manikin, but the battle is still winnable at low levels—this copy of Kuja is very bad at dealing with Wind Shear if you perform the attack just above or below the manikin. This battle is worth a ton of EXP if you end up winning through a dozen or so Wind Shears! The rare Exdeath manikin that shows up nearby after a 3-star rating isn't as nasty—by the time you run back through Destiny Odyssey V again, you've likely mastered Holy and unlocked Flare, along with learning Flood. Since this manikin is passive, these tools are effective, even if the enemy is still a higher level. This Exdeath copy may sometimes defend, but won't take many other countermeasures, making the fight underwhelming when compared to most ultimate battle piece brawls. The boss, Golbez, won't present a problem if you were able to deal with the expert Kuja battle piece earlier on.

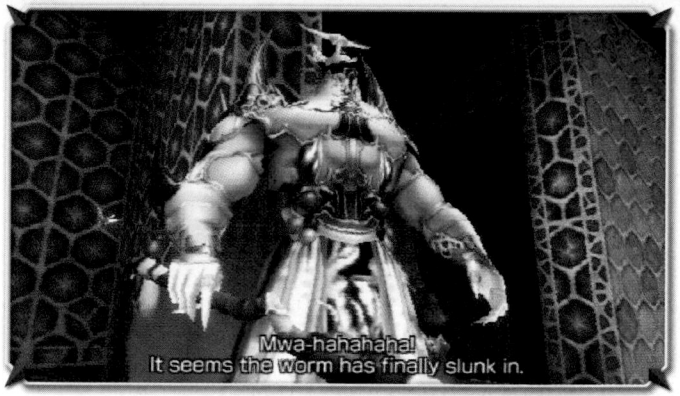

Mwa-hahahaha!
It seems the worm has finally slunk in.

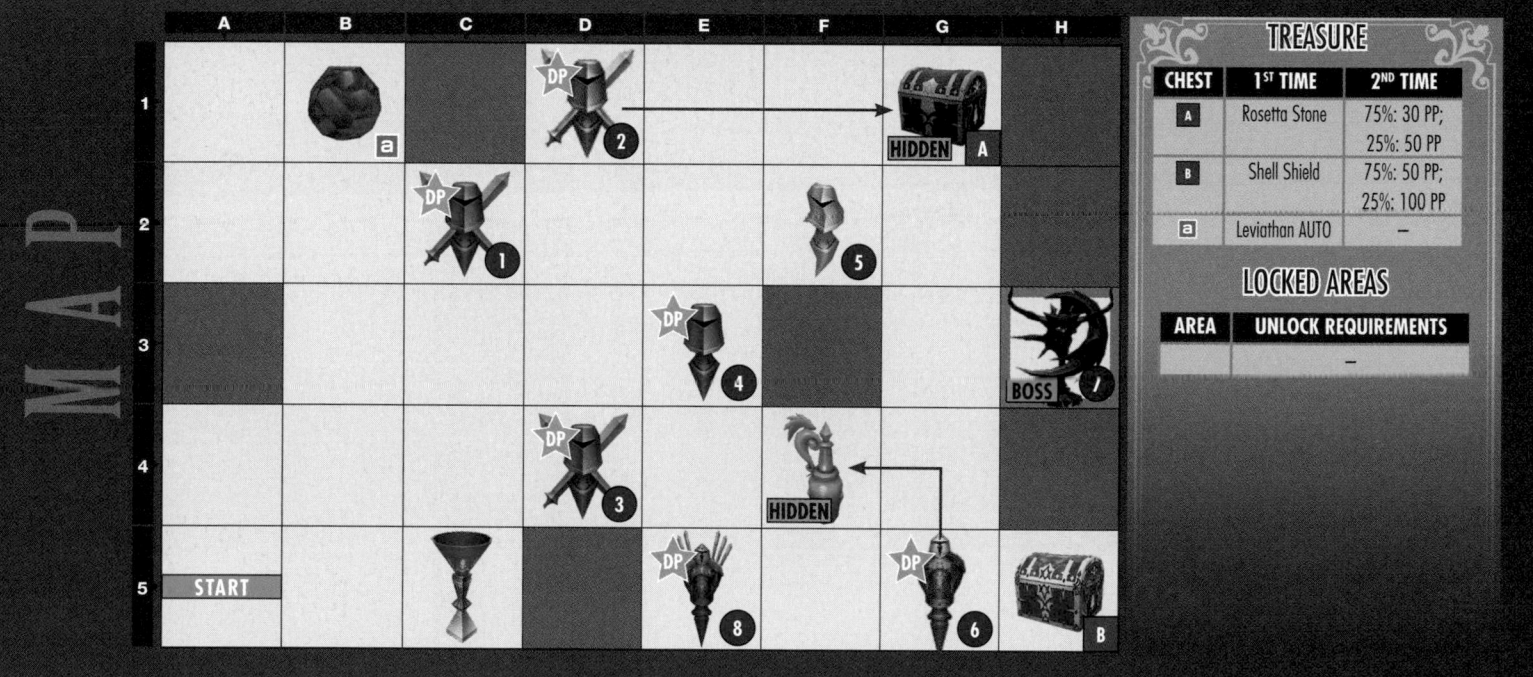

TREASURE

CHEST	1ST TIME	2ND TIME
A	Rosetta Stone	75%: 30 PP; 25%: 50 PP
B	Shell Shield	75%: 50 PP; 25%: 100 PP
a	Leviathan AUTO	—

LOCKED AREAS

AREA	UNLOCK REQUIREMENTS
	—

DP EFFICIENCY ROUTE

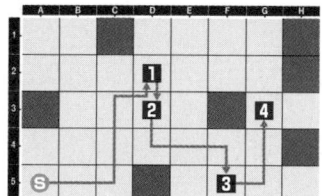

A trio of two-part battle chains leads to maximum DP here, but a previous 3-star rating is required to spawn the rare battle piece. First, head to D-2 and chain battle pieces ① and ②—you'll be forced into combat immediately by battle piece ② upon arrival. Next, head down to D-3 and chain battle pieces ③ and ④. Finally, head between the expert and ultimate battle pieces and chain them before heading to the Stigma of Chaos for the boss fight.

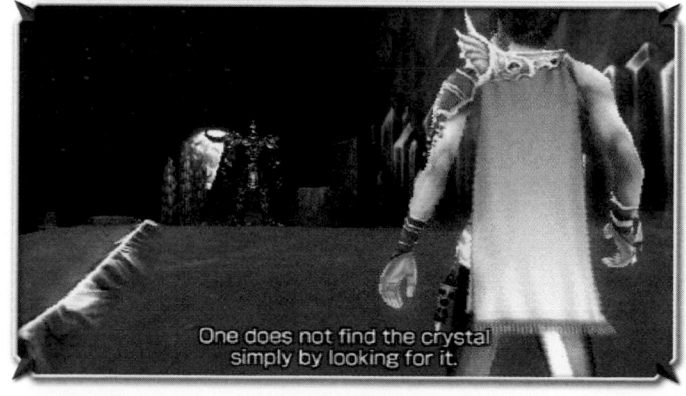

One does not find the crystal simply by looking for it.

BATTLE PIECE DATA

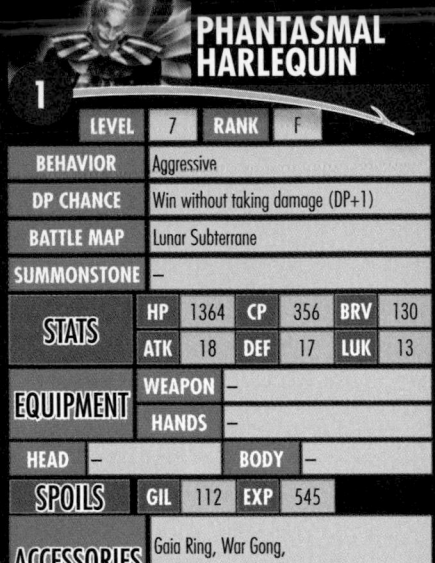

1 PHANTASMAL HARLEQUIN

LEVEL	7	RANK	F

BEHAVIOR	Aggressive
DP CHANCE	Win without taking damage (DP+1)
BATTLE MAP	Lunar Subterrane
SUMMONSTONE	—

STATS	HP	1364	CP	356	BRV	130
	ATK	18	DEF	17	LUK	13

EQUIPMENT	WEAPON	—
	HANDS	—

HEAD	—	BODY	—

SPOILS	GIL	112	EXP	545

ACCESSORIES	Gaia Ring, War Gong, [BRV] BRV ≥ Base Value x8

2 FALLACIOUS TREE

LEVEL	8	RANK	F

BEHAVIOR	Evader
DP CHANCE	Critical hit within 10 seconds (DP+1)
BATTLE MAP	World of Darkness
SUMMONSTONE	—

STATS	HP	1424	CP	357	BRV	136
	ATK	18	DEF	21	LUK	14

EQUIPMENT	WEAPON	—
	HANDS	—

HEAD	—	BODY	—

SPOILS	GIL	112	EXP	569

ACCESSORIES	Gaia Ring, War Gong, Battle Chant, [BRV] BRV ≥ Base Value x7

3 TRANSIENT LION

LEVEL	3	RANK	G

BEHAVIOR	Evader
DP CHANCE	BRV Break within 10 seconds (DP+1)
BATTLE MAP	World of Darkness
SUMMONSTONE	—

STATS	HP	1121	CP	332	BRV	107
	ATK	12	DEF	14	LUK	11

EQUIPMENT	WEAPON	—
	HANDS	—

HEAD	—	BODY	—

SPOILS	GIL	112	EXP	448

ACCESSORIES	Gaia Ring, War Gong, [BRV] BRV ≥ Base Value x8

4 IMAGINARY SOLDIER

LEVEL	3	RANK	G

BEHAVIOR	Evader
DP CHANCE	Win within 10 seconds (DP+1)
BATTLE MAP	Lunar Subterrane
SUMMONSTONE	—

STATS	HP	1121	CP	332	BRV	107
	ATK	13	DEF	15	LUK	11

EQUIPMENT	WEAPON	—
	HANDS	—

HEAD	—	BODY	—

SPOILS	GIL	112	EXP	448

5 IMITATION LIEGEMAN

LEVEL	8	RANK	C

BEHAVIOR	Summoner
DP CHANCE	—
BATTLE MAP	Order's Sanctuary
SUMMONSTONE	Tiamat

STATS	HP	1	CP	338	BRV	495
	ATK	19	DEF	13	LUK	14

EQUIPMENT	WEAPON	—
	HANDS	Cracked Shield

HEAD	Heavy Helm	BODY	Rusted Armor

SPOILS	GIL	112	EXP	2848

ACCESSORIES	The Rotten, Soul of the Sovereign

6 CAPRICIOUS REAPER

LEVEL	16	RANK	C

BEHAVIOR	Conservative
DP CHANCE	Win battle (DP+1)
BATTLE MAP	Order's Sanctuary
SUMMONSTONE	—

STATS	HP	1909*	CP	348	BRV	250
	ATK	38	DEF	27*	LUK	18

EQUIPMENT	WEAPON	[Rank 4]
	HANDS	Power Armlet

HEAD	Plumed Hat	BODY	Poncho

SPOILS	GIL	112	EXP	0

7 GOLBEZ

LEVEL	10	RANK	D

BEHAVIOR	Survivor
DP CHANCE	—
BATTLE MAP	Lunar Subterrane
SUMMONSTONE	—

STATS	HP	2035	CP	341	BRV	147
	ATK	23	DEF	23	LUK	15

EQUIPMENT	WEAPON	Rod
	HANDS	—

HEAD	—	BODY	Bronze Armor

SPOILS	GIL	168	EXP	3090

8 FALLACIOUS TREE

LEVEL	26	RANK	B

BEHAVIOR	Calm
DP CHANCE	Win battle (DP+2)
BATTLE MAP	Order's Sanctuary
SUMMONSTONE	—

STATS	HP	3621	CP	375	BRV	297
	ATK	52	DEF	55	LUK	23

EQUIPMENT	WEAPON	Rod of Wisdom
	HANDS	[Rank 3]

HEAD	Knight Helm	BODY	Mythril Armor

SPOILS	GIL	336	EXP	0

ACCESSORIES	Gaia Ring, War Gong, [BRV] BRV ≥ Base Value x8

* Denotes use of the base value (for stats that vary).

DESTINY ODYSSEY V-4

STARTING DP **5** | MAX FINISHING **5** | ENGAGEMENTS **6**

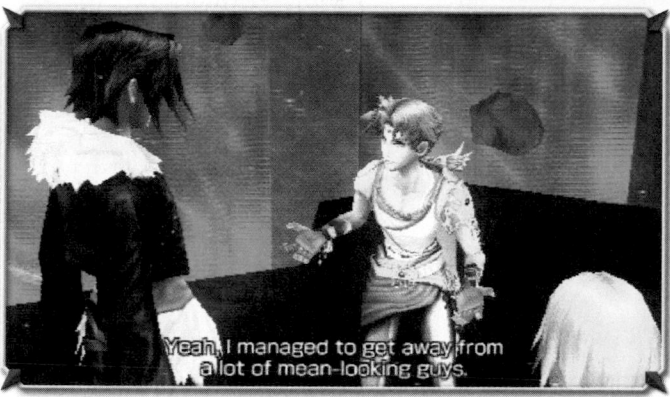

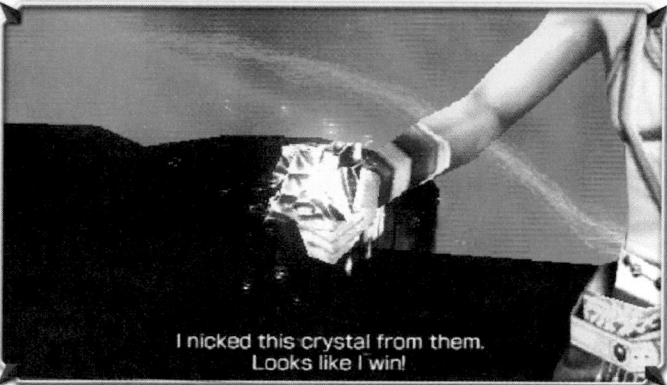

This level is composed of criss-crossing paths, dotted with battle pieces. A Locked Area that only disappears after a 2-star rating bars the way to treasure chest **B**, which contains a Rosetta Stone. Treasure chest **C** appears near the Stigma of Chaos only after achieving a 4-star rating. Apart from these variations, this level is pretty straightforward, and ends without a boss fight.

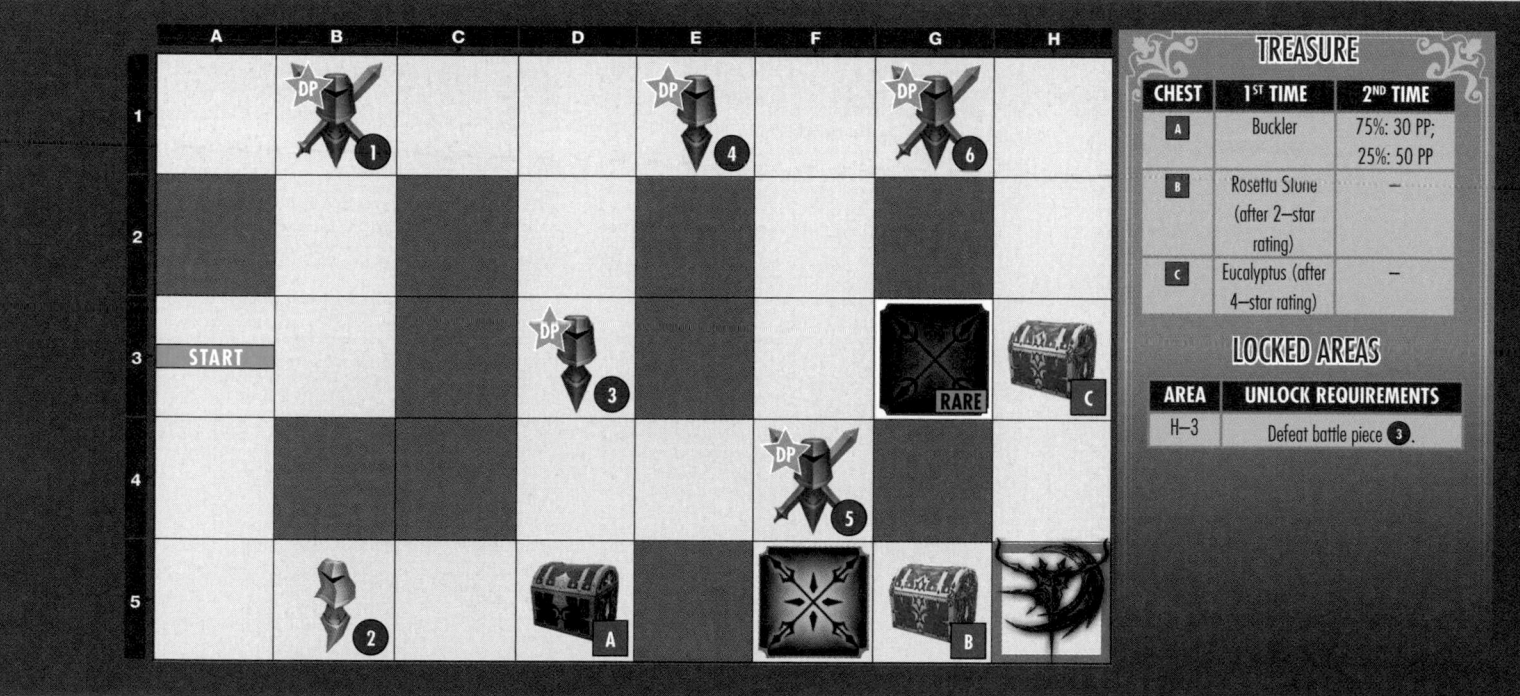

TREASURE

CHEST	1ST TIME	2ND TIME
A	Buckler	75%: 30 PP; 25%: 50 PP
B	Rosetta Stone (after 2–star rating)	—
C	Eucalyptus (after 4–star rating)	—

LOCKED AREAS

AREA	UNLOCK REQUIREMENTS
H–3	Defeat battle piece ❸.

DP EFFICIENCY ROUTE

It's a bit of a rollercoaster here, when going for max DP. From the start, head upward and engage battle piece ❶. Then, loop down to take on battle piece ❸. Next, go after battle piece ❺. Finally, head back upward and chain battle pieces ❹ and ❻ before descending to the Stigma of Chaos. Note that if you've recently acquired a 4-star rating here, but haven't yet collected rare treasure chest **C**, this chest blocks the way and prevents max DP. If you've previously opened the 2-star chest containing the Rosetta Stone, though, you can take an alternate route to the exit.

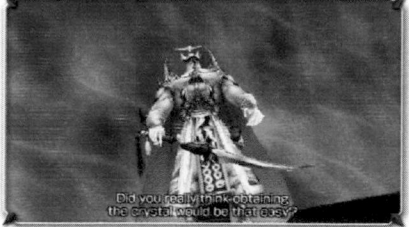

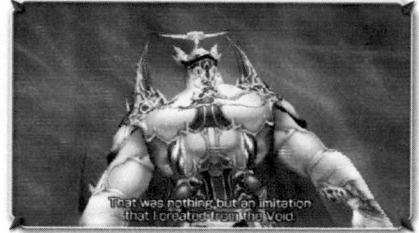

BATTLE PIECE DATA

1 FALLACIOUS TREE

LEVEL	10	RANK	E

BEHAVIOR	Normal
DP CHANCE	Win without taking damage (DP+1)
BATTLE MAP	Kefka's Tower
SUMMONSTONE	—

STATS	HP	1545	CP	359	BRV	147
	ATK	20	DEF	23	LUK	15

EQUIPMENT	WEAPON	—
	HANDS	—

HEAD	—	BODY	—

SPOILS	GIL	140	EXP	309

ACCESSORIES	Gaia Ring, War Gong, Battle Chant, [BRV] BRV ≥ Base Value x7

2 IMITATION LIEGEMAN

LEVEL	8	RANK	B

BEHAVIOR	Summoner
DP CHANCE	—
BATTLE MAP	Lunar Subterrane
SUMMONSTONE	Tiamat

STATS	HP	1	CP	338	BRV	136*
	ATK	19	DEF	20*	LUK	14

EQUIPMENT	WEAPON	—
	HANDS	Cracked Shield

HEAD	[Rank 5]	BODY	Rusted Armor

SPOILS	GIL	140	EXP	2848

ACCESSORIES	The Rotten, Soul of the Sovereign

3 COUNTERFEIT WRAITH

LEVEL	4	RANK	G

BEHAVIOR	Normal
DP CHANCE	Win within 10 seconds (DP+1)
BATTLE MAP	Ultimecia's Castle
SUMMONSTONE	Phoenix

STATS	HP	1182	CP	353	BRV	113
	ATK	13	DEF	15	LUK	12

EQUIPMENT	WEAPON	—
	HANDS	—

HEAD	—	BODY	—

SPOILS	GIL	140	EXP	236

4 PHANTASMAL GIRL

LEVEL	5	RANK	G

BEHAVIOR	Evader
DP CHANCE	Critical hit within 10 seconds (DP+1)
BATTLE MAP	Ultimecia's Castle
SUMMONSTONE	—

STATS	HP	1242	CP	335	BRV	118
	ATK	16	DEF	15	LUK	12

EQUIPMENT	WEAPON	—
	HANDS	—

HEAD	—	BODY	—

SPOILS	GIL	140	EXP	248

* Denotes use of the base value (for stats that vary).

5 FALSE STALWART

LEVEL	10	RANK	E

BEHAVIOR	Evader
DP CHANCE	Win without losing HP (DP+1)
BATTLE MAP	Lunar Subterrane
SUMMONSTONE	—

STATS	HP	1545	CP	341	BRV	147
	ATK	22	DEF	23	LUK	15

EQUIPMENT	WEAPON	—
	HANDS	—

HEAD	—	BODY	—

SPOILS	GIL	140	EXP	309

ACCESSORIES	Gaia Ring, War Gong, [BRV] BRV ≥ Base Value x8

6 IMAGINARY CHAMPION

LEVEL	11	RANK	E

BEHAVIOR	Evader
DP CHANCE	BRV Break within 10 seconds (DP+1)
BATTLE MAP	World of Darkness
SUMMONSTONE	—

STATS	HP	1606	CP	342	BRV	153
	ATK	21	DEF	22	LUK	15

EQUIPMENT	WEAPON	—
	HANDS	—

HEAD	—	BODY	—

SPOILS	GIL	140	EXP	321

ACCESSORIES	Gaia Ring, War Gong, [BRV] BRV ≥ Base Value x8

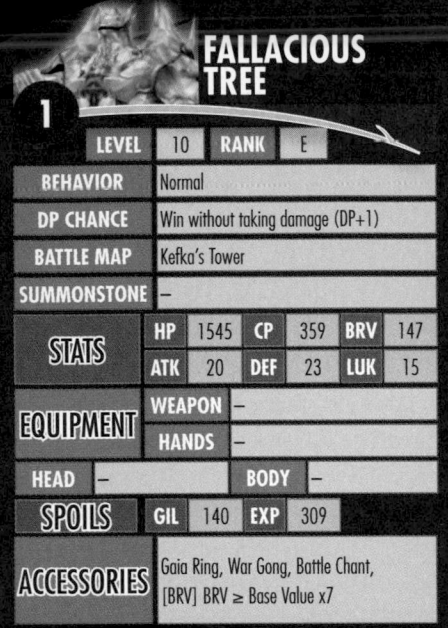
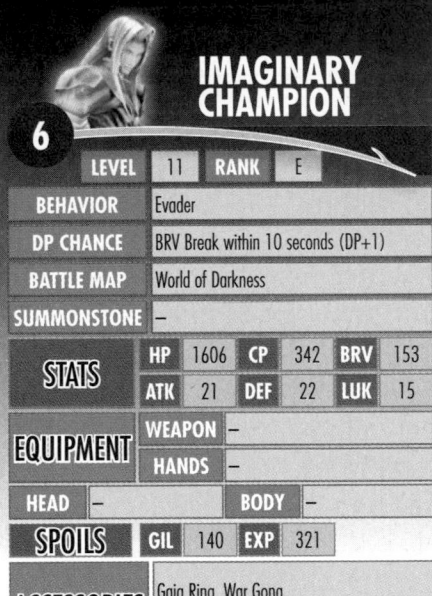

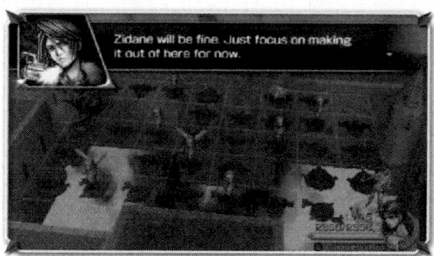
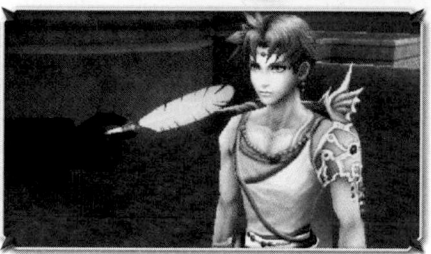
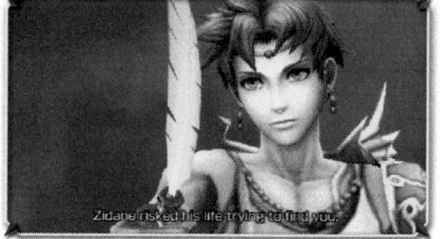

The last level places a gauntlet of battle pieces between Bartz and the Stigma of Chaos. The path to the exit is clear; it's just a matter of deciding how much combat you want along the way. The battles with DP Chances are clustered in the middle, while some extra battles are available along the fringe, including one that, upon victory, spawns treasure chest **B** in the upper left corner. A 3-star rating generates ultimate battle piece **9** in the center of the level, while a 4-star rating spawns treasure chest **C** along the top. The ultimate battle piece is a strong crystal version of Bartz himself. However, this foe is quite predictable, making it less difficult than you might expect—run around the foe just a few steps away, and it will almost always use Soul Eater, Wind Shear, or Paladin Force, all of which can be easily avoided on reaction simply by running backward. Then, you can hit the manikin with either Flood or Holy into Flare while it recovers from its failed attack. Wash, rinse, repeat. Exdeath, the boss, is a lumbering fiend who uses the Atomos summon to absorb your bravery whenever you damage Exdeath's HP. This can be dangerous because beating the stuffing from Exdeath while he's under the influence of this summon only gives him huge comeback potential when (and if) he finally hits you back! Between Atomos and Exdeath's powerful innate defensive abilities, it might be best to wait out the Atomos timer. Try to inflict Break on Exdeath so you can take him down with one successful HP attack when the Atomos timer is up.

MAP

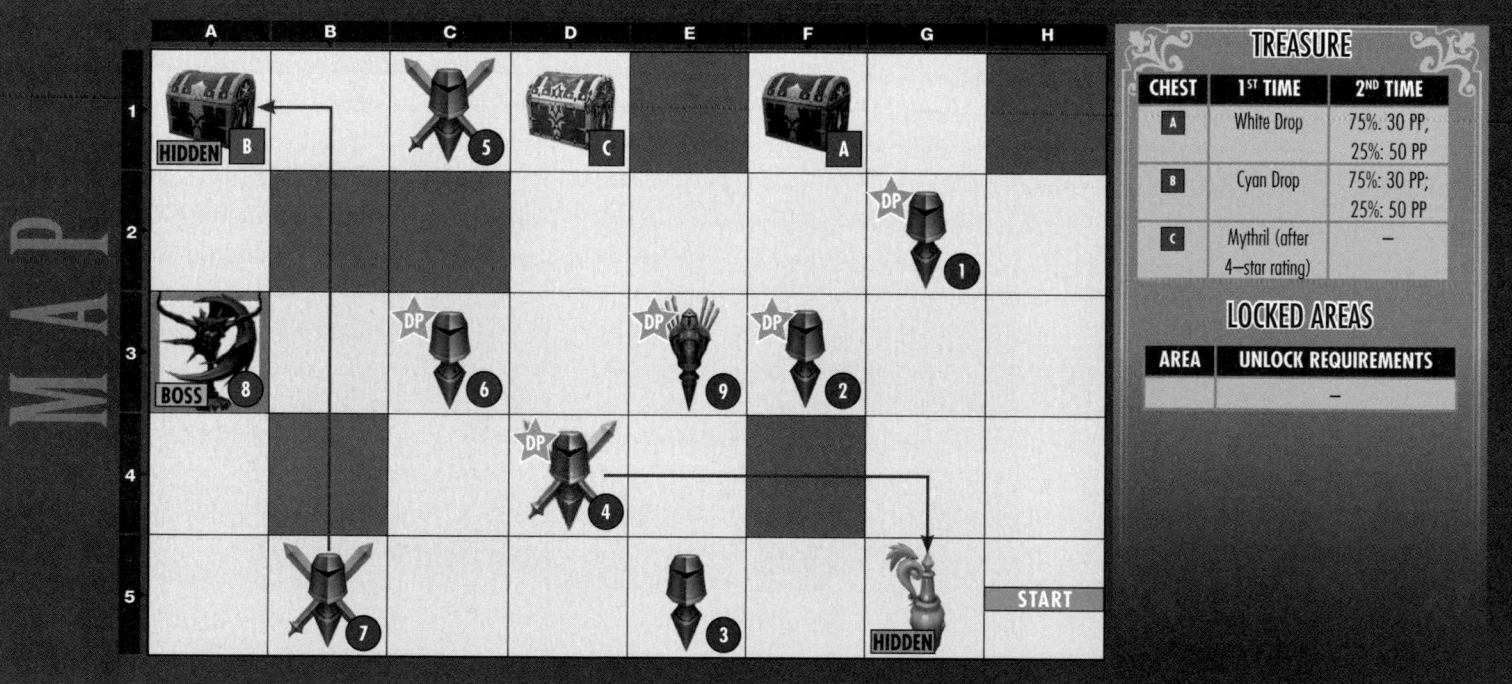

TREASURE		
CHEST	1ST TIME	2ND TIME
A	White Drop	75%. 30 PP; 25%: 50 PP
B	Cyan Drop	75%: 30 PP; 25%: 50 PP
C	Mythril (after 4-star rating)	—

LOCKED AREAS

AREA	UNLOCK REQUIREMENTS
	—

DP EFFICIENCY ROUTE

As with many levels, achieving max DP here is possible only after obtaining a 3-star rating, which causes a rare battle piece to appear directly in the thick of things. From the outset, head to G-3 and chain battle pieces **1** and **2**. The first must be defeated within ten seconds, while the second requires a fast critical hit. This means you can't just use the fight against battle piece

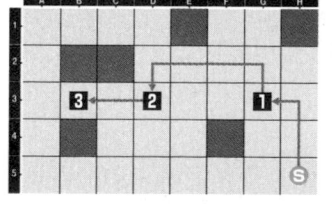

1 to build up EX Force for an easy critical hit via EX Mode against battle piece **2**. Instead, you'll have to either hit battle piece **2** with an immediate HP attack followed by a bravery attack while bravery recovers, or you'll have to block their bravery attack and counter with your own while they stagger. After this chain, move to D-3, where you'll immediately be forced into another chain by red battle piece **4**. The only requirement here is to keep your foe away from EX Cores, which nicely dovetails into hitting battle piece **6** with an EX Burst within 10 seconds. Against the rare ultimate battle piece, all you have to do is win—though this might be a tall order in and of itself, depending on your level! After this three-part chain is complete, head to the Stigma of Chaos.

BATTLE PIECE DATA

1 — IMITATION DESPOT

LEVEL	6	RANK	G

BEHAVIOR	Normal
DP CHANCE	Win within 10 seconds (DP+1)
BATTLE MAP	World of Darkness
SUMMONSTONE	–

STATS	HP	1303	CP	336	BRV	171
	ATK	16	DEF	18	LUK	13

EQUIPMENT	WEAPON	–
	HANDS	–

HEAD	Plumed Hat	BODY	–

SPOILS	GIL	168	EXP	130

2 — COUNTERFEIT WRAITH

LEVEL	7	RANK	G

BEHAVIOR	Blocker
DP CHANCE	Critical hit within 10 seconds (DP+1)
BATTLE MAP	Lunar Subterrane
SUMMONSTONE	Magic Pot

STATS	HP	1364	CP	356	BRV	130
	ATK	16	DEF	18	LUK	13

EQUIPMENT	WEAPON	–
	HANDS	–

HEAD	–	BODY	–

SPOILS	GIL	168	EXP	136

3 — TRANSIENT LION

LEVEL	7	RANK	G

BEHAVIOR	Blocker
DP CHANCE	–
BATTLE MAP	Ultimecia's Castle
SUMMONSTONE	Phoenix

STATS	HP	1364	CP	337	BRV	130
	ATK	16	DEF	18	LUK	13

EQUIPMENT	WEAPON	–
	HANDS	–

HEAD	–	BODY	–

SPOILS	GIL	168	EXP	136

4 — PHANTASMAL HARLEQUIN

LEVEL	12	RANK	E

BEHAVIOR	Evader
DP CHANCE	Keep foe from getting EX Cores (DP+1)
BATTLE MAP	The Rift
SUMMONSTONE	–

STATS	HP	1667	CP	361	BRV	159
	ATK	23	DEF	22	LUK	16

EQUIPMENT	WEAPON	–
	HANDS	–

HEAD	–	BODY	–

SPOILS	GIL	168	EXP	166

ACCESSORIES	Gaia Ring, War Gong, [BRV] BRV ≥ Base Value x8

5 — IMAGINARY CHAMPION

LEVEL	13	RANK	E

BEHAVIOR	Aggressive
DP CHANCE	–
BATTLE MAP	Kefka's Tower
SUMMONSTONE	Titan

STATS	HP	1727	CP	344	BRV	165
	ATK	23	DEF	24	LUK	16

EQUIPMENT	WEAPON	–
	HANDS	–

HEAD	–	BODY	–

SPOILS	GIL	168	EXP	172

ACCESSORIES	Gaia Ring, War Gong, [BRV] BRV ≥ Base Value x8

6 — FALSE STALWART

LEVEL	7	RANK	G

BEHAVIOR	Blocker
DP CHANCE	EX Burst within 10 seconds (DP+1)
BATTLE MAP	Kefka's Tower
SUMMONSTONE	–

STATS	HP	1364	CP	337	BRV	130
	ATK	19	DEF	20	LUK	13

EQUIPMENT	WEAPON	–
	HANDS	–

HEAD	–	BODY	–

SPOILS	GIL	168	EXP	136

7 — DELUSORY WARLOCK

LEVEL	12	RANK	E

BEHAVIOR	Evader
DP CHANCE	–
BATTLE MAP	Lunar Subterrane
SUMMONSTONE	–

STATS	HP	1667	CP	343	BRV	159
	ATK	22	DEF	24	LUK	16

EQUIPMENT	WEAPON	–
	HANDS	–

HEAD	–	BODY	–

SPOILS	GIL	168	EXP	166

ACCESSORIES	Gaia Ring, War Gong, [BRV] BRV ≥ Base Value x8

8 — EXDEATH

LEVEL	15	RANK	D

BEHAVIOR	Cautious
DP CHANCE	–
BATTLE MAP	The Rift
SUMMONSTONE	Atomos

STATS	HP	2458	CP	364	BRV	230
	ATK	33	DEF	29	LUK	17

EQUIPMENT	WEAPON	Oak Staff
	HANDS	–

HEAD	Iron Helm	BODY	Iron Armor

SPOILS	GIL	252	EXP	4620

ACCESSORIES	Gaia Ring, Phoenix Down, [HP] HP = 1, [HP] Near Death, [HP] Near Loss

9 — FALLACIOUS WANDERER

LEVEL	29	RANK	B

BEHAVIOR	Vicious
DP CHANCE	Win battle (DP+2)
BATTLE MAP	The Rift
SUMMONSTONE	Leviathan

STATS	HP	2697*	CP	378	BRV	257*
	ATK	39*	DEF	40*	LUK	24

EQUIPMENT	WEAPON	[Rank 5]
	HANDS	[Rank 4]

HEAD	[Rank 6]	BODY	[Rank 4]

SPOILS	GIL	336	EXP	0

ACCESSORIES	Gaia Ring, War Gong, [BRV] BRV ≥ Base Value x8

* Denotes use of the base value (for stats that vary).

DESTINY ODYSSEY V

Difficulty

DESTINY ODYSSEY VI
STRENGTH FOR WHOM?

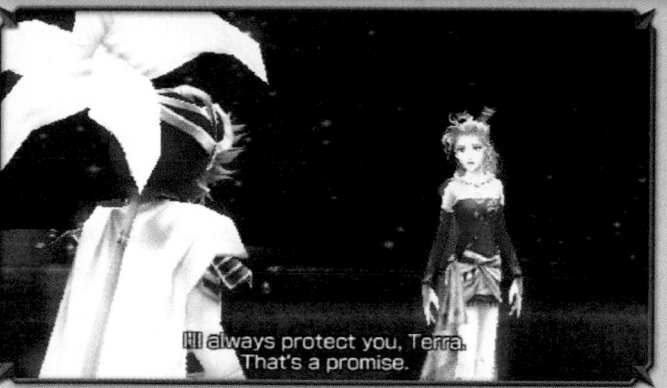

Prerequisite: Finish Prologue

I'll always protect you, Terra.
That's a promise.

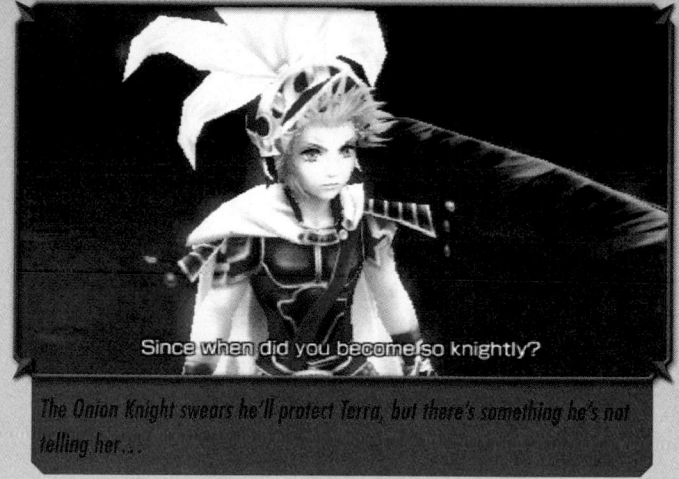

Since when did you become so knightly?

The Onion Knight swears he'll protect Terra, but there's something he's not telling her...

REWARDS

At the end of each level, rewards are available if you finish with a positive number of Destiny Points, or DP. This walkthrough includes miniature level maps that indicate the most efficient route to take through a given level, in order to maximize DP.

LEVEL COMPLETION

Remaining DP	1st Time	2nd Time
7	Rosetta Stone	300 PP
6	Snowscepter	200 PP
5	Flamescepter	120 PP
4	Deathgaze	80 PP
3	1000 gil	50 PP
2	600 gil	30 PP
1	300 gil	20 PP
0	100 gil	10 PP

At the end of each set of levels, you'll receive rewards based on your performance. Story Points, or SP, are awarded after each level based on remaining DP and HP, as well as the number of engagements undertaken. Points are penalized for retries, or for a DP total that dips into negatives. If you miss out on a desired bonus on the first playthrough, don't worry—SP is cumulative across multiple playthroughs.

DESTINY ODYSSEY VI COMPLETION

Star Rating	SP Required	Award
☆	100	New skill
☆☆	200	Special areas unlocked
☆☆☆	300	Rare battle pieces spawned
☆☆☆☆	400	Rare treasure chests spawned
–	500 SP, then every 500 SP extra	100 PP

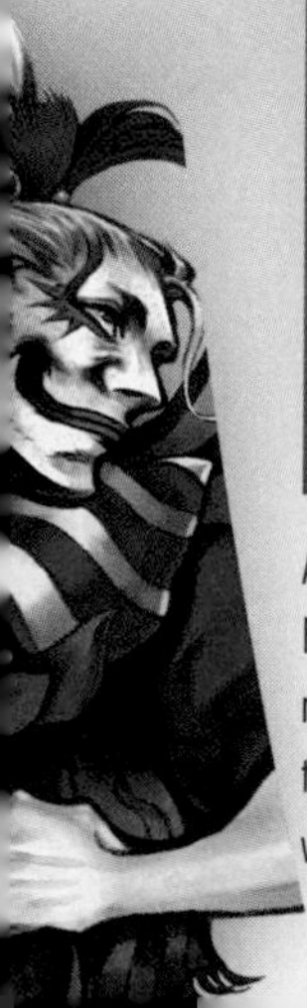

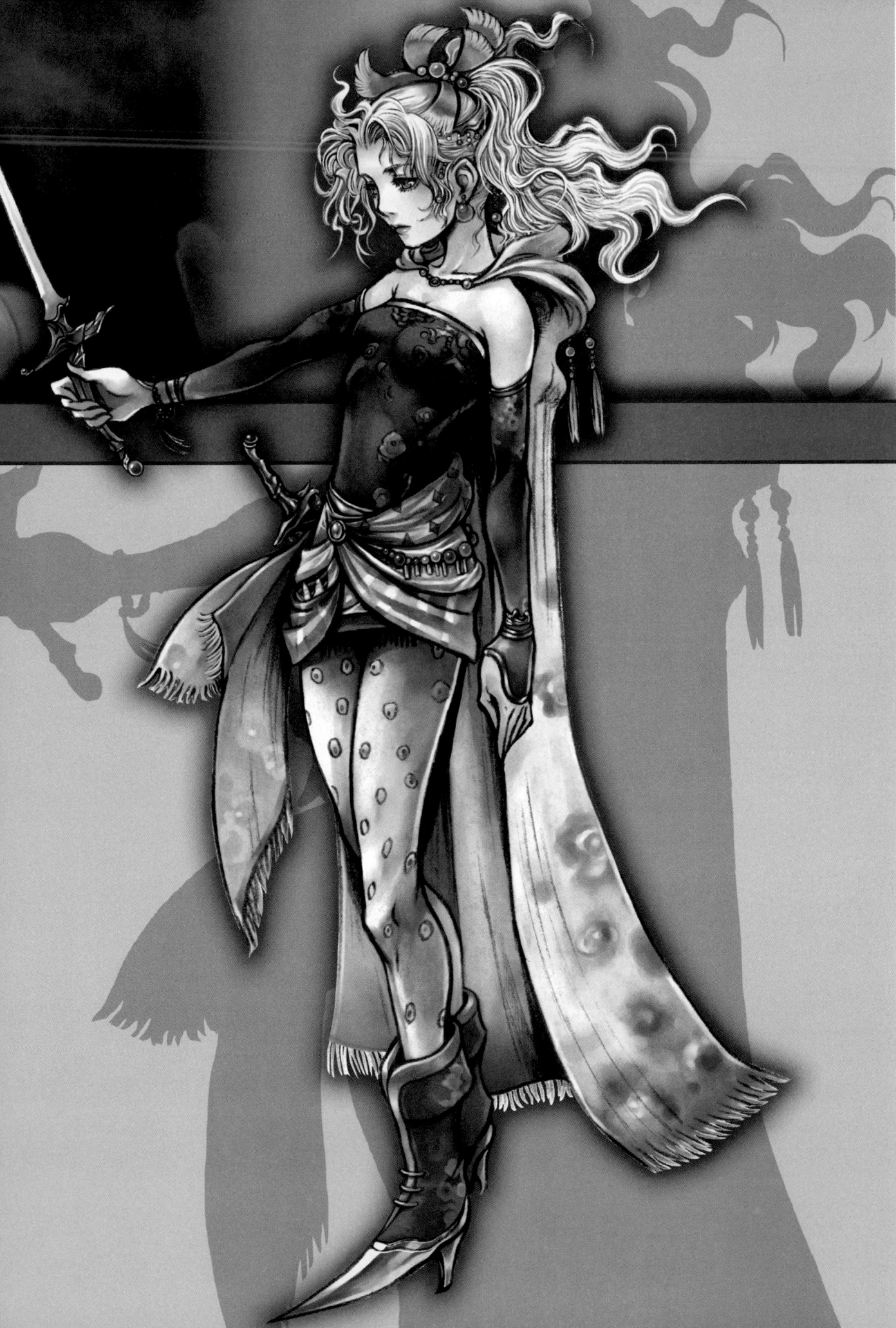

DESTINY ODYSSEY VI

STARTING DP	MAX FINISHING	ENGAGEMENTS
5	3	7

Terra's combat style differs from that of her friends. She largely fights from long range, with a focus on magic attacks. She even learns Reverse Free Air Dash extremely early, at level 2, to enhance her ability to run and strike from afar. Most of Terra's levels consist of two large, nebulous "room" areas, with small bottlenecks between them. This first level has quite a few encounters with weak foes, allowing acclimation to Terra's abilities. Beware red battle piece ④, which engages you when you pass by whether you're ready or not! Engaging the Stigma of Chaos will destroy it without a boss fight, leading to the next level.

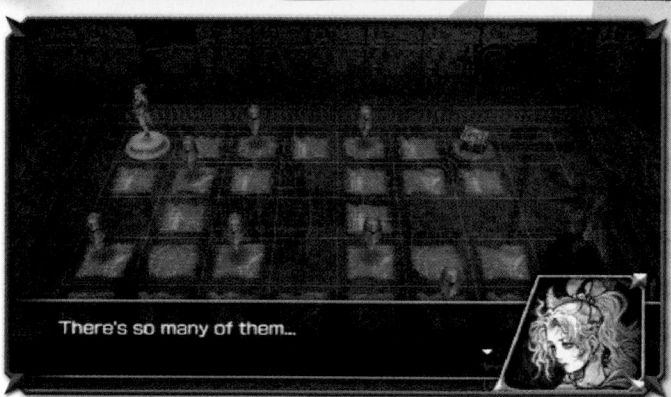

There's so many of them...

MAP

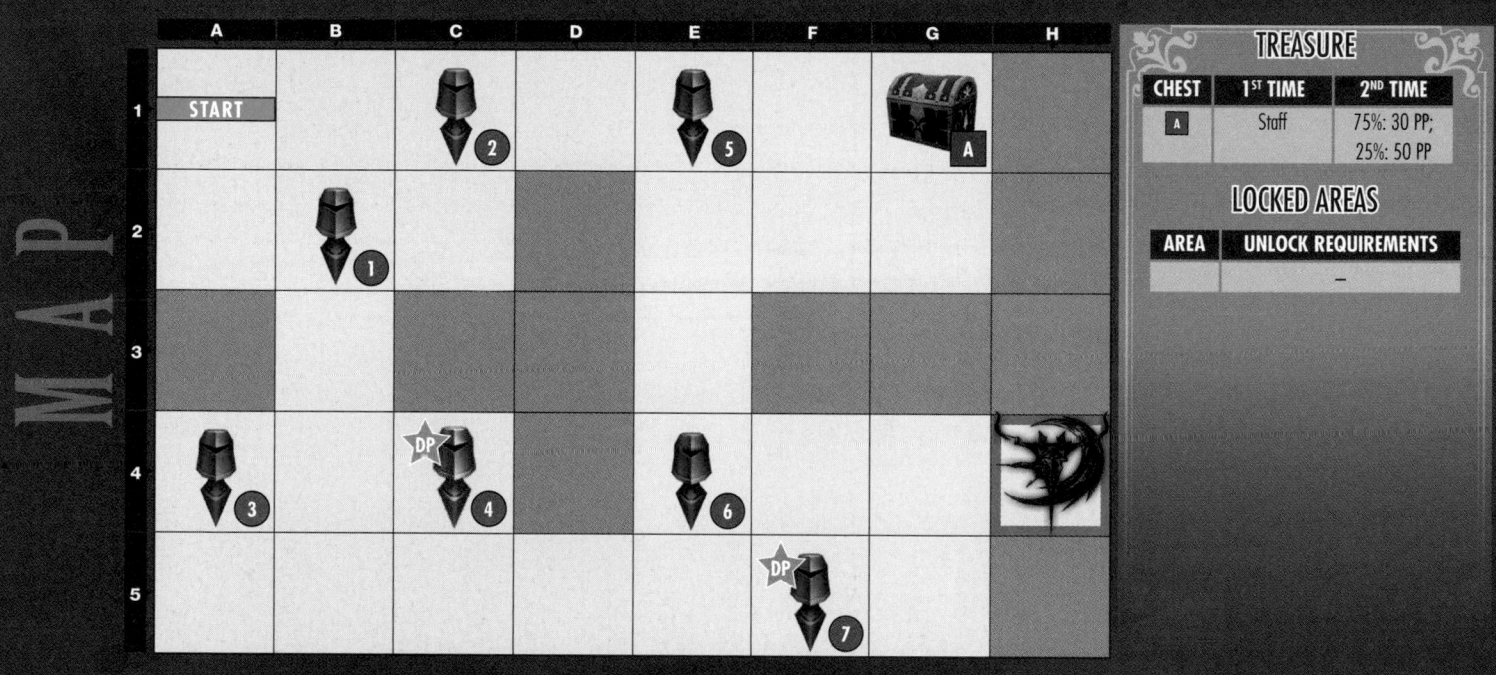

TREASURE

CHEST	1ST TIME	2ND TIME
A	Staff	75%: 30 PP; 25%: 50 PP

LOCKED AREAS

AREA	UNLOCK REQUIREMENTS
	—

DP EFFICIENCY ROUTE

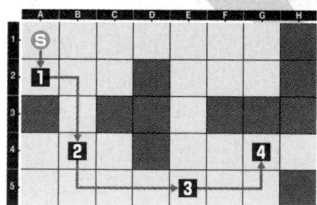

From the start, defeat battle piece ① and then head to the lower portion of the level (alternatively, you can chain battle piece ② with battle piece ① for extra EXP without using any extra Destiny Points). Upon passing battle piece ④ you'll be forced into a chain with it, along with battle piece ③. Defeat them, then head to E-5 for a chain with battle pieces ⑥ and ⑦ before breaking the Stigma of Chaos and ending the level.

BATTLE PIECE DATA

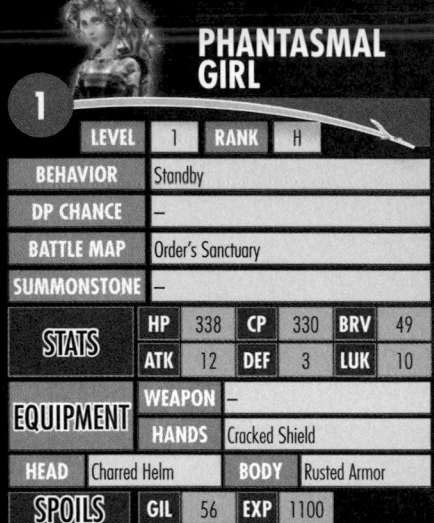

1. PHANTASMAL GIRL

LEVEL	1	RANK	H

BEHAVIOR	Standby
DP CHANCE	–
BATTLE MAP	Order's Sanctuary
SUMMONSTONE	–

STATS	HP	338	CP	330	BRV	49
	ATK	12	DEF	3	LUK	10

EQUIPMENT	WEAPON	–		
	HANDS	Cracked Shield		
HEAD	Charred Helm	BODY	Rusted Armor	

SPOILS	GIL	56	EXP	1100

2. DELUSORY KNIGHT

LEVEL	2	RANK	H

BEHAVIOR	Aggressive
DP CHANCE	–
BATTLE MAP	Lunar Subterrane
SUMMONSTONE	–

STATS	HP	399	CP	331	BRV	55
	ATK	11	DEF	4	LUK	11

EQUIPMENT	WEAPON	–		
	HANDS	Cracked Shield		
HEAD	Charred Helm	BODY	Rusted Armor	

SPOILS	GIL	56	EXP	1167

3. FALSE HERO

LEVEL	2	RANK	H

BEHAVIOR	Aggressive
DP CHANCE	–
BATTLE MAP	Lunar Subterrane
SUMMONSTONE	–

STATS	HP	399	CP	331	BRV	55
	ATK	12	DEF	7	LUK	11

EQUIPMENT	WEAPON	–		
	HANDS	Cracked Shield		
HEAD	Charred Helm	BODY	Rusted Armor	

SPOILS	GIL	56	EXP	1167

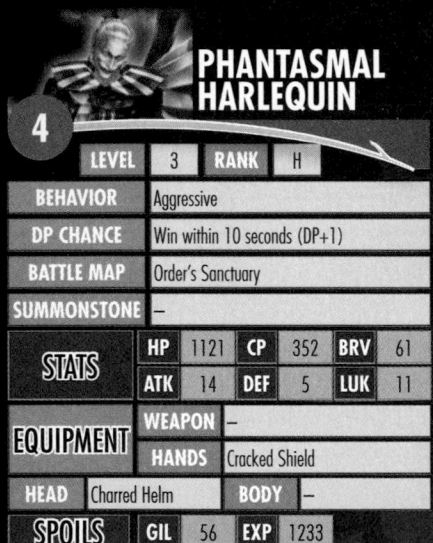

4. PHANTASMAL HARLEQUIN

LEVEL	3	RANK	H

BEHAVIOR	Aggressive
DP CHANCE	Win within 10 seconds (DP+1)
BATTLE MAP	Order's Sanctuary
SUMMONSTONE	–

STATS	HP	1121	CP	352	BRV	61
	ATK	14	DEF	5	LUK	11

EQUIPMENT	WEAPON	–		
	HANDS	Cracked Shield		
HEAD	Charred Helm	BODY	–	

SPOILS	GIL	56	EXP	1233

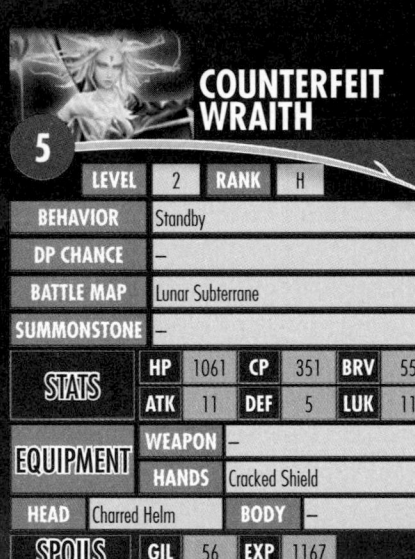

5. COUNTERFEIT WRAITH

LEVEL	2	RANK	H

BEHAVIOR	Standby
DP CHANCE	–
BATTLE MAP	Lunar Subterrane
SUMMONSTONE	–

STATS	HP	1061	CP	351	BRV	55
	ATK	11	DEF	5	LUK	11

EQUIPMENT	WEAPON	–		
	HANDS	Cracked Shield		
HEAD	Charred Helm	BODY	–	

SPOILS	GIL	56	EXP	1167

6. IMITATION DESPOT

LEVEL	3	RANK	H

BEHAVIOR	Aggressive
DP CHANCE	–
BATTLE MAP	Order's Sanctuary
SUMMONSTONE	–

STATS	HP	1121	CP	332	BRV	61
	ATK	13	DEF	7	LUK	11

EQUIPMENT	WEAPON	–		
	HANDS	Cracked Shield		
HEAD	Charred Helm	BODY	–	

SPOILS	GIL	56	EXP	1233

7. EPHEMERAL PHANTOM

LEVEL	2	RANK	H

BEHAVIOR	Aggressive
DP CHANCE	BRV Break within 10 seconds (DP+1)
BATTLE MAP	Lunar Subterrane
SUMMONSTONE	–

STATS	HP	399	CP	331	BRV	55
	ATK	14	DEF	6	LUK	11

EQUIPMENT	WEAPON	–		
	HANDS	Cracked Shield		
HEAD	Charred Helm	BODY	Rusted Armor	

SPOILS	GIL	56	EXP	1167

DESTINY ODYSSEY VI

DESTINY ODYSSEY VI-2

STARTING DP	MAX FINISHING	ENGAGEMENTS
5	4	6

The Potion right by the start of this level is a trap of sorts—grabbing it leads to a chain against hidden battle piece ⑥. Open the Locked Area in the middle by defeating battle piece ②, likely during a chain that also involves battle piece ①. Treasure chest Ⓐ is tucked away behind another duo of battle pieces in the lower left corner of the level. Finally, the Demon Wall Summonstone can be found here, but only after a 2-star rating, so the gold Locked Area disappears.

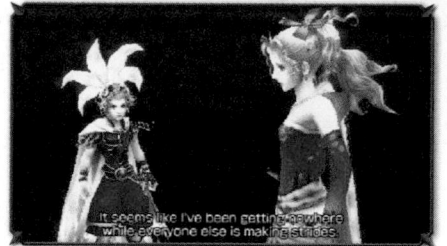

It seems like I've been getting anywhere while everyone else is making strides.

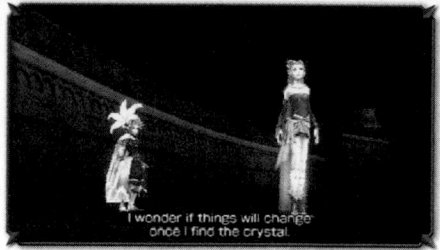

I wonder if things will change once I find the crystal.

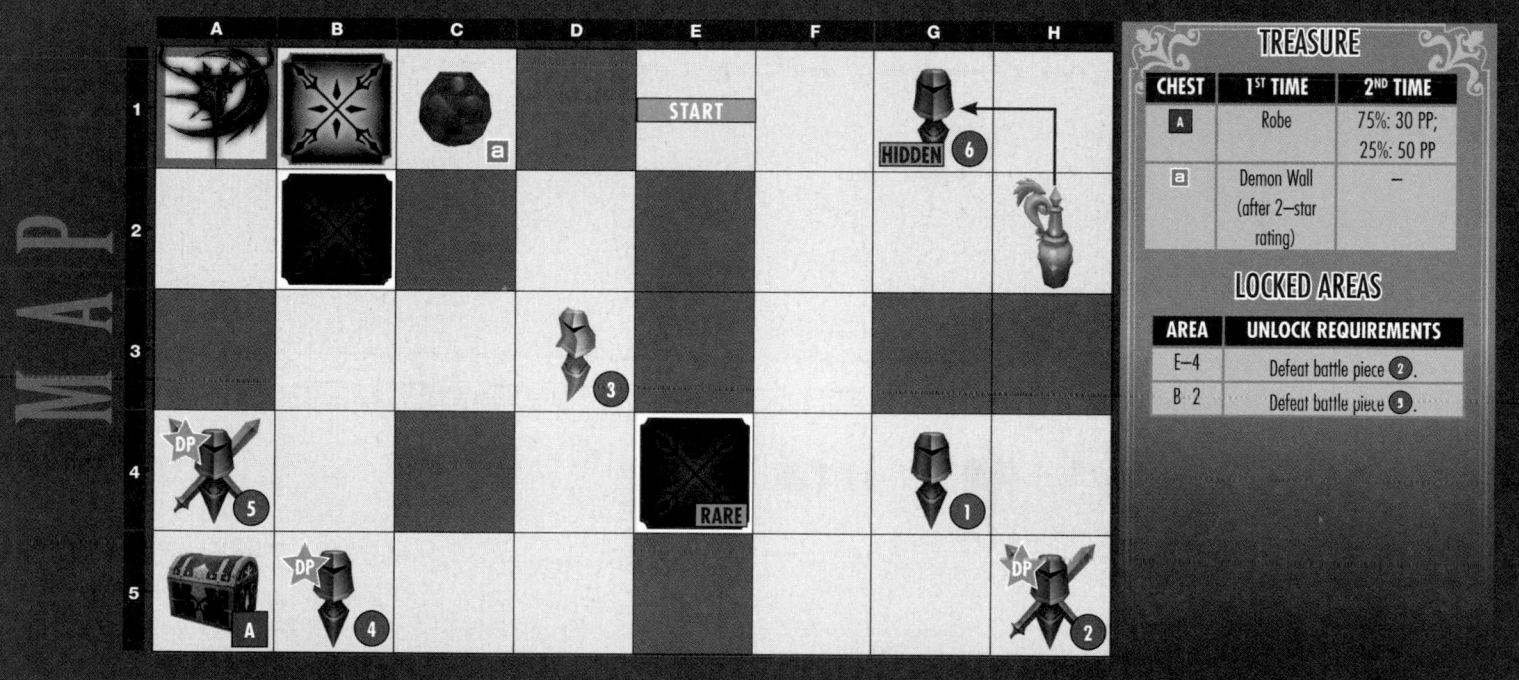

TREASURE

CHEST	1ST TIME	2ND TIME
Ⓐ	Robe	75%: 30 PP; 25%: 50 PP
ⓐ	Demon Wall (after 2–star rating)	—

LOCKED AREAS

AREA	UNLOCK REQUIREMENTS
E–4	Defeat battle piece ②.
B–2	Defeat battle piece ⑤.

DP EFFICIENCY ROUTE

Move down to battle pieces ① and ②, chaining them. After battle piece ② falls, the Locked Area barring the way to the other half of the stage disappears. If you prefer, you can

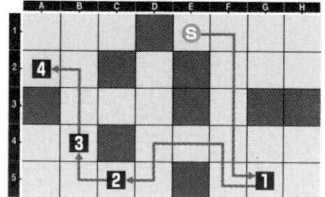

also chain battle pieces ④ and ⑤ from B-4, but this will require fighting battle piece ③. The Locked Area blocking the Stigma of Chaos disappears after defeating battle piece ⑤.

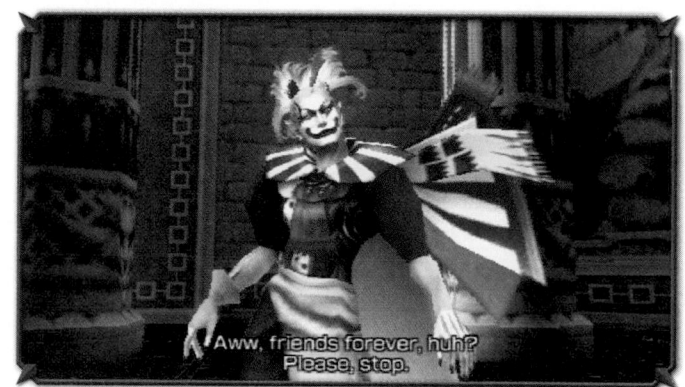

Aww, friends forever, huh? Please, stop.

BATTLE PIECE DATA

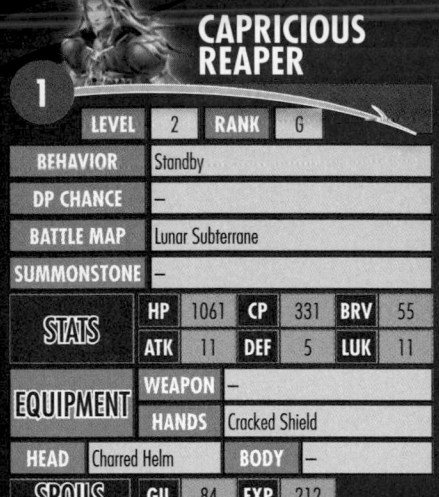

1 CAPRICIOUS REAPER

LEVEL 2 **RANK** G	
BEHAVIOR	Standby
DP CHANCE	–
BATTLE MAP	Lunar Subterrane
SUMMONSTONE	–

STATS	HP	1061	CP	331	BRV	55
	ATK	11	DEF	5	LUK	11

EQUIPMENT	**WEAPON**	–	
	HANDS	Cracked Shield	
HEAD	Charred Helm	**BODY**	–

SPOILS	GIL	84	EXP	212

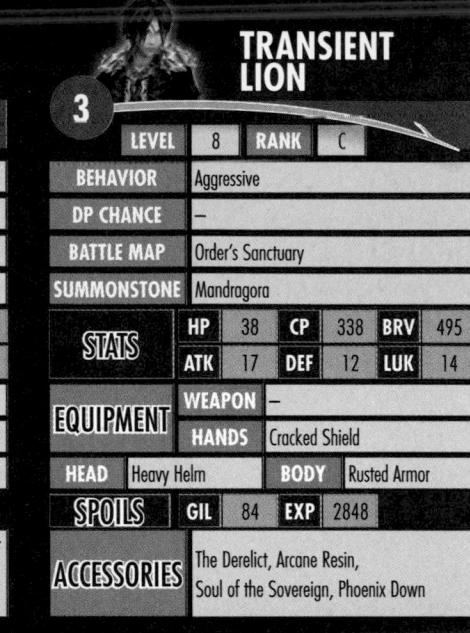

2 PHANTASMAL HARLEQUIN

LEVEL 7 **RANK** F	
BEHAVIOR	Aggressive
DP CHANCE	Win within 10 seconds (DP+1)
BATTLE MAP	Dream's End
SUMMONSTONE	–

STATS	HP	1364	CP	356	BRV	130
	ATK	18	DEF	9	LUK	13

EQUIPMENT	**WEAPON**	–	
	HANDS	Cracked Shield	
HEAD	–	**BODY**	–

SPOILS	GIL	84	EXP	272

ACCESSORIES	Gaia Ring, [Time] After 30 Seconds, [Time] After 60 Seconds, [Time] After 90 Seconds, [Time] After 120 Seconds, [Time] After 180 Seconds

3 TRANSIENT LION

LEVEL 8 **RANK** C	
BEHAVIOR	Aggressive
DP CHANCE	–
BATTLE MAP	Order's Sanctuary
SUMMONSTONE	Mandragora

STATS	HP	38	CP	338	BRV	495
	ATK	17	DEF	12	LUK	14

EQUIPMENT	**WEAPON**	–	
	HANDS	Cracked Shield	
HEAD	Heavy Helm	**BODY**	Rusted Armor

SPOILS	GIL	84	EXP	2848

ACCESSORIES	The Derelict, Arcane Resin, Soul of the Sovereign, Phoenix Down

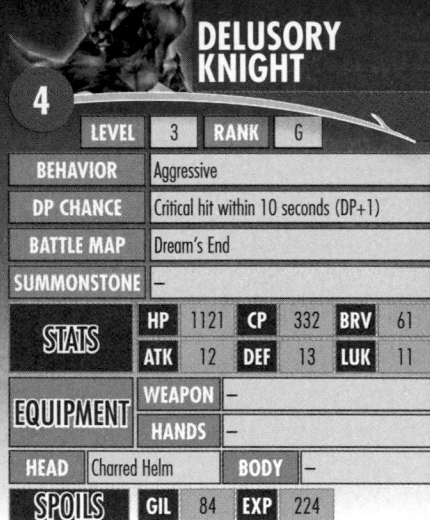

4 DELUSORY KNIGHT

LEVEL 3 **RANK** G	
BEHAVIOR	Aggressive
DP CHANCE	Critical hit within 10 seconds (DP+1)
BATTLE MAP	Dream's End
SUMMONSTONE	–

STATS	HP	1121	CP	332	BRV	61
	ATK	12	DEF	13	LUK	11

EQUIPMENT	**WEAPON**	–	
	HANDS	–	
HEAD	Charred Helm	**BODY**	–

SPOILS	GIL	84	EXP	224

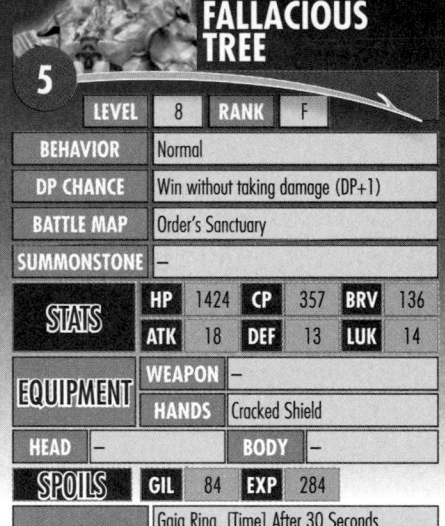

5 FALLACIOUS TREE

LEVEL 8 **RANK** F	
BEHAVIOR	Normal
DP CHANCE	Win without taking damage (DP+1)
BATTLE MAP	Order's Sanctuary
SUMMONSTONE	–

STATS	HP	1424	CP	357	BRV	136
	ATK	18	DEF	13	LUK	14

EQUIPMENT	**WEAPON**	–	
	HANDS	Cracked Shield	
HEAD	–	**BODY**	–

SPOILS	GIL	84	EXP	284

ACCESSORIES	Gaia Ring, [Time] After 30 Seconds, [Time] After 60 Seconds, [Time] After 90 Seconds, [Time] After 120 Seconds

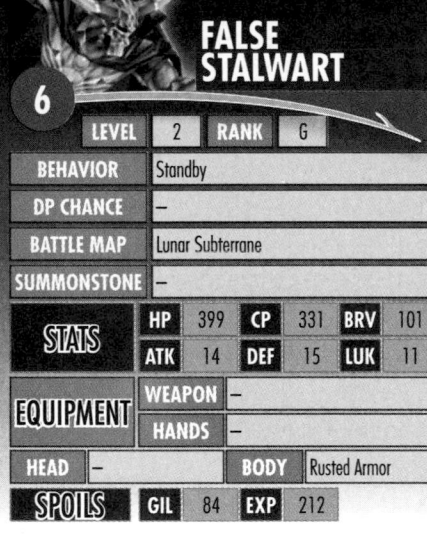

6 FALSE STALWART

LEVEL 2 **RANK** G	
BEHAVIOR	Standby
DP CHANCE	–
BATTLE MAP	Lunar Subterrane
SUMMONSTONE	–

STATS	HP	399	CP	331	BRV	101
	ATK	14	DEF	15	LUK	11

EQUIPMENT	**WEAPON**	–	
	HANDS	–	
HEAD	–	**BODY**	Rusted Armor

SPOILS	GIL	84	EXP	212

For the first part of this level, you'll have no choice—you can only assault battle pieces ➊ and ➋. However, after defeating piece ➋, you'll have a few options. You can proceed further right in the stage, or go through the Locked Area that opens up to grab treasure chest ▣ and chain battle piece ➌. Expert battle piece ➏ may seem tough at first—this Ultimecia manikin will probably be around three times your level the first time through! But, as with many characters armed with long-range attacks, Terra has an easier time with this challenge than you might expect. Hide behind the moon rocks and pepper the foe with Flood. The enemy dodges most of the time, but not *all* the time—and if you keep up the Flood onslaught, the enemy also won't ever get a chance to chase you down behind the rocks you're using as cover. The boss here is something of a surprise. He'll dodge or block incoming attacks often, and is quick to go after EX Cores. The biggest openings to strike come from avoiding his attacks. In particular, watch out for his homing HP attack, Braver. Dodge it, then hit him while he's vulnerable.

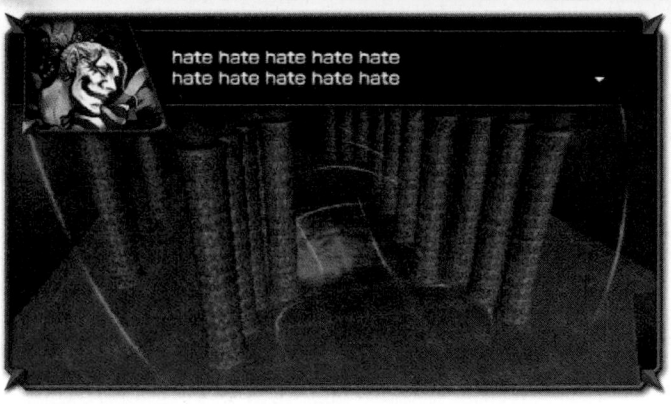

hate hate hate hate hate
hate hate hate hate hate

MAP

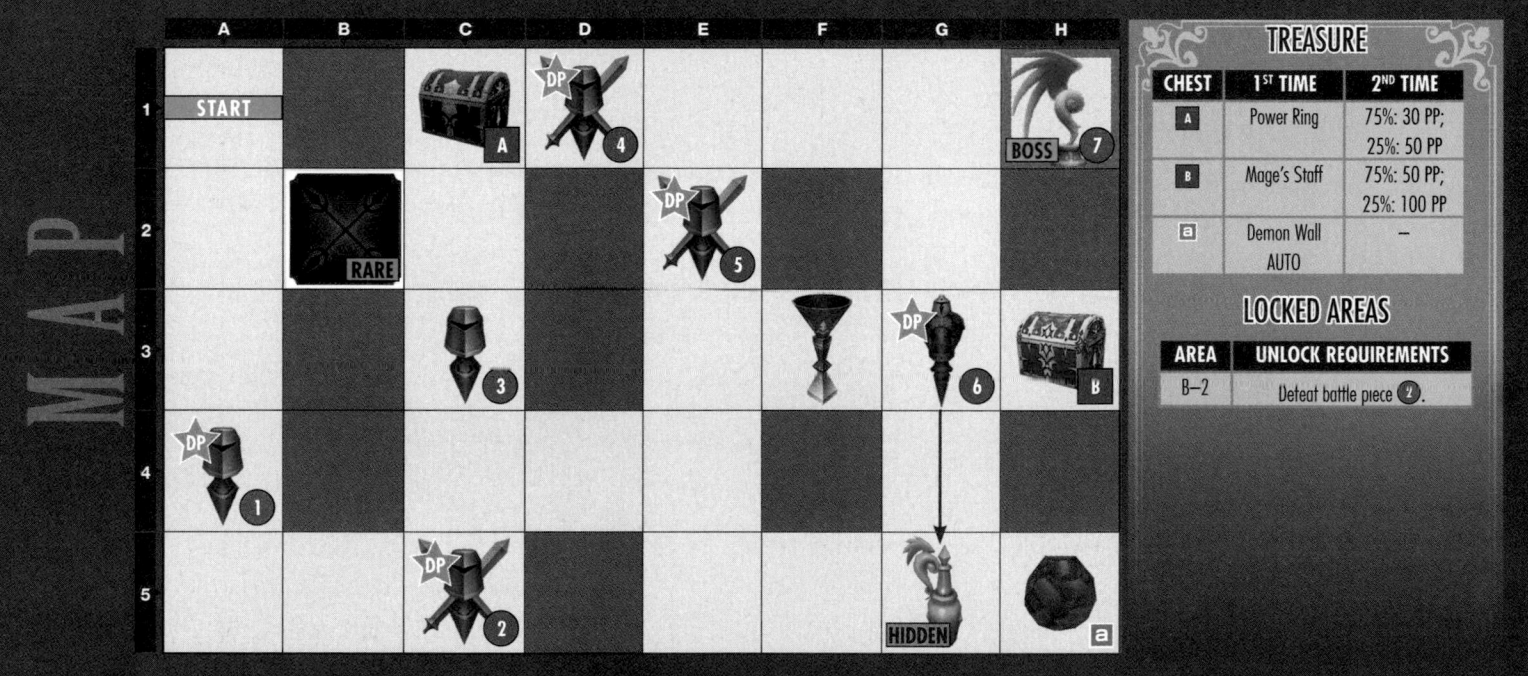

TREASURE		
CHEST	1ST TIME	2ND TIME
A	Power Ring	75%: 30 PP; 25%: 50 PP
B	Mage's Staff	75%: 50 PP; 25%: 100 PP
a	Demon Wall AUTO	—

LOCKED AREAS

AREA	UNLOCK REQUIREMENTS
B–2	Defeat battle piece ➋

DP EFFICIENCY ROUTE

From the start, head down and engage battle piece ➊, followed by battle piece ➋. Then, move to G-4 and engage expert battle piece ➏. A Potion spawns right behind you after this battle, and you can take it without sacrificing DP. After refilling HP and EX Force, head up to E-1 for a chain with battle pieces ➍ and ➎. After that, move to the exit in the upper right corner of the board.

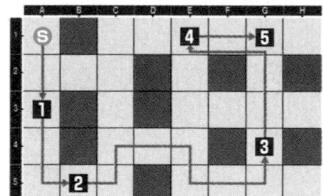

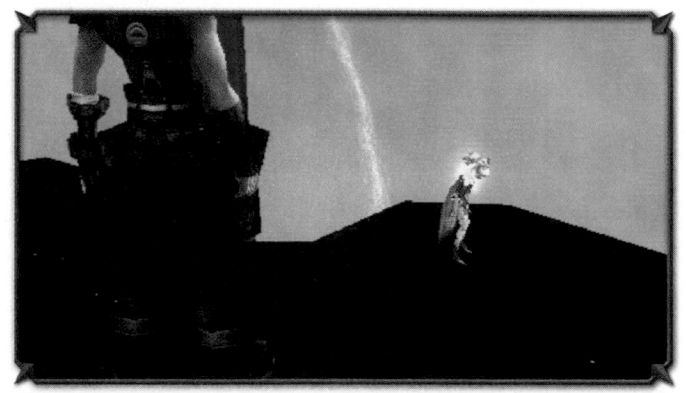

BATTLE PIECE DATA

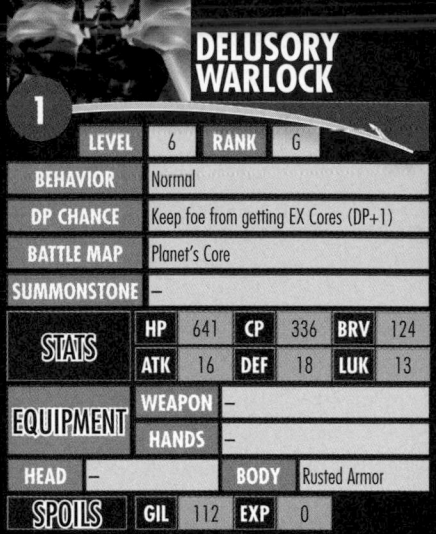

1 DELUSORY WARLOCK

LEVEL	6	RANK	G

BEHAVIOR	Normal
DP CHANCE	Keep foe from getting EX Cores (DP+1)
BATTLE MAP	Planet's Core
SUMMONSTONE	—

STATS	HP	641	CP	336	BRV	124
	ATK	16	DEF	18	LUK	13

EQUIPMENT	WEAPON	—		
	HANDS	—		
HEAD	—		BODY	Rusted Armor

SPOILS	GIL	112	EXP	0

2 EPHEMERAL PHANTOM

LEVEL	10	RANK	E

BEHAVIOR	Aggressive
DP CHANCE	Win without taking damage (DP+1)
BATTLE MAP	Dream's End
SUMMONSTONE	—

STATS	HP	1545	CP	341	BRV	147
	ATK	22	DEF	14	LUK	15

EQUIPMENT	WEAPON	—		
	HANDS	Cracked Shield		
HEAD	—		BODY	—

SPOILS	GIL	112	EXP	0

ACCESSORIES	Gaia Ring, [Time] After 30 Seconds, [Time] After 60 Seconds, [Time] After 90 Seconds, [Time] After 120 Seconds

3 FALLACIOUS TREE

LEVEL	5	RANK	G

BEHAVIOR	Evader
DP CHANCE	—
BATTLE MAP	Lunar Subterrane
SUMMONSTONE	—

STATS	HP	1242	CP	354	BRV	72
	ATK	15	DEF	18	LUK	12

EQUIPMENT	WEAPON	—		
	HANDS	—		
HEAD	Charred Helm		BODY	—

SPOILS	GIL	112	EXP	0

4 PHANTASMAL HARLEQUIN

LEVEL	8	RANK	E

BEHAVIOR	Evader
DP CHANCE	Win within 10 seconds (DP+1)
BATTLE MAP	Planet's Core
SUMMONSTONE	—

STATS	HP	1424	CP	357	BRV	136
	ATK	19	DEF	10	LUK	14

EQUIPMENT	WEAPON	—		
	HANDS	Cracked Shield		
HEAD	—		BODY	—

SPOILS	GIL	112	EXP	0

ACCESSORIES	Gaia Ring, [Time] After 30 Seconds, [Time] After 60 Seconds, [Time] After 90 Seconds, [Time] After 120 Seconds, [Time] After 180 Seconds

5 CAPRICIOUS REAPER

LEVEL	10	RANK	E

BEHAVIOR	Aggressive
DP CHANCE	BRV Break within 10 seconds (DP+1)
BATTLE MAP	Order's Sanctuary
SUMMONSTONE	—

STATS	HP	1545	CP	341	BRV	147
	ATK	19	DEF	13	LUK	15

EQUIPMENT	WEAPON	—		
	HANDS	Cracked Shield		
HEAD	—		BODY	—

SPOILS	GIL	112	EXP	0

ACCESSORIES	Gaia Ring, [Time] After 30 Seconds, [Time] After 60 Seconds, [Time] After 90 Seconds, [Time] After 120 Seconds

6 TRANSIENT WITCH

LEVEL	18	RANK	C

BEHAVIOR	Survivor
DP CHANCE	Win battle (DP+1)
BATTLE MAP	Lunar Subterrane
SUMMONSTONE	—

STATS	HP	2030*	CP	350	BRV	193*
	ATK	41	DEF	27*	LUK	19

EQUIPMENT	WEAPON	[Rank 3]		
	HANDS	Power Armlet		
HEAD	[Rank 4]		BODY	Cotton Robes

SPOILS	GIL	112	EXP	0

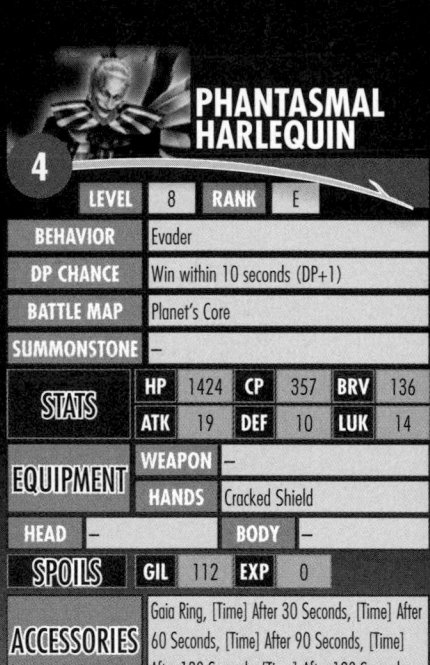

7 CLOUD

LEVEL	12	RANK	F

BEHAVIOR	Cautious
DP CHANCE	—
BATTLE MAP	Planet's Core
SUMMONSTONE	—

STATS	HP	2035	CP	343	BRV	159
	ATK	27	DEF	24	LUK	16

EQUIPMENT	WEAPON	Buster Sword		
	HANDS	—		
HEAD	—		BODY	Leather Armor

SPOILS	GIL	168	EXP	3334

* Denotes use of the base value (for stats that vary).

STARTING DP	MAX FINISHING	ENGAGEMENTS
4	5 (+2 after 3-star rating)	6 (+1 after 3-star rating)

This level features a wall of foes blocking the exit from Terra. Returning after a 2-star rating opens the way to a Rosetta Stone, squirreled away in treasure chest **A** in the upper right. After a 4-star rating, treasure chest **A** appears at the bottom of the level. A 3-star rating spawns ultimate battle piece **7**, a very rough version of Kefka. This manikin counters most of Terra's abilities very effectively. Holy is blocked and reflected right back at you more often than not, and Tornado will almost always be avoided. This Kefka copy has one weak point in its defense—it doesn't deal with Blizzara very well. When it's far away, fire Blizzara at it repeatedly, both to build up bravery and to interrupt the dangerous HP attacks that this manikin uses from afar. This strategy is doubly effective during EX Mode, where Terra can fire spells back-to-back thanks to Chainspell. Once you have enough bravery built up to make going for HP attacks worth it, lock your bravery, if possible, with Alexander, then use Flood on the manikin. Sure, it may dodge this attack often, but like any CPU opponent, it won't dodge it 100% of the time. This is much safer than trying to land Tornado up close, since the manikin is very dangerous at close range, and it is quite good at evading your attacks before decimating you with Havoc Wing.

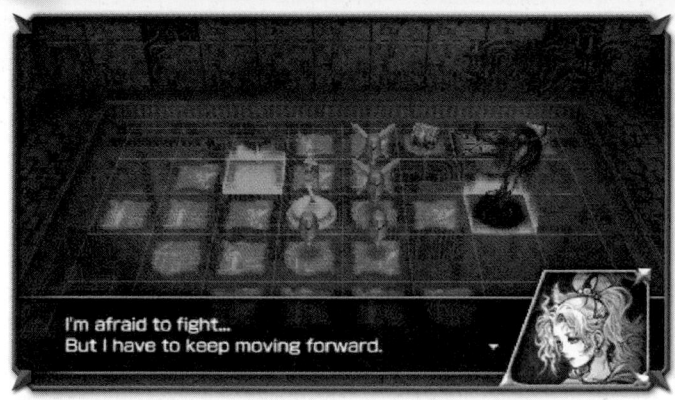

I'm afraid to fight...
But I have to keep moving forward.

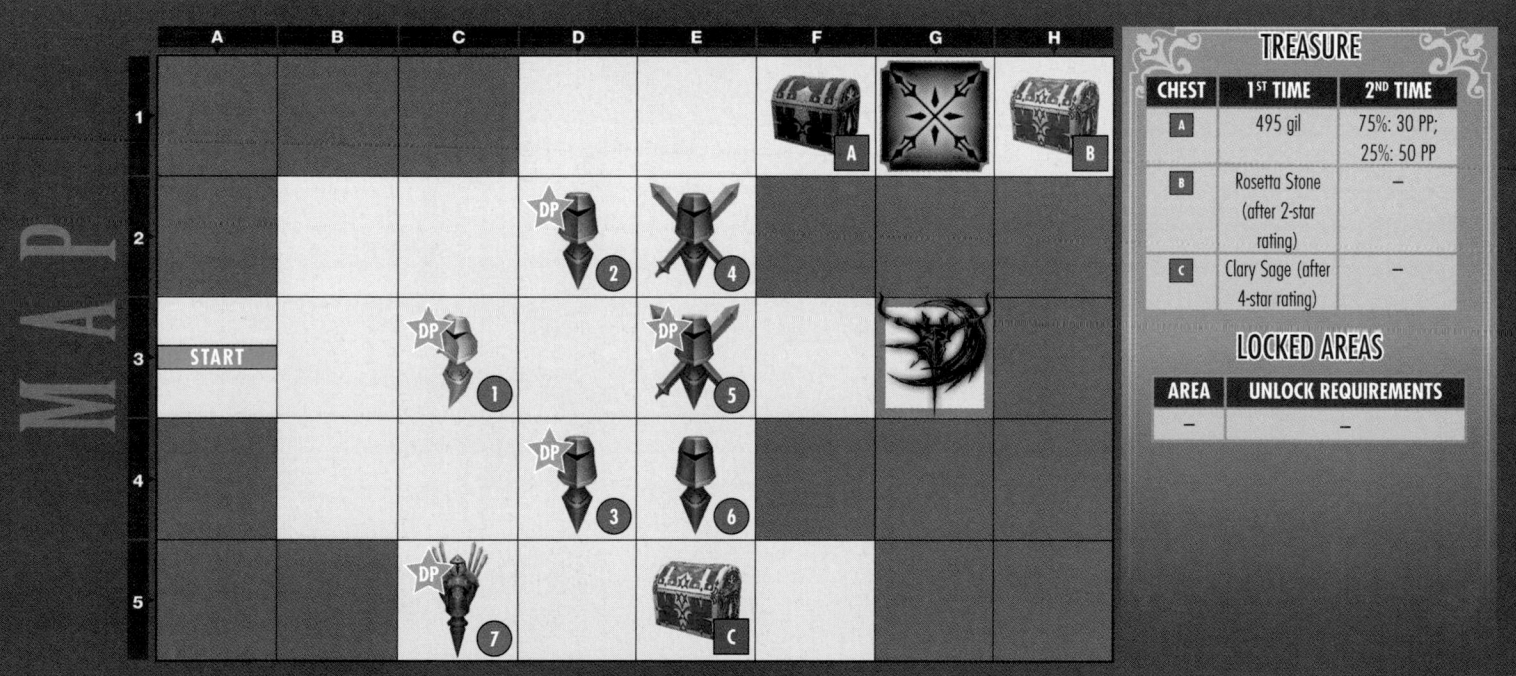

MAP

TREASURE

CHEST	1ST TIME	2ND TIME
A	495 gil	75%: 30 PP; 25%: 50 PP
B	Rosetta Stone (after 2-star rating)	–
C	Clary Sage (after 4-star rating)	–

LOCKED AREAS

AREA	UNLOCK REQUIREMENTS
–	–

DP EFFICIENCY ROUTE

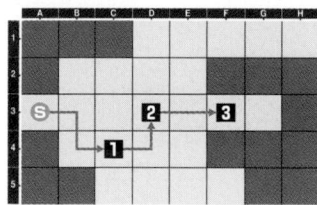

Maximizing DP here must wait until you've already cleared Destiny Odyssey VI with at least a 3-star rating, so that rare battle piece **7** spawns. However, once this piece is present, it's pretty simple. From the start, head to C-4 and chain battle pieces **1**, **3**, and **7**. After that, go to D-3 to chain battle pieces **2** and **5**. Battle piece **2** requires an EX Burst within 10 seconds to score the DP Chance, so save up EX Force during the first battle chain so you'll have it ready to go. After the two chains are complete, head to the Stigma of Chaos to complete the level.

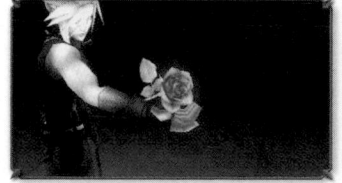

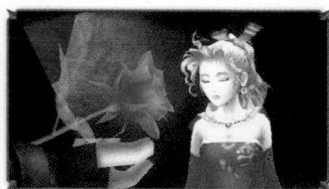

BATTLE PIECE DATA

1 TRANSIENT LION

LEVEL	11	RANK	B

BEHAVIOR	Aggressive
DP CHANCE	Critical hit within 10 seconds (DP+1)
BATTLE MAP	Crystal World
SUMMONSTONE	Mandragora

STATS	HP	47	CP	342	BRV	153*
	ATK	20	DEF	22*	LUK	15

EQUIPMENT	WEAPON	—
	HANDS	Cracked Shield

HEAD	[Rank 5]	BODY	Rusted Armor

SPOILS	GIL	140	EXP	3212

ACCESSORIES	The Derelict, Arcane Resin, Soul of the Sovereign, Phoenix Down

2 COUNTERFEIT WRAITH

LEVEL	6	RANK	G

BEHAVIOR	Aggressive
DP CHANCE	EX Burst within 10 seconds (DP+1)
BATTLE MAP	Order's Sanctuary
SUMMONSTONE	—

STATS	HP	1303	CP	355	BRV	124
	ATK	15	DEF	17	LUK	13

EQUIPMENT	WEAPON	—
	HANDS	—

HEAD	—	BODY	—

SPOILS	GIL	140	EXP	0

3 IMITATION DESPOT

LEVEL	6	RANK	G

BEHAVIOR	Evader
DP CHANCE	Wall Rush within 10 seconds (DP+1)
BATTLE MAP	Dream's End
SUMMONSTONE	Leviathan AUTO

STATS	HP	641	CP	336	BRV	124
	ATK	16	DEF	18	LUK	13

EQUIPMENT	WEAPON	—
	HANDS	—

HEAD	—	BODY	Rusted Armor

SPOILS	GIL	140	EXP	0

4 FALSE STALWART

LEVEL	12	RANK	E

BEHAVIOR	Aggressive
DP CHANCE	—
BATTLE MAP	Kefka's Tower
SUMMONSTONE	—

STATS	HP	1667	CP	343	BRV	159
	ATK	24	DEF	17	LUK	16

EQUIPMENT	WEAPON	—
	HANDS	Cracked Shield

HEAD	—	BODY	—

SPOILS	GIL	140	EXP	0

ACCESSORIES	Gaia Ring, [Time] After 30 Seconds, [Time] After 60 Seconds, [Time] After 90 Seconds, [Time] After 120 Seconds

5 PHANTASMAL HARLEQUIN

LEVEL	12	RANK	E

BEHAVIOR	Standby
DP CHANCE	Win within 10 seconds (DP+1)
BATTLE MAP	Lunar Subterrane
SUMMONSTONE	—

STATS	HP	1667	CP	361	BRV	159
	ATK	23	DEF	14	LUK	16

EQUIPMENT	WEAPON	—
	HANDS	Cracked Shield

HEAD	—	BODY	—

SPOILS	GIL	140	EXP	0

ACCESSORIES	Gaia Ring, [Time] After 30 Seconds, [Time] After 60 Seconds, [Time] After 90 Seconds, [Time] After 120 Seconds, [Time] After 180 Seconds

6 FALSE HERO

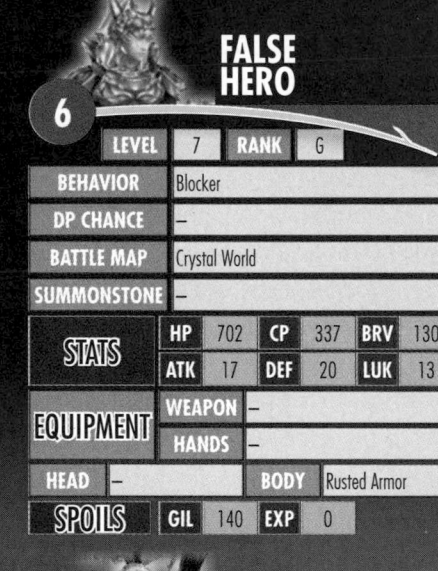

LEVEL	7	RANK	G

BEHAVIOR	Blocker
DP CHANCE	—
BATTLE MAP	Crystal World
SUMMONSTONE	—

STATS	HP	702	CP	337	BRV	130
	ATK	17	DEF	20	LUK	13

EQUIPMENT	WEAPON	—
	HANDS	—

HEAD	—	BODY	Rusted Armor

SPOILS	GIL	140	EXP	0

7 PHANTASMAL HARLEQUIN

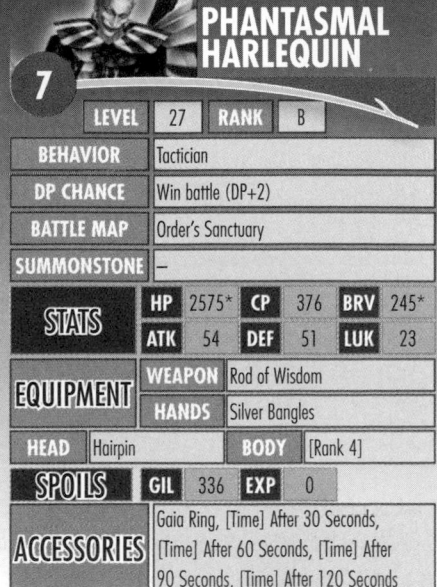

LEVEL	27	RANK	B

BEHAVIOR	Tactician
DP CHANCE	Win battle (DP+2)
BATTLE MAP	Order's Sanctuary
SUMMONSTONE	—

STATS	HP	2575*	CP	376	BRV	245*
	ATK	54	DEF	51	LUK	23

EQUIPMENT	WEAPON	Rod of Wisdom
	HANDS	Silver Bangles

HEAD	Hairpin	BODY	[Rank 4]

SPOILS	GIL	336	EXP	0

ACCESSORIES	Gaia Ring, [Time] After 30 Seconds, [Time] After 60 Seconds, [Time] After 90 Seconds, [Time] After 120 Seconds

* Denotes use of the base value (for stats that vary).

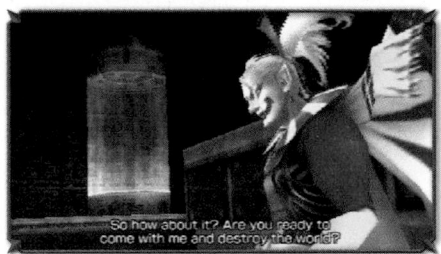
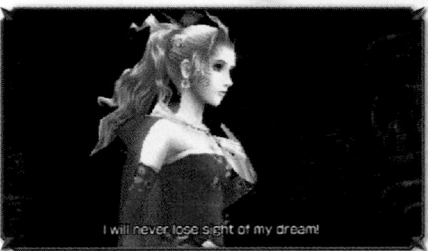
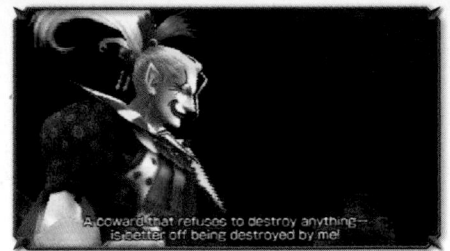

Terra's final level doesn't completely open up until you return. A 4-star rating spawns treasure chest **C** on the second half of the map. The 3-star rating you'll get along the way also spawns rare battle piece **9** nearby. This ultimate battle piece is a crystal copy of Terra. Like most rare battle pieces, it's very powerful, but in this particular fight, you have a decent advantage, given Terra's tools. Note the square corner rooms in the upper reaches of the stage, where EX Cores often spawn—this foe has a terrible time avoiding Tornado when in the same square area as you, and just as bad a time avoiding Flood when in a different one. Beware the false Terra's own Tornado when you're close, and use the stage to your advantage to put walls between you and your foe at longer ranges, negating the manikin's ranged magic attacks. This particular Terra manikin is not as inclined to use attacks that ignore walls. Kefka, the boss, is a different story. He frequently uses Trine to strike at your HP from anywhere, even behind walls or across the stage. Don't commit to any actions that take an inordinate amount of time when he's far away, and be ready to dodge. If he uses Forsaken Null, interrupt his attack with Blizzara. When bravery is built up, attack him from behind walls with Flood, or use Tornado in close quarters, especially if he's cornered in the upper reaches of the stage. However, beware his Magic Pot summon, which can instantly match his bravery to yours.

MAP

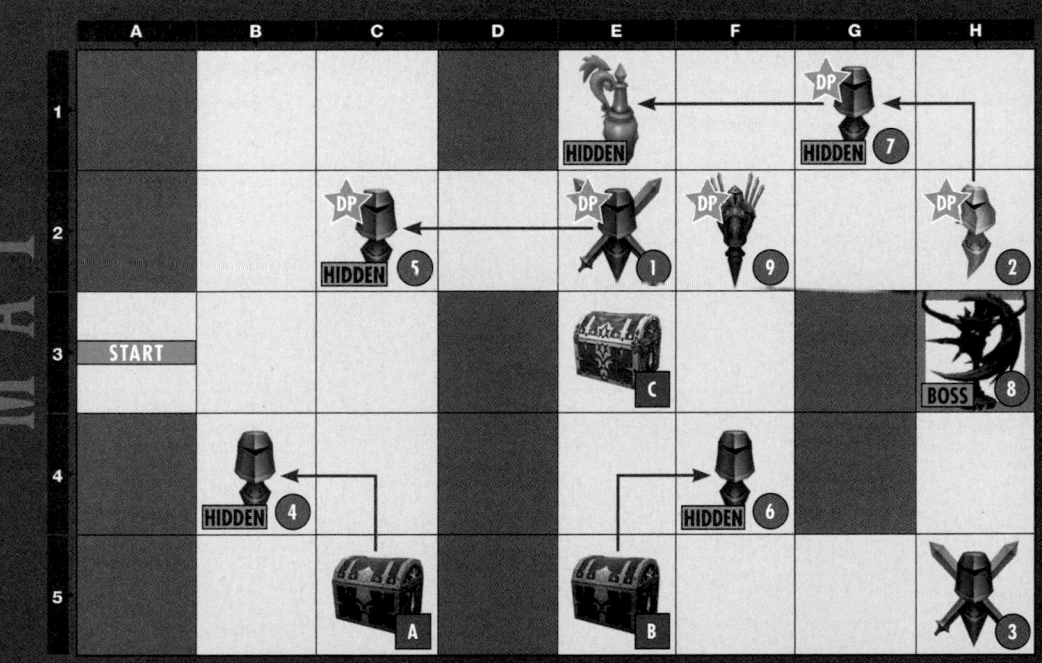

TREASURE		
CHEST	1ST TIME	2ND TIME
A	[EX] EX Mode	10 PP
B	Rosetta Stone	75%: 30 PP; 25%: 50 PP
C	Mythril (after 4-star rating)	—

LOCKED AREAS

AREA	UNLOCK REQUIREMENTS
	—

DP EFFICIENCY ROUTE

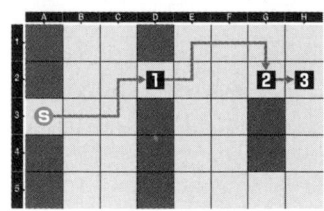

Like the level before it, max DP can't be accomplished here until after a 3-star rating on a previous playthrough of Destiny Odyssey VI. Once that's done, and rare battle piece **9** has spawned, open the level by heading to D-2 and engaging battle piece **1**. This causes a chain with battle piece **5**, hidden right behind you. After that, head to G-2 for another chain, this time against battle pieces **2**, **7**, and **9**. After these pieces are dispensed with and all the Destiny Points are gathered, head to the Stigma of Chaos for the boss fight and the end of Terra's chapter.

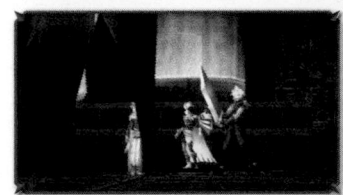
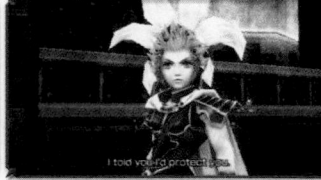
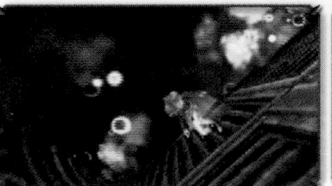
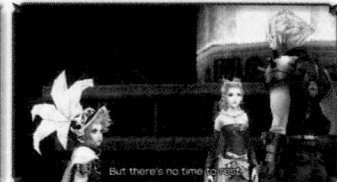

BATTLE PIECE DATA

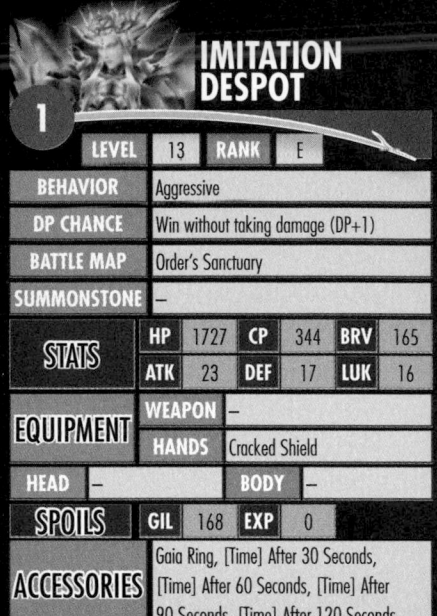

1 — IMITATION DESPOT

LEVEL	13	RANK	E

BEHAVIOR	Aggressive
DP CHANCE	Win without taking damage (DP+1)
BATTLE MAP	Order's Sanctuary
SUMMONSTONE	–

STATS	HP	1727	CP	344	BRV	165
	ATK	23	DEF	17	LUK	16

EQUIPMENT	WEAPON	–		
	HANDS	Cracked Shield		
HEAD	–		BODY	–

SPOILS	GIL	168	EXP	0

ACCESSORIES	Gaia Ring, [Time] After 30 Seconds, [Time] After 60 Seconds, [Time] After 90 Seconds, [Time] After 120 Seconds

2 — TRANSIENT LION

LEVEL	14	RANK	B

BEHAVIOR	Aggressive
DP CHANCE	Critical hit within 10 seconds (DP+1)
BATTLE MAP	Order's Sanctuary
SUMMONSTONE	Mandragora

STATS	HP	56	CP	345	BRV	597
	ATK	23	DEF	18	LUK	17

EQUIPMENT	WEAPON	–		
	HANDS	Cracked Shield		
HEAD	Heavy Helm	BODY	Rusted Armor	

SPOILS	GIL	168	EXP	3576

ACCESSORIES	The Derelict, Arcane Resin, Soul of the Sovereign, Phoenix Down

3 — FALSE STALWART

LEVEL	14	RANK	C

BEHAVIOR	Blocker
DP CHANCE	–
BATTLE MAP	Crystal World
SUMMONSTONE	–

STATS	HP	1788	CP	345	BRV	170
	ATK	26	DEF	19	LUK	17

EQUIPMENT	WEAPON	–		
	HANDS	Cracked Shield		
HEAD	–		BODY	–

SPOILS	GIL	168	EXP	0

ACCESSORIES	Gaia Ring, [Time] After 30 Seconds, [Time] After 60 Seconds, [Time] After 90 Seconds, [Time] After 120 Seconds

4 — EPHEMERAL PHANTOM

LEVEL	9	RANK	G

BEHAVIOR	Evader
DP CHANCE	–
BATTLE MAP	Kefka's Tower
SUMMONSTONE	–

STATS	HP	1485	CP	339	BRV	141
	ATK	21	DEF	21	LUK	14

EQUIPMENT	WEAPON	–		
	HANDS	–		
HEAD	–		BODY	–

SPOILS	GIL	168	EXP	0

5 — FALLACIOUS TREE

LEVEL	9	RANK	G

BEHAVIOR	Blocker
DP CHANCE	BRV Break within 10 seconds (DP+1)
BATTLE MAP	Crystal World
SUMMONSTONE	–

STATS	HP	1485	CP	358	BRV	141
	ATK	19	DEF	22	LUK	14

EQUIPMENT	WEAPON	–		
	HANDS	–		
HEAD	–		BODY	–

SPOILS	GIL	168	EXP	0

6 — CAPRICIOUS REAPER

LEVEL	8	RANK	G

BEHAVIOR	Aggressive
DP CHANCE	–
BATTLE MAP	Lunar Subterrane
SUMMONSTONE	–

STATS	HP	762	CP	338	BRV	136
	ATK	17	DEF	19	LUK	14

EQUIPMENT	WEAPON	–		
	HANDS	–		
HEAD	–		BODY	Rusted Armor

SPOILS	GIL	168	EXP	0

7 — DELUSORY WARLOCK

LEVEL	9	RANK	G

BEHAVIOR	Aggressive
DP CHANCE	Wall Rush within 10 seconds (DP+1)
BATTLE MAP	Lunar Subterrane
SUMMONSTONE	Iron Giant

STATS	HP	1485	CP	339	BRV	141
	ATK	19	DEF	21	LUK	14

EQUIPMENT	WEAPON	–		
	HANDS	–		
HEAD	–		BODY	–

SPOILS	GIL	168	EXP	0

* Denotes use of the base value (for stats that vary).

8 — KEFKA

LEVEL	17	RANK	D

BEHAVIOR	Extreme
DP CHANCE	–
BATTLE MAP	Kefka's Tower
SUMMONSTONE	Magic Pot

STATS	HP	2450	CP	366	BRV	283
	ATK	36	DEF	28	LUK	18

EQUIPMENT	WEAPON	Guard Stick		
	HANDS	–		
HEAD	Plumed Hat	BODY	Cotton Robes	

SPOILS	GIL	252	EXP	4925

ACCESSORIES	Gaia Ring, [Combat] Pre–Bravery Attack, [Combat] Pre–Bravery Damage, [Combat] Pre–HP Attack, [Combat] Pre–HP Damage, [HP] HP = 100%

9 — PHANTASMAL GIRL

LEVEL	30	RANK	B

BEHAVIOR	Calm
DP CHANCE	Win battle (DP+2)
BATTLE MAP	Kefka's Tower
SUMMONSTONE	Demon Wall

STATS	HP	2757*	CP	365	BRV	263*
	ATK	62	DEF	58	LUK	25

EQUIPMENT	WEAPON	Rod of Wisdom		
	HANDS	[Rank 4]		
HEAD	[Rank 6]	BODY	[Rank 4]	

SPOILS	GIL	336	EXP	0

ACCESSORIES	Gaia Ring, [Time] After 30 Seconds, [Time] After 60 Seconds, [Time] After 90 Seconds, [Time] After 120 Seconds

DESTINY ODYSSEY VI

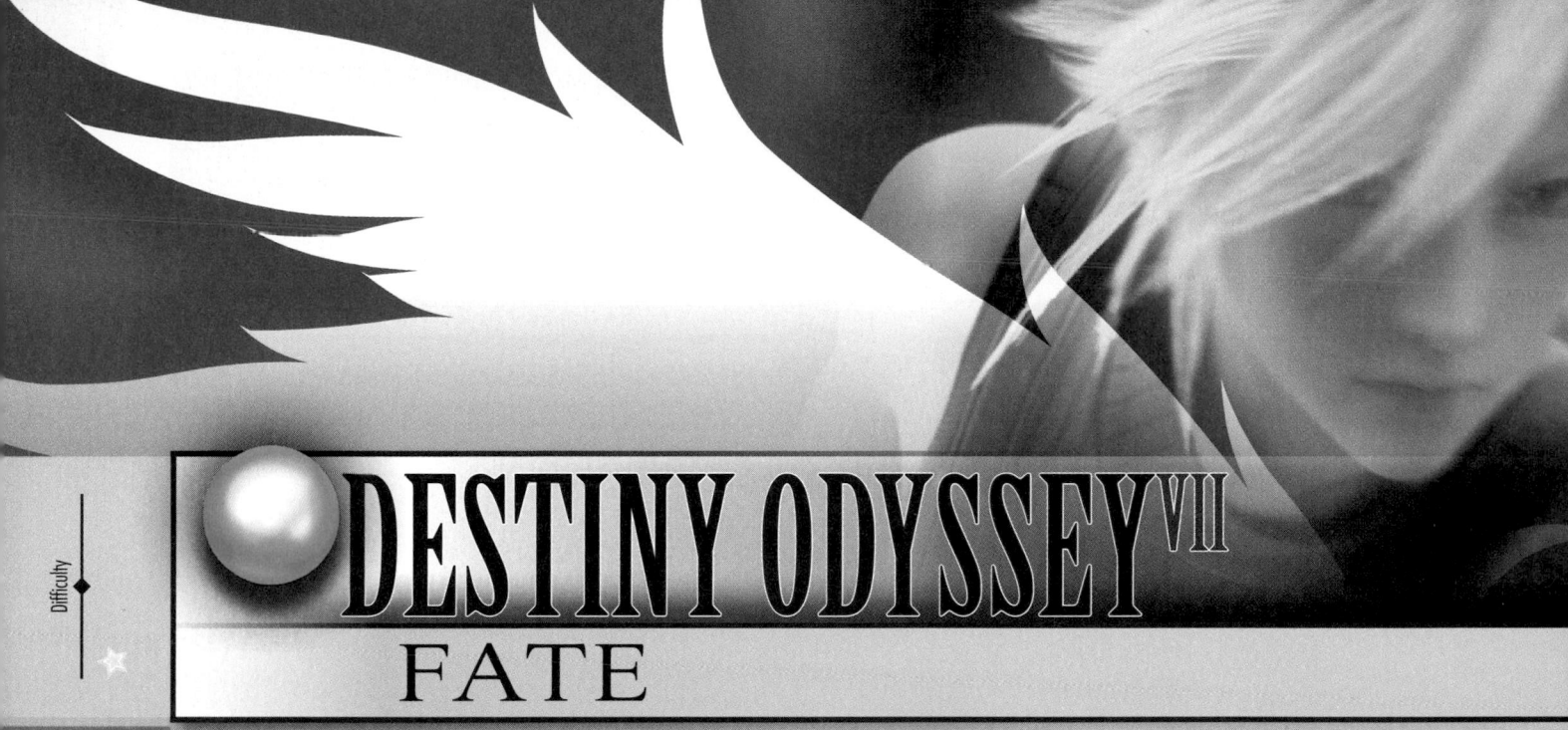

DESTINY ODYSSEY VII
FATE

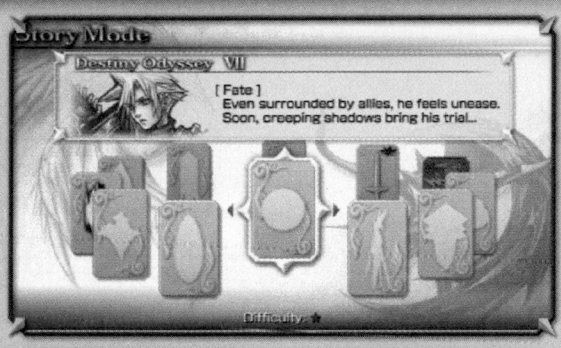

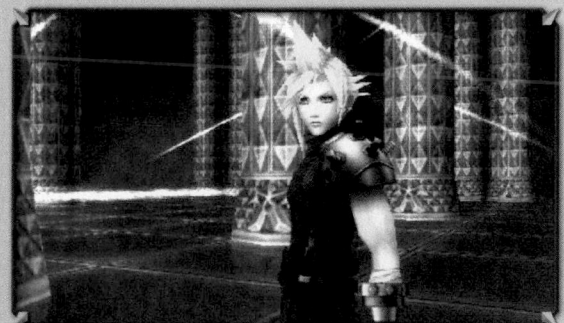

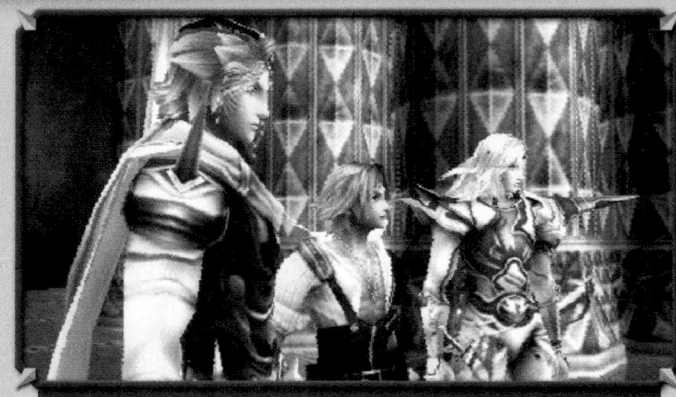

Cloud searches for his crystal with Firion, Cecil, and Tidus. Not sharing his friends' enthusiasm for the fight, a weary Cloud seeks a reason to perpetuate the seemingly endless struggle...

Difficulty

Prerequisite — Finish Prologue

REWARDS

At the end of each level, rewards are available if you finish with a positive number of Destiny Points, or DP. This walkthrough includes miniature level maps that indicate the most efficient route to take through a given level, in order to maximize DP.

LEVEL COMPLETION

REMAINING DP				2ND TIME
7		Rosetta Stone		300 PP
6		Flamberge		200 PP
5	1ST TIME	Zweihander		120 PP
4		Typhon		80 PP
3		1000 gil		50 PP
2		600 gil		30 PP
1		300 gil		20 PP
0		100 gil		10 PP

DESTINY ODYSSEY VII COMPLETION

STAR RATING		SP REQUIRED	AWARD
☆		100	New skill
☆ ☆		200	Special areas unlocked
☆ ☆ ☆		300	Rare battle pieces spawned
☆ ☆ ☆ ☆		400	Rare treasure chests spawned
—		500 SP, then every 500 SP extra	100 PP

At the end of each set of levels, you'll receive rewards based on your performance. Story Points, or SP, are awarded after each level based on remaining DP, HP, and the number of engagements undertaken. Points are penalized for retries, or a DP total that dips into negatives. If you miss out on a desired bonus on the first playthrough, don't fret—SP is cumulative across multiple playthroughs.

DESTINY ODYSSEY VII

STARTING DP	**MAX FINISHING**	**ENGAGEMENTS**
5	3	4

Chapter difficulty primarily involves the number of encounters across a character's stages. Cloud has a relatively low number, and ends several stages without a boss fight. His stages are also fairly simple, and he's a capable fighter. His Slashing Blow and Braver attacks are enough to beat most opposition easily. Slashing Blow can often be repeated over and over against enemies, depending on the position they end up in after the first two hits. Perform a neutral dodge (■ + ✗ without any ● input) after the first two hits of Slashing Blow, and sometimes you'll be in position to use Slashing Blow again right away, before the enemy can recover. Sometimes it helps to dodge towards the enemy's new position.

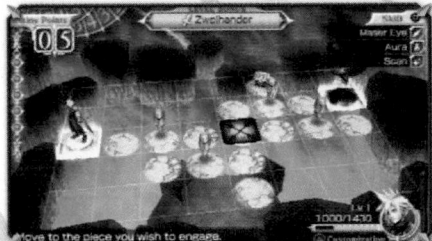

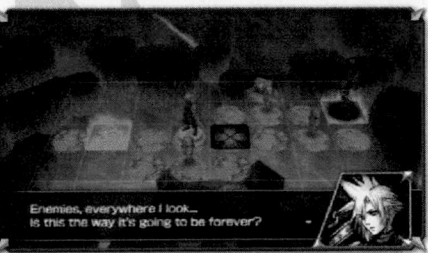

MAP

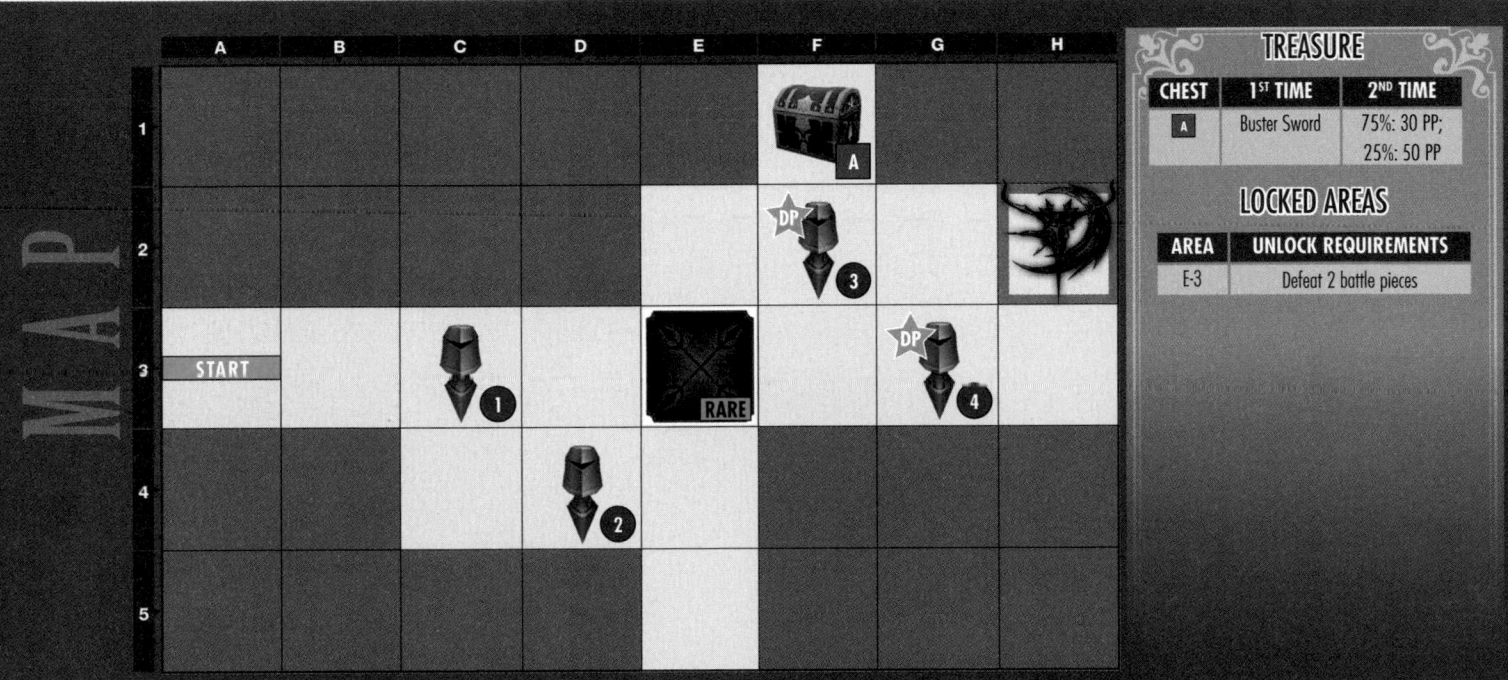

TREASURE

CHEST	1ST TIME	2ND TIME
A	Buster Sword	75%: 30 PP; 25%: 50 PP

LOCKED AREAS

AREA	UNLOCK REQUIREMENTS
E-3	Defeat 2 battle pieces

DP EFFICIENCY ROUTE

A straight shot across is the only route here. You'll have to fight all battle pieces: the first group of two to remove the Locked Area, and the second group of two in a chain, before the exit.

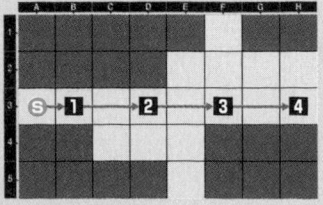

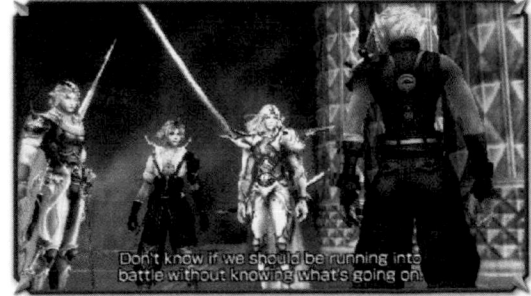

Don't know if we should be running into battle without knowing what's going on.

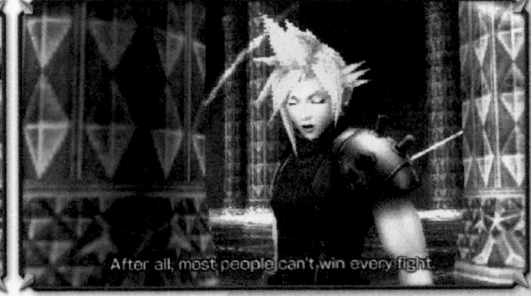

After all, most people can't win every fight.

BATTLE PIECE DATA

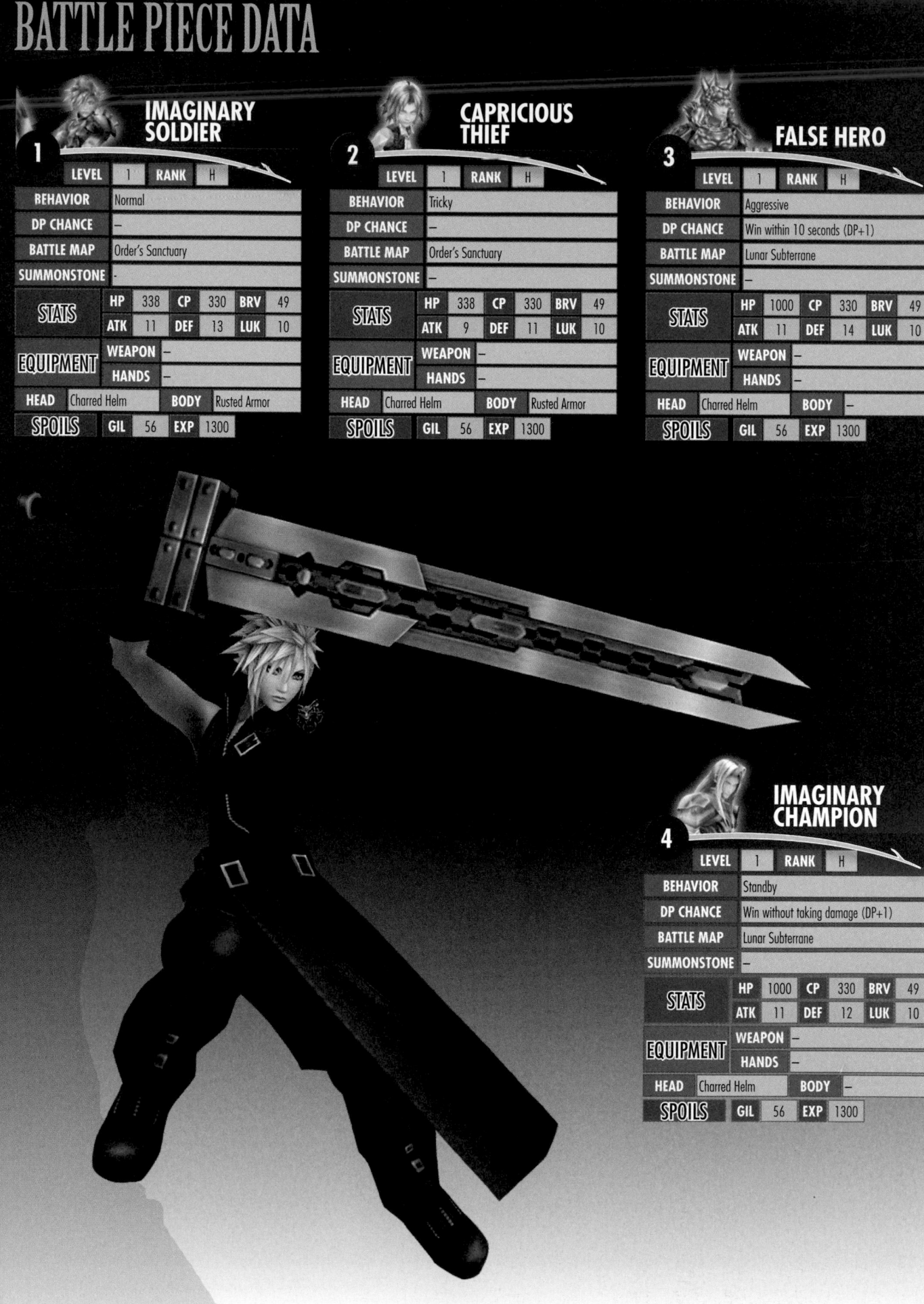

1 — IMAGINARY SOLDIER

LEVEL	1	RANK	H

BEHAVIOR	Normal
DP CHANCE	—
BATTLE MAP	Order's Sanctuary
SUMMONSTONE	—

STATS	HP	338	CP	330	BRV	49
	ATK	11	DEF	13	LUK	10

EQUIPMENT	WEAPON	—
	HANDS	—

HEAD	Charred Helm	BODY	Rusted Armor

SPOILS	GIL	56	EXP	1300

2 — CAPRICIOUS THIEF

LEVEL	1	RANK	H

BEHAVIOR	Tricky
DP CHANCE	—
BATTLE MAP	Order's Sanctuary
SUMMONSTONE	—

STATS	HP	338	CP	330	BRV	49
	ATK	9	DEF	11	LUK	10

EQUIPMENT	WEAPON	—
	HANDS	—

HEAD	Charred Helm	BODY	Rusted Armor

SPOILS	GIL	56	EXP	1300

3 — FALSE HERO

LEVEL	1	RANK	H

BEHAVIOR	Aggressive
DP CHANCE	Win within 10 seconds (DP+1)
BATTLE MAP	Lunar Subterrane
SUMMONSTONE	—

STATS	HP	1000	CP	330	BRV	49
	ATK	11	DEF	14	LUK	10

EQUIPMENT	WEAPON	—
	HANDS	—

HEAD	Charred Helm	BODY	—

SPOILS	GIL	56	EXP	1300

4 — IMAGINARY CHAMPION

LEVEL	1	RANK	H

BEHAVIOR	Standby
DP CHANCE	Win without taking damage (DP+1)
BATTLE MAP	Lunar Subterrane
SUMMONSTONE	—

STATS	HP	1000	CP	330	BRV	49
	ATK	11	DEF	12	LUK	10

EQUIPMENT	WEAPON	—
	HANDS	—

HEAD	Charred Helm	BODY	—

SPOILS	GIL	56	EXP	1300

DESTINY ODYSSEY VII

DESTINY ODYSSEY VII-2

Like the first level, this board has a straight, clear path to the Stigma of Chaos, although you can take a slight detour near the start for an extra battle and a treasure chest. Later on in this level, Magic Pot will be up for grabs. This is one of the most useful and game-changing summons. It's only available after getting at least a 2-star rating through previous Destiny Odyssey VII runs.

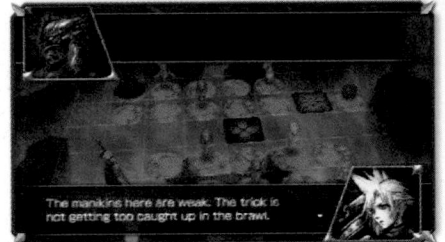
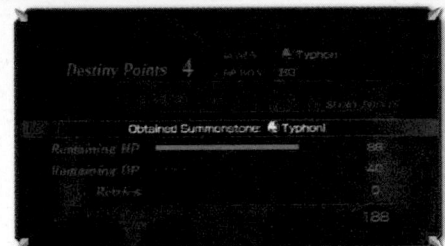

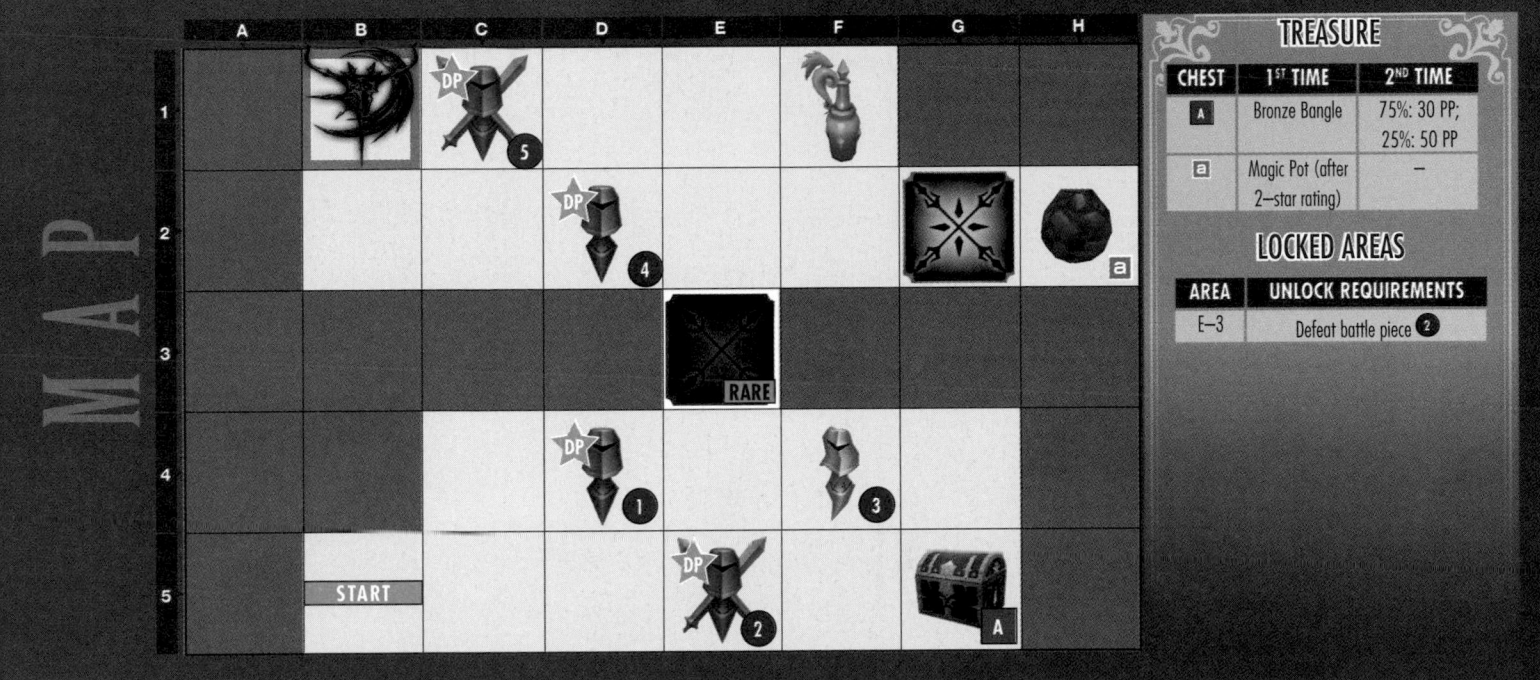

TREASURE

CHEST	1ST TIME	2ND TIME
A	Bronze Bangle	75%: 30 PP; 25%: 50 PP
a	Magic Pot (after 2–star rating)	—

LOCKED AREAS

AREA	UNLOCK REQUIREMENTS
E–3	Defeat battle piece ②

DP EFFICIENCY ROUTE

A straight shot across is the only route here. You'll have to fight all battle pieces: the first group of two to remove the Locked Area, and the second group of two in a chain, before the exit.

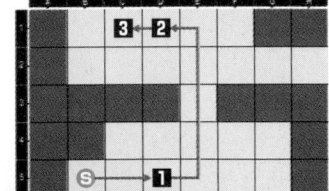

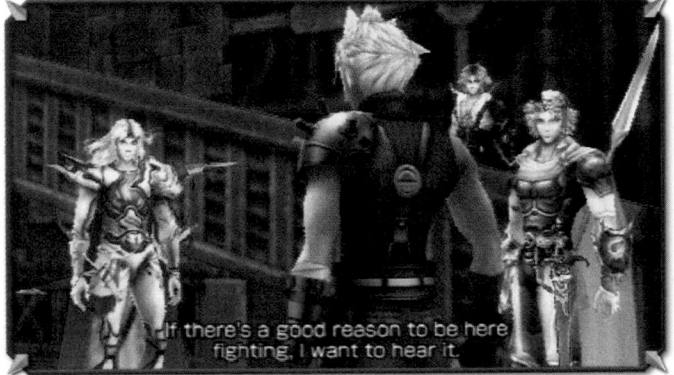

If there's a good reason to be here fighting, I want to hear it.

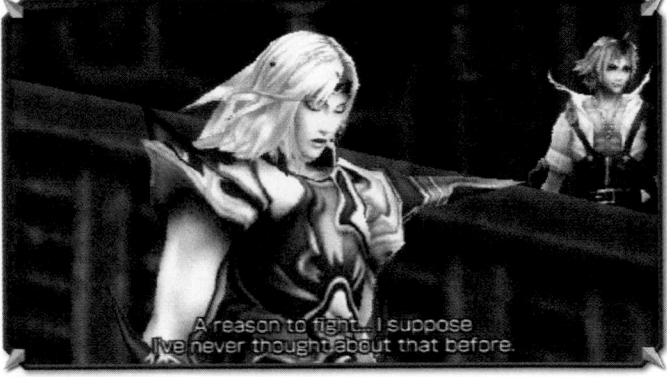

A reason to fight... I suppose I've never thought about that before.

BATTLE PIECE DATA

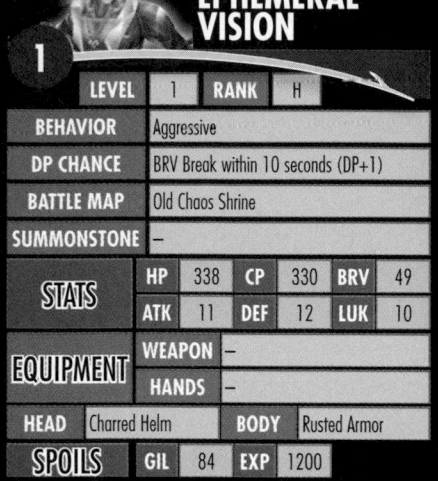

1 EPHEMERAL VISION

LEVEL	1	RANK	H

BEHAVIOR	Aggressive
DP CHANCE	BRV Break within 10 seconds (DP+1)
BATTLE MAP	Old Chaos Shrine
SUMMONSTONE	—

STATS	HP	338	CP	330	BRV	49
	ATK	11	DEF	12	LUK	10

EQUIPMENT	WEAPON	—
	HANDS	—

HEAD	Charred Helm	BODY	Rusted Armor

SPOILS	GIL	84	EXP	1200

* Denotes use of the base value (for stats that vary).

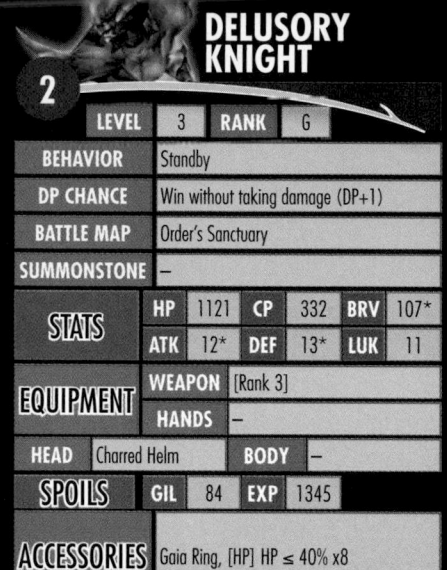

2 DELUSORY KNIGHT

LEVEL	3	RANK	G

BEHAVIOR	Standby
DP CHANCE	Win without taking damage (DP+1)
BATTLE MAP	Order's Sanctuary
SUMMONSTONE	—

STATS	HP	1121	CP	332	BRV	107*
	ATK	12*	DEF	13*	LUK	11

EQUIPMENT	WEAPON	[Rank 3]
	HANDS	—

HEAD	Charred Helm	BODY	—

SPOILS	GIL	84	EXP	1345

ACCESSORIES	Gaia Ring, [HP] HP ≤ 40% x8

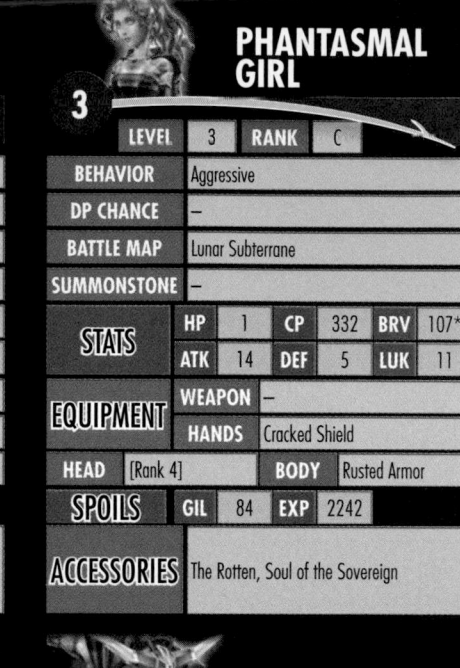

3 PHANTASMAL GIRL

LEVEL	3	RANK	C

BEHAVIOR	Aggressive
DP CHANCE	—
BATTLE MAP	Lunar Subterrane
SUMMONSTONE	—

STATS	HP	1	CP	332	BRV	107*
	ATK	14	DEF	5	LUK	11

EQUIPMENT	WEAPON	—
	HANDS	Cracked Shield

HEAD	[Rank 4]	BODY	Rusted Armor

SPOILS	GIL	84	EXP	2242

ACCESSORIES	The Rotten, Soul of the Sovereign

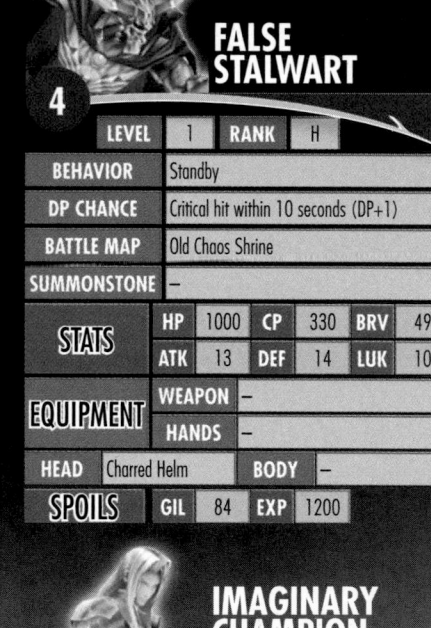

4 FALSE STALWART

LEVEL	1	RANK	H

BEHAVIOR	Standby
DP CHANCE	Critical hit within 10 seconds (DP+1)
BATTLE MAP	Old Chaos Shrine
SUMMONSTONE	—

STATS	HP	1000	CP	330	BRV	49
	ATK	13	DEF	14	LUK	10

EQUIPMENT	WEAPON	—
	HANDS	—

HEAD	Charred Helm	BODY	—

SPOILS	GIL	84	EXP	1200

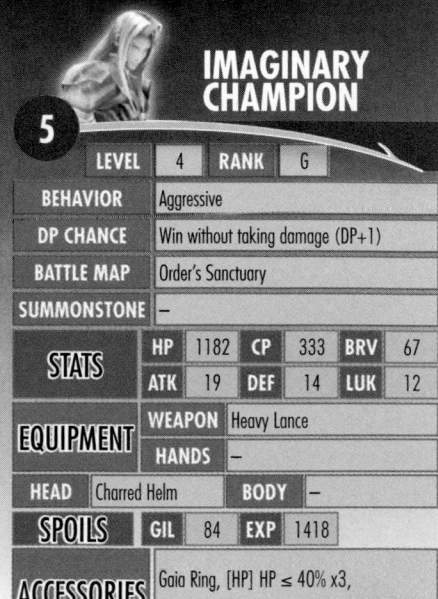

5 IMAGINARY CHAMPION

LEVEL	4	RANK	G

BEHAVIOR	Aggressive
DP CHANCE	Win without taking damage (DP+1)
BATTLE MAP	Order's Sanctuary
SUMMONSTONE	—

STATS	HP	1182	CP	333	BRV	67
	ATK	19	DEF	14	LUK	12

EQUIPMENT	WEAPON	Heavy Lance
	HANDS	—

HEAD	Charred Helm	BODY	—

SPOILS	GIL	84	EXP	1418

ACCESSORIES	Gaia Ring, [HP] HP ≤ 40% x3, [HP] Near Death x4

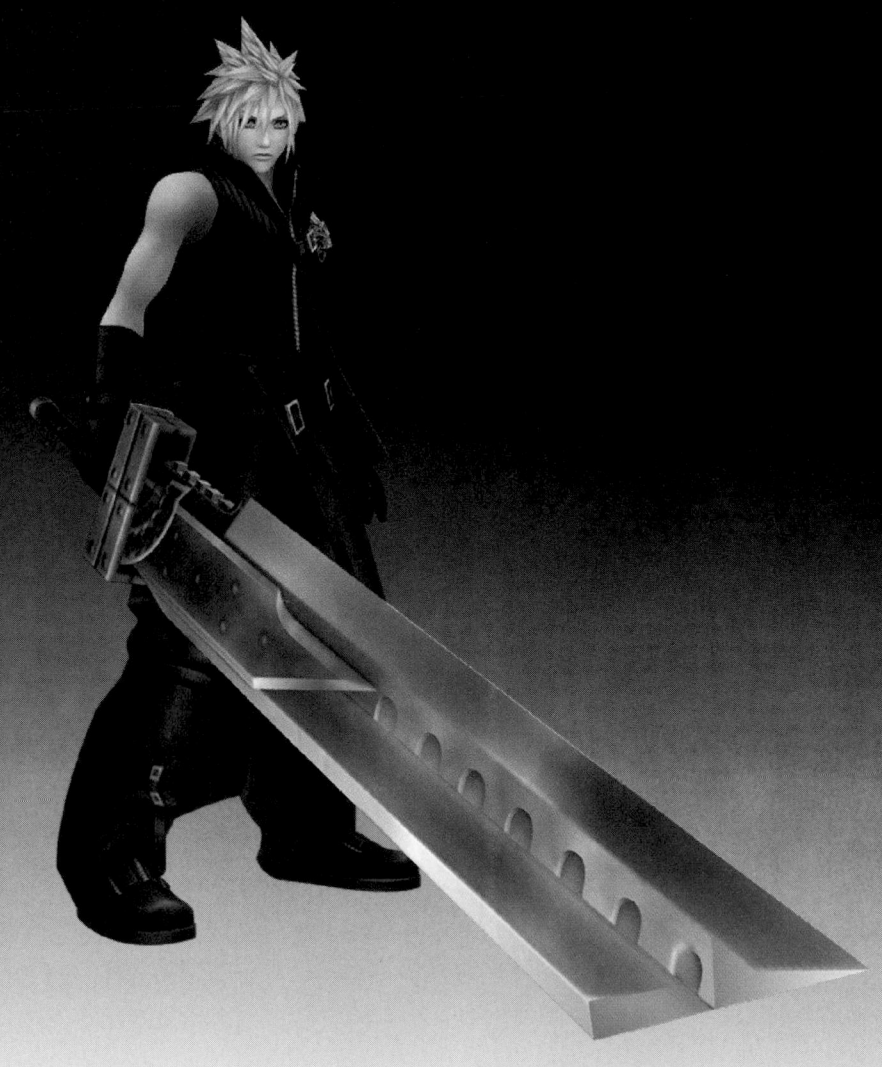

Here, you can choose between exploring the whole board for battles and treasure, or simply taking the south route through three battle pieces before the exit. Battle piece ❶ may seem formidable on your first playthrough, but don't worry. Despite being an expert piece with a decent level, this copy of Jecht is very predictable. Dodge his attacks up close, then nail him with counterattacks while he recovers. Remember to grab the special sword for Cloud; it's hidden away in the treasure chest behind this piece.

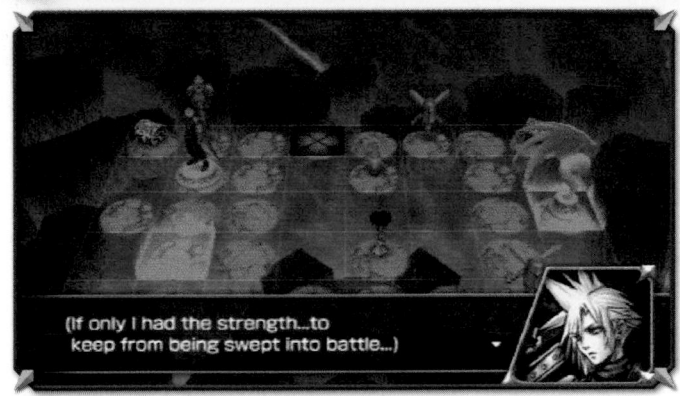

(If only I had the strength...to keep from being swept into battle...)

MAP

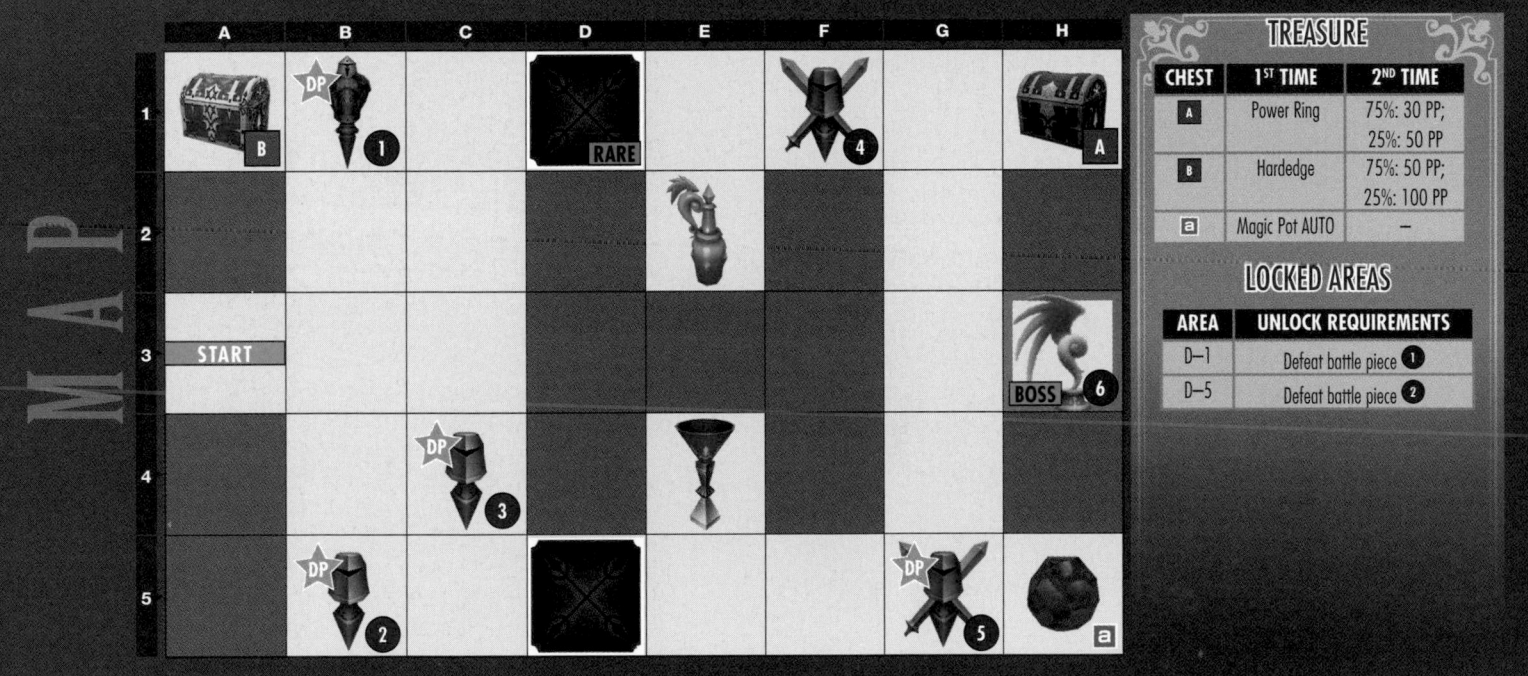

TREASURE

CHEST	1ST TIME	2ND TIME
B	Power Ring	75%: 30 PP; 25%: 50 PP
B	Hardedge	75%: 50 PP; 25%: 100 PP
a	Magic Pot AUTO	—

LOCKED AREAS

AREA	UNLOCK REQUIREMENTS
D–1	Defeat battle piece ❶
D–5	Defeat battle piece ❷

DP EFFICIENCY ROUTE

Execute a chain against battle pieces ❷ and ❸. This tactic scores 2 DP while opening the Locked Area at D-5. Cross over to battle piece ❺ for another DP Chance before heading to the boss.

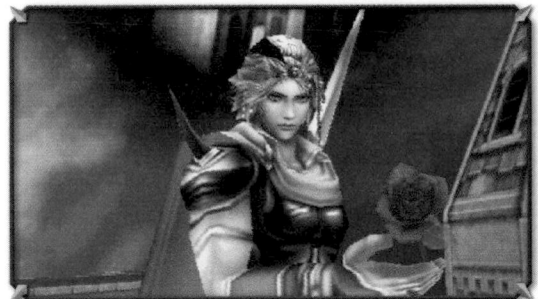

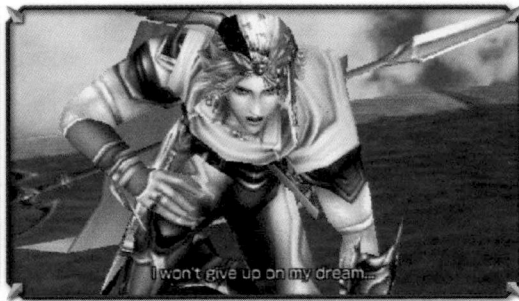

I won't give up on my dream...

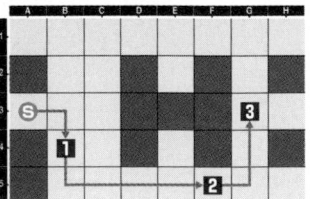

BATTLE PIECE DATA

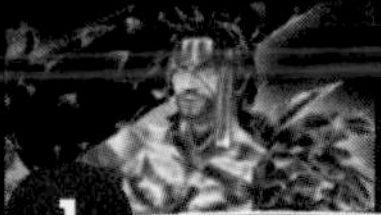

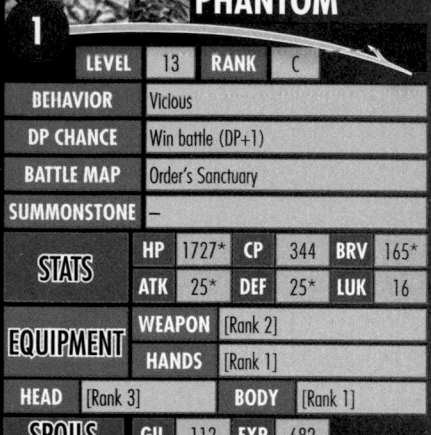

1 EPHEMERAL PHANTOM

LEVEL	13	RANK	C

BEHAVIOR	Vicious
DP CHANCE	Win battle (DP+1)
BATTLE MAP	Order's Sanctuary
SUMMONSTONE	–

STATS	HP	1727*	CP	344	BRV	165*
	ATK	25*	DEF	25*	LUK	16

EQUIPMENT	WEAPON	[Rank 2]
	HANDS	[Rank 1]
HEAD	[Rank 3]	BODY	[Rank 1]

SPOILS	GIL	112	EXP	682

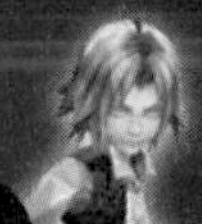

2 CAPRICIOUS THIEF

LEVEL	1	RANK	H

BEHAVIOR	Tricky
DP CHANCE	Win without taking damage (DP+1)
BATTLE MAP	The Rift
SUMMONSTONE	–

STATS	HP	1000	CP	330	BRV	49
	ATK	9	DEF	11	LUK	10

EQUIPMENT	WEAPON	–
	HANDS	–
HEAD	Charred Helm	BODY	–

SPOILS	GIL	112	EXP	1200

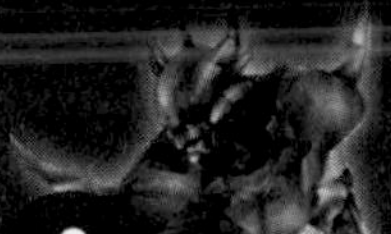

3 DELUSORY KNIGHT

LEVEL	1	RANK	H

BEHAVIOR	Tricky
DP CHANCE	BRV Break within 10 seconds (DP+1)
BATTLE MAP	Lunar Subterrane
SUMMONSTONE	–

STATS	HP	1000	CP	330	BRV	95
	ATK	10	DEF	11	LUK	10

EQUIPMENT	WEAPON	–
	HANDS	–
HEAD	–	BODY	–

SPOILS	GIL	112	EXP	1200

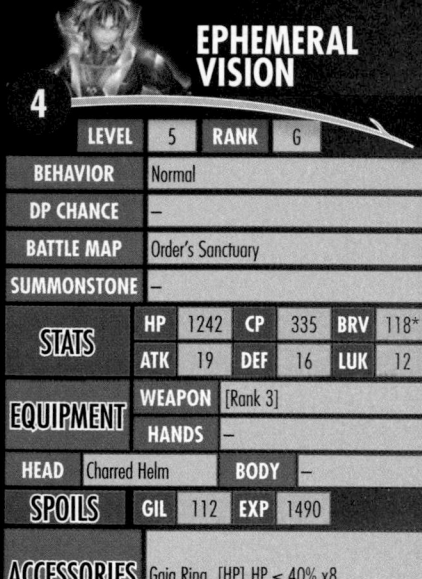

4 EPHEMERAL VISION

LEVEL	5	RANK	G

BEHAVIOR	Normal
DP CHANCE	–
BATTLE MAP	Order's Sanctuary
SUMMONSTONE	–

STATS	HP	1242	CP	335	BRV	118*
	ATK	19	DEF	16	LUK	12

EQUIPMENT	WEAPON	[Rank 3]
	HANDS	–
HEAD	Charred Helm	BODY	–

SPOILS	GIL	112	EXP	1490

ACCESSORIES	Gaia Ring, [HP] HP ≤ 40% x8

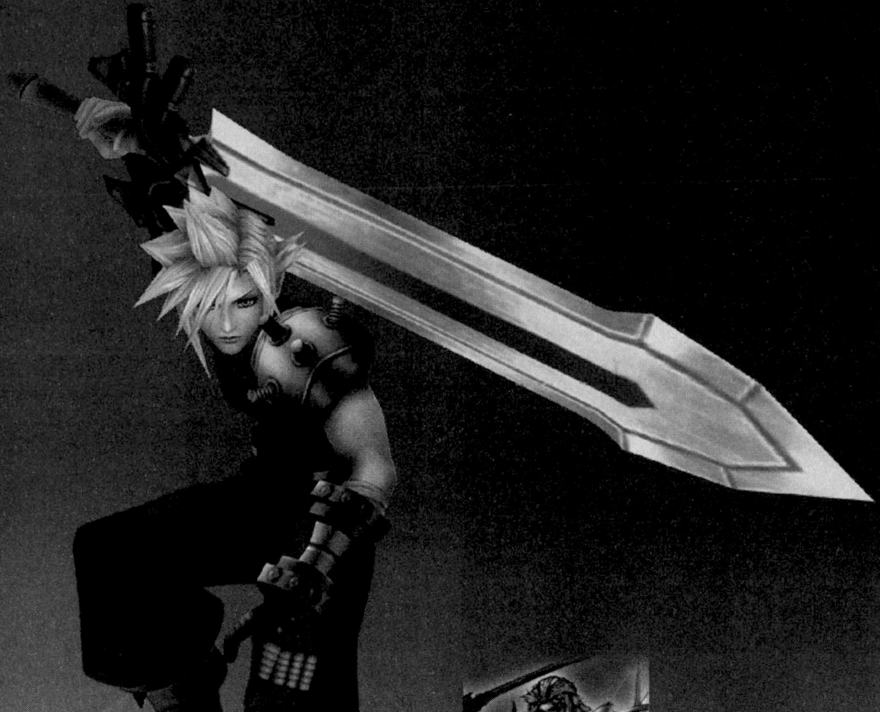

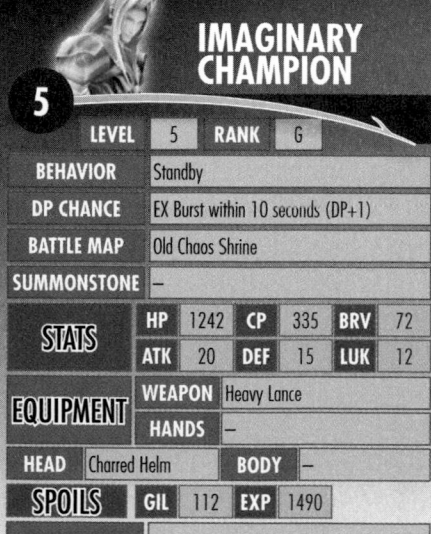

5 IMAGINARY CHAMPION

LEVEL	5	RANK	G

BEHAVIOR	Standby
DP CHANCE	EX Burst within 10 seconds (DP+1)
BATTLE MAP	Old Chaos Shrine
SUMMONSTONE	–

STATS	HP	1242	CP	335	BRV	72
	ATK	20	DEF	15	LUK	12

EQUIPMENT	WEAPON	Heavy Lance
	HANDS	–
HEAD	Charred Helm	BODY	–

SPOILS	GIL	112	EXP	1490

ACCESSORIES	Gaia Ring, [HP] HP ≤ 40% x3, [HP] Near Death x4

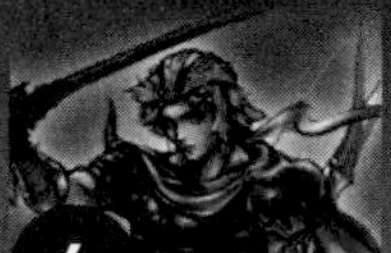

6 FIRION

LEVEL	7	RANK	E

BEHAVIOR	Tactician
DP CHANCE	–
BATTLE MAP	The Rift
SUMMONSTONE	–

STATS	HP	1732	CP	337	BRV	130
	ATK	23	DEF	18	LUK	13

EQUIPMENT	WEAPON	Spear
	HANDS	–
HEAD	–	BODY	Leather Armor

SPOILS	GIL	168	EXP	1364

* Denotes use of the base value (for stats that vary).

DESTINY ODYSSEY VII

	STARTING DP	MAX FINISHING	ENGAGEMENTS
	5	5 (+2 after 3-star rating)	6 (+1 after 3-star rating)

After three levels without secrets, this one has them all. The Rosetta Stone tucked away in a treasure chest behind the Locked Area at D-1 is only accessible after achieving a 2-star rating. A 3-star rating generates ultimate battle piece ⑦. This fight is against a particularly nasty Sephiroth manikin. This creature focuses on building bravery, and it's very good at it, so look to use Carbuncle to steal bravery when your foe has a threatening amount, making you equally lethal. A 4-star rating places a rare treasure chest at H-1.

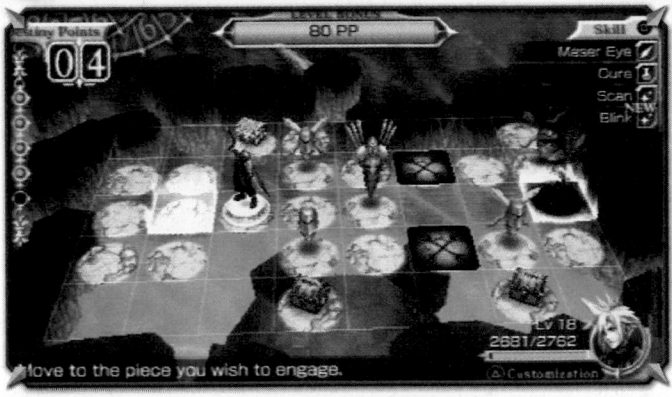

MAP

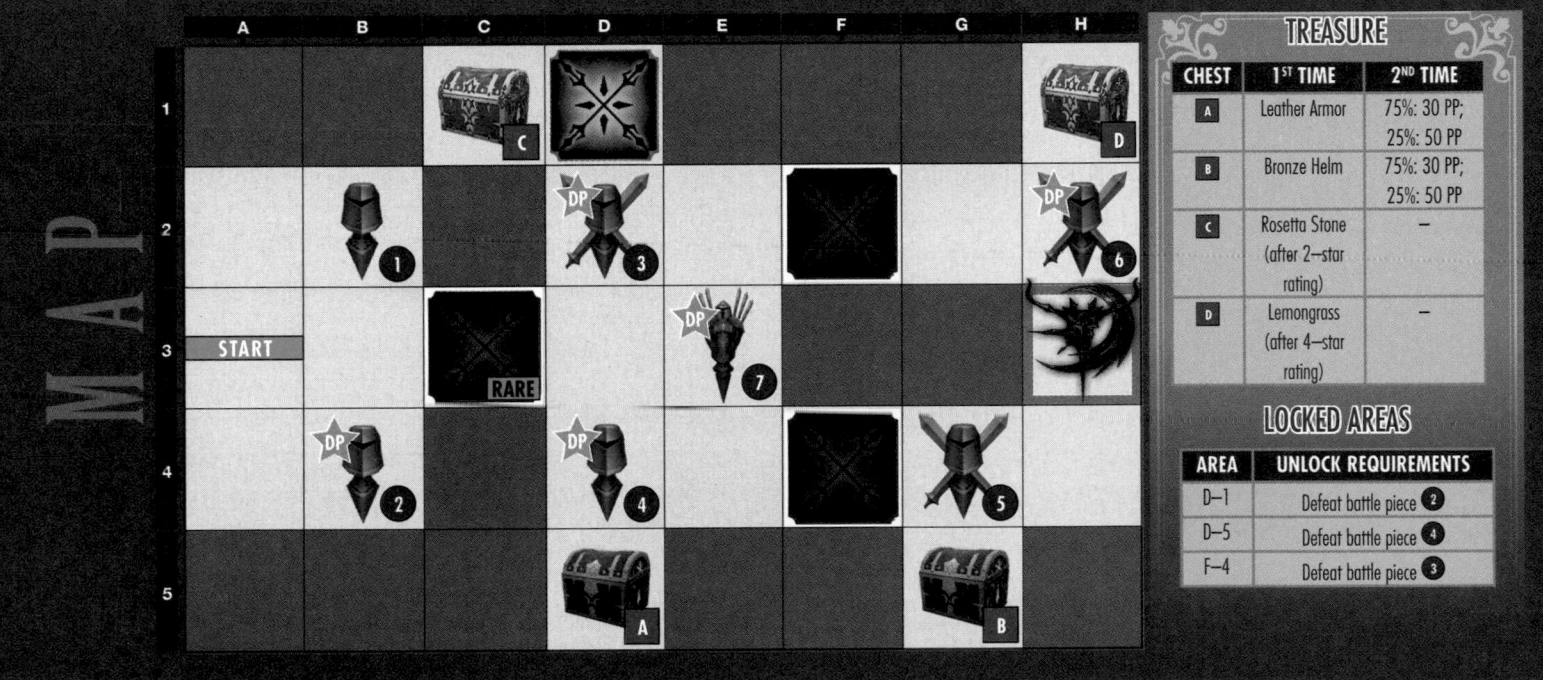

TREASURE

CHEST	1ST TIME	2ND TIME
A	Leather Armor	75%: 30 PP; 25%: 50 PP
B	Bronze Helm	75%: 30 PP; 25%: 50 PP
C	Rosetta Stone (after 2-star rating)	–
D	Lemongrass (after 4-star rating)	–

LOCKED AREAS

AREA	UNLOCK REQUIREMENTS
D–1	Defeat battle piece ②
D–5	Defeat battle piece ④
F–4	Defeat battle piece ③

DP EFFICIENCY ROUTE

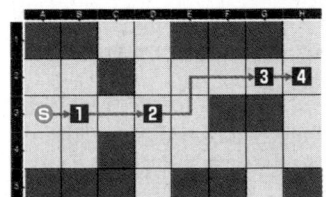

Getting Max DP here must wait until you already have a 3-star rating, so the rare battle piece spawns. This piece is worth +2 DP just for beating it. Start battle chains from B-3, then D-3. Afterwards, engage battle piece ⑥ before exiting the level.

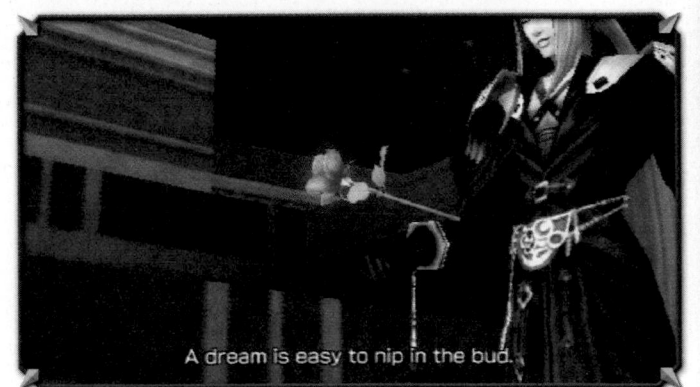

A dream is easy to nip in the bud.

BATTLE PIECE DATA

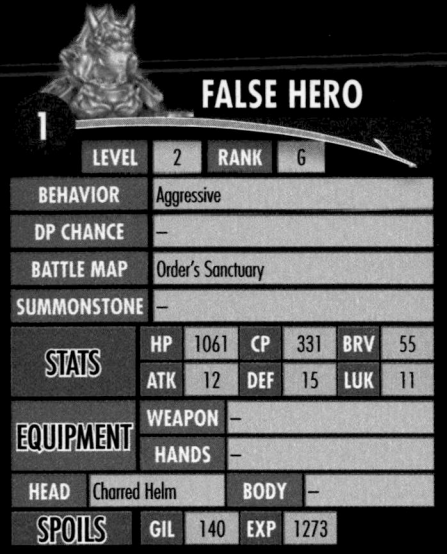
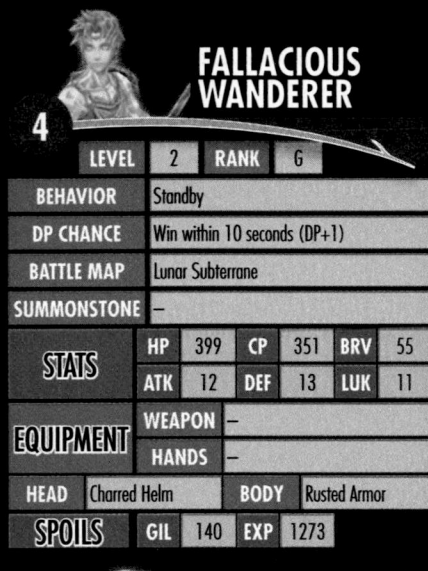

1 — FALSE HERO

LEVEL	2	RANK	G

BEHAVIOR	Aggressive
DP CHANCE	—
BATTLE MAP	Order's Sanctuary
SUMMONSTONE	—

STATS						
	HP	1061	CP	331	BRV	55
	ATK	12	DEF	15	LUK	11

EQUIPMENT		
WEAPON	—	
HANDS	—	
HEAD	Charred Helm	BODY	—

SPOILS	GIL	140	EXP	1273

2 — PHANTASMAL HARLEQUIN

LEVEL	2	RANK	G

BEHAVIOR	Tricky
DP CHANCE	BRV Break within 10 seconds (DP+1)
BATTLE MAP	World of Darkness
SUMMONSTONE	—

STATS						
	HP	339	CP	351	BRV	101
	ATK	13	DEF	12	LUK	11

EQUIPMENT		
WEAPON	—	
HANDS	—	
HEAD	—	BODY	Rusted Armor

SPOILS	GIL	140	EXP	1273

3 — IMITATION LIEGEMAN

LEVEL	7	RANK	F

BEHAVIOR	Standby
DP CHANCE	Keep foe from getting EX Cores (DP+1)
BATTLE MAP	The Rift
SUMMONSTONE	—

STATS						
	HP	1364*	CP	337	BRV	130*
	ATK	18*	DEF	19*	LUK	13

EQUIPMENT		
WEAPON	[Rank 3]	
HANDS	—	
HEAD	Charred Helm	BODY	—

SPOILS	GIL	140	EXP	1636

ACCESSORIES	Gaia Ring, [HP] HP ≤ 40% x8

4 — FALLACIOUS WANDERER

LEVEL	2	RANK	G

BEHAVIOR	Standby
DP CHANCE	Win within 10 seconds (DP+1)
BATTLE MAP	Lunar Subterrane
SUMMONSTONE	—

STATS						
	HP	399	CP	351	BRV	55
	ATK	12	DEF	13	LUK	11

EQUIPMENT		
WEAPON	—	
HANDS	—	
HEAD	Charred Helm	BODY	Rusted Armor

SPOILS	GIL	140	EXP	1273

5 — IMAGINARY CHAMPION

LEVEL	8	RANK	F

BEHAVIOR	Aggressive
DP CHANCE	—
BATTLE MAP	World of Darkness
SUMMONSTONE	—

STATS						
	HP	1424	CP	338	BRV	90
	ATK	29	DEF	19*	LUK	14

EQUIPMENT		
WEAPON	[Rank 4]	
HANDS	—	
HEAD	Charred Helm	BODY	—

SPOILS	GIL	140	EXP	1708

ACCESSORIES	Gaia Ring, [HP] HP ≤ 40% x3, [HP] Near Death x4

6 — PHANTASMAL HARLEQUIN

LEVEL	8	RANK	F

BEHAVIOR	Tricky
DP CHANCE	Wall Rush within 10 seconds (DP+1)
BATTLE MAP	The Rift
SUMMONSTONE	—

STATS						
	HP	1424*	CP	357	BRV	136*
	ATK	19*	DEF	18*	LUK	14

EQUIPMENT		
WEAPON	[Rank 4]	
HANDS	—	
HEAD	Charred Helm	BODY	—

SPOILS	GIL	140	EXP	1708

ACCESSORIES	Gaia Ring, [HP] HP ≤ 40% x8

7 — IMAGINARY CHAMPION

LEVEL	23	RANK	B

BEHAVIOR	Conservative
DP CHANCE	Win battle (DP+2)
BATTLE MAP	Order's Sanctuary
SUMMONSTONE	—

STATS						
	HP	2333*	CP	356	BRV	279*
	ATK	51	DEF	49	LUK	21

EQUIPMENT		
WEAPON	Uchigatana	
HANDS	[Rank 3]	
HEAD	[Rank 3]	BODY	[Rank 4]

SPOILS	GIL	336	EXP	0

ACCESSORIES	Gaia Ring, [HP] HP ≤ 40% x8

* Denotes use of the base value (for stats that vary).

DESTINY ODYSSEY VII

DESTINY ODYSSEY VII-5

The Cloud copy at C-5 only appears after achieving a 3-star rating. This fierce opponent doesn't have many weaknesses, and often evades or counters your attacks. Magic Pot can help turn the tables on its aggression. A Potion appears at B-4 after you've defeated four battle pieces, and it can come in handy before proceeding to the Stigma of Chaos. Sephiroth, the boss, has accessories that grant him enormous staying potential. Avoid his dangerous linear moves by dodging laterally, then hit him while he recovers.

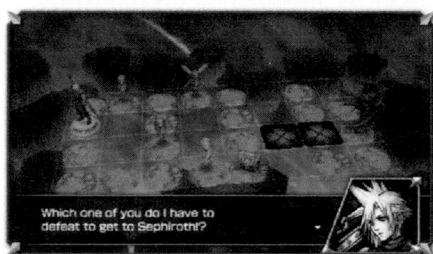

Which one of you do I have to defeat to get to Sephiroth!?

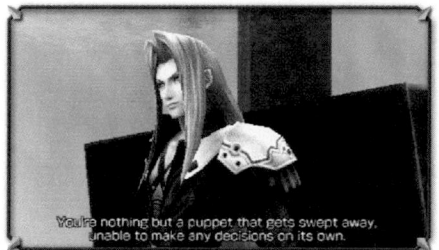

You're nothing but a puppet that gets swept away, unable to make any decisions on its own.

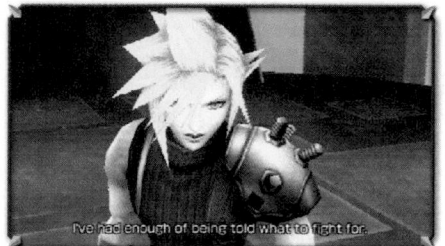

I've had enough of being told what to fight for.

MAP

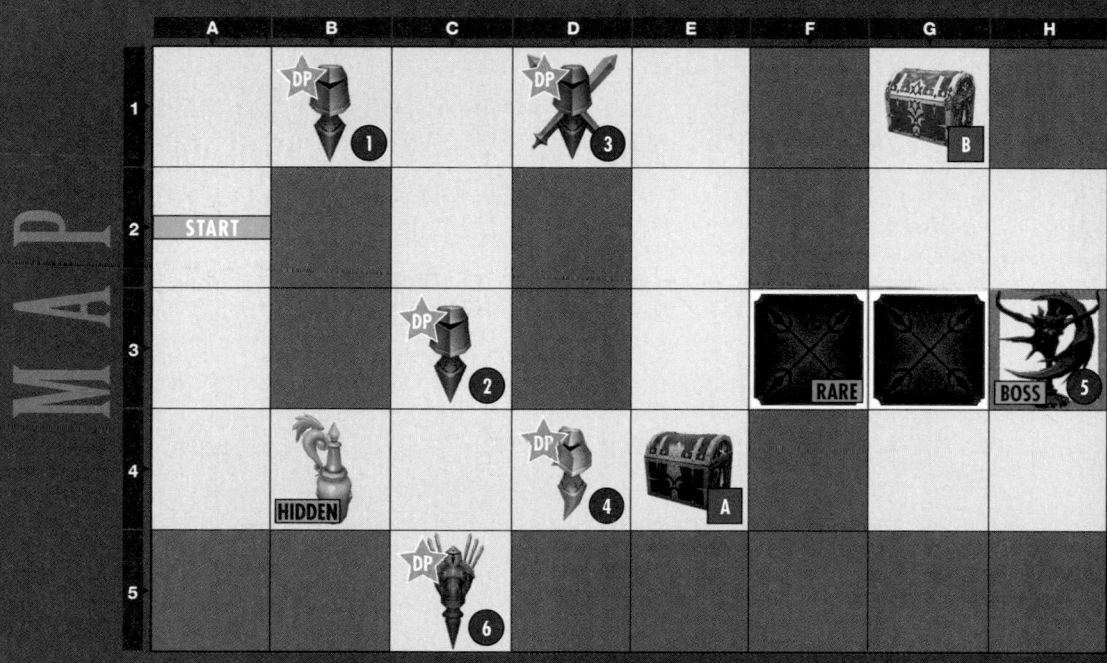

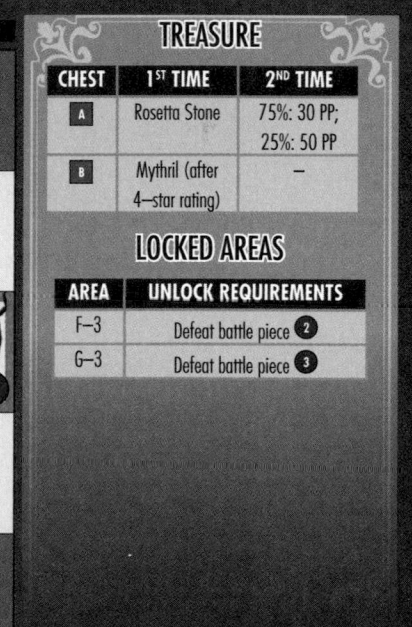

TREASURE

CHEST	1ST TIME	2ND TIME
A	Rosetta Stone	75%: 30 PP; 25%: 50 PP
B	Mythril (after 4-star rating)	–

LOCKED AREAS

AREA	UNLOCK REQUIREMENTS
F-3	Defeat battle piece ②
G-3	Defeat battle piece ③

DP EFFICIENCY ROUTE

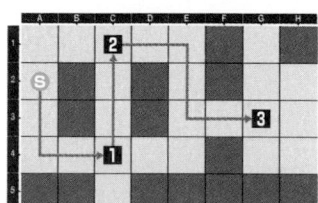

Like the previous level, this one requires a 3-star rating for the ultimate battle piece to spawn. Start a lengthy chain against the three battle pieces adjacent to C-4 before going for another chain from C-1. The way to the boss is now open.

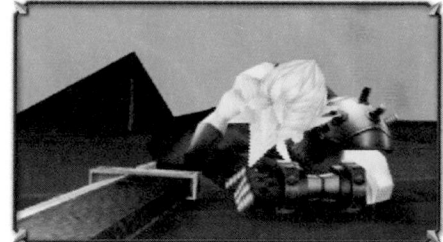

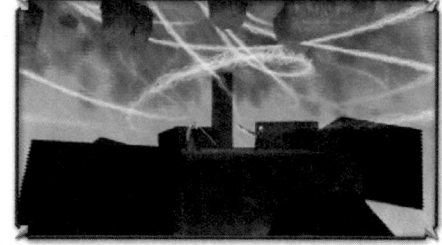

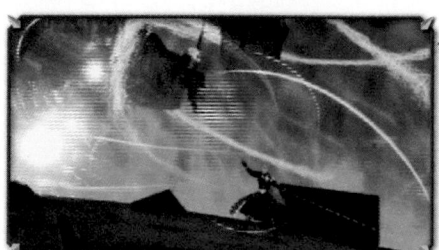

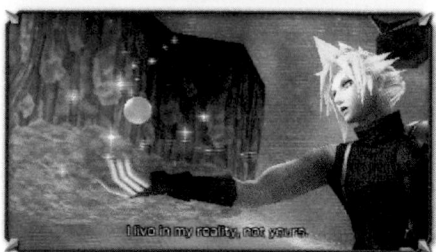

I live in my reality, not yours.

BATTLE PIECE DATA

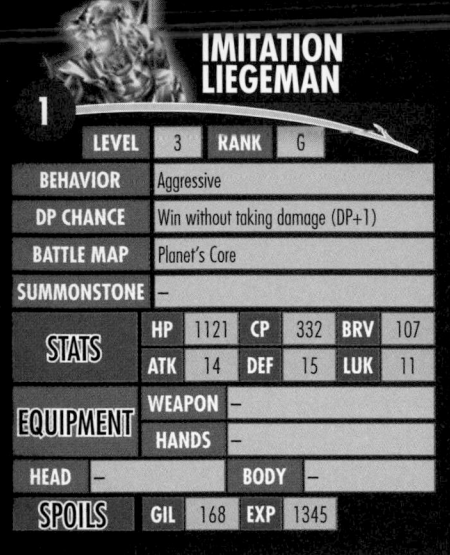

1 — IMITATION LIEGEMAN

LEVEL	3	RANK	G

BEHAVIOR	Aggressive
DP CHANCE	Win without taking damage (DP+1)
BATTLE MAP	Planet's Core
SUMMONSTONE	—

STATS	HP	1121	CP	332	BRV	107
	ATK	14	DEF	15	LUK	11

EQUIPMENT	WEAPON	—
	HANDS	—

HEAD	—		BODY	—

SPOILS	GIL	168	EXP	1345

2 — FALSE STALWART

LEVEL	3	RANK	G

BEHAVIOR	Evader
DP CHANCE	Win within 10 seconds (DP+1)
BATTLE MAP	World of Darkness
SUMMONSTONE	—

STATS	HP	1121	CP	332	BRV	107
	ATK	15	DEF	16	LUK	11

EQUIPMENT	WEAPON	—
	HANDS	—

HEAD	—		BODY	—

SPOILS	GIL	168	EXP	1345

3 — FALLACIOUS WANDERER

LEVEL	10	RANK	F

BEHAVIOR	Evader
DP CHANCE	Win without taking damage (DP+1)
BATTLE MAP	Lunar Subterrane
SUMMONSTONE	—

STATS	HP	1545*	CP	359	BRV	101
	ATK	20*	DEF	21*	LUK	15

EQUIPMENT	WEAPON	[Rank 4]
	HANDS	—

HEAD	Charred Helm		BODY	—

SPOILS	GIL	168	EXP	1854

ACCESSORIES	Gaia Ring, [HP] HP ≤ 40% x8

4 — PHANTASMAL GIRL

LEVEL	10	RANK	B

BEHAVIOR	Aggressive
DP CHANCE	BRV Break within 10 seconds (DP+1)
BATTLE MAP	The Rift
SUMMONSTONE	—

STATS	HP	1	CP	341	BRV	702
	ATK	21	DEF	12	LUK	15

EQUIPMENT	WEAPON	—
	HANDS	Cracked Shield

HEAD	Tiara		BODY	Rusted Armor

SPOILS	GIL	168	EXP	3090

ACCESSORIES	The Rotten, Soul of the Sovereign

5 — SEPHIROTH

LEVEL	12	RANK	D

BEHAVIOR	Calm
DP CHANCE	—
BATTLE MAP	Planet's Core
SUMMONSTONE	Demon Wall

STATS	HP	2095	CP	343	BRV	168
	ATK	27	DEF	24	LUK	16

EQUIPMENT	WEAPON	Katana
	HANDS	—

HEAD	Bronze Helm		BODY	Bronze Armor

SPOILS	GIL	252	EXP	4167

ACCESSORIES	Gaia Ring, Phoenix Down, [HP] HP = 1, [HP] Near Death, [HP] Near Loss

6 — IMAGINARY SOLDIER

LEVEL	27	RANK	B

BEHAVIOR	Valiant
DP CHANCE	Win battle (DP+2)
BATTLE MAP	Planet's Core
SUMMONSTONE	Magic Pot

STATS	HP	2575*	CP	361	BRV	245*
	ATK	37*	DEF	39*	LUK	23

EQUIPMENT	WEAPON	[Rank 4]
	HANDS	[Rank 3]

HEAD	[Rank 5]		BODY	Poncho

SPOILS	GIL	336	EXP	1409

ACCESSORIES	Gaia Ring, [HP] HP ≤ 40% x8

* Denotes use of the base value (for stats that vary).

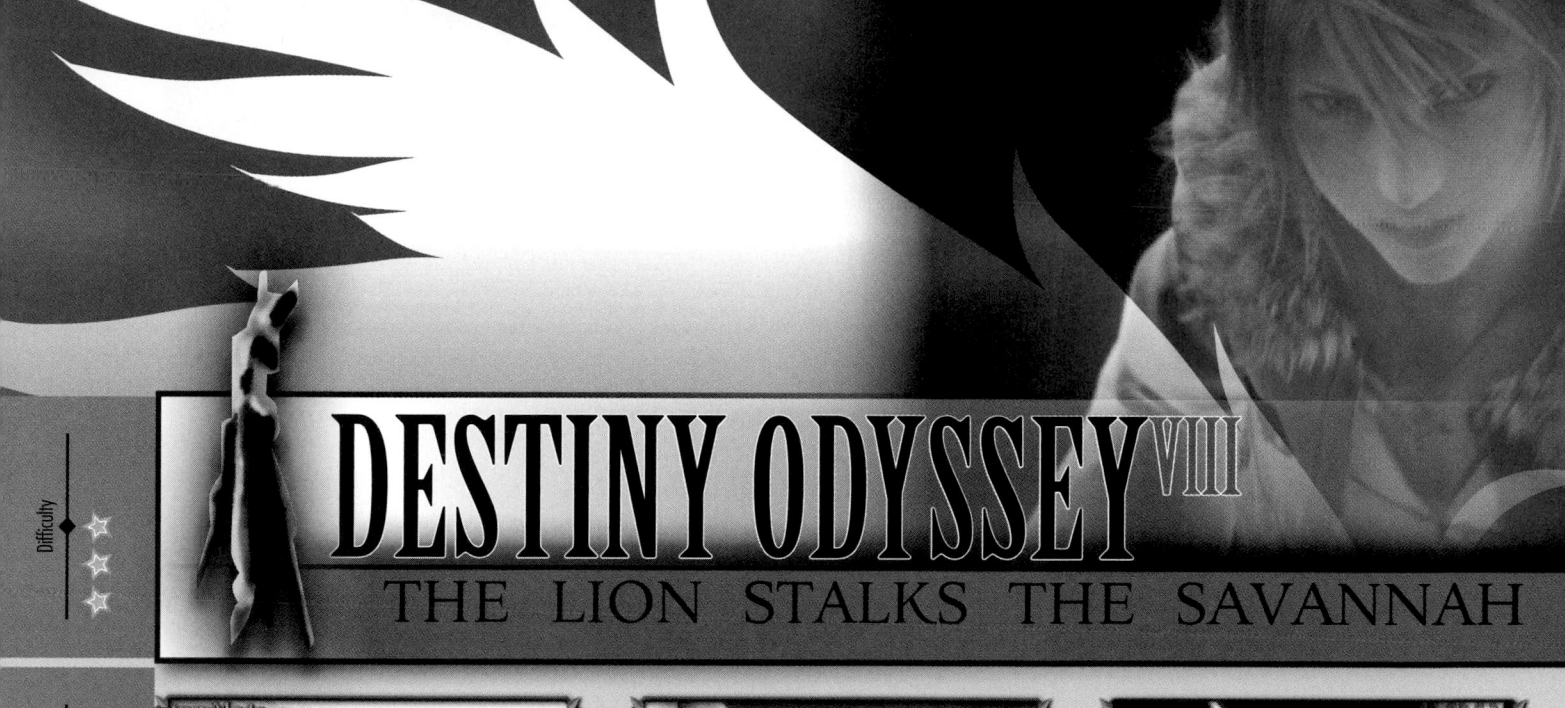

DESTINY ODYSSEY VIII
THE LION STALKS THE SAVANNAH

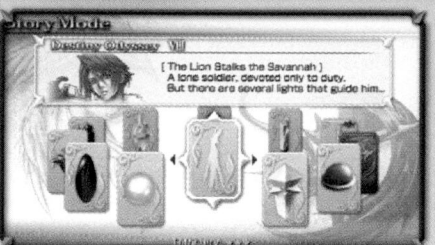

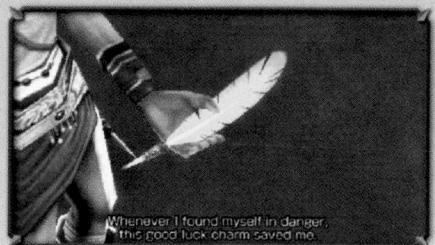

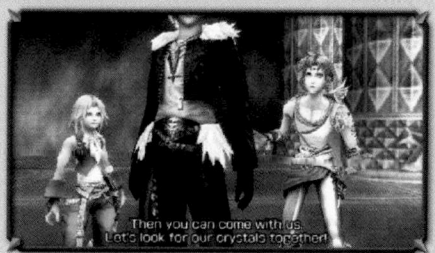

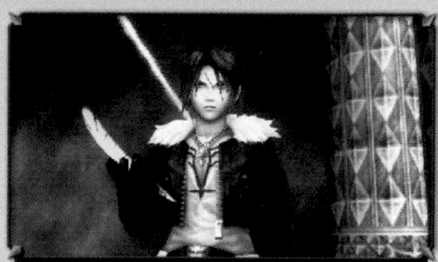

To say Squall is aloof to his allies would be selling him short. He declines to join them on their search, and is hesitant to accept a gift from Bartz. Squall doesn't feel he needs a little help from his friends to get by…

REWARDS

At the end of each level, rewards are available if you finish with a positive number of Destiny Points, or DP. This walkthrough includes miniature level maps that indicate the most efficient route to take through a given level, in order to maximize DP.

LEVEL COMPLETION

REMAINING DP	1ST TIME		2ND TIME	
7		Rosetta Stone		300 PP
6		Icebrand		200 PP
5		Flametongue		120 PP
4		PuPu		80 PP
3		1000 gil		50 PP
2		600 gil		30 PP
1		300 gil		20 PP
0		100 gil		10 PP

At the end of each set of levels, you'll receive rewards based on your performance. Story Points, or SP, are awarded after each level based on remaining DP and HP, as well as the number of engagements undertaken. Points are penalized for retries, or for a DP total that dips into negatives. If you miss out on a desired bonus on the first playthrough, don't worry—SP is cumulative across multiple playthroughs.

DESTINY ODYSSEY VIII COMPLETION

STAR RATING	SP REQUIRED	AWARD
★	100	New skill
★ ★	200	Special areas unlocked
★ ★ ★	300	Rare battle pieces spawned
★ ★ ★ ★	400	Rare treasure chests spawned
—	500 SP, then every 500 SP extra	100 PP

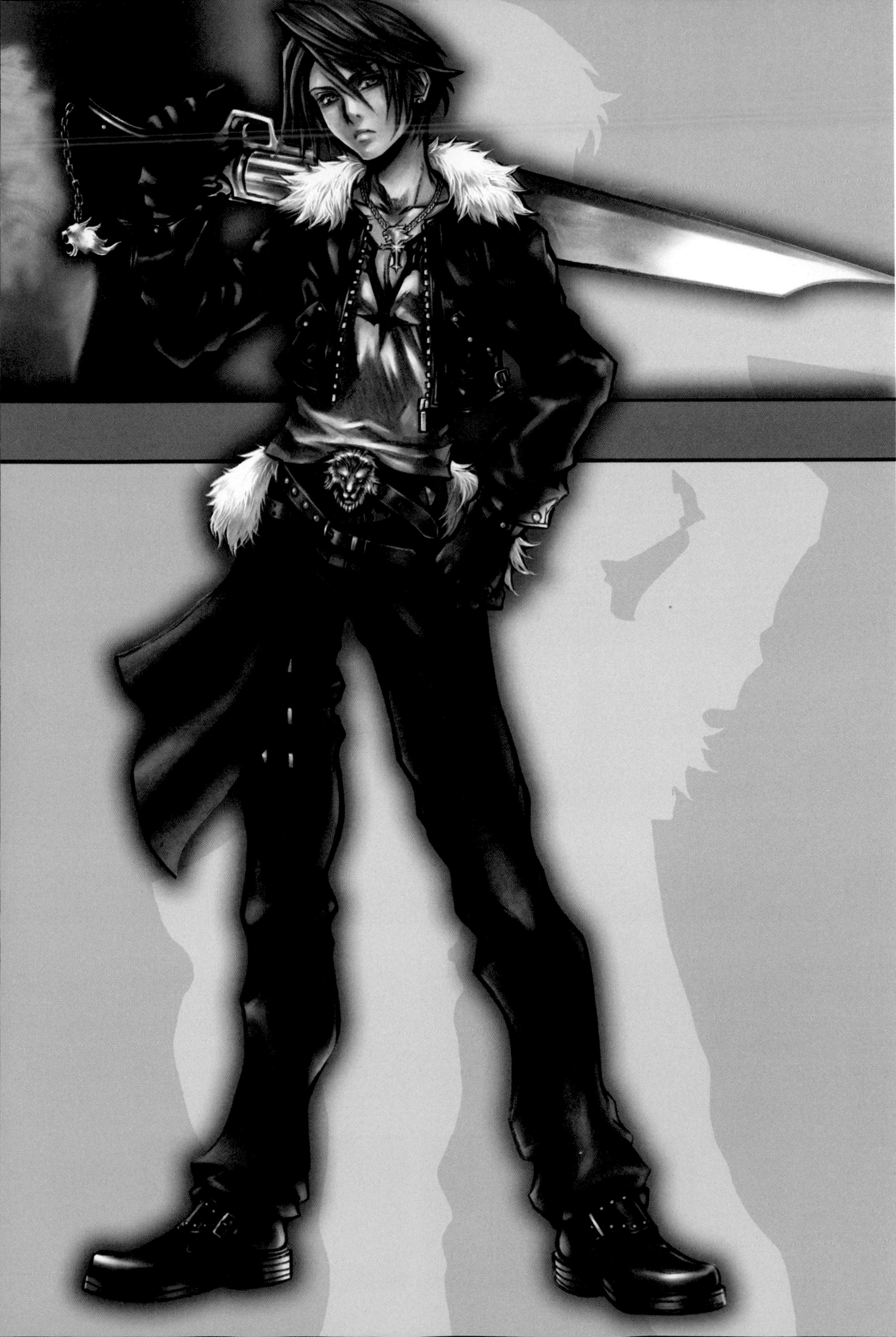

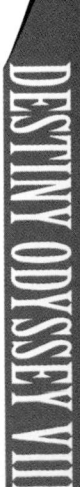

DESTINY ODYSSEY VIII

STARTING DP	MAX FINISHING	ENGAGEMENTS
5	3	6

Squall's levels begin largely unpopulated, but eventually become the most convoluted levels of all once the chips start to fall. Engaging most battle pieces or cracking most treasure chests, Potions, and Elixirs will cause more pieces to appear on the stage, often right next to your position. Be mindful of this, and plan your route using the following maps. Squall's style is unique, because unlike most combatants, he focuses almost exclusively on close-quarters combat. Use Air Dash to shorten the distance to your foe quickly, then either dodge past your enemy's up-close offense to strike from behind, block your opponent's bravery attacks and go for critical hit counterattacks, or dance on the edge of your foe's range and wait for your opponent to grow overzealous and miss with an attack before striking.

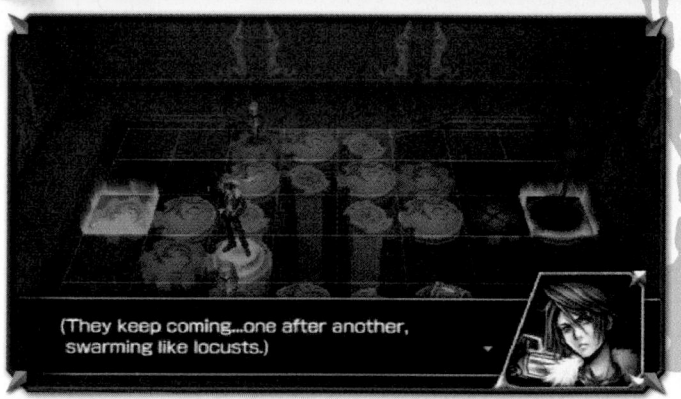

(They keep coming...one after another, swarming like locusts.)

MAP

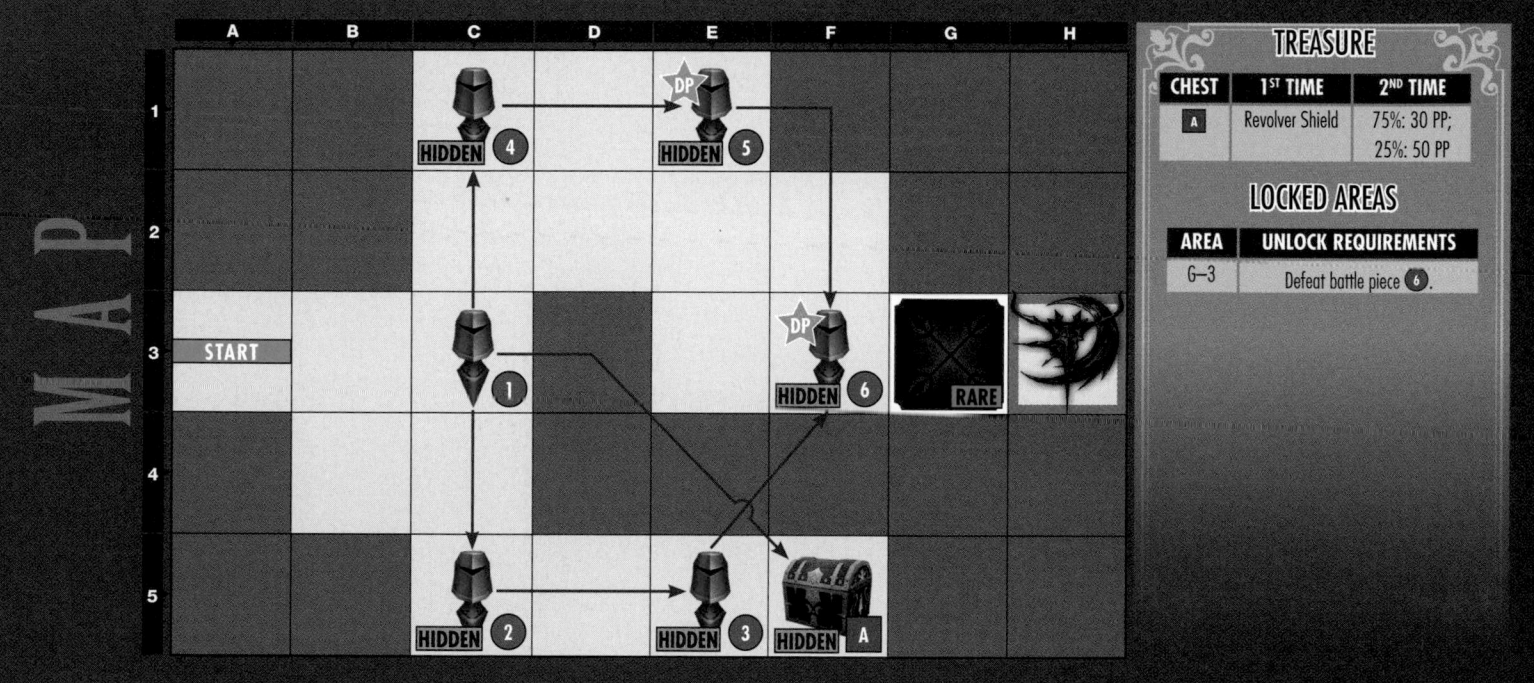

TREASURE

CHEST	1ST TIME	2ND TIME
A	Revolver Shield	75%: 30 PP; 25%: 50 PP

LOCKED AREAS

AREA	UNLOCK REQUIREMENTS
G–3	Defeat battle piece 6.

DP EFFICIENCY ROUTE

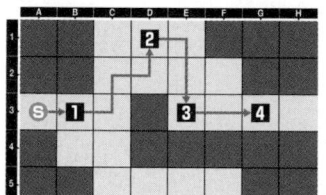

In Squall's levels, more so than others, you must be in exactly the right place to cause chains and conserve DP. Since most battle pieces don't spawn until you've defeated others, you can't just visually verify that you are in the right place for a chain by squeezing between multiple, already visible pieces. From the start, defeat battle piece ❶, which spawns piece ❹. Then, move to D-1 to engage battle piece ❹, which leads to a chain with battle piece ❺. Defeating battle piece ❺ spawns piece ❻, which is not only the last DP Chance available, but also opens the way to the Stigma of Chaos upon defeat.

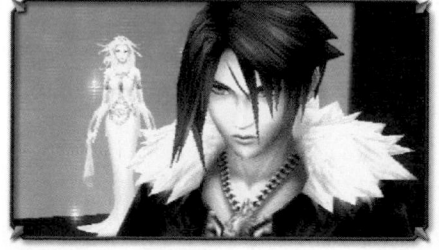

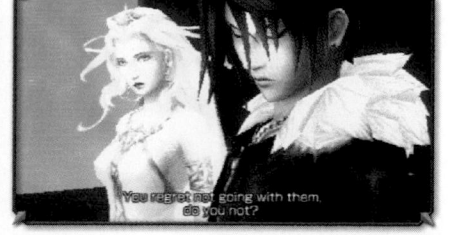

(You regret not going with them, do you not?)

BATTLE PIECE DATA

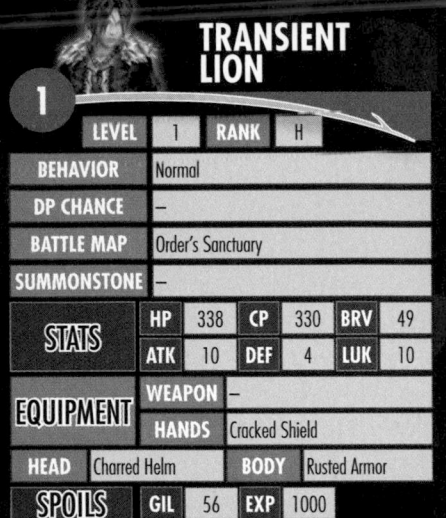

1 TRANSIENT LION

LEVEL	1	RANK	H

BEHAVIOR	Normal
DP CHANCE	–
BATTLE MAP	Order's Sanctuary
SUMMONSTONE	–

STATS	HP	338	CP	330	BRV	49
	ATK	10	DEF	4	LUK	10

EQUIPMENT	WEAPON	–	
	HANDS	Cracked Shield	
HEAD	Charred Helm	BODY	Rusted Armor

SPOILS	GIL	56	EXP	1000

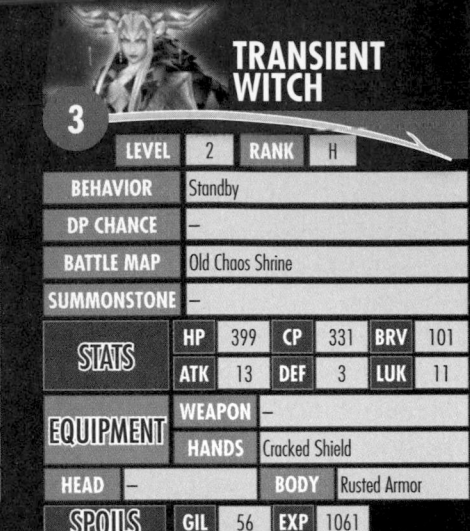

2 EPHEMERAL VISION

LEVEL	1	RANK	H

BEHAVIOR	Tricky
DP CHANCE	–
BATTLE MAP	Order's Sanctuary
SUMMONSTONE	–

STATS	HP	338	CP	330	BRV	49
	ATK	11	DEF	4	LUK	10

EQUIPMENT	WEAPON	–	
	HANDS	Cracked Shield	
HEAD	Charred Helm	BODY	Rusted Armor

SPOILS	GIL	56	EXP	1000

3 TRANSIENT WITCH

LEVEL	2	RANK	H

BEHAVIOR	Standby
DP CHANCE	–
BATTLE MAP	Old Chaos Shrine
SUMMONSTONE	–

STATS	HP	399	CP	331	BRV	101
	ATK	13	DEF	3	LUK	11

EQUIPMENT	WEAPON	–	
	HANDS	Cracked Shield	
HEAD	–	BODY	Rusted Armor

SPOILS	GIL	56	EXP	1061

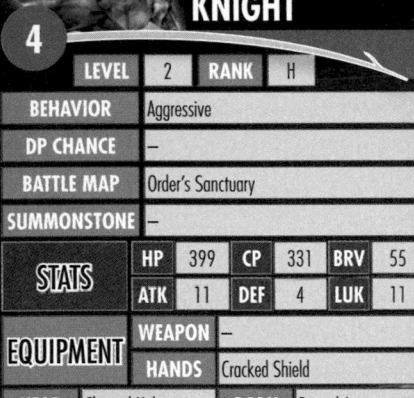

4 DELUSORY KNIGHT

LEVEL	2	RANK	H

BEHAVIOR	Aggressive
DP CHANCE	–
BATTLE MAP	Order's Sanctuary
SUMMONSTONE	–

STATS	HP	399	CP	331	BRV	55
	ATK	11	DEF	4	LUK	11

EQUIPMENT	WEAPON	–	
	HANDS	Cracked Shield	
HEAD	Charred Helm	BODY	Rusted Armor

SPOILS	GIL	56	EXP	1061

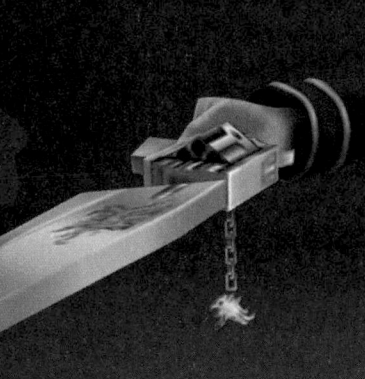

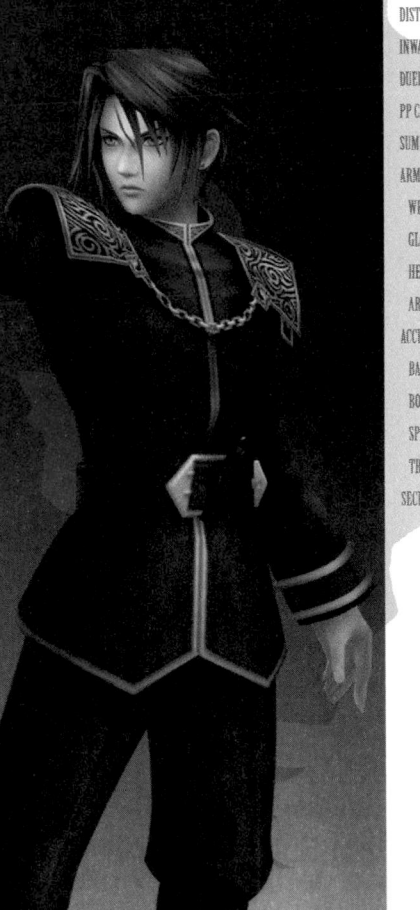

5 PHANTASMAL GIRL

LEVEL	2	RANK	H

BEHAVIOR	Standby
DP CHANCE	BRV Break within 10 seconds (DP+1)
BATTLE MAP	Old Chaos Shrine
SUMMONSTONE	–

STATS	HP	399	CP	331	BRV	55
	ATK	13	DEF	4	LUK	11

EQUIPMENT	WEAPON	–	
	HANDS	Cracked Shield	
HEAD	Charred Helm	BODY	Rusted Armor

SPOILS	GIL	56	EXP	1061

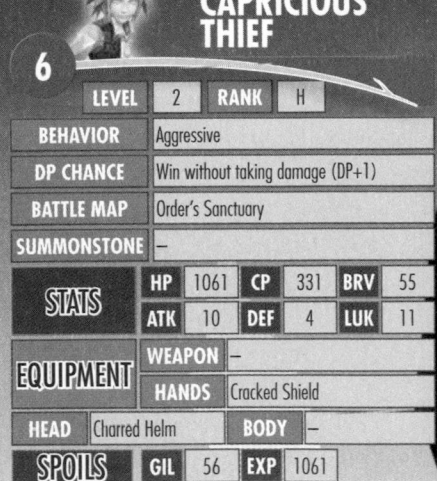

6 CAPRICIOUS THIEF

LEVEL	2	RANK	H

BEHAVIOR	Aggressive
DP CHANCE	Win without taking damage (DP+1)
BATTLE MAP	Order's Sanctuary
SUMMONSTONE	–

STATS	HP	1061	CP	331	BRV	55
	ATK	10	DEF	4	LUK	11

EQUIPMENT	WEAPON	–	
	HANDS	Cracked Shield	
HEAD	Charred Helm	BODY	–

SPOILS	GIL	56	EXP	1061

DESTINY ODYSSEY VIII

Squall's second level is more of the same, with most battle pieces hidden until they are uncovered through battles with other foes. After returning with at least a 2-star rating from a previous Destiny Odyssey VIII run, the Bahamut Summonstone can be found in the lower reaches of the level. The Locked Area in front of the Stigma of Chaos doesn't unlock until defeating battle piece ④, which itself must be uncovered by defeating pieces ① and ② in turn. Along the way, you might as well chain battle piece ⑤ when it appears, especially if you have any kind of EXP bonus active, since this piece gives a ton of EXP. However, beware its incredibly high bravery!

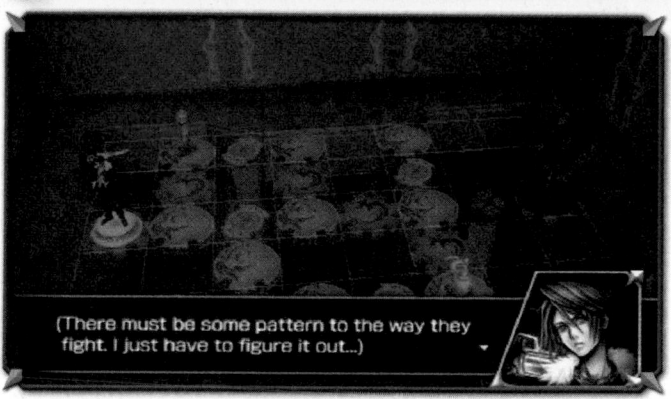

(There must be some pattern to the way they fight. I just have to figure it out...)

MAP

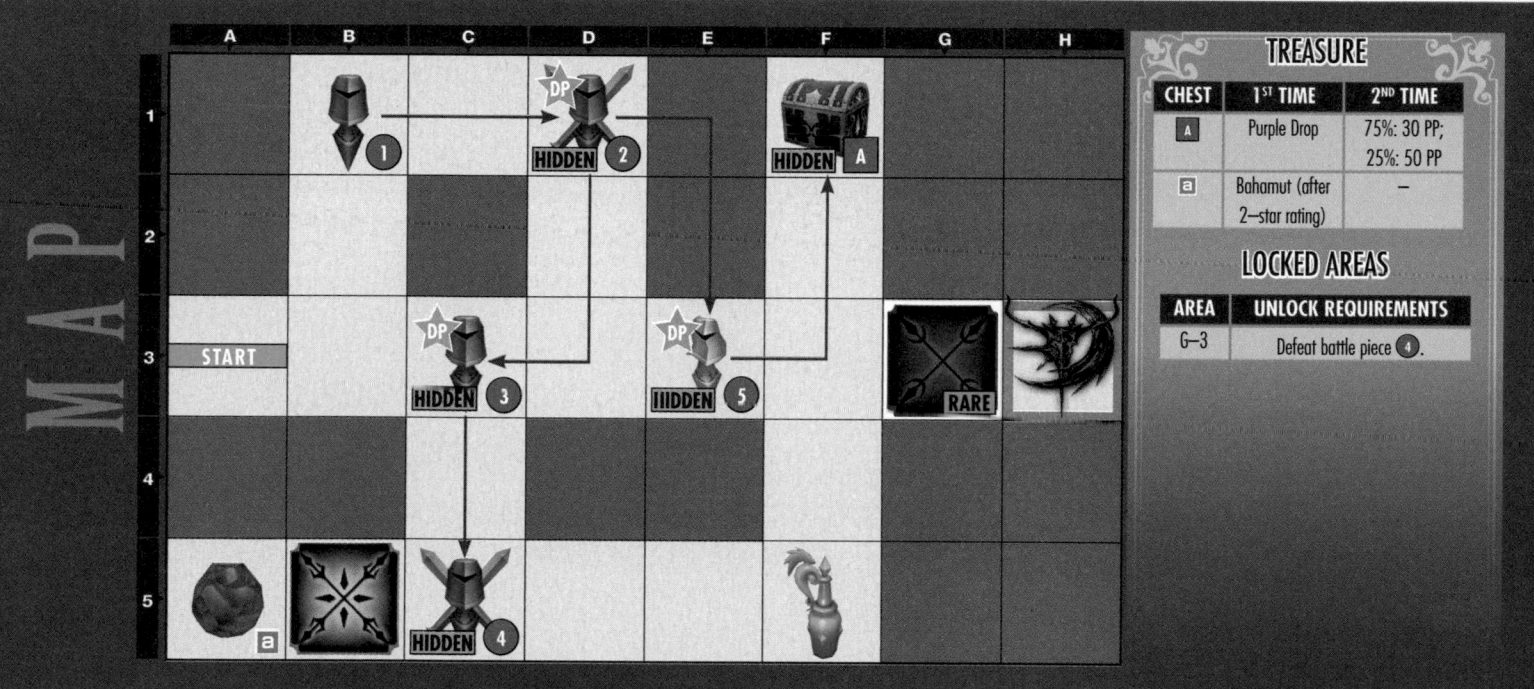

TREASURE

CHEST	1ST TIME	2ND TIME
A	Purple Drop	75%: 30 PP; 25%: 50 PP
a	Bahamut (after 2–star rating)	–

LOCKED AREAS

AREA	UNLOCK REQUIREMENTS
G–3	Defeat battle piece ④.

DP EFFICIENCY ROUTE

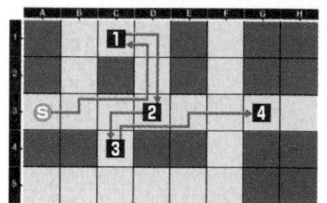

Loop around to C-1 to engage battle piece ①. After winning this fight, battle piece ② appears right behind you, presenting the level's first DP Chance. Winning here spawns battle pieces ③ and ⑤, so head down to D-3 to chain both of them. This action spawns battle piece ④ toward the bottom of the level. While this piece doesn't offer a DP Chance, its defeat opens the Locked Area in front of the Stigma of Chaos. Defeat this piece to gain access to the exit.

BATTLE PIECE DATA

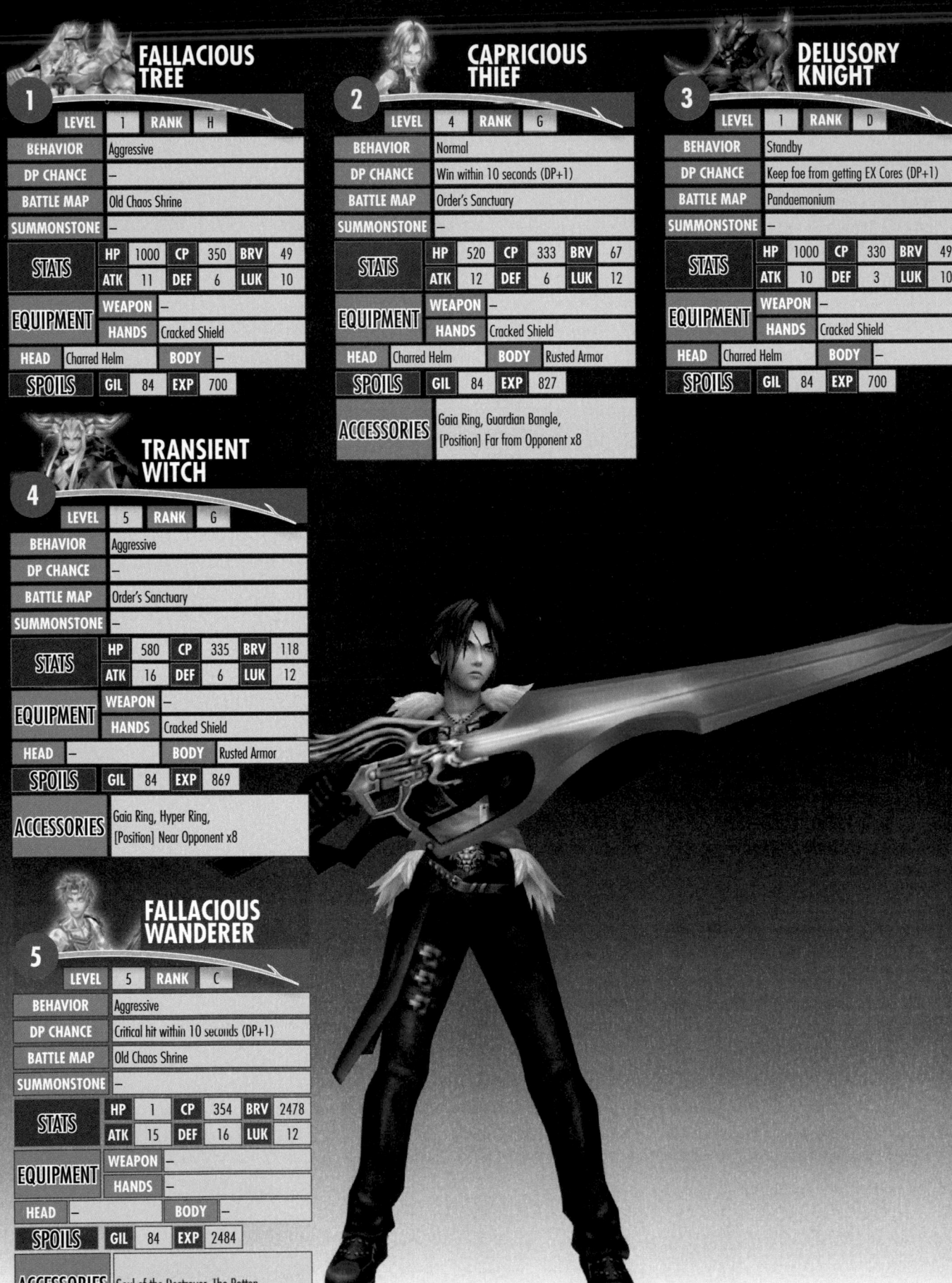

1 FALLACIOUS TREE

LEVEL	1	RANK	H

BEHAVIOR	Aggressive
DP CHANCE	–
BATTLE MAP	Old Chaos Shrine
SUMMONSTONE	–

STATS	HP	1000	CP	350	BRV	49
	ATK	11	DEF	6	LUK	10

EQUIPMENT	WEAPON	–
	HANDS	Cracked Shield
HEAD	Charred Helm	BODY	–

SPOILS	GIL	84	EXP	700

2 CAPRICIOUS THIEF

LEVEL	4	RANK	G

BEHAVIOR	Normal
DP CHANCE	Win within 10 seconds (DP+1)
BATTLE MAP	Order's Sanctuary
SUMMONSTONE	–

STATS	HP	520	CP	333	BRV	67
	ATK	12	DEF	6	LUK	12

EQUIPMENT	WEAPON	–
	HANDS	Cracked Shield
HEAD	Charred Helm	BODY	Rusted Armor

SPOILS	GIL	84	EXP	827

ACCESSORIES	Gaia Ring, Guardian Bangle, [Position] Far from Opponent x8

3 DELUSORY KNIGHT

LEVEL	1	RANK	D

BEHAVIOR	Standby
DP CHANCE	Keep foe from getting EX Cores (DP+1)
BATTLE MAP	Pandaemonium
SUMMONSTONE	–

STATS	HP	1000	CP	330	BRV	49
	ATK	10	DEF	3	LUK	10

EQUIPMENT	WEAPON	–
	HANDS	Cracked Shield
HEAD	Charred Helm	BODY	–

SPOILS	GIL	84	EXP	700

4 TRANSIENT WITCH

LEVEL	5	RANK	G

BEHAVIOR	Aggressive
DP CHANCE	–
BATTLE MAP	Order's Sanctuary
SUMMONSTONE	–

STATS	HP	580	CP	335	BRV	118
	ATK	16	DEF	6	LUK	12

EQUIPMENT	WEAPON	–
	HANDS	Cracked Shield
HEAD	–	BODY	Rusted Armor

SPOILS	GIL	84	EXP	869

ACCESSORIES	Gaia Ring, Hyper Ring, [Position] Near Opponent x8

5 FALLACIOUS WANDERER

LEVEL	5	RANK	C

BEHAVIOR	Aggressive
DP CHANCE	Critical hit within 10 seconds (DP+1)
BATTLE MAP	Old Chaos Shrine
SUMMONSTONE	–

STATS	HP	1	CP	354	BRV	2478
	ATK	15	DEF	16	LUK	12

EQUIPMENT	WEAPON	–
	HANDS	–
HEAD	–	BODY	–

SPOILS	GIL	84	EXP	2484

ACCESSORIES	Soul of the Destroyer, The Rotten

The AUTO version of Bahamut can be found in the lower left corner of this level, on your very first run through Destiny Odyssey VIII. The fastest route through this level involves cascading battle piece victories until battle piece ④ appears and is defeated, opening a Locked Area along the lower route to the exit. Continuing on to battle pieces ⑤ and ⑥ opens the way to a treasure chest in the upper reaches of the level, while blocking the lower path with a Potion. Similar to the previous level, this one features an adversary with very threatening bravery, who also bestows copious EXP when defeated—strange battle piece ③. You've likely learned Beat Fang by now, and Kuja, the boss, is very susceptible to having his bravery broken if you punish him with Beat Fang to Wall Rush him into the ground. Follow up with Rough Divide from a fair distance or Aerial Circle from up close to end the battle easily.

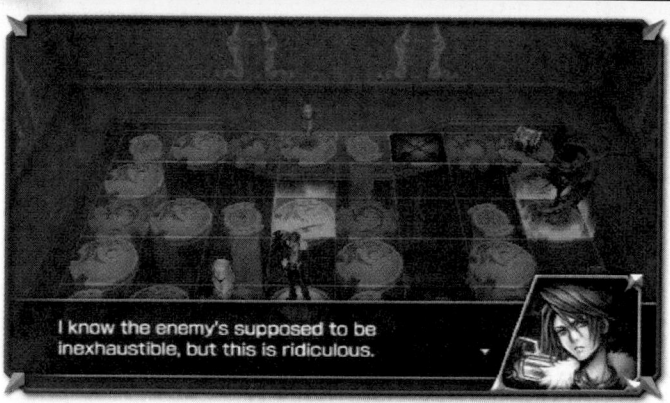

I know the enemy's supposed to be inexhaustible, but this is ridiculous.

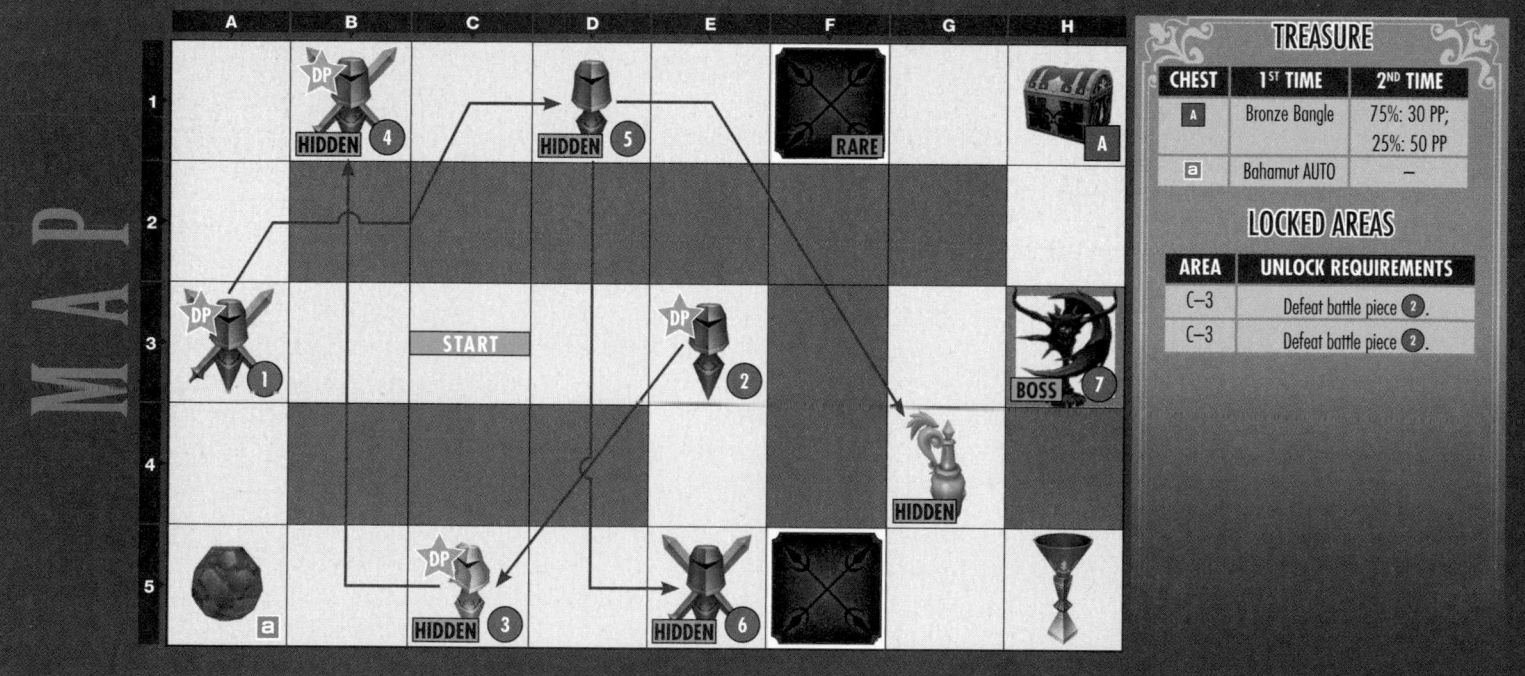

TREASURE

CHEST	1ST TIME	2ND TIME
A	Bronze Bangle	75%: 30 PP; 25%: 50 PP
a	Bahamut AUTO	—

LOCKED AREAS

AREA	UNLOCK REQUIREMENTS
C–3	Defeat battle piece ②.
C–3	Defeat battle piece ②.

DP EFFICIENCY ROUTE

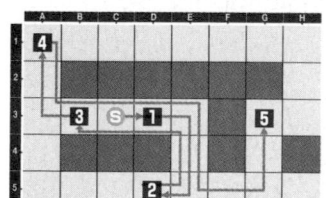

The most efficient route here is quite circuitous. At first, slide right one square and engage battle piece ②. Winning here spawns battle piece ③, which is the next target. Next, take on battle piece ①. If you don't have a full EX Gauge, build it up before the end of this battle. For the last battle of the stage before the boss, head upward and defeat battle piece ④ with a quick EX Burst, scoring the final DP Chance and opening the way to the Stigma of Chaos and Kuja.

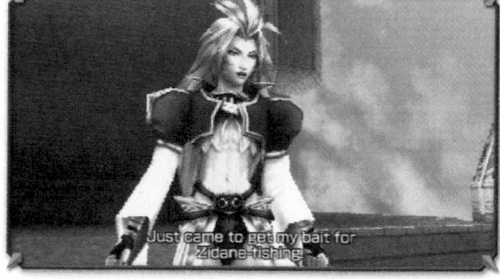

Just came to get my bait for Zidane-fishing.

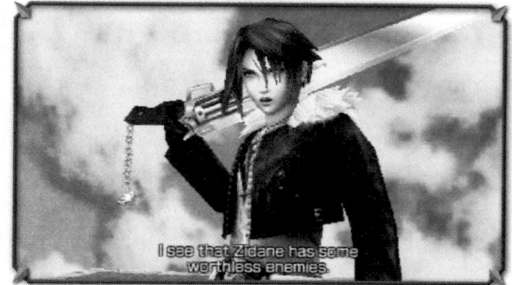

I see that Zidane has some worthless enemies.

BATTLE PIECE DATA

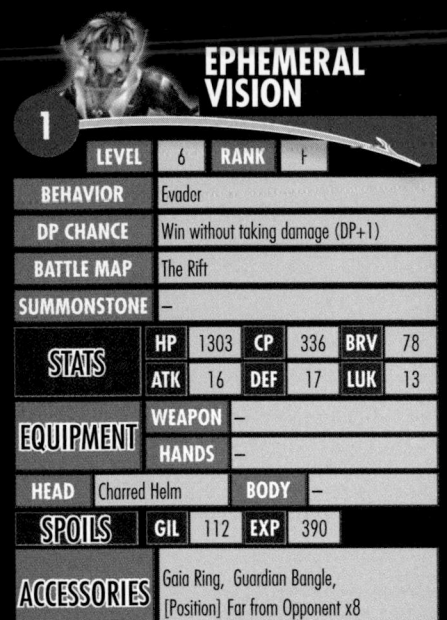

1 EPHEMERAL VISION

LEVEL	6	RANK	F

BEHAVIOR	Evader
DP CHANCE	Win without taking damage (DP+1)
BATTLE MAP	The Rift
SUMMONSTONE	–

STATS	HP	1303	CP	336	BRV	78
	ATK	16	DEF	17	LUK	13

EQUIPMENT	WEAPON	–
	HANDS	–

HEAD	Charred Helm	BODY	–

SPOILS	GIL	112	EXP	390

ACCESSORIES	Gaia Ring, Guardian Bangle, [Position] Far from Opponent x8

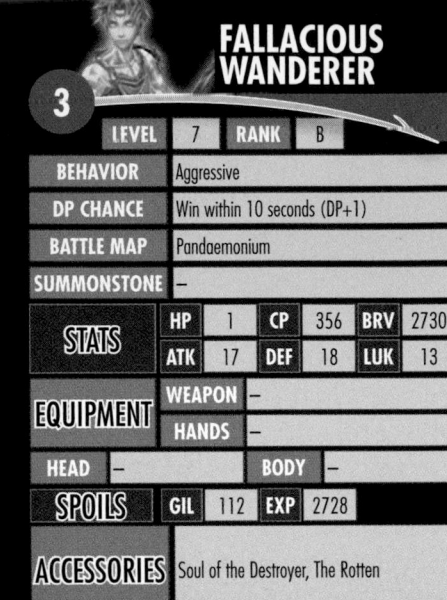

2 DELUSORY KNIGHT

LEVEL	2	RANK	G

BEHAVIOR	Evader
DP CHANCE	BRV Break within 10 seconds (DP+1)
BATTLE MAP	Order's Sanctuary
SUMMONSTONE	–

STATS	HP	1061	CP	331	BRV	55
	ATK	11	DEF	12	LUK	11

EQUIPMENT	WEAPON	–
	HANDS	–

HEAD	Charred Helm	BODY	–

SPOILS	GIL	112	EXP	318

3 FALLACIOUS WANDERER

LEVEL	7	RANK	B

BEHAVIOR	Aggressive
DP CHANCE	Win within 10 seconds (DP+1)
BATTLE MAP	Pandaemonium
SUMMONSTONE	–

STATS	HP	1	CP	356	BRV	2730
	ATK	17	DEF	18	LUK	13

EQUIPMENT	WEAPON	–
	HANDS	–

HEAD	–	BODY	–

SPOILS	GIL	112	EXP	2728

ACCESSORIES	Soul of the Destroyer, The Rotten

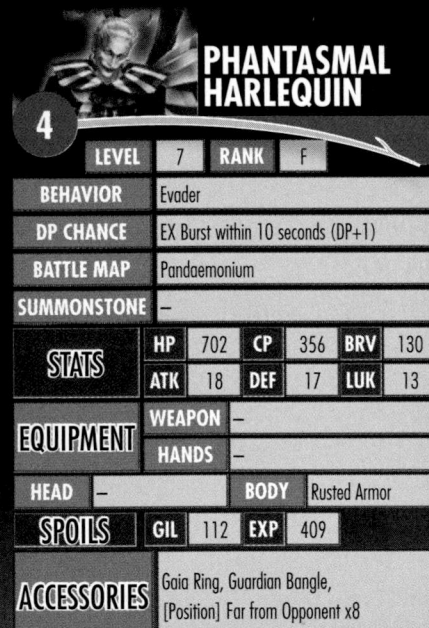

4 PHANTASMAL HARLEQUIN

LEVEL	7	RANK	F

BEHAVIOR	Evader
DP CHANCE	EX Burst within 10 seconds (DP+1)
BATTLE MAP	Pandaemonium
SUMMONSTONE	–

STATS	HP	702	CP	356	BRV	130
	ATK	18	DEF	17	LUK	13

EQUIPMENT	WEAPON	–
	HANDS	–

HEAD	–	BODY	Rusted Armor

SPOILS	GIL	112	EXP	409

ACCESSORIES	Gaia Ring, Guardian Bangle, [Position] Far from Opponent x8

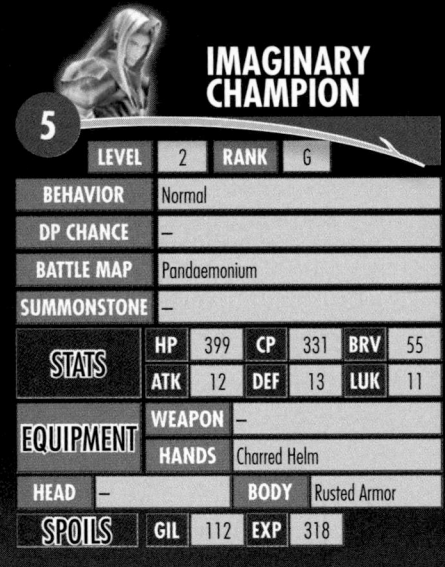

5 IMAGINARY CHAMPION

LEVEL	2	RANK	G

BEHAVIOR	Normal
DP CHANCE	–
BATTLE MAP	Pandaemonium
SUMMONSTONE	–

STATS	HP	399	CP	331	BRV	55
	ATK	12	DEF	13	LUK	11

EQUIPMENT	WEAPON	–
	HANDS	Charred Helm

HEAD	–	BODY	Rusted Armor

SPOILS	GIL	112	EXP	318

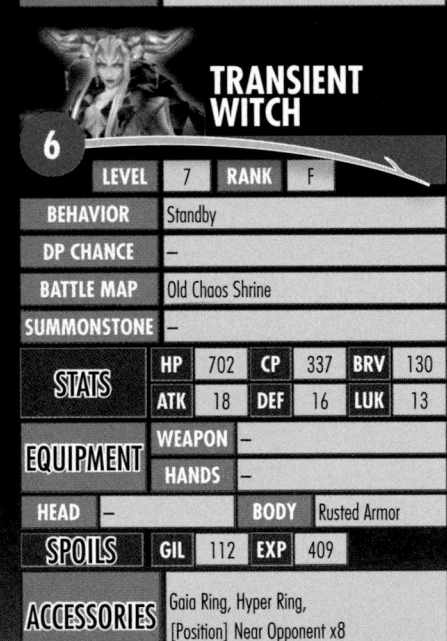

6 TRANSIENT WITCH

LEVEL	7	RANK	F

BEHAVIOR	Standby
DP CHANCE	–
BATTLE MAP	Old Chaos Shrine
SUMMONSTONE	–

STATS	HP	702	CP	337	BRV	130
	ATK	18	DEF	16	LUK	13

EQUIPMENT	WEAPON	–
	HANDS	–

HEAD	–	BODY	Rusted Armor

SPOILS	GIL	112	EXP	409

ACCESSORIES	Gaia Ring, Hyper Ring, [Position] Near Opponent x8

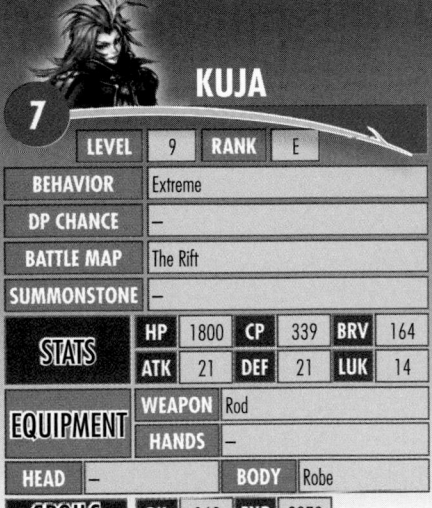

7 KUJA

LEVEL	9	RANK	E

BEHAVIOR	Extreme
DP CHANCE	–
BATTLE MAP	The Rift
SUMMONSTONE	–

STATS	HP	1800	CP	339	BRV	164
	ATK	21	DEF	21	LUK	14

EQUIPMENT	WEAPON	Rod
	HANDS	–

HEAD	–	BODY	Robe

SPOILS	GIL	168	EXP	2970

DESTINY ODYSSEY VIII-4

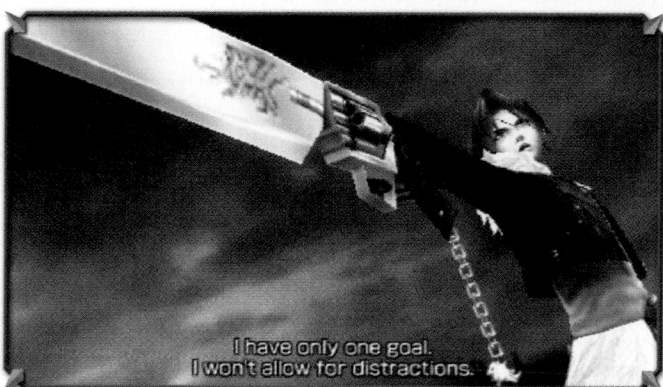

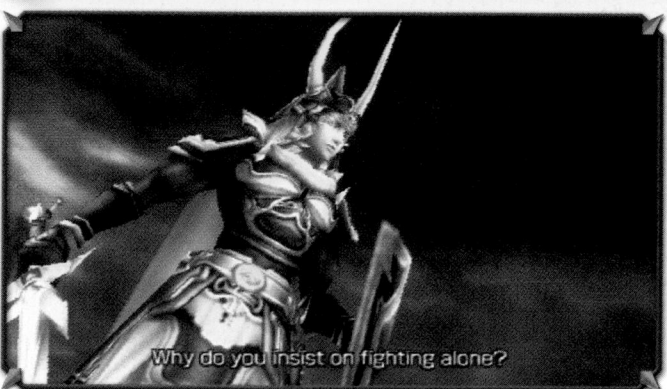

This level has a number of wrinkles, depending on your approach as well as your results on any previous playthroughs. Expert battle piece 6 only appears after you defeat two other battle pieces on the level. The treasure chest in the upper left corner can only be acquired after earning a 2-star rating, while treasure chest D only appears after a 4-star rating. Ultimate battle piece 9 also only appears after a 3-star rating. Expert battle piece 6 (a Garland manikin) is strong, but can be bested by using Beat Fang. In fact, if you can knock him into the floor with Beat Fang just off the ground, you can usually perform this attack over and over—typically, he cannot break free of this. Ultimate battle piece 9 is powerful as well, but also falls prey to some repetitive tactics—if you can dodge past this Ultimecia manikin's barrage of needle-like bravery attacks, you can stick it with Beat Fang and slap it into the ground. From here, just like against the fake Garland mentioned before, you can often simply repeat Beat Fang immediately, and the manikin will fall for it again. However, this foe blocks on occasion, so dodge as soon as possible when it does and look for another opening to use Beat Fang. Collect EX Cores when they are available and attempt an EX Burst once the Beat Fang barrage finally causes a Bravery Break. Against the boss, watch out for his bravery attacks, which lead easily into HP finishers. The boss isn't afraid to use these, especially if he snags enough EX Force to enter EX Mode. Beat him to EX Cores and strike after dodging his attacks to win.

MAP

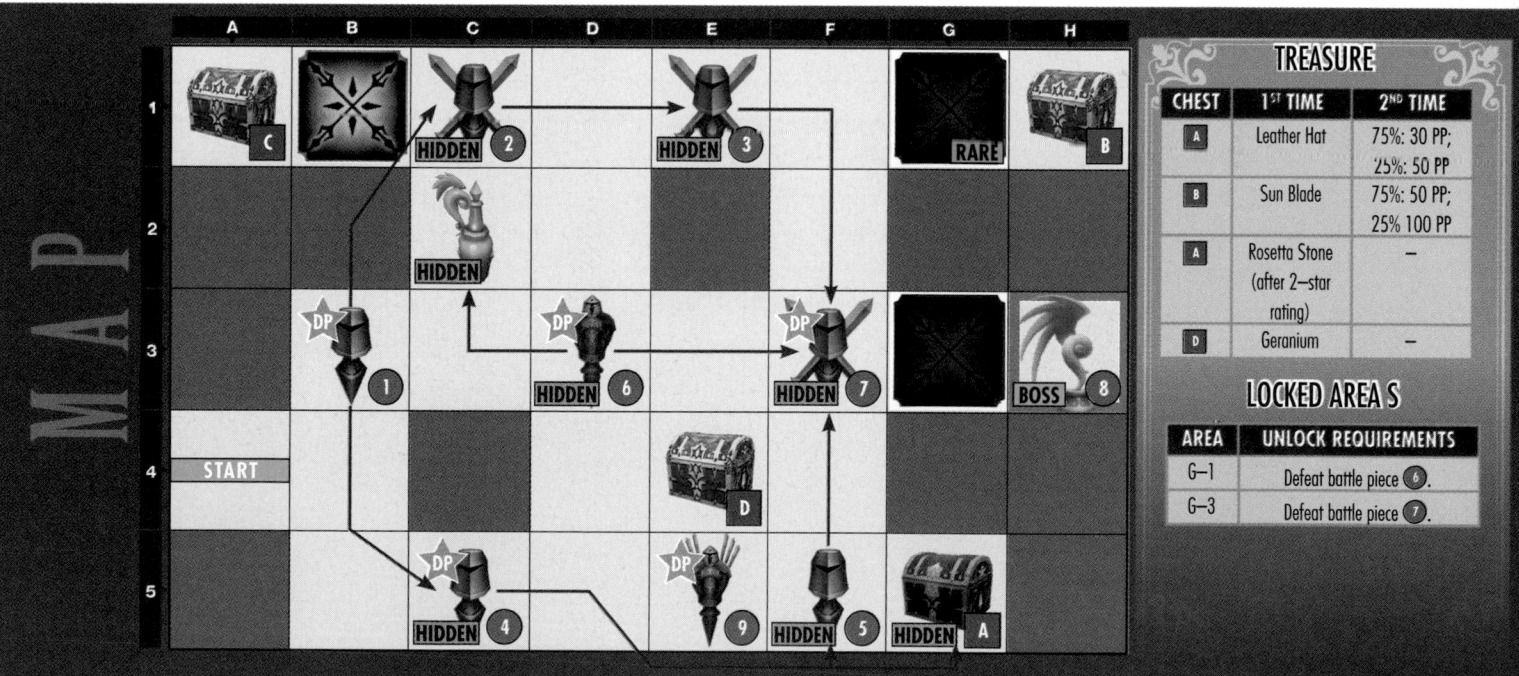

TREASURE

CHEST	1ST TIME	2ND TIME
A	Leather Hat	75%: 30 PP; 25%: 50 PP
B	Sun Blade	75%: 50 PP; 25% 100 PP
A	Rosetta Stone (after 2-star rating)	—
D	Geranium	—

LOCKED AREAS

AREA	UNLOCK REQUIREMENTS
G-1	Defeat battle piece 6.
G-3	Defeat battle piece 7.

DP EFFICIENCY ROUTE

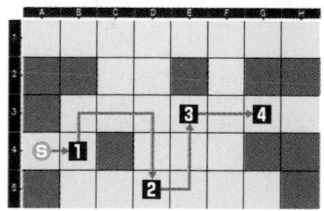

Max DP here requires a previous 3-star rating, so that ultimate battle piece 9 spawns. Also, you must either have previously acquired the rare treasure chest from a 4-star rating, or not yet have spawned it. Once these conditions are in place, begin by defeating battle piece 1, which spawns battle piece 4. Head to D-5 to chain battle pieces 4 and 9. Expert battle piece 6 spawns during this battle chain. Head up to E-4 to chain battle pieces 6 and 7. Defeating battle piece 7 opens the way to the exit, which is your next and final stop.

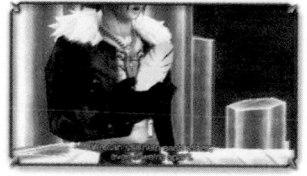

BATTLE PIECE DATA

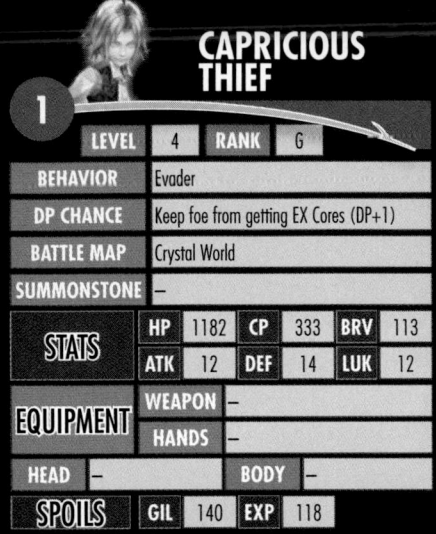

1 CAPRICIOUS THIEF

LEVEL	4	RANK	G

BEHAVIOR	Evader
DP CHANCE	Keep foe from getting EX Cores (DP+1)
BATTLE MAP	Crystal World
SUMMONSTONE	—

STATS	HP	1182	CP	333	BRV	113
	ATK	12	DEF	14	LUK	12

EQUIPMENT	WEAPON	—
	HANDS	—

HEAD	—	BODY	—

SPOILS	GIL	140	EXP	118

2 FALLACIOUS TREE

LEVEL	8	RANK	F

BEHAVIOR	Aggressive
DP CHANCE	—
BATTLE MAP	The Rift
SUMMONSTONE	—

STATS	HP	762	CP	357	BRV	90
	ATK	18	DEF	13	LUK	14

EQUIPMENT	WEAPON	—
	HANDS	Cracked Shield

HEAD	Charred Helm	BODY	Rusted Armor

SPOILS	GIL	140	EXP	142

ACCESSORIES	Gaia Ring, Guardian Bangle, [Position] Far from Opponent x8

3 PHANTASMAL GIRL

LEVEL	9	RANK	F

BEHAVIOR	Tricky
DP CHANCE	—
BATTLE MAP	Pandaemonium
SUMMONSTONE	—

STATS	HP	1485	CP	339	BRV	95
	ATK	20	DEF	19	LUK	14

EQUIPMENT	WEAPON	—
	HANDS	—

HEAD	Charred Helm	BODY	—

SPOILS	GIL	140	EXP	148

ACCESSORIES	Gaia Ring, Guardian Bangle, [Position] Far from Opponent x8

4 PHANTASMAL HARLEQUIN

LEVEL	4	RANK	G

BEHAVIOR	Standby
DP CHANCE	Win within 10 seconds (DP+1)
BATTLE MAP	The Rift
SUMMONSTONE	—

STATS	HP	1182	CP	353	BRV	113
	ATK	15	DEF	14	LUK	12

EQUIPMENT	WEAPON	—
	HANDS	—

HEAD	—	BODY	—

SPOILS	GIL	140	EXP	118

5 EPHEMERAL PHANTOM

LEVEL	3	RANK	G

BEHAVIOR	Aggressive
DP CHANCE	—
BATTLE MAP	Pandaemonium
SUMMONSTONE	—

STATS	HP	459	CP	332	BRV	107
	ATK	15	DEF	15	LUK	11

EQUIPMENT	WEAPON	—
	HANDS	—

HEAD	—	BODY	Rusted Armor

SPOILS	GIL	140	EXP	112

6 FALSE STALWART

LEVEL	17	RANK	C

BEHAVIOR	Tactician
DP CHANCE	Win battle (DP+1)
BATTLE MAP	Crystal World
SUMMONSTONE	—

STATS	HP	1970*	CP	349	BRV	188*
	ATK	29*	DEF	30*	LUK	18

EQUIPMENT	WEAPON	[Rank 3]
	HANDS	[Rank 2]

HEAD	[Rank 4]	BODY	[Rank 2]

SPOILS	GIL	140	EXP	0

7 TRANSIENT WITCH

LEVEL	9	RANK	F

BEHAVIOR	Aggressive
DP CHANCE	Critical hit within 10 seconds (DP+1)
BATTLE MAP	Old Chaos Shrine
SUMMONSTONE	—

STATS	HP	1485	CP	339	BRV	95
	ATK	20	DEF	18	LUK	14

EQUIPMENT	WEAPON	—
	HANDS	—

HEAD	Charred Helm	BODY	—

SPOILS	GIL	140	EXP	148

ACCESSORIES	Gaia Ringm, Hyper Ring, [Position] Near Opponent x8

8 WARRIOR OF LIGHT

LEVEL	11	RANK	E

BEHAVIOR	Valiant
DP CHANCE	—
BATTLE MAP	Crystal World
SUMMONSTONE	Ifrit

STATS	HP	2034	CP	342	BRV	178
	ATK	25	DEF	25	LUK	15

EQUIPMENT	WEAPON	Broadsword
	HANDS	—

HEAD	Bronze Helm	BODY	Bronze Armor

SPOILS	GIL	252	EXP	1606

9 TRANSIENT WITCH

LEVEL	25	RANK	B

BEHAVIOR	Survivor
DP CHANCE	Win battle (DP+2)
BATTLE MAP	Order's Sanctuary
SUMMONSTONE	—

STATS	HP	2454*	CP	359	BRV	359*
	ATK	52	DEF	48	LUK	22

EQUIPMENT	WEAPON	Rod of Wisdom
	HANDS	Silver Bangles

HEAD	Hairpin	BODY	[Rank 4]

SPOILS	GIL	336	EXP	2454

ACCESSORIES	Gaia Ring, Guardian Bangle, [Position] Far from Opponent x8

* Denotes use of the base value (for stats that vary).

DESTINY ODYSSEY VIII

DESTINY ODYSSEY VIII-5

Squall's final level features battle pieces spawning out of thin air once again, in reaction to the defeat of others. This time, however, they won't force you into unexpected battle chains. Coming here with a 3-star or better rating spawns a rare battle piece, and a 4-star rating results in a rare treasure chest. Rare, ultimate battle piece ⑧ is a facsimile of Squall himself. This manikin can use many of the same tricks you've likely used to get here—dodging attacks and replying with Beat Fang, using Rough Divide from afar, Aerial Circle from up close—so you'll just have to play solidly to win. The Squall manikin is very quick about reacting to EX Core spawns and going after them, so be attentive and beat it to the punch. If you're of a lower level than this foe (which is likely the first time you run into it), inflicting BRV Break without being in EX Mode to confer extra power and critical hits proves to be incredibly tough, so you'll need that EX Force to survive. It's also useful if you get caught in an attack you fear may break your bravery, since activating EX Mode acts as a combo breaker. Against the boss, Ultimecia, you can use the stage itself against many of her attacks—hiding behind pillars or under and over floors can block many of her projectile-based assaults. Up close, Squall is the more formidable opponent, so draw cautiously near or dodge through one of her attacks before attacking.

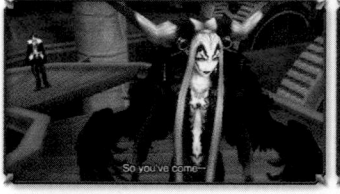
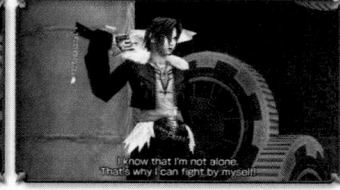
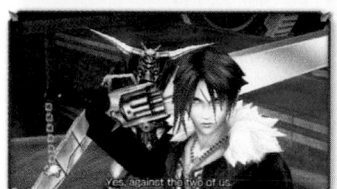
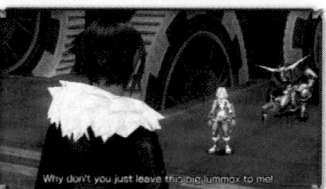

MAP

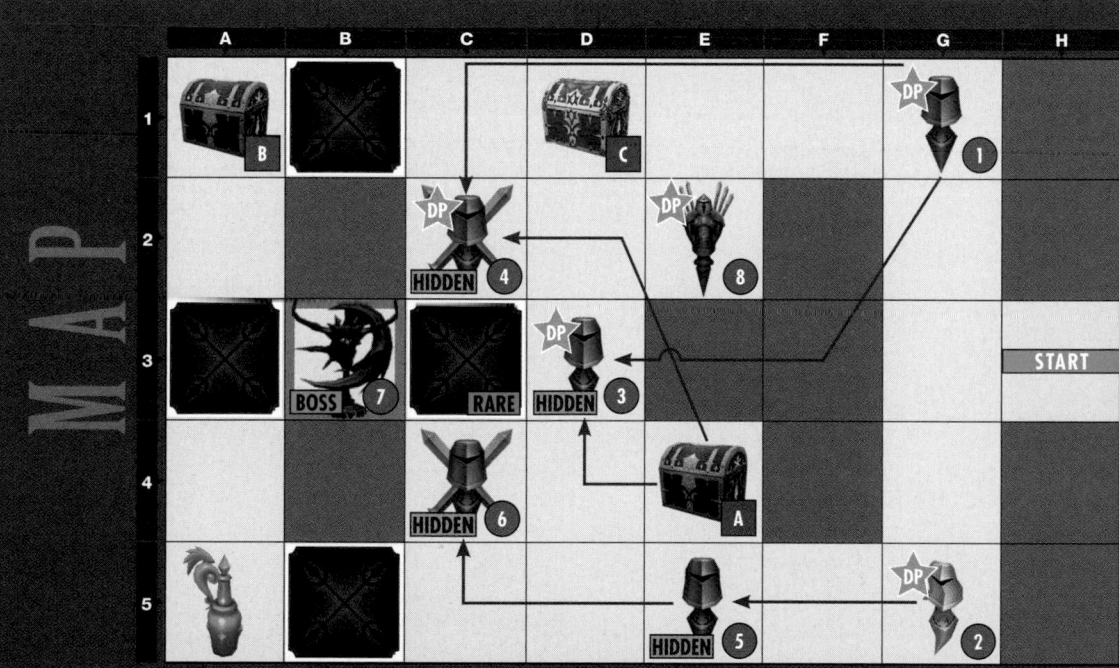

TREASURE

CHEST	1ST TIME	2ND TIME
A	Guard Ring	75%: 30 PP; 25%: 50 PP
B	Rosetta Stone	75%: 30 PP; 25%: 50 PP
C	Mythril	—

LOCKED AREAS

AREA	UNLOCK REQUIREMENTS
C–3	Defeat 5 battle pieces
B–1	Defeat battle piece ⑥
B–5	Defeat battle piece ②
A–3	Defeat battle piece ④

DP EFFICIENCY ROUTE

Like many later levels, going for max DP here must be done after garnering a 3-star rating, so that a rare battle piece shows up, but either before a 4-star rating or after grabbing the rare treasure chest that a 4-star rating spawns. If the rare treasure chest is actually on the board, it blocks your way at one point, forcing you to burn a Destiny Point you wouldn't have to otherwise. With the right conditions in place, begin by heading upward to defeat battle piece ①, then back down to defeat battle piece ②. Afterward, head to D-2, where you can chain battle pieces ③, ④, and ⑧. The DP Chance for Battle Piece ④ requires an EX Burst within 10 seconds, so be sure to save up EX Force before this fight. After the 3-part chain is complete, head to the Stigma of Chaos for Squall's showdown with Ultimecia.

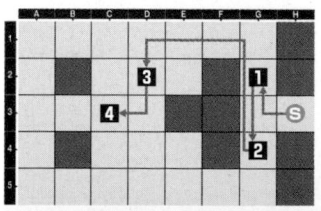
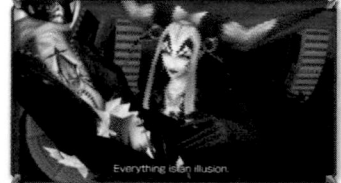
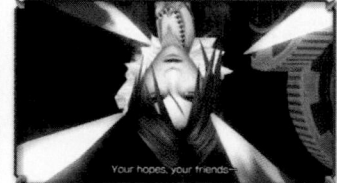
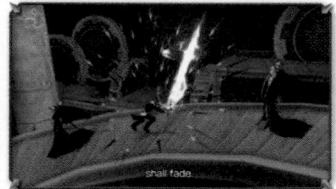
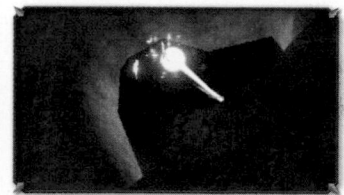

BATTLE PIECE DATA

1 IMAGINARY CHAMPION

LEVEL	6	RANK	G

BEHAVIOR	Blocker
DP CHANCE	Win without taking damage (DP+1)
BATTLE MAP	Pandaemonium
SUMMONSTONE	—

STATS	HP	641	CP	336	BRV	124
	ATK	16	DEF	17	LUK	13

EQUIPMENT	WEAPON	—
	HANDS	—
HEAD		BODY	Rusted Armor

SPOILS	GIL	168	EXP	0

2 FALLACIOUS WANDERER

LEVEL	11	RANK	B

BEHAVIOR	Aggressive
DP CHANCE	Critical hit within 10 seconds (DP+1)
BATTLE MAP	Order's Sanctuary
SUMMONSTONE	Odin

STATS	HP	1	CP	360	BRV	3213
	ATK	21	DEF	22	LUK	15

EQUIPMENT	WEAPON	—
	HANDS	—
HEAD		BODY	—

SPOILS	GIL	168	EXP	3212

ACCESSORIES	Soul of the Destroyer, The Rotten

3 EPHEMERAL PHANTOM

LEVEL	6	RANK	G

BEHAVIOR	Blocker
DP CHANCE	Win within 10 seconds (DP+1)
BATTLE MAP	The Rift
SUMMONSTONE	Atomos

STATS	HP	1303	CP	336	BRV	124
	ATK	18	DEF	18	LUK	13

EQUIPMENT	WEAPON	—
	HANDS	—
HEAD	—	BODY	—

SPOILS	GIL	168	EXP	0

4 PHANTASMAL HARLEQUIN

LEVEL	12	RANK	E

BEHAVIOR	Evader
DP CHANCE	EX Burst within 10 seconds (DP+1)
BATTLE MAP	Crystal World
SUMMONSTONE	—

STATS	HP	1667	CP	361	BRV	159
	ATK	23	DEF	22	LUK	16

EQUIPMENT	WEAPON	—
	HANDS	—
HEAD	—	BODY	—

SPOILS	GIL	168	EXP	0

ACCESSORIES	Gaia Ring, Guardian Bangle, [Position] Far from Opponent x8

5 PHANTASMAL GIRL

LEVEL	5	RANK	G

BEHAVIOR	Evader
DP CHANCE	—
BATTLE MAP	Ultimecia's Castle
SUMMONSTONE	—

STATS	HP	1242	CP	335	BRV	72
	ATK	16	DEF	15	LUK	12

EQUIPMENT	WEAPON	—
	HANDS	—
HEAD	Charred Helm	BODY	—

SPOILS	GIL	168	EXP	0

6 FALLACIOUS TREE

LEVEL	11	RANK	E

BEHAVIOR	Blocker
DP CHANCE	—
BATTLE MAP	The Rift
SUMMONSTONE	—

STATS	HP	1606	CP	360	BRV	153
	ATK	21	DEF	24	LUK	15

EQUIPMENT	WEAPON	—
	HANDS	—
HEAD	—	BODY	—

SPOILS	GIL	168	EXP	0

ACCESSORIES	Gaia Ring, Guardian Bangle, [Position] Far from Opponent x8

7 ULTIMECIA

LEVEL	14	RANK	D

BEHAVIOR	Cautious
DP CHANCE	—
BATTLE MAP	Ultimecia's Castle
SUMMONSTONE	Lich

STATS	HP	2171	CP	345	BRV	280
	ATK	33	DEF	24	LUK	17

EQUIPMENT	WEAPON	Guard Stick
	HANDS	—
HEAD	Hairpin	BODY	Cotton Robes

SPOILS	GIL	336	EXP	4470

ACCESSORIES	Gaia Ring, Phoenix Down, [HP] HP = 1, [HP] Near Death, [HP] Near Loss

8 TRANSIENT LION

LEVEL	28	RANK	B

BEHAVIOR	Conservative
DP CHANCE	Win battle (DP+2)
BATTLE MAP	Ultimecia's Castle
SUMMONSTONE	—

STATS	HP	2636*	CP	362	BRV	251*
	ATK	37*	DEF	39*	LUK	24

EQUIPMENT	WEAPON	[Rank 4]
	HANDS	[Rank 3]
HEAD	[Rank 5]	BODY	Poncho

SPOILS	GIL	336	EXP	2636

ACCESSORIES	Gaia Ring, Hyper Ring, [Position] Near Opponent x8

* Denotes use of the base value (for stats that vary).

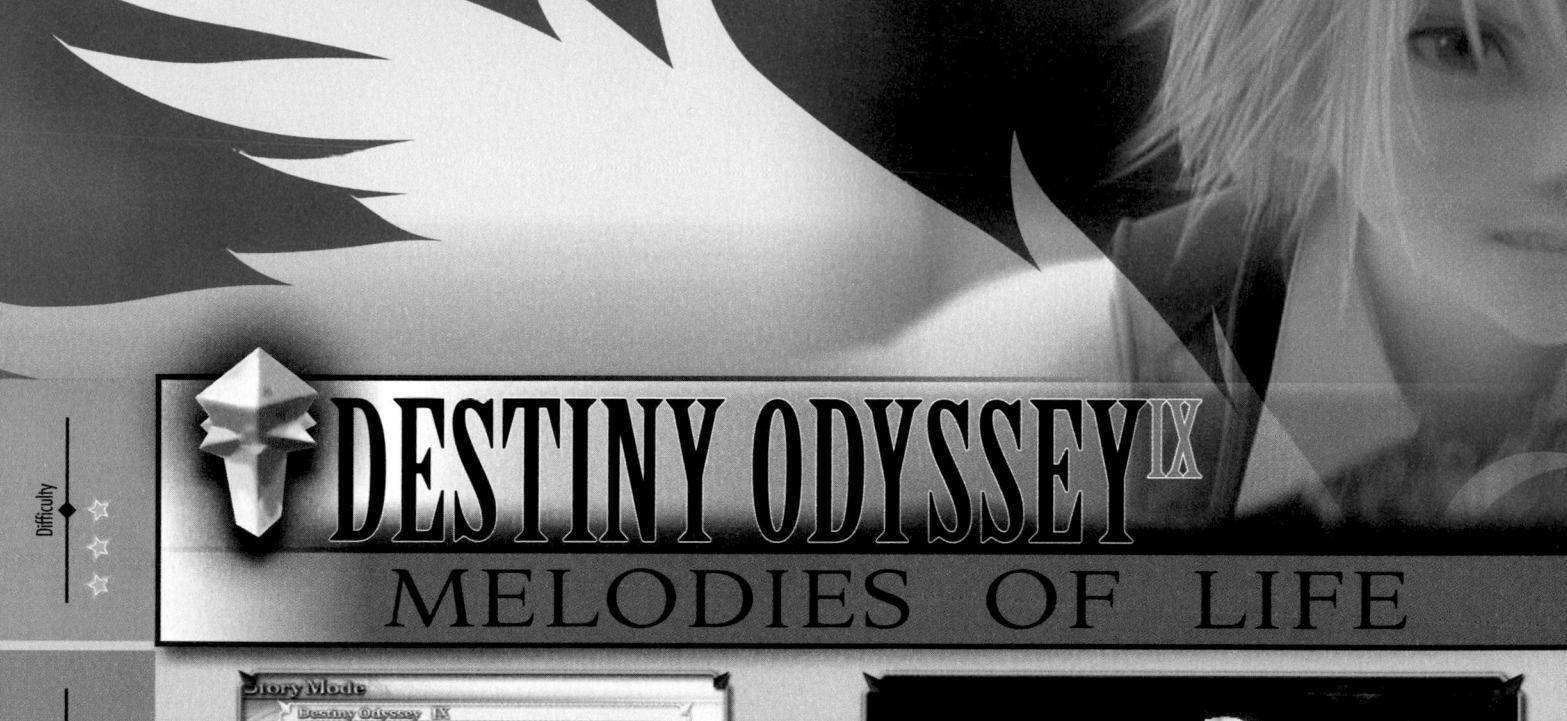

DESTINY ODYSSEY IX
MELODIES OF LIFE

Difficulty ☆☆☆

Prerequisite ◆ Finish Prologue

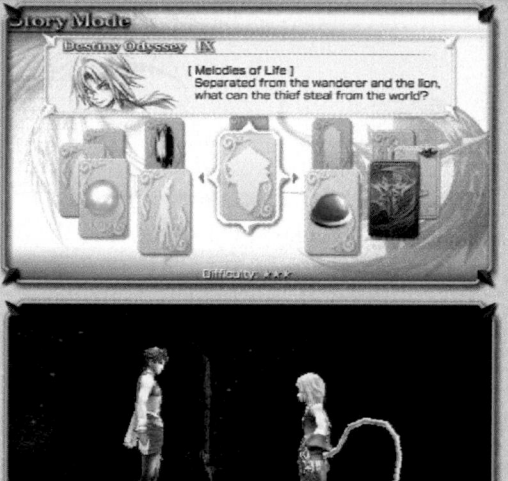

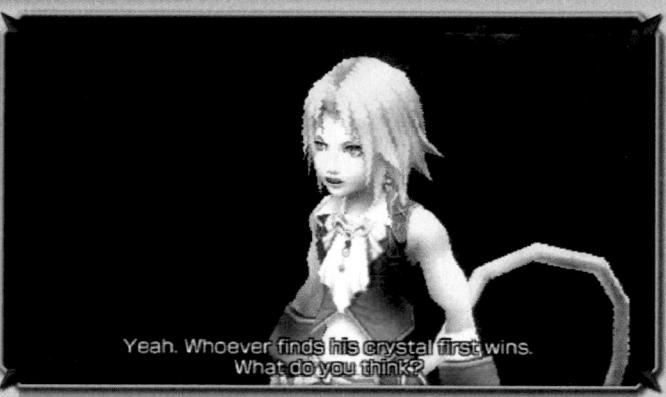

Yeah. Whoever finds his crystal first wins. What do you think?

Injecting some levity into the otherwise dirge-like proceedings, Zidane and Bartz challenge each other to a race to their respective crystals.

REWARDS

At the end of each level, rewards are available if you finish with a positive number of Destiny Points, or DP. This walkthrough includes miniature level maps that indicate the most efficient route to take through a given level, in order to maximize DP.

LEVEL COMPLETION

REMAINING DP		1ST TIME		2ND TIME
7	Rosetta Stone		300 PP	
6	Mage Masher		200 PP	
5	Main Gauche		120 PP	
4	Cactuar		80 PP	
3	1000 gil		50 PP	
2	600 gil		30 PP	
1	300 gil		20 PP	
0	100 gil		10 PP	

DESTINY ODYSSEY IX COMPLETION

STAR RATING	SP REQUIRED	AWARD
☆	100	New skill
☆☆	200	Special areas unlocked
☆☆☆	300	Rare battle pieces spawned
☆☆☆☆	400	Rare treasure chests spawned
–	500 SP, then every 500 SP extra	100 PP

At the end of each set of levels, you'll receive rewards based on your performance. Story Points, or SP, are awarded after each level based on remaining DP, HP, and the number of engagements undertaken. Points are penalized for retries, or for a DP total that dips into negatives. If you miss out on a desired bonus on the first playthrough, don't fret—SP is cumulative across multiple playthroughs.

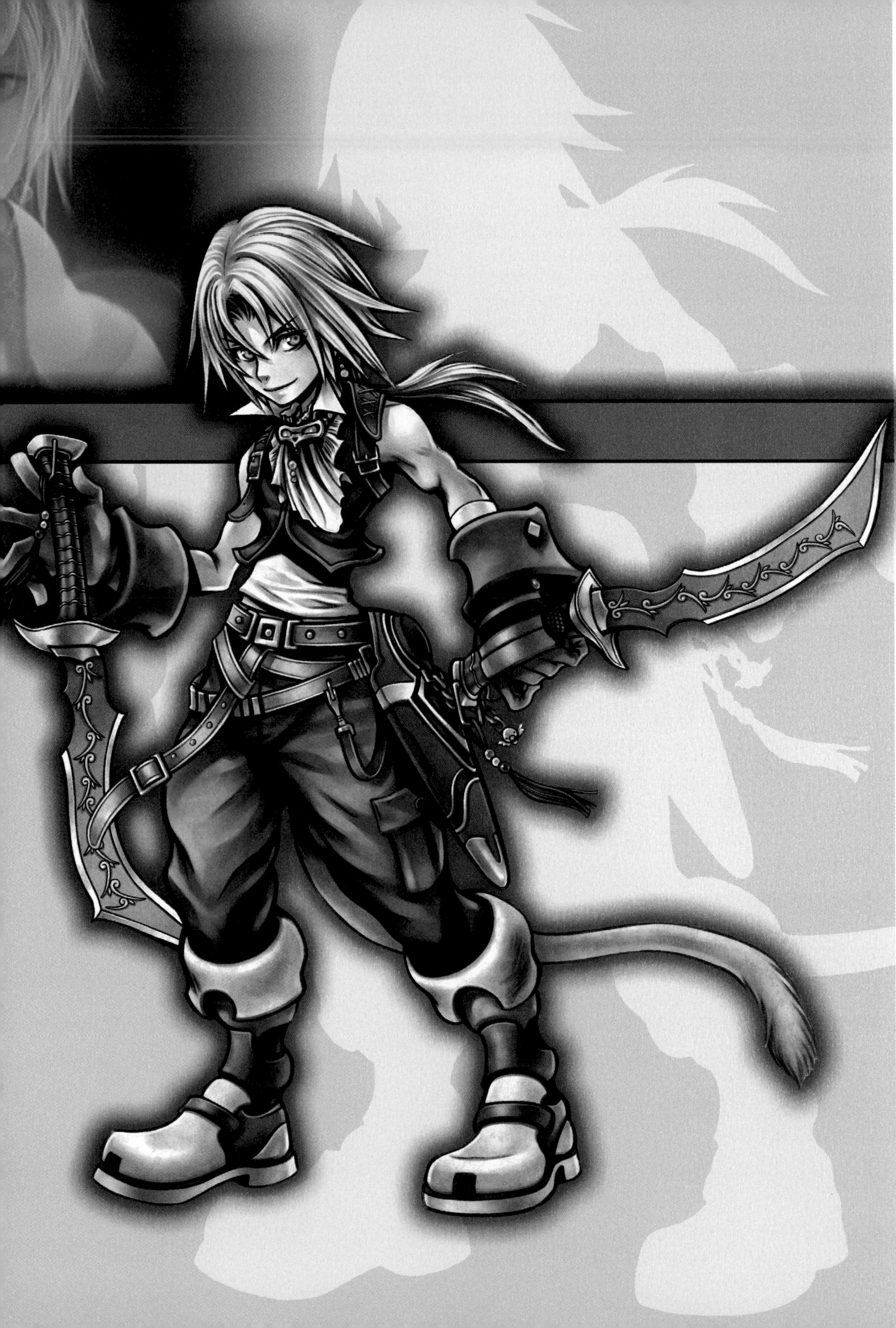

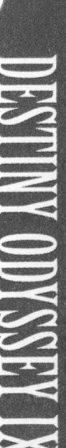

DESTINY ODYSSEY IX

	STARTING DP	MAX FINISHING	ENGAGEMENTS
	5	3	5

Zidane's levels begin largely uncomplicated, but defeating battle pieces and opening treasure chests often spawns more battle pieces far away. Zidane is well-equipped to defeat his foes—on top of his innate triple jump (or a 10-part jump during EX Mode!) and his well-rounded arsenal even at low levels, his Tidal Flame often presents problems for CPU-controlled opponents. When in doubt during Zidane's chapter, get on flat ground and just use Tidal Flame over and over. More often than not, foes then try to dodge over and over, only to mess up eventually.

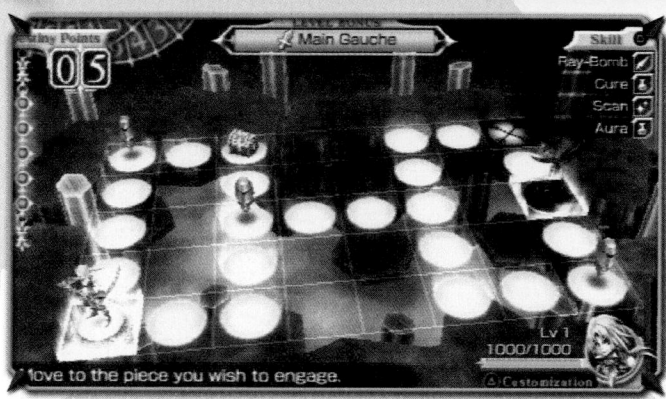

MAP

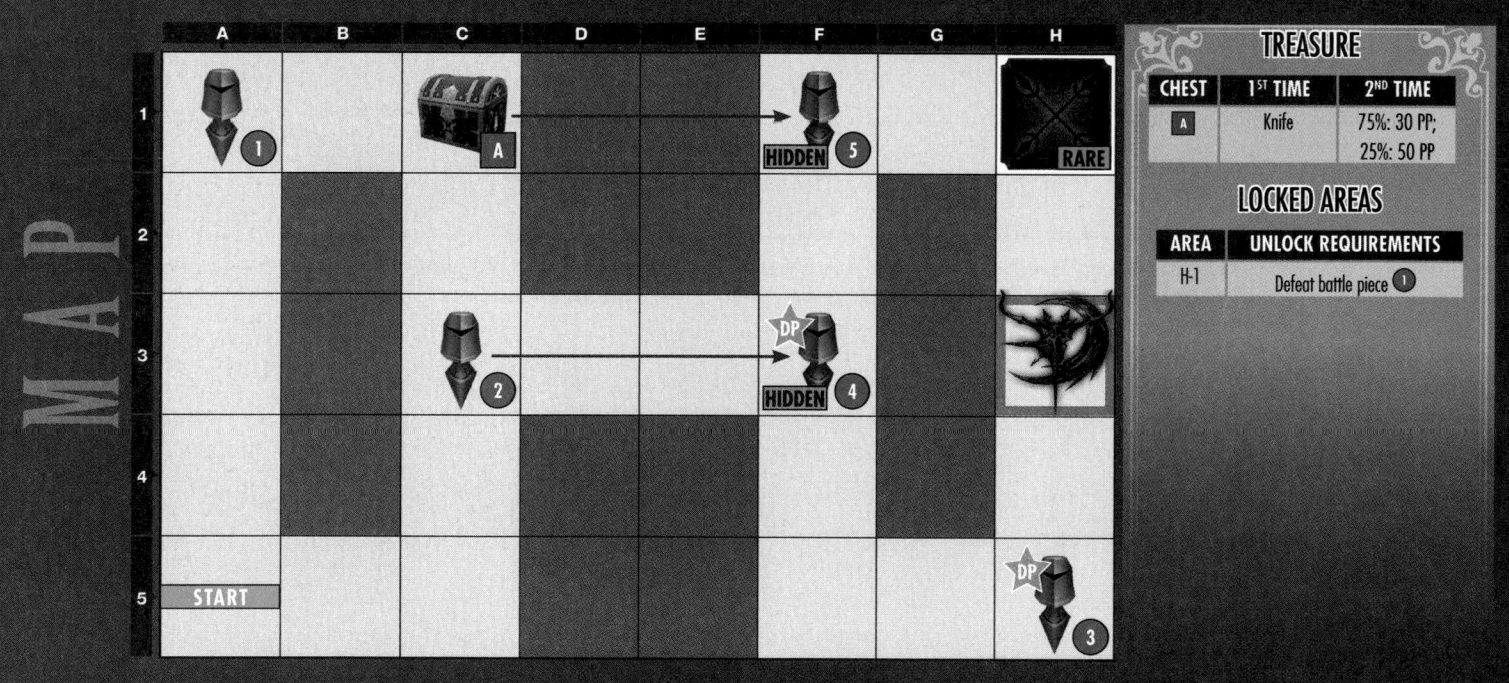

TREASURE

CHEST	1ST TIME	2ND TIME
A	Knife	75%: 30 PP; 25%: 50 PP

LOCKED AREAS

AREA	UNLOCK REQUIREMENTS
H-1	Defeat battle piece ①

DP EFFICIENCY ROUTE

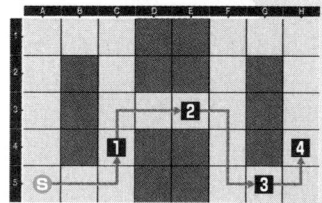

The fastest route here simply involves hugging the lowest boundary of the level. Save EX Force against battle pieces ② and ④, so you can activate EX Mode and score a guaranteed critical hit quickly against battle piece ③.

BATTLE PIECE DATA

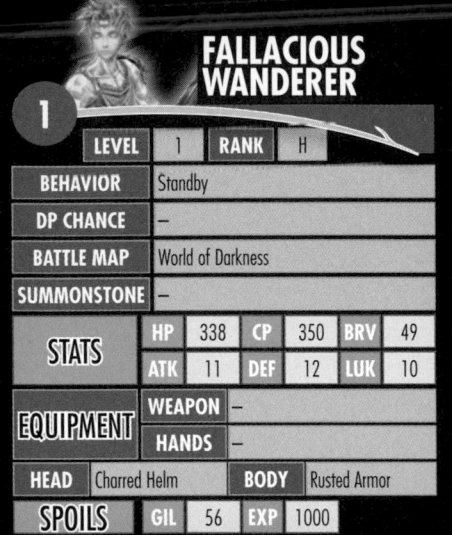

1 FALLACIOUS WANDERER

LEVEL	1	RANK	H

BEHAVIOR	Standby
DP CHANCE	—
BATTLE MAP	World of Darkness
SUMMONSTONE	—

STATS	HP	338	CP	350	BRV	49
	ATK	11	DEF	12	LUK	10

EQUIPMENT	WEAPON	—
	HANDS	—

HEAD	Charred Helm	BODY	Rusted Armor

SPOILS	GIL	56	EXP	1000

2 CAPRICIOUS THIEF

LEVEL	1	RANK	H

BEHAVIOR	Normal
DP CHANCE	—
BATTLE MAP	Order's Sanctuary
SUMMONSTONE	—

STATS	HP	338	CP	330	BRV	49
	ATK	9	DEF	11	LUK	10

EQUIPMENT	WEAPON	—
	HANDS	—

HEAD	Charred Helm	BODY	Rusted Armor

SPOILS	GIL	56	EXP	1000

3 CAPRICIOUS REAPER

LEVEL	2	RANK	H

BEHAVIOR	Aggressive
DP CHANCE	Critical hit within 10 seconds (DP+1)
BATTLE MAP	Order's Sanctuary
SUMMONSTONE	—

STATS	HP	1061	CP	331	BRV	101
	ATK	11	DEF	13	LUK	11

EQUIPMENT	WEAPON	—
	HANDS	—

HEAD	—	BODY	—

SPOILS	GIL	56	EXP	1061

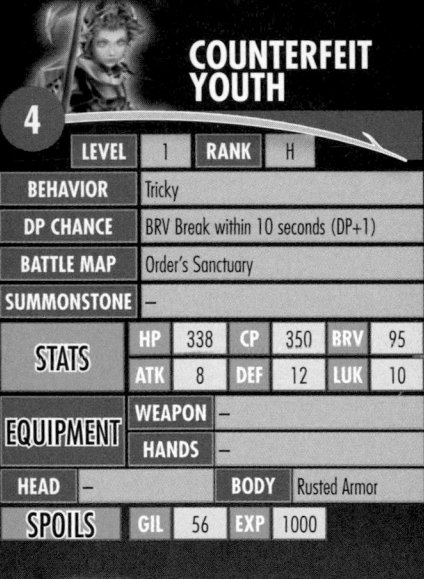

4 COUNTERFEIT YOUTH

LEVEL	1	RANK	H

BEHAVIOR	Tricky
DP CHANCE	BRV Break within 10 seconds (DP+1)
BATTLE MAP	Order's Sanctuary
SUMMONSTONE	—

STATS	HP	338	CP	350	BRV	95
	ATK	8	DEF	12	LUK	10

EQUIPMENT	WEAPON	—
	HANDS	—

HEAD	—	BODY	Rusted Armor

SPOILS	GIL	56	EXP	1000

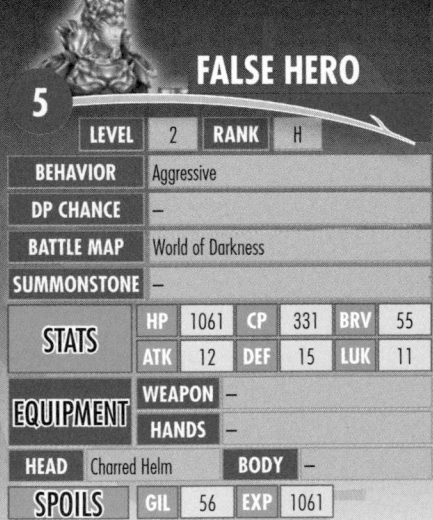

5 FALSE HERO

LEVEL	2	RANK	H

BEHAVIOR	Aggressive
DP CHANCE	—
BATTLE MAP	World of Darkness
SUMMONSTONE	—

STATS	HP	1061	CP	331	BRV	55
	ATK	12	DEF	15	LUK	11

EQUIPMENT	WEAPON	—
	HANDS	—

HEAD	Charred Helm	BODY	—

SPOILS	GIL	56	EXP	1061

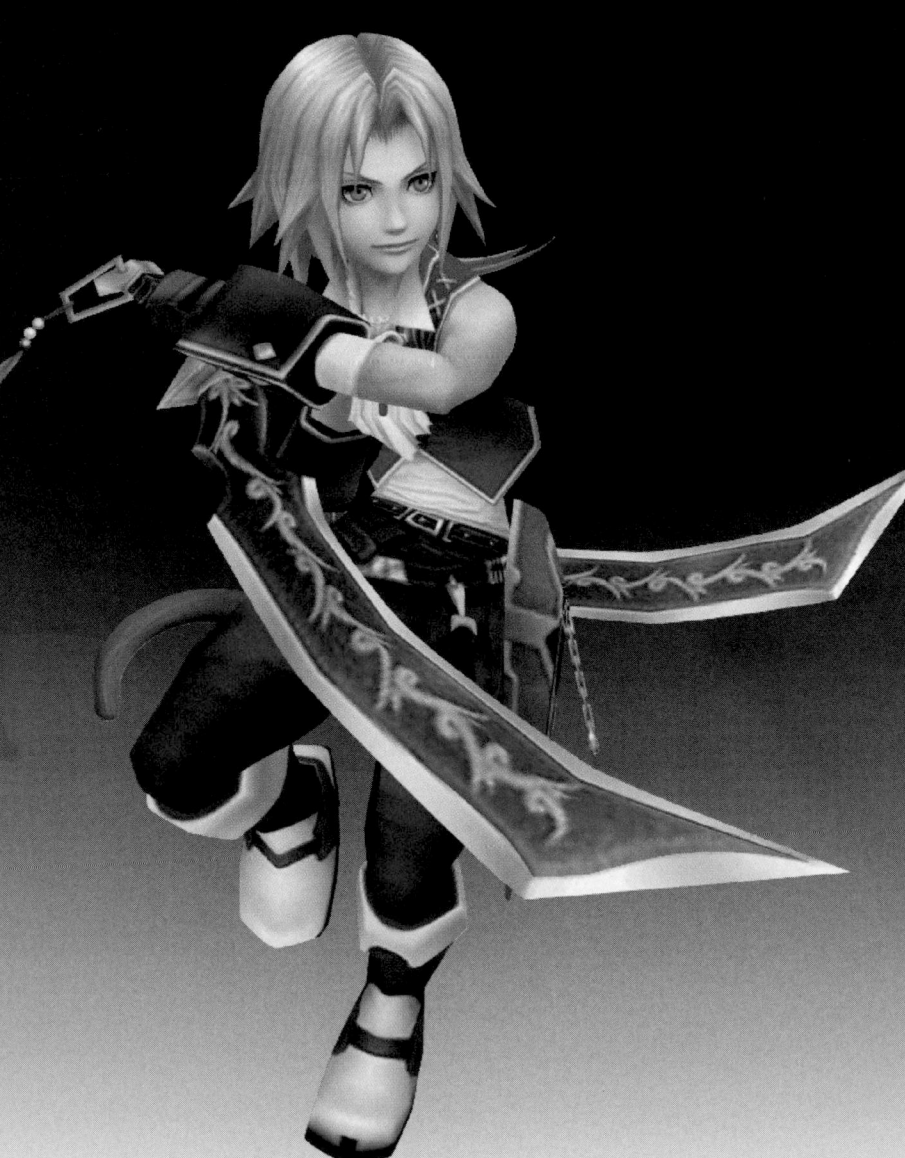

STARTING DP	MAX FINISHING	ENGAGEMENTS
4	4	5

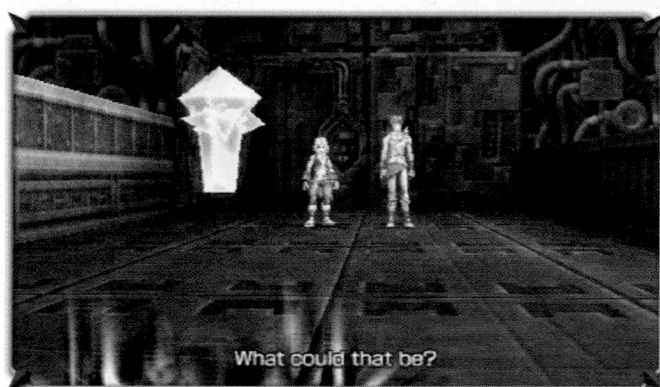

What could that be?

This is another straightforward level, where engaging pieces at the beginning reveals more near the end. Watch out for battle piece ④, which engages you first if you get close to it. Opening treasure chest Ⓐ will spawn a strange battle piece, which provides a large EXP bonus, as always. The Alexander Summonstone can be found here during a return trip, after a 2-star rating. This useful summon freezes your bravery for a little while on command. This is best done after boosting your bravery to a very high amount, such as after inflicting Break on your opponent.

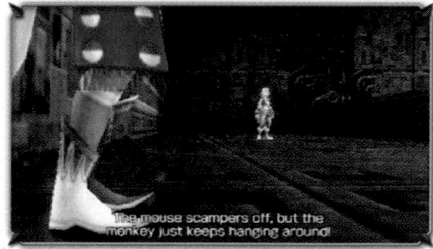

The mouse scampers off, but the monkey just keeps hanging around!

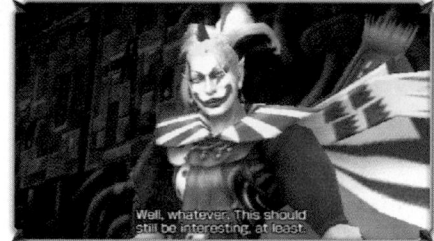

Well, whatever. This should still be interesting, at least.

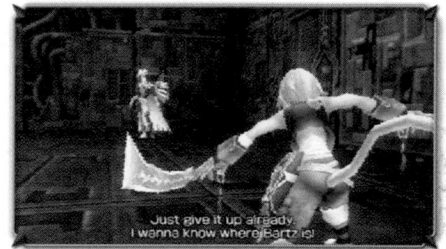

Just give it up already. I wanna know where Bartz is!

MAP

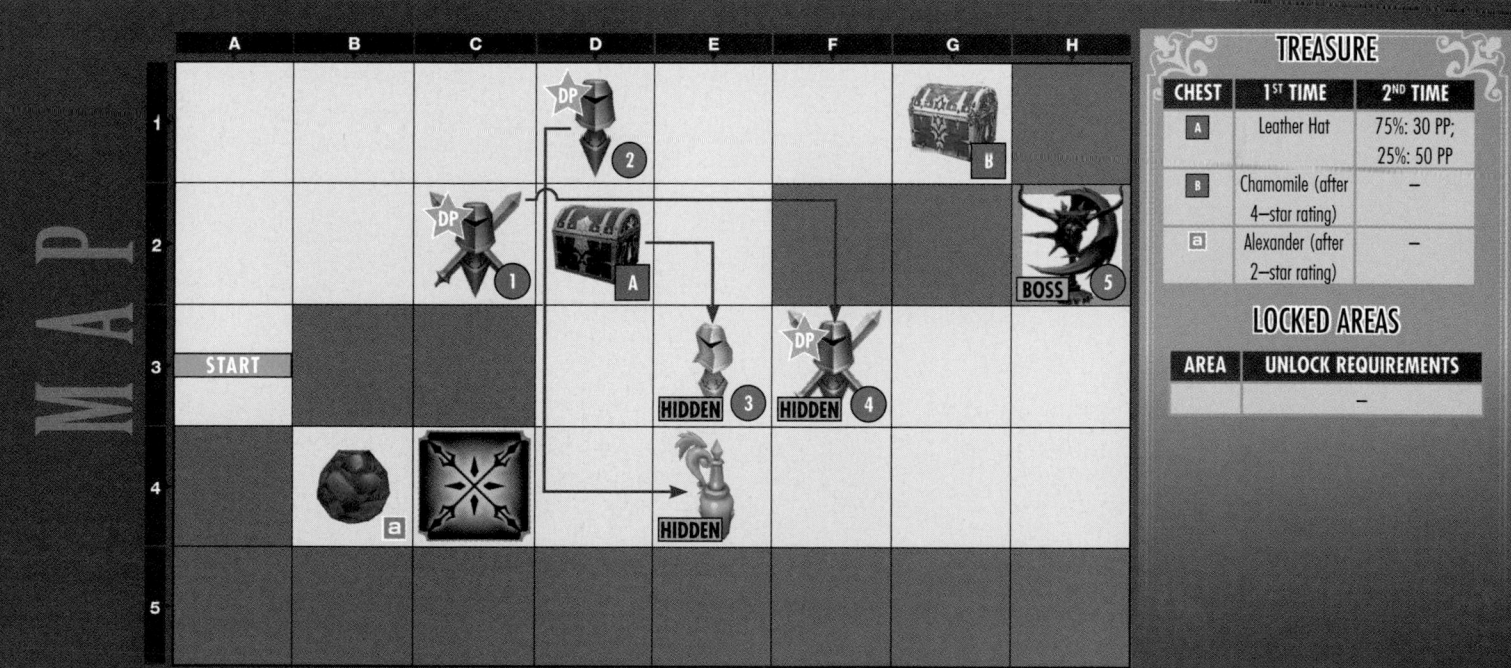

TREASURE

CHEST	1ST TIME	2ND TIME
A	Leather Hat	75%: 30 PP; 25%: 50 PP
B	Chamomile (after 4–star rating)	–
a	Alexander (after 2–star rating)	–

LOCKED AREAS

AREA	UNLOCK REQUIREMENTS
	–

DP EFFICIENCY ROUTE

Begin this level by chaining battle pieces ① and ② (possibly building a full EX Gauge to make the DP Chance against ② easier; otherwise, try blocking and countering an early attack). Defeating battle piece ② spawns battle piece ④ further toward the exit. Defeat this foe within 10 seconds for the final DP Chance, before heading to the boss.

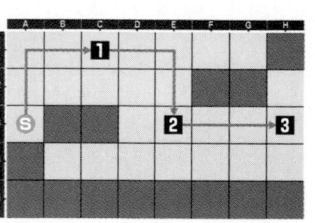

BATTLE PIECE DATA

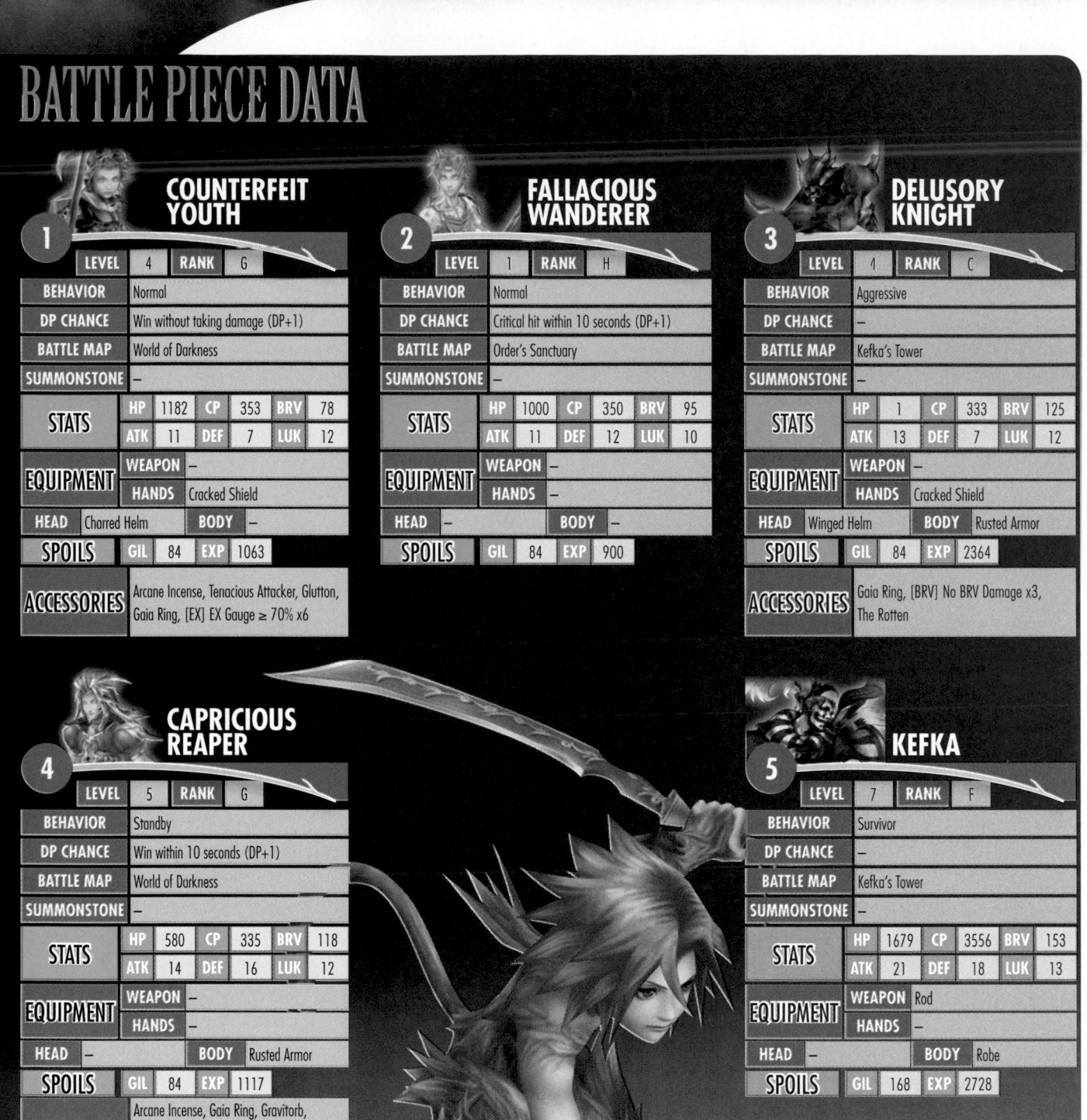

1 COUNTERFEIT YOUTH

LEVEL	4	RANK	G

BEHAVIOR	Normal
DP CHANCE	Win without taking damage (DP+1)
BATTLE MAP	World of Darkness
SUMMONSTONE	–

STATS	HP	1182	CP	353	BRV	78
	ATK	11	DEF	7	LUK	12

EQUIPMENT	WEAPON	–
	HANDS	Cracked Shield

HEAD	Charred Helm	BODY	–

SPOILS	GIL	84	EXP	1063

ACCESSORIES	Arcane Incense, Tenacious Attacker, Glutton, Gaia Ring, [EX] EX Gauge ≥ 70% x6

2 FALLACIOUS WANDERER

LEVEL	1	RANK	H

BEHAVIOR	Normal
DP CHANCE	Critical hit within 10 seconds (DP+1)
BATTLE MAP	Order's Sanctuary
SUMMONSTONE	–

STATS	HP	1000	CP	350	BRV	95
	ATK	11	DEF	12	LUK	10

EQUIPMENT	WEAPON	–
	HANDS	–

HEAD		BODY	–

SPOILS	GIL	84	EXP	900

3 DELUSORY KNIGHT

LEVEL	1	RANK	C

BEHAVIOR	Aggressive
DP CHANCE	–
BATTLE MAP	Kefka's Tower
SUMMONSTONE	–

STATS	HP	1	CP	333	BRV	125
	ATK	13	DEF	7	LUK	12

EQUIPMENT	WEAPON	–
	HANDS	Cracked Shield

HEAD	Winged Helm	BODY	Rusted Armor

SPOILS	GIL	84	EXP	2364

ACCESSORIES	Gaia Ring, [BRV] No BRV Damage x3, The Rotten

4 CAPRICIOUS REAPER

LEVEL	5	RANK	G

BEHAVIOR	Standby
DP CHANCE	Win within 10 seconds (DP+1)
BATTLE MAP	World of Darkness
SUMMONSTONE	–

STATS	HP	580	CP	335	BRV	118
	ATK	14	DEF	16	LUK	12

EQUIPMENT	WEAPON	–
	HANDS	–

HEAD	–	BODY	Rusted Armor

SPOILS	GIL	84	EXP	1117

ACCESSORIES	Arcane Incense, Gaia Ring, Gravitorb, Pearl Necklace, [EX] EX Core Present x2, [EX] EX Gauge ≥ 70% x4

5 KEFKA

LEVEL	7	RANK	F

BEHAVIOR	Survivor
DP CHANCE	–
BATTLE MAP	Kefka's Tower
SUMMONSTONE	–

STATS	HP	1679	CP	3556	BRV	153
	ATK	21	DEF	18	LUK	13

EQUIPMENT	WEAPON	Rod
	HANDS	–

HEAD	–	BODY	Robe

SPOILS	GIL	168	EXP	2728

This level is a bit more complex. Four Locked Areas surround the Stigma of Chaos. You can open a direct route to the exit by defeating either battle piece ❹ or ❺. Battle piece ❷ is an expert fight against a Golbez manikin that trumps you in level your first time through. These fights can be rough on certain characters, but not Zidane. Because Golbez's primary bravery attacks are relatively easy to avoid, and because manikins in general have an awful time dealing with Tidal Flame, you should be able to win this encounter during your initial playthrough without too much trouble. Don't forget to acquire the AUTO version of the Alexander Summonstone, tucked away here in the top left corner.

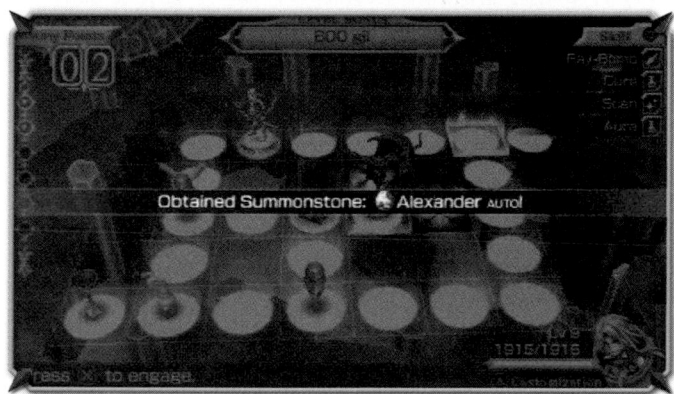

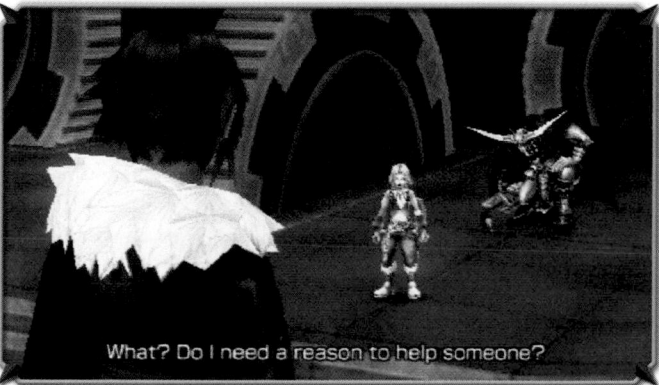

MAP

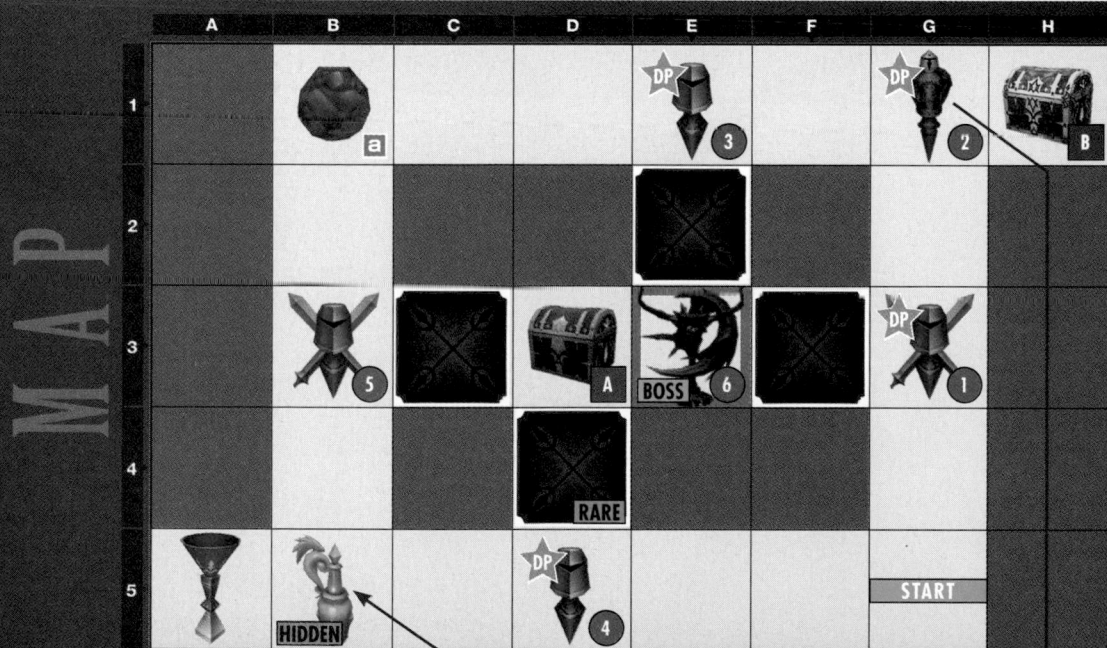

TREASURE

CHEST	1ST TIME	2ND TIME
A	Green Drop	75%: 30 PP; 25%: 50 PP
B	Triton's Dagger	75%: 50 PP; 25%: 100 PP
a	Alexander AUTO	—

LOCKED AREAS

AREA	UNLOCK REQUIREMENTS
D–4	Defeat battle piece ❸
F–3	Defeat battle piece ❺
E–2	Defeat battle piece ❹
C–3	Defeat battle piece ❶

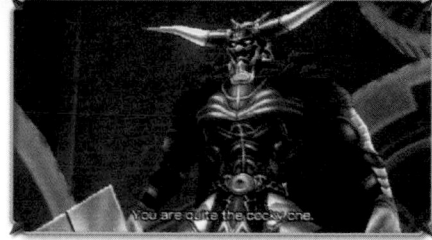

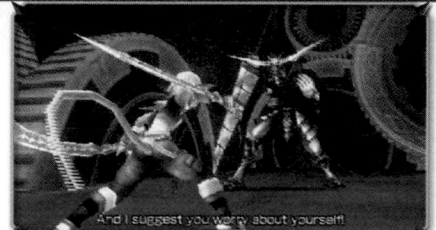

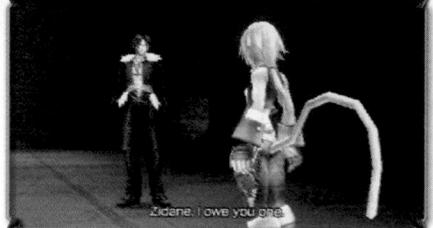

DP EFFICIENCY ROUTE

The first order of business here is to defeat battle piece ❹, which opens a route to the exit near the top of the level. Travel along the right edge after that, defeating battle pieces ❶, ❷, and ❸ on the way.

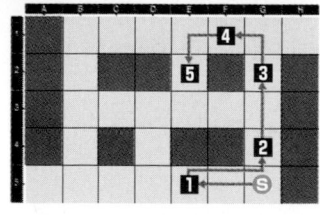

BATTLE PIECE DATA

1 — IMITATION DESPOT

LEVEL	7	RANK	F

BEHAVIOR	Evader
DP CHANCE	BRV Break within 10 seconds (DP+1)
BATTLE MAP	World of Darkness
SUMMONSTONE	–

STATS	HP	1364	CP	337	BRV	84
	ATK	17	DEF	19	LUK	13

EQUIPMENT	WEAPON	–
	HANDS	–

HEAD	Charred Helm	BODY	–

SPOILS	GIL	112	EXP	954

ACCESSORIES	Arcane Incense, Tenacious Attacker, Glutton, Gaia Ring, [EX] EX Gauge ≥ 70% x6

2 — DELUSORY WARLOCK

LEVEL	15	RANK	C

BEHAVIOR	Valiant
DP CHANCE	Win battle (DP+1)
BATTLE MAP	World of Darkness
SUMMONSTONE	–

STATS	HP	1848*	CP	347	BRV	176*
	ATK	25*	DEF	27*	LUK	17

EQUIPMENT	WEAPON	[Rank 3]
	HANDS	[Rank 2]

HEAD	[Rank 4]	BODY	[Rank 2]

SPOILS	GIL	112	EXP	0

3 — TRANSIENT LION

LEVEL	2	RANK	G

BEHAVIOR	Aggressive
DP CHANCE	Win within 10 seconds (DP+1)
BATTLE MAP	Ultimecia's Castle
SUMMONSTONE	–

STATS	HP	1061	CP	331	BRV	55
	ATK	11	DEF	13	LUK	11

EQUIPMENT	WEAPON	–
	HANDS	–

HEAD	Charred Helm	BODY	–

SPOILS	GIL	112	EXP	742

4 — FALSE HERO

LEVEL	3	RANK	G

BEHAVIOR	Standby
DP CHANCE	Wall Rush within 10 seconds (DP+1)
BATTLE MAP	World of Darkness
SUMMONSTONE	–

STATS	HP	1121	CP	332	BRV	107
	ATK	13	DEF	16	LUK	11

EQUIPMENT	WEAPON	–
	HANDS	–

HEAD	–	BODY	–

SPOILS	GIL	112	EXP	784

* Denotes use of the base value (for stats that vary).

5 — CAPRICIOUS REAPER

LEVEL	8	RANK	F

BEHAVIOR	Evader
DP CHANCE	–
BATTLE MAP	Kefka's Tower
SUMMONSTONE	–

STATS	HP	1424	CP	338	BRV	136
	ATK	17	DEF	11	LUK	14

EQUIPMENT	WEAPON	–
	HANDS	Cracked Shield

HEAD	–	BODY	–

SPOILS	GIL	112	EXP	996

ACCESSORIES	Arcane Incense, Gaia Ring, Gravitorb, Pearl Necklace, [EX] EX Core Present x2, [EX] EX Gauge ≥ 70% x4

6 — GARLAND

LEVEL	9	RANK	F

BEHAVIOR	Vicious
DP CHANCE	–
BATTLE MAP	Ultimecia's Castle
SUMMONSTONE	–

STATS	HP	1913	CP	339	BRV	141
	ATK	32	DEF	20	LUK	14

EQUIPMENT	WEAPON	Light Axe
	HANDS	–

HEAD	–	BODY	Bronze Armor

SPOILS	GIL	252	EXP	2970

ACCESSORIES	Muscle Belt x2, Champion Belt, [Position] Near Opponent x2, [Combat] Attacking Bravery

DESTINY ODYSSEY IX-4

STARTING DP	5	MAX FINISHING	5 (+2 after 3-star rating)	ENGAGEMENTS	5 (+1 after 3-star rating)

A few aspects of this level only reveal themselves after you've already beaten Destiny Odyssey with a sufficient star rating. After a 2-star rating, a Rosetta Stone can be found at the bottom right corner of the level. After a 3-star rating, an ultimate battle piece that represents a nasty Kuja manikin appears near the starting point. This foe uses Kuja's HP attacks repeatedly, so beware of this piece whenever you move near it. Be ready to dodge backward or laterally. Finally, after a 4-star rating, a treasure chest containing Mythril appears in the upper right corner of the stage. Watch out for the red battle piece near the exit, as it engages you whether or not you had any interest in battle!

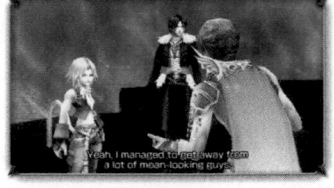

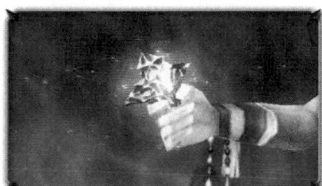

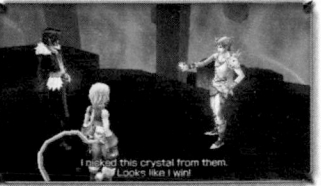

MAP

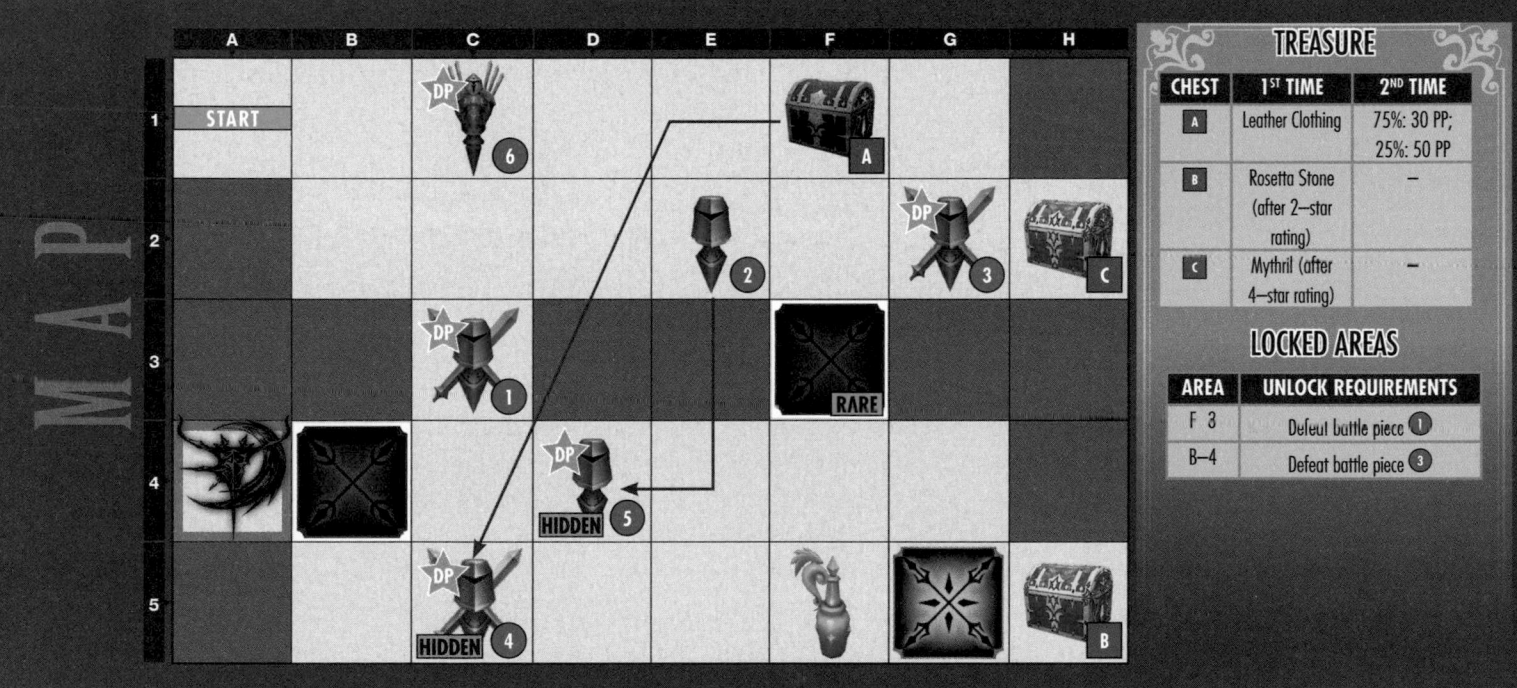

TREASURE

CHEST	1ST TIME	2ND TIME
A	Leather Clothing	75%: 30 PP; 25%: 50 PP
B	Rosetta Stone (after 2-star rating)	—
C	Mythril (after 4-star rating)	—

LOCKED AREAS

AREA	UNLOCK REQUIREMENTS
F 3	Defeat battle piece ①
B—4	Defeat battle piece ③

DP EFFICIENCY ROUTE

Maximum DP is only possible here after a 3-star rating, and requires quite a circuitous route. From the start, move between battle piece ① and rare battle piece ⑥, chaining them for their DP Chances. The Locked Area at F-3 then disappears, allowing you to slip through to grid square F-2. From here, open the treasure chest, which consequently spawns battle piece ④ while starting a chain with pieces ② and ③. After the battles, head to D-5 to chain battle pieces ④ and ⑤. The DP Chance against battle piece ④ requires a fast EX Burst, so build a full EX Gauge during previous fights.

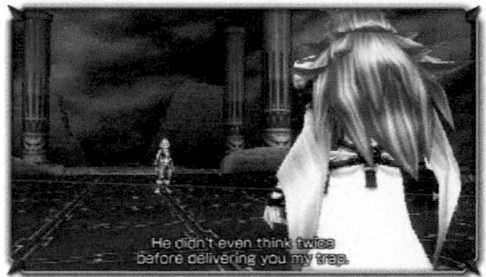

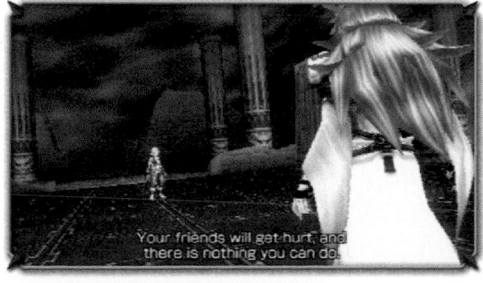

BATTLE PIECE DATA

1 TRANSIENT LION

LEVEL	9	RANK	F

BEHAVIOR	Evader
DP CHANCE	Win without taking damage (DP+1)
BATTLE MAP	Dream's End
SUMMONSTONE	–

STATS	HP	1485	CP	339	BRV	95
	ATK	18	DEF	12	LUK	14

EQUIPMENT	WEAPON	–
	HANDS	Cracked Shield

HEAD	Charred Helm	BODY	–

SPOILS	GIL	140	EXP	742

ACCESSORIES	Arcane Incense, Tenacious Attacker, Glutton, Gaia Ring, [EX] EX Gauge ≥ 70% x6

2 TRANSIENT WITCH

LEVEL	9	RANK	G

BEHAVIOR	Standby
DP CHANCE	–
BATTLE MAP	Kefka's Tower
SUMMONSTONE	Shiva

STATS	HP	1485	CP	339	BRV	141
	ATK	20	DEF	18	LUK	14

EQUIPMENT	WEAPON	–
	HANDS	–

HEAD	–	BODY	–

SPOILS	GIL	140	EXP	742

3 FALLACIOUS TREE

LEVEL	9	RANK	F

BEHAVIOR	Evader
DP CHANCE	Keep foe from getting EX Cores (DP+1)
BATTLE MAP	World of Darkness
SUMMONSTONE	–

STATS	HP	823	CP	358	BRV	141
	ATK	19	DEF	22	LUK	14

EQUIPMENT	WEAPON	–
	HANDS	–

HEAD	–	BODY	Rusted Armor

SPOILS	GIL	140	EXP	742

ACCESSORIES	Arcane Incense, Tenacious Attacker, Glutton, Gaia Ring, [EX] EX Gauge ≥ 70% x6

4 CAPRICIOUS REAPER

LEVEL	11	RANK	F

BEHAVIOR	Aggressive
DP CHANCE	EX Burst within 10 seconds (DP+1)
BATTLE MAP	Ultimecia's Castle
SUMMONSTONE	–

STATS	HP	944	CP	342	BRV	153
	ATK	20	DEF	22	LUK	15

EQUIPMENT	WEAPON	–
	HANDS	–

HEAD	–	BODY	Rusted Armor

SPOILS	GIL	140	EXP	803

ACCESSORIES	Arcane Incense, Gaia Ring, Gravitorb, Pearl Necklace, [EX] EX Core Present x2, [EX] EX Gauge ≥ 70% x4

5 EPHEMERAL PHANTOM

LEVEL	4	RANK	G

BEHAVIOR	Normal
DP CHANCE	Win within 10 seconds (DP+1)
BATTLE MAP	Dream's End
SUMMONSTONE	–

STATS	HP	1182	CP	333	BRV	113
	ATK	16	DEF	16	LUK	12

EQUIPMENT	WEAPON	–
	HANDS	–

HEAD	–	BODY	–

SPOILS	GIL	140	EXP	591

6 CAPRICIOUS REAPER

LEVEL	25	RANK	B

BEHAVIOR	Vicious
DP CHANCE	Win battle (DP+2)
BATTLE MAP	Order's Sanctuary
SUMMONSTONE	–

STATS	HP	2454*	CP	359	BRV	234*
	ATK	50	DEF	50	LUK	22

EQUIPMENT	WEAPON	Rod of Wisdom
	HANDS	Silver Bangles

HEAD	Hairpin	BODY	[Rank 4]

SPOILS	GIL	336	EXP	0

ACCESSORIES	Arcane Incense, Tenacious Attacker, Glutton, Gaia Ring, [EX] EX Gauge ≥ 70% x6

* Denotes use of the base value (for stats that vary).

DESTINY ODYSSEY — IX-5

A veritable gauntlet of Locked Areas and battle pieces must be braved to reach the Stigma of Chaos here, followed by a boss fight with Kuja. Ultimate battle piece **7** appears after a 3-star rating. This evil copy of Zidane is formidable, with a balanced attack and the Alexander Summonstone. If this foe inflicts Break, it will use Alexander to freeze its bravery at a very high level. Obviously, this is extremely dangerous, so play cautiously. A summon like Magic Pot also helps, as you

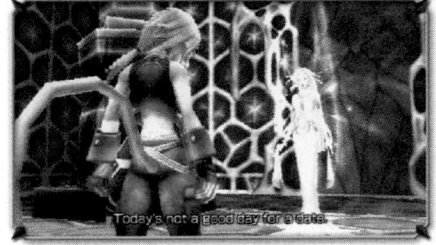
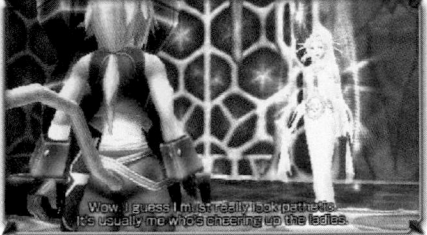

can simply copy the manikin's high bravery and go toe-to-toe with high-stakes attacks. Kuja, the boss, uses a different summoning approach—if his bravery gets low, such as just after hitting you with an HP attack, he'll use Carbuncle to match your bravery with his low total.

MAP

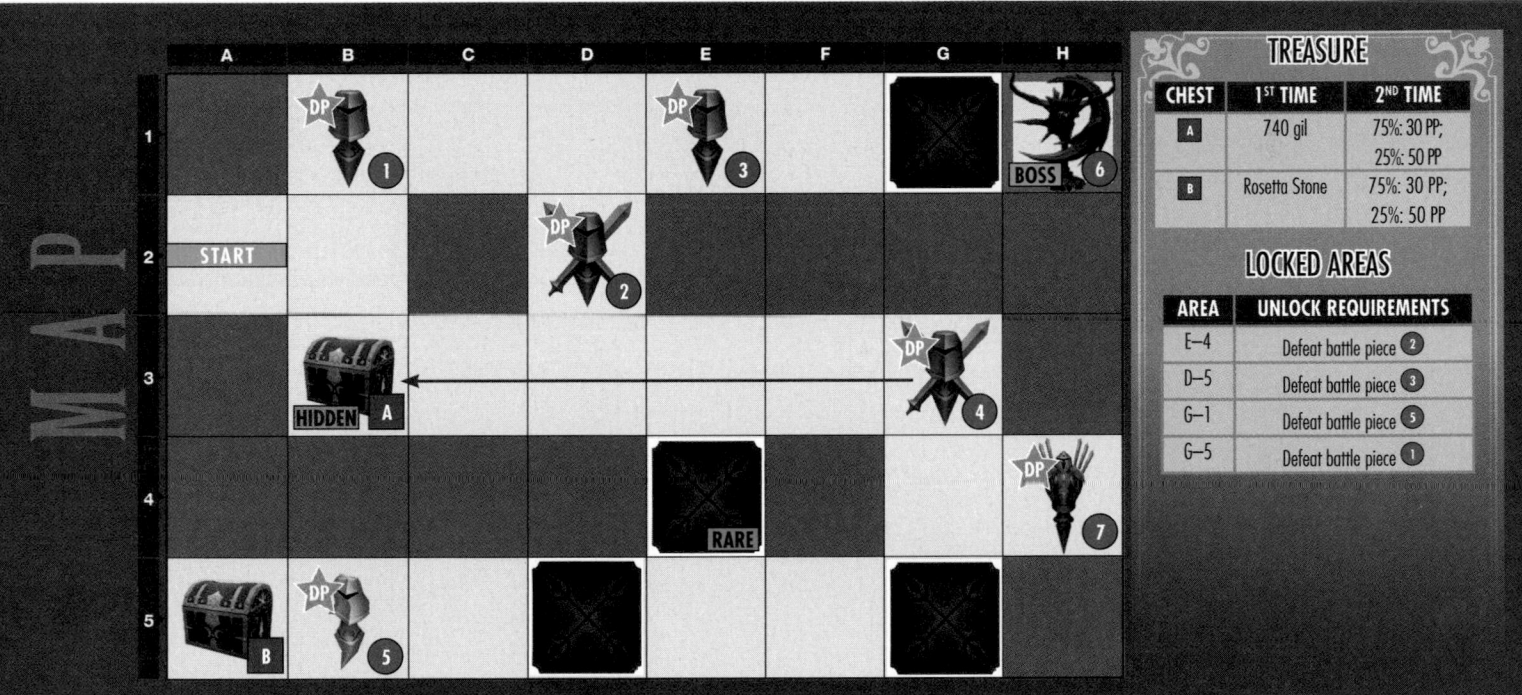

TREASURE

CHEST	1ST TIME	2ND TIME
A	740 gil	75%: 30 PP; 25%: 50 PP
B	Rosetta Stone	75%: 30 PP; 25%: 50 PP

LOCKED AREAS

AREA	UNLOCK REQUIREMENTS
E—4	Defeat battle piece ②
D—5	Defeat battle piece ③
G—1	Defeat battle piece ⑤
G—5	Defeat battle piece ①

DP EFFICIENCY ROUTE

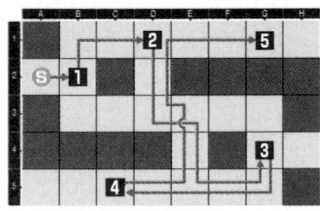

Another roundabout route is required for all the DP Chances in this level. After tackling battle piece ①, chain battle pieces ② and ③. Not only do all these pieces have DP Chances, but they also open up crucial Locked Areas lower in the stage. Head through the newly opened areas to grid square G-4, where you can chain battle pieces ④ and ⑦ (after a 3-star rating). Now there's just one stop left before the boss—battle piece ⑤, for the final DP Chance.

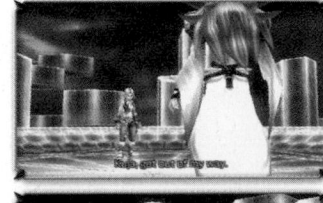
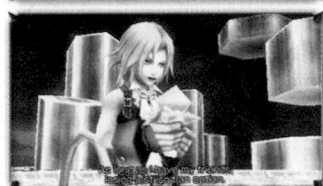
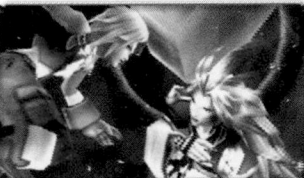
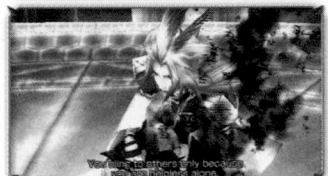

BATTLE PIECE DATA

1 — COUNTERFEIT WRAITH

LEVEL	5	RANK	G

BEHAVIOR	Blocker
DP CHANCE	Win within 10 seconds (DP+1)
BATTLE MAP	Ultimecia's Castle
SUMMONSTONE	Titan

STATS	HP	1242	CP	354	BRV	72
	ATK	14	DEF	8	LUK	12

EQUIPMENT	WEAPON	—
	HANDS	Cracked Shield

HEAD	Charred Helm	BODY	—

SPOILS	GIL	168	EXP	496

2 — IMITATION DESPOT

LEVEL	10	RANK	E

BEHAVIOR	Blocker
DP CHANCE	Win without taking damage (DP+1)
BATTLE MAP	Dream's End
SUMMONSTONE	

STATS	HP	1545	CP	341	BRV	101
	ATK	20	DEF	22	LUK	15

EQUIPMENT	WEAPON	—
	HANDS	

HEAD	Charred Helm	BODY	—

SPOILS	GIL	168	EXP	618

ACCESSORIES	Arcane Incense, Tenacious Attacker, Glutton, Gaia Ring, [EX] EX Gauge ≥ 70% x6

3 — EPHEMERAL PHANTOM

LEVEL	6	RANK	G

BEHAVIOR	Blocker
DP CHANCE	Keep foe from getting EX Cores (DP+1)
BATTLE MAP	Crystal World
SUMMONSTONE	Malboro

STATS	HP	1303	CP	336	BRV	78
	ATK	18	DEF	18	LUK	13

EQUIPMENT	WEAPON	—
	HANDS	

HEAD	Charred Helm	BODY	—

SPOILS	GIL	168	EXP	521

4 — FALLACIOUS TREE

LEVEL	11	RANK	E

BEHAVIOR	Blocker
DP CHANCE	BRV Break within 10 seconds (DP+1)
BATTLE MAP	Kefka's Tower
SUMMONSTONE	—

STATS	HP	1606	CP	360	BRV	153
	ATK	21	DEF	24	LUK	15

EQUIPMENT	WEAPON	—
	HANDS	

HEAD	—	BODY	—

SPOILS	GIL	168	EXP	642

ACCESSORIES	Arcane Incense, Tenacious Attacker, Glutton, Gaia Ring, [EX] EX Gauge ≥ 70% x6

5 — DELUSORY KNIGHT

LEVEL	6	RANK	B

BEHAVIOR	Aggressive
DP CHANCE	Critical hit within 10 seconds (DP+1)
BATTLE MAP	World of Darkness
SUMMONSTONE	

STATS	HP	1	CP	336	BRV	136
	ATK	15	DEF	9	LUK	13

EQUIPMENT	WEAPON	—
	HANDS	Cracked Shield

HEAD	Mythril Helm	BODY	Rusted Armor

SPOILS	GIL	168	EXP	2606

ACCESSORIES	Gaia Ring, [BRV] No BRV Damage x3, The Rotten

6 — KUJA

LEVEL	14	RANK	E

BEHAVIOR	Conservative
DP CHANCE	—
BATTLE MAP	Crystal World
SUMMONSTONE	Carbuncle

STATS	HP	2268	CP	345	BRV	265
	ATK	31	DEF	26	LUK	17

EQUIPMENT	WEAPON	Guard Stick
	HANDS	—

HEAD	Plumed Hat	BODY	Cotton Robes

SPOILS	GIL	336	EXP	4470

ACCESSORIES	Earring x2, Star Earring, [Position] Far from Opponent x2

7 — CAPRICIOUS THIEF

LEVEL	28	RANK	B

BEHAVIOR	Tactician
DP CHANCE	Win battle (DP+2)
BATTLE MAP	Crystal World
SUMMONSTONE	Alexander

STATS	HP	2636*	CP	362	BRV	251*
	ATK	36*	DEF	51*	LUK	24

EQUIPMENT	WEAPON	[Rank 4]
	HANDS	Silver Bangles

HEAD	[Rank 5]	BODY	Poncho

SPOILS	GIL	336	EXP	0

ACCESSORIES	Arcane Incense, Tenacious Attacker, Glutton, Gaia Ring, [EX] EX Gauge ≥ 70% x6

* Denotes use of the base value (for stats that vary).

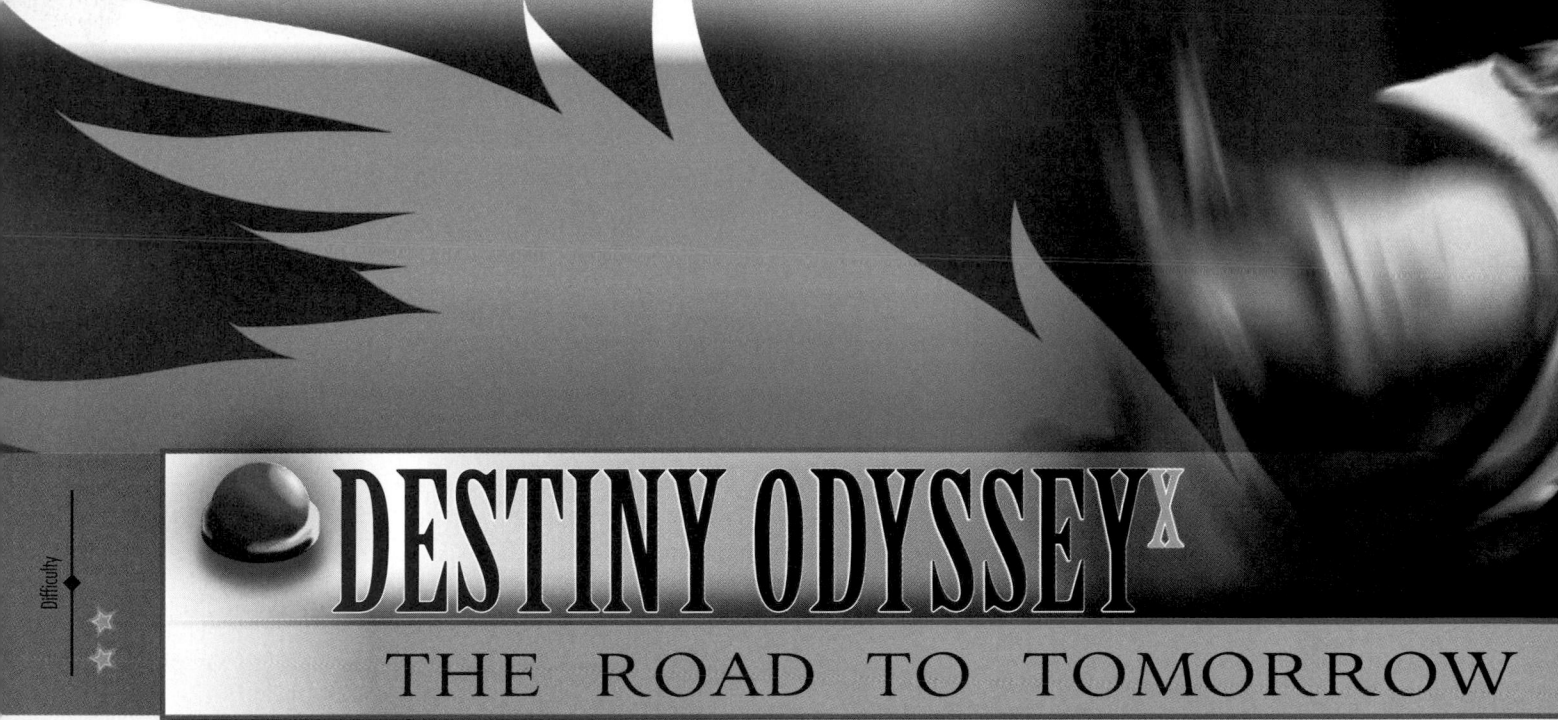

DESTINY ODYSSEY X
THE ROAD TO TOMORROW

Story Mode

Destiny Odyssey X

[The Road to Tomorrow]
Different from bonds and dreams,
there is only one reason he fights...

Difficulty ★★

Tidus, the young man with the heart of an unflinching ace—

Traveling in search of his crystal,
he spurs on his companions with his cheerful disposition.
But his eyes were only on one man's back—
his father, Jecht—
now an enemy sided with Chaos.

Tidus must someday break clear
of his father's giant shadow...

REWARDS

At the end of each level, rewards are available if you finish with a positive number of Destiny Points, or DP. This walkthrough includes miniature level maps that indicate the most efficient route to take through a given level, in order to maximize DP.

LEVEL COMPLETION

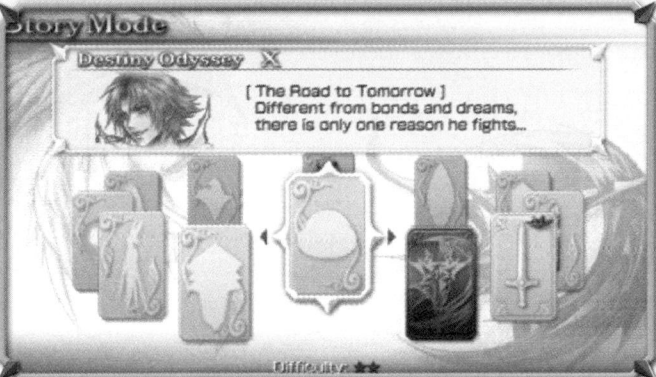

REMAINING DP		1ST TIME		2ND TIME
7		Rosetta Stone		300 PP
6		Winged Helm		200 PP
5		Barbut		120 PP
4		Behemoth		80 PP
3		1000 gil		50 PP
2		600 gil		30 PP
1		300 gil		20 PP
0		100 gil		10 PP

At the end of each set of levels, you'll receive rewards based on your performance. Story Points, or SP, are awarded after each level based on remaining DP, HP, and the number of engagements undertaken. Points are penalized for retries, or for a DP total that dips into negatives. If you miss out on a desired bonus on the first playthrough, don't worry—SP is cumulative across multiple playthroughs.

DESTINY ODYSSEY X COMPLETION

STAR RATING		SP REQUIRED		AWARD
★		100		New skill
★★		200		Special areas unlocked
★★★		300		Rare battle pieces spawned
★★★★		400		Rare treasure chests spawned
—		500 SP, then every 500 SP extra		100 PP

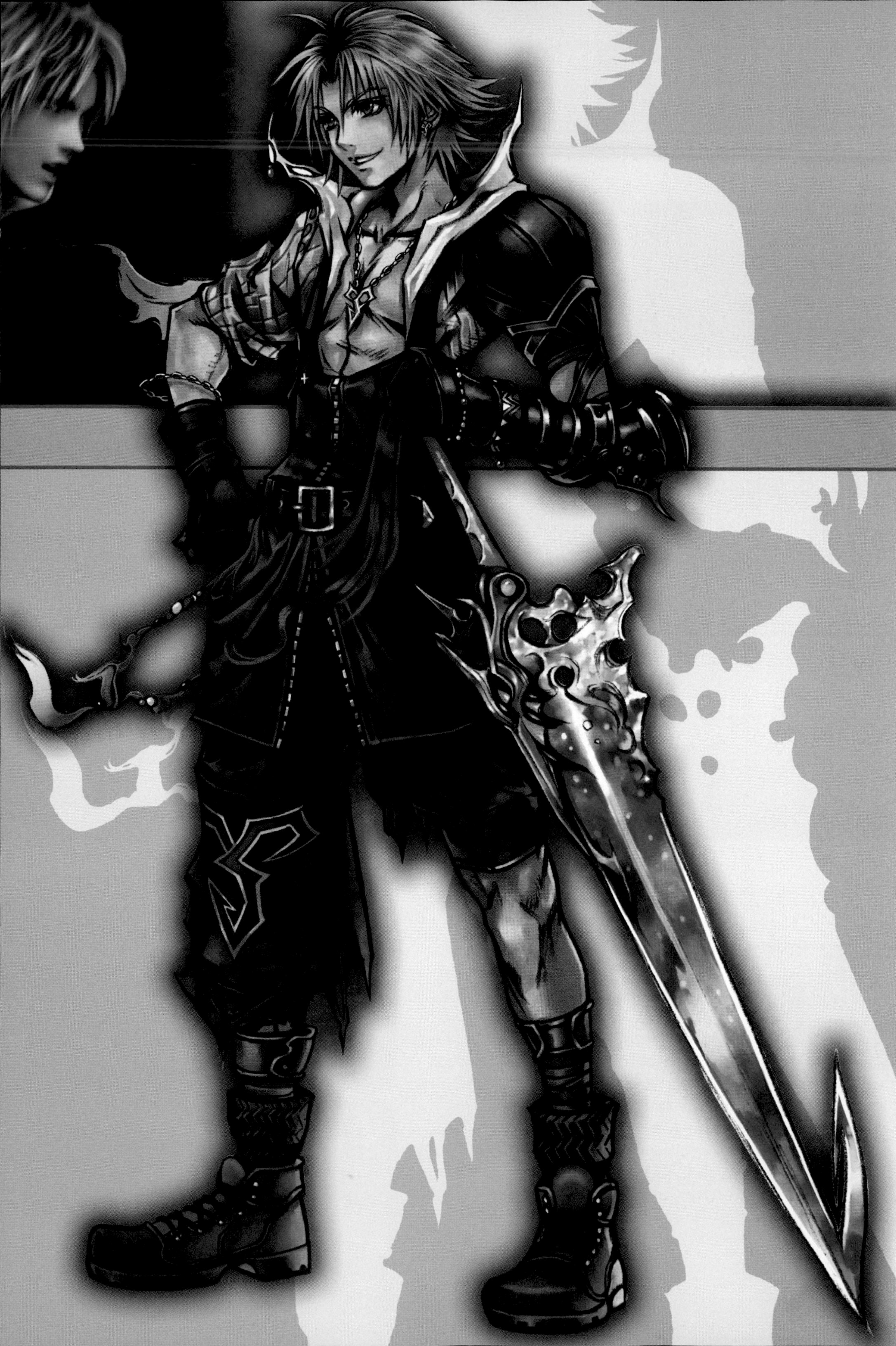

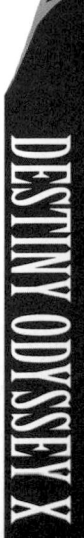

DESTINY ODYSSEY X

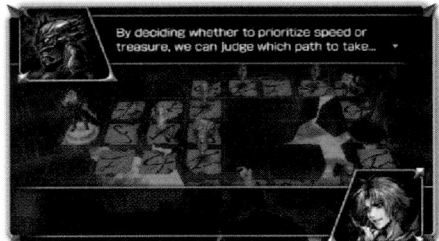

By deciding whether to prioritize speed or treasure, we can judge which path to take...

Hunting for his father with Firion and Cecil doesn't come naturally to Tidus, for obvious reasons. Fortunately, Cecil understands the difficulties of a struggle with kin. Tidus's levels have a high number of encounters, but the manikins are mostly weak, and don't yield much EXP. There are also no Locked Areas—what you see is what you get. You can choose between simply taking a straight path to the Stigma of Chaos or clearing out all the battle pieces on a level to build AP, EXP, and gil.

MAP

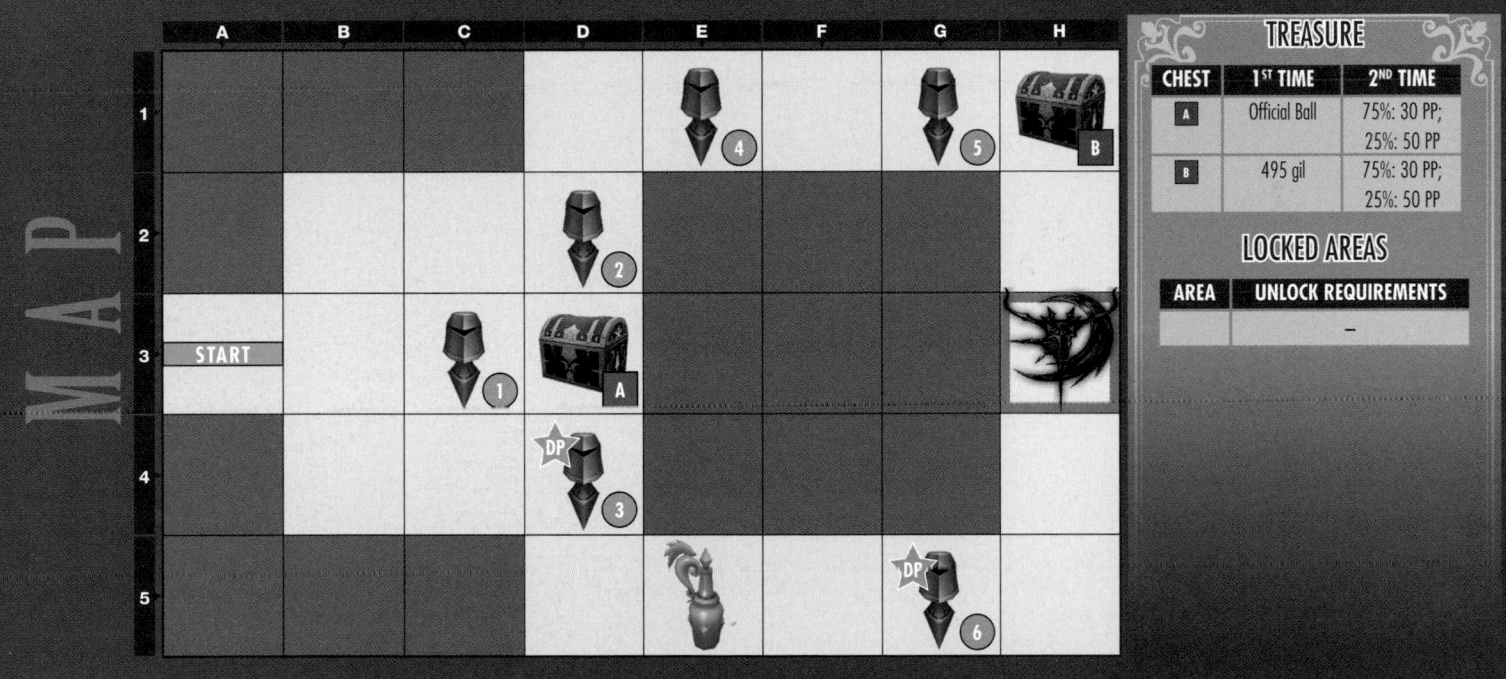

CHEST	1ST TIME	2ND TIME
A	Official Ball	75%: 30 PP; 25%: 50 PP
B	495 gil	75%: 30 PP; 25%: 50 PP

LOCKED AREAS

AREA	UNLOCK REQUIREMENTS
	–

DP EFFICIENCY ROUTE

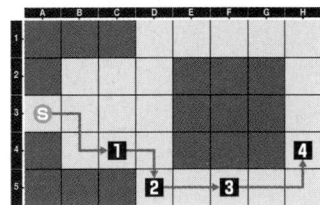

Each level of Tidus's story has two distinct routes: one with more DP Chances, and another with more engagements and easier access to treasure. Whenever you are going to take the longer route, you might as well clear the whole stage. When going for maximum DP, follow the routes listed here. On this stage, there is no way to avoid consuming the Potion along the lower route. Score both DP chances around it, then head to the Stigma of Chaos, clearing the level. Be sure to save EX Force for the last battle piece at G-5, since this DP Chance requires an EX Burst within 10 seconds.

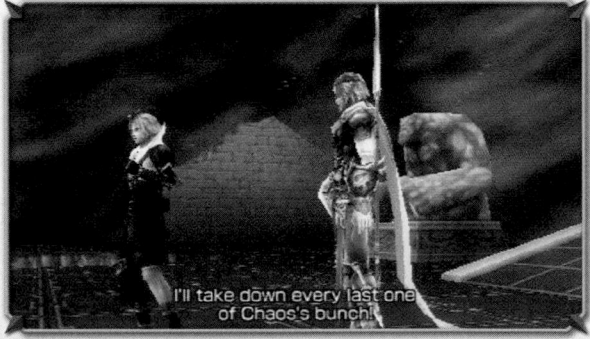

I'll take down every last one of Chaos's bunch!

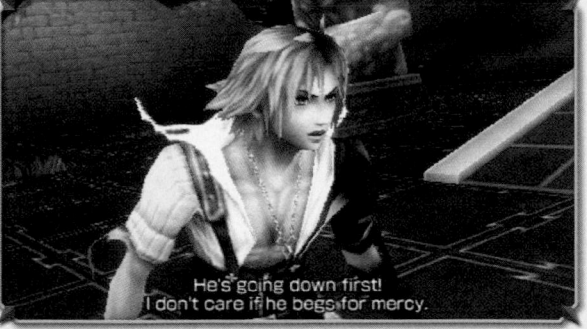

He's going down first! I don't care if he begs for mercy.

BATTLE PIECE DATA

1 EPHEMERAL VISION
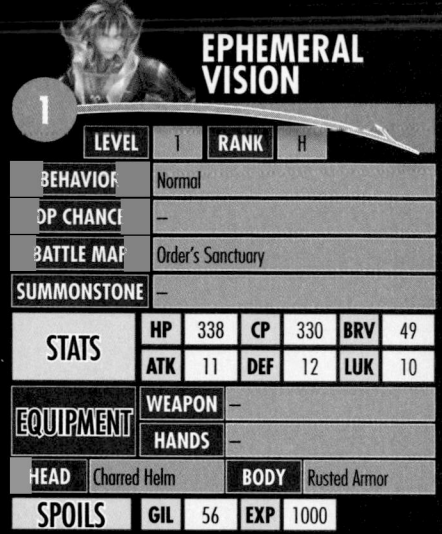

LEVEL	1	RANK	H

BEHAVIOR	Normal
DP CHANCE	—
BATTLE MAP	Order's Sanctuary
SUMMONSTONE	—

STATS	HP	338	CP	330	BRV	49
	ATK	11	DEF	12	LUK	10

EQUIPMENT	WEAPON	—
	HANDS	—

HEAD	Charred Helm	BODY	Rusted Armor

SPOILS	GIL	56	EXP	1000

2 COUNTERFEIT YOUTH

LEVEL	1	RANK	H

BEHAVIOR	Aggressive
DP CHANCE	—
BATTLE MAP	Order's Sanctuary
SUMMONSTONE	—

STATS	HP	338	CP	350	BRV	49
	ATK	8	DEF	12	LUK	10

EQUIPMENT	WEAPON	—
	HANDS	—

HEAD	Charred Helm	BODY	Rusted Armor

SPOILS	GIL	56	EXP	1000

3 FALLACIOUS WANDERER

LEVEL	1	RANK	H

BEHAVIOR	Tricky
DP CHANCE	Wall Rush within 10 seconds (DP+1)
BATTLE MAP	Lunar Subterrane
SUMMONSTONE	—

STATS	HP	338	CP	350	BRV	95
	ATK	11	DEF	12	LUK	10

EQUIPMENT	WEAPON	—
	HANDS	—

HEAD	—	BODY	Rusted Armor

SPOILS	GIL	56	EXP	1000

4 IMAGINARY SOLDIER
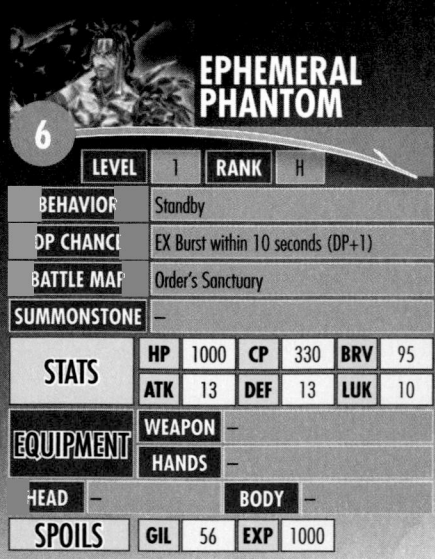

LEVEL	2	RANK	H

BEHAVIOR	Tricky
DP CHANCE	—
BATTLE MAP	Lunar Subterrane
SUMMONSTONE	—

STATS	HP	399	CP	331	BRV	65
	ATK	12	DEF	14	LUK	11

EQUIPMENT	WEAPON	—
	HANDS	—

HEAD	Charred Helm	BODY	Rusted Armor

SPOILS	GIL	56	EXP	1061

5 FALSE HERO
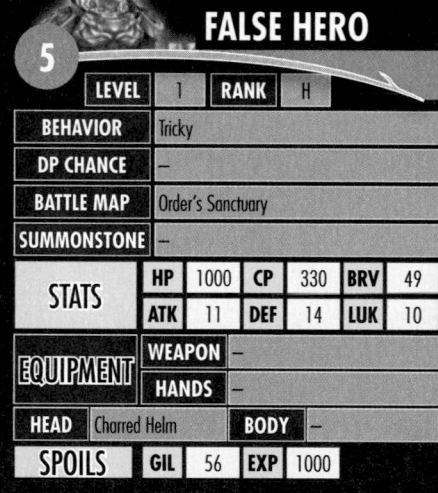

LEVEL	1	RANK	H

BEHAVIOR	Tricky
DP CHANCE	—
BATTLE MAP	Order's Sanctuary
SUMMONSTONE	—

STATS	HP	1000	CP	330	BRV	49
	ATK	11	DEF	14	LUK	10

EQUIPMENT	WEAPON	—
	HANDS	—

HEAD	Charred Helm	BODY	—

SPOILS	GIL	56	EXP	1000

6 EPHEMERAL PHANTOM

LEVEL	1	RANK	H

BEHAVIOR	Standby
DP CHANCE	EX Burst within 10 seconds (DP+1)
BATTLE MAP	Order's Sanctuary
SUMMONSTONE	—

STATS	HP	1000	CP	330	BRV	95
	ATK	13	DEF	13	LUK	10

EQUIPMENT	WEAPON	—
	HANDS	—

HEAD	—	BODY	—

SPOILS	GIL	56	EXP	1000

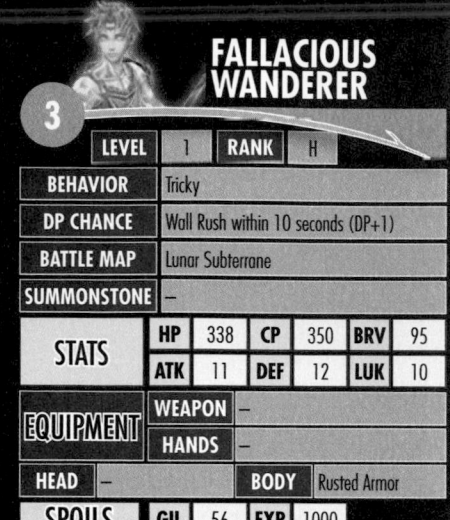

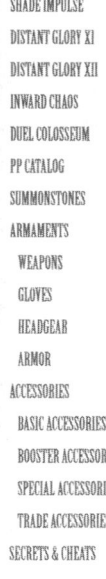

DESTINY ODYSSEY X

DESTINY ODYSSEY

STARTING DP	MAX FINISHING	ENGAGEMENTS
4	4	8

Both treasure chests here hold gear that you probably already have, unless Tidus's Destiny Odyssey is the first one that you chose to tackle. Your route selection, then, is mostly dependent on whether or not you want to go for DP Chances—there are more on the route to the right. After a 2-star rating is achieved on prior runs, the Magus Sisters Summonstone also becomes available here.

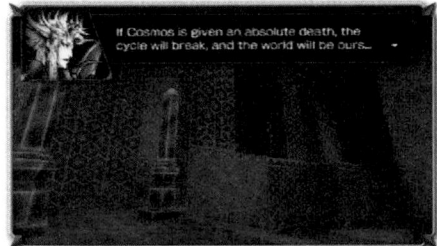

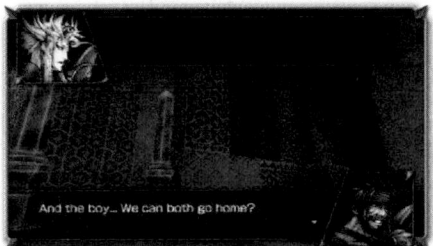

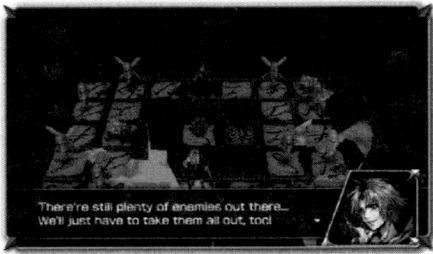

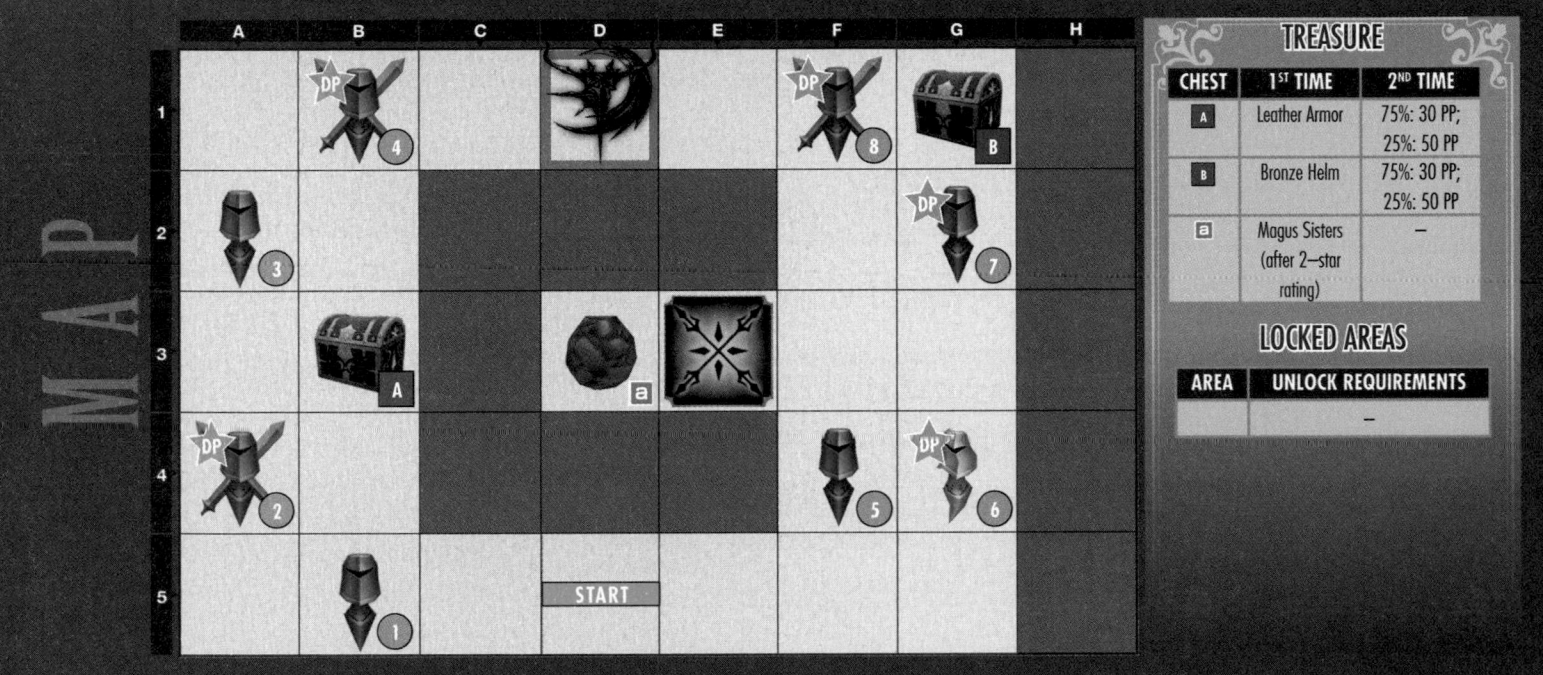

TREASURE

CHEST	1ST TIME	2ND TIME
A	Leather Armor	75%: 30 PP; 25%: 50 PP
B	Bronze Helm	75%: 30 PP; 25%: 50 PP
a	Magus Sisters (after 2—star rating)	—

LOCKED AREAS

AREA	UNLOCK REQUIREMENTS
	—

DP EFFICIENCY ROUTE

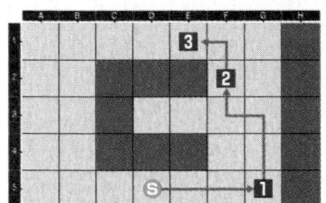

Engage the battle piece at G-4 before moving up to chain the battle pieces around treasure chest **B**. Scoring a critical hit against battle piece **6** right away can be tricky, since you won't have a prior chance to build up EX Force here to ensure critical hits in EX Mode. Furthermore, this foe starts out with 1 HP, so going for a quick HP attack followed by a bravery attack while your bravery recovers (which is a guaranteed critical hit) is also out. Instead, you must try to block one of the manikin's bravery attacks, then strike back while the fiend staggers.

BATTLE PIECE DATA

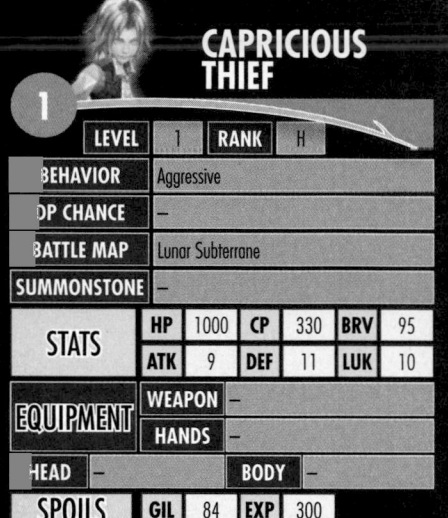

1 CAPRICIOUS THIEF

LEVEL	1	RANK	H
BEHAVIOR	Aggressive		
DP CHANCE	—		
BATTLE MAP	Lunar Subterrane		
SUMMONSTONE	—		

STATS	HP	1000	CP	330	BRV	95
	ATK	9	DEF	11	LUK	10

EQUIPMENT	WEAPON	—
	HANDS	—

HEAD	—	BODY	—

SPOILS	GIL	84	EXP	300

2 IMAGINARY SOLDIER

LEVEL	4	RANK	G*
BEHAVIOR	Aggressive		
DP CHANCE	Win without losing HP (DP+1)		
BATTLE MAP	Order's Sanctuary		
SUMMONSTONE	—		

STATS	HP	1182	CP	333	BRV	140
	ATK	14	DEF	9	LUK	12

EQUIPMENT	WEAPON	—
	HANDS	Cracked Shield

HEAD	Knight Helm	BODY	—

SPOILS	GIL	84	EXP	354

ACCESSORIES	Elven Mantle, Spirit Stanchion, Battle Boots, Mindcrush, [HP] HP ≤ 40% x3, [HP] Near Death x3

3 FALLACIOUS WANDERER

LEVEL	1	RANK	H
BEHAVIOR	Aggressive		
DP CHANCE	—		
BATTLE MAP	The Rift		
SUMMONSTONE	—		

STATS	HP	1000	CP	350	BRV	95
	ATK	11	DEF	12	LUK	10

EQUIPMENT	WEAPON	—
	HANDS	—

HEAD	—	BODY	—

SPOILS	GIL	84	EXP	300

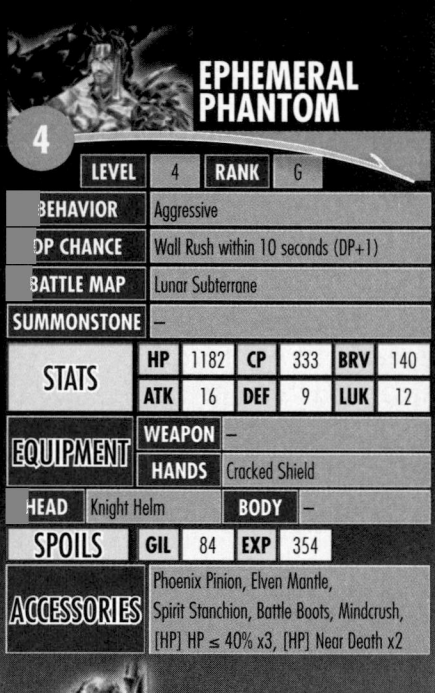

4 EPHEMERAL PHANTOM

LEVEL	4	RANK	G
BEHAVIOR	Aggressive		
DP CHANCE	Wall Rush within 10 seconds (DP+1)		
BATTLE MAP	Lunar Subterrane		
SUMMONSTONE	—		

STATS	HP	1182	CP	333	BRV	140
	ATK	16	DEF	9	LUK	12

EQUIPMENT	WEAPON	—
	HANDS	Cracked Shield

HEAD	Knight Helm	BODY	—

SPOILS	GIL	84	EXP	354

ACCESSORIES	Phoenix Pinion, Elven Mantle, Spirit Stanchion, Battle Boots, Mindcrush, [HP] HP ≤ 40% x3, [HP] Near Death x2

5 FALSE STALWART

LEVEL	1	RANK	H
BEHAVIOR	Standby		
DP CHANCE	—		
BATTLE MAP	Order's Sanctuary		
SUMMONSTONE	—		

STATS	HP	1000	CP	330	BRV	95
	ATK	13	DEF	14	LUK	10

EQUIPMENT	WEAPON	—
	HANDS	—

HEAD	—	BODY	—

SPOILS	GIL	84	EXP	300

8 COUNTERFEIT YOUTH

LEVEL	4	RANK	G
BEHAVIOR	Standby		
DP CHANCE	Win without taking damage (DP+1)		
BATTLE MAP	The Rift		
SUMMONSTONE	—		

STATS	HP	1085	CP	353	BRV	175
	ATK	11	DEF	7	LUK	12

EQUIPMENT	WEAPON	—
	HANDS	Cracked Shield

HEAD	Hairpin	BODY	—

SPOILS	GIL	84	EXP	354

ACCESSORIES	Elven Mantle, Spirit Stanchion, Battle Boots, Mindcrush, [HP] HP ≤ 40% x3, [HP] Near Death x3

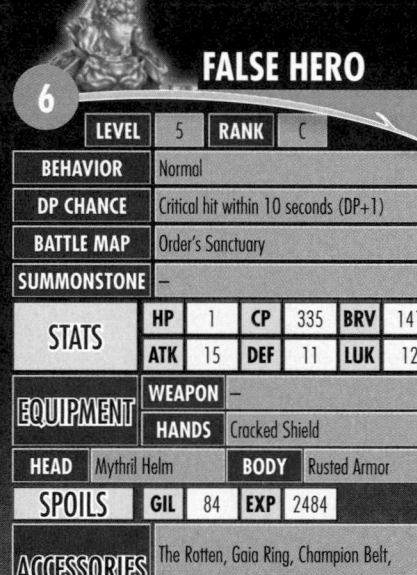

6 FALSE HERO

LEVEL	5	RANK	C
BEHAVIOR	Normal		
DP CHANCE	Critical hit within 10 seconds (DP+1)		
BATTLE MAP	Order's Sanctuary		
SUMMONSTONE	—		

STATS	HP	1	CP	335	BRV	141
	ATK	15	DEF	11	LUK	12

EQUIPMENT	WEAPON	—
	HANDS	Cracked Shield

HEAD	Mythril Helm	BODY	Rusted Armor

SPOILS	GIL	84	EXP	2484

ACCESSORIES	The Rotten, Gaia Ring, Champion Belt, [Position] Near Opponent x5

7 IMITATION LIEGEMAN

LEVEL	1	RANK	H
BEHAVIOR	Tricky		
DP CHANCE	Win within 10 seconds (DP+1)		
BATTLE MAP	Lunar Subterrane		
SUMMONSTONE	—		

STATS	HP	1000	CP	330	BRV	95
	ATK	12	DEF	13	LUK	10

EQUIPMENT	WEAPON	—
	HANDS	

HEAD	—	BODY	—

SPOILS	GIL	84	EXP	300

The expert battle piece at G-5 may be too tough for the first playthrough. This Kefka manikin is very nasty, and despite the large number of encounters in Tidus's chapter, you probably won't be past level 6 or 7 yet. Take the north route through the stage, saving the southern route for return trips, when Tidus is beefier. When you do go after this rough enemy, note that EX Cores show up more frequently during the fight, thanks to one of the accessories the manikin has equipped. During the boss fight against The Emperor, beware his roving Flare attack—that ball of fire seeks you out for a long time.

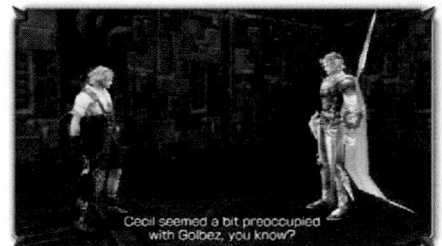

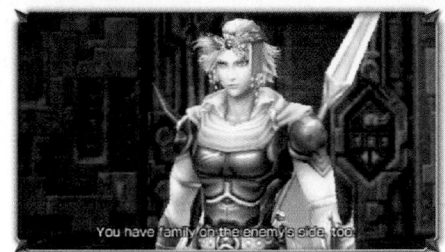

MAP

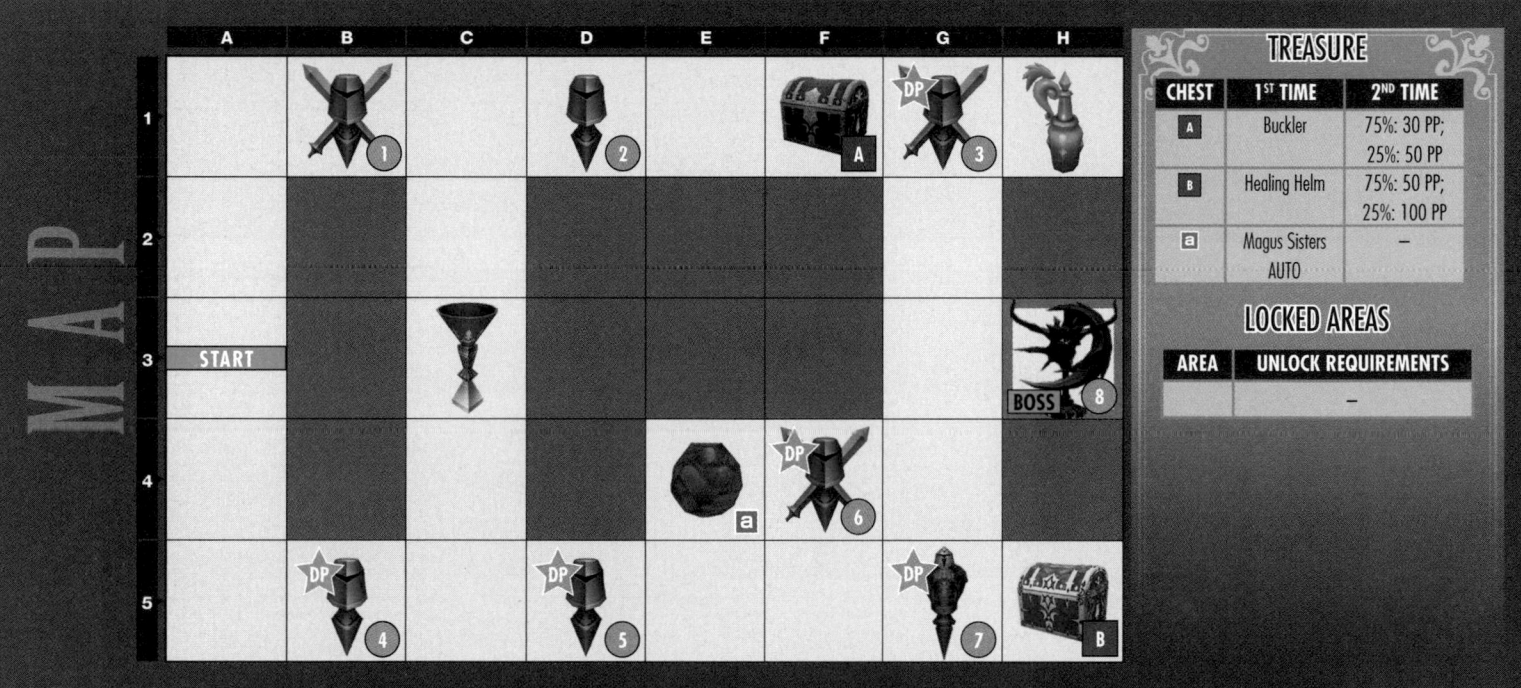

TREASURE

CHEST	1ST TIME	2ND TIME
A	Buckler	75%: 30 PP; 25%: 50 PP
B	Healing Helm	75%: 50 PP; 25%: 100 PP
a	Magus Sisters AUTO	—

LOCKED AREAS

AREA	UNLOCK REQUIREMENTS
	—

DP EFFICIENCY ROUTE

After inflicting BRV Break on battle piece 4 within 10 seconds, spend some time waiting for EX Cores before you win the battle. A full EX Force gauge is invaluable against both battle piece 5 and 6—the former to use EX Mode to ensure critical hits, and the latter to land a quick EX Burst. If you use EX Mode against battle piece 5, you might want to fight battle piece 7 before 6, so you can again collect EX Force in anticipation of the following fight. After clearing these DP Chances, head to the Stigma of Chaos and the boss fight with The Emperor.

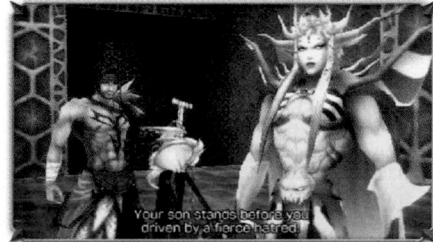

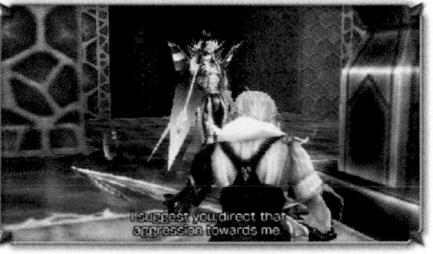

BATTLE PIECE DATA

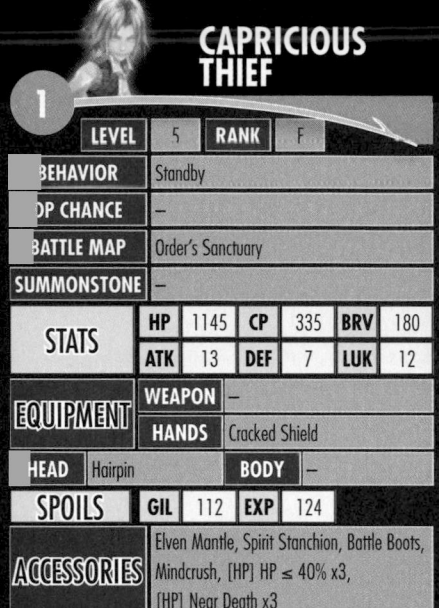

1. CAPRICIOUS THIEF

LEVEL	5	RANK	F

BEHAVIOR	Standby
DP CHANCE	–
BATTLE MAP	Order's Sanctuary
SUMMONSTONE	–

STATS	HP	1145	CP	335	BRV	180
	ATK	13	DEF	7	LUK	12

EQUIPMENT	WEAPON	–
	HANDS	Cracked Shield

HEAD	Hairpin	BODY	–

SPOILS	GIL	112	EXP	124

ACCESSORIES	Elven Mantle, Spirit Stanchion, Battle Boots, Mindcrush, [HP] HP ≤ 40% x3, [HP] Near Death x3

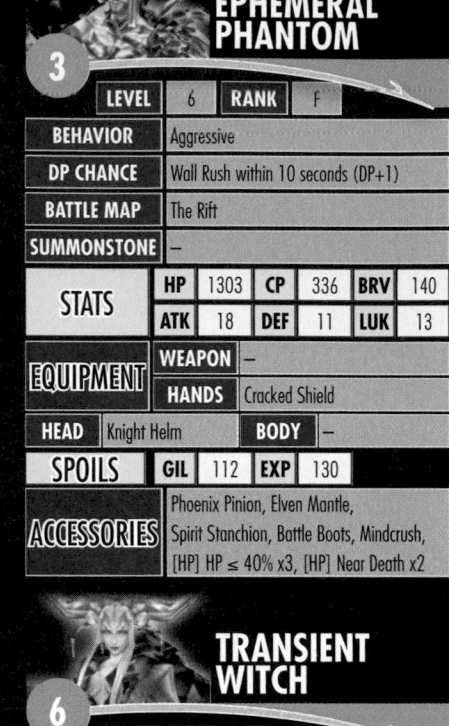

2. COUNTERFEIT WRAITH

LEVEL	2	RANK	G

BEHAVIOR	Standby
DP CHANCE	–
BATTLE MAP	Pandaemonium
SUMMONSTONE	–

STATS	HP	399	CP	351	BRV	101
	ATK	11	DEF	13	LUK	11

EQUIPMENT	WEAPON	–
	HANDS	–

HEAD	–	BODY	Rusted Armor

SPOILS	GIL	112	EXP	106

3. EPHEMERAL PHANTOM

LEVEL	6	RANK	F

BEHAVIOR	Aggressive
DP CHANCE	Wall Rush within 10 seconds (DP+1)
BATTLE MAP	The Rift
SUMMONSTONE	–

STATS	HP	1303	CP	336	BRV	140
	ATK	18	DEF	11	LUK	13

EQUIPMENT	WEAPON	–
	HANDS	Cracked Shield

HEAD	Knight Helm	BODY	–

SPOILS	GIL	112	EXP	130

ACCESSORIES	Phoenix Pinion, Elven Mantle, Spirit Stanchion, Battle Boots, Mindcrush, [HP] HP ≤ 40% x3, [HP] Near Death x2

4. FALLACIOUS WANDERER

LEVEL	2	RANK	G

BEHAVIOR	Normal
DP CHANCE	BRV Break within 10 seconds (DP+1)
BATTLE MAP	Pandaemonium
SUMMONSTONE	–

STATS	HP	1061	CP	351	BRV	55
	ATK	12	DEF	13	LUK	11

EQUIPMENT	WEAPON	–
	HANDS	–

HEAD	Charred Helm	BODY	–

SPOILS	GIL	112	EXP	106

5. IMAGINARY SOLDIER

LEVEL	3	RANK	G

BEHAVIOR	Normal
DP CHANCE	Critical hit within 10 seconds (DP+1)
BATTLE MAP	Order's Sanctuary
SUMMONSTONE	–

STATS	HP	1121	CP	332	BRV	61
	ATK	13	DEF	15	LUK	11

EQUIPMENT	WEAPON	–
	HANDS	–

HEAD	Charred Helm	BODY	–

SPOILS	GIL	112	EXP	112

6. TRANSIENT WITCH

LEVEL	6	RANK	F

BEHAVIOR	Aggressive
DP CHANCE	EX Burst within 10 seconds (DP+1)
BATTLE MAP	The Rift
SUMMONSTONE	–

STATS	HP	1206	CP	336	BRV	186
	ATK	17	DEF	7	LUK	13

EQUIPMENT	WEAPON	–
	HANDS	Cracked Shield

HEAD	Hairpin	BODY	–

SPOILS	GIL	112	EXP	130

ACCESSORIES	Elven Mantle, Spirit Stanchion, Battle Boots, Mindcrush, [HP] HP ≤ 40% x3, [HP] Near Death x3

7. PHANTASMAL HARLEQUIN

LEVEL	14	RANK	C

BEHAVIOR	Conservative
DP CHANCE	Win battle (DP+1)
BATTLE MAP	Lunar Subterrane
SUMMONSTONE	–

STATS	HP	1786*	CP	363	BRV	170*
	ATK	33	DEF	24*	LUK	17

EQUIPMENT	WEAPON	[Rank 2]
	HANDS	Bronze Bangle

HEAD	Hairpin	BODY	[Rank 1]

SPOILS	GIL	112	EXP	2145

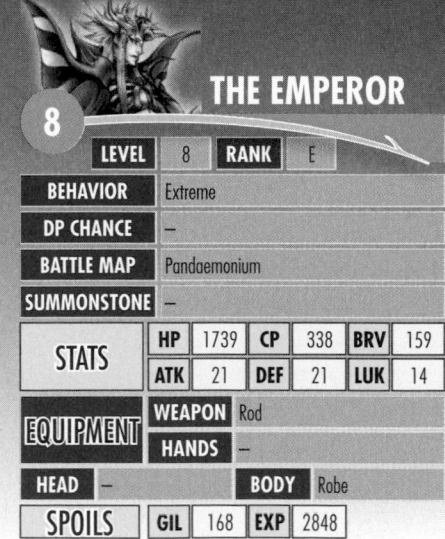

8. THE EMPEROR

LEVEL	8	RANK	E

BEHAVIOR	Extreme
DP CHANCE	–
BATTLE MAP	Pandaemonium
SUMMONSTONE	–

STATS	HP	1739	CP	338	BRV	159
	ATK	21	DEF	21	LUK	14

EQUIPMENT	WEAPON	Rod
	HANDS	–

HEAD	–	BODY	Robe

SPOILS	GIL	168	EXP	2848

* Denotes use of the base value (for stats that vary).

DESTINY ODYSSEY

X-4

STARTING DP	**MAX FINISHING**	**ENGAGEMENTS**
4	5 (+2 after 3-star rating)	8 (+1 after 3-star rating)

Again, this level has two clear routes. The lower path has far more going on once you have cleared Destiny Odyssey X once or twice before and uncovered all the hidden board pieces. After a 2-star rating, you can find a Rosetta Stone in treasure chest **C**. After a 3-star rating, a tough Jecht manikin appears at F-5. This unholy copy of Tidus's dear old dad uses bravery attacks at the beginning of the battle, so block his attacks and counter with bravery attacks of your own. Breaking the manikin's bravery with critical hits in this manner (and perhaps boosting your bravery further with a summon like Ifrit or Behemoth) goes a long way toward defeating this tough opponent. Finally, a rare treasure chest appears right by the Stigma of Chaos after achieving a 4-star rating.

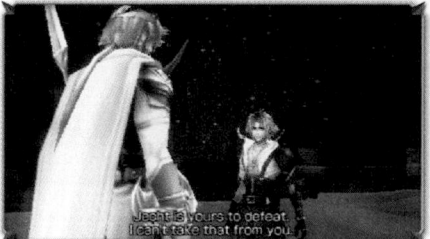

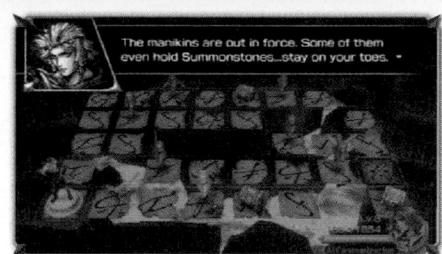

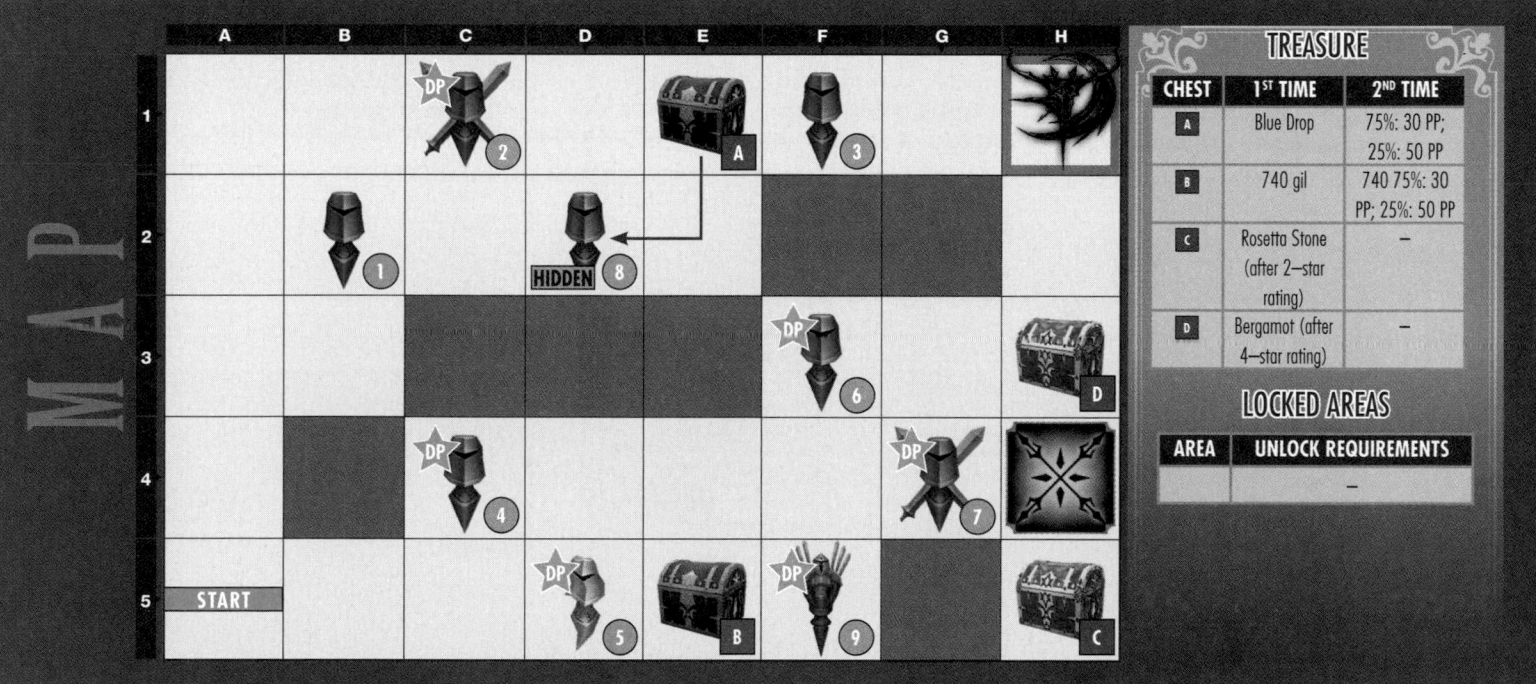

TREASURE

CHEST	1ST TIME	2ND TIME
A	Blue Drop	75%: 30 PP; 25%: 50 PP
B	740 gil	740 75%: 30 PP; 25%: 50 PP
C	Rosetta Stone (after 2–star rating)	–
D	Bergamot (after 4–star rating)	–

LOCKED AREAS

AREA	UNLOCK REQUIREMENTS
	–

DP EFFICIENCY ROUTE

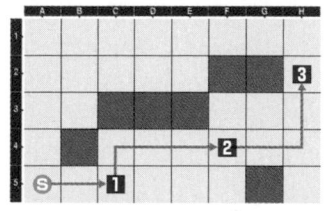

Max DP can only occur on this level either after you have achieved a 3-star rating but before a 4-star rating, or after you've achieved a 4-star rating *and* grabbed the rare treasure chest at H-3. This is because you need the rare battle piece to spawn, but the rare treasure chest must be absent. In either case, chain battle pieces ④ and ⑤, then battle pieces ⑥, ⑦, and ⑨. Save EX Force heading into the fight with battle piece ⑦, so you can enter EX Mode immediately and go for a quick EX Burst. Scoring the DP Chance against ultimate battle piece ⑨ simply requires that you win the fight, which is admittedly a tall order until Tidus is around level 25.

BATTLE PIECE DATA

1. COUNTERFEIT WRAITH

LEVEL	3	RANK	G

BEHAVIOR	Evader
DP CHANCE	—
BATTLE MAP	Kefka's Tower
SUMMONSTONE	—

STATS	HP	1121	CP	352	BRV	107
	ATK	12	DEF	14	LUK	11

EQUIPMENT	WEAPON	—
	HANDS	—

HEAD	—	BODY	—

SPOILS	GIL	140	EXP	0

2. DELUSORY WARLOCK

LEVEL	7	RANK	F

BEHAVIOR	Evader
DP CHANCE	BRV Break within 10 seconds (DP+1)
BATTLE MAP	Pandaemonium
SUMMONSTONE	—

STATS	HP	1364	CP	337	BRV	146
	ATK	17	DEF	12	LUK	13

EQUIPMENT	WEAPON	—
	HANDS	Cracked Shield

HEAD	Knight Helm	BODY	—

SPOILS	GIL	140	EXP	0

ACCESSORIES	Elven Mantle, Spirit Stanchion, Battle Boots, Mindcrush, [HP] HP ≤ 40% x3, [HP] Near Death x3

3. TRANSIENT WITCH

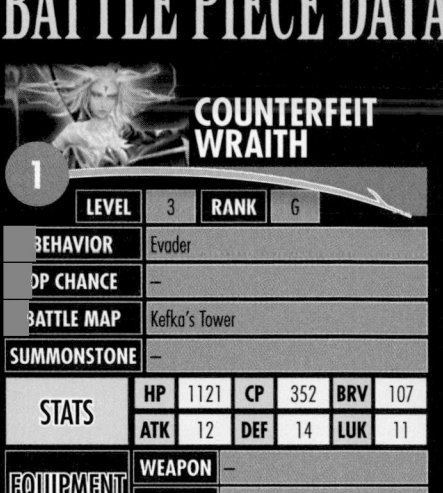

LEVEL	3	RANK	G

BEHAVIOR	Standby
DP CHANCE	—
BATTLE MAP	Lunar Subterrane
SUMMONSTONE	Ultros

STATS	HP	1121	CP	332	BRV	107
	ATK	14	DEF	12	LUK	11

EQUIPMENT	WEAPON	—
	HANDS	—

HEAD	—	BODY	—

SPOILS	GIL	140	EXP	0

4. COUNTERFEIT YOUTH

LEVEL	2	RANK	G

BEHAVIOR	Evader
DP CHANCE	Win within 10 seconds (DP+1)
BATTLE MAP	Lunar Subterrane
SUMMONSTONE	—

STATS	HP	1061	CP	351	BRV	101
	ATK	9	DEF	13	LUK	11

EQUIPMENT	WEAPON	—
	HANDS	—

HEAD	—	BODY	—

SPOILS	GIL	140	EXP	0

5. FALSE HERO

LEVEL	9	RANK	B

BEHAVIOR	Aggressive
DP CHANCE	Wall Rush within 10 seconds (DP+1)
BATTLE MAP	Kefka's Tower
SUMMONSTONE	—

STATS	HP	1	CP	339	BRV	184
	ATK	19	DEF	15	LUK	14

EQUIPMENT	WEAPON	—
	HANDS	Cracked Shield

HEAD	Heavy Helm	BODY	Rusted Armor

SPOILS	GIL	140	EXP	2970

ACCESSORIES	The Rotten,, Gaia Ring, Champion Belt, [Position] Near Opponent x5

6. IMITATION LIEGEMAN

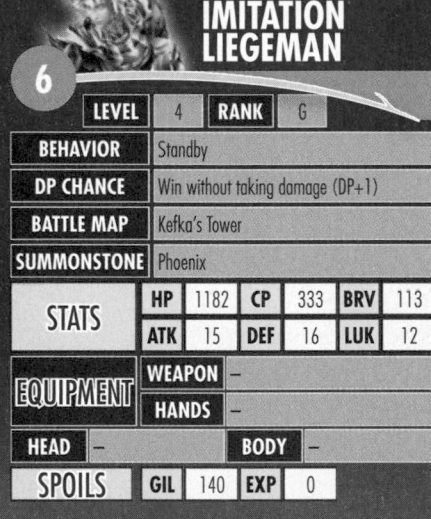

LEVEL	4	RANK	G

BEHAVIOR	Standby
DP CHANCE	Win without taking damage (DP+1)
BATTLE MAP	Kefka's Tower
SUMMONSTONE	Phoenix

STATS	HP	1182	CP	333	BRV	113
	ATK	15	DEF	16	LUK	12

EQUIPMENT	WEAPON	—
	HANDS	—

HEAD	—	BODY	—

SPOILS	GIL	140	EXP	0

7. EPHEMERAL PHANTOM

LEVEL	9	RANK	F

BEHAVIOR	Evader
DP CHANCE	EX Burst within 10 seconds (DP+1)
BATTLE MAP	Pandaemonium
SUMMONSTONE	—

STATS	HP	1485	CP	339	BRV	141*
	ATK	21	DEF	21*	LUK	14

EQUIPMENT	WEAPON	—
	HANDS	Cracked Shield

HEAD	[Rank 4]	BODY	—

SPOILS	GIL	140	EXP	0

ACCESSORIES	Phoenix Pinion, Elven Mantle, Spirit Stanchion, Battle Boots, Mindcrush, [HP] HP ≤ 40% x3, [HP] Near Death x2

8. CAPRICIOUS THIEF

LEVEL	3	RANK	G

BEHAVIOR	Evader
DP CHANCE	—
BATTLE MAP	Dream's End
SUMMONSTONE	—

STATS	HP	1121	CP	332	BRV	107
	ATK	11	DEF	13	LUK	11

EQUIPMENT	WEAPON	—
	HANDS	—

HEAD	—	BODY	—

SPOILS	GIL	140	EXP	0

9. EPHEMERAL PHANTOM

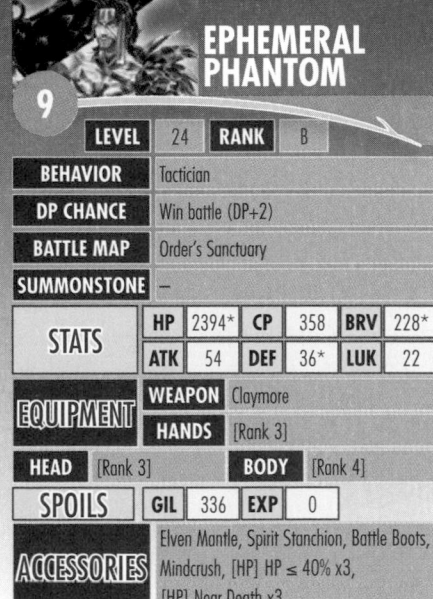

LEVEL	24	RANK	B

BEHAVIOR	Tactician
DP CHANCE	Win battle (DP+2)
BATTLE MAP	Order's Sanctuary
SUMMONSTONE	—

STATS	HP	2394*	CP	358	BRV	228*
	ATK	54	DEF	36*	LUK	22

EQUIPMENT	WEAPON	Claymore
	HANDS	[Rank 3]

HEAD	[Rank 3]	BODY	[Rank 4]

SPOILS	GIL	336	EXP	0

ACCESSORIES	Elven Mantle, Spirit Stanchion, Battle Boots, Mindcrush, [HP] HP ≤ 40% x3, [HP] Near Death x3

* Denotes use of the base value (for stats that vary).

DESTINY ODYSSEY

X-5

STARTING DP 4	**MAX FINISHING** 5 (+2 after 3-star rating)	**ENGAGEMENTS** 7 (+1 after 3-star rating)	

As with the previous level, this one features a lower route that becomes more crowded the higher your star rating is. The facsimile of Tidus that appears after achieving a 3-star rating is certainly not a slouch. This manikin has a balanced attack, dodges often, and makes good decisions. Don't hesitate to soften it up pre-battle with skills like Ray-Bomb. Bring a summon into the fight who steals or builds bravery in order to get the most from HP attacks when you can land them. Up close, you can often bait this foe into whiffing Hop Step and Energy Rain, which provides an opportunity to strike back. Against Jecht, the boss, be watchful for Triumphant Grasp and Jecht Blade up close—dodge either attack, then punish Jecht while he recovers.

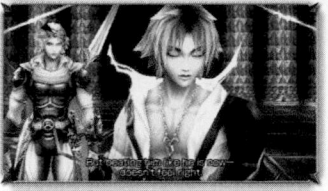
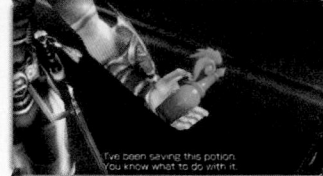
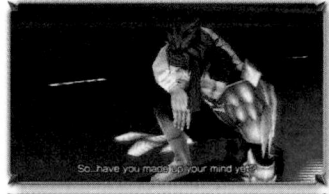
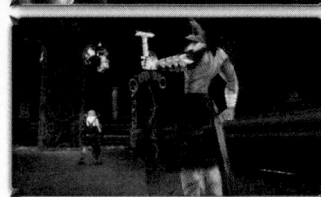
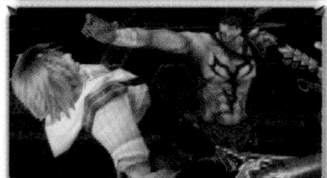
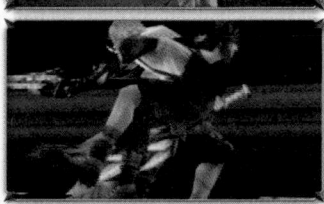

MAP

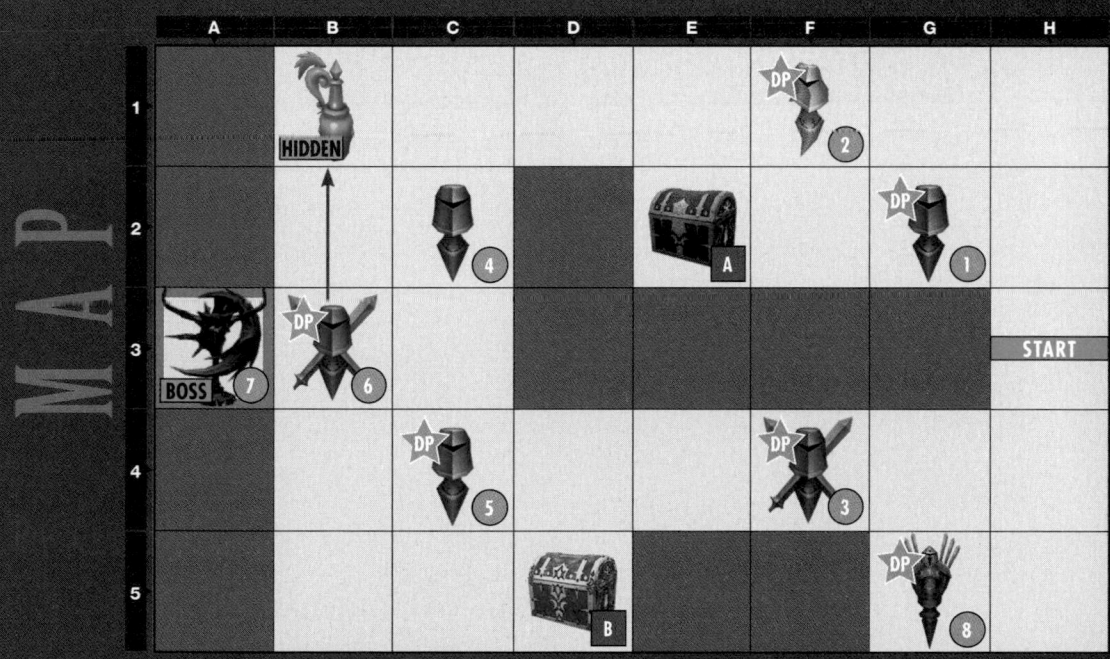

TREASURE

CHEST	1ST TIME	2ND TIME
A	Rosetta Stone	75%: 30 PP; 25%: 50 PP
B	Mythril (after 4-star rating)	–

LOCKED AREAS

AREA	UNLOCK REQUIREMENTS
	–

DP EFFICIENCY ROUTE

This is the only level for Tidus where a chain full of DP Chances is available right at the beginning along both paths. Therefore, after achieving a 3-star rating (but before a 4-star rating, or after obtaining the contents of the rare 4-star treasure chest, so it's no longer in the way). The best way to get a high DP total here is to chain the two battle pieces at the beginning of the upper path before proceeding to the exit along the lower route. Battle piece 6 only shows up after a prior 3-star rating.

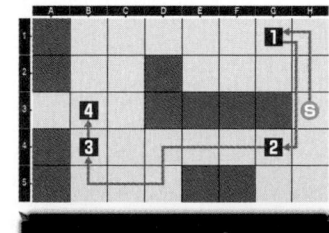
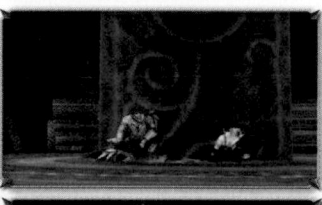
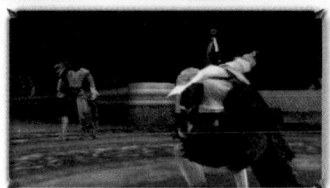
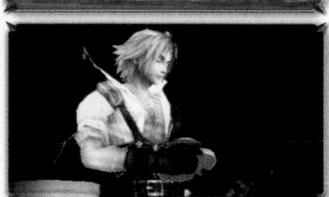

BATTLE PIECE DATA

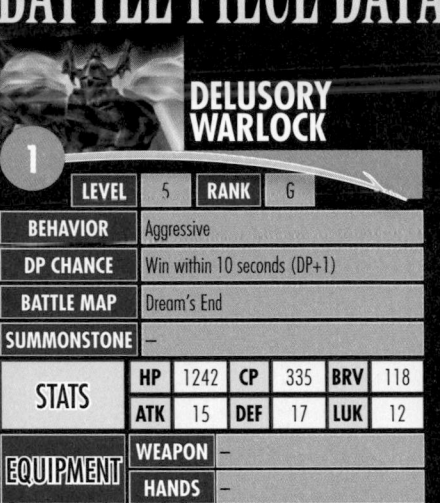

1 — DELUSORY WARLOCK

LEVEL	5	RANK G
BEHAVIOR	Aggressive	
DP CHANCE	Win within 10 seconds (DP+1)	
BATTLE MAP	Dream's End	
SUMMONSTONE	–	

STATS: HP 1242 | CP 335 | BRV 118 | ATK 15 | DEF 17 | LUK 12

EQUIPMENT: WEAPON – | HANDS – | HEAD – | BODY –

SPOILS: GIL 168 | EXP 0

2 — FALSE HERO

LEVEL	10	RANK B
BEHAVIOR	Aggressive	
DP CHANCE	Critical hit within 10 seconds (DP+1)	
BATTLE MAP	Lunar Subterrane	
SUMMONSTONE	–	

STATS: HP 1 | CP 341 | BRV 176 | ATK 20 | DEF 16 | LUK 15

EQUIPMENT: WEAPON – | HANDS Cracked Shield | HEAD Heavy Helm | BODY Rusted Armor

SPOILS: GIL 168 | EXP 3090

ACCESSORIES: The Rotten, Gaia Ring, Champion Belt, [Position] Near Opponent x5

3 — IMITATION LIEGEMAN

LEVEL	10	RANK F
BEHAVIOR	Evader	
DP CHANCE	Win without taking damage (DP+1)	
BATTLE MAP	Pandaemonium	
SUMMONSTONE	–	

STATS: HP 1545 | CP 341 | BRV 147* | ATK 21 | DEF 22* | LUK 15

EQUIPMENT: WEAPON – | HANDS Cracked Shield | HEAD [Rank 4] | BODY –

SPOILS: GIL 168 | EXP 0

ACCESSORIES: Elven Mantle, Spirit Stanchion, Battle Boots, Mindcrush, [HP] HP ≤ 40% x3, [HP] Near Death x3

4 — COUNTERFEIT WRAITH

LEVEL	5	RANK G
BEHAVIOR	Aggressive	
DP CHANCE	–	
BATTLE MAP	The Rift	
SUMMONSTONE	–	

STATS: HP 1242 | CP 354 | BRV 118 | ATK 14 | DEF 16 | LUK 12

EQUIPMENT: WEAPON – | HANDS – | HEAD – | BODY –

SPOILS: GIL 168 | EXP 803

5 — FALSE STALWART

LEVEL	6	RANK G
BEHAVIOR	Aggressive	
DP CHANCE	EX Burst within 10 seconds (DP+1)	
BATTLE MAP	Dream's End	
SUMMONSTONE	–	

STATS: HP 1303 | CP 336 | BRV 124 | ATK 18 | DEF 19 | LUK 13

EQUIPMENT: WEAPON – | HANDS – | HEAD – | BODY –

SPOILS: GIL 168 | EXP 0

6 — IMITATION DESPOT

LEVEL	11	RANK F
BEHAVIOR	Tricky	
DP CHANCE	BRV Break within 10 seconds (DP+1)	
BATTLE MAP	Kefka's Tower	
SUMMONSTONE	–	

STATS: HP 1606* | CP 342 | BRV 153* | ATK 21 | DEF 15 | LUK 15

EQUIPMENT: WEAPON – | HANDS Cracked Shield | HEAD [Rank 4] | BODY –

SPOILS: GIL 168 | EXP 0

ACCESSORIES: Elven Mantle, Spirit Stanchion, Battle Boots, Mindcrush, [HP] HP ≤ 40% x3, [HP] Near Death x3

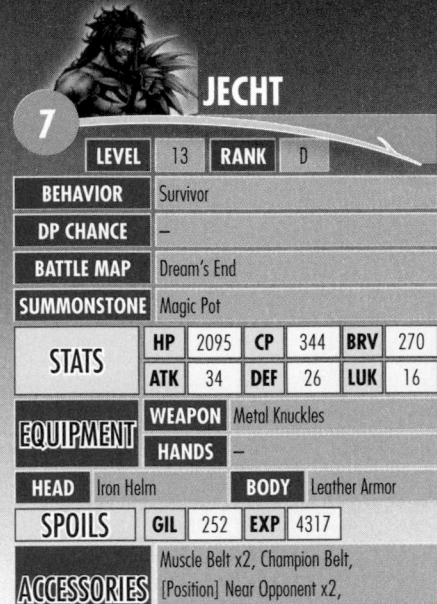

7 — JECHT

LEVEL	13	RANK D
BEHAVIOR	Survivor	
DP CHANCE	–	
BATTLE MAP	Dream's End	
SUMMONSTONE	Magic Pot	

STATS: HP 2095 | CP 344 | BRV 270 | ATK 34 | DEF 26 | LUK 16

EQUIPMENT: WEAPON Metal Knuckles | HANDS – | HEAD Iron Helm | BODY Leather Armor

SPOILS: GIL 252 | EXP 4317

ACCESSORIES: Muscle Belt x2, Champion Belt, [Position] Near Opponent x2, [Combat] Attacking Bravery

8 — EPHEMERAL VISION

LEVEL	27	RANK B
BEHAVIOR	Valiant	
DP CHANCE	Win battle (DP+2)	
BATTLE MAP	Dream's End	
SUMMONSTONE	Magus Sisters	

STATS: HP 2575* | CP 361 | BRV 245* | ATK 55 | DEF 38* | LUK 23

EQUIPMENT: WEAPON [Rank 4] | HANDS [Rank 3] | HEAD [Rank 5] | BODY Poncho

SPOILS: GIL 336 | EXP 0

ACCESSORIES: Elven Mantle, Spirit Stanchion, Battle Boots, Mindcrush, [HP] HP ≤ 40% x3, [HP] Near Death x3

* Denotes use of the base value (for stats that vary).

SHADE IMPULSE ¹
A TRUTH LOST

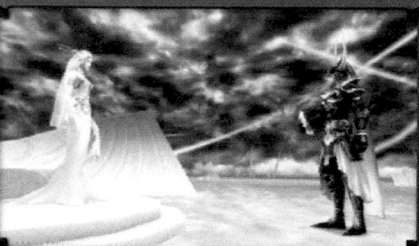

After finishing any Destiny Odyssey chapter, you'll see what happens once the forces of Cosmos collect each crystal.

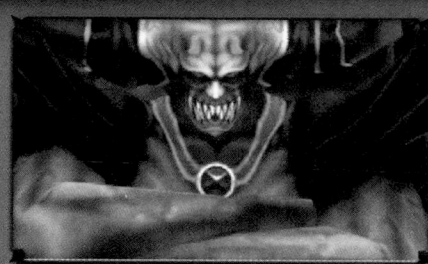

Contrary to what the heroes expect to happen, the collection of the crystals seems to transform the Sanctuary of Cosmos into a hellish landscape, wreathed in flame. The god of discord himself— Chaos—finally appears.

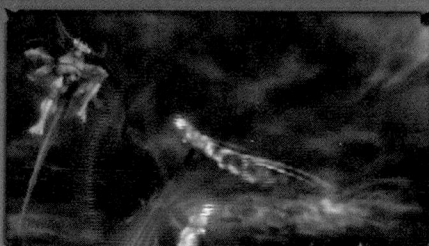

Astonishingly, he defeats Cosmos, and she vanishes! Has hunting down the crystals only taken the enormous conflict down a tragic alley rather than helping end it? The story continues in Shade Impulse…

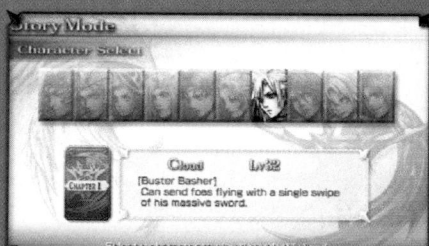

Any character aligned with Cosmos can be selected for battle in the Shade Impulse chapters. Four total Shade Impulse chapters lead up to the final confrontation with Chaos himself.

REWARDS

At the end of each level, rewards are available if you finish with a positive number of Destiny Points, or DP. This walkthrough includes miniature level maps that indicate the most efficient route to take through a given level, in order to maximize DP.

LEVEL COMPLETION

REMAINING DP		1ˢᵀ TIME		2ᴺᴰ TIME
7		Rosetta Stone		300 PP
6		Warlord's Gauntlets		200 PP
5		Warlord's Soul		120 PP
4		Lich		80 PP
3		3000 gil		50 PP
2		1800 gil		30 PP
1		900 gil		20 PP
0		300 gil		10 PP

At the end of each set of levels, you'll receive rewards based on your performance. Story Points, or SP, are awarded after each level based on remaining DP and HP, as well as the number of engagements undertaken. Points are penalized for retries, or for a DP total that dips into negatives. If you miss out on a desired bonus on the first playthrough, don't worry—SP is cumulative across multiple playthroughs.

DESTINY ODYSSEY X COMPLETION

STAR RATING	SP REQUIRED	AWARD
☆	300	New skill
☆ ☆	200	Special areas unlocked
☆ ☆ ☆	300	Rare battle pieces spawned
☆ ☆ ☆ ☆	400	Rare treasure chests spawned
–	500 SP, then every 500 SP extra	100 PP

(Ω) VARIATIONS

Stages in Shade Impulse take on a new, more menacing character. The stages themselves become threats, changing over time and lashing out at nearby c▮▮▮ instead of being static for each stage, bravery is dynamic here, and changes based on different factors. After first encountering each (Ω) stage in Shade Impulse, that stage becomes available in the PP Catalog for use in other gameplay modes.

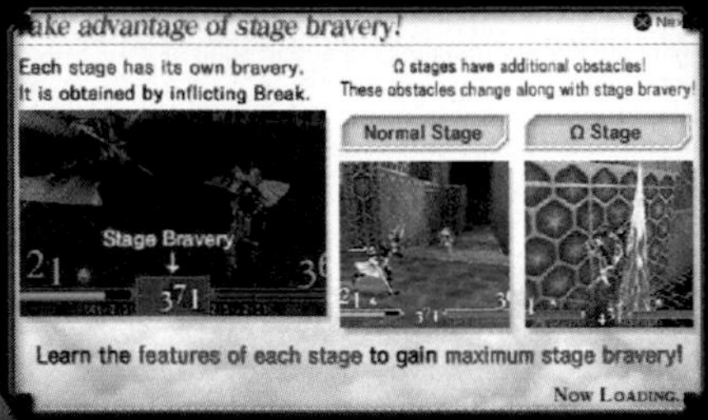

Take advantage of stage bravery!
Each stage has its own bravery. It is obtained by inflicting Break.
Ω stages have additional obstacles! These obstacles change along with stage bravery!

| Normal Stage | Ω Stage |

Stage Bravery
21 → 371 39

Learn the features of each stage to gain maximum stage bravery!

Now Loading.

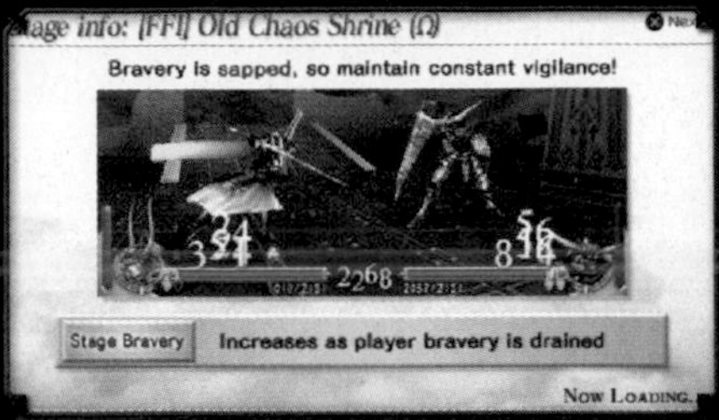

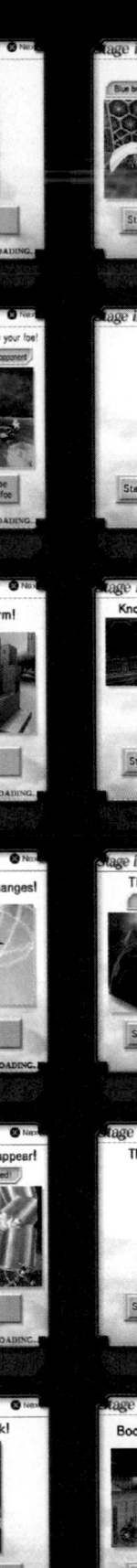

Stage info: [FFI] Old Chaos Shrine (Ω)
Bravery is sapped, so maintain constant vigilance!

| Stage Bravery | Increases as player bravery is drained |

Now Loading.

Old Chaos Shrine (Ω)

Stage info: [FFII] Pandaemonium (Ω)
Keep track of the safe areas!

Blue bricks are normal | Red bricks are dangerous | Gray stone is safe

| Stage Bravery | Increases when players are hit by spikes |

Now Loading.

Pandaemonium (Ω)

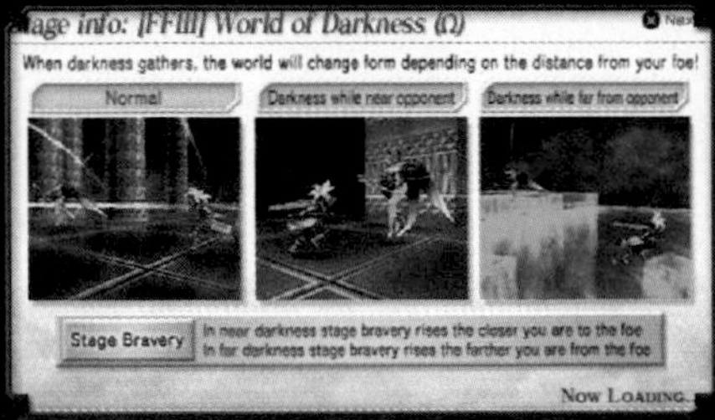

Stage info: [FFIII] World of Darkness (Ω)
When darkness gathers, the world will change form depending on the distance from your foe!

Normal | Darkness while near opponent | Darkness while far from opponent

| Stage Bravery | In near darkness stage bravery rises the closer you are to the foe / In far darkness stage bravery rises the farther you are from the foe |

Now Loading.

World of Darkness (Ω)

Stage info: [FFIV] Lunar Subterrane (Ω)
Try to destroy things in the stage!

| Stage Bravery | Rises when environment destroyed; bonuses for chained destruction |

Now Loading.

Lunar Subterrane (Ω)

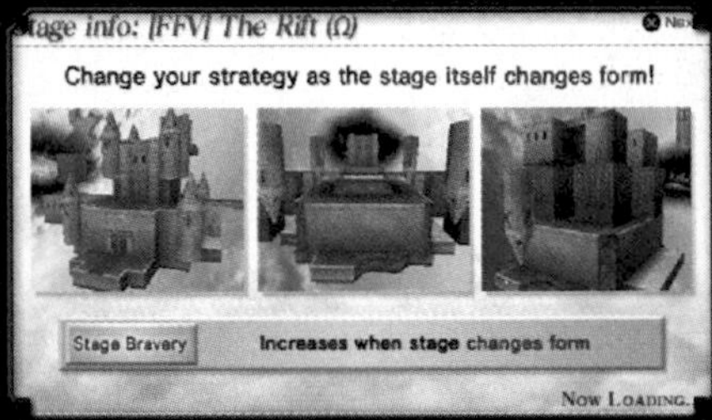

Stage info: [FFV] The Rift (Ω)
Change your strategy as the stage itself changes form!

| Stage Bravery | Increases when stage changes form |

Now Loading.

The Rift (Ω)

Stage info: [FFVI] Kefka's Tower (Ω)
Knock foes into bursts of Magitek steam to send them flying!

| Stage Bravery | Increases when Magitek steam blows |

Now Loading.

Kefka's Tower (Ω)

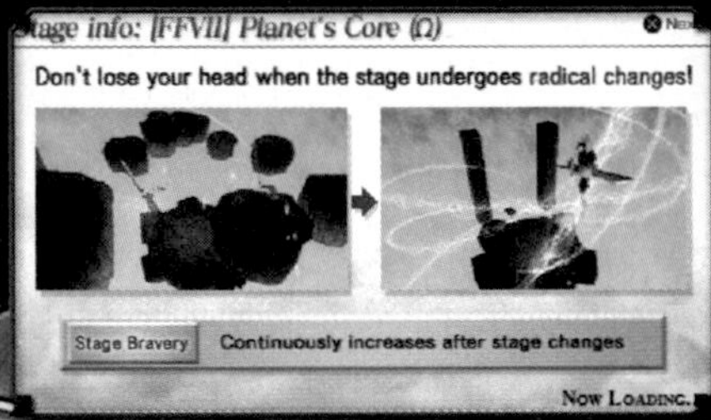

Stage info: [FFVII] Planet's Core (Ω)
Don't lose your head when the stage undergoes radical changes!

| Stage Bravery | Continuously increases after stage changes |

Now Loading.

Planet's Core (Ω)

Stage info: [FFVIII] Ultimecia's Castle (Ω)
Time Compression has begun... Let luck be your guide!

Gears deal damage! | Destroyed things reappear!

| Stage Bravery | Randomly changes during time compression |

Now Loading.

Ultimecia's Castle (Ω)

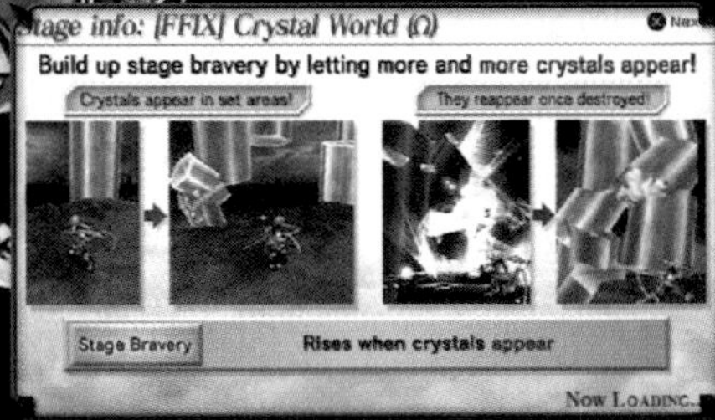

Stage info: [FFIX] Crystal World (Ω)
Build up stage bravery by letting more and more crystals appear!

Crystals appear in set areas! | They reappear once destroyed!

| Stage Bravery | Rises when crystals appear |

Now Loading.

Crystal World (Ω)

Stage info: [FFX] Dream's End (Ω)
There's no holding back...It's time for an all-out battle!

| Stage Bravery | Rises along with connecting attacks |

Now Loading.

Dream's End (Ω)

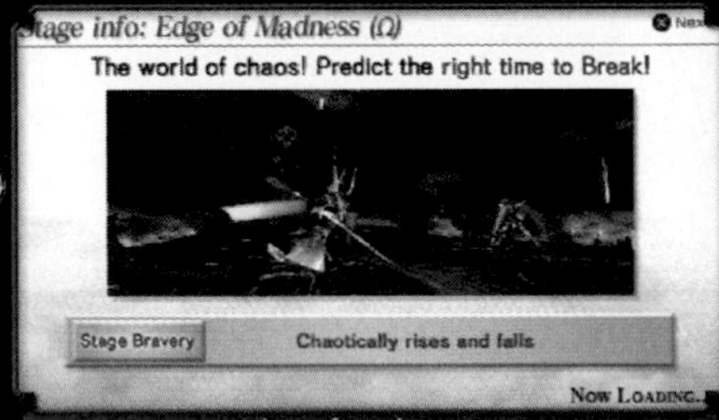

Stage info: Edge of Madness (Ω)
The world of chaos! Predict the right time to Break!

| Stage Bravery | Chaotically rises and falls |

Now Loading.

Edge of Madness (Ω)

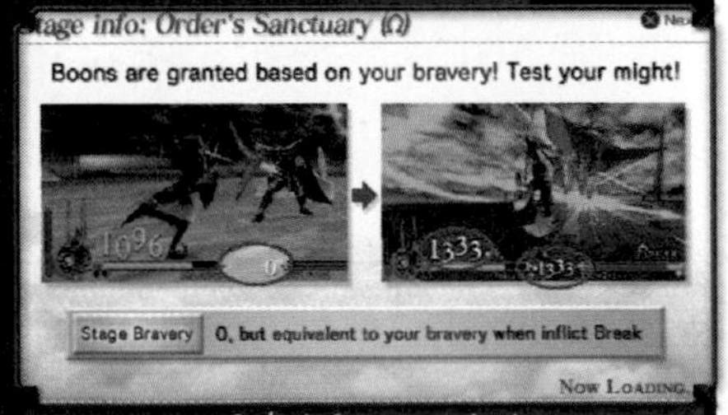

Stage info: Order's Sanctuary (Ω)
Boons are granted based on your bravery! Test your might!

| Stage Bravery | 0, but equivalent to your bravery when inflict Break |

Now Loading.

Order's Sanctuary (Ω)

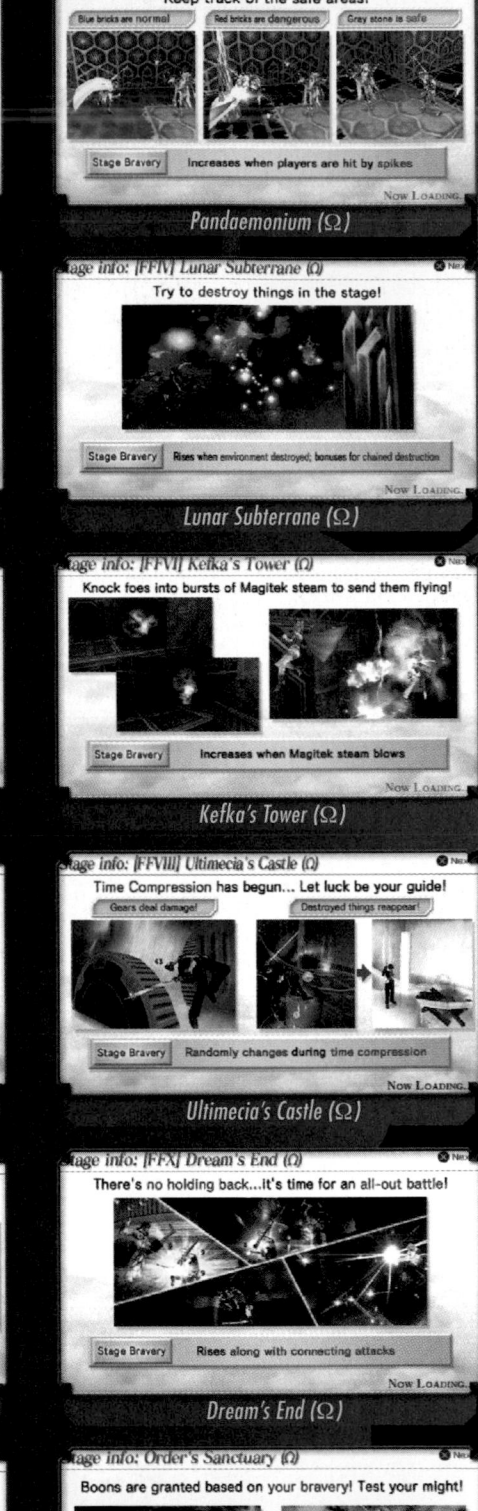

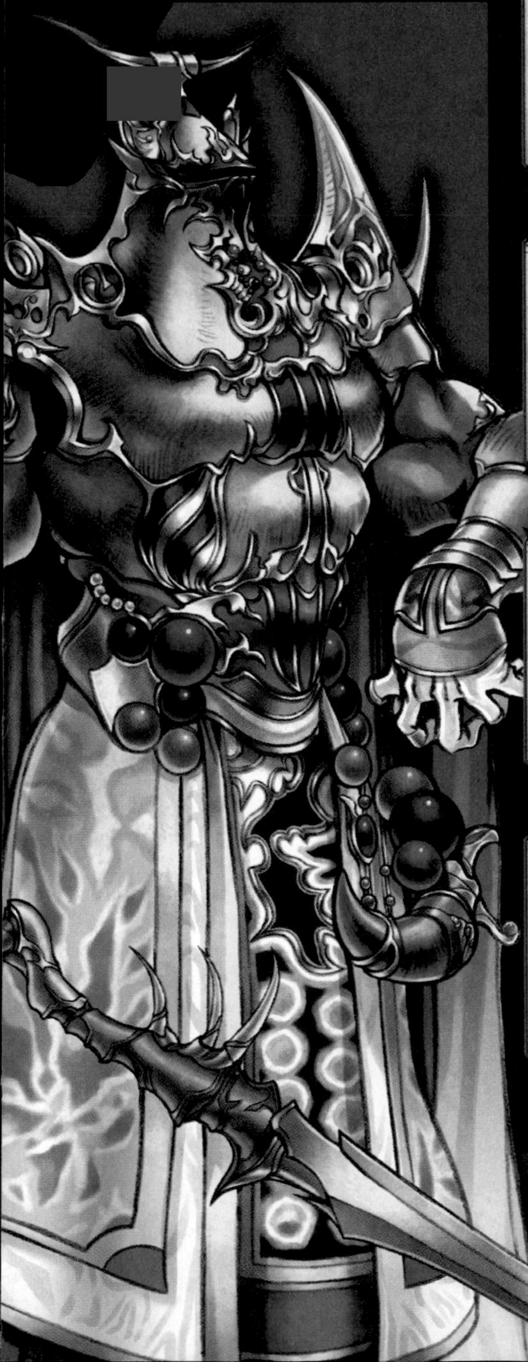

SHADE IMPULSE I

The stakes rise in the story in Shade Impulse, and the combat intensifies as well. Battle pieces represent higher level, more vicious opponents. Their behavior is more tactical than their Destiny Odyssey counterparts, and their equipment improved. They also pack Summonstones and accessories far more often. Various tricks and traps from Destiny Odyssey chapters show up on certain levels. Also, the ultimate battle pieces revealed by 3-star ratings for repeat completions are *much* tougher than the usual competition, with levels approaching 100. If you can manage to win, you'll gain massive EXP from these fights. There's difficulty to match, if you're not within a few levels of these adversaries, they'll be able to BRV Break your character easily. This can lead to repeated, frustrating one-shot losses to bravery attacks that combo into HP strikes. Sometimes, rather than relying on strategy, you'll just need more levels and better equipment. This first Shade Impulse level doesn't have this danger, but it does have a tight cluster of foes who can create a four-part battle chain. The Stigma of Chaos only appears after defeating at least two enemies, while treasure chest B only appears after defeating all six.

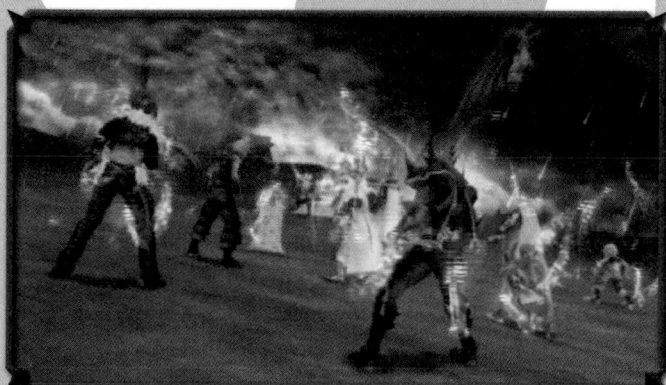
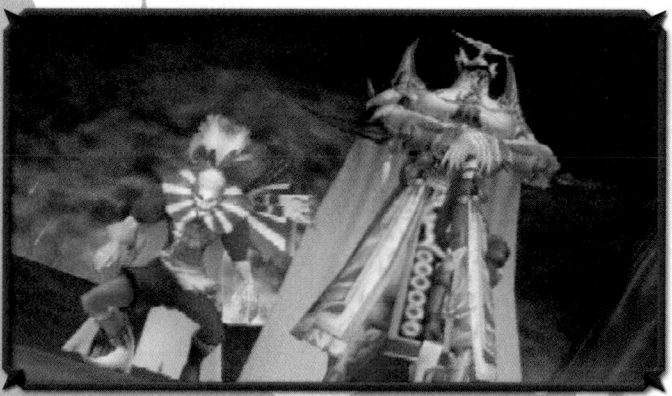

MAP

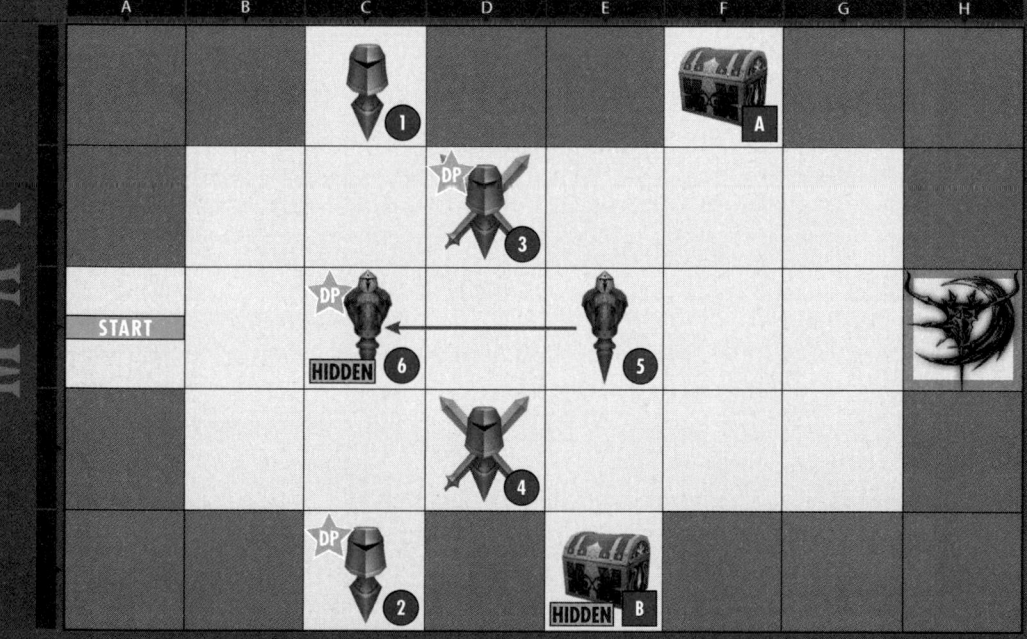

TREASURE

CHEST	1ST TIME	2ND TIME
A	Valor Incense	50%: 50 PP; 25%: Geranium; 20%: Ylang Ylang; 5%: Valor Resin
B	Gold (after defeating all 6 battle pieces)	50%: 50 PP; 25%: Rosemary; 20%: Tea Tree; 5%: Arcane Resin

LOCKED AREAS

AREA	UNLOCK REQUIREMENTS
—	—

DP EFFICIENCY ROUTE

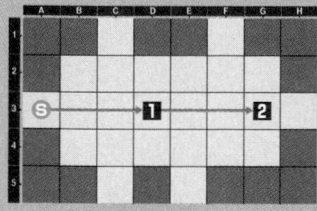

You can maximize Destiny Points here by executing a straight shot across the level along with one four-part battle chain. Head across and engage battle pieces 3, 4, and 5. Battle piece 6 spawns, closing off the exit from this quartet of foes, once battle piece 5 is defeated. Only battle pieces 3 and 6 have DP Chances. After the chain is done, head to the exit.

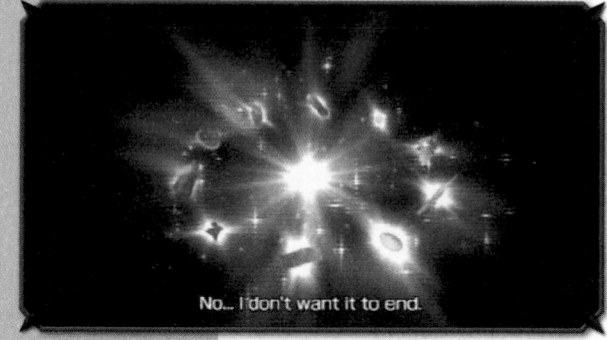

No... I don't want it to end.

BATTLE PIECE DATA

1 FALSE HERO

LEVEL	8	RANK	G

BEHAVIOR	Standby
DP CHANCE	–
BATTLE MAP	Old Chaos Shrine (Ω)
SUMMONSTONE	–

STATS	HP	1424	CP	338	BRV	136
	ATK	18	DEF	21	LUK	14

EQUIPMENT	WEAPON	–
	HANDS	–

HEAD	–	BODY	–

SPOILS	GIL	308	EXP	427

2 DELUSORY KNIGHT

LEVEL	9	RANK	G

BEHAVIOR	Aggressive
DP CHANCE	Win without taking damage (DP+1)
BATTLE MAP	Pandaemonium (Ω)
SUMMONSTONE	–

STATS	HP	1485	CP	339	BRV	141
	ATK	18	DEF	19	LUK	14

EQUIPMENT	WEAPON	–
	HANDS	–

HEAD	–	BODY	–

SPOILS	GIL	308	EXP	445

4 PHANTASMAL GIRL

LEVEL	15	RANK	F

BEHAVIOR	Aggressive
DP CHANCE	Win without losing HP (DP+1)
BATTLE MAP	Old Chaos Shrine (Ω)
SUMMONSTONE	–

STATS	HP	1848*	CP	347	BRV	176*
	ATK	26	DEF	25	LUK	17

EQUIPMENT	WEAPON	–
	HANDS	–

HEAD	[Rank 5]	BODY	–

SPOILS	GIL	308	EXP	554

ACCESSORIES	Force Begets Courage, Gravitorb, Ivory Choker, [HP] HP ≤ 40% x3 [HP] Near Death x3

4 IMAGINARY CHAMPION

LEVEL	14	RANK	E

BEHAVIOR	Standby
DP CHANCE	–
BATTLE MAP	World of Darkness (Ω)
SUMMONSTONE	–

STATS	HP	1788	CP	345	BRV	203
	ATK	24	DEF	26	LUK	17

EQUIPMENT	WEAPON	–
	HANDS	–

HEAD	[Rank 4]	BODY	–

SPOILS	GIL	308	EXP	536

ACCESSORIES	Force Begets Courage, Gravitorb, Ivory Choker, [HP] HP ≤ 40% x3, [HP] Near Death x3

5 FALSE STALWART

LEVEL	26	RANK	C

BEHAVIOR	Vicious
DP CHANCE	–
BATTLE MAP	Pandaemonium (Ω)
SUMMONSTONE	Atomos

STATS	HP	2515*	CP	360	BRV	297
	ATK	56	DEF	54	LUK	23

EQUIPMENT	WEAPON	[Rank 5]
	HANDS	[Rank 3]

HEAD	[Rank 3]	BODY	[Rank 4]

SPOILS	GIL	308	EXP	0

ACCESSORIES	Gaia Ring, Hyper Ring, [HP] HP ≤ 40% x6, [HP] Near Death x2

6 TRANSIENT LION

LEVEL	27	RANK	C

BEHAVIOR	Tactician
DP CHANCE	Critical hit within 10 seconds (DP+1)
BATTLE MAP	Old Chaos Shrine (Ω)
SUMMONSTONE	Magus Sisters

STATS	HP	2575*	CP	361	BRV	245*
	ATK	36*	DEF	38*	LUK	23

EQUIPMENT	WEAPON	[Rank 4]
	HANDS	[Rank 3]

HEAD	[Rank 5]	BODY	Poncho

SPOILS	GIL	308	EXP	0

ACCESSORIES	Champion Belt, Muscle Belt, [Position] Near Opponent x6 [Time] After 90 Seconds

* Denotes use of the base value (for stats that vary).

SHADE IMPULSE

1-2

STARTING DP	MAX FINISHING	ENGAGEMENTS
5	4	8

This level's narrow pathways restrict movement until battle pieces and Locked Areas are removed. Battle piece ❸, right by the start, opens the Locked Area in the lower left upon defeat. To unlock the area in the upper right, clear at least a 2-star rating on previous runs of Shade Impulse 1. This area bars access to the summon beast Scarmiglione, and is flanked by two expert battle pieces. Kefka stands in wait as a sort of mid-boss on this level, offering +2 DP upon defeat, but you can skip fighting him if you like by taking the low or high routes to the Stigma of Chaos in the bottom right.

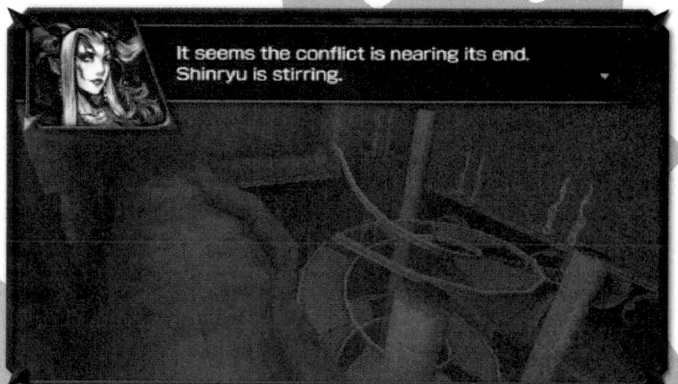

It seems the conflict is nearing its end. Shinryu is stirring.

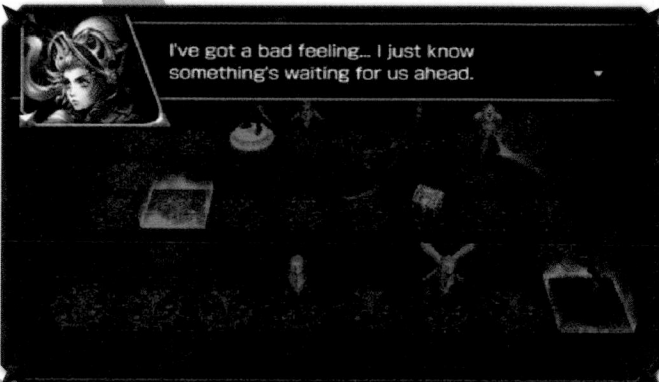

I've got a bad feeling... I just know something's waiting for us ahead.

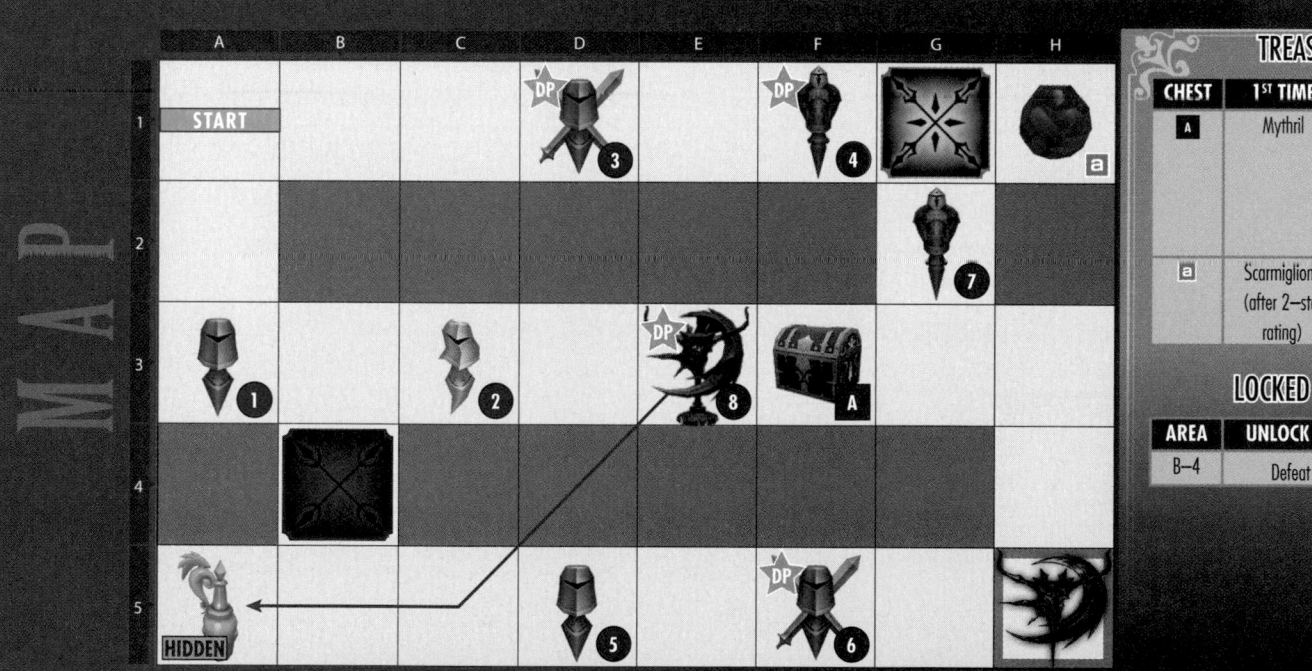

TREASURE

CHEST	1ST TIME	2ND TIME
A	Mythril	50%: 50 PP; 25%: Bergamot; 20%: Eucalyptus; 5%: Destruction Resin
a	Scarmiglione (after 2-star rating)	—

LOCKED AREAS

AREA	UNLOCK REQUIREMENTS
B–4	Defeat battle piece ❸

DP EFFICIENCY ROUTE

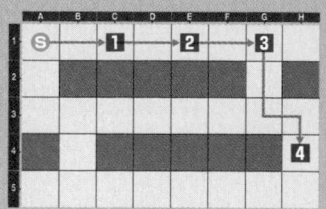

You'll need to return to this map after a 2-star rating for max DP here, so that the Locked Area in the upper right disappears. Move to the right and defeat battle pieces ❸, ❹, and ❼ in turn before heading to the exit. While the DP Chance for the first fight against piece ❸ requires a win within 20 seconds, the second fight against piece ❹ requires an EX Burst within 10 seconds. Build EX Force in a short time through a combination of the Aura skill and whatever you can collect during the first short fight, bolstered with accessories that increase EX Core appearance and EX Force absorption.

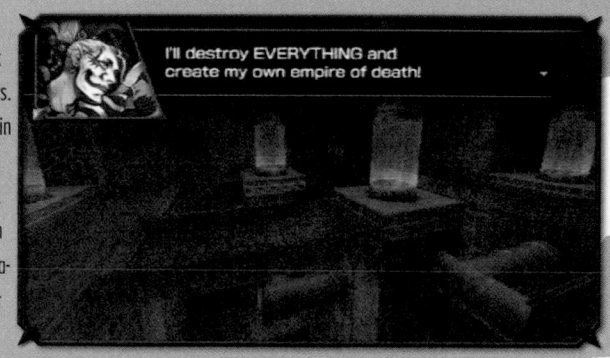

I'll destroy EVERYTHING and create my own empire of death!

BATTLE PIECE DATA

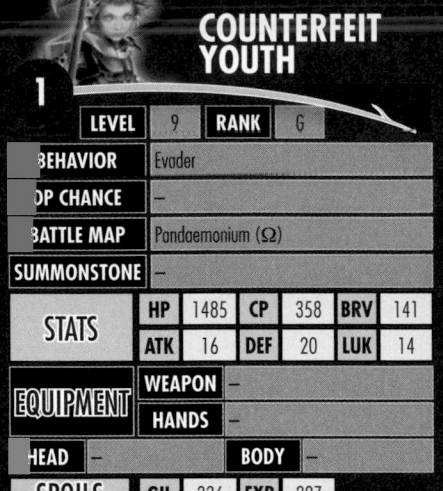

1 COUNTERFEIT YOUTH

LEVEL	9	RANK	G

BEHAVIOR	Evader
DP CHANCE	–
BATTLE MAP	Pandaemonium (Ω)
SUMMONSTONE	–

STATS	HP	1485	CP	358	BRV	141
	ATK	16	DEF	20	LUK	14

EQUIPMENT	WEAPON	–
	HANDS	–

HEAD	–	BODY	–

SPOILS	GIL	336	EXP	297

2 EPHEMERAL VISION

LEVEL	16	RANK	B

BEHAVIOR	Aggressive
DP CHANCE	–
BATTLE MAP	World of Darkness (Ω)
SUMMONSTONE	–

STATS	HP	1	CP	348	BRV	182*
	ATK	26	DEF	27*	LUK	18

EQUIPMENT	WEAPON	–
	HANDS	–

HEAD	[Rank 6]	BODY	–

SPOILS	GIL	336	EXP	3818

ACCESSORIES	Arcane Resin, The Rotten, Gaia Ring, [Position] Near Opponent x5

3 FALLACIOUS TREE

LEVEL	15	RANK	E

BEHAVIOR	Standby
DP CHANCE	Win within 20 seconds (DP+1)
BATTLE MAP	World of Darkness (Ω)
SUMMONSTONE	–

STATS	HP	1848	CP	364	BRV	176
	ATK	25	DEF	42	LUK	17

EQUIPMENT	WEAPON	–
	HANDS	Heavy Shield

HEAD	–	BODY	–

SPOILS	GIL	336	EXP	369

ACCESSORIES	Hyper Ring, Guardian Bangle, [HP] Near Loss x6

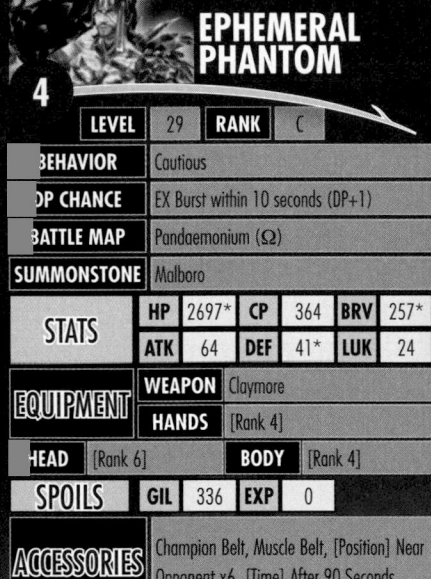

4 EPHEMERAL PHANTOM

LEVEL	29	RANK	C

BEHAVIOR	Cautious
DP CHANCE	EX Burst within 10 seconds (DP+1)
BATTLE MAP	Pandaemonium (Ω)
SUMMONSTONE	Malboro

STATS	HP	2697*	CP	364	BRV	257*
	ATK	64	DEF	41*	LUK	24

EQUIPMENT	WEAPON	Claymore
	HANDS	[Rank 4]

HEAD	[Rank 6]	BODY	[Rank 4]

SPOILS	GIL	336	EXP	0

ACCESSORIES	Champion Belt, Muscle Belt, [Position] Near Opponent x6, [Time] After 90 Seconds

5 CAPRICIOUS THIEF

LEVEL	9	RANK	G

BEHAVIOR	Aggressivew1485
DP CHANCE	339
BATTLE MAP	141
SUMMONSTONE	17

STATS	HP	19	CP	14	BRV	–
	ATK	–	DEF	–	LUK	–

EQUIPMENT	WEAPON	336
	HANDS	297

HEAD		BODY	

SPOILS	GIL		EXP	

6 CAPRICIOUS REAPER

LEVEL	16	RANK	F

BEHAVIOR	Aggressive
DP CHANCE	Win without taking damage (DP+1)
BATTLE MAP	Pandaemonium (Ω)
SUMMONSTONE	–

STATS	HP	2041	CP	348	BRV	182
	ATK	25	DEF	40	LUK	18

EQUIPMENT	WEAPON	–
	HANDS	[Rank 5]

HEAD	–	BODY	–

SPOILS	GIL	336	EXP	381

ACCESSORIES	Hyper Ring, Guardian Bangle, [HP] HP = 100% x6

7 DELUSORY KNIGHT

LEVEL	28	RANK	C

BEHAVIOR	Conservative
DP CHANCE	Wall Rush within 10 seconds (DP+1)
BATTLE MAP	The Rift (Ω)
SUMMONSTONE	Mandragora

STATS	HP	2636*	CP	362	BRV	251*
	ATK	37*	DEF	38*	LUK	24

EQUIPMENT	WEAPON	[Rank 5]
	HANDS	[Rank 3]

HEAD	[Rank 3]	BODY	[Rank 4]

SPOILS	GIL	336	EXP	0

ACCESSORIES	Gaia Ring, Guardian Bangle, [HP] HP = 100% x3, [HP] HP ≥ 80% x5

8 KEFKA

LEVEL	18	RANK	E

BEHAVIOR	Tactician
DP CHANCE	Win battle (DP+2)
BATTLE MAP	Kefka's Tower (Ω)
SUMMONSTONE	Iron Giant

STATS	HP	2762	CP	367	BRV	296
	ATK	41	DEF	42	LUK	19

EQUIPMENT	WEAPON	Healing Rod
	HANDS	Silver Bangles

HEAD	Hairpin	BODY	Poncho

SPOILS	GIL	1428	EXP	4060

ACCESSORIES	Star Earring, Earring, [Position] Far from Opponent x6, [Time] After 90 Seconds

* Denotes use of the base value (for stats that vary).

SHADE IMPULSE

1-3

STARTING DP	MAX FINISHING	ENGAGEMENTS
6	**5** (+2 after 3-star rating)	**7** (+1 after 3-star rating)

Like Onion Knight's Destiny Odyssey, this level is blanketed with shrouded Enigma Areas. Their contents are only revealed when you engage them. The Sight skill can remove them as well, if available. 3-star and 4-star ratings here reveal battle piece **8** and treasure chest **A**. Battle piece **8** is a crystal version of Warrior of Light, at a very high level. If you're not near his level, it's likely he'll inflict Break on you with nearly any bravery attack, sometimes leading right into a combo finish with Bitter End or Rune Saber. Also look out for Shield of Light, which deflects bravery attacks during its startup period. Dodge behind the manikin and hit him in the back as he recovers.

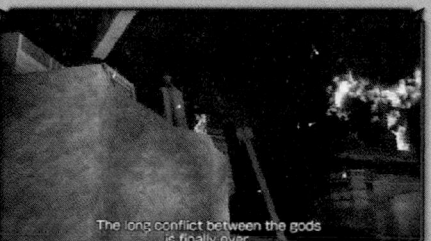
The long conflict between the gods is finally over.

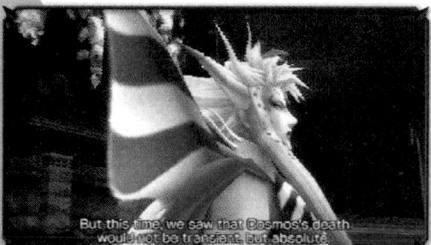
But this time, we saw that Cosmos's death would not be transient, but absolute.

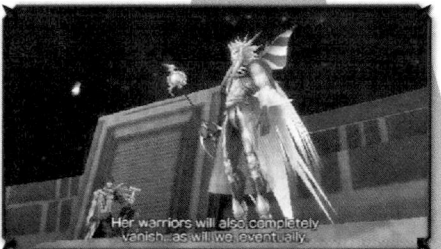
Her warriors will also completely vanish, as will we eventually.

MAP

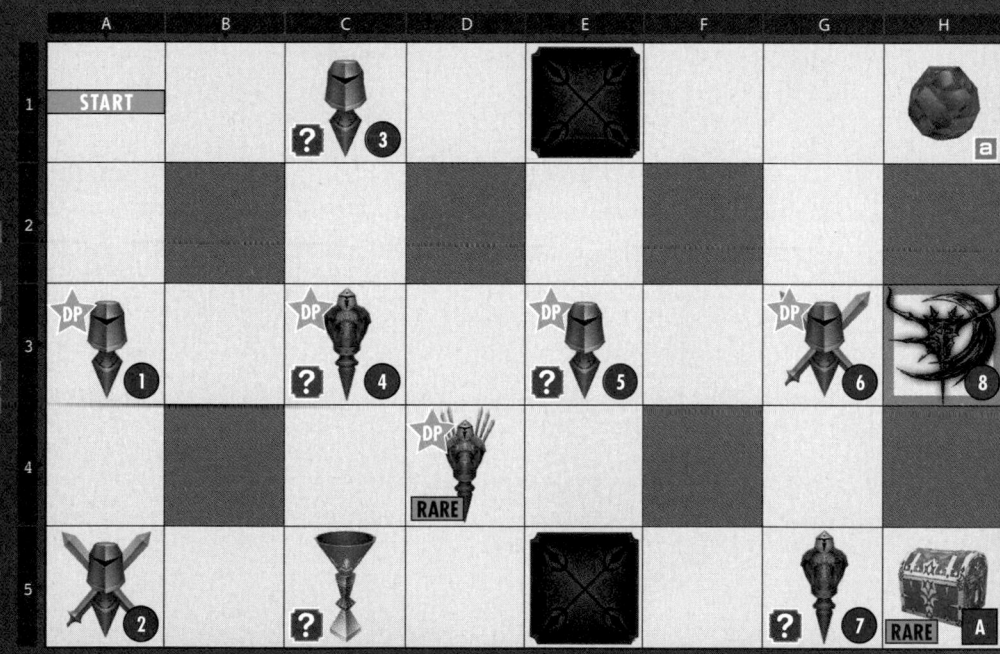

TREASURE

CHEST	1ST TIME	2ND TIME
A	Gold (after 4-star rating)	—
a	Odin AUTO	—

LOCKED AREAS

AREA	UNLOCK REQUIREMENTS
E–1	Defeat battle piece **2**
E–5	Defeat battle piece **3**

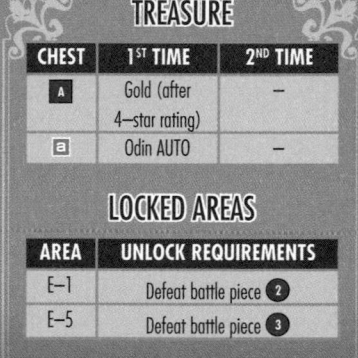

DP EFFICIENCY ROUTE

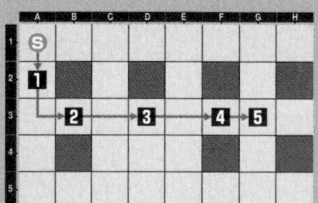

Battle piece **8** must be present to draw the most Destiny Points from this level. This piece doesn't appear until you have a 3-star rating from previous completions. Once it's here, start by heading down to battle piece **1** for the first DP Chance. Afterward, simply head right toward the exit, taking out battle piece **4**, then chaining battle pieces **5** and **8**, then finally taking on battle piece **6** along the way.

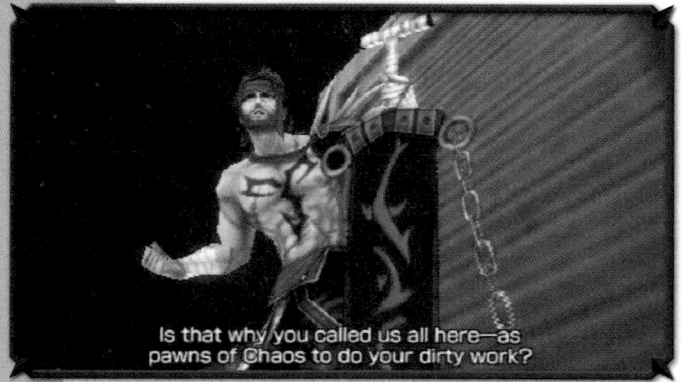
Is that why you called us all here—as pawns of Chaos to do your dirty work?

BATTLE PIECE DATA

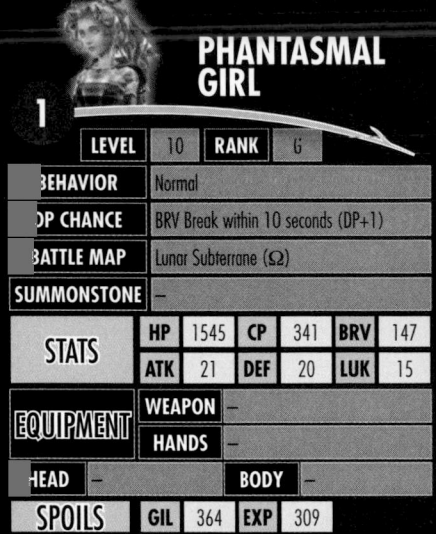

1 PHANTASMAL GIRL

LEVEL	10	RANK	G

BEHAVIOR	Normal
DP CHANCE	BRV Break within 10 seconds (DP+1)
BATTLE MAP	Lunar Subterrane (Ω)
SUMMONSTONE	–

STATS	HP	1545	CP	341	BRV	147
	ATK	21	DEF	20	LUK	15

EQUIPMENT	WEAPON	–
	HANDS	–

HEAD	–	BODY	–

SPOILS	GIL	364	EXP	309

2 COUNTERFEIT WRAITH

LEVEL	18	RANK	F

BEHAVIOR	Standby
DP CHANCE	–
BATTLE MAP	The Rift (Ω)
SUMMONSTONE	Leviathan AUTO

STATS	HP	2030*	CP	367	BRV	323*
	ATK	35	DEF	29*	LUK	19

EQUIPMENT	WEAPON	[Rank 2]
	HANDS	Bronze Bangle

HEAD	Hairpin	BODY	Cotton Robes

SPOILS	GIL	364	EXP	406

ACCESSORIES	Arcane Incense, Gravitorb, Attractorb x2, [Position] Far from Opponent x6

3 FALLACIOUS WANDERER

LEVEL	10	RANK	G

BEHAVIOR	Normal
DP CHANCE	–
BATTLE MAP	The Rift (Ω)
SUMMONSTONE	–

STATS	HP	1545	CP	359	BRV	147
	ATK	20	DEF	21	LUK	15

EQUIPMENT	WEAPON	–
	HANDS	–

HEAD	–	BODY	–

SPOILS	GIL	364	EXP	309

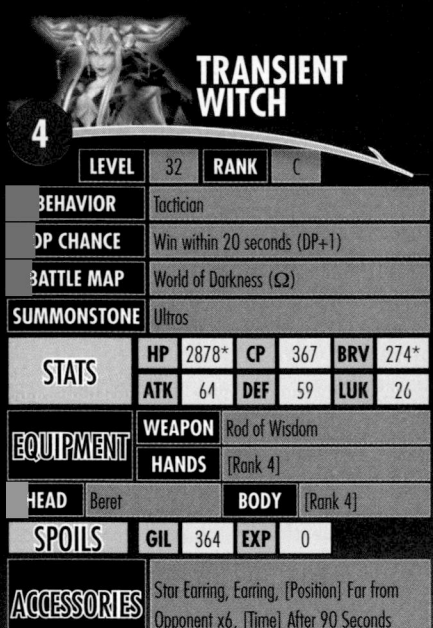

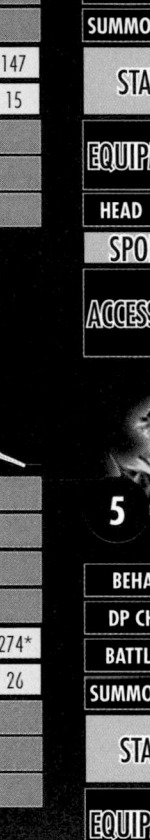

4 TRANSIENT WITCH

LEVEL	32	RANK	C

BEHAVIOR	Tactician
DP CHANCE	Win within 20 seconds (DP+1)
BATTLE MAP	World of Darkness (Ω)
SUMMONSTONE	Ultros

STATS	HP	2878*	CP	367	BRV	274*
	ATK	61	DEF	59	LUK	26

EQUIPMENT	WEAPON	Rod of Wisdom
	HANDS	[Rank 4]

HEAD	Beret	BODY	[Rank 4]

SPOILS	GIL	364	EXP	0

ACCESSORIES	Star Earring, Earring, [Position] Far from Opponent x6, [Time] After 90 Seconds

5 IMITATION LIEGEMAN

LEVEL	12	RANK	F

BEHAVIOR	Blocker
DP CHANCE	Battlegen within 10 seconds (DP+1)
BATTLE MAP	World of Darkness (Ω)
SUMMONSTONE	–

STATS	HP	1667	CP	343	BRV	159
	ATK	23	DEF	24	LUK	16

EQUIPMENT	WEAPON	–
	HANDS	–

HEAD	–	BODY	–

SPOILS	GIL	364	EXP	333

6 EPHEMERAL PHANTOM

LEVEL	19	RANK	F

BEHAVIOR	Normal
DP CHANCE	Keep foe from getting EX Cores (DP+1)
BATTLE MAP	Lunar Subterrane (Ω)
SUMMONSTONE	–

STATS	HP	2091*	CP	351	BRV	199*
	ATK	31*	DEF	31*	LUK	19

EQUIPMENT	WEAPON	[Rank 2]
	HANDS	[Rank 1]

HEAD	[Rank 3]	BODY	Chainmail

SPOILS	GIL	364	EXP	418

ACCESSORIES	Arcane Incense, Gravitorb, Attractorb x2, [Position] Far from Opponent x6

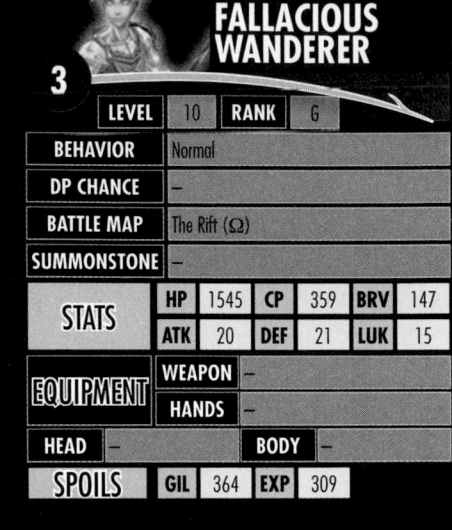

7 IMITATION DESPOT

LEVEL	31	RANK	C

BEHAVIOR	Valiant
DP CHANCE	–
BATTLE MAP	World of Darkness (Ω)
SUMMONSTONE	Magic Pot

STATS	HP	2818*	CP	366	BRV	268*
	ATK	41*	DEF	43*	LUK	25

EQUIPMENT	WEAPON	[Rank 6]
	HANDS	[Rank 4]

HEAD	[Rank 4]	BODY	[Rank 5]

SPOILS	GIL	364	EXP	0

ACCESSORIES	Gaia Ring, Hyper Ring, [HP] HP ≤ 40% x6, [HP] Near Death x2

8 FALSE HERO

LEVEL	78	RANK	S

BEHAVIOR	Vicious
DP CHANCE	Win battle (DP+2)
BATTLE MAP	Order's Sanctuary (Ω)
SUMMONSTONE	Rubicante

STATS	HP	7880	CP	423	BRV	540*
	ATK	88*	DEF	91*	LUK	49

EQUIPMENT	WEAPON	[Rank 13]
	HANDS	[Rank 11]

HEAD	Platinum Helm	BODY	[Rank 12]

SPOILS	GIL	476	EXP	0

ACCESSORIES	Gaia Ring, Guardian Bangle, [HP] HP = 100% x3, [HP] HP ≥ 80% x5

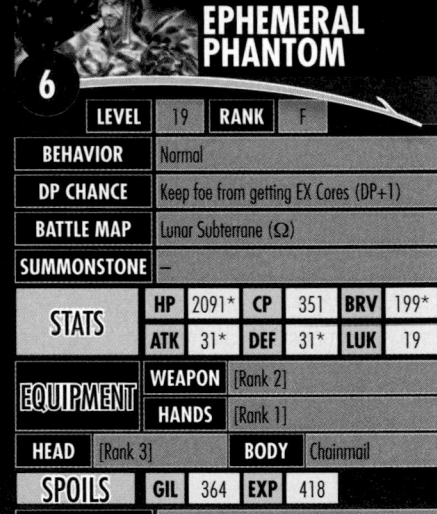

* Denotes use of the base value (for stats that vary).

SHADE IMPULSE 1

SHADE IMPULSE

1-4

STARTING DP	MAX FINISHING	ENGAGEMENTS
4	5	7

A wall of foes stands between the start and the finish of this level. Defeating these foes removes all of the Locked Areas on the right side of the stage. These block access to the exit, Jecht serving as a mid-boss, and the treasure chest behind Jecht. After achieving at least a 2-star rating on Shade Impulse 1, look for a Diamond behind the gold Locked Area along the bottom. Jecht provides +2 DP simply for winning the battle, so he's worth going after even if you're not usually concerned about Destiny Points.

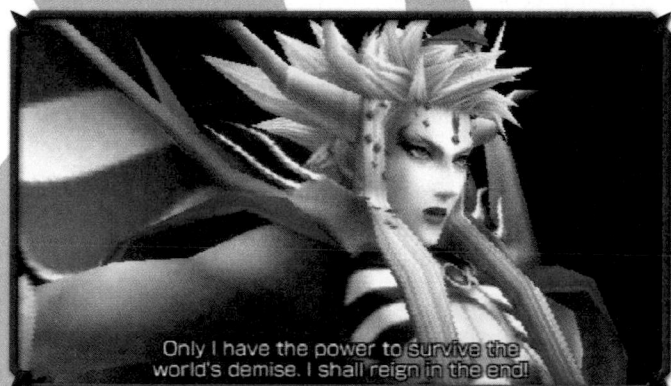

Only I have the power to survive the world's demise. I shall reign in the end!

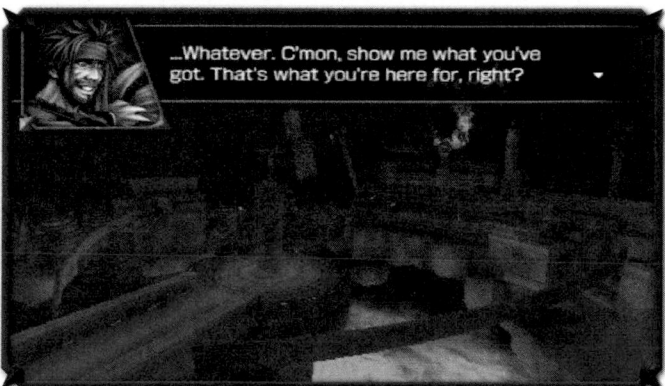

...Whatever. C'mon, show me what you've got. That's what you're here for, right?

MAP

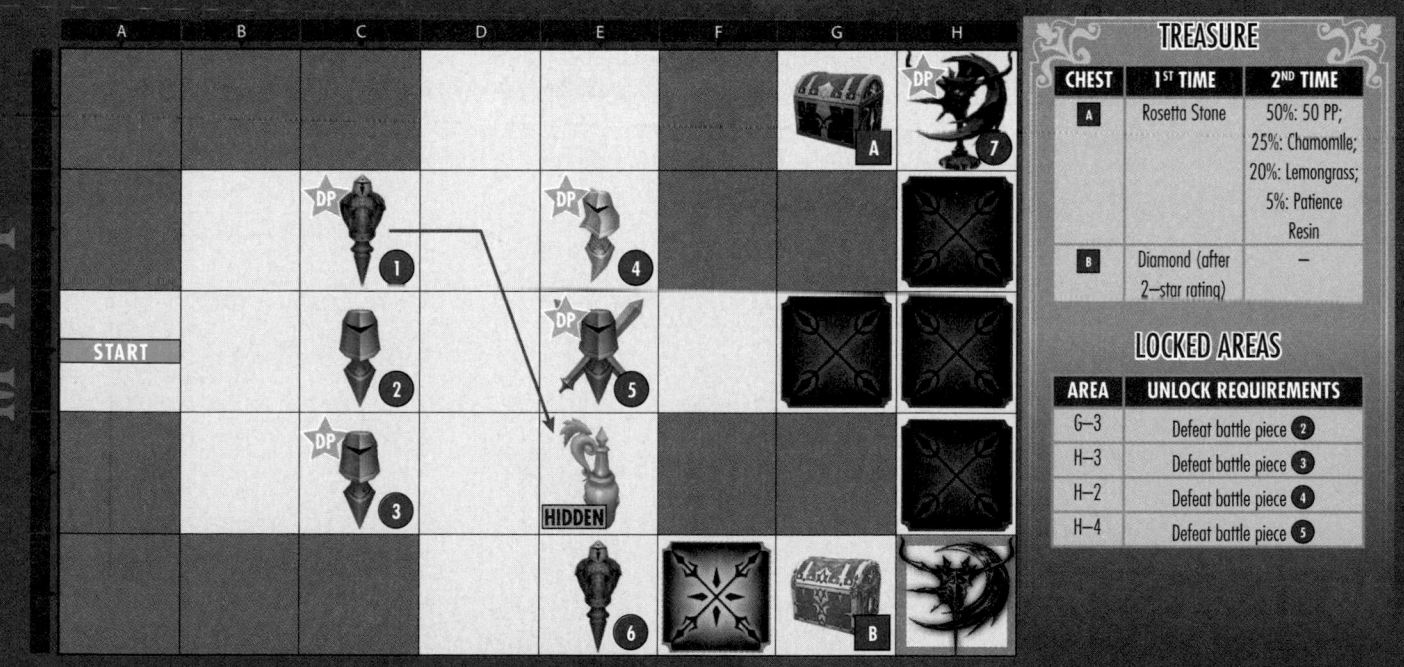

TREASURE

CHEST	1ST TIME	2ND TIME
A	Rosetta Stone	50%: 50 PP; 25%: Chamomlle; 20%: Lemongrass; 5%: Patience Resin
B	Diamond (after 2-star rating)	—

LOCKED AREAS

AREA	UNLOCK REQUIREMENTS
G–3	Defeat battle piece ②
H–3	Defeat battle piece ③
H–2	Defeat battle piece ④
H–4	Defeat battle piece ⑤

DP EFFICIENCY ROUTE

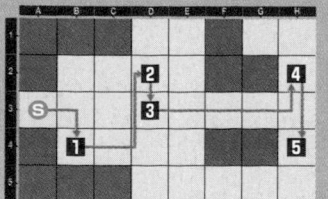

You'll clear out all but one battle piece to max out DP on this level. Start by engaging battle piece ③. Winning here opens the way to stand between the other clustered battle pieces, chaining them in pairs. Chain pieces ① and ④, then ② and ⑤. Battle piece ① has an unusual DP Chance condition—achieve a booster accessory multiplier of x8.0 or greater. Obviously, this requires advance planning, so shuffle your accessories if necessary before instigating the chain. Once battle pieces ① through ⑤ are defeated, the way is open to engage Jecht for 2 more DP before exiting.

BATTLE PIECE DATA

1 EPHEMERAL VISION

LEVEL	33	RANK	C

BEHAVIOR	Extreme
DP CHANCE	Booster accessory multiplier ≥ 8x (DP+1)
BATTLE MAP	Lunar Subterrane (Ω)
SUMMONSTONE	Titan

STATS	HP	2939*	CP	368	BRV	280*
	ATK	43*	DEF	44*	LUK	26

EQUIPMENT	WEAPON	[Rank 6]
	HANDS	[Rank 4]

HEAD	[Rank 4]	BODY	[Rank 5]

SPOILS	GIL	448	EXP	0

ACCESSORIES	Gaia Ring, Guardian Bangle, [HP] HP = 100% x3, [HP] HP ≥ 80% x5

2 IMAGINARY SOLDIER

LEVEL	11	RANK	F

BEHAVIOR	Evader
DP CHANCE	—
BATTLE MAP	Lunar Subterrane (Ω)
SUMMONSTONE	—

STATS	HP	1606	CP	342	BRV	153
	ATK	21	DEF	23	LUK	15

EQUIPMENT	WEAPON	—
	HANDS	—

HEAD	—	BODY	—

SPOILS	GIL	448	EXP	160

3 CAPRICIOUS REAPER

LEVEL	9	RANK	G

BEHAVIOR	Normal
DP CHANCE	Battlegen within 10 seconds (DP+1)
BATTLE MAP	The Rift (Ω)
SUMMONSTONE	—

STATS	HP	1485	CP	339	BRV	141
	ATK	18	DEF	20	LUK	14

EQUIPMENT	WEAPON	—
	HANDS	—

HEAD	—	BODY	—

SPOILS	GIL	448	EXP	148

4 PHANTASMAL GIRL

LEVEL	20	RANK	B

BEHAVIOR	Aggressive
DP CHANCE	Critical hit within 10 seconds (DP+1)
BATTLE MAP	Lunar Subterrane (Ω)
SUMMONSTONE	—

STATS	HP	1	CP	353	BRV	879
	ATK	31	DEF	30	LUK	20

EQUIPMENT	WEAPON	—
	HANDS	—

HEAD	Beret	BODY	—

SPOILS	GIL	448	EXP	4302

ACCESSORIES	The Rotten, Soul of the Sovereign

5 IMAGINARY CHAMPION

LEVEL	19	RANK	E

BEHAVIOR	Normal
DP CHANCE	Win without taking damage (DP+1)
BATTLE MAP	Old Chaos Shrine (Ω)
SUMMONSTONE	Ramuh

STATS	HP	2091	CP	351	BRV	199
	ATK	43	DEF	30	LUK	19

EQUIPMENT	WEAPON	Uchigatana
	HANDS	—

HEAD	—	BODY	—

SPOILS	GIL	448	EXP	209

ACCESSORIES	Gaia Ring, [HP] HP ≤ 40% x3, [HP] Near Death x4

6 FALSE STALWART

LEVEL	34	RANK	C

BEHAVIOR	Survivor
DP CHANCE	—
BATTLE MAP	The Rift (Ω)
SUMMONSTONE	Tiamat

STATS	HP	3000*	CP	370	BRV	286*
	ATK	46*	DEF	47*	LUK	27

EQUIPMENT	WEAPON	[Rank 5]
	HANDS	[Rank 4]

HEAD	[Rank 6]	BODY	[Rank 4]

SPOILS	GIL	448	EXP	0

ACCESSORIES	Gaia Ring, Hyper Ring, [HP] HP ≤ 40% x6, [HP] Near Death x2

7 JECHT

LEVEL	22	RANK	E

BEHAVIOR	Vicious
DP CHANCE	Win battle (DP+2)
BATTLE MAP	Dream's End (Ω)
SUMMONSTONE	Carbuncle

STATS	HP	3241	CP	355	BRV	308
	ATK	52	DEF	48	LUK	21

EQUIPMENT	WEAPON	Darksteel Claws
	HANDS	Silver Bangles

HEAD	Knight Helm	BODY	Mythril Vest

SPOILS	GIL	1764	EXP	4544

ACCESSORIES	Gaia Ring, Guardian Bangle, [HP] HP = 100% x3, [HP] HP ≥ 80% x5

* Denotes use of the base value (for stats that vary).

SHADE IMPULSE 1

SHADE IMPULSE

1-5

STARTING DP	MAX FINISHING	ENGAGEMENTS
4	**5** (+2 after 3-star rating)	**7** (+1 after 3-star rating)

The last Shade Impulse 1 level again clusters a number of foes between the start and the Stigma of Chaos. If you have sufficient star rating, you may also find an extra battle piece and treasure chest. Ultimate battle piece **8** is a fierce imposter of Garland. Watch out for Blaze from afar, and Cyclone or Earthquake up close. At point-blank range on the ground, you can bait this manikin into using Earthquake, allowing you to dodge backward before punishing its missed attack. However, if you try to take the initiative and attack first you may be blocked more often than not. This foe can easily Break your bravery, giving itself bravery totals nearing 9999. Using Magic Pot here to match its high-reward attacks doesn't work, since it can respond to your summon with a Scarmiglione summon, instantly reducing your bravery to 0. You'll simply have to play it straight. The boss, Exdeath, should present no problem if you've come this far already. After completing Shade Impulse 1, you can move on to Shade Impulse 2. You can also purchase all the alternate (Ω) stages you've encountered so far in the PP Catalog.

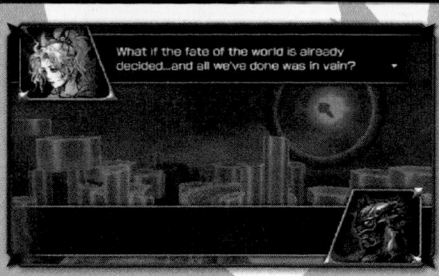

MAP

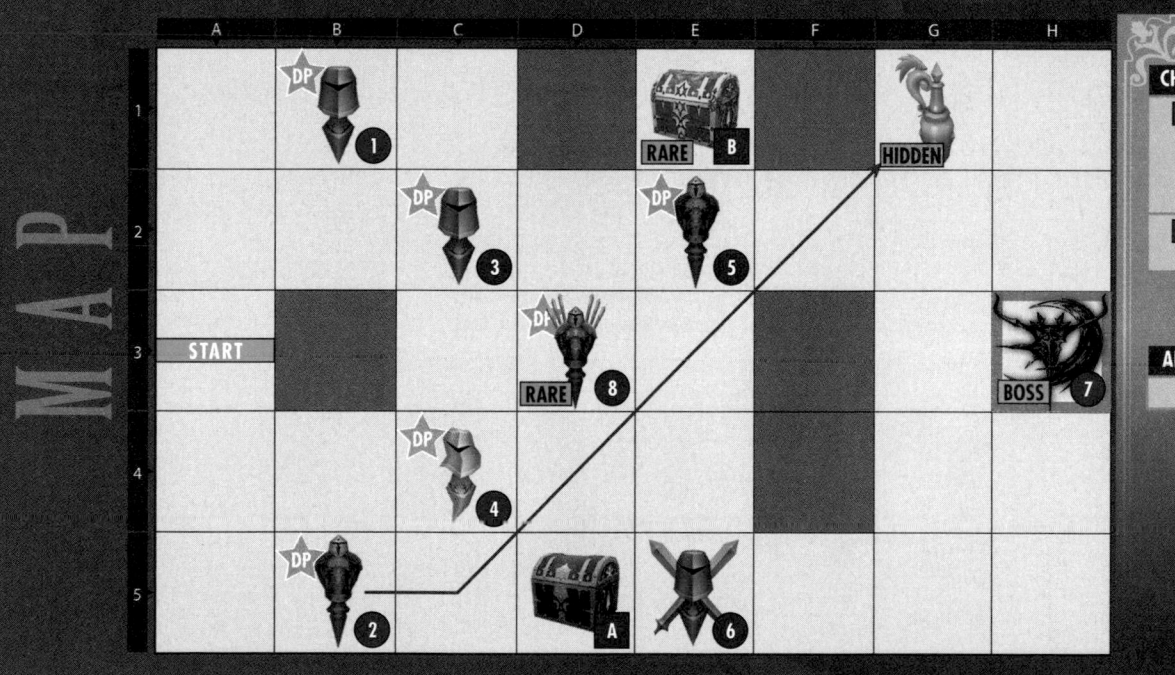

TREASURE

CHEST	1ST TIME	2ND TIME
A	Ivory Choker	50%: 50 PP; 25%: Ylang Ylang; 20%: Rosemary; 5%: Life Resin
B	Gold (after 4—star rating)	-

LOCKED AREAS

AREA	UNLOCK REQUIREMENTS
–	–

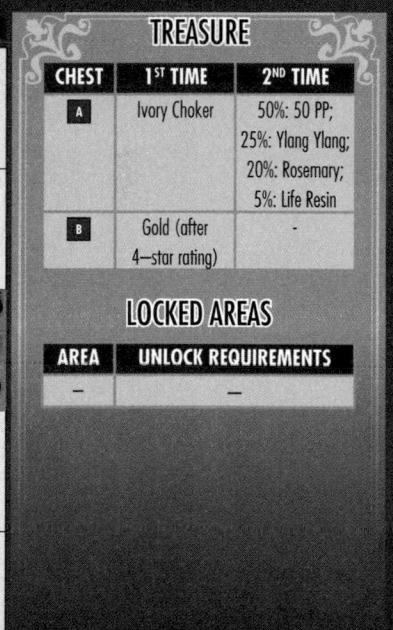

DP EFFICIENCY ROUTE

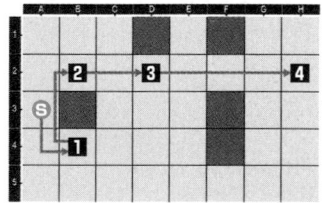

After returning with a 3-star or better rating so that battle piece **8** shows up, begin by engaging battle pieces **2** and **4**. After scoring both DP Chances, head upward to chain battle pieces **1** and **3**. Follow this up by moving right to chain battle pieces **5** and **8**. After taking down all these DP Chances, it's time to head to Exdeath, the boss.

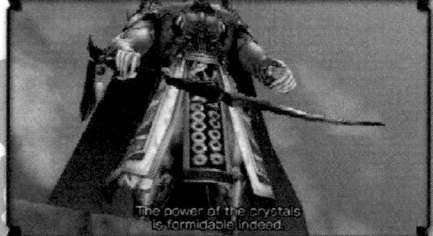

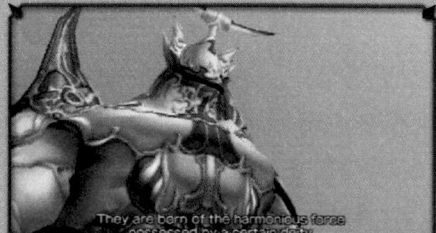

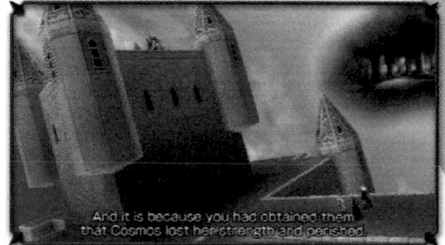

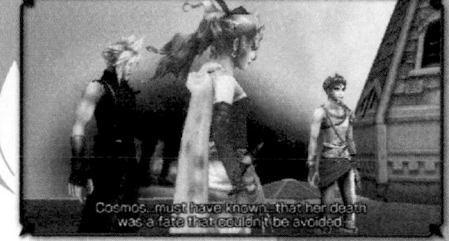

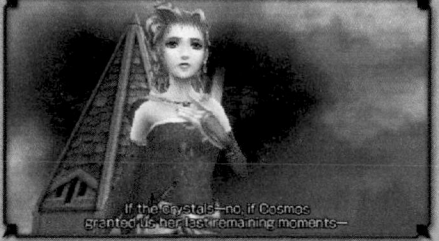

BATTLE PIECE DATA

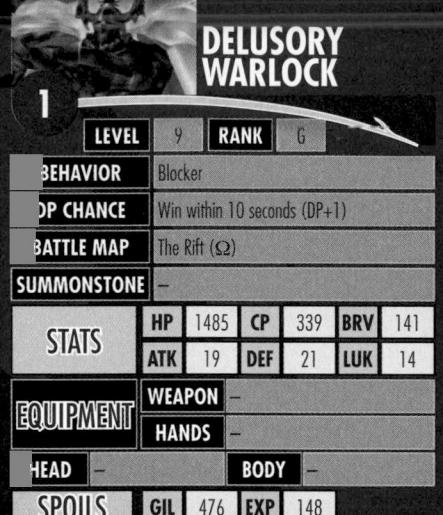

1 DELUSORY WARLOCK

LEVEL	9	RANK	G

BEHAVIOR	Blocker
DP CHANCE	Win within 10 seconds (DP+1)
BATTLE MAP	The Rift (Ω)
SUMMONSTONE	–

STATS	HP	1485	CP	339	BRV	141
	ATK	19	DEF	21	LUK	14

EQUIPMENT	WEAPON	–
	HANDS	–

HEAD	–	BODY	–

SPOILS	GIL	476	EXP	148

2 EPHEMERAL PHANTOM

LEVEL	36	RANK	C

BEHAVIOR	Calm
DP CHANCE	Keep foe from getting EX Cores (DP+1)
BATTLE MAP	Pandaemonium (Ω)
SUMMONSTONE	Ramuh

STATS	HP	3121*	CP	372	BRV	297*
	ATK	48*	DEF	48*	LUK	28

EQUIPMENT	WEAPON	[Rank 7]
	HANDS	[Rank 5]

HEAD	[Rank 5]	BODY	[Rank 6]

SPOILS	GIL	476	EXP	0

ACCESSORIES	Gaia Ring, Guardian Bangle, [HP] HP = 100% x3, [HP] HP ≥ 80% x5

3 PHANTASMAL HARLEQUIN

LEVEL	12	RANK	F

BEHAVIOR	Aggressive
DP CHANCE	Critical hit within 10 seconds (DP+1)
BATTLE MAP	Old Chaos Shrine (Ω)
SUMMONSTONE	–

STATS	HP	1667	CP	361	BRV	159
	ATK	23	DEF	22	LUK	16

EQUIPMENT	WEAPON	–
	HANDS	–

HEAD	–	BODY	–

SPOILS	GIL	476	EXP	166

4 FALSE HERO

LEVEL	22	RANK	B

BEHAVIOR	Aggressive
DP CHANCE	Wall Rush within 10 seconds (DP+1)
BATTLE MAP	Old Chaos Shrine (Ω)
SUMMONSTONE	–

STATS	HP	1	CP	355	BRV	216*
	ATK	32	DEF	36	LUK	21

EQUIPMENT	WEAPON	–
	HANDS	–

HEAD	[Rank 7]	BODY	–

SPOILS	GIL	476	EXP	4544

ACCESSORIES	The Rotten, Gaia Ring, Champion Belt, [Position] Near Opponent x5

5 TRANSIENT WITCH

LEVEL	37	RANK	C

BEHAVIOR	Valiant
DP CHANCE	Win without losing HP (DP+1)
BATTLE MAP	The Rift (Ω)
SUMMONSTONE	Kraken

STATS	HP	3181*	CP	373	BRV	303*
	ATK	48*	DEF	46*	LUK	28

EQUIPMENT	WEAPON	[Rank 6]
	HANDS	[Rank 5]

HEAD	[Rank 7]	BODY	[Rank 5]

SPOILS	GIL	476	EXP	0

ACCESSORIES	Gaia Ring, Hyper Ring, [HP] HP ≤ 40% x6, [HP] Near Death x2

6 COUNTERFEIT YOUTH

LEVEL	21	RANK	E

BEHAVIOR	Aggressive
DP CHANCE	–
BATTLE MAP	Old Chaos Shrine (Ω)
SUMMONSTONE	Bahamut

STATS	HP	2212*	CP	370	BRV	211*
	ATK	28*	DEF	32*	LUK	20

EQUIPMENT	WEAPON	[Rank 2]
	HANDS	[Rank 1]

HEAD	Hairpin	BODY	Chainmail

SPOILS	GIL	476	EXP	221

ACCESSORIES	Gaia Ring, War Gong, [BRV] BRV ≥ Base Value x8

7 EXDEATH

LEVEL	24	RANK	E

BEHAVIOR	Valiant
DP CHANCE	–
BATTLE MAP	The Rift (Ω)
SUMMONSTONE	Lich

STATS	HP	3301	CP	373	BRV	301
	ATK	51	DEF	53	LUK	22

EQUIPMENT	WEAPON	Mythril Rod
	HANDS	Knight's Shield

HEAD	Mythril Helm	BODY	Knight's Armor

SPOILS	GIL	2100	EXP	5985

ACCESSORIES	Gaia Ring, Hyper Ring, [HP] HP ≤ 40% x6, [HP] Near Death x2

8 FALSE STALWART

LEVEL	81	RANK	S

BEHAVIOR	Tactician
DP CHANCE	Win battle (DP+2)
BATTLE MAP	Order's Sanctuary (Ω)
SUMMONSTONE	Scarmiglione

STATS	HP	8093	CP	427	BRV	557*
	ATK	93*	DEF	94*	LUK	50

EQUIPMENT	WEAPON	[Rank 12]
	HANDS	[Rank 11]

HEAD	[Rank 13]	BODY	Mirror Mail

SPOILS	GIL	476	EXP	0

ACCESSORIES	Champion Belt, Muscle Belt, [Position] Near Opponent x6, [Time] After 90 Second

* Denotes use of the base value (for stats that vary).

SHADE IMPULSE I

SHADE IMPULSE ²
THE SCHEMERS

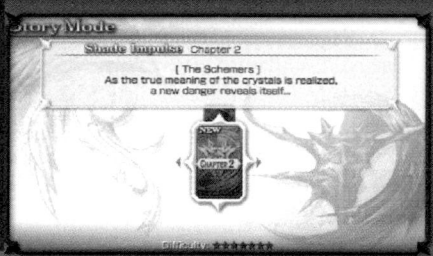

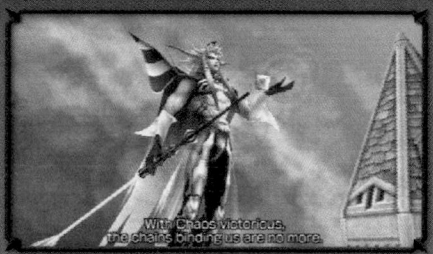

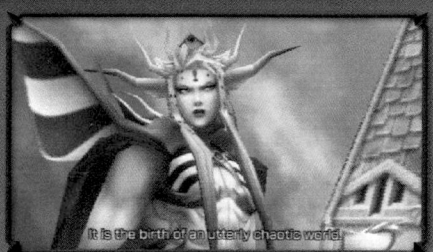

REWARDS

At the end of each level, rewards are available if you finish with a positive number of Destiny Points, or DP. This walkthrough includes miniature level maps that indicate the most efficient route to take through a given level, in order to maximize DP.

LEVEL COMPLETION

REMAINING DP		1ST TIME		2ND TIME
7		Rosetta Stone		300 PP
6		Warblade		200 PP
5		Warlord's Corselet		120 PP
4		Marilith		80 PP
3		4000 gil		50 PP
2		2400 gil		30 PP
1		1200 gil		20 PP
0		400 gil		10 PP

At the end of each set of levels, you'll receive rewards based on your performance. Story Points, or SP, are awarded after each level based on remaining DP and HP, as well as the number of engagements undertaken. Points are penalized for retries, or for a DP total that dips into negatives. If you miss out on a desired bonus on the first playthrough, don't worry—SP is cumulative across multiple playthroughs.

SHADE IMPULSE 2 COMPLETION

STAR RATING		SP REQUIRED		AWARD
☆		300		New skill
☆ ☆		200		Special areas unlocked
☆ ☆ ☆		300		Rare battle pieces spawned
☆ ☆ ☆ ☆		400		Rare treasure chests spawned
–		500 SP, then every 500 SP extra		100 PP

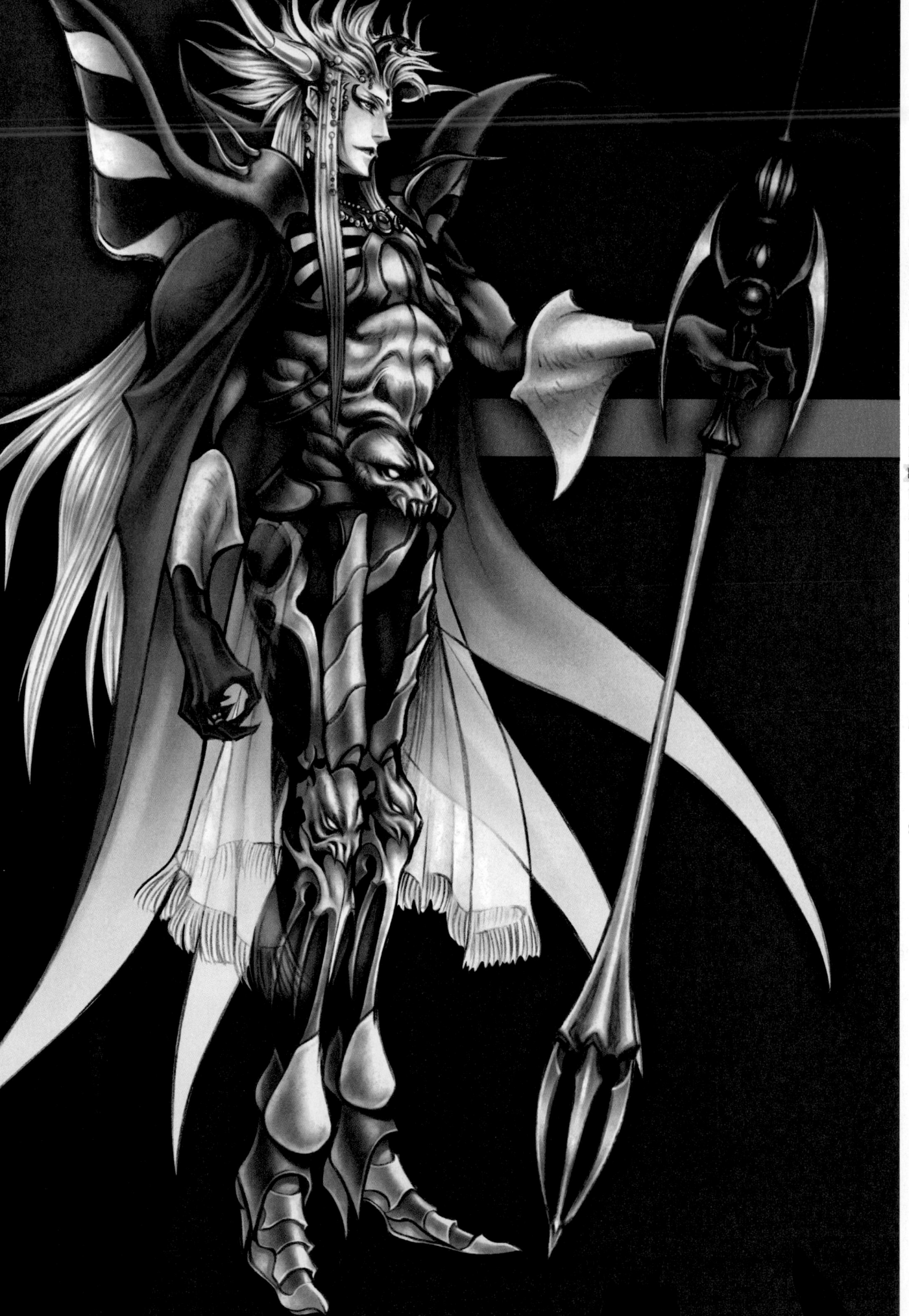

SHADE IMPULSE 2

SHADE IMPULSE

2-1

STARTING DP	MAX FINISHING	ENGAGEMENTS
4	3	7

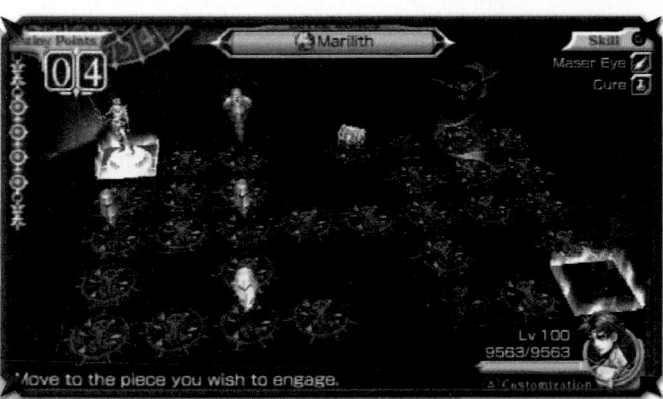

Just as experienced in the levels during Squall's Destiny Odyssey chapter, battle pieces can appear all over the place after defeating others. This doesn't ever trap you in unexpected battle chains here, however. Kuja serves as a mid-boss, fighting on a Crystal World stage that continually collapses and re-forms. Defeating him awards +2 Destiny Points and uncovers a hidden treasure chest in the bottom left. Battle piece ❹ must be defeated to open the way to another treasure chest near Kuja.

MAP

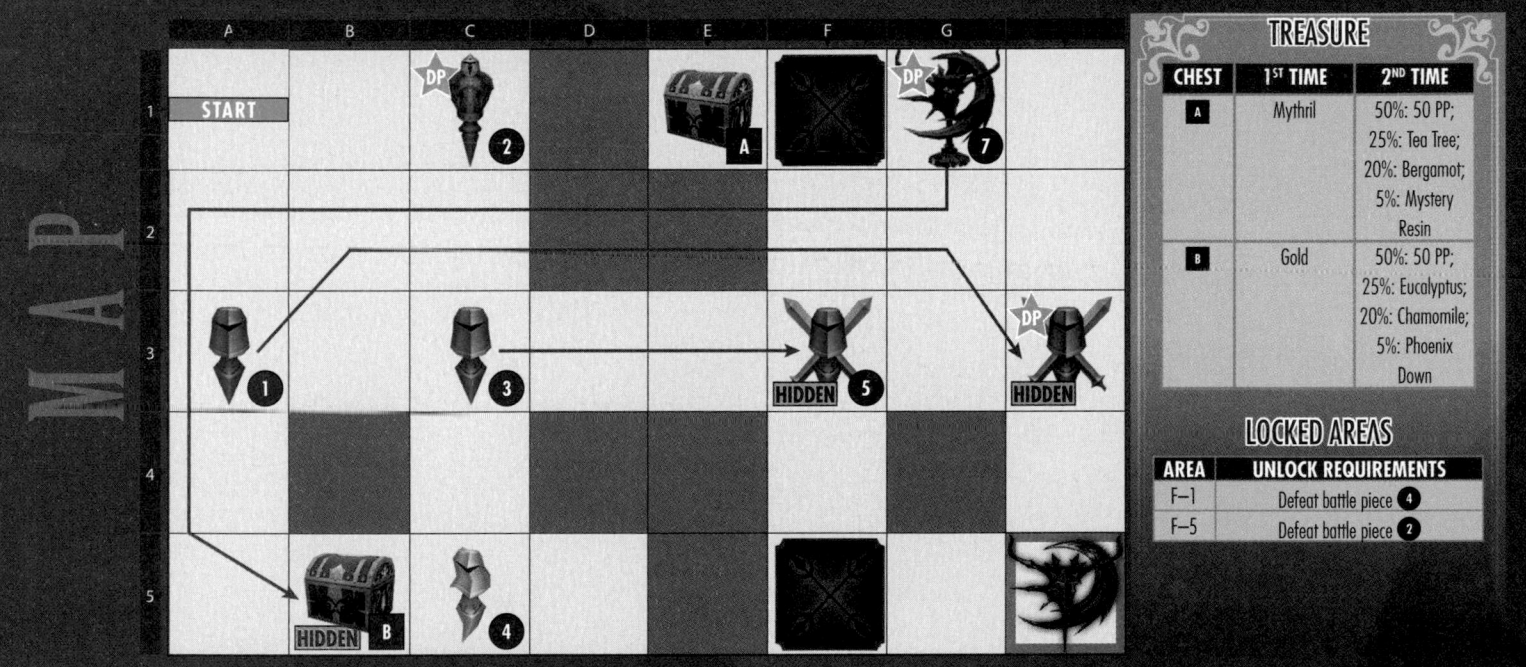

TREASURE

CHEST	1ST TIME	2ND TIME
A	Mythril	50%: 50 PP; 25%: Tea Tree; 20%: Bergamot; 5%: Mystery Resin
B	Gold	50%: 50 PP; 25%: Eucalyptus; 20%: Chamomile; 5%: Phoenix Down

LOCKED AREAS

AREA	UNLOCK REQUIREMENTS
F—1	Defeat battle piece ❹
F—5	Defeat battle piece ❷

DP EFFICIENCY ROUTE

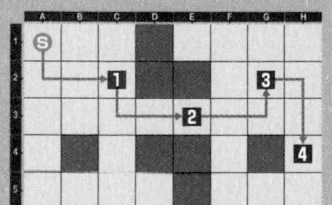

Head to C-2 and chain battle pieces ❷ and ❸. Destroying battle piece ❸ spawns battle piece ❺ further down the path. Defeat battle piece ❺, then defeat battle piece ❼. Afterward, move to the Stigma of Chaos.

BATTLE PIECE DATA

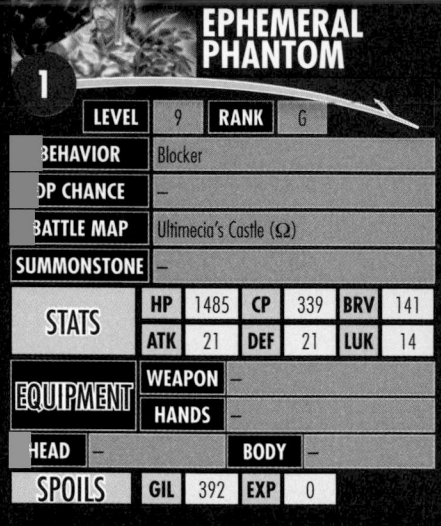

1 EPHEMERAL PHANTOM

LEVEL	9	RANK	G

BEHAVIOR	Blocker
DP CHANCE	–
BATTLE MAP	Ultimecia's Castle (Ω)
SUMMONSTONE	–

STATS	HP	1485	CP	339	BRV	141
	ATK	21	DEF	21	LUK	14

EQUIPMENT	WEAPON	–
	HANDS	–

HEAD	–	BODY	–

SPOILS	GIL	392	EXP	0

2 FALLACIOUS WANDERER

LEVEL	39	RANK	C

BEHAVIOR	Survivor
DP CHANCE	Win without losing HP (DP+1)
BATTLE MAP	Kefka's Tower (Ω)
SUMMONSTONE	Ifrit

STATS	HP	3303*	CP	388	BRV	315*
	ATK	49*	DEF	50*	LUK	29

EQUIPMENT	WEAPON	[Rank 6]
	HANDS	[Rank 5]

HEAD	[Rank 7]	BODY	[Rank 5]

SPOILS	GIL	392	EXP	0

ACCESSORIES	Gaia Ring, Hyper Ring, [HP] HP ≤ 40% x6, [HP] Near Death x2

3 DELUSORY KNIGHT

LEVEL	9	RANK	G

BEHAVIOR	Standby
DP CHANCE	–
BATTLE MAP	Kefka's Tower (Ω)
SUMMONSTONE	–

STATS	HP	1485	CP	339	BRV	141
	ATK	18	DEF	19	LUK	14

EQUIPMENT	WEAPON	–
	HANDS	–

HEAD	–	BODY	–

SPOILS	GIL	392	EXP	0

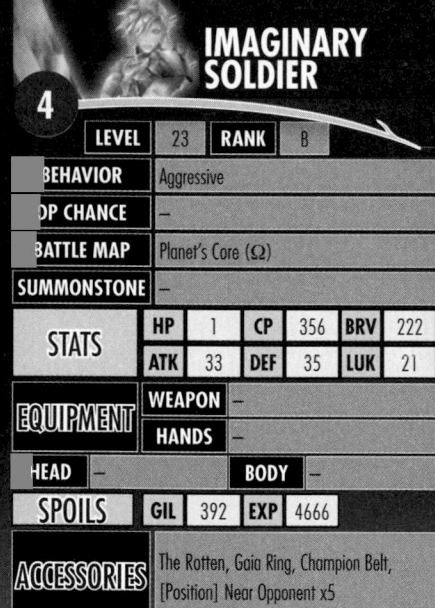

4 IMAGINARY SOLDIER

LEVEL	23	RANK	B

BEHAVIOR	Aggressive
DP CHANCE	–
BATTLE MAP	Planet's Core (Ω)
SUMMONSTONE	–

STATS	HP	1	CP	356	BRV	222
	ATK	33	DEF	35	LUK	21

EQUIPMENT	WEAPON	–
	HANDS	–

HEAD	–	BODY	–

SPOILS	GIL	392	EXP	4666

ACCESSORIES	The Rotten, Gaia Ring, Champion Belt, [Position] Near Opponent x5

5 CAPRICIOUS THIEF

LEVEL	24	RANK	F

BEHAVIOR	Normal
DP CHANCE	–
BATTLE MAP	Crystal World (Ω)
SUMMONSTONE	–

STATS	HP	2394*	CP	358	BRV	228*
	ATK	32*	DEF	34*	LUK	22

EQUIPMENT	WEAPON	[Rank 3]
	HANDS	[Rank 2]

HEAD	[Rank 4]	BODY	Poncho

SPOILS	GIL	392	EXP	0

ACCESSORIES	Arcane Incense, Tenacious Attacker, Glutton Gaia Ring, [EX] EX Gauge ≥ 70% x6

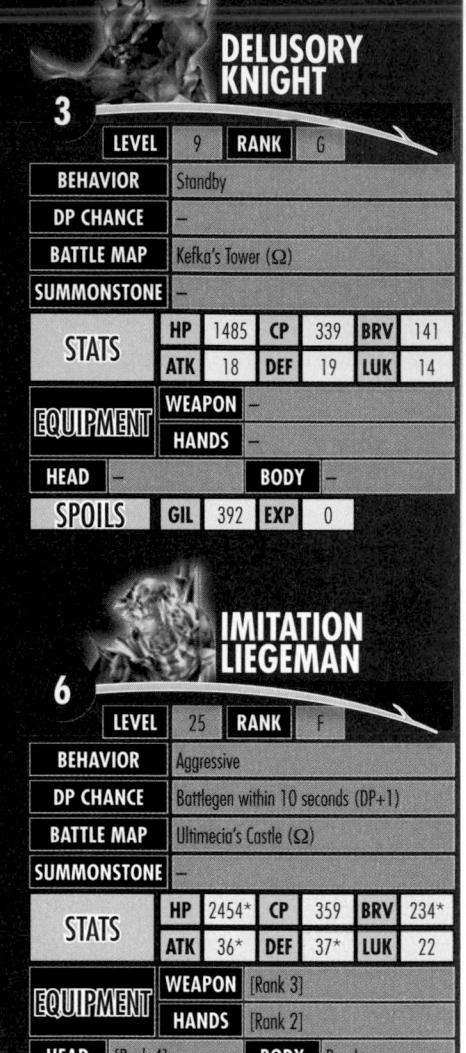

6 IMITATION LIEGEMAN

LEVEL	25	RANK	F

BEHAVIOR	Aggressive
DP CHANCE	Battlegen within 10 seconds (DP+1)
BATTLE MAP	Ultimecia's Castle (Ω)
SUMMONSTONE	–

STATS	HP	2454*	CP	359	BRV	234*
	ATK	36*	DEF	37*	LUK	22

EQUIPMENT	WEAPON	[Rank 3]
	HANDS	[Rank 2]

HEAD	[Rank 4]	BODY	Poncho

SPOILS	GIL	392	EXP	0

ACCESSORIES	Arcane Incense, Tenacious Attacker, Glutton Gaia Ring, [EX] EX Gauge ≥ 70% x6

7 KUJA

LEVEL	27	RANK	E

BEHAVIOR	Survivor
DP CHANCE	Win battle (DP+2)
BATTLE MAP	Crystal World (Ω)
SUMMONSTONE	Magic Pot

STATS	HP	3366	CP	361	BRV	388
	ATK	53	DEF	51	LUK	23

EQUIPMENT	WEAPON	Mage Masher
	HANDS	Silver Bangles

HEAD	Green Beret	BODY	Silk Robes

SPOILS	GIL	2520	EXP	5150

ACCESSORIES	Gaia Ring, Hyper Ring, [HP] HP ≤ 40% x6, [HP] Near Death x2

* Denotes use of the base value (for stats that vary).

STARTING DP	MAX FINISHING	ENGAGEMENTS
4	4	10

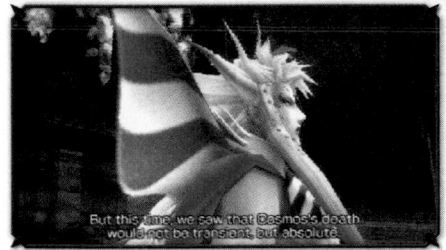

Many pieces here are shrouded with Enigma Areas, like with Onion Knight's Destiny Odyssey levels. Cagnazzo's Summon-stone is squirreled away behind a Locked Area that only disappears after completing Shade Impulse 2 with at least a 2-star rating. There isn't a mid-boss here, or any new pieces after higher star ratings. However, combat is present in abundance, and you can choose between either cleaning all pieces out for EXP or heading straight for the exit.

MAP

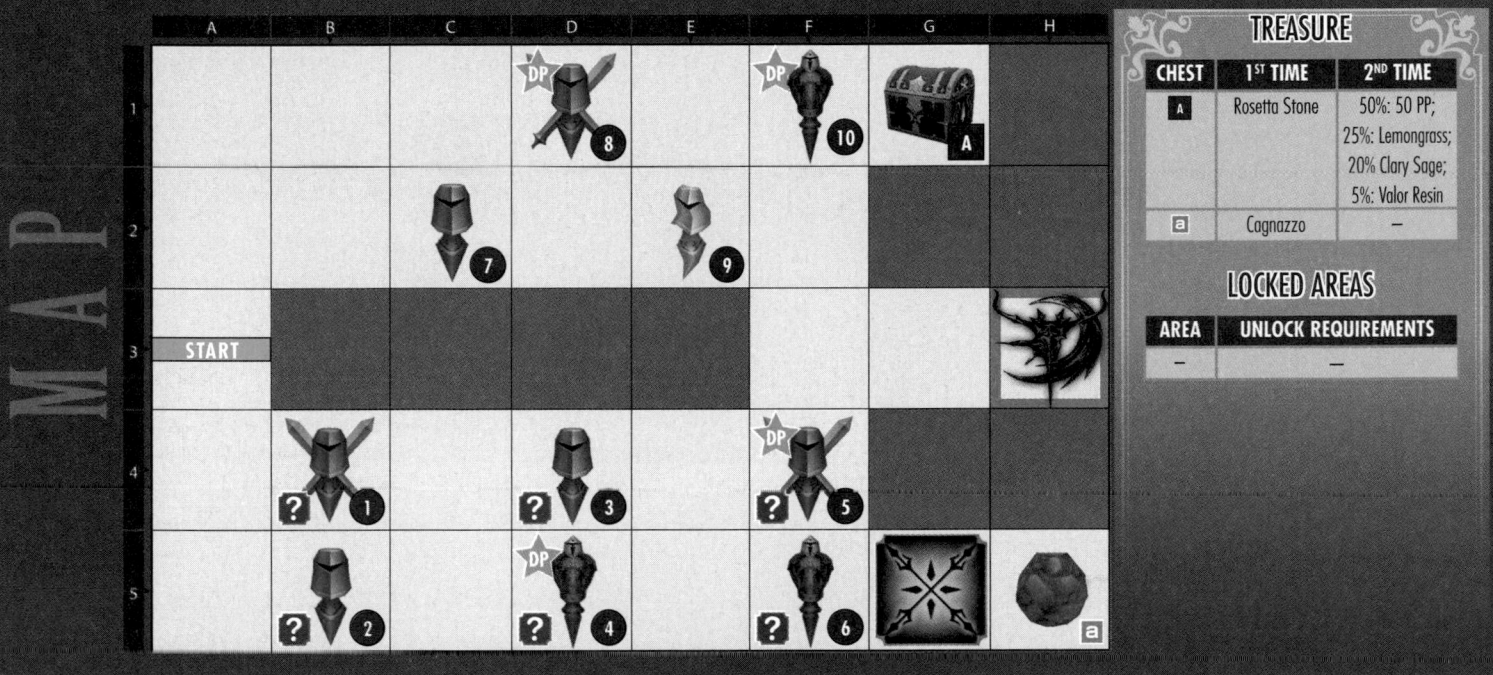

TREASURE

CHEST	1ST TIME	2ND TIME
A	Rosetta Stone	50%: 50 PP; 25%: Lemongrass; 20% Clary Sage; 5%: Valor Resin
a	Cagnazzo	—

LOCKED AREAS

AREA	UNLOCK REQUIREMENTS
—	—

BATTLE PIECE DATA

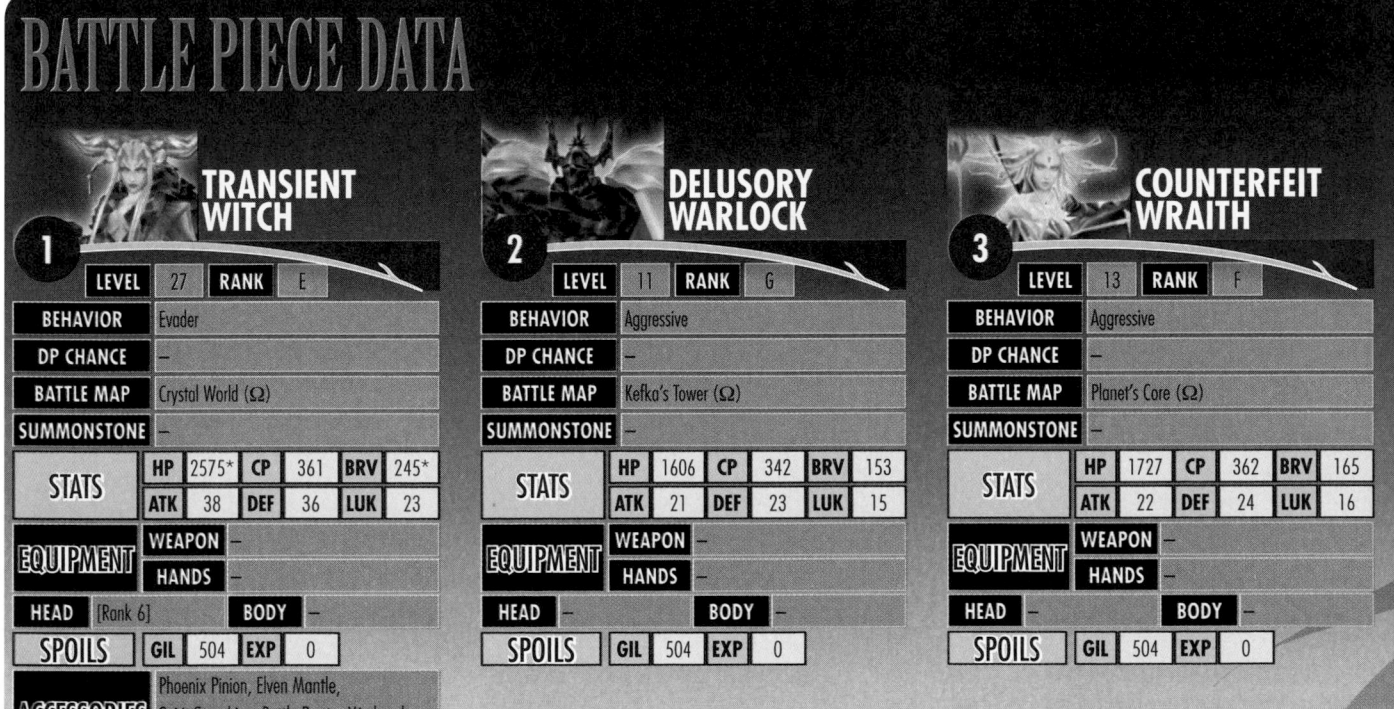

1 TRANSIENT WITCH

LEVEL	27	RANK	E

BEHAVIOR	Evader
DP CHANCE	—
BATTLE MAP	Crystal World (Ω)
SUMMONSTONE	—

STATS	HP	2575*	CP	361	BRV	245*
	ATK	38	DEF	36	LUK	23

EQUIPMENT	WEAPON	—
	HANDS	—

HEAD	[Rank 6]	BODY	—

SPOILS	GIL	504	EXP	0

ACCESSORIES	Phoenix Pinion, Elven Mantle, Spirit Stanchion, Battle Boots, Mindcrush, [HP] HP ≤ 40% x3, [HP] Near Death x2

2 DELUSORY WARLOCK

LEVEL	11	RANK	G

BEHAVIOR	Aggressive
DP CHANCE	—
BATTLE MAP	Kefka's Tower (Ω)
SUMMONSTONE	—

STATS	HP	1606	CP	342	BRV	153
	ATK	21	DEF	23	LUK	15

EQUIPMENT	WEAPON	—
	HANDS	—

HEAD	—	BODY	—

SPOILS	GIL	504	EXP	0

3 COUNTERFEIT WRAITH

LEVEL	13	RANK	F

BEHAVIOR	Aggressive
DP CHANCE	—
BATTLE MAP	Planet's Core (Ω)
SUMMONSTONE	—

STATS	HP	1727	CP	362	BRV	165
	ATK	22	DEF	24	LUK	16

EQUIPMENT	WEAPON	—
	HANDS	—

HEAD	—	BODY	—

SPOILS	GIL	504	EXP	0

* Denotes use of the base value (for stats that vary).

BATTLE PIECE DATA

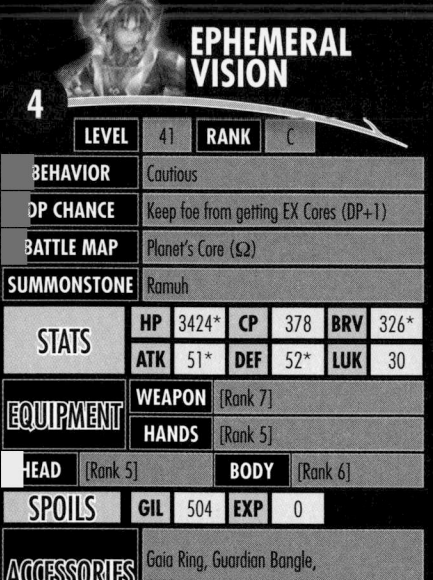

4 EPHEMERAL VISION

LEVEL	41	RANK C
BEHAVIOR	Cautious	
DP CHANCE	Keep foe from getting EX Cores (DP+1)	
BATTLE MAP	Planet's Core (Ω)	
SUMMONSTONE	Ramuh	

STATS						
	HP	3424*	CP	378	BRV	326*
	ATK	51*	DEF	52*	LUK	30

EQUIPMENT	WEAPON	[Rank 7]
	HANDS	[Rank 5]

HEAD	[Rank 5]	BODY	[Rank 6]

SPOILS	GIL	504	EXP	0

ACCESSORIES	Gaia Ring, Guardian Bangle, [HP] HP = 100% x3, [HP] HP ≥ 80% x5

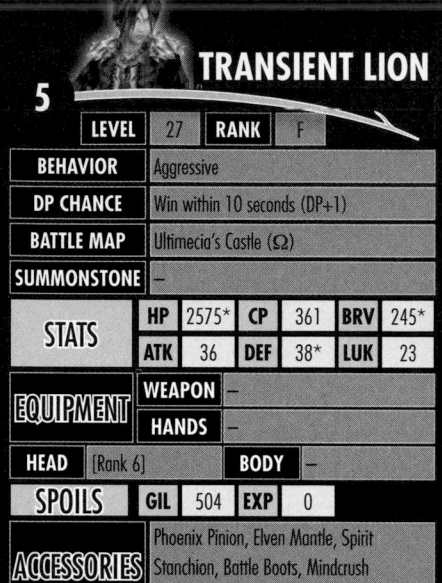

5 TRANSIENT LION

LEVEL	27	RANK F
BEHAVIOR	Aggressive	
DP CHANCE	Win within 10 seconds (DP+1)	
BATTLE MAP	Ultimecia's Castle (Ω)	
SUMMONSTONE	—	

STATS						
	HP	2575*	CP	361	BRV	245*
	ATK	36	DEF	38*	LUK	23

EQUIPMENT	WEAPON	—
	HANDS	—

HEAD	[Rank 6]	BODY	—

SPOILS	GIL	504	EXP	0

ACCESSORIES	Phoenix Pinion, Elven Mantle, Spirit Stanchion, Battle Boots, Mindcrush [HP] HP ≤ 40% x3, [HP] Near Death x2

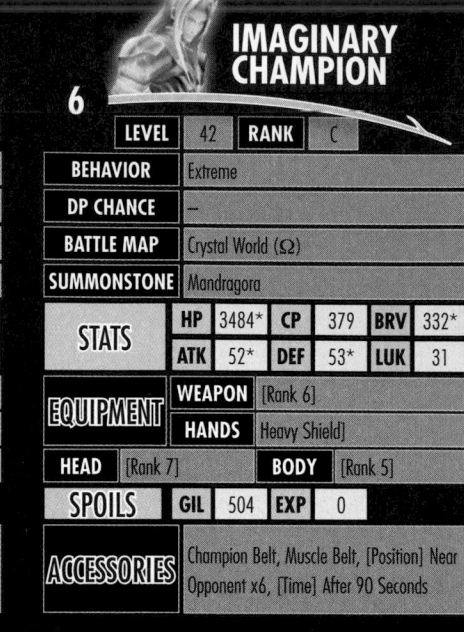

6 IMAGINARY CHAMPION

LEVEL	42	RANK C
BEHAVIOR	Extreme	
DP CHANCE	—	
BATTLE MAP	Crystal World (Ω)	
SUMMONSTONE	Mandragora	

STATS						
	HP	3484*	CP	379	BRV	332*
	ATK	52*	DEF	53*	LUK	31

EQUIPMENT	WEAPON	[Rank 6]
	HANDS	Heavy Shield]

HEAD	[Rank 7]	BODY	[Rank 5]

SPOILS	GIL	504	EXP	0

ACCESSORIES	Champion Belt, Muscle Belt, [Position] Near Opponent x6, [Time] After 90 Seconds

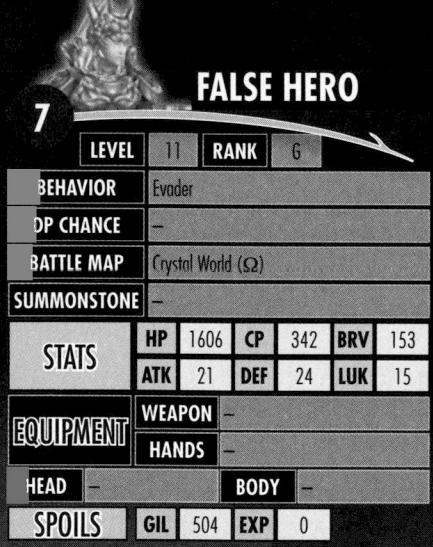

7 FALSE HERO

LEVEL	11	RANK G
BEHAVIOR	Evader	
DP CHANCE	—	
BATTLE MAP	Crystal World (Ω)	
SUMMONSTONE	—	

STATS						
	HP	1606	CP	342	BRV	153
	ATK	21	DEF	24	LUK	15

EQUIPMENT	WEAPON	—
	HANDS	—

HEAD		BODY	—

SPOILS	GIL	504	EXP	0

8 COUNTERFEIT WRAITH

LEVEL	28	RANK F
BEHAVIOR	Normal	
DP CHANCE	Wall Rush within 10 seconds (DP+1)	
BATTLE MAP	Dream's End (Ω)	
SUMMONSTONE	Ifrit	

STATS						
	HP	2636*	CP	377	BRV	251*
	ATK	37	DEF	39	LUK	24

EQUIPMENT	WEAPON	—
	HANDS	—

HEAD	[Rank 6]	BODY	—

SPOILS	GIL	504	EXP	0

ACCESSORIES	Phoenix Pinion, Elven Mantle, Spirit Stanchion, Battle Boots, Mindcrush, [HP] HP ≤ 40% x3, [HP] Near Death x2

9 FALLACIOUS WANDERER

LEVEL	27	RANK B
BEHAVIOR	Aggressive	
DP CHANCE	Critical hit within 10 seconds (DP+1)	
BATTLE MAP	Crystal World (Ω)	
SUMMONSTONE	Odin	

STATS						
	HP	1	CP	376	BRV	5145
	ATK	37	DEF	38	LUK	23

EQUIPMENT	WEAPON	—
	HANDS	—

HEAD	—	BODY	—

SPOILS	GIL	504	EXP	5150

ACCESSORIES	Soul of the Destroyer, The Rotten

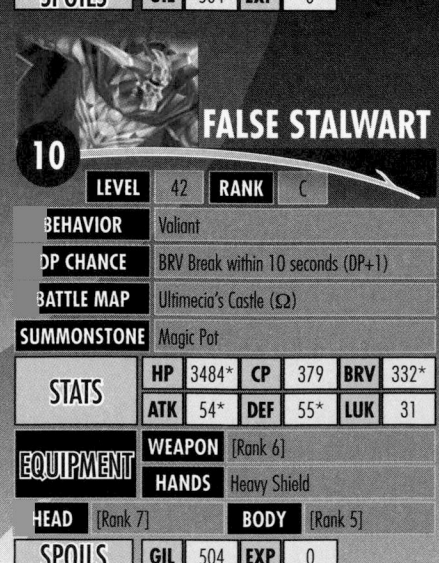

10 FALSE STALWART

LEVEL	42	RANK C
BEHAVIOR	Valiant	
DP CHANCE	BRV Break within 10 seconds (DP+1)	
BATTLE MAP	Ultimecia's Castle (Ω)	
SUMMONSTONE	Magic Pot	

STATS						
	HP	3484*	CP	379	BRV	332*
	ATK	54*	DEF	55*	LUK	31

EQUIPMENT	WEAPON	[Rank 6]
	HANDS	Heavy Shield

HEAD	[Rank 7]	BODY	[Rank 5]

SPOILS	GIL	504	EXP	0

ACCESSORIES	Gaia Ring, Hyper Ring, [HP] HP ≤ 40% x6, [HP] Near Death x2

DP EFFICIENCY ROUTE

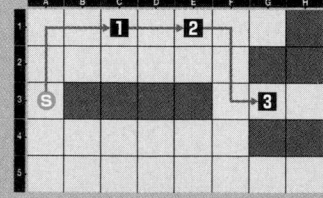

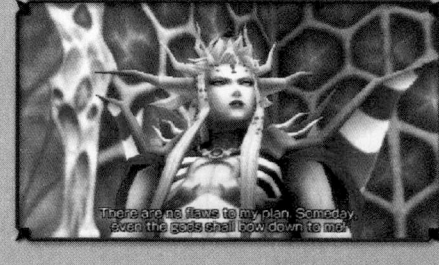

No special star rating is required for maximum Destiny Points on this level. Chain battle pieces **8** and **7** first before following up with **9** and **10**. Continue on to the exit after dispatching this pair of chains.

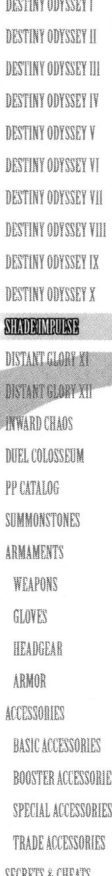

SHADE IMPULSE 2

SHADE IMPULSE

2-3

STARTING DP	MAX FINISHING	ENGAGEMENTS
4	**5** (+2 after .3-star rating)	**8** (+1 after 3-star rating)

Again, many pieces are covered with Enigma Areas. If you aren't concerned with Destiny Points on your first time through, you can just grab Odin's Summonstone from the upper right corner and head for the exit without a single battle. After achieving a 4-star Shade Impulse 2 rating, a treasure chest appears in the bottom left. The mid-boss, Cloud of Darkness, guards this chest's position. Battle piece ⑨, near Odin, shows up only after a 3-star rating. This crystal version of Warrior of Light is very strong and doesn't leave many openings. If you're at a much lower level than this foe, you'll have little chance of winning through simple attacks or BRV Break. Instead, you can try letting the enemy inflict Break on *you*, giving the manikin foe a giant pool of bravery. Then, steal it with Magic Pot. The enemy then counters this with Cagnazzo, but this is an awful move for him, since this only freezes the bravery you just stole.

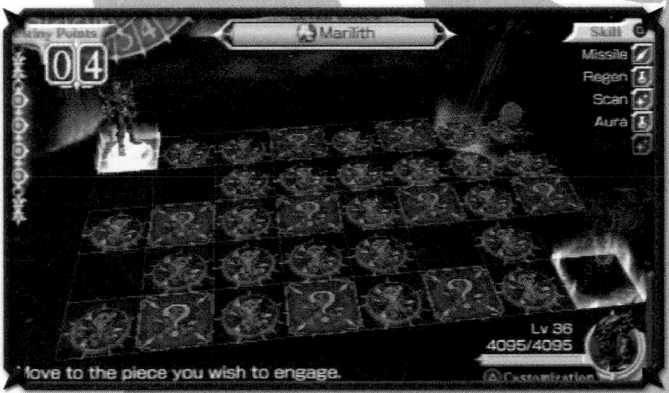

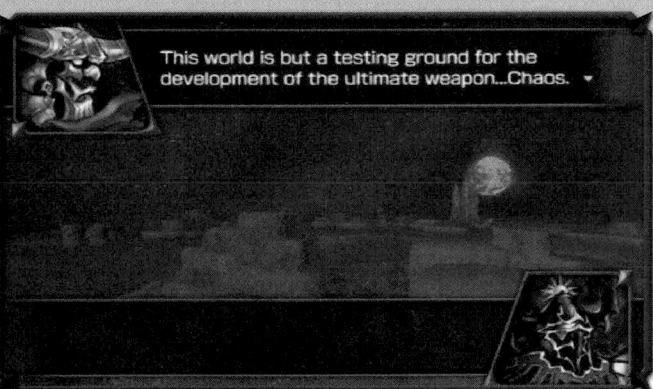

MAP

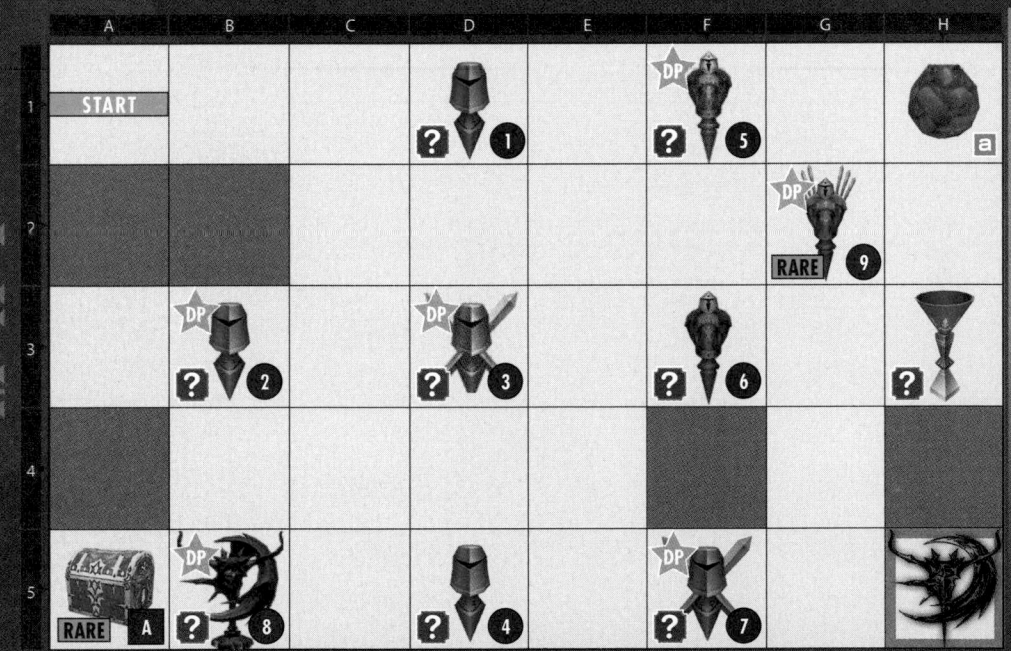

TREASURE

CHEST	1ST TIME	2ND TIME
A	Gold (after 4-star rating)	–
a	Odin	–

LOCKED AREAS

AREA	UNLOCK REQUIREMENTS
–	–

DP EFFICIENCY ROUTE

Full DP here requires the presence of the rare, ultimate battle piece. This means returning to Shade Impulse 2 after a 3-star rating. Start by heading downward and chaining battle pieces ⑧ and ②. Next, move to F-2 and chain battle pieces ⑤, ⑥, and ⑨. You can build your EX Gauge during the fight with battle piece ⑥ to ensure a quick victory against battle piece ⑤. After this chain, engage the mid-boss, a level 31 Cloud of Darkness, and head for the exit.

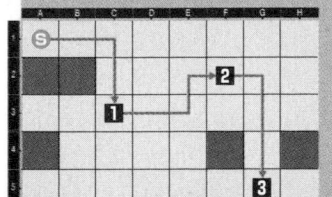

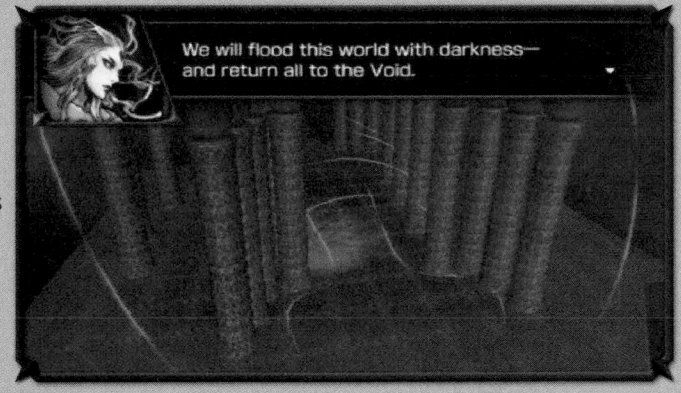

BATTLE PIECE DATA

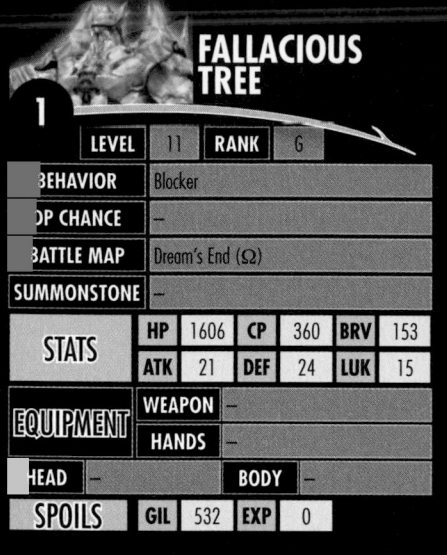

1 FALLACIOUS TREE

LEVEL	11	RANK	6

BEHAVIOR	Blocker
DP CHANCE	–
BATTLE MAP	Dream's End (Ω)
SUMMONSTONE	–

STATS	HP	1606	CP	360	BRV	153
	ATK	21	DEF	24	LUK	15

EQUIPMENT	WEAPON	–
	HANDS	–
HEAD		BODY	–

SPOILS	GIL	532	EXP	0

2 EPHEMERAL PHANTOM

LEVEL	13	RANK	F

BEHAVIOR	Normal
DP CHANCE	Win without taking damage (DP+1)
BATTLE MAP	Dream's End (Ω)
SUMMONSTONE	–

STATS	HP	1727	CP	344	BRV	165
	ATK	25	DEF	25	LUK	16

EQUIPMENT	WEAPON	–
	HANDS	–
HEAD		BODY	–

SPOILS	GIL	532	EXP	0

3 COUNTERFEIT YOUTH

LEVEL	28	RANK	F

BEHAVIOR	Normal
DP CHANCE	Battlegen within 10 seconds (DP+1)
BATTLE MAP	Ultimecia's Castle (Ω)
SUMMONSTONE	–

STATS	HP	2636*	CP	377	BRV	251*
	ATK	35*	DEF	39*	LUK	24

EQUIPMENT	WEAPON	[Rank 3]
	HANDS	[Rank 2]
HEAD	[Rank 4]	BODY	Poncho

SPOILS	GIL	532	EXP	0

ACCESSORIES	Defense Cuff x4, [HP] Near Death x2

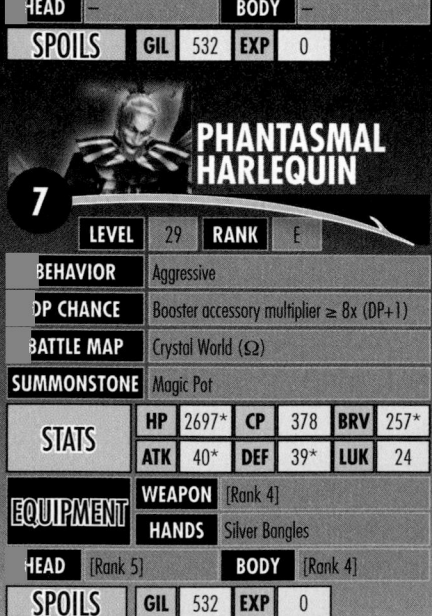

4 IMAGINARY SOLDIER

LEVEL	14	RANK	F

BEHAVIOR	Blocker
DP CHANCE	–
BATTLE MAP	Crystal World (Ω)
SUMMONSTONE	–

STATS	HP	1788	CP	345	BRV	170
	ATK	24	DEF	26	LUK	17

EQUIPMENT	WEAPON	–
	HANDS	–
HEAD	–	BODY	–

SPOILS	GIL	532	EXP	0

5 EPHEMERAL VISION

LEVEL	44	RANK	B

BEHAVIOR	Tactician
DP CHANCE	Win within 20 seconds (DP+1)
BATTLE MAP	Ultimecia's Castle (Ω)
SUMMONSTONE	Ifrit

STATS	HP	3605*	CP	382	BRV	343*
	ATK	54*	DEF	55*	LUK	32

EQUIPMENT	WEAPON	[Rank 8]
	HANDS	[Rank 6]
HEAD	[Rank 6]	BODY	[Rank 7]

SPOILS	GIL	532	EXP	0

ACCESSORIES	Gaia Ring, Hyper Ring, [HP] HP ≤ 40% x6, [HP] Near Death x2

6 CAPRICIOUS REAPER

LEVEL	45	RANK	B

BEHAVIOR	Extreme
DP CHANCE	–
BATTLE MAP	Ultimecia's Castle (Ω)
SUMMONSTONE	Ultros

STATS	HP	3666*	CP	383	BRV	349*
	ATK	54*	DEF	56*	LUK	32

EQUIPMENT	WEAPON	Wizard's Rod
	HANDS	[Rank 6]
HEAD	Red Cap	BODY	Traveler's Vestment

SPOILS	GIL	532	EXP	0

ACCESSORIES	Gaia Ring, Guardian Bangle, [HP] HP = 100% x3, [HP] HP ≥ 80% x5

7 PHANTASMAL HARLEQUIN

LEVEL	29	RANK	E

BEHAVIOR	Aggressive
DP CHANCE	Booster accessory multiplier ≥ 8x (DP+1)
BATTLE MAP	Crystal World (Ω)
SUMMONSTONE	Magic Pot

STATS	HP	2697*	CP	378	BRV	257*
	ATK	40*	DEF	39*	LUK	24

EQUIPMENT	WEAPON	[Rank 4]
	HANDS	Silver Bangles
HEAD	[Rank 5]	BODY	[Rank 4]

SPOILS	GIL	532	EXP	0

ACCESSORIES	Black Cape x4, [HP] Near Death x2

* Denotes use of the base value (for stats that vary).

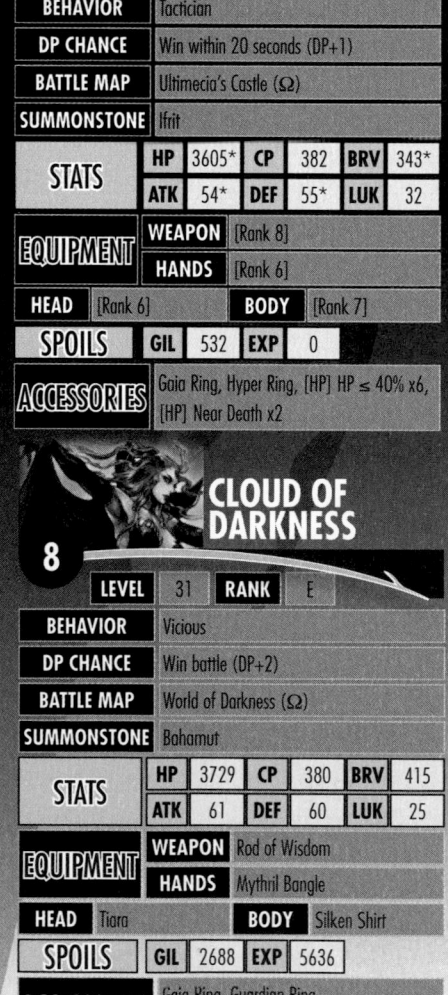

8 CLOUD OF DARKNESS

LEVEL	31	RANK	E

BEHAVIOR	Vicious
DP CHANCE	Win battle (DP+2)
BATTLE MAP	World of Darkness (Ω)
SUMMONSTONE	Bahamut

STATS	HP	3729	CP	380	BRV	415
	ATK	61	DEF	60	LUK	25

EQUIPMENT	WEAPON	Rod of Wisdom
	HANDS	Mythril Bangle
HEAD	Tiara	BODY	Silken Shirt

SPOILS	GIL	2688	EXP	5636

ACCESSORIES	Gaia Ring, Guardian Ring, [HP] HP = 100% x3, [HP] HP ≥ 80% x5

9 FALSE HERO

LEVEL	86	RANK	S

BEHAVIOR	Conservative
DP CHANCE	Win battle (DP+2)
BATTLE MAP	Order's Sanctuary (Ω)
SUMMONSTONE	Cagnazzo

STATS	HP	6150*	CP	433	BRV	586*
	ATK	96*	DEF	99*	LUK	53

EQUIPMENT	WEAPON	[Rank 14]
	HANDS	[Rank 12]
HEAD	[Rank 12]	BODY	[Rank 13]

SPOILS	GIL	672	EXP	0

ACCESSORIES	Gaia Ring, Hyper Ring, [HP] HP ≤ 40% x6, [HP] Near Death x2

SHADE IMPULSE 2

This board behaves like one of Squall's levels, with most encounters generating another battle piece far away. A Locked Area that opens after a 2-star rating blocks access to a treasure chest, but no new pieces appear after a rating of three stars or better. Golbez, the mid-boss, appears after defeating battle piece ④. Approaching him as Cecil reveals a cutscene before battle.

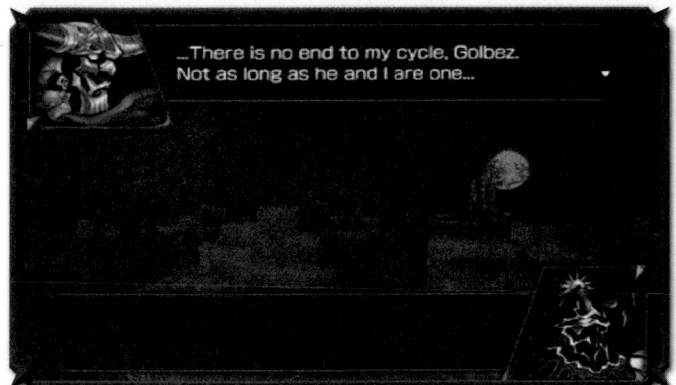

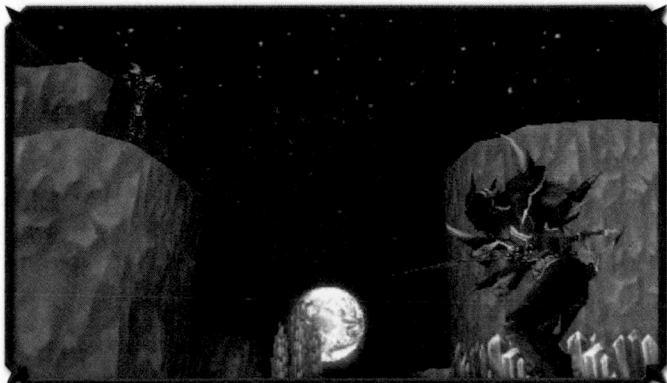

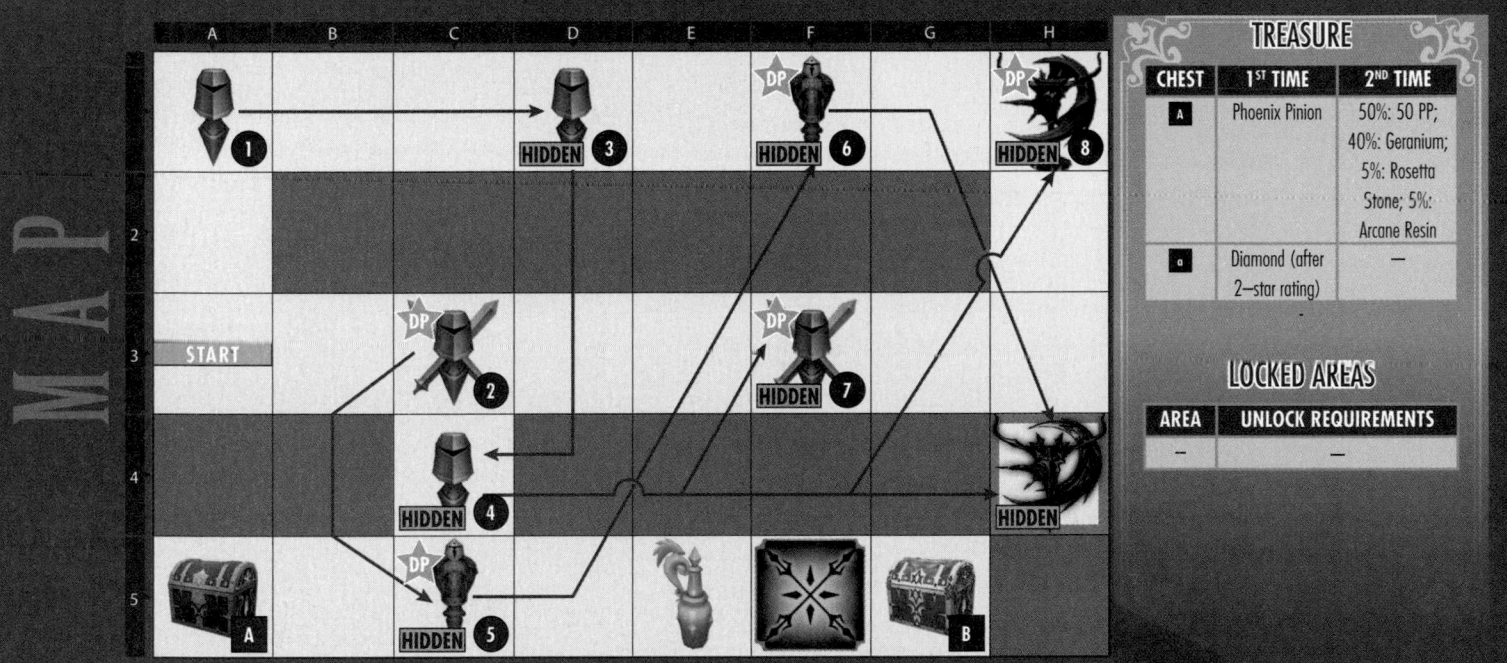

TREASURE

CHEST	1ST TIME	2ND TIME
A	Phoenix Pinion	50%: 50 PP; 40%: Geranium; 5%: Rosetta Stone; 5%: Arcane Resin
B	Diamond (after 2—star rating)	—

LOCKED AREAS

AREA	UNLOCK REQUIREMENTS
—	—

DP EFFICIENCY ROUTE

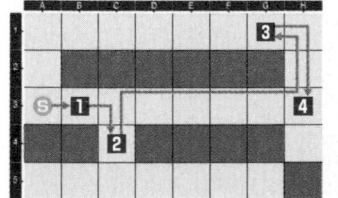

Engage battle piece ② and defeat it within 10 seconds. The next target is battle piece ⑤. The DP Chance during this fight requires an EX Burst within 10 seconds, so you'll have to prepare beforehand with accessories, skills, and as much EX Force as you can collect during the previous fight. Defeating battle piece ⑤ reveals battle piece ⑥. Head up to piece ⑥ and engage it before heading to the Stigma of Chaos, finishing the level.

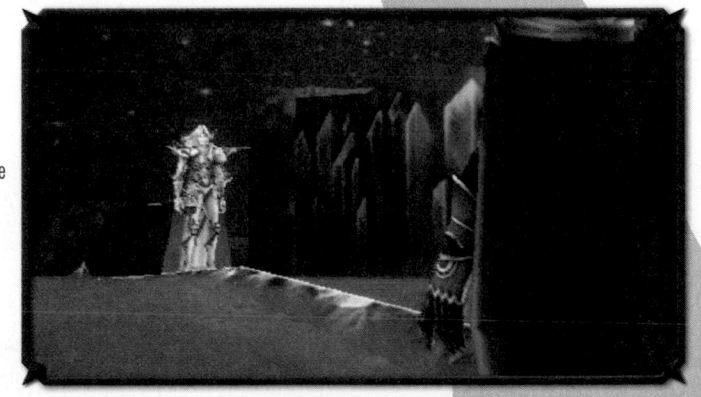

BATTLE PIECE DATA

1 PHANTASMAL GIRL

LEVEL	13	RANK	F		

BEHAVIOR	Normal
DP CHANCE	–
BATTLE MAP	Crystal World (Ω)
SUMMONSTONE	–

STATS	HP	1727	CP	344	BRV	165
	ATK	24	DEF	23	LUK	16

EQUIPMENT	WEAPON	–
	HANDS	–

HEAD	–		BODY	–

SPOILS	GIL	560	EXP	0

2 DELUSORY KNIGHT

LEVEL	31	RANK	E		

BEHAVIOR	Normal
DP CHANCE	Win within 10 seconds (DP+1)
BATTLE MAP	Kefka's Tower (Ω)
SUMMONSTONE	PuPu

STATS	HP	2818*	CP	366	BRV	268*
	ATK	40*	DEF	41*	LUK	25

EQUIPMENT	WEAPON	[Rank 4]
	HANDS	Knight's Shield

HEAD	Heavy Helm		BODY	[Rank 4]

SPOILS	GIL	560	EXP	0

ACCESSORIES	Gaia Ring, Hyper Ring, [Position] Near Opponent x8

3 EPHEMERAL VISION

LEVEL	11	RANK	G		

BEHAVIOR	Evader
DP CHANCE	–
BATTLE MAP	Crystal World (Ω)
SUMMONSTONE	–

STATS	HP	1606	CP	342	BRV	153
	ATK	21	DEF	22	LUK	15

EQUIPMENT	WEAPON	–
	HANDS	–

HEAD	–		BODY	–

SPOILS	GIL	560	EXP	0

4 FALSE STALWART

LEVEL	15	RANK	F		

BEHAVIOR	Evader
DP CHANCE	–
BATTLE MAP	Kefka's Tower (Ω)
SUMMONSTONE	–

STATS	HP	1848	CP	347	BRV	176
	ATK	27	DEF	28	LUK	17

EQUIPMENT	WEAPON	–
	HANDS	–

HEAD	–		BODY	–

SPOILS	GIL	560	EXP	0

5 TRANSIENT WITCH

LEVEL	46	RANK	B		

BEHAVIOR	Extreme
DP CHANCE	EX Burst within 10 seconds (DP+1)
BATTLE MAP	Dream's End (Ω)
SUMMONSTONE	Kraken

STATS	HP	3727*	CP	384	BRV	355*
	ATK	57*	DEF	55*	LUK	33

EQUIPMENT	WEAPON	[Rank 7]
	HANDS	[Rank 6]

HEAD	[Rank 8]		BODY	Traveler's Vestment

SPOILS	GIL	560	EXP	0

ACCESSORIES	Star Earring, Earring, [Position] Far from Opponent x6, [Time] After 90 Seconds

6 IMAGINARY CHAMPION

LEVEL	47	RANK	B		

BEHAVIOR	Conservative
DP CHANCE	Keep foe from getting EX Cores (DP+1)
BATTLE MAP	Crystal World (Ω)
SUMMONSTONE	Carbuncle

STATS	HP	3787*	CP	385	BRV	361*
	ATK	57*	DEF	58*	LUK	33

EQUIPMENT	WEAPON	[Rank 8]
	HANDS	[Rank 6]

HEAD	[Rank 6]		BODY	[Rank 7]

SPOILS	GIL	560	EXP	0

ACCESSORIES	Gaia Ring, Hyper Ring, [HP] HP ≤ 40% x6, [HP] Near Death x2

7 FALSE HERO

LEVEL	31	RANK	F		

BEHAVIOR	Aggressive
DP CHANCE	Win without taking damage (DP+1)
BATTLE MAP	Dream's End (Ω)
SUMMONSTONE	–

STATS	HP	2818*	CP	366	BRV	357
	ATK	41*	DEF	44*	LUK	25

EQUIPMENT	WEAPON	[Rank 4]
	HANDS	[Rank 3]

HEAD	Heavy Helm		BODY	[Rank 4]

SPOILS	GIL	560	EXP	0

ACCESSORIES	Gaia Ring, Hyper Ring, [Position] Near Opponent x8

8 GOLBEZ

LEVEL	33	RANK	E		

BEHAVIOR	Calm
DP CHANCE	Win battle (DP+2)
BATTLE MAP	Lunar Subterrane (Ω)
SUMMONSTONE	Shiva

STATS	HP	3811	CP	368	BRV	386
	ATK	66	DEF	63	LUK	26

EQUIPMENT	WEAPON	Claymore
	HANDS	Gauntlets

HEAD	Heavy Helm		BODY	Linen Cuirass

SPOILS	GIL	2856	EXP	5878

ACCESSORIES	Gaia Ring, Hyper Ring, [HP] HP ≤ 40% x6, [HP] Near Death x2

* Denotes use of the base value (for stats that vary).

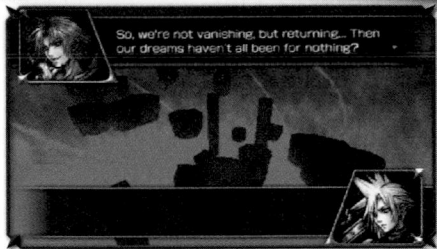

2-5

STARTING DP	MAX FINISHING	ENGAGEMENTS
5	5 (+2 after 3-star rating)	10 (+1 after 3-star rating)

The level begins with a wall of three battle pieces blocking your passage. Defeating any of these three reveals three more pieces further down the path; in turn, defeating any of these three pieces spawns three *more* near the Stigma of Chaos! A 3-star rating spawns an ultimate battle piece between the first two of these groups, while a 4-star rating spawns a rare treasure chest just above the first group. The ultimate battle piece is a powerful manikin of Garland, armed with the Rubicante summon. As with other high level battle pieces, winning with a lower level character can involve gaming the system a bit rather than actually besting your foe in combat. If he inflicts BRV Break on you, his bravery can approach or match 9999—a terrific total to copy with Magic Pot. Then, it's just a matter of landing a single hit. The Emperor stands with the Stigma of Chaos as boss of Shade Impulse 2. The halls of Pandaemonium are cramped spaces that don't favor The Emperor's projectiles. When he initiates his ranged attacks, just dance behind a wall or down another corridor and wait out his assault.

MAP

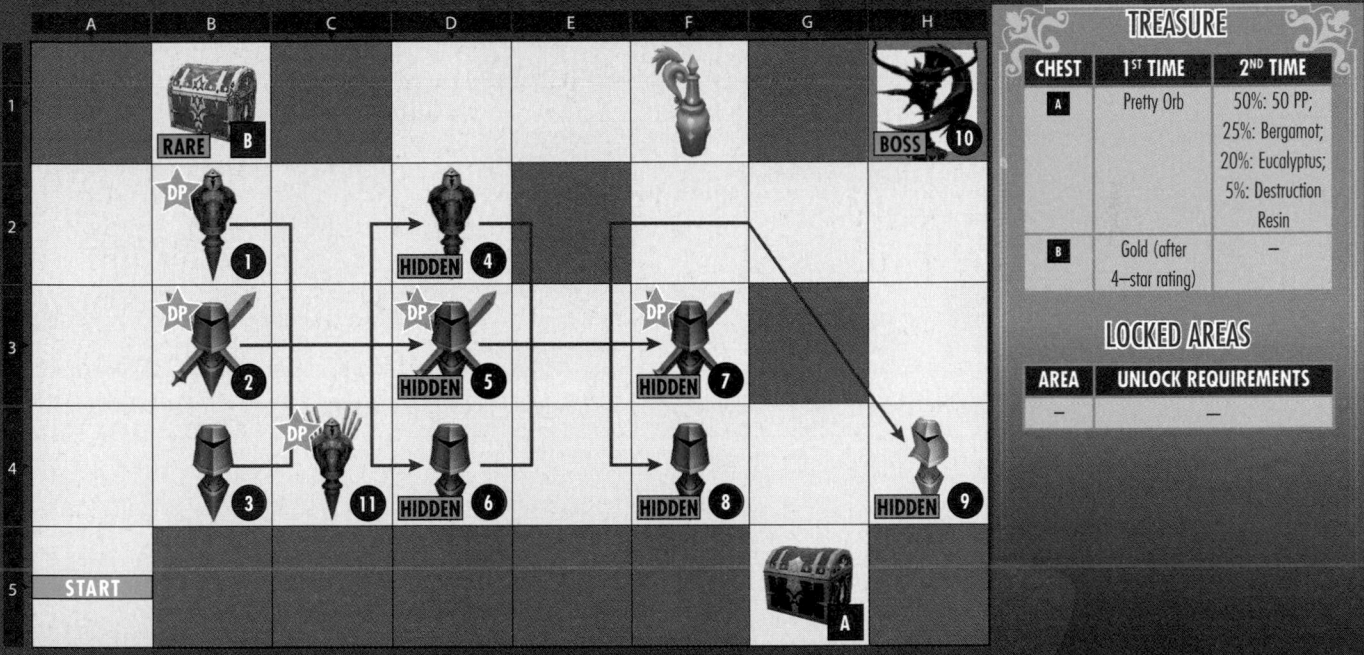

TREASURE

CHEST	1ST TIME	2ND TIME
A	Pretty Orb	50%: 50 PP; 25%: Bergamot; 20%: Eucalyptus; 5%: Destruction Resin
B	Gold (after 4-star rating)	—

LOCKED AREAS

AREA	UNLOCK REQUIREMENTS
—	—

BATTLE PIECE DATA

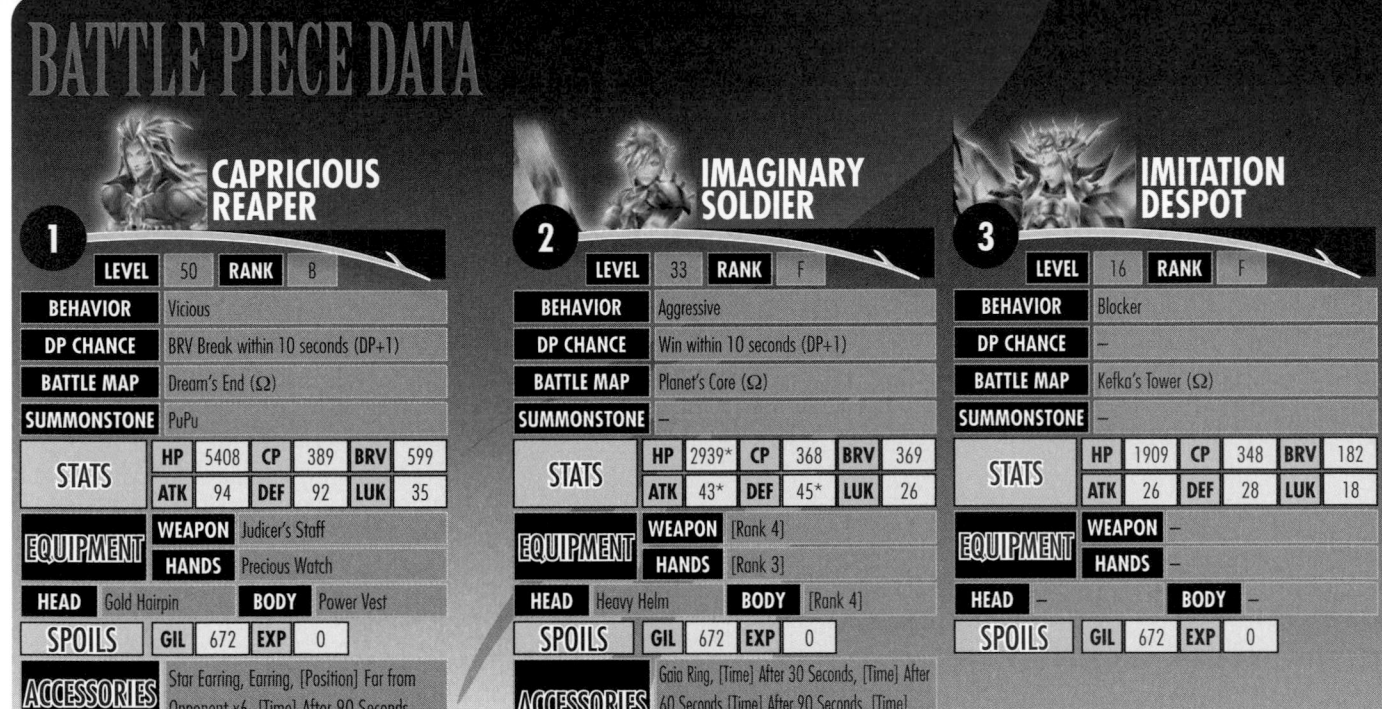

1 CAPRICIOUS REAPER

LEVEL	50
RANK	B
BEHAVIOR	Vicious
DP CHANCE	BRV Break within 10 seconds (DP+1)
BATTLE MAP	Dream's End (Ω)
SUMMONSTONE	PuPu

STATS	HP	5408	CP	389	BRV	599
	ATK	94	DEF	92	LUK	35

EQUIPMENT	WEAPON	Judicer's Staff
	HANDS	Precious Watch

HEAD	Gold Hairpin	BODY	Power Vest

SPOILS	GIL	672	EXP	0

ACCESSORIES	Star Earring, Earring, [Position] Far from Opponent x6, [Time] After 90 Seconds

2 IMAGINARY SOLDIER

LEVEL	33
RANK	F
BEHAVIOR	Aggressive
DP CHANCE	Win within 10 seconds (DP+1)
BATTLE MAP	Planet's Core (Ω)
SUMMONSTONE	—

STATS	HP	2939*	CP	368	BRV	369
	ATK	43*	DEF	45*	LUK	26

EQUIPMENT	WEAPON	[Rank 4]
	HANDS	[Rank 3]

HEAD	Heavy Helm	BODY	[Rank 4]

SPOILS	GIL	672	EXP	0

ACCESSORIES	Gaia Ring, [Time] After 30 Seconds, [Time] After 60 Seconds, [Time] After 90 Seconds, [Time] After 120 Seconds, [Time] After 180 Seconds

3 IMITATION DESPOT

LEVEL	16
RANK	F
BEHAVIOR	Blocker
DP CHANCE	—
BATTLE MAP	Kefka's Tower (Ω)
SUMMONSTONE	—

STATS	HP	1909	CP	348	BRV	182
	ATK	26	DEF	28	LUK	18

EQUIPMENT	WEAPON	—
	HANDS	—

HEAD	—	BODY	—

SPOILS	GIL	672	EXP	0

BATTLE PIECE DATA

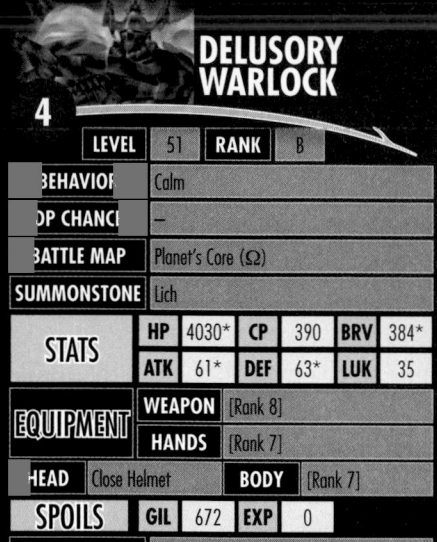

4 DELUSORY WARLOCK

LEVEL	51	RANK	B

BEHAVIOR	Calm
DP CHANCE	—
BATTLE MAP	Planet's Core (Ω)
SUMMONSTONE	Lich

STATS	HP	4030*	CP	390	BRV	384*
	ATK	61*	DEF	63*	LUK	35

EQUIPMENT	WEAPON	[Rank 8]
	HANDS	[Rank 7]

HEAD	Close Helmet	BODY	[Rank 7]

SPOILS	GIL	672	EXP	0

ACCESSORIES	Gaia Ring, Guardian Bangle, [HP] HP = 100% x3, [HP] HP ≥ 80% x5

5 PHANTASMAL HARLEQUIN

LEVEL	34	RANK	E

BEHAVIOR	Normal
DP CHANCE	Win without taking damage (DP+1)
BATTLE MAP	Dream's End (Ω)
SUMMONSTONE	Kraken

STATS	HP	3000*	CP	383	BRV	286*
	ATK	45*	DEF	44*	LUK	27

EQUIPMENT	WEAPON	[Rank 4]
	HANDS	Silver Bangles

HEAD	[Rank 5]	BODY	[Rank 4]

SPOILS	GIL	672	EXP	0

ACCESSORIES	Gaia Ring, [Time] After 30 Seconds, [Time] After 60 Seconds, [Time] After 90 Seconds, [Time] After 120 Seconds, [Time] After 180 Seconds

6 TRANSIENT LION

LEVEL	14	RANK	F

BEHAVIOR	Aggressive
DP CHANCE	—
BATTLE MAP	Dream's End (Ω)
SUMMONSTONE	—

STATS	HP	1788	CP	345	BRV	170
	ATK	23	DEF	25	LUK	17

EQUIPMENT	WEAPON	
	HANDS	

HEAD		BODY	—

SPOILS	GIL	672	EXP	0

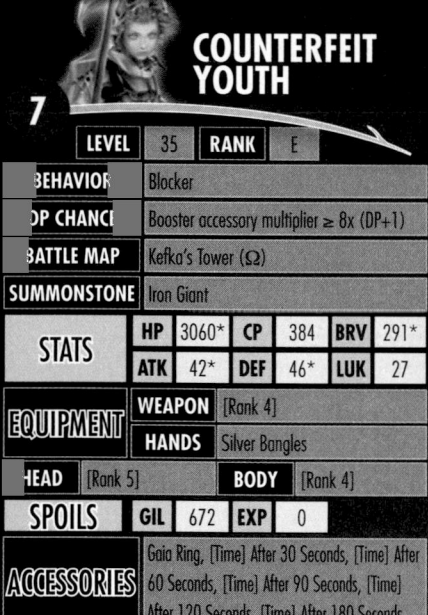

7 COUNTERFEIT YOUTH

LEVEL	35	RANK	E

BEHAVIOR	Blocker
DP CHANCE	Booster accessory multiplier ≥ 8x (DP+1)
BATTLE MAP	Kefka's Tower (Ω)
SUMMONSTONE	Iron Giant

STATS	HP	3060*	CP	384	BRV	291*
	ATK	42*	DEF	46*	LUK	27

EQUIPMENT	WEAPON	[Rank 4]
	HANDS	Silver Bangles

HEAD	[Rank 5]	BODY	[Rank 4]

SPOILS	GIL	672	EXP	0

ACCESSORIES	Gaia Ring, [Time] After 30 Seconds, [Time] After 60 Seconds, [Time] After 90 Seconds, [Time] After 120 Seconds, [Time] After 180 Seconds

8 EPHEMERAL PHANTOM

LEVEL	15	RANK	F

BEHAVIOR	Blocker
DP CHANCE	—
BATTLE MAP	Dream's End (Ω)
SUMMONSTONE	—

STATS	HP	1848	CP	347	BRV	176
	ATK	27	DEF	27	LUK	17

EQUIPMENT	WEAPON	
	HANDS	

HEAD	—	BODY	—

SPOILS	GIL	672	EXP	0

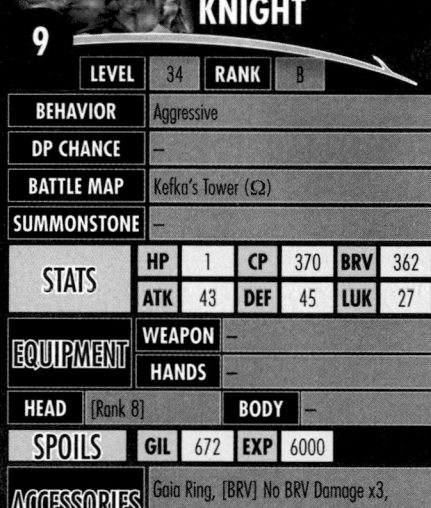

9 DELUSORY KNIGHT

LEVEL	34	RANK	B

BEHAVIOR	Aggressive
DP CHANCE	—
BATTLE MAP	Kefka's Tower (Ω)
SUMMONSTONE	—

STATS	HP	1	CP	370	BRV	362
	ATK	43	DEF	45	LUK	27

EQUIPMENT	WEAPON	—
	HANDS	—

HEAD	[Rank 8]	BODY	—

SPOILS	GIL	672	EXP	6000

ACCESSORIES	Gaia Ring, [BRV] No BRV Damage x3, The Rotten

10 THE EMPEROR

LEVEL	37	RANK	E

BEHAVIOR	Tactician
DP CHANCE	—
BATTLE MAP	Pandaemonium (Ω)
SUMMONSTONE	Marilith

STATS	HP	4153	CP	373	BRV	512
	ATK	73	DEF	71	LUK	28

EQUIPMENT	WEAPON	Golden Staff
	HANDS	Hyper Wrist

HEAD	Beret	BODY	Wizard's Robes

SPOILS	GIL	3024	EXP	7952

ACCESSORIES	Gaia Ring, Guardian Bangle, [HP] HP = 100% x3, [HP] HP ≥ 80% x5

11 FALSE STALWART

LEVEL	90	RANK	S

BEHAVIOR	Cautious
DP CHANCE	Win battle (DP+2)
BATTLE MAP	Order's Sanctuary (Ω)
SUMMONSTONE	Rubicante

STATS	HP	6393*	CP	437	BRV	609*
	ATK	102*	DEF	103*	LUK	55

EQUIPMENT	WEAPON	[Rank 13]
	HANDS	[Rank 12]

HEAD	Kaiser Helm	BODY	[Rank 12]

SPOILS	GIL	672	EXP	0

ACCESSORIES	Champion Belt, Muscle Belt, [Position] Near Opponent x6, [Time] After 90 Seconds

DP EFFICIENCY ROUTE

You'll need a 3-star rating on previous runs of Shade Impulse 2 in order to get the max amount of Destiny Points here. Head upward and engage battle piece ❶ first. This opens the way to grid square C-3, from which you can chain battle pieces ❷, ❺, and ⓫. After this chain, arrange your accessories so you can get a multiplier of 8x or greater from accessories before engaging battle piece ❼. After this fight, head to the boss.

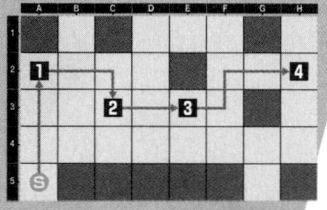

* Denotes use of the base value (for stats that vary).

SHADE IMPULSE 2

SHADE IMPULSE ³
WHILE TIME GROWS SHORT

Difficulty

Prerequisite

Finish Shade Impulse 2

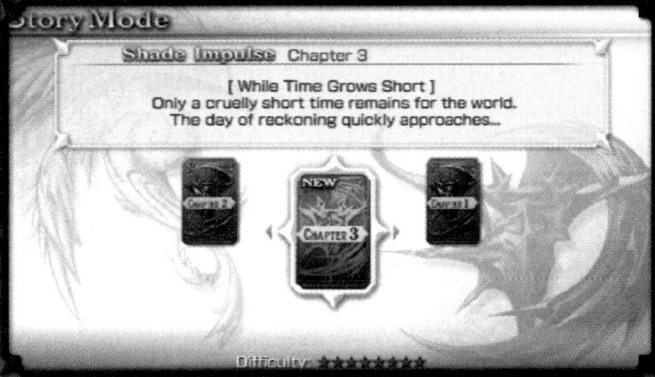

Story Mode

Shade Impulse Chapter 3

[While Time Grows Short]
Only a cruelly short time remains for the world.
The day of reckoning quickly approaches...

Chapter 2   NEW CHAPTER 3   Chapter 1

Difficulty: ★★★★★★★

REWARDS

At the end of each level, rewards are available if you finish with a positive number of Destiny Points, or DP. This walkthrough includes miniature level maps that indicate the most efficient route to take through a given level, in order to maximize DP.

LEVEL COMPLETION

REMAINING DP		1ST TIME		2ND TIME
7		Rosetta Stone		300 PP
6		Scarmiglione's Fang		200 PP
5		Barbariccia's Wristlet		120 PP
4		Kraken		80 PP
3		5000 gil		50 PP
2		3000 gil		30 PP
1		1500 gil		20 PP
0		500 gil		10 PP

At the end of each set of levels, you'll receive rewards based on your performance. Story Points, or SP, are awarded after each level based on remaining DP and HP, as well as the number of engagements undertaken. Points are penalized for retries, or for a DP total that dips into negatives. If you miss out on a desired bonus on the first playthrough, don't worry—SP is cumulative across multiple playthroughs.

SHADE IMPULSE 3 COMPLETION

STAR RATING		SP REQUIRED		AWARD
☆		300		New skill
☆ ☆		200		Special areas unlocked
☆ ☆ ☆		300		Rare battle pieces spawned
☆ ☆ ☆ ☆		400		Rare treasure chests spawned
—		500 SP, then every 500 SP extra		100 PP

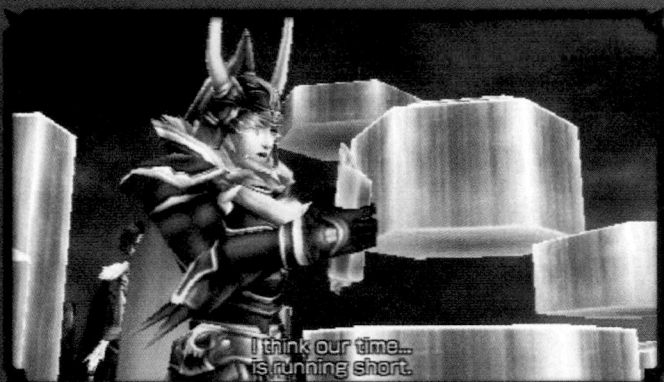

I think our time...
is running short.

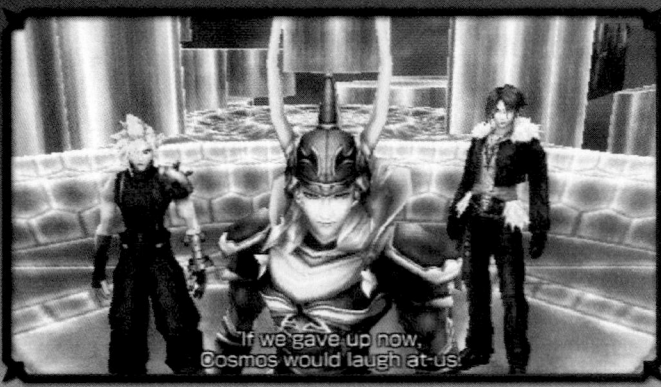

If we gave up now,
Cosmos would laugh at us!

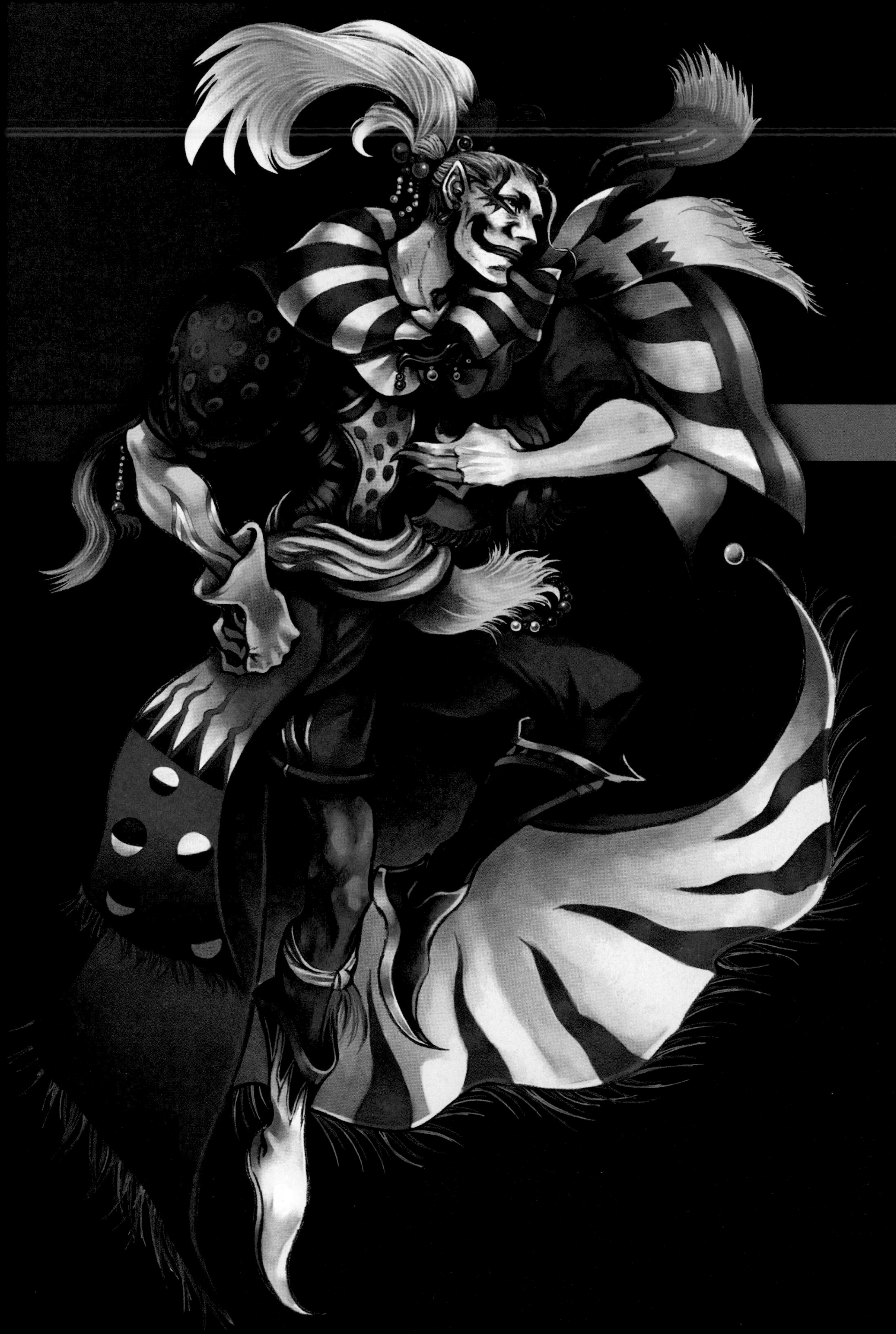

SHADE IMPULSE 3

As the conflict reaches its climax, enemies grow more dangerous. On the first level of Shade Impulse 3, you'll encounter six foes clustered before the exit. Defeating all six of them reveals treasure chest **B**. Reaching the Stigma of Chaos ends the level without a boss fight.

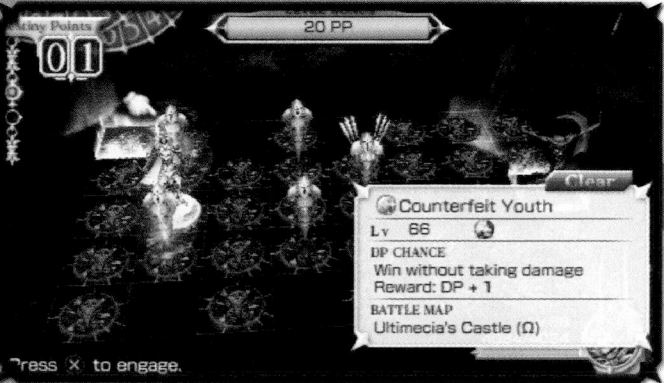

Counterfeit Youth
Lv 66
DP CHANCE
Win without taking damage
Reward: DP + 1
BATTLE MAP
Ultimecia's Castle (Ω)

Press X to engage.

M A P

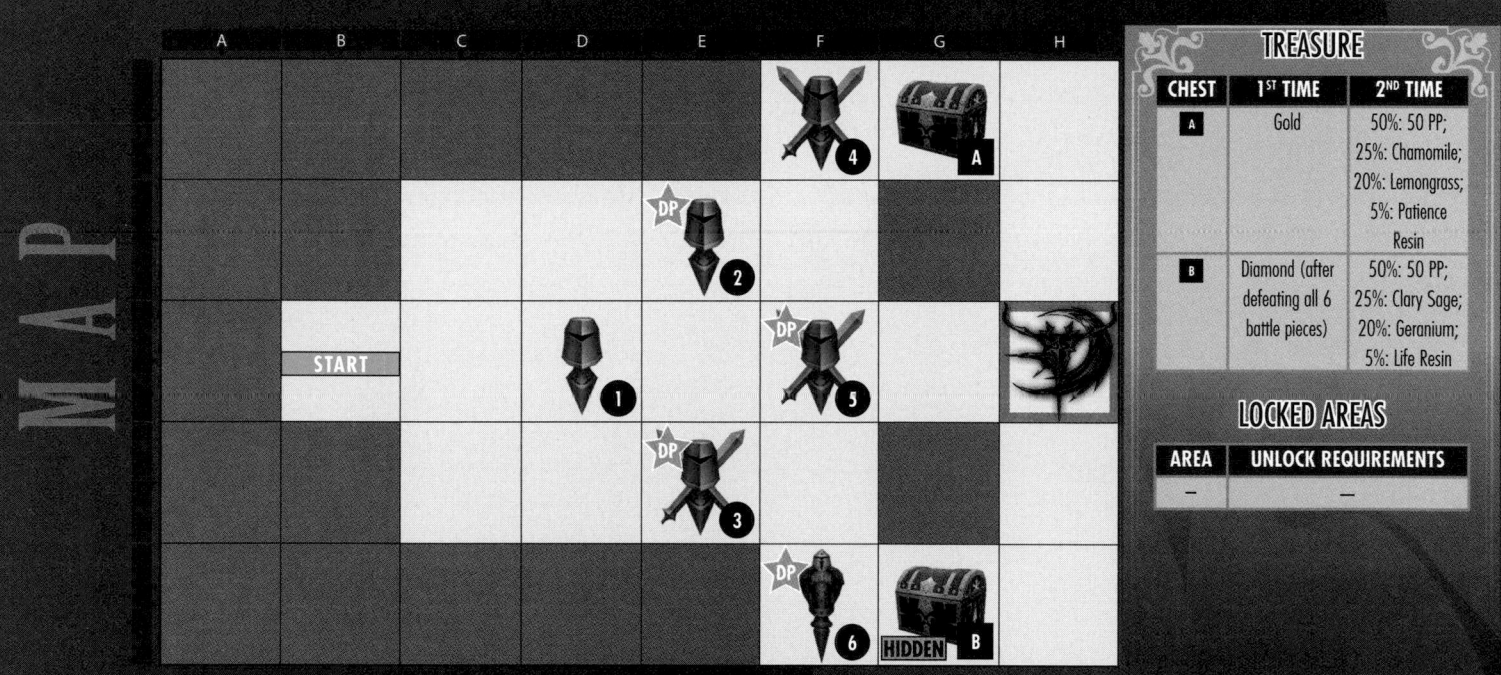

TREASURE

CHEST	1ST TIME	2ND TIME
A	Gold	50%: 50 PP; 25%: Chamomile; 20%: Lemongrass; 5%: Patience Resin
B	Diamond (after defeating all 6 battle pieces)	50%: 50 PP; 25%: Clary Sage; 20%: Geranium; 5%: Life Resin

LOCKED AREAS

AREA	UNLOCK REQUIREMENTS
—	—

DP EFFICIENCY ROUTE

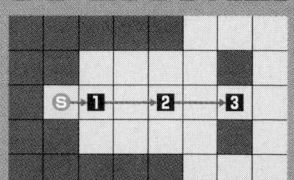

A straight shot across this level results in the maximum amount of Destiny Points. Take out battle piece ❶ first, which allows you to squeeze between pieces ❷, ❸, and ❺. Take these pieces out in a three-part battle chain, scoring each DP Chance along the way. Plan ahead for battle piece ❺—the DP Chance requirement here is a booster accessory multiplier of 8.0 or greater. After clearing out the chain, head to the Stigma of Chaos to end the level.

BATTLE PIECE DATA

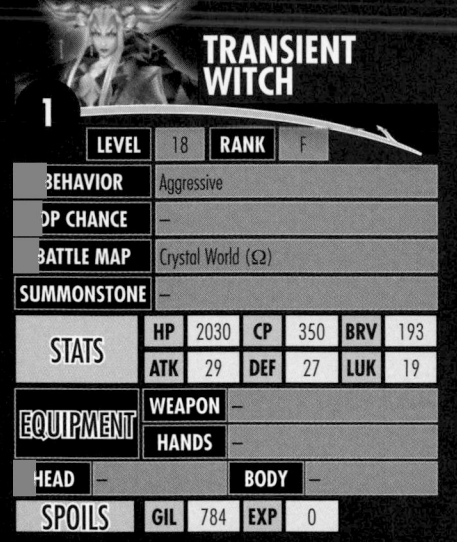

1 TRANSIENT WITCH

LEVEL	18	RANK	F

BEHAVIOR	Aggressive
DP CHANCE	—
BATTLE MAP	Crystal World (Ω)
SUMMONSTONE	—

STATS	HP	2030	CP	350	BRV	193
	ATK	29	DEF	27	LUK	19

EQUIPMENT	WEAPON	—
	HANDS	—

HEAD	—	BODY	—

SPOILS	GIL	784	EXP	0

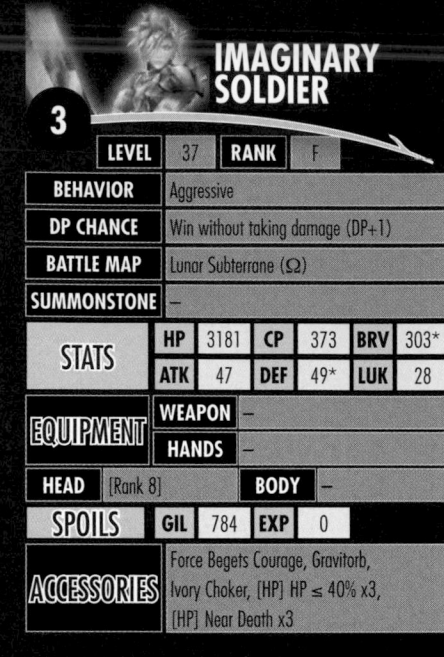

2 COUNTERFEIT WRAITH

LEVEL	19	RANK	F

BEHAVIOR	Standby
DP CHANCE	Win within 10 seconds (DP+1)
BATTLE MAP	Pandaemonium (Ω)
SUMMONSTONE	—

STATS	HP	2091	CP	368	BRV	199
	ATK	28	DEF	30	LUK	19

EQUIPMENT	WEAPON	—
	HANDS	—

HEAD	—	BODY	—

SPOILS	GIL	784	EXP	0

3 IMAGINARY SOLDIER

LEVEL	37	RANK	F

BEHAVIOR	Aggressive
DP CHANCE	Win without taking damage (DP+1)
BATTLE MAP	Lunar Subterrane (Ω)
SUMMONSTONE	—

STATS	HP	3181	CP	373	BRV	303*
	ATK	47	DEF	49*	LUK	28

EQUIPMENT	WEAPON	—
	HANDS	—

HEAD	[Rank 8]	BODY	—

SPOILS	GIL	784	EXP	0

ACCESSORIES	Force Begets Courage, Gravitorb, Ivory Choker, [HP] HP ≤ 40% x3, [HP] Near Death x3

4 FALLACIOUS WANDERER

LEVEL	38	RANK	F

BEHAVIOR	Standby
DP CHANCE	—
BATTLE MAP	Dream's End (Ω)
SUMMONSTONE	—

STATS	HP	3242	CP	387	BRV	309*
	ATK	48*	DEF	49	LUK	29

EQUIPMENT	WEAPON	[Rank 8]
	HANDS	—

HEAD	—	BODY	—

SPOILS	GIL	784	EXP	0

ACCESSORIES	Gaia Ring, [HP] HP ≤ 40% x3, [HP] Near Death x4

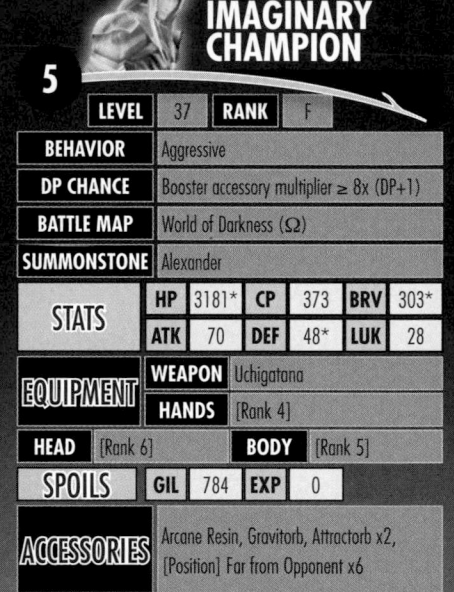

5 IMAGINARY CHAMPION

LEVEL	37	RANK	F

BEHAVIOR	Aggressive
DP CHANCE	Booster accessory multiplier ≥ 8x (DP+1)
BATTLE MAP	World of Darkness (Ω)
SUMMONSTONE	Alexander

STATS	HP	3181*	CP	373	BRV	303*
	ATK	70	DEF	48*	LUK	28

EQUIPMENT	WEAPON	Uchigatana
	HANDS	[Rank 4]

HEAD	[Rank 6]	BODY	[Rank 5]

SPOILS	GIL	784	EXP	0

ACCESSORIES	Arcane Resin, Gravitorb, Attractorb x2, [Position] Far from Opponent x6

6 CAPRICIOUS THIEF

LEVEL	53	RANK	B

BEHAVIOR	Tactician
DP CHANCE	Win within 20 seconds (DP+1)
BATTLE MAP	Old Chaos Shrine (Ω)
SUMMONSTONE	Ramuh

STATS	HP	4151*	CP	393	BRV	395*
	ATK	98	DEF	94	LUK	36

EQUIPMENT	WEAPON	Rising Sun
	HANDS	[Rank 7]

HEAD	Gold Hairpin	BODY	[Rank 8]

SPOILS	GIL	784	EXP	0

ACCESSORIES	Gaia Ring, Guardian Bangle, [HP] HP = 100% x3, [HP] HP ≥ 80% x5

* Denotes use of the base value (for stats that vary).

SHADE IMPULSE 3

On this level, you'll begin smack in the middle of a large group of foes. Possible battle chains lie in every direction. Squall's nemesis Ultimecia waits on the left edge of the level, serving as a mid-boss. Behind her is a golden Locked Area that hides away Rubicante, leader of the four fiends. His services can be acquired after returning to Shade Impulse 3 with a 2-star rating or better. If you want to blaze through this level quickly, simply defeat battle pieces ❹ and ❺ before heading to the Stigma of Chaos.

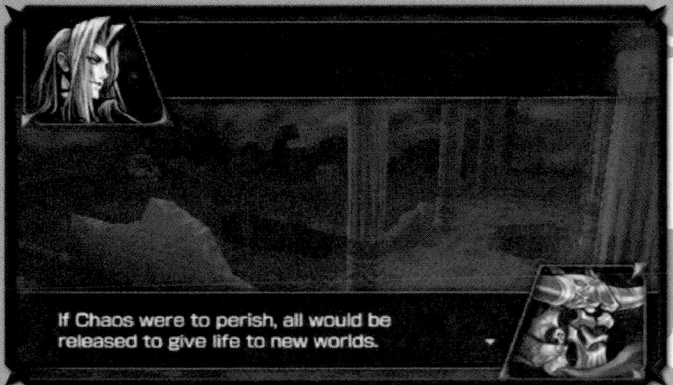

If Chaos were to perish, all would be released to give life to new worlds.

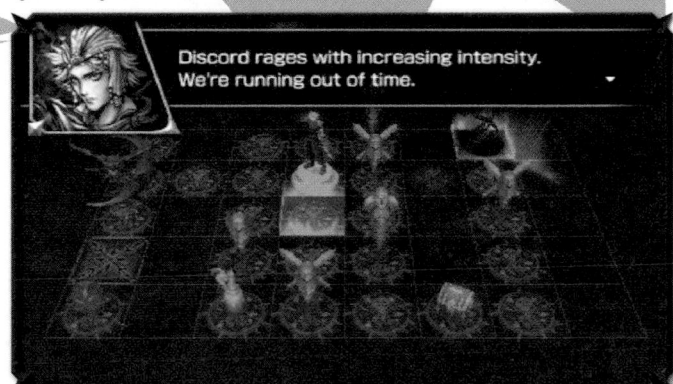

Discord rages with increasing intensity. We're running out of time.

MAP

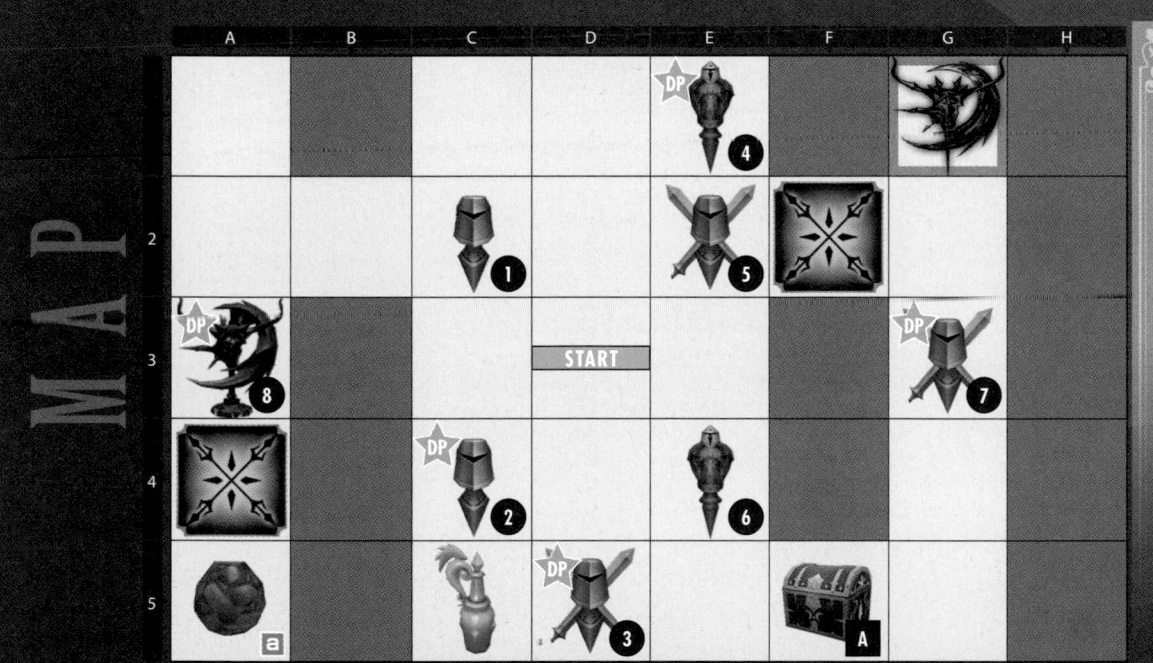

TREASURE

CHEST	1ST TIME	2ND TIME
A	Phoenix Down	50%: 50 PP; 25%: Ylang Ylang; 20%: Rosetta Stone; 5%: Mystery Resin
a	Rubicante (after 2-star rating)	—

LOCKED AREAS

AREA	UNLOCK REQUIREMENTS
F–2	Defeat battle piece ❹

DP EFFICIENCY ROUTE

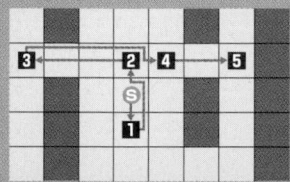

Maximizing DP here requires a long and winding path. From the outset, move down and engage battle pieces ❷, ❸, and ❻ in a chain. Afterward, head upward and chain battle pieces ❶ and ❺. Neither offers a DP Chance, but you'll have to clear both to progress. Once these pieces are cleared, head left and take on Ultimecia, who offers +2 DP upon defeat. Then, fight battle piece ❹ to open the Locked Area that blocks the way to the exit. Move to G-2 and defeat battle piece ❼ before engaging the Stigma of Chaos.

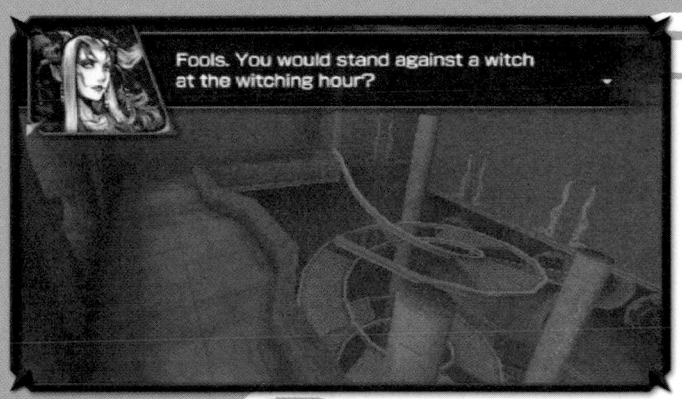

Fools. You would stand against a witch at the witching hour?

BATTLE PIECE DATA

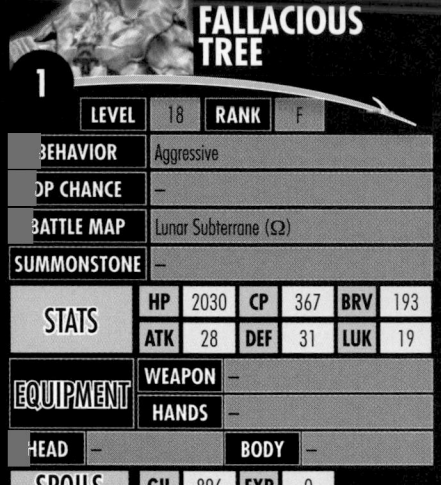

1 FALLACIOUS TREE

LEVEL	18	RANK	F

BEHAVIOR	Aggressive
DP CHANCE	–
BATTLE MAP	Lunar Subterrane (Ω)
SUMMONSTONE	–

STATS	HP	2030	CP	367	BRV	193
	ATK	28	DEF	31	LUK	19

EQUIPMENT	WEAPON	–
	HANDS	–

HEAD	–	BODY	–

SPOILS	GIL	896	EXP	0

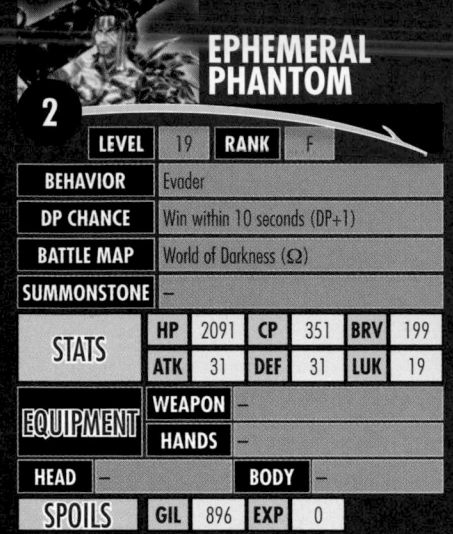

2 EPHEMERAL PHANTOM

LEVEL	19	RANK	F

BEHAVIOR	Evader
DP CHANCE	Win within 10 seconds (DP+1)
BATTLE MAP	World of Darkness (Ω)
SUMMONSTONE	–

STATS	HP	2091	CP	351	BRV	199
	ATK	31	DEF	31	LUK	19

EQUIPMENT	WEAPON	–
	HANDS	–

HEAD	–	BODY	–

SPOILS	GIL	896	EXP	0

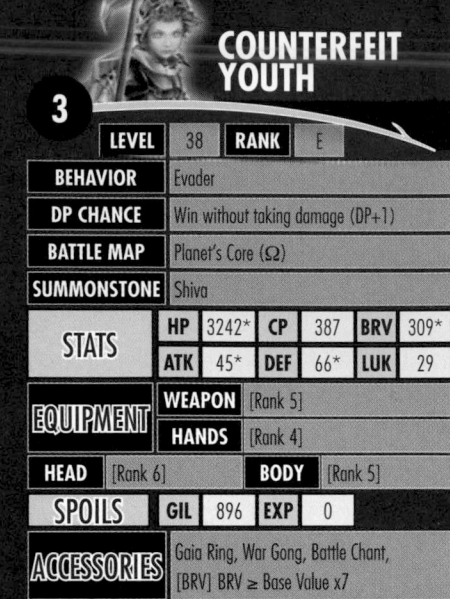

3 COUNTERFEIT YOUTH

LEVEL	38	RANK	E

BEHAVIOR	Evader
DP CHANCE	Win without taking damage (DP+1)
BATTLE MAP	Planet's Core (Ω)
SUMMONSTONE	Shiva

STATS	HP	3242*	CP	387	BRV	309*
	ATK	45*	DEF	66*	LUK	29

EQUIPMENT	WEAPON	[Rank 5]
	HANDS	[Rank 4]

HEAD	[Rank 6]	BODY	[Rank 5]

SPOILS	GIL	896	EXP	0

ACCESSORIES	Gaia Ring, War Gong, Battle Chant, [BRV] BRV ≥ Base Value x7

4 FALSE HERO

LEVEL	55	RANK	B

BEHAVIOR	Calm
DP CHANCE	Win within 20 seconds (DP+1)
BATTLE MAP	Old Chaos Shrine (Ω)
SUMMONSTONE	Kraken

STATS	HP	4272*	CP	395	BRV	407*
	ATK	65*	DEF	68*	LUK	37

EQUIPMENT	WEAPON	[Rank 9]
	HANDS	[Rank 7]

HEAD	[Rank 7]	BODY	[Rank 8]

SPOILS	GIL	896	EXP	0

ACCESSORIES	Champion Belt, Muscle Belt, [Position] Near Opponent x6, [Time] After 90 Seconds

5 FALSE STALWART

LEVEL	38	RANK	E

BEHAVIOR	Aggressive
DP CHANCE	–
BATTLE MAP	Pandaemonium (Ω)
SUMMONSTONE	–

STATS	HP	3242	CP	374	BRV	309
	ATK	78	DEF	51	LUK	29

EQUIPMENT	WEAPON	[Rank 8]
	HANDS	–

HEAD	–	BODY	–

SPOILS	GIL	896	EXP	0

ACCESSORIES	Arcane Incense, Gaia Ring, Gravitorb, Pearl Necklace, [EX] EX Core Present x2, [EX] EX Gauge ≥ 70% x4

6 PHANTASMAL HARLEQUIN

LEVEL	54	RANK	B

BEHAVIOR	Valiant
DP CHANCE	–
BATTLE MAP	Ultimecia's Castle (Ω)
SUMMONSTONE	Tiamat

STATS	HP	4211*	CP	403	BRV	401*
	ATK	65*	DEF	64*	LUK	37

EQUIPMENT	WEAPON	[Rank 8]
	HANDS	[Rank 7]

HEAD	[Rank 9]	BODY	[Rank 7]

SPOILS	GIL	896	EXP	0

ACCESSORIES	Star Earring, Earring, [Position] Far from Opponent x6, [Time] After 90 Seconds

7 PHANTASMAL GIRL

LEVEL	39	RANK	F

BEHAVIOR	Standby
DP CHANCE	Win without taking damage (DP+1)
BATTLE MAP	Dream's End (Ω)
SUMMONSTONE	–

STATS	HP	3303*	CP	376	BRV	315*
	ATK	71	DEF	67	LUK	29

EQUIPMENT	WEAPON	Rod of Wisdom
	HANDS	[Rank 4]

HEAD	[Rank 6]	BODY	[Rank 5]

SPOILS	GIL	896	EXP	0

ACCESSORIES	Gaia Ring, Guardian Bangle, [Position] Far from Opponent x8

8 ULTIMECIA

LEVEL	40	RANK	E

BEHAVIOR	Extreme
DP CHANCE	Win battle (DP+2)
BATTLE MAP	Ultimecia's Castle (Ω)
SUMMONSTONE	Leviathan

STATS	HP	4335	CP	377	BRV	506
	ATK	72	DEF	72	LUK	30

EQUIPMENT	WEAPON	Rod of Wisdom
	HANDS	Hyper Wrist

HEAD	Tiara	BODY	Wizard's Robes

SPOILS	GIL	3528	EXP	6726

ACCESSORIES	Gaia Ring, Guardian Bangle, [HP] = 100% x3, [HP] ≥ 80% x5

* Denotes use of the base value (for stats that vary).

SHADE IMPULSE 3

SHADE IMPULSE

3-3

STARTING DP	2	
MAX FINISHING	5	(+2 after 3-star rating)
ENGAGEMENTS	6	(+1 after 3-star rating)

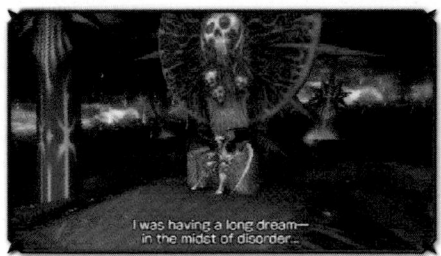
I was having a long dream— in the midst of disorder...

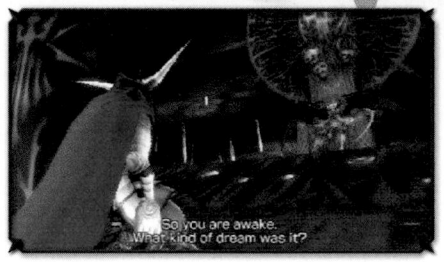
So you are awake. What kind of dream was it?

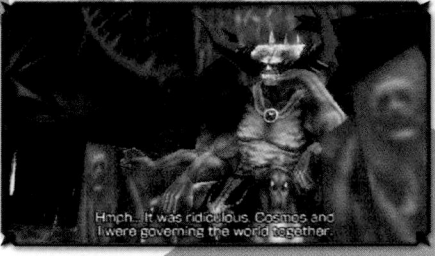
Hmph... It was ridiculous. Cosmos and I were governing the world together.

Here, toward the end, is one of the more unusual levels in the game. This board is simply a corridor lined with optional encounters. If you like, you can simply cross over to the Stigma of Chaos and move on to the next level. Stick around, however, and you can gain many opportunities for combat and treasure. Even more unusual, most DP Chance encounters on this level offer +2 DP upon success, for battle pieces that aren't ultimate versions. The *actual* ultimate battle piece that shows up here after a 3-star rating gives *+3* DP upon defeat! This level also houses two Summonstones for the taking—Ramuh AUTO along the bottom, and Barbariccia, one of the four fiends, along the top. Ultimate battle piece **7** is a high-level crystal version of Warrior of Light. This manikin is extremely strong, but fortunately it is predictable. If you get close and attack right away, it almost always blocks. It's best not to attack directly. If you get close but then pause for just one second, it will almost always attack. Of course, you can then avoid the attack by dodging directly at the manikin. You'll end up behind it, free to strike its back. If it attacks unexpectedly and manages to launch you into the air, be ready to dodge Rune Saber at the last second—its combo into this attack is not guaranteed.

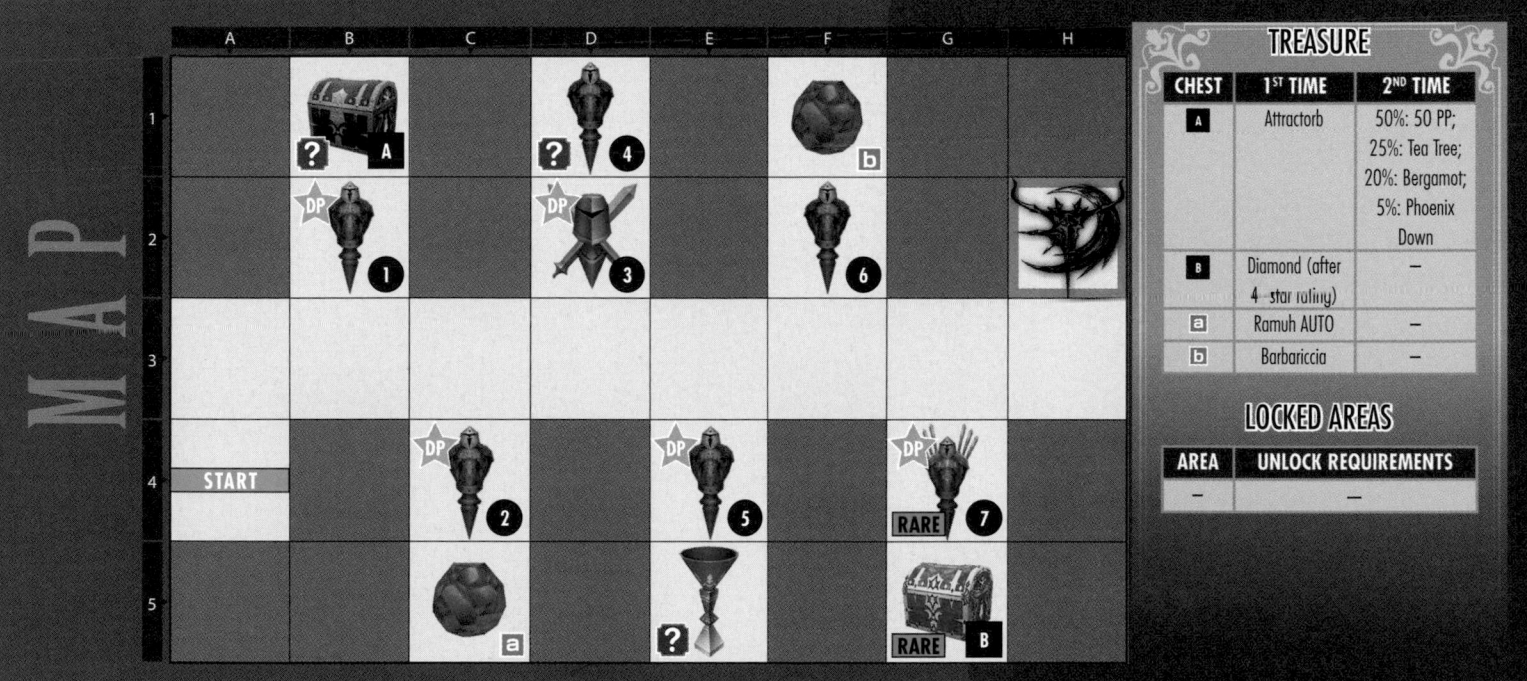

TREASURE

CHEST	1ST TIME	2ND TIME
A	Attractorb	50%: 50 PP; 25%: Tea Tree; 20%: Bergamot; 5%: Phoenix Down
B	Diamond (after 4-star rating)	—
a	Ramuh AUTO	—
b	Barbariccia	—

LOCKED AREAS

AREA	UNLOCK REQUIREMENTS
—	—

DP EFFICIENCY ROUTE

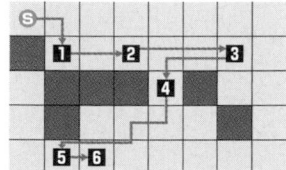

Destiny Points can't be maxed out here until battle piece **7** shows up after returning with a 3-star rating. Once this piece is in place, simply proceed down the line, knocking down each DP Chance in turn.

BATTLE PIECE DATA

1 TRANSIENT LION

LEVEL	57	RANK	B

BEHAVIOR	Tactician
DP CHANCE	Win without taking damage (DP+2)
BATTLE MAP	The Rift (Ω)
SUMMONSTONE	Magic Pot

STATS	HP	4393*	CP	397	BRV	418*
	ATK	66*	DEF	68*	LUK	38

EQUIPMENT	WEAPON	[Rank 9]
	HANDS	[Rank 8]

HEAD	[Rank 10]	BODY	[Rank 8]

SPOILS	GIL	1260	EXP	0

ACCESSORIES	Champion Belt, Muscle Belt, [Position] Near Opponent x6, [Time] After 90 Seconds

2 IMITATION LIEGEMAN

LEVEL	55	RANK	B

BEHAVIOR	Valiant
DP CHANCE	Win within 20 seconds (DP+2)
BATTLE MAP	Kefka's Tower (Ω)
SUMMONSTONE	Tiamat

STATS	HP	4272*	CP	395	BRV	407*
	ATK	66*	DEF	67*	LUK	37

EQUIPMENT	WEAPON	[Rank 8]
	HANDS	[Rank 7]

HEAD	[Rank 9]	BODY	[Rank 7]

SPOILS	GIL	1260	EXP	0

ACCESSORIES	Gaia Ring, Hyper Ring, [HP] HP ≤ 40% x6, [HP] Near Death x2

3 IMAGINARY CHAMPION

LEVEL	41	RANK	E

BEHAVIOR	Blocker
DP CHANCE	Win within 10 seconds (DP+1)
BATTLE MAP	Old Chaos Shrine (Ω)
SUMMONSTONE	–

STATS	HP	3424*	CP	378	BRV	326*
	ATK	74	DEF	52*	LUK	30

EQUIPMENT	WEAPON	Uchigatana
	HANDS	[Rank 4]

HEAD	[Rank 6]	BODY	[Rank 5]

SPOILS	GIL	1260	EXP	0

ACCESSORIES	Gaia Ring, [Time] After 30 Seconds, [Time] After 60 Seconds, [Time] After 90 Seconds, [Time] After 120 Seconds, [Time] After 180 Seconds

4 DELUSORY KNIGHT

LEVEL	59	RANK	B

BEHAVIOR	Conservative
DP CHANCE	–
BATTLE MAP	World of Darkness (Ω)
SUMMONSTONE	Atomos

STATS	HP	4514*	CP	400	BRV	430*
	ATK	68*	DEF	69*	LUK	39

EQUIPMENT	WEAPON	[Rank 9]
	HANDS	[Rank 8]

HEAD	Crystal Helm	BODY	[Rank 8]

SPOILS	GIL	1260	EXP	0

ACCESSORIES	Star Earring, Earring, [Position] Far from Opponent x6, [Time] After 90 Seconds

5 IMITATION DESPOT

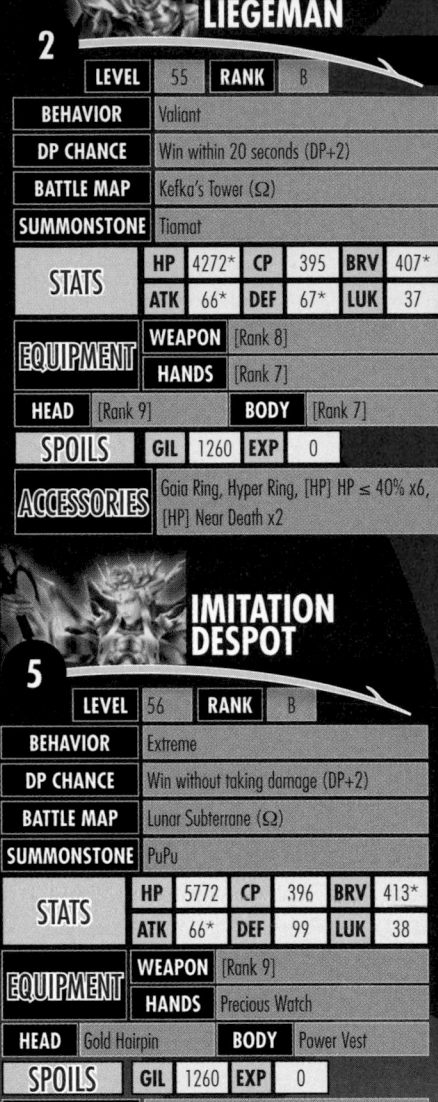

LEVEL	56	RANK	B

BEHAVIOR	Extreme
DP CHANCE	Win without taking damage (DP+2)
BATTLE MAP	Lunar Subterrane (Ω)
SUMMONSTONE	PuPu

STATS	HP	5772	CP	396	BRV	413*
	ATK	66*	DEF	99	LUK	38

EQUIPMENT	WEAPON	[Rank 9]
	HANDS	Precious Watch

HEAD	Gold Hairpin	BODY	Power Vest

SPOILS	GIL	1260	EXP	0

ACCESSORIES	Gaia Ring, Guardian Bangle, [HP] HP = 100% x3, [HP] HP ≥ 80% x5

6 DELUSORY WARLOCK

LEVEL	58	RANK	B

BEHAVIOR	Survivor
DP CHANCE	Win within 20 seconds (DP+2)
BATTLE MAP	Ultimecia's Castle (Ω)
SUMMONSTONE	Iron Giant

STATS	HP	4454*	CP	399	BRV	424*
	ATK	68*	DEF	70*	LUK	39

EQUIPMENT	WEAPON	[Rank 10]
	HANDS	[Rank 8]

HEAD	[Rank 8]	BODY	[Rank 9]

SPOILS	GIL	1260	EXP	0

ACCESSORIES	Gaia Ring, Hyper Ring, [HP] HP ≤ 40% x6, [HP] Near Death x2

7 FALSE HERO

LEVEL	94	RANK	S

BEHAVIOR	Tactician
DP CHANCE	Win battle (DP+3)
BATTLE MAP	Order's Sanctuary (Ω)
SUMMONSTONE	Barbariccia

STATS	HP	9184	CP	442	BRV	632*
	ATK	104*	DEF	107*	LUK	57

EQUIPMENT	WEAPON	[Rank 15]
	HANDS	[Rank 13]

HEAD	[Rank 13]	BODY	Vishnu Vest

SPOILS	GIL	1764	EXP	0

ACCESSORIES	Gaia Ring, Guardian Bangle, [HP] HP = 100% x3, [HP] HP ≥ 80% x5

* Denotes use of the base value (for stats that vary).

SHADE IMPULSE 3

SHADE IMPULSE 3-4

As with a few other levels, the pieces here are mostly shrouded in blue Enigma Areas. Use Sight (if available) to reveal their contents, or consult the maps provided here. Sephiroth serves as a mid-boss on this stage, providing a unique cutscene if you approach him while using Cloud. Behind Sephiroth is a golden Locked Area that only disappears after a 2-star rating. This Locked Area bars the way to a treasure chest containing Gold.

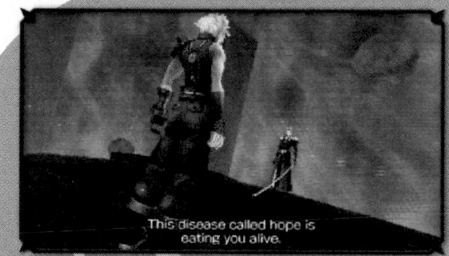

This disease called hope is eating you alive.

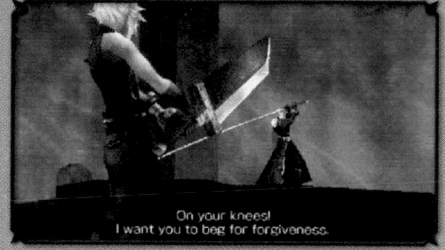

On your knees! I want you to beg for forgiveness.

MAP

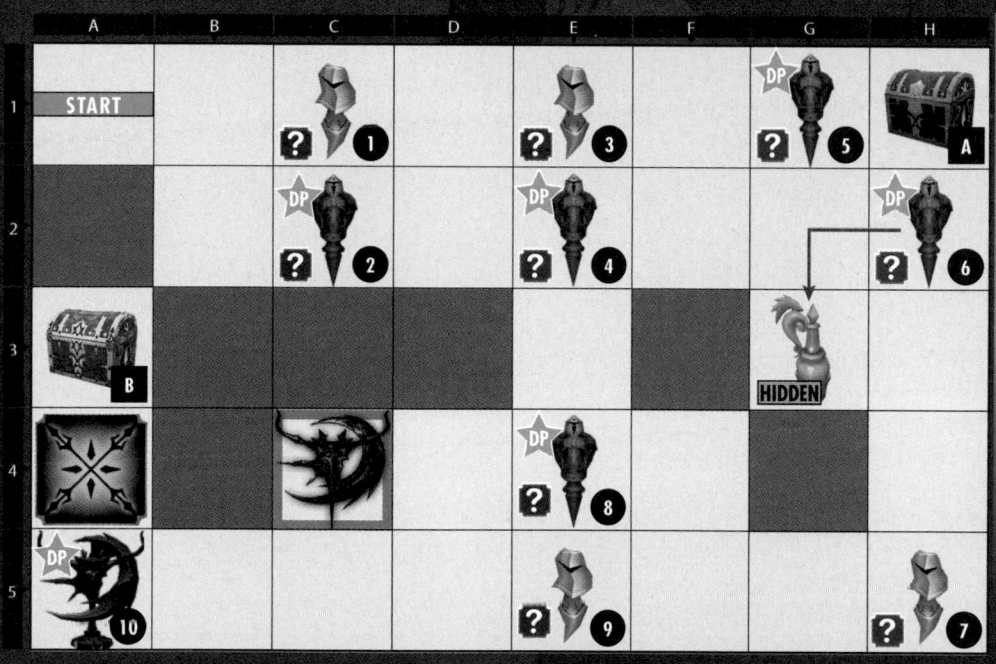

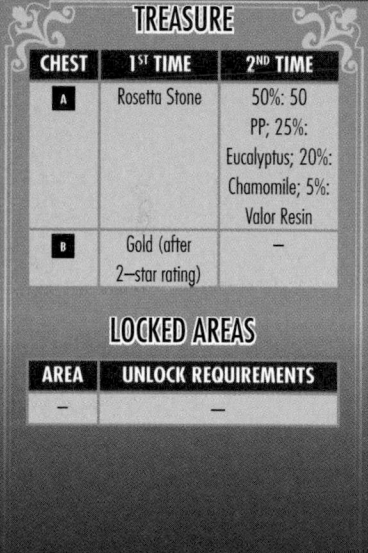

TREASURE

CHEST	1ST TIME	2ND TIME
A	Rosetta Stone	50%: 50 PP; 25%: Eucalyptus; 20%: Chamomile; 5%: Valor Resin
B	Gold (after 2–star rating)	—

LOCKED AREAS

AREA	UNLOCK REQUIREMENTS
—	—

BATTLE PIECE DATA

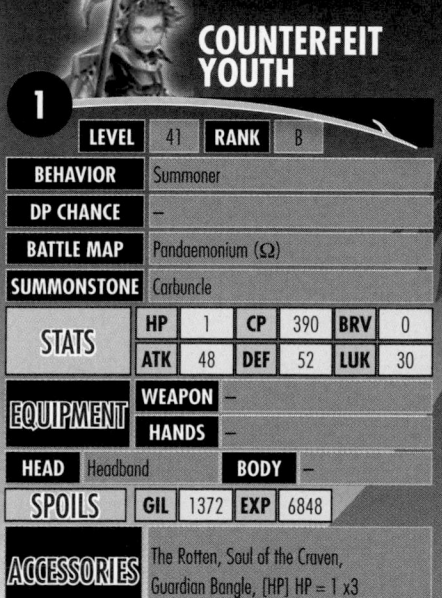

1 COUNTERFEIT YOUTH

LEVEL	41	RANK	B

BEHAVIOR	Summoner
DP CHANCE	—
BATTLE MAP	Pandaemonium (Ω)
SUMMONSTONE	Carbuncle

STATS

HP	1	CP	390	BRV	0
ATK	48	DEF	52	LUK	30

EQUIPMENT

WEAPON	—
HANDS	—

HEAD	Headband	BODY	—

SPOILS

GIL	1372	EXP	6848

ACCESSORIES The Rotten, Soul of the Craven, Guardian Bangle, [HP] HP = 1 x3

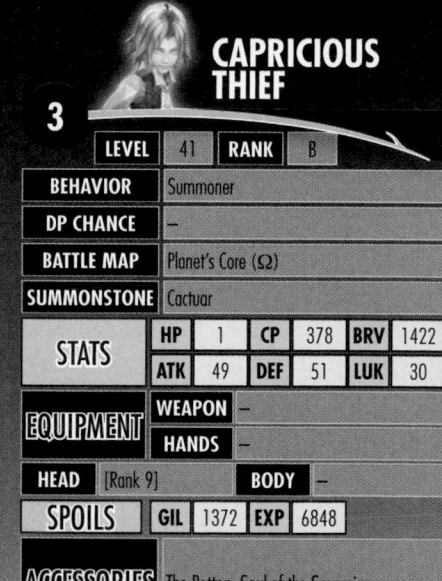

2 PHANTASMAL HARLEQUIN

LEVEL	62	RANK	A

BEHAVIOR	Vicious
DP CHANCE	Win within 20 seconds (DP+1)
BATTLE MAP	Crystal World (Ω)
SUMMONSTONE	PuPu

STATS

HP	4696*	CP	411	BRV	447*
ATK	112	DEF	107	LUK	41

EQUIPMENT

WEAPON	Judicer's Staff
HANDS	[Rank 8]

HEAD	[Rank 10]	BODY	Power Vest

SPOILS

GIL	1372	EXP	0

ACCESSORIES Gaia Ring, Guardian Bangle, [HP] HP = 100% x3, [HP] HP ≥ 80% x5

3 CAPRICIOUS THIEF

LEVEL	41	RANK	B

BEHAVIOR	Summoner
DP CHANCE	—
BATTLE MAP	Planet's Core (Ω)
SUMMONSTONE	Cactuar

STATS

HP	1	CP	378	BRV	1422
ATK	49	DEF	51	LUK	30

EQUIPMENT

WEAPON	—
HANDS	—

HEAD	[Rank 9]	BODY	—

SPOILS

GIL	1372	EXP	6848

ACCESSORIES The Rotten, Soul of the Sovereign

BATTLE PIECE DATA

4 FALSE STALWART

LEVEL	63	RANK	A

BEHAVIOR	Cautious
DP CHANCE	Win within 10 seconds (DP+1)
BATTLE MAP	Kefka's Tower (Ω)
SUMMONSTONE	Titan

STATS	HP	4757*	CP	405	BRV	590
	ATK	116	DEF	112	LUK	41

EQUIPMENT	WEAPON	Crystal Lance
	HANDS	[Rank 8]

HEAD	[Rank 8]	BODY	[Rank 9]

SPOILS	GIL	1372	EXP	0

ACCESSORIES	Gaia Ring, Hyper Ring, [HP] HP ≤ 40% x6, [HP] Near Death x2

5 COUNTERFEIT WRAITH

LEVEL	63	RANK	A

BEHAVIOR	Calm
DP CHANCE	Win without taking damage (DP+1)
BATTLE MAP	Ultimecia's Castle (Ω)
SUMMONSTONE	Mandragora

STATS	HP	4757*	CP	412	BRV	453*
	ATK	111	DEF	109	LUK	41

EQUIPMENT	WEAPON	Judicer's Staff, [Rank 8], [Rank
	HANDS	10], Power Vest

HEAD	1372	BODY	0

SPOILS	GIL	Gaia	EXP	Ring

ACCESSORIES	Hyper Ring, [HP] HP ≤ 40% x6, [HP] Near Death x2

6 CAPRICIOUS REAPER

LEVEL	64	RANK	A

BEHAVIOR	Survivor
DP CHANCE	Win within 20 seconds (DP+1)
BATTLE MAP	Dream's End (Ω)
SUMMONSTONE	Tiamat

STATS	HP	4817*	CP	406	BRV	459*
	ATK	73*	DEF	75*	LUK	42

EQUIPMENT	WEAPON	[Rank 10]
	HANDS	[Rank 9]

HEAD	Cat—ear Hood	BODY	[Rank 9]

SPOILS	GIL	1372	EXP	0

ACCESSORIES	Star Earring, Earring, [Position] Far from Opponent x6, [Time] After 90 Seconds

7 IMITATION LIEGEMAN

LEVEL	42	RANK	B

BEHAVIOR	Summoner
DP CHANCE	—
BATTLE MAP	The Rift (Ω)
SUMMONSTONE	Tiamat

STATS	HP	1	CP	379	BRV	1440
	ATK	53	DEF	54	LUK	31

EQUIPMENT	WEAPON	—
	HANDS	—

HEAD	[Rank 9]	BODY	—

SPOILS	GIL	1372	EXP	6968

ACCESSORIES	The Rotten, Soul of the Sovereign

8 TRANSIENT WITCH

LEVEL	65	RANK	A

BEHAVIOR	Vicious
DP CHANCE	Win within 20 seconds (DP+1)
BATTLE MAP	The Rift (Ω)
SUMMONSTONE	Magus Sisters

STATS	HP	6840	CP	407	BRV	465*
	ATK	120	DEF	115	LUK	42

EQUIPMENT	WEAPON	[Rank 11]
	HANDS	[Rank 9]

HEAD	[Rank 9]	BODY	Ninja Gear

SPOILS	GIL	1372	EXP	0

ACCESSORIES	Star Earring, Earring, [Position] Far from Opponent x6, [Time] After 90 Seconds

9 TRANSIENT LION

LEVEL	42	RANK	B

BEHAVIOR	Aggressive
DP CHANCE	—
BATTLE MAP	Lunar Subterrane (Ω)
SUMMONSTONE	Mandragora

STATS	HP	174	CP	379	BRV	332*
	ATK	51	DEF	53*	LUK	31

EQUIPMENT	WEAPON	—
	HANDS	—

HEAD	[Rank 9]	BODY	—

SPOILS	GIL	1372	EXP	6968

ACCESSORIES	The Derelict, Arcane Resin, Soul of the Sovereign, Phoenix Down

* Denotes use of the base value (for stats that vary).

10 SEPHIROTH

LEVEL	44	RANK	E

BEHAVIOR	Conservative
DP CHANCE	Win battle (DP+2)
BATTLE MAP	Planet's Core (Ω)
SUMMONSTONE	Phoenix

STATS	HP	4942	CP	382	BRV	447
	ATK	86	DEF	88	LUK	32

EQUIPMENT	WEAPON	Warblade
	HANDS	Force Shield

HEAD	Burgonet	BODY	Golden Armor

SPOILS	GIL	3864	EXP	7210

ACCESSORIES	Gaia Ring, Hyper Ring, [HP] HP ≤ 40% x6, [HP] Near Death x2

DP EFFICIENCY ROUTE

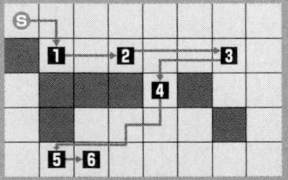

To gain maximum DP here, you should only focus on the battle pieces with DP Chances. Start off by attacking battle piece ❷, which is hidden in the lower of the shrouded areas close to the start. Defeating this piece opens the way to engage battle piece ❹, the next in line. After this piece is defeated as well, head to G-2 for a battle chain with battle pieces ❺ and ❻. A Potion appears after battle piece ❻ falls, and from this position you can grab it without using any DP. Head next to E-3 to attack battle piece ❽. After this, all that's left is to defeat Sephiroth before heading to the exit.

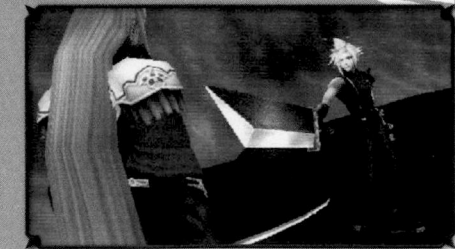

* Denotes use of the base value (for stats that vary).

SHADE IMPULSE

3-5

STARTING DP	MAX FINISHING	ENGAGEMENTS
2	4 (+3 after 3-star rating)	7 (+1 after 3-star rating)

The final level of Shade Impulse 3 is just as odd in layout as the third. From the start, you can simply move to the Stigma of Chaos and initiate the boss battle with Garland. Opening the chest along the way, however, immediately spawns four expert battle pieces, throwing you into a battle chain with two of them. Clearing all four of these expert pieces then generates two more expert battle pieces, along with treasure chest **B** in the upper right area. A Potion also spawns along the bottom, offering refreshment if desired. All of these pieces approach or exceed level 70, while Garland, the boss, is only level 45. This should figure into your decision—if your level is low, it's wise to just cross to Garland and complete Shade Impulse 3. The expert battle pieces (along with ultimate battle piece **7**, which spawns only during return trips after a 3-star rating) are best left for a time when your level is more comparable. Ultimate battle piece **7** is a ferocious manikin of Garland, who is much harder than the real thing. This foe can break lower level characters easily, and can respond to summons with its own, reducing bravery to 0. This foe also blocks any aggressive actions unless it is engaged in its own. By getting close, you can often provoke it into using Earthquake or Cyclone. These attacks leave it open if you get away quickly.

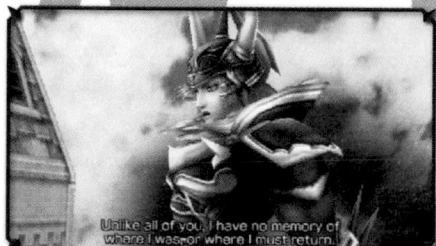

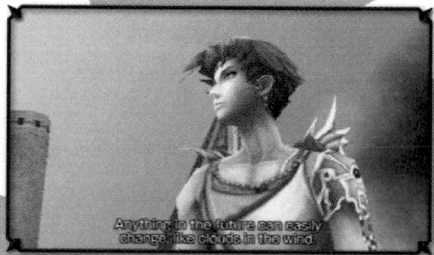

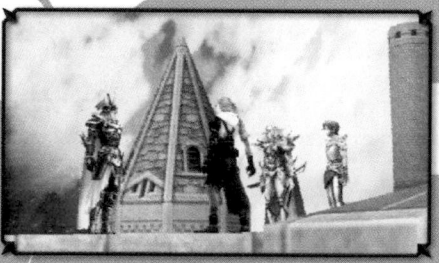

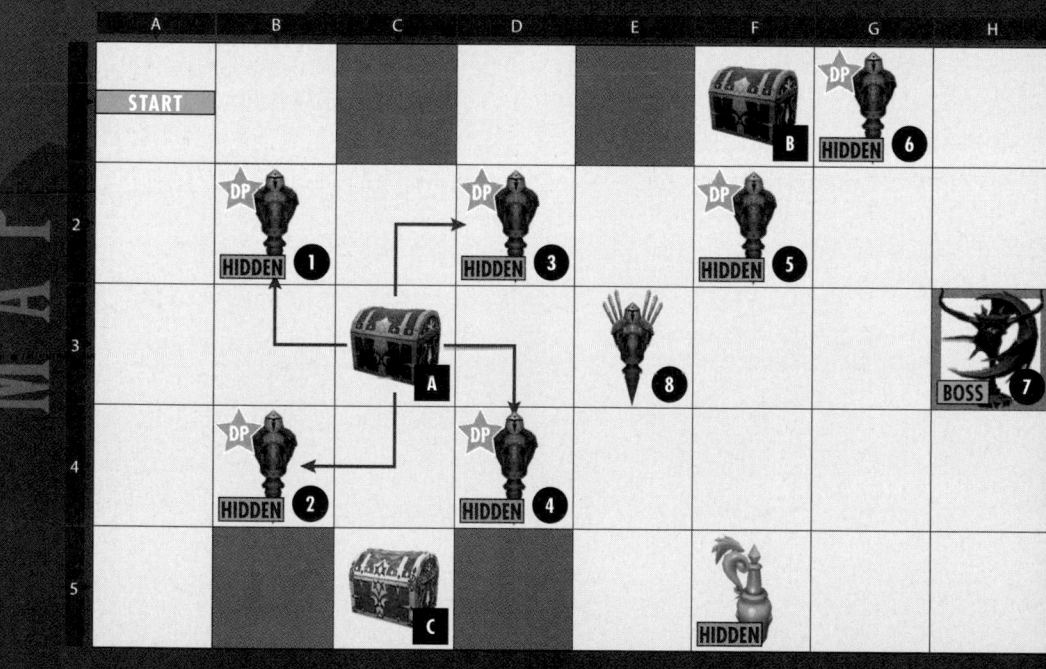

TREASURE

CHEST	1ST TIME	2ND TIME
A	Arcane Incense	85%: 10 PP; 5%: Geranium; 5%: Ylang Ylang; 5%: Destruction Resin
B	Gold (after 4 battle pieces are defeated)	50%: 50 PP; 25%: Rosemary; 20%: 300 PP; 5%: Rosetta Stone
C	Diamond (after 4-star rating)	

LOCKED AREAS

AREA	UNLOCK REQUIREMENTS
—	—

DP EFFICIENCY ROUTE

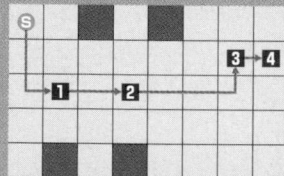

For the most DP here, you must make ultimate battle piece **8** appear, which means coming back after a 3-star rating. Head to B-3 and open the treasure chest. This action spawns the first four battle pieces, forcing you into a chain with pieces **1** and **2**. Defeat them, then move to D-3 and chain pieces **3**, **4**, and **8**. With them out of the way, battle pieces **5** and **6** spawn. They are your next target, so head to G-2 for the final chain before engaging the Stigma of Chaos for the boss fight. Just about all the DP Chances involve winning without losing HP or winning without getting hit at all, so stay on your toes!

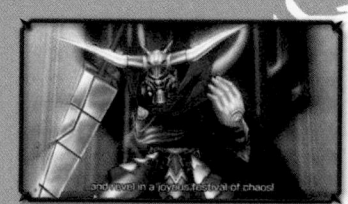

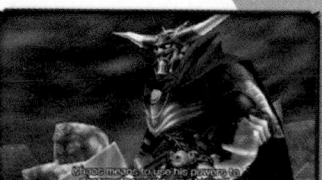

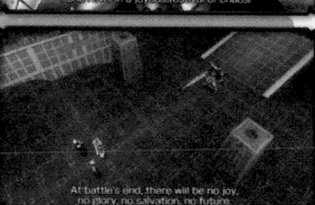

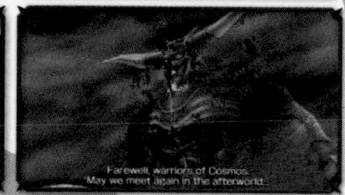

BATTLE PIECE DATA

1 COUNTERFEIT YOUTH

LEVEL	66	RANK A

BEHAVIOR	Extreme
DP CHANCE	Win without taking damage (DP+1)
BATTLE MAP	Ultimecia's Castle (Ω)
SUMMONSTONE	Demon Wall

STATS	HP	4938*	CP	415	BRV	470*
	ATK	73*	DEF	77*	LUK	43

EQUIPMENT	WEAPON	[Rank 11]
	HANDS	[Rank 9]

HEAD	[Rank 9]	BODY	[Rank 10]

SPOILS	GIL	1764	EXP	0

ACCESSORIES	Champion Belt, Muscle Belt, [Position] Near Opponent x6, [Time] After 90 Seconds

2 IMITATION DESPOT

LEVEL	67	RANK A

BEHAVIOR	Conservative
DP CHANCE	Win without taking damage (DP+1)
BATTLE MAP	Kefka's Tower (Ω)
SUMMONSTONE	Shiva

STATS	HP	4999*	CP	410	BRV	476*
	ATK	77*	DEF	79*	LUK	43

EQUIPMENT	WEAPON	[Rank 10]
	HANDS	[Rank 9]

HEAD	Cat–ear Hood	BODY	[Rank 9]

SPOILS	GIL	1764	EXP	0

ACCESSORIES	Gaia Ring, Hyper Ring, [HP] HP ≤ 40% x6, [HP] Near Death x2

3 PHANTASMAL GIRL

LEVEL	68	RANK A

BEHAVIOR	Cautious
DP CHANCE	Win without losing HP (DP+1)
BATTLE MAP	World of Darkness (Ω)
SUMMONSTONE	Lich

STATS	HP	7022	CP	411	BRV	482*
	ATK	123	DEF	119	LUK	44

EQUIPMENT	WEAPON	[Rank 11]
	HANDS	[Rank 9]

HEAD	[Rank 9]	BODY	Ninja Gear

SPOILS	GIL	1764	EXP	0

ACCESSORIES	Gaia Ring, Guardian Bangle, [HP] HP = 100% x3, [HP] HP ≥ 80% x5

4 FALLACIOUS TREE

LEVEL	69	RANK A

BEHAVIOR	Tactician
DP CHANCE	Win without taking damage (DP+1)
BATTLE MAP	Pandaemonium (Ω)
SUMMONSTONE	Marilith

STATS	HP	5120*	CP	418	BRV	701
	ATK	123	DEF	124	LUK	44

EQUIPMENT	WEAPON	Staff of the Magi
	HANDS	Demon Gloves

HEAD	Close Helmet	BODY	[Rank 10]

SPOILS	GIL	1764	EXP	0

ACCESSORIES	Gaia Ring, Hyper Ring, [HP] HP ≤ 40% x6, [HP] Near Death x2

5 FALSE STALWART

LEVEL	71	RANK A

BEHAVIOR	Valiant
DP CHANCE	Win without taking damage (DP+1)
BATTLE MAP	The Rift (Ω)
SUMMONSTONE	Bahamut

STATS	HP	7487	CP	414	BRV	668
	ATK	133	DEF	84*	LUK	45

EQUIPMENT	WEAPON	[Rank 12]
	HANDS	Crystal Shield

HEAD	Crystal Helm	BODY	Mirror Mail

SPOILS	GIL	1764	EXP	0

ACCESSORIES	Champion Belt, Muscle Belt, [Position] Near Opponent x6, [Time] After 90 Seconds

6 DELUSORY WARLOCK

LEVEL	70	RANK A

BEHAVIOR	Survivor
DP CHANCE	Win without losing HP (DP+1)
BATTLE MAP	Crystal World (Ω)
SUMMONSTONE	Carbuncle

STATS	HP	5181*	CP	413	BRV	685
	ATK	80*	DEF	82*	LUK	45

EQUIPMENT	WEAPON	[Rank 10]
	HANDS	Demon Gloves

HEAD	Platinum Helm	BODY	[Rank 9]

SPOILS	GIL	1764	EXP	0

ACCESSORIES	Gaia Ring, Guardian Bangle, [HP] HP = 100% x3 , [HP] HP ≥ 80% x5

7 GARLAND

LEVEL	45	RANK D

BEHAVIOR	Valiant
DP CHANCE	–
BATTLE MAP	Old Chaos Shrine (Ω)
SUMMONSTONE	Alexander

STATS	HP	5041	CP	383	BRV	470
	ATK	90	DEF	89	LUK	32

EQUIPMENT	WEAPON	Francisca
	HANDS	Force Shield

HEAD	Sallet	BODY	Survival Vest

SPOILS	GIL	4032	EXP	9165

ACCESSORIES	Champion Belt, Muscle Belt, [Position] Near Opponent x6, [Time] After 90 Seconds

8 FALSE STALWART

LEVEL	99	RANK S

BEHAVIOR	Valiant
DP CHANCE	Win battle (DP+3)
BATTLE MAP	Order's Sanctuary (Ω)
SUMMONSTONE	Scarmiglione

STATS	HP	9487	CP	448	BRV	910*
	ATK	179	DEF	112*	LUK	59

EQUIPMENT	WEAPON	[Rank 15]
	HANDS	Aegis Shield

HEAD	[Rank 15]	BODY	Vishnu Vest

SPOILS	GIL	1764	EXP	0

ACCESSORIES	Gaia Ring, Hyper Ring, [HP] HP ≤ 40% x6, [HP] Near Death x2

* Denotes use of the base value (for stats that vary).

SHADE IMPULSE 4
THE DECISIVE BATTLE

REWARDS

Shade Impulse 4 is the only chapter where you do not accrue or expend Destiny Points. The march toward Chaos is the utter focus!

Shade Impulse 4 also lacks Story Points and the rewards they bestow.

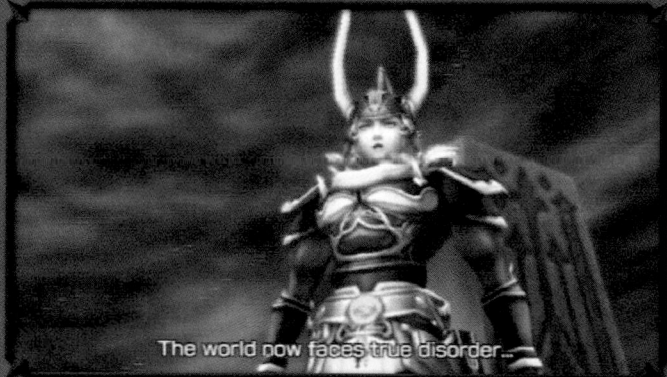

The world now faces true disorder...

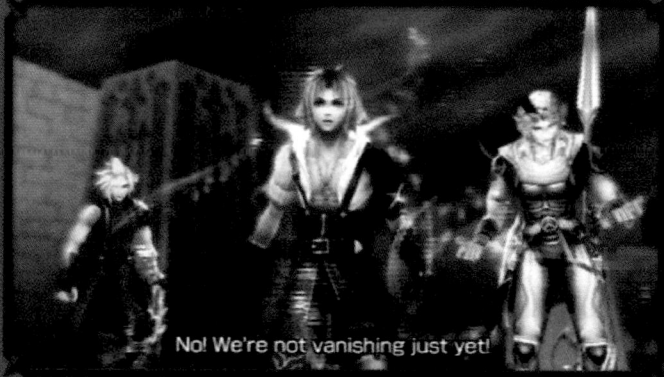

No! We're not vanishing just yet!

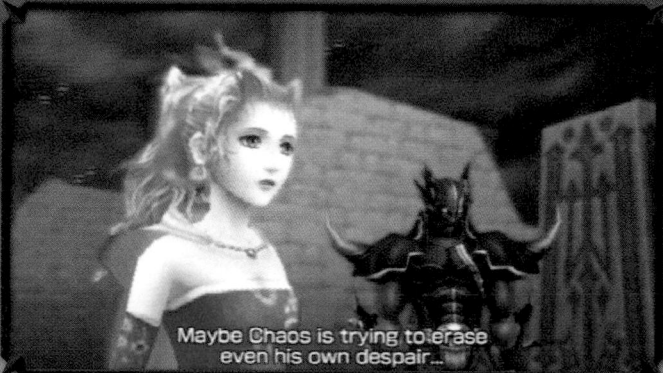

Maybe Chaos is trying to erase even his own despair...

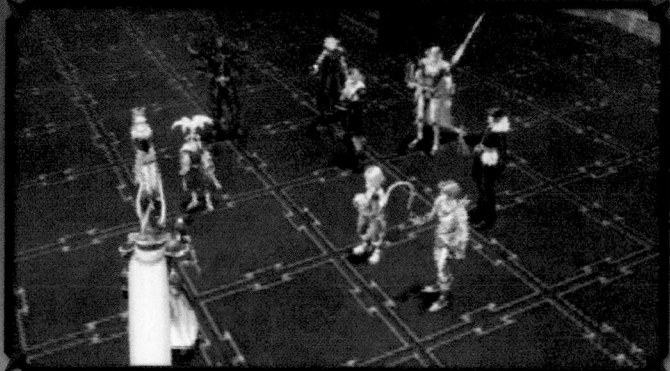

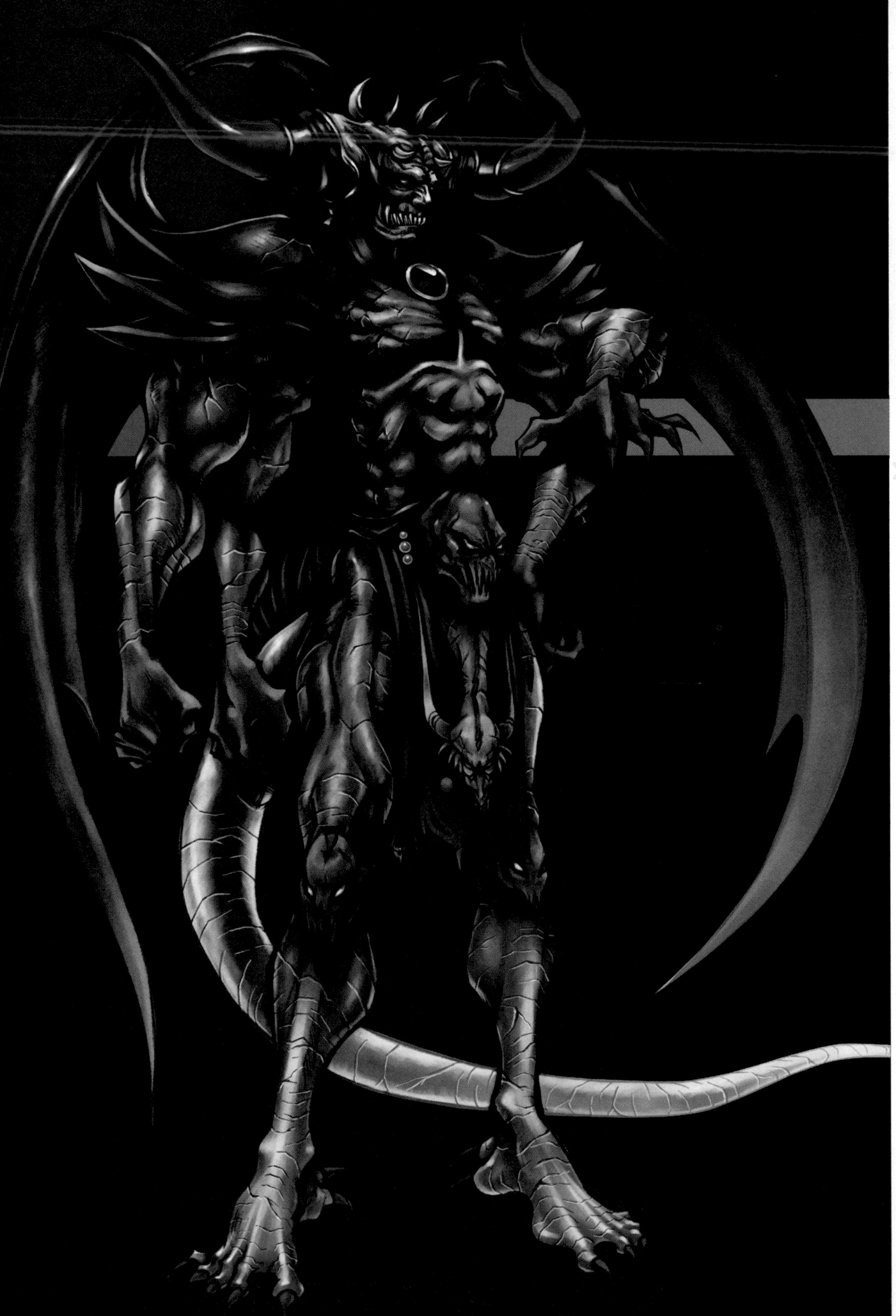

SHADE IMPULSE 4

SHADE IMPULSE

STARTING DP	MAX FINISHING	ENGAGEMENTS
0	0	5

There are no Locked Areas or unexpected traps in Shade Impulse 4. There are simply a handful of encounters on the two levels leading to Chaos himself. With everything you've gone through in previous Shade Impulse and Destiny Odyssey chapters, these fights should be easy enough. Our heroes are contemplative as each of the last manikins are pushed aside, musing about the long journey here as well as the possibility that soon nothing may exist or matter. All Shade Impulse 4 battles before Chaos take place on the Order's Sanctuary (Ω) stage. Don't forget to snag the Ramuh Summonstone, hidden in the lower left portion of the level.

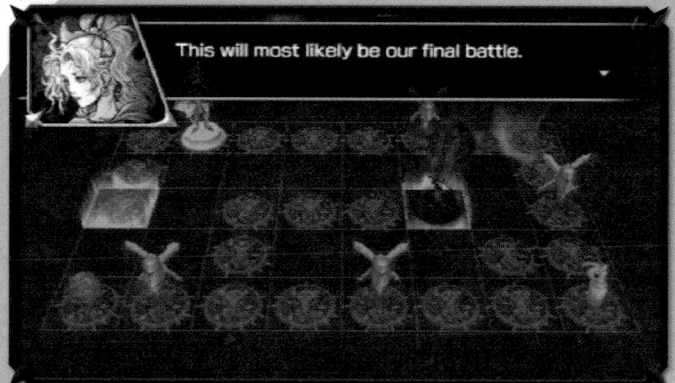

This will most likely be our final battle.

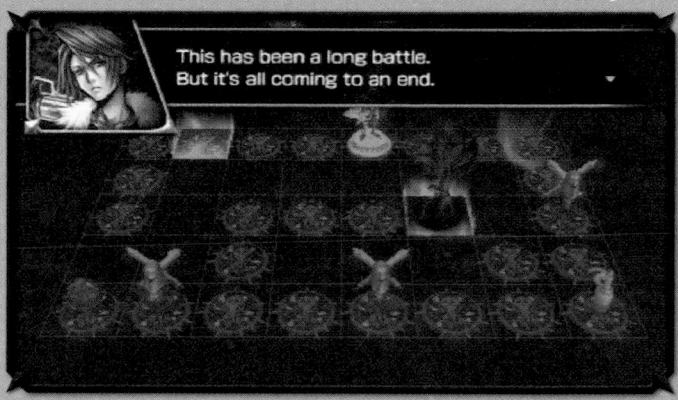

This has been a long battle.
But it's all coming to an end.

MAP

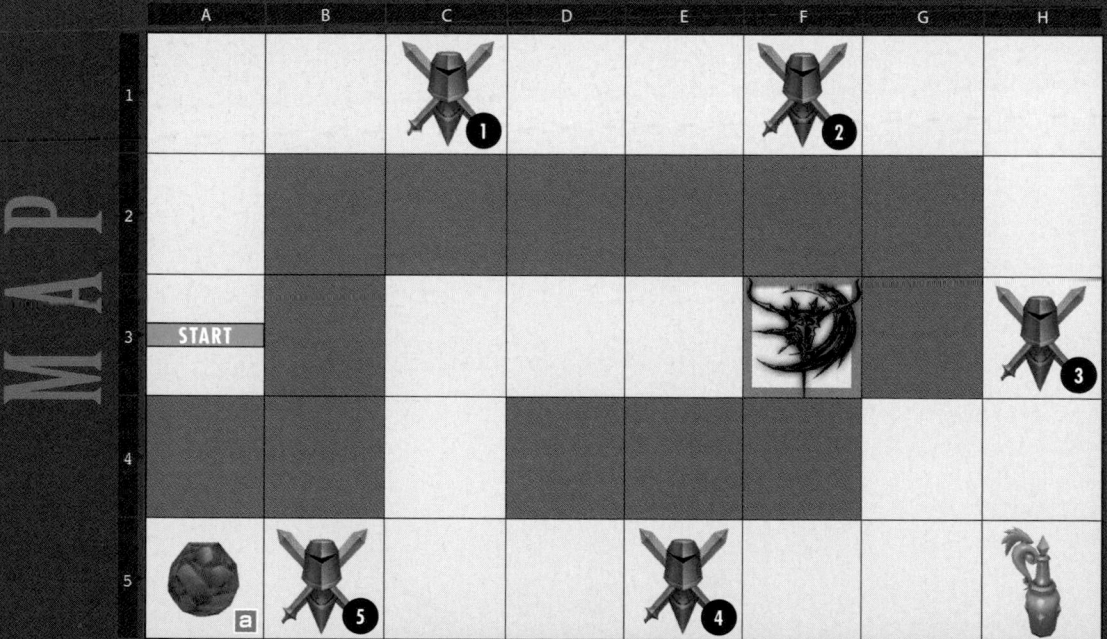
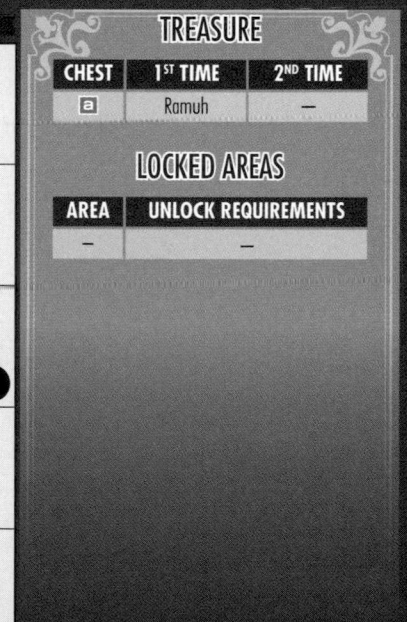

TREASURE

CHEST	1ST TIME	2ND TIME
a	Ramuh	—

LOCKED AREAS

AREA	UNLOCK REQUIREMENTS
—	—

DP EFFICIENCY ROUTE

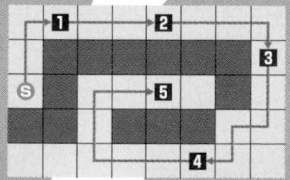

Destiny Points aren't a factor for Shade Impulse 4, so this is simply the most expeditious route through the level. Shade Impulse 4-1 isn't rife with options and alternate paths; the only encounters you can skip are with the Potion, and the battle with piece 5 and the Summonstone it guards.

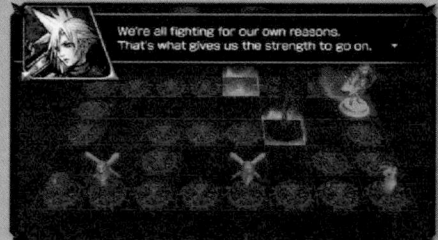

We're all fighting for our own reasons.
That's what gives us the strength to go on.

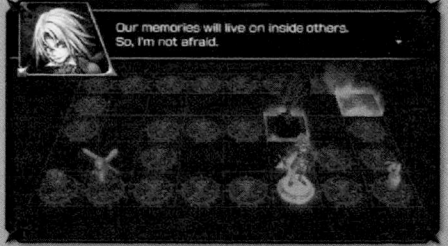

Our memories will live on inside others.
So, I'm not afraid.

BATTLE PIECE DATA

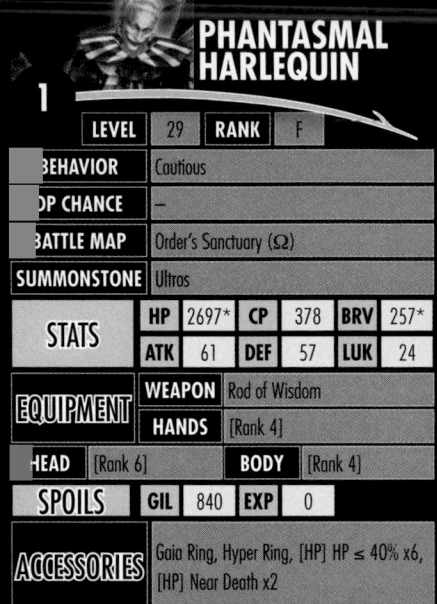

1 PHANTASMAL HARLEQUIN

LEVEL	29	RANK	F

BEHAVIOR	Cautious
DP CHANCE	–
BATTLE MAP	Order's Sanctuary (Ω)
SUMMONSTONE	Ultros

STATS	HP	2697*	CP	378	BRV	257*
	ATK	61	DEF	57	LUK	24

EQUIPMENT	WEAPON	Rod of Wisdom
	HANDS	[Rank 4]

HEAD	[Rank 6]	BODY	[Rank 4]

SPOILS	GIL	840	EXP	0

ACCESSORIES	Gaia Ring, Hyper Ring, [HP] HP ≤ 40% x6, [HP] Near Death x2

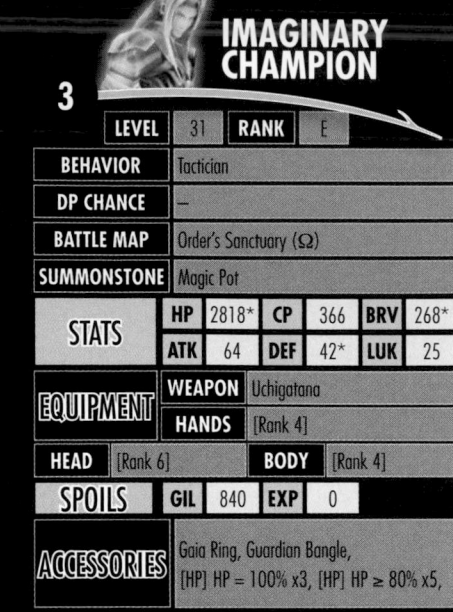

2 TRANSIENT WITCH

LEVEL	29	RANK	F

BEHAVIOR	Conservative
DP CHANCE	–
BATTLE MAP	Order's Sanctuary (Ω)
SUMMONSTONE	Kraken

STATS	HP	2697*	CP	364	BRV	257*
	ATK	62	DEF	38*	LUK	24

EQUIPMENT	WEAPON	[Rank 6]
	HANDS	[Rank 4]

HEAD	[Rank 4]	BODY	[Rank 5]

SPOILS	GIL	840	EXP	0

ACCESSORIES	Star Earring, Earring, [Position] Far from Opponent x6, [Time] After 90 Seconds

3 IMAGINARY CHAMPION

LEVEL	31	RANK	E

BEHAVIOR	Tactician
DP CHANCE	–
BATTLE MAP	Order's Sanctuary (Ω)
SUMMONSTONE	Magic Pot

STATS	HP	2818*	CP	366	BRV	268*
	ATK	64	DEF	42*	LUK	25

EQUIPMENT	WEAPON	Uchigatana
	HANDS	[Rank 4]

HEAD	[Rank 6]	BODY	[Rank 4]

SPOILS	GIL	840	EXP	0

ACCESSORIES	Gaia Ring, Guardian Bangle, [HP] HP = 100% x3, [HP] HP ≥ 80% x5,

4 CAPRICIOUS REAPER

LEVEL	28	RANK	F

BEHAVIOR	Valiant
DP CHANCE	–
BATTLE MAP	Order's Sanctuary (Ω)
SUMMONSTONE	Mandragora

STATS	HP	2636*	CP	362	BRV	251*
	ATK	54	DEF	39*	LUK	24

EQUIPMENT	WEAPON	[Rank 4]
	HANDS	Silver Bangles

HEAD	[Rank 5]	BODY	Poncho

SPOILS	GIL	840	EXP	0

ACCESSORIES	Star Earring, Earring, [Position] Far from Opponent x6, [Time] After 90 Seconds

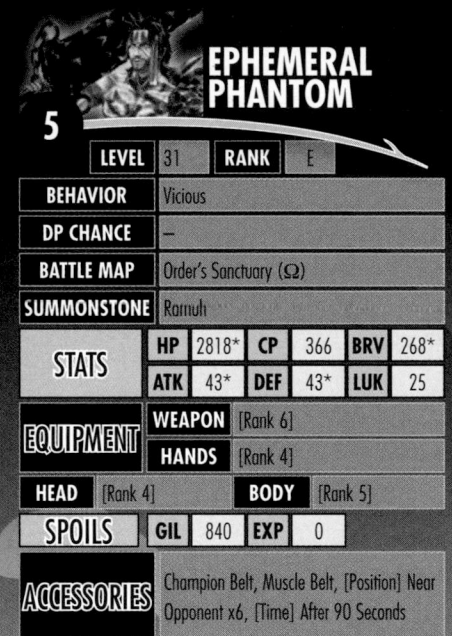

5 EPHEMERAL PHANTOM

LEVEL	31	RANK	E

BEHAVIOR	Vicious
DP CHANCE	–
BATTLE MAP	Order's Sanctuary (Ω)
SUMMONSTONE	Ramuh

STATS	HP	2818*	CP	366	BRV	268*
	ATK	43*	DEF	43*	LUK	25

EQUIPMENT	WEAPON	[Rank 6]
	HANDS	[Rank 4]

HEAD	[Rank 4]	BODY	[Rank 5]

SPOILS	GIL	840	EXP	0

ACCESSORIES	Champion Belt, Muscle Belt, [Position] Near Opponent x6, [Time] After 90 Seconds

* Denotes use of the base value (for stats that vary).

SHADE IMPULSE 4

4-2

STARTING DP	MAX FINISHING	ENGAGEMENTS
0	0	6

And so the stage is set for the final battle. Here again, a small group of crystal pretenders stand before the Stigma of Chaos. Tiamat can be found in the upper reaches of the level, behind battle piece ❹. Be sure to check the Customization Menu to ensure you're wearing the best equipment and accessories. Likewise, equip your favorite summon for a hard fight. Once you're properly outfitted, quaff the Potion tucked away on the bottom edge of the level, refilling HP and EX Force to full. Then, engage the Stigma of Chaos and prepare for the final battle!

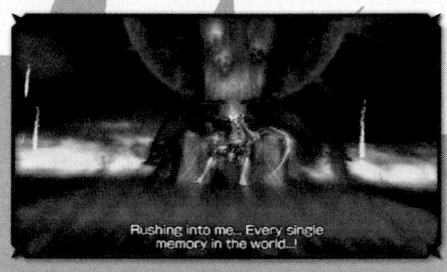

Rushing into me... Every single memory in the world...!

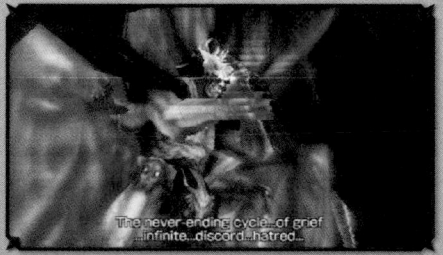

The never-ending cycle...of grief ...infinite...discord...hatred...

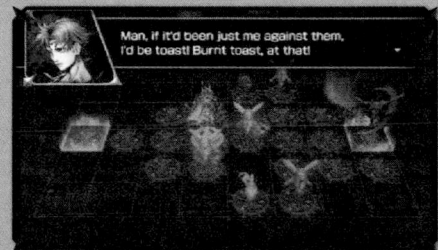

Man, if it'd been just me against them, I'd be toast! Burnt toast, at that!

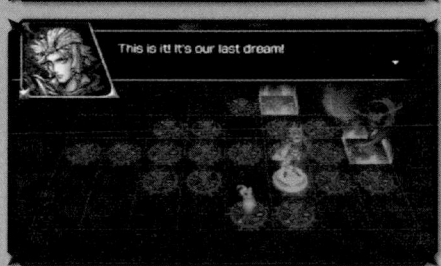

This is it! It's our last dream!

MAP

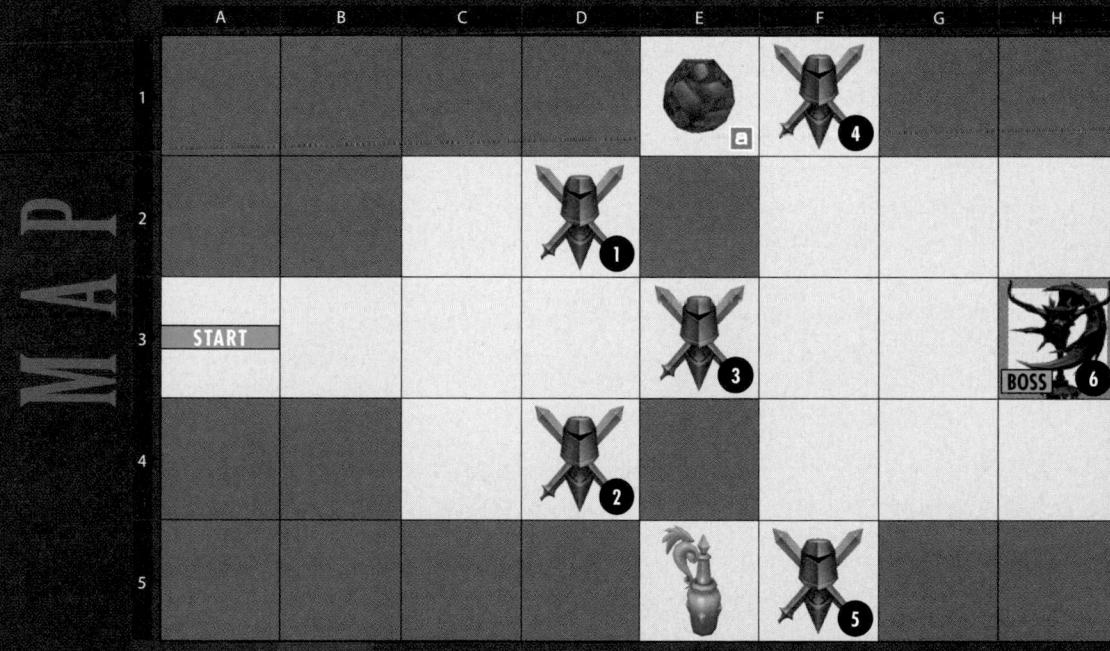
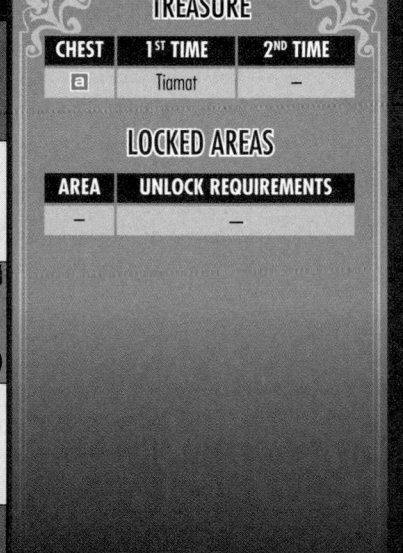

TREASURE

CHEST	1ST TIME	2ND TIME
a	Tiamat	—

LOCKED AREAS

AREA	UNLOCK REQUIREMENTS
—	—

DP EFFICIENCY ROUTE

The quickest path to Chaos is a straight line. Head to D-3 and engage battle pieces ❶, ❷, and ❸ in a three-part battle chain. Having dispensed with these manikins, make a beeline for the god of discord himself.

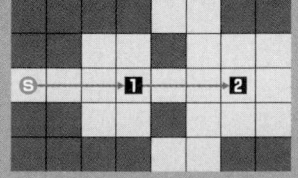

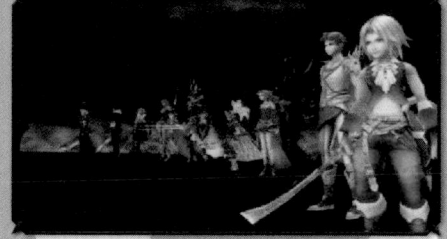

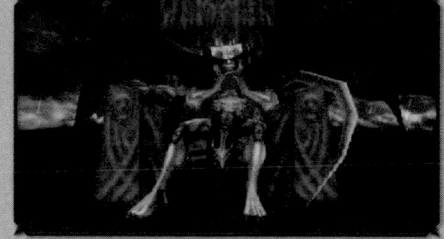

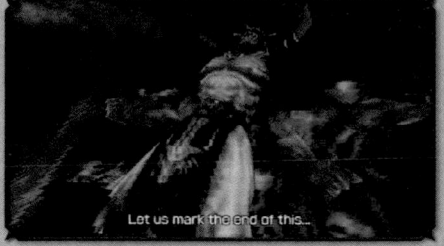

Let us mark the end of this...

BATTLE PIECE DATA

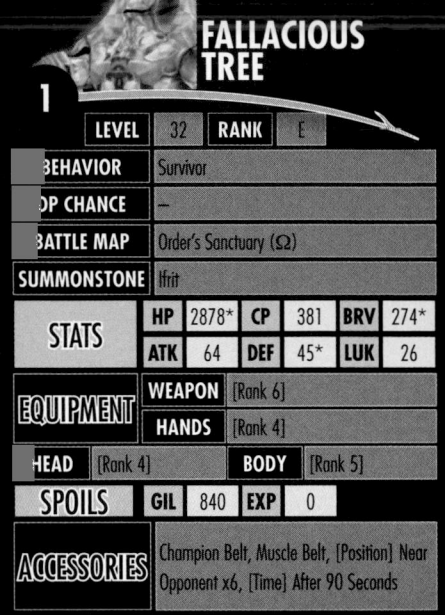

1 FALLACIOUS TREE

LEVEL	32	RANK	E

BEHAVIOR	Survivor
DP CHANCE	–
BATTLE MAP	Order's Sanctuary (Ω)
SUMMONSTONE	Ifrit

STATS	HP	2878*	CP	381	BRV	274*
	ATK	64	DEF	45*	LUK	26

EQUIPMENT	WEAPON	[Rank 6]
	HANDS	[Rank 4]

HEAD	[Rank 4]	BODY	[Rank 5]

SPOILS	GIL	840	EXP	0

ACCESSORIES	Champion Belt, Muscle Belt, [Position] Near Opponent x6, [Time] After 90 Seconds

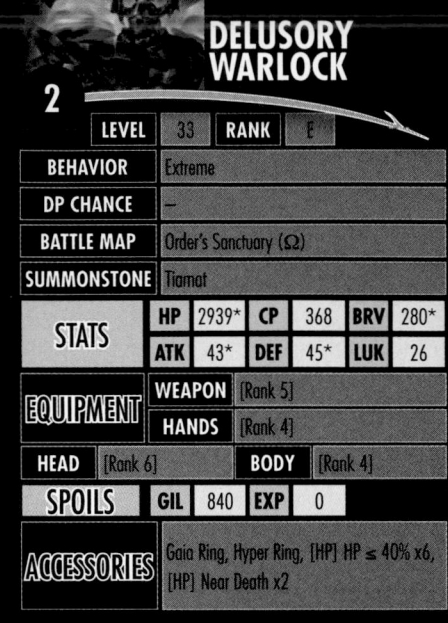

2 DELUSORY WARLOCK

LEVEL	33	RANK	E

BEHAVIOR	Extreme
DP CHANCE	–
BATTLE MAP	Order's Sanctuary (Ω)
SUMMONSTONE	Tiamat

STATS	HP	2939*	CP	368	BRV	280*
	ATK	43*	DEF	45*	LUK	26

EQUIPMENT	WEAPON	[Rank 5]
	HANDS	[Rank 4]

HEAD	[Rank 6]	BODY	[Rank 4]

SPOILS	GIL	840	EXP	0

ACCESSORIES	Gaia Ring, Hyper Ring, [HP] HP ≤ 40% x6, [HP] Near Death x2

3 COUNTERFEIT WRAITH

LEVEL	34	RANK	E

BEHAVIOR	Tactician
DP CHANCE	–
BATTLE MAP	Order's Sanctuary (Ω)
SUMMONSTONE	Titan

STATS	HP	3000*	CP	383	BRV	286*
	ATK	65	DEF	45*	LUK	27

EQUIPMENT	WEAPON	[Rank 6]
	HANDS	[Rank 4]

HEAD	[Rank 4]	BODY	[Rank 5]

SPOILS	GIL	840	EXP	0

ACCESSORIES	Gaia Ring, Guardian Bangle, [HP] HP = 100% x3, [HP] HP ≥ 80% x5

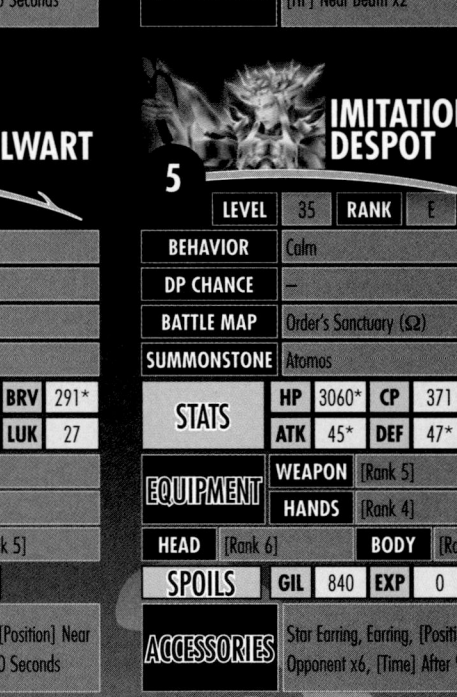

4 FALSE STALWART

LEVEL	35	RANK	E

BEHAVIOR	Valiant
DP CHANCE	–
BATTLE MAP	Order's Sanctuary (Ω)
SUMMONSTONE	PuPu

STATS	HP	3060*	CP	371	BRV	291*
	ATK	47*	DEF	48*	LUK	27

EQUIPMENT	WEAPON	[Rank 6]
	HANDS	[Rank 4]

HEAD	[Rank 4]	BODY	[Rank 5]

SPOILS	GIL	840	EXP	0

ACCESSORIES	Champion Belt, Muscle Belt, [Position] Near Opponent x6, [Time] After 90 Seconds

5 IMITATION DESPOT

LEVEL	35	RANK	E

BEHAVIOR	Calm
DP CHANCE	–
BATTLE MAP	Order's Sanctuary (Ω)
SUMMONSTONE	Atomos

STATS	HP	3060*	CP	371	BRV	291*
	ATK	45*	DEF	47*	LUK	27

EQUIPMENT	WEAPON	[Rank 5]
	HANDS	[Rank 4]

HEAD	[Rank 6]	BODY	[Rank 4]

SPOILS	GIL	840	EXP	0

ACCESSORIES	Star Earring, Earring, [Position] Far from Opponent x6, [Time] After 90 Seconds

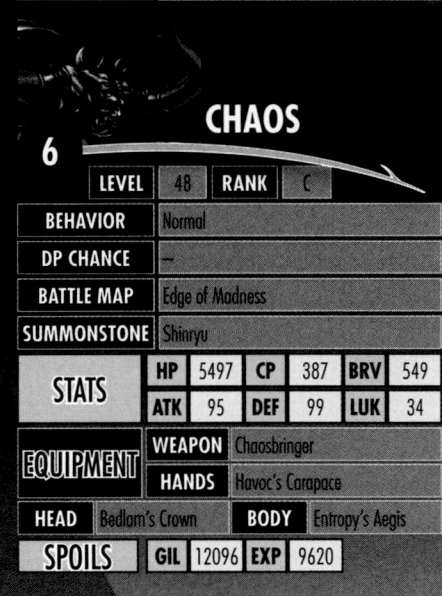

6 CHAOS

LEVEL	48	RANK	C

BEHAVIOR	Normal
DP CHANCE	–
BATTLE MAP	Edge of Madness
SUMMONSTONE	Shinryu

STATS	HP	5497	CP	387	BRV	549
	ATK	95	DEF	99	LUK	34

EQUIPMENT	WEAPON	Chaosbringer
	HANDS	Havoc's Carapace

HEAD	Bedlam's Crown	BODY	Entropy's Aegis

SPOILS	GIL	12096	EXP	9620

* Denotes use of the base value (for stats that vary).

CHAOS

The long-awaited battle is finally upon you. The fate of the world is decided here on this small, circular stage in front of the throne of Chaos, surrounded by the roiling, infernal landscape. The confined space makes it difficult to get any reprieve from the assault of the god of discord, as there's only so far to flee in any given direction. Watch for EX Cores that spawn right in front of the throne.

If this doesn't sound rough enough, consider this—Chaos must be defeated *three times in a row*, and he grows more aggressive and powerful after each defeat! You have no such luxury—lose to any form of Chaos and you'll have to start all over. But keep in mind that Shade Impulse 4 has no Destiny Points or Story Points to worry about. If you lose, select "Flee" instead of "Retry." This allows you to reevaluate your equipment and summons if desired, while keeping any EXP earned by hitting Chaos with HP attacks. This way, even if you lose several times, you'll at least gain levels, making subsequent attempts easier.

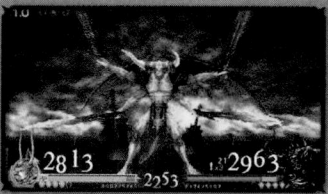 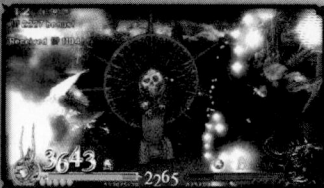

You can make things easier on yourself through a few insurance policies. Entering the battle with a full EX Gauge is a big help. EX Mode is very useful against Chaos, not so much for a potential EX Burst, but rather for the vastly increased rate of critical hits on bravery attacks. This makes it much easier to inflict Break on him. Taking along the right summon is also crucial. Rather than bringing along a monster that augments offense directly, try bringing one that can help safeguard your life. If Chaos's bravery is high enough to ensure a killshot against you, while your own bravery is much lower, Carbuncle can instantly bring him down to your level and buy you some time. This is especially helpful just after he inflicts Break on you—either flee until Break wears off or tag him with an HP attack to negate Break status, then immediately use Carbuncle.

Voila: his bravery drops from very dangerous quadruple digits to near 0. With the tables turned and his bravery so low, this presents an ideal time to inflict Break on Chaos. Along the same lines, Phoenix and Demon Wall can shield your bravery, preventing Break status. Whichever summon you choose, pace yourself using it. Remember, Chaos has three forms, and while he can use his Shinryu summon multiple times, you can still only use yours once. A solid gameplan might involve using EX Mode immediately against his first form, hopefully pushing quickly through to his second. Then, on the second form, be mindful of opportunities to use your summon to escape a tight spot or avoid defeat. Finally, certain accessories like Phoenix Pinions can be helpful in buying an extra stay of execution when things look grim.

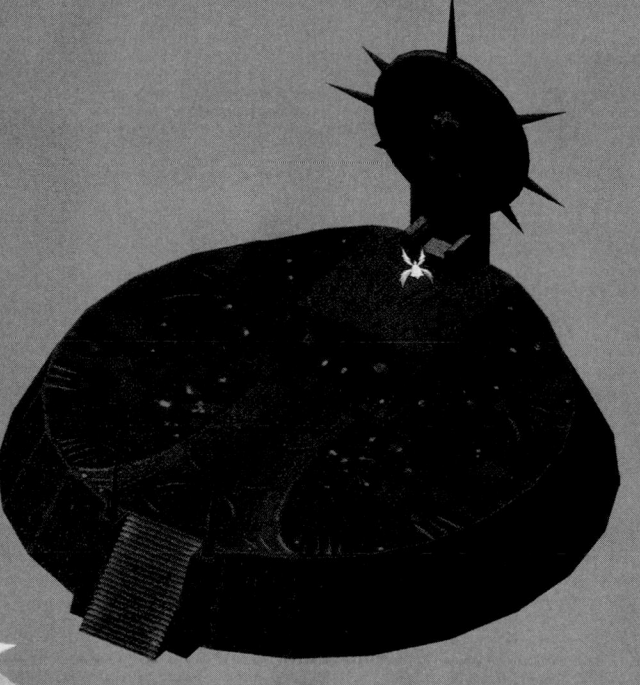

The Edge of Madness

His bravery attacks cut a wide swath, but most are relatively easy to deal with, and don't lead directly to finishing HP attacks. His bravery swipes in the air or on the ground are easy to block and counter if he starts them from a few steps away. When he takes to the air, watch out for his diving kick—be ready to dodge or block. His flame pillars and fireballs are also avoidable through dodging or blocking. You won't actually gain an advantage from blocking the diving kick or flaming pillars, but you won't take any damage either. Taking bravery damage is not really the issue, however. The true threat are the brutal HP attacks of Chaos. They are all avoidable on reaction, but you must react exactly right to avoid withering damage. Just dodging in whichever direction doesn't work as it will against most normal characters. Consistently avoiding his HP attacks is essential to success, as otherwise he'll simply deal too much damage to handle, and he's only truly vulnerable after missing one of his attacks—he will otherwise almost always dodge or block.

HP ATTACKS

NAME	NOTES
Condemn	Chaos draws in nearby foes before damaging them with a great vertical pillar of flame. Dodge backward, away from Chaos, to avoid it.
Divine Punishment	Chaos forms a vortex of flame around his foe, before striking with swords of flames. If the swords strike successful, Chaos continues his assault with an aerial combo. You mustn't touch the pillar of flame, then dodge the flaming swords to avoid this attack. Stay motionless to avoid touching the initial flames, then use a neutral dodge then a lateral dodge to avoid the sword strikes. If far away, simply dash directly at Chaos to avoid the entire attack. If nearby, you'll have to stand motionless amongst the flames, then dodge the swords at the end.
Soul of Oblivion	Chaos draws in energy for a long time before blowing fire directly at his foe. Almost unlimited range—to avoid this, either charge directly for Chaos and hit him to interrupt the charging period, or get as far away as possible on both a horizontal and vertical axis. There's no *guarantee* that this attack will miss at any range if you don't directly interrupt Chaos, but sometimes the attack will fail at odd angles or extreme distance.

NAME	NOTES
Demonsdance	Chaos teleports directly above his foe and drops on them five times. This attack can hit repeatedly, but also has many gaps where it can be escaped. Be watchful for Chaos to appear overhead, then dodge at the last second over and over until the attack ceases.
Scarlet Rain	Chaos causes the floor of the stage to explode into flame, then hurls volleys of small fireballs before throwing a final, large fireball. Dodge or jump upward initially, then block the small fireballs before dodging the big one.
Utter Chaos	Chaos grows to an enormous size and attacks with one of the huge swords seen in the background. Vertical slashes can be avoided by dodging laterally, while horizontal slashes can be avoided by increasing altitude.
Brink of Delusion	This attack always follows Utter Chaos. The stage will be nuked in areas indicated by flashing circles. Get out of these areas to avoid taking damage.

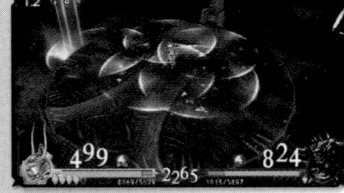
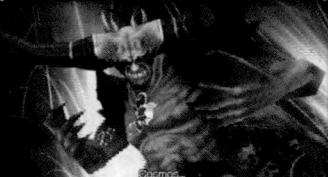
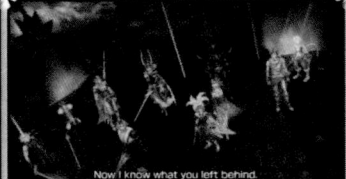
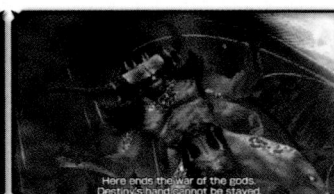

GAME COMPLETION

When the main conflict is resolved, a trove of goodies is revealed. The Duel Colosseum becomes available, along with many new items in the PP Catalog. And two new chapters unveil themselves when the main story is finished—the tales of Distant Glory. Distant Glory XI is opened when you finish Shade Impulse and five of the Destiny Odyssey chapters. Distant Glory XII is opened after you finish Shade Impulse and ten of the Destiny Odyssey chapters.

SHADE IMPULSE 4

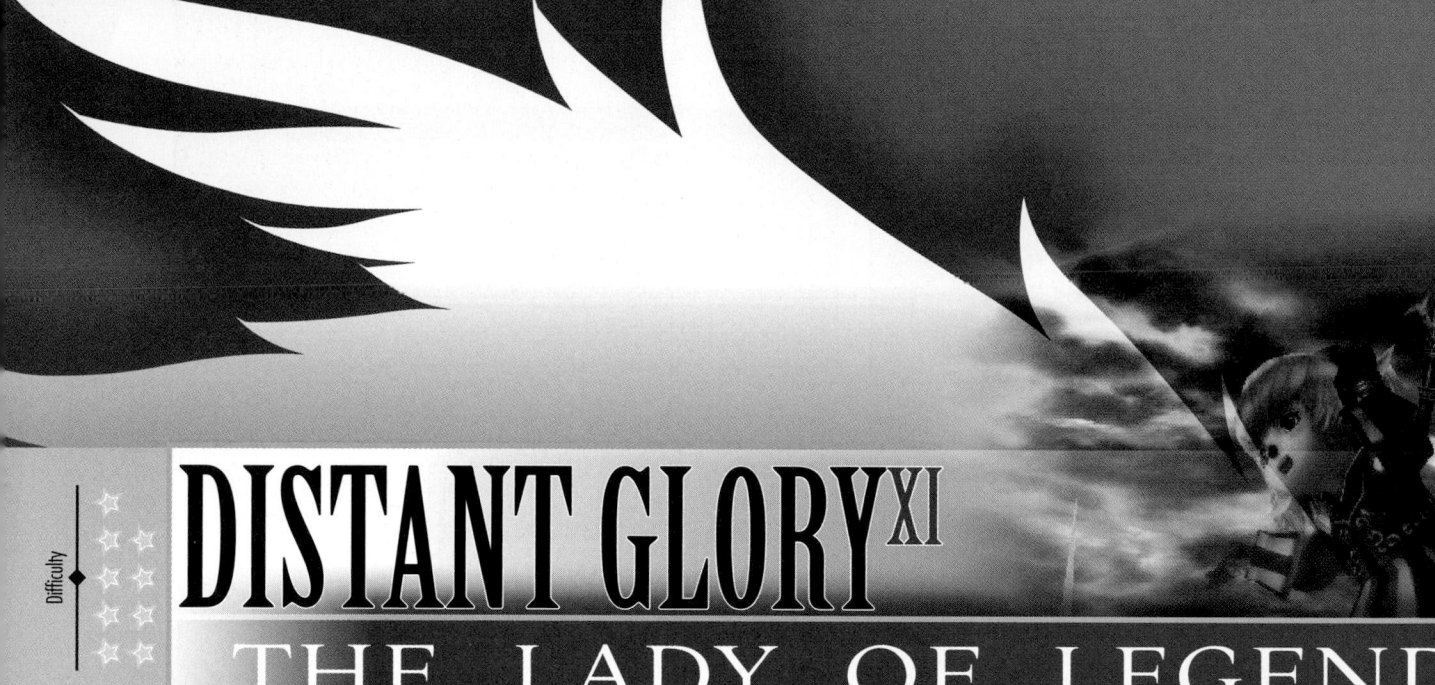

DISTANT GLORY XI
THE LADY OF LEGEND

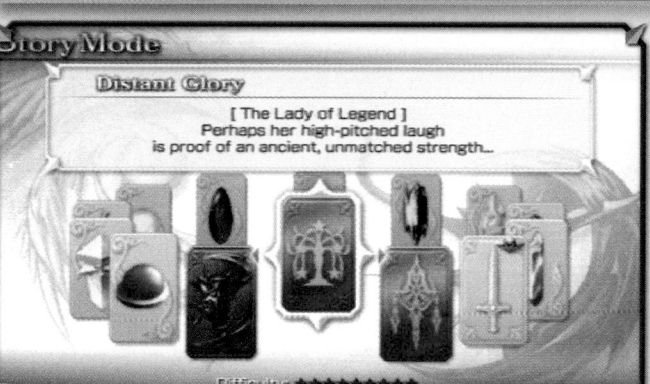

Story Mode

Distant Glory

[The Lady of Legend]
Perhaps her high-pitched laugh
is proof of an ancient, unmatched strength...

Difficulty: ★★★★★★★★★

Up until now, only Cosmos-aligned characters could be used in Story Mode. However, for the Distant Glory levels, you can choose any character you like, including Chaos-aligned fiends.

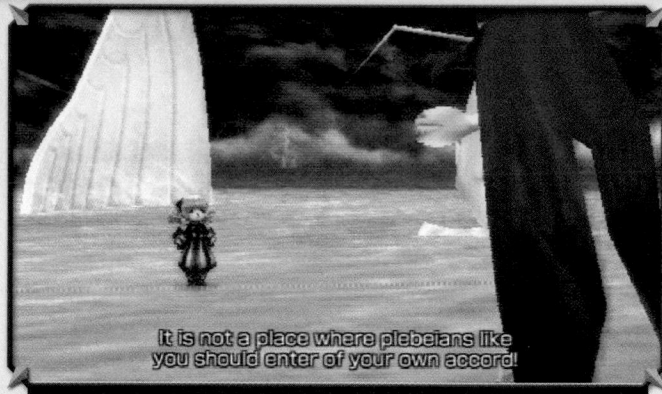

It is not a place where plebeians like you should enter of your own accord!

As veterans of Final Fantasy XI remember, Shantotto speaks jovially in frequently caustic poetry. More of her creative disdain is found throughout missions for the nation of Windurst, alongside displays of her tremendous magical power.

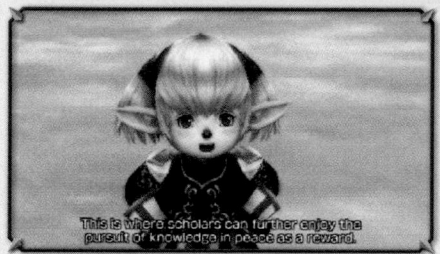

This is where scholars can further enjoy the pursuit of knowledge in peace as a reward.

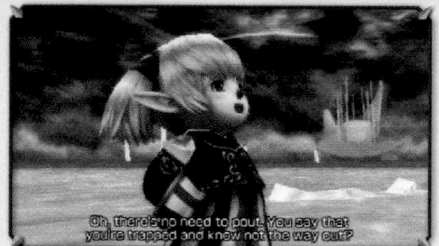

Oh, there's no need to pout. You say that you're trapped and know not the way out?

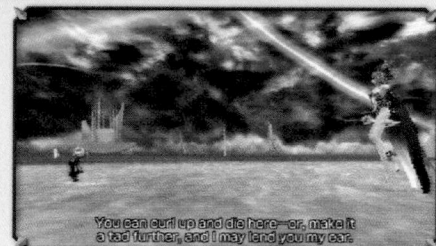

You can curl up and die here—or, make it a tad further, and I may lend you my ear.

REWARDS

At the end of each level, rewards are available if you finish with a positive number of Destiny Points, or DP. This walkthrough includes miniature level maps that indicate the most efficient route to take through a given level, in order to maximize DP.

LEVEL COMPLETION

REMAINING DP		1ST TIME		2ND TIME
7		Rosetta Stone	300 PP	
6		Heike's Shield	200 PP	
5		Heike's Helm	120 PP	
4		Chocobo	80 PP	
3		Crystal	50 PP	
2		Diamond	30 PP	
1		4000 gil	20 PP	
0		2000 gil	10 PP	

DISTANT GLORY XI COMPLETION

STAR RATING	SP REQUIRED	AWARD
★	300	Special areas unlocked
★★	200	Rare battle pieces spawned
★★★	300	Rare treasure chests spawned
★★★★	500 SP, then every 500 SP extra	100 PP
–	–	–

At the end of each set of levels, you'll receive rewards based on your performance. Story Points, or SP, are awarded after each level based on remaining DP and HP, as well as the number of engagements undertaken. Points are penalized for retries, or for a DP total that dips into negatives. If you miss out on a desired bonus on the first playthrough, don't worry—SP is cumulative across multiple playthroughs.

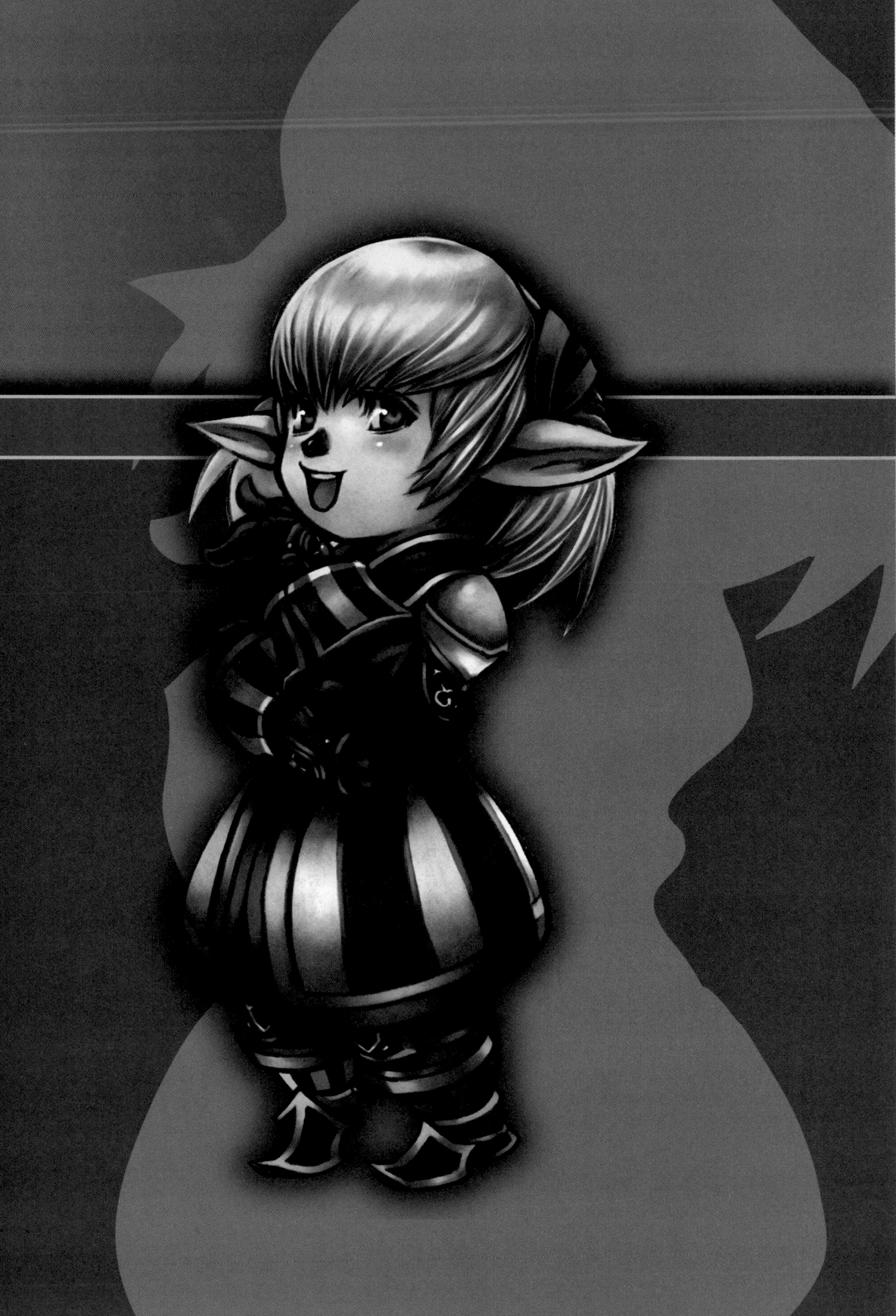

DISTANT GLORY XI

DISTANT GLORY

Shantotto's levels are a little like Squall's: defeating the battle pieces visible at the beginning reveals more pieces farther away. The new pieces offer encounters with Cosmos-aligned characters. The Stigma of Chaos on each level won't appear until all the standard battle pieces are defeated—no skipping fights here. The difficulty rating for Distant Glory is a little deceptive. Sure, the going will be rough if you try bringing a low-level character through, but playing Distant Glory to begin with means you finished Shade Impulse, and any character sufficiently leveled and geared to trudge across Shade Impulse should breeze through Distant Glory. Those who crave a challenge need not worry: Inward Chaos is a different story.

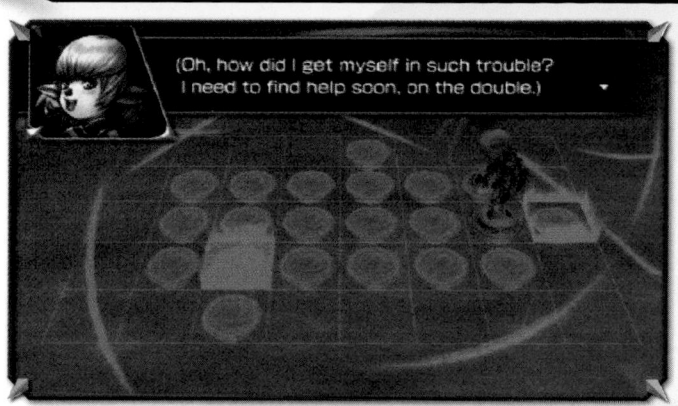

(Oh, how did I get myself in such trouble? I need to find help soon, on the double.)

MAP

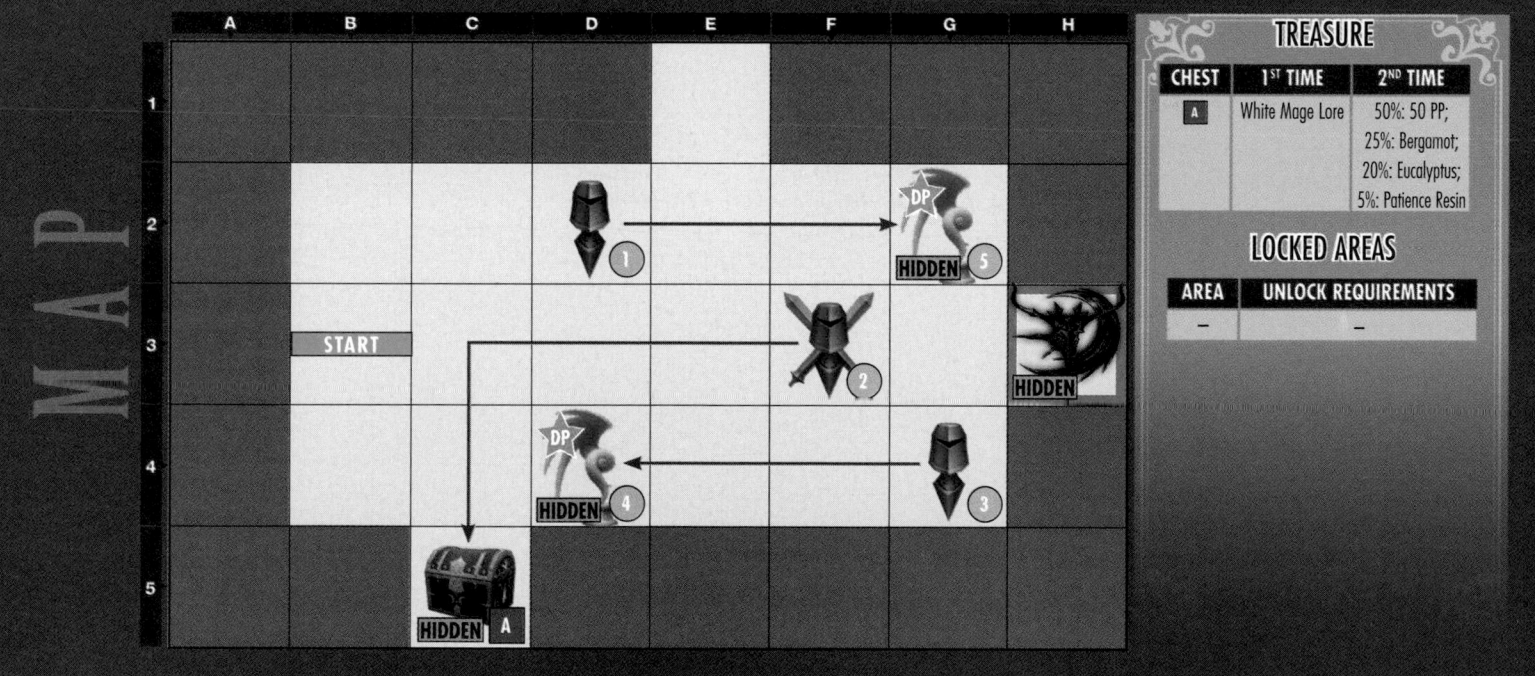

TREASURE

CHEST	1ST TIME	2ND TIME
A	White Mage Lore	50%: 50 PP;
		25%: Bergamot;
		20%: Eucalyptus;
		5%: Patience Resin

LOCKED AREAS

AREA	UNLOCK REQUIREMENTS
—	—

DP EFFICIENCY ROUTE

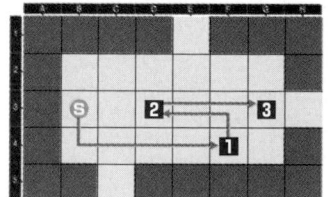

From the start, head to F-4 for a two-part battle chain with battle pieces ② and ③. Neither of these fights offers a DP Chance, but defeating piece ③ spawns Cosmos piece ④. Next, move to D-3 to chain battle piece ① and Cosmos piece ④. When piece ① falls, Cosmos piece ⑤ appears. The final order of business is to head to G-3 before defeating Cosmos piece ⑤. The Stigma of Chaos here doesn't actually appear until every enemy on the level falls. Finishing the last foe from G-3 means you won't have to expend any Destiny Points traipsing to the exit.

BATTLE PIECE DATA

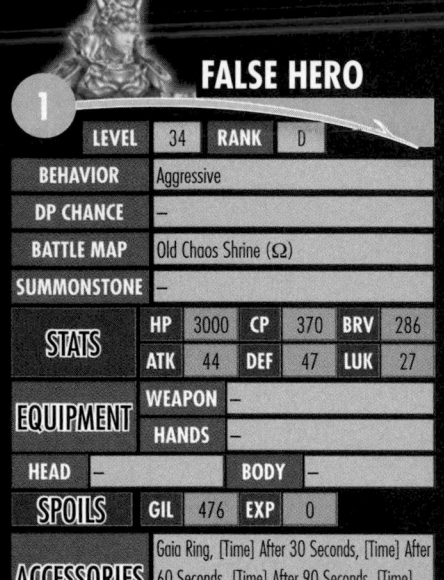

1 FALSE HERO

LEVEL	34	RANK	D

BEHAVIOR	Aggressive
DP CHANCE	—
BATTLE MAP	Old Chaos Shrine (Ω)
SUMMONSTONE	—

STATS	HP	3000	CP	370	BRV	286
	ATK	44	DEF	47	LUK	27

EQUIPMENT	WEAPON	—
	HANDS	—
HEAD	—	BODY	—

SPOILS	GIL	476	EXP	0

ACCESSORIES	Gaia Ring, [Time] After 30 Seconds, [Time] After 60 Seconds, [Time] After 90 Seconds, [Time] After 120 Seconds, [Time] After 180 Seconds

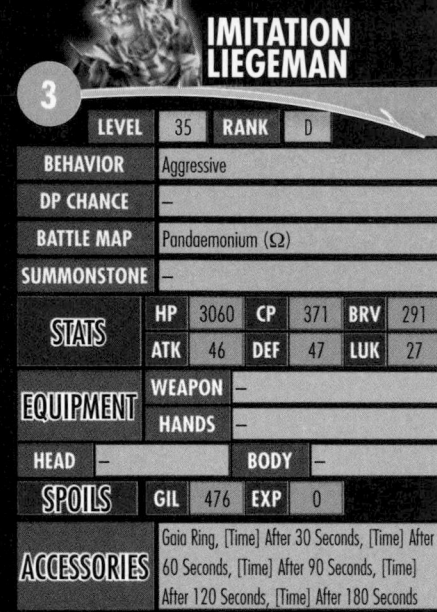

2 LADY OF ANTIQUITY

LEVEL	43	RANK	E

BEHAVIOR	Standby
DP CHANCE	—
BATTLE MAP	Order's Sanctuary (Ω)
SUMMONSTONE	—

STATS	HP	3545	CP	421	BRV	338
	ATK	55	DEF	52	LUK	31

EQUIPMENT	WEAPON	—
	HANDS	—
HEAD	—	BODY	—

SPOILS	GIL	476	EXP	0

ACCESSORIES	Gaia Ring, [Time] After 30 Seconds, [Time] After 60 Seconds, [Time] After 90 Seconds, [Time] After 120 Seconds, [Time] After 180 Seconds

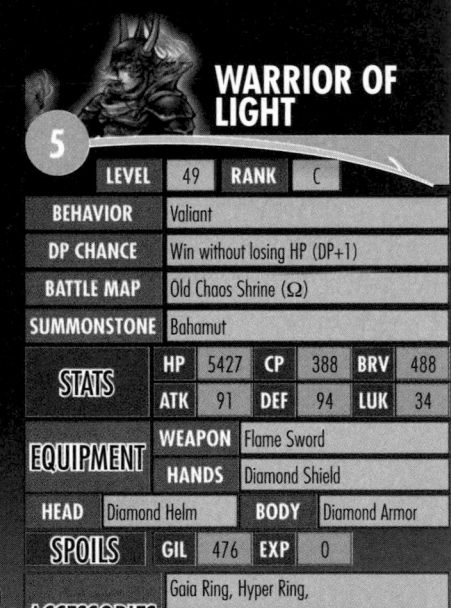

3 IMITATION LIEGEMAN

LEVEL	35	RANK	D

BEHAVIOR	Aggressive
DP CHANCE	—
BATTLE MAP	Pandaemonium (Ω)
SUMMONSTONE	—

STATS	HP	3060	CP	371	BRV	291
	ATK	46	DEF	47	LUK	27

EQUIPMENT	WEAPON	—
	HANDS	—
HEAD	—	BODY	—

SPOILS	GIL	476	EXP	0

ACCESSORIES	Gaia Ring, [Time] After 30 Seconds, [Time] After 60 Seconds, [Time] After 90 Seconds, [Time] After 120 Seconds, [Time] After 180 Seconds

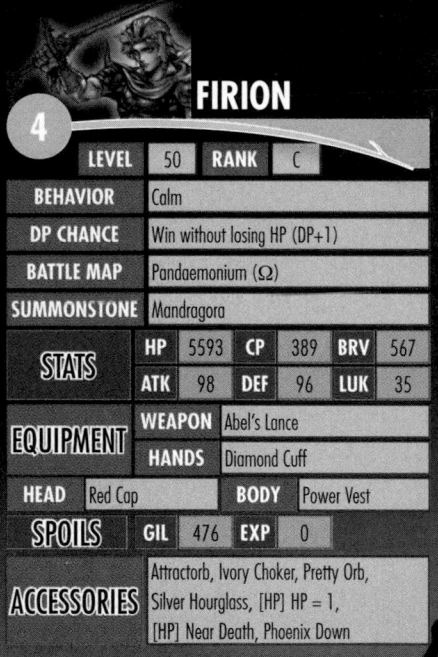

4 FIRION

LEVEL	50	RANK	C

BEHAVIOR	Calm
DP CHANCE	Win without losing HP (DP+1)
BATTLE MAP	Pandaemonium (Ω)
SUMMONSTONE	Mandragora

STATS	HP	5593	CP	389	BRV	567
	ATK	98	DEF	96	LUK	35

EQUIPMENT	WEAPON	Abel's Lance
	HANDS	Diamond Cuff
HEAD	Red Cap	BODY	Power Vest

SPOILS	GIL	476	EXP	0

ACCESSORIES	Attractorb, Ivory Choker, Pretty Orb, Silver Hourglass, [HP] HP = 1, [HP] Near Death, Phoenix Down

5 WARRIOR OF LIGHT

LEVEL	49	RANK	C

BEHAVIOR	Valiant
DP CHANCE	Win without losing HP (DP+1)
BATTLE MAP	Old Chaos Shrine (Ω)
SUMMONSTONE	Bahamut

STATS	HP	5427	CP	388	BRV	488
	ATK	91	DEF	94	LUK	34

EQUIPMENT	WEAPON	Flame Sword
	HANDS	Diamond Shield
HEAD	Diamond Helm	BODY	Diamond Armor

SPOILS	GIL	476	EXP	0

ACCESSORIES	Gaia Ring, Hyper Ring, [Position] Near Opponent x2, [Combat] Chasing, [Position] In Midair

STARTING DP	MAX FINISHING	ENGAGEMENTS
4	4	5

All five battle pieces here must be defeated to reveal the exit. The Atomos Summonstone can be found behind the golden Locked Area, after achieving at least a 1-star rating on previous runs of this Distant Glory chapter.

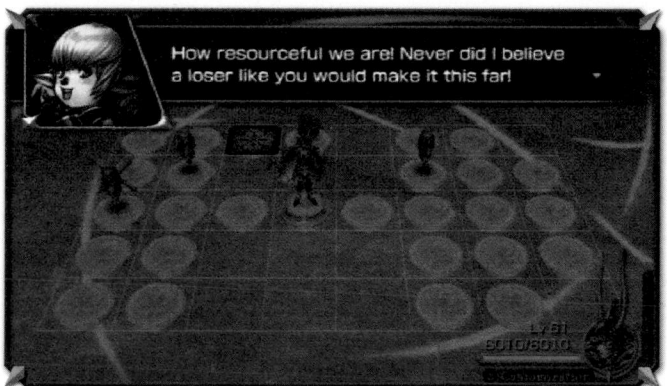

How resourceful we are! Never did I believe a loser like you would make it this far!

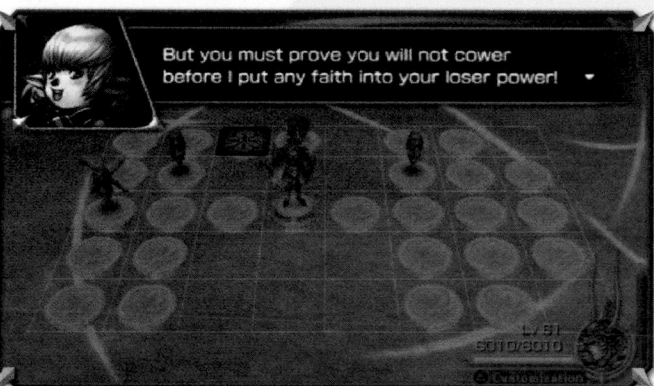

But you must prove you will not cower before I put any faith into your loser power!

MAP

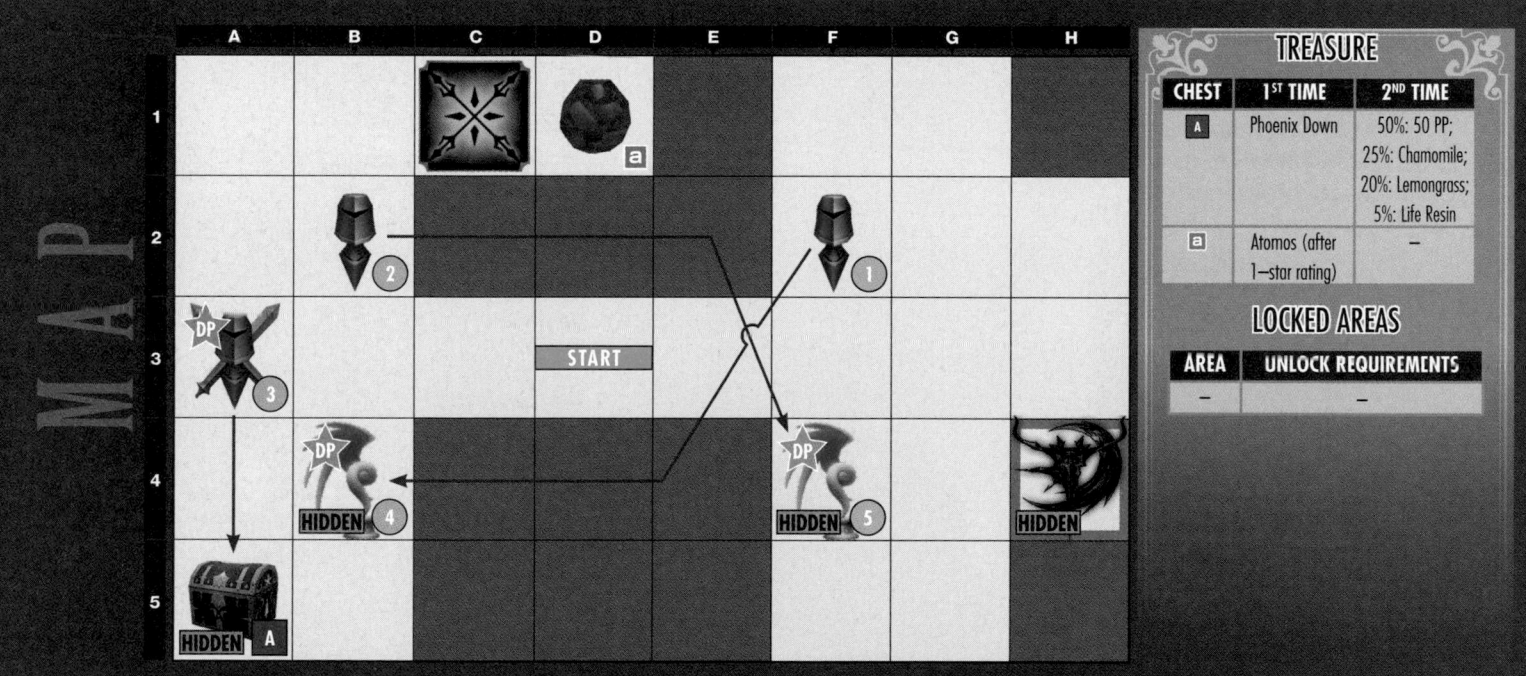

TREASURE

CHEST	1ST TIME	2ND TIME
A	Phoenix Down	50%: 50 PP; 25%: Chamomile; 20%: Lemongrass; 5%: Life Resin
a	Atomos (after 1-star rating)	—

LOCKED AREAS

AREA	UNLOCK REQUIREMENTS
—	—

DP EFFICIENCY ROUTE

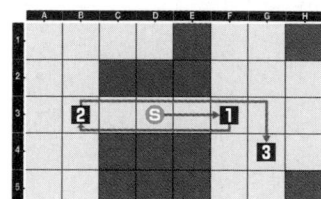

Start off the action here by defeating battle piece ①. This causes Cosmos piece ④ to spawn near battle pieces ② and ③. Next, prepare for a three-part chain against these foes. Defeating battle piece ② during this chain spawns Cosmos piece ⑤ back across the stage. Once the battle chain is over, head to G-4 to engage Cosmos piece ⑤. Once this foe falls, the Stigma of Chaos materializes right next to you.

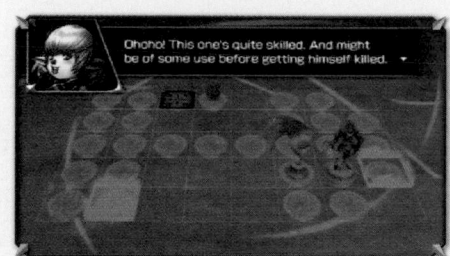

Ohoho! This one's quite skilled. And might be of some use before getting himself killed.

BATTLE PIECE DATA

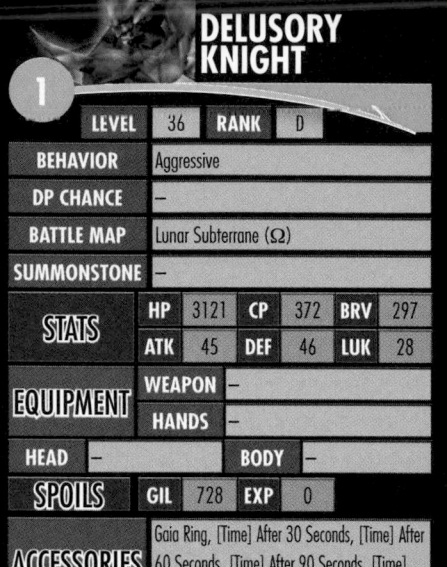

1 DELUSORY KNIGHT

LEVEL	36	RANK	D

BEHAVIOR	Aggressive
DP CHANCE	–
BATTLE MAP	Lunar Subterrane (Ω)
SUMMONSTONE	–

STATS	HP	3121	CP	372	BRV	297
	ATK	45	DEF	46	LUK	28

EQUIPMENT	WEAPON	–
	HANDS	–

HEAD	–	BODY	–

SPOILS	GIL	728	EXP	0

ACCESSORIES	Gaia Ring, [Time] After 30 Seconds, [Time] After 60 Seconds, [Time] After 90 Seconds, [Time] After 120 Seconds, [Time] After 180 Seconds

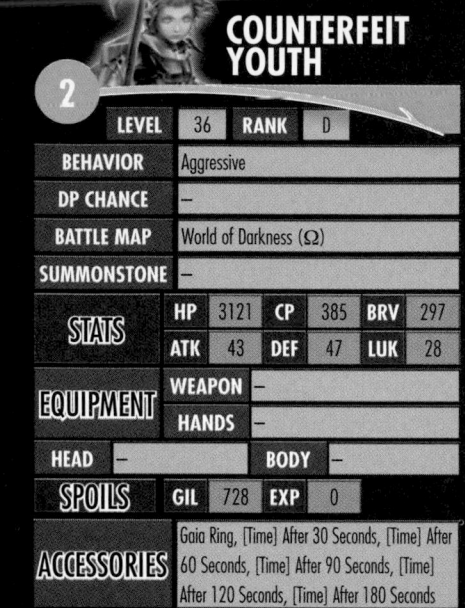

2 COUNTERFEIT YOUTH

LEVEL	36	RANK	D

BEHAVIOR	Aggressive
DP CHANCE	–
BATTLE MAP	World of Darkness (Ω)
SUMMONSTONE	–

STATS	HP	3121	CP	385	BRV	297
	ATK	43	DEF	47	LUK	28

EQUIPMENT	WEAPON	–
	HANDS	–

HEAD	–	BODY	–

SPOILS	GIL	728	EXP	0

ACCESSORIES	Gaia Ring, [Time] After 30 Seconds, [Time] After 60 Seconds, [Time] After 90 Seconds, [Time] After 120 Seconds, [Time] After 180 Seconds

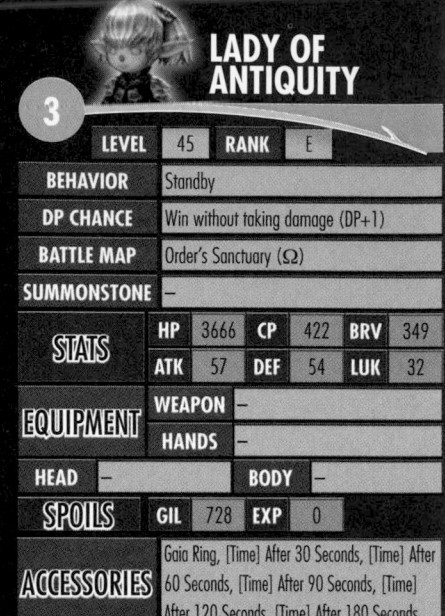

3 LADY OF ANTIQUITY

LEVEL	45	RANK	E

BEHAVIOR	Standby
DP CHANCE	Win without taking damage (DP+1)
BATTLE MAP	Order's Sanctuary (Ω)
SUMMONSTONE	–

STATS	HP	3666	CP	422	BRV	349
	ATK	57	DEF	54	LUK	32

EQUIPMENT	WEAPON	–
	HANDS	–

HEAD	–	BODY	–

SPOILS	GIL	728	EXP	0

ACCESSORIES	Gaia Ring, [Time] After 30 Seconds, [Time] After 60 Seconds, [Time] After 90 Seconds, [Time] After 120 Seconds, [Time] After 180 Seconds

4 CECIL

LEVEL	52	RANK	C

BEHAVIOR	Survivor
DP CHANCE	Wall Rush within 10 seconds (DP+1)
BATTLE MAP	Lunar Subterrane (Ω)
SUMMONSTONE	Barbariccia

STATS	HP	5791	CP	391	BRV	527
	ATK	98	DEF	99	LUK	36

EQUIPMENT	WEAPON	Mythgraven Blade
	HANDS	Diamond Shield

HEAD	Diamond Helm	BODY	Diamond Armor

SPOILS	GIL	728	EXP	0

ACCESSORIES	Gaia Ring, Champion Belt, Hyperstar, [Opponent] In Midair x2

5 ONION KNIGHT

LEVEL	51	RANK	C

BEHAVIOR	Tactician
DP CHANCE	Wall Rush within 10 seconds (DP+1)
BATTLE MAP	World of Darkness (Ω)
SUMMONSTONE	Kraken

STATS	HP	5654	CP	400	BRV	573
	ATK	94	DEF	97	LUK	35

EQUIPMENT	WEAPON	Tyrfing
	HANDS	Diamond Cuff

HEAD	Red Cap	BODY	Power Vest

SPOILS	GIL	728	EXP	0

ACCESSORIES	Gaia Ring, [HP] HP = 100%, [BRV] No BRV Damage, [HP] HP = 1, [HP] Near Death, Phoenix Down

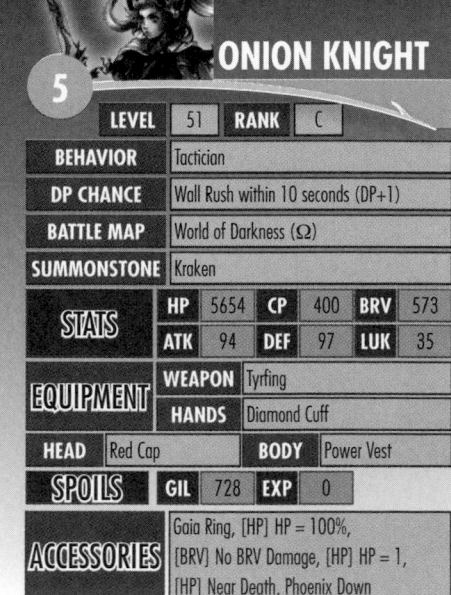

DISTANT GLORY XI

STARTING DP	MAX FINISHING	ENGAGEMENTS
5	5	5
	(+2 after 2-star rating)	(+1 after 2-star rating)

Once again, all standard foes must fall for the Stigma of Chaos to appear. The rare battle piece that spawns after a 2-star rating isn't required, however. This rare battle piece guards a rare treasure chest, which only spawns after a 3-star rating. This chest contains Bard Lore, one of the "lore" items. Like Rosetta Stones, these items can be traded under the "etc" category of the Shop to augment the active character. They allow combatants to wield equipment that they can't otherwise. Rare, ultimate battle piece ⑥ is a feisty, high-level crystal copy of Shantotto. Stature is no indicator of strength, since this manikin is a pint-sized terror. Its high attack allows it to inflict Break on you easily, and it can chain magic attacks one after the other, making any stray hit extremely dangerous and potentially fatal. The easiest way to win, especially at a lower level, is to bring along Magic Pot. If the manikin has a huge bravery total, which is almost inevitable, steal it and use it against the manikin.

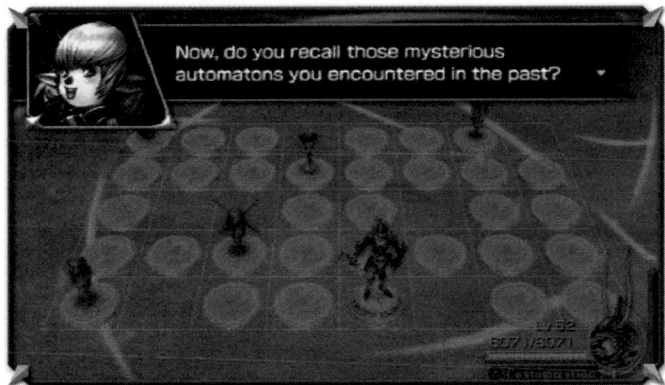

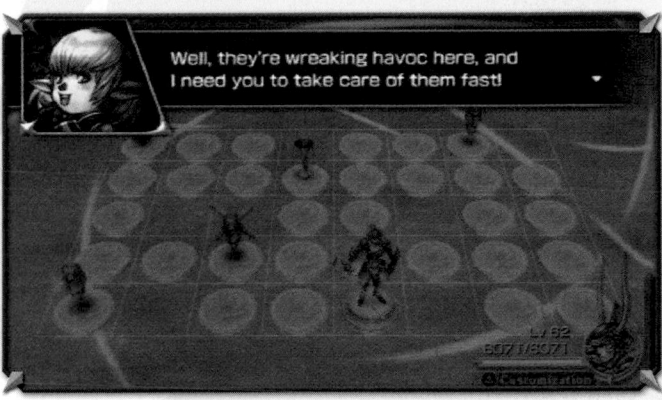

MAP

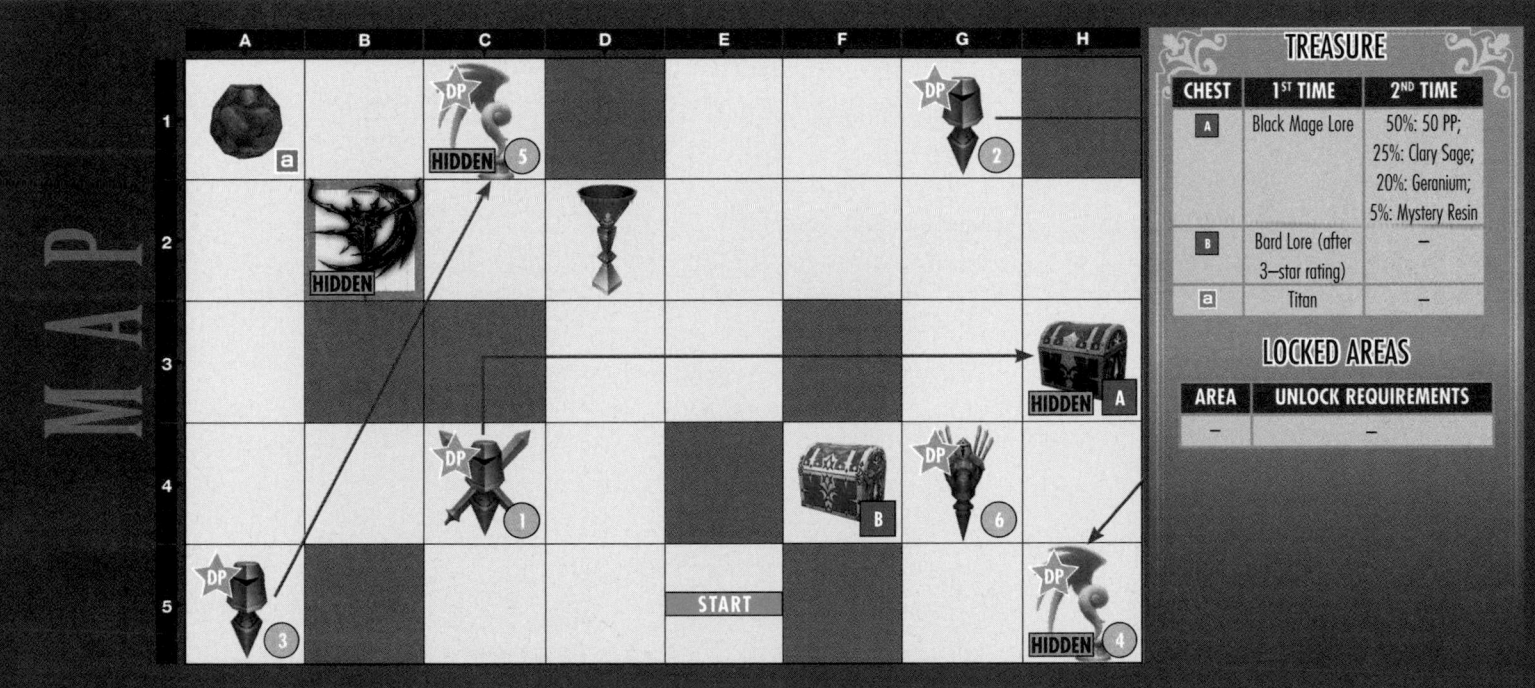

TREASURE

CHEST	1ST TIME	2ND TIME
A	Black Mage Lore	50%: 50 PP; 25%: Clary Sage; 20%: Geranium; 5%: Mystery Resin
B	Bard Lore (after 3—star rating)	—
a	Titan	—

LOCKED AREAS

AREA	UNLOCK REQUIREMENTS
—	—

DP EFFICIENCY ROUTE

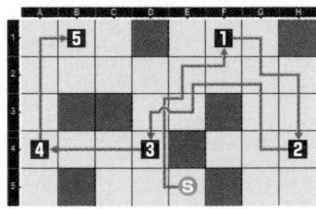

You'll need a 2-star rating on a previous completion to maximize DP here, and you should have already collected the Summonstone in the upper left as well. With these out of the way, begin by heading to the upper right to defeat battle piece ②. This causes Cosmos piece ① to spawn nearby, next to ultimate battle piece ⑥. Head down to H-4 to start a battle chain against these two foes. Afterward, move to defeat battle pieces ① and ③, clearing a path to defeat Cosmos piece ⑤ immediately before shattering the Stigma of Chaos.

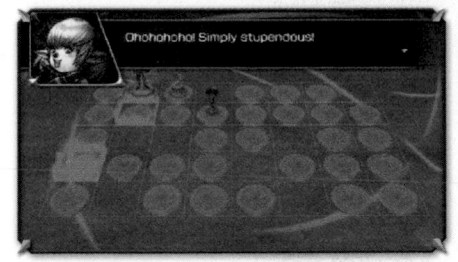

BATTLE PIECE DATA

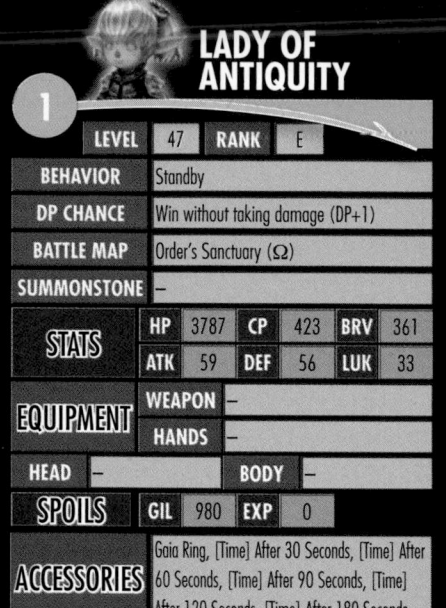

1 — LADY OF ANTIQUITY

- **LEVEL:** 47 **RANK:** E
- **BEHAVIOR:** Standby
- **DP CHANCE:** Win without taking damage (DP+1)
- **BATTLE MAP:** Order's Sanctuary (Ω)
- **SUMMONSTONE:** –
- **STATS:** HP 3787 | CP 423 | BRV 361 | ATK 59 | DEF 56 | LUK 33
- **EQUIPMENT:** WEAPON – | HANDS – | HEAD – | BODY –
- **SPOILS:** GIL 980 | EXP 0
- **ACCESSORIES:** Gaia Ring, [Time] After 30 Seconds, [Time] After 60 Seconds, [Time] After 90 Seconds, [Time] After 120 Seconds, [Time] After 180 Seconds

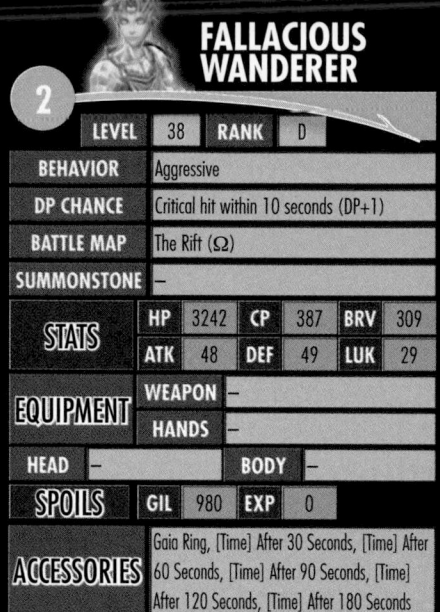

2 — FALLACIOUS WANDERER

- **LEVEL:** 38 **RANK:** D
- **BEHAVIOR:** Aggressive
- **DP CHANCE:** Critical hit within 10 seconds (DP+1)
- **BATTLE MAP:** The Rift (Ω)
- **SUMMONSTONE:** –
- **STATS:** HP 3242 | CP 387 | BRV 309 | ATK 48 | DEF 49 | LUK 29
- **EQUIPMENT:** WEAPON – | HANDS – | HEAD – | BODY –
- **SPOILS:** GIL 980 | EXP 0
- **ACCESSORIES:** Gaia Ring, [Time] After 30 Seconds, [Time] After 60 Seconds, [Time] After 90 Seconds, [Time] After 120 Seconds, [Time] After 180 Seconds

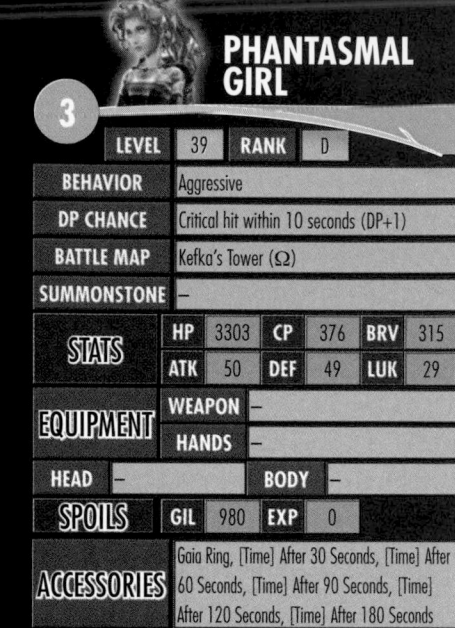

3 — PHANTASMAL GIRL

- **LEVEL:** 39 **RANK:** D
- **BEHAVIOR:** Aggressive
- **DP CHANCE:** Critical hit within 10 seconds (DP+1)
- **BATTLE MAP:** Kefka's Tower (Ω)
- **SUMMONSTONE:** –
- **STATS:** HP 3303 | CP 376 | BRV 315 | ATK 50 | DEF 49 | LUK 29
- **EQUIPMENT:** WEAPON – | HANDS – | HEAD – | BODY –
- **SPOILS:** GIL 980 | EXP 0
- **ACCESSORIES:** Gaia Ring, [Time] After 30 Seconds, [Time] After 60 Seconds, [Time] After 90 Seconds, [Time] After 120 Seconds, [Time] After 180 Seconds

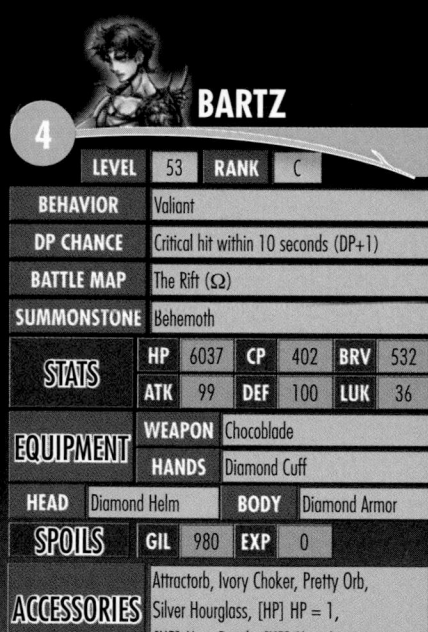

4 — BARTZ

- **LEVEL:** 53 **RANK:** C
- **BEHAVIOR:** Valiant
- **DP CHANCE:** Critical hit within 10 seconds (DP+1)
- **BATTLE MAP:** The Rift (Ω)
- **SUMMONSTONE:** Behemoth
- **STATS:** HP 6037 | CP 402 | BRV 532 | ATK 99 | DEF 100 | LUK 36
- **EQUIPMENT:** WEAPON Chocoblade | HANDS Diamond Cuff | HEAD Diamond Helm | BODY Diamond Armor
- **SPOILS:** GIL 980 | EXP 0
- **ACCESSORIES:** Attractorb, Ivory Choker, Pretty Orb, Silver Hourglass, [HP] HP = 1, [HP] Near Death, [HP] Near Loss

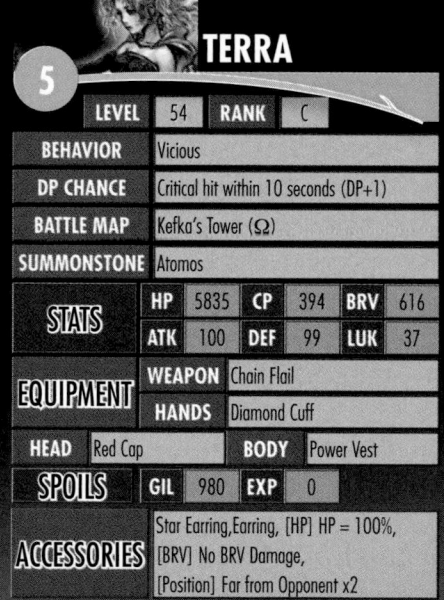

5 — TERRA

- **LEVEL:** 54 **RANK:** C
- **BEHAVIOR:** Vicious
- **DP CHANCE:** Critical hit within 10 seconds (DP+1)
- **BATTLE MAP:** Kefka's Tower (Ω)
- **SUMMONSTONE:** Atomos
- **STATS:** HP 5835 | CP 394 | BRV 616 | ATK 100 | DEF 99 | LUK 37
- **EQUIPMENT:** WEAPON Chain Flail | HANDS Diamond Cuff | HEAD Red Cap | BODY Power Vest
- **SPOILS:** GIL 980 | EXP 0
- **ACCESSORIES:** Star Earring, Earring, [HP] HP = 100%, [BRV] No BRV Damage, [Position] Far from Opponent x2

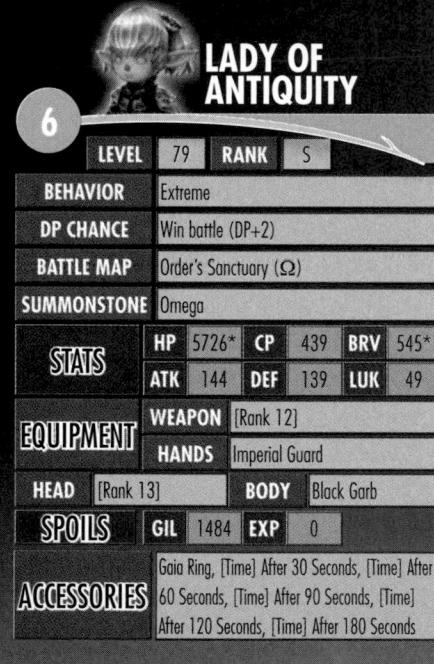

6 — LADY OF ANTIQUITY

- **LEVEL:** 79 **RANK:** S
- **BEHAVIOR:** Extreme
- **DP CHANCE:** Win battle (DP+2)
- **BATTLE MAP:** Order's Sanctuary (Ω)
- **SUMMONSTONE:** Omega
- **STATS:** HP 5726* | CP 439 | BRV 545* | ATK 144 | DEF 139 | LUK 49
- **EQUIPMENT:** WEAPON [Rank 12] | HANDS Imperial Guard | HEAD [Rank 13] | BODY Black Garb
- **SPOILS:** GIL 1484 | EXP 0
- **ACCESSORIES:** Gaia Ring, [Time] After 30 Seconds, [Time] After 60 Seconds, [Time] After 90 Seconds, [Time] After 120 Seconds, [Time] After 180 Seconds

DISTANT GLORY

XI-4

Like all of Shantotto's levels, you must defeat all battle pieces to reveal the Stigma of Chaos. Along the way you'll have an opportunity to open treasure chest **A**, which appears after defeating battle piece ③. Behind battle piece ③ is treasure chest **B**, but this can only be acquired after returning with a 1-star rating.

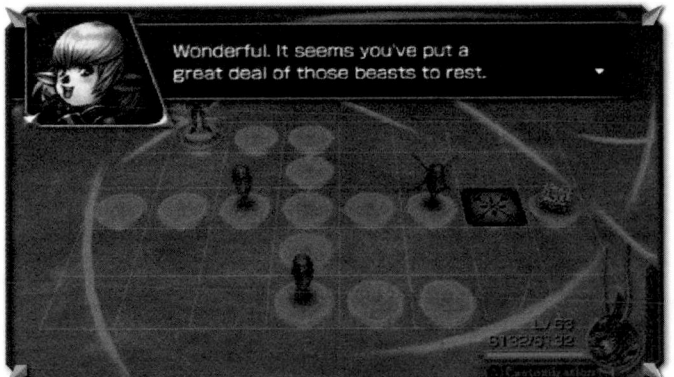

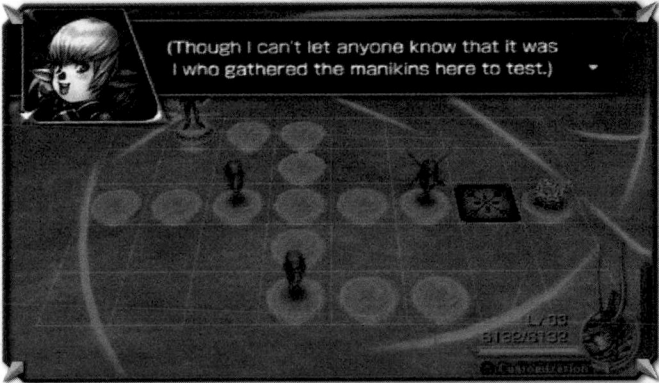

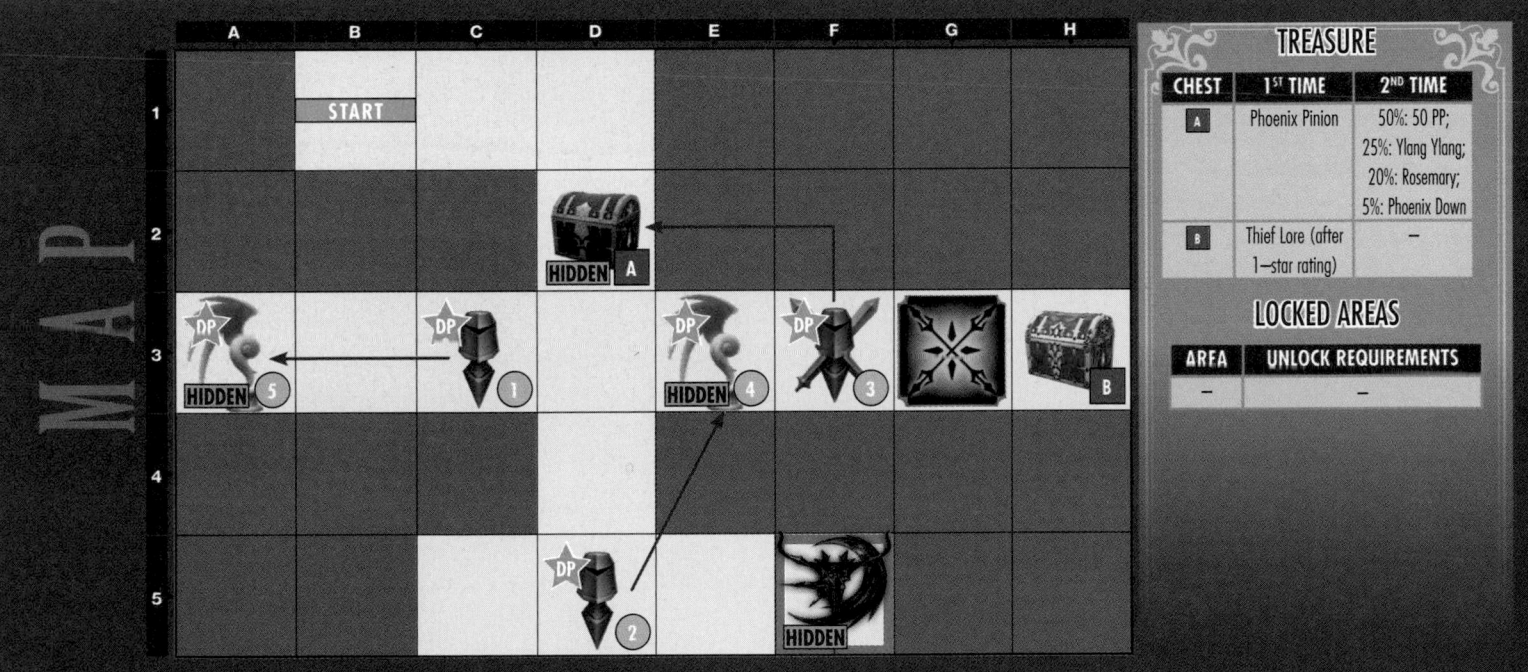

TREASURE

CHEST	1ST TIME	2ND TIME
A	Phoenix Pinion	50%: 50 PP; 25%: Ylang Ylang; 20%: Rosemary; 5%: Phoenix Down
B	Thief Lore (after 1-star rating)	—

LOCKED AREAS

AREA	UNLOCK REQUIREMENTS
—	—

DP EFFICIENCY ROUTE

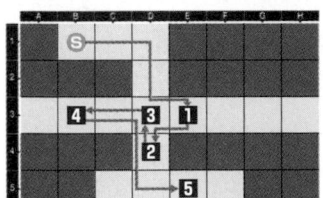

The first target is battle piece ③. Next, take out battle piece ②. Both these pieces have a DP Chance, and their defeat sets up a two-part chain between battle piece ① and Cosmos piece ④ at D-3. This chain is your next target; feel free to grab the treasure chest here as well, as it won't cost any extra DP. After piece ① falls in the chain, Cosmos piece ⑤ spawns behind it. Defeating this final piece spawns the Stigma of Chaos.

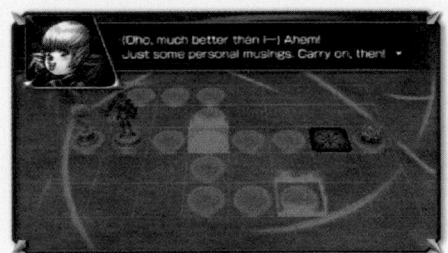

BATTLE PIECE DATA

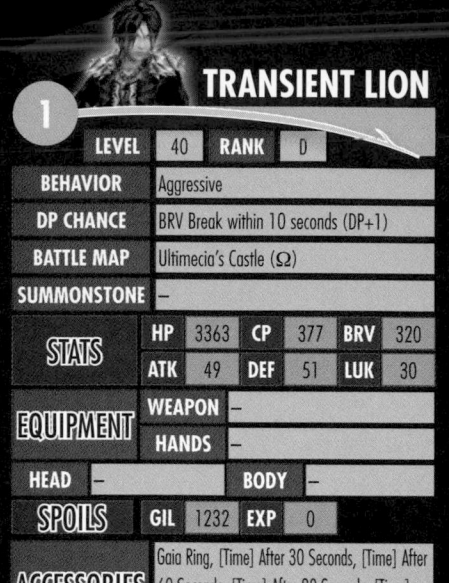

1 TRANSIENT LION

LEVEL	40 **RANK** D
BEHAVIOR	Aggressive
DP CHANCE	BRV Break within 10 seconds (DP+1)
BATTLE MAP	Ultimecia's Castle (Ω)
SUMMONSTONE	–

STATS

HP	3363	CP	377	BRV	320
ATK	49	DEF	51	LUK	30

EQUIPMENT

WEAPON	–
HANDS	–
HEAD	–	BODY	–

SPOILS | GIL 1232 | EXP 0

ACCESSORIES Gaia Ring, [Time] After 30 Seconds, [Time] After 60 Seconds, [Time] After 90 Seconds, [Time] After 120 Seconds, [Time] After 180 Seconds

2 IMAGINARY SOLDIER

LEVEL	39 **RANK** D
BEHAVIOR	Aggressive
DP CHANCE	BRV Break within 10 seconds (DP+1)
BATTLE MAP	Planet's Core (Ω)
SUMMONSTONE	–

STATS

HP	3303	CP	376	BRV	315
ATK	49	DEF	51	LUK	29

EQUIPMENT

WEAPON	–
HANDS	–
HEAD	–	BODY	–

SPOILS | GIL 1232 | EXP 0

ACCESSORIES Gaia Ring, [Time] After 30 Seconds, [Time] After 60 Seconds, [Time] After 90 Seconds, [Time] After 120 Seconds, [Time] After 180 Seconds

3 LADY OF ANTIQUITY

LEVEL	59 **RANK** E
BEHAVIOR	Standby
DP CHANCE	Win without taking damage (DP+1)
BATTLE MAP	Order's Sanctuary (Ω)
SUMMONSTONE	–

STATS

HP	4514	CP	429	BRV	430
ATK	71	DEF	68	LUK	39

EQUIPMENT

WEAPON	–
HANDS	–
HEAD	–	BODY	–

SPOILS | GIL 1232 | EXP 0

ACCESSORIES Gaia Ring, [Time] After 30 Seconds, [Time] After 60 Seconds, [Time] After 90 Seconds, [Time] After 120 Seconds, [Time] After 180 Seconds

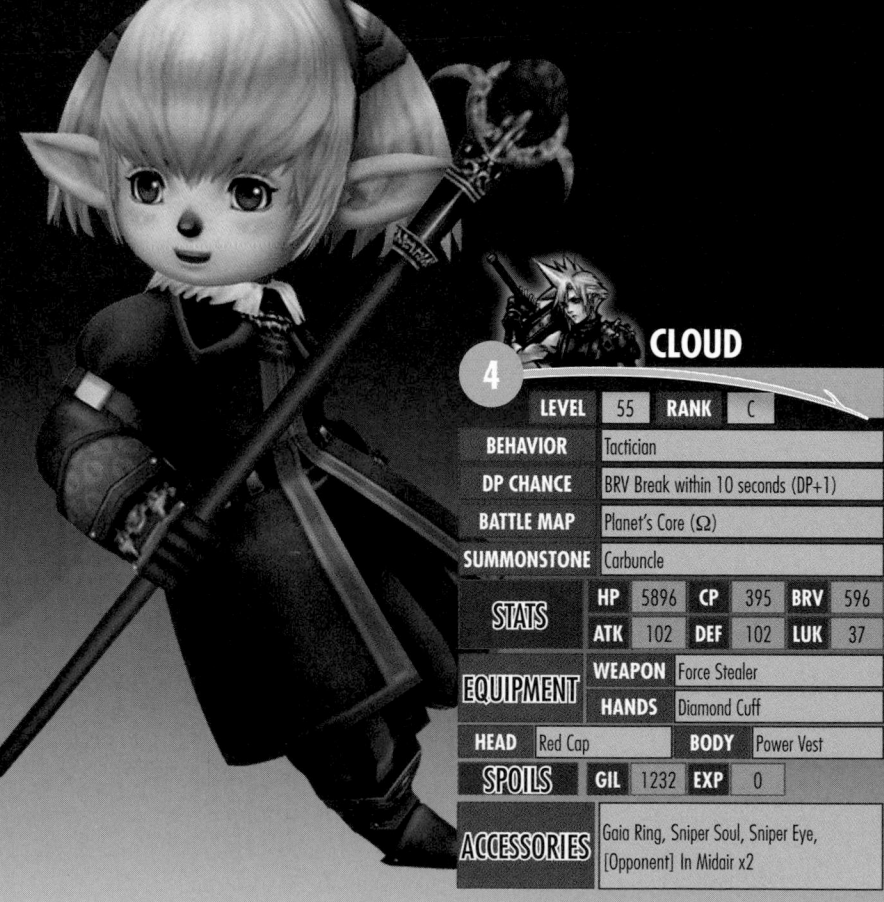

4 CLOUD

LEVEL	55 **RANK** C
BEHAVIOR	Tactician
DP CHANCE	BRV Break within 10 seconds (DP+1)
BATTLE MAP	Planet's Core (Ω)
SUMMONSTONE	Carbuncle

STATS

HP	5896	CP	395	BRV	596
ATK	102	DEF	102	LUK	37

EQUIPMENT

WEAPON	Force Stealer
HANDS	Diamond Cuff
HEAD	Red Cap	BODY	Power Vest

SPOILS | GIL 1232 | EXP 0

ACCESSORIES Gaia Ring, Sniper Soul, Sniper Eye, [Opponent] In Midair x2

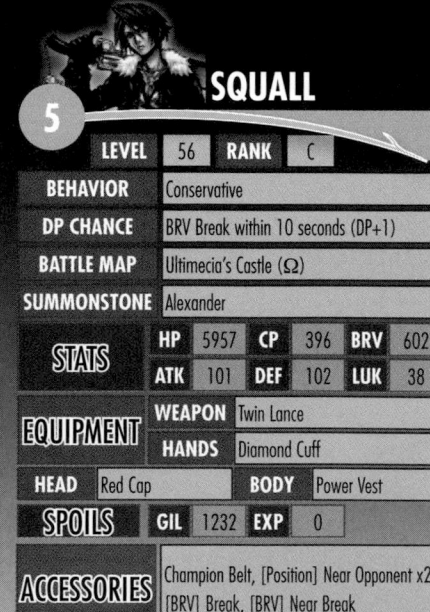

5 SQUALL

LEVEL	56 **RANK** C
BEHAVIOR	Conservative
DP CHANCE	BRV Break within 10 seconds (DP+1)
BATTLE MAP	Ultimecia's Castle (Ω)
SUMMONSTONE	Alexander

STATS

HP	5957	CP	396	BRV	602
ATK	101	DEF	102	LUK	38

EQUIPMENT

WEAPON	Twin Lance
HANDS	Diamond Cuff
HEAD	Red Cap	BODY	Power Vest

SPOILS | GIL 1232 | EXP 0

ACCESSORIES Champion Belt, [Position] Near Opponent x2, [BRV] Break, [BRV] Near Break

Treasure chest **A** only appears after defeating three battle pieces, while the Stigma of Chaos requires that you fell the four standard pieces before it appears. Rare battle piece **6**, spawned by a 2-star rating, is a manikin impersonating Gabranth, the wounded antihero of *Final Fantasy XII* who also serves as the antagonist of Distant Glory: Redemption of the Warrior. Like any ultimate battle piece, his stats and level are high, so he'll inflict Break on you easily if you let him connect with bravery attacks. If he does manage to cause Break, wait it out, then use Magic Pot to steal his undoubtedly high bravery total. Gabranth likes to use EX Charge to fill his EX Force from afar. Dash in immediately when he does this and hit him with your best shot. The boss, Shantotto, chains powerful magic together if you give her a chance, so dodge when you see her casting a spell. Shantotto can be acquired for use from the PP Catalog after winning this battle.

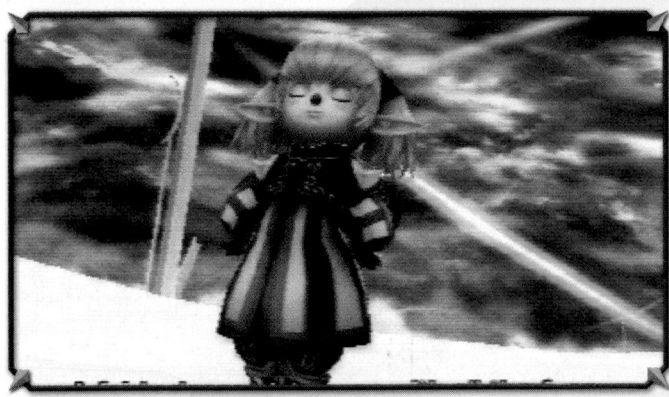

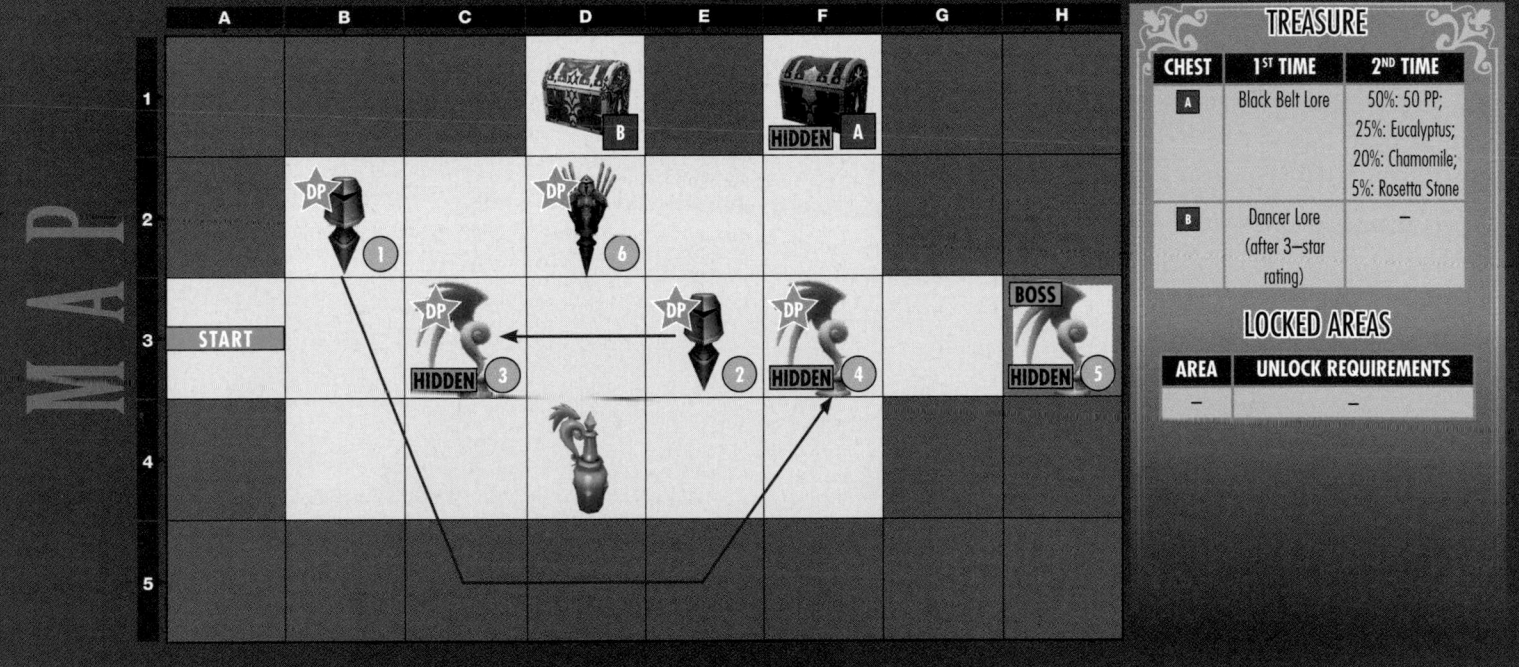

TREASURE

CHEST	1ST TIME	2ND TIME
A	Black Belt Lore	50%: 50 PP; 25%: Eucalyptus; 20%: Chamomile; 5%: Rosetta Stone
B	Dancer Lore (after 3—star rating)	—

LOCKED AREAS

AREA	UNLOCK REQUIREMENTS
—	—

DP EFFICIENCY ROUTE

Max DP can't be achieved here until after a 2-star rating, which causes battle piece **6** to spawn. Once the rare piece is in place, begin by heading to D-3. Here, you can start a chain with either battle piece **2** or **6**; Cosmos piece **3** will appear and continue the chain after battle piece **2** disappears. After this three-part battle chain, head to C-2 to take on battle piece **1**. Getting rid of this piece spawns Cosmos piece **4**. Move to F-2 to both defeat Cosmos piece **4** and open treasure chest **A**. Finally, head to the exit for the boss fight with Shantotto. Apart from rare battle piece **6**, every DP Chance on this level requires an EX Burst within 10 seconds.

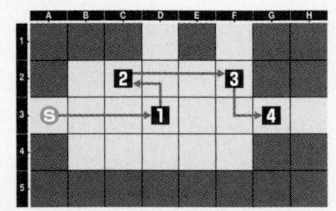

Maintaining enough EX Force to always be ready for the next battle is quite challenging. One way to tip the scales in your favor is to wear appropriate equipment; weapons like Rune Blade and accessories like Dragonfly Orb, Cyan Drop, and Victory Pendant help keep EX Force at a high level. The Aura skill, if available, can charge 50% of the EX Gauge when desired, and the Potion on the stage can be used to fill the gauge up completely. Just be sure to use Aura or the Potion when it will not expend extra DP. The Arcane Incense and Arcane Resin accessories can also be equipped to fill some of the gauge in between stages—just be sure to replace these accessories after each battle, as they'll break upon use.

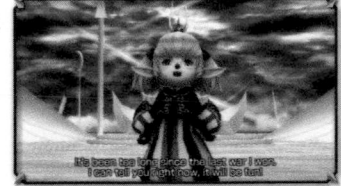

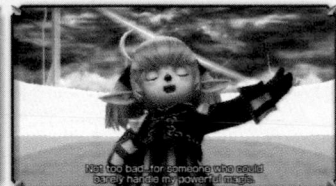

BATTLE PIECE DATA

1 — CAPRICIOUS THIEF

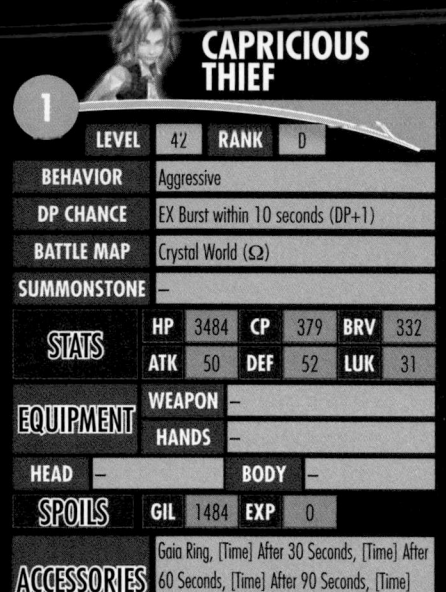

LEVEL	42	RANK	D

BEHAVIOR	Aggressive
DP CHANCE	EX Burst within 10 seconds (DP+1)
BATTLE MAP	Crystal World (Ω)
SUMMONSTONE	—

STATS	HP	3484	CP	379	BRV	332
	ATK	50	DEF	52	LUK	31

EQUIPMENT	WEAPON	—
	HANDS	—
HEAD	—	BODY	—

SPOILS	GIL	1484	EXP	0

ACCESSORIES	Gaia Ring, [Time] After 30 Seconds, [Time] After 60 Seconds, [Time] After 90 Seconds, [Time] After 120 Seconds, [Time] After 180 Seconds

2 — EPHEMERAL VISION

LEVEL	43	RANK	D

BEHAVIOR	Aggressive
DP CHANCE	EX Burst within 10 seconds (DP+1)
BATTLE MAP	Dream's End (Ω)
SUMMONSTONE	—

STATS	HP	3545	CP	381	BRV	338
	ATK	53	DEF	54	LUK	31

EQUIPMENT	WEAPON	—
	HANDS	—
HEAD	—	BODY	—

SPOILS	GIL	1484	EXP	0

ACCESSORIES	Gaia Ring, [Time] After 30 Seconds, [Time] After 60 Seconds, [Time] After 90 Seconds, [Time] After 120 Seconds, [Time] After 180 Seconds

3 — TIDUS

LEVEL	58	RANK	C

BEHAVIOR	Cautious
DP CHANCE	EX Burst within 10 seconds (DP+1)
BATTLE MAP	Dream's End (Ω)
SUMMONSTONE	Rubicante

STATS	HP	6366	CP	399	BRV	551
	ATK	105	DEF	111	LUK	39

EQUIPMENT	WEAPON	Striker
	HANDS	Rune Armlet
HEAD	Close Helmet	BODY	Assassin's Vest

SPOILS	GIL	1484	EXP	0

ACCESSORIES	Gaia Ring, Champion Belt, [Combat] Chasing x2, [Position] In Midair

4 — ZIDANE

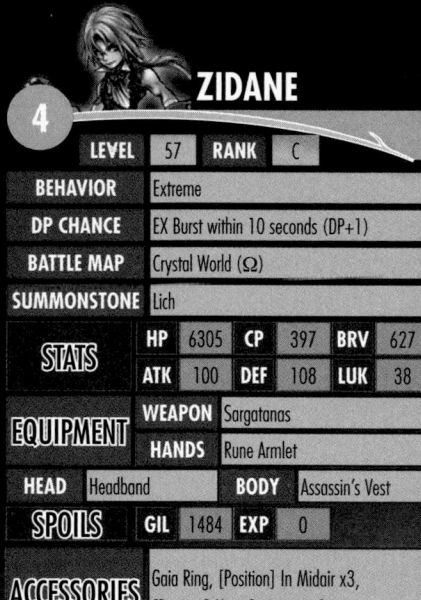

LEVEL	57	RANK	C

BEHAVIOR	Extreme
DP CHANCE	EX Burst within 10 seconds (DP+1)
BATTLE MAP	Crystal World (Ω)
SUMMONSTONE	Lich

STATS	HP	6305	CP	397	BRV	627
	ATK	100	DEF	108	LUK	38

EQUIPMENT	WEAPON	Sargatanas
	HANDS	Rune Armlet
HEAD	Headband	BODY	Assassin's Vest

SPOILS	GIL	1484	EXP	0

ACCESSORIES	Gaia Ring, [Position] In Midair x3, [Position] Near Opponent x2

5 — SHANTOTTO

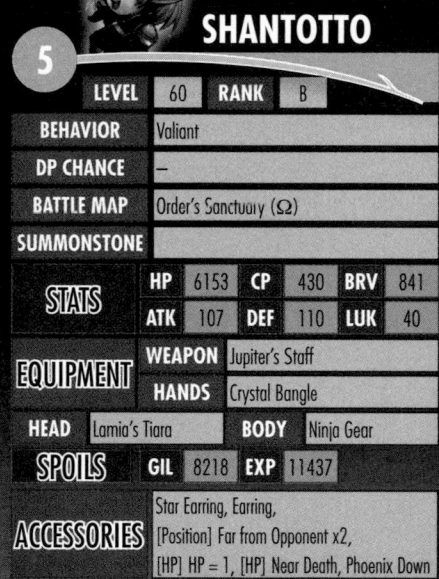

LEVEL	60	RANK	B

BEHAVIOR	Valiant
DP CHANCE	—
BATTLE MAP	Order's Sanctuary (Ω)
SUMMONSTONE	

STATS	HP	6153	CP	430	BRV	841
	ATK	107	DEF	110	LUK	40

EQUIPMENT	WEAPON	Jupiter's Staff
	HANDS	Crystal Bangle
HEAD	Lamia's Tiara	BODY	Ninja Gear

SPOILS	GIL	8218	EXP	11437

ACCESSORIES	Star Earring, Earring, [Position] Far from Opponent x2, [HP] HP = 1, [HP] Near Death, Phoenix Down

6 — WARRIOR OF ANTIQUITY

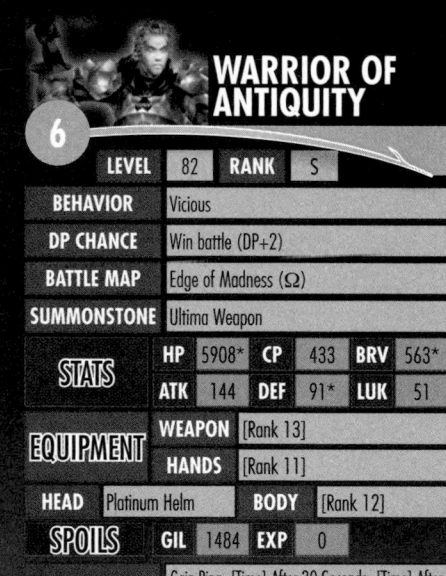

LEVEL	82	RANK	S

BEHAVIOR	Vicious
DP CHANCE	Win battle (DP+2)
BATTLE MAP	Edge of Madness (Ω)
SUMMONSTONE	Ultima Weapon

STATS	HP	5908*	CP	433	BRV	563*
	ATK	144	DEF	91*	LUK	51

EQUIPMENT	WEAPON	[Rank 13]
	HANDS	[Rank 11]
HEAD	Platinum Helm	BODY	[Rank 12]

SPOILS	GIL	1484	EXP	0

ACCESSORIES	Gaia Ring, [Time] After 30 Seconds, [Time] After 60 Seconds, [Time] After 90 Seconds, [Time] After 120 Seconds, [Time] After 180 Seconds

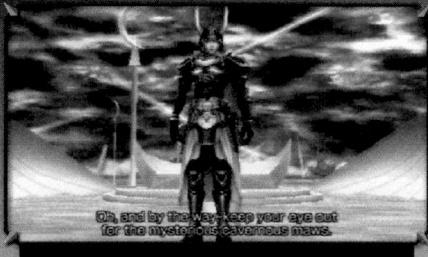

More Cavernous Maws, and Shantotto couplets, are found in Final Fantasy XI: Wings of the Goddess.

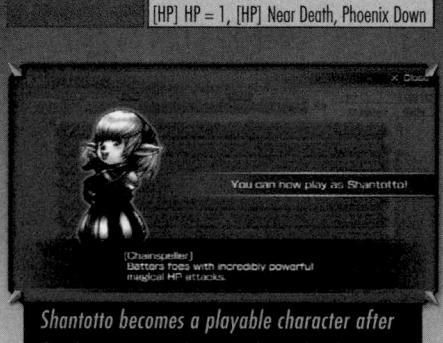

Shantotto becomes a playable character after finishing Distant Glory XI: The Lady of Legend. Be sure to purchase her services from the PP Catalog! Once you've finished both versions of Distant Glory, the final challenge— Inward Chaos—appears in Story Mode.

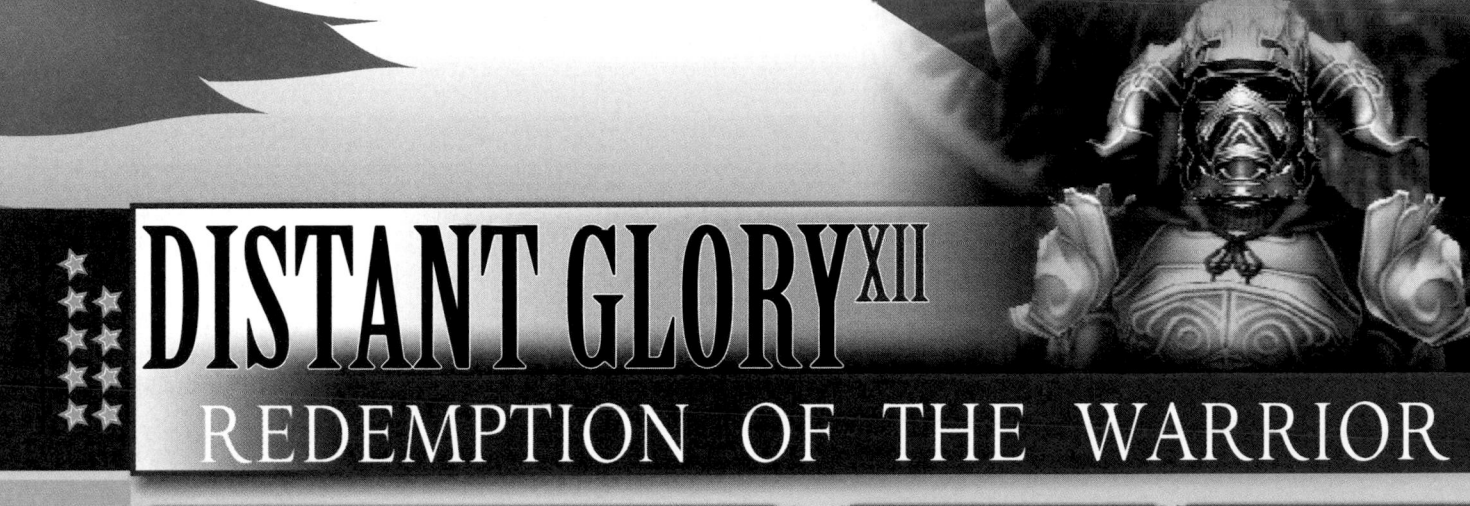

DISTANT GLORY XII
REDEMPTION OF THE WARRIOR

Prerequisite

Finish Shade Impulse 4 and ten Destiny Odyssey Chapters

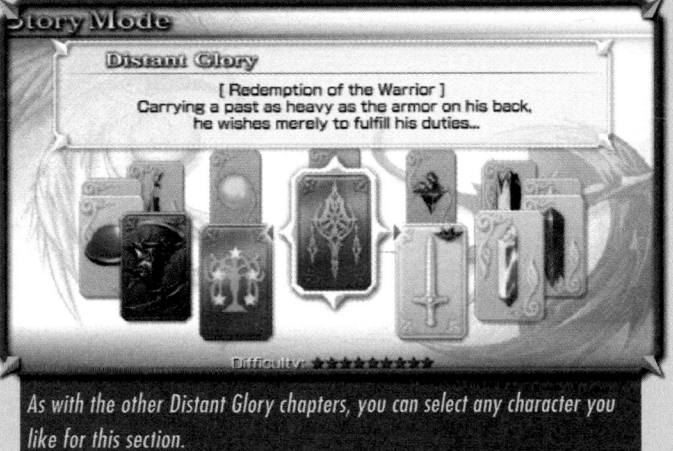

Story Mode

Distant Glory

[Redemption of the Warrior]
Carrying a past as heavy as the armor on his back, he wishes merely to fulfill his duties...

Difficulty: ★★★★★★★★★

As with the other Distant Glory chapters, you can select any character you like for this section.

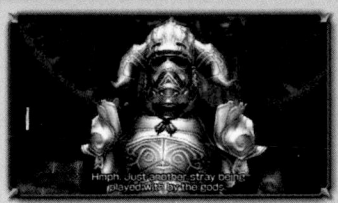

Hmph. Just another stray being played with by the gods.

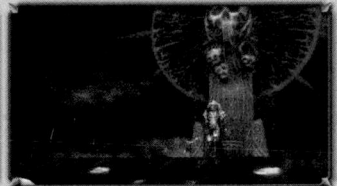

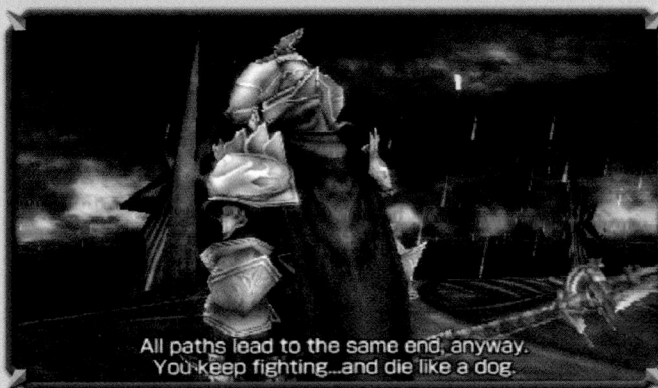

All paths lead to the same end, anyway. You keep fighting...and die like a dog.

Judge Gabranth is an instrument of the corrupt Vayne Solidor, but he is not all bad—like Golbez, he is tortured by a disgraceful past.

REWARDS

At the end of each level, rewards are available if you finish with a positive number of Destiny Points, or DP. This walkthrough includes miniature level maps that indicate the most efficient route to take through a given level, in order to maximize DP.

LEVEL COMPLETION

REMAINING DP			2ND TIME
7		Rosetta Stone	300 PP
6		Heike's Blade	200 PP
5		Heike's Armor	120 PP
4	1ST TIME	Asura	80 PP
3		Crystal	50 PP
2		Diamond	30 PP
1		4000 gil	20 PP
0		2000 gil	10 PP

DISTANT GLORY XII COMPLETION

STAR RATING	SP REQUIRED	AWARD
★	300	Special areas unlocked
★★	200	Rare battle pieces spawned
★★★	300	Rare treasure chests spawned
★★★★	500 SP, then every 500 SP extra	100 PP
–	–	–

At the end of each set of levels, you'll receive rewards based on your performance. Story Points, or SP, are awarded after each level based on remaining DP and HP, as well as the number of engagements undertaken. Points are penalized for retries, or for a DP total that dips into negatives. If you miss out on a desired bonus on the first playthrough, don't worry—SP is cumulative across multiple playthroughs.

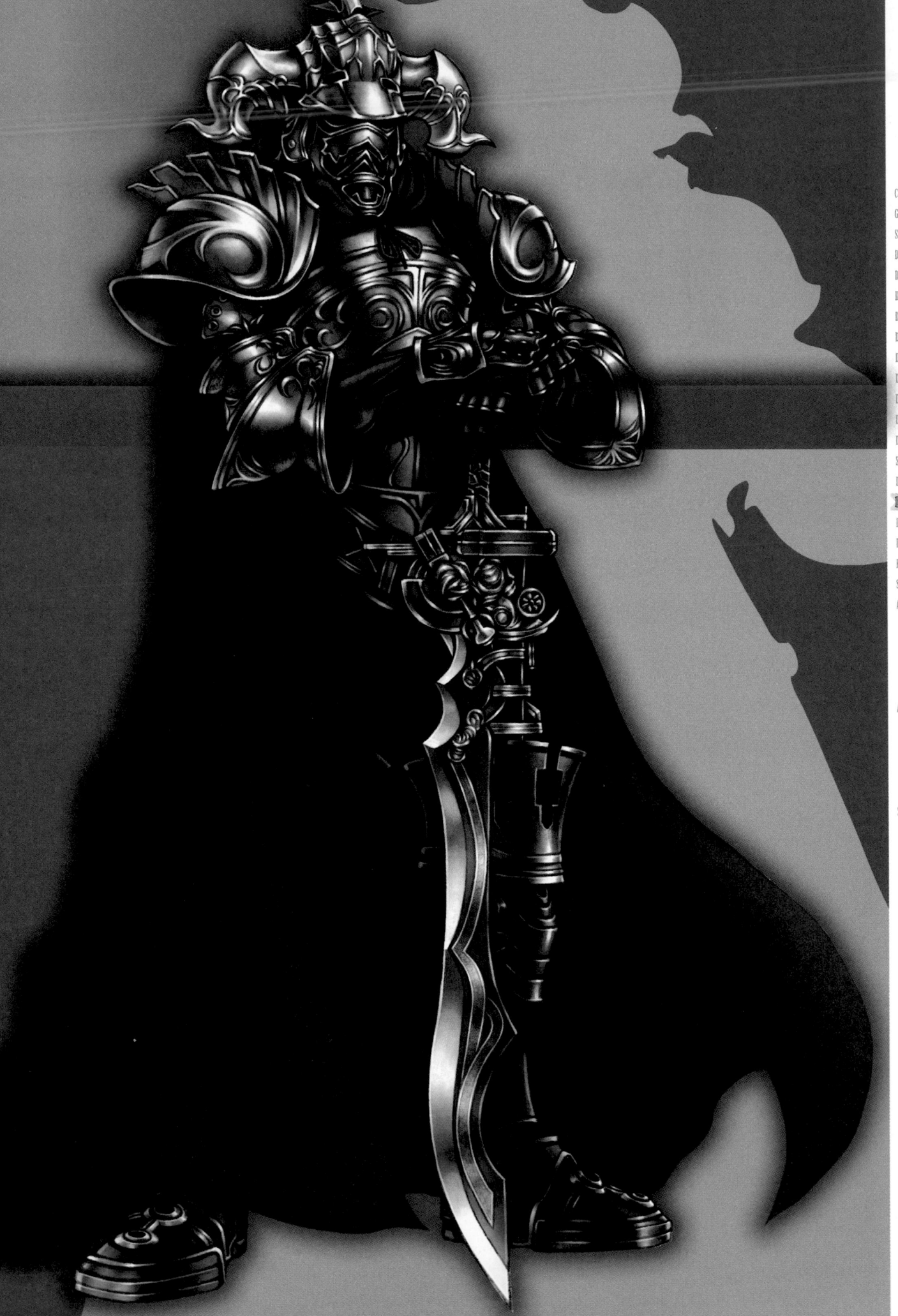

DISTANT GLORY XI

DISTANT GLORY

STARTING DP 4
MAX FINISHING 3
ENGAGEMENTS 5

On Gabranth's levels, defeating the initial battle pieces reveals Stigma of Chaos pieces that represent fights against Chaos-aligned foes. As with Shantotto's levels during the other chapter of Distant Glory, every foe must go; the Stigma of Chaos signifying the end of each level won't appear until all battle pieces on a level are defeated, except for rare battle pieces spawned after a 2-star rating. Bring along a character built up enough to tackle Shade Impulse, and most combat situations should not present a problem—except for those extra-powerful rare battle pieces.

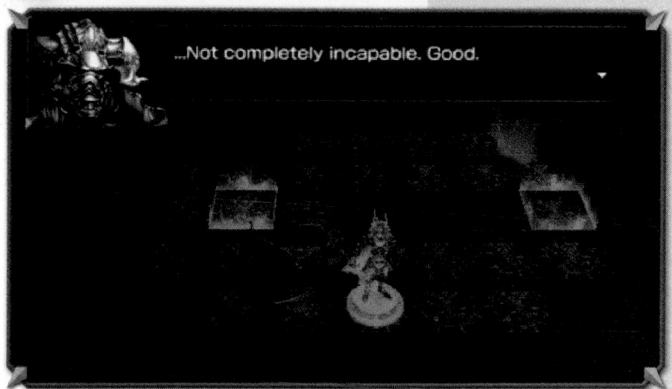

...Not completely incapable. Good.

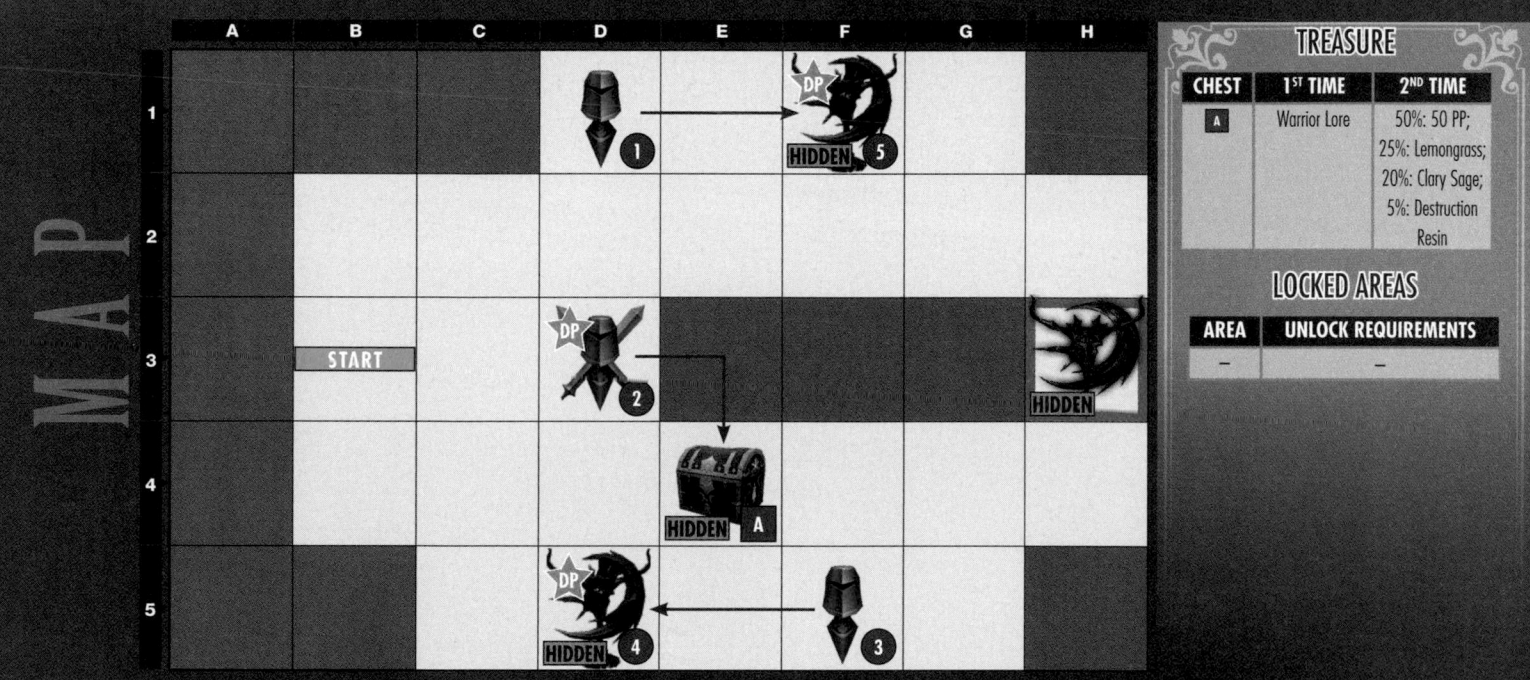

TREASURE

CHEST	1ST TIME	2ND TIME
A	Warrior Lore	50%: 50 PP; 25%: Lemongrass; 20%: Clary Sage; 5%: Destruction Resin

LOCKED AREAS

AREA	UNLOCK REQUIREMENTS
—	—

DP EFFICIENCY ROUTE

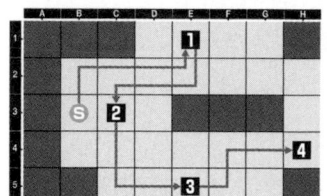

Head to E-1 to engage battle piece ❶. Crush this piece to cause a battle chain with Stigma of Chaos ❺. Afterward, defeat battle piece ❷. Move to E-5 and begin a battle chain with piece ❸, followed by Stigma of Chaos ❹, by opening treasure chest Ⓐ. DP Chances against the Stigmas of Chaos here require quick Battlegen activation, so accessories like Sunrise are helpful.

BATTLE PIECE DATA

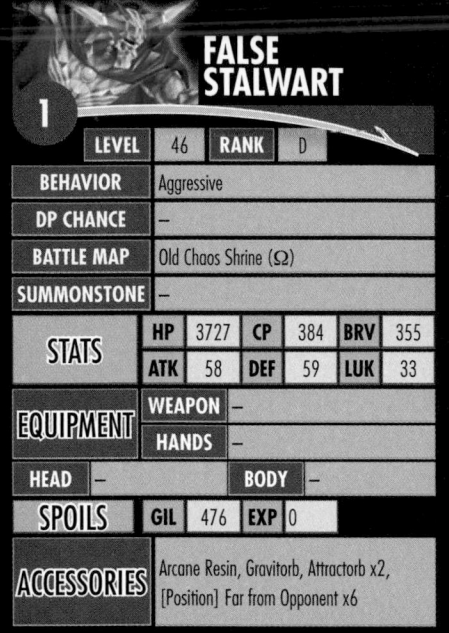

1 FALSE STALWART

LEVEL	46	RANK	D

BEHAVIOR	Aggressive
DP CHANCE	—
BATTLE MAP	Old Chaos Shrine (Ω)
SUMMONSTONE	—

STATS	HP	3727	CP	384	BRV	355
	ATK	58	DEF	59	LUK	33

EQUIPMENT	WEAPON	—
	HANDS	—

HEAD	—	BODY	—

SPOILS	GIL	476	EXP	0

ACCESSORIES	Arcane Resin, Gravitorb, Attractorb x2, [Position] Far from Opponent x6

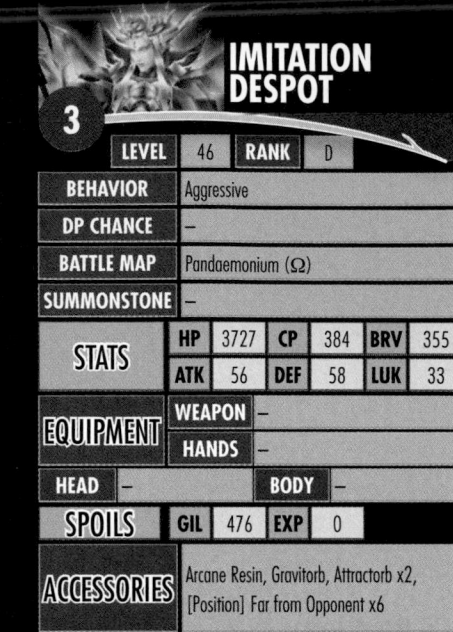

2 WARRIOR OF ANTIQUITY

LEVEL	54	RANK	E

BEHAVIOR	Standby
DP CHANCE	Win without taking damage (DP+1)
BATTLE MAP	Edge of Madness (Ω)
SUMMONSTONE	—

STATS	HP	4211	CP	408	BRV	401
	ATK	62	DEF	63	LUK	37

EQUIPMENT	WEAPON	—
	HANDS	—

HEAD	—	BODY	—

SPOILS	GIL	476	EXP	0

ACCESSORIES	Arcane Resin, Gravitorb, Attractorb x2, [Position] Far from Opponent x6

3 IMITATION DESPOT

LEVEL	46	RANK	D

BEHAVIOR	Aggressive
DP CHANCE	—
BATTLE MAP	Pandaemonium (Ω)
SUMMONSTONE	—

STATS	HP	3727	CP	384	BRV	355
	ATK	56	DEF	58	LUK	33

EQUIPMENT	WEAPON	—
	HANDS	—

HEAD	—	BODY	—

SPOILS	GIL	476	EXP	0

ACCESSORIES	Arcane Resin, Gravitorb, Attractorb x2, [Position] Far from Opponent x6

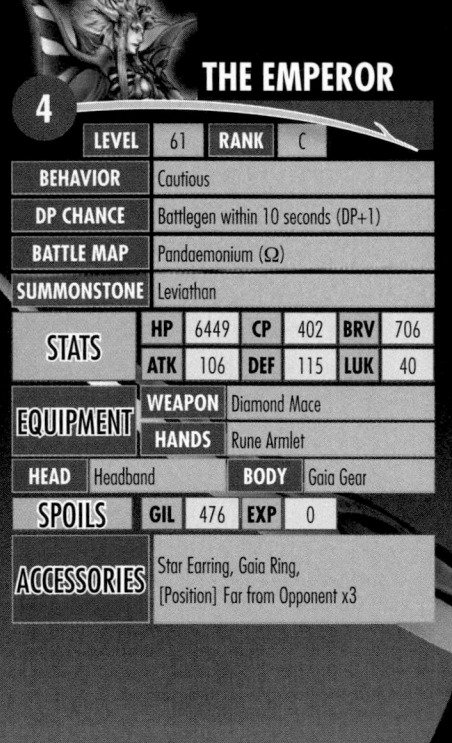

4 THE EMPEROR

LEVEL	61	RANK	C

BEHAVIOR	Cautious
DP CHANCE	Battlegen within 10 seconds (DP+1)
BATTLE MAP	Pandaemonium (Ω)
SUMMONSTONE	Leviathan

STATS	HP	6449	CP	402	BRV	706
	ATK	106	DEF	115	LUK	40

EQUIPMENT	WEAPON	Diamond Mace
	HANDS	Rune Armlet

HEAD	Headband	BODY	Gaia Gear

SPOILS	GIL	476	EXP	0

ACCESSORIES	Star Earring, Gaia Ring, [Position] Far from Opponent x3

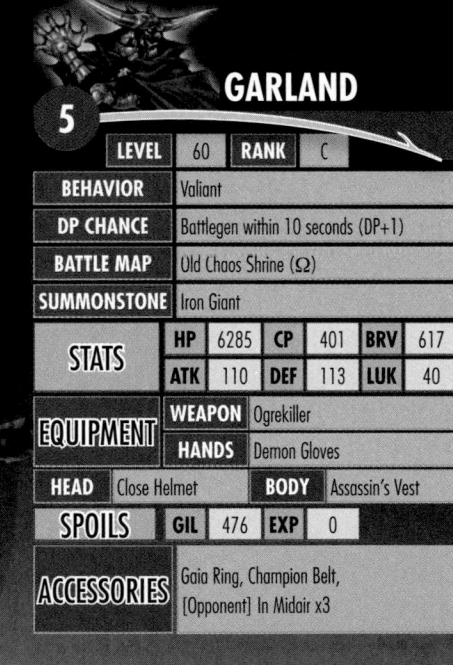

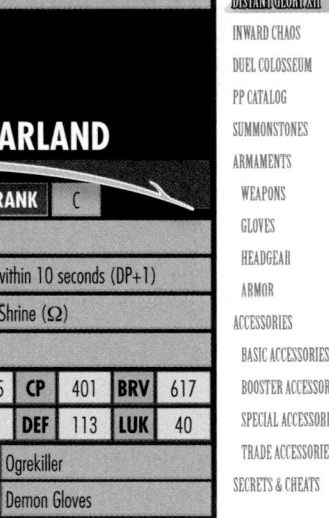

5 GARLAND

LEVEL	60	RANK	C

BEHAVIOR	Valiant
DP CHANCE	Battlegen within 10 seconds (DP+1)
BATTLE MAP	Old Chaos Shrine (Ω)
SUMMONSTONE	Iron Giant

STATS	HP	6285	CP	401	BRV	617
	ATK	110	DEF	113	LUK	40

EQUIPMENT	WEAPON	Ogrekiller
	HANDS	Demon Gloves

HEAD	Close Helmet	BODY	Assassin's Vest

SPOILS	GIL	476	EXP	0

ACCESSORIES	Gaia Ring, Champion Belt, [Opponent] In Midair x3

Again, every battle piece must be defeated to make the exit appear. The golden Locked Area at E-1 disappears after a 1-star rating on previous playthroughs of this Distant Glory chapter. Behind it, you can find the Gilgamesh Summonstone.

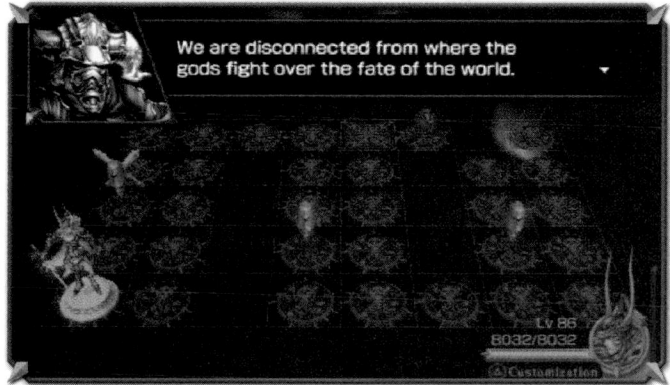

We are disconnected from where the gods fight over the fate of the world.

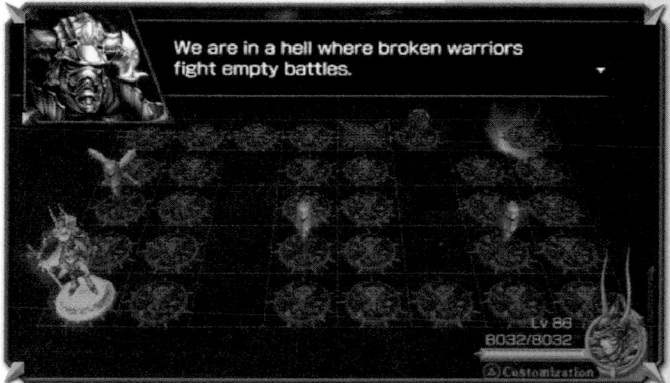

We are in a hell where broken warriors fight empty battles.

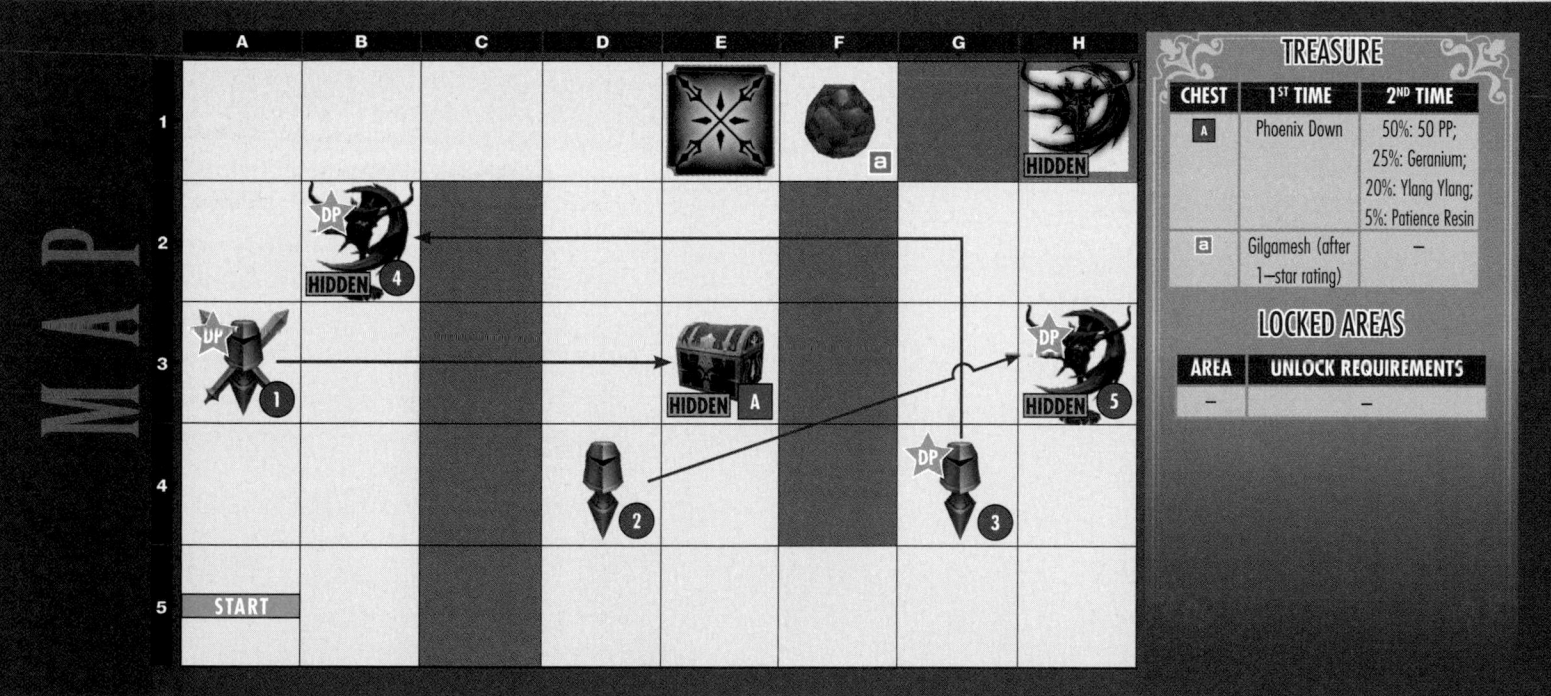

TREASURE		
CHEST	1ST TIME	2ND TIME
A	Phoenix Down	50%: 50 PP; 25%: Geranium; 20%: Ylang Ylang; 5%: Patience Resin
a	Gilgamesh (after 1—star rating)	—

LOCKED AREAS	
AREA	UNLOCK REQUIREMENTS
—	—

DP EFFICIENCY ROUTE

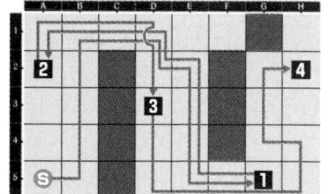

This is one of few levels where you have the run of the place from the beginning. Take advantage of this by moving all the way across the stage to take on battle piece ③. Beating this piece sets up a battle chain against battle piece ① and Stigma of Chaos ④ all the way back near the beginning. Clear this battle chain, and you can then head to D-3 to pop treasure chest A and fight battle piece ②. Finally, move to H-2 to take down Stigma of Chaos ⑤, which spawns the exit directly behind you.

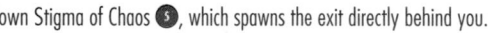

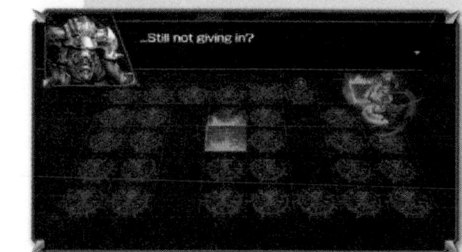

...Still not giving in?

BATTLE PIECE DATA

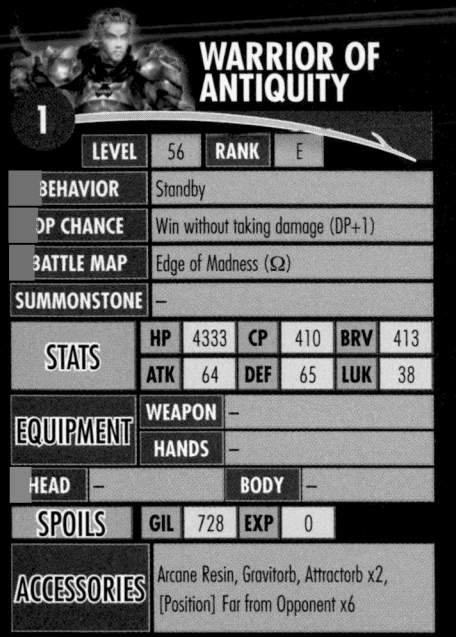

1 WARRIOR OF ANTIQUITY

LEVEL	56	RANK	E

BEHAVIOR	Standby
DP CHANCE	Win without taking damage (DP+1)
BATTLE MAP	Edge of Madness (Ω)
SUMMONSTONE	—

STATS	HP	4333	CP	410	BRV	413
	ATK	64	DEF	65	LUK	38

EQUIPMENT	WEAPON	—
	HANDS	—
HEAD	—	BODY	—

SPOILS	GIL	728	EXP	0

ACCESSORIES	Arcane Resin, Gravitorb, Attractorb x2, [Position] Far from Opponent x6

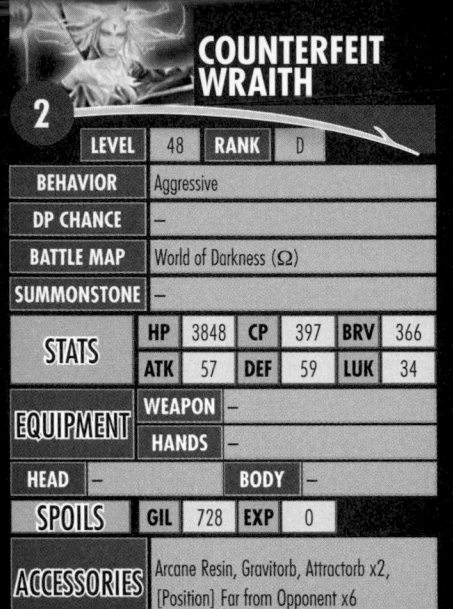

2 COUNTERFEIT WRAITH

LEVEL	48	RANK	D

BEHAVIOR	Aggressive
DP CHANCE	—
BATTLE MAP	World of Darkness (Ω)
SUMMONSTONE	—

STATS	HP	3848	CP	397	BRV	366
	ATK	57	DEF	59	LUK	34

EQUIPMENT	WEAPON	—
	HANDS	—
HEAD	—	BODY	—

SPOILS	GIL	728	EXP	0

ACCESSORIES	Arcane Resin, Gravitorb, Attractorb x2, [Position] Far from Opponent x6

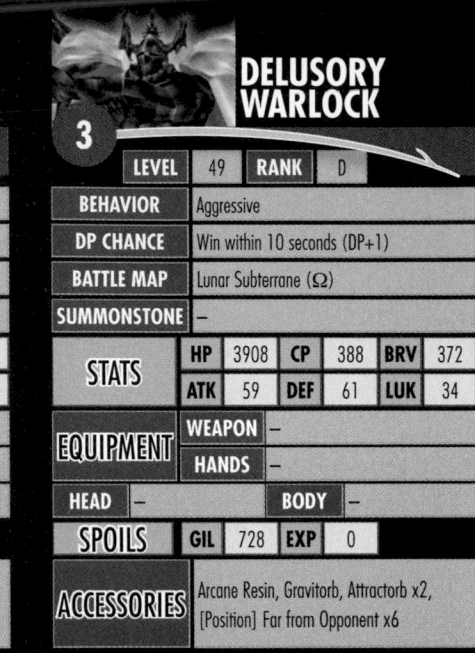

3 DELUSORY WARLOCK

LEVEL	49	RANK	D

BEHAVIOR	Aggressive
DP CHANCE	Win within 10 seconds (DP+1)
BATTLE MAP	Lunar Subterrane (Ω)
SUMMONSTONE	—

STATS	HP	3908	CP	388	BRV	372
	ATK	59	DEF	61	LUK	34

EQUIPMENT	WEAPON	—
	HANDS	—
HEAD	—	BODY	—

SPOILS	GIL	728	EXP	0

ACCESSORIES	Arcane Resin, Gravitorb, Attractorb x2, [Position] Far from Opponent x6

4 GOLBEZ

LEVEL	63	RANK	C

BEHAVIOR	Valiant
DP CHANCE	Win within 30 seconds (DP+1)
BATTLE MAP	Lunar Subterrane (Ω)
SUMMONSTONE	Marilith

STATS	HP	6652	CP	405	BRV	634
	ATK	108	DEF	118	LUK	41

EQUIPMENT	WEAPON	Lilith Rod
	HANDS	Demon Gloves
HEAD	Close Helmet	BODY	Assassin's Vest

SPOILS	GIL	728	EXP	0

ACCESSORIES	Gravitorb, Pearl Necklace, Dragonfly Orb, Gold Hourglass, [HP] HP = 1, [HP] Near Death, Phoenix Down

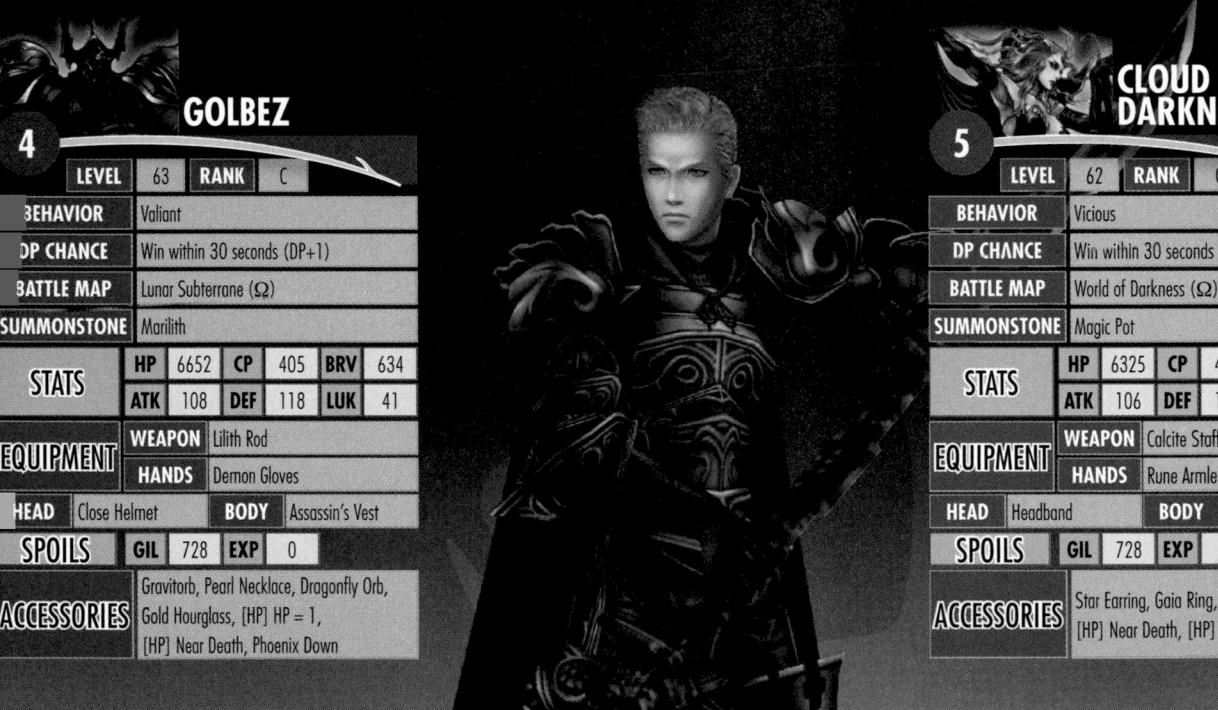

5 CLOUD OF DARKNESS

LEVEL	62	RANK	C

BEHAVIOR	Vicious
DP CHANCE	Win within 30 seconds (DP+1)
BATTLE MAP	World of Darkness (Ω)
SUMMONSTONE	Magic Pot

STATS	HP	6325	CP	411	BRV	738
	ATK	106	DEF	114	LUK	41

EQUIPMENT	WEAPON	Calcite Staff
	HANDS	Rune Armlet
HEAD	Headband	BODY	Gaia Gear

SPOILS	GIL	728	EXP	0

ACCESSORIES	Star Earring, Gaia Ring, [HP] HP = 1, [HP] Near Death, [HP] Near Loss

DISTANT GLORY XII-3

The Iron Giant Summonstone is out in the open in the upper right on this level. Treasure chests appear after defeating battle piece ③, and after returning with a 3-star rating. Ultimate battle piece ⑥ appears near the chests after returning with a 2-star rating. This fight is against a very powerful Shantotto manikin. This manikin will dodge incoming attacks consistently, while actively trying to use Bind to freeze you in place. From there, any of its HP attack spell chains can cause big problems for you. Even at a very high level, she can inflict Break status easily, gaining huge bravery totals. Luckily, this means Magic Pot can save the day. It is only really vulnerable to attack if you dodge one of its spells and end up near this powerful manikin before it finishes casting.

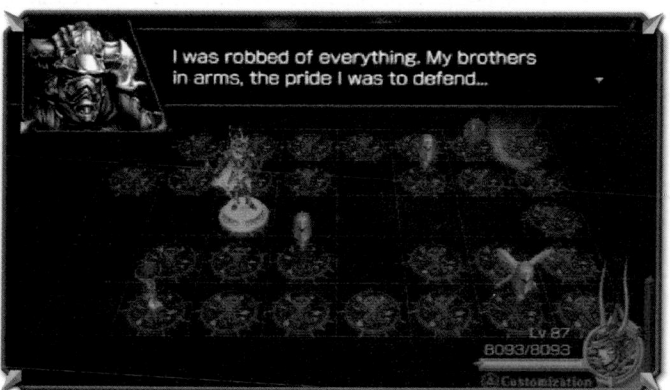

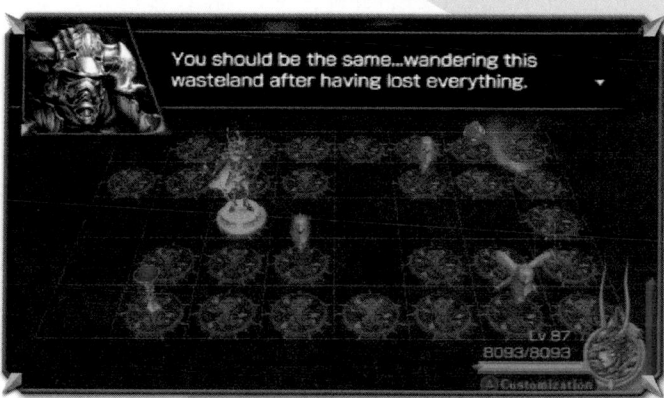

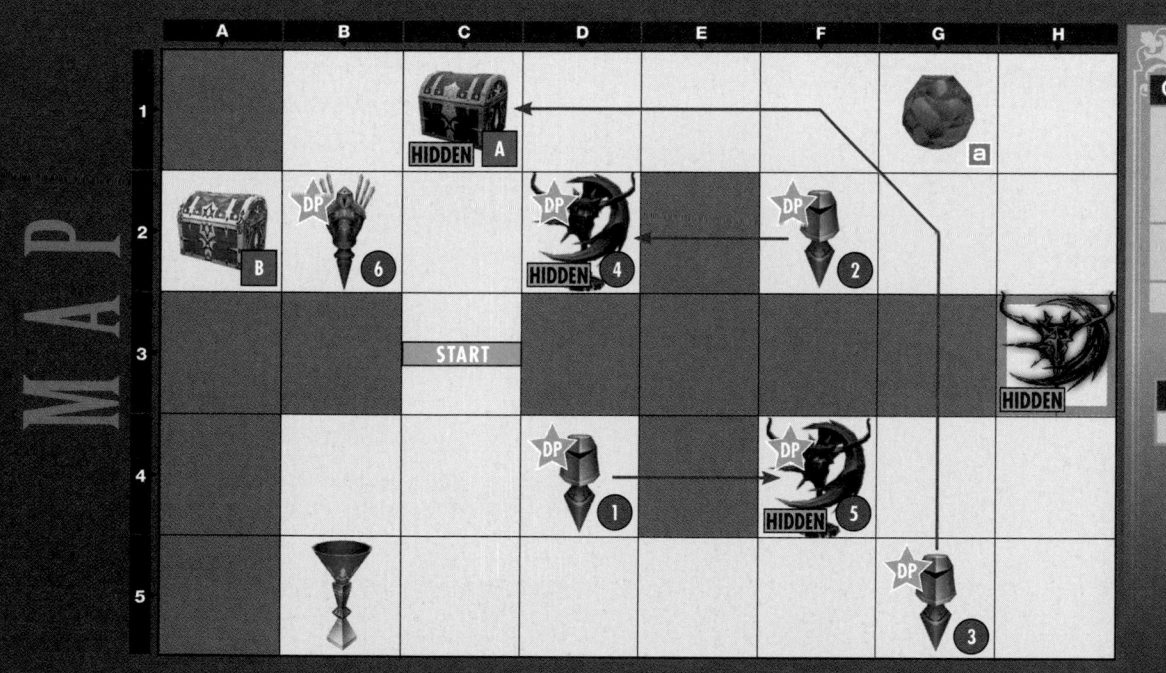

TREASURE

CHEST	1ST TIME	2ND TIME
A	Knight Lore	50%: 50 PP; 25%: Rosemary; 20%: Tea Tree; 5%: Life Resin
B	Ninja Lore (after 3-star rating)	—
a	Iron Giant	—

LOCKED AREAS

AREA	UNLOCK REQUIREMENTS
—	—

DP EFFICIENCY ROUTE

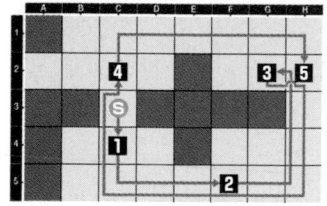

You'll need to return after a 2-star rating to maximize Destiny Points here. Open by moving one grid square from the start to engage battle piece ①. Winning here sets up a two-part battle chain at F-5 with battle piece ③ and Stigma of Chaos ⑤. The next target is battle piece ②, along with Iron Giant if he's still waiting. The stage is now set for a two-part battle chain with battle piece ⑥ and Stigma of Chaos ④ at C-2. Treasure chest A can be collected, too. After this chain, head to the exit.

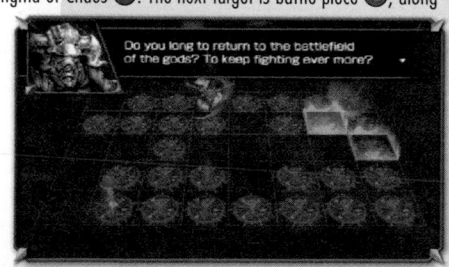

BATTLE PIECE DATA

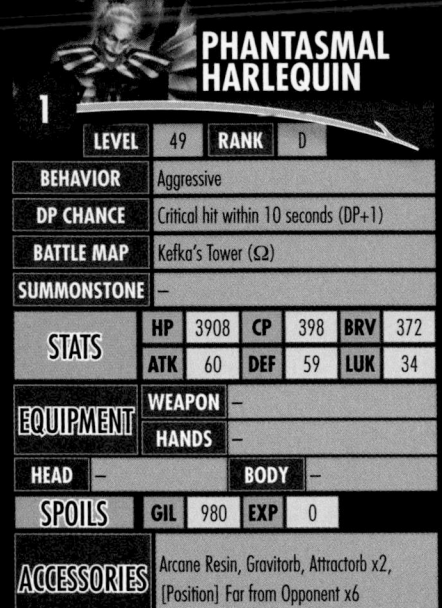

1 PHANTASMAL HARLEQUIN

LEVEL	49	RANK	D

BEHAVIOR	Aggressive
DP CHANCE	Critical hit within 10 seconds (DP+1)
BATTLE MAP	Kefka's Tower (Ω)
SUMMONSTONE	–

STATS	HP	3908	CP	398	BRV	372
	ATK	60	DEF	59	LUK	34

EQUIPMENT	WEAPON	–
	HANDS	–

HEAD	–	BODY	–

SPOILS	GIL	980	EXP	0

ACCESSORIES	Arcane Resin, Gravitorb, Attractorb x2, [Position] Far from Opponent x6

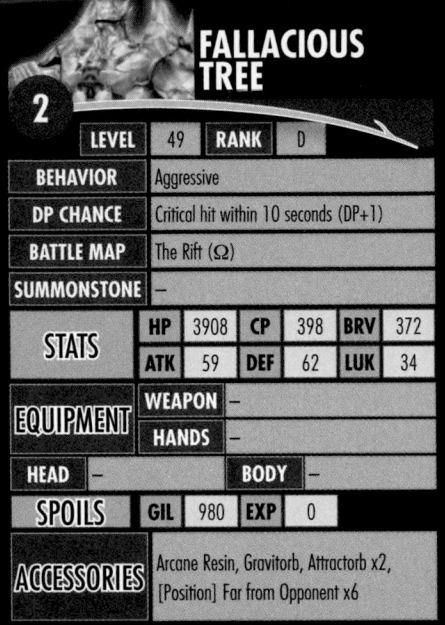

2 FALLACIOUS TREE

LEVEL	49	RANK	D

BEHAVIOR	Aggressive
DP CHANCE	Critical hit within 10 seconds (DP+1)
BATTLE MAP	The Rift (Ω)
SUMMONSTONE	–

STATS	HP	3908	CP	398	BRV	372
	ATK	59	DEF	62	LUK	34

EQUIPMENT	WEAPON	–
	HANDS	–

HEAD	–	BODY	–

SPOILS	GIL	980	EXP	0

ACCESSORIES	Arcane Resin, Gravitorb, Attractorb x2, [Position] Far from Opponent x6

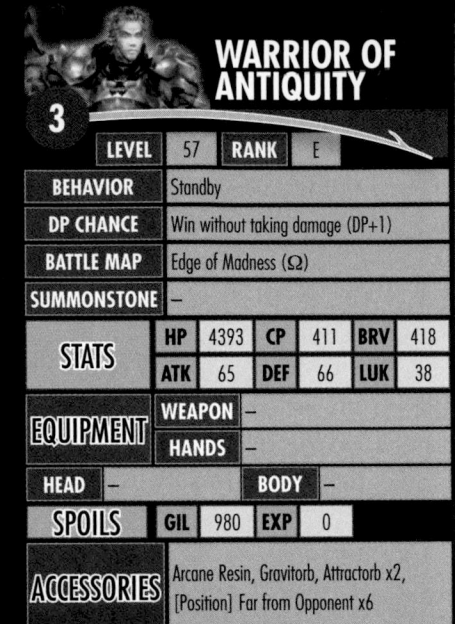

3 WARRIOR OF ANTIQUITY

LEVEL	57	RANK	E

BEHAVIOR	Standby
DP CHANCE	Win without taking damage (DP+1)
BATTLE MAP	Edge of Madness (Ω)
SUMMONSTONE	–

STATS	HP	4393	CP	411	BRV	418
	ATK	65	DEF	66	LUK	38

EQUIPMENT	WEAPON	–
	HANDS	–

HEAD	–	BODY	–

SPOILS	GIL	980	EXP	0

ACCESSORIES	Arcane Resin, Gravitorb, Attractorb x2, [Position] Far from Opponent x6

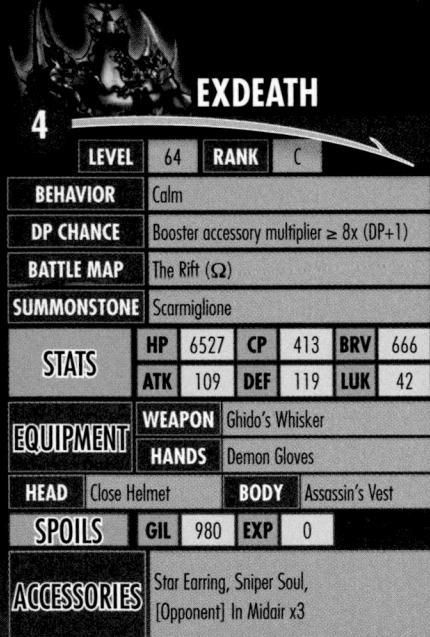

4 EXDEATH

LEVEL	64	RANK	C

BEHAVIOR	Calm
DP CHANCE	Booster accessory multiplier ≥ 8x (DP+1)
BATTLE MAP	The Rift (Ω)
SUMMONSTONE	Scarmiglione

STATS	HP	6527	CP	413	BRV	666
	ATK	109	DEF	119	LUK	42

EQUIPMENT	WEAPON	Ghido's Whisker
	HANDS	Demon Gloves

HEAD	Close Helmet	BODY	Assassin's Vest

SPOILS	GIL	980	EXP	0

ACCESSORIES	Star Earring, Sniper Soul, [Opponent] In Midair x3

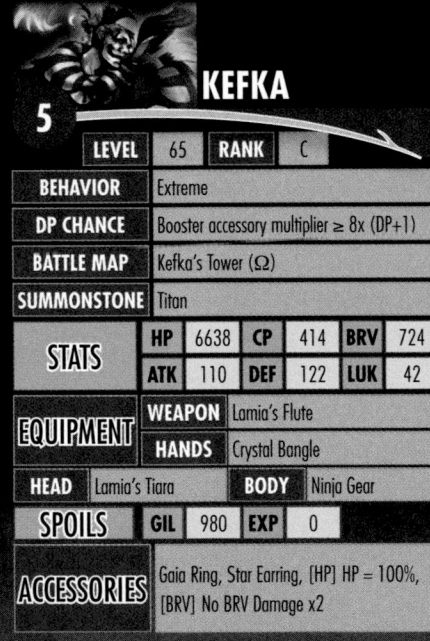

5 KEFKA

LEVEL	65	RANK	C

BEHAVIOR	Extreme
DP CHANCE	Booster accessory multiplier ≥ 8x (DP+1)
BATTLE MAP	Kefka's Tower (Ω)
SUMMONSTONE	Titan

STATS	HP	6638	CP	414	BRV	724
	ATK	110	DEF	122	LUK	42

EQUIPMENT	WEAPON	Lamia's Flute
	HANDS	Crystal Bangle

HEAD	Lamia's Tiara	BODY	Ninja Gear

SPOILS	GIL	980	EXP	0

ACCESSORIES	Gaia Ring, Star Earring, [HP] HP = 100%, [BRV] No BRV Damage x2

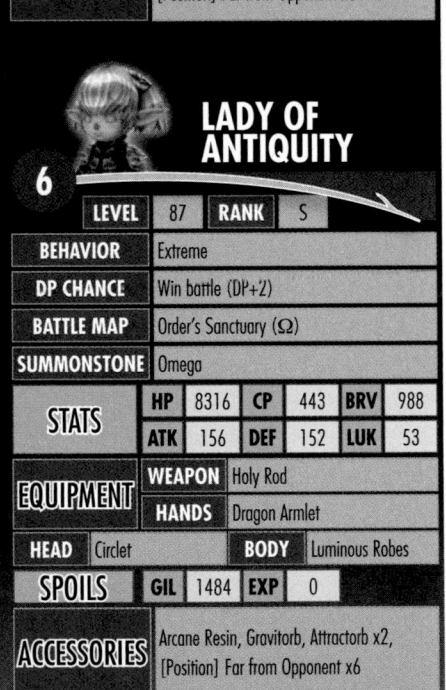

6 LADY OF ANTIQUITY

LEVEL	87	RANK	S

BEHAVIOR	Extreme
DP CHANCE	Win battle (DP+2)
BATTLE MAP	Order's Sanctuary (Ω)
SUMMONSTONE	Omega

STATS	HP	8316	CP	443	BRV	988
	ATK	156	DEF	152	LUK	53

EQUIPMENT	WEAPON	Holy Rod
	HANDS	Dragon Armlet

HEAD	Circlet	BODY	Luminous Robes

SPOILS	GIL	1484	EXP	0

ACCESSORIES	Arcane Resin, Gravitorb, Attractorb x2, [Position] Far from Opponent x6

DISTANT GLORY

All battle pieces must be crushed to spawn the Stigma of Chaos, which also serves as the exit. Dragoon Lore (another of the "lore" items that allow fighters to use equipment they can't otherwise) is found behind the space where a golden Locked Area rests, before a 1-star rating or better. Treasure chest **A** is revealed when battle piece **3** is defeated.

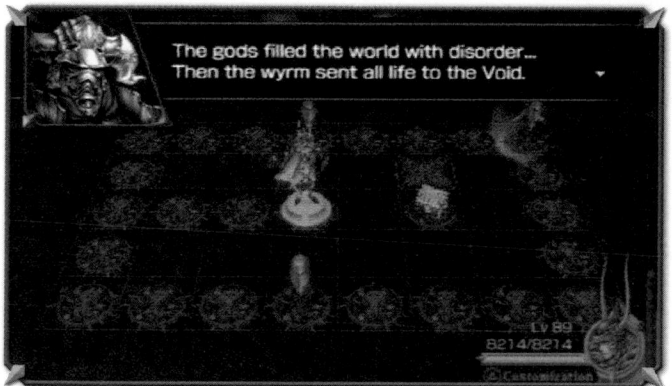

The gods filled the world with disorder...
Then the wyrm sent all life to the Void.

Lv 89
8214/8214
Customization

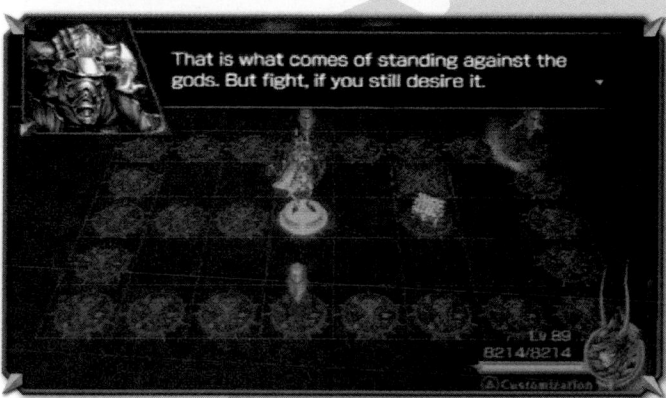

That is what comes of standing against the gods. But fight, if you still desire it.

Lv 89
8214/8214
Customization

MAP

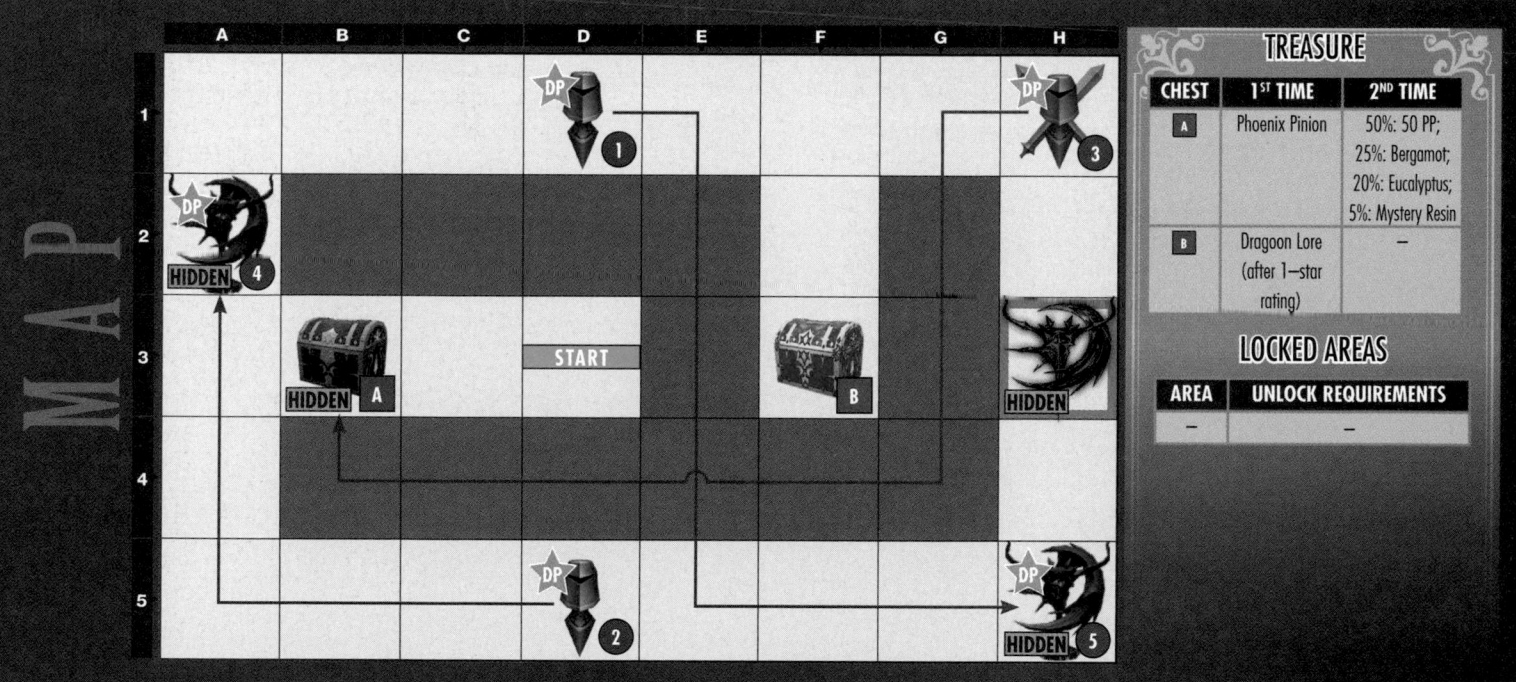

TREASURE

CHEST	1ST TIME	2ND TIME
A	Phoenix Pinion	50%: 50 PP; 25%: Bergamot; 20%: Eucalyptus; 5%: Mystery Resin
B	Dragoon Lore (after 1–star rating)	—

LOCKED AREAS

AREA	UNLOCK REQUIREMENTS
—	—

DP EFFICIENCY ROUTE

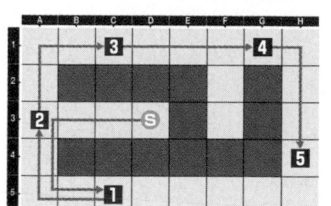

You'll skirt the circumference of the level here. Begin by taking out battle piece **2**, then Stigma of Chaos **4**. Next, move to battle piece **1**, then piece **3** beyond it. The final order of business is to move to H-4 and engage Stigma of Chaos **5**. After it falls, the exit appears behind you.

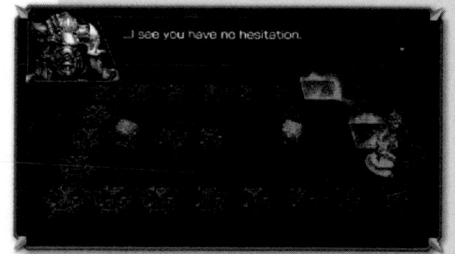

...I see you have no hesitation.

BATTLE PIECE DATA

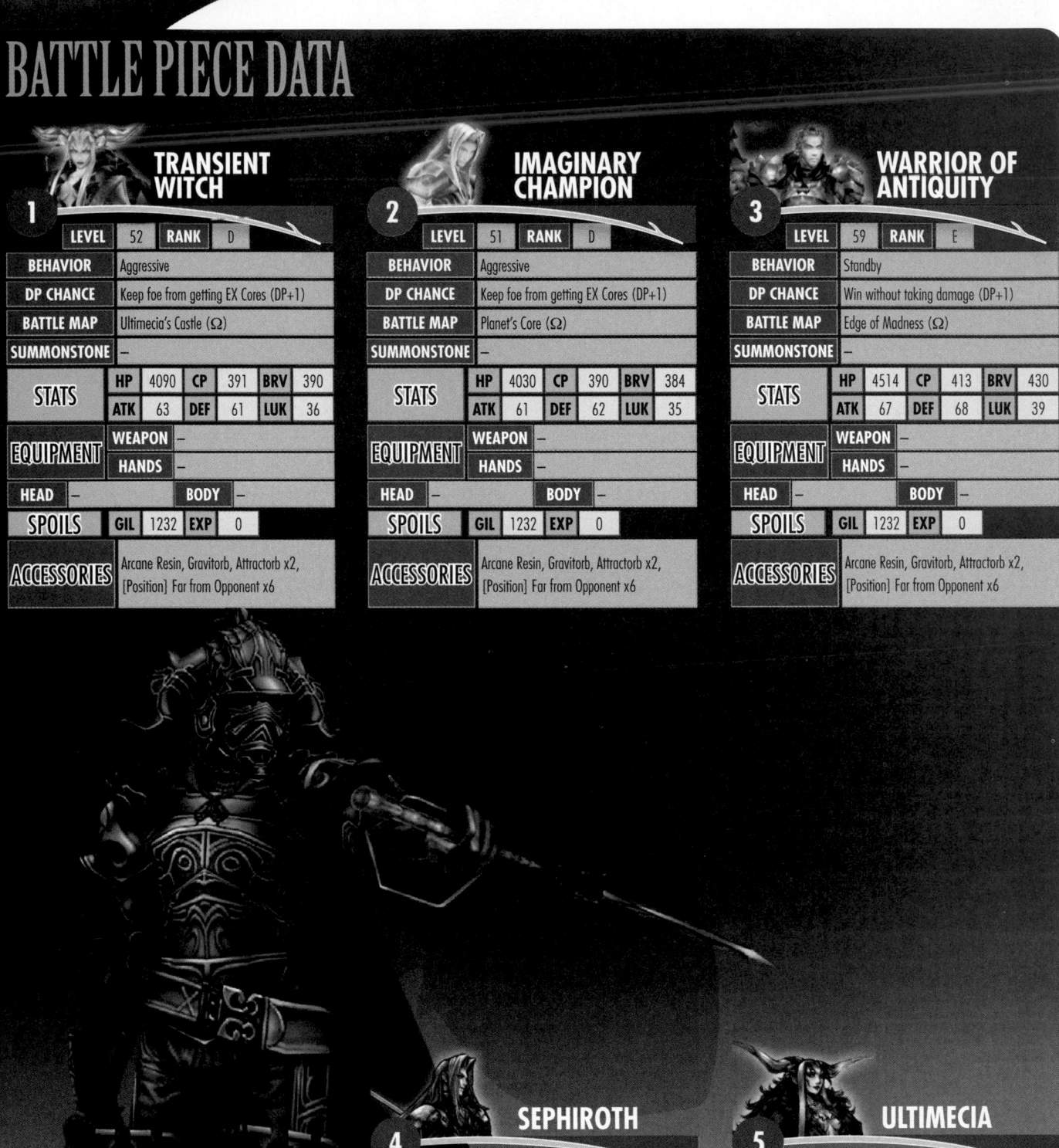

1 — TRANSIENT WITCH

LEVEL 52   **RANK** D

BEHAVIOR	Aggressive
DP CHANCE	Keep foe from getting EX Cores (DP+1)
BATTLE MAP	Ultimecia's Castle (Ω)
SUMMONSTONE	–

STATS

HP	4090	CP	391	BRV	390
ATK	63	DEF	61	LUK	36

EQUIPMENT

WEAPON	–
HANDS	–
HEAD	–
BODY	–

SPOILS — GIL 1232   EXP 0

ACCESSORIES — Arcane Resin, Gravitorb, Attractorb x2, [Position] Far from Opponent x6

2 — IMAGINARY CHAMPION

LEVEL 51   **RANK** D

BEHAVIOR	Aggressive
DP CHANCE	Keep foe from getting EX Cores (DP+1)
BATTLE MAP	Planet's Core (Ω)
SUMMONSTONE	–

STATS

HP	4030	CP	390	BRV	384
ATK	61	DEF	62	LUK	35

EQUIPMENT

WEAPON	–
HANDS	–
HEAD	–
BODY	–

SPOILS — GIL 1232   EXP 0

ACCESSORIES — Arcane Resin, Gravitorb, Attractorb x2, [Position] Far from Opponent x6

3 — WARRIOR OF ANTIQUITY

LEVEL 59   **RANK** E

BEHAVIOR	Standby
DP CHANCE	Win without taking damage (DP+1)
BATTLE MAP	Edge of Madness (Ω)
SUMMONSTONE	–

STATS

HP	4514	CP	413	BRV	430
ATK	67	DEF	68	LUK	39

EQUIPMENT

WEAPON	–
HANDS	–
HEAD	–
BODY	–

SPOILS — GIL 1232   EXP 0

ACCESSORIES — Arcane Resin, Gravitorb, Attractorb x2, [Position] Far from Opponent x6

4 — SEPHIROTH

LEVEL 66   **RANK** C

BEHAVIOR	Survivor
DP CHANCE	Keep foe from getting EX Cores (DP+1)
BATTLE MAP	Planet's Core (Ω)
SUMMONSTONE	Shiva

STATS

HP	7002	CP	408	BRV	639
ATK	113	DEF	124	LUK	43

EQUIPMENT

WEAPON	Masamune Blade
HANDS	Crystal Shield
HEAD	Crystal Helm
BODY	Crystal Armor

SPOILS — GIL 1232   EXP 0

ACCESSORIES — Gaia Ring, Champion Belt, Guardian Bangle

5 — ULTIMECIA

LEVEL 67   **RANK** C

BEHAVIOR	Tactician
DP CHANCE	Keep foe from getting EX Cores (DP+1)
BATTLE MAP	Ultimecia's Castle (Ω)
SUMMONSTONE	PuPu

STATS

HP	6944	CP	410	BRV	735
ATK	113	DEF	122	LUK	43

EQUIPMENT

WEAPON	Valkyrie
HANDS	Crystal Bangle
HEAD	Lamia's Tiara
BODY	Ninja Gear

SPOILS — GIL 1232   EXP 0

ACCESSORIES — Star Earring, [Position] Far from Opponent x2, [HP] HP = 1, [HP] Near Death, Phoenix Down

DISTANT GLORY　　XII-5

The final level of Gabranth's chapter again requires that all battle pieces are subdued for the final Stigma of Chaos to appear. Treasure chest **A** also only appears after defeating three battle pieces, while the Potion nearby only appears after defeating four pieces. Rare treasure chest **B**, containing Samurai Lore, appears after a 3-star rating. Ultimate battle piece **6**, which appears after a 2-star rating, stands guard in front of this rare chest. This manikin of Gabranth is very strong, but remember that Gabranth can only use HP attacks during EX Mode. The manikin begins with a full EX Gauge thanks to his Arcane Resin, but if you make it past his first EX Mode activation it must collect EX Cores or use EX Charge to regain EX Force. Beat the manikin to the EX Cores, dashing in and attacking when it uses EX Charge. If it does happen to reactivate EX Mode, just run away and wait it out. These same tactics work against the actual Judge Magister, who acts as the boss of the chapter.

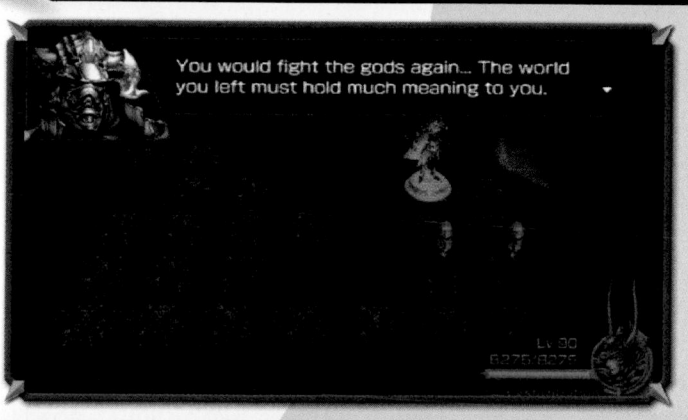

> You would fight the gods again... The world you left must hold much meaning to you.

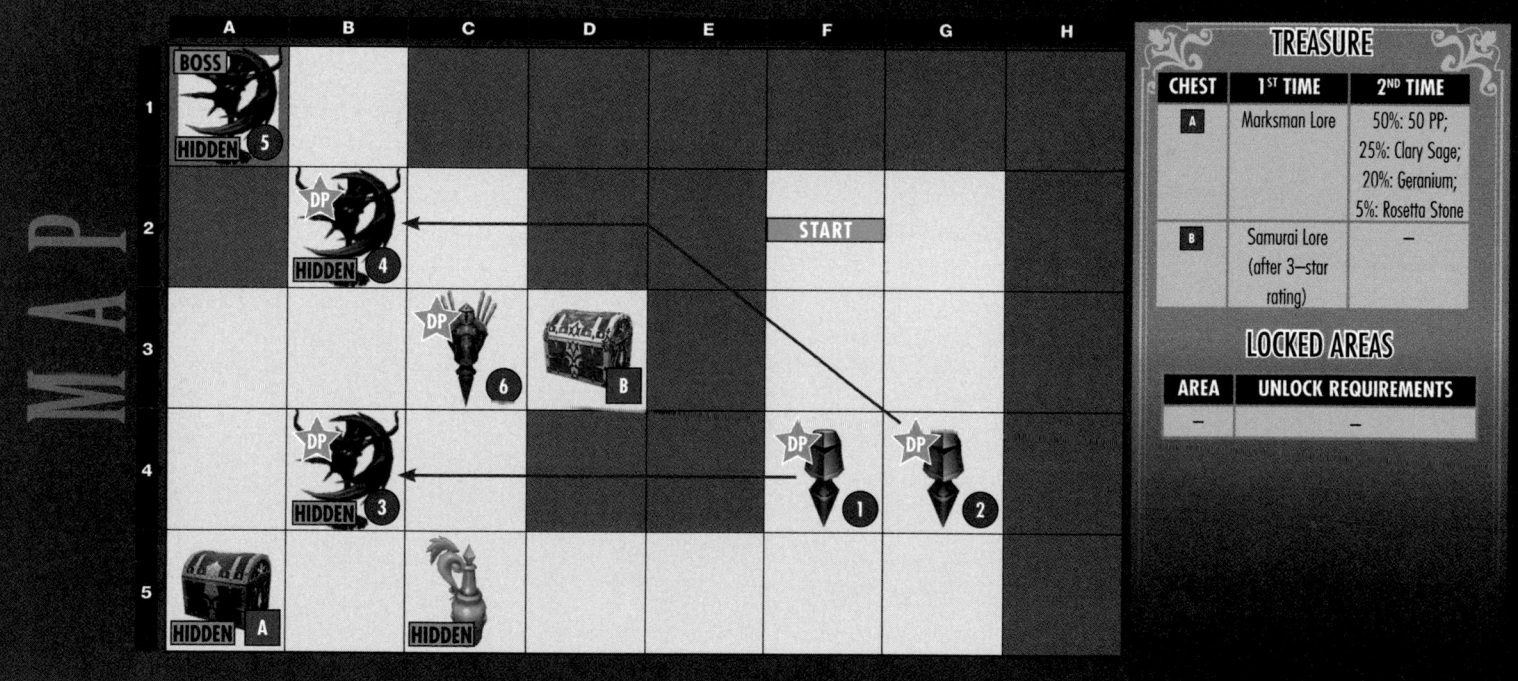

MAP

	A	B	C	D	E	F	G	H
1	BOSS / HIDDEN **5**							
2		DP / HIDDEN **4**				START		
3			DP **6**	B (chest)				
4		DP / HIDDEN **3**				DP **1**	DP **2**	
5	A (chest) HIDDEN	HIDDEN (Potion)						

TREASURE

CHEST	1ST TIME	2ND TIME
A	Marksman Lore	50%: 50 PP; 25%: Clary Sage; 20%: Geranium; 5%: Rosetta Stone
B	Samurai Lore (after 3-star rating)	–

LOCKED AREAS

AREA	UNLOCK REQUIREMENTS
–	–

DP EFFICIENCY ROUTE

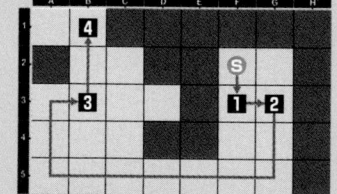

Getting the most DP from this level requires returning after a 2-star rating. This way, ultimate battle piece **6** will appear. With this piece in place, the action is straightforward. Take out battle pieces **1** and **2** near the start, then head to B-3 for a brutal three-part chain against Stigmas of Chaos **3** and **4**, and ultimate battle piece **6**.

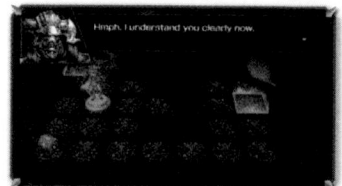
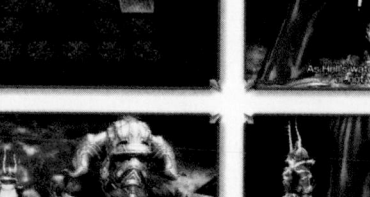
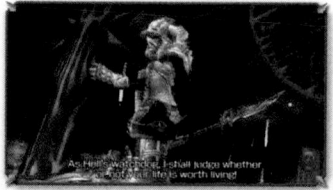
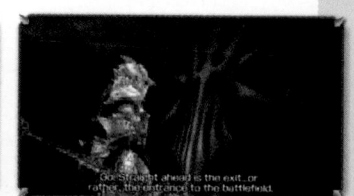
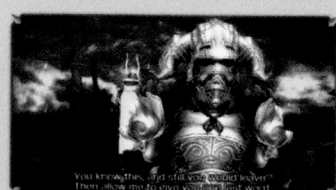
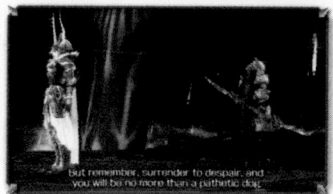
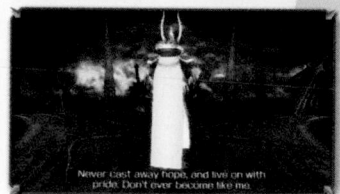
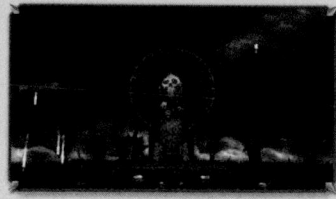

BATTLE PIECE DATA

1 CAPRICIOUS REAPER

LEVEL	53	RANK	D

BEHAVIOR	Aggressive
DP CHANCE	Win without taking damage (DP+1)
BATTLE MAP	Crystal World (Ω)
SUMMONSTONE	–

STATS	HP	4151	CP	393	BRV	395
	ATK	62	DEF	64	LUK	36

EQUIPMENT	WEAPON	–
	HANDS	–
HEAD	–	BODY	–

SPOILS	GIL	1484	EXP	0

ACCESSORIES	Arcane Resin, Gravitorb, Attractorb x2, [Position] Far from Opponent x6

2 EPHEMERAL PHANTOM

LEVEL	54	RANK	D

BEHAVIOR	Aggressive
DP CHANCE	Win without taking damage (DP+1)
BATTLE MAP	Dream's End (Ω)
SUMMONSTONE	–

STATS	HP	4211	CP	394	BRV	401
	ATK	66	DEF	66	LUK	37

EQUIPMENT	WEAPON	–
	HANDS	–
HEAD	–	BODY	–

SPOILS	GIL	1484	EXP	0

ACCESSORIES	Arcane Resin, Gravitorb, Attractorb x2, [Position] Far from Opponent x6

3 KUJA

LEVEL	68	RANK	C

BEHAVIOR	Conservative
DP CHANCE	Win without losing HP (DP+1)
BATTLE MAP	Crystal World (Ω)
SUMMONSTONE	Tiamat

STATS	HP	7005	CP	411	BRV	741
	ATK	112	DEF	125	LUK	44

EQUIPMENT	WEAPON	Punisher
	HANDS	Crystal Bangle
HEAD	Lamia's Tiara	BODY	Ninja Gear

SPOILS	GIL	1484	EXP	0

ACCESSORIES	Star Earring, Hyper Ring, [Position] Near Opponent x2, [Position] Far from Opponent x2

4 JECHT

LEVEL	69	RANK	C

BEHAVIOR	Tactician
DP CHANCE	Win without losing HP (DP+1)
BATTLE MAP	Dream's End (Ω)
SUMMONSTONE	Malboro

STATS	HP	7218	CP	412	BRV	709
	ATK	117	DEF	127	LUK	44

EQUIPMENT	WEAPON	Kaiser Knuckles
	HANDS	Crystal Bangle
HEAD	Crystal Helm	BODY	Crystal Vest

SPOILS	GIL	1484	EXP	0

ACCESSORIES	Gaia Ring, Champion Belt, [Position] Near Opponent x2, [Opponent] In Midair

5 GABRANTH

LEVEL	72	RANK	B

BEHAVIOR	Calm
DP CHANCE	–
BATTLE MAP	Edge of Madness (Ω)
SUMMONSTONE	Omega

STATS	HP	7548	CP	424	BRV	689
	ATK	116	DEF	128	LUK	46

EQUIPMENT	WEAPON	Demonsbane
	HANDS	Crystal Shield
HEAD	Platinum Helm	BODY	Mirror Mail

SPOILS	GIL	8218	EXP	13255

ACCESSORIES	Gold Hourglass, Silver Hourglass x2, [HP] HP = 100%, [BRV] No BRV Damage x2, [HP] HP = 1, [HP] Near Death, Phoenix Down

6 WARRIOR OF ANTIQUITY

LEVEL	90	RANK	S

BEHAVIOR	Vicious
DP CHANCE	Win battle (DP+2)
BATTLE MAP	Edge of Madness (Ω)
SUMMONSTONE	Ultima Weapon

STATS	HP	9003	CP	441	BRV	609*
	ATK	98*	DEF	99*	LUK	55

EQUIPMENT	WEAPON	[Rank 14]
	HANDS	[Rank 12]
HEAD	[Rank 12]	BODY	[Rank 13]

SPOILS	GIL	1484	EXP	0

ACCESSORIES	Arcane Resin, Gravitorb, Attractorb x2, [Position] Far from Opponent x6

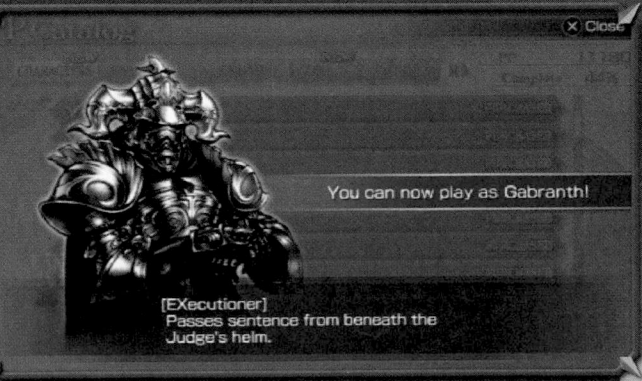

You can now play as Gabranth!

[EXecutioner]
Passes sentence from beneath the Judge's helm.

Complete this chapter of Distant Glory to unlock Gabranth in the PP Catalog. This Judge Magister of Ivalice fights differently than the rest of the cast. Gabranth builds EX Force at will through EX Charge, and can only execute HP attacks during EX Mode.

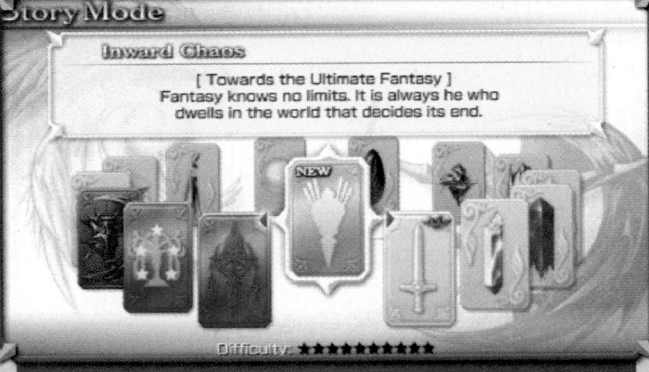

Story Mode

Inward Chaos

[Towards the Ultimate Fantasy]
Fantasy knows no limits. It is always he who dwells in the world that decides its end.

NEW

Difficulty: ★★★★★★★★★★

Once both tales of Distant Glory are finished, Inward Chaos becomes accessible!

INWARD CHAOS
TOWARDS THE ULTIMATE FANTASY

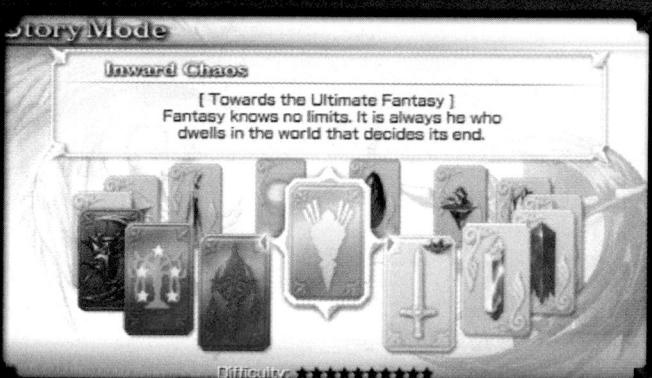

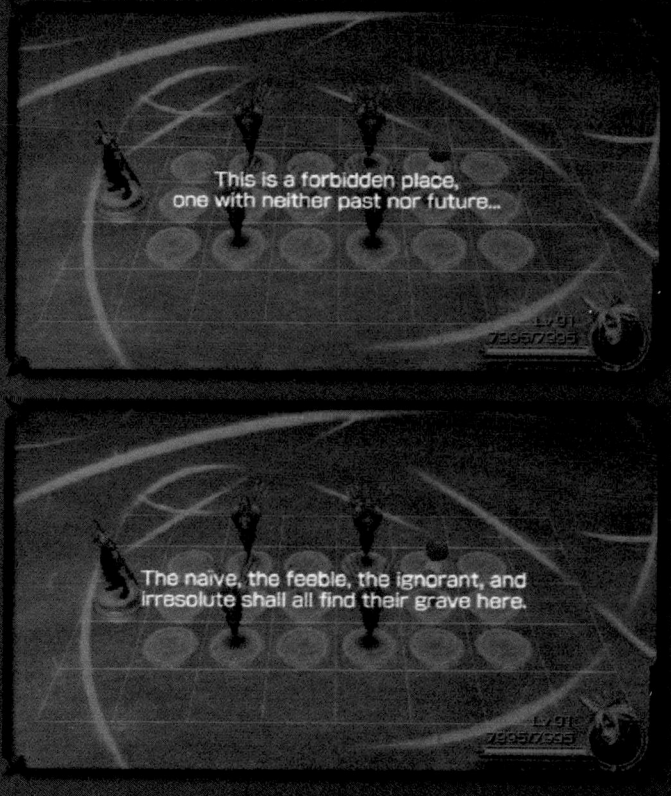

With all other challenges in Story Mode met and defeated, the road to the final challenge is paved. Inward Chaos is a menagerie of incredibly stout nemeses, arranged to test you by no less than the wyrm Shinryu itself. At the very end of Inward Chaos waits an incarnation of the god Chaos who makes the version you fought during Shade Impulse 4 seem like a pile of down pillows. Finish Inward Chaos to obtain access to purchase the Genji set of equipment from the PP Catalog.

REWARDS

At the end of each level, rewards are available if you finish with a positive number of Destiny Points, or DP. This walkthrough includes miniature level maps that indicate the most efficient route to take through a given level, in order to maximize DP.

LEVEL COMPLETION

REMAINING DP	1ST TIME	2ND TIME
2	Adamantite	300 PP
1	Ultima Weapon	200 PP
0	Mallet	120 PP

INWARD CHAOS COMPLETION

STAR RATING	SP REQUIRED	AWARD
–	800 SP, then every 800 SP extra	100 PP

At the end of each set of levels, you'll receive rewards based on your performance. Story Points, or SP, are awarded after each level based on remaining DP and HP, as well as the number of engagements undertaken. Points are penalized for retries, or for a DP total that dips into negatives. If you miss out on a desired bonus on the first playthrough, don't worry—SP is cumulative across multiple playthroughs.

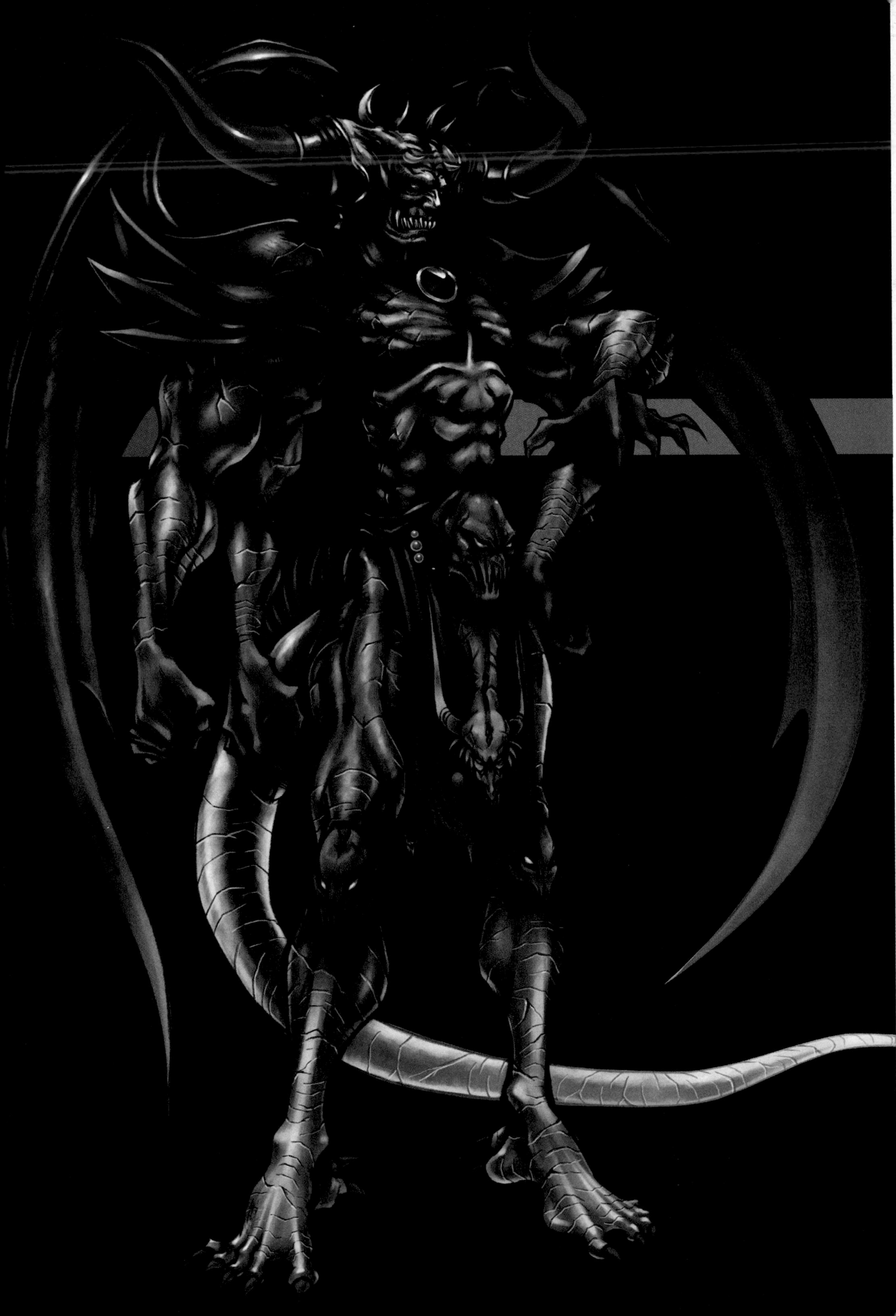

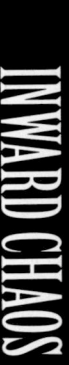

INWARD CHAOS

STARTING DP	MAX FINISHING	ENGAGEMENTS
1	1	4

Shade Impulse and Distant Glory are fairly challenging, but mid-level characters can finish those chapters without much difficulty. Inward Chaos is a different story. Every single foe found throughout this final chapter is stronger in power than the rare, ultimate enemies found in any other chapter. Adversaries range in level from 92 to 110, with summons, accessories, and equipment to match.

To have a chance here, you'll need a character at least as beefy. If you've come this far, and especially if you've taken time to unlock higher star ratings along the way, you probably have a character or two approaching lv.100, ready for the challenge. At lv.100, each character learns the extra abilities EXP to HP, EXP to Bravery, and EXP to EX Force. As EXP gain is irrelevant at lv.100, these abilities are a great boon. Because foes react more intelligently compared to other chapters, it also helps to bring a character whose attacks give the CPU trouble regardless of behavior type. Warrior of Light (Shield Strike to Bitter End), Cecil (Dark Flame), Zidane (Tidal Flame), and Shantotto (Aero, Thunder) are a few good examples. You can also use summons like Magic Pot, Alexander, Kraken, and Carbuncle to skew things drastically in your favor during hard fights—just don't lean on this strategy against Bartz during Inward Chaos 2, since he'll use Scarmiglione's Curse to negate your summon while reducing your bravery to 0. Keep your skills in mind, also. Cure, Aura, Missile, and Ray-Bomb can keep you healthy while softening up targets before you engage. Finally, no enemy is avoidable—the Stigma of Chaos signifying the end of each level doesn't appear until every battle piece is removed. Finally, note the background music during Inward Chaos—the tune that plays during a given stage is taken directly from the opening of its respective *Final Fantasy* title!

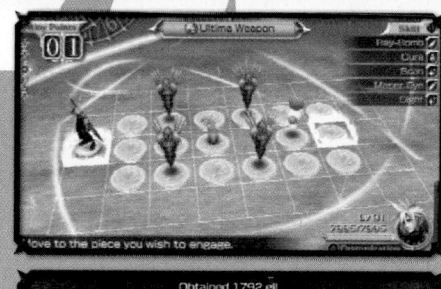

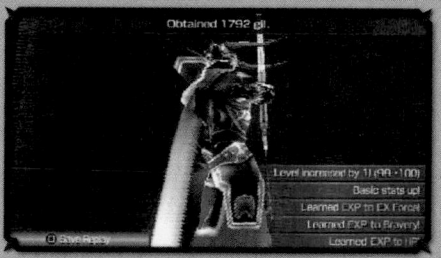

MAP

TREASURE		
CHEST	1ST TIME	2ND TIME
a	Moogle	Superslick or 300 PP

LOCKED AREAS

AREA	UNLOCK REQUIREMENTS
–	–

DP EFFICIENCY ROUTE

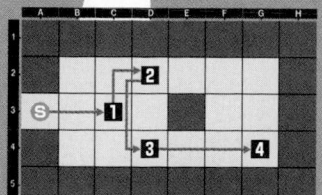

The combat is the challenge during Inward Chaos, so the DP Chances for the entire chapter all simply involve winning each battle. This works out, since you're already forced to fight every battle because the exits to each level won't appear until all foes are slain. Here, you'll want to chain battle pieces ❶ and ❷ before taking on ❸ and ❹ individually. Find the Potion positioned in the midst of the foes such that you can use it without expending an extra Destiny Point. Head to the Stigma of Chaos once all four foes are defeated.

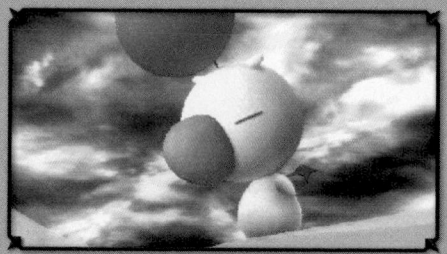

BATTLE PIECE DATA

1 WARRIOR OF LIGHT

LEVEL	92
RANK	S
BEHAVIOR	Valiant
DP CHANCE	Win battle (DP+1)
BATTLE MAP	Old Chaos Shrine (Ω)
SUMMONSTONE	Iron Giant

STATS					
HP	9049	CP	440	BRV	888
ATK	165	DEF	173	LUK	56

EQUIPMENT		
WEAPON	Braveheart	
HANDS	Borghertz's Hands	
HEAD	Grand Helm	
BODY	Brigandine	

SPOILS			
GIL	1792	EXP	0

ACCESSORIES: Gaia Ring, Hyper Ring x2, [Combat] Chasing x2, [Position] In Midair, [Position] Near Opponent x3

2 FIRION

LEVEL	93
RANK	S
BEHAVIOR	Calm
DP CHANCE	Win battle (DP+1)
BATTLE MAP	Pandaemonium (Ω)
SUMMONSTONE	Leviathan

STATS					
HP	9109	CP	441	BRV	854
ATK	168	DEF	173	LUK	56

EQUIPMENT		
WEAPON	Longinus	
HANDS	Hero's Shield	
HEAD	Grand Helm	
BODY	Brigandine	

SPOILS			
GIL	1792	EXP	0

ACCESSORIES: Attractorb, Gravitorb, Pearl Necklace, Dragonfly Orb, Back–Breaking Straw, Gold Hourglass, Victory Pendant, [HP] HP = 1, [HP] Near Death, Phoenix Down

3 ONION KNIGHT

LEVEL	94
RANK	S
BEHAVIOR	Tactician
DP CHANCE	Win battle (DP+1)
BATTLE MAP	World of Darkness (Ω)
SUMMONSTONE	Magic Pot

STATS					
HP	9017	CP	443	BRV	941
ATK	165	DEF	172	LUK	57

EQUIPMENT		
WEAPON	Royal Sword	
HANDS	Blurry Moon	
HEAD	Dueling Mask	
BODY	Brave Suit	

SPOILS			
GIL	1792	EXP	0

ACCESSORIES: Gaia Ring, Hyper Ring x2, [HP] HP = 100%, [BRV] No BRV Damage x2, [HP] HP = 1, [HP] Near Death, Phoenix Down

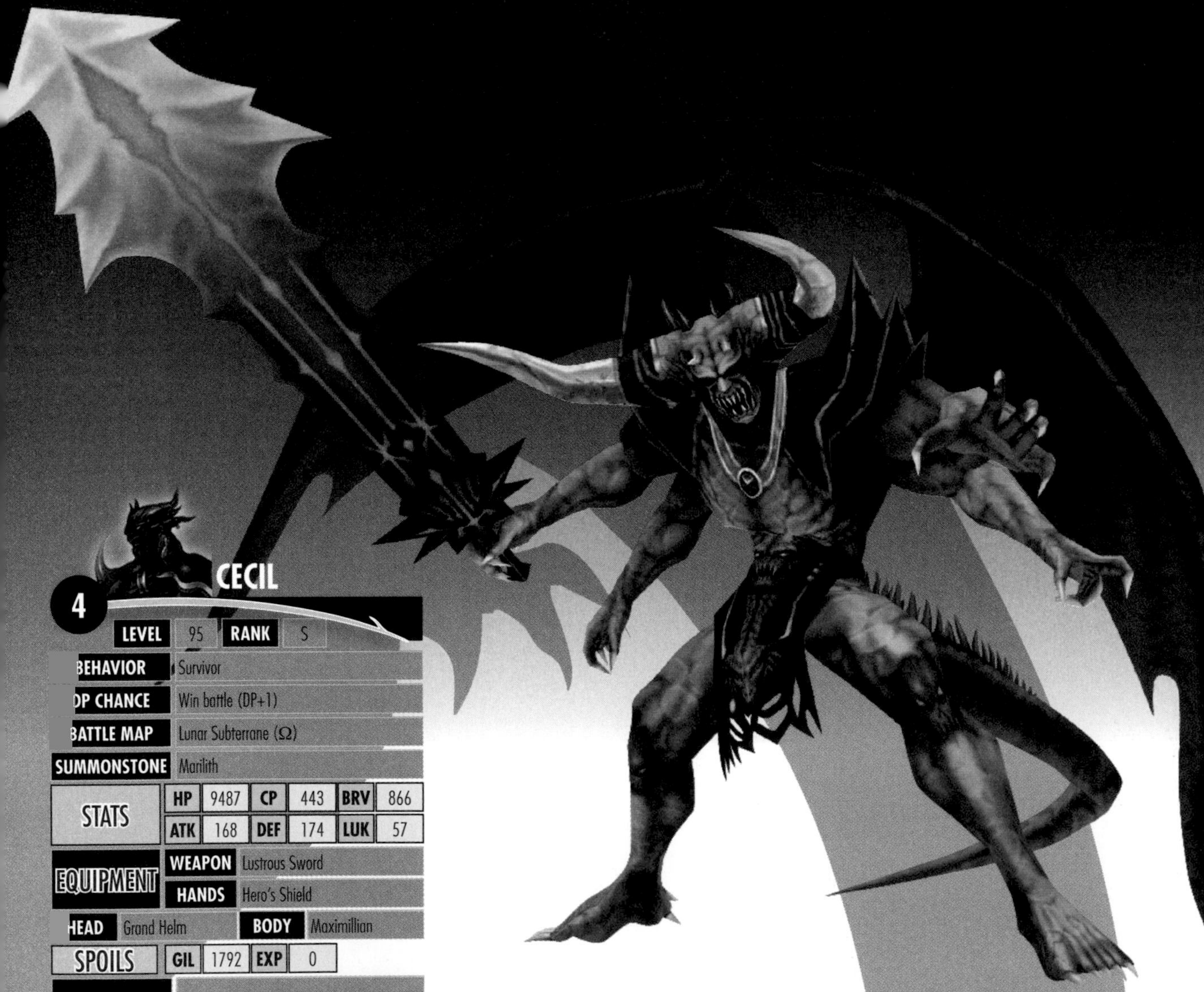

4 CECIL

LEVEL	95
RANK	S
BEHAVIOR	Survivor
DP CHANCE	Win battle (DP+1)
BATTLE MAP	Lunar Subterrane (Ω)
SUMMONSTONE	Marilith

STATS					
HP	9487	CP	443	BRV	866
ATK	168	DEF	174	LUK	57

EQUIPMENT		
WEAPON	Lustrous Sword	
HANDS	Hero's Shield	
HEAD	Grand Helm	
BODY	Maximillian	

SPOILS			
GIL	1792	EXP	0

ACCESSORIES: Gaia Ring, Hyper Ring x2, Champion Belt, Muscle Belt x2, Hyperstar, Booster x2

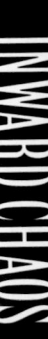

INWARD CHAOS

INWARD CHAOS 2

Intelligent use of EX Force is vital to success throughout Inward Chaos. A full EX Gauge is an insurance policy, since EX Mode activation can be used to escape from an attack in progress. Many accessories (Arcane Resin, Ivory Choker, Pretty Orb, and so on) help build EX Force more quickly, and the EXP to EX Force ability can speed the process along too. However, keep in mind that only one of the abilities that converts EXP to either EX Force, BRV, or HP can be equipped at a time—so weigh which is most valuable to you. Potions and the Aura skill are also helpful for building EX Force. EX Mode often offers special benefits depending on character, along with a vastly increased critical hit rate. Breaking the bravery of Inward Chaos enemies can be like kicking water uphill, so the extra criticals help. You might forego activating EX Mode until you're using it as a combo breaker of sorts; once EX Mode is active, you might pass up using EX Burst in favor of staying in EX Mode, reaping the rewards of extra criticals and Regen of either HP (naturally) or bravery (equip Bravery Regen ability).

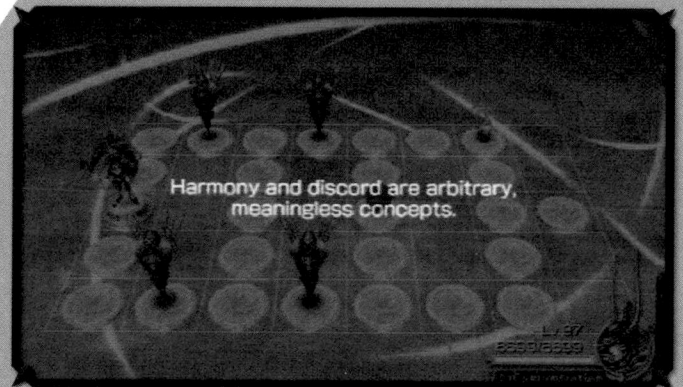

Harmony and discord are arbitrary, meaningless concepts.

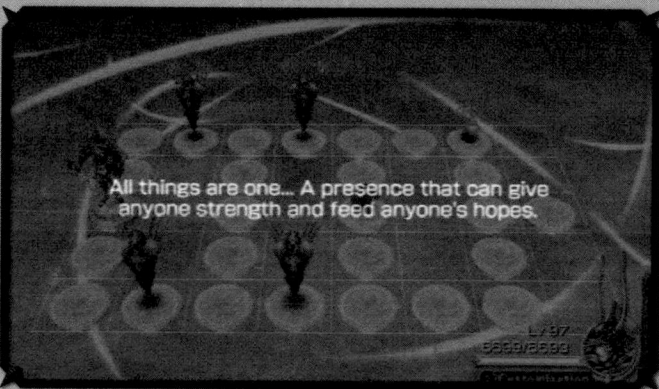

All things are one... A presence that can give anyone strength and feed anyone's hopes.

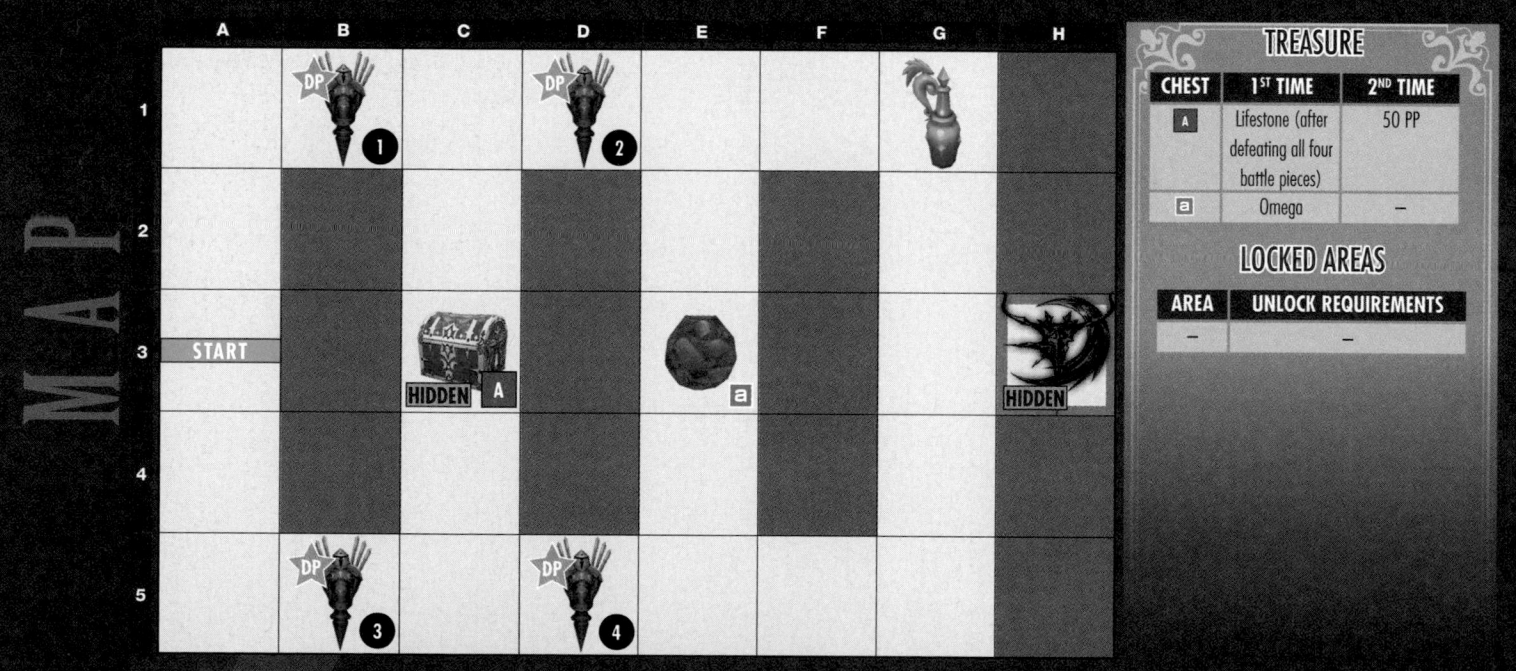

TREASURE

CHEST	1ST TIME	2ND TIME
A	Lifestone (after defeating all four battle pieces)	50 PP
a	Omega	–

LOCKED AREAS

AREA	UNLOCK REQUIREMENTS
–	–

DP EFFICIENCY ROUTE

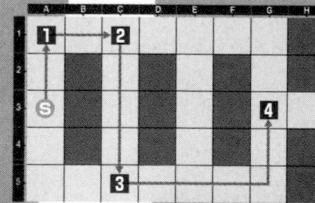

Engage battle piece ❶ first so you can move beyond it and engage battle piece ❷. Finally, engage in a two-part battle chain with battle pieces ❸ and ❹. The exit appears when all four pieces are subdued.

BATTLE PIECE DATA

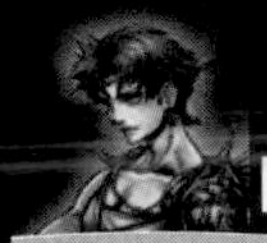

1 BARTZ

LEVEL	96	RANK	S

BEHAVIOR	Valiant
DP CHANCE	Win battle (DP+1)
BATTLE MAP	The Rift (Ω)
SUMMONSTONE	Scarmiglione

STATS	HP	9138	CP	445	BRV	952
	ATK	170	DEF	174	LUK	58

EQUIPMENT	WEAPON	Dayspring
	HANDS	Blurry Moon

HEAD	Dueling Mask	BODY	Brave Suit

SPOILS	GIL	1792	EXP	0

ACCESSORIES	Attractorb, Gravitorb, Pearl Necklace, Dragonfly Orb, Back-Breaking Straw, Gold Hourglass, Victory Pendant, [HP] HP = 1, [HP] Near Death, [HP] Near Loss

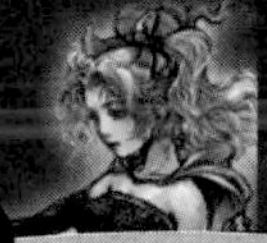

2 TERRA

LEVEL	97	RANK	S

BEHAVIOR	Vicious
DP CHANCE	Win battle (DP+1)
BATTLE MAP	Kefka's Tower (Ω)
SUMMONSTONE	Titan

STATS	HP	8943	CP	446	BRV	1117
	ATK	170	DEF	174	LUK	58

EQUIPMENT	WEAPON	Morning Star
	HANDS	Seydlitz

HEAD	Royal Crown	BODY	Rainbow Robes

SPOILS	GIL	1792	EXP	0

ACCESSORIES	Star Earring, Earring x2, [HP] HP = 100%, [BRV] No BRV Damage x2, [Position] Far from Opponent x3

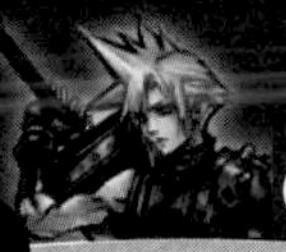

3 CLOUD

LEVEL	98	RANK	S

BEHAVIOR	Tactician
DP CHANCE	Win battle (DP+1)
BATTLE MAP	Planet's Core (Ω)
SUMMONSTONE	Shiva

STATS	HP	9719	CP	447	BRV	883
	ATK	172	DEF	178	LUK	59

EQUIPMENT	WEAPON	Butterfly Edge
	HANDS	Seydlitz

HEAD	Grand Helm	BODY	Brigandine

SPOILS	GIL	1792	EXP	0

ACCESSORIES	Gaia Ring, Hyper Ring x2, Sniper Soul, Sniper Eye x2, [Opponent] In Midair x3

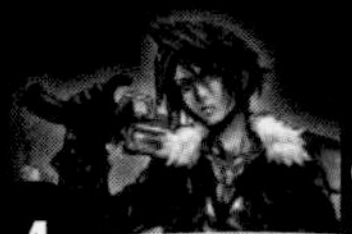

4 SQUALL

LEVEL	99	RANK	S

BEHAVIOR	Conservative
DP CHANCE	Win battle (DP+1)
BATTLE MAP	Ultimecia's Castle (Ω)
SUMMONSTONE	PuPu

STATS	HP	9655	CP	448	BRV	910
	ATK	171	DEF	184	LUK	59

EQUIPMENT	WEAPON	Punishment
	HANDS	Hero's Shield

HEAD	Grand Helm	BODY	Brigandine

SPOILS	GIL	1792	EXP	0

ACCESSORIES	Champion Belt, Muscle Belt x2, [Position] Near Opponent x3, [BRV] Break, [BRV] Near Break x2

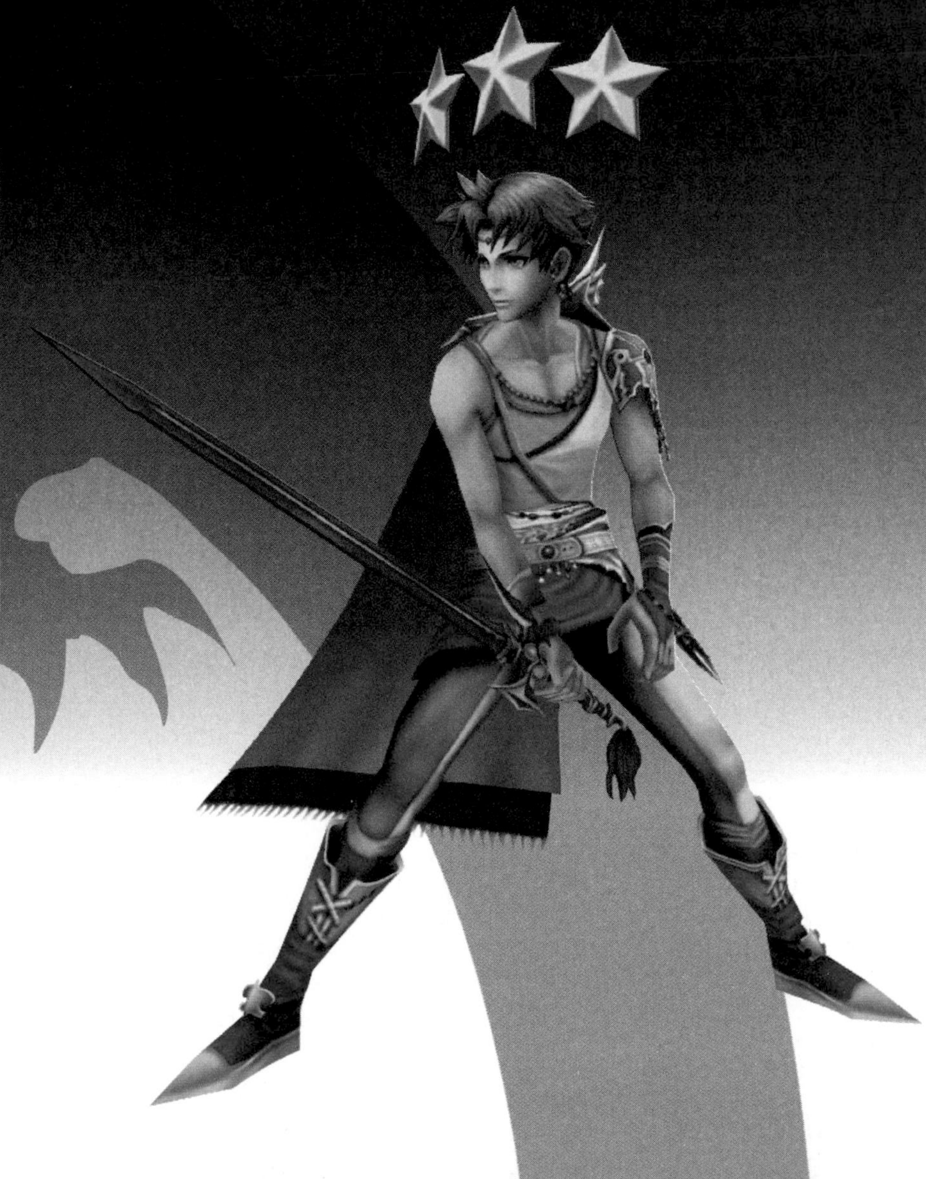

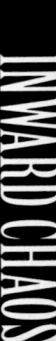

INWARD CHAOS

Foes inhabiting Inward Chaos come equipped with fantastic weapons and huge attack totals. Enemies throughout the five levels can easily inflict Break on you if they land a solid bravery attack or two. If they strike you with a bravery attack that hits multiple times, forget it—Break is assured. This immediately puts their bravery in the realm of 6000~9999, making every adversary extremely dangerous. If your foe ends a bravery attack with an HP attack finisher, you may be looking at what amounts to a frustrating one-hit loss! Accessories like Phoenix Down and Phoenix Pinion give you a second chance after receiving a deathblow, but are in limited supply and break after use. Solid equipment and accessories reduce your risk; happily, these foes sometimes drop the very pieces they're wearing upon defeat. The higher your luck stat, the more likely the drop. If you're seeking endgame drops for a particular character, find and fight that same character wherever he or she is in Inward Chaos. If the foe drops nothing after being defeated, pause the game and select "Quit Level Progression," then "Retry Level." Fight the enemy again, repeating until successful. You can also play the Duel Colosseum mode to gain this elite gear.

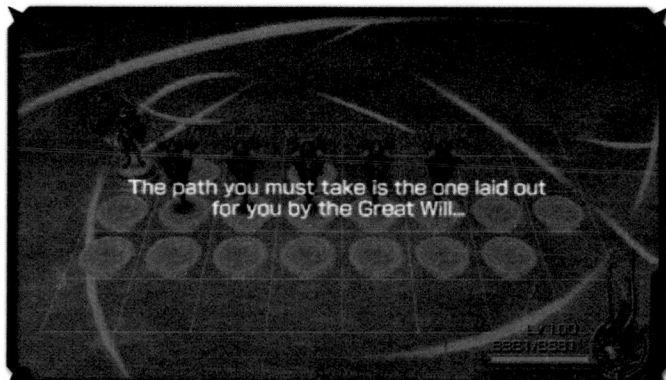

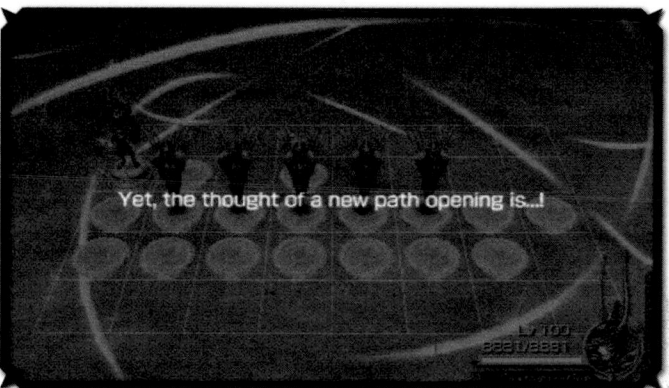

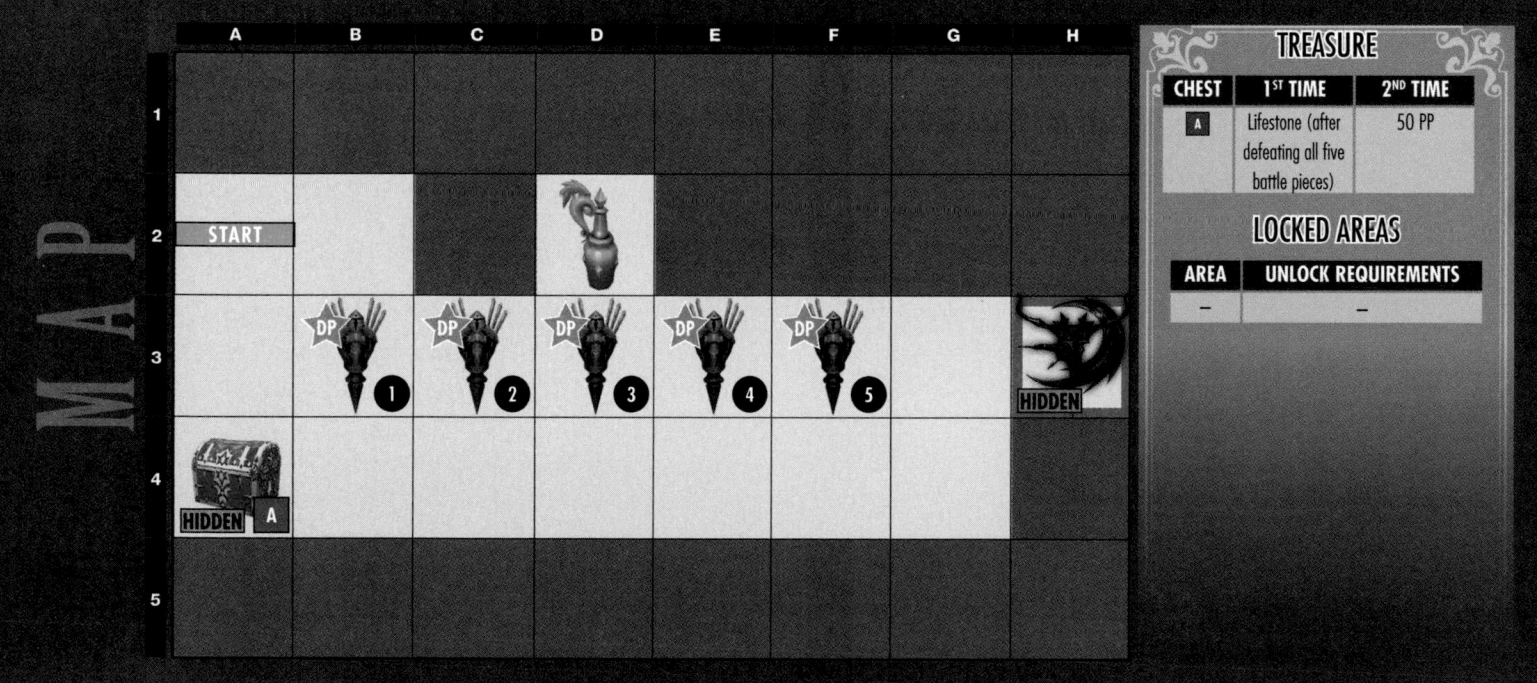

TREASURE		
CHEST	1ST TIME	2ND TIME
A	Lifestone (after defeating all five battle pieces)	50 PP

LOCKED AREAS	
AREA	UNLOCK REQUIREMENTS
–	–

DP EFFICIENCY ROUTE

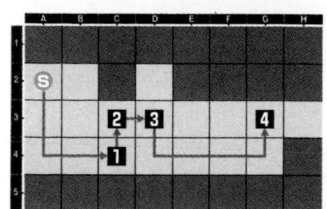

Battle piece **2** is the first target here. After it's defeated, a space opens at C-3. Move to this area to chain battle pieces **1** and **3**. Once they're down, move one square right to engage battle piece **4**. The Potion can be used if needed here, too. Finally, move to G-3 to engage battle piece **5**. When it falls, the exit appears right behind you.

BATTLE PIECE DATA

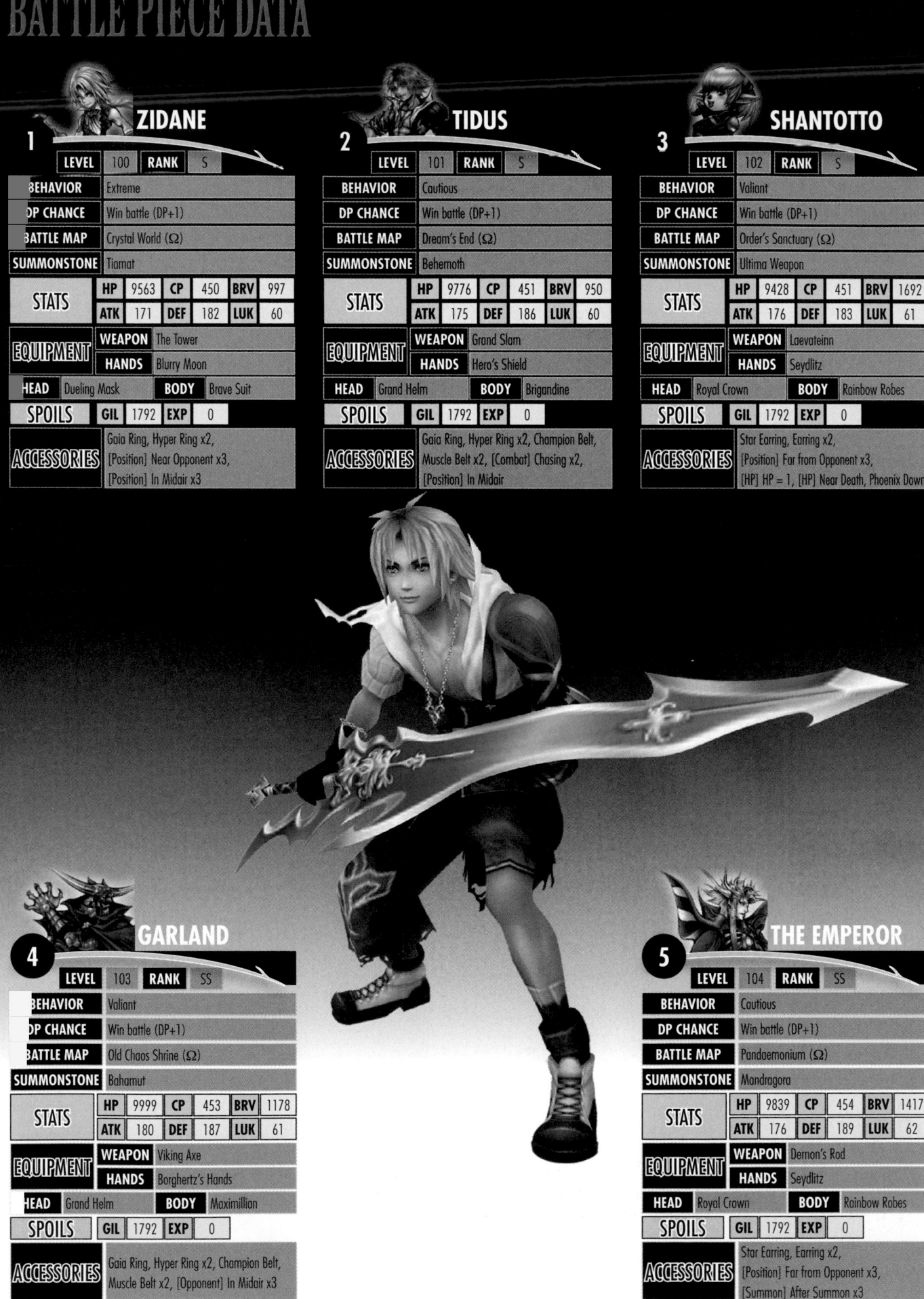

1 ZIDANE

LEVEL	100	RANK	S

BEHAVIOR	Extreme
DP CHANCE	Win battle (DP+1)
BATTLE MAP	Crystal World (Ω)
SUMMONSTONE	Tiamat

STATS	HP	9563	CP	450	BRV	997
	ATK	171	DEF	182	LUK	60

EQUIPMENT	WEAPON	The Tower
	HANDS	Blurry Moon

HEAD	Dueling Mask	BODY	Brave Suit

SPOILS	GIL	1792	EXP	0

ACCESSORIES	Gaia Ring, Hyper Ring x2, [Position] Near Opponent x3, [Position] In Midair x3

2 TIDUS

LEVEL	101	RANK	S

BEHAVIOR	Cautious
DP CHANCE	Win battle (DP+1)
BATTLE MAP	Dream's End (Ω)
SUMMONSTONE	Behemoth

STATS	HP	9776	CP	451	BRV	950
	ATK	175	DEF	186	LUK	60

EQUIPMENT	WEAPON	Grand Slam
	HANDS	Hero's Shield

HEAD	Grand Helm	BODY	Brigandine

SPOILS	GIL	1792	EXP	0

ACCESSORIES	Gaia Ring, Hyper Ring x2, Champion Belt, Muscle Belt x2, [Combat] Chasing x2, [Position] In Midair

3 SHANTOTTO

LEVEL	102	RANK	S

BEHAVIOR	Valiant
DP CHANCE	Win battle (DP+1)
BATTLE MAP	Order's Sanctuary (Ω)
SUMMONSTONE	Ultima Weapon

STATS	HP	9428	CP	451	BRV	1692
	ATK	176	DEF	183	LUK	61

EQUIPMENT	WEAPON	Laevateinn
	HANDS	Seydlitz

HEAD	Royal Crown	BODY	Rainbow Robes

SPOILS	GIL	1792	EXP	0

ACCESSORIES	Star Earring, Earring x2, [Position] Far from Opponent x3, [HP] HP = 1, [HP] Near Death, Phoenix Down

4 GARLAND

LEVEL	103	RANK	SS

BEHAVIOR	Valiant
DP CHANCE	Win battle (DP+1)
BATTLE MAP	Old Chaos Shrine (Ω)
SUMMONSTONE	Bahamut

STATS	HP	9999	CP	453	BRV	1178
	ATK	180	DEF	187	LUK	61

EQUIPMENT	WEAPON	Viking Axe
	HANDS	Borghertz's Hands

HEAD	Grand Helm	BODY	Maximillian

SPOILS	GIL	1792	EXP	0

ACCESSORIES	Gaia Ring, Hyper Ring x2, Champion Belt, Muscle Belt x2, [Opponent] In Midair x3

5 THE EMPEROR

LEVEL	104	RANK	SS

BEHAVIOR	Cautious
DP CHANCE	Win battle (DP+1)
BATTLE MAP	Pandaemonium (Ω)
SUMMONSTONE	Mandragora

STATS	HP	9839	CP	454	BRV	1417
	ATK	176	DEF	189	LUK	62

EQUIPMENT	WEAPON	Demon's Rod
	HANDS	Seydlitz

HEAD	Royal Crown	BODY	Rainbow Robes

SPOILS	GIL	1792	EXP	0

ACCESSORIES	Star Earring, Earring x2, [Position] Far from Opponent x3, [Summon] After Summon x3

INWARD CHAOS

STARTING DP	MAX FINISHING	ENGAGEMENTS
1	2	5

Summons can easily tip the scales against most of these enemies. Due to their advanced behavior and strong defense, Bravery Break can be hard to inflict directly. Meanwhile, as discussed previously, it's pretty easy for them to inflict Break on you, regardless of your level or outfitting. This ends up as something of a double-edged sword. Their otherwise horrifying bravery total approaching 9999 becomes savory when you bring along Magic Pot or Kraken. These summons are great equalizers, allowing wins where wins are otherwise unlikely—let the enemies build up bravery until it surpasses their HP, while avoiding HP attacks—of course. Victory is then just a matter of stealing their bravery with either summon, then landing a single HP attack.

You'll have to do one better against foes packing a Phoenix Down or Phoenix Pinion, as they'll survive with 1 HP, but the victory is still far easier than grinding it out straight up. The caveat to winning with this method is that it only goes so far, as Magic Pot and Kraken are expended after two uses each, and must rest in order to recharge. You can close the gap by using Magic Pot AUTO while these summons are shelved. Assuming Magic Pot is used for two battles, then Kraken for two, then Magic Pot AUTO for three, you'll only have one battle to win with a different summon before Magic Pot is charged and ready to begin the cycle again. Only Bartz during Inward Chaos 2 can thwart an attempt to flip bravery. And remember that Chaos, the final opponent of Inward Chaos, must be defeated three times in a row, so bravery flipping ultimately only helps for one of the fights.

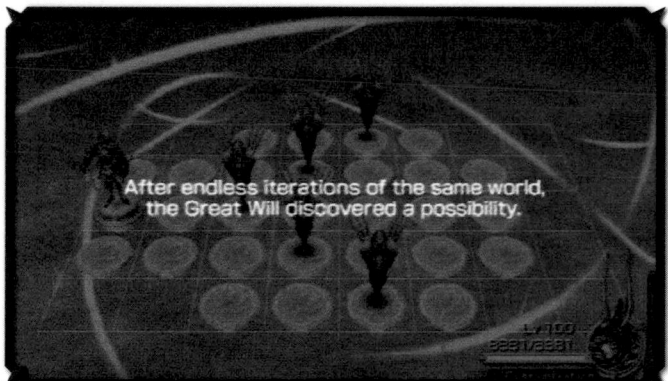

After endless iterations of the same world, the Great Will discovered a possibility.

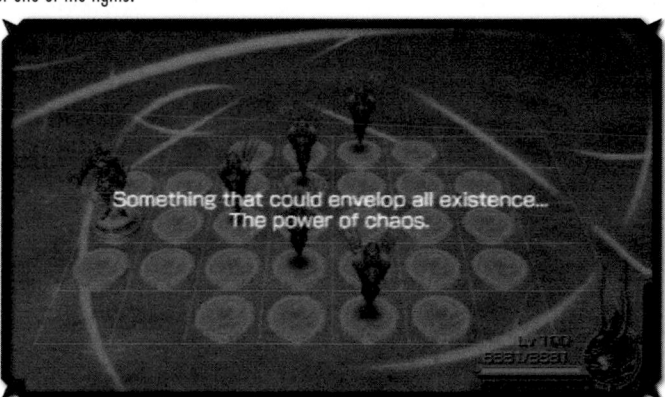

Something that could envelop all existence... The power of chaos.

MAP

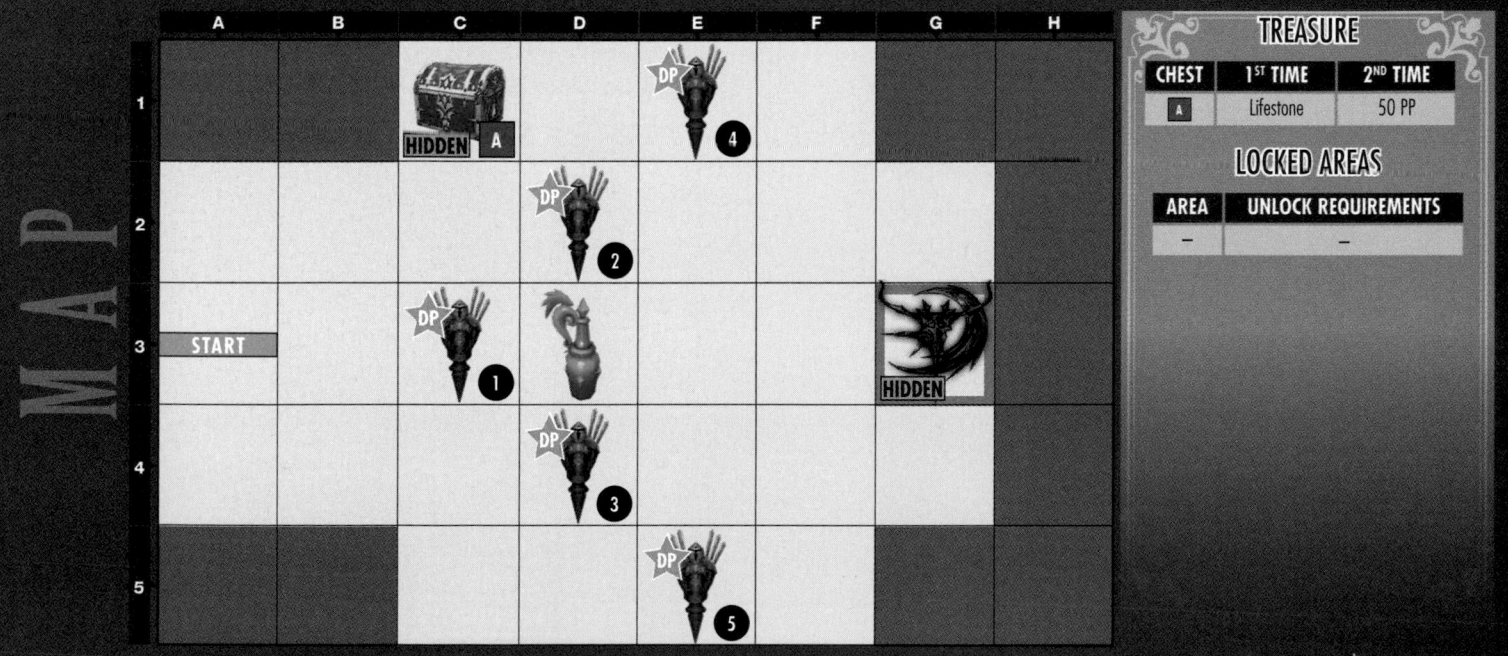

TREASURE

CHEST	1ST TIME	2ND TIME
A	Lifestone	50 PP

LOCKED AREAS

AREA	UNLOCK REQUIREMENTS
—	—

DP EFFICIENCY ROUTE

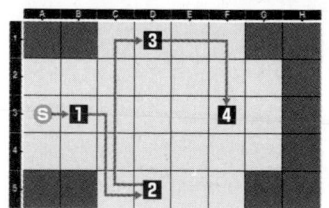

From the start, move right slightly to take on battle piece ❶. After it falls, head down to D-5 to engage battle pieces ❸ and ❺ in a two-part chain. Next, move to D-1 to chain battle pieces ❷ and ❹. Once these are both defeated, treasure chest Ⓐ appears right next to you while the exit materializes to the right.

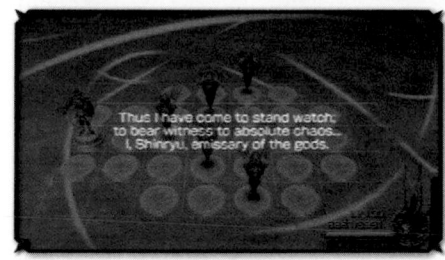

Thus I have come to stand watch, to bear witness to absolute chaos... I, Shinryu, emissary of the gods.

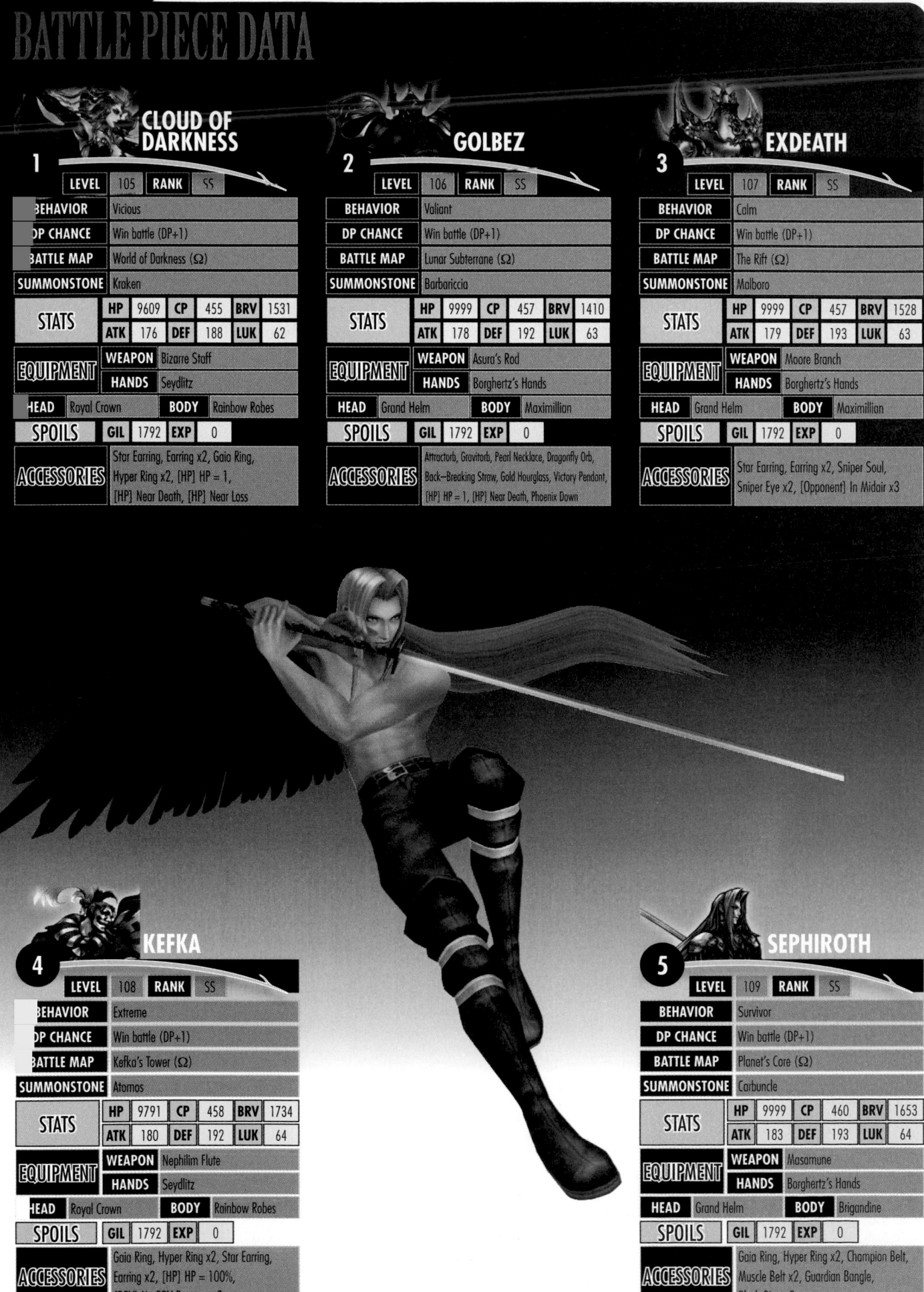

BATTLE PIECE DATA

1 CLOUD OF DARKNESS

LEVEL	105	RANK	SS

BEHAVIOR	Vicious
DP CHANCE	Win battle (DP+1)
BATTLE MAP	World of Darkness (Ω)
SUMMONSTONE	Kraken

STATS	HP	9609	CP	455	BRV	1531
	ATK	176	DEF	188	LUK	62

EQUIPMENT	WEAPON	Bizarre Staff
	HANDS	Seydlitz

HEAD	Royal Crown	BODY	Rainbow Robes

SPOILS	GIL	1792	EXP	0

ACCESSORIES	Star Earring, Earring x2, Gaia Ring, Hyper Ring x2, [HP] HP = 1, [HP] Near Death, [HP] Near Loss

2 GOLBEZ

LEVEL	106	RANK	SS

BEHAVIOR	Valiant
DP CHANCE	Win battle (DP+1)
BATTLE MAP	Lunar Subterrane (Ω)
SUMMONSTONE	Barbariccia

STATS	HP	9999	CP	457	BRV	1410
	ATK	178	DEF	192	LUK	63

EQUIPMENT	WEAPON	Asura's Rod
	HANDS	Borghertz's Hands

HEAD	Grand Helm	BODY	Maximillian

SPOILS	GIL	1792	EXP	0

ACCESSORIES	Attractorb, Gravitorb, Pearl Necklace, Dragonfly Orb, Back-Breaking Straw, Gold Hourglass, Victory Pendant, [HP] HP = 1, [HP] Near Death, Phoenix Down

3 EXDEATH

LEVEL	107	RANK	SS

BEHAVIOR	Calm
DP CHANCE	Win battle (DP+1)
BATTLE MAP	The Rift (Ω)
SUMMONSTONE	Malboro

STATS	HP	9999	CP	457	BRV	1528
	ATK	179	DEF	193	LUK	63

EQUIPMENT	WEAPON	Moore Branch
	HANDS	Borghertz's Hands

HEAD	Grand Helm	BODY	Maximillian

SPOILS	GIL	1792	EXP	0

ACCESSORIES	Star Earring, Earring x2, Sniper Soul, Sniper Eye x2, [Opponent] In Midair x3

4 KEFKA

LEVEL	108	RANK	SS

BEHAVIOR	Extreme
DP CHANCE	Win battle (DP+1)
BATTLE MAP	Kefka's Tower (Ω)
SUMMONSTONE	Atomos

STATS	HP	9791	CP	458	BRV	1734
	ATK	180	DEF	192	LUK	64

EQUIPMENT	WEAPON	Nephilim Flute
	HANDS	Seydlitz

HEAD	Royal Crown	BODY	Rainbow Robes

SPOILS	GIL	1792	EXP	0

ACCESSORIES	Gaia Ring, Hyper Ring x2, Star Earring, Earring x2, [HP] HP = 100%, [BRV] No BRV Damage x2

5 SEPHIROTH

LEVEL	109	RANK	SS

BEHAVIOR	Survivor
DP CHANCE	Win battle (DP+1)
BATTLE MAP	Planet's Core (Ω)
SUMMONSTONE	Carbuncle

STATS	HP	9999	CP	460	BRV	1653
	ATK	183	DEF	193	LUK	64

EQUIPMENT	WEAPON	Masamune
	HANDS	Borghertz's Hands

HEAD	Grand Helm	BODY	Brigandine

SPOILS	GIL	1792	EXP	0

ACCESSORIES	Gaia Ring, Hyper Ring x2, Champion Belt, Muscle Belt x2, Guardian Bangle, Block Ring x2

INWARD CHAOS

First, note that treasure chest **A** contains Chemist Lore. This treasure chest only appears after defeating all four battle pieces on this stage. This lore item allows a character to learn the ability to use machine weapons from the Shop. Normally, no character can equip machines! As with all other levels of Inward Chaos, the Stigma of Chaos appears after defeating every battle piece. This time it's not the exit, but a boss fight with a lv.110 version of Chaos. While his behavior, equipment, and abilities are identical to his Shade Impulse 4 incarnation, he far outstrips his earlier counterpart in ferocity. You'll have to beat him three consecutive times as before. If you have any skills left that damage enemies prior to battle, unload them on Chaos before engaging.

Entering this battle equipped with the Magic Pot Summonstone and sporting a full EX Gauge is strongly advised. If necessary, chug the Potion at C-5 pre-battle to fill HP and EX Force. Like the climax of Shade Impulse 4, dodging and punishing his HP attacks is absolutely critical. If you are hit with Divine Punishment or Soul of Oblivion, the fight is probably over, or close to it. Save a full EX Gauge and use it expressly to interrupt a deathblow, then land an EX Burst if possible. Keep a watchful eye out for EX Cores to replenish EX Force. If you land a deathblow during EX Mode prior to the EX Burst, intentionally cancel the EX Burst opportunity with ●. Your EX Force for the next form of Chaos then carries over, wherever it was. If you use an unnecessary EX Burst, you'll start against the next form with an empty EX Gauge. If you've brought along Magic Pot, save it for the third form. Beating forms one and two doesn't matter if you lose to the third form, so it's best to backload your arsenal, saving the best firepower for last.

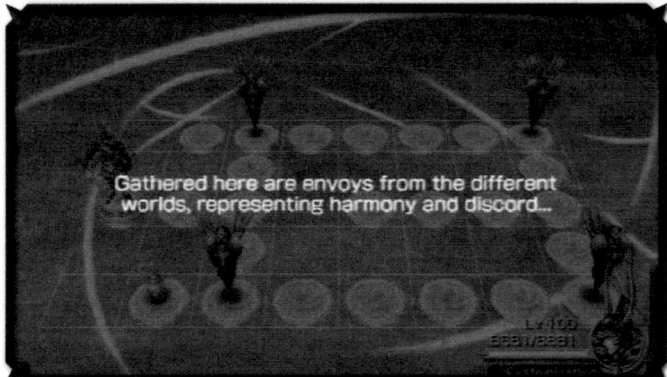

Gathered here are envoys from the different worlds, representing harmony and discord...

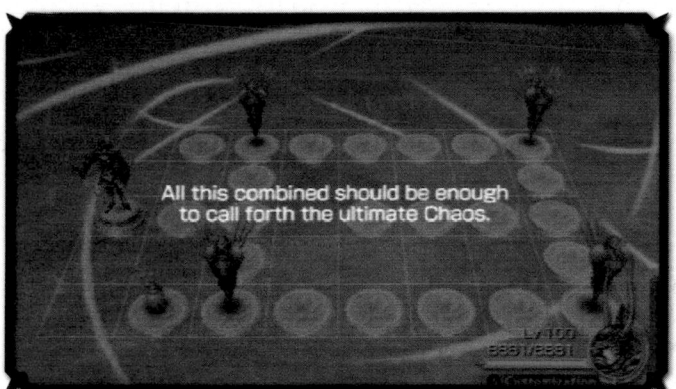

All this combined should be enough to call forth the ultimate Chaos.

MAP

	A	B	C	D	E	F	G	H
1			DP ❶					DP ❸
2								
3	START	HIDDEN A			BOSS / HIDDEN ❺			
4								
5		Potion	DP ❷					DP ❹

TREASURE

CHEST	1ST TIME	2ND TIME
A	Chemist Lore (after defeating all four battle pieces)	50 PP

LOCKED AREAS

AREA	UNLOCK REQUIREMENTS
–	–

DP EFFICIENCY ROUTE

Battle pieces here are spread to the four corners, meaning you'll simply have to trudge to each and take them on one at a time. Begin with battle piece ❶ in the upper left before moving down to battle piece ❷. Afterward, head right and engage battle piece ❹, then battle piece ❸. The Stigma of Chaos, this time representing Chaos himself, spawns in the center of the level once all four surrounding battle pieces are defeated.

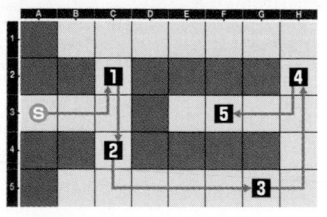

BATTLE PIECE DATA

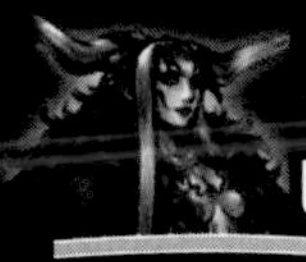

1 ULTIMECIA

LEVEL	110	RANK	SS

BEHAVIOR	Tactician
DP CHANCE	Win battle (DP+1)
BATTLE MAP	Ultimecia's Castle (Ω)
SUMMONSTONE	Alexander

STATS	HP	9999	CP	462	BRV	1899
	ATK	183	DEF	192	LUK	65

EQUIPMENT	WEAPON	Cardinal
	HANDS	Seydlitz

HEAD	Royal Crown	BODY	Rainbow Robes

SPOILS	GIL	1792	EXP	0

ACCESSORIES	Star Earring, Earring x2, [Position] Far from Opponent x3, [HP] HP = 1, [HP] Near Death, Phoenix Down

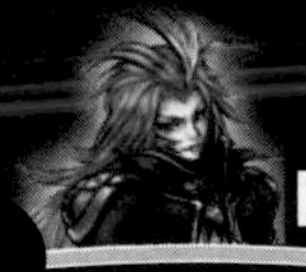

2 KUJA

LEVEL	110	RANK	SS

BEHAVIOR	Conservative
DP CHANCE	Win battle (DP+1)
BATTLE MAP	Crystal World (Ω)
SUMMONSTONE	Lich

STATS	HP	9999	CP	462	BRV	1899
	ATK	181	DEF	194	LUK	65

EQUIPMENT	WEAPON	Whale Whisker
	HANDS	Seydlitz

HEAD	Royal Crown	BODY	Rainbow Robes

SPOILS	GIL	1792	EXP	0

ACCESSORIES	Star Earring, Earring x2, [Position] Near Opponent x3, [Position] Far from Opponent x3

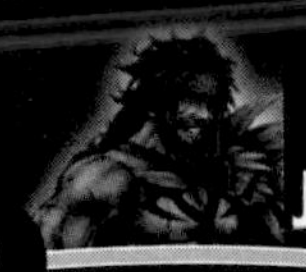

3 JECHT

LEVEL	110	RANK	SS

BEHAVIOR	Tactician
DP CHANCE	Win battle (DP+1)
BATTLE MAP	Dream's End (Ω)
SUMMONSTONE	Rubicante

STATS	HP	9999	CP	462	BRV	1774
	ATK	185	DEF	195	LUK	65

EQUIPMENT	WEAPON	Sin's Talon
	HANDS	Seydlitz

HEAD	Grand Helm	BODY	Brigandine

SPOILS	GIL	1792	EXP	0

ACCESSORIES	Gaia Ring, Hyper Ring x2, Champion Belt, Muscle Belt x2, [Position] Near Opponent x3

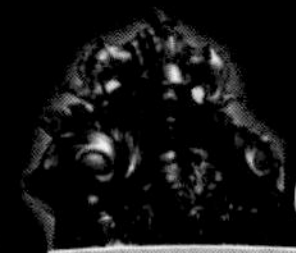

4 GABRANTH

LEVEL	110	RANK	SS

BEHAVIOR	Vicious
DP CHANCE	Win battle (DP+1)
BATTLE MAP	Order's Sanctuary (Ω)
SUMMONSTONE	Omega

STATS	HP	9999	CP	459	BRV	1697
	ATK	182	DEF	192	LUK	65

EQUIPMENT	WEAPON	Deathbringer
	HANDS	Highway Star

HEAD	Grand Helm	BODY	Maximillian

SPOILS	GIL	1792	EXP	0

ACCESSORIES	Gold Hourglass, Silver Hourglass x2, [HP] HP = 100%, [BRV] No BRV Damage x2, [HP] HP = 1, [HP] Near Death, Phoenix Down

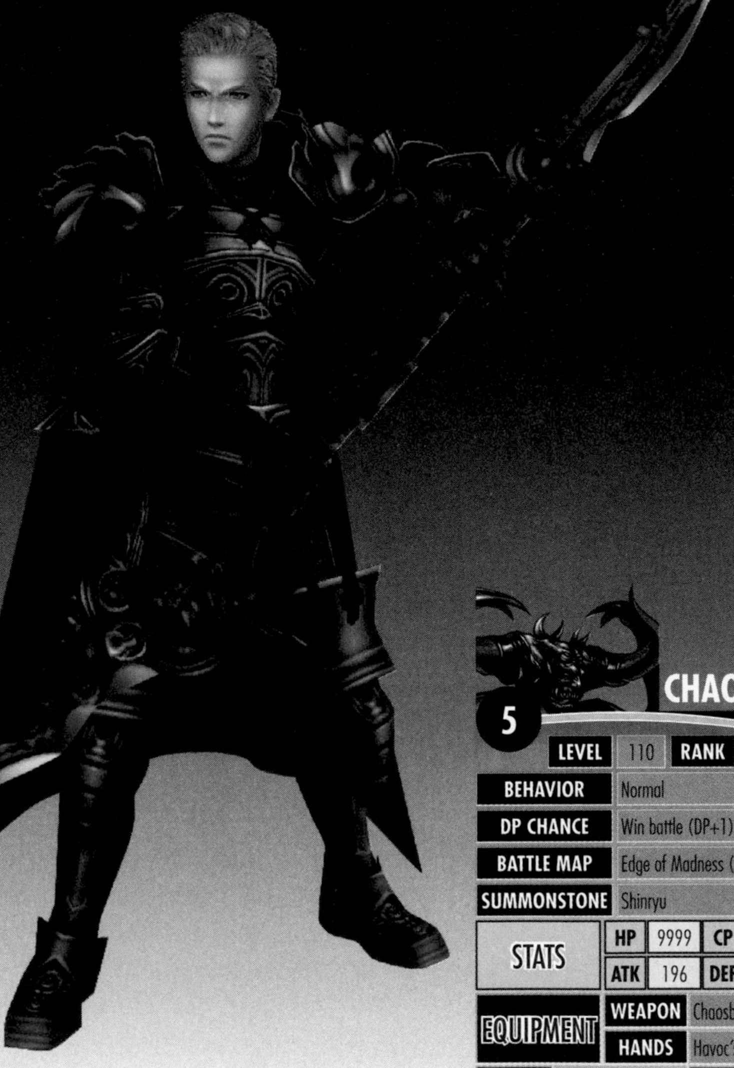

5 CHAOS

LEVEL	110	RANK	SS

BEHAVIOR	Normal
DP CHANCE	Win battle (DP+1)
BATTLE MAP	Edge of Madness (Ω)
SUMMONSTONE	Shinryu

STATS	HP	9999	CP	462	BRV	1809
	ATK	196	DEF	202	LUK	65

EQUIPMENT	WEAPON	Chaosbringer
	HANDS	Havoc's Carapace

HEAD	Bedlam's Crown	BODY	Entropy's Aegis

SPOILS	GIL	25200	EXP	19010

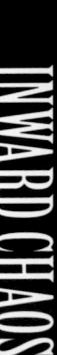

INWARD CHAOS

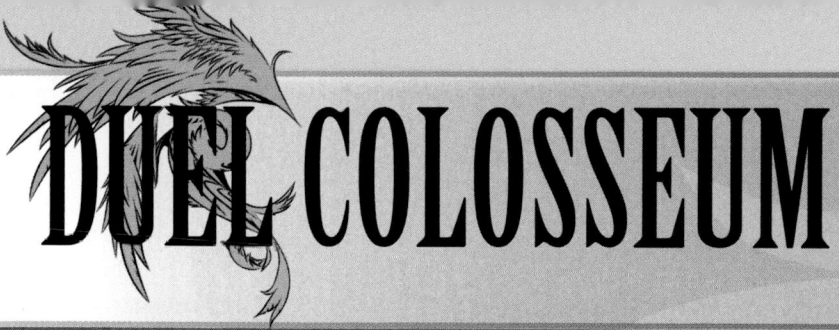

DUEL COLOSSEUM

The Duel Colosseum is unlocked after the completion of Shade Impulse Chapter 4. This unique mode is packed with useful items, difficult foes who hold rare equipment, and a random factor that makes every trip an interesting one.

COLOSSEUM BASICS

When you enter the Colosseum, you'll choose a single character and you won't have an opportunity to switch until you opt to end your game. The Duel Colosseum never ends; you can keep at it for as long as you want, although if you run out of cards, you'll be left with no option but to head to the exit. Whether you're leaving under duress or at the end of a long and successful run, you'll get to keep every treasure you bought with your Colosseum medals and earn an additional prize of PP if you have medals left over.

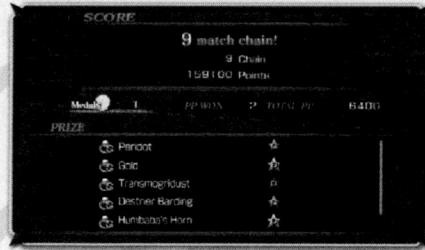

CHOOSE YOUR COURSE

There are five different Duel Colosseum courses: Airship, Falcon, Invincible, Lunar Whale, and Blackjack. Each course has tougher foes than the one before it and a different assortment of prizes, but the courses play out in the exact same way. The Airship and Falcon courses are initially selectable, but the Invincible and Lunar Whale courses must be unlocked from the PP Catalog. The Blackjack Course can also be unlocked from the PP Catalog, but you won't get the option until you complete the Inward Chaos Story Mode.

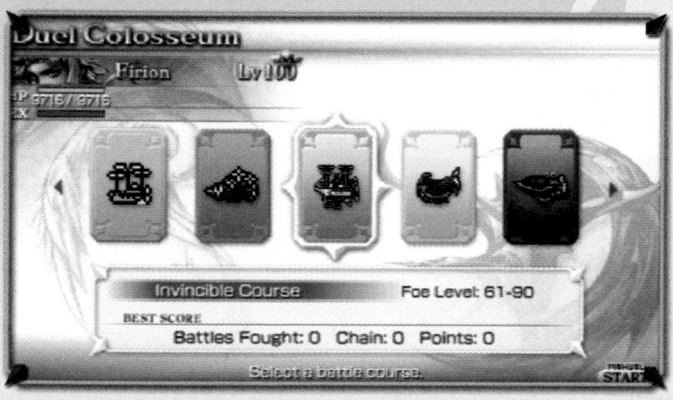

DRAWING CARDS

When you begin your Duel Colosseum game, you'll be dealt a hand of three cards, along with the Exit Card (which you only play when you're ready to exit the Colosseum). When you play a card, the other cards in your hand typically get discarded, and you'll draw the next three cards from the bottomless deck. To the right of your hand, you can see the backs of the cards in the deck, allowing you to tell when Treasure and Job Cards are coming (but not which ones).

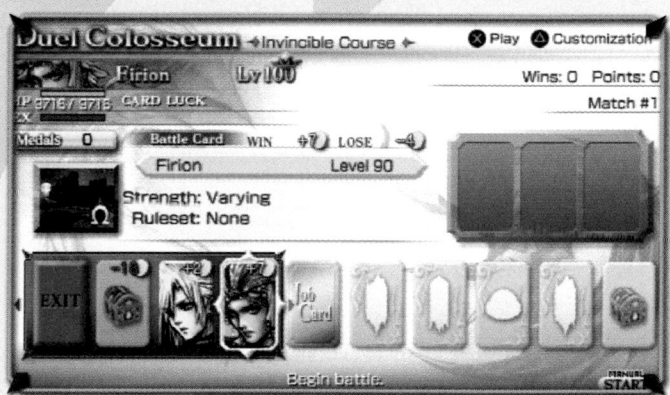

Battle Cards: Battle Cards depict the face of an enemy that you can battle to earn medals. Highlight the card to see the level of your foe and the foe's strength, as well as the battlefield on which you'll fight and any special rulesets. Above that information you'll see the amount of medals you'll earn for a victory and the amount you'll lose for a loss.

Treasure Cards: You earn medals from Battle Cards and spend them on Treasure Cards. When you select a Treasure Card, you'll see the item it contains, the amount of that item you're already holding, and its medal cost. Try to keep a healthy supply of medals around so you'll always be able to buy new items when they roll around.

Job Cards: On the right side of the screen you'll find the "Job Cells," an area with three slots for Job Cards. Job Cards change the rules of the game (typically in your favor) by making battles worth more medals, making treasure cheaper, providing regular healing, and so on. You can only fit three Job Cards into your Job Cells, so once you fill up the three slots, the next Job Card you take will cause the oldest Job Card to be discarded.

CARD LUCK

In the upper-left corner of the screen, your Card Luck is measured in blue stars. As you win battles, particularly against strong foes, your Card Luck rises, and as you lose, it falls. Card Luck determines the rarity level of Treasure Cards that appear and the difficulty level of Battle Cards, gradually raising both the risks and rewards as you play. Job Cards also appear more frequently as your luck rises. You can manipulate Card Luck with certain Job Cards, but you should resist the temptation to do so if you're having trouble against the Battle Cards you are currently being dealt.

RISKS AND REWARDS OF COMBAT

If you fail to defeat a Battle Card, you stand to lose much more than a few medals. Whenever you lose a battle, your hand size shrinks by one (or, if you have a Knight Card in your Job Cell, it becomes inactive). The smaller your hand, the fewer your options, and the closer you get to playing that Exit Card. The only perk to losing is getting your HP completely refilled. When you win a battle, you instead get only 30% of your Max HP refilled, while your EX Gauge stays exactly as it was at the end of the fight.

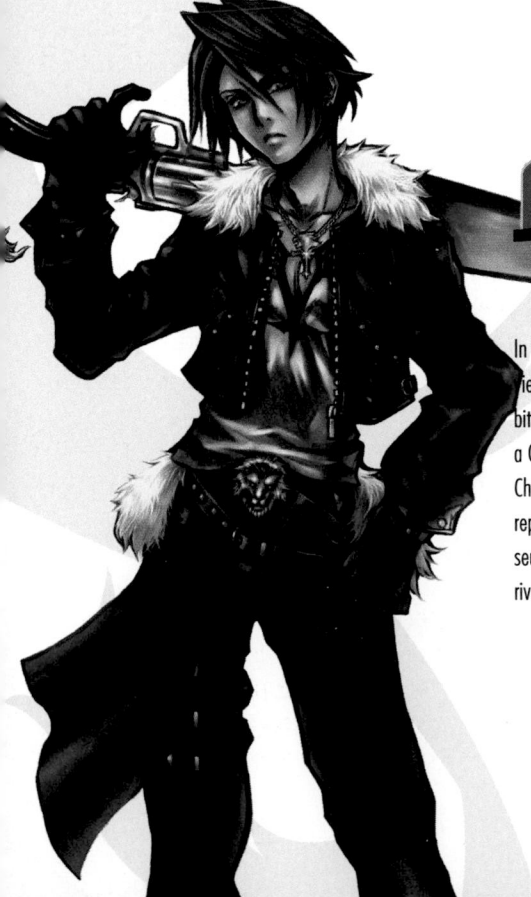

SPECIAL BATTLE CARDS

There are three special types of Battle Cards. You'll see them more and more frequently as your Card Luck rises.

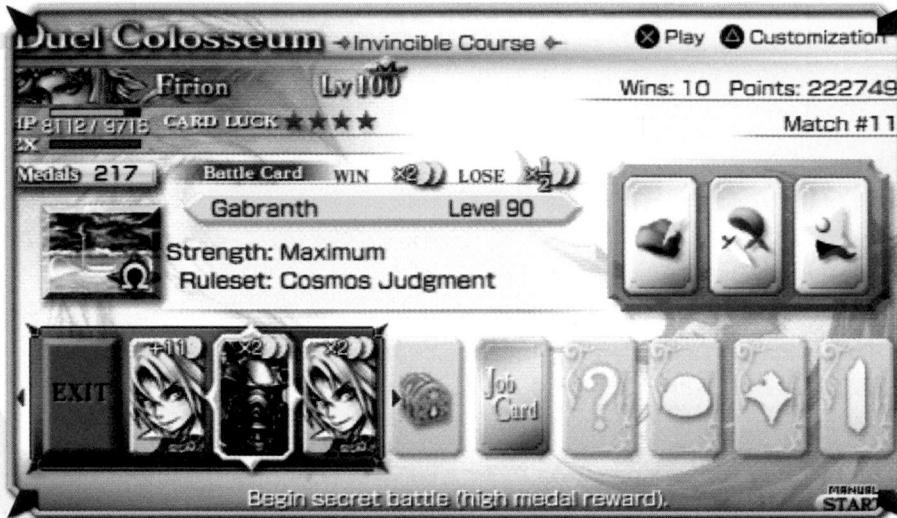

Boss Cards: These stay in your hand until you play them, and typically contain more challenging foes. Deal with them promptly, or their presence can severely limit your options each turn.

Chaos Cards: When Chaos appears, he's always a Boss Card. You'll have to fight the full three rounds of the battle to get it out of your hand. At least he's worth a nice pile of medals!

Secret Cards: Secret Cards are like normal Battle Cards, but they offer a much sweeter deal. Beat them and your current medal total doubles; lose and it drops by one half.

EARNING CHAOS REPORTS

In the Museum (available from the Main Menu), you can view the Chaos Reports and Cosmos Reports that provide a bit more story for each of the game's combatants. To earn a Cosmos character's report, you must beat Shade Impulse Chapter 4 with that character. However, to earn a Chaos report, you have to take that character into the Duel Colosseum and beat the Boss Card of that character's Cosmos rival (the hero character from the same game).

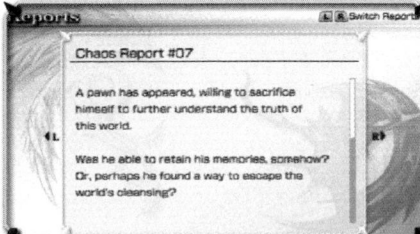

GETTING A JOB

Job Cards twist the rules of the Colosseum to an extent that can radically change the way you play the game. Once played, a Job Card goes to the "Job Cells" on the right side of the screen. Most Job Cards have a continuous effect as long as they're there, but some cards have a one-use effect and then just clog up space in the Job Cells (Job Cards without active effects turn grey).

The best Job Card is probably the Knight; whether you're looking for Treasure Cards or rare item drops, you always have more options with a larger hand. The Knight Card also effectively protects you from having your hand size permanently reduced (although losing "kills" the Knight Card, forcing you to cycle through your jobs to get rid of it and open up another space). Not all Job Cards are helpful; in addition to bad conditions like Frog, you can trap yourself by playing cards like Red Mage at the wrong time. Always think a few steps ahead before you play a Job Card!

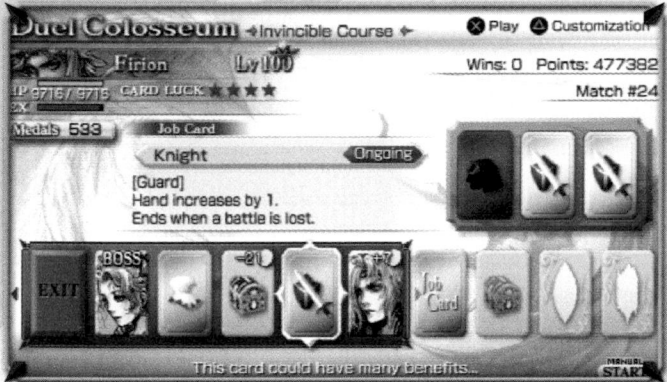

ONE-USE JOB CARDS

Dragoon: Discards your hand and draws another hand, which will also have a Dragoon Card in it. The Dragoon lets you continuously filter your hand, but clogs up your Job Cells with spent Dragoon Cards. This is a great card to play early in order to get you to your first Knight Card, but don't use it if you like the jobs you already have.

Mimic: Turns into a random Job Card when it enters the Job Cells. Most Job Cards have positive effects, but there's a chance it could backfire by turning into a Status Ailment Card or an untimely Red Mage Card.

Monk: Causes the next batch of Battle Cards you draw to be at the lowest possible strength for your course. This is only useful when challenging difficult courses.

Samurai: Discards all Boss or Chaos Battle Cards in your hand. This is a godsend on difficult courses when your hand fills up with battles you know you can't win.

Summoner: Fills your hands with Job Cards and half-price Treasure Cards. This is a great effect when you don't have a lot of continuous Job Cards that you want to keep.

CONTINUOUS JOB CARDS

Black Mage: The Black Mage causes you to draw Secret Battle Cards (Battle Cards that double your medals when defeated) more frequently.

Blue Mage: The Blue Mage causes you to draw Job Cards more frequently. If your Job Cells are empty or you'd like to rotate out what you have, this dramatically increases your Job Card options.

Chemist: The Chemist ends the effects of any Status Ailment Job Cards in your Job Cells and keeps any further Status Ailment Job Cards from being drawn.

Knight: Increases your hand size by 1. If you lose a battle, the effect ends and the Knight card turns inactive, but you will not suffer the usual penalty of a permanent hand-size reduction. If you can find them, you'll want one or two of these in your Job Cells at all times.

Mystic Knight: Card Luck rises more quickly. As with the Time Mage, this leads you to both rarer Treasure Cards and harder foes.

Ninja: While the Ninja is in your Job Cells, you won't lose medals or Card Luck for losing battles. This isn't as powerful as it sounds, since you'll still suffer the hand-size reduction penalty for losses, but it's a nice insurance policy to have when challenging a Secret Battle Card on a tough course.

Ranger: The Ranger adds 5 medals to the prize pool of every Battle Card. This is a fantastic effect to draw early in the game, but less important later when you'll be getting most of your medals by doubling up with Secret Battle Cards.

Red Mage: The Red Mage reduces the cost of all Treasure Cards to 0. It also causes cards to stay in your hand until played, so you only draw one new card per turn. This is an extraordinarily powerful effect, but it can be disastrous when you don't get many Treasure Cards and have to choose a tough battle each and every turn. (Remember, you can't turn the effect off until you play three more Job Cards, which could take 50 or more turns to show up with the Red Mage in effect.) You generally shouldn't play this unless you have a Thief Card or were just about ready to head to the exit.

Thief: The Thief lets you draw Treasure Cards more often. Don't play it until you've amassed a nice stock of medals, or you'll quickly run out of medals and space in your hand. If you can get a Thief and a Red Mage in your Job Cells together, you can go on one hell of a shopping spree.

Time Mage: The Time Mage increases your Card Luck to five stars. That'll make rare Treasure Cards appear earlier than usual, but it also means tougher Battle Cards.

White Mage: The White Mage refills your HP when played and sticks around to completely refill your HP after each subsequent battle.

STATUS AILMENT JOB CARDS

Imp (Ongoing): The Job Cards in your Job Cells have no effect.

Mini (Ongoing): HP does not refill after battle, even if you also have a White Mage in your Job Cells.

Pig (One-Use): You lose half of your medal supply.

Toad (Ongoing): Treasure Cards are no longer drawn.

TREASURE HUNTING IN THE COLOSSEUM

Each course has its own unique selection of treasures, typically consisting of 30-40 rare trade ingredients and an exclusive series of weapons and armaments. In the PP Catalog, you can buy options that add the trade accessories in each of the first four courses to the shop, but to buy those accessories, you'll need to be able to trade one more of the Elixirs that are found only in that course.

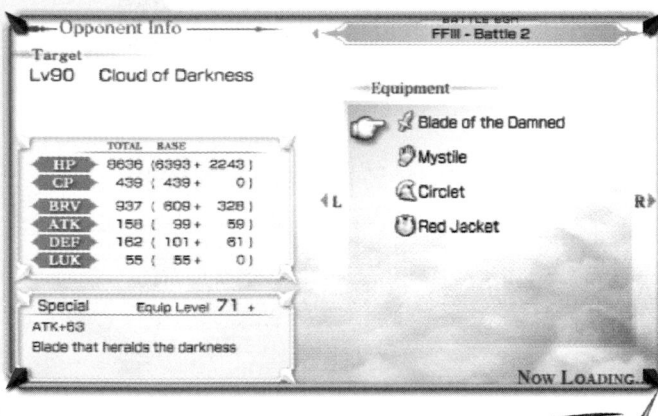

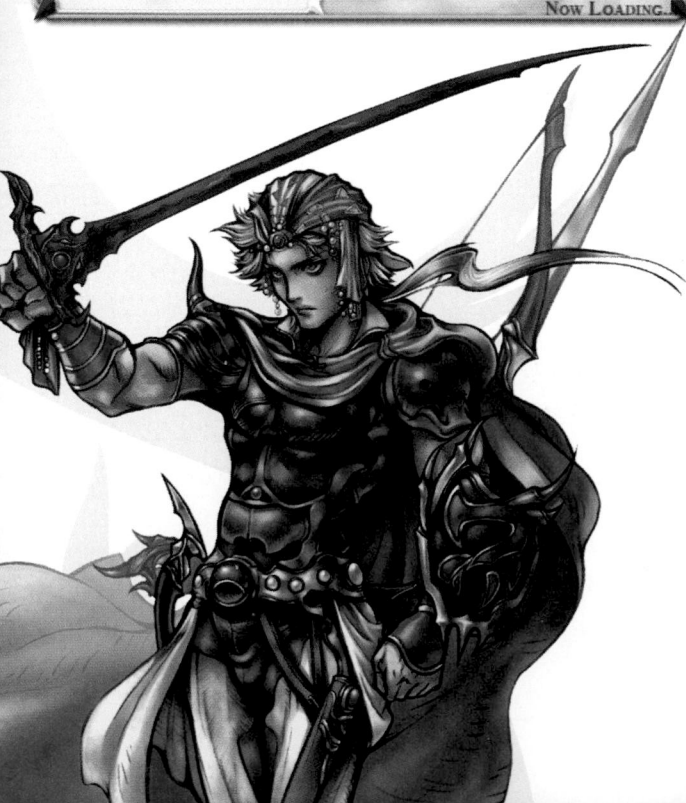

RARE ITEM DROPS

Unlike the first four courses, the Blackjack course offers only a small assortment of special accessories and an occasional Rosetta Stone in its meager supply of Treasure Cards. The appeal of that course is not the Treasure Cards, but the unique and powerful equipment wielded by the foes in the Battle Cards.

The Duel Colosseum is a great place to hunt for item drops, particularly on both the Blackjack and Lunar Whale Courses. Keep an eye out for foes who have "Equipment" or (better yet) "Antiquities" listed by their strength; you know for sure that they're packing some of the best gear in the game. But even normal foes may hold a piece of Lufenian gear or other not-for-sale treats. Remember that you can't leave the Colosseum without quitting your game, so buy a bunch of Item Drop Rate Up (10 pack) from the PP Catalog well in advance!

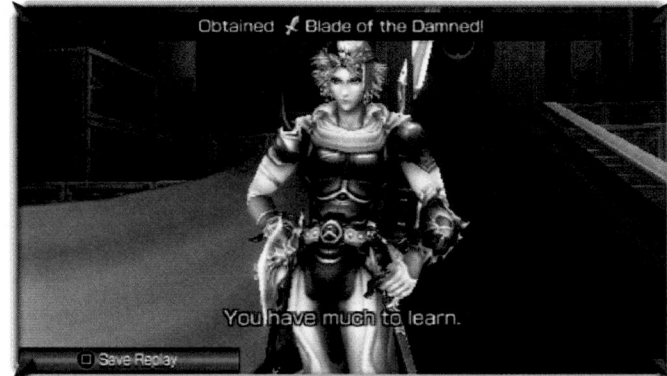

WHAT DO ELIXIRS DO?

Each of the first four courses has its own flavor of Elixir: Dusty Elixir, Elixir, Hi-Elixir, and Megalixir, respectively. These items have no inherent use, but if you buy the "Shop - X Course Added" items from the PP Catalog, you'll be able to trade your Elixirs for any trade accessory from the same course. For example, instead of spending three hours in the Invincible Course hunting for that elusive set of Djinn Scales you need, spend your medals on Hi-Elixirs. You can then buy "Shop - Invincible Course Added" from the PP Catalog and trade three Hi-Elixirs for a set of Djinn Scales in the shop.

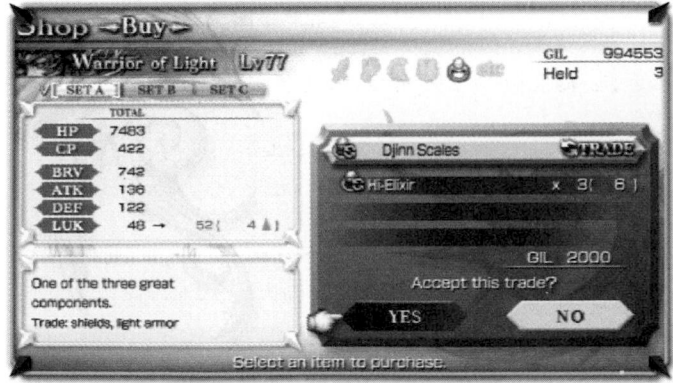

DUEL COLOSSEUM

WHAT DOES TRANSMOGRIDUST DO?

Transmogridust pops up a lot in the Duel Colosseum, but that's fine—you'll need a lot of it. Transmogridust appears in scores of recipes, and one (the Super Ribbon) requires a full 99 doses of the stuff. At only 3 medals to buy, Transmogridust is a welcome sight in the Colosseum, as it allows you to cheaply burn through a hand while getting a useful trade accessory out of the deal.

WHAT DO PEBBLES DO?

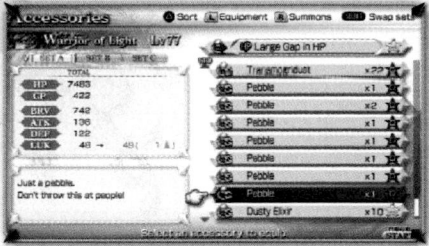

Pebbles aren't actually a single item—there are ten different ones, they just happen to have the exact same name. (This is why you can buy several of them and it may still say "Held x 0.")

When equipped as an accessory, Pebbles effectively have Accessory Breakability: 20% and will eventually shatter at the end of a battle. When they do, you'll find a hidden treasure inside. Nine of the ten contain items from the familiar herb series: Rosemary, Geranium, Lemongrass, etc. These items are easily acquired and are no great treat. But the tenth holds a Growth Seed, which is the key ingredient in the Growth Egg, a special accessory that provides a 20% EXP boost and won't break like Chocobo accessories do. Incidentally, the Pebbles that contain the Growth Seed will always be the lowest Pebbles in your accessory inventory. They also seem to have a lower rate of breakage, so you may want to equip a Mallet to speed things along.

COURSE DETAILS

With so many rare items locked away in the Duel Colosseum, you'll want to spend some time in each of the courses to fill out your inventory of rare items and trade accessories. The list of treasures for each can be found below.

AIRSHIP COURSE

With enemies between level 1 and 30, the Airship Course is a fantastic way to level up newly unlocked characters who are starting from scratch. You can put a lot of the treasures you'll find to immediate use by swapping them at the shop for new gear for your fighters. The exclusive "Flavor of Life" series of gear (Frying Pan, Toque Blanche, Kitchen Timer, and Iron Apron) makes for some particularly excellent finds.

ITEMS

ITEM	MEDAL COST
Frying Pan	17
Toque Blanche	17
Kitchen Timer	8
Iron Apron	13

ACCESSORIES

ACCESSORY	MEDAL COST
Transmogridust	3
Bergamot	8
Chamomile	8
Clary Sage	8
Eucalyptus	8
Geranium	8
Lemongrass	8
Rosemary	8
Tea Tree	8
Ylang Ylang	8
Gold	11
Mythril	11
Aquamarine	13
Bird Feather	13
Ichthon Scales	13
Iron Carapace	13
Large Fang	13
Large Horn	13
Splinter	18
Pebble	15
Beast Bone	18
Charger Barding	18
Dusty Elixir	18

ACCESSORY	MEDAL COST
Emerald	18
Quality Branch	13
White Stone	18
Yensa Scales	18
Wind Stone	21
Black Stone	22
Black Tiger Fang	22
Lamia Scales	22
Lumber	22
Moonstone	22
Summoner's Horn	22
Unknown's Bone	22
Giant Feather	27
Gigas Bone	27
Great Serpent's Fang	27
Great Serpentskin	27
Ruby	27
Spirit Stone	27
Thorny Lumber	27
Wyvern's Horn	27
Water Stone	28
Lifestone	35

FALCON COURSE

Item hunters will have a field day on the Falcon Course, which is intended for levels 31-60. In addition to the entire "Force of the Resolute" series of weapons—which convert EX Force intro bravery when worn as a set—you can find the two missing items in the Elemental Archfiend series (which you began picking up as DP Prizes in Shade Impulse Chapter 3). As always, there are plenty of exclusive trade accessories to find as well.

ITEMS

ITEM	MEDAL COST
Nail Bat	17
Skull Wristlet	17
Spirit Band	8
Bomber Jacket	13
Rubicante's Cowl	10
Cagnazzo's Carapace	10

ACCESSORIES

ACCESSORY	MEDAL COST
Transmogridust	3
Chimera Fang	8
Demon Feather	8
Landshark Scales	8
Mako Stone	8
Nue Bone	8
Peridot	8
Quality Lumber	8
Taurus Horn	8
Wormskin	8
Crystal	11
Diamond	11
Gold	11
Pebble	15
Ancient Bone	18
Destrier Barding	18
Elixir	18
Fallen Angel Feather	18
Leviathan Scales	18
Levistone	18
Lizard Horn	18
Mistletoe	18

ACCESSORY	MEDAL COST
Sapphire	18
Throat Wolf Fang	18
Wind Stone	21
Big Tree	22
Dewdrop Pebble	22
Emperor Scales	22
Humbaba's Horn	22
Mammoth Tusk	22
Opal	22
Royal Wing	22
Shadow Bone	22
Diablos's Wing	27
Giant Turtle Shell	27
Godfighter Scales	27
Ixion Horn	27
Spiritwood	27
Stone of the Condemner	27
Topaz	27
Wargod Bone	27
Water Stone	28
Lifestone	35

INVINCIBLE COURSE

The Invincible Course is intended for levels 61-90, so don't overlook the opportunity to unlock it from the PP Catalog once you have a character in that range. The Invincible Course has a smaller selection of treasures than the two previous courses, but there's plenty here that's worth your while. The "Imp's Blessing" series of items is a particular highlight, since they can be equipped by any character in the game.

ITEMS

ITEM	MEDAL COST
Impartisan	17
Tortoise Shield	17
Saucer	8
Reed Cloak	13

ACCESSORIES

ACCESSORY	MEDAL COST
Transmogridust	3
Crystal	11
Dragonstone	13
Dragonwood	13
Land Dragon Bone	13
Sea Serpent Scales	13
Wind Drake Horn	13
Wyrm Carapace	13
Wyrmstone	13
Wyvern Wing	13
Pebble	15
Hi-Elixir	18
Wind Stone	21
Blessed Barding	22
Blessed Gem	22
Holy Fang	22

ACCESSORY	MEDAL COST
Holystone	22
Sacred Beast Scales	22
Sacred Beast Wing	22
Saint's Bone	22
Unicorn Horn	22
Aged Turtle Shell	27
Beastlord Fang	27
Beastlord Horn	27
Blood-Darkened Bone	27
Djinn Scales	27
Garuda's Wing	27
Goddess's Magicite	27
Lapis Lazuli	27
Revival Tree	27
Water Stone	28
Lifestone	35

LUNAR WHALE COURSE

The challenge climbs sharply in the Lunar Whale Course, where enemies can reach levels as high as 120! You'll have to endure them to acquire the ingredients needed to create each character's best weapon, as well as the Tomes that are used in the highest-tier basic accessories.

If you're not into trading, you can pick up the four pieces of equipment in the exceptional Snowpetal series, but their Treasure Cards won't be easy to find, since they are rarer than similar armaments have been in past courses.

Lucky characters can also pick up pieces of Lufenian gear as item drops.

ITEMS

ACCESSORY	MEDAL COST
Lunate Armlet	17
Blue Moon	17
Snowflake Sweater	8
Chaplet	13

ACCESSORIES

ACCESSORY	MEDAL COST
Transmogridust	3
Tome of Kings	13
Tome of Lies	13
Tome of Love	13
Tome of Memories	13
Tome of Men	13
Tome of Mysteries	13
Tome of Shadows	13
Tome of Silence	13
Tome of Souls	13
Tome of the Farplane	13
Tome of the Masters	13
Tome of the Orator	13
Pebble	15
Ancient Turtle Shell	18
Bahamut's Wing	18
Behemoth Horn	18
Eden's Scales	18
Hero's Bone	18
Iifa Tree	18
Maduin's Fang	18
Megalixir	18
Sky Jewel	18
Supreme Gem	18
Wind Stone	21
Boiling Blood	27
Fanatic's Leer	27
Fayth's Dream	27
Gates of Judgment	27
Gears of Time	27
God of Destruction	27
Guiding Light	27
Life of the Planet	27
Lone Heart	27
Lust for Power	27
Medal of Honor	27
Onion	27
Power of the Void	27
Roaming Clouds	27
Splendor of the Wind	27
The Youth's Dream	27
Theater Ticket	27
True Past	27
Twin Form	27
Unshelled Bullet	27
Veiled Magic	27
Wheel of Darkness	27
Water Stone	28
Lifestone	35
Pink Tail	56

BLACKJACK COURSE

The Blackjack Course is the game's greatest challenge, where enemies can reach as high as level 150! Fortunately, you needn't spend a lot of time here to get all the best treasures, as there are only a handful of items available in Treasure Cards. The real treats come as item drops, and even the merely level 100 enemies tend to be decked out in Lufenian armaments and wielding the game's finest weapons for your item-dropping convenience.

ACCESSORY	MEDAL COST
Arcane Resin	3
Destruction Resin	3
Mystery Resin	3
Patience Resin	3
Phoenix Down	3
Phoenix Pinion	3
Valor Resin	3
Rosetta Stone	30

PP CATALOG

You earn PP for almost every fight you engage in, and you can spend it in a PP Catalog that contains well over 200 unlockable characters, collectibles, and options. New entries unlock regularly, usually after beating certain Story Mode chapters.

CHARACTERS

ALTERNATE LOOKS

Once unlocked, you can switch any character to his or her alternate look by pressing ▲ in the Customization menu.

CATALOG ITEM	PP COST	LISTING CONDITION
Alternate Look - Warrior of Light	300	Unlock Catalog
Alternate Look - Garland	300	Unlock Garland
Alternate Look - Firion	300	Unlock Catalog
Alternate Look - The Emperor	300	Unlock The Emperor
Alternate Look - Onion Knight	300	Unlock Catalog
Alternate Look - Cloud of Darkness	300	Unlock Cloud of Darkness
Alternate Look - Cecil	300	Unlock Catalog
Alternate Look - Golbez	300	Unlock Golbez
Alternate Look - Bartz	300	Unlock Catalog
Alternate Look - Exdeath	300	Unlock Exdeath
Alternate Look - Terra	300	Unlock Catalog
Alternate Look - Kefka	300	Unlock Kefka
Alternate Look - Cloud	300	Unlock Catalog
Alternate Look - Sephiroth	300	Unlock Sephiroth
Alternate Look - Squall	300	Unlock Catalog
Alternate Look - Ultimecia	300	Unlock Ultimecia
Alternate Look - Zidane	300	Unlock Catalog
Alternate Look - Kuja	300	Unlock Kuja
Alternate Look - Tidus	300	Unlock Catalog
Alternate Look - Jecht	300	Unlock Jecht
Alternate Look - Shantotto	300	Unlock Shantotto
Alternate Look - Gabranth	300	Unlock Gabranth

UNLOCKABLE CHARACTERS

In addition to the game's ten initially selectable heroes, you can unlock all of the Chaos characters as well as a pair of secret characters from *Final Fantasy* XI and XII.

CATALOG ITEM	PP COST	LISTING CONDITION
Garland	500	Unlock Catalog
The Emperor	500	Unlock Catalog
Cloud of Darkness	500	Unlock Catalog
Golbez	500	Unlock Catalog
Exdeath	500	Unlock Catalog
Kefka	500	Unlock Catalog
Sephiroth	500	Unlock Catalog
Ultimecia	500	Unlock Catalog
Kuja	500	Unlock Catalog
Jecht	500	Unlock Catalog
Shantotto	1,000	Clear Distant Glory: The Lady of Legend
Gabranth	1,000	Clear Distant Glory: Redemption of the Warrior

ENCOUNTER VOICES

These options unlock the whole list of pre-battle taunts characters use to greet each other. You can hear them in Museum.

CATALOG ITEM	PP COST	LISTING CONDITION
Encounter Voice - Warrior of Light	100	Unlock Catalog
Encounter Voice - Garland	100	Unlock Garland
Encounter Voice - Firion	100	Unlock Catalog
Encounter Voice - The Emperor	100	Unlock The Emperor
Encounter Voice - Onion Knight	100	Unlock Catalog
Encounter Voice - Cloud of Darkness	100	Unlock Cloud of Darkness
Encounter Voice - Cecil	100	Unlock Catalog
Encounter Voice - Golbez	100	Unlock Golbez
Encounter Voice - Bartz	100	Unlock Catalog
Encounter Voice - Exdeath	100	Unlock Exdeath
Encounter Voice - Terra	100	Unlock Catalog
Encounter Voice - Kefka	100	Unlock Kefka
Encounter Voice - Cloud	100	Unlock Catalog
Encounter Voice - Sephiroth	100	Unlock Sephiroth
Encounter Voice - Squall	100	Unlock Catalog
Encounter Voice - Ultimecia	100	Unlock Ultimecia
Encounter Voice - Zidane	100	Unlock Catalog
Encounter Voice - Kuja	100	Unlock Kuja
Encounter Voice - Tidus	100	Unlock Catalog
Encounter Voice - Jecht	100	Unlock Jecht
Encounter Voice - Shantotto	100	Unlock Shantotto
Encounter Voice - Gabranth	100	Unlock Gabranth
Encounter Voice - Chaos	100	Clear Shade Impulse Chapter 4

COMBAT VOICES

These options unlock the rest of the voice samples used in combat, as well as some bonus utterances from Golbez and Exdeath.

CATALOG ITEM	PP COST	LISTING CONDITION
Voice - Warrior of Light	100	Unlock Catalog
Voice - Garland	100	Unlock Garland
Voice - Firion	100	Unlock Catalog
Voice - The Emperor	100	Unlock The Emperor
Voice - Onion Knight	100	Unlock Catalog
Voice - Cloud of Darkness	100	Unlock Cloud of Darkness
Voice - Cecil	100	Unlock Catalog
Voice - Golbez	100	Unlock Golbez
Voice - Bartz	100	Unlock Catalog
Voice - Exdeath	100	Unlock Exdeath
Voice - Terra	100	Unlock Catalog
Voice - Kefka	100	Unlock Kefka
Voice - Cloud	100	Unlock Catalog
Voice - Sephiroth	100	Unlock Sephiroth
Voice - Squall	100	Unlock Catalog
Voice - Ultimecia	100	Unlock Ultimecia
Voice - Zidane	100	Unlock Catalog
Voice - Kuja	100	Unlock Kuja
Voice - Tidus	100	Unlock Catalog
Voice - Jecht	100	Unlock Jecht
Voice - Shantotto	100	Unlock Shantotto
Voice - Gabranth	100	Unlock Gabranth
Voice - Chaos	100	Clear Shade Impulse Chapter 4
Secret Voice - Golbez	300	Reach level 100 as Golbez
Secret Voice - Exdeath	300	Reach level 100 as Exdeath

SYSTEM
GAME MODE UPGRADES

The game modes in *DISSIDIA FINAL FANTASY* are always evolving with new rules, courses, and expanded options that can be unlocked in the PP Catalog.

CATALOG ITEM	PP COST	LISTING CONDITION
Story Mode - Skill Slots Lv 1	500	Clear three Destiny Odyssey Chapters
Story Mode - Skill Slots Lv 2	500	Clear six Destiny Odysseys Chapters*
Arcade Mode - Hard Mode Unlocked	3,000	Unlock Catalog
Arcade Mode - Time Attack Unlocked	10,000	Clear Shade Impulse Chapter 4
Colosseum - Invincible Course Unlocked	500	Clear Shade Impulse Chapter 4
Colosseum - Lunar Whale Course Unlocked	1,000	Clear Shade Impulse Chapter 4
Colosseum - Blackjack Course Unlocked	2,000	Clear Inward Chaos
Online Match - Gain AP After Loss	300	Unlock Catalog
Online Match - Gain Gil After Loss	300	Unlock Catalog
Online Match - Gain Item After Loss	300	Unlock Catalog
Online Match - Gain Accessories After Loss	300	Unlock Catalog
Online Match - Battlegen OK	300	Unlock Catalog
Ghost Match - Battlegen OK	300	Unlock Catalog
Trade Component Drop OK	100	Clear Shade Impulse Chapter 4
Ruleset - Cosmos Judgment	50	Complete a Cosmos Judgment battle (in Duel Colosseum, for example)
Ruleset - Chaos Judgment	50	Complete a Chaos Judgment battle (in Duel Colosseum, for example)
Ruleset - Double Judgment	50	Unlock Cosmos Judgment and Chaos Judgment rulesets
Chaos in Quick Battle	100	Clear Shade Impulse Chapter 4

*Must also purchase previous level of skill

UNLOCKABLE STAGES

You'll encounter most of these stages during the Shade Impulse Story Mode, and you can then unlock them for use in Quick Battle and Online Communication modes.

CATALOG ITEM	PP COST	LISTING CONDITION
Stage - Old Chaos Shrine (Ω)	100	Battle in this stage during Shade Impulse
Stage - Pandaemonium (Ω)	100	Battle in this stage during Shade Impulse
Stage - World of Darkness (Ω)	100	Battle in this stage during Shade Impulse
Stage - Lunar Subterrane (Ω)	100	Battle in this stage during Shade Impulse
Stage - The Rift (Ω)	100	Battle in this stage during Shade Impulse
Stage - Kefka's Tower (Ω)	100	Battle in this stage during Shade Impulse
Stage - Dream's End (Ω)	100	Battle in this stage during Shade Impulse
Stage - Planet's Core (Ω)	100	Battle in this stage during Shade Impulse
Stage - Ultimecia's Castle (Ω)	100	Battle in this stage during Shade Impulse
Stage - Crystal World (Ω)	100	Battle in this stage during Shade Impulse
Stage - Order's Sanctuary (Ω)	100	Battle in this stage during Shade Impulse
Stage - Edge of Madness	100	Battle Chaos during Shade Impulse
Stage - Edge of Madness (Ω)	100	Battle in this stage during Duel Colosseum or Distant Glory

LEVEL CAP BOOSTS

These boosts allow you to level up the CPU in Quick Battle matches, for players who are either seeking a greater challenge or who wish to use exploits to level up new characters quickly.

CATALOG ITEM	PP COST	LISTING CONDITION
CPU Level Cap +10	100	Unlock Catalog
CPU Level Cap +20	100	Unlock Catalog*
CPU Level Cap +30	100	Unlock Catalog*
CPU Level Cap +40	100	Character at level 30+*
CPU Level Cap +50	100	Character at level 30+*
CPU Level Cap +60	100	Character at level 30+*
CPU Level Cap +70	100	Character at level 50+*
CPU Level Cap +80	100	Character at level 50+*
CPU Level Cap +90	100	Character at level 50+*
CPU Level Cap +100	100	Character at level 70+*

*Must also purchase previous level of skill

CUTSCENES

It's not cheap, but you can unlock all of the in-game events for the Museum's cutscene viewer in one fell swoop.

CATALOG ITEM	PP COST	LISTING CONDITION
Unlock all Cutscenes	20,000	Clear Shade Impulse Chapter 4

CALENDAR

BONUS UPGRADES

The Icon Likelihood catalog entries raise the frequency of calendar bonuses, while the others strengthen the bonuses themselves.

CATALOG ITEM	PP COST	LISTING CONDITION
EXP Icon Boost Lv 2	50	Unlock Catalog
EXP Icon Boost Lv 3	100	Unlock Catalog*
EXP Icon Boost Lv 4	150	Unlock Catalog*
EXP Icon Boost Lv 5	200	Unlock Catalog*
EXP Icon Boost Lv 6	250	Clear all Destiny Odyssey Chapters*
EXP Icon Boost Lv 7	300	Clear all Destiny Odyssey Chapters*
EXP Icon Boost Lv 8	350	Clear all Destiny Odyssey Chapters*
EXP Icon Boost Lv 9	400	Clear all Destiny Odyssey Chapters*
EXP Icon Boost Lv 10	500	Clear all Destiny Odyssey Chapters*
PP Icon Boost Lv 2	100	Unlock Catalog
PP Icon Boost Lv 3	300	Unlock Catalog*
Gil Icon Boost Lv 2	50	Unlock Catalog
Gil Icon Boost Lv 3	100	Unlock Catalog*
Gil Icon Boost Lv 4	150	Unlock Catalog*
Gil Icon Boost Lv 5	200	Unlock Catalog*
Gil Icon Boost Lv 6	250	Clear all Destiny Odyssey Chapters*

CATALOG ITEM	PP COST	LISTING CONDITION
Gil Icon Boost Lv 7	300	Clear all Destiny Odyssey Chapters*
Gil Icon Boost Lv 8	350	Clear all Destiny Odyssey Chapters*
Gil Icon Boost Lv 9	400	Clear all Destiny Odyssey Chapters*
Gil Icon Boost Lv 10	500	Clear all Destiny Odyssey Chapters*
AP Icon Boost Lv 2	100	Unlock Catalog
AP Icon Boost Lv 3	300	Clear all Destiny Odyssey Chapters*
Icon Likelihood Lv 2	50	Unlock Catalog
Icon Likelihood Lv 3	100	Unlock Catalog*
Icon Likelihood Lv 4	150	Unlock Catalog*
Icon Likelihood Lv 5	200	Unlock Catalog*
Icon Likelihood Lv 6	250	Clear all Destiny Odyssey Chapters*
Icon Likelihood Lv 7	300	Clear all Destiny Odyssey Chapters*
Icon Likelihood Lv 8	350	Clear all Destiny Odyssey Chapters*
Icon Likelihood Lv 9	400	Clear all Destiny Odyssey Chapters*
Icon Likelihood Lv 10	500	Clear all Destiny Odyssey Chapters*

*Must also purchase previous level of skill

ICONS

PLAYER ICONS

These Player Icon packs will give you more designs to use on your friend card.

CATALOG ITEM	PP COST	LISTING CONDITION
No. 007-010 (Final Fantasy I) Set of 4	250	Unlock Catalog
No. 011-014 (Final Fantasy I) Set of 4	250	Clear 3 Destiny Odyssey Chapters
No. 015-018 (Final Fantasy I) Set of 4	250	Clear 6 Destiny Odyssey Chapters
No. 019-022 (Final Fantasy I) Set of 4	250	Clear 9 Destiny Odyssey Chapters
No. 030-034 (Final Fantasy II) Set of 5	310	Unlock Catalog
No. 039-043 (Final Fantasy II) Set of 5	310	Clear 4 Destiny Odyssey Chapters
No. 044-047 (Final Fantasy II) Set of 4	250	Clear 7 Destiny Odyssey Chapters
No. 048-051 (Final Fantasy II) Set of 4	250	Clear 9 Destiny Odyssey Chapters
No. 054-057 (Final Fantasy III) Set of 4	250	Unlock Catalog
No. 058-061 (Final Fantasy III) Set of 4	250	Clear 5 Destiny Odyssey Chapters
No. 062-065 (Final Fantasy III) Set of 4	250	Clear 8 Destiny Odyssey Chapters
No. 066-069 (Final Fantasy III) Set of 4	250	Clear 8 Destiny Odyssey Chapters
No. 070-072 (Final Fantasy III) Set of 3	190	Clear 9 Destiny Odyssey Chapters
No. 075-077 (Final Fantasy III) Set of 3	190	Clear Shade Impulse Chapter 1
No. 082-085 (Final Fantasy IV) Set of 4	250	Clear 3 Destiny Odyssey Chapters
No. 086-089 (Final Fantasy IV) Set of 4	250	Clear 3 Destiny Odyssey Chapters
No. 090-093 (Final Fantasy IV) Set of 4	250	Clear 6 Destiny Odyssey Chapters
No. 097-100 (Final Fantasy IV) Set of 4	250	Clear 6 Destiny Odyssey Chapters
No. 101-104 (Final Fantasy IV) Set of 4	250	Clear 9 Destiny Odyssey Chapters
No. 105-108 (Final Fantasy IV) Set of 4	250	Clear 9 Destiny Odyssey Chapters
No. 109-112 (Final Fantasy IV) Set of 4	250	Clear Shade Impulse Chapter 1
No. 113-115 (Final Fantasy IV) Set of 3	190	Clear Shade Impulse Chapter 1
No. 117-119 (Final Fantasy IV) Set of 3	190	Clear Shade Impulse Chapter 2
No. 127-129 (Final Fantasy V) Set of 3	190	Clear 4 Destiny Odyssey Chapters
No. 130-133 (Final Fantasy V) Set of 4	250	Clear 4 Destiny Odyssey Chapters
No. 134-136 (Final Fantasy V) Set of 3	310	Clear 7 Destiny Odyssey Chapters
No. 137-140 (Final Fantasy V) Set of 4	250	Clear 7 Destiny Odyssey Chapters
No. 141-144 (Final Fantasy V) Set of 4	250	Clear 9 Destiny Odyssey Chapters
No. 145-147 (Final Fantasy V) Set of 3	190	Clear 9 Destiny Odyssey Chapters
No. 148-150 (Final Fantasy V) Set of 3	250	Clear Shade Impulse Chapter 1
No. 151-154 (Final Fantasy V) Set of 4	250	Clear Shade Impulse Chapter 2
No. 165-168 (Final Fantasy VI) Set of 4	250	Clear 5 Destiny Odyssey Chapters
No. 169-172 (Final Fantasy VI) Set of 4	250	Clear 5 Destiny Odyssey Chapters
No. 173-176 (Final Fantasy VI) Set of 4	250	Clear 8 Destiny Odyssey Chapters
No. 179-182 (Final Fantasy VI) Set of 4	250	Clear 8 Destiny Odyssey Chapters
No. 183-186 (Final Fantasy VI) Set of 4	250	Clear 9 Destiny Odyssey Chapters
No. 187-190 (Final Fantasy VI) Set of 4	250	Clear 9 Destiny Odyssey Chapters
No. 191-194 (Final Fantasy VI) Set of 4	250	Clear Shade Impulse Chapter 2
No. 195-198 (Final Fantasy VI) Set of 4	250	Clear Shade Impulse Chapter 2
No. 199-202 (Final Fantasy VI) Set of 4	250	Clear Shade Impulse Chapter 2
No. 210-213 (Final Fantasy VII) Set of 4	250	Clear 6 Destiny Odyssey Chapters
No. 214-217 (Final Fantasy VII) Set of 4	250	Clear Shade Impulse Chapter 3
No. 220-223 (Final Fantasy VII) Set of 4	250	Clear Shade Impulse Chapter 3
No. 224-227 (Final Fantasy VIII) Set of 4	250	Clear Shade Impulse Chapter 3
No. 232-235 (Final Fantasy IX) Set of 4	250	Clear 8 Destiny Odyssey Chapters
No. 236-238 (Final Fantasy IX) Set of 3	250	Clear Shade Impulse Chapter 3
No. 240-242 (Final Fantasy X) Set of 3	190	Clear 9 Destiny Odyssey Chapters
No. 243-245 (Final Fantasy X) Set of 3	190	Clear Shade Impulse Chapter 3
No. 247-250 (Final Fantasy XI) Set of 4	190	Clear Distant Glory: The Lady of Legend
No. 251-254 (Final Fantasy XI) Set of 4	250	Clear Distant Glory: The Lady of Legend
No. 255-258 (Final Fantasy XII) Set of 4	250	Clear Distant Glory: The Lady of Legend
No. 259-261 (Final Fantasy XII) Set of 3	250	Clear Distant Glory: Redemption of the Warrior
No. 262-264 (Final Fantasy XII) Set of 3	190	Clear Distant Glory: Redemption of the Warrior

ETC.

TEMPORARY BOOSTS

These modest boosts to Battlegen rates (+0.5%) and item drop rates (+1%) are must-buys for item hunters. You can buy each item repeatedly and cache up to 100 instances of each.

CATALOG ITEM	PP COST	LISTING CONDITION
Item Drop Rate Up	30	Unlock Catalog
Battlegen Rate Up	30	Unlock Catalog
Item Drop Rate Up (10 pack)	300	Unlock Catalog
Battlegen Rate Up (10 pack)	300	Unlock Catalog

SHOP STOCK ADDITIONS

You can update the shop's stock lists with the trade accessories found in the Duel Colosseum courses, as well as new and exclusive items in two rare series.

CATALOG ITEM	PP COST	LISTING CONDITION
Shop - Pretty Princess Series Added	800	Clear Shade Impulse Chapter 4 with Cloud
Shop - Genji Series Added	800	Clear Inward Chaos
Shop - Diamond Ring Added	100	Clear Shade Impulse Chapter 4
Shop - Airship Course Added	100	Clear Shade Impulse Chapter 4
Shop - Falcon Course Added	100	Clear Shade Impulse Chapter 4
Shop - Invincible Course Added	100	Purchase Invincible Course
Shop - Lunar Whale Course Added	100	Purchase Lunar Whale Course

FRIEND REWARD BOOSTS

When you re-encounter a friend who's been battling against your friend card ghost, you'll receive Friend Rewards based on your ghost's performance. Buying these raises the Friend Reward gil as well as the PP cap.

CATALOG ITEM	PP COST	LISTING CONDITION
Friend Reward Boost Lv 1	100	Unlock Catalog
Friend Reward Boost Lv 2	100	Unlock Catalog*
Friend Reward Boost Lv 3	200	Unlock Catalog*
Friend Reward Boost Lv 4	200	Unlock Catalog*
Friend Reward Boost Lv 5	300	Unlock Catalog*
Friend Reward Boost Lv 6	300	Unlock Catalog*
Friend Reward Boost Lv 7	400	Clear all Destiny Odyssey Chapters*
Friend Reward Boost Lv 8	500	Clear all Destiny Odyssey Chapters*
Friend Reward Boost Lv 9	700	Clear all Destiny Odyssey Chapters*
Friend Reward Boost Lv 10	1000	Clear all Destiny Odyssey Chapters*

*Must also purchase previous level of skill

ADDITIONAL PLAY PLANS

These new play plans allow you to focus your energy on leveling (Black Chocobo) or earning accessories (Fat Chocobo), even in short play sessions.

CATALOG ITEM	PP COST	LISTING CONDITION
Play Plan - Black Chocobo Course	300	Clear all Destiny Odyssey Chapters
Play Plan - Fat Chocobo Course	300	Clear all Destiny Odyssey Chapters

CLASSIC MUSIC TRACKS

Once you unlock one of these straight-from-the-game music tracks, you can either listen to it in the Museum or as in-game battle music.

CATALOG ITEM	PP COST	LISTING CONDITION
BGM - FFI - Town	500	Clear Shade Impulse Chapter 4
BGM - FFII - The Rebel Army	500	Clear Shade Impulse Chapter 4
BGM - FFIII - The Crystal Tower	500	Clear Shade Impulse Chapter 4
BGM - FFIV - The Red Wings	500	Clear Shade Impulse Chapter 4
BGM - FFV - The Decisive Battle	500	Clear Shade Impulse Chapter 4
BGM - FFVI - Dancing Mad	500	Clear Shade Impulse Chapter 4
BGM - FFVII - Opening - Bombing Mission	500	Clear Shade Impulse Chapter 4
BGM - FFVIII - The Man with the Machine Gun	500	Clear Shade Impulse Chapter 4
BGM - FFIX - The Darkness of Eternity	500	Clear Shade Impulse Chapter 4
BGM - FFX - Fight with Seymour	500	Clear Shade Impulse Chapter 4
BGM - FFXI - Awakening	500	Clear Distant Glory: The Lady of Legend
BGM - FFXII - Fight to the Death	500	Clear Distant Glory: Redemption of the Warrior

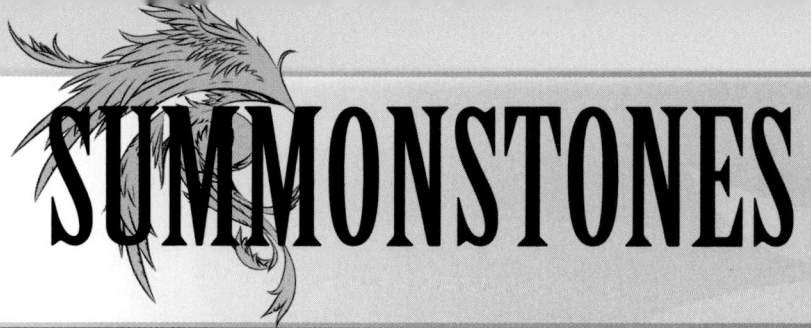

SUMMONSTONES

A timely summon can cement your victory or turn a losing battle around. There are over fifty different Summonstones to collect, and you'll find all of them in the game's Story Mode chapters.

SOME FAVORITE SUMMONSTONES:

NAME	NOTES
IFRIT (AUTO)	When battling weaker foes, Ifrit's timely bravery boost often allows you to finish your foes in a single hit.
ALEXANDER (AUTO)	Alexander's ability triggers right when you need it, giving you around fifteen seconds in which you can score HP Attacks without losing your bravery. With this skill, it only takes one or two hits to finish the fight.
MAGIC POT	There's no easier way to turn a losing battle around than to steal your foe's potentially fatal bravery total. Stick with the manual version; the auto one can mess you up as often as it helps.
CARBUNCLE (AUTO)	Useful when you connect with an HP attack or when your opponent breaks your bravery.
DEATHGAZE	Everyone's bravery hits a multiple of 5 at some point. Keep your eye on the corner of the screen so you don't miss a free Bravery Break opportunity.
SCARMIGLIONE	When playing with a friend, expect to see a lot of Ifrit, Behemoth, and Magic Pot Summonstones. Scarmiglione makes your opponents' strategies backfire by zeroing out their bravery as soon as it's raised.

AUTO SUMMONS

There are both auto and manual versions of the twelve summons listed below. Effects with timed durations are typically more powerful when used manually, but auto summons allow beginning players to execute powerful effects without having to pay attention to yet another battlefield factor. Even experienced players may prefer auto summons for their superior use/charge stats; all auto summons can be used three times (once per battle), and subsequently require only three battles to recharge.

IFRIT

USE	3	CHARGE	3
EFFECT	Your bravery is boosted to 150%.		
AUTO SUMMON	When you gain stage bravery		
LOCATION	Destiny Odyssey I map 3		

SHIVA

USE	3	CHARGE	3
EFFECT	Opponent's bravery temporarily prevented from rising.		
AUTO SUMMON	When opponent's bravery = 0		
LOCATION	Destiny Odyssey II map 3		

RAMUH

USE	3	CHARGE	3
EFFECT	Opponent's Summons are temporarily sealed.		
AUTO SUMMON	When opponent gains stage bravery		
LOCATION	Shade Impulse Chapter 3 map 3		

CARBUNCLE

USE	3	CHARGE	3
EFFECT	Opponent's bravery becomes equal to your bravery.		
AUTO SUMMON	When your bravery = 0		
LOCATION	Destiny Odyssey IV map 2		

MAGIC POT

USE	3	CHARGE	3
EFFECT	Your bravery becomes equal to opponent's bravery.		
AUTO SUMMON	When opponent's bravery = 3x base bravery		
LOCATION	Destiny Odyssey VII map 3		

DEMON WALL

USE	3	CHARGE	3
EFFECT	Your bravery is temporarily shielded (does not fall due to Bravery Attacks).		
AUTO SUMMON	When your bravery = 50% of base bravery		
LOCATION	Destiny Odyssey IV map 3		

MAGUS SISTERS

USE	3	CHARGE	3
EFFECT	Opponent's current bravery is halved and opponent's base bravery is temporarily halved.		
AUTO SUMMON	When opponent gains stage bravery		
LOCATION	Destiny Odyssey X map 3		

ODIN

USE	3	CHARGE	3
EFFECT	50% chance of inflicting Bravery Break upon opponent.		
AUTO SUMMON	When near death		
LOCATION	Shade Impulse Chapter 1 map 3		

PHOENIX

USE	3	CHARGE	3
EFFECT	You are temporarily protected from Bravery Break, and your bravery is restored to base value.		
AUTO SUMMON	When your bravery = half of base value		
LOCATION	Destiny Odyssey III map 3		

ALEXANDER

USE	3	CHARGE	3
EFFECT	Your bravery is temporarily frozen.		
AUTO SUMMON	When you gain stage bravery		
LOCATION	Destiny Odyssey IX map 3		

LEVIATHAN

USE	3	CHARGE	3
EFFECT	Opponent's bravery temporarily decreases (by roughly 20 points per second).		
AUTO SUMMON	When opponent gains stage bravery		
LOCATION	Destiny Odyssey V map 3		

BAHAMUT

USE	3	CHARGE	3
EFFECT	Your bravery temporarily rises (by roughly 20 points per second).		
AUTO SUMMON	When your bravery = half of base value		
LOCATION	Destiny Odyssey VIII map 3		

MANUAL SUMMONS

You can trigger manual summons at will by pressing 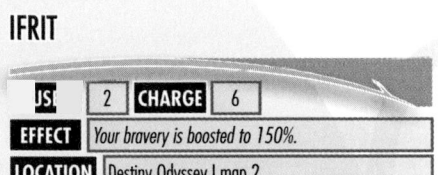 and ● together. However, you pay a steep price for the privilege of using your summons whenever you like; all of the summons listed below can only be used twice before they require a six-battle charging period. Notable exceptions are Omega and Ultima Weapon, which require a ten-battle charging period after each use!

IFRIT

USE	2	CHARGE	6

EFFECT Your bravery is boosted to 150%.

LOCATION Destiny Odyssey I map 2

SHIVA

USE	2	CHARGE	6

EFFECT Opponent's bravery temporarily prevented from rising. (Duration longer than auto version.)

LOCATION Destiny Odyssey II map 2

RAMUH

USE	2	CHARGE	6

EFFECT Opponent's summons are temporarily sealed. (Duration longer than auto version.)

LOCATION Shade Impulse Chapter 4 map 1

CARBUNCLE

USE	2	CHARGE	6

EFFECT Opponent's bravery becomes equal to your bravery.

LOCATION Destiny Odyssey IV map 2

MAGIC POT

USE	2	CHARGE	6

EFFECT Your bravery becomes equal to opponent's bravery.

LOCATION Destiny Odyssey VII map 2

DEMON WALL

USE	2	CHARGE	6

EFFECT Your bravery is temporarily shielded (does not fall due to bravery attacks). (Duration longer than auto version.)

LOCATION Destiny Odyssey IV map 2

MAGUS SISTERS

USE	2	CHARGE	6

EFFECT Opponent's current bravery is halved and opponent's base bravery is temporarily halved. (Duration longer than auto version.)

LOCATION Destiny Odyssey X map 2

ODIN

USE	2	CHARGE	6

EFFECT 50% chance of inflicting Bravery Break upon opponent.

LOCATION Shade Impulse Chapter 2 map 3

PHOENIX

USE	2	CHARGE	6

EFFECT You are temporarily protected from Bravery Break, and your bravery is restored to base value. (Duration longer than auto version.)

LOCATION Destiny Odyssey III map 2

ALEXANDER

USE	2	CHARGE	6

EFFECT Your bravery is temporarily frozen. (Duration longer than auto version.)

LOCATION Destiny Odyssey IX map 2

LEVIATHAN

USE	2	CHARGE	6

EFFECT Opponent's bravery temporarily decreases (by roughly 40 points per second).

LOCATION Destiny Odyssey V map 2

BAHAMUT

USE	2	CHARGE	6

EFFECT Your bravery temporarily rises (by roughly 40 points per second).

LOCATION Destiny Odyssey VIII map 2

CHOCOBO

USE	2	CHARGE	6

EFFECT The digits of both fighters' bravery values are randomly shuffled.

LOCATION DP Prize: Distant Glory: The Lady of Legend

MOOGLE

USE	2	CHARGE	6

EFFECT Randomly selects and uses the ability of another summon.

LOCATION Inward Chaos map 1

MANDRAGORA

USE	2	CHARGE	6

EFFECT Temporarily enables rapid bravery regeneration (up to your base bravery value).

LOCATION DP Prize: Destiny Odyssey I

BOMB

USE	2	CHARGE	6

EFFECT After 10 seconds, costs opponent an amount of bravery equal to your current bravery.

LOCATION DP Prize: Destiny Odyssey IV

ASURA

USE	2	CHARGE	6

EFFECT Randomly either destroys opponent's Summonstone, forces opponent to use it, or temporarily seals it.

LOCATION DP Prize: Distant Glory: Redemption of the Warrior

TITAN

USE	2	CHARGE	6

EFFECT For a period of time, your bravery triples whenever you take HP damage.

LOCATION Distant Glory: The Lady of Legend map 3

ACCESSORIES

ATOMOS

USE	2	CHARGE	6

EFFECT For a period of time, you absorb an equal amount of bravery from your opponent whenever you take HP damage.

LOCATION Distant Glory: The Lady of Legend map 2

IRON GIANT

USE	2	CHARGE	6

EFFECT For a period of time, your opponent's bravery is halved whenever you deal HP damage.

LOCATION Distant Glory: Redemption of the Warrior map 3

CACTUAR

USE	2	CHARGE	6

EFFECT Reduces opponent's bravery by 1,000.

LOCATION DP Prize: Destiny Odyssey IX

TONBERRY

USE	2	CHARGE	6

EFFECT After a set period of time, opponent loses bravery equal to the amount of HP damage you've taken this battle.

LOCATION DP Prize: Destiny Odyssey V

MALBORO

USE	2	CHARGE	6

EFFECT For a period of time, continuously reduces opponent's bravery. The closer you are, the greater the reduction.

LOCATION DP Prize: Destiny Odyssey II

ULTROS

USE	2	CHARGE	6

EFFECT For a period of time, opponent cannot see either combatant's bravery totals.

LOCATION DP Prize: Destiny Odyssey III

TYPHON

USE	2	CHARGE	6

EFFECT A randomly chosen digit of opponent's bravery total is reduced to 0.

LOCATION DP Prize: Destiny Odyssey VII

DEATHGAZE

USE	2	CHARGE	6

EFFECT If opponent's bravery total is a multiple of 5, inflicts Bravery Break.

LOCATION DP Prize: Destiny Odyssey IV

BEHEMOTH

USE	2	CHARGE	6

EFFECT Doubles your bravery, but afterwards temporarily drops your bravery by 60 per second.

LOCATION DP Prize: Destiny Odyssey X

PUPU

USE	2	CHARGE	6

EFFECT Halves your bravery, but afterwards temporarily rises your bravery by 60 per second.

LOCATION DP Prize: Destiny Odyssey VIII

LICH

USE	2	CHARGE	6

EFFECT After a period of time, opponent's bravery falls to 0.

LOCATION DP Prize: Shade Impulse Chapter 1

MARILITH

USE	2	CHARGE	6

EFFECT After a period of time, opponent's bravery is frozen for around 30 seconds.

LOCATION DP Prize: Shade Impulse Chapter 2

KRAKEN

USE	2	CHARGE	6

EFFECT After a period of time, you trade bravery values with your opponent.

LOCATION DP Prize: Shade Impulse Chapter 3

TIAMAT

USE	2	CHARGE	6

EFFECT After a period of time, your bravery triples.

LOCATION Shade Impulse Chapter 4 map 2

SCARMIGLIONE

USE	2	CHARGE	6

EFFECT When opponent calls a summon, his or her bravery falls to 0.

LOCATION Shade Impulse Chapter 1 map 2

CAGNAZZO

USE	2	CHARGE	6

EFFECT After opponent calls a summon, his or her bravery is temporarily frozen.

LOCATION Shade Impulse Chapter 2 map 2

BARBARICCIA

USE	2	CHARGE	6

EFFECT When opponent calls a summon, his or her bravery swaps with yours.

LOCATION Shade Impulse Chapter 3 map 3

RUBICANTE

USE	2	CHARGE	6

EFFECT When opponent calls a summon, your bravery is tripled.

LOCATION Shade Impulse Chapter 3 map 2

GILGAMESH

USE	2	CHARGE	6

EFFECT Usually triples your bravery, but may randomly reduce it to 1.

LOCATION Distant Glory: Redemption of the Warrior map 2

ULTIMA WEAPON

USE	1	CHARGE	10

EFFECT Inflicts Bravery Break on opponent after a period of time.

LOCATION DP Prize: Inward Chaos

OMEGA

USE	1	CHARGE	10

EFFECT For a short period of time, opponent's bravery is cut in half every second.

LOCATION Inward Chaos map 2

ARMAMENTS

There are over 400 weapons and armaments in *DISSIDIA: FINAL FANTASY*, and collecting them all proves to be one of the game's greatest challenges. In the following section, you'll find full stats for each item, as well as the easiest means with which to acquire them. Happy hunting!

UNDERSTANDING THE ENTRIES

WEAPON TYPES

Not every character can use every type of equipment. Each category begins with a chart that shows which characters can wield or wear that particular armament. Characters are presented in game order, with Cosmos characters on top, and Chaos characters below. Some characters also have exclusive items that can be found at the end of each section.

MEANS OF ACQUISITION

There are five ways in which you can acquire items. The easiest method is listed for each item entry in the section that follows.

Find: When an item can be found in a chest in a Story Mode chapter, the description will reveal the chapter name and particular map. Note that some chests may not appear until certain conditions are met, but you can find full details in the appropriate walkthrough section.

DP Prize: Some items can be won as a reward for having substantial amounts of leftover Destiny Points at the end of a Story Mode map. The applicable Story Mode chapter is listed here.

Shop: The vast majority of weapons can be purchased at the shop, although certain conditions may need to be fulfilled before the listing appears. (See "Shop Updates" below for more details.)

Card: Some items appear as treasure cards that can be purchased with medals in the Duel Colosseum. The course in which you can find the treasure card is listed.

Drop: There's a small chance that enemies you fight may drop one of their armaments, and it's possible to get the vast majority of game items this way. But earning specific items through drops is time-consuming and unpredictable, so item-drop information is listed only when it's the only known means of acquiring the item. When such items appear as enemy equipment in the Duel Colosseum, the easiest course where they commonly appear will be listed.

SHOP STOCK CONDITIONS

The shop deals in most of the game's items, but you'll first need to make the listing appear by fulfilling one of the six conditions listed below. The best items often require the exchange of certain trade accessories as well as cash; these "recipes" are listed for each purchasable item.

Initially available: This item is in stock as soon as the game shop opens its virtual doors.

Once found: The shop won't stock this item until you find it elsewhere, typically in a Story Mode chapter. That's not much help, but since you can only find each piece of equipment once, this is the only way to make duplicates for trade purposes.

Character at Lv X: Many items only appear when a character who is capable of equipping that item reaches a set minimum level, usually seven levels lower than the minimum level necessary to equip it.

Ingredient acquired: Most recipes appear when you've acquired one or more of the ingredients necessary to trade for it. Some listings appear when you find any ingredient, while others only appear when a single specific ingredient is acquired.

Buy X from PP Catalog: When certain conditions are met, the "Etc." section of the PP Catalog will offer options like "Shop - Genji Series Added." Purchasing these catalog entries unlocks the listings for certain items.

Password recipe: Items with this appearance condition do not appear in the shop until you enter a special password in the personal message section of your Friend Card. The developers plan to reveal these passwords in the weeks and months following the game's release.

COMBINATION EFFECTS

You'll find the full abilities of each item in its entry. Abilities like "Glorious Gold (1/3)" count as 1 of 3 parts of a combination special effect. To make the effect active, you'll need to simultaneously equip two other items with the Glorious Gold ability. Here is the full list of non-artifact item combination effects:

EFFECT NAME	PARTS	ABILITY
Adamant Chains	3	BRV Boost on Dodge +30%, Midair Evasion Boost
All Glories Must Fade	4	Initial EX Force +100%, EX Mode Duration -50%
Allure of Honey	4	Battlegen Rate x 1.5, Drop Rate x 1.5
Blessed Crystal	3	EX Force Absorption +20%, EX Core Absorption +20%
Dazzling Diamond	3	AP +100%
Elemental Archfiend	4	BRV up on evasion/block/Quickmove/stage destruction
Flavor of Life	4	Regen +100%
Force of the Resolute	4	EX Core & EX Force to BRV, EX Force Absorption + 30%
Glorious Gold	3	Gil +50%
Imp's Blessing	4	EX Intake Range +15m
Mystic Mythril	3	EX Mode Duration +30%
Power of Darkness	3	Wall Rush BRV Damage +20%, Wall Rush HP Damage +20%
Pride of the Titans	3	HP +750, BRV +100
Snowpetal	3	Magic Counter Strength +300%, BRV Boost on Block +30%
Soul of Yamato	3	LUK +3, Regen +20%, HP to BRV, EX Core Appearance Boost
Uniter	4	BRV Recovery +200%
Whisper of the Wyrm	3	Physical Defense +10%, Magic Defense +10%
Wisdom of Lufenia	3	EX Gauge Depletion +15% (Depletes EX Gauge of opponent on successful hit)

WEAPONS

SWORDS

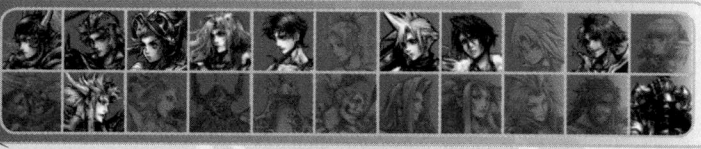

NAME	EQUIP LEVEL	ACQUIRE	HP	BRV	ATK	DEF	RANK	ABILITIES	COST	INGREDIENT 1	QUANTITY	INGREDIENT 2	QUANTITY	INGREDIENT 3	QUANTITY
Broadsword	1	Find: Prologue map 3 Shop: Initially available	—	—	4	—	—	(none)	1,000	—	—	—	—	—	—
Sun Blade	1	Find: Destiny Odyssey VIII map 4 Shop: Once found	—	—	4	—	—	Initial Bravery +20%	1,000	Broadsword	1	Bless Shard	1	Transmogridust	2
Iron Sword	8	Shop: Character at Lv 3	—	—	9	—	2	(none)	2,000	—	—	—	—	—	—
Serpent Sword	15	Shop: Character at Lv 8	—	—	13	—	3	(none)	3,700	—	—	—	—	—	—
Flametongue	15	DP Prize: Destiny Odyssey VIII Shop: Once found	—	—	13	—	3	Initial Bravery +20%	3,700	Broadsword	1	Bless Shard	1	Transmogridust	4
Mythril Sword	22	Shop: Ingredient acquired	—	—	18	—	4	Mystic Mythril (1/3)	6,050	Iron Sword	1	Mythril	1		
Icebrand	22	DP Prize: Destiny Odyssey VIII Shop: Once found	—	—	18	—	4	Initial Bravery +20%	6,050	Iron Sword	1	Lithe Shard	1	Transmogridust	8
Mythril Sword+	8	Shop: Ingredient acquired	—	—	18	—	4	Mystic Mythril (1/3)	6,050	Mythril Sword	1	Geranium	1	Transmogridust	2

SWORDS (CONTINUED)

NAME	EQUIP LEVEL	ACQUIRE	HP	BRV	ATK	DEF	RANK	ABILITIES	COST	INGREDIENT 1	QUANTITY	INGREDIENT 2	QUANTITY	INGREDIENT 3	QUANTITY
Saber	29	Shop: Character at Lv 22	—	—	22	—	5	(none)	8,400	—	—	—	—	—	—
Rapier	36	Shop: Character at Lv 29	—	—	27	—	—	(none)	10,750	—	—	—	—	—	—
Gold Sword	36	Shop: Ingredient acquired	—	—	27	—	—	Glorious Gold (1/3)	10,750	Saber	1	Gold	1	—	—
Gold Sword+	22	Shop: Ingredient acquired	—	—	27	—	—	Glorious Gold (1/3)	10,750	Gold Sword	1	White Stone	1	Transmogridust	3
Ancient Sword	36	Shop: Ingredient acquired	—	—	27	—	—	Initial Bravery +20%	10,750	Sun Blade	1	Black Stone	1	—	—
Estoc	43	Shop: Character at Lv 36	—	—	31	—	7	(none)	13,100	—	—	—	—	—	—
Diamond Sword	50	Shop: Ingredient acquired	—	—	36	—	8	Dazzling Diamond (1/3)	15,460	Rapier	1	Diamond	1	—	—
Coral Sword	50	Shop: Character at Lv 43	—	—	36	—	—	Initial Bravery +20%	15,460	Rapier	1	Spirit Stone	1	Transmogridust	1
Diamond Sword+	36	Shop: Ingredient acquired	—	—	36	—	8	Dazzling Diamond (1/3)	15,460	Diamond Sword	1	Black Stone	1	Transmogridust	4
Rune Blade	57	Shop: Character at Lv 50	—	—	40	—	9	Initial Bravery +30%	17,810	Estoc	1	Levistone	1	Mako Stone	2
Crystal Sword	64	Shop: Ingredient acquired	—	—	45	—	—	Blessed Crystal (1/3)	20,160	Diamond Sword	1	Crystal	1	Dewdrop Pebble	3
Defender	64	Shop: Ingredient acquired	—	—	45	—	—	Initial Bravery +30%	20,160	Coral Sword	1	Dewdrop Pebble	3	Transmogridust	4
Enhancer	71	Shop: Ingredient acquired	—	—	49	—	—	Initial Bravery +30%	22,510	Rune Blade	1	Stone of the Condemner	3	Crimson Powder	4
Falchion	78	Shop: Character at Lv 71	—	—	54	—	—	(none)	32,310	—	—	—	—	—	—
Dragon Slayer	78	Shop: Ingredient acquired	—	—	54	—	12	Initial Bravery +30% Whisper of the Wyrm (1/3)	24,860	Flametongue	1	Wyrmstone	3	Protect Shard	3
Save the Queen	85	Shop: Ingredient acquired	—	—	58	—	13	Initial Bravery +40%	27,220	Enhancer	1	Blessed Gem	4	Magnet Shard	1
Brave Blade	92	Shop: Ingredient acquired	—	—	63	—	14	Initial Bravery +40%	29,570	Icebrand	1	Goddess's Magicite	5	Red Gem	1
Excalibur	99	Shop: Ingredient acquired	—	—	67	—	—	Initial Bravery +50%	31,920	Save the Queen	1	Supreme Gem	5	—	—
Excalipoor	99	Shop: Password Recipe	—	—	68	—	—	Physical Damage -100%	31,920	Cancer Recipe	1	Dragon Seal	1	Chocograph	1
Wyrmhero Blade	99	Shop: Password Recipe	—	—	67	—	—	"Legendary blade held by many"	31,920	Aquarius Recipe	1	Crystal Eye	1	Al Bhed Primer	1
Lufenian Saber	99	Drop: Lunar Whale Course	—	—	67	—	—	Wisdom of Lufenia (1/3)	(not sold)	—	—	—	—	—	—
Excalibur II	99	Drop: Blackjack Course	—	—	67	—	15	EXP+100%	(not sold)	—	—	—	—	—	—

DAGGERS

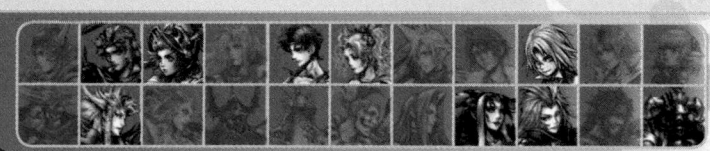

NAME	EQUIP LEVEL	ACQUIRE	HP	BRV	ATK	DEF	RANK	ABILITIES	COST	INGREDIENT 1	QUANTITY	INGREDIENT 2	QUANTITY	INGREDIENT 3	QUANTITY
Knife	1	Find: Destiny Odyssey IX map 1 Shop: Initially available	—	—	3	—	—	(none)	450	—	—	—	—	—	—
Triton's Dagger	1	Find: Destiny Odyssey IX map 3 Shop: Once found	—	—	3	—	—	Initial EX Force +15%	450	Knife	1	Power Shard	1	Transmogridust	2
Dagger	8	Shop: Character at Lv 2	—	—	8	—	2	(none)	1,450	—	—	—	—	—	—
Khukuri	15	Shop: Character at Lv 8	—	—	12	—	3	(none)	3,150	—	—	—	—	—	—
Main Gauche	15	DP Prize: Destiny Odyssey IX Shop: Once found	—	—	12	—	3	Initial EX Force +15%	3,150	Knife	1	Power Shard	1	Transmogridust	4
Mage Masher	22	DP Prize: Destiny Odyssey IX Shop: Once found	—	—	17	—	4	Initial EX Force +15%	5,500	Dagger	1	Resilience Shard	1	Transmogridust	8
Piercing Dagger	36	Shop: Character at Lv 29	—	—	26	—	6	(none)	10,200	—	—	—	—	—	—
Man-Eater	36	Shop: Ingredient acquired	—	—	26	—	—	Initial EX Force +15%	10,200	Triton's Dagger	1	Black Tiger Fang	1	—	—
Air Knife	50	Shop: Character at Lv 43	—	—	35	—	—	Initial EX Force +15%	14,910	Piercing Dagger	1	Great Serpent's Fang	1	Transmogridust	1
Assassin's Dagger	64	Shop: Ingredient acquired	—	—	44	—	10	Initial EX Force +20%	19,610	Main Gauche	1	Mammoth Tusk	3	Transmogridust	4
Orichalcum Dirk	71	Shop: Ingredient acquired	—	—	48	—	11	Initial EX Force +20%	21,960	Air Knife	1	Mammoth Tusk	6	Orange Gem	1
Valiant Knife	78	Shop: Character at Lv 71	—	—	53	—	—	(none)	29,310	—	—	—	—	—	—
Gladius	92	Shop: Ingredient acquired	—	—	62	—	14	Initial EX Force +25%	29,020	Mage Masher	1	Beastlord Fang	5	Orange Gem	1
Zwill Crossblade	99	Shop: Ingredient acquired	—	—	66	—	—	Initial EX Force +30%	31,370	Air Knife	1	Maduin's Fang	5	—	—
Adamant Knife	99	Shop: Ingredient acquired	—	—	66	—	—	Initial EX Force +30% Adamant Chains (1/3)	31,370	Orichalcum Dirk	1	Adamantite	1	—	—
Chicken Knife	99	Shop: Password Recipe	—	—	66	—	—	BRV Boost on Quickmove +2%	31,370	Libra Recipe	1	Omega Badge	1	Sphere	1
Lufenian Dagger	99	Drop: Lunar Whale Course	—	—	66	—	—	Wisdom of Lufenia (1/3)	(not sold)	—	—	—	—	—	—

GREATSWORDS

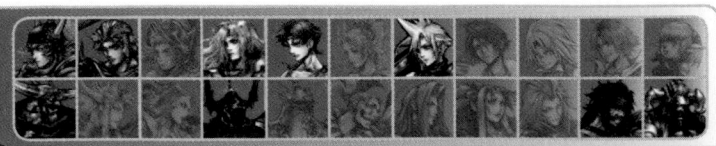

NAME	EQUIP LEVEL	ACQUIRE	HP	BRV	ATK	DEF	RANK	ABILITIES	COST	INGREDIENT 1	QUANTITY	INGREDIENT 2	QUANTITY	INGREDIENT 3	QUANTITY
Longsword	1	Find: Destiny Odyssey V map 1 Shop: Once found	—	—	5	—	—	(none)	1,830	—	—	—	—	—	—
Hardedge	1	Find: Destiny Odyssey VII map 3 Shop: Once found	—	—	5	—	—	Physical Damage +10%	1,830	Longsword	1	Gale Shard	1	Transmogridust	2
Greatsword	8	Shop: Character at Lv 3	—	—	10	—	2	(none)	2,830	—	—	—	—	—	—
Zweihander	15	DP Prize: Destiny Odyssey VII Shop: Once found	—	—	14	—	3	Physical Damage +10%	4,520	Longsword	1	Gale Shard	1	Transmogridust	4
Flamberge	22	DP Prize: Destiny Odyssey VII Shop: Once found	—	—	19	—	4	Physical Damage +10%	6,870	Greatsword	1	Oath Shard	1	Transmogridust	8
Claymore	29	Shop: Character at Lv 22	—	—	23	—	5	(none)	9,230	—	—	—	—	—	—
Inferno Sword	36	Shop: Ingredient acquired	—	—	28	—	6	Physical Damage +10%	11,580	Hardedge	1	Unknown's Bone	1	—	—
Ogrenix	50	Shop: Character at Lv 43	—	—	37	—	8	Physical Damage +10%	16,280	Zweihander	1	Gigas Bone	1	Transmogridust	1
Nail Bat	57	Card: DC Falcon Course	—	—	41	—	9	Force of the Resolute (1/4)	(not sold)	—	—	—	—	—	—
Apocalypse	71	Shop: Ingredient acquired	—	—	50	—	—	Physical Damage +15%	23,340	Flamberge	1	Wargod Bone	3	Yellow Gem	1
Royal Swordsman's Blade	78	Shop: Character at Lv 71	—	—	55	—	12	(none)	35,310	—	—	—	—	—	—
Ragnarok	99	Shop: Ingredient acquired	—	—	68	—	—	Physical Damage +25%	32,750	Apocalypse	1	Hero's Bone	5	—	—
Lufenia's Edge	99	Drop: Lunar Whale Course	—	—	68	—	—	Wisdom of Lufenia (1/3)	(not sold)	—	—	—	—	—	—

KATANA

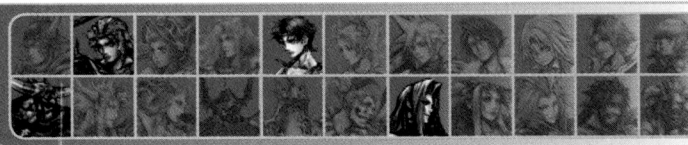

NAME	EQUIP LEVEL	ACQUIRE	HP	BRV	ATK	DEF	RANK	ABILITIES	COST	INGREDIENT 1	QUANTITY	INGREDIENT 2	QUANTITY	INGREDIENT 3	QUANTITY
Katana	1	Shop: Initially available	—	—	5	—	—	(none)	1,000	—	—	—	—	—	—
Nodachi	24	Shop: Ingredient acquired	—	—	19	—	4	EX Intake Range +2m	6,050	Katana	1	Large Horn	1	—	—
Uchigatana	31	Shop: Character at Lv 24	—	—	23	—	5	(none)	8,400	—	—	—	—	—	—
Warblade	45	DP Prize: Shade Impulse Ch 2	—	—	32	—	—	Uniter (1/4)	(not sold)	—	—	—	—	—	—
Kiku-ichimonji	53	Shop: Character at Lv 43	—	—	37	—	8	EX Intake Range +2m	15,460	Uchigatana	1	Wyvern Horn	1	Transmogridust	1
Murasame	60	Shop: Character at Lv 50	—	—	41	—	—	EX Intake Range +3m	17,810	Kiku-ichimonji	1	Lizard Horn	1	Taurus Horn	2
Heike's Blade	81	DP Prize: Distant Glory: RotW	—	—	55	—	12	All Glories Must Fade (1/4)	(not sold)	—	—	—	—	—	—
Kazekiri	88	Shop: Ingredient acquired	—	—	59	—	—	EX Intake Range +4m	27,220	Murasame	1	Unicorn Horn	4	Orange Gem	1
Heaven's Cloud	100	Shop: Ingredient acquired	—	—	68	—	15	EX Intake Range +6m	31,920	Kazekiri	1	Behemoth Horn	5	—	—

ARMAMENTS

KATANA (CONTINUED)

NAME	EQUIP LEVEL	ACQUIRE	HP	BRV	ATK	DEF	RANK	ABILITIES	COST	INGREDIENT 1	QUANTITY	INGREDIENT 2	QUANTITY	INGREDIENT 3	QUANTITY
Piggy's Stick	100	Shop: Password Recipe	—	200	68	—	15	BRV Recovery -80%	31,920	Capricorn Recipe	1	Tintinnabulum	1	Strategy Guide	1
Lufenian Katana	100	Drop: Lunar Whale Course	—	—	68	—	15	Wisdom of Lufenia (1/3)	(not sold)	—	—	—	—	—	—
Genji Blade	100	Shop: Buy "Genji Series Added" in PP Catalog Drop: Lunar Whale Course	—	—	68	—	—	Soul of Yamato (1/3)	31,920	Heike's Blade	1	Behemoth Horn	5	Titan Crystal	5

SPEARS

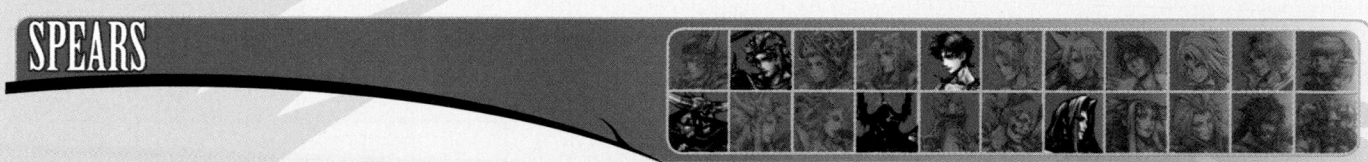

NAME	EQUIP LEVEL	ACQUIRE	HP	BRV	ATK	DEF	RANK	ABILITIES	COST	INGREDIENT 1	QUANTITY	INGREDIENT 2	QUANTITY	INGREDIENT 3	QUANTITY
Spear	1	Find: Destiny Odyssey II map 1 Shop: Initially available	—	—	5	-1	—	(none)	1,000	—	—	—	—	—	—
Scorpion	2	Find: Destiny Odyssey II map 3 Shop: Initially available	—	—	5	-1	—	Wall Rush BRV Damage +20%	1,000	Spear	1	Magnet Shard	1	Transmogridust	2
Javelin	9	Shop: Character at Lv 2	—	—	10	-1	—	(none)	2,000	—	—	—	—	—	—
Heavy Lance	16	Shop: Character at Lv 9	—	—	14	-1	—	(none)	3,700	—	—	—	—	—	—
Flame Lance	16	DP Prize: Destiny Odyssey II Shop: Once found	—	—	14	-1	3	Wall Rush BRV Damage +20%	3,700	Spear	1	Magnet Shard	1	Transmogridust	4
Mythril Spear	23	Shop: Ingredient acquired	—	—	19	-1	4	Mystic Mythril (1/3)	6,050	Javelin	1	Mythril	1	—	—
Ice Lance	23	DP Prize: Destiny Odyssey II Shop: Once found	—	—	19	-1	4	Wall Rush BRV Damage +20%	6,050	Javelin	1	Healing Shard	1	Transmogridust	8
Mythril Spear	9	Shop: Ingredient acquired	—	—	19	-1	4	Mystic Mythril (1/3)	6,050	Mythril Spear	1	Bergamot	1	Transmogridust	2
Obelisk	37	Shop: Character at Lv 30	—	—	28	-1	6	(none)	10,750	—	—	—	—	—	—
Wind Spear	37	Shop: Ingredient acquired	—	—	28	-1	6	Wall Rush BRV Damage +20%	10,750	Scorpion	1	Summoner's Horn	1	—	—
Partisan	44	Shop: Character at Lv 37	—	—	32	-1	—	(none)	13,100	—	—	—	—	—	—
Crystal Lance	65	Shop: Ingredient acquired	—	—	46	-1	—	Blessed Crystal (1/3)	20,160	Obelisk	1	Crystal	1	Humbaba's Horn	3
Trident	72	Shop: Ingredient acquired	—	—	50	-1	—	Wall Rush BRV Damage +30%	22,510	Partisan	1	Ixion Horn	3	Blue Gem	1
Radiant Lance	79	Shop: Character at Lv 72	—	—	55	-1	12	(none)	32,310	—	—	—	—	—	—
Wyvern Lance	79	Shop: Ingredient acquired	—	—	55	-1	12	Wall Rush BRV Damage +30% Whisper of the Wyrm (1/3)	24,860	Flame Lance	1	Wind Drake Horn	3	Recovery Shard	1
Holy Lance	86	Shop: Ingredient acquired	—	—	59	-1	13	Wall Rush BRV Damage +40%	27,220	Crystal Lance	1	Unicorn Horn	3	Titan Shard	1
Gae Bolg	93	Shop: Ingredient acquired	—	—	64	-1	—	Wall Rush BRV Damage +40%	29,570	Ice Lance	1	Beastlord Horn	5	Yellow Gem	1
Gungnir	100	Shop: Ingredient acquired	—	—	68	-1	15	Wall Rush BRV Damage +50%	31,920	Holy Lance	1	Behemoth Horn	5	—	—
Lufenian Lance	100	Drop: DC Lunar Whale Course	—	—	68	-1	—	Wisdom of Lufenia (1/3)	(not sold)	—	—	—	—	—	—

AXES

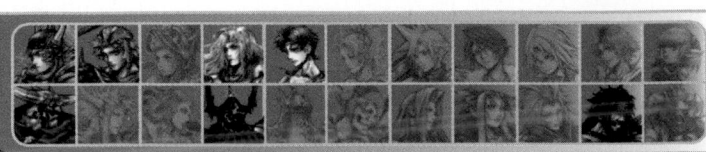

NAME	EQUIP LEVEL	ACQUIRE	HP	BRV	ATK	DEF	RANK	ABILITIES	COST	INGREDIENT 1	QUANTITY	INGREDIENT 2	QUANTITY	INGREDIENT 3	QUANTITY
Axe	1	Shop: Initially available	—	—	6	-2	—	(none)	1,000	—	—	—	—	—	—
Slasher	1	Find: Destiny Odyssey I map 4 Shop: Once found	—	—	6	-2	—	Wall Rush HP Damage +5%	1,000	Axe	1	Protect Shard	1	Transmogridust	2
Light Axe	8	Shop: Character at Lv 3	—	—	11	-2	2	(none)	2,000	—	—	—	—	—	—
Battle Axe	15	Shop: Character at Lv 8	—	—	15	-2	3	(none)	3,700	—	—	—	—	—	—
Tomahawk	15	DP Prize: Destiny Odyssey I Shop: Once found	—	—	15	-2	3	Wall Rush HP Damage +5%	3,700	Axe	1	Protect Shard	1	Transmogridust	4
Mythril Axe	22	Shop: Ingredient acquired	—	—	20	-2	4	Mystic Mythril (1/3)	6,050	Light Axe	1	Mythril	2	—	—
Dwarven Axe	22	DP Prize: Destiny Odyssey I Shop: Once found	—	—	20	-2	4	Wall Rush HP Damage +5%	6,050	Light Axe	1	Strength Shard	1	Transmogridust	8
Mythril Axe+	8	Shop: Ingredient acquired	—	—	20	-2	4	Mystic Mythril (1/3)	6,050	Mythril Axe	1	Rosemary	1	Transmogridust	2
Death Sickle	36	Shop: Ingredient acquired	—	—	29	-2	6	Wall Rush HP Damage +5%	10,750	Slasher	1	Unknown's Bone	1	—	—
Francisca	43	Shop: Character at Lv 36	—	—	33	-2	7	(none)	13,100	—	—	—	—	—	—
Rune Axe	57	Shop: Character at Lv 50	—	—	42	-2	—	Wall Rush HP Damage +10%	17,810	Tomahawk	1	Ancient Bone	1	Nue Bone	2
Giant's Axe	85	Shop: Ingredient acquired	—	—	60	-2	13	Wall Rush HP Damage +20% Pride of the Titans (1/3)	27,220	Dwarven Axe	1	Saint's Bone	4	Cyan Gem	1
Earthbreaker	99	Shop: Ingredient acquired	—	—	69	-2	—	Wall Rush HP Damage +30%	31,920	Giant's Axe	1	Hero's Bone	5	—	—
Lufenian Axe	99	Drop: Lunar Whale Course	—	—	69	-2	15	Wisdom of Lufenia (1/3)	(not sold)	—	—	—	—	—	—

RODS

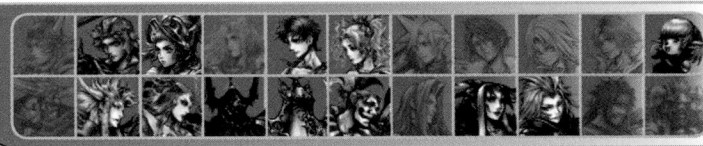

NAME	EQUIP LEVEL	ACQUIRE	HP	BRV	ATK	DEF	RANK	ABILITIES	COST	INGREDIENT 1	QUANTITY	INGREDIENT 2	QUANTITY	INGREDIENT 3	QUANTITY
Rod	1	Find: Destiny Odyssey III map 5 Shop: Initially available	62	—	3	1	—	(none)	1,000	—	—	—	—	—	—
Full Metal Staff	3	Find: Destiny Odyssey III map 3 Shop: Once found	62	—	3	1	—	Magic Damage +10%	1,000	Rod	1	Recovery Shard	1	Transmogridust	2
Guard Stick	10	Shop: Character at Lv 3	80	—	8	1	2	(none)	2,000	—	—	—	—	—	—
Healing Rod	17	Shop: Character at Lv 10	97	—	12	1	3	(none)	3,700	—	—	—	—	—	—
Flame Rod	17	DP Prize: Destiny Odyssey III Shop: Once found	97	—	12	1	—	Magic Damage +10%	3,700	Rod	1	Recovery Shard	1	Transmogridust	4
Mythril Rod	24	Shop: Ingredient acquired	115	—	17	1	4	Mystic Mythril (1/3)	6,050	Guard Stick	1	Mythril	1	—	—
Ice Rod	24	DP Prize: Destiny Odyssey III Shop: Once found	115	—	17	1	4	Magic Damage +10%	6,050	Guard Stick	1	Mana Shard	1	Transmogridust	8
Mythril Rod+	10	Shop: Ingredient acquired	115	—	17	1	4	Mystic Mythril (1/3)	6,050	Mythril Rod	1	Tea Tree	1	Transmogridust	2
Rod of Wisdom	31	Shop: Character at Lv 24	132	—	21	1	5	(none)	8,400	—	—	—	—	—	—
Faerie Rod	38	Shop: Ingredient acquired	150	—	26	1	—	Magic Damage +10%	10,750	Full Metal Staff	1	Moonstone	1	—	—

ARMAMENTS

RODS (CONTINUED)

NAME	EQUIP LEVEL	ACQUIRE	HP	BRV	ATK	DEF	RANK	ABILITIES	COST	INGREDIENT 1	QUANTITY	INGREDIENT 2	QUANTITY	INGREDIENT 3	QUANTITY
Wizard's Rod	15	Shop: Character at Lv 38	167	—	30	1	7	(none)	13,100	—	—	—	—	—	—
Crown Scepter	67	Shop: Ingredient acquired	220	—	44	1	10	Magic Damage +15%	20,160	Flame Rod	1	Opal	3	Purple Gem	1
Holy Rod	88	Shop: Ingredient acquired	272	—	57	1	—	Magic Damage +20%	27,220	Ice Rod	1	Holystone	4	Purple Gem	1
Stardust Rod	100	Shop: Ingredient acquired	307	—	66	1	—	Magic Damage +25%	31,920	Holy Rod	1	Sky Jewel	5	—	—
Lufenian Rod	100	Drop: Lunar Whale Course	307	—	66	1	—	Wisdom of Lufenia (1/3)	(not sold)	—	—	—	—	—	—

STAVES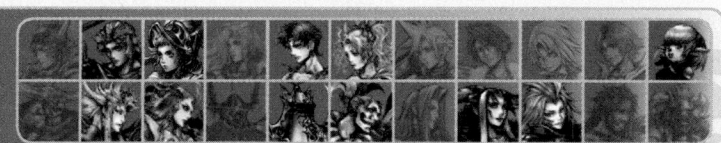

NAME	EQUIP LEVEL	ACQUIRE	HP	BRV	ATK	DEF	RANK	ABILITIES	COST	INGREDIENT 1	QUANTITY	INGREDIENT 2	QUANTITY	INGREDIENT 3	QUANTITY
Staff	1	Find: Destiny Odyssey VI map 1 / Shop: Initially available	—	11	3	—	—	(none)	1,000	—	—	—	—	—	—
Mage's Staff	1	Find: Destiny Odyssey VI map 3 / Shop: Once found	—	11	3	—	—	EX Mode Duration +10%	1,000	Staff	1	Amplification Shard	1	Transmogridust	2
Oak Staff	8	Shop: Character at Lv 3	—	13	8	—	2	(none)	2,000	—	—	—	—	—	—
Healing Staff	15	Shop: Character at Lv 8	—	15	12	—	3	(none)	3,700	—	—	—	—	—	—
Flamescepter	15	DP Prize: Destiny Odyssey VI / Shop: Once found	—	15	12	—	3	EX Mode Duration +10%	3,700	Staff	1	Amplification Shard	1	Transmogridust	4
Power Staff	22	Shop: Ingredient acquired	—	17	17	—	4	EX Mode Duration +10%	6,050	Staff	1	Strength Powder	3	—	—
Snowscepter	22	DP Prize: Destiny Odyssey VI / Shop: Once found	—	17	17	—	4	EX Mode Duration +10%	6,050	Oak Staff	1	Allure Shard	1	Transmogridust	8
Golden Staff	36	Shop: Ingredient acquired	—	22	26	—	6	Glorious Gold (1/3)	10,750	Oak Staff	1	Gold	1	—	—
Golden Staff+	22	Shop: Ingredient acquired	—	22	26	—	6	Glorious Gold (1/3)	10,750	Golden Staff	1	Splinter	1	Transmogridust	3
Elder Staff	36	Shop: Ingredient acquired	—	22	26	—	6	EX Mode Duration +10%	10,750	Mage's Staff	1	Lumber	1	—	—
Rune Staff	50	Shop: Character at Lv 43	—	26	35	—	—	EX Mode Duration +10%	15,460	Healing Staff	1	Thorny Lumber	1	Transmogridust	1
Judicer's Staff	57	Shop: Character at Lv 50	—	28	39	—	9	EX Mode Duration +20%	17,810	Flamescepter	1	Mistletoe	1	Quality Lumber	2
Staff of the Magi	71	Shop: Ingredient acquired	—	32	48	—	11	EX Mode Duration +20%	22,510	Rune Staff	1	Spiritwood	3	White Gem	1
Eight-fluted Pole	78	Shop: Character at Lv 71	—	34	53	—	12	(none)	32,310	—	—	—	—	—	—
Staff of Light	78	Shop: Ingredient acquired	—	34	53	—	12	EX Mode Duration +20%	24,860	Snowscepter	1	Dragonwood	3	Luck Shard	1
Zeus Mace	92	Shop: Ingredient acquired	—	38	62	—	—	EX Mode Duration +30%	29,570	Staff of the Magi	1	Revival Tree	5	Green Gem	1
Nirvana	99	Shop: Ingredient acquired	—	40	66	—	—	EX Mode Duration +40%	31,920	Staff of Light	1	Iifa Tree	5	—	—
Lufenian Staff	99	Drop: Lunar Whale Course	—	40	66	—	—	Wisdom of Lufenia (1/3)	(not sold)	—	—	—	—	—	—
Fire Book	99	Drop: Blackjack Course	—	40	66	—	—	Regen +75%	(not sold)	—	—	—	—	—	—

THROWN

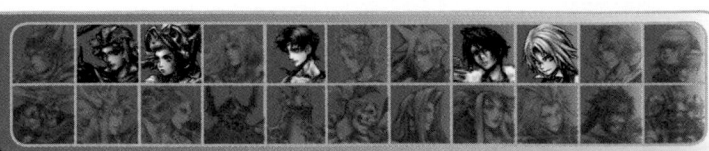

NAME	EQUIP LEVEL	ACQUIRE	HP	BRV	ATK	DEF	RANK	ABILITIES	COST	INGREDIENT 1	QUANTITY	INGREDIENT 2	QUANTITY	INGREDIENT 3	QUANTITY
Juji Shuriken	15	Shop: Character at Lv 8	—	-15	14	—	—	(none)	3,700	—	—	—	—	—	—
Boomerang	22	Shop: Character at Lv 15	—	-17	19	—	4	(none)	6,050	—	—	—	—	—	—
Chakram	22	Shop: Ingredient acquired	—	-17	19	—	4	EX Force Absorption +10%	6,050	Boomerang	1	Large Fang	1	—	—
Pinwheel	29	Shop: Character at Lv 22	—	-19	23	—	5	(none)	8,400	—	—	—	—	—	—
Frying Pan	29	Card: Airship Course Drop: Stiltzkin 4 Friend Card	—	-19	23	—	5	Flavor of Life (1/4)	(not sold)	—	—	—	—	—	—
Moonring Blade	43	Shop: Character at Lv 36	—	-24	32	—	—	(none)	13,100	—	—	—	—	—	—
Rising Sun	57	Shop: Character at Lv 50	—	-28	41	—	9	EX Force Absorption +15%	17,810	Pinwheel	1	Throat Wolf Fang	1	Chimera Fang	2
Fuma Shuriken	85	Shop: Ingredient acquired	—	-36	59	—	—	EX Force Absorption +20%	27,220	Rising Sun	1	Holy Fang	4	Red Gem	1
Cleaver	99	Shop: Ingredient acquired	—	-40	68	—	—	EX Force Absorption +30%	31,920	Fuma Shuriken	1	Beastlord Fang	5	—	—
Star of Lufenia	99	Drop: Lunar Whale Course	—	-40	68	—	—	Wisdom of Lufenia (1/3)	(not sold)	—	—	—	—	—	—

GRAPPLING

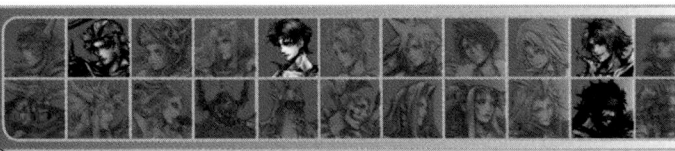

NAME	EQUIP LEVEL	ACQUIRE	HP	BRV	ATK	DEF	RANK	ABILITIES	COST	INGREDIENT 1	QUANTITY	INGREDIENT 2	QUANTITY	INGREDIENT 3	QUANTITY
Leather Gloves	1	Shop: Initially available	—	23	4	—	—	(none)	1,550	—	—	—	—	—	—
Metal Knuckles	15	Shop: Character at Lv 8	—	31	13	—	—	(none)	4,250	—	—	—	—	—	—
Mythril Claw	22	Shop: Ingredient acquired	—	35	18	—	4	Mystic Mythril (1/3)	6,600	Metal Knuckles	1	Mythril	1	—	—
Mythril Claw+	8	Shop: Ingredient acquired	—	35	18	—	4	Mystic Mythril (1/3)	6,600	Mythril Claw	1	Ylang Ylang	1	Transmogridust	2
Darksteel Claws	22	Shop: Ingredient acquired	—	35	18	—	4	Chase BRV Damage +20%	6,600	Metal Knuckles	1	Iron Carapace	1	—	—
Sonic Knuckles	36	Shop: Character at Lv 29	—	44	27	—	6	(none)	11,300	—	—	—	—	—	—
Tigerfangs	57	Shop: Character at Lv 50	—	56	40	—	—	Chase BRV Damage +30%	18,360	Sonic Knuckles	1	Destrier Barding	1	Wormskin	2
Cat Claws	64	Shop: Ingredient acquired	—	60	45	—	—	Chase BRV Damage +30%	20,710	Tigerfangs	1	Giant Turtleshell	3	Transmogridust	5
Scarmiglione's Fang	64	DP Prize: Shade Impulse 3	—	60	45	—	—	Elemental Archfiend (1/4)	(not sold)	—	—	—	—	—	—
Godhand	92	Shop: Ingredient acquired	—	77	63	—	—	Chase BRV Damage +40%	30,120	Cat Claws	1	Aged Turtle Shell	5	Blue Gem	1
Premium Heart	99	Shop: Ingredient acquired	—	81	67	—	—	Chase BRV Damage +50%	32,470	Godhand	1	Ancient Turtle Shell	5	—	—
Lufenian Claw	99	Drop: Lunar Whale Course	—	81	67	—	—	Wisdom of Lufenia (1/3)	(not sold)	—	—	—	—	—	—

ARMAMENTS

INSTRUMENT

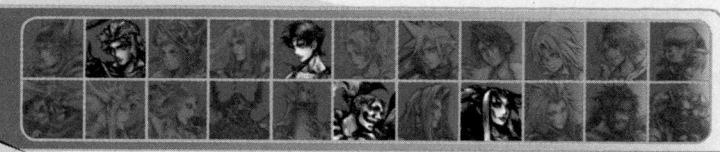

INSTRUMENTS	EQUIP LEVEL	ACQUIRE	HP	BRV	ATK	DEF	RANK	ABILITIES	COST	INGREDIENT 1	QUANTITY	INGREDIENT 2	QUANTITY	INGREDIENT 3	QUANTITY
Diamond Bell	22	Shop: Character at Lv 15	—	—	16	2	4	(none)	6,050	—	—	—	—	—	—
Gaia Bell	22	Shop: Ingredient acquired	—	—	16	2	4	EX Core Absorption +10%	6,050	Diamond Bell	1	Quality Branch	1	—	—
Rune Bell	50	Shop: Character at Lv 43	—	—	34	2	—	EX Core Absorption +10%	15,460	Diamond Bell	1	Thorny Lumber	1	Transmogridust	1
Dream Harp	64	Shop: Ingredient acquired	—	—	43	2	—	EX Core Absorption +15%	20,160	Rune Bell	1	Big Tree	3	Transmogridust	5
Lamia Harp	78	Shop: Ingredient acquired	—	—	52	2	—	EX Core Absorption +15%	24,860	Dream Harp	1	Dragonwood	3	Amplification Shard	1
Apollo's Harp	92	Shop: Ingredient acquired	—	—	61	2	—	EX Core Absorption +20%	29,570	Lamia Harp	1	Revival Tree	5	Cyan Gem	1
Loki's Lute	99	Shop: Ingredient acquired	—	—	65	2	—	EX Core Absorption +30%	31,920	Apollo's Harp	1	Iifa Tree	5	—	—
Lufenian Lute	99	Drop: Lunar Whale Course	—	—	65	2	—	Wisdom of Lufenia (1/3)	(not sold)	—	—	—	—	—	—

SPECIAL (GENERAL)

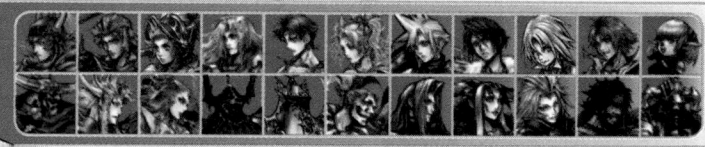

NAME	EQUIP LEVEL	ACQUIRE	HP	BRV	ATK	DEF	RANK	ABILITIES	COST	INGREDIENT 1	QUANTITY	INGREDIENT 2	QUANTITY	INGREDIENT 3	QUANTITY
Cursed Blade	22	Drop: Stiltzkin 5 Friend Card	—	—	31	—	7	"Blade that heralds the darkness"	(not sold)	—	—	—	—	—	—
Impartisan	85	Card: Invincible Course	—	—	58	—	13	Imp's Blessing (1/4)	(not sold)	—	—	—	—	—	—
Blade of the Damned	71	Drop: Lunar Whale Course	—	—	63	—	14	"Blade that heralds the darkness"	(not sold)	—	—	—	—	—	—
Ultima Weapon	99	Drop: Lunar Whale Course	—	—	68	—	—	More powerful when HP is full	31,920	Pisces Recipe	1	Noah's Lute	1	Whisperweed	1

SPECIAL (PRETTY PRINCESS)

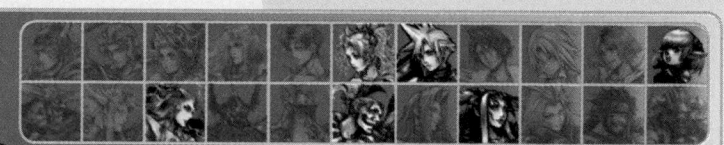

NAME	EQUIP LEVEL	ACQUIRE	HP	BRV	ATK	DEF	RANK	ABILITIES	COST	INGREDIENT 1	QUANTITY	INGREDIENT 2	QUANTITY	INGREDIENT 3	QUANTITY
Sexy Cologne	43	Shop: Buy "Pretty Princess Series Added" in PP Catalog	—	—	31	—	7	Allure of Honey (1/4)	13,100	Spirit Stone	5	Gale Shard	2	—	—

MACHINE

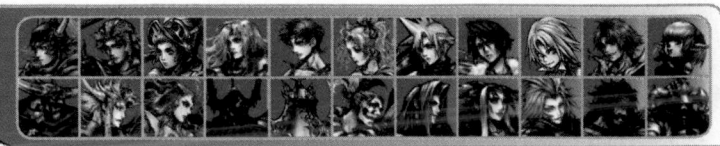

"No character can naturally equip machines, but anyone can learn how to do so by buying "Use Machines" at the shop. (Use Machines becomes available after acquiring Chemist Lore in the Inward Chaos Story Mode.)

NAME	EQUIP LEVEL	ACQUIRE	HP	BRV	ATK	DEF	RANK	ABILITIES	COST	INGREDIENT 1	QUANTITY	INGREDIENT 2	QUANTITY	INGREDIENT 3	QUANTITY
Machine Gun	96	Shop: Acquire Mallet as Inward Chaos DP Prize	-307	81	67	—	—	Accessory Breakability +5% Wall Rush BRV Damage +30%	31,920	Mallet	1	Supreme Gem	5	—	—

COSMOS-SIDE EXCLUSIVES

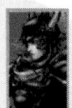

WARRIOR OF LIGHT

NAME	EQUIP LEVEL	ACQUIRE	HP	BRV	ATK	DEF	RANK	ABILITIES	COST	INGREDIENT 1	QUANTITY	INGREDIENT 2	QUANTITY	INGREDIENT 3	QUANTITY
Flame Sword	50	Shop: Ingredient acquired	—	—	36	—	—	Defense +5%	15,460	Rapier	1	Spirit Stone	3	Protect Shard	2
Braveheart	92	Shop: Ingredient acquired	—	—	63	—	14	Defense +10%	29,570	Flame Sword	1	Goddess's Magicite	5	Protect Crystal	3
Barbarian's Sword	100	Shop: Ingredient acquired	—	—	68	—	15	Defense +15% Minor Counterattack Effect	31,920	Braveheart	1	Guiding Light	5	Protect Orb	5

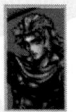

FIRION

NAME	EQUIP LEVEL	ACQUIRE	HP	BRV	ATK	DEF	RANK	ABILITIES	COST	INGREDIENT 1	QUANTITY	INGREDIENT 2	QUANTITY	INGREDIENT 3	QUANTITY
Abel's Lance	51	Shop: Ingredient acquired	—	—	37	-1	—	Extra HP to BRV	15,460	Partisan	1	Wyvern Horn	3	Magnet Shard	2
Longinus	93	Shop: Ingredient acquired	—	—	64	-1	—	Extra HP to BRV	29,570	Abel's Lance	1	Beastlord Horn	5	Magnet Crystal	3
Wild Rose	100	Shop: Ingredient acquired	—	—	69	-1	—	Extra HP to BRV Minor Counterattack Effect	31,920	Longinus	1	The Youth's Dream	5	Magnet Orb	5

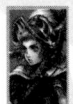

ONION KNIGHT

NAME	EQUIP LEVEL	ACQUIRE	HP	BRV	ATK	DEF	RANK	ABILITIES	COST	INGREDIENT 1	QUANTITY	INGREDIENT 2	QUANTITY	INGREDIENT 3	QUANTITY
Tyrfing	50	Shop: Ingredient acquired	—	—	36	—	—	Damage +5%	15,460	Rapier	1	Spirit Stone	3	Recovery Shard	2
Royal Sword	92	Shop: Ingredient acquired	—	—	63	—	—	Damage +10%	29,570	Tyrfing	1	Goddess's Magicite	5	Recovery Crystal	3
Onion Sword	100	Shop: Ingredient acquired	—	—	68	—	—	Damage +15% Major Gambler's Spirit Effect	31,920	Royal Sword	1	Onion	5	Recovery Orb	5

ARMAMENTS

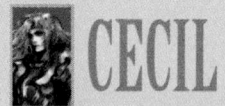

CECIL

NAME	EQUIP LEVEL	ACQUIRE	HP	BRV	ATK	DEF	RANK	ABILITIES	COST	INGREDIENT 1	QUANTITY	INGREDIENT 2	QUANTITY	INGREDIENT 3	QUANTITY
Dark Sword	1	Find: DOIV map 1	—	—	4	—	—	Power of Darkness (1/3)	(not sold)	—	—	—	—	—	—
Mythgraven Blade	50	Shop: Ingredient acquired	—	—	37	—	—	[When Paladin] DEF +1	16,280	Dark Sword	1	Gigas Bone	3	Titan Shard	2
Lustrous Sword	92	Shop: Ingredient acquired	—	—	64	—	—	[When Paladin] DEF +2	30,390	Mythgraven Blade	1	Blood-Darkened Bone	5	Titan Crystal	3
Lightbringer	100	Shop: Ingredient acquired	—	—	69	—	—	[When Paladin] DEF +2 Minor Sneak Attack Effect	32,750	Lustrous Sword	1	Twin Form	5	Titan Orb	5
Cimmerian Edge	100	Shop: Ingredient acquired	—	—	69	—	—	[When Dark Knight] ATK +2 Minor Counterattack Effect	32,750	Lustrous Sword	1	Twin Form	5	Titan Orb	5

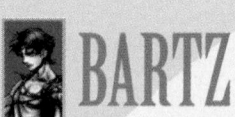

BARTZ

NAME	EQUIP LEVEL	ACQUIRE	HP	BRV	ATK	DEF	RANK	ABILITIES	COST	INGREDIENT 1	QUANTITY	INGREDIENT 2	QUANTITY	INGREDIENT 3	QUANTITY
Chocoblade	50	Shop: Ingredient acquired	—	—	36	—	8	Regen +30%	15,460	Rapier	1	Spirit Stone	3	Luck Shard	2
Dayspring	92	Shop: Ingredient acquired	—	—	63	—	—	Regen +40%	29,570	Chocoblade	1	Goddess's Magicite	5	Luck Crystal	3
Dorgann's Blade	100	Shop: Ingredient acquired	—	—	68	—	—	Regen +50% Cat Nip Effect	31,920	Dayspring	1	Splendor of the Wind	5	Luck Orb	5

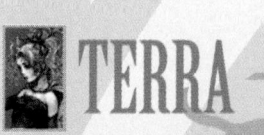

TERRA

NAME	EQUIP LEVEL	ACQUIRE	HP	BRV	ATK	DEF	RANK	ABILITIES	COST	INGREDIENT 1	QUANTITY	INGREDIENT 2	QUANTITY	INGREDIENT 3	QUANTITY
Chain Flail	50	Shop: Ingredient acquired	—	26	35	—	—	Magic Defense +30%	15,460	Healing Staff	1	Thorny Lumber	3	Amplification Shard	2
Morning Star	92	Shop: Ingredient acquired	—	38	62	—	—	Magic Defense +40%	29,570	Chain Flail	1	Revival Tree	5	Amplification Crystal	3
Maduin's Horn	100	Shop: Ingredient acquired	—	40	67	—	—	Magic Defense +50% Minor Anti-EX Effect	31,920	Morning Star	1	Veiled Magic	5	Amplification Orb	5

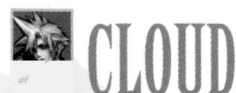 CLOUD

NAME	EQUIP LEVEL	ACQUIRE	HP	BRV	ATK	DEF	RANK	ABILITIES	COST	INGREDIENT 1	QUANTITY	INGREDIENT 2	QUANTITY	INGREDIENT 3	QUANTITY
Buster Sword	1	Find: DOVII map 1	—	—	5	—	—	(none)	(not sold)	—	—	—	—	—	—
Force Stealer	50	Shop: Ingredient acquired	—	—	37	—	—	Wall Rush HP Damage +10%	16,280	Buster Sword	1	Gigas Bone	3	Gale Shard	2
Butterfly Edge	92	Shop: Ingredient acquired	—	—	64	—	—	Wall Rush HP Damage +20%	30,390	Force Stealer	1	Blood-Darkened Bone	5	Gale Crystal	3
Fenrir	100	Shop: Ingredient acquired	—	—	69	—	—	Wall Rush HP Damage +30% Minor Sneak Attack Effect	32,750	Butterfly Edge	1	True Past	5	Gale Orb	5

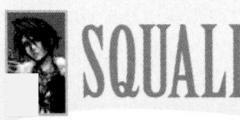 SQUALL

NAME	EQUIP LEVEL	ACQUIRE	HP	BRV	ATK	DEF	RANK	ABILITIES	COST	INGREDIENT 1	QUANTITY	INGREDIENT 2	QUANTITY	INGREDIENT 3	QUANTITY
Revolver	1	Find: DOVIII map 1	—	—	4	—	—	(none)	(not sold)	—	—	—	—	—	—
Twin Lance	50	Shop: Ingredient acquired	—	—	36	—	—	EX Core Absorption +15%	15,460	Revolver	1	Spirit Stone	3	Bless Shard	2
Punishment	92	Shop: Ingredient acquired	—	—	63	—	—	EX Core Absorption +20%	29,570	Twin Lance	1	Goddess's Magicite	5	Bless Crystal	3
Lionheart	100	Shop: Ingredient acquired	—	—	68	—	—	EX Core Absorption +30% Minor Sneak Attack Effect	31,920	Punishment	1	Unshelled Bullet	5	Bless Orb	5

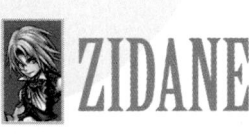 ZIDANE

NAME	EQUIP LEVEL	ACQUIRE	HP	BRV	ATK	DEF	RANK	ABILITIES	COST	INGREDIENT 1	QUANTITY	INGREDIENT 2	QUANTITY	INGREDIENT 3	QUANTITY
Sargatanas	50	Shop: Ingredient acquired	—	—	35	—	—	BRV Boost on Dodge +10%	14,910	Pinwheel	1	Great Serpent's Fang	3	Power Shard	2
The Tower	92	Shop: Ingredient acquired	—	—	62	—	—	BRV Boost on Dodge +15%	29,020	Sargatanas	1	Beastlord Fang	5	Power Crystal	3
Ozma's Splinter	100	Shop: Ingredient acquired	—	—	67	—	—	BRV Boost on Dodge +20% Major Gambler's Spirit Effect	31,370	The Tower	1	Theater Ticket	5	Power Orb	5

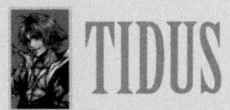

TIDUS

NAME	EQUIP LEVEL	ACQUIRE	HP	BRV	ATK	DEF	RANK	ABILITIES	COST	INGREDIENT 1	QUANTITY	INGREDIENT 2	QUANTITY	INGREDIENT 3	QUANTITY
Official Ball	1	Find: DOX map 1	—	-11	5	—	—	(none)	(not sold)	—	—	—	—	—	—
Striker	50	Shop: Ingredient acquired	—	-26	37	—	—	BRV Boost on Dodge +10%	15,460	Official Ball	1	Great Serpent's Fang	3	Guts Shard	2
Grand Slam	92	Shop: Ingredient acquired	—	-38	64	—	—	BRV Boost on Dodge +15%	29,570	Striker	1	Beastlord Fang	5	Guts Crystal	3
World Champion	100	Shop: Ingredient acquired	—	-40	69	—	—	BRV Boost on Dodge +20% Cat Nip Effect	31,920	Grand Slam	1	Fayth's Dream	5	Guts Orb	5

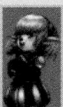

SHANTOTTO

NAME	EQUIP LEVEL	ACQUIRE	HP	BRV	ATK	DEF	RANK	ABILITIES	COST	INGREDIENT 1	QUANTITY	INGREDIENT 2	QUANTITY	INGREDIENT 3	QUANTITY
Jupiter's Staff	50	Shop: Ingredient acquired	—	26	35	—	—	Initial BRV +20%	15,460	Healing Staff	1	Thorny Lumber	3	Quickstrike Shard	2
Laevateinn	92	Shop: Ingredient acquired	—	38	62	—	—	Initial BRV +30%	29,570	Jupiter's Staff	1	Revival Tree	5	Quickstrike Crystal	3
Claustrum	100	Shop: Ingredient acquired	—	40	67	—	—	Initial BRV +40% Major Gambler's Spirit Effect	31,920	Laevateinn	1	Boiling Blood	5	Quickstrike Orb	5

CHAOS-SIDE EXCLUSIVES

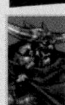

GARLAND

NAME	EQUIP LEVEL	ACQUIRE	HP	BRV	ATK	DEF	RANK	ABILITIES	COST	INGREDIENT 1	QUANTITY	INGREDIENT 2	QUANTITY	INGREDIENT 3	QUANTITY
Ogrekiller	50	Shop: Ingredient acquired	—	—	38	-2	—	EX Force Absorption +15%	15,460	Francisca	1	Gigas Bone	3	Strength Shard	2
Viking Axe	92	Shop: Ingredient acquired	—	—	65	-2	—	EX Force Absorption +20%	29,570	Ogrekiller	1	Blood-Darkened Bone	5	Strength Crystal	3
Gigant Axe	100	Shop: Ingredient acquired	—	—	70	-2	—	EX Force Absorption +30% Minor Anti-EX Effect	31,920	Viking Axe	1	Wheel of Darkness	5	Strength Orb	5

THE EMPEROR

NAME	EQUIP LEVEL	ACQUIRE	HP	BRV	ATK	DEF	RANK	ABILITIES	COST	INGREDIENT 1	QUANTITY	INGREDIENT 2	QUANTITY	INGREDIENT 3	QUANTITY
Diamond Mace	53	Shop: Ingredient acquired	185	—	35	1	—	EX Intake Range +2m	15,460	Wizard's Rod	1	Ruby	3	Healing Shard	2
Demon's Rod	95	Shop: Ingredient acquired	290	—	62	1	—	EX Intake Range +4m	29,570	Diamond Mace	1	Lapis Lazuli	5	Healing Crystal	3
Mateus's Malice	100	Shop: Ingredient acquired	307	—	67	1	—	EX Intake Range +6m Minor Anti-EX Effect	31,920	Demon's Rod	1	Lust for Power	5	Healing Orb	5

CLOUD OF DARKNESS

NAME	EQUIP LEVEL	ACQUIRE	HP	BRV	ATK	DEF	RANK	ABILITIES	COST	INGREDIENT 1	QUANTITY	INGREDIENT 2	QUANTITY	INGREDIENT 3	QUANTITY
Calcite Staff	50	Shop: Ingredient acquired	—	26	35	—	—	BRV Recovery +50%	15,460	Healing Staff	1	Thorny Lumber	3	Mana Shard	2
Bizarre Staff	92	Shop: Ingredient acquired	—	38	62	—	—	BRV Recovery +75%	29,570	Calcite Staff	1	Revival Tree	5	Mana Crystal	3
Everdark	100	Shop: Ingredient acquired	—	40	67	—	—	BRV Recovery +100% Major Gambler's Spirit Effect	31,920	Bizarre Staff	1	Roaming Clouds	5	Mana Orb	5

GOLBEZ

NAME	EQUIP LEVEL	ACQUIRE	HP	BRV	ATK	DEF	RANK	ABILITIES	COST	INGREDIENT 1	QUANTITY	INGREDIENT 2	QUANTITY	INGREDIENT 3	QUANTITY
Lilith Rod	53	Shop: Ingredient acquired	185	—	35	1	8	Damage +5%	15,460	Wizard's Rod	1	Ruby	3	Destruction Shard	2
Asura's Rod	95	Shop: Ingredient acquired	290	—	62	1	—	Damage +10%	29,570	Lilith Rod	1	Lapis Lazuli	5	Destruction Crystal	3
Zeromus Shard	100	Shop: Ingredient acquired	307	—	67	1	—	Damage +15% Back to the Wall Effect	31,920	Asura's Rod	1	Lone Heart	5	Destruction Orb	5

EXDEATH

NAME	EQUIP LEVEL	ACQUIRE	HP	BRV	ATK	DEF	RANK	ABILITIES	COST	INGREDIENT 1	QUANTITY	INGREDIENT 2	QUANTITY	INGREDIENT 3	QUANTITY
Ghido's Whisker	50	Shop: Ingredient acquired	—	26	35	—	—	BRV Boost on Block +10%	15,460	Healing Staff	1	Thorny Lumber	3	Reflex Shard	2
Moore Branch	92	Shop: Ingredient acquired	—	38	62	—	—	BRV Boost on Block +15%	29,570	Ghido's Whisker	1	Revival Tree	5	Reflex Crystal	3
Enuo's Scourge	100	Shop: Ingredient acquired	—	40	67	—	—	BRV Boost on Block +20% Riposte Effect	31,920	Moore Branch	1	Power of the Void	5	Reflex Orb	5

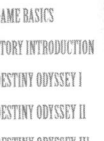

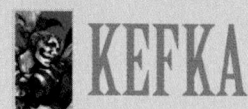

KEFKA

NAME	EQUIP LEVEL	ACQUIRE	HP	BRV	ATK	DEF	RANK	ABILITIES	COST	INGREDIENT 1	QUANTITY	INGREDIENT 2	QUANTITY	INGREDIENT 3	QUANTITY
Lamia's Flute	50	Shop: Ingredient acquired	—	—	34	2	7	Initial EX Force +15%	15,460	Diamond Bell	1	Thorny Lumber	3	Allure Shard	2
Nephilim Flute	92	Shop: Ingredient acquired	—	—	61	2	—	Initial EX Force +20%	29,570	Lamia's Flute	1	Revival Tree	5	Allure Crystal	3
Dancing Mad	100	Shop: Ingredient acquired	—	—	66	2	—	Initial EX Force +25% Back to the Wall Effect	31,920	Nephilim Flute	1	Fanatic's Leer	5	Allure Orb	5

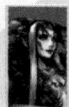

SEPHIROTH

NAME	EQUIP LEVEL	ACQUIRE	HP	BRV	ATK	DEF	RANK	ABILITIES	COST	INGREDIENT 1	QUANTITY	INGREDIENT 2	QUANTITY	INGREDIENT 3	QUANTITY
Masamune Blade	53	Shop: Ingredient acquired	—	—	37	—	8	Damage +5%	15,460	Uchigatana	1	Wyvern Horn	3	Oath Shard	2
Masamune	95	Shop: Ingredient acquired	—	—	64	—	—	Damage +10%	29,570	Masamune Blade	1	Beastlord Horn	5	Oath Crystal	3
One-Winged Angel	100	Shop: Ingredient acquired	—	—	69	—	—	Damage +15% Minor Sneak Attack Effect	31,920	Masamune	1	Life of the Planet	5	Oath Orb	5

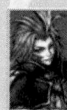

ULTIMECIA

NAME	EQUIP LEVEL	ACQUIRE	HP	BRV	ATK	DEF	RANK	ABILITIES	COST	INGREDIENT 1	QUANTITY	INGREDIENT 2	QUANTITY	INGREDIENT 3	QUANTITY
Valkyrie	53	Shop: Ingredient acquired	185	—	35	1	—	EX Force Absorption +15%	15,460	Pinwheel	1	Ruby	3	Lithe Shard	2
Cardinal	95	Shop: Ingredient acquired	290	—	62	1	—	EX Force Absorption +20%	29,570	Valkyrie	1	Lapis Lazuli	5	Lithe Crystal	3
Shooting Star	100	Shop: Ingredient acquired	307	—	67	1	—	EX Force Absorption +30% Back to the Wall Effect	31,920	Cardinal	1	Gears of Time	5	Lithe Orb	5

KUJA

NAME	EQUIP LEVEL	ACQUIRE	HP	BRV	ATK	DEF	RANK	ABILITIES	COST	INGREDIENT 1	QUANTITY	INGREDIENT 2	QUANTITY	INGREDIENT 3	QUANTITY
Punisher	53	Shop: Ingredient acquired	185	—	35	1	—	EX Force Absorption +15%	15,460	Wizard's Rod	1	Ruby	3	Resilience Shard	2
Whale Whisker	95	Shop: Ingredient acquired	290	—	62	1	—	EX Force Absorption +20%	29,570	Punisher	1	Lapis Lazuli	5	Resilience Crystal	3
Terra's Legacy	100	Shop: Ingredient acquired	307	—	67	1	—	EX Force Absorption +30% Back to the Wall Effect	31,920	Whale Whisker	1	God of Destruction	5	Resilience Orb	5

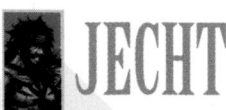

JECHT

NAME	EQUIP LEVEL	ACQUIRE	HP	BRV	ATK	DEF	RANK	ABILITIES	COST	INGREDIENT 1	QUANTITY	INGREDIENT 2	QUANTITY	INGREDIENT 3	QUANTITY
Kaiser Knuckles	50	Shop: Ingredient acquired	—	52	36	—	—	Wall Rush HP Defense +50%	16,010	Sonic Knuckles	1	Great Serpentskin	3	Crimson Shard	2
Sin's Talon	92	Shop: Ingredient acquired	—	77	63	—	—	Wall Rush HP Defense +50%	30,120	Kaiser Knuckles	1	Aged Turtle Shell	5	Crimson Crystal	3
Sin's Fang	100	Shop: Ingredient acquired	—	81	68	—	—	Wall Rush HP Defense +75% Minor Sneak Attack Effect	32,470	Sin's Talon	1	Medal of Honor	5	Crimson Orb	5

GABRANTH

NAME	EQUIP LEVEL	ACQUIRE	HP	BRV	ATK	DEF	RANK	ABILITIES	COST	INGREDIENT 1	QUANTITY	INGREDIENT 2	QUANTITY	INGREDIENT 3	QUANTITY
Demonsbane	50	Shop: Ingredient acquired	—	—	36	—	—	EX Mode Duration +20%	15,460	Rapier	1	Spirit Stone	3	Time Shard	2
Deathbringer	92	Shop: Ingredient acquired	—	—	63	—	14	EX Mode Duration +30%	29,570	Demonsbane	1	Goddess's Magicite	5	Time Crystal	3
Chaos Blade	100	Shop: Ingredient acquired	—	—	68	—	—	EX Mode Duration +40% Minor Counterattack Effect	31,920	Deathbringer	1	Gates of Judgment	5	Time Orb	5

GLOVES

PARRYING

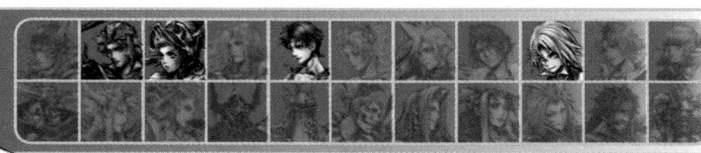

NAME	EQUIP LEVEL	ACQUIRE	HP	BRV	ATK	DEF	RANK	ABILITIES	COST	INGREDIENT 1	QUANTITY	INGREDIENT 2	QUANTITY	INGREDIENT 3	QUANTITY
Kunai	1	Find: Destiny Odyssey II map 4 Shop: Initially available	—	—	1	4	1	(none)	1,830	—	—	—	—	—	—
Wakizashi	8	Shop: Character at Lv 4	—	—	1	9	2	(none)	2,830	—	—	—	—	—	—
Kodachi	22	Shop: Character at Lv 15	—	—	1	17	4	(none)	6,870	—	—	—	—	—	—
Sakura	22	Shop: Ingredient acquired	—	—	1	17	4	BRV Boost on Block +5%	6,870	Kodachi	1	Large Fang	1	—	—
Shinobi-Gatana	36	Shop: Character at Lv 29	—	—	1	26	—	(none)	11,580	—	—	—	—	—	—
Sasuke	57	Shop: Character at Lv 50	—	—	1	41	—	BRV Boost on Block +10%	18,630	Shinobi-Gatana	1	Throat Wolf Fang	1	Chimera Fang	2
Kagenui	85	Shop: Ingredient acquired	—	—	1	61	—	BRV Boost on Block +15%	28,040	Sasuke	1	Holy Fang	4	Green Gem	1
Blurry Moon	99	Shop: Ingredient acquired	—	—	1	72	—	(none)	32,750	Kagenui	1	Maduin's Fang	5	—	—
Lufenian Dirk	99	Drop: Lunar Whale Course	—	—	1	72	—	Wisdom of Lufenia (1/3)	(not sold)	—	—	—	—	—	—

ARMAMENTS

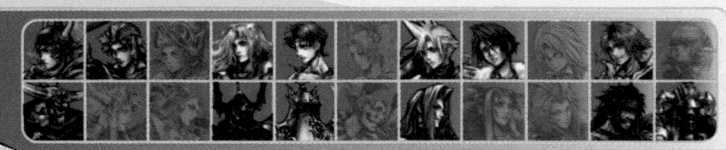

NAME	EQUIP LEVEL	ACQUIRE	HP	BRV	ATK	DEF	RANK	ABILITIES	COST	INGREDIENT 1	QUANTITY	INGREDIENT 2	QUANTITY	INGREDIENT 3	QUANTITY
Buckler	1	Find: Destiny Odyssey X map 3 / Shop: Initially available	—	—	—	5	1	(none)	1,000	—	—	—	—	—	—
Shell Shield	1	Find: Destiny Odyssey V map 3 / Shop: Once found	—	—	—	5	1	Wall Rush HP Defense +20%	1,000	Buckler	1	Luck Shard	1	Transmogridust	2
Iron Shield	8	Shop: Character at Lv 3	—	—	—	10	2	(none)	2,000	—	—	—	—	—	—
Knight's Shield	15	Shop: Character at Lv 8	—	—	—	14	3	(none)	3,700	—	—	—	—	—	—
Flame Shield	15	DP Prize: Destiny Odyssey V / Shop: Once found	—	—	—	14	3	Wall Rush HP Defense +20%	3,700	Buckler	1	Luck Shard	1	Transmogridust	4
Mythril Shield	22	Shop: Ingredient acquired	—	—	—	18	4	Mystic Mythril (1/3)	6,050	Iron Shield	1	Mythril	2	—	—
Ice Shield	22	DP Prize: Destiny Odyssey V / Shop: Once found	—	—	—	18	4	Wall Rush HP Defense +20%	6,050	Iron Shield	1	Reflex Shard	1	Transmogridust	8
Mythril Shield+	8	Shop: Ingredient acquired	—	—	—	18	4	Mystic Mythril (1/3)	6,050	Mythril Shield	1	Eucalyptus	1	Transmogridust	2
Heavy Shield	29	Shop: Character at Lv 22	—	—	—	23	5	(none)	8,400	—	—	—	—	—	—
Golden Shield	36	Shop: Ingredient acquired	—	—	—	27	—	Glorious Gold (1/3)	10,750	Knight's Shield	1	Gold	2	—	—
Golden Shield+	22	Shop: Ingredient acquired	—	—	—	27	—	Glorious Gold (1/3)	10,750	Golden Shield	1	Yensa Scales	1	Transmogridust	3
Demon Shield	36	Shop: Ingredient acquired	—	—	—	27	6	Wall Rush HP Defense +20%	10,750	Shell Shield	1	Lamia Scales	1	—	—
Force Shield	43	Shop: Character at Lv 36	—	—	—	32	7	(none)	13,100	—	—	—	—	—	—
Diamond Shield	50	Shop: Ingredient acquired	—	—	—	36	8	Dazzling Diamond (1/3)	15,460	Heavy Shield	1	Diamond	2	—	—
Diamond Shield+	36	Shop: Ingredient acquired	—	—	—	36	8	Dazzling Diamond (1/3)	15,460	Diamond Shield	1	Lamia Scales	1	Transmogridust	4
Crystal Shield	64	Shop: Ingredient acquired	—	—	—	46	—	Blessed Crystal (1/3)	20,160	Force Shield	1	Crystal	2	Emperor Scales	3
Lustrous Shield	71	Shop: Ingredient acquired	—	—	—	52	11	(none)	22,510	Force Shield	1	Godfighter Scales	3	Blue Gem	1
Dragon Shield	78	Shop: Ingredient acquired	—	—	—	56	12	Whisper of the Wyrm (1/3)	24,860	Flame Shield	1	Sea Serpent Scales	3	Gale Shard	1
Heike's Shield	78	DP Prize: Distant Glory: TLoL / Drop: Lunar Whale Course	—	—	—	56	12	All Glories Must Fade (1/4)	(not sold)	—	—	—	—	—	—
Thunder Shield	85	Shop: Ingredient acquired	—	—	—	62	13	(none)	27,220	Lustrous Shield	1	Sacred Beast Scales	4	Bless Shard	1
Aegis Shield	92	Shop: Ingredient acquired	—	—	—	67	—	Wall Rush HP Defense +40%	29,570	Ice Shield	1	Djinn Scales	5	Purple Gem	1
Hero's Shield	99	Shop: Ingredient acquired	—	—	—	73	—	(none)	31,920	Thunder Shield	1	Eden's Scales	5	—	—
Adamant Shield	99	Shop: Ingredient acquired	—	—	—	73	—	Adamant Chains (1/3)	31,920	Crystal Shield	1	Adamantite	1	—	—
Ensanguined Shield	99	Shop: Password Recipe	—	—	—	73	—	Initial HP -95% Initial Bravery -100%	31,920	Taurus Recipe	1	Wyvern Egg	1	Snowboard	1
Lufenian Shield	99	Drop: Lunar Whale Course	—	—	—	73	—	Wisdom of Lufenia (1/3)	(not sold)	—	—	—	—	—	—
Genji Shield	99	Shop: Buy "Genji Series Added" in PP Catalog / Drop: Lunar Whale Course	—	—	—	73	—	Soul of Yamato (1/3)	31,920	Heike's Shield	1	Eden's Scales	5	Time Crystal	5

BANGLES

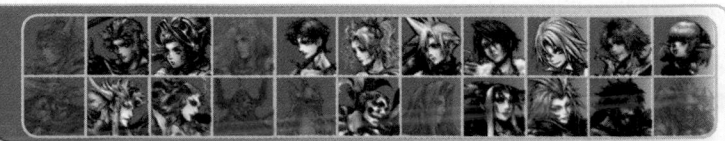

NAME	EQUIP LEVEL	ACQUIRE	HP	BRV	ATK	DEF	RANK	ABILITIES	COST	INGREDIENT 1	QUANTITY	INGREDIENT 2	QUANTITY	INGREDIENT 3	QUANTITY
Bronze Bangle	1	Find: Destiny Odyssey VII map 2 / Find: Destiny Odyssey VIII map 3 / Shop: Initially available	62	—	—	4	1	(none)	1,000	—	—	—	—	—	—
Power Armlet	8	Shop: Character at Lv 3	80	—	—	9	2	(none)	2,000	—	—	—	—	—	—
Silver Bangles	15	Shop: Character at Lv 8	97	—	—	13	3	(none)	3,700	—	—	—	—	—	—
Mythril Bangle	22	Shop: Ingredient acquired	115	—	—	17	4	Mystic Mythril (1/3)	6,050	Power Armlet	1	Mythril	1	—	—
Mythril Bangle+	8	Shop: Ingredient acquired	115	—	—	17	4	Mystic Mythril (1/3)	6,050	Mythril Bangle	1	Tea Tree	1	Transmogridust	2
Chocobracelet	22	Shop: Ingredient acquired	115	—	—	17	4	Regen +25%	6,050	Silver Bangles	1	Aquamarine	1	—	—
Hyper Wrist	29	Shop: Character at Lv 22	132	—	—	22	5	(none)	8,400	—	—	—	—	—	—
Kitchen Timer	29	Card: Airship Course / Drop: Stiltzkin 4 Friend Card	132	—	—	22	5	Flavor of Life (1/4)	(not sold)	—	—	—	—	—	—
Gold Bangle	36	Shop: Ingredient acquired	150	—	—	26	6	Glorious Gold (1/3)	10,750	Silver Bangles	1	Gold	1	—	—
Gold Bangle+	22	Shop: Ingredient acquired	150	—	—	26	6	Glorious Gold (1/3)	10,750	Gold Bangle	1	Emerald	1	Transmogridust	3
Precious Watch	43	Shop: Character at Lv 36	167	—	—	31	7	(none)	13,100	—	—	—	—	—	—
Diamond Cuff	50	Shop: Ingredient acquired	185	—	—	35	8	Dazzling Diamond (1/3)	15,460	Hyper Wrist	1	Diamond	1	—	—
Diamond Cuff+	36	Shop: Ingredient acquired	185	—	—	35	8	Dazzling Diamond (1/3)	15,460	Diamond Cuff	1	Moonstone	1	Transmogridust	4
Rune Armlet	57	Shop: Character at Lv 50	202	—	—	41	9	(none)	17,810	Hyper Wrist	1	Sapphire	1	Peridot	2
Skull Wristlet	57	Card: Falcon Course	202	—	—	41	9	Force of the Resolute (1/4)	(not sold)	—	—	—	—	—	—
Crystal Bangle	64	Shop: Ingredient acquired	220	—	—	45	—	Blessed Crystal (1/3)	20,160	Precious Watch	1	Crystal	1	Opal	3
Barbariccia's Wristlet	64	DP Prize: Shade Impulse 3	220	—	—	45	—	Elemental Archfiend (1/4)	(not sold)	—	—	—	—	—	—
Imperial Guard	71	Shop: Ingredient acquired	237	—	—	51	—	(none)	22,510	Precious Watch	1	Topaz	3	Recovery Powder	4
Dragon Armlet	78	Shop: Ingredient acquired	255	—	—	55	—	Whisper of the Wyrm (1/3)	24,860	Rune Armlet	1	Dragonstone	3	Power Shard	1
Protective Armlet	85	Shop: Ingredient acquired	272	—	—	61	—	(none)	27,220	Imperial Guard	1	Holystone	4	Guts Shard	1
Mystile	92	Shop: Ingredient acquired	290	—	—	66	—	(none)	29,570	Dragon Armlet	1	Lapis Lazuli	5	White Gem	1
Seydlitz	99	Shop: Ingredient acquired	207	—	—	72	—	(none)	31,920	Protective Armlet	1	Sky Jewel	5	—	—
Blue Moon	99	Card: Lunar Whale Course	307	—	—	72	—	Snowpetal (1/3)	(not sold)	—	—	—	—	—	—
Lufenian Bangle	99	Drop: Lunar Whale Course	307	—	—	72	—	Wisdom of Lufenia (1/3)	(not sold)	—	—	—	—	—	—

GAUNTLETS

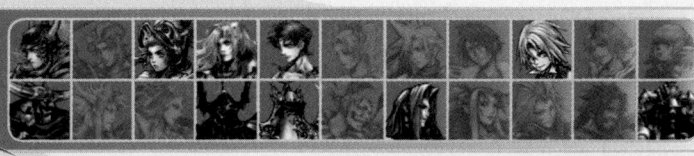

NAME	EQUIP LEVEL	ACQUIRE	HP	BRV	ATK	DEF	RANK	ABILITIES	COST	INGREDIENT 1	QUANTITY	INGREDIENT 2	QUANTITY	INGREDIENT 3	QUANTITY
Hide Armlet	1	Find: Destiny Odyssey III map 3 Shop: Initially available	—	11	—	4	1	(none)	1,000	—	—	—	—	—	—
Iron Armlet	8	Shop: Character at Lv 3	—	13	—	9	2	(none)	2,000	—	—	—	—	—	—
Gauntlets	22	Shop: Character at Lv 15	—	17	—	17	4	(none)	6,050	—	—	—	—	—	—
Battle Gloves	22	Shop: Ingredient acquired	—	17	—	17	4	Magic Counter Strength +20%	6,050	Gauntlets	1	Iron Carapace	1	—	—
Gold Armlet	36	Shop: Ingredient acquired	—	22	—	26	6	Glorious Gold (1/3)	10,750	Gauntlets	1	Gold	1	—	—
Gold Armlet+	22	Shop: Ingredient acquired	—	22	—	26	6	Glorious Gold (1/3)	10,750	Gold Armlet	1	Charger Barding	1	Transmogridust	3
Warlord's Gauntlets	43	DP Prize: Shade Impulse 1 Drop: Stiltzkin 2 Friend Card	—	24	—	31	7	Uniter (1/4)	(not sold)	—	—	—	—	—	—
Demon Gloves	57	Shop: Character at Lv 50	—	28	—	41	—	(none)	17,810	Gauntlets	1	Destrier Barding	1	Wormskin	2
Thief Gloves	71	Shop: Ingredient acquired	—	32	—	51	11	Drop Rate x 1.2	22,510	Demon Gloves	1	Giant Turtleshell	3	Titan Powder	4
Dragon Gloves	78	Shop: Ingredient acquired	—	34	—	55	12	Whisper of the Wyrm (1/3)	24,860	Thief Gloves	1	Wyrm Carapace	3	Quickstrike Crystal	1
Giant's Gloves	85	Shop: Ingredient acquired	—	36	—	61	13	Pride of the Titans (1/3)	27,220	Dragon Gloves	1	Blessed Barding	4	Purple Gem	1
Lunate Armlet	99	Card: Lunar Whale Course	—	40	—	72	—	Snowpetal (1/3)	(not sold)	—	—	—	—	—	—
Borghertz's Hands	99	Shop: Ingredient acquired	—	40	—	72	—	(none)	31,920	Giant's Gloves	1	Ancient Turtle Shell	5	—	—
Lufenian Gauntlets	99	Drop: Lunar Whale Course	—	40	—	72	—	Wisdom of Lufenia (1/3)	(not sold)	—	—	—	—	—	—

SPECIAL (GENERAL)

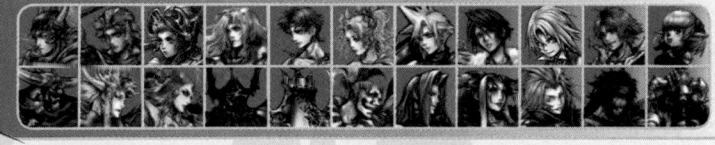

NAME	EQUIP LEVEL	ACQUIRE	HP	BRV	ATK	DEF	RANK	ABILITIES	COST	INGREDIENT 1	QUANTITY	INGREDIENT 2	QUANTITY	INGREDIENT 3	QUANTITY
Tortoise Shield	85	Card: Invincible Course	—	—	—	62	—	Imp's Blessing (1/4)	(not sold)	—	—	—	—	—	—

SPECIAL (PRETTY PRINCESS)

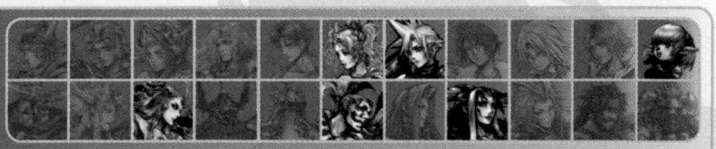

NAME	EQUIP LEVEL	ACQUIRE	HP	BRV	ATK	DEF	RANK	ABILITIES	COST	INGREDIENT 1	QUANTITY	INGREDIENT 2	QUANTITY	INGREDIENT 3	QUANTITY
Member's Card	43	Shop: Buy "Pretty Princess Series Added" in PP Catalog	—	—	—	32	7	Allure of Honey (1/4)	13,100	Great Serpent's Fang	5	Amplification Shard	2	—	—

MACHINE

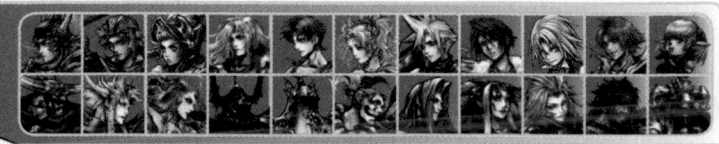

*No character can naturally equip machines, but anyone can learn how to do so by buying "Use Machines" at the shop. (Use Machines becomes available after acquiring Chemist Lore in the Inward Chaos Story Mode.)

NAME	EQUIP LEVEL	ACQUIRE	HP	BRV	ATK	DEF	RANK	ABILITIES	COST	INGREDIENT 1	QUANTITY	INGREDIENT 2	QUANTITY	INGREDIENT 3	QUANTITY
Chainsaw	96	Shop: Acquire Mallet as Inward Chaos DP Prize	-307	81	—	73	—	Accessory Breakability +5% Wall Rush HP Damage +20%	31,920	Mallet	1	Eden's Scales	5	—	—

COSMOS-SIDE EXCLUSIVES

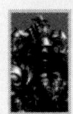

CECIL

NAME	EQUIP LEVEL	ACQUIRE	HP	BRV	ATK	DEF	RANK	ABILITIES	COST	INGREDIENT 1	QUANTITY	INGREDIENT 2	QUANTITY	INGREDIENT 3	QUANTITY
Dark Shield	1	Find: Destiny Odyssey IV map 3	—	—	—	5	—	Power of Darkness (1/3)	(not sold)	—	—	—	—	—	—

CHAOS-SIDE EXCLUSIVES

GABRANTH

NAME	EQUIP LEVEL	ACQUIRE	HP	BRV	ATK	DEF	RANK	ABILITIES	COST	INGREDIENT 1	QUANTITY	INGREDIENT 2	QUANTITY	INGREDIENT 3	QUANTITY
Highway Star	100	Shop: Ingredient acquired	—	—	1	72	—	EX Force Absorption +10%	32,750	Deathbringer	1	Gates of Judgment	5	Time Orb	5

HEADGEAR

HATS

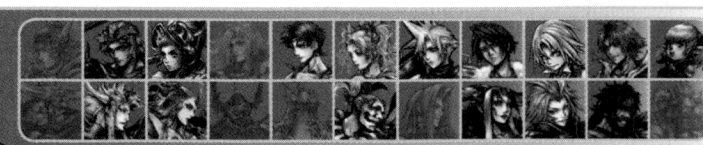

NAME	EQUIP LEVEL	ACQUIRE	HP	BRV	ATK	DEF	RANK	ABILITIES	COST	INGREDIENT 1	QUANTITY	INGREDIENT 2	QUANTITY	INGREDIENT 3	QUANTITY
Leather Hat	1	Find: Destiny Odyssey VIII map 4 Find: Destiny Odyssey IX map 2 Shop: Initially available	—	48	—	—	—	(none)	500	—	—	—	—	—	—
Plumed Hat	8	Shop: Initially available	—	68	—	—	—	(none)	1,000	—	—	—	—	—	—
Wizard's Hat	22	Shop: Character at Lv 15	—	108	—	—	4	(none)	3,020	—	—	—	—	—	—
Green Beret	22	Shop: Ingredient acquired	—	108	—	—	4	BRV Boost on Dodge +5%	3,020	Wizard's Hat	1	Bird Feather	1	—	—

ARMAMENTS

HATS (CONTINUED)

NAME	EQUIP LEVEL	ACQUIRE	HP	BRV	ATK	DEF	RANK	ABILITIES	COST	INGREDIENT 1	QUANTITY	INGREDIENT 2	QUANTITY	INGREDIENT 3	QUANTITY
Toque Blanche	29	Card: Airship Course Drop: Stiltzkin 4 Friend Card	—	128	—	—	5	Flavor of Life (1/4)	(not sold)	—	—	—	—	—	—
Beret	36	Shop: Character at Lv 29	—	148	—	—	6	(none)	5,380	—	—	—	—	—	—
Red Cap	50	Shop: Character at Lv 43	—	189	—	—	8	(none)	7,730	Wizard's Hat	1	Giant Feather	1	Transmogridust	1
Headband	57	Shop: Character at Lv 50	—	209	—	—	9	(none)	8,900	Beret	1	Fallen Angel Feather	1	Demon Feather	2
Spirit Band	57	Card: Falcon Course	—	209	—	—	9	Force of the Resolute (1/4)	(not sold)	—	—	—	—	—	—
Rubicante's Cowl	64	Card: Falcon Course	—	229	—	—	10	Elemental Archfiend (1/4)	(not sold)	—	—	—	—	—	—
Tiger Mask	78	Shop: Ingredient acquired	—	269	—	—	—	BRV Boost on Dodge +5%	12,430	Red Cap	1	Wyvern Wing	3	White Gem	1
Thief's Cap	85	Shop: Ingredient acquired	—	290	—	—	—	Drop Rate x 1.2	13,610	Headband	1	Sacred Beast Wing	4	Strength Shard	1
Black Cowl	92	Shop: Ingredient acquired	—	310	—	—	—	(none)	14,780	Tiger Mask	1	Garuda's Wing	5	Allure Crystal	3
Dueling Mask	99	Shop: Ingredient acquired	—	330	—	—	—	(none)	15,960	Thief's Cap	1	Bahamut's Wing	5	—	—
Lufenian Cap	99	Drop: Lunar Whale Course	—	330	—	—	—	Wisdom of Lufenia (1/3)	(not sold)	—	—	—	—	—	—
Chaplet	99	Card: Lunar Whale Course	—	330	—	—	—	Snowpetal (1/3)	(not sold)	—	—	—	—	—	—

HAIRPINS

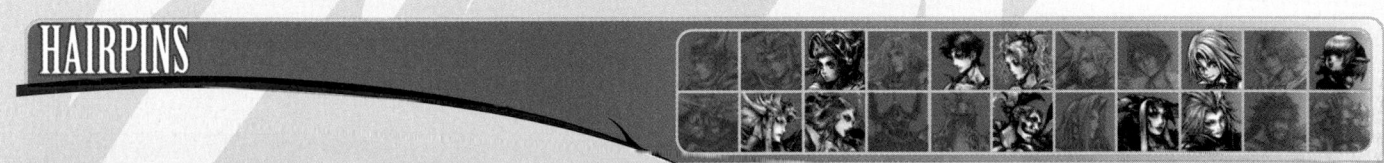

NAME	EQUIP LEVEL	ACQUIRE	HP	BRV	ATK	DEF	RANK	ABILITIES	COST	INGREDIENT 1	QUANTITY	INGREDIENT 2	QUANTITY	INGREDIENT 3	QUANTITY
Hairpin	15	Shop: Character at Lv 8	-97	103	—	—	—	(none)	1,850	—	—	—	—	—	—
Extension	22	Shop: Ingredient acquired	-115	125	—	—	4	BRV Recovery +25%	3,020	Hairpin	1	Aquamarine	1	—	—
Mythril Hairpin	22	Shop: Ingredient acquired	-115	125	—	—	4	Mystic Mythril (1/3)	3,020	Hairpin	1	Mythril	1	—	—
Tiara	29	Shop: Character at Lv 22	-132	147	—	—	5	(none)	4,200	—	—	—	—	—	—
Gold Hairpin+	22	Shop: Ingredient acquired	-150	170	—	—	6	Glorious Gold (1/3)	5,380	Gold Hairpin	1	Emerald	1	Transmogridust	3
Gold Hairpin	43	Shop: Ingredient acquired	-167	193	—	—	7	Glorious Gold (1/3)	6,550	Hairpin	1	Gold	1	—	—
Diamond Hairpin	50	Shop: Ingredient acquired	-185	215	—	—	8	Dazzling Diamond (1/3)	7,730	Tiara	1	Diamond	1	—	—
Lamia's Tiara	64	Shop: Ingredient acquired	-220	259	—	—	10	BRV Recovery +50%	10,080	Tiara	1	Opal	3	Transmogridust	5
Crystal Hairpin	64	Shop: Ingredient acquired	-220	259	—	—	10	Blessed Crystal (1/3)	10,080	Tiara	1	Crystal	1	—	—
Cat-ear Hood	71	Shop: Ingredient acquired	-237	281	—	—	—	(none)	11,260	Lamia's Tiara	1	Topaz	3	Bless Powder	4
Hypnocrown	85	Shop: Ingredient acquired	-272	326	—	—	15	BRV Recovery +75%	13,610	Cat-ear Hood	1	Holystone	4	Healing Shard	1
Circlet	92	Shop: Ingredient acquired	-290	348	—	—	—	BRV Recovery +75%	14,780	Hypnocrown	1	Lapis Lazuli	5	Oath Crystal	3
Royal Crown	99	Shop: Ingredient acquired	-307	370	—	—	—	(none)	15,960	Circlet	1	Sky Jewel	5	—	—
Thornlet	99	Shop: Password recipe	—	500	—	—	—	BRV Boost on Dodge -3% BRV Boost on Block -5%	15,960	Leo Recipe	1	Delicious Fish	1	Nethicite	1
Lufenian Hairpin	99	Drop: Lunar Whale Course	-307	370	—	—	—	Wisdom of Lufenia (1/3)	(not sold)	—	—	—	—	—	—

HELMS

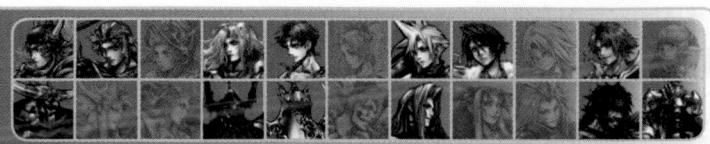

NAME	EQUIP LEVEL	ACQUIRE	HP	BRV	ATK	DEF	RANK	ABILITIES	COST	INGREDIENT 1	QUANTITY	INGREDIENT 2	QUANTITY	INGREDIENT 3	QUANTITY
Bronze Helm	1	Find: Destiny Odyssey VII map 4 Find: Destiny Odyssey X map 2 Shop: Initially available	—	25	—	1	—	(none)	780	—	—	—	—	—	—
Healing Helm	1	Find: Destiny Odyssey X map 3 Shop: Once found	—	25	—	1	—	Chase BRV Defense +20%	780	Bronze Helm	1	Guts Shard	1	Transmogridust	2
Iron Helm	8	Shop: Character at Lv 3	—	41	—	1	—	(none)	1,280	—	—	—	—	—	—
Knight Helm	15	Shop: Character at Lv 8	—	57	—	1	3	(none)	2,120	—	—	—	—	—	—
Barbut	15	DP Prize: Destiny Odyssey X Shop: Once found	—	57	—	1	3	Chase BRV Defense +20%	2,120	Bronze Helm	1	Guts Shard	1	Transmogridust	4
Mythril Helm	22	Shop: Ingredient acquired	—	73	—	1	4	Mystic Mythril (1/3)	3,300	Iron Helm	1	Mythril	1	—	—
Winged Helm	22	DP Prize: Destiny Odyssey X Shop: Once found	—	73	—	1	4	Chase BRV Defense +20%	3,300	Iron Helm	1	Crimson Shard	1	Transmogridust	8
Mythril Helm+	8	Shop: Ingredient acquired	—	73	—	1	4	Mystic Mythril (1/3)	3,300	Mythril Helm	1	Geranium	1	Transmogridust	2
Heavy Helm	29	Shop: Character at Lv 22	—	89	—	1	5	(none)	4,480	—	—	—	—	—	—
Golden Helm	36	Shop: Ingredient acquired	—	104	—	1	6	Glorious Gold (1/3)	5,650	Knight Helm	1	Gold	1	—	—
Golden Helm+	22	Shop: Ingredient acquired	—	104	—	1	6	Glorious Gold (1/3)	5,650	Golden Helm	1	White Stone	1	Transmogridust	3
Burgonet	36	Shop: Character at Lv 29	—	104	—	1	6	Chase BRV Defense +20%	5,650	Healing Helm	1	Black Stone	1	—	—
Warlord's Soul	43	DP Prize: Shade Impulse 1 Drop: Stiltzkin 2 Friend Card	—	121	—	1	7	Uniter (1/4)	(not sold)	—	—	—	—	—	—
Sallet	43	Shop: Character at Lv 36	—	121	—	1	7	(none)	6,830	—	—	—	—	—	—
Diamond Helm	50	Shop: Ingredient acquired	—	137	—	1	8	Dazzling Diamond (1/3)	8,000	Heavy Helm	1	Diamond	1	—	—
Diamond Helm+	50	Shop: Ingredient acquired	—	137	—	1	8	Dazzling Diamond (1/3)	8,000	Diamond Helm	1	Black Stone	1	Transmogridust	4
Close Helmet	57	Shop: Character at Lv 50	—	153	—	1	—	(none)	9,180	Sallet	1	Levistone	1	Mako Stone	2
Crystal Helm	64	Shop: Ingredient acquired	—	169	—	1	—	Blessed Crystal (1/3)	10,360	Sallet	1	Crystal	1	Dewdrop Pebble	3
Platinum Helm	71	Shop: Ingredient acquired	—	184	—	1	—	(none)	11,530	Barbut	1	Stone of the Condemner	3	Healing Powder	4
Dragon's Crest	78	Shop: Ingredient acquired	—	200	—	1	12	Whisper of the Wyrm (1/3)	12,710	Close Helmet	1	Wyrmstone	3	Mana Shard	1
Heike's Helm	78	DP Prize: Distant Glory: TLoL Drop: Lunar Whale Course	—	200	—	1	12	All Glories Must Fade (1/4)	(not sold)	—	—	—	—	—	—
Giant's Helm	85	Shop: Ingredient acquired	—	217	—	1	13	Pride of the Titans (1/3)	13,880	Platinum Helm	1	Blessed Gem	4	Destruction Shard	1
Kaiser Helm	92	Shop: Ingredient acquired	—	233	—	1	—	(none)	15,060	Winged Helm	1	Goddess's Magicite	5	Lithe Crystal	3
Grand Helm	99	Shop: Ingredient acquired	—	249	—	1	15	(none)	16,240	Giant's Helm	1	Supreme Gem	5	—	—
Adamant Helm	99	Shop: Ingredient acquired	—	249	—	1	15	Adamant Chains (1/3)	16,240	Crystal Helm	1	Adamantite	1	—	—
Lufenian Helm	99	Drop: Lunar Whale Course	—	249	—	1	—	Wisdom of Lufenia (1/3)	(not sold)	—	—	—	—	—	—
Genji Helm	99	Shop: Buy "Genji Series Added" in PP Catalog Drop: Lunar Whale Course	—	249	—	1	—	Soul of Yamato (1/3)	16,240	Heike's Helm	1	Supreme Gem	5	Chaos Crystal	2

RIBBONS

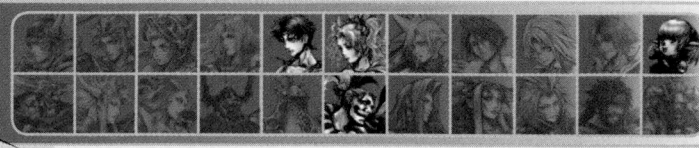

NAME	EQUIP LEVEL	ACQUIRE	HP	BRV	ATK	DEF	RANK	ABILITIES	COST	INGREDIENT 1	QUANTITY	INGREDIENT 2	QUANTITY	INGREDIENT 3	QUANTITY
Ribbon	78	Shop: Ingredient acquired	-255	303	—	—	—	Accessory Breakability -20%	12,430	Cat-ear Hood	1	Wyvern Wing	3	Transmogridust	16
Super Ribbon	99	Shop: Ingredient acquired	-307	370	—	—	—	Accessory Breakability -30%	15,960	Ribbon	1	Bahamut's Wing	5	Transmogridust	99

SPECIAL (GENERAL)

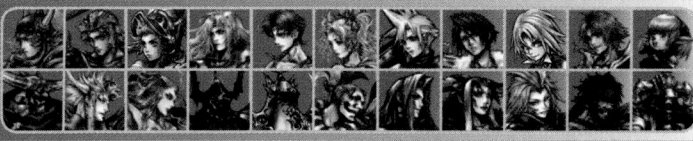

NAME	EQUIP LEVEL	ACQUIRE	HP	BRV	ATK	DEF	RANK	ABILITIES	COST	INGREDIENT 1	QUANTITY	INGREDIENT 2	QUANTITY	INGREDIENT 3	QUANTITY
Saucer	85	Card: Invincible Course	—	290	—	—	13	Imp's Blessing (1/4)	(not sold)	—	—	—	—	—	—

SPECIAL (PRETTY PRINCESS)

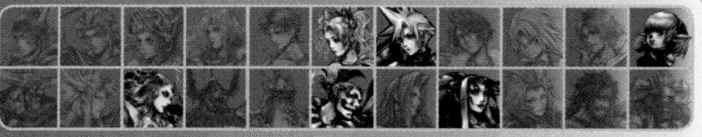

NAME	EQUIP LEVEL	ACQUIRE	HP	BRV	ATK	DEF	RANK	ABILITIES	COST	INGREDIENT 1	QUANTITY	INGREDIENT 2	QUANTITY	INGREDIENT 3	QUANTITY
Blonde Wig	43	Shop: Buy "Pretty Princess Series Added" in PP Catalog	—	169	—	—	7	Allure of Honey (1/4)	6,550	Ruby	5	Allure Shard	2	—	—

MACHINE

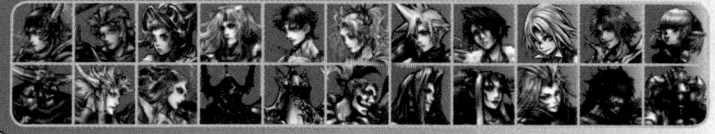

*No character can naturally equip machines, but anyone can learn how to do so by buying "Use Machines" at the shop. (Use Machines becomes available after acquiring Chemist Lore in the Inward Chaos Story Mode.)

NAME	EQUIP LEVEL	ACQUIRE	HP	BRV	ATK	DEF	RANK	ABILITIES	COST	INGREDIENT 1	QUANTITY	INGREDIENT 2	QUANTITY	INGREDIENT 3	QUANTITY
Drill	96	Shop: Acquire Mallet as Inward Chaos DP Prize	-307	411	—	—	—	Accessory Breakability +5% Chase BRV Damage +30%	15,960	Mallet	1	Behemoth Horn	5	—	—

COSMOS-SIDE EXCLUSIVES

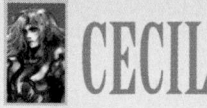 ## CECIL

NAME	EQUIP LEVEL	ACQUIRE	HP	BRV	ATK	DEF	RANK	ABILITIES	COST	INGREDIENT 1	QUANTITY	INGREDIENT 2	QUANTITY	INGREDIENT 3	QUANTITY
Dark Helm	1	Find: Destiny Odyssey IV map 4	—	25	—	1	—	Power of Darkness (1/3)	(not sold)	—	—	—	—	—	—

ARMOR

CLOTHING

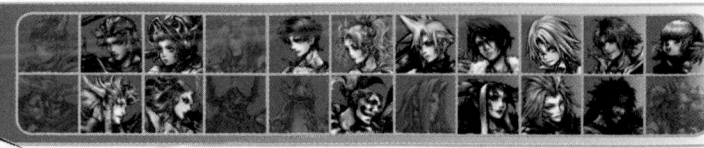

NAME	EQUIP LEVEL	ACQUIRE	HP	BRV	ATK	DEF	RANK	ABILITIES	COST	INGREDIENT 1	QUANTITY	INGREDIENT 2	QUANTITY	INGREDIENT 3	QUANTITY
Leather Clothing	1	Find: Destiny Odyssey IX map 4 Shop: Initially available	313	—	—	—	1	(none)	400	—	—	—	—	—	—
Poncho	13	Shop: Character Lv 6	635	—	—	—	—	(none)	2,420	—	—	—	—	—	—
Silken Shirt	20	Shop: Character Lv 13	796	—	—	—	4	(none)	4,190	—	—	—	—	—	—
Bard's Tunic	20	Shop: Ingredient acquired	796	—	—	—	4	Stage Defense +25%	4,190	Poncho	1	Bird Feather	1	—	—
Kenpo Gi	27	Shop: Character Lv 20	956	—	—	—	5	(none)	5,950	—	—	—	—	—	—
Black Belt's Gi	41	Shop: Character Lv 34	1278	—	—	—	7	(none)	9,480	—	—	—	—	—	—
Power Vest	48	Shop: Character Lv 43	1439	—	—	—	8	Stage Defense +25%	11,240	Kenpogi	1	Giant Feather	1	Transmogridust	1
Bomber Jacket	55	Card: Falcon Course	1599	—	—	—	9	Force of the Resolute (1/4)	(not sold)	—	—	—	—	—	—
Ninja Gear	62	Shop: Ingredient acquired	1760	—	—	—	—	(none)	14,770	Black Belt's Gi	1	Royal Wing	3	Transmogridust	5
Black Garb	69	Shop: Ingredient acquired	1921	—	—	—	—	(none)	16,530	Power Vest	1	Diablos's Wing	3	Yellow Gem	1
Red Jacket	83	Shop: Ingredient acquired	2243	—	—	—	—	(none)	20,060	Ninja Gear	1	Sacred Beast Wing	4	Reflex Shard	1
Snowflake Sweater	96	Card: Lunar Whale Course	2564	—	—	—	—	Snowpetal (1/3)	(not sold)	—	—	—	—	—	—
Brave Suit	96	Shop: Ingredient acquired	2564	—	—	—	—	Chase BRV Defense +40%	23,590	Black Garb	1	Bahamut's Wing	5	—	—
Lufenian Jacket	96	Drop: Lunar Whale Course	2564	—	—	—	—	Wisdom of Lufenia (1/3)	(not sold)	—	—	—	—	—	—

ROBE

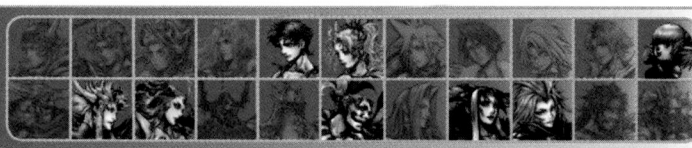

NAME	EQUIP LEVEL	ACQUIRE	HP	BRV	ATK	DEF	RANK	ABILITIES	COST	INGREDIENT 1	QUANTITY	INGREDIENT 2	QUANTITY	INGREDIENT 3	QUANTITY
Robe	1	Find: Destiny Odyssey VI map 2 Shop: Initially available	253	23	—	—	1	(none)	750	—	—	—	—	—	—
Cotton Robes	6	Shop: Character Lv 3	400	27	—	—	—	(none)	1,500	—	—	—	—	—	—
Silk Robes	20	Shop: Character Lv 13	694	35	—	—	4	(none)	4,540	—	—	—	—	—	—
Sage's Surplice	20	Shop: Ingredient acquired	694	35	—	—	4	Magic Defense +10%	4,540	Silk Robes	1	Bird Feather	1	—	—
Wizard's Robes	27	Shop: Character Lv 20	840	39	—	—	5	(none)	6,300	—	—	—	—	—	—
Traveler's Vestment	34	Shop: Character Lv 27	987	44	—	—	—	(none)	8,060	—	—	—	—	—	—
Gaia Gear	55	Shop: Character Lv 50	1427	56	—	—	9	Magic Defense +15%	13,360	Wizard's Robe	1	Fallen Angel Feather	1	Demon Feather	2
Luminous Robes	76	Shop: Ingredient acquired	1868	69	—	—	—	Magic Defense +15%	18,650	Traveler's Vestment	1	Wyvern Wing	3	Yellow Gem	1
Lordly Robes	90	Shop: Ingredient acquired	2161	77	—	—	—	(none)	22,180	Gaia Gear	1	Garuda's Wing	5	Resilience Crystal	3
Rainbow Robes	96	Shop: Ingredient acquired	2308	81	—	—	—	Magic Defense +20%	23,940	Luminous Robes	1	Bahamut's Wing	5	—	—
Lufenian Robes	96	Drop: Lunar Whale Course	2308	81	—	—	—	Wisdom of Lufenia (1/3)	(not sold)	—	—	—	—	—	—

ARMAMENTS

LIGHT ARMOR

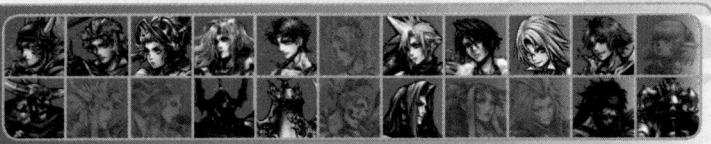

NAME	EQUIP LEVEL	ACQUIRE	HP	BRV	ATK	DEF	RANK	ABILITIES	COST	INGREDIENT 1	QUANTITY	INGREDIENT 2	QUANTITY	INGREDIENT 3	QUANTITY
Leather Armor	1	Find: Destiny Odyssey II map 2 Find: Destiny Odyssey VII map 4 Find: Destiny Odyssey X map 2 Shop: Initially available	368	—	—	—	1	(none)	750	—	—	—	—	—	—
Chainmail	8	Shop: Character Lv 3	536	—	—	—	2	(none)	1,500	—	—	—	—	—	—
Mythril Vest	22	Shop: Ingredient acquired	872	—	—	—	4	Mystic Mythril (1/3)	4,540	Leather Armor	1	Mythril	2	—	—
Mythril Vest+	8	Shop: Ingredient acquired	877	—	—	—	4	Mystic Mythril (1/3)	4,540	Mythril Vest	1	Eucalyptus	1	Transmogridust	2
Linen Cuirass	22	Shop: Ingredient acquired	872	—	—	—	4	Wall Rush BRV Defense +20%	4,540	Chainmail	1	Ichthon Scales	1	—	—
Iron Apron	29	Card: Airship Course Drop: Stiltzkin 4 Friend Card	1039	—	—	—	5	Flavor of Life (1/4)	(not sold)	—	—	—	—	—	—
Golden Vest	36	Shop: Ingredient acquired	1207	—	—	—	6	Glorious Gold (1/3)	8,060	Chainmail	1	Gold	2	—	—
Golden Vest+	22	Shop: Ingredient acquired	1207	—	—	—	6	Glorious Gold (1/3)	8,060	Golden Vest	1	Yensa Scales	1	Transmogridust	3
Survival Vest	43	Shop: Character Lv 36	1375	—	—	—	7	(none)	9,830	—	—	—	—	—	—
Diamond Vest	50	Shop: Ingredient acquired	1543	—	—	—	8	Dazzling Diamond (1/3)	11,590	Survival Vest	1	Diamond	2	—	—
Assassin's Vest	57	Shop: Character Lv 50	1710	—	—	—	9	(none)	13,360	Survival Vest	1	Leviathan Scales	1	Landshark Scales	2
Crystal Vest	64	Shop: Ingredient acquired	1878	—	—	—		Blessed Crystal (1/3)	15,120	Survival Vest	1	Crystal	2	Emperor Scales	3
Cagnazzo's Carapace	64	Card: Falcon Course	1878	—	—	—	—	Elemental Archfiend (1/4)	(not sold)	—	—	—	—	—	—
Mirage Vest	78	Shop: Ingredient acquired	2214	—	—	—	12	Wall Rush BRV Defense +30%	18,650	Assassin's Vest	1	Sea Serpent Scales	3	Oath Powder	4
Vishnu Vest	92	Shop: Ingredient acquired	2549	—	—	—	—	(none)	22,180	Mirage Vest	1	Eden's Scales	5	Crimson Crystal	3
Brigandine	99	Shop: Ingredient acquired	2717	—	—	—	—	Wall Rush BRV Defense +40%	23,940	Vishnu Vest	1	Lone Heart	5	—	—
Lufenian Vest	99	Drop: Lunar Whale Course	2717	—	—	—	—	Wisdom of Lufenia (1/3)	(not sold)	—	—	—	—	—	—
Adamant Vest	99	Shop: Ingredient acquired	2717	—	—	—	—	Adamant Chains (1/3)	23,940	Crystal Armor	1	Adamantite	1	—	—

HEAVY ARMOR

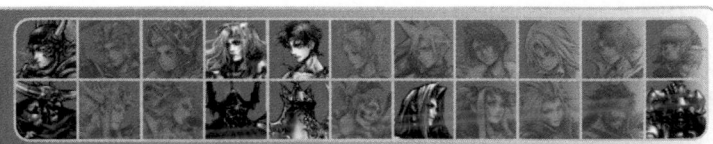

NAME	EQUIP LEVEL	ACQUIRE	HP	BRV	ATK	DEF	RANK	ABILITIES	COST	INGREDIENT 1	QUANTITY	INGREDIENT 2	QUANTITY	INGREDIENT 3	QUANTITY
Bronze Armor	1	Find: Destiny Odyssey I map 2 / Shop: Initially available	428	—	—	—	—	(none)	1,200	—	—	—	—	—	—
Shell Armor	2	Find: Destiny Odyssey IV map 4 / Shop: Once found	428	—	—	—	—	Physical Defense +10%	1,200	Bronze Armor	1	Titan Shard	1	Transmogridust	2
Iron Armor	9	Shop: Character Lv 4	610	—	—	—	2	(none)	1,950	—	—	—	—	—	—
Knight's Armor	16	Shop: Character Lv 9	792	—	—	—	3	(none)	3,220	—	—	—	—	—	—
Flame Armor	16	DP Prize: Destiny Odyssey IV / Shop: Once found	792	—	—	—	3	Physical Defense +10%	3,220	Bronze Armor	1	Titan Shard	1	Transmogridust	4
Mythril Armor	23	Shop: Ingredient acquired	974	—	—	—	4	Mystic Mythril (1/3)	4,990	Iron Armor	1	Mythril	2	—	—
Ice Armor	23	DP Prize: Destiny Odyssey IV / Shop: Once found	974	—	—	—	4	Physical Defense +10%	4,990	Iron Armor	1	Destruction Shard	1	Transmogridust	8
Mythril Armor+	9	Shop: Ingredient acquired	974	—	—	—	4	Mystic Mythril (1/3)	4,990	Mythril Armor	1	Rosemary	1	Transmogridust	2
Heavy Armor	30	Shop: Character Lv 23	1155	—	—	—	5	(none)	6,750	—	—	—	—	—	—
Golden Armor	37	Shop: Ingredient acquired	1337	—	—	—	6	Glorious Gold (1/3)	8,510	Knight's Armor	1	Gold	2	—	—
Golden Armor+	23	Shop: Ingredient acquired	1337	—	—	—	6	Glorious Gold (1/3)	8,510	Golden Armor	1	Beast Bone	1	Transmogridust	3
Shielded Armor	37	Shop: Ingredient acquired	1337	—	—	—	—	Physical Defense +10%	8,510	Shell Armor	1	Unknown's Bone	1		
Warlord's Corselet	44	DP Prize: Shade Impulse 2	1519	—	—	—	7	Uniter (1/4)	(not sold)	—	—	—	—	—	—
Diamond Armor	51	Shop: Ingredient acquired	1701	—	—	—	8	Dazzling Diamond (1/3)	12,040	Heavy Armor	1	Diamond	2	—	—
Diamond Armor+	37	Shop: Ingredient acquired	1701	—	—	—	8	Dazzling Diamond (1/3)	12,040	Diamond Armor	1	Unknown's Bone	1	Transmogridust	4
Demon Mail	58	Shop: Character Lv 50	1882	—	—	—	9	(none)	13,810	Heavy Armor	1	Ancient Bone	1	Nue Bone	2
Crystal Armor	65	Shop: Ingredient acquired	2064	—	—	—	—	Blessed Crystal (1/3)	15,570	Survival Vest	1	Crystal	2	Shadow Bone	3
Mirror Mail	72	Shop: Ingredient acquired	2246	—	—	—	—	Magic Counter Strength +30%	17,330	Flame Armor	1	Wargod Bone	3	Cyan Gem	1
Dragon Mail	79	Shop: Ingredient acquired	2428	—	—	—	12	Whisper of the Wyrm (1/3)	19,100	Demon Mail	1	Land Dragon Bone	3	Allure Shard	1
Heike's Armor	79	DP Prize: Distant Glory: RotW / Drop: Lunar Whale Course	2428	—	—	—	12	All Glories Must Fade (1/4)	(not sold)	—	—	—	—	—	—
Giant's Harness	86	Shop: Ingredient acquired	2610	—	—	—	13	Pride of the Titans (1/3)	20,860	Ice Armor	1	Saint's Bone	4	Cyan Gem	1
Genji Armor	100	Shop: Buy "Genji Series Added" in PP Catalog / Drop: DC Lunar Whale Course	2973	—	—	—	—	Soul of Yamato (1/3)	24,390	Heike's Armor	1	Hero's Bone	5	Oath Crystal	5
Maximillian	100	Shop: Ingredient acquired	2973	—	—	—	—	Physical Defense +20%	24,390	Dragon Mail	1	Blood-Darkened Bone	5	—	—
Bone Mail	100	Shop: Password recipe	2973	—	—	—	—	Cannot Take EX Core / Cannot Take EX Force	24,390	Scorpio Recipe	1	Wild Rose	1	GF Eden	1
Lufenian Armor	100	Drop: Lunar Whale Course	2973	—	—	—	—	Wisdom of Lufenia (1/3)	(not sold)	—	—	—	—	—	—

ARMAMENTS

SPECIAL (GENERAL)

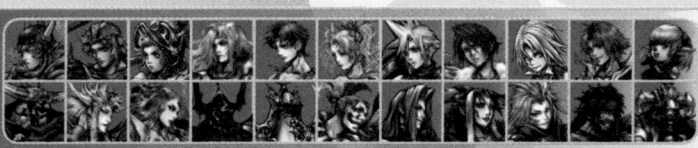

NAME	EQUIP LEVEL	ACQUIRE	HP	BRV	ATK	DEF	RANK	ABILITIES	COST	INGREDIENT 1	QUANTITY	INGREDIENT 2	QUANTITY	INGREDIENT 3	QUANTITY
Reed Cloak	85	Card: Invincible Course	2610	—	—	—	13	Imp's Blessing (1/4)	(not sold)	—	—	—	—	—	—

SPECIAL (PRETTY PRINCESS)

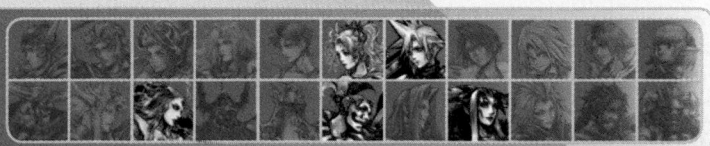

NAME	EQUIP LEVEL	ACQUIRE	HP	BRV	ATK	DEF	RANK	ABILITIES	COST	INGREDIENT 1	QUANTITY	INGREDIENT 2	QUANTITY	INGREDIENT 3	QUANTITY
Silk Dress	43	Shop: Buy "Pretty Princess Series Added" in PP Catalog	1519	—	—	—	7	Allure of Honey (1/4)	9,830	Giant Feather	5	Quickstrike Shard	2	—	—

MACHINE

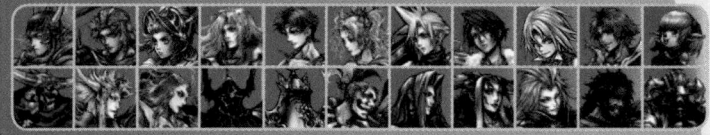

*No character can naturally equip machines, but anyone can learn how to do so by buying "Use Machines" at the shop. (Use Machines becomes available after acquiring Chemist Lore in the Inward Chaos Story Mode.)

NAME	EQUIP LEVEL	ACQUIRE	HP	BRV	ATK	DEF	RANK	ABILITIES	COST	INGREDIENT 1	QUANTITY	INGREDIENT 2	QUANTITY	INGREDIENT 3	QUANTITY
Auto Crossbow	96	Shop: Acquire Mallet as Inward Chaos DP Prize	2666	81	—	—	—	Accessory Breakability +5% Physical Damage +15%	23,940	Mallet	1	Hero's Bone	5	—	—

COSMOS-SIDE EXCLUSIVES

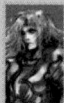 ## CECIL

NAME	EQUIP LEVEL	ACQUIRE	HP	BRV	ATK	DEF	RANK	ABILITIES	COST	INGREDIENT 1	QUANTITY	INGREDIENT 2	QUANTITY	INGREDIENT 3	QUANTITY
Dark Armor	2	Find: Destiny Odyssey IV map 2	428	—	—	—		Power of Darkness (1/3)	(not sold)	—	—	—	—	—	—

ACCESSORIES

There are over 500 accessories in *DISSIDIA FINAL FANTASY*. Some are powerful tools that will help you defeat your foes, while others are mere ingredients to be traded for other weapons, armor, and accessories.

UNDERSTANDING THE ACCESSORY ENTRIES

ACCESSORY TYPES

Basic: Basic accessories typically provide a modest boost to one of your characters' offensive or defensive capabilities. This boost can be further enhanced by equipping booster accessories.

Booster: Booster accessories modify the power of basic accessories by multiplying their power by a preset rate whenever some condition is met. The key to using a booster is picking the conditions that are likely to be met most often in the situation in which you'll want the boost.

Special: Special accessories differ from basic accessories in several ways. They cannot be modified by booster accessories, they may have multiple abilities, and some of them have a chance of breaking at the end of any battle.

Trade: Trade accessories offer a modest stat boost, but are intended primarily to be traded—not to be worn. There are over 300 trade accessories, and you'll need a large variety of them if you hope to acquire most of the game's best items and accessories at the shop.

MEANS OF ACQUISITION

There are several ways in which you can acquire accessories. The easiest methods are listed here. (Note: Some accessories cannot be obtained, and are only seen on CPU opponents. These accessories are omitted from the list.)

Find: When an item can be found in a chest in a Story Mode chapter, its entry reveals the chapter name and particular map. Some chests in the Shade Impulse and Distant Glory Story Mode chapters may randomly contain accessories when they're opened for a second time and beyond, but the odds of any single accessory appearing can be as low as 5%. Note that some chests may not appear until certain conditions are met, but you can find full details in the appropriate walkthrough section.

Prize: Booster and trade accessories are common prizes in *DISSIDIA FINAL FANTASY*. You can receive them for having extra DP at the end of Story Mode chapters, for completing in-game accomplishments, and for beating any challenge in Arcade Mode.

Battlegen: There are roughly 100 trade accessories that can only be earned through Battlegen. Each character has three or four items that you can randomly earn by hitting them with Bravery Breaks, HP attacks, or EX Bursts. Each stage also has an exclusive item that you can randomly create by destroying parts of the stage.

In the Online Lobby, players who have unlocked "Online - Battlegen OK" and "Ghost Match - Battlegen OK" will find that in addition to these preset Battlegen accessories, they can create any accessory that their foe has equipped. Theoretically, you can earn any accessory this way, but only the accessories held by the Stiltzkin (whose friend cards you can earn through Mognet correspondence—see the Secrets and Cheats section) are called out in the following charts.

Shop: Some accessories can be purchased at the shop, although certain conditions may need to be fulfilled before the listing appears. (See The "Etc." Shop on the next page for more details.)

Card: Many accessories appear as treasure cards that can be purchased with medals in the Duel Colosseum. The course in which you can find the treasure card is listed.

Other: There are a few accessories that can only be earned through other methods, such as Mognet correspondence, or from your daily play plan.

SHOP STOCK CONDITIONS

Before you can buy an accessory from the shop, you'll need to make its listing appear by fulfilling one of the four conditions listed below. Virtually all accessories require the exchange of trade accessories as well as cash; these "recipes" are listed for each purchasable item.

Once found: The shop won't stock this accessory until you find it elsewhere, typically in a Story Mode chapter.

Ingredient acquired: Most booster accessory and special accessory recipes appear when you've acquired one or more of the ingredients necessary to trade for it. Some listings appear once you've found any ingredient, while others only appear when a single specific ingredient is acquired.

Buy X from PP Catalog: When certain conditions are met, the "Etc." section of the PP Catalog will offer options like "Shop - Falcon Course Added." Purchasing such catalog entries unlocks most of the trade accessories (but none of the items) available in that Duel Colosseum course. To buy these accessories, you'll typically need to trade whichever elixir variant is found in the same Duel Colosseum course.

Password recipe: Accessories with this appearance condition do not appear in the shop until you enter a special password in the personal message section of your friend card. The developers plan to reveal these passwords in the weeks and months following the game's release.

ACCESSORY RANKS

Each accessory has a rank that roughly describes its quality and rarity, and determines how many copies of that accessory a character can have equipped at once.

RANK	EQUIP LIMIT
☆ ("S")	1
☆ ("A")	2
☆ ("B")	3
☆ ("C")	4
☆ ("D")	No limit

THE "ETC." SHOP

The final section of the shop does not sell items or accessories, but character abilities. To unlock the listings, you must acquire the single trade-accessory ingredient in each of the recipes. The full stock of the "etc." section is shown below.

NAME	ACQUIRE	COST	INGREDIENT 1	QUANTITY
Extra Slot	Adds 1 accessory slot	1,000	Rosetta Stone	1
Level Up	Adds 1 level	1,000	Chocobo Cologne	1
Command Battle Boost	Strengthens command-battle	1,000	Rosetta Stone	1
Equip Swords	Enables sword use	1,000	Warrior Lore	1
Equip Daggers	Enables dagger use	1,000	Thief Lore	1
Equip Greatswords	Enables greatsword use	1,000	Knight Lore	1
Equip Katana	Enables katana use	1,000	Samurai Lore	1
Equip Spears	Enables spear use	1,000	Dragoon Lore	1
Equip Axes	Enables axe use	1,000	Marksman Lore	1
Equip Rods	Enables rod use	1,000	Black Mage Lore	1
Equip Staves	Enables staff use	1,000	White Mage Lore	1
Use Thrown Weapons	Enables thrown weapon use	1,000	Ninja Lore	1
Use Grappling Weapons	Enables grappling weapon use	1,000	Black Belt Lore	1
Use Instruments	Enables instrument use	1,000	Bard Lore	1
Use Parrying Weapons	Enables parrying weapon use	1,000	Ninja Lore	1
Equip Shields	Enables shield use	1,000	Knight Lore	1
Equip Bangles	Enables bangle use	1,000	Bard Lore	1
Equip Gauntlets	Enables gauntlet use	1,000	Samurai Lore	1
Equip Hats	Enables hat use	1,000	Thief Lore	1
Equip Hairpins	Enables hairpin use	1,000	White Mage Lore	1
Equip Helms	Enables helm use	1,000	Marksman Lore	1
Equip Ribbons	Enables ribbon use	1,000	Dancer Lore	1
Equip Clothing	Enables clothing use	1,000	Black Belt Lore	1
Equip Robes	Enables robe use	1,000	Black Mage Lore	1
Equip Light Armor	Enables light armor use	1,000	Dragoon Lore	1
Equip Heavy Armor	Enables heavy armor use	1,000	Warrior Lore	1
Use Machines	Enables machine use	1,000	Chemist Lore	1

BASIC ACCESSORIES

NAME	RANK	ACQUIRE	ABILITIES	COST	INGREDIENT 1	QUANTITY	INGREDIENT 2	QUANTITY	INGREDIENT 3	QUANTITY
Power Ring	☆	Find: Destiny Odyssey Prologue Find: Destiny Odyssey I map 1 Find: Destiny Odyssey VI map 3 Find: Destiny Odyssey VII map 3 Shop: Ingredient acquired	Damage +5%	300	Strength Powder	2	Red Drop	1	—	—
Hyper Ring	☆	Battlegen: Stiltzkin 2, 3, 6, 7 or 8 friend card [Bravery Break] Shop: Ingredient acquired	Damage +10%	1,000	Strength Powder	3	Strength Shard	2	—	—
Gaia Ring	☆	Battlegen: Stiltzkin 2, 3, 6, 7 or 8 friend card [Bravery Break] Shop: Ingredient acquired	Damage +15%	1,800	Strength Shard	3	Crimson Shard	2	Strength Crystal	2
Guard Ring	☆	Find: Destiny Odyssey IV map 5 Find: Destiny Odyssey VIII map 5 Shop: Ingredient acquired	Wall Rush Defense +10%	1,000	Protect Powder	2	Orange Drop	1	—	—

NAME	RANK	ACQUIRE	ABILITIES	COST	INGREDIENT 1	QUANTITY	INGREDIENT 2	QUANTITY	INGREDIENT 3	QUANTITY
Block Ring	☆	Shop: Ingredient acquired	Wall Rush Defense +20%	1,800	Protect Powder	3	Protect Shard	2	—	—
Guardian Bangle	☆	Shop: Ingredient acquired	Defense +5%	1,800	Protect Shard	3	Orange Gem	2	Protect Crystal	2
Attractorb	☆	Find: Shade Impulse Ch 3 map 3 / Shop: Ingredient acquired	EX Intake Range +2m	1,000	Magnet Powder	2	—	—	—	—
Gravitorb	☆	Battlegen: Stiltzkin 4 or 5 friend card [EX Burst] / Shop: Ingredient acquired	EX Intake Range +3m	1,800	Magnet Shard	3	Magnet Crystal	2	Tome of Souls	3
Ivory Choker	☆	Find: Shade Impulse Ch 1 map 5 / Shop: Ingredient acquired	EX Force Absorption +15%	1,000	Bless Powder	2	—	—	—	—
Pearl Necklace	☆	Battlegen: Stiltzkin 4 or 5 friend card [Bravery Break] / Shop: Ingredient acquired	EX Force Absorption +30%	1,800	Bless Shard	3	Bless Crystal	2	Tome of Men	5
Pretty Orb	☆	Find: Shade Impulse Ch 2 map 5 / Shop: Ingredient acquired	EX Core Absorption +15%	1,000	Amplification Powder	2	—	—	—	—
Dragonfly Orb	☆	Battlegen: Stiltzkin 4 or 5 friend card [HP Attack] / Shop: Ingredient acquired	EX Core Absorption +30%	1,800	Amplification Shard	3	Amplification Crystal	2	Tome of Silence	5
Silver Hourglass	☆	Shop: Ingredient acquired	EX Mode Duration +10%	1,000	Time Shard	3	—	—	—	—
Gold Hourglass	☆	Battlegen: Stiltzkin 4 or 5 friend card [Stage damage] / Shop: Ingredient acquired	EX Mode Duration +20%	1,800	Time Shard	3	Time Crystal	2	Tome of the Orator	5
Pendant	☆	Shop: Ingredient acquired	EX Core Appearance Boost	1,000	Allure Powder	2	—	—	—	—
Victory Pendant	☆	Battlegen: Stiltzkin 4 or 5 friend card [EX Burst] / Shop: Ingredient acquired	Big EX Core Appearance Boost	1,800	Allure Shard	3	Allure Crystal	2	Tome of the Masters	5
Muscle Belt	☆	Battlegen: Stiltzkin 3 or 6 friend card [Bravery Break] / Shop: Ingredient acquired	Physical Damage +15%	1,300	Crimson Powder	2	—	—	—	—
Champion Belt	☆	Battlegen: Stiltzkin 3 or 6 friend card [Bravery Break] / Shop: Ingredient acquired	Physical Damage +25%	1,900	Crimson Shard	3	Crimson Crystal	2	Tome of the Orator	5
Earring	☆	Battlegen: Stiltzkin 1 or 8 friend card [HP attack] / Shop: Ingredient acquired	Magic Damage +15%	1,300	Mana Powder	2	—	—	—	—
Star Earring	☆	Battlegen: Stiltzkin 1 or 8 friend card [HP attack] / Shop: Ingredient acquired	Magic Damage +25%	1,900	Mana Shard	3	Mana Crystal	2	Tome of the Masters	5
Protect Stud	☆	Shop: Ingredient acquired	Physical Defense +5%	1,300	Resilience Powder	2	Orange Drop	1	—	—
Defense Cuff	☆	Shop: Ingredient acquired	Physical Defense +10%	1,900	Resilience Shard	3	Protect Shard	2	Resilience Crystal	2
White Cape	☆	Shop: Ingredient acquired	Magic Defense +5%	1,300	Reflex Powder	1	Mana Powder	1	—	—
Black Cape	☆	Shop: Ingredient acquired	Magic Defense +10%	1,900	Resilience Powder	3	Reflex Shard	2	Mana Crystal	2
Angel Brooch	☆	Shop: Ingredient acquired	Stage Defense +20%	1,000	Resilience Powder	1	Allure Powder	1	—	—
Angel Wings	☆	Shop: Ingredient acquired	Stage Defense +30%	1,800	Resilience Shard	2	Allure Shard	2	Tome of Souls	3
Zephyr Cloak	☆	Shop: Ingredient acquired	BRV Boost on Dodge +3%	1,300	Resilience Powder	1	Guts Powder	1	—	—
Elven Mantle	☆	Shop: Ingredient acquired	BRV Boost on Dodge +6%	1,900	Resilience Shard	2	Guts Shard	2	Guts Crystal	1
Heart's Ease	☆	Shop: Ingredient acquired	BRV Boost on Block +5%	1,300	Guts Powder	1	Protect Powder	1	—	—
Spirit Stanchion	☆	Shop: Ingredient acquired	BRV Boost on Block +10%	1,900	Guts Shard	2	Protect Shard	2	Lithe Shard	1
Bravery Orb	☆	Shop: Ingredient acquired	BRV Recovery +20%	1,000	Recovery Powder	2			—	—
Bravery Elemental	☆	Shop: Ingredient acquired	BRV Recovery +40%	1,800	Recovery Shard	2	Guts Shard	2	Recovery Crystal	1
Reflect Strand	☆	Shop: Ingredient acquired	Magic Counter Strength +20%	1,000	Reflex Powder	2			—	—
Mirrored Chain	☆	Shop: Ingredient acquired	Magic Counter Strength +40%	1,800	Reflex Shard	3	Reflex Crystal	2	Tome of Memories	5
Booster	☆	Battlegen: Stiltzkin 3 friend card [Stage damage] / Shop: Ingredient acquired	Wall Rush BRV Damage +10%	1,300	Gale Powder	2	—	—	—	—
Hyperstar	☆	Battlegen: Stiltzkin 3 friend card [Stage damage] / Shop: Ingredient acquired	Wall Rush BRV Damage +20%	1,900	Gale Shard	3	Gale Crystal	2	Tome of Shadows	4
Sniper Eye	☆	Shop: Ingredient acquired	Wall Rush HP Damage +10%	1,300	Destruction Powder	2	—	—	—	—
Sniper Soul	☆	Shop: Ingredient acquired	Wall Rush HP Damage +20%	1,900	Destruction Shard	3	Destruction Crystal	2	Tome of Mysteries	5
Defense Veil	☆	Shop: Ingredient acquired	Wall Rush BRV Defense +20%	1,300	Lithe Powder	2	—	—	—	—
Mystery Veil	☆	Shop: Ingredient acquired	Wall Rush BRV Defense +30%	1,900	Lithe Shard	3	Lithe Crystal	2	Tome of Love	3
Decoy	☆	Shop: Ingredient acquired	Wall Rush HP Defense +20%	1,300	Resilience Powder	2	—	—	—	—

ACCESSORIES

NAME	RANK	ACQUIRE	ABILITIES	COST	INGREDIENT 1	QUANTITY	INGREDIENT 2	QUANTITY	INGREDIENT 3	QUANTITY
Scapegoat	☆	Shop: Ingredient acquired	Wall Rush HP Defense +30%	1,900	Resilience Shard	3	Resilience Crystal	2	Tome of Souls	3
Jet Engine	☆	Shop: Ingredient acquired	Chase BRV Damage +10%	1,300	Power Powder	2	—	—	—	—
Rocket Engine	☆	Shop: Ingredient acquired	Chase BRV Damage +20%	1,900	Power Shard	3	Power Crystal	2	Tome of Lies	5
Amulet	☆	Shop: Ingredient acquired	Chase BRV Defense +10%	1,300	Gale Powder	1	Lithe Powder	1	—	—
Golden Amulet	☆	Shop: Ingredient acquired	Chase BRV Defense +20%	1,900	Gale Shard	2	Lithe Shard	2	Tome of Kings	3
Mindhrenk	☆	Shop: Ingredient acquired	BRV boost when stage elements destroyed +2%	1,300	Destruction Powder	1	Gale Powder	1	—	—
Mindcrush	☆	Shop: Ingredient acquired	BRV boost when stage elements destroyed +4%	1,900	Destruction Shard	2	Gale Shard	2	Tome of Men	5
Angel's Bell	☆	Shop: Ingredient acquired	Regen +10%	1,000	Healing Powder	2	—	—	—	—
Archangel's Bell	☆	Shop: Ingredient acquired	Regen +20%	1,800	Healing Shard	3	Healing Crystal	2	Tome of Shadows	4
Sunrise	☆	Shop: Ingredient acquired	Battlegen Rate x 1.2	1,000	Allure Powder	1	Luck Powder	1	Power Powder	1
Moonrise	☆	Shop: Ingredient acquired	Battlegen Rate x 1.5	1,800	Allure Shard	2	Power Shard	2	Luck Crystal	1
Battle Chant	☆	Shop: Ingredient acquired	Chase BRV Damage +15%, Defense -10%	1,300	Chaos Shard	2	—	—	—	—
War Gong	☆	Shop: Ingredient acquired	Chase BRV Damage +30%, Defense -20%	1,900	Chaos Crystal	2	Chaos Orb	2	Entropy's Birth	2
Dismay Shock	☆	Shop: Ingredient acquired	EX Gauge Depletion +4%	1,900	Bless Crystal	2	Destruction Crystal	2	Chaos Crystal	2
Despair Shock	☆	Shop: Ingredient acquired	EX Gauge Depletion +8%	2,000	Bless Orb	3	Destruction Orb	3	Chaos Orb	3
Safety Bit	☆	Shop: Ingredient acquired	Last Chance +1%	1,300	Phoenix Down	3	Phoenix Pinion	3	—	—
Safety Ring	☆	Shop: Ingredient acquired	Last Chance +2%	1,800	Safety Bit	1	Phoenix Down	3	Phoenix Pinion	3
Smiting Soul	☆	Shop: Ingredient acquired	Iai Strike +2% (May randomly inflict Break)	2,000	Entropy's Birth	3	Chaos Crystal	3	Chaos Orb	1

BOOSTER ACCESSORIES

NAME	RANK	ACQUIRE	BOOST CONDITION	EFFECT	COST	INGREDIENT 1	QUANTITY	INGREDIENT 2	QUANTITY	INGREDIENT 3	QUANTITY
[HP] HP = 100%	☆	Prize: Accomplishment 002 Battlegen: Stiltzkin 2 friend card [HP attack]	When your HP is 100%	1.5 times	(not sold)	—	—	—	—	—	—
[HP] HP ≥ 80%	☆	Prize: Accomplishment 024	When you have at least 80% of your HP	1.2 times	(not sold)	—	—	—	—	—	—
[HP] HP ≤ 40%	☆	Prize: Accomplishment 036	When you have 40% or loss of your HP	1.2 times	(not sold)	—	—	—	—	—	—
[HP] HP is 50-70%	☆	Prize: Accomplishment 064	When your HP is 50-70%	1.2 times	(not sold)	—	—	—	—	—	—
[HP] HP = 1	☆	Prize: Accomplishment 013 Battlegen: Stiltzkin 2, 4, 5, or 8 friend card [HP attack]	When you have 1 HP	1.5 times	(not sold)	—	—	—	—	—	—
[HP] Near Death	☆	Prize: Accomplishment 003 Battlegen: Stiltzkin 2, 4, 5, or 8 friend card [HP attack]	When you are near death	1.5 times	(not sold)	—	—	—	—	—	—
[HP] Near Loss	☆	Prize: Accomplishment 005 Battlegen: Stiltzkin 4 or 8 friend card [HP attack]	When you are in danger of losing in 1 hit	1.5 times	(not sold)	—	—	—	—	—	—
[HP] Large Gap in HP	☆	Prize: Accomplishment 044	When HP gap between you and foe is at least 2,000 points	1.5 times	(not sold)	—	—	—	—	—	—
[HP] Small Gap in HP	☆	Prize: Accomplishment 045	When HP gap between you and foe is under 200 points	1.5 times	(not sold)	—	—	—	—	—	—
[HP] HP is a Multiple of 2	☆	Prize: Accomplishment 068	When your HP is a multiple of 2	1.1 times	(not sold)	—	—	—	—	—	—
[HP] HP is a Multiple of 3	☆	Prize: Accomplishment 070	When your HP is a multiple of 3	1.2 times	(not sold)	—	—	—	—	—	—
[HP] HP is a Multiple of 4	☆	Prize: Accomplishment 072	When your HP is a multiple of 4	1.3 times	(not sold)	—	—	—	—	—	—
[HP] HP is a Multiple of 5	☆	Prize: Accomplishment 073	When your HP is a multiple of 5	1.4 times	(not sold)	—	—	—	—	—	—

NAME	RANK	ACQUIRE	BOOST CONDITION	EFFECT	COST	INGREDIENT 1	QUANTITY	INGREDIENT 2	QUANTITY	INGREDIENT 3	QUANTITY
[HP] HP is a Prime Number	☆	Prize: Accomplishment 075	When your HP is a prime number	1.5 times	(not sold)	—	—	—	—	—	—
[Bravery] BRV ≥ Base Value	☆	Prize: Accomplishment 032	When your BRV is its base value or higher	1.2 times	(not sold)	—	—	—	—	—	—
[Bravery] BRV ≤ Base Value	☆	Prize: Accomplishment 034	When your BRV is its base value or lower	1.2 times	(not sold)	—	—	—	—	—	—
[Bravery] Break	☆	Prize: Accomplishment 008	When you are suffering from Break	1.5 times	(not sold)	—	—	—	—	—	—
[Bravery] Near Break	☆	Prize: Accomplishment 009	When you are in danger of Break	1.5 times	(not sold)	—	—	—	—	—	—
[Bravery] Victory Chance	☆	Prize: Accomplishment 004	When you have a chance to win	1.5 times	(not sold)	—	—	—	—	—	—
[Bravery] Large Gap in BRV	☆	Prize: Accomplishment 046	When BRV gap between you and foe is at least 1,000 points	1.5 times	(not sold)	—	—	—	—	—	—
[Bravery] Small Gap in BRV	☆	Prize: Accomplishment 047	When BRV gap between you and foe is under 200 points	1.5 times	(not sold)	—	—	—	—	—	—
[Bravery] No BRV Damage	☆	Prize: Accomplishment 092 Battlegen: Stiltzkin 2 friend card [Bravery Break]	When you haven't taken BRV damage	1.5 times	(not sold)	—	—	—	—	—	—
[Bravery] BRV = 0	☆	Prize: Accomplishment 086	When your BRV is 0	1.5 times	(not sold)	—	—	—	—	—	—
[Bravery] BRV is a Multiple of 2	☆	Prize: Accomplishment 077	When your BRV is a multiple of 2	1.1 times	(not sold)	—	—	—	—	—	—
[Bravery] BRV is a Multiple of 3	☆	Prize: Accomplishment 078	When your BRV is a multiple of 3	1.2 times	(not sold)	—	—	—	—	—	—
[Bravery] BRV is a Multiple of 4	☆	Prize: Accomplishment 079	When your BRV is a multiple of 4	1.3 times	(not sold)	—	—	—	—	—	—
[Bravery] BRV is a Multiple of 5	☆	Prize: Accomplishment 081	When your BRV is a multiple of 5	1.4 times	(not sold)	—	—	—	—	—	—
[Bravery] BRV is a Prime Number	☆	Prize: Accomplishment 084	When your BRV is a prime number	1.5 times	(not sold)	—	—	—	—	—	—
[EX] Full EX Gauge	☆	Prize: Accomplishment 041	When your EX Gauge is full	1.5 times	(not sold)	—	—	—	—	—	—
[EX] Empty EX Gauge	☆	Prize: Accomplishment 017	When your EX Gauge is empty	1.5 times	(not sold)	—	—	—	—	—	—
[EX] EX Gauge ≥ 70%	☆	Prize: Accomplishment 022	When your EX Gauge is at least 70% full	1.2 times	(not sold)	—	—	—	—	—	—
[EX] EX Gauge ≤ 30%	☆	Prize: Accomplishment 080	When your EX Gauge is at most 30% full	1.2 times	(not sold)	—	—	—	—	—	—
[EX] EX Core Present	☆	Prize: Accomplishment 098	When EX Core is present	1.5 times	(not sold)	—	—	—	—	—	—
[Summon] After Summon	☆	Prize: Accomplishment 020	Once you have used a summon	1.5 times	(not sold)	—	—	—	—	—	—
[Summon] Summon Unused	☆	Prize: Accomplishment 021	When you have not yet used a summon	1.5 times	(not sold)	—	—	—	—	—	—
[Combat] Standing Still	☆	Prize: Accomplishment 037	When you are standing still	1.3 times	(not sold)	—	—	—	—	—	—
[Combat] In Motion	☆	Prize: Accomplishment 012	When you are moving	1.2 times	(not sold)	—	—	—	—	—	—
[Combat] Attacking Bravery	☆	Prize: Accomplishment 014	While performing a BRV attack	1.2 times	(not sold)	—	—	—	—	—	—
[Combat] Attacking HP	☆	Prize: Accomplishment 018	While performing an HP attack	1.2 times	(not sold)	—	—	—	—	—	—
[Combat] Taking Damage	☆	Prize: Accomplishment 042	While taking damage	1.2 times	(not sold)	—	—	—	—	—	—
[Combat] Blocking	☆	Prize: Accomplishment 088	While blocking	1.2 times	(not sold)	—	—	—	—	—	—
[Combat] Evading	☆	Prize: Accomplishment 087	While evading	1.2 times	(not sold)	—	—	—	—	—	—
[Combat] Quickmove	☆	Prize: Accomplishment 056	During Quickmove	1.2 times	(not sold)	—	—	—	—	—	—
[Combat] Chasing	☆	Prize: Accomplishment 057 Battlegen: Stiltzkin 7 friend card [Stage damage]	While performing a chase attack	1.3 times	(not sold)	—	—	—	—	—	—

ACCESSORIES

NAME	RANK	ACQUIRE	BOOST CONDITION	EFFECT	COST	INGREDIENT 1	QUANTITY	INGREDIENT 2	QUANTITY	INGREDIENT 3	QUANTITY
[EX] EX Mode	☆	Prize: Accomplishment 039	While you are in EX Mode	1.3 times	(not sold)	—	—	—	—	—	—
[Combat] Pre-Bravery Attack	☆	Prize: Accomplishment 050	When you haven't yet performed a BRV attack	1.5 times	(not sold)	—	—	—	—	—	—
[Combat] Pre-Bravery Damage	☆	Prize: Accomplishment 051	When you haven't yet hit with a bravery attack	1.2 times	(not sold)	—	—	—	—	—	—
[Combat] Pre-HP Attack	☆	Prize: Accomplishment 052	When you haven't yet performed an HP attack	1.5 times	(not sold)	—	—	—	—	—	—
[Combat] Pre-HP Damage	☆	Prize: Accomplishment 053	When you haven't yet hit with an HP attack	1.2 times	(not sold)	—	—	—	—	—	—
[Position] On the Ground	☆	Prize: Accomplishment 010	When you are on the ground	1.2 times	(not sold)	—	—	—	—	—	—
[Position] In Midair	☆	Prize: Accomplishment 011 Battlegen: Stiltzkin 7 friend card [Stage damage]	When you are in midair	1.2 times	(not sold)	—	—	—	—	—	—
[Position] Near Opponent	☆	Prize: Accomplishment 006 Battlegen: Stiltzkin 7 friend card [Stage damage]	While near opponent	1.2 times	(not sold)	—	—	—	—	—	—
[Position] Far from Opponent	☆	Prize: Accomplishment 007 Battlegen: Stiltzkin 1 friend card [Stage damage]	While far from opponent	1.2 times	(not sold)	—	—	—	—	—	—
[Position] Above Opponent	☆	Prize: Accomplishment 090	While higher than opponent	1.2 times	(not sold)	—	—	—	—	—	—
[Position] Below Opponent	☆	Prize: Accomplishment 093	While lower than opponent	1.2 times	(not sold)	—	—	—	—	—	—
[Position] On Ground, Foe in Midair	☆	Prize: Accomplishment 061	When opponent is in midair and you are on the ground	1.5 times	(not sold)	—	—	—	—	—	—
[Time] After 30 Seconds	☆	Prize: Accomplishment 030	30 seconds after battle starts	1.2 times	(not sold)	—	—	—	—	—	—
[Level] Large Gap in Level	☆	Prize: Accomplishment 048	When at least a 20 level gap with opponent	1.5 times	(not sold)	—	—	—	—	—	—
[Level] Small Gap in Level	☆	Prize: Accomplishment 049	When at most a 3 level gap with opponent	1.2 times	(not sold)	—	—	—	—	—	—
[Level] Level ≤ 3	☆	Prize: Accomplishment 001	When your level is 3 or under	2 times	(not sold)	—	—	—	—	—	—
[Level] Level 10-19	☆	Prize: Accomplishment 095	When your level is 10-19	1.5 times	(not sold)	—	—	—	—	—	—
[Level] Level 20-29	☆	Prize: Accomplishment 096	When your level is 20-29	1.2 times	(not sold)	—	—	—	—	—	—
[Level] Level 30-39	☆	Prize: Accomplishment 097	When your level is 30-39	1.2 times	(not sold)	—	—	—	—	—	—
[Level] Level 40-49	☆	Prize: Accomplishment 083	When your level is 40-49	1.2 times	(not sold)	—	—	—	—	—	—
[Level] Level 50-59	☆	Prize: Accomplishment 065	When your level is 50-59	1.2 times	(not sold)	—	—	—	—	—	—
[Level] Level 60-69	☆	Prize: Accomplishment 067	When your level is 60-69	1.2 times	(not sold)	—	—	—	—	—	—
[Level] Level 70-79	☆	Prize: Accomplishment 015	When your level is 70-79	1.2 times	(not sold)	—	—	—	—	—	—
[Level] Level 80-89	☆	Prize: Accomplishment 082	When your level is 80-89	1.2 times	(not sold)	—	—	—	—	—	—
[Level] Level 90-99	☆	Prize: Accomplishment 019	When your level is 90-99	1.2 times	(not sold)	—	—	—	—	—	—
[Level] Level 100	☆	Prize: Accomplishment 066	When your level is 100	1.2 times	(not sold)	—	—	—	—	—	—
[Level] Level = Multiple of 2	☆	Prize: Accomplishment 085	When your level is a multiple of 2	1.1 times	(not sold)	—	—	—	—	—	—
[Level] Level = Multiple of 3	☆	Prize: Accomplishment 016	When your level is a multiple of 3	1.2 times	(not sold)	—	—	—	—	—	—
[Level] Level = Multiple of 4	☆	Prize: Accomplishment 062	When your level is a multiple of 4	1.2 times	(not sold)	—	—	—	—	—	—
[Level] Level = Multiple of 5	☆	Prize: Accomplishment 063	When your level is a multiple of 5	1.2 times	(not sold)	—	—	—	—	—	—
[Level] Level is a Prime Number	☆	Prize: Accomplishment 060	When your level is a prime number	1.5 times	(not sold)	—	—	—	—	—	—

NAME	RANK	ACQUIRE	BOOST CONDITION	EFFECT	COST	INGREDIENT 1	QUANTITY	INGREDIENT 2	QUANTITY	INGREDIENT 3	QUANTITY
[Opponent] HP = 100%	☆	Prize: Accomplishment 069	When opponent's HP is 100%	1.5 times	(not sold)	—	—	—	—	—	—
[Opponent] Near Death	☆	Prize: Accomplishment 071	When opponent is near death	1.5 times	(not sold)	—	—	—	—	—	—
[Opponent] Near Loss	☆	Prize: Accomplishment 074	When opponent is near loss	1.5 times	(not sold)	—	—	—	—	—	—
[Opponent] BRV ≥ Base Value	☆	Prize: Accomplishment 033	When opponent's BRV is its base value or higher	1.2 times	(not sold)	—	—	—	—	—	—
[Opponent] BRV ≤ Base Value	☆	Prize: Accomplishment 035	When opponent's BRV is its base value or lower	1.2 times	(not sold)	—	—	—	—	—	—
[Opponent] Break	☆	Prize: Accomplishment 028	When opponent is suffering from Break	1.5 times	(not sold)	—	—	—	—	—	—
[Opponent] Near Break	☆	Prize: Accomplishment 029	When opponent is in danger of Break	1.5 times	(not sold)	—	—	—	—	—	—
[Opponent] Victory Chance	☆	Prize: Accomplishment 094	When opponent has a chance to win	1.5 times	(not sold)	—	—	—	—	—	—
[Opponent] EX Gauge Full	☆	Prize: Accomplishment 055	When opponent's EX Gauge is full	1.5 times	(not sold)	—	—	—	—	—	—
[Opponent] EX Gauge ≥ 70%	☆	Prize: Accomplishment 023	When opponent's EX Gauge is at least 70% full	1.5 times	(not sold)	—	—	—	—	—	—
[Opponent] After Summon	☆	Prize: Accomplishment 100	Once opponent has used a summon	1.5 times	(not sold)	—	—	—	—	—	—
[Opponent] Summon Unused	☆	Prize: Accomplishment 102	When opponent hasn't used a summon	1.5 times	(not sold)	—	—	—	—	—	—
[Opponent] In Motion	☆	Prize: Accomplishment 054	While opponent is moving	1.2 times	(not sold)	—	—	—	—	—	—
[Opponent] Attacking Bravery	☆	Prize: Accomplishment 038	While opponent performs a BRV attack	1.2 times	(not sold)	—	—	—	—	—	—
[Opponent] Attacking HP	☆	Prize: Accomplishment 076	While opponent performs an HP attack	1.2 times	(not sold)	—	—	—	—	—	—
[Opponent] Taking Damage	☆	Prize: Accomplishment 043	While opponent takes damage	1.2 times	(not sold)	—	—	—	—	—	—
[Opponent] Chasing	☆	Prize: Accomplishment 059	While opponent performs a chase attack	1.3 times	(not sold)	—	—	—	—	—	—
[Opponent] EX Mode	☆	Prize: Accomplishment 040	While opponent is in EX Mode	1.3 times	(not sold)	—	—	—	—	—	—
[Opponent] Pre-Bravery Damage	☆	Prize: Accomplishment 089	While opponent hasn't connected with a BRV attack	1.5 times	(not sold)	—	—	—	—	—	—
[Opponent] Pre-HP Damage	☆	Prize: Accomplishment 091	While opponent hasn't connected with an HP attack	1.5 times	(not sold)	—	—	—	—	—	—
[Opponent] On the Ground	☆	Prize: Accomplishment 099	While opponent is on the ground	1.2 times	(not sold)	—	—	—	—	—	—
[Opponent] In Midair	☆	Prize: Accomplishment 101 Battlegen: Stiltzkin 6 friend card [Stage damage]	While opponent is in midair	1.2 times	(not sold)	—	—	—	—	—	—
[Opponent] HP ≥ 70%	☆	Prize: Accomplishment 026	When opponent has at least 70% HP	1.2 times	(not sold)	—	—	—	—	—	—
[Opponent] HP ≤ 30%	☆	Prize: Accomplishment 027	When opponent has 30% HP or less	1.2 times	(not sold)	—	—	—	—	—	—
[Opponent] HP = 1	☆	Prize: Accomplishment 025	When opponent has 1 HP	1.5 times	(not sold)	—	—	—	—	—	—
[Opponent] No BRV Damage	☆	Prize: Accomplishment 031	When opponent hasn't taken BRV damage	1.5 times	(not sold)	—	—	—	—	—	—
[Opponent] EX Gauge ≤ 30%	☆	Prize: Accomplishment 058	When opponent's EX Gauge is under 30%	1.2 times	(not sold)	—	—	—	—	—	—
Easy Come, Easy Go	☆	Shop: Password recipe	Right after battle starts: After 30 seconds:	2.5 times 0.5 times	2,000	Sagittarius Recipe	1	Carnelian Signet	1	Shinra Card Key	1
Strong Against Adversity	☆	Shop: Password recipe	When HP is 1: When over 1% HP:	3 times 0.5 times	2,000	Virgo Recipe	1	Warp Cube	1	Occult Fan	1

ACCESSORIES

SPECIAL ACCESSORIES

NAME	RANK	ACQUIRE	ABILITIES	COST	INGREDIENT 1	QUANTITY	INGREDIENT 2	QUANTITY	INGREDIENT 3	QUANTITY
Lucky Charm	☆	Shop: Ingredient acquired	LUK +4 Summon Recharge +1	1,000	Yellow Drop	1	Luck Powder	2	—	—
Rabbit's Foot	☆	Shop: Ingredient acquired	LUK +8 Summon Recharge +2	1,800	Yellow Gem	2	Luck Shard	2	Luck Crystal	1
Desert Boots	☆	Shop: Ingredient acquired	BRV Boost on Quickmove +1%	1,300	Guts Powder	1	Quickstrike Shard	1		
Battle Boots	☆	Shop: Ingredient acquired	BRV Boost on Quickmove +2%	1,900	Guts Shard	2	Quickstrike Crystal	2	Tome of Silence	5
White Drop	☆	Find: Destiny Odyssey III map 5 Find: Destiny Odyssey V map 5 Battlegen: Stiltzkin 1 friend card [Bravery Break]	EX Force Absorption +10%	(not sold)	—	—	—	—	—	—
Red Drop	☆	Find: Destiny Odyssey III map 1 Battlegen: Stiltzkin 8 friend card [Bravery Break]	ATK +1	(not sold)	—	—	—	—	—	—
Orange Drop	☆	Find: Destiny Odyssey II map 5 Battlegen: Stiltzkin 7 friend card [HP attack]	DEF +1	(not sold)	—	—	—	—	—	—
Yellow Drop	☆	Find: Destiny Odyssey III map 2 Battlegen: Stiltzkin 6 friend card [HP attack]	LUK +1	(not sold)	—	—	—	—	—	—
Green Drop	☆	Find: Destiny Odyssey IX map 3 Battlegen: Stiltzkin 5 friend card [Stage damage]	HP +100	(not sold)	—	—	—	—	—	—
Blue Drop	☆	Find: Destiny Odyssey X map 4 Battlegen: Stiltzkin 3 friend card [Stage damage]	BRV +20	(not sold)	—	—	—	—	—	—
Cyan Drop	☆	Find: Destiny Odyssey V map 5 Battlegen: Stiltzkin 2 friend card [EX Burst]	Initial EX Force +10%	(not sold)	—	—	—	—	—	—
Purple Drop	☆	Find: Destiny Odyssey VIII map 2 Battlegen: Stiltzkin 4 friend card [EX Burst]	Regen +5%	(not sold)	—	—	—	—	—	—
Red Gem	☆	Battlegen: Stiltzkin 8 friend card or any other online opponent with a RED ID [Bravery Break]	ATK +2	(not sold)	—	—	—	—	—	—
Orange Gem	☆	Battlegen: Stiltzkin 7 friend card or any other online opponent with a ORG ID [Bravery Break]	DEF +2	(not sold)	—	—	—	—	—	—
Yellow Gem	☆	Battlegen: Stiltzkin 6 friend card or any other online opponent with a YEL ID [HP attack]	LUK +2	(not sold)	—	—	—	—	—	—
Green Gem	☆	Battlegen: Stiltzkin 5 friend card or any other online opponent with a GRN ID [HP attack]	HP +300	(not sold)	—	—	—	—	—	—
Blue Gem	☆	Battlegen: Stiltzkin 3 friend card or any other online opponent with a BLU ID [Stage damage]	BRV +60	(not sold)	—	—	—	—	—	—
Cyan Gem	☆	Battlegen: Stiltzkin 2 friend card or any other online opponent with a SKY ID [Stage damage]	Initial EX Force +20%	(not sold)	—	—	—	—	—	—
Purple Gem	☆	Battlegen: Stiltzkin 4 friend card or any other online opponent with a PUR ID [EX Burst]	Regen +10%	(not sold)	—	—	—	—	—	—
White Gem	☆	Battlegen: Stiltzkin 1 friend card or any other online opponent with a WHT ID [EX Burst]	EX Force Absorption +20%	(not sold)	—	—	—	—	—	—
Hero's Spirit	☆	Shop: Ingredient acquired	CP +20	1,300	Lucky Charm	1	Guard Ring	1	—	—
Hero's Essence	☆	Shop: Ingredient acquired	CP +40	1,600	Rabbit's Foot	1	Block Ring	1	—	—
Back to the Wall	☆	Shop: Ingredient acquired	Initial HP -90%	1,900	Life Resin	3	Mystery Resin	3	—	—
Tenacious Attacker	☆	Shop: Ingredient acquired	Absorb EX Force during attacks	1,900	Attractorb	1	Muscle Belt	1	—	—
Blazing Totema	☆	Shop: Ingredient acquired	Absorb EX Force after summoning Summon Recharge +2	1,900	Glutton	1	Tenacious Attacker	1	—	—
Growth Egg	☆	Shop: Ingredient acquired	Experience Value +20%	1,900	Growth Seed	1	Chocobo Wing	3	Chocobo Feather	1

NAME	RANK	ACQUIRE	ABILITIES	COST	INGREDIENT 1	QUANTITY	INGREDIENT 2	QUANTITY	INGREDIENT 3	QUANTITY
Strength Begets Courage	☆	Shop: Ingredient acquired	Extra HP to BRV	1,900	Life Resin	3	Archangel's Bell	1	Tome of Memories	5
Force Begets Courage	☆	Shop: Ingredient acquired	EX Core & EX Force to BRV	1,900	Spirit Stanchion	1	Pearl Necklace	1	Tome of Silence	5
Vengeful Soul	☆	Shop: Ingredient acquired	Eye for an Eye: Add bravery to damage when reflecting a magical HP attack	1,900	Mirrored Chain	1	Star Earring	1	Tome of Shadows	4
Rebellious Soul	☆	Shop: Ingredient acquired	Bonecrusher: BRV increases by 30% of max HP when near death	1,900	Gaia Ring	1	Rabbit's Foot	1	Tome of Memories	5
Final Position	☆	Shop: Ingredient acquired	BRV Last Chance: Can endure one attack that would inflict Break with 0 BRV	1,900	Guts Crystal	1	Luck Shard	3	Moonflow	3
Final Decision	☆	Shop: Ingredient acquired	BRV Combo Chance: Can endure one combo that would inflict Break with 0 BRV	1,900	Guts Crystal	1	Power Shard	3	Moonflow	3
Destroyer	☆	Shop: Ingredient acquired	No Chance: Disables opponent's "Chance" effects	1,900	Star's Core	3	Phoenix Pinion	3	—	—
Glutton	☆	Shop: Ingredient acquired	Absorb EX Force when taking damage	2,000	Gravitorb	1	Pearl Necklace	1	Tome of Shadows	4
Great Gospel	☆	Shop: Ingredient acquired	Regen +20% BRV Recovery +50% BRV Boost on Quickmove +1%	2,000	Bravery Elemental	1	Battle Boots	1	Tome of Love	3
Steel Curtain	☆	Shop: Ingredient acquired	Wall Rush BRV Defense +30% Wall Rush HP Defense +30%	2,000	Mystery Veil	1	Scapegoat	1	Tome of Kings	3
Berserker Ring	☆	Shop: Ingredient acquired	Wall Rush BRV Damage +20% Wall Rush HP Damage +20%	2,000	Sniper Soul	1	Hyperstar	1	Tome of Mysteries	5
Close to You	☆	Shop: Ingredient acquired	Absorb EX Force during attacks Absorb EX Force when damaged Absorb EX Force after summoning	2,000	Gravitorb	1	Dragonfly Orb	1	Tome of the Masters	5
Center of the World	☆	Shop: Ingredient acquired	EX Intake Range +2m EX Force Absorption +15% EX Core Absorption +15%	2,000	Pearl Necklace	1	Dragonfly Orb	1	Tome of Souls	3
First to Victory	☆	Shop: Ingredient acquired	Initial EX Force +25% Initial Bravery +25%	2,000	Arcane Resin	6	Valor Resin	3	Tome of Mysteries	5
Hero's Seal	☆	Shop: Ingredient acquired	Initial Bravery +50%	2,000	Valor Incense	6	Valor Resin	3	Tome of Love	3
Beckoning Cat	☆	Shop: Ingredient acquired	Gil +20% AP +100% PP +20%	2,000	Rabbit's Foot	1	Mog's Amulet	1	Tome of Kings	3
Sturm und Drang	☆	Shop: Ingredient acquired	Physical Damage +20% Wall Rush BRV Damage +10% Chase BRV Damage +10%	2,000	Champion Belt	1	Hyperstar	1	Tome of Lies	5
Soul of Thamasa	☆	Shop: Ingredient acquired	Magic Damage +20% Wall Rush BRV Damage +10% Chase BRV Damage +10%	2,000	Star Earring	1	Rocket Engine	1	Tome of the Farplane	5
Fake Mustache	☆	Shop: Ingredient acquired	LUK +10 EX Core Appearance Boost	2,000	Victory Pendant	1	Rabbit's Foot	1	Tome of Men	5
Back-Breaking Straw	☆	Battlegen: Stiltzkin 4 or 5 friend card [HP attack] Shop: Ingredient acquired	BRV Boost on Dodge +3% BRV Boost on Block +5% BRV Boost on Quickmove +1%	2,000	Elven Mantle	1	Spirit Stanchion	1	Tome of the Orator	5
Phoenix Down	☆	Find: Distant Glory: TLoL map 2 Find: Shade Impulse Ch 3 map 2 Battlegen: Stiltzkin 2 or 5 friend card [HP attack] Card: Blackjack Course Shop: Ingredient acquired	Last Chance: Endure killing blow with 1 HP Breaks upon use	1,000	Blackcrystal Sliver	1	Star's Core	1	Moonflow	1
Phoenix Pinion	☆	Find: Distant Glory: TLoL map 4 Find: Distant Glory: RotW map 4 Find: Shade Impulse Ch 2 map 4 Card: Blackjack Course Shop: Ingredient acquired	Second Chance: When HP=0, convert BRV to HP Breaks upon use	1,500	Phoenix Down	1	Demon Soul	1	Order of Emptiness	1
Valor Incense	☆	Find: Shade Impulse Ch 1 map 1 Shop: Ingredient acquired	Initial Bravery +100% Accessory Breakability: 100%	1,000	Sealed Darkness	1	Guts Powder	2	—	—

ACCESSORIES

NAME	RANK	ACQUIRE	ABILITIES	COST	INGREDIENT 1	QUANTITY	INGREDIENT 2	QUANTITY	INGREDIENT 3	QUANTITY
Valor Resin	☆	Find: Shade Impulse/Distant Glory previously opened chests Card: Blackjack Course Shop: Ingredient acquired	Initial Bravery +200% Accessory Breakability: 100%	2,000	Sealed Darkness	3	Geranium	1	Rosemary	1
Arcane Incense	★	Find: Shade Impulse Ch 3 map 5 Shop: Ingredient acquired	Initial EX Force +25% Accessory Breakability: 100%	1,000	Moon Stone	1	Oath Powder	2		
Arcane Resin	☆	Find: Shade Impulse/Distant Glory previously opened chests Card: Blackjack Course Shop: Ingredient acquired	Initial EX Force +100% Accessory Breakability: 100%	2,000	Moon Stone	3	Amplification Powder	1	Bergamot	1
Destruction Incense	☆	Find: Shade Impulse previously opened chests Shop: Ingredient acquired	ATK +4 Accessory Breakability: 100%	1,000	Voidshard	1	Strength Powder	2		
Destruction Resin	☆	Find: Shade Impulse/Distant Glory previously opened chests Card: Blackjack Course Shop: Ingredient acquired	ATK +8 Accessory Breakability: 100%	2,000	Voidshard	3	Crimson Shard	5	Chamomile	1
Patience Incense	☆	Find: Shade Impulse previously opened chests Shop: Ingredient acquired	DEF +4 Accessory Breakability: 100%	1,000	Magicite Shard	1	Protect Powder	2		
Patience Resin	☆	Find: Shade Impulse/Distant Glory previously opened chests Card: Blackjack Course Shop: Ingredient acquired	DEF +8 Accessory Breakability: 100%	2,000	Magicite Shard	3	Clary Sage	1	Ylang Ylang	1
Life Incense	☆	Shop: Ingredient acquired	HP +500 Accessory Breakability: 100%	1,000	Materia	1	Titan Powder	2		
Life Resin	☆	Find: Shade Impulse/Distant Glory previously opened chests Shop: Ingredient acquired	HP +1,000 Accessory Breakability: 100%	2,000	Materia	3	Healing Shard	2	Tea Tree	1
Mystery Incense	☆	Find: Shade Impulse previously opened chests Shop: Ingredient acquired	LUK +8 Accessory Breakability: 100%	1,000	Time Warp	1	Luck Powder	2		
Mystery Resin	☆	Find: Shade Impulse/Distant Glory previously opened chests Card: Blackjack Course Shop: Ingredient acquired	LUK +16 Accessory Breakability: 100%	2,000	Time Warp	3	Eucalyptus	1	Lemongrass	1
Chocobo Down	☆	Play Plan: Casual Gamer or Treasure Hunter	Experience Value +20% Accessory Breakability: 30%	(not sold)	—	—	—	—	—	—
Chocobo Wing	☆	Play Plan: Average Gamer or Treasure Hunter	Experience Value +50% Accessory Breakability: 30%	(not sold)	—	—	—	—	—	—
Chocobo Feather	☆	Play Plan: Hardcore Gamer or Treasure Hunter	Experience Value +100% Accessory Breakability: 30%	(not sold)	—	—	—	—	—	—
Superslick	☆	Mognet: Message attachment	Battlegen Rate x 1.5 Accessory Breakability: 30%	(not sold)	—	—	—	—	—	—
Mog's Amulet	☆	Mognet: Message attachment	Drop Rate x 1.5 Accessory Breakability: 30%	(not sold)	—	—	—	—	—	—
Diamond Ring	☆	Shop: Buy "Diamond Ring Added" in PP Catalog	AP +300% Accessory Breakability: 100%	10,000	—	—	—	—	—	—
Miracle Shoes	☆	Shop: Password recipe	ATK +1, DEF +1, LUK +1	2,000	Aries Recipe	1	Rosetta Stone	1		
Dangerously Lucky	☆	Shop: Password recipe	Last Chance: Endure killing blow with 1 HP Breaks upon use Drop Rate x 1.75	2,000	Gemini Recipe	1	Gnomish Bread	1	Automaton Parts	1

TRADE ACCESSORIES (IN ALPHABETICAL ORDER)

With over 300 trade accessories in all, it can be hard to find the one you need in the game-order list, so they've been re-ordered alphabetically here. If you're looking to fill in the gaps in your collection, you'll find a game-order list (names only) after this alphabetical catalog.

NAME	RANK	ACQUIRE	ABILITIES	COST	INGREDIENT 1	QUANTITY	INGREDIENT 2	QUANTITY	INGREDIENT 3	QUANTITY
Adamantite	☆	DP Prize: Inward Chaos / Shop: Ingredient acquired	LUK +4	2,000	Pink Tail	1	—	—	—	—
Aged Turtle Shell	☆	Card: Invincible Course / Shop: Buy "Invincible Course Added" in PP Catalog	LUK +4	2,000	Hi-Elixir	3	—	—	—	—
Al Bhed Primer	☆	Shop: Password required	LUK +4	(not sold)	—	—	—	—	—	—
Allure Crystal	☆	Battlegen: Kefka [EX Burst] (After successful Allure Shard Battlegen)	EX Core Appearance Boost	(not sold)	—	—	—	—	—	—
Allure Orb	☆	Battlegen: Kefka [Bravery Break] (After successful Allure Crystal Battlegen)	EX Core Appearance Boost	(not sold)	—	—	—	—	—	—
Allure Powder	☆	Battlegen: Kefka [Bravery Break]	EX Core Appearance Boost	(not sold)	—	—	—	—	—	—
Allure Shard	☆	Battlegen: Kefka [HP attack] (After successful Allure Powder Battlegen)	EX Core Appearance Boost	(not sold)	—	—	—	—	—	—
Amplification Crystal	☆	Battlegen: Terra [HP attack] (After successful Amplification Shard Battlegen)	EX Core Absorption +10%	(not sold)	—	—	—	—	—	—
Amplification Orb	☆	Battlegen: Terra [EX Burst] (After successful Amplification Crystal Battlegen)	EX Core Absorption +10%	(not sold)	—	—	—	—	—	—
Amplification Powder	☆	Battlegen: Terra [Bravery Break]	EX Core Absorption +10%	(not sold)	—	—	—	—	—	—
Amplification Shard	☆	Battlegen: Terra [Bravery Break] (After successful Amplification Powder Battlegen)	EX Core Absorption +10%	(not sold)	—	—	—	—	—	—
Ancient Bone	☆	Card: Falcon Course / Shop: Buy "Falcon Course Added" in PP Catalog	LUK +2	1,500	Elixir	1	—	—	—	—
Ancient Turtle Shell	☆	Card: Lunar Whale Course / Shop: Buy "Lunar Whale Course Added" in PP Catalog	LUK +4	2,000	Megalixir	2	—	—	—	—
Aquamarine	☆	Card: Airship Course / Shop: Buy "Airship Course Added" in PP Catalog	LUK +1	1,000	Dusty Elixir	1	—	—	—	—
Aquarius Recipe	☆	Shop: Password required	(none)	(not sold)	—	—	—	—	—	—
Aries Recipe	☆	Shop: Password required	(none)	(not sold)	—	—	—	—	—	—
Automaton Parts	☆	Shop: Password required	LUK +4	(not sold)	—	—	—	—	—	—
Bahamut's Wing	☆	Card: Lunar Whale Course / Shop: Buy "Lunar Whale Course Added" in PP Catalog	LUK +4	2,000	Megalixir	2	—	—	—	—
Bard Lore	☆	Find: Distant Glory TLoL map 3 / Shop: Once found	LUK +4	2,000	Wind Stone	1	Water Stone	1	Lifestone	1
Beast Bone	☆	Card: Airship Course / Shop: Buy "Airship Course Added" in PP Catalog	LUK +1	1,000	Dusty Elixir	1	—	—	—	—
Beastlord Fang	☆	Card: Invincible Course / Shop: Buy "Invincible Course Added" in PP Catalog	LUK +4	2,000	Hi-Elixir	3	—	—	—	—
Beastlord Horn	☆	Card: Invincible Course / Shop: Buy "Invincible Course Added" in PP Catalog	LUK +4	2,000	Hi-Elixir	3	—	—	—	—
Behemoth Horn	☆	Card: Lunar Whale Course / Shop: Buy "Lunar Whale Course Added" in PP Catalog	LUK +4	2,000	Megalixir	2	—	—	—	—
Bergamot	☆	Find: Destiny Odyssey II map 4 / Find: Destiny Odyssey X map 4 / Find: Shade Impulse/Distant Glory previously opened chests / Find: When equipped Pebble accessory breaks / Card: Airship Course / Shop: Buy "Airship Course Added" in PP Catalog	LUK +1	2,000	—	—	—	—	—	—
Big Tree	☆	Card: Falcon Course / Shop: Buy "Falcon Course Added" in PP Catalog	LUK +3	1,600	Elixir	2	—	—	—	—
Bird Feather	☆	Card: Airship Course / Shop: Buy "Airship Course Added" in PP Catalog	LUK +1	1,000	Dusty Elixir	1	—	—	—	—

ACCESSORIES

NAME	RANK	ACQUIRE	ABILITIES	COST	INGREDIENT 1	QUANTITY	INGREDIENT 2	QUANTITY	INGREDIENT 3	QUANTITY
Black Belt Lore	☆	Find: Distant Glory: TLoL map 5 Shop: Once found	LUK +4	2,000	Wind Stone	1	Water Stone	1	Lifestone	1
Black Mage Lore	☆	Find: Distant Glory: TLoL map 3 Shop: Once found	LUK +4	2,000	Wind Stone	1	Water Stone	1	Lifestone	1
Black Stone	☆	Card: Airship Course Shop: Buy "Airship Course Added" in PP Catalog	LUK +2	1,000	Dusty Elixir	2	—	—	—	—
Black Tiger Fang	☆	Card: Airship Course Shop: Buy "Airship Course Added" in PP Catalog	LUK +2	1,000	Dusty Elixir	2	—	—	—	—
Blackcrystal Sliver	☆	Battlegen: Old Chaos Shrine [stage damage]	LUK +2	(not sold)	—	—	—	—	—	—
Bless Crystal	☆	Battlegen: Squall [EX Burst] (After successful Bless Shard Battlegen)	EX Force Absorption +10%	(not sold)	—	—	—	—	—	—
Bless Orb	☆	Battlegen: Squall [Bravery Break] (After successful Bless Crystal Battlegen)	EX Force Absorption +10%	(not sold)	—	—	—	—	—	—
Bless Powder	☆	Battlegen: Squall [Bravery Break]	EX Force Absorption +10%	(not sold)	—	—	—	—	—	—
Bless Shard	☆	Battlegen: Squall [HP attack] (After successful Bless Powder Battlegen)	EX Force Absorption +10%	(not sold)	—	—	—	—	—	—
Blessed Barding	☆	Card: Invincible Course Shop: Buy "Invincible Course Added" in PP Catalog	LUK +3	2,000	Hi-Elixir	2	—	—	—	—
Blessed Gem	☆	Card: Invincible Course Shop: Buy "Invincible Course Added" in PP Catalog	LUK +3	2,000	Hi-Elixir	2	—	—	—	—
Blood-Darkened Bone	☆	Card: Invincible Course Shop: Buy "Invincible Course Added" in PP Catalog	LUK +4	2,000	Hi-Elixir	3	—	—	—	—
Boiling Blood	☆	Card: Lunar Whale Course Shop: Buy "Lunar Whale Course Added" in PP Catalog	LUK +4	2,000	Megalixir	4	—	—	—	—
Cancer Recipe	☆	Shop: Password required	(none)	(not sold)	—	—	—	—	—	—
Capricorn Recipe	☆	Shop: Password required	(none)	(not sold)	—	—	—	—	—	—
Carnelian Signet	☆	Shop: Password required	LUK +4	(not sold)	—	—	—	—	—	—
Chamomile	☆	Find: Destiny Odyssey IX map 2 Find: Shade Impulse/Distant Glory previously opened chests Find: When equipped Pebble accessory breaks Card: Airship Course Shop: Buy "Airship Course Added" in PP Catalog	LUK +1	2,000	—	—				—
Chaos Crystal	☆	Battlegen: Chaos [HP attack] (After successful Chaos Shard Battlegen)	ATK +1, DEF -1	(not sold)	—	—	—	—	—	—
Chaos Orb	☆	Battlegen: Chaos [Bravery Break] (After successful Chaos Crystal Battlegen)	ATK +1, DEF -1	(not sold)	—	—	—	—	—	—
Chaos Shard	☆	Battlegen: Chaos [EX Burst]	ATK +1, DEF -1	(not sold)	—	—	—	—	—	—
Charger Barding	☆	Card: Airship Course Shop: Buy "Airship Course Added" in PP Catalog	LUK +1	1,000	Dusty Elixir	1	—	—	—	—
Chemist Lore	☆	Find: Inward Chaos map 5 Shop: Once found	LUK +4	2,000	Wind Stone	1	Water Stone	1	Lifestone	1
Chimera Fang	☆	Card: Falcon Course Shop: Buy "Falcon Course Added" in PP Catalog	LUK +2	1,300	Elixir	1	—	—	—	—
Chocobo Cologne	☆	Prize: Arcade Mode (Normal Mode)	LUK +4	(not sold)	—	—	—	—	—	—
Chocograph	☆	Shop: Password required	LUK +4	(not sold)	—	—	—	—	—	—
Clary Sage	☆	Find: Destiny Odyssey VI map 4 Find: Shade Impulse/Distant Glory previously opened chests Find: When equipped Pebble accessory breaks Card: Airship Course Shop: Buy "Airship Course Added" in PP Catalog	LUK +1	2,000	—	—				—
Crimson Crystal	☆	Battlegen: Jecht [HP attack] (After successful Crimson Shard Battlegen)	Physical Damage +10%	(not sold)	—	—	—	—	—	—
Crimson Orb	☆	Battlegen: Jecht [Bravery Break] (After successful Crimson Crystal Battlegen)	Physical Damage +10%	(not sold)	—	—	—	—	—	—
Crimson Powder	☆	Battlegen: Jecht [Bravery Break]	Physical Damage +10%	(not sold)	—	—	—	—	—	—
Crimson Shard	☆	Battlegen: Jecht [HP attack] (After successful Crimson Powder Battlegen)	Physical Damage +10%	(not sold)	—	—	—	—	—	—

NAME	RANK	ACQUIRE	ABILITIES	COST	INGREDIENT 1	QUANTITY	INGREDIENT 2	QUANTITY	INGREDIENT 3	QUANTITY
Crystal	☆	DP Prize: Distant Glory: TLoL and RotW Card: Falcon and Invincible Courses	LUK +4	(not sold)	—	—	—	—	—	—
Crystal Eye	☆	Shop: Password required	LUK +4	(not sold)	—	—	—	—	—	—
Dancer Lore	☆	Find: Distant Glory TLoL map 5 Shop: Once found	LUK +4	2,000	Wind Stone	1	Water Stone	1	Lifestone	1
Delicious Fish	☆	Shop: Password required	LUK +4	(not sold)	—	—	—	—	—	—
Demon Feather	☆	Card: Falcon Course Shop: Buy "Falcon Course Added" in PP Catalog	LUK +2	1,300	Elixir	1	—	—	—	—
Demon Soul	☆	Battlegen: Pandaemonium [stage damage]	LUK +2	(not sold)	—	—	—	—	—	—
Destrier Barding	☆	Card: Falcon Course Shop: Buy "Falcon Course Added" in PP Catalog	LUK +2	1,500	Elixir	1	—	—	—	—
Destruction Crystal	☆	Battlegen: Golbez [EX Burst] (After successful Destruction Shard Battlegen)	Wall Rush HP Damage +5%	(not sold)	—	—	—	—	—	—
Destruction Orb	☆	Battlegen: Golbez [Bravery Break] (After successful Destruction Crystal Battlegen)	Wall Rush HP Damage +5%	(not sold)	—	—	—	—	—	—
Destruction Powder	☆	Battlegen: Golbez [Bravery Break]	Wall Rush HP Damage +5%	(not sold)	—	—	—	—	—	—
Destruction Shard	☆	Battlegen: Golbez [HP attack] (After successful Destruction Powder Battlegen)	Wall Rush HP Damage +5%	(not sold)	—	—	—	—	—	—
Dewdrop Pebble	☆	Card: Falcon Course Shop: Buy "Falcon Course Added" in PP Catalog	LUK +3	1,600	Elixir	2	—	—	—	—
Diablos's Wing	☆	Card: Falcon Course Shop: Buy "Falcon Course Added" in PP Catalog	LUK +3	1,800	Elixir	3	—	—	—	—
Diamond	☆	Find: Shade Impulse Chapters 1, 2, and 3 DP Prize: Distant Glory: TLoL and RotW Card: Falcon Course	LUK +3	(not sold)	—	—	—	—	—	—
Djinn Scales	☆	Card: Invincible Course Shop: Buy "Invincible Course Added" in PP Catalog	LUK +4	2,000	Hi-Elixir	3	—	—	—	—
Dragon Seal	☆	Shop: Password required	LUK +4	(not sold)	—	—	—	—	—	—
Dragonstone	☆	Card: Invincible Course Shop: Buy "Invincible Course Added" in PP Catalog	LUK +3	1,900	Hi-Elixir	1	—	—	—	—
Dragonwood	☆	Card: Invincible Course Shop: Buy "Invincible Course Added" in PP Catalog	LUK +3	1,900	Hi-Elixir	1	—	—	—	—
Dragoon Lore	☆	Find: Distant Glory: RotW map 4 Shop: Once found	LUK +4	2,000	Wind Stone	1	Water Stone	1	Lifestone	1
Dusty Elixir	☆	Card: Airship Course Shop: Buy "Airship Course Added" in PP Catalog	LUK +4	(not sold)	—	—	—	—	—	—
Eden's Scales	☆	Card: Lunar Whale Course Shop: Buy "Lunar Whale Course Added" in PP Catalog	LUK +4	2,000	Megalixir	2	—	—	—	—
Elixir	☆	Prize: Arcade Mode (Time Attack - based on performance) Card: Falcon Course Shop: Buy "Falcon Course Added" in PP Catalog	LUK +4	(not sold)	—	—	—	—	—	—
Emerald	☆	Card: Airship Course Shop: Buy "Airship Course Added" in PP Catalog	LUK +1	1,000	Dusty Elixir	1	—	—	—	—
Emperor Scales	☆	Card: Falcon Course Shop: Buy "Falcon Course Added" in PP Catalog	LUK +3	1,600	Elixir	2	—	—	—	—
Entropy's Birth	☆	Battlegen: Edge of Madness [stage damage]	LUK +2	(not sold)	—	—	—	—	—	—
Eucalyptus	☆	Find: Destiny Odyssey V map 4 Find: Shade Impulse/Distant Glory previously opened chests Find: When equipped Pebble accessory breaks Card: Airship Course Shop: Buy "Airship Course Added" in PP Catalog	LUK +1	2,000	—	—	—	—	—	—
Fallen Angel Feather	☆	Card: Falcon Course Shop: Buy "Falcon Course Added" in PP Catalog	LUK +2	1,500	Elixir	1	—	—	—	—
Fanatic's Leer	☆	Card: Lunar Whale Course Shop: Buy "Lunar Whale Course Added" in PP Catalog	LUK +4	2,000	Megalixir	4	—	—	—	—

ACCESSORIES

NAME	RANK	ACQUIRE	ABILITIES	COST	INGREDIENT 1	QUANTITY	INGREDIENT 2	QUANTITY	INGREDIENT 3	QUANTITY
Fayth's Dream	☆	Card: Lunar Whale Course Shop: Buy "Lunar Whale Course Added" in PP Catalog	LUK +4	2,000	Megalixir	4	—	—	—	—
Gale Crystal	☆	Battlegen: Cloud [HP attack] (After successful Gale Shard Battlegen)	Wall Rush BRV Damage +5%	(not sold)	—	—	—	—	—	—
Gale Orb	☆	Battlegen: Cloud [Bravery Break] (After successful Gale Crystal Battlegen)	Wall Rush BRV Damage +5%	(not sold)	—	—	—	—	—	—
Gale Powder	☆	Battlegen: Cloud [Bravery Break]	Wall Rush BRV Damage +5%	(not sold)	—	—	—	—	—	—
Gale Shard	☆	Battlegen: Cloud [HP attack] (After successful Gale Powder Battlegen)	Wall Rush BRV Damage +5%	(not sold)	—	—	—	—	—	—
Garuda's Wing	☆	Card: Invincible Course Shop: Buy "Invincible Course Added" in PP Catalog	LUK +4	2,000	Hi-Elixir	3	—	—	—	—
Gates of Judgment	☆	Card: Lunar Whale Course Shop: Buy "Lunar Whale Course Added" in PP Catalog	LUK +4	2,000	Megalixir	4	—	—	—	—
Gears of Time	☆	Card: Lunar Whale Course Shop: Buy "Lunar Whale Course Added" in PP Catalog	LUK +4	2,000	Megalixir	4	—	—	—	—
Gemini Recipe	☆	Shop: Password required	(none)	(not sold)	—	—	—	—	—	—
Geranium	☆	Find: Destiny Odyssey VIII map 4 Find: Shade Impulse/Distant Glory previously opened chests Find: When equipped Pebble accessory breaks Card: Airship Course Shop: Buy "Airship Course Added" in PP Catalog	LUK +1	2,000	—	—	—	—	—	—
GF Eden	☆	Shop: Password required	LUK +4	(not sold)	—	—	—	—	—	—
Giant Feather	☆	Card: Airship Course Shop: Buy "Airship Course Added" in PP Catalog	LUK +2	1,200	Dusty Elixir	3	—	—	—	—
Giant Turtleshell	☆	Card: Falcon Course Shop: Buy "Falcon Course Added" in PP Catalog	LUK +3	1,800	Elixir	3	—	—	—	—
Gigas Bone	☆	Card: Airship Course Shop: Buy "Airship Course Added" in PP Catalog	LUK +2	1,200	Dusty Elixir	3	—	—	—	—
Gnomish Bread	☆	Shop: Password required	LUK +4	(not sold)	—	—	—	—	—	—
God of Destruction	☆	Card: Lunar Whale Course Shop: Buy "Lunar Whale Course Added" in PP Catalog	LUK +4	2,000	Megalixir	4	—	—	—	—
Goddess's Magicite	☆	Card: Invincible Course Shop: Buy "Invincible Course Added" in PP Catalog	LUK +4	2,000	Hi-Elixir	3	—	—	—	—
Godfighter Scales	☆	Card: Falcon Course Shop: Buy "Falcon Course Added" in PP Catalog	LUK +3	1,800	Elixir	3	—	—	—	—
Gold	☆	Find: Shade Impulse Chapters 1, 2, and 3 Card: Airship and Falcon Courses	LUK +2	(not sold)	—	—	—	—	—	—
Great Serpent's Fang	☆	Card: Airship Course Shop: Buy "Airship Course Added" in PP Catalog	LUK +2	1,200	Dusty Elixir	3	—	—	—	—
Great Serpentskin	☆	Card: Airship Course Shop: Buy "Airship Course Added" in PP Catalog	LUK +2	1,200	Dusty Elixir	3	—	—	—	—
Growth Seed	☆	Find: When equipped Pebble accessory breaks	LUK +1	(not sold)	—	—	—	—	—	—
Guiding Light	☆	Card: Lunar Whale Course Shop: Buy "Lunar Whale Course Added" in PP Catalog	LUK +4	2,000	Megalixir	4	—	—	—	—
Guts Crystal	☆	Battlegen: Tidus [HP attack] (After successful Guts Shard Battlegen)	BRV +10	(not sold)	—	—	—	—	—	—
Guts Orb	☆	Battlegen: Tidus [Bravery Break] (After successful Guts Crystal Battlegen)	BRV +10	(not sold)	—	—	—	—	—	—
Guts Powder	☆	Battlegen: Tidus [Bravery Break]	BRV +10	(not sold)	—	—	—	—	—	—
Guts Shard	☆	Battlegen: Tidus [HP attack] (After successful Guts Powder Battlegen)	BRV +10	(not sold)	—	—	—	—	—	—
Healing Crystal	☆	Battlegen: The Emperor [HP attack] (After successful Healing Shard Battlegen)	Regen +5%	(not sold)	—	—	—	—	—	—
Healing Orb	☆	Battlegen: The Emperor [Bravery Break] (After successful Healing Crystal Battlegen)	Regen +5%	(not sold)	—	—	—	—	—	—
Healing Powder	☆	Battlegen: The Emperor [Bravery Break]	Regen +5%	(not sold)	—	—	—	—	—	—

NAME	RANK	ACQUIRE	ABILITIES	COST	INGREDIENT 1	QUANTITY	INGREDIENT 2	QUANTITY	INGREDIENT 3	QUANTITY
Healing Shard	☆	Battlegen: The Emperor [HP attack] (After successful Healing Powder Battlegen)	Regen +5%	(not sold)	—	—	—	—	—	—
Hero's Bone	☆	Card: Lunar Whale Course Shop: Buy "Lunar Whale Course Added" in PP Catalog	LUK +4	2,000	Megalixir	2	—	—	—	—
Hi-Elixir	☆	Prize: Arcade Mode (Time Attack - based on performance) Card: Invincible Course Shop: Buy "Invincible Course Added" in PP Catalog	LUK +4	(not sold)	—	—	—	—	—	—
Holy Fang	☆	Card: Invincible Course Shop: Buy "Invincible Course Added" in PP Catalog	LUK +3	2,000	Hi-Elixir	2	—	—	—	—
Holystone	☆	Card: Invincible Course Shop: Buy "Invincible Course Added" in PP Catalog	LUK +3	2,000	Hi-Elixir	2	—	—	—	—
Humbaba's Horn	☆	Card: Falcon Course Shop: Buy "Falcon Course Added" in PP Catalog	LUK +3	1,600	Elixir	2	—	—	—	—
Ichthon Scales	☆	Card: Airship Course Shop: Buy "Airship Course Added" in PP Catalog	LUK +1	1,000	Dusty Elixir	1	—	—	—	—
Iifa Tree	☆	Card: Lunar Whale Course Shop: Buy "Lunar Whale Course Added" in PP Catalog	LUK +4	2,000	Megalixir	2	—	—	—	—
Iron Carapace	☆	Card: Airship Course Shop: Buy "Airship Course Added" in PP Catalog	LUK +1	1,000	Dusty Elixir	1	—	—	—	—
Ixion Horn	☆	Card: Falcon Course Shop: Buy "Falcon Course Added" in PP Catalog	LUK +3	1,800	Elixir	3	—	—	—	—
Knight Lore	☆	Find: Distant Glory: RotW map 3 Shop: Once found	LUK +4	2,000	Wind Stone	1	Water Stone	1	Lifestone	1
Lamia Scales	☆	Card: Airship Course Shop: Buy "Airship Course Added" in PP Catalog	LUK +2	1,000	Dusty Elixir	2	—	—	—	—
Land Dragon Bone	☆	Card: Invincible Course Shop: Buy "Invincible Course Added" in PP Catalog	LUK +3	1,900	Hi-Elixir	1	—	—	—	—
Landshark Scales	☆	Card: Falcon Course Shop: Buy "Falcon Course Added" in PP Catalog	LUK +2	1,300	Elixir	1	—	—	—	—
Lapis Lazuli	☆	Card: Invincible Course Shop: Buy "Invincible Course Added" in PP Catalog	LUK +4	2,000	Hi-Elixir	3	—	—	—	—
Large Fang	☆	Card: Airship Course Shop: Buy "Airship Course Added" in PP Catalog	LUK +1	1,000	Dusty Elixir	1	—	—	—	—
Large Horn	☆	Card: Airship Course Shop: Buy "Airship Course Added" in PP Catalog	LUK +1	1,000	Dusty Elixir	1	—	—	—	—
Lemongrass	☆	Find: Destiny Odyssey VII map 4 Find: Shade Impulse/Distant Glory previously opened chests Find: When equipped Pebble accessory breaks Card: Airship Course Shop: Buy "Airship Course Added" in PP Catalog	LUK +1	2,000	—	—	—	—	—	—
Leo Recipe	☆	Shop: Password required	(none)	(not sold)	—	—	—	—	—	—
Leviathan Scales	☆	Card: Falcon Course Shop: Buy "Falcon Course Added" in PP Catalog	LUK +2	1,500	Elixir	1	—	—	—	—
Levistone	☆	Card: Falcon Course Shop: Buy "Falcon Course Added" in PP Catalog	LUK +2	1,500	Elixir	1	—	—	—	—
Libra Recipe	☆	Shop: Password required	(none)	(not sold)	—	—	—	—	—	—
Life of the Planet	☆	Card: Lunar Whale Course Shop: Buy "Lunar Whale Course Added" in PP Catalog	LUK +4	2,000	Megalixir	4	—	—	—	—
Lifestone	☆	Prize: Arcade Mode (Hard Mode) Card: Airship, Falcon, Invincible, and Lunar Whale Courses	LUK +4	(not sold)	—	—	—	—	—	—
Lithe Crystal	☆	Battlegen: Ultimecia [HP attack] (After successful Lithe Shard Battlegen)	Wall Rush BRV Defense +5%	(not sold)	—	—	—	—	—	—
Lithe Orb	☆	Battlegen: Ultimecia [Bravery Break] (After successful Lithe Crystal Battlegen)	Wall Rush BRV Defense +5%	(not sold)	—	—	—	—	—	—

ACCESSORIES

NAME	RANK	ACQUIRE	ABILITIES	COST	INGREDIENT 1	QUANTITY	INGREDIENT 2	QUANTITY	INGREDIENT 3	QUANTITY
Lithe Powder	☆	Battlegen: Ultimecia [Bravery Break]	Wall Rush BRV Defense +5%	(not sold)	—	—	—	—	—	—
Lithe Shard	☆	Battlegen: Ultimecia [HP attack] (After successful Lithe Powder Battlegen)	Wall Rush BRV Defense +5%	(not sold)	—	—	—	—	—	—
Lizard Horn	☆	Card: Falcon Course Shop: Buy "Falcon Course Added" in PP Catalog	LUK +2	1,500	Elixir	1	—	—	—	—
Lone Heart	☆	Card: Lunar Whale Course Shop: Buy "Lunar Whale Course Added" in PP Catalog	LUK +4	2,000	Megalixir	4	—	—	—	—
Luck Crystal	☆	Battlegen: Bartz [HP attack] (After successful Luck Shard Battlegen)	LUK +1	(not sold)	—	—	—	—	—	—
Luck Orb	☆	Battlegen: Bartz [Bravery Break] (After successful Luck Crystal Battlegen)	LUK +1	(not sold)	—	—	—	—	—	—
Luck Powder	☆	Battlegen: Bartz [Bravery Break]	LUK +1	(not sold)	—	—	—	—	—	—
Luck Shard	☆	Battlegen: Bartz [HP attack] (After successful Luck Powder Battlegen)	LUK +1	(not sold)	—	—	—	—	—	—
Lumber	☆	Card: Airship Course Shop: Buy "Airship Course Added" in PP Catalog	LUK +2	1,000	Dusty Elixir	2	—	—	—	—
Lust for Power	☆	Card: Lunar Whale Course Shop: Buy "Lunar Whale Course Added" in PP Catalog	LUK +4	2,000	Megalixir	4	—	—	—	—
Maduin's Fang	☆	Card: Lunar Whale Course Shop: Buy "Lunar Whale Course Added" in PP Catalog	LUK +4	2,000	Megalixir	2	—	—	—	—
Magicite Shard	☆	Battlegen: Kefka's Tower [stage damage]	LUK +2	(not sold)	—	—	—	—	—	—
Magnet Crystal	☆	Battlegen: Firion [EX Burst] (After successful Magnet Shard Battlegen)	EX Intake Range +1m	(not sold)	—	—	—	—	—	—
Magnet Orb	☆	Battlegen: Firion [Bravery Break] (After successful Magnet Crystal Battlegen)	EX Intake Range +1m	(not sold)	—	—	—	—	—	—
Magnet Powder	☆	Battlegen: Firion [Bravery Break]	EX Intake Range +1m	(not sold)	—	—	—	—	—	—
Magnet Shard	☆	Battlegen: Firion [HP attack] (After successful Magnet Powder Battlegen)	EX Intake Range +1m	(not sold)	—	—	—	—	—	—
Mako Stone	☆	Card: Falcon Course Shop: Buy "Falcon Course Added" in PP Catalog	LUK +2	1,300	Elixir	1	—	—	—	—
Mallet	☆	DP Prize: Inward Chaos Battlegen: Ultimecia's Castle [stage damage] (After won as DP prize)	Accessory Breakability +20%	(not sold)	—	—	—	—	—	—
Mammoth Tusk	☆	Card: Falcon Course Shop: Buy "Falcon Course Added" in PP Catalog	LUK +3	1,600	Elixir	2	—	—	—	—
Mana Crystal	☆	Battlegen: Cloud of Darkness [EX Burst] (After successful Mana Shard Battlegen)	Magic Damage +10%	(not sold)	—	—	—	—	—	—
Mana Orb	☆	Battlegen: Cloud of Darkness [Bravery Break] (After successful Mana Crystal Battlegen)	Magic Damage +10%	(not sold)	—	—	—	—	—	—
Mana Powder	☆	Battlegen: Cloud of Darkness [Bravery Break]	Magic Damage +10%	(not sold)	—	—	—	—	—	—
Mana Shard	☆	Battlegen: Cloud of Darkness [HP attack] (After successful Mana Powder Battlegen)	Magic Damage +10%	(not sold)	—	—	—	—	—	—
Marksman Lore	☆	Find: Distant Glory: RotW map 5 Shop: Once found	LUK +4	2,000	Wind Stone	1	Water Stone	1	Lifestone	1
Materia	☆	Battlegen: Planet's Core [stage damage]	LUK +2	(not sold)	—	—	—	—	—	—
Medal of Honor	☆	Card: Lunar Whale Course Shop: Buy "Lunar Whale Course Added" in PP Catalog	LUK +4	2,000	Megalixir	4	—	—	—	—
Megalixir	☆	Prize: Arcade Mode (Time Attack - based on performance) Card: Lunar Whale Course Shop: Buy "Lunar Whale Course Added" in PP Catalog	LUK +4	(not sold)	—	—	—	—	—	—
Mistletoe	☆	Card: Falcon Course Shop: Buy "Falcon Course Added" in PP Catalog	LUK +2	1,500	Elixir	1	—	—	—	—
Moon Stone	☆	Battlegen: Lunar Subterrane [stage damage]	LUK +2	(not sold)	—	—	—	—	—	—
Moonflow	☆	Battlegen: Dream's End [stage damage]	LUK +2	(not sold)	—	—	—	—	—	—
Moonstone	☆	Card: Airship Course Shop: Buy "Airship Course Added" in PP Catalog	LUK +2	1,000	Dusty Elixir	2	—	—	—	—

NAME	RANK	ACQUIRE	ABILITIES	COST	INGREDIENT 1	QUANTITY	INGREDIENT 2	QUANTITY	INGREDIENT 3	QUANTITY
Mythril	★	Find: Most Story Mode chapters Card: Airship Course	LUK +1	(not sold)	—	—	—	—	—	—
Nethicite	★	Shop: Password required	LUK +4	(not sold)	—	—	—	—	—	—
Ninja Lore	★	Find: Distant Glory: RotW map 3 Shop: Once found	LUK +4	2,000	Wind Stone	1	Water Stone	1	Lifestone	1
Noah's Lute	★	Shop: Password required	LUK +4	(not sold)	—	—	—	—	—	—
Nue Bone	★	Card: Falcon Course Shop: Buy "Falcon Course Added" in PP Catalog	LUK +2	1,300	Elixir	1	—	—	—	—
Oath Crystal	★	Battlegen: Sephiroth [EX Burst] (After successful Oath Shard Battlegen)	Initial EX Force +5%	(not sold)	—	—	—	—	—	—
Oath Orb	★	Battlegen: Sephiroth [Bravery Break] (After successful Oath Crystal Battlegen)	Initial EX Force +5%	(not sold)	—	—	—	—	—	—
Oath Powder	★	Battlegen: Sephiroth [Bravery Break]	Initial EX Force +5%	(not sold)	—	—	—	—	—	—
Oath Shard	★	Battlegen: Sephiroth [HP attack] (After successful Oath Powder Battlegen)	Initial EX Force +5%	(not sold)	—	—	—	—	—	—
Occult Fan	★	Shop: Password required	LUK +4	(not sold)	—	—	—	—	—	—
Omega Badge	★	Shop: Password required	LUK +4	(not sold)	—	—	—	—	—	—
Onion	★	Card: Lunar Whale Course Shop: Buy "Lunar Whale Course Added" in PP Catalog	LUK +4	2,000	Megalixir	4	—	—	—	—
Opal	★	Card: Falcon Course Shop: Buy "Falcon Course Added" in PP Catalog	LUK +3	1,600	Elixir	2	—	—	—	—
Order of Emptiness	★	Battlegen: Order's Sanctuary [stage damage]	LUK +2	(not sold)	—	—	—	—	—	—
Pebble	★	Card: Airship, Falcon, Invincible, and Lunar Whale Courses	LUK +1	(not sold)	—	—	—	—	—	—
Peridot	★	Card: Falcon Course Shop: Buy "Falcon Course Added" in PP Catalog	LUK +2	1,300	Elixir	1	—	—	—	—
Pink Tail	★	Card: Lunar Whale Course	LUK +4	(not sold)	—	—	—	—	—	—
Pisces Recipe	★	Shop: Password required	(none)	(not sold)	—	—	—	—	—	—
Power Crystal	★	Battlegen: Zidane [HP attack] (After successful Power Shard Battlegen)	Chase BRV Damage +5%	(not sold)	—	—	—	—	—	—
Power of the Void	★	Card: Lunar Whale Course Shop: Buy "Lunar Whale Course Added" in PP Catalog	LUK +4	2,000	Megalixir	4	—	—	—	—
Power Orb	★	Battlegen: Zidane [Bravery Break] (After successful Power Crystal Battlegen)	Chase BRV Damage +5%	(not sold)	—	—	—	—	—	—
Power Powder	★	Battlegen: Zidane [Bravery Break]	Chase BRV Damage +5%	(not sold)	—	—	—	—	—	—
Power Shard	★	Battlegen: Zidane [HP attack] (After successful Power Powder Battlegen)	Chase BRV Damage +5%	(not sold)	—	—	—	—	—	—
Protect Crystal	★	Battlegen: Warrior of Light [HP attack] (After successful Protect Shard Battlegen)	DEF +1	(not sold)	—	—	—	—	—	—
Protect Orb	★	Battlegen: Warrior of Light [Bravery Break] (After successful Protect Crystal Battlegen)	DEF +1	(not sold)	—	—	—	—	—	—
Protect Powder	★	Battlegen: Warrior of Light [Bravery Break]	DEF +1	(not sold)	—	—	—	—	—	—
Protect Shard	★	Battlegen: Warrior of Light [HP attack] (After successful Protect Powder Battlegen)	DEF +1	(not sold)	—	—	—	—	—	—
Quality Branch	★	Card: Airship Course Shop: Buy "Airship Course Added" in PP Catalog	LUK +1	1,000	Dusty Elixir	1	—	—	—	—
Quality Lumber	★	Card: Falcon Course Shop: Buy "Falcon Course Added" in PP Catalog	LUK +2	1,300	Elixir	1	—	—	—	—
Quickstrike Crystal	★	Battlegen: Shantotto [HP attack] (After successful Quickstrike Shard Battlegen)	Initial Bravery +10%	(not sold)	—	—	—	—	—	—
Quickstrike Orb	★	Battlegen: Shantotto [Bravery Break] (After successful Quickstrike Crystal Battlegen)	Initial Bravery +10%	(not sold)	—	—	—	—	—	—
Quickstrike Shard	★	Battlegen: Shantotto [HP attack] (After completing Distant Glory: TLoL)	Initial Bravery +10%	(not sold)	—	—	—	—	—	—
Recovery Crystal	★	Battlegen: Onion Knight [EX Burst] (After successful Recovery Shard Battlegen)	BRV Recovery +10%	(not sold)	—	—	—	—	—	—
Recovery Orb	★	Battlegen: Onion Knight [Bravery Break] (After successful Recovery Crystal Battlegen)	BRV Recovery +10%	(not sold)	—	—	—	—	—	—
Recovery Powder	★	Battlegen: Onion Knight [Bravery Break]	BRV Recovery +10%	(not sold)	—	—	—	—	—	—

ACCESSORIES

NAME	RANK	ACQUIRE	ABILITIES	COST	INGREDIENT 1	QUANTITY	INGREDIENT 2	QUANTITY	INGREDIENT 3	QUANTITY
Recovery Shard	☆	Battlegen: Onion Knight [HP attack] (After successful Recovery Powder Battlegen)	BRV Recovery +10%	(not sold)	—	—	—	—	—	—
Reflex Crystal	☆	Battlegen: Exdeath [HP attack] (After successful Reflex Shard Battlegen)	Magic Counter Strength +10%	(not sold)	—	—	—	—	—	—
Reflex Orb	☆	Battlegen: Exdeath [Bravery Break] (After successful Reflex Crystal Battlegen)	Magic Counter Strength +10%	(not sold)	—	—	—	—	—	—
Reflex Powder	☆	Battlegen: Exdeath [Bravery Break]	Magic Counter Strength +10%	(not sold)	—	—	—	—	—	—
Reflex Shard	☆	Battlegen: Exdeath [HP attack] (After successful Reflex Powder Battlegen)	Magic Counter Strength +10%	(not sold)	—	—	—	—	—	—
Resilience Crystal	☆	Battlegen: Kuja [HP attack] (After successful Resilience Shard Battlegen)	Wall Rush HP Defense +5%	(not sold)	—	—	—	—	—	—
Resilience Orb	☆	Battlegen: Kuja [Bravery Break] (After successful Resilience Crystal Battlegen)	Wall Rush HP Defense +5%	(not sold)	—	—	—	—	—	—
Resilience Powder	☆	Battlegen: Kuja [Bravery Break]	Wall Rush HP Defense +5%	(not sold)	—	—	—	—	—	—
Resilience Shard	☆	Battlegen: Kuja [HP attack] (After successful Resilience Powder Battlegen)	Wall Rush HP Defense +5%	(not sold)	—	—	—	—	—	—
Revival Tree	☆	Card: Invincible Course Shop: Buy "Invincible Course Added" in PP Catalog	LUK +4	2,000	Hi-Elixir	3	—	—	—	—
Roaming Clouds	☆	Card: Lunar Whale Course Shop: Buy "Lunar Whale Course Added" in PP Catalog	LUK +4	2,000	Megalixir	4	—	—	—	—
Rosemary	☆	Find: Destiny Odyssey I map 3 Find: Shade Impulse/Distant Glory previously opened chests Find: When equipped Pebble accessory breaks Card: Airship Course Shop: Buy "Airship Course Added" in PP Catalog	LUK +1	2,000	—	—	—	—	—	—
Rosetta Stone	☆	Find: Most Story Mode chapters DP Prize: Most Story Mode chapters Card: Blackjack Course Shop: Ingredient acquired	LUK +4	2,000	Wind Stone	1	Water Stone	1	Lifestone	1
Royal Wing	☆	Card: Falcon Course Shop: Buy "Falcon Course Added" in PP Catalog	LUK +3	1,600	Elixir	2	—	—	—	—
Ruby	☆	Card: Airship Course Shop: Buy "Airship Course Added" in PP Catalog	LUK +2	1,200	Dusty Elixir	3	—	—	—	—
Sacred Beast Scales	☆	Card: Invincible Course Shop: Buy "Invincible Course Added" in PP Catalog	LUK +3	2,000	Hi-Elixir	2	—	—	—	—
Sacred Beast Wing	☆	Card: Invincible Course Shop: Buy "Invincible Course Added" in PP Catalog	LUK +3	2,000	Hi-Elixir	2	—	—	—	—
Sagittarius Recipe	☆	Shop: Password required	(none)	(not sold)	—	—	—	—	—	—
Saint's Bone	☆	Card: Invincible Course Shop: Buy "Invincible Course Added" in PP Catalog	LUK +3	2,000	Hi-Elixir	2	—	—	—	—
Samurai Lore	☆	Find: Distant Glory: RotW map 5 Shop: Once found	LUK +4	2,000	Wind Stone	1	Water Stone	1	Lifestone	1
Sapphire	☆	Card: Falcon Course Shop: Buy "Falcon Course Added" in PP Catalog	LUK +2	1,500	Elixir	1	—	—	—	—
Scorpio Recipe	☆	Shop: Password required	(none)	(not sold)	—	—	—	—	—	—
Sea Serpent Scales	☆	Card: Invincible Course Shop: Buy "Invincible Course Added" in PP Catalog	LUK +3	1,900	Hi-Elixir	1	—	—	—	—
Sealed Darkness	☆	Battlegen: World of Darkness [stage damage]	LUK +2	(not sold)	—	—	—	—	—	—
Shadow Bone	☆	Card: Falcon Course Shop: Buy "Falcon Course Added" in PP Catalog	LUK +3	1,600	Elixir	2	—	—	—	—
Shinra Card Key	☆	Shop: Password required	LUK +4	(not sold)	—	—	—	—	—	—
Sky Jewel	☆	Card: Lunar Whale Course Shop: Buy "Lunar Whale Course Added" in PP Catalog	LUK +4	2,000	Megalixir	2	—	—	—	—
Snowboard	☆	Shop: Password required	LUK +4	(not sold)	—	—	—	—	—	—
Sphere	☆	Shop: Password required	LUK +4	(not sold)	—	—	—	—	—	—

NAME	RANK	ACQUIRE	ABILITIES	COST	INGREDIENT 1	QUANTITY	INGREDIENT 2	QUANTITY	INGREDIENT 3	QUANTITY
Spirit Stone	★	Card: Airship Course Shop: Buy "Airship Course Added" in PP Catalog	LUK +2	1,200	Dusty Elixir	3	—	—	—	—
Spiritwood	☆	Card: Falcon Course Shop: Buy "Falcon Course Added" in PP Catalog	LUK +3	1,800	Elixir	3	—	—	—	—
Splendor of the Wind	☆	Card: Lunar Whale Course Shop: Buy "Lunar Whale Course Added" in PP Catalog	LUK +4	2,000	Megalixir	4	—	—	—	—
Splinter	☆	Card: Airship Course Shop: Buy "Airship Course Added" in PP Catalog	LUK +1	1,000	Dusty Elixir	1	—	—	—	—
Star's Core	☆	Battlegen: Crystal World [stage damage]	LUK +2	(not sold)	—	—	—	—	—	—
Stone of the Condemner	☆	Card: Falcon Course Shop: Buy "Falcon Course Added" in PP Catalog	LUK +3	1,800	Elixir	3	—	—	—	—
Strategy Guide	☆	Shop: Password required	LUK +4	(not sold)	—	—	—	—	—	—
Strength Crystal	☆	Battlegen: Garland [HP attack] (After successful Strength Shard Battlegen)	ATK +1	(not sold)	—	—	—	—	—	—
Strength Orb	☆	Battlegen: Garland [Bravery Break] (After successful Strength Crystal Battlegen)	ATK +1	(not sold)	—	—	—	—	—	—
Strength Powder	☆	Battlegen: Garland [Bravery Break]	ATK +1	(not sold)	—	—	—	—	—	—
Strength Shard	☆	Battlegen: Garland [HP attack] (After successful Strength Powder Battlegen)	ATK +1	(not sold)	—	—	—	—	—	—
Summoner's Horn	☆	Card: Airship Course Shop: Buy "Airship Course Added" in PP Catalog	LUK +2	1,000	Dusty Elixir	2	—	—	—	—
Supreme Gem	☆	Card: Lunar Whale Course Shop: Buy "Lunar Whale Course Added" in PP Catalog	LUK +4	2,000	Megalixir	2	—	—	—	—
Taurus Horn	☆	Card: Falcon Course Shop: Buy "Falcon Course Added" in PP Catalog	LUK +2	1,300	Elixir	1	—	—	—	—
Taurus Recipe	☆	Shop: Password required	(none)	(not sold)	—	—	—	—	—	—
Tea Tree	☆	Find: Destiny Odyssey III map 4 Find: Shade Impulse/Distant Glory previously opened chests Find: When equipped Pebble accessory breaks Card: Airship Course Shop: Buy "Airship Course Added" in PP Catalog	LUK +1	2,000	—	—	—	—	—	—
The Youth's Dream	☆	Card: Lunar Whale Course Shop: Buy "Lunar Whale Course Added" in PP Catalog	LUK +4	2,000	Megalixir	4	—	—	—	—
Theater Ticket	☆	Card: Lunar Whale Course Shop: Buy "Lunar Whale Course Added" in PP Catalog	LUK +4	2,000	Megalixir	4	—	—	—	—
Thief Lore	☆	Find: Distant Glory: TLoL map 4 Shop: Once found	LUK +4	2,000	Wind Stone	1	Water Stone	1	Lifestone	1
Thorny Lumber	☆	Card: Airship Course Shop: Buy "Airship Course Added" in PP Catalog	LUK +2	1,200	Dusty Elixir	3	—	—	—	—
Throat Wolf Fang	☆	Card: Falcon Course Shop: Buy "Falcon Course Added" in PP Catalog	LUK +2	1,500	Elixir	1	—	—	—	—
Time Crystal	☆	Battlegen: Gabranth [HP attack] (After successful Time Shard Battlegen)	EX Mode Duration +5%	(not sold)	—	—	—	—	—	—
Time Orb	☆	Battlegen: Gabranth [EX Burst] (After successful Time Crystal Battlegen)	EX Mode Duration +5%	(not sold)	—	—	—	—	—	—
Time Shard	☆	Battlegen: Gabranth [Bravery Break] (After completing Distant Glory: RotW)	EX Mode Duration +5%	(not sold)	—	—	—	—	—	—
Time Warp	☆	Battlegen: Ultimecia's Castle [stage damage]	LUK +2	(not sold)	—	—	—	—	—	—
Tintinnabulum	☆	Shop: Password required	LUK +4	(not sold)	—	—	—	—	—	—
Titan Crystal	☆	Battlegen: Cecil [HP attack] (After successful Titan Shard Battlegen)	HP +50	(not sold)	—	—	—	—	—	—
Titan Orb	☆	Battlegen: Cecil [Bravery Break] (After successful Titan Crystal Battlegen)	HP +50	(not sold)	—	—	—	—	—	—
Titan Powder	☆	Battlegen: Cecil [Bravery Break]	HP +50	(not sold)	—	—	—	—	—	—
Titan Shard	☆	Battlegen: Cecil [HP attack] (After successful Titan Powder Battlegen)	HP +50	(not sold)	—	—	—	—	—	—
Tome of Kings	☆	Card: Lunar Whale Course Shop: Buy "Lunar Whale Course Added" in PP Catalog	LUK +3	1,900	Hi-Elixir	1	—	—	—	—

ACCESSORIES

NAME	RANK	ACQUIRE	ABILITIES	COST	INGREDIENT 1	QUANTITY	INGREDIENT 2	QUANTITY	INGREDIENT 3	QUANTITY
Tome of Lies	☆	Card: Lunar Whale Course Shop: Buy "Lunar Whale Course Added" in PP Catalog	LUK +4	2,000	Megalixir	3	—	—	—	—
Tome of Love	☆	Card: Lunar Whale Course Shop: Buy "Lunar Whale Course Added" in PP Catalog	LUK +3	1,800	Elixir	3	—	—	—	—
Tome of Memories	☆	Card: Lunar Whale Course Shop: Buy "Lunar Whale Course Added" in PP Catalog	LUK +4	2,000	Megalixir	3	—	—	—	—
Tome of Men	☆	Card: Lunar Whale Course Shop: Buy "Lunar Whale Course Added" in PP Catalog	LUK +4	2,000	Megalixir	3	—	—	—	—
Tome of Mysteries	☆	Card: Lunar Whale Course Shop: Buy "Lunar Whale Course Added" in PP Catalog	LUK +4	2,000	Megalixir	3	—	—	—	—
Tome of Shadows	☆	Card: Lunar Whale Course Shop: Buy "Lunar Whale Course Added" in PP Catalog	LUK +3	2,000	Hi-Elixir	2	—	—	—	—
Tome of Silence	☆	Card: Lunar Whale Course Shop: Buy "Lunar Whale Course Added" in PP Catalog	LUK +4	2,000	Megalixir	3	—	—	—	—
Tome of Souls	☆	Card: Lunar Whale Course Shop: Buy "Lunar Whale Course Added" in PP Catalog	LUK +3	1,600	Elixir	2	—	—	—	—
Tome of the Farplane	☆	Card: Lunar Whale Course Shop: Buy "Lunar Whale Course Added" in PP Catalog	LUK +4	2,000	Megalixir	3	—	—	—	—
Tome of the Masters	☆	Card: Lunar Whale Course Shop: Buy "Lunar Whale Course Added" in PP Catalog	LUK +4	2,000	Megalixir	3	—	—	—	—
Tome of the Orator	☆	Card: Lunar Whale Course Shop: Buy "Lunar Whale Course Added" in PP Catalog	LUK +4	2,000	Megalixir	3	—	—	—	—
Topaz	☆	Card: Falcon Course Shop: Buy "Falcon Course Added" in PP Catalog	LUK +3	1,800	Elixir	3	—	—	—	—
Transmogridust	☆	Prize: Arcade Mode (Time Attack) Card: Airship, Falcon, Invincible, and Lunar Whale Courses	LUK +1	(not sold)	—	—	—	—	—	—
True Past	☆	Card: Lunar Whale Course Shop: Buy "Lunar Whale Course Added" in PP Catalog	LUK +4	2,000	Megalixir	4	—	—	—	—
Twin Form	☆	Card: Lunar Whale Course Shop: Buy "Lunar Whale Course Added" in PP Catalog	LUK +4	2,000	Megalixir	4	—	—	—	—
Unicorn Horn	☆	Card: Invincible Course Shop: Buy "Invincible Course Added" in PP Catalog	LUK +3	2,000	Hi-Elixir	2	—	—	—	—
Unknown's Bone	☆	Card: Airship Course Shop: Buy "Airship Course Added" in PP Catalog	LUK +2	1,000	Dusty Elixir	2	—	—	—	—
Unshelled Bullet	☆	Card: Lunar Whale Course Shop: Buy "Lunar Whale Course Added" in PP Catalog	LUK +4	2,000	Megalixir	4	—	—	—	—
Veiled Magic	☆	Card: Lunar Whale Course Shop: Buy "Lunar Whale Course Added" in PP Catalog	LUK +4	2,000	Megalixir	4	—	—	—	—
Virgo Recipe	☆	Shop: Password required	(none)	(not sold)	—	—	—	—	—	—
Voidshard	☆	Battlegen: The Rift [stage damage]	LUK +2	(not sold)	—	—	—	—	—	—
Wargod Bone	☆	Card: Falcon Course Shop: Buy "Falcon Course Added" in PP Catalog	LUK +3	1,800	Elixir	3	—	—	—	—
Warp Cube	☆	Shop: Password required	LUK +4	(not sold)	—	—	—	—	—	—
Warrior Lore	☆	Find: Distant Glory: RotW map 1 Shop: Once found	LUK +4	2,000	Wind Stone	1	Water Stone	1	Lifestone	1
Water Stone	☆	Prize: Arcade Mode (Hard Mode) Card: Airship, Falcon, Invincible, and Lunar Whale Courses	LUK +3	(not sold)	—	—	—	—	—	—

NAME	RANK	ACQUIRE	ABILITIES	COST	INGREDIENT 1	QUANTITY	INGREDIENT 2	QUANTITY	INGREDIENT 3	QUANTITY
Wheel of Darkness	★	Card: Lunar Whale Course Shop: Buy "Lunar Whale Course Added" in PP Catalog	LUK +4	2,000	Megalixir	4	—	—	—	—
Whisperweed	☆	Shop: Password required	LUK +4	(not sold)	—	—	—	—	—	—
White Mage Lore	☆	Find: Distant Glory: TLoL map 1 Shop: Once found	LUK +4	2,000	Wind Stone	1	Water Stone	1	Lifestone	1
White Stone	☆	Card: Airship Course Shop: Buy "Airship Course Added" in PP Catalog	LUK +1	1,000	Dusty Elixir	1	—	—	—	—
Wild Rose	☆	Shop: Password required	LUK +4	(not sold)	—	—	—	—	—	—
Wind Drake Horn	☆	Card: Invincible Course Shop: Buy "Invincible Course Added" in PP Catalog	LUK +3	1,900	Hi-Elixir	1	—	—	—	—
Wind Stone	☆	Prize: Arcade Mode (Hard Mode) Card: Airship, Falcon, Invincible, and Lunar Whale Courses	LUK +2	(not sold)	—	—	—	—	—	—
Wormskin	☆	Card: Falcon Course Shop: Buy "Falcon Course Added" in PP Catalog	LUK +2	1,300	Elixir	1	—	—	—	—
Wyrm Carapace	☆	Card: Invincible Course Shop: Buy "Invincible Course Added" in PP Catalog	LUK +3	1,900	Hi-Elixir	1	—	—	—	—
Wyrmstone	☆	Card: Invincible Course Shop: Buy "Invincible Course Added" in PP Catalog	LUK +3	1,900	Hi-Elixir	1	—	—	—	—
Wyvern Egg	☆	Shop: Password required	LUK +4	(not sold)	—	—	—	—	—	—
Wyvern Horn	☆	Card: Airship Course Shop: Buy "Airship Course Added" in PP Catalog	LUK +2	1,200	Dusty Elixir	3	—	—	—	—
Wyvern Wing	☆	Card: Invincible Course Shop: Buy "Invincible Course Added" in PP Catalog	LUK +3	1,900	Hi-Elixir	1	—	—	—	—
Yensa Scales	☆	Card: Airship Course Shop: Buy "Airship Course Added" in PP Catalog	LUK +1	1,000	Dusty Elixir	1	—	—	—	—
Ylang Ylang	☆	Find: Destiny Odyssey IV map 3 Find: Shade Impulse/Distant Glory previously opened chests Find: When equipped Pebble accessory breaks Card: Airship Course Shop: Buy "Airship Course Added" in PP Catalog	LUK +1	2,000	—	—	—	—	—	—

TRADE ACCESSORY LIST (IN GAME ORDER)

NAME	NAME	NAME	NAME	NAME
Rosetta Stone	Pink Tail	Luck Shard	Guts Shard	Destruction Crystal
Mythril	Growth Seed	Luck Crystal	Guts Crystal	Destruction Orb
Gold	Chocobo Cologne	Luck Orb	Guts Orb	Reflex Powder
Diamond	Protect Powder	Amplification Powder	Quickstrike Shard	Reflex Shard
Crystal	Protect Shard	Amplification Shard	Quickstrike Crystal	Reflex Crystal
Adamantite	Protect Crystal	Amplification Crystal	Quickstrike Orb	Reflex Orb
Warrior Lore	Protect Orb	Amplification Orb	Strength Powder	Allure Powder
Thief Lore	Magnet Powder	Gale Powder	Strength Shard	Allure Shard
Knight Lore	Magnet Shard	Gale Shard	Strength Crystal	Allure Crystal
Dragoon Lore	Magnet Crystal	Gale Crystal	Strength Orb	Allure Orb
Marksman Lore	Magnet Orb	Gale Orb	Healing Powder	Oath Powder
Black Belt Lore	Recovery Powder	Bless Powder	Healing Shard	Oath Shard
Samurai Lore	Recovery Shard	Bless Shard	Healing Crystal	Oath Crystal
Bard Lore	Recovery Crystal	Bless Crystal	Healing Orb	Oath Orb
White Mage Lore	Recovery Orb	Bless Orb	Mana Powder	Lithe Powder
Black Mage Lore	Titan Powder	Power Powder	Mana Shard	Lithe Shard
Ninja Lore	Titan Shard	Power Shard	Mana Crystal	Lithe Crystal
Dancer Lore	Titan Crystal	Power Crystal	Mana Orb	Lithe Orb
Chemist Lore	Titan Orb	Power Orb	Destruction Powder	Resilience Powder
Mallet	Luck Powder	Guts Powder	Destruction Shard	Resilience Shard

ACCESSORIES

TRADE ACCESSORY LIST (CONTINUED)

NAME	NAME	NAME	NAME	NAME
Resilience Crystal	Land Dragon Bone	Blessed Barding	Tea Tree	Dusty Elixir
Resilience Orb	Saint's Bone	Aged Turtle Shell	Eucalyptus	Elixir
Crimson Powder	Blood-Darkened Bone	Ancient Turtle Shell	Lemongrass	Hi-Elixir
Crimson Shard	Hero's Bone	Aquamarine	Tome of Souls	Megalixir
Crimson Crystal	Large Horn	Emerald	Tome of Love	Crystal Eye
Crimson Orb	Summoner's Horn	Moonstone	Tome of Kings	Warp Cube
Time Shard	Wyvern Horn	Ruby	Tome of Shadows	Wild Rose
Time Crystal	Taurus Horn	Peridot	Tome of Memories	Wyvern Egg
Time Orb	Lizard Horn	Sapphire	Tome of Mysteries	Noah's Lute
Chaos Shard	Humbaba's Horn	Opal	Tome of Lies	Gnomish Bread
Chaos Crystal	Ixion Horn	Topaz	Tome of the Farplane	Carnelian Signet
Chaos Orb	Wind Drake Horn	Dragonstone	Tome of Men	Whisperweed
Order of Emptiness	Unicorn Horn	Holystone	Tome of Silence	Dragon Seal
Blackcrystal Sliver	Beastlord Horn	Lapis Lazuli	Tome of the Orator	Omega Badge
Demon Soul	Behemoth Horn	Sky Jewel	Tome of the Masters	Delicious Fish
Sealed Darkness	Large Fang	Ichthon Scales	Guiding Light	Tintinnabulum
Moon Stone	Black Tiger Fang	Yensa Scales	Wheel of Darkness	Snowboard
Voidshard	Great Serpent's Fang	Lamia Scales	The Youth's Dream	Shinra Card Key
Magicite Shard	Chimera Fang	Landshark Scales	Lust for Power	Occult Fan
Materia	Throat Wolf Fang	Leviathan Scales	Onion	GF Eden
Time Warp	Mammoth Tusk	Emperor Scales	Roaming Clouds	Chocograph
Star's Core	Holy Fang	Godfighter Scales	Twin Form	Strategy Guide
Moonflow	Beastlord Fang	Sea Serpent Scales	Lone Heart	Sphere
Entropy's Birth	Maduin's Fang	Sacred Beast Scales	Splendor of the Wind	Al Bhed Primer
White Stone	Quality Branch	Djinn Scales	Power of the Void	Automaton Parts
Black Stone	Splinter	Eden's Scales	Veiled Magic	Nethicite
Spirit Stone	Lumber	Bird Feather	Fanatic's Leer	Aries Recipe
Mako Stone	Thorny Lumber	Giant Feather	True Past	Taurus Recipe
Levistone	Quality Lumber	Demon Feather	Life of the Planet	Gemini Recipe
Dewdrop Pebble	Mistletoe	Fallen Angel Feather	Unshelled Bullet	Cancer Recipe
Stone of the Condemner	Big Tree	Royal Wing	Gears of Time	Leo Recipe
Wyrmstone	Spiritwood	Diablos's Wing	Theater Ticket	Virgo Recipe
Blessed Gem	Dragonwood	Wyvern Wing	God of Destruction	Libra Recipe
Goddess's Magicite	Revival Tree	Sacred Beast Wing	Fayth's Dream	Scorpio Recipe
Supreme Gem	Iifa Tree	Garuda's Wing	Medal of Honor	Sagittarius Recipe
Beast Bone	Iron Carapace	Bahamut's Wing	Boiling Blood	Capricorn Recipe
Unknown's Bone	Charger Barding	Geranium	Gates of Judgment	Aquarius Recipe
Gigas Bone	Great Serpentskin	Rosemary	Wind Stone	Pisces Recipe
Nue Bone	Wormskin	Bergamot	Water Stone	
Ancient Bone	Destrier Barding	Chamomile	Lifestone	
Shadow Bone	Giant Turtleshell	Clary Sage	Transmogridust	
Wargod Bone	Wyrm Carapace	Ylang Ylang	Pebble	

SECRETS & CHEATS

THE SECRET EPILOGUE

DISSIDIA FINAL FANTASY has a secret epilogue scene that can only be viewed by players who unlock every Cosmos and Chaos Report. To unlock the Cosmos Reports, you'll need to beat Shade Impulse Chapter 4 with every Cosmos character (except Shantotto, who has no report). To unlock the Chaos Reports, you'll need to use every Chaos character (except Gabranth) in the Duel Colosseum, and have them each beat a Boss card of their Cosmos-side counterpart.

When you have all the reports, you can find the secret scene as #222 in the Museum's Cutscenes viewer.

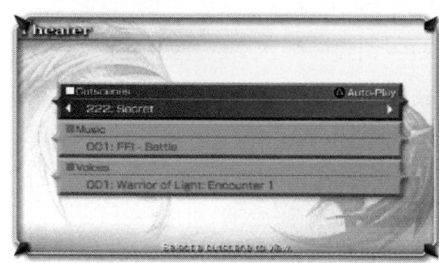

POWER-LEVELING TECHNIQUES

With 22 characters to master, it's natural to want to speed the leveling process along. There are several exploits that can allow you to do this.

POWER-LEVELING SOLO — CHOCOBO

METHOD

Set your PSP internal clock to make it your Bonus Day. Next, set your play plan to Hardcore or Grind-lover, and fight easy battles until your chocobo hits the maximum x5 EXP bonus. Then, take on a tough but beatable opponent in the Quick Battle mode. After you win and the game autosaves the EXP, AP, PP, and items you earned, a menu will pop up asking if you want to return to the setup screen, have a rematch, etc. Instead of choosing an option, hit the Home button on your PSP to quit the game. Then, reload your file and battle again—you'll find that all of your earnings were saved, but that the chocobo hasn't taken a step, so you can fight repeatedly with the same x5 EXP bonus. Also, if you purchase a single Item Drop Rate Up and Battlegen Rate Up from the PP Catalog, they will never be removed from your stock for as long as you use this trick.

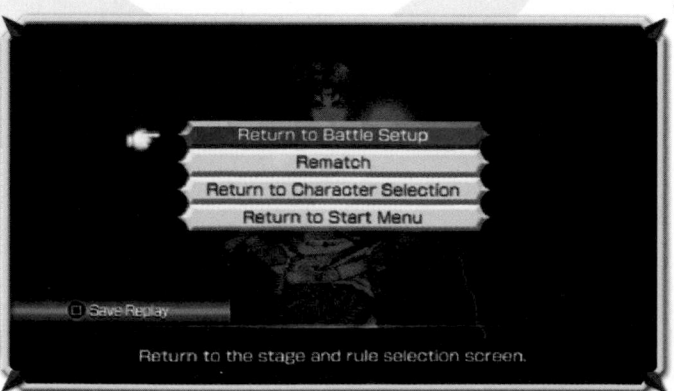

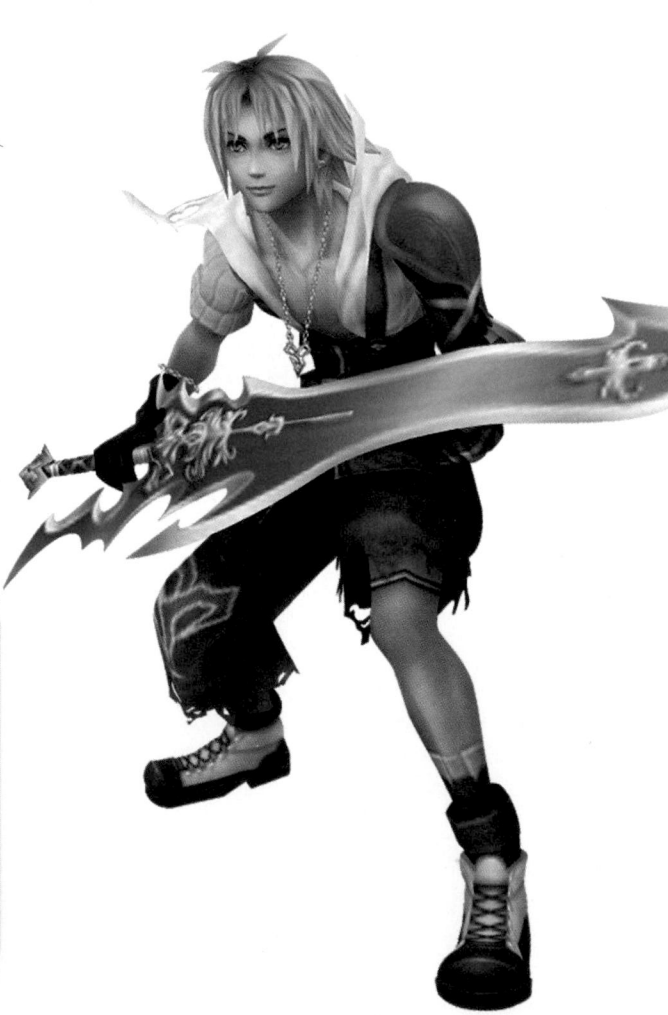

POWER-LEVELING SOLO—EXDEATH

METHOD

Who's the best opponent to fight when you want to level up? How about a level 100 Exdeath? Believe it or not, you can beat him at level 1, although it won't even matter if you don't—all you need to do is score a single hit to gain 50 or more levels in a single fight. It's a good idea to choose Exdeath since he isn't very aggressive and uses clearly telegraphed, easy to dodge attacks. But if you find that he's a difficult opponent for the character you want to level up, feel free to choose someone else. Either way, the prep is the same:

- If it isn't your Bonus Day, set your PSP internal clock to make it so.

- Unlock Exdeath and all the CPU Level Cap options in the PP Catalog. (You'll need at least one character at or above level 50 to buy CPU Level Cap +90, or (better yet) one at level 70+ to buy CPU Level Cap +100.)

- Make sure you have the Magic Pot Summonstone (*not* Magic Pot Auto) from Cloud's Destiny Odyssey VII chapter, and check that it's fully charged.

- With your play plan at Hardcore or Grind-lover, fight a bunch of easy battles until your chocobo hits its maximum x5 bonus opportunity. (Players who aren't too familiar with Exdeath should use this opportunity to fight him at normal levels and practice dodging his attacks.)

- When you're ready to fight, set Magic Pot as your character's summon (if you have Kraken, put that in reserve), and equip all the Chocobo accessories and Growth Eggs you can to further boost your EXP.

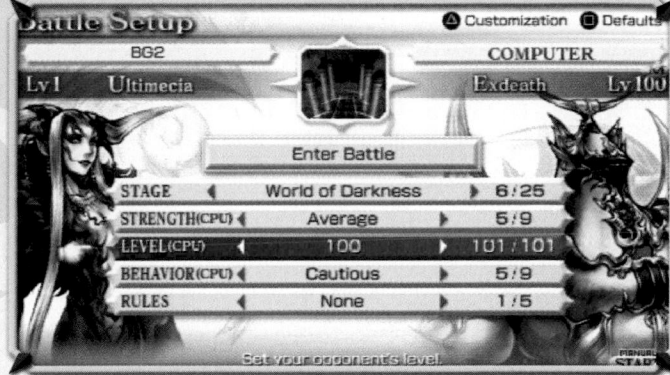

When you're ready, set up a quick battle with a level 100 Exdeath (or whoever). The higher you set his strength, the more EXP you'll get, but less experienced players should set him to Average to make landing a hit easier. The World of Darkness is a good stage, since it's easy to hide behind the columns when waiting out a Bravery Break. Set Exdeath's behavior to Cautious, so that he'll use long-ranged bravery attacks instead of constantly attacking your HP.

If you want to go for the win, allow Exdeath to hit you with a bravery attack. (Keep your distance, and he'll use a bravery projectile attack. Let it knock you into something so he won't be able to follow up with a chase.) Hide behind the pillars until you recover from Bravery Break, then use Magic Pot to copy his 9,999 bravery total. All you need to do now is land an HP attack! Sometimes Exdeath's summon will trigger to cut down your bravery or keep him alive, so you may not be able to win the fight, but you'll still get plenty of EXP.

Win or lose, press the Home button after the game autosaves (at the menu that offers Return to Battle Setup, Rematch, etc.) so you can come back and fight him again without your chocobo having moved from the x5 bonus. Of course, you'll need to recharge your Magic Pot after the second fight. Kraken has a similar effect (although you have to wait 20 seconds before it triggers), so that allows you to do it two more times.

POWER-LEVELING WITH A FRIEND

Two players working together can power-level with the Friend Card system by making high level, easily beaten ghosts and trading them with their friends. Just take your highest level character and use the Ability menu to deselect all of its attacks except for the one HP attack that's easiest to avoid. (Long-range spells paired with a long casting time, like Cloud's Meteorain, are ideal.) Give the character any accessories and equipment your friends might want as item drops, then make it your ghost in your Friend Card Settings menu. If the ghost's HP attack is easily avoidable, your friends should be able to win (eventually) with even a low level character. Summonstones like Magic Pot and Carbuncle can make this significantly easier.

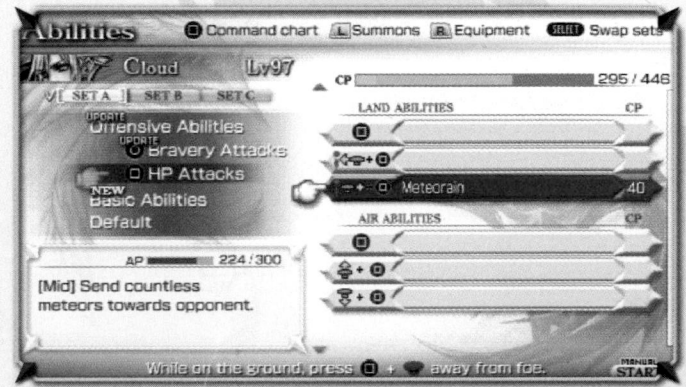

POWER-LEVELING YOUR ABILITIES

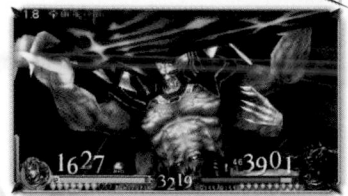

The problem with leveling up quickly is that your character ends up with very few AP. You can't grind for AP quite as easily, but there are a few tricks you can use. First of all, once you unlock Chaos, you can set him to level 1 and fight him repeatedly in the Quick Battle menu. There are three phases to Chaos, so you'll get triple the AP.

Equip everything that gives you an AP bonus: the combination effect of a full set of Diamond gear provides a 100% bonus, as does the Beckoning Cat accessory, and the breakable (but re-buyable) Diamond Ring provides a whopping 300% boost. You'll get AP bonuses on your Bonus Day as well as two extra AP for completing the AP chance in each quick battle.

SECRET PASSWORDS

The following passwords can be entered into the personal message section of your Friend Card to receive the listed rewards. Use the NA Ver. passwords for the North American version of the game and use the EU Ver. Passwords for the European version of the game. Many more passwords will be released by the developer after the game's release. Enjoy!

REWARDS	NA VER.	EU VER.
Player Icon: Chocobo (FF5)	58205 2436	62942 36172
Player Icon: Moogle (FF5)	13410 3103	84626 93120
Capricorn Recipe	87032 2642	6199 27495
Aquarius Recipe	39275 40667	3894 27509
Pisces Recipe	5310 62973	15812 2748
Friend Card: Matoya	39392 58263	1849 16360
Friend Card: Ninja	27481 73856	46490 11483
Friend Card: Fusoya	2943 2971	2971 2943
Friend Card: Siegfried	2015 1231	25496 12772
Friend Card: Vivi	37842 27940	70271 8560
Friend Card: Auron	12982 28499	33705 59603

CHEATING UP ARTIFACT ABILITIES

When you find an artifact through online play and it has the hammer-and-feather icon, you can rename it in the Artifacts menu to generate a new ability. The game won't autosave until you press ● to leave the Artifacts menu, so if the ability you generate is not to your liking, you can hit the Home button on your PSP to quit the game without saving, and then reload and rename it again. (The ability has no connection to the name, so even if you give it the same name, you'll generate a different ability.)

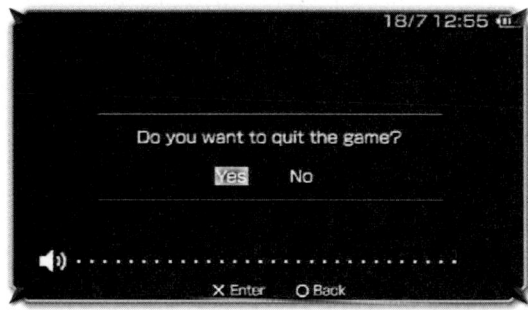

HACKING MOGNET

The letters you receive through Mognet aren't just for fun; they're a valuable source of PP, accessories, and Stiltzkin Friend Cards. But the moogles' trivia questions are difficult, and it's never clear what the right answer is to their personal questions. Read on to find out what to say and how often to log on if you want to get the best rewards.

You'll typically receive two pieces of mail per day: one blue and one yellow. Blue mail arrives based on your play patterns, but yellow mail (which consists of personal correspondence with three different moogles) arrives at random. When you've completed all of the yellow mail sequences outlined below, they cycle in repetition, giving you a second chance to provide the right answers.

THE STILTZKIN FRIEND CARDS

Mognet is the only way to get the friend cards for the eight Stiltzkin. Each Stiltzkin comes with an exclusive Player Icon, and if you can't play online, collecting these friend cards is also the only way you'll be able to Battlegen the eight colored gems that are needed for much of the game's best equipment. Stiltzkin 4 also provides an early crack at some of the Duel Colosseum-exclusive armaments, while Stiltzkin 5 may drop the rare and powerful Cursed Blade, which isn't available anywhere else in the game. If you've purchased the "Ghost Match - Battlegen OK" entry from the PP Catalog, you'll also be able to Battlegen a number of valuable accessories from the Stiltzkins.

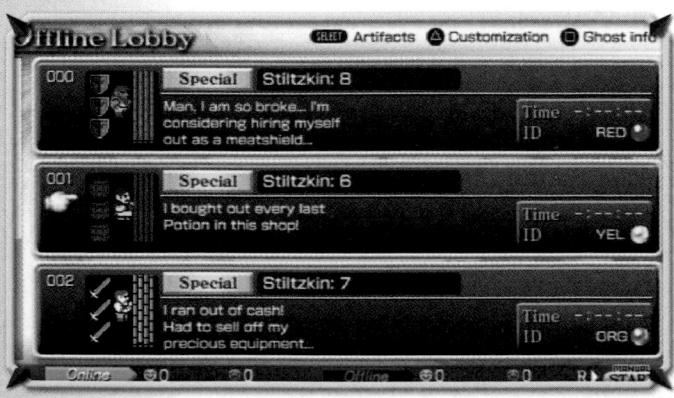

STILTZKIN 1 (WHT)

EXDEATH LV 45		
ITEMS	Wizard's Rod	
	Precious Watch	
	Gold Hairpin	
	Black Belt's Gi	
BATTLEGEN ACCESSORIES	HP	Earring
	HP	Star Earring
	Stage	[Position] Far from Opponent
	BRV	White Drop

STILTZKIN 2 (SKY)

ONION KNIGHT LV 45		
ITEMS	Moonring Blade	
	Warlord's Gauntlets	
	Warlord's Soul	
	Black Belt Gi	
BATTLEGEN ACCESSORIES	BRV	Gaia Ring
	BRV	Hyper Ring
	HP	[HP] HP = 100%
	BRV	[Bravery] No BRV Damage
	HP	[HP] HP = 1
	HP	[HP] Near Death
	HP	Phoenix Down
	EX	Cyan Drop

STILTZKIN 3 (BLU)

CECIL LV 38		
ITEMS	Francisca	
	Force Shield	
	Sallet	
	Survival Vest	
BATTLEGEN ACCESSORIES	BRV	Gaia Ring
	BRV	Hyper Ring
	BRV	Champion Belt
	BRV	Muscle Belt
	Stage	Hyperstar
	Stage	Booster
	Stage	Blue Drop

STILTZKIN 4 (PUR)

BARTZ LV 31		
ITEMS	Frying Pan	
	Kitchen Timer	
	Toque Blanche	
	Iron Apron	
BATTLEGEN ACCESSORIES	EX	Gravitorb
	BRV	Pearl Necklace
	HP	Dragonfly Orb
	HP	Back-Breaking Straw
	Stage	Gold Hourglass
	EX	Victory Pendant
	HP	[HP] HP =1
	HP	[HP] Near Death
	HP	[HP] Near Loss
	EX	Purple Drop

STILTZKIN 5 (GRN)

GOLBEZ LV 38		
ITEMS	Cursed Blade	
	Force Shield	
	Sallet	
	Survival Vest	
BATTLEGEN ACCESSORIES	EX	Gravitorb
	BRV	Pearl Necklace
	HP	Dragonfly Orb
	HP	Back-Breaking Straw
	Stage	Gold Hourglass
	EX	Victory Pendant
	HP	[HP] HP =1
	HP	[HP] Near Death
	HP	Phoenix Down
	Stage	Green Drop

STILTZKIN 6 (YEL)

GARLAND LV 24		
ITEMS	Dwarven Axe	
	Mythril Shield	
	Mythril Helm	
	Mythril Armor	
BATTLEGEN ACCESSORIES	BRV	Gaia Ring
	BRV	Hyper Ring
	BRV	Champion Belt
	BRV	Muscle Belt
	Stage	[Opponent] In Midair
	HP	Yellow Drop

STILTZKIN 7 (ORG)

WARRIOR OF LIGHT LV 24		
ITEMS	Flamberge	
	Mythril Shield	
	Mythril Helm	
	Mythril Armor	
BATTLEGEN ACCESSORIES	BRV	Gaia Ring
	BRV	Hyper Ring
	Stage	[Combat] Chasing
	Stage	[Stage] In Midair
	Stage	[Stage] Near Opponent
	HP	Orange Drop

STILTZKIN 8 (RED)

GARLAND LV 24		
ITEMS	Ice Rod	
	Mythril Bangle+	
	Wizard's Hat	
	Silk Robes	
BATTLEGEN ACCESSORIES	HP	Star Earring
	HP	Earring
	BRV	Gaia Ring
	BRV	Hyper Ring
	HP	[HP] HP = 1
	HP	[HP] Near Death
	HP	[HP] Near Loss
	BRV	Red Drop

THE MOGNET HEAD OFFICE

The blue letters you receive are from the Mognet head office, and typically consist of basic gameplay tips. But the moogles are always keeping track of how often you play, and will reward you for either playing daily or letting a long period of time elapse between games. It's easy to manipulate them by changing your PSP Date & Time Settings; clock-tweakers can easily log twenty days straight (earning seven of the eight Stiltzkin Friend Cards) in less than an hour. You'll receive the messages listed here every time the conditions are met, even if you've already received the same letter.

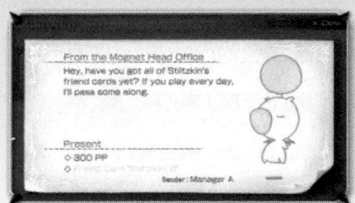

MAIL CONDITION	PRIZES
Play 5 days straight	300 PP, Friend Card "Stiltzkin: 8"
Receive 10 total letters	30 PP, Friend Card "Stiltzkin: 4"
Play 10 days straight	300 PP, Friend Card "Stiltzkin: 5"
Play 15 days straight	Friend Card "Stiltzkin: 3," Friend Card "Stiltzkin: 4"
Play 20 days straight	Friend Card "Stiltzkin: 1," Friend Card "Stiltzkin: 2"
Play after not playing for 6 to 28 days	300 PP
Play after not playing for over 28 days	300 PP + Mog's Amulet

MOGSTACHE'S *FINAL FANTASY* QUIZZES

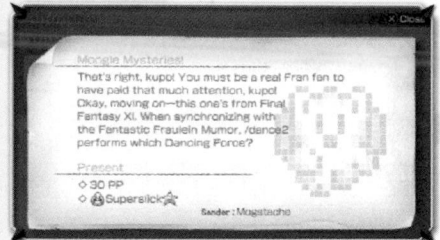

While other moogles seek friendship or advice, Mogstache wants only to test your knowledge of obscure *Final Fantasy* trivia. He has three different quizzes, which could come in any order. Each quiz consists of three or four questions; if you get the right answer, you'll earn a Superslick accessory and the right to move on to the next question in the next day's mail. The prize for providing all the correct answers is a Stiltzkin Friend Card. But Mogstache is a strict quizmaster; if you give him a single wrong answer, the quiz ends abruptly.

MOOGLE RAGTIME!

[FFII] Put these *Final Fantasy* II events in order: (A) Obtain Egil's Torch, (B) Obtain the Goddess's Bell, (C) Talk to the giant beaver.

C > B > A	RIGHT: 30 PP + Superslick
B > C > A	WRONG: 30 PP + quiz ends
A > C > B	WRONG: 30 PP + quiz ends

[FFIV] In *Final Fantasy* IV, which country didn't have a crystal?

Damcyan	WRONG: 30 PP + quiz ends
Fabul	WRONG: 30 PP + quiz ends
Baron	RIGHT: 30 PP + Superslick

[FFVII] *Final Fantasy* VII had the Gold Saucer amusement park, right? Which of the following games was not on the 2nd floor of Wonder Square?

G-Bike	WRONG: 30 PP + quiz ends
Mog's House	WRONG: 30 PP + quiz ends
Mega Sumo	RIGHT: 30 PP + Superslick

[FFVIII] In the Laguna story, during the Centra Crater battle, what DOESN'T Laguna grumble?

"I have to go to the bathroom!"	WRONG: 30 PP + quiz ends
"The bottom o' my feet are itchhhy!"	RIGHT: 30 PP + Friend Card "Stiltzkin: 1"
"The tip o' my nose itchesss!"	WRONG: 30 PP + quiz ends

MOOGLE QUIZ!

[FFVI] How about that aria Celes sang, eh? All you've got to do is fill in the blank, kupo!
"I am thankful, my beloved,
For your tenderness and grace.
I see in your eyes, (   ),
All doubts and fears erased!"

So gentle and wise	RIGHT: 30 PP + Superslick
They look just like pies	WRONG: 30 PP + quiz ends
Such beauty and joy	WRONG: 30 PP + quiz ends

[FFV] When you started learning [the piano], you heard a metronome…when did you stop hearing it?

Piano Lesson 4	WRONG: 30 PP + quiz ends
Piano Lesson 5	RIGHT: 30 PP + Superslick
Piano Lesson 6	WRONG: 30 PP + quiz ends

[FFIX] In "I Want to Be Your Canary"…the heroine Cornelia's fiance, Schneider, is prince of what country?

Canaan	WRONG: 30 PP + quiz ends
Sasune	RIGHT: 30 PP + Friend Card "Stiltzkin: 5"
Argus	WRONG: 30 PP + quiz ends

MOOGLE MYSTERIES!

[FFXII] When lifting the seal on Eruyt Village in the Golmore Jungle, Fran does a certain action… What is it, kupo?

She traces something in the air.	RIGHT: 30 PP + Superslick
She sings a mysterious song.	WRONG: 30 PP + quiz ends
She lights incense and candles.	WRONG: 30 PP + quiz ends

[FFXI] When synchronizing with the Fantastic Fraulein Mumor, /dance2 performs which Dancing Force?

Neo Crystal Jig!!!	WRONG: 30 PP + quiz ends
Lovely Miracle Waltz!!!	RIGHT: 30 PP + Superslick
Shining Summer Samba!!!	WRONG: 30 PP + quiz ends

[FFIX] Fill in the blank:
"Gemini thought by the river:
'I will sing her a song.'
(   ), but
he hoped his song would reach her."

He watched the sunset from the cape	WRONG: 30 PP + quiz ends
The sun had almost set on the sea	WRONG: 30 PP + quiz ends
He didn't know where she was	RIGHT: 30 PP + Friend Card "Stiltzkin: 2"

MOGSTACHE'S MOOGLE REPORTS

When he isn't busy quizzing you, Mogstache will be happy to answer your moogle-related questions. There are no right or wrong answers here; he'll send you a follow-up letter with some PP no matter what you ask.

WHICH DO YOU WANT TO KNOW ABOUT, KUPO?

Final Fantasy III Moogles	30 PP
Final Fantasy V Moogles	30 PP
Final Fantasy VI Moogles	30 PP

Which are your favorite moogles, kupo?

Gaia Moogles	30 PP
Vana'diel Moogles	30 PP
Ivalice Moogles	30 PP

BENJAMIN'S TRAVELS

Benjamin is eager to see the world, but wants advice from you on how to do it and where to go. Use the charts below to identify the answer(s) that result in successful adventures for Benjamin and additional rewards for you.

THE TRAVELING MOOGLE

Where should I go, kupo?

Information gathering in town!	30 PP
Treasure hunting in the caves!	30 PP
Just go east.	30 PP

What should I not forget, kupo?

Be careful with your money.	30 PP + Superslick
All you need is blazing passion!	30 PP
Everything's more fun with friends!	30 PP

BENJAMIN'S BIG ADVENTURE

What castle do you recommend, kupo?

A giant, three-tiered castle.	30 PP
One that can hide under the desert.	30 PP
A pretty one hidden in the mountains.	30 PP

If I wanna relax with nature, kupo...

...try diving in the river!	30 PP + Superslick
...try swimming in a lake!	30 PP
...try meditating by the sea!	30 PP + Friend Card "Stiltzkin: 6"

BENJAMIN'S FIRST MISSION

My first mission, should I choose to accept it:

Sneaking into a castle basement!	30 PP
Deep forest rescue!	30 PP
Breaking into a mansion!	30 PP

You've got to want...

...a super-rare treasure!	30 PP
...to meet a special person!	30 PP + Friend Card "Stiltzkin: 3"
...to be stronger than anyone else!	30 PP + Friend Card "Stiltzkin: 8"

BENJAMIN'S WILD GOOSE CHASE

Benjamin's on the trail of a thief and wants your advice. It doesn't matter what you say to him; after both exchanges, he'll mail you again to express his gratitude with a Mog's Amulet.

You seen anyone blue, kupo!?

I've seen a dragoon dressed in blue!	30 PP
I've seen a bounty hunter wearing blue!	30 PP
I've seen a young noble wearing blue!	30 PP

Who's the animal crook!?

Some sweet-talking cat girl, I bet.	30 PP
Some wolf-looking guy, I bet.	30 PP
Some giant moogle, I bet.	30 PP

WON'T YOU BE LINALY'S PEN PAL?

Linaly wants to be your pen pal. She's a sweet enough moogle, but she's a little sensitive. You'll need to be mindful of her feelings to get a friend card, but if you already have it, you can make more PP by being rude.

PEN PAL LINALY, PART I

Will you exchange letters with me, kupo?

If you tell me something happy, sure.	30 PP + Superslick
I'd love to.	30 PP
Nope, I'm kinda busy.	30 PP + Superslick + correspondence ends

[Follow-up if you agreed to exchange letters] What sort of friends do you have, kupo?

Strong friends.	30 PP
Cheerful friends.	30 PP
Friends who hate being alone.	30 PP

PEN PAL LINALY, PART II

Random letters are...

exciting!	30 PP + Friend Card "Stiltzkin: 7"
annoying.	30 PP
thrilling!	30 PP + Friend Card "Stiltzkin: 7"

[If you answered "exciting" or "thrilling"] What would you like?

Superslick	30 PP + Superslick
Moogle Pom-pom	30 PP
Moogle Nose	30 PP

[If you answered "annoying"] Why do you read these letters?

Sometimes I just feel like it.	30 PP
I get PP.	30 PP + 300 PP
I just wanted to check the calendar.	(nothing)

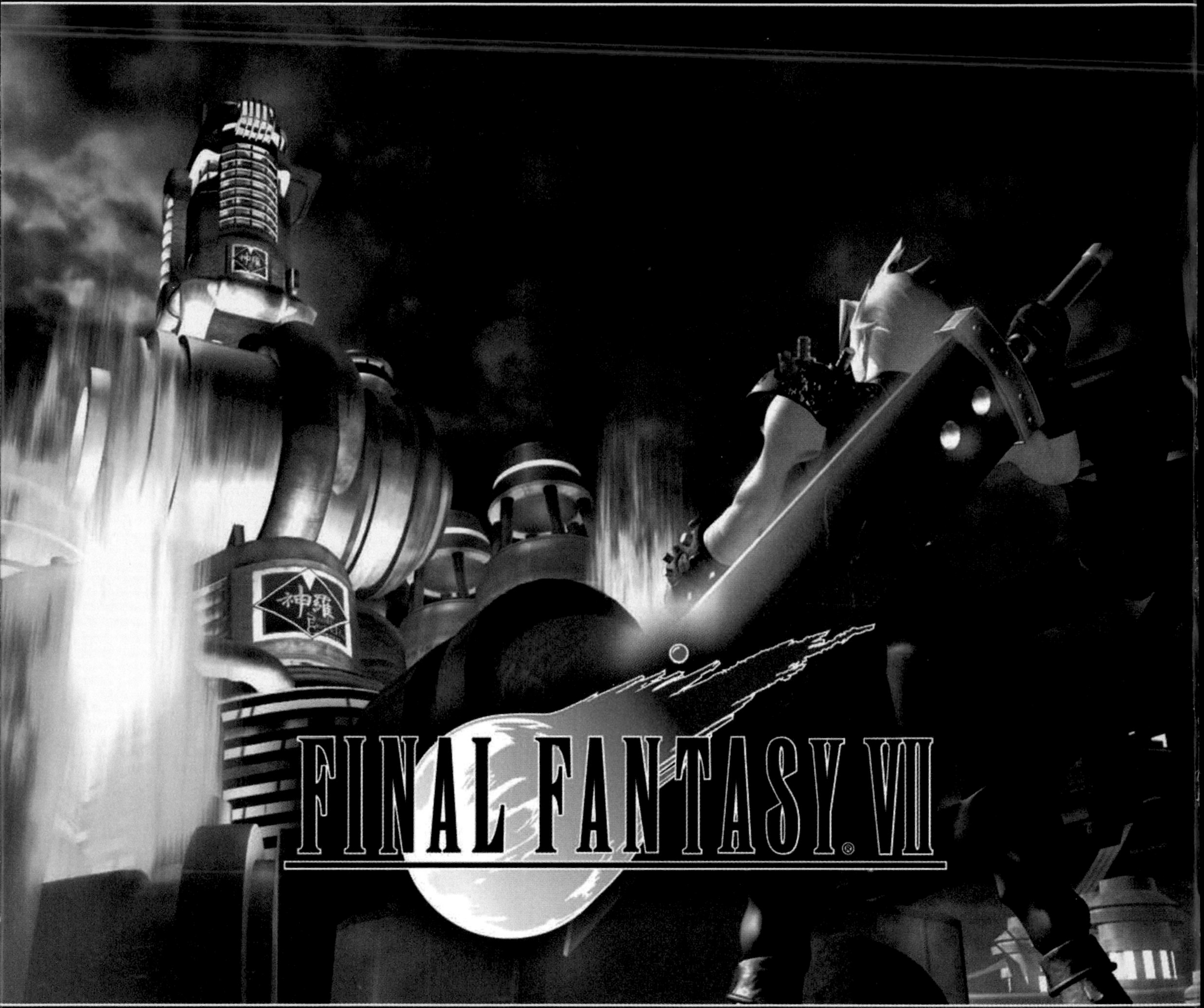

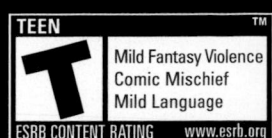
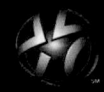

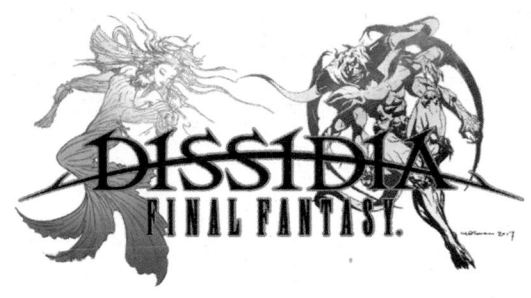

OFFICIAL STRATEGY GUIDE

Written by Joe Epstein and Casey Loe

ISBN: 978-0-7440-1142-5
Printing Code: The rightmost double-digit number is the year of the book's printing; the rightmost single-digit number is the number of the book's printing. For example, 09-1 shows that the first printing of the book occurred in 2009.
11 10 09 08   4 3 2 1
Printed in the USA.

BRADYGAMES STAFF

Publisher
David Waybright

Editor-In-Chief
H. Leigh Davis

Licensing Manager
Mike Degler

Marketing Manager
Debby Neubauer

International Translations
Brian Saliba

CREDITS

Senior Development Editor
Chris Hausermann

Screenshot Editor
Michael Owen

Lead Book Designer
Doug Wilkins

Book Designer
Colin King

Production Designer
Wil Cruz

Editorial Assistant
Angela Blau

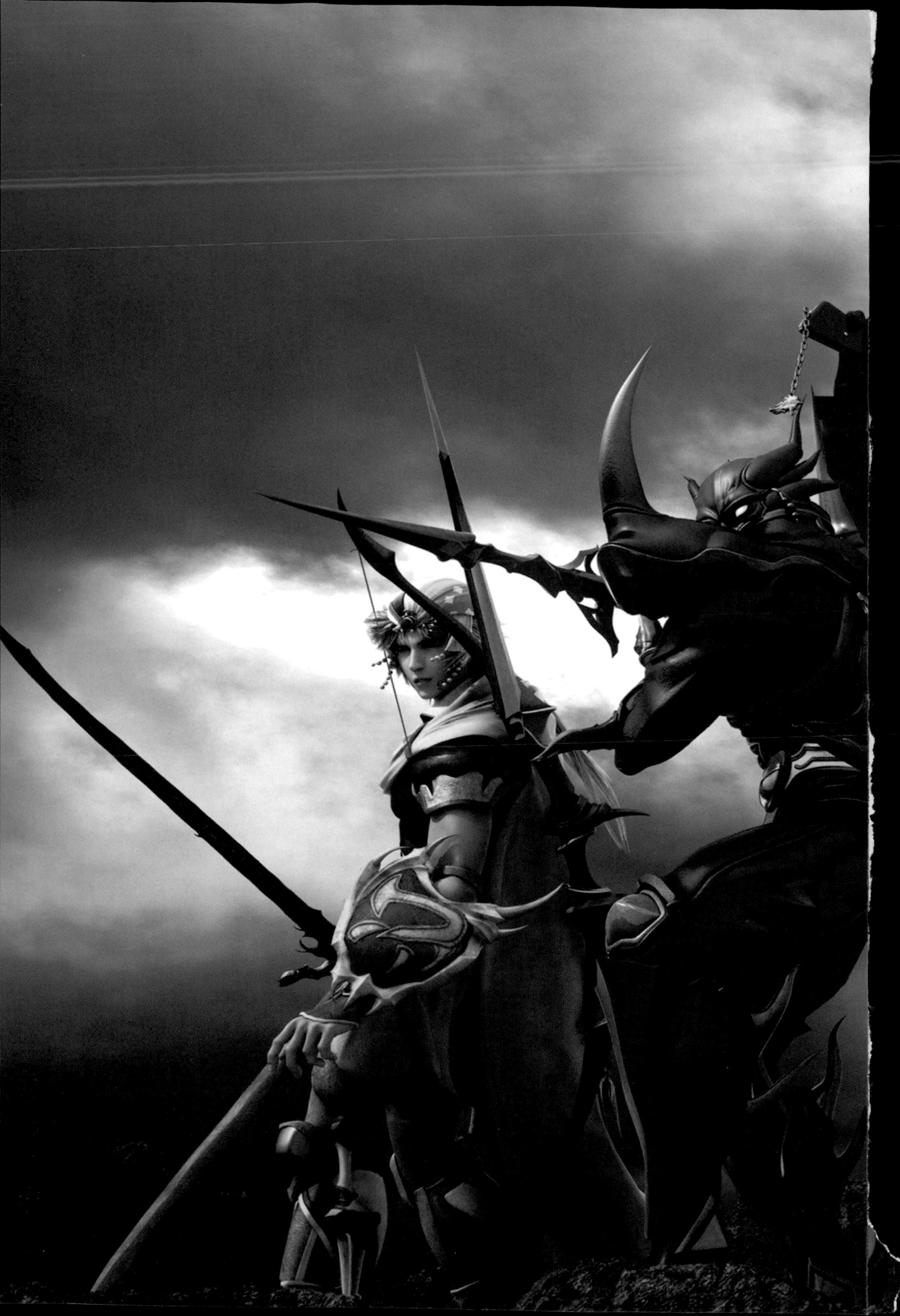

1 Shadow
nal Fantasy VI}
lock from PP Catalog

2 Edgar
al Fantasy VI}
ock from PP Catalog

3 Sabin
al Fantasy VI}
k from PP Catalog

Celes
l Fantasy VI}
ck from PP Catalog

Strago
l Fantasy VI}
ck from PP Catalog

6 Relm
nal Fantasy VI}
ock from PP Catalog

87 Setzer
inal Fantasy VI}
nlock from PP Catalog

8 Mog
al Fantasy VI}
ck from PP Catalog

Gau
l Fantasy VI}
ck from PP Catalog

Gogo
l Fantasy VI}
k from PP Catalog

Umaro
al Fantasy VI}
ck from PP Catalog

2 Biggs & Wedge
nal Fantasy VI}
nlock from PP Catalog

93 Banon
Final Fantasy VI}
Inlock from PP Catalog

94 Leo
{Final Fantasy VI}
nlock from PP Catalog

95 Ultros
inal Fantasy VI}
ock from PP Catalog

96 Typhon
nal Fantasy VI}
ck from PP Catalog

97 Chadarnook
inal Fantasy VI}
nlock from PP Catalog

98 Fiend
inal Fantasy VI}
lock from PP Catalog

99 Goddess
inal Fantasy VI}
lock from PP Catalog

00 Demon
inal Fantasy VI}
lock from PP Catalog

201 Cactuar
{Final Fantasy VI}
Unlock from PP Catalog

202 Kefka
{Final Fantasy VI}
Unlock from PP Catalog

203 Kefka
{Final Fantasy VI}
Prize: Accomplishment 108

204 Siegfried
{Final Fantasy VI}
Prize: Accomplishment 151

205 Imp
{Final Fantasy VI}
Prize: Accomplishment 129

206 Mysidian Rabbit
{Final Fantasy VI}
Prize: Accomplishment 131

207 Maria (Celes)
{Final Fantasy VI}
Prize: Accomplishment 132

208 The Blackjack
{Final Fantasy VI}
Prize: Accomplishment 141

209 Cloud
{Final Fantasy VII}
Initially available

210 Barret
{Final Fantasy VII}
Unlock from PP Catalog

211 Tifa
{Final Fantasy VII}
Unlock from PP Catalog

212 Aerith
{Final Fantasy VII}
Unlock from PP Catalog

213 Red XIII
{Final Fantasy VII}
Unlock from PP Catalog

214 Yuffie
{Final Fantasy VII}
Unlock from PP Catalog

215 Cait Sith
{Final Fantasy VII}
Unlock from PP Catalog

216 Vincent
{Final Fantasy VII}
Unlock from PP Catalog

217 Cid
{Final Fantasy VII}
Unlock from PP Catalog

218 Sephiroth
{Final Fantasy VII}
Prize: Accomplishment 109

219 Squall
{Final Fantasy VIII}
Initially available

220 Zell
{Final Fantasy VIII}
Unlock from PP Catalog

221 Irvine
{Final Fantasy VIII}
Unlock from PP Catalog

222 Quistis
{Final Fantasy VIII}
Unlock from PP Catalog

223 Rinoa
{Final Fantasy VIII}
Unlock from PP Catalog

224 Selphie
{Final Fantasy VIII}
Unlock from PP Catalog

225 Laguna
{Final Fantasy VIII}
Unlock from PP Catalog

226 Kiros
{Final Fantasy VIII}
Unlock from PP Catalog

227 Ward
{Final Fantasy VIII}
Unlock from PP Catalog

228 Seifer
{Final Fantasy VIII}
Prize: Accomplishment 110

229 Edea
{Final Fantasy VIII}
Prize: Accomplishment 127

230 Chocobo World
{Final Fantasy VIII}
Prize: Accomplishment 133

231 Zidane
{Final Fantasy IX}
Initially available

232 Vivi
{Final Fantasy IX}
Unlock from PP Catalog

233 Garnet
{Final Fantasy IX}
Unlock from PP Catalog

234 Steiner
{Final Fantasy IX}
Unlock from PP Catalog

235 Freya
{Final Fantasy IX}
Unlock from PP Catalog

236 Quina
{Final Fantasy IX}
Unlock from PP Catalog

237 Eiko
{Final Fantasy IX}
Unlock from PP Catalog

238 Amarant
{Final Fantasy IX}
Unlock from PP Catalog

239 Tidus
{Final Fantasy X}
Initially available

240 Yuna
{Final Fantasy X}
Unlock from PP Catalog

241 Wakka
{Final Fantasy X}
Unlock from PP Catalog

242 Lulu
{Final Fantasy X}
Unlock from PP Catalog

243 Kimahri
{Final Fantasy X}
Unlock from PP Catalog

244 Auron
{Final Fantasy X}
Unlock from PP Catalog

245 Rikku
{Final Fantasy X}
Unlock from PP Catalog

246 Seymour
{Final Fantasy X}
Prize: Accomplishment 112

247 Hume Male
{Final Fantasy XI}
Unlock from PP Catalog

248 Hume Female
{Final Fantasy XI}
Unlock from PP Catalog

249 Elvaan Male
{Final Fantasy XI}
Unlock from PP Catalog

250 Elvaan Female
{Final Fantasy XI}
Unlock from PP Catalog

251 Tarutaru Male
{Final Fantasy XI}
Unlock from PP Catalog

252 Tarutaru Female
{Final Fantasy XI}
Unlock from PP Catalog

253 Mithra
{Final Fantasy XI}
Unlock from PP Catalog

254 Galka
{Final Fantasy XI}
Unlock from PP Catalog

255 Vaan
{Final Fantasy XII}
Unlock from PP Catalog

256 Dalthier
{Final Fantasy XII}
Unlock from PP Catalog

257 Fran
{Final Fantasy XII}
Unlock from PP Catalog

258 Basch
{Final Fantasy XII}
Unlock from PP Catalog

259 Ashe
{Final Fantasy XII}
Unlock from PP Catalog

260 Penelo
{Final Fantasy XII}
Unlock from PP Catalog

261 Larsa
{Final Fantasy XII}
Unlock from PP Catalog

262 Reks
{Final Fantasy XII}
Unlock from PP Catalog

263 Vossler
{Final Fantasy XII}
Unlock from PP Catalog

264 Reddas
{Final Fantasy XII}
Unlock from PP Catalog

265 Warrior of Light
Initially available

266 Firion
Initially available

267 Onion Knight
Initially available

268 Cecil
Initially available

269 Bartz
Initially available

270 Terra
Initially available

271 Cloud
Initially available

272 Squall
Initially available

273 Zidane
Initially available

274 Tidus
Initially available

275 Garland
Prize: Accomplishment 113

276 The Emperor
Prize: Accomplishment 114

277 Cloud of Darkness
Prize: Accomplishment 115

278 Golbez
Prize: Accomplishment 116

279 Exdeath
Prize: Accomplishment 117

280 Kefka
Prize: Accomplishment 118

281 Sephiroth
Prize: Accomplishment 119

282 Ultimecia
Prize: Accomplishment 120

283 Kuja
Prize: Accomplishment 121

284 Jecht
Prize: Accomplishment 122

285 Cosmos
Prize: Accomplishment 125

286 Chaos
Prize: Accomplishment 143

287 Shantotto
Prize: Accomplishment 123

288 Gabranth
Prize: Accomplishment 124

289 Moai Statue
{Final Fantasy V}
Mognet: Stiltzkin 1 Friend Card

290 Floating Continent
{Final Fantasy III}
Mognet: Stiltzkin 2 Friend Card

291 Tent
{Final Fantasy IV}
Mognet: Stiltzkin 3 Friend Card

292 Crystal
{Final Fantasy V}
Mognet: Stiltzkin 4 Friend Card

293 Treasure Chest
{Final Fantasy III}
Mognet: Stiltzkin 5 Friend Card

294 Item Shop
{Final Fantasy I}
Mognet: Stiltzkin 6 Friend Card

295 Weapon Shop
{Final Fantasy I}
Mognet: Stiltzkin 7 Friend Card

296 Armor Shop
{Final Fantasy I}
Mognet: Stiltzkin 8 Friend Card

[Not Numbered]
Final Fantasy Agito XIII
Prize: Password Friend Card

[Not Numbered]
Final Fantasy Agito XIII
Prize: Password Friend Card

[Not Numbered]
Final Fantasy Versus XIII
Prize: Password Friend Card

[Not Numbered]
Final Fantasy Versus XIII
Prize: Password Friend Card

[Not Numbered]
Final Fantasy XIII
Prize: Password Friend Card

[Not Numbered]
Final Fantasy XIII
Prize: Password Friend Card

[Not Numbered]
Chocobo {Final Fantasy V}
Prize: Password Friend Card

[Not Numbered]
Moogle {Final Fantasy V}
Prize: Password Friend Card

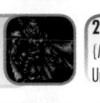

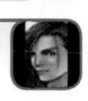

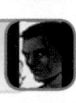

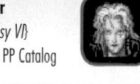

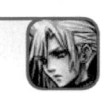

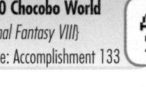

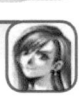

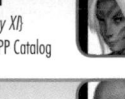

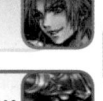

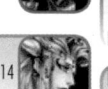

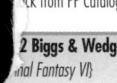

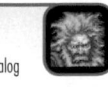

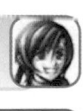

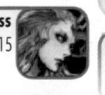

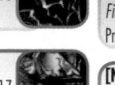

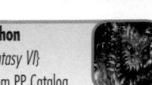

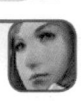

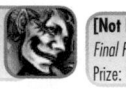

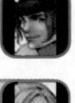

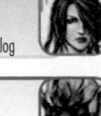

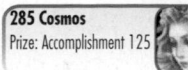

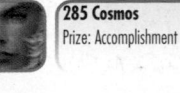

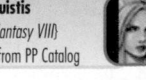

055 Monk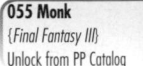
{Final Fantasy III}
Unlock from PP Catalog

056 White Mage
{Final Fantasy III}
Unlock from PP Catalog

057 Black Mage
{Final Fantasy III}
Unlock from PP Catalog

058 Red Mage
{Final Fantasy III}
Unlock from PP Catalog

059 Ranger
{Final Fantasy III}
Unlock from PP Catalog

060 Knight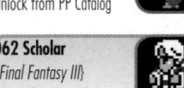
{Final Fantasy III}
Unlock from PP Catalog

061 Thief
{Final Fantasy III}
Unlock from PP Catalog

062 Scholar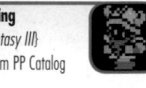
{Final Fantasy III}
Unlock from PP Catalog

063 Geomancer
{Final Fantasy III}
Unlock from PP Catalog

064 Dragoon
{Final Fantasy III}
Unlock from PP Catalog

065 Viking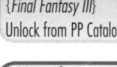
{Final Fantasy III}
Unlock from PP Catalog

066 Black Belt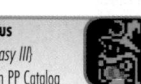
{Final Fantasy III}
Unlock from PP Catalog

067 Dark Knight
{Final Fantasy III}
Unlock from PP Catalog

068 Illusionist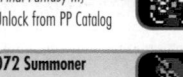
{Final Fantasy III}
Unlock from PP Catalog

069 Bard
{Final Fantasy III}
Unlock from PP Catalog

070 Magus
{Final Fantasy III}
Unlock from PP Catalog

071 Devout
{Final Fantasy III}
Unlock from PP Catalog

072 Summoner
{Final Fantasy III}
Unlock from PP Catalog

073 Sage
{Final Fantasy III}
Prize: Accomplishment 137

074 Ninja
{Final Fantasy III}
Prize: Accomplishment 138

075 Garuda
{Final Fantasy III}
Unlock from PP Catalog

076 Nepto Dragon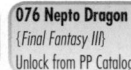
{Final Fantasy III}
Unlock from PP Catalog

077 Hein
{Final Fantasy III}
Unlock from PP Catalog

078 Xande
{Final Fantasy III}
Prize: Accomplishment 135

079 Ahriman
{Final Fantasy III}
Prize: Accomplishment 148

080 Cloud of Darkness
{Final Fantasy III}
Prize: Accomplishment 105

081 Cecil (Dark Knight) / Battle
{Final Fantasy IV}
Initially available

082 Cecil / Battle
{Final Fantasy IV}
Unlock from PP Catalog

083 Kain / Battle
{Final Fantasy IV}
Unlock from PP Catalog

084 Rydia (Child) / Battle
{Final Fantasy IV}
Unlock from PP Catalog

085 Rydia / Battle
{Final Fantasy IV}
Unlock from PP Catalog

086 Tellah / Battle
{Final Fantasy IV}
Unlock from PP Catalog

087 Edward / Battle
{Final Fantasy IV}
Unlock from PP Catalog

088 Rosa / Battle
{Final Fantasy IV}
Unlock from PP Catalog

089 Yang / Battle
{Final Fantasy IV}
Unlock from PP Catalog

090 Palom / Battle
{Final Fantasy IV}
Unlock from PP Catalog

091 Porom / Battle
{Final Fantasy IV}
Unlock from PP Catalog

092 Cid / Battle
{Final Fantasy IV}
Unlock from PP Catalog

093 Edge / Battle
{Final Fantasy IV}
Unlock from PP Catalog

094 Fusoya / Battle
{Final Fantasy IV}
Prize: Accomplishment 145

095 Golbez / Battle
{Final Fantasy IV}
Prize: Accomplishment 134

096 Cecil (Dark Knight)
{Final Fantasy IV}
Initially available

097 Cecil
{Final Fantasy IV}
Unlock from PP Catalog

098 Kain
{Final Fantasy IV}
Unlock from PP Catalog

099 Rydia (Child)
{Final Fantasy IV}
Unlock from PP Catalog

100 Rydia
{Final Fantasy IV}
Unlock from PP Catalog

101 Tellah
{Final Fantasy IV}
Unlock from PP Catalog

102 Edward
{Final Fantasy IV}
Unlock from PP Catalog

103 Rosa
{Final Fantasy IV}
Unlock from PP Catalog

104 Yang
{Final Fantasy IV}
Unlock from PP Catalog

105 Palom
{Final Fantasy IV}
Unlock from PP Catalog

106 Porom
{Final Fantasy IV}
Unlock from PP Catalog

107 Cid
{Final Fantasy IV}
Unlock from PP Catalog

108 Edge
{Final Fantasy IV}
Unlock from PP Catalog

109 Fusoya
{Final Fantasy IV}
Unlock from PP Catalog

110 Flan Princess
{Final Fantasy IV}
Unlock from PP Catalog

111 Mist Dragon
{Final Fantasy IV}
Unlock from PP Catalog

112 Calcabrina
{Final Fantasy IV}
Unlock from PP Catalog

113 Golbez
{Final Fantasy IV}
Unlock from PP Catalog

114 Zemus
{Final Fantasy IV}
Unlock from PP Catalog

115 Zeromus
{Final Fantasy IV}
Unlock from PP Catalog

116 Zeromus
{Final Fantasy IV}
Prize: Accomplishment 106

117 Pig
{Final Fantasy IV}
Unlock from PP Catalog

118 Toad
{Final Fantasy IV}
Unlock from PP Catalog

119 Mini
{Final Fantasy IV}
Unlock from PP Catalog

120 Namingway
{Final Fantasy IV}
Prize: Accomplishment 128

121 Red Wings
{Final Fantasy IV}
Prize: Accomplishment 139

122 Bartz / Freelancer
{Final Fantasy V}
Initially available

123 Lenna / Freelancer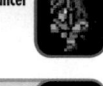
{Final Fantasy V}
Initially available

124 Galuf / Freelancer
{Final Fantasy V}
Initially available

125 Faris / Freelancer
{Final Fantasy V}
Initially available

126 Krile / Freelancer
{Final Fantasy V}
Initially available

127 Bartz / Knight
{Final Fantasy V}
Unlock from PP Catalog

128 Lenna / Monk
{Final Fantasy V}
Unlock from PP Catalog

129 Galuf / Thief
{Final Fantasy V}
Unlock from PP Catalog

130 Krile / Dragoon
{Final Fantasy V}
Unlock from PP Catalog

131 Faris / Ninja
{Final Fantasy V}
Unlock from PP Catalog

132 Galuf / Samurai
{Final Fantasy V}
Unlock from PP Catalog

133 Krile / Berserker
{Final Fantasy V}
Unlock from PP Catalog

134 Lenna / Ranger
{Final Fantasy V}
Unlock from PP Catalog

135 Faris / Mystic Knight
{Final Fantasy V}
Unlock from PP Catalog

136 Krile / White Mage
{Final Fantasy V}
Unlock from PP Catalog

137 Bartz / Black Mage
{Final Fantasy V}
Unlock from PP Catalog

138 Lenna / Time Mage
{Final Fantasy V}
Unlock from PP Catalog

139 Faris / Summoner
{Final Fantasy V}
Unlock from PP Catalog

140 Lenna / Blue Mage
{Final Fantasy V}
Unlock from PP Catalog

141 Faris / Red Mage
{Final Fantasy V}
Unlock from PP Catalog

142 Galuf / Beastmaster
{Final Fantasy V}
Unlock from PP Catalog

143 Galuf / Chemist
{Final Fantasy V}
Unlock from PP Catalog

144 Krile / Geomancer
{Final Fantasy V}
Unlock from PP Catalog

145 Bartz / Bard
{Final Fantasy V}
Unlock from PP Catalog

146 Bartz / Dancer
{Final Fantasy V}
Unlock from PP Catalog

147 Bartz / Mimic
{Final Fantasy V}
Unlock from PP Catalog

148 Magic Pot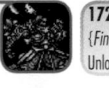
{Final Fantasy V}
Unlock from PP Catalog

149 Tonberry
{Final Fantasy V}
Unlock from PP Catalog

150 Mover
{Final Fantasy V}
Unlock from PP Catalog

151 Gilgamesh
{Final Fantasy V}
Unlock from PP Catalog

152 Exdeath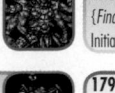
{Final Fantasy V}
Unlock from PP Catalog

153 Necrophobe
{Final Fantasy V}
Unlock from PP Catalog

154 Famed Mimic Gogo
{Final Fantasy V}
Unlock from PP Catalog

155 Exdeath
{Final Fantasy V}
Prize: Accomplishment 144

156 Neo Exdeath
{Final Fantasy V}
Prize: Accomplishment 107

157 Gilgamesh
{Final Fantasy V}
Prize: Accomplishment 140

158 Omega
{Final Fantasy V}
Prize: Accomplishment 149

159 The Dawn Warriors
{Final Fantasy V}
Prize: Accomplishment 142

160 Sage Ghido
{Final Fantasy V}
Prize: Accomplishment 130

161 Mr. Clio
{Final Fantasy V}
Prize: Accomplishment 111

162 Boko
{Final Fantasy V}
Prize: Accomplishment 150

163 Terra / Battle
{Final Fantasy VI}
Initially available

164 Terra (Esper) / Battle
{Final Fantasy VI}
Prize: Accomplishment 147

165 Locke / Battle
{Final Fantasy VI}
Unlock from PP Catalog

166 Cyan / Battle
{Final Fantasy VI}
Unlock from PP Catalog

167 Shadow / Battle
{Final Fantasy VI}
Unlock from PP Catalog

168 Edgar / Battle
{Final Fantasy VI}
Unlock from PP Catalog

169 Sabin / Battle
{Final Fantasy VI}
Unlock from PP Catalog

170 Celes / Battle
{Final Fantasy VI}
Unlock from PP Catalog

171 Strago / Battle
{Final Fantasy VI}
Unlock from PP Catalog

172 Relm / Battle
{Final Fantasy VI}
Unlock from PP Catalog

173 Setzer / Battle
{Final Fantasy VI}
Unlock from PP Catalog

174 Mog / Battle
{Final Fantasy VI}
Unlock from PP Catalog

175 Gau / Battle
{Final Fantasy VI}
Unlock from PP Catalog

176 Umaro / Battle
{Final Fantasy VI}
Unlock from PP Catalog

177 Gogo / Battle
{Final Fantasy VI}
Prize: Accomplishment 136

178 Terra
{Final Fantasy VI}
Initially available

179 Locke
{Final Fantasy VI}
Unlock from PP Catalog

180 Cyan
{Final Fantasy VI}
Unlock from PP Catalog

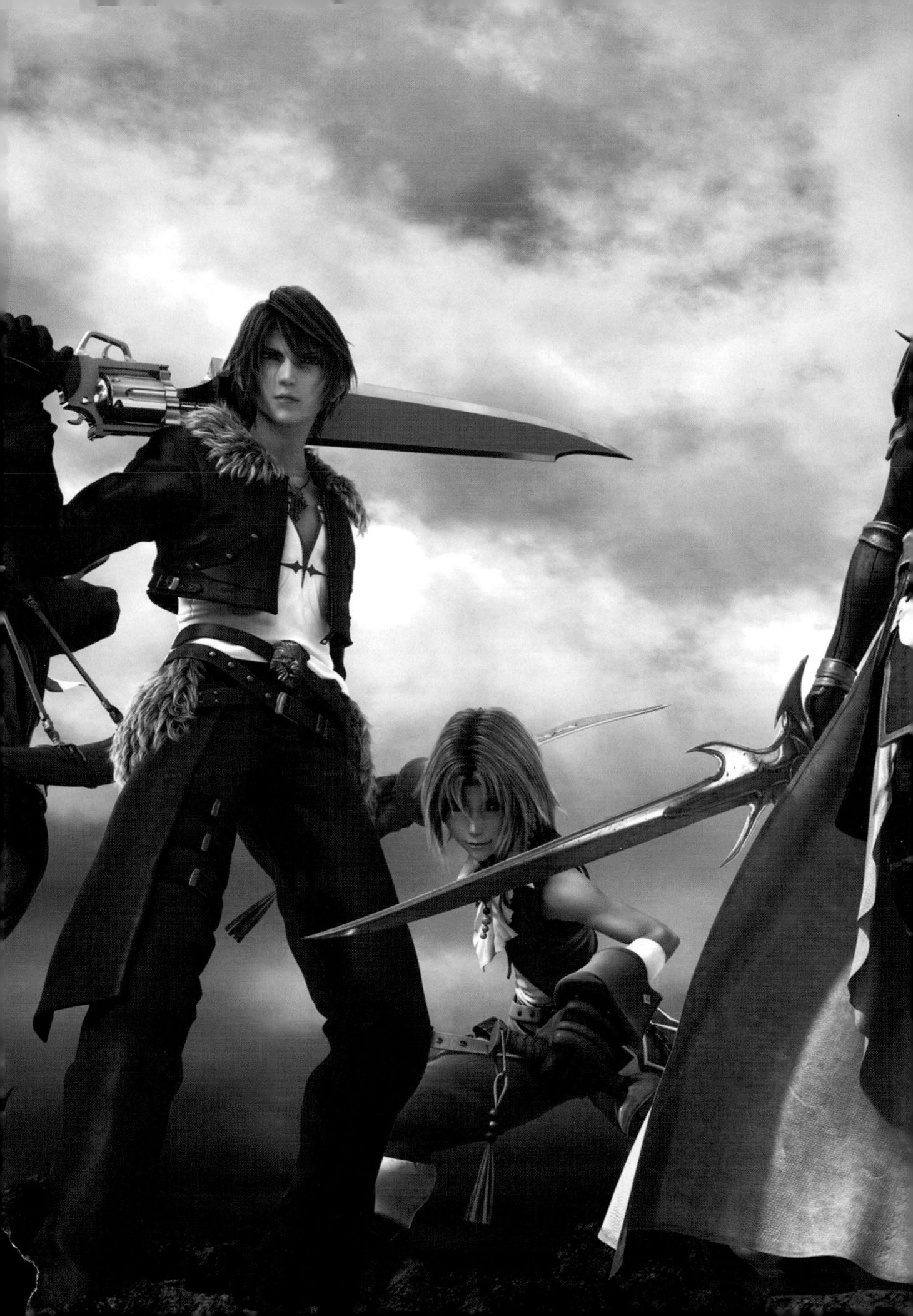

Number	Name	Requirement	Result	Reward
125	The Day the World Ended	Hint: Destroy the ultimate Chaos. (Clear Inward Chaos Story Mode.)	Listing appears at completion	Player Icon 285
126	The Crimson Soul	Battlegen the Red Gem. (From an online opponent or ghost card with a RED ID.)	Listing appears after completing Inward Chaos Story Mode	Player Icon 025
127	The Saffron Soul	Battlegen the Orange Gem. (From an online opponent or ghost card with an ORG ID.)	Listing appears after completing Inward Chaos Story Mode	Player Icon 229
128	The Canary Soul	Battlegen the Yellow Gem. (From an online opponent or ghost card with a YEL ID.)	Listing appears after completing Inward Chaos Story Mode	Player Icon 120
129	The Viridian Soul	Battlegen the Green Gem. (From an online opponent or ghost card with a GRN ID.)	Listing appears after completing Inward Chaos Story Mode	Player Icon 205
130	The Cerulean Soul	Battlegen the Blue Gem. (From an online opponent or ghost card with a BLU ID.)	Listing appears after completing Inward Chaos Story Mode	Player Icon 160
131	The Azure Soul	Battlegen the Cyan Gem. (From an online opponent or ghost card with a SKY ID.)	Listing appears after completing Inward Chaos Story Mode	Player Icon 206
132	The Tyrian Soul	Battlegen the Purple Gem. (From an online opponent or ghost card with a PUR ID.)	Listing appears after completing Inward Chaos Story Mode	Player Icon 207
133	The Ivory Soul	Battlegen the White Gem. (From an online opponent or ghost card with a WHT ID.)	Listing appears after completing Inward Chaos Story Mode	Player Icon 230
134	Carnage	Hint: Countless fallen in your wake. (Win at least 3,000 battles.)	Listing appears at 50% completion	Player Icon 095
135	Vengeance of the Fallen	Hint: An unshakable fixation. (Lose at least 500 battles.)	Listing appears at 50% completion	Player Icon 078
136	The Directionless Truthseeker	Hint: Beyond all limitations. (Earn at least 1,000,000 EXP with level-100 characters.)	Listing appears at 50% completion	Player Icon 177
137	The Broken Leader	Hint: The value of life. (Deal at least 25,000,000 points of damage.)	Listing appears at 50% completion	Player Icon 073
138	Clash of the Valiant	Hint: The proof of courage. (Claim at least 30,000,000 points of bravery.)	Listing appears at 50% completion	Player Icon 074
139	The Neverending March	Hint: Go anywhere, everywhere, near and far. (Travel at least 800 kilometers.)	Listing appears at 50% completion	Player Icon 121
140	Core Grabber	Hint: The powerful bluish-white crystals. (Collect at least 1,000 EX Cores.)	Listing appears at 50% completion	Player Icon 157
141	Olympic Medalist	Hint: All that glitters. (Collect at least 5,000 Duel Colosseum medals.)	Listing appears at 50% completion	Player Icon 208
142	A Single Answer	Hint: The end of the journey. (Reach level 100 with all characters.)	Listing appears after completing Inward Chaos Story Mode	Player Icon 159
143	He Who Covets Jewels	Hint: Unintentional destruction. (Break at least 100 accessories.)	Listing appears at 50% completion	Player Icon 286
144	Now I Am the Master	Hint: No more need for training. (Master at least 1,000 abilities.)	Listing appears at 50% completion	Player Icon 155
145	The Ravenous Collector	Hint: The perfect collection of weapons. (Acquire all armaments except for password-only items.)	Listing appears after completing Inward Chaos Story Mode	Player Icon 094
146	My Road to El Dorado	Hint: The perfect collection of jewelry. (Acquire all accessories except for password-only items.)	Listing appears after completing Inward Chaos Story Mode	Player Icon 023
147	Tamer of the Gods	Hint: Trust in the totems. (Acquire all Summonstones.)	Listing appears at 50% completion	Player Icon 164
148	Something from Nothing	Hint: The maven's trade. (Have a trade accessory surplus of at least 1,000,000 gil.)	Listing appears at 50% completion	Player Icon 079
149	I Love Dissidia	Hint: Happy days with Dissidia. (Play for at least 15 days straight.)	Listing appears after completing Inward Chaos Story Mode	Player Icon 158
150	Wings of Icarus	Hint: What a flightless bird dreams of. (Achieve a play plan "Lucky" value of 100%.)	Listing appears after completing Inward Chaos Story Mode	Player Icon 162
151	Favored Customer	Hint: Help the shop window catch the eye. (Shop stock percentage of 100%.)	Listing appears at 50% completion	Player Icon 204

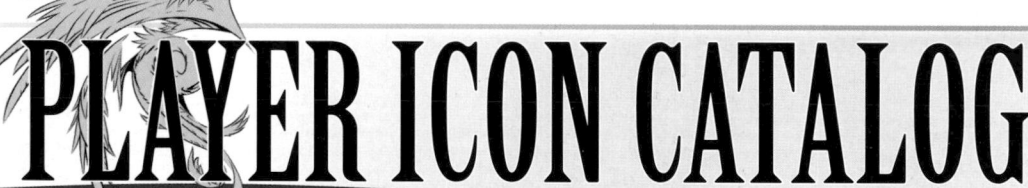

PLAYER ICON CATALOG

There are over 300 Player Icons that you can choose as your Friend Card Icon, representing every game in the Final Fantasy series. While several of these icons are initially available, you can unlock hundreds more by completing accomplishments, entering secret passwords, and unlocking them from the PP Catalog.

001 Fighter
{*Final Fantasy I*}
Initially available

002 Thief
{*Final Fantasy I*}
Initially available

003 Monk
{*Final Fantasy I*}
Initially available

004 Red Mage
{*Final Fantasy I*}
Initially available

005 White Mage
{*Final Fantasy I*}
Initially available

006 Black Mage
{*Final Fantasy I*}
Initially available

007 Knight
{*Final Fantasy I*}
Unlock from PP Catalog

008 Ninja
{*Final Fantasy I*}
Unlock from PP Catalog

009 Master
{*Final Fantasy I*}
Unlock from PP Catalog

010 Red Wizard
{*Final Fantasy I*}
Unlock from PP Catalog

011 White Wizard
{*Final Fantasy I*}
Unlock from PP Catalog

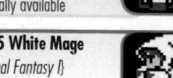

012 Black Wizard
{*Final Fantasy I*}
Unlock from PP Catalog

013 Goblin
{*Final Fantasy I*}
Unlock from PP Catalog

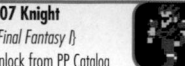

014 Sahagin
{*Final Fantasy I*}
Unlock from PP Catalog

015 Ochu
{*Final Fantasy I*}
Unlock from PP Catalog

016 Mindflayer
{*Final Fantasy I*}
Unlock from PP Catalog

017 Evil Eye
{*Final Fantasy I*}
Unlock from PP Catalog

018 Garland
{*Final Fantasy I*}
Unlock from PP Catalog

019 Lich
{*Final Fantasy I*}
Unlock from PP Catalog

020 Marilith
{*Final Fantasy I*}
Unlock from PP Catalog

021 Kraken
{*Final Fantasy I*}
Unlock from PP Catalog

022 Tiamat
{Final Fantasy I}
Unlock from PP Catalog

023 Death Machine
{*Final Fantasy I*}
Prize: Accomplishment 146

024 Chaos
{*Final Fantasy I*}
Prize: Accomplishment 103

025 Matoya
{*Final Fantasy I*}
Prize: Accomplishment 126

026 Firion/Battle
{*Final Fantasy II*}
Initially available

027 Maria/Battle
{*Final Fantasy II*}
Initially available

028 Guy/Battle
{*Final Fantasy II*}
Initially available

029 Leon/Battle
{*Final Fantasy II*}
Initially available

030 Minwu/Battle
{*Final Fantasy II*}
Unlock from PP Catalog

031 Josef/Battle
{*Final Fantasy II*}
Unlock from PP Catalog

032 Gordon/Battle
{*Final Fantasy II*}
Unlock from PP Catalog

033 Leila/Battle
{*Final Fantasy II*}
Unlock from PP Catalog

034 Richard/Battle
{*Final Fantasy II*}
Unlock from PP Catalog

035 Firion
{*Final Fantasy II*}
Initially available

036 Maria
{*Final Fantasy II*}
Initially available

037 Guy
{*Final Fantasy II*}
Initially available

038 Leon
{*Final Fantasy II*}
Initially available

039 Minwu
{*Final Fantasy II*}
Unlock from PP Catalog

040 Josef
{*Final Fantasy II*}
Unlock from PP Catalog

041 Gordon
{*Final Fantasy II*}
Unlock from PP Catalog

042 Leila
{*Final Fantasy II*}
Unlock from PP Catalog

043 Richard
{*Final Fantasy II*}
Unlock from PP Catalog

044 Bomb
{*Final Fantasy II*}
Unlock from PP Catalog

045 Malboro
{*Final Fantasy II*}
Unlock from PP Catalog

046 Iron Giant
{*Final Fantasy II*}
Unlock from PP Catalog

047 Adamantoise
{*Final Fantasy II*}
Unlock from PP Catalog

048 Behemoth
{*Final Fantasy II*}
Unlock from PP Catalog

049 Astaroth
{*Final Fantasy II*}
Unlock from PP Catalog

050 Beelzebub
{*Final Fantasy II*}
Unlock from PP Catalog

051 The Emperor
{*Final Fantasy II*}
Unlock from PP Catalog

052 The Emperor
{*Final Fantasy II*}
Prize: Accomplishment 104

053 Onion Knight
{*Final Fantasy III*}
Initially available

054 Warrior
{*Final Fantasy III*}
Unlock from PP Catalog

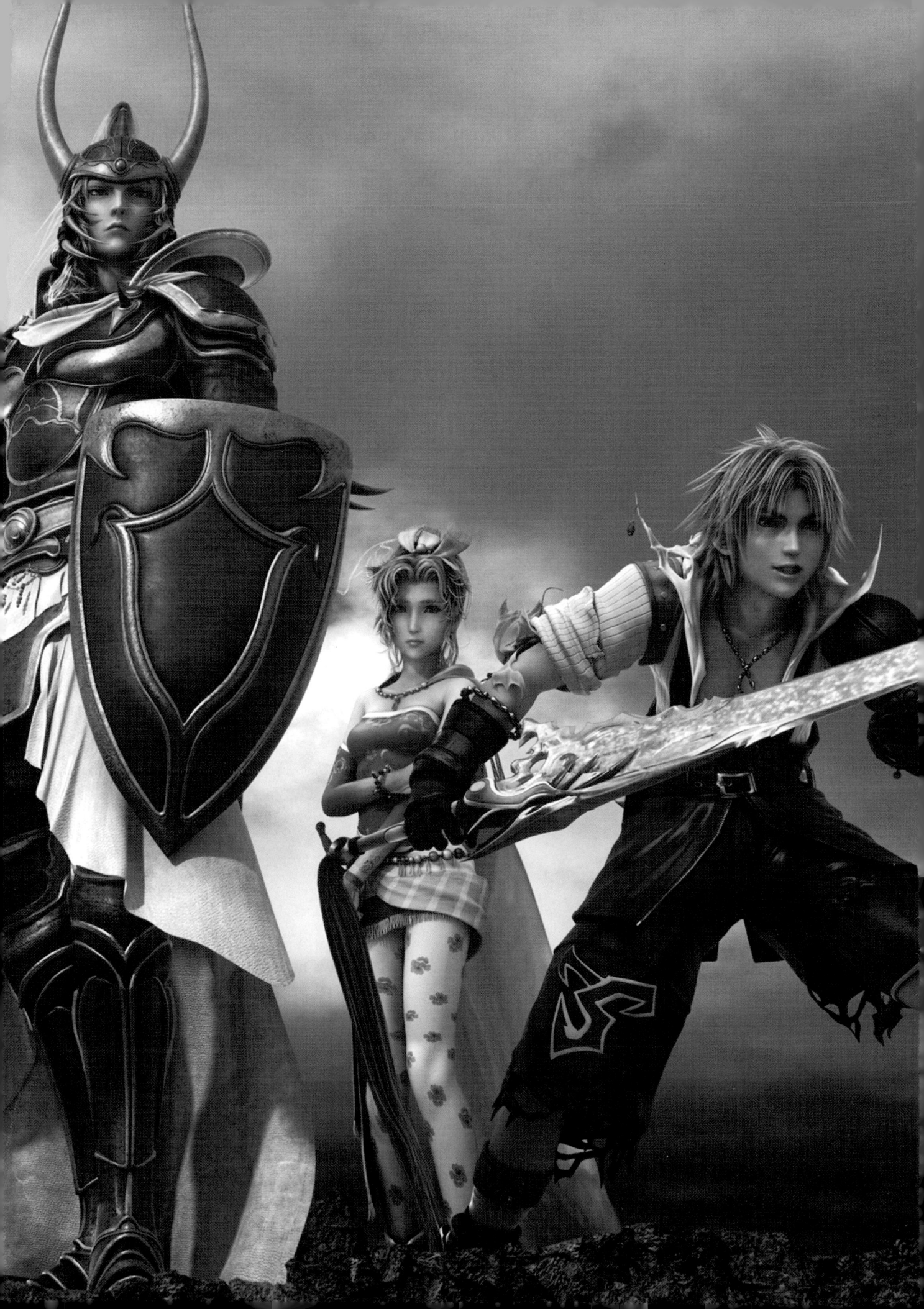

Number	Name	Requirement	Result	Reward
052	Impulse: Final Fantasy IX	Clear any Shade Impulse chapter with Zidane.	Listing appears after clearing Shade Impulse Chapter 4	[Combat] Pre-HP Attack
053	Impulse: Final Fantasy X	Clear any Shade Impulse chapter with Tidus.	Listing appears after clearing Shade Impulse Chapter 4	[Combat] Pre-HP Damage
054	Shade Impulse Completed	Have each character clear at least one Shade Impulse chapter.	Listing appears upon completion	[Opponent] In Motion
055	Acting Impulsively	Clear a Shade Impulse chapter at least 10 times.	Listing appears at 50% completion	[Opponent] EX Gauge Full
056	Treasure Hunter	Open at least 200 treasure chests.	Listing appears at 50% completion	[Combat] Quickmove
057	Unswerving Path	Finish Story Mode levels with a combined 100 DP remaining.	Listing appears at 50% completion	[Combat] Chasing
058	One for the Record Books	Duel Colosseum, Lunar Whale course: achieve 10 consecutive wins.	Listing appears at 50% completion	[Opponent] EX Gauge ≤ 30%
059	Pugilist Pointillist	Duel Colosseum, Lunar Whale course: earn 100,000 points.	Listing appears at 50% completion	[Opponent] Chasing
060	Veteran Duelist	Duel Colosseum, Lunar Whale course: fight at least 100 battles.	Listing appears at 50% completion	[Level] Level is a Prime Number
061	Time Attacker	Clear an Arcade Mode Time Attack within 1,200 seconds.	Listing appears after clearing Shade Impulse Chapter 4	[Position] On Ground, Foe in Midair
062	Hope They're All Gold	Win at least 100 medals in the Duel Colosseum.	Listing appears at 50% completion	[Level] Level = Multiple of 4
063	Accolades of the Gladiator	Gain at least 20 awards in one Duel Colosseum playthrough.	Listing appears at 50% completion	[Level] Level = Multiple of 5
064	The Strongest Link	Have one character reach at least level 20.	Listing appears after clearing any Destiny Odyssey	[HP] HP is 50-70%
065	The Strongest Link	Have one character reach at least level 50.	Listing appears after clearing Shade Impulse Chapter 1	[Level] Level 50-59
066	The Strongest Link	Have one character reach at least level 100.	Listing appears after clearing Shade Impulse Chapter 4	[Level] Level 100
067	On the Level	Have all characters reach level 50.	Listing appears at 50% completion	[Level] Level 60-69
068	A Fistful of Gil	Receive at least 200,000 gil.	Listing appears at 50% completion	[HP] HP is a Multiple of 2
069	A Fistful of Gil	Receive at least 5,000,000 gil.	Listing appears at 50% completion	[Opponent] HP = 100%
070	It's Got AP-peal	Receive at least 30,000 AP.	Listing appears at 50% completion	[HP] HP is a Multiple of 3
071	It's Got AP-peal	Receive at least 100,000 AP.	Listing appears at 50% completion	[Opponent] Near Death
072	Bonus Round	Have a successful AP bonus at least 100 times.	Listing appears at 50% completion	[HP] HP is a Multiple of 4
073	PP Baron	Earn at least 5,000 PP.	Listing appears at 50% completion	[HP] HP is a Multiple of 5
074	PP Baron	Earn at least 10,000 PP.	Listing appears at 50% completion	[Opponent] Near Loss
075	Cast of Thousands	Earn access to a total of 22 playable characters.	Listing appears at 11 playable characters	[HP] HP is a Prime Number
076	In Vogue	Obtain alternate look of all characters.	Listing appears after clearing Shade Impulse Chapter 4	[Opponent] Attacking HP
077	Jack of All Trades	Master more than 150 abilities.	Listing appears at 50% completion	[Bravery] BRV is a Multiple of 2
078	Loaded for Bear	Obtain at least 100 items.	Listing appears at 50% completion	[Bravery] BRV is a Multiple of 3
079	Fashion Conscious	Obtain at least 100 accessories.	Listing appears at 50% completion	[Bravery] BRV is a Multiple of 4
080	A Little Help from My Friends	Obtain at least 30 summons.	Listing appears at 50% completion	[EX] EX Gauge ≤ 30%
081	Mass Production	Battlegen at least 300 times.	Listing appears at 50% completion	[Bravery] BRV is a Multiple of 5
082	Mass Production	Battlegen at least 1,000 times.	Listing appears at 50% completion	[Level] Level 80-89
083	Battlegenesis Does	Battlegen an item from each character.	Listing appears after completing all Destiny Odysseys	[Level] Level 40-49
084	Productive Battling	In one battle, create 5 accessories.	Listing appears after creating three accessories in one battle	[Bravery] BRV is a Prime Number
085	Boosteriffic!	Attain a booster accessory multiplier of at least 8.	Listing appears at 50% completion	[Level] Level = Multiple of 2
086	Bull in a China Shop	Break at least 10 accessories.	Listing appears at 50% completion	[Bravery] BRV = 0
087	'Tis Better to Receive	Obtain at least 20 dropped items.	Listing appears at 50% completion	[Combat] Evading
088	The Blessings of Mercantilism	Trade at least 100 times (at the shop).	Listing appears at 50% completion	[Combat] Blocking
089	Arbitrageur	Have a trade accessory surplus of at least 100,000 gil.	Listing appears at 50% completion	[Opponent] Pre-Bravery Damage
090	Special Delivery	Receive at least 10 letters from moogles.	Listing appears at 50% completion	[Position] Above Opponent
091	Special Delivery	Receive at least 100 letters from moogles.	Listing appears at 50% completion	[Opponent] Pre-HP Damage
092	The Daily Grind	Play for at least 5 days straight.	Listing appears at completion	[Bravery] No BRV Damage
093	A Long Road	Completed 7 days after first creating your save file.	Listing appears at 50% completion	[Position] Below Opponent
094	A Long Road	Completed 30 days after first creating your save file.	Listing appears at 50% completion	[Opponent] Victory Chance
095	A Good Plan	Clear The Casual Gamer play plan.	Listing appears at start of game	[Level] Level 10-19
096	A Good Plan	Clear The Average Gamer play plan.	Listing appears at start of game	[Level] Level 20-29
097	A Good Plan	Clear The Hardcore Gamer play plan.	Listing appears at start of game	[Level] Level 30-39
098	Clover-Covered Rabbit's Foot	Achieve a play plan "Lucky" value of 50%.	Listing appears at completion	[EX] EX Core Present
099	Restocker's Paradise	Shop stock percentage of at least 50%.	Listing appears at 50% completion	[Opponent] On the Ground
100	Hey, Big Spender	Spend at least 100,000 gil at the shop.	Listing appears at 50% completion	[Opponent] After Summon
101	Collect Them All	PP Catalog at least 50% complete.	Listing appears at 50% completion	[Opponent] In Midair
102	Catalog Shopper	Spend at least 3,000 PP in the PP Catalog.	Listing appears at 50% completion	[Opponent] Summon Unused
103	Reprisal on the Hero	Hint: The hero's gravestone. (Defeat Warrior of Light 30 times.)	Listing appears at 50% completion	Player Icon 024
104	The Thwarted Liegeman	Hint: The liegeman's gravestone. (Defeat Firion 30 times.)	Listing appears at 50% completion	Player Icon 052
105	The Foiled Youth	Hint: The youth's gravestone. (Defeat Onion Knight 30 times.)	Listing appears at 50% completion	Player Icon 080
106	The Vanquished Knight	Hint: The knight's gravestone. (Defeat Cecil 30 times.)	Listing appears at 50% completion	Player Icon 116
107	The Wanderer's End	Hint: The traveler's gravestone. (Defeat Bartz 30 times.)	Listing appears at 50% completion	Player Icon 156
108	The Girl's Last Laugh	Hint: The girl's gravestone. (Defeat Terra 30 times.)	Listing appears at 50% completion	Player Icon 203
109	What Slayed the Soldier	Hint: The soldier's gravestone. (Defeat Cloud 30 times.)	Listing appears at 50% completion	Player Icon 218
110	The Lion's Snare	Hint: The lion's gravestone. (Defeat Squall 30 times.)	Listing appears at 50% completion	Player Icon 228
111	What Defeated the Thief	Hint: The pirate's gravestone. (Defeat Zidane 30 times.)	Listing appears at 50% completion	Player Icon 161
112	What Banished the Vision	Hint: The dreamer's gravestone. (Defeat Tidus 30 times.)	Listing appears at 50% completion	Player Icon 246
113	Reprisal on the Stalwart	Hint: The stalwart's gravestone. (Defeat Garland 30 times.)	Listing appears at 50% completion	Player Icon 275
114	The Thwarted Despot	Hint: The despot's gravestone. (Defeat the Emperor 30 times.)	Listing appears at 50% completion	Player Icon 276
115	The Foiled Wraith	Hint: The wraith's gravestone. (Defeat Cloud of Darkness 30 times.)	Listing appears at 50% completion	Player Icon 277
116	The Vanquished Warlock	Hint: The warlock's gravestone. (Defeat Golbez 30 times.)	Listing appears at 50% completion	Player Icon 278
117	What Felled the Mighty Tree	Hint: The great tree's gravestone. (Defeat Exdeath 30 times.)	Listing appears at 50% completion	Player Icon 279
118	The Harlequin's Last Laugh	Hint: The harlequin's gravestone. (Defeat Kefka 30 times.)	Listing appears at 50% completion	Player Icon 280
119	What Slayed the Champion	Hint: The champion's gravestone. (Defeat Sephiroth 30 times.)	Listing appears at 50% completion	Player Icon 281
120	The Witch's Snare	Hint: The witch's gravestone. (Defeat Ultimecia 30 times.)	Listing appears at 50% completion	Player Icon 282
121	What Defeated the Reaper	Hint: The reaper's gravestone. (Defeat Kuja 30 times.)	Listing appears at 50% completion	Player Icon 283
122	What Banished the Phantom	Hint: The phantom's gravestone. (Defeat Jecht 30 times.)	Listing appears at 50% completion	Player Icon 284
123	What Bested the Lady	Hint: The lady's gravestone. (Defeat Shantotto 30 times.)	Listing appears at 50% completion	Player Icon 287
124	What Bested the Warrior	Hint: The warrior's gravestone. (Defeat Gabranth 30 times.)	Listing appears at 50% completion	Player Icon 288

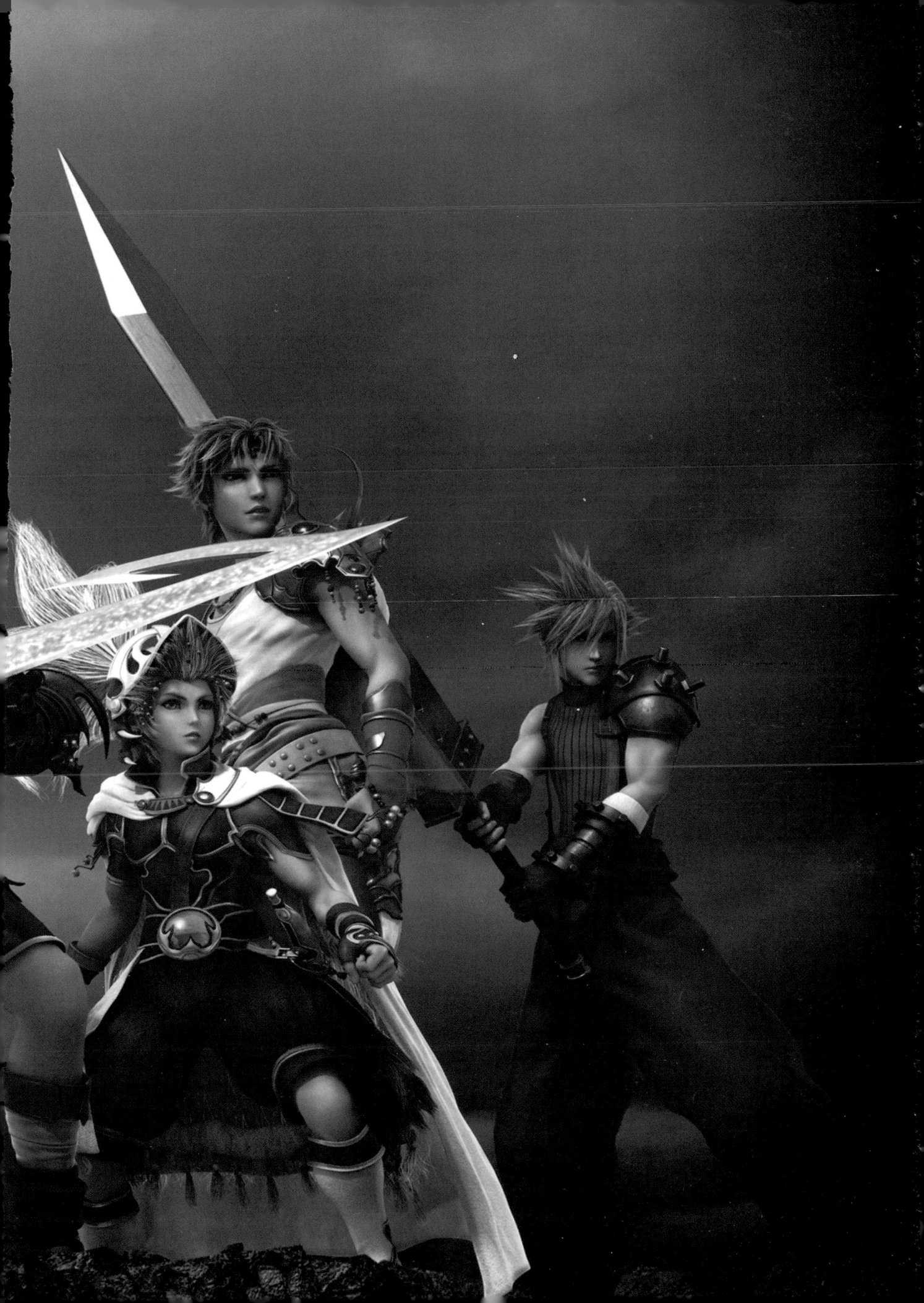

ACCOMPLISHMENTS

Although battling through Story Mode may reveal the ending, the true test of *DISSIDIA FINAL FANTASY* mastery is completing accomplishments. Like the achievements and trophies on other game consoles, accomplishments are awarded when you complete a certain task, usually performing an action (such as attacking, blocking, or beating a specific character) a certain amount of times. Most accomplishments are hidden until they are halfway achieved, or until some other condition is met. The listing condition for each accomplishment is shown in the following section, but note that is not necessary to reveal a listing before you complete it.

You'll receive a different booster accessory as a reward for completing each of the first 101 accomplishments. The final 50 accomplishments are known as secret accomplishments, and instead offer exclusive player icons as rewards. These secret accomplishments are more difficult to complete, and offer only vague hints instead of explicit directions. More specific instructions for each of them are included in this table.

Number	Name	Requirement	Result	Reward
001	The End of the Beginning	Clear the Prologue.	Listing appears at start of game	[Level] Level ≤ 3
002	Odyssey: Final Fantasy I	Clear Destiny Odyssey I with Warrior of Light.	Listing appears after clearing any Destiny Odyssey	[HP] HP = 100%
003	Odyssey: Final Fantasy II	Clear Destiny Odyssey II with Firion.	Listing appears after clearing any Destiny Odyssey	[HP] Near Death
004	Odyssey: Final Fantasy III	Clear Destiny Odyssey III with Onion Knight.	Listing appears after clearing any Destiny Odyssey	[Bravery] Victory Chance
005	Odyssey: Final Fantasy IV	Clear Destiny Odyssey IV with Cecil.	Listing appears after clearing any Destiny Odyssey	[HP] Near Loss
006	Odyssey: Final Fantasy V	Clear Destiny Odyssey V with Bartz.	Listing appears after clearing any Destiny Odyssey	[Position] Near Opponent
007	Odyssey: Final Fantasy VI	Clear Destiny Odyssey VI with Terra.	Listing appears after clearing any Destiny Odyssey	[Position] Far from Opponent
008	Odyssey: Final Fantasy VII	Clear Destiny Odyssey VII with Cloud.	Listing appears after clearing any Destiny Odyssey	[Bravery] Break
009	Odyssey: Final Fantasy VIII	Clear Destiny Odyssey VIII with Squall.	Listing appears after clearing any Destiny Odyssey	[Bravery] Near Break
010	Odyssey: Final Fantasy IX	Clear Destiny Odyssey IX with Zidane.	Listing appears after clearing any Destiny Odyssey	[Position] On the Ground
011	Odyssey: Final Fantasy X	Clear Destiny Odyssey X with Tidus.	Listing appears after clearing any Destiny Odyssey	[Position] In Midair
012	At Odyssey's End	Clear all Destiny Odysseys.	Listing appears after clearing any five Destiny Odysseys	[Combat] In Motion
013	The Odyssey	Clear a Destiny Odyssey at least 30 times.	Listing appears after clearing a Destiny Odyssey fifteen times	[HP] HP = 1
014	I Love a Brawl	Participate in at least 300 battles.	Listing appears at start of game	[Combat] Attacking Bravery
015	I Love a Brawl	Participate in at least 1,000 battles.	Listing appears at 50% completion	[Level] Level 70-79
016	Battle 'Em All	Fight against every character.	Listing appears after clearing Shade Impulse Chapter 4	[Level] Level = Multiple of 3
017	World Warrior	Fight on every stage.	Listing appears after clearing all Destiny Odysseys	[EX] Empty EX Gauge
018	The Road to Conquest	Win at least 300 battles.	Listing appears at start of game	[Combat] Attacking HP
019	The Road to Conquest	Win at least 500 battles.	Listing appears at 50% completion	[Level] Level 90-99
020	Hard Habit to Break	Play for at least 15 hours.	Listing appears at start of game	[Summon] After Summon
021	Time for Some Action	Battle for at least 10 hours.	Listing appears at start of game	[Summon] Summon Unused
022	Two Piece and a Biscuit	Deal at least 100,000 points of damage.	Listing appears at start of game	[EX] EX Gauge ≥ 70%
023	Two Piece and a Biscuit	Deal at least 1,500,000 points of damage.	Listing appears at 50% completion	[Opponent] EX Gauge ≥ 70%
024	The Most Valiant of All	Gain at least 50,000 points of bravery.	Listing appears at start of game	[HP] HP ≥ 80%
025	The Most Valiant of All	Gain at least 2,000,000 points of bravery.	Listing appears at 50% completion	[Opponent] HP = 1
026	Test One's Mettle	Deliver at least 1,500 bravery attacks.	Listing appears at start of game	[Opponent] HP ≥ 70%
027	Test One's Mettle	Deliver at least 30,000 bravery attacks.	Listing appears at 50% completion	[Opponent] HP ≤ 30%
028	Hit Where It Hurts	Deliver at least 300 HP attacks.	Listing appears at start of game	[Opponent] Break
029	Hit Where It Hurts	Deliver at least 10,000 HP attacks.	Listing appears at 50% completion	[Opponent] Near Break
030	Road Trip	Travel at least 100 kilometers.	Listing appears at 50% completion	[Time] After 30 Seconds
031	Road Trip	Travel at least 150 kilometers.	Listing appears at 50% completion	[Opponent] No BRV Damage
032	Impenetrable Defense	Successfully block at least 1,000 blows.	Listing appears at 50% completion	[BRV] BRV ≥ Base Value
033	Impenetrable Defense	Successfully block at least 5,000 blows.	Listing appears at 50% completion	[Opponent] BRV ≥ Base Value
034	Artful Dodger	Successfully dodge at least 1,000 times.	Listing appears at 50% completion	[BRV] BRV ≤ Base Value
035	Artful Dodger	Successfully dodge at least 5,000 times.	Listing appears at 50% completion	[Opponent] BRV ≤ Base Value
036	Core Blimey	Collect at least 50 EX Cores.	Listing appears at 50% completion	[HP] HP ≤ 40%
037	Core Blimey	Collect at least 300 EX Cores.	Listing appears at 50% completion	[Combat] Standing Still
038	Modus EX-perandi	Enter EX Mode at least 100 times.	Listing appears at 50% completion	[Opponent] Attacking Bravery
039	Rejuvenation	Regenerate at least 10,000 HP.	Listing appears at 50% completion	[EX] EX Mode
040	Rejuvenation	Regenerate at least 1,000,000 HP.	Listing appears at 50% completion	[Opponent] EX Mode
041	Go Out With a Bang	Finish a match with an EX Burst at least 30 times.	Listing appears at 50% completion	[EX] Full EX Gauge
042	Earth-Unfriendly	Damage the stage at least 1,000 times.	Listing appears at 50% completion	[Combat] Taking Damage
043	Earth-Unfriendly	Damage the stage at least 20,000 times.	Listing appears at 50% completion	[Opponent] Taking Damage
044	Impulse: Final Fantasy I	Clear any Shade Impulse chapter with Warrior of Light.	Listing appears after clearing Shade Impulse Chapter 4	[HP] Large Gap in HP
045	Impulse: Final Fantasy II	Clear any Shade Impulse chapter with Firion.	Listing appears after clearing Shade Impulse Chapter 4	[HP] Small Gap in HP
046	Impulse: Final Fantasy III	Clear any Shade Impulse chapter with Onion Knight.	Listing appears after clearing Shade Impulse Chapter 4	[Bravery] Large Gap in BRV
047	Impulse: Final Fantasy IV	Clear any Shade Impulse chapter with Cecil.	Listing appears after clearing Shade Impulse Chapter 4	[Bravery] Small Gap in BRV
048	Impulse: Final Fantasy V	Clear any Shade Impulse chapter with Bartz.	Listing appears after clearing Shade Impulse Chapter 4	[Level] Large Gap in Level
049	Impulse: Final Fantasy VI	Clear any Shade Impulse chapter with Terra.	Listing appears after clearing Shade Impulse Chapter 4	[Level] Small Gap in Level
050	Impulse: Final Fantasy VII	Clear any Shade Impulse chapter with Cloud.	Listing appears after clearing Shade Impulse Chapter 4	[Combat] Pre-Bravery Attack
051	Impulse: Final Fantasy VIII	Clear any Shade Impulse chapter with Squall.	Listing appears after clearing Shade Impulse Chapter 4	[Combat] Pre-Bravery Damage

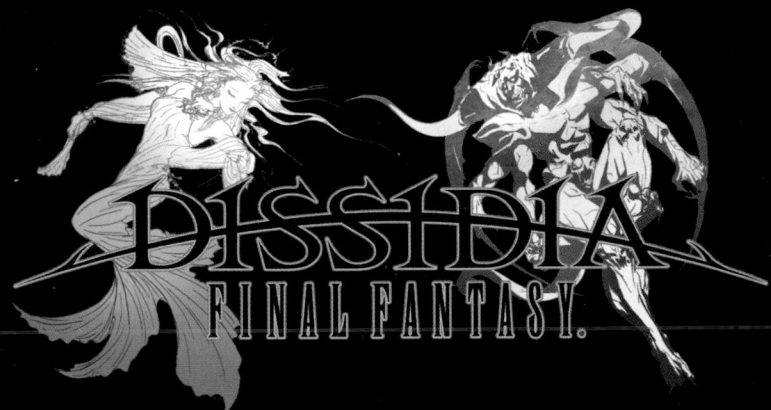

BRADYGAMES

SQUARE ENIX ®